American Freedom

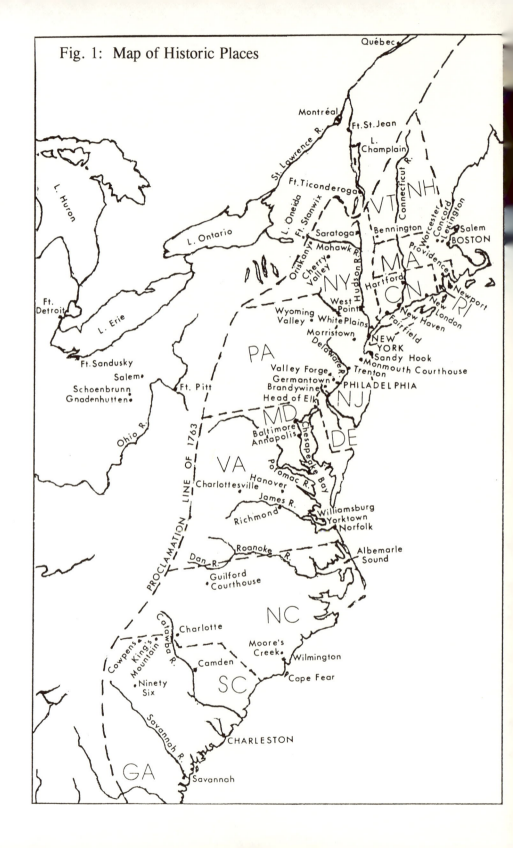

Fig. 1: Map of Historic Places

American Freedom

The Fight for People's Rights from Colonial Petitions to Modern Courtrooms

by
Frank C. Manak III

QuidPro Publishing
Hudson, Ohio

Library of Congress Cataloging-in-Publication Data

Manak, Frank C.
    American freedom : the fight for people's rights from colonial petitions to modern courtrooms / Frank Manak ; editor, Cheryl Brooke -- 1 st ed.
    p. cm.
    Preassigned LCCN 95-60858
    ISBN 0-9666508-0-8
    Includes bibliographical references and index.

    1. United States--Politics and government. 2. Political science--United States--History. 3. United States--History--Revolution, 1775-1783. 4. United States--History--Constitutional period, 1789-1809. I. Title.

JK54.M36 1998   320'.0973
                             QBI98-1116

Cover design: Roberta Dickinson
Editor: Cheryl Brooke
       Department of English
       Cleveland State University

Copyright © 1998, Frank C. Manak III
All rights reserved.
No part of this book may be reproduced or transmitted in any form or by any means without prior written permission from the publisher, except by a reviewer who wishes to quote brief passages for inclusion in a magazine, newspaper or broadcast.

Printed in the United States of America
Printing number
10 9 8 7 6 5 4 3 2 1

For volume pricing and discounts contact:
QuidPro Publishing Company
Suite L7, 110 West Streetsboro Street
Hudson OH 44236-2709
Telephone (330) 528-3004

Dedication

In the Kingdom of Bohemia in 1872, Martin Kletečka was a builder and operator of flour mills. He was my great-great grandfather. My parents said that Martin would spend his spare time reading about the wonderful conditions in post-Civil War America. He was impressed by the freedoms enjoyed by the American people, such as their freedom of speech and press, freedom of religion, freedom from arbitrary searches of their homes by police, freedom from arbitrary police arrest and freedom from laws that treat people unequally because of race, religion or nationality.

The Czech people of Bohemia had no such freedoms under their ruler, the Austrian emperor Franz Josef. All the key positions in their local government were held by Germans. All their schools were under the control of the Catholic Church, and their teachers were forbidden to teach many events of Czech history. The Czech language was forbidden in all schools and government offices.

Many people were arrested for criticizing the emperor. They had much to criticize. The emperor was more concerned with Prussia's expanding control of various German duchies than with the well-being of his own people. His war against Prussia in 1866 had resulted in the Prussian invasion of Bohemia and the loss of many Czech lives. In 1871, the emperor promised that Bohemia would be given the status of a federal republic, similar to that of Hungary. However, he reneged on his promise and continued to treat the Czechs as second-class people.

Fig. 2: MARTIN KLETEČKA (1806-1877)

Fig. 3: PRESIDENT BENEŠ, MAYOR BURTON
AND FRANK C. MANAK, JR. AT THE CZECH CULTURAL GARDEN
IN CLEVELAND (MARCH 1938)

Dedication

So at the age of sixty-six, Martin left the wooded hills of southern Bohemia and came to America with the families of three of his five daughters, one of whom was my mother's grandmother. His other two daughters, including my father's grandmother, came two years later.

In the spring of 1939, after Hitler's armies had taken over Czechoslovakia, the Czechoslovak president Eduard Beneš came to America and visited a number of cities, including Cleveland, where my family lived. He had come to encourage America to stop Hitler before the Nazi leader made the whole world subject to his will and deprived everyone of the freedoms proclaimed by the United States Constitution. My father was president of Cleveland's Czech Cultural Garden at the time. Along with Mayor Harold Burton of Cleveland, who later became a justice of the United States Supreme Court, he and a gathering of Czech people gave President Beneš an enthusiastic reception in the Czech Cultural Garden. They were surrounded by statues and busts of the great freedom fighters of Czech history. My Grandfather Manak had donated a bust of the Czech newspaper editor, Karel Havlíček. Unfortunately, America did not heed President Beneš's call. By December 1941, when it did finally enter the Second World War, millions of people had lost their lives or freedom.

In 1993, my wife and I traveled to Prague, the capital of the Czech Republic, where my son and daughter-in-law were living. The city was vibrant with activity. Buildings were being restored to their old glory. I saw thousands of energetic young people working to create better lives for themselves. Then, I saw a grave marker that had been placed in front of the famous statue of King Wenceslas on Wenceslas Square. It was inscribed with the words, "Obetem Komunismo," meaning "The Death of Communism." Next to the marker was a picture of a young man who had died in 1968, protesting the Russian tanks that had driven into Prague to force the Czechoslovak president Alexander Dubček out of office.

I dedicate this book to my parents, Frank and Frances Manak and their ancestors, who gave me the opportunity to live in the United States of America, where the basic purpose of the government is to protect every person's life, liberty and property and where all political action must center on that purpose. My parents gave me other things that have helped me live a healthy, happy and productive life. However, most of them would not have mattered had I lived in another place where a political agenda such as Naziism, Fascism or Communism took precedence over the protection of people.

I am a patent attorney. In many respects, this book is outside the scope of my law practice. However, all branches of law, including patent law, relate to rights proclaimed in the United States Constitution. Patents and copyrights also played a role in establishing America's independence. The Boston Tea Party, which started the final chain of events that led to the Declaration of Independence, was a protest not only against a British tax on tea but against an unlawful patent granted to the British East India Company. In 1776, Tom Paine assigned the copyright of his pamphlet, *Common Sense*, to the Continental Congress. A half million copies were sold that year, exhorting Americans to declare their independence. The Congress used the copyright royalties to finance the first part of the War of Independence.

I live with my wife Patricia in Hudson, Ohio. My son Charles, his wife Evelyne and their son Anton now live in Budapest, Hungary. My daughter Christine, her husband Zackary Edmonds and their children Matthew and Hannah live in Lexington, Massachusetts. My daughter Noël lives in Washington, D.C. I do not know where in the world they will live in the future, but I hope they will be places governed by the principles of freedom that Americans have fought to preserve for over two hundred years.

Frank C. Manak III
Hudson, Ohio
December 1997

Contents

Introduction   3

Chapter 1   The Rights of Englishmen and the Realities of British Government   7
- A. James Otis, 7
- B. Patrick Henry, 10
- C. The Law of Nature and Life, Liberty and Property, 12
- D. John Wilkes, 20
- E. The Power of Parliament, 23
- F. The Sons of Liberty, 28
- G. A Test of Wills, 41

Chapter 2   Reconciliation or Confrontation?   48
- A. A Calm before the Storm, 48
- B. The *Gaspée* Incident, 48
- C. The Committees of Correspondence, 49
- D. The Boston Tea Party, 51
- E. The Intolerable Acts, 56
- F. The Colonists Respond, 58
- G. The First Continental Congress, 60

Chapter 3   To Arms! To Arms!   70
- A. The Preparations for War, 70
- B. Lexington and Concord, 75
- C. The Williamsburg Gunpowder Incident, 76
- D. The Green Mountain Boys and Fort Ticonderoga, 79
- E. The Second Continental Congress, 82
- F. Bunker Hill, 83
- G. Another Petition and More Fighting, 84

Chapter 4   The Declaration of Independence   88
- A. A Call for *Common Sense*, 88
- B. The People Respond, 90

Chapter 5 The War of Independence 99
A. Patriots and Loyalists, 99
B. The War and the Soldiers, 102
C. Long Island and Manhattan Island, 103
D. White Plains, Fort Lee and Fort Washington, 108
E. Trenton and Princeton, 110
F. Lake Champlain, Bennington, Fort Stanwix and Saratoga, 114
G. Brandywine, Germantown and Valley Forge, 120
H. The French Alliance, 127
I. Philadelphia and Monmouth Court House, 130
J. The War at Sea, 134
K. The Western Front, 138
L. Savannah, Charleston and Camden, 140
M. The Treason of Benedict Arnold, 143
N. King's Mountain, Cowpens and Guilford Court House, 148
O. Victory at Yorktown, 154
P. The Conclusion of the War, 164
Q. The War and the People, 167

Chapter 6 The New Nation Struggles 174
A. The Articles of Confederation, 174
B. The Problems of Government under the Articles, 176

Chapter 7 The United States Constitution 179
A. The Annapolis Meeting, 179
B. The Constitutional Convention, 181
C. The United States Government Compared to the British Government, 193
D. Federalists and Antifederalists, 194
E. The Constitution Becomes the Law of the Land, 197

Chapter 8 Religious Freedom 199
A. The Development of Religious Freedom in the Thirteen Colonies, 199
  1. *Virginia*, 200
  2. *New England*, 202
  3. *New York*, 214
  4. *Pennsylvania, Delaware and New Jersey*, 222
  5. *Maryland*, 227
  6. *The Carolinas and Georgia*, 233
  7. *The "Great Awakening" Revival*, 238

B. The Expansion of Religious Freedom between 1775 and 1790, 248
C. The Virginia Statute for Religious Freedom, 268
D. Religious Freedom According to the First Amendment, 282

Chapter 9 The Bill of Rights   296
A. The Absolute Rights of Life, Liberty and Property, 296
  1. *The Right of Personal Security*, 301
  2. *The Right of Liberty*, 304
  3. *The Right of Property*, 309
  4. *The Auxiliary Rights for the Protection of Life, Liberty and Property*, 311
  5. *Summary*, 315
B. The Absolute Duties of People, 317
  1. *Religious Duties*, 317
  2. *The Equivalent Protection Principle*, 321
  3. *The Control of What Goes in the Mind and Body*, 322
  4. *The Control of Body Integrity*, 324
  5. *The Control of Life and Death*, 332
  6. *The Control of People's Sex Lives*, 343
C. Free Speech and Press, 349
  1. *Early Struggles for the Right of Free Speech and Press*, 349
  2. *Political Speech and the Protection of Government*, 360
  3. *Prior Restraint and Post-Publication Liability*, 364
  4. *The Right of Peaceable Assembly*, 369
  5. *Fighting Words and Hate Speech*, 370
  6. *Non-Verbal Communications*, 375
  7. *The Right of the Public to Attend Criminal Trials*, 379
  8. *Freedom of Speech on the Internet*, 382
D. Summary, 386

Chapter 10 The Fourteenth Amendment   389
A. Background, 389
B. The Adoption of the Fourteenth Amendment, 391
C. The Meaning of Section 1, 398
D. The Privileges and Immunities and Life, Liberty and Property Clauses, 409
  1. *The Slaughter-House Decision*, 410
  2. *Life after the Slaughter-House*, 415
  3. *The Lochner Era*, 427
  4. *Liberty beyond Lochner*, 435

　　　　5. The Selective Incorporation Era, 449
　　　　6. The Right of a Criminal Suspect to Be Informed
　　　　　　of His Rights, 458
　　　　7. Fundamental Rights Guaranteed in the Main Body
　　　　　　of the Constitution, 461
　　　　8. Summary and Further Comment on Incorporation, 462
　　E. The Equal Protection Clause, 475
　　　　1. Background, 475
　　　　2. Equal Protection from the Civil War to World War II, 492
　　　　3. The Japanese Internment Cases, 505
　　　　4. Past Wrongs Corrected, 511
　　　　5. The Slow Pace of School Desegregation, 522
　　　　6. The Civil Rights Acts, 534
　　　　7. Affirmative Action, 544
　　　　8. The California Civil Rights Initiative, 567
　　　　9. The Equal Rights of Women, 571
　　　　10. Homosexual Marriages, 584
　　　　11. Summary, 595

Chapter 11　Religion in the Public Schools　　　596
　　A. Religious Instruction, 596
　　B. School Prayers and Bible Verses, 600
　　C. The Definition of "Religion", 613
　　D. Religion in Extracurricular Activities, 626
　　E. Graduation Prayers, 634
　　F. Religious Music and Holiday Celebrations, 647
　　G. Evolution and Other Controversial Subjects, 656
　　　　1. Darwin's Theory, 656
　　　　2. The "Monkey" Trial, 659
　　　　3. The Recent Cases, 676
　　　　4. Science versus Religion, 688
　　H. Teaching Values, 689
　　I. Establishment of Religion versus Free Exercise of Religion, 695

Chapter 12　The Nature and Purpose of Government　　　697
　　A. The Nature of Government, 698
　　B. The Purpose of Government, 706

Appendices

BL	A Biography of Sir William Blackstone	713
BL1	Blackstone on the Nature of Laws	718
BL2	Blackstone on the Countries Subject to the Laws of England	743
BL3	Blackstone on the Absolute Rights of Individuals	745
BL4	Blackstone on Slavery	770
BL5	Blackstone on Religion	775
BL6	Blackstone on Freedom of the Press	800
BL7	Blackstone on Monopolies	803
A	Selected Chapters of the Magna Charta (1215)	805
B	The Petition of Right (1628)	806
C	The Massachusetts Body of Liberties (Selected Sections) (1641)	809
D	Agreement Proposed by the Levellers (Selected Sections) (1649)	815
E	The English Declaration of Rights (First Part) (1689)	818
F	Locke on Civil Government (1690) and Religion (1689)	820
G	Massachusetts Assembly Memorial Footnote (1764)	839
H	Resolutions of the Stamp Act Congress (1765)	841
I	*A Vindication of the British Colonies* (Selected Section), by James Otis (1765)	843
J	*The Rights of the Colonists*, by Sam Adams (1772)	845
K	The Declaration and Resolves by the First Continental Congress (1774)	849
L	The Declaration of Independence (1776)	853
M	A Bill of Memorial and Remonstrance against Religious Assessments Presented to the Virginia General Assembly (1785)	856
N	The Virginia Statute for Religious Freedom (1786)	863
O	The United States Constitution (Selected Sections and Amendments, 1787, 1789)	865
P	The Rights of Women (Seneca Falls Declaration) (1848)	874

Notes to Chapters 878
Bibliography 909
Index 919
  A. People, Groups and Private Organizations, 919
  B. Places and Events, 927
  C. Nations, States and Government Agencies, Laws and Documents, 931
  D. Legal Rights, Philosophies, Religions, and Other Subjects, 937
  E. Table of Cases, 940

Map and Pictures

Fig. 1	Map of Historic Places	ii
Fig. 2	Martin Klatečka (1806-1877)	vi
Fig. 3	President Beneš, Mayor Burton and Frank C. Manak, Jr. at the Cleveland Czech Cultural Garden (March 1938)	vi
Fig. 4	A Colonial Newspaper Protests the Stamp Act	30
Fig. 5	The Boston Tea Party	57
Fig. 6	"To Arms! To Arms! The British Are Coming!"	77
Fig. 7	The Battle of Lexington	77
Fig. 8	Ethan Allen Demands the Surrender of Ft. Ticonderoga	82
Fig. 9	Washington Crossing the Delaware	113
Fig. 10	The Winter at Valley Forge	125
Fig. 11	Franklin Is Presented to King Louis XVI and Queen Marie Antoinette of France	128
Fig. 12	Molly Pitcher Takes Over for Her Fallen Husband	133

Figures 4-12 are copies of pictures reproduced by permission from *The American Revolution: A Picture Sourcebook* by John Grafton, Dover Pictorial Archive Series (New York: Dover Publications, 1975).

Tables

1	Religious Freedom in the Thirteen Colonies in 1775	250
2	Religious Freedom in the Thirteen States and Vermont in 1790	251
3	The Historical Background of the Bill of Rights	464-465
4	Estimated Number of Black and White People in the United States in 1790	479
5	The Relationships between Blackstone's Terms of Art	712

American Freedom

Extremism in defense of liberty is no vice!
Moderation in pursuit of justice is no virtue!

--Barry Goldwater
(1909-1998)

Introduction

For the past two centuries, millions of people have come to America from all over the world. They have come to enjoy the freedom promised by the Declaration of Independence, the Constitution and the Bill of Rights. In recent years, however, Americans have come to hold different views of what that freedom is.

To some Americans, freedom is the right to send their children to a public school where each day opens with a Judeo-Christian prayer and scripture reading. To others, freedom is the right to send their children to a public school where all spiritual beliefs are treated equally and none is presented as true or false.

To some Americans, freedom is the right to die if they are suffering from terminal illness and their future holds nothing but unbearable pain and suffering. To others, freedom is the right to live in a society that holds every human life sacred and allows no one to take his own life before he dies of a natural cause.

To some Americans, freedom is the right to protest against their government by burning the American flag. To others, freedom is the right to live in a society that respects the national flag and its values and protects that flag from desecration.

Americans are divided on other freedom issues, including the right to a quality public education, racial equality and affirmative action, the right to bear arms, women's rights, abortion, gay rights, the rights of criminal defendants and the proper role of the courts in resolving these disputes. They are divided on these issues because they have different views of the kind of government that was established by the United States Constitution. They also disagree on the reasons why the American colonists declared their independence from Great Britain and adopted that constitution.

The purpose of this book is to clarify these issues and to show the relationship between the colonial fight for independence and the modern courtroom battles over the rights guaranteed by the Constitution.

Some historians say that before the Declaration of Independence, most colonists were content to live under British rule but were angry with their local governments. They say that a few wealthy colonists led the protests against the British leaders to advance their own importance or to deflect the average person's anger away from his local government. Others, defenders of the British imperial system, say the colonists went to war because they did not appreciate the benefits of British protection and were therefore unwilling to pay the cost of that protection. Some religious fundamentalists contend the war was caused by the decaying morals of British leaders who were humanists and suppressing the Bible-based American value system. Some environmentalists and Indian rights activists say the war was caused by American frontiersmen filled with greed, who wanted to take over Indian lands and exploit their natural resources but who were thwarted by British laws against western settlement. This is only a partial list of recent views expressed by various historians and political groups.

There may be truth in all these contentions. However, they are overshadowed by the reason that was repeated many times by the colonists themselves. They said in their Declaration of Independence that they were entitled to certain "unalienable Rights," among which were "Life, Liberty and the pursuit of Happiness." They also said the British government had destroyed these rights through "a history of repeated injuries and usurpations," which they listed in the Declaration. Finally, they said that those circumstances required that they abolish their ties to the British government and institute a new government.

Modern liberal scholars have questioned whether the Declaration of Independence truly reflects the views held by most American colonists in 1776. The Declaration was not submitted to a popular vote and so we can not know exactly how many colonists would have signed it had they had the opportunity. However, the events presented in this book show that a very large number of colonists, including nearly all their elected leaders, were angry because the British government was depriving them of their "unalienable rights." In 1776, when their population was a little over two million, the colonists bought a half million copies of Tom Paine's pamphlet, *Common Sense*. That pamphlet urged them to declare their independence and to form a new government that guaranteed "freedom and property to all men, and above all things the free exercise of religion." Most of Paine's readers were persuaded by his pamphlet. That was a major reason why the delegates to the Continental Congress voted in favor of independence.

The colonists did not always act in ways that were proper or free of hypocrisy. They smuggled tea and molasses to avoid British tariffs. Their protests sometimes led to riots, in which property was stolen and destroyed. After the colonists won the War of Independence, many of them continued to hold black people as slaves. These black people did not gain the rights that they should have gained as a result of that war.

Nevertheless, the American colonists set many good examples. They persisted in asserting their rights, in spite of British attempts to intimidate them by military occupation, blockades and oppressive laws. They persevered through a very difficult war, one that they often seemed certain of losing. They also established a constitution that limited the powers of their new government and guaranteed personal freedoms that are valued today by people all over the world. These include not only freedoms that the English common law had recognized but freedoms that others could only dream of, including religious freedom and freedom of speech and press. Finally, their statement in the Declaration of Independence that "all men are created equal" inspired Abraham Lincoln and other Americans to fight for the elimination of slavery. After the Civil War, the United States added amendments to its Constitution ending slavery and giving everyone the right of equal protection of the laws.

Another clause added to the Constitution after the Civil War said that no state shall "deprive any person of his life, liberty or property, without due process of law." The United States Supreme

Court has held that this clause requires state governments to respect most of the rights listed in the Constitution's Bill of Rights, which were originally binding only on the federal government. Modern conservative scholars argue that this clause is not entitled to such a broad meaning. However, they do not realize how consistent the Court's interpretations are with the American founding fathers' understanding of the absolute rights of personal security, personal liberty and private property. The early Americans had learned of these rights from the Oxford law professor William Blackstone, who had described them in his *Commentaries on the Laws of England*. They believed they had even broader absolute rights than Blackstone had recognized, particularly with regard to the freedoms of religion, speech and press.

On the other hand, many liberal scholars have wrongly questioned the motives of the men who wrote the Declaration of Independence and the Bill of Rights. They stress the importance of the Bill of Rights today, yet they say the colonists did not fight the War of Independence because they were concerned about their "unalienable rights." Clearly, they do not understand the importance that the colonists placed on freedom from arbitrary government. We must appreciate the validity of the colonial challenges to British oppression to understand the freedom they claimed in the Bill of Rights. Liberal scholars also question the wisdom of relying on documents and events of the past to resolve today's modern conflicts. They fail to realize that any lasting organization of people must be based on a mutual understanding of rights and responsibilities. A just and stable government must therefore be based on an enduring social contract. In the United States, that contract is its two-hundred-year-old written Constitution. Government must adjust to the changing needs of people, but it must also retain its basic nature. That nature, like the nature of people, is the one inherited from the past.

For these reasons, we should know the story of the fight for American freedom, from the first colonial protests to the Bill of Rights. We should also know how this legacy has shaped the modern courtroom decisions that define American freedom.

1

The Rights of Englishmen and the Realities of British Government

On July 4, 1776, the American colonists declared their independence from Great Britain. They said their action had become necessary because the British government would not recognize their "unalienable Rights," including their rights to "Life, Liberty and the pursuit of Happiness." For more than a decade before that celebrated event, the colonists had claimed that the British government was violating their rights in many ways. Their homes were no longer their own: not only were they being searched without proper warrants, but they were used to quarter British soldiers. Their property was being taken without their being given the opportunity to be heard before judges. They were being punished for criticizing the British government and being forced to pay taxes not authorized by their elected representatives.

A. James Otis

These conditions had not always existed in America. The troubles began in 1760, when the British government decided it had to raise more revenue from its American colonies than it had in the past. It had incurred large debts during the Seven Years War against France and Austria and its American counterpart, the French and Indian War. The British were also faced with the expense of defending the American territory taken from France during the French and Indian War.

The colonists were already paying a tariff on molasses imported from England, imposed under the Sugar Act of 1733. That law also forbade them to buy molasses from other nations. However, the British authorities had not been enforcing the law. Smuggling had therefore become a way of life for many colonists. In Massachusetts, the economic well-being of nearly everyone depended on it: sixty distillers were making rum from molasses smuggled from the French and Dutch colonies in the West Indies. They did not want to buy the lower quality English molasses or pay the taxes due under the Sugar Act.

To stop the smuggling and increase the taxes collected from the colonists, British customs officers applied to the Massachusetts Superior Court for writs of assistance--blanket licenses to search anyone's property for smuggled molasses. The colonists knew the smuggling was wrong, but they did not believe that the customs officers were justified in forcibly entering anyone's home at any time they pleased. Therefore, the Boston merchants retained a young attorney, James Otis, to oppose the writs. In a hearing on February 24, 1761 in the State House on the corner of the present State and Washington Streets in Boston, Otis argued that

> one of the most essential branches of English liberty is the freedom of one's house. A man's house is his castle. This writ, if it should be declared legal, would totally annihilate this privilege. Custom-house officers may enter our houses, when they please; we are commanded to permit their entry. Their menial servants may enter, may break locks, bars, and every thing in their way; and whether they break through malice or revenge, no man, no court, can inquire. Bare suspicion without oath is sufficient.[1]

Otis argued that the writs of assistance were void because "An act against the Constitution is void," and "An act against natural equity is void." The spectators in the courtroom cheered. Sensing that a decision against the merchants might cause a riot, Chief Justice Thomas Hutchinson delayed ruling on the matter and wrote to

England for advice. A year later, after being told that the courts in England were issuing similar writs called "general warrants," the Superior Court ruled that the writs were valid. The Boston customs officers were therefore able to search anyone's house for smuggled molasses without proving to a judge that they had probable cause for such a search.[2]

Another young attorney was sitting in the Superior Court gallery watching Otis argue his case. John Adams, who was to become the second president of the United States, later wrote of the event, "Then and there was the first scene of the first act of opposition to the arbitrary claims of Great Britain. Then and there the child of Independence was born." He explained that the American Revolution was brought about before the war began:

> The Revolution was in the minds and hearts of the people; a change in their religious sentiments of their duties and obligations. While the king, and all in authority under him, were believed to govern in justice and mercy, according to the laws and constitution derived to them from the God of nature and transmitted to them by their ancestors, they thought themselves bound to pray for the king and queen and all the royal family, and all in authority under them, as ministers ordained of God for their good; but when they saw those powers renouncing all principles of authority, and bent upon the destruction of all the securities of their lives, liberties and properties, they thought it their duty to pray for the continental congress and all the thirteen State congresses, &c.
>
> There might be, and there were others who thought less about religion and conscience, but had certain habitual sentiments of allegiance and loyalty derived from their education; but believing allegiance and protection to be reciprocal, when protection was withdrawn, they thought their allegiance was dissolved.[3]

Otis's stirring speech against the writs of assistance gained him election to the Massachusetts House of Representatives. There he convinced his fellow legislators that they had the right to approve all decisions relating to the colony's affairs. When the royal governor of Massachusetts appropriated several hundred pounds to send an armed ship to Newfoundland to protect English fisheries from French invasion, Otis pushed through a House resolution of protest. He said that if the legislators gave up their right to appropriate revenue, Massachusetts might as well be ruled by the king of France instead of George III. Upon hearing these words, another legislator accused Otis of treason.[4]

B. Patrick Henry

While James Otis was captivating audiences in Massachusetts, another young attorney was becoming active in Virginia politics. Patrick Henry gained fame in a case involving an Anglican parson who claimed he had been underpaid for his services. Because the Anglican Church was still supported by Virginia's colonial government, the plantation owners of each parish were required to contribute to their parson's wages. The wages were paid in tobacco, not money, and the amount fixed by law was sixteen thousand pounds of tobacco per year. A deputy sheriff collected the tobacco from the plantation owners of each parish and delivered it to the parson. When there was a bad harvest, many believed the amount due the parson was not fair. His allotment was worth more, while everyone else's income was less. To remedy that situation, the Virginia House of Burgesses passed the Two Penny Act in 1758. The Act required each parson to accept a wage of two pennies for every pound of tobacco due him, even though the current market value of most tobacco was about six pennies a pound. However, because the king had not approved this new law, many members of the clergy challenged its validity and sued for the value of the tobacco due them under the old law.

Reverend James Maury of Hanover County was one of the clergy who filed a suit demanding damages from the local deputy sheriff who had underpaid him. At a trial in the town of Hanover in November 1763, the judge ruled in Maury's favor and set the date of December 1 for a jury hearing on the damages. The deputy sheriff was desperate because he could not find an experienced lawyer to represent him at this hearing. So he hired Patrick Henry, a novice attorney who was the son of the judge presiding over the case.

Not to be confused with the judge's brother, the Anglican Reverend Patrick Henry, the young attorney Patrick Henry was a member of the New Lights, a religious group that preached against the rituals and teachings of the established Anglican Church. His mother and her father were also New Lights, and when he was younger, they had taken him to hear the famous evangelist Samuel Davies preach that free people should never be taxed to support a religion they did not believe to be true. Some people thought that Davies was loud and offensive, but Patrick Henry was impressed by his style and sought to emulate it.

Fortunately for the young attorney and his client, three of the jurors were also New Lights and one was his cousin. They listened intently as Henry argued,

> We have heard a great deal about the benevolence and holy zeal of our reverend clergy. But how is this manifested? Do they feed the hungry and clothe the naked? Oh, no, gentlemen! These rapacious harpies would, were their power equal to their will, snatch from the hearth of their honest parishioner his last hoe-cake, from the widow and her orphan children her last milch cow! The last bed--nay, the last blanket--from the lying-in woman![5]

Henry also explained that his client had complied with the Two Penny Act. Although the king had not approved the act, Henry argued that the king had a duty to approve it because it was a reasonable law made for the protection of people's property. The king's failure to approve the law therefore violated the social contract whereby the king was obliged to protect the people and they were obliged to obey him. If the king did not fulfill his obligation, said Henry, he was no longer fit to rule the people. Instead, he was a mere tyrant. The jury could therefore ignore the king's failure to approve the law. Upon hearing that argument, the opposing counsel exclaimed, "The gentleman has spoken treason!"[6]

The crowd, however, loved the speech. The jury took only a moment to decide the damages--a grand total of a penny! Patrick

Henry was carried out of the courtroom on the shoulders of the spectators. The next year, he added 164 clients to his law practice; the following year, he was elected to the House of Burgesses.

C. The Law of Nature and Life, Liberty and Property

The rights asserted by James Otis and Patrick Henry were not novel concepts. They had been recognized for a long time as basic principles of English government. In 1765, Sir William Blackstone explained the fundamental rights of Englishmen in the first volume of his *Commentaries on the Laws of England*.[7] He said these rights were based on the law of nature, to which all government laws had to conform and which the English pediatrician and philosopher John Locke had explained in his *Second Essay Concerning Civil Government*, published in 1690.[8]

In his essay, Locke told of the primary state of nature in which primitive people live without any government. In that circumstance, each person has certain God-given rights relating to the enjoyment of his life, liberty and property. Because he must enforce those rights himself, he is often at war with other people who try to take them away. Locke said that people therefore gather into communities and form governments by entering into social contracts. By these contracts, they delegate their power of enforcing their God-given rights to one or more community leaders. These community leaders then have the power to make laws and punish violators by taking away one or more aspects of their life, liberty and property. However, these leaders do not have unlimited power, because they can recieve only the power that the people themselves have in a state of nature. In that state, said Locke, each person has only the power over the life, liberty and property of other people that is necessary "for the preservation of himself and the rest of mankind." Therefore, all government power is subject to the same limitation (App. F, par. 135).[9] By Blackstone's time, Locke's natural law principles were well known on both sides of the Atlantic.

Many people questioned Locke's thesis that governments derive their power from formal contracts entered into by primitive peoples. Blackstone was one of those people. However, he said that these contracts are implied when people stay together out of "the sense of their weakness and imperfection." They recognize that in order to stay together, "the whole should protect all its parts, and that every part should pay obedience to the will of the whole" (BL1, 47-48).[10] They therefore agree to obey government laws that are for their mutual protection and benefit.

Blackstone also said these government laws are subordinate to God's laws, both His law of nature and the revealed law of His holy scriptures: "if any human law should allow or injoin us to commit it [that is, violate God's natural or revealed law], we are bound to transgress that human law, or else we must offend both the natural and the divine" (BL1, 43; see also BL1, 41). The immutable law of nature vests people with certain absolute rights relating to their life, liberty and property, which they are entitled to enjoy whether they are living in a state of nature or in a society controlled by an organized government (BL3, 120, 119). Blackstone explained these absolute rights and put them under the headings of "personal security," which includes the right of life (BL3, 125-130), "personal liberty" (BL3, 130-134) and "private property" (BL3, 134-136). Because the main purpose of human government is to maintain and preserve these absolute rights, he argued, the laws that government makes to enforce the relative rights and duties between people for their mutual protection and benefit are secondary to this main purpose (BL3, 120). That means that when legislators, judges, prosecutors and police make and enforce laws designed to prevent people from violating each other's relative rights and duties, they must do so without violating their absolute rights.

The idea that people had absolute rights began in the days when the Saxon kings ruled England. Most Saxon kings were weak rulers and had a hard time controlling the powerful lords of their kingdom. They were therefore forced to recognize that these lords had certain rights of land ownership that no king could take away.

The Saxon king Edward the Confessor issued a code of laws that described these rights.[11]

This situation changed when William the Conqueror came across the sea from Normandy, invaded England and defeated King Harold at the Battle of Hastings in 1066. He took away most of the property of the Saxon lords and made his own soldiers the chief lords. King William and the kings who succeeded him exercised tight control over these lords. In the early 1200s, King John levied oppressive taxes on the lords to finance his wars in France. He also seized church property and had his enemies tortured and murdered. The lords and bishops feared this king would take away all their rights, as William the Conqueror had done when he gave the Saxon lords' property to their ancestors. They believed that in order to restore order, security and happiness in the kingdom, the king had to recognize that each landowner had certain fundamental rights-- rights that no one could take away.

In 1215, the lords and bishops threatened civil war and forced King John to sign the Magna Charta. Chapter 52 of this charter said, using the royal "we," "If any have been disseised or dispossessed by us, without a legal verdict of their peers, of their lands, castles, liberties, or rights, we will immediately restore these things to them; . . . ." (App. A). These rights were confirmed in the First Great Charters of Henry III and Edward I in 1216 and 1297, respectively,[12] and they were elaborated upon in several fourteenth-century statutes (BL3, 131, 134).

These early charters and laws protected only the rights of "freemen," which in those times was a technical feudal term that meant only a few large landowners. The charters and laws did not protect the rights of people who were bound in feudal service to these landowners. As time passed, however, more people became freemen, and they realized the value of the rights proclaimed in the ancient charters and laws. They demanded that their representatives in Parliament protect these rights. In 1601, some people petitioned Parliament to rescind several patents that Queen Elizabeth had recently granted her courtiers. These patents gave the courtiers the exclusive right to make, use and sell products and processes that had been known to everyone for a long time. The patents therefore deprived the common people of their freedom to engage in their usual trades. To avoid a Parliamentary showdown, the queen was forced to cancel some of the patents.[13]

Parliament's own acts were challenged in 1610. Chief Justice Edward Coke of the King's Bench said in *Bonham's Case*, "when an Act of Parliament is against common right and reason, or repugnant, or impossible to be performed, the common law will control it and adjudge such Act to be void."[14] At Coke's urging, Parliament enacted the Statute of Monopolies in 1623, which declared that all monopolies were void except for patents on inventions of new products and processes (BL7). Coke also convinced Parliament to enact the Petition of Right in 1628, which confirmed that no man could be put to death, taken, imprisoned or put out of his lands or tenements without a trial conducted according to due process of law. The Petition of Right also forbade the imposition of taxes not consented to by Parliament and the quartering of soldiers in private houses (App. B).

In America, the Plymouth Colony settlers proclaimed similar rights in their Great Fundamentals of Government, published in 1636. The Massachusetts Bay settlers proclaimed their rights in the Massachusetts Body of Liberties of 1641 (App. C).

Not all attempts to claim people's rights were successful. In 1647, during peace negotiations to end the English Civil War, a group of reformers calling themselves "Levellers" published a proposed agreement between the English people and their government (App. D). The purpose of the agreement was to heal the emotional wounds incurred by both sides during the war and to establish conditions for a lasting peace. In addition to proclaiming many rights that had already been established, the agreement added a ban against capital punishment except for murder and like crimes, the right to free exercise of religion, the right to refuse to pay for the support of religious ministers, and the right of a person accused of a crime to be represented by counsel and to refuse to testify at his trial. The agreement presumed that the people had the right to form their own government and it set limits on the powers of that government. All privileges based on class were to be abolished and every adult man was to have the right to vote. Unfortunately, these ideas were regarded as too extreme and the authors were imprisoned in the Tower of London.

After the English Revolution of 1688, Parliament passed the English Declaration of Rights, which restated many of the rights declared in the Petition of Right of 1628. It also declared the right of people to bear arms for their defense and their right to petition the king for redress of grievances. It said the king could not raise armies in times of peace without the consent of Parliament, nor could he impose cruel or unusual punishments or require excessive bail (App. E).

One of the purposes of the English Declaration of Rights was to justify to the world the English Revolution of 1688, which deposed the Catholic King James II in favor of the Protestant King William III. John Locke also sought to justify this event by writing two essays on government in 1690. He supported many of the arguments in his *Second Essay* with quotations from *The Laws of Ecclesiastical Polity* (1594, 1597, 1648) by the English theologian and philosopher Richard Hooker. Although Hooker was primarily concerned with defending the Anglican religious traditions against those of the Puritans and Roman Catholics, he also laid out principles of civil government that Locke used in constructing his social contract theory. These principles included government by consent of the governed and government's subservience to the law of God and the law of nature.

Locke also relied on the works of a Dutch lawyer, Hugo Grotius, and a German lawyer living in Sweden, Samuel Freiherr von Pufendorf. Grotius suggested in his essay *On the Law of War and Peace* (1625) that all nations are bound by a natural law derived from the nature of man. Pufendorf published two books, *Of the Law and Nature of Nations* (1672) and *The Whole Duty of Man According to the Law of Nature* (1673), which claimed that every person has a right to equality and freedom based on his human dignity. He said there is no such person as a natural slave because all master-servant relationships are based on contracts.

Another scholar who preceded Locke was the English politician Algernon Sidney, but his famous work, *Discourses Concerning Civil Government*, was not published until 1698. Sidney had been beheaded in 1683 for participating in a plot to assassinate King Charles II, after a manuscript of his *Discourses* had been introduced at his trial showing that he believed in the right of revolution to achieve social justice.

Locke's natural law principles inspired other people to write about them and apply them to the political issues of the day. In 1697, John Trenchard and Walter Moyle published a pamphlet castigating William III's standing armies and proclaiming there was "no worse state of thraldom than a military power in any government, unchecked and uncontrolled by a civil power." In 1719, Trenchard teamed with a young Scotsman, Thomas Gordon, to write two series of pamphlets, the *Independent Whig* and *Cato's Letters*. These pamphlets became widely known on both sides of the Atlantic for their searing criticism of British politics and England's religious establishment. Bernard Bailyn said in his *Ideological Origins of the American Revolution* that "the writings of Trenchard and Gordon ranked with the treatises of Locke as the most authoritative statement of the nature of political liberty and above Locke as an exposition of the social sources and threats that it faced."[15]

Other British philosophers who influenced American thought were Bishop Benjamin Hoadly, Joseph Priestly and Catharine Macaulay. Hoadly published pamphlets during the early 1700s that repudiated the Anglican doctrines of the church visible, of the divine right of civil and religious leaders and of passive obedience. Priestly was a clergyman, political philosopher and scientist who wrote during the late 1700s. He was best known for his discovery of oxygen in 1774, but in 1769 he published an *Essay on the First Principles of Government, and on the Nature of Political, Civil and Religious Liberty*. Macaulay, a Scottish historian, espoused the ideals of republican government in her eight-volume *History of England from the Ascension of James I to That of the Brunswick Line*, published between 1763 and 1783. In 1775, she endorsed the

American colonial protests against the Québec Act and taxation without representation in her *Address to the People of England, Scotland and Ireland*.

Across the Channel, the philosophers of the French Enlightenment, Baron Charles-Louis Montesquieu, Voltaire and Jean-Jacques Rousseau, were also writing books and essays on the nature of government. In 1748, Montesquieu said in his *Spirit of the Laws* that the three basic forms of government were the republic based on virtue, the monarchy based on honor and the despotic state based on fear. He also said that government best promotes liberty when its legislative, executive and judicial powers are separated into three independent branches. Voltaire wrote a variety of literary and historical works and was best known in America as a critic of religious oppression and authoritarian government. A great admirer of the Quakers, in 1734 he wrote in his *Lettres philosophiques* that William Penn had established "that golden age of which men talk so much and which probably has never existed anywhere except in Pennsylvania."[16] Rousseau said that all men had been free and equal in a state of nature and they were therefore entitled to be free and equal participants in their civil societies. In his *Discourse on the Origin of Inequality* in 1755, he explored the reasons why men were not free and equal in most societies. Then in 1762, he suggested in *The Social Contract* that men could regain their freedom and equality by a social contract in which they gave up all their natural rights to a republican government in exchange for equal civil rights. Rousseau's social contract was similar to Locke's, except that it involved a complete surrender of every man's natural rights. Most Americans disagreed with Rousseau on that point. However, his concepts of equality and democracy became embodied in the statement in the American Declaration of Independence that "all men are created equal" and in the closing words of Lincoln's Gettysburg address, "that government of the people, by the people and for the people, shall not perish from the earth."

Elsewhere in Europe, a prominent Swiss lawyer, Emmerich de Vattel, published *The Law of Nations* in 1758, which applied the

Enlightenment principles of natural law, liberty and equality to international relations. In 1764, a young Italian criminologist, Cesare Beccaria, published a treatise entitled *Crimes and Punishment*, in which he criticized the use of torture to gain confessions, secret trials and brutal punishments. Beccaria's proposals for reform quickly became part of the general call for government reform that was sweeping Europe and America.

When the British government began asserting greater control over American affairs in the 1760s, the colonists began circulating newspapers and pamphlets claiming that their natural rights were being violated by the British government. These papers and pamphlets cited the works of Locke, Trenchard, Gordon and the other European philosophers and reform advocates. Some of the more famous pamphlets were Richard Bland's *The Colonel Dismounted: Or the Rector Vindicated* (Williamsburg, 1764), James Otis's *The Rights of the British Colonies Asserted and Proved* (Boston, 1764), John Dickinson's *Letters from a Farmer in Pennsylvania* (Philadelphia, 1768) and Sam Adams's *The Rights of the Colonists* (Boston, 1772) (App. J).[17]

Without Blackstone's four-volume *Commentaries on the Laws of England*, however, the Americans would have been mere dissenters defying the lawful authority of their British governors. Blackstone showed that the British were the unlawful actors in the colonial conflicts. He explained the same rights of life, liberty and property that the colonists were asserting and said they were absolute rights that originated from the law of nature, not from any law of human government (BL3, 120). They were not the mere gifts of Parliament, to be given or taken on the whim of a majority vote. They were the pre-existing, natural rights of all people, and all governments were bound to observe them (BL1, 41, 42-43). These statements carried great weight because Blackstone was a highly respected legal scholar, especially among British royalty and nobility. He was solicitor general to the queen and a conservative Tory member of Parliament. In 1770, the year after he had published the last of his *Commentaries*, King George III knighted him for his scholarship and appointed him judge of the Common

Pleas Court. Even if had they desired to do so, the king and his counselors could not have turned around and attacked Blackstone's account of the absolute rights of people.

From the moment the first volume was published in 1765, Blackstone's *Commentaries* were well received in America. In a speech to the House of Commons in 1775, Edmund Burke said he had heard that nearly as many copies of Blackstone had been sold in America as in England.[18] The books were purchased by not only lawyers but, as Burke called them, "smatterers in law." Blackstone's biographer Lewis Warden estimates that twenty-five hundred sets of the *Commentaries* were sold in America before the Declaration of Independence was signed.[19] According to the publisher's subscription list, sixteen purchasers became signers of the Declaration and six became signers of the Constitution. In the backwoods county of Dunmore, Virginia (now Shenandoah County), a boy named John Marshall read all four volumes of the *Commentaries* before he turned sixteen in 1771. He then read them three more times before taking his bar exam.[20] Marshall later became chief justice of the United States Supreme Court. The noted historian Daniel J. Boorstin wrote,

> Blackstone was to American law what Noah Webster's blue-back speller was to be to American literacy. With nothing more than the four volumes of the *Commentaries* at hand, anyone--however far from ancient professional centers, from courts or legislatures--could become an amateur lawyer. Blackstone was a godsend to the rising American, to the ambitious backwoodsman and the aspiring politician.[21]

While the British government was depriving them of their basic rights of life, liberty and property, it was only natural that thousands of Americans would want to learn more about those rights by reading Blackstone's *Commentaries*.

D. John Wilkes

While the American colonists were asserting their rights, a major controversy over the same rights was taking place in England.

Many Englishmen resented the way the new king, George III, was meddling in the affairs of Parliament and misusing his royal prerogative. He was securing votes for his proposed laws and ministerial candidates by various forms of bribery, including promises to grant titles of nobility to members of the House of Commons. In that manner, the young king was able to elevate his allies in the House of Commons to permanent positions in the House of Lords, while those who opposed him still had to seek re-election in order to hold on to their positions.

During this time, a newspaper called *The North Briton* published a series of articles that criticized the king and his ministers. One issue said the ministers had given too many concessions to France in the peace treaty ending the Seven Years War. It called them "tools of despotism and corruption." Then, on April 23, 1763, *The North Briton No. 45* did the unthinkable. It criticized the king's address to Parliament. It also warned that

> [t]he prerogative of the crown is to exert the constitutional powers entrusted to it in a way, not of blind favor and partiality, but of wisdom and judgment. . . . The people too have *their* prerogative.[22]

Prime Minister George Grenville was so incensed he ordered his secretary of state to obtain a general warrant to find and arrest everyone connected with the paper. High government officials tore through private homes, seizing papers and arresting nearly fifty people. John Wilkes, a member of Parliament, was among those arrested. When he refused to answer questions, he was sent to the Tower of London. Wilkes protested that the general warrant was illegal and claimed Parliamentary privilege. Chief Justice Pratt of the House of Lords agreed and ordered his release.

Wilkes also sued the secretary of state and the arresting officer for trespass, on the ground that their general warrant was illegal. Chief Justice Pratt again intervened and instructed the Common Pleas Court to rule that the general warrants were illegal. The jury awarded Wilkes £5,000 damages, £4,000 to be paid by the secretary of state for issuing the illegal warrant and £1,000 to be paid by the officer who made the illegal search of Wilkes's private home. The verdict was rendered in 1763, only a year after the Massachusetts Superior Court had ruled that British customs officials could use general warrants to search the homes of American colonists.

In 1765, the House of Lords ruled that general warrants were illegal in the case of *Entick v. Carrington and Three Other King's Messengers*.[23] These were general search warrants that government officials had used to gain entry to a private home and break open desks and boxes of papers. The House of Lords upheld a jury verdict that the officials had committed a trespass against the owner of the house. In 1766, the House of Commons passed a special resolution condemning general warrants as "illegal and obnoxious."

In the first volume of his *Commentaries*, Blackstone said that a warrant or some other authorization by a judge was required before a person could be detained in prison. That was one of the basic rights of liberty, he said, explaining it as follows:

> To make imprisonment lawful, it must either be, by process from the courts of judicature, or by warrant from some legal officer, having authority to commit to prison: which warrant must be in writing, under the hand and seal of the magistrate, and express the causes of the commitment, in order to be examined into (if necessary) upon a *habeas corpus*. (BL3, 132-133)

In his fourth volume, published in 1769, Blackstone addressed the issue of whether a general warrant satisfied the warrant requirement that he had described in his first volume:

> A *general* warrant to apprehend all persons suspected, without naming or particularly describing any person in special, is illegal and void for its uncertainty; for it is the duty of the magistrate, and ought not to be left to the officer, to judge the ground of suspicion. And a warrant to apprehend all persons guilty of a crime therein specified, is no legal warrant: for the point, upon which its authority rests, is a fact to be decided on a subsequent trial; namely, whether the person apprehended thereupon is really guilty or not. It is therefore no warrant at all: for it will not justify the officer who acts under it; . . . .[24]

Thus, within eight years after James Otis had challenged their validity in the Massachusetts Superior Court, general warrants were declared illegal and obnoxious by the House of Lords, the House of Commons and queen's solicitor general.

Meanwhile, John Wilkes became a national hero. Parliament voted to expel him and send him into exile for his libelous publications, but in 1768, he returned to England to campaign for another seat. He was elected, expelled, elected again and expelled again. He was also thrown into prison for publishing an obscene parody of Pope's *Essay on Man*, called *Essay on Woman*. After his release from prison, he was elected Lord Mayor of London and elected again to Parliament. The news of Wilkes's trials and tribulations was followed closely by the American colonists, and these events played a major role in shaping American views on searches and seizures of private property, arrests of criminal suspects and freedom of the press.

E. The Power of Parliament

On October 7, 1763, while the people of England were debating the ethics and wisdom of the king and his ministers, King George proclaimed that no colonists would be permitted to settle west of the Appalachian Mountains.[25] Most colonists saw this order, confining them to their coastal regions, as an attempt to thwart their desire to develop their own economies and become less dependent on trade with England.

The following year, Parliament tried to capitalize on Britain's captive colonial trade by passing the Revenue Act. That act reduced the duties on molasses but more than made up for the reduction with new duties on wine, silk and linen. Most colonists viewed these duties as an unfair burden. Many also believed that Parliament had no right to tax them because of their ancient right to be taxed only by consent of their elected representatives. That right had originated in the Confirmation Charter of King Edward I, granted in 1297, which said that for no business from henceforth, shall we take such manner of aids, tasks, and taxes of our kingdom, but by the common consent of all the realm, and for the common profit thereof; saving the ancient aids and taxes accustomed.[26]

Some colonists also objected to the Revenue Act because it provided that accused violators could be tried in the admiralty courts, where there were no jury trials. The right of trial by jury had been established in Chapter 52 of the Magna Charta, which said that if any people had been disseised or dispossessed, without a legal verdict of their peers, of their lands, castles, liberties or rights, those things would be immediately restored to them (App. A).

The Revenue Act caught the attention of a group of Bostonians who were ready to criticize the British government at every opportunity. Their leader was Sam Adams, a second cousin of John Adams. Sam Adams had spent most of his time in tavern political debates, while the malt liquor business he had inherited from his father deteriorated. In the 1750s, he formed a political action club whose newspaper earned the nickname the "Whippingpost," because of its criticism of local royal governors. He also gained the following of several young Harvard intellectuals, including Dr. Joseph Warren and Benjamin Church. However, most people paid little attention to Adams and his followers until 1764.

In May of that year, Adams introduced a resolution at a Boston town meeting that called for repeal of the Revenue Act. He argued that the Act set a dangerous precedent because Parliament might eventually tax everything the colonists owned. The resolution passed and was sent to the Massachusetts House of Representatives. James Otis led the House debates on the matter and was appointed to send a letter to the colony's London agent, Jasper Mauduit, telling him to seek Parliament's repeal of the new law. The letter included Adams's resolution, which contained the following paragraph:

> But what still heightens our apprehensions is that these unexpected proceedings may be preparatory to new taxations upon us: for if our

trade be taxed, why not our lands? Why not the produce of our lands and everything we possess and make use of? This we apprehend annihilates our charter right to govern and tax ourselves. It strikes at our British privileges, which, as we have never forfeited them, we hold in common with our fellow subjects who are natives of Britain: if taxes are laid upon us in any shape without our having a legal representation where they are laid, are we not reduced from the character of free subjects to the miserable state of tributary slaves?

In the main body of his letter, Otis argued that the colonists were entitled to the absolute rights of Englishmen, including the exclusive right to tax themselves, because those rights were derived from the law of nature and were guaranteed by the colonial charters:

> The absolute rights of Englishmen, as frequently declared in Parliament, from Magna Carta to this time, are the rights of *personal security*, *personal liberty*, and of *private property*. .
> The allegiance of British subjects being natural, perpetual, and inseparable from their persons, let them be in what country they may, their rights are also natural, inherent, and perpetual.
> By the laws of nature and of nations, the voice of universal reason, and of God, when a nation takes possession of a desert, uncultivated, and uninhabited country, or purchases of savages, as was the case with far the greatest part of the British settlements, the colonists, transplanting themselves and their posterity, though separated from the principal establishment of the mother country, naturally became part of the state with its ancient possessions, and entitled to all the essential rights of the mother country. This is not only confirmed by the practice of the ancients but by the moderns ever since the discovery of America. Frenchmen, Spaniards, and Portugals are no greater slaves abroad than at home; and hitherto Britons have been as free on one side of the Atlantic as on the other: and it is humbly hoped that His Majesty and the Parliament will in their wisdom be graciously pleased to continue the colonists in this happy state.
> It is presumed that upon these principles the colonists have been by their several charters declared natural subjects and entrusted with the power of making *their own laws*, not repugnant to the laws of England, and with *the power of taxing themselves*. . . . .

Otis then explained that he was not questioning the general power of Parliament to govern the colonies, but he was asserting that its power was limited by certain fundamental principles that the judges of England had recognized were part of Britain's unwritten constitution:

> The question is not upon the general power or right of Parliament, but whether it is not circumscribed within some equitable and reasonable bounds. 'Tis hoped it will not be considered as a new doctrine that even the authority of the Parliament of *Great Britain* is circumscribed by certain bounds which if exceeded their acts become those of mere *power* without *right*, and consequently void. The judges of England have declared in favor of these sentiments when they expressly declare that *acts against the fundamental principles of the British constitution are void.*‡ [See App. G for full text of Otis's footnote] This doctrine is agreeable to the law of nature and nations, and to the divine dictates of natural and revealed religion. It is contrary to reason that the supreme power should have the right to alter the constitution. This would imply that those who are entrusted with sovereignty by the people have a right to do as they please.[27]

Copies of Otis's letter were sent to other colonies. Otis also published a pamphlet entitled *The Rights of the British Colonies Asserted and Proved* (Boston, 1764), which said that Parliament could regulate the affairs of the colonists but only to the extent that it did not violate their fundamental rights. These rights included their freedom from taxation of any kind, except by colonial legislatures in which they had representatives, and their freedom from the jurisdiction of admiralty judges who "can take just what they please." Another Boston lawyer, Oxenbridge Thacher, published a pamphlet entitled *The Sentiments of a British American* (Boston, 1764), which also argued that Parliament had no right to tax the colonists or to try their violations of the tax laws in the admiralty courts. Thacher explained his objections to the admiralty courts as follows:

> The power therein given the courts of admiralty alarms them greatly. The common law is the birthright of every subject, and trial

by jury a most darling privilege. So deemed our ancestors in ancient times, long before the colonies were begun to be planted.[28] . . . In this particular the colonists are put under a quite different law from all the rest of the King's subjects: jurisdiction is nowhere else given to court of admiralty of matters so foreign from their connusance. In some things the colonists have been long subject to this cruel yoke, and have indeed fully experienced its galling nature. Loud complaints have been long made by them of the oppressions of these courts, their exorbitant fees, and the little justice the subject may expect from them in cases of seizures. Let me mention one thing that is notorious: these courts have assumed (I know not by what law) a commission of five per cent to the judge on all seizures condemned. What chance does the subject stand for his right upon the best claim when the judge, condemning, is to have a hundred or perhaps five hundred pounds, and acquitting, less than twenty shillings? . . .

But in the act we are considering, the power of these courts is even much enlarged and made still more grievous. For it is thereby enacted that the seizor may inform in any court of admiralty for the particular colony, or in any court of admiralty to be appointed over all America, at his pleasure. Thus a malicious seizor may take the goods of any man, ever so lawfully and duly imported, and carry the trial of the cause to a thousand miles distance, where for mere want of ability to follow, the claimer shall be incapable of defending his right. At the same time an hardship is laid upon the claimer; this claim is not to be admitted or heard until he find sureties to prosecute, who are to be of known ability in the place where security is given. And he, being unknown in a place so distance from home, whatever be his estate, shall be incapable of producing such sureties. . . . And if the judge of admiralty will certify that there was probable cause of seizure, no action shall be maintained by the claimant though his goods on trial appear to be ever so duly imported and liable to no sort of forfeiture, and he hath been forced to expend ever so much in defense of them. This last regulation is peculiarly confined to America.[29]

Colonists outside Massachusetts also published pamphlets criticizing the Revenue Act. The Rhode Island and Connecticut legislatures issued pamphlets written by their respective governors, Stephen Hopkins and Thomas Fitch. Like Thacher, Hopkins attacked the law's enforcement provisions that extended the powers of the admiralty courts. Hopkins and Fitch both criticized the law's unfair economic burden, but they did not say that Parliament had no right to tax the colonists, as Adams, Otis and Thacher had said. In *The Rights of the Colonies Examined* (Providence, 1764), Hopkins acknowledged that Parliament had the power to regulate certain general matters concerning the colonies, such as money, paper credit and commerce between each colony and the rest of the empire. That power included duties on colonial imports. Governor Fitch of Connecticut reached the same conclusion in *Reasons Why the British Colonies in America Should Not Be Charged with Internal Taxes* (New Haven, 1764) by arguing that Parliament had the power to regulate the external affairs of the colonies, while their internal affairs were the exclusive province of their local legislatures. Richard Bland of Virginia made the same distinction in *The Colonel Dismounted, or the Rector Vindicated?* (Williamsburg, 1764), a pamphlet that defended Virginia's right to enforce its Two Penny Act relating to the salaries paid to Anglican parsons.[30]

The colonial pamphlets thus criticized the British government for a variety of reasons, and not all of them questioned Parliament's power to tax their imported goods. Most colonists agreed, however, that Parliament had no power to tax the goods they made and sold to each other, because that was an internal matter for their own legislatures to decide.

F. The Sons of Liberty

Prime Minister Grenville did not think that Parliament's taxing powers were limited in any respect. Near the end of 1764, he also concluded that Britain needed more money from the colonies than the Revenue Act would provide. He therefore recommended that Parliament repeal the Revenue Act and substitute a tax system that would cover a wider range of goods and a larger number of colonists. Parliament approved Grenville's new plan, and on March 22, 1765, it passed the Stamp Act.

The Stamp Act was the first British tax law that covered products that the colonists made and sold to each other. Every sheet of every copy of a newspaper or pamphlet was taxed a shilling (twelve pence).[31] Two shillings were assessed on every advertisement in a newspaper or pamphlet, four pence on every one-year calendar, two pounds (forty shillings) on every school diploma and one shilling on every deck of playing cards. The new law also imposed taxes on various kinds of commercial paper used by the colonists in the conduct of their businesses, including bonds for securing the payment of money, shipping documents and titles to land and other property. A special sheet of stamped paper had to be attached to all products and documents subject to the tax. If commercial paper subject to the tax did not have the stamped paper attached, the courts were directed to rule the transaction void. Like the Revenue Act, violations of the Stamp Act could be tried in admiralty courts, where there was no trial by jury.

The Stamp Act told the colonists that Parliament was not listening to them. All the arguments and concerns they had voiced during the previous year had been to no avail. Some members of Parliament voted against the Stamp Act because they knew the colonists would be angry. One member, Colonel Isaac Barré, who had served with the British army in America, predicted that the Stamp Act would cause trouble, because similar acts had "caused the blood of those *sons of liberty* [emphasis added] to recoil within them."[32]

The Stamp Act was not to take effect until November 1, 1765. However, the colonists began protesting as soon they heard the news in May 1765. *The Maryland Gazette* carried the headline, "Thunderstruck."[33] The news publishers were upset because they were among the hardest hit by the tax. Some questioned whether the colonial freedom of the press was under attack. *The Pennsylvania Journal and Weekly Advertiser* said it would be forced to suspend publication because of the new law. In New York City, town criers circulated copies of the Stamp Act with the headline, "The folly of England, and the ruin of America."[34]

On May 29, 1765, the twenty-nine-year-old Patrick Henry, in his ninth day in the Virginia House of Burgesses, introduced a set of resolutions protesting the Stamp Act and claiming that Parliament had no right to tax Virginians without the consent of their elected representatives. Henry reminded his colleagues that their charter of 1606 had guaranteed that all Virginia colonists and their descendants would enjoy their English liberties "as if they had been abiding and born within this our realm of England." At the end of his speech, Henry proclaimed, "Caesar had his Brutus, Charles the First his Cromwell and George the Third may profit by their example!" Cries of "Treason!" rang out, to which he replied, "If this be treason, make the most of it!" The Virginia assembly responded by passing most of Henry's resolutions on the following day.

In cities throughout the colonies, groups of middle-class citizens, taking a cue from Barré's speech and calling themselves "Sons of Liberty," organized demonstrations against the Stamp Act. Riots broke out in Boston, Newport, New York City and Charleston. Homes of government officials were attacked and looted.

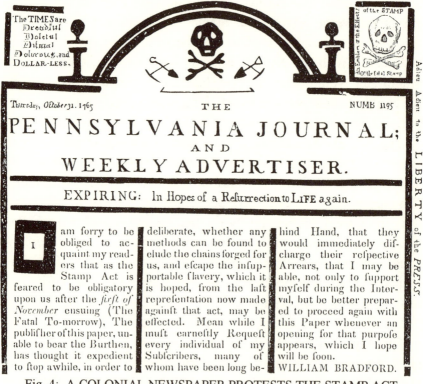

Fig. 4: A COLONIAL NEWSPAPER PROTESTS THE STAMP ACT

Sam Adams disclaimed responsibility for the Boston riots. However, he and his friends had probably put up the clever display that led to one of them. One morning in August 1765, the citizens of Boston awoke to find an elm tree across from Boylston Square decorated with an effigy of Andrew Oliver, the newly appointed stamp tax collector for the colony. Also hanging from the tree was a boot, which everyone understood to represent Lord Bute, a former prime minister who was the companion of King George's mother and one of his most trusted advisors. Popping from the top of the boot was a dummy dressed as the devil and holding a copy of the Stamp Act. A crowd gathered around the tree and some people invited others to bow down before the dummy and have it stamp their goods. At dusk, forty to fifty tradesmen cut down Oliver's effigy and carried it through the streets of Boston to his house, where they lit a bonfire and tore down his gazebo. They also entered his house, where they did more damage. Fortunately, Oliver had been forewarned and had escaped with his family to a safe hiding place.[35]

Later that month, another riot broke out in Boston. The colonists burned the records of the Vice Admiralty Court, where evidence of smuggling had been kept. They also broke into the home of the tax collector's brother-in-law, Lieutenant Governor Thomas Hutchinson, the same person who had upheld the validity of writs of assistance when he was chief justice of the Superior Court. The rioting colonists destroyed Hutchinson's furniture, paintings and part of his library of books and manuscripts.[36] Hutchinson had a large collection of original documents relating to the early history of the New England colonies, including transcripts of the trial of his great-great grandmother, the Puritan dissenter Anne Hutchinson. Fortunately, many of these documents survived.

After receiving the Virginia House resolutions, the Massachusetts House of Representatives voted on June 8 to send a letter to the other colonies, recommending a joint congress to discuss the problems created by the Stamp Act. Nine colonies sent delegates to the Stamp Act Congress, which convened in the New York City Hall on October 7, 1765. The Virginia, North Carolina and

Georgia legislatures were not able to appoint delegates because their governors would not authorize them to meet. The New Jersey and Delaware governors also refused to convene their legislatures, but they met informally and selected delegates who paid their own way. The New Hampshire legislature did not send anyone but announced that it would sign any resolution adopted by the congress. On October 19, 1765, the Stamp Act Congress adopted thirteen resolutions addressed to King George III. These asserted that Parliament had no power to impose taxes on the colonists or to extend the jurisdiction of the admiralty courts as provided by the Act (App. H, pars. VI and VIII).

In addition to the resolutions by the Stamp Act Congress and the Virginia House of Burgesses, other resolutions were published by the Massachusetts House of Representatives, the town of Braintree, Massachusetts and the court of Northampton County, Virginia.[37] Sam Adams wrote the Massachusetts House resolution and John Adams the Braintree resolution.

At the same time, some colonists circulated pamphlets that defended Parliament's power to tax them. One of these pamphlets was a printed form of a letter that had been written by Martin Howard of Halifax, Nova Scotia, to a friend in Rhode Island in February 1765. A prominent attorney who had once lived in Rhode Island, Howard argued that Parliament could tax the American colonists because they were virtually represented in Parliament, in the same way as the non-voting people of England were represented. An Englishman had to own land in order to vote, so even wealthy copyholders and leaseholders could not choose representatives to Parliament. That meant, said Howard,

> [a] worthless freeholder of forty shillings per annum can vote for a member of Parliament, whereas a merchant, though worth one hundred pounds sterling, if it consist of only his personal effects, has no vote at all. But yet let no one suppose that the interest of the latter is not equally the object of Parliamentary attention with the latter.[38]

Several months later, a pamphlet by Soame Jenyns, an English member of Parliament, pointed out that even some landowners, including those in Birmingham, Leeds and Manchester, could not vote in Parliamentary elections. Jenyns did not argue that these people were virtually represented. He simply said the facts proved that not all Englishmen were free of taxation without representation, as the Americans were claiming. He then commented,

> I am well aware that I shall hear Locke, Sidney, Selden, and many other great names quoted to prove that every Englishman, whether he has a right to vote for a representative or not, is still represented in the British Parliament; in which opinion they all agree. On what principle of common sense this opinion is founded I comprehend not, but on the authority of such respectable names I shall not acknowledge its truth; but then I will ask one question, and on that I will rest the whole merits of the cause. Why does not this imaginary representation extend to America as well as over the whole island of Great Britain? If it can travel 300 miles, why not 3,000? If it can jump over rivers and mountains, why cannot it sail over the ocean? If the towns of Manchester and Birmingham, sending no representatives to Parliament, are notwithstanding there represented, why are not the cities of Albany and Boston equally represented in that assembly? Are they not alike British subjects? Are they not Englishmen? Or are they only Englishmen when they solicit for protection, but not Englishmen when taxes are required to enable this country to protect them?[39]

Thomas Whately and William Knox, British politicians who later served as undersecretaries of state, also published pamphlets claiming the colonists were virtually represented in Parliament. Whately cited the long-standing postal fees the colonists had paid as evidence that they had accepted Parliament's power to levy internal taxes. He apparently did not appreciate the difference between a government tax on products and services that people deliver to each other and a postage fee that people pay for hiring the government to deliver their mail. Knox based his argument on Parliament's supreme authority over the colonies, which included its unlimited power to tax. He did recommend, however, that because members of Parliament would not suffer from oppressive laws applied to Americans, "a peculiar tenderness be observed in laying taxes on the colonies."[40]

In March 1765, James Otis responded to Howard's virtual representation argument with a pamphlet entitled *A Vindication of the British Colonies*. He said the non-voting people of England "are justly deemed as represented. They have all fathers, brothers, friends, or neighbors in the House of Commons, and many *ladies* have husbands there. Few of the members have any of these endearing ties to America." In October 1765, a Maryland lawyer, Daniel Dulany, answered the Jenyns, Whately and Knox pamphlets. He said the lessees, copyholders and other non-voting classes should not be considered ineligible to vote because they could acquire the right to vote by buying land near where they lived. These non-voting classes of people also had the same interests as those who could vote because of their mutual connection among neighbors, friends and relations. This inseparable connection gave the non-voting people security against oppression--the same oppression would fall on the voters and their chosen representatives. Dulany also pointed out that the English non-voters had no actual representatives in any legislature having the power to levy taxes. Excusing these people from taxation would therefore excuse them from all taxes while they reaped the benefits of a government paid for by their own friends and neighbors, who were also providing their security against oppression. Dulany said these reasons provided the only possible justification for holding the non-electors of England virtually represented in Parliament. Because none of these reasons applied to the American colonists, they could not be said to be virtually represented.[41]

Otis presented another argument that showed why the American colonists viewed the taxation question as an extremely important matter. Howard had said that representation in Parliament would avail the colonists very little, "unless you can suppose that a few American members could bias the deliberations of the whole British legislature." He obviously assumed that the two million people in America would not be represented in the same proportion as the six million people then living in England, nor would the Americans' future representation reflect their anticipated population increase. Otis answered that though a representation would avail the colonies very little in this generation, yet to posterity it might be an invaluable blessing. It may also in future ages be very beneficial to Great Britain. Is it to be believed that when a continent of 3000 miles in length shall have more inhabitants than there are at this day in Great Britain, France and Ireland, perhaps all of Europe, they will be quite content with the bare name of British subjects, and to the end of time supinely acquiesce in laws made, as it may happen, against their interest by an assembly 3000 miles beyond the sea, and where, should they agree with the sentiments of the Halifax gentleman, it may be thought that an admission of an American member would "sully and defile the purity of the whole body"? One hundred years will give this continent more inhabitants than there are in the three kingdoms.[42]

The stamp taxes took effect on November 1, 1765. Later that month, copies of the first volume of Blackstone's *Commentaries* were sent to America. Blackstone confirmed one of the absolute rights of property:

[N]o subject of England can be constrained to pay any aids or taxes, even for the defence of the realm or the support of government, but such as are imposed by his own consent, or that of his representatives in parliament. (BL3, 135)

Although he did not explain how non-voting Englishmen gave their consent to be taxed, Blackstone admitted the rules governing Parliamentary elections were arbitrary. In his chapter "Of the Parliament," he said, "[I]f any alteration might be wished or suggested in the present frame of parliaments, it should be in favour of a more complete representation of the people." On the other hand, Blackstone did not believe this was a pressing problem, because "there is hardly a free agent but what is entitled to a vote in some place or other in the kingdom."[43] He seemed to be oblivious to the American situation.

On the day the Stamp Act took effect, New Yorkers flew their flags at half mast to proclaim the death of American freedom. The New York Sons of Liberty burned an effigy of their unpopular lieutenant governor, Cadwallader Colden. They also burned his carriages and the house of a British army officer. Throughout the colonies, most people ignored the Act and went on with their business as usual, without buying the required stamped paper. Some refused in protest, while others were afraid of retribution by the Sons of Liberty. Most colonial merchants also refused to ship or receive goods from England, as they followed through on the Stamp Act Congress's threat in its Resolution XI "[t]hat the restrictions imposed by the several late Acts of Parliament on the trade of these colonies will render them unable to purchase the Manufactures of Great Britain" (App. H).

Meanwhile, agents of the colonial legislatures were in London lobbying to get the Stamp Act repealed. Benjamin Franklin represented the Pennsylvania legislature. Many members of Parliament were sympathetic to their cause, especially after the new prime minister, the Marquess of Rockingham, announced that he favored repeal. He believed that the difficulties of enforcing the new law were not worth the ill feelings it was causing in both England and America. The London merchants joined the repeal movement with a petition to Parliament. Their businesses depended so much on trade with America, it said, that "nothing less than its utter ruin is apprehended, without the immediate interposition of parliament."[44]

Parliament took up a bill to repeal the Stamp Act in January 1766. The debate featured two former prime ministers, George Grenville and William Pitt. Pitt said in defense of the colonists,

> I have been charged with giving birth to sedition in America. I rejoice that America has resisted. . . . The gentleman asks, "When were the colonies emancipated?" But I desire to know, when were they made slaves?[45]

Pitt also disputed the contention that the American colonists were virtually represented in Parliament, using the same arguments that Otis and Dulany had put forth.[46]

On February 22, 1766, Parliament repealed the Stamp Act, 274 votes to 134. On March 18, however, it passed the Declaratory Act, proclaiming that whereas the American colonies had passed certain resolutions "derogatory to the legislative authority of Parliament, and inconsistent with the dependency of the said colonies . . . ," the king and parliament had full power to make laws for the colonies "in all cases whatsoever."[47] That implied to the colonists that Parliament had no obligation to respect their basic rights. To make matters worse, Blackstone said in the first volume of his *Commentaries* that the American colonists were not entitled to enjoy the common law rights that were "the birthright of every English subject." That apparently included the rights that he described in his chapter entitled "The Absolute Rights of Individuals." He explained that America had been inhabited by other people, namely the Indians, and therefore the laws of those people, not the English common law, originally applied to the American colonists. He then reasoned that when the British government had replaced the governments of the Indians, it had gained the power to repeal the Indian laws and make other laws. By saying the common law did not apply in America, Blackstone gave the impression that the British authorities could enforce these other laws without regard to the absolute rights of the colonists. In contrast, the British authorities had to respect the common-law rights of people in territories that were previously uninhabited, because the common law guaranteeing those people's rights came into force as soon as the British occupied their territories (BL2, 104-105).

Because it rejected the colonists' claims to their fundamental rights, the Declaratory Act appeared to say that when the colonists settled the American territories, Parliament gained the power to take away the rights of both the Indians and the colonists. Some might say the colonists deserved that treatment because they had stolen the lands of the Indians. However, in many cases the colonists had paid the Indians for their land. In the cases where they had not, their act of conquest was a joint act between the colonists and the British government. Neither party was therefore in a position to question the morality of the other. Also, the colonists did not have to prove they deserved their fundamental rights; they were inalienable rights derived from the social contract basis of all government. They were also derived from the Magna

Charta, which the noble descendants of William the Conqueror's army had forced King John to sign in order to preserve their rights in property taken from the Saxons. Many of the American colonial charters granted by the English kings had guaranteed that all the colonists and their descendants would retain the English rights guaranteed by the Magna Charta. Blackstone also said that the absolute rights of individuals to life, liberty and property were vested in people by the immutable law of nature and that every man is entitled to enjoy those rights whether out of society or in it (BL3, 120, 119). He said the law of nature is superior to all other laws, is binding all over the globe, in all countries at all times, and that no human laws are of any validity if contrary to the law of nature (BL1, 41). Finally, he said that people are bound to disobey human laws that force them to violate the law of nature (BL1, 42-43).[48] The British treatment of their American colonies also conflicted with the philosophy of Emmerich de Vattel who had written in his *Law of Nations*,

> When a nation takes possession of a different country and settles a colony there, that country, though separated from the principal establishment, or mother country, naturally becomes part of the state equally with its ancient possessions. Whenever the political laws or treaties make no distinction between them everything said of the territory of a nation ought also to extend to its colonies. (App. G)

Martin Howard agreed with de Vattel's statement. He conceded in his *Halifax Letter* that the rights "of life, liberty and estate, are secured to us by the common law, which is every subject's birthright, whether born in Great Britain, on the ocean, or in the colonies; and it is in this sense we are said to enjoy all the rights and privileges of Englishmen."[49] However, he said the personal rights of the colonists were different from their political rights: their power to govern themselves by their own legislatures, spelled out in their various colonial charters, was subject to revocation by Parliament.

In his *Vindication* pamphlet, Otis interpreted Howard's letter to mean that Parliament could revoke the colonists' rights of personal security, personal liberty and private property. He cited Blackstone's statement that these rights are "are the absolute liberties of Englishmen" (App. I)[50] and argued that they were not mere privileges that Parliament could take away arbitrarily. Otis apparently overlooked Howard's concession that the colonists were as much entitled to these rights as any Englishman.

The real disagreement between Howard and Otis was over the nature and breadth of these rights. Howard said the right of the colonists to be taxed only by their elected representatives had not been violated because they were virtually represented in Parliament. Otis said the colonists were not virtually represented because they had "no endearing ties" to the members of Parliament. Howard also said that "the new instituted court of admiralty and the power given the seizor" (to deny the right of trial by jury and to issue general warrants) was justified because, if

> customs are due the crown; if illicit commerce is to be put an end to as ruinous to the welfare of the nation . . . [and if] these ends could not be compassed or obtained in the common and ordinary way, tell me, what could the government do but to apply a remedy desperate as the disease?[51]

Many colonists, including Otis, had an answer to that question. They had never surrendered their absolute rights to any government. They were therefore determined to resist all attempts by the British government to exceed its "common and ordinary" powers, regardless of the consequences.

In 1767, more disputes arose over Parliament's authority to govern the colonies. The Quartering Act, passed by Parliament in 1765, required all colonial governments to house British soldiers and furnish them with supplies, including beer and rum. When two regiments of British soldiers arrived in New York City in 1766, the colonial Assembly complied with the Quartering Act in most respects, but it refused to provide a few supplies, including the beer and rum. Parliament therefore passed a law on July 2, 1767, declaring that all laws passed by the New York Assembly after October 1, 1767 would be void, unless and until the Assembly fully complied with the Quartering Act. In one of his *Letters from a Pennsylvania Farmer*, dated November 5, 1767, John Dickinson argued that when Parliament forced the colonists to give supplies to the British soldiers, under penalty of voiding the acts of their own legislatures, it had chosen yet another way of imposing taxes on them without their consent. The law suspending the acts of the New York Assembly, he said, therefore violated the natural liberty of the colonists.[52]

The New York Assembly law had been sponsored by Britain's new chancellor of the exchequer, Charles Townshend, known as "Champaign Charlie" because of his entertaining speeches in Parliament after the cocktail hour. He also sponsored the Townshend Revenue Act, passed June 29, 1967, which taxed the colonists on imported paper, paint, lead, glass, wine and tea. Because the taxes applied only to imported products, this law was arguably within Parliament's power to regulate commerce between the colonies and the rest of the empire. However, it provided for writs of assistance

> to authorize and impower the officers of his Majesty's customs to enter and go into any house, warehouse, shop, cellar, or other place in the *British* colonies or plantations in *America*, [and] to search for and seize prohibited and uncustomed goods, ...[53]

Another Townshend Act, the Trade and Navigation Act, empowered the admiralty courts to try violations of the Townshend Revenue Act. Mercy Otis Warren, the sister of James Otis, criticized the Townshend Acts in her 1805 history book, saying the admiralty courts

> were vested with certain powers that dispensed with the mode of trial by jury, annihilated the privileges of Englishmen, and placed the liberty of every man in the hand of a petty officer of the customs. By warrant of a writ of assistance from the governor or lieutenant governor, any officer of the revenue was authorized to enter the dwelling of the most respectable inhabitant on the smallest suspicion of a concealment of contraband goods, and to insult, search or seize, with impunity.[54]

These writs of assistance, or "general warrants," had been declared illegal by the House of Lords in 1765, and "illegal and obnoxious" by the House of Commons in 1766. Warren also pointed out that Blackstone, "in his excellent commentaries on the laws of England, has observed, 'that trial by jury and the liberties of the people went out together.'"[55] Parliament apparently did not believe the American colonists were entitled to these fundamental rights.

The Townshend Revenue Act also directed that a portion of the revenues collected from the colonists be use to pay the salaries of the colonial governors and judges. That removed their salaries from the control of the colonial legislatures. Another Townshend Act made the judges' salaries dependent on the number of convictions they ordered.

In spite of colonists' concerns over these issues, their protests against the Townshend Acts were not as violent as their protests against the Stamp Act. Sam Adams told his followers, "No mobs, no confusions, no tumult." They concentrated instead on pamphlets, letters and petitions. On February 11, 1768, the Massachusetts House of Representatives sent a petition to King George telling him why the Townshend Acts violated their fundamental rights and asking that they be repealed. Written by James Otis and Sam Adams, the petition argued that Parliament had no power to levy taxes on American imports if their sole purpose were to generate revenue rather than regulate trade. The petition also questioned "whether any People can be said to enjoy any degree of Freedom" if the king should determine the salaries of the governor and the judges "without the Consent of the people & at their expense."[56]

G. A Test of Wills

In his *Commentaries*, Blackstone said that every individual had the right to petition the king or parliament for "the redress of grievances" (BL3, 138-139). He listed that right among the auxiliary rights necessary for securing the basic rights of personal security, liberty and property. However, King George and his ministers considered the Massachusetts petition an affront to their absolute right to govern the colonies. They were also upset that copies of the petition were being circulated throughout the colonies. Lord Hillsborough, who held the newly created post of British secretary for the colonies, demanded that the Massachusetts House of Representatives repeal its petition and recant what it had said. He also ordered the Massachusetts governor to dissolve the legislature if it did not carry out his command.[57]

No one knows what might have happened had the king merely denied the Massachusetts petition. The Massachusetts House refused to cower under the British threat of reprisal. On June 21, 1768, it voted ninety-two to seventeen to confirm its petition. On the following day, the House was dissolved by Massachusetts Governor Francis Bernard.

The conflict between the colonists and the British government thus took on another dimension. No longer were the issues confined to taxes, warrants and jury trials. The colonists were now defending their rights to petition the king, to speak freely and to assert all their rights as free Englishmen. They sought to identify themselves with John Wilkes, who was currently trying to regain his seat in Parliament. The Massachusetts Sons of Liberty sent Wilkes two turtles. One weighed forty-five pounds, because the battle cry of the Wilkes campaign was "45," short for the *North Briton No. 45*, the newspaper that had started the Wilkes controversy. The other turtle weighed forty-seven pounds, so that the weight of the two turtles combined was ninety-two pounds. Ninety-two was the number of Massachusetts legislators who had voted to confirm their petition to King George. A Boston silversmith, Paul Revere, made a silver bowl engraved with a dedication to the "Immortal 92," as well as other slogans, including "Wilkes and Liberty" and "No General Warrants." The South Carolina Assembly sent fifteen hundred pounds to the Wilkes campaign for his re-election to Parliament.[58]

While the Massachusetts House had been debating its response to the British threats of reprisal, another conflict was taking place in the Boston Harbor. In May 1768, a fifty-gun British battleship, the

Romney, arrived in the Boston harbor to help enforce the customs laws. A month later, while the *Romney* stood by, British customs officials seized the merchant ship *Liberty*, owned by one of Boston's wealthiest merchants, John Hancock. The seizure was based on a customs inspector's statement that he had boarded the *Liberty* during the previous month and the ship's captain had held him captive inside a cabin while casks of undeclared wine were unloaded. Unfortunately, by the time the inspector told his story, the ship's captain had died and was not available to refute what the inspector had said. The captain's presence probably would not have mattered anyway, because the customs agents seized the ship without a court hearing.

The seizure of the *Liberty* without a court hearing violated another right proclaimed by Blackstone:

> To bereave a man of life, or by violence to confiscate his estate, without accusation or trial, would be so gross and notorious and act of despotism, as must at once convey the alarm of tyranny throughout the whole kingdom. (BL3, 131-132)

In addition, he said that this basic right of property had been a long-standing principle of English law:

> Upon this principle the great charter has declared that no freeman shall be disseised, or divested, of his freehold, or of his liberties, or free customs, but by the judgment of his peers, or by the law of the land. And by a variety of antient statutes it is enacted, that no man's lands or goods shall be seized into the king's hands, against the great charter, and the law of the land; and that no man shall be disinherited, nor put out of his franchises or freehold, unless he be duly brought to answer, and be forejudged by course of law; and if any thing be done to the contrary, it shall be redressed, and holden for none. (BL3, 134-135)

On the other hand, Blackstone had also implied that Americans were not entitled to the absolute rights of Englishmen. The people of Boston were tired of debating that question. They could not stand by and watch one of their leading businessmen suffer the loss of his ship and cargo. John Adams calculated that a thousand

Boston families were dependent on Hancock's business for their daily support. As the customs agents towed away the *Liberty*, a crowd of colonists gathered at a nearby dock and protested. When they had the opportunity, they attacked and beat several customs agents. They also grabbed a private pleasure boat belonging to a customs official and carted it off to the Boston Common, where they burned it. They then went to the homes of two customs officials. Several windows were broken. Finally, one of the colonial leaders was able to calm the group, crying, "We will defend our liberties and property by the strength of our arm and the help of our God. To your tents, O Israel!"[59] The angry crowd went home peacefully, but determined to fight another day.

In addition to fighting the Townshend Acts with petitions and demonstrations, many colonists boycotted products imported from England. On November 20, 1767, the effective date of the Revenue Act, Sam Adams and the Sons of Liberty started the boycott by asking people on the streets of Boston to sign non-importation agreements. The movement spread throughout the colonies, but it was more successful in the north than in the south. By 1769, imports were down by almost fifty percent in Massachusetts, Pennsylvania and New Jersey and by over eighty percent in New York. Some people made greater sacrifices than others. The students at Yale gave up wine, while the Harvard students gave up tea.[60]

In 1768, Massachusetts Governor Bernard claimed that some merchants who had signed boycott agreements were stealing goods off the piers and selling them through secret deals. A newspaper friendly to the governor published the names of suspected merchants. Sam Adams believed that Bernard was not only relaying this information back to Lord Hillsborough in London but exaggerating the colony's law-and-order problems in order to justify a request for British troops similar to those stationed in New York City. One of Adams's lieutenants, Dr. Joseph Warren, wrote a letter to the governor that was published in the *Boston Gazette*. It said,

We have known for a long time your enmity in this province. We have had full proof of your cruelty to a loyal people. No age has, perhaps, furnished a more glaring instance of obstinate perseverance in the path of malice.[61]

Warren concluded the letter with a statement that the governor was "totally abandoned to wickedness," and signed it "A True Patriot." Bernard was so upset upon reading it that he asked the House of Representatives to punish the author. The House declined to act, saying, "Although defaming a man, public or private, is certainly an outrage, yet freedom of the newspapers to tell lies on public men is so associated with their power to tell the truth that we think it impolitic to attempt by law to punish such lying."[62]

Throughout the summer of 1768, Bernard denied that he had requested British troops to occupy Boston. However, when a British officer arrived from Halifax to make preparations in early September, all the people of Boston realized the soldiers were coming. The Sons of Liberty erected a tall pole on the top of Beacon Hill, with a turpentine barrel tied to the top of the pole. They announced that when the troops were sighted, the barrel would be ignited to warn everyone. As the word spread, the story of what would happen began to grow. Someone reported that the lighted barrel was designed to signal thirty thousand men who were being gathered around Boston, ready to storm the city, seize the governor and lieutenant governor, plunder the city treasury and fly a new flag from the Liberty Tree.

The leaders of the Sons of Liberty, Sam Adams and James Otis, called a town meeting on September 12 in Faneuil Hall to discuss the colony's response to the arrival of the British troops. Adams and Otis believed that standing armies were illegal, except when the people gave their consent, and they hoped the people of Boston would consent to an army of their own to show their resistance. As people filed into the hall on the night of the meeting, they saw the town's stock of muskets and balls, which had been hauled in from nearby storehouses. When the hall was filled with people, Otis and Adams urged that the muskets and balls be passed out to those who needed them for protection. Their proposal was voted down, but another one passed. The assembly voted to call a convention of all the towns in the colony to decide what action ought to be taken.

Most people in the other towns, particularly those in the western part of Massachusetts, were not alarmed at the prospect of a few British regiments coming to Boston. They were certainly not prepared to take up arms to fight them. When only seventy delegates showed up at the convention on September 22, Otis and Adams knew their resistance plans were doomed. The delegates voted merely to send a message to the king that he regard their meeting as "a fresh token of the loyalty of our respective towns to His Majesty."[63] Many colonists, however, waited anxiously to see what would happen when the British soldiers arrived. In some parts of the countryside, a few farmers could be seen exercising their arms and performing other drill movements.

On October 1, 1768, two British regiments totaling a thousand men arrived in Boston and paraded through the city without a major incident. The barrel at the top of the pole on Beacon Hill was never lit because it had been empty all the time. At their Castle William headquarters, the customs commissioners set off skyrockets and rejoiced with a song that derided the timid colonists:

> Yankee Doodle came to town, a-riding on a pony.
> He stuck a feather in his hat and called it macaroni.
> Yankee Doodle, keep it up! Yankee Doodle, dandy!
> Mind the music and the step, and with the girls be handy!

Several years later, that song acquired a new meaning when American soldiers began singing it as they marched into battles against the British, and the term "Yankee" became a badge of honor.

Early in 1769, Governor Bernard wrote Lord Hillsborough that he thought several leaders of the Sons of Liberty, including Sam Adams, had committed treason. Hillsborough told Bernard to send proof and Bernard replied with several affidavits. The attorney general reviewed them and concluded that Adams and others had come "within a hair's breadth" of treason, but the evidence was insufficient to prosecute them. Bernard's failed attempt to hang the Sons of Liberty leaders for treason widened the gulf between him and all the people of Massachusetts.

Parliament's attitude toward the colonial problems was also changing. English merchants were losing money and thousands of English workers were losing their jobs because of the colonial boycott. Both the voting and the non-voting people of England urged Parliament to make peace with the American colonists. Some demanded that Governor Bernard be recalled. In July, one regiment of British soldiers left Boston for Halifax and another regiment received orders to return to Ireland. Governor Bernard received his orders as well. His ship sailed from Boston on July 31, 1769.

However, two British regiments remained in Boston, and so did the two in New York. In January 1770, some of the soldiers in New York City cut down a liberty pole and piled the pieces in front of the local headquarters of the Sons of Liberty. A riot followed in which one colonist was killed. In March, several Boston colonists threw snowballs at a sentry standing near the Massachusetts State House. The main guard was called to the rescue, causing a larger crowd to gather. For about half an hour, the soldiers pointed their rifles at the colonists, while the colonists surrounded the soldiers and taunted them, throwing stones and other objects. They were angry because the soldiers had been working in the dockyards and other places, taking jobs away from colonial workers. They also resented having to quarter the soldiers in their homes. At last, one of the soldiers could not tolerate the taunting any longer. He fired his rifle. Several other soldiers then fired their rifles. Five colonists were killed, including Crispus Attucks, a black man who was one of the leaders. The event became known as the "Boston Massacre."

Fortunately, the violence in New York and Boston did not spread further, because it was overshadowed by news that Parliament had repealed most of the Townshend taxes. However, a small tax on tea remained to remind the colonists of Parliament's supremacy.

2

Reconciliation or Confrontation?

A. A Calm before the Storm

After the Townshend Acts were repealed, a peaceful atmosphere prevailed for a while in the colonies. Improved economic conditions helped ease the tensions. Sam Adams and the Sons of Liberty were almost rebels without a cause. However, the British government continued to place large numbers of soldiers in America to remind the colonists who was in control. Many colonists resented living under the watchful eye of the British army; resentment became antagonism in 1772 when Parliament resumed its practice of setting the pay of colonial governors and judges, thus removing them from the control of the colonial legislatures.

B. The *Gaspée* Incident

On June 10, 1772, tensions further increased when a group of colonists burned a British naval ship, the *Gaspée*, which had been patrolling Rhode Island's Narragansett Bay looking for smugglers. The ship became vulnerable to attack when it ran aground on a sandy ridge close to the shore. Not only did the colonists burn the ship, but they beat the captain and crew. When the news reached London, the British ministers announced that when the culprits were caught they would be brought to England for non-jury trials. They also reminded the colonists that English law provided the death penalty for anyone found guilty of destroying a part of a British naval vessel.[1]

The *Gaspée* incident concerned the colonists for a long time because the British investigators were not able to identify who had burned the ship. The colonial newspapers focused on the unfairness of the British response. They claimed the British ministers were "worse than Egyptian tyrants" because they were threatening "courts of inquisition."[2]

The threats by the British ministers violated a number of principles that had been described by Blackstone in his *Commentaries*. In his first volume, he said that people accused of crimes were entitled to jury trials as part of their rights of liberty and property (BL3, 130-131, 134). He elaborated on that entitlement in his third volume, saying,

> Upon these accounts the trial by jury ever has been, and I trust ever will be, looked upon as the glory of the English law. And, if it has so great an advantage over others in regulating civil property, how much must that advantage be heightened, when it is applied to criminal cases! . . . [I]t is the most transcendent privilege which any subject can enjoy, or wish for, that he cannot be affected either in his property, his liberty, or his person, but by the unanimous consent of twelve of his neighbors and equals.[3]

Blackstone also said, regarding the absolute right of personal security, that the death penalty was to be imposed only "upon the highest necessity" (BL3, 129). The destruction of a naval vessel was a serious crime, but many questioned whether the death penalty was an appropriate punishment.

The colonists also thought the British ministers were violating their rights by threatening to take all accused persons to London for trial. Blackstone said, regarding the absolute right of liberty, that

> no power on earth, except authority of parliament, can send any subject of England *out of* the land against his will; no not even a criminal. For exile, or transportation, is a punishment unknown to the common law; . . . . (BL3, 133)

C. The Committees of Correspondence

The fires of colonial protest thus began burning once again. On November 2, 1772, Sam Adams made a motion at a Boston town meeting to organize a committee of correspondence "to state the rights of the colonists and of this Province in particular, as men, as Christians, and as subjects; and to the several towns and to the world." Adams then drafted a declaration of these rights and presented them at a meeting on November 20. The declaration said, in part,

> Among the natural rights of the colonists are these: first, a right to life; second, to liberty; third, to property; together with the right to support and defend them in the best manner they can. These are evident branches of, rather than deductions from, the duty of self-preservation, commonly called the first law of nature....
>
> The natural liberty of man, by entering into society, is abridged or restrained so far only as is necessary for the great end of society, the best good of the whole....
>
> Magna Charta itself is in substance but a constrained declaration or proclamation and promulgation in the name of the King, Lords and Commons, of the sense the latter had of their original, inherent, indefeasible natural rights, as also those of free citizens equally perdurable with one another. That great author, that great jurist, and even that court writer, Mr. Justice Blackstone, holds that this recognition was justly obtained of King John sword in hand [BL3, 123-124]. And peradventure it must be one day sword in hand again rescued and preserved from total destruction and oblivion....
>
> The absolute rights of Englishmen and all freemen, in or out of civil society, are principally personal security, personal liberty, and private property....
>
> "The legislative cannot justly assume to itself a power to rule by extempore arbitrary decrees; but it is bound to see that justice is dispensed, and that the rights of the subjects be decided by promulgated, standing, and known laws, and authorized *independent judges*"; that is, independent, as far as possible, of prince and people. "There should be one rule of justice for rich and poor, for the favorite at court, and the countryman at the plough."
>
> Third, the supreme power cannot justly take from any man any part of his property, without his consent in person or by his representative. (App. J)

This declaration was then published in pamphlet form and distributed throughout the colonies.

In addition to the Boston Committee of Correspondence, Sam Adams organized committees of correspondence in eighty towns in Massachusetts. Their purpose was to publicize the rights of the colonists, monitor violations of these rights by British officials and spread the news of these violations throughout the colonies.

In Virginia, the House of Burgesses appointed a standing committee of correspondence that was headed by Patrick Henry and included Thomas Jefferson. Such committees were organized in other colonies and eventually they formed a network that was useful in coordinating colonial responses to later acts of British oppression.

D. The Boston Tea Party

In the following year, relations between the British government and its American colonies completely unraveled. The controversy centered on the special trade and tax privileges that had been granted by the British government to the East India Company. The protests against these privileges led to the event that came to be known as the "Boston Tea Party."

By a 1709 charter, Parliament had granted a patent to the East India Company gaving it a monopoly on all goods shipped between England and the far east, including India.[4] Colonial businessmen had always resented the British government's practice of granting such patents, which were not for the protection of new inventions but were perpetual monopolies arbitrarily granted to politically powerful companies. The Puritan founders of Massachusetts had legislated against these monopolies in their *Body of Liberties* of 1641 (App. C, sec. 9).[5] The East India Company was a prime example of their unfairness. A few owners of the East India Company had gained tremendous wealth, while all other Englishmen had been denied the opportunity of trading directly with over half the people of the world.

Before 1773, the Americans had been insulated from the East India Company's monopoly because the Company had to sell its oriental goods at public auctions in England.[6] Independent merchants were able to buy these goods in bulk in England and then ship them to the colonies for sale either to wholesalers or to retailers. Many enterprising colonists therefore had an ample opportunity to make a profit.

However, in 1773, the East India Company was facing financial ruin owing to poor management, a recession and excessive dividends to its stockholders. Parliament therefore passed the Tea Act, granting the East India Company permission to ship its large surplus of tea directly to the American colonies. The act also gave the Company permission to set up its own distribution agents in America. In Massachusetts, the Company appointed five agents, all with close ties to the royal governor. Two were his sons, one was his nephew and the other two were friends.[7] Parliament also granted the Company a full drawback of English duties otherwise payable on tea shipped to America. That drawback was partly offset by the relatively small Townshend tax on American tea imports, but the net tax advantage was still sufficient to enable the East India company to set the price of its tea below that of the tea smuggled into American ports from other nations.

Colonial merchants immediately recognized the threat posed by the Tea Act. The power of the East India Company's monopoly was being unlawfully extended to America.[8] All legitimate tea suppliers, except the East India Company and its agents, would have to close their doors. They would not be able to compete because their only source was the East India tea bought at auction in England; this tea was not subject to the duty drawback granted the East India Company. The tea smugglers would also have trouble competing. If the Tea Act were successful, Parliament might well decide to grant the East India Company or other British companies the right to monopolize American trade in other products. That prospect alarmed the merchants because the American colonies were but a string of seaports whose economies were based on foreign trade. If there were no competition in this trade, everyone would be paying higher prices for all their necessities.

Other colonists protested against the Tea Act for a different reason. They were concerned about the continuation of the Townshend tax on tea shipped to America. The Tea Act reduced the total tax on East India tea because of the drawback on the English duty, but that reduction was exactly what concerned many colonists. Previously, the total tax on the East India tea was so high that very few colonists bought it; instead, they settled for sassafras tea or smuggled tea or stopped drinking the beverage. Thus, the total revenue from the Townshend tax was very small. By canceling the large English tax on the East India tea but allowing the smaller American tax to remain, the Tea Act threatened to increase the amount of East India tea bought by the colonists and also the amount of taxes collected from them by the British government. That prospect again raised the question of whether Parliament had the right to tax the colonists without the approval of their elected representatives. Furthermore, by allowing the East India Company to ship its tea to its exclusive agents in America rather than requiring the Company to selling it to other firms at English auctions, the Tea Act made the Company a prime example of British oppression and an easy target for an American protest against all taxes imposed by Parliament.

The first ships carrying East India tea under the new act arrived in Charleston, South Carolina, in late 1773. The local Sons of Liberty intervened and were able to have the tea locked in a warehouse. In New York and Philadelphia, the colonists convinced the captains to turn their ships around and go back to England. In Boston, however, such efforts failed because of the animosity between Massachusetts Governor Thomas Hutchinson and his fellow colonists.

There was a long history of conflicts between Governor Hutchinson and the people of Massachusetts. First, there was the controversy over the writs of assistance when he was chief justice of the Massachusetts Superior Court in the early 1760s. Then there were the Stamp Act riots of 1765, in which mobs of protesters had wrecked his home and furnishings, as well as those of his brother-in-law Andrew Oliver. Most recently, the Massachusetts House of Representatives had sent King George a petition to remove him and his brother-in-law from their positions as governor and lieutenant governor of the colony. The petition was based on "hateful discords" arising from recently publicized letters that Hutchinson and Oliver had written to one of the king's advisors, Thomas Whately, in 1768. Hutchinson had said in one of the letters, "there must be an abridgment of what are called English liberties. I doubt whether it is possible to project a system of government in which a colony three thousand miles distant shall enjoy all the liberty of the parent state." The petition to remove Hutchinson and Oliver because of the ill will generated by this statement was still pending before the king's privy council.[9] With his job on the line, Hutchinson was determined to govern Massachusetts with an iron hand and to prove that he was the right man to enforce the king's law and order.

When the ship *Dartmouth* carrying East India tea entered the Boston harbor on Sunday, November 28, Sam Adams had notices posted all over the colony:

> Friends, Brethren, Countrymen--That worst of plagues, the detested tea shipped for this port by the East India Company, is now arrived in this harbor. The hour of destruction, or manly opposition to the machinations of tyranny, stares you in the face.[10]

The next day, five to six thousand people gathered in Faneuil Hall, next to the present Quincy Market in Boston. Because the hall was not big enough to hold the crowd, the convention moved to the Old South Meeting House, on the corner of the present Washington and Milk Streets. One of the first items on the agenda was the appointment of a committee that included Paul Revere to watch the wharf day and night to make sure that no tea was unloaded. The convention then debated how to prevent any unloading, while causing the least harm to innocent people. One of the owners of the *Dartmouth*, a Quaker named Francis Rotch, explained his predicament. The customs agents would not let his

Chapter 2   Reconciliation or Confrontation?   55

ship leave the harbor until he had unloaded it and paid the tax. He also had to pay the tax within twenty days after entering the harbor or the customs agents would have the authority to sink his ship, tea and all. Therefore, if the convention did not work out a solution by December 17, Rotch would be forced to unload the tea or face losing his ship.

For over two weeks the convention deliberated. The farmers from the outlying areas stayed to see how the matter would be resolved because they had little else to do in the middle of winter and they knew that some action had to be taken by mid-December. Meanwhile, several more ships arrived in the Boston harbor with East India tea. The convention sent a delegation to Governor Hutchinson to ask him to allow these ships to leave the harbor without paying the tax. The governor denied their request, saying he had to abide by his legal obligation to have the customs agents collect the tax once the tea entered the harbor. The convention also sent a delegation to the East India agents to ask them to resign their commissions so they would not be able to accept delivery of the tea. Being close friends and relatives of the governor, the agents likewise refused. They said that it would be a breach of their duty to the East India Company to resign their commissions under these circumstances.

Finally, the hour of decision arrived. On the afternoon of December 16, a huge crowd, estimated to include a major portion of Boston's twenty thousand residents and several thousand others from the surrounding countryside, met in and around the Old South Meeting House.[11] Rotch was asked to make one last appeal to Governor Hutchinson for a pass out of the harbor. As evening approached, Rotch returned, saying the governor had denied his pass. After some commotion, Sam Adams announced, "This meeting can do nothing more to save the country." Suddenly, forty to fifty men dressed as Indians entered the hall. Someone shouted, "Boston harbor a teapot tonight!" As the crowd began to leave the hall, John Hancock sensed the anarchy toward which they were headed. He shouted, "Let every man do that which is right in his own eyes!"[12]

Led by the Indian masqueraders, the crowd made its way down to Griffin's Wharf, where the Congress Street Bridge is now located. It was low tide and the "Indians" easily boarded the tea-loaded ships. For several hours, they broke open the tea chests and shoveled the tea into the harbor. By nine o'clock, their work was done. Three hundred and forty-two chests of tea had been dumped in the harbor.[13]

E. The Intolerable Acts

When the news of the "tea party" reached London, the British ministers were aghast at the colonists' bold defiance of their authority. This clearly was not an isolated incident of vandalism by a few outlaws. It was a show of force planned by a convention of thousands of people. King George and the Parliament knew that they could not take this matter lightly; if they did, they might lose control of all the American colonies. They decided to respond with their own show of force.

Between March and June of 1774, Parliament passed a series of laws designed to bring the Massachusetts rebels to their knees. The British called these laws the "Coercive Acts" but the colonists called them the "Intolerable Acts." The Boston Port Act closed the port of Boston to all ships bearing goods, wares or merchandise. The Massachusetts Government Act took away the right of the colony's House of Representatives to appoint the governor's council. Henceforth, the council members were to be appointed by the king and most other public officials were to be appointed by the governor, who was in turn appointed by the king. The committees of correspondence were ordered to disband. The Administration of Justice Act provided that persons accused of capital crimes were to be taken to England for trial, raising again the colonists' complaint that any removal from their homeland violated their fundamental rights (BL3, 133). The Québec Act transferred all the colonial territories west of the Appalachian Mountains and north of the Ohio River to the colony of Québec, depriving many colonies of western lands that had been granted by their charters. Finally, the Quartering Act gave all colonial governors the power to order the

Chapter 2   Reconciliation or Confrontation?   57

Fig. 5: THE BOSTON TEA PARTY

quartering of British soldiers in private homes. This act was contrary to the English law that said that "no soldier shall be quartered on the subject without his consent."[14]

Of all the Intolerable Acts, the Boston Port Act had the greatest impact. It imposed a military occupation and blockade on Boston that was not to be lifted until the tea dumped in the Boston harbor was paid for and the king was satisfied that "peace and obedience to the laws was restored. The blockade would surely devastate Boston's economy. Even some members of Parliament thought that they had gone too far. One member, Edmund Burke, wrote to the New York Correspondence Committee,

> The rendering the Means of Subsistence of a Whole City dependent on the King's private pleasure, even after the payment of a fine and satisfaction made, was without Precedent, and of a most dangerous example.[15]

F. The Colonists Respond

The news of the Intolerable Acts traveled fast through the colonies' committees of correspondence. Many colonies rushed aid to the Bostonians. South Carolina sent provisions worth £2,700 sterling. Virginia sent corn, wheat and flour. The Virginia House of Burgesses passed a resolution on May 27 that denounced the military occupation of Boston as a "hostile invasion" and designated June 1, 1774, the date the Port Act was to take effect, as a "day of fasting, humiliation and prayer."[16]

To prevent further resolutions from passing, Governor Dunmore of Virginia dissolved the House of Burgesses. Its members therefore adjourned to the Raleigh Tavern in Williamsburg, where they made plans to contact the correspondence committees in all the colonies and call a joint congress to determine how to respond to the Intolerable Acts. A committee of fifty-one New York citizens had already expressed the need for such a congress in a letter to the Boston Committee of Correspondence dated May 23. The correspondence committees in all the colonies except Georgia thought that a congress was a good idea and agreed to send delegates.

On July 26, 1774, the freeholders of Albemarle County, Virginia adopted a resolution claiming that only the local legislatures of the colonists, "duly appointed with their own consent," could govern them. Another resolution claimed that the "natural and legal rights" of the colonists had been violated by the act of Parliament that

Chapter 2   Reconciliation or Confrontation?   59

blockaded Boston. "[A]ll such assumptions of unlawful power," they said, "are dangerous to the right of the British Empire in general"; they would be ever ready to join with their fellow subjects "in executing all those rightful powers which God has given us, for the reestablishment and guaranteeing such their constitutional rights, when, where, and by whomsoever invaded." To that end, they instructed their deputies to the Virginia Convention, scheduled the next week in Williamsburg, to recommend a colonial agreement to stop all trade with Great Britain.[17] The author of these resolves was Thomas Jefferson, one of the two deputies that the freeholders had chosen to send to the Convention. He had represented Albemarle County for five years in the House of Burgesses.

In addition to drafting resolves for his neighboring freeholders, Jefferson wrote a sixty-five-hundred-word resolution for the Virginia Convention. The resolution was later entitled "A Summary View of the Rights of British America." It described the "many unwarrantable incroachments and usurpations, attempted to be made by the legislature of one part of the empire, upon those rights which god and the laws have given equally and independently to all." It also blamed the king for many encroachments. Jefferson restated most of them two years later when he drafted the Declaration of Independence. The resolution concluded with the following statement:

> We are willing on our part to sacrifice every thing which reason can ask to the restoration of that tranquility for which all must wish. On their part let them be ready to establish union on a generous plan. Let them name their terms, but let them be just. Accept of every commercial preference it is in our power to give for such things as we can raise for their use, or they make for ours. But let them not think to exclude us from going to other markets, to dispose of those commodities which they cannot use, nor to supply those wants which they cannot supply. Still less let it be proposed that our properties within our territories shall be taxed or regulated by any power on earth but our own. The god who gave us life, gave us liberty at the same time: the hand of force may destroy, but cannot disjoin them.[18]

Jefferson became too ill to go to Williamsburg, but he sent his resolution to the convention by courier.

The convention did not adopt Jefferson's resolution. The delegates were afraid to put their names on a document that was so critical of the king and so firm in its assertion of the natural rights of liberty and self government. However, a Williamsburg printer published the resolution as a pamphlet and it was reprinted in Philadelphia and London before the end of the year, naming the author as "A Native, and Member of the House of Burgesses."[19]

In place of Jefferson's resolution, the Virginia Convention approved a set of instructions to its delegates to the general congress in Philadelphia, scheduled for the following month. The instructions said, "The end of government would be defeated by the British Parliament exercising a power over the lives, the property, and the liberty of American subjects who are not, and from their local circumstances cannot be, there represented." The document listed the Intolerable Acts as examples of Parliament's unlawful exercise of such a power. It also said the Virginians were willing to enter into an agreement to stop all imports from Great Britain after November 1, 1774 and all exports to Great Britain after August 10, 1775 if the colonial grievances had not been redressed by those dates.[20]

G. The First Continental Congress

The First Continental Congress convened in Carpenters' Hall in Philadelphia on September 5, 1774 and met for seven weeks. With the proceedings of this congress, the official record of the proceedings of the present United States Congress begins. The fifty-six delegates chose as their president Peyton Randolph, the speaker of the Virginia House of Burgesses. Their only objective was to end the injustices of the Intolerable Acts and settle their differences with the British government. As John Adams said, there was no man among them "who would not be happy to see accommodation with Britain."[21]

Chapter 2   Reconciliation or Confrontation?

Early on, Joseph Galloway, a conservative delegate from Pennsylvania, proposed that the Congress offer a compromise plan to Parliament whereby the power to tax the colonies would reside in a legislature composed of British and American representatives. Galloway's plan was rejected because it did not resolve the matter of whether the colonists were entitled to all of the rights of Englishmen, nor did it address the current blockade of Boston.

The convention took a radical turn when Paul Revere rode in from Boston with news that the Massachusetts colonists had set up their own government and that on September 9 a convention of towns in Suffolk County, which included Boston, had passed a list of "Suffolk Resolves," drafted by Dr. Joseph Warren. The members of the Congress listened intently while the Resolves were read. They declared the Intolerable Acts to be "the arbitrary will of a licentious minister" and said the people of Massachusetts should collect their own taxes and withhold them from the royal governor until the Intolerable Acts were repealed. The Resolves also recommended that an armed militia be formed to protect the people of Massachusetts from the British troops. After the reading, Galloway commented that the Resolves amounted to a declaration of war. However, most of the delegates gathered around their friends from Massachusetts to express their sympathy and support. They immediately adopted the Suffolk Resolves as those of the Continental Congress, without changing a word.

The delegates also agreed to a compact called "The Continental Association" whereby they would boycott all imports from England on December 1, 1774 if by that date Parliament had not repealed the Intolerable Acts. They agreed to stop exports to England on September 10, 1775 if the Intolerable Acts were still in force on that date. Local committees were organized in the colonies to enforce the compact. In many colonies, the committees of correspondence took over this function. The New York delegates did not vote for the boycott and Georgia did not send delegates to the Congress, but people in those colonies organized their own committees to make sure that everyone adhered to the agreement.[22]

On October 14, 1774, the Congress adopted a Declaration and Resolves (App. K) asserting that the colonists were entitled to all the rights of Englishmen, contrary to what Blackstone had said in his *Commentaries* (BL2). The Declaration listed the rights that the British government had recently violated, including the right of trial by jury, the right to be free of soldiers quartered in their homes and the right to be free of taxes not consented to by their elected representatives.

The Declaration also named the recent acts of Parliament that violated their rights. One of these was the Québec Act. The Continental Congress explained its objection to this law more fully in its address "To the people of Great Britain," drafted by John Jay and adopted October 24th. It said,

> ... [W]e think the Legislature of Great Britain is not authorized by the constitution to establish a religion, fraught with sanguinary and impious tenets, or to erect an arbitrary form of government, in any quarter of the globe.[23]

This criticism was directed not toward the Church of England but toward the Catholic Church that dominated Québec. The Québec Act allowed both Catholics and Protestants to practice their religions and recognized both the Catholic Church and the Anglican Church as established churches in Canada. It also sanctioned the continuation of the Catholic seigneuries, feudal estates created by the French before the British had taken over in 1759. About one-fourth of the seigneuries were owned by clergy acting on behalf of the Catholic Church.[24] Most of the other seigneurs were military officers who held their positions on the condition that they provide military service to the provincial government.

The Congress's main objection to the Québec Act was that it perpetuated the French civil law. That law allowed the seigneurs to treat their tenants, or "habitants," as feudal serfs, thus depriving them of the basic rights accorded most other British subjects. Each habitant was always on call to perform forced labor or military service for his government, without pay.[25] Only the seigneurs and the clergy were happy with the new law.[26] Outside the colony, neighboring colonists worried that the British government might impose the same autocratic rule on them. They were particularly concerned because the Québec Act extended the borders of Québec down the western side of the Appalachian Mountains to the Ohio River, so that it enveloped the western sides of the New York, Pennsylvania and Virginia colonies.

The Continental Congress therefore said in its address to the people of Great Britain that

> by another Act the dominion of Canada is to be so extended, modeled, and governed, as that being disunited from us, detached from our interests, by civil as well as religious prejudices, that by their numbers daily swelling with Catholic emigrants from Europe, and by their devotion to Administration, so friendly to their religion, they might become formidable to us, and on occasion, be fit instruments in the hands of power, to reduce the ancient free Protestant Colonies to the same state of slavery with themselves.[27]

The address also elaborated on other rights asserted in the Declaration and Resolves and made the following appeal:

> We believe there is yet much virtue, much justice, and much public spirit in the English nation. To that justice we now appeal. You have been told that we are seditious, impatient of government, and desirous of independence. Be assured that these are not facts, but calumnies. Permit us to be as free as yourselves, and we shall ever esteem a union with you to be our greatest glory, and our greatest happiness; we shall ever be ready to contribute all in our power to the welfare of the empire; we shall consider your enemies as our enemies, and your interest as our own.
>
> But if you are determined that your ministers shall wantonly sport with the rights of mankind; if neither the voice of justice, the dictates of the law, the principles of the constitution, or the suggestions of humanity can restrain your hands from shedding human blood in such an impious cause, we must then tell you that we will never submit to be hewers of wood or drawers of water for any ministry or nation in the world.
>
> Place us in the same situation that we were at the close of the last war, and our former harmony will be restored.[28]

In its last session on October 26, the Congress voted to send a letter to the people of Québec, asking them to join the other colonies in their protest of British laws that were depriving everyone of their rights. The letter listed five great rights,

> without which a people cannot be free and happy, and under the protecting and encouraging influence of which, these colonies have hitherto so amazingly flourished and increased. These are the rights, a profligate Ministry are now striving, by force of arms, to ravish from us, and which we are, with one mind, resolved never to resign but with our lives.

According to the letter, these rights were the following:

(1) "the right of the people having a share in their own government by their representatives chosen by themselves," by which no portion of their property "can legally be taken from them, but with their own full and free consent" (see BL3, 135-136);

(2) the right of trial by jury (see BL3, 130-131, 134);

(3) the right of any person who is imprisoned to "immediately obtain a writ, termed a Habeas Corpus, from a Judge, whose sworn duty it is to grant it, and thereupon procure any illegal restraint to be quickly enquired into and redressed" (see BL3, 131);

(4) the right "of holding lands by the tenure of easy rents, and not by rigorous and oppressive services, frequently forcing the possessors from their families and their business, to perform what ought to be done in all well regulated states, by men hired for the purpose"; and

(5) the right of freedom of the press (see BL6).[29]

The delegates also resolved to convene a second congress on May 10, 1775.

Most of the rights asserted by the First Continental Congress were based on fundamental principles of English government. In its Declaration and Resolves (App. K), it asserted the right of a person to be free of taxes except by the consent of his elected representatives (Resolve 4, based on BL3, 135), the right of an accused to a trial by jury (Resolve 5, based on BL3, 130-131, 134), the right to petition the king (Resolve 8, based on BL3, 138), the right of the people to be free of standing armies in times of peace (Resolve 9, based on App. E) and the right a person to be free of soldiers quartered in his house (Final Resolve, Par. 6, based on App. E).

However, the Congress also expanded some of these rights. In Resolve 1, it declared that the colonists had never ceded to any sovereign power the right to dispose of their life, liberty or property without their consent. It thereby asserted that people had not only the right to consent to taxation but also the right to have their elected representatives consent to all government control. The Congress carried this principle forward in Resolve 4, in which it asserted that the locally elected colonial legislatures, and not Parliament, had the power to legislate in matters "of taxation and internal polity." In Resolve 8, it said that the colonists not only had the right to petition the king, but also the right "to peaceably assemble" in order to consider the grievances upon which they might petition. In Resolve 9, it interpreted the guarantee of the English Declaration of Rights--that there be no standing army in time of peace without the consent of Parliament--to mean that each colony had the right to be free of a standing army in time of peace "without the consent of the legislature of that colony." In its address to the people of Great Britain, the Congress asserted that "the Legislature of Great Britain is not authorized by the constitution to establish a religion, . . ." In its letter to the people of Québec, it asserted that the right of free press was one of "the five great rights." Another of those five great rights was the right "of holding lands by the tenure of easy rents, and not by rigorous and oppressive services." In his chapter, "Of the modern English

Tenures," Blackstone had said that "the oppressive or military part of the feodal constitution was happily done away, ..."[30] However, Parliament did not believe, as the Continental Congress did, that the abolishment of oppressive tenures in England created such a fundamental right that the same tenures could not be preserved in America, as, for example, in the colony of Québec.

Of all the new and expanded rights asserted by the Congress, the most controversial was the right of the colonies to govern themselves without the interference of Parliament, except in the regulation of external commerce (Resolve 4). At the end of the English Civil War in 1649, the Levelers had recognized the right of the people to govern themselves when they proposed a constitution that put the supreme authority of English government in an assembly of four hundred representatives elected by the people (App. D, sec. I). However, Oliver Cromwell had rejected that proposal because he wanted to hold to hold the supreme authority as Lord Protector of England. John Locke had said that the people cannot "be bound by any laws but such as are enacted by those whom they have chosen and authorized to make laws for them" (App. F, par. 141). However, Parliament had never recognized this natural right of people.

Immediately after the Congress adjourned, a New York rector of the Church of England, Samuel Seabury, published a series of pamphlets aimed at convincing New York farmers that the Continental Congress had not acted in their best interests.[31] He signed his name "A Westchester Farmer." Seabury's arguments were answered in two pamphlets, published by "A Friend of America" and "A Sincere Friend of America." The friend turned out to be Alexander Hamilton, a seventeen-year-old student at King's College (now Columbia University). In his first pamphlet, *A Full Vindication of the Measures of Congress*, Hamilton attacked Seabury's position that Parliament had the absolute right to govern the colonies without any limitations:

> What then is the subject of our controversy with the mother country?---It is this, whether we shall preserve that security to our lives and

properties, which the law of nature, the genius of the British Constitution, and our charters afford us; or whether we shall resign them into the hands of the British House of Commons, which is no more privileged to dispose of them than the Grand Mogul?[32]

"Farmer" Seabury answered Hamilton's pamphlet with another pamphlet, in which he confused the natural rights that people reserve to themselves when they submit to a governmental authority with the natural rights that they have in a state of nature:

> I wish you had explicitly declared to the public your ideas of the natural rights of mankind. Man in a state of nature may be considered as perfectly free from all restraints of law and government; and then the weak must submit to the strong. From such a state, I confess, I have a violent aversion. I think the form of government we lately enjoyed a much more eligible state to live in, and cannot help regretting our having lost it by the equity, wisdom, and authority of the Congress, who have introduced in the room of it confusion and violence, where all must submit to the power of a mob.[33]

In his second pamphlet, *The Farmer Refuted*, Hamilton tried to explain Locke's basic principles of government to Farmer Seabury, using extensive quotations from Blackstone's *Commentaries*. He also accused the Farmer of making the same errors that the philosopher Thomas Hobbes had made. According to Hamilton, Hobbes had said that man was, in a state of nature,

> perfectly free from all restraint of *law* and *government*. Moral obligation, according to him, is derived from the introduction of civil society; and there is no virtue, but what is purely artificial,--the mere contrivance of politicians, for the maintenance of social intercourse. But the reason he ran into this absurd and impious doctrine, was, that he disbelieved the existence of an intelligent superintending principle, who is the governor, and will be the final judge of the universe.
> As you, sometimes, swear *by him that made you*, I conclude, your sentiment does not correspond with his, in that which is the basis of the doctrine, you both agree in; and this makes it impossible to imagine whence this congruity between you arises. To grant, that there is a

supreme intelligence, who rules the world, and has established laws to regulate the actions of his creatures; and, still, to assert, that man, in a state of nature, may be considered as perfectly free from all restraints of *law* and *government*, appear in common understanding, altogether irreconcilable.

Good and wise men, in all ages, have embraced a very dissimilar theory. They have supposed, that the deity, from the relations, we stand in, to himself and to each other, has constituted an external and immutable law; which is, indispensibly, obligatory upon all mankind, prior to any human institution whatever.

This what is called the law of nature, "which, being coeval with mankind, and dictated by God himself, is, of course, superior in obligation to any other. It is binding over all the globe, in all countries, and at all times. No human laws are of any validity, if contrary to this; and such of them as are valid, derive all their authority, mediately, or immediately, from this original." BLACKSTONE [BL1, 41].

Upon this law, depend the natural rights of mankind, the supreme being gave existence to man, together with the means of preserving and beautifying that existence. He endowed him with rational faculties, by the help of which, to discern and pursue such things, as were consistent with his duty and interest, and invested him with an inviolable right to personal liberty, and personal safety.

Hence, in a state of nature, no man had any *moral* power to deprive another of his life, limbs, property or liberty; nor the least authority to command, or exact obedience from him; except that which arose from the ties of consanguinity.

Hence also, the origin of all civil government, justly established, must be a voluntary compact, between the rulers and the ruled; and must be liable to such limitations, as are necessary for the security of the *absolute rights* of the latter; for what original title can any man or set of men have, to govern others, except their own consent? To usurp dominion over a people, in their own despite, or to grasp at a more extensive power than they are willing to entrust, is to violate that law of nature, which gives every man a right to his personal liberty; and can, therefore, confer no obligation or obedience.

"The principle aim of society is to protect individuals, in the enjoyment of those absolute rights, which were vested in them by the immutable laws of nature; but which could not be preserved, in peace, without that mutual assistance, and intercourse, which is gained by the

Chapter 2 Reconciliation or Confrontation? 69

institution of friendly and social communities. Hence it follows, that the first and primary end of human laws, is to maintain and regulate these *absolute rights* of individuals." BLACKSTONE [BL3, 120].[34]

Seabury acknowledged that individuals have certain rights and freedoms. However, he said, "In every government there must be a supreme, absolute authority lodged somewhere." In the case of the British Empire, he said, that was the king, the House of Lords and the House of Commons. Seabury therefore believed that the colonists should confine their grievances to peaceful petitions and resolutions to these supreme authorities.[35] Blackstone had agreed that in all governments there must be "a supreme, irresistible, absolute, uncontrolled authority, in which the *jura summi imperii*, or the rights of sovereignty, reside" (BL1, 49), but he also said, regarding the absolute rights of individuals, that

> to vindicate these rights, when actually attacked, the subjects of England are entitled, in the first place, to the regular administration and free course of justice in the courts of law; next to the right of petitioning the king and parliament for redress of grievances; and lastly to the right of having and using arms for self-preservation and defense. (BL3, 140)

3

To Arms! To Arms!

A. The Preparations for War

One right that the colonists did not mention in their letters or Declaration and Resolves was their right to bear arms. Blackstone said that this right was among those rights that secure the basic rights of personal security, liberty and property. He explained it as follows:

> The fifth and last auxiliary right of the subject, that I shall at present mention, is that of having arms for their defence, suitable to their condition and degree, and such as are allowed by law. Which is also declared by the same statute 1 W.&M. st.2.c.2 and is indeed a public allowance, under due restrictions, of the natural right of resistance and self-preservation, when the sanctions of society and laws are found insufficient to restrain the violence of oppression. (BL3, 139)

An example of a "due restriction" of the right to bear arms was the Statute of Northampton, 2 Edw. III, c.3, which forbade a person to disturb the public peace by carrying a dangerous or unusual weapon.[1] However, the Massachusetts colonists could claim that their peace had already been disturbed and the sanctions of their society and laws had become "insufficient to restrain the violence of oppression." Their main commercial center, Boston, had been occupied by four thousand British soldiers. The civilian population of the town was only twenty thousand. The soldiers had replaced the civilian government. Lieutenant General Thomas Gage was now both the governor and the captain-general of the colony. British naval ships had surrounded the town and blockaded it. Because of the blockade, the people of Boston were starving. The fish caught in Massachusetts Bay had been their main source of food, but no fishing vessels were allowed to land at the city's piers. No goods of any kind could be transported to Boston by water. Instead, they had to be carried over the long, narrow isthmus that was Boston's only connection to the mainland. One person wrote,

> The fishermen of Marblehead, when they bestowed quintals of dried fish on the poor of Boston, were obliged to transport their offerings in waggons by a circuit of thirty miles.[2]

The Massachusetts colonists outside Boston therefore exercised their right to bear arms by organizing a militia during the winter of 1774-75. Their purpose was to prevent the British troops from extending the blockade beyond Boston. They called themselves "Minutemen" because they were prepared to grab their arms on a minute's notice whenever they heard news of a British attack. In addition to arms owned by individual soldiers, the Minutemen stockpiled an assortment of cannon, cannonballs and other ammunition.

The Minutemen were supervised by the "Massachusetts Provincial Congress," which was the name taken by the former Massachusetts House of Representatives after it had been dissolved by the colony's British governor. John Hancock presided over the Congress, which sometimes met in Salem and sometimes in Concord. Dr. Joseph Warren was chairman of the Congress' Committee of Safety and also the leader and organizer of the Minutemen.

While the colonists were demanding their rights as Englishmen and arming themselves to defend those rights, Parliament spent that winter debating what should be done to restore order in America. Former prime minister William Pitt came out of retirement to argue for concessions to the colonies. He had read the Declaration and Resolves adopted by the Continental Congress and was impressed by how well they stated the principles of English liberty. He said to the House of Lords, "When your lordships look at the papers transmitted from America, when you consider their decency, firmness and wisdom, you cannot but respect their cause and wish to make it your own." He called for the removal of Gage's troops from Boston, saying, "You may call them an army of safety and of guard. But they are in truth an army of impotence and contempt, and to make the folly equal to the disgrace, they are an army of irritation and vexation." He also moved to have Parliament repeal of the Intolerable Acts and renounce forever its right to tax the colonists, saying, "We shall be forced ultimately to retract. Let us retract while we can, not when we must."[3]

In the House of Commons, Edmund Burke pushed for repeal of the Boston Port Act, the Massachusetts Government Act and the Administration of Justice Act. He also said that the American colonists should be accorded all the rights of Englishmen. After all, he said, 250 years before, Henry VIII had given those rights to the Welsh, even though they "spoke a language in no way resembling that of His Majesty's English subjects." Burke then asked, "Are not the people of America as much Englishmen as the Welsh?"[4] He also proposed to remove the tea tax, as well as all other direct taxes on the colonists. Instead, he suggested, Parliament could renew the practice of requesting grants of "supplies and aids" from the colonial legislatures. He pointed out that the American legislatures had always complied in the past with such requests with "cheerfulness and sufficiency."[5] In summarizing his plea for compromise, he said,

> All government, indeed every human benefit and enjoyment, every virtue, and every prudent act, is founded on compromise and barter. We balance inconveniences; we give and we take; we remit some rights, that we may enjoy others; and we choose rather to be happy citizens than subtle disputants. As we must give away some natural liberty to enjoy civil advantages, so we must sacrifice some civil liberties for the advantages to be derived from the communion and fellowship of a great empire. But, in all fair dealings, the thing bought must bear some proportion to the purchase paid. None will barter away the immediate jewel of his soul. . . . But although there are some amongst us who think our Constitution wants many improvements to make it a complete system of liberty, perhaps none who are of that opinion would think it is right to aim at such improvement by disturbing his country, and risking everything that is dear to him. In every

arduous enterprise we consider what we are to lose, as well as what we are to gain; and the more and better stake of liberty every people possess, the less they will hazard in vain attempt to make it more. These are *the cords of man*.[6]

However, the House of Commons voted down Burke's proposals by a margin of two to one. The majority in both houses of Parliament believed that war was the best way to resolve the matter and that the victory would easily be England's. John Montague, the Earl of Sandwich, said confidently that the American soldiers would be undisciplined and cowardly. In fact, said Montague, the larger their army, the easier it would be to defeat them. Parliament therefore voted down all proposals to repeal the Intolerable Acts or to remove the troops from Boston.[7]

Prime Minister Lord North led the fight in Parliament to vote down all the proposals to reach a compromise with the colonists. He did, however, approach Benjamin Franklin to see if he could settle the American dispute privately. Through intermediaries, North suggested to Franklin that he would be handsomely rewarded if he could successfully mediate the latest dispute. He even promised him an £1,800 advance payment. Franklin refused the bribe but continued to negotiate with the British ministers. At one point, he offered to pay for the tea dumped in the Boston harbor from his own funds if Parliament would repeal the Intolerable Acts and pull the British troops out of Boston. The ministers refused his offer and the negotiations failed. Sadly, Franklin sailed home to Philadelphia to join his countrymen for the fight of their lives.[8]

Lord North then made another attempt to pressure the colonists into submission. He introduced the New England Restraining Act, which forbade the residents of Massachusetts, New Hampshire, Rhode Island and Connecticut to trade with any part of the world except Great Britain and Ireland. It also forbade the people of those colonies to fish off the coasts of Newfoundland and Nova Scotia. The Act was signed into law March 30, 1775.

On March 20, 1775, the Virginia Revolutionary Convention met at St. John's Church in Richmond to ratify the acts of the First Continental Congress and decide what to do next. George

Washington, Thomas Jefferson, Patrick Henry and the brothers Richard Henry Lee and Francis Lightfoot Lee were present. On the third day of the meeting, Patrick Henry stunned everyone by proposing that they organize a militia to defend Virginia in case of war. He addressed the convention chairman Peyton Randolph:

> Sir, we have done everything that could be done to avert the storm which is now coming on. We have petitioned; we have remonstrated; we have supplicated; we have prostrated ourselves before the throne and have implored its interposition to arrest the tyrannical hands of the Ministry and Parliament. Our petitions have been slighted; our remonstrances have produced additional violence and insult; our supplications have been disregarded; and we have been spurned with contempt, from the foot of the throne. In vain, after these things, may we indulge the fond hope of peace and reconciliation.
>
> There is no longer any room for hope. If we wish to be free; if we mean to preserve inviolate those inestimable privileges for which we have so long been contending; if we mean not basely to abandon the noble struggle in which we have so long engaged, and which we have pledged ourselves never to abandon, until the glorious object of our contest shall be obtained; we must fight! I repeat, sir, we must fight! An appeal to arms and to the God of Hosts is all that is left us!
>
> They tell us, sir . . . that we are weak, unable to cope with so formidable an adversary. But when shall we be stronger? Will it be next week, or next year? Will it be when we are totally disarmed, and when a British guard shall be stationed in every house? . . . Three million people, armed in the holy cause of liberty, and in such a country as that which we possess, are invincible to any force which our enemy can send against us.
>
> Besides, sir, we shall not fight our battles alone. There is a just God who presides over the destinies of nations, and who will raise up friends to fight our battles for us. The battle, sir, is not to the strong alone; it is to the vigilant, the active, the brave. Besides, sir, we have no election. If we were base enough to desire it, it is now too late to retire from the contest. There is no retreat but in submission and slavery! Our chains are forged. Their clanking may be heard on the plains of Boston! The war is inevitable. And let it come! I repeat, sir, let it come!

It is vain, sir, to extenuate the matter. Gentlemen may cry peace, peace. But there is no peace. The war has actually begun! The next gale that sweeps from the north will bring to our ears the clash of resounding arms! Our brethren are already in the field! Why do we stand here idle? What is it that gentlemen wish? What would they have? Is life so dear or peace so sweet, as to be purchased at the price of chains and slavery?

Forbid it, Almighty God! I know not what course others may take. But as for me, give me liberty--or give me death![9]

The sanctuary was silent.[10] Everyone knew they had to prepare for war.

B. Lexington and Concord

There is a time to pray and a time to fight. This is the time to fight.
--John Peter Gabriel Muhlenberg, 1775 sermon

While Patrick Henry was exhorting his fellow Virginians, the British commander in Boston, General Gage, was making plans to raid the ammunition depot of the Minutemen in Concord. He also wanted to capture the rebel leaders John Hancock and Sam Adams, who were headquartered in Lexington, on the road from Boston to Concord. The pressure on Gage to execute his plans increased when the ship *Nautilus* arrived in Boston with a message from the British colonial secretary that the rebel army should be attacked soon before its commanders had more time to organize.[11] However, the Minutemen had a network of spies and messengers ready to warn their troops in Concord and Lexington of an impending attack.

On the night of April 18, 1775, a light signal from the steeple of Christ's Church in Boston warned the Charlestown residents across the harbor that the British were coming toward them in boats.[12] Paul Revere and William Dawes rode from Boston to Lexington by different routes, shouting, "To arms! To arms! The British are coming!" Samuel Prescott joined them in Lexington and the three rode toward Concord to warn the people there. On the way,

Revere was captured by British soldiers and Dawes was thrown from his horse, but Prescott reached Concord to give the warning.

Early the next morning, six hundred British soldiers arrived at Lexington and were confronted by seventy armed Minutemen farmers.[13] The British commander yelled, "Disperse ye rebels, disperse!" A shot was fired and more shots followed. By the time the shooting stopped, eight Minutemen had given their lives for the cause of freedom. The British soldiers searched for Hancock and Adams, but they had been forewarned by Paul Revere and were safely on their way to Philadelphia.

The British then marched to Concord, where they set fire to several buildings and destroyed five hundred pounds of cannon balls.[14] However, they found little else because the Minutemen had carted most their weapons and ammunition to distant hiding places. About a hundred British soldiers continued searching north of Concord, but they were turned back at the North Bridge by three to four hundred Minutemen.[15] After that, the British retreated to Boston, but they were attacked by the sniper fire of Minutemen hiding along the wooded roadsides. British soldiers searched private homes for the snipers, taking plunder as they went along. By the end of the day, they had suffered seventy-three killed and two hundred wounded. The Americans had lost forty-nine killed and forty-six wounded.[16] The war had begun. General Gage had carried out his orders to engage the rebels.

C. The Williamsburg Gunpowder Incident

Two days later, early in the morning of April 21, British soldiers from the schooner *H.M.S. Magdalen* crept from their ship's mooring on the James River into the Virginia capital of Williamsburg. They opened the town's public arms magazine and carted off fifteen half-barrels of gunpowder. The royal governor, Lord Dunmore, had procured keys to the magazine from the keeper and had given them to the soldiers. When local guards saw what was happening, they began beating their drums. Alarmed, most of the townspeople arose from their beds and gathered at the market-

Chapter 3 — To Arms! To Arms!

Fig. 6: "TO ARMS! TO ARMS! THE BRITISH ARE COMING!"

Fig. 7: THE BATTLE OF LEXINGTON

marketsquare adjacent the magazine. Their leaders calmed them down and said they would confront the governor immediately.[17]

At the mansion called the "Governor's Palace," a delegation headed by House of Burgesses Speaker Peyton Randolph, colonial Treasurer Robert Carter Nicholas and Williamsburg Mayor John Dixon told Governor Dunmore that the powder belonged to the people of the colony, not to the crown. They demanded an explanation and the return of their powder. The governor said he was surprised by the adverse public reaction. He explained that he had taken the powder only to protect it from a rumored slave uprising. He promised to return it promptly if and when it was needed. The delegates accepted his explanation and his promise. They did not want to prolong the dispute because they feared it would delay their travel plans to the Second Continental Congress, scheduled in Philadelphia in early May. They also believed their best response would be to list incident among the grievances that the Congress would be sending to King George.

When news of the gunpowder incident reached the other counties in Virginia, local leaders organized volunteer militia companies and rode toward Williamsburg to protect their capital city. On April 29, over six hundred mounted men met at Fredericksburg. The evening before, they had heard the news of the battles at Lexington and Concord. Those events seemed too similar their experience at Williamsburg to be a coincidence. Many feared the British were preparing to attack their homes and families. However, Speaker Randolph convinced a representative committee of soldiers that such was not the case and they should disband. They did so but pledged to defend "at a moment's warning . . . this or any sister colony, from unjust and wicked invasion."[18]

Not everyone chose to be so cooperative. The company from Hanover County to the south of Fredericksburg did not disband. Led by Patrick Henry, its 150 soldiers continued to march until they reached Doncastle's Ordinary, about fifteen miles from Williamsburg. British Captain George Montagu, commander of the *H.M.S. Fowey* on the York River, responded with a threat to bombard Yorktown. When they heard the news, some of the residents fled their homes. Henry's goal was to capture the governor's receiver general, Richard Corbin, and force him to pay for the powder. Corbin's son-in-law, Carter Braxton, intervened and offered Henry a bill of exchange for £330 to settle the matter. Henry refused but accepted a note signed by Thomas Nelson, Jr., a prominent merchant and planter from Yorktown. He then sent a message to Nicholas suggesting that he bring his men into Williamsburg to protect the public treasury. After Nicholas coldly replied that his services were not needed, Henry finally sent his men home.[19]

D. The Green Mountain Boys and Fort Ticonderoga

In the land that later became the state of Vermont, the people had started their own war of independence. A dispute had been raging for twenty years over conflicting royal land grants to the colonies of New York and New Hampshire. Originally, the eastern New York boundary had been defined by the Connecticut River, which now divides New Hampshire from the state of Vermont. However, in the 1740s, the British Royal Council and the solicitor general ruled that the western boundary of the New Hampshire colony was a line running only twenty miles east of the Hudson River. King George II ordered the royal governor of New Hampshire, Benning Wentworth, to plant settlers in the lands west of the Connecticut River and to establish a garrison of soldiers at Fort Dummer on the west bank of the river. That proved to be a satisfactory arrangement during the French and Indian Wars of the 1740s and '50s. However, the New York government persisted in its claim to the same territory. In 1764, upon a recommendation by the British Board of Trade, King George III decreed that this beautiful land, dominated by the Green Mountains, belonged to New York. By that time, Governor Wentworth of New Hampshire had already sold many tracts of the same land to New England farmers, and these farmers had settled on the land with their families.[20] Unfortunately, the decree did not say whether the land had always belonged to New York, but London officials often referred to the decree as a "transfer" to New York.[21]

During this struggle for control of the Green Mountains, Benning Wentworth had taken full advantage of the fact that the colonists in New York and the British officials were preoccupied with other matters, such as the war with the French and the Indians. For example, he once sent a petition to London presenting the New Hampshire side of the dispute, without sending a copy to the New York officials. Historians have described his tactics as fraudulent and deceitful. Perhaps many of the farmers buying land from Wentworth knew how he was operating. Nevertheless, Wentworth's land grants were pursuant to the authority vested in him by of the king of England. Therefore, in 1764, when the New York government repudiated the New Hampshire grants and threatened to chase the farmers off their lands, most of the farmers refused to move. Unlike the lawyers and merchants of Boston, few if any of these backwoods people could have quoted the Magna Charta or Blackstone in support of their claims. They simply believed they had a God-given right to their farmlands.

The New York government did not try hard to chase the Hampshire grants farmers off their lands. It also failed to send judges and law enforcement officers to the Green Mountains. However, between 1765 and 1775, it sold over two million acres of the same lands to New Yorkers, who tried to rent the lands to tenant farmers. Few people were interested in renting these lands because the Hampshire grants farmers were still living on them.

From 1765 to 1769, the Green Mountains were in a state of anarchy. Then in 1769, Ethan Allen, a Connecticut farmer and land speculator, came with a large extended family and seized control of the territory. In 1770, he organized the men of various towns into militia companies of Green Mountain Boys and became the unofficial territorial governor. He said his actions were based on "the law of self-preservation." He wrote, "Self preservation makes it necessary that the said Inhabitants hold together, and defend themselves against this excrable Cunning of New York;" otherwise, he said, they would be reduced to poverty and "by terms inslav'd."[22]

From 1770 to 1774, Allen said that he would recognize New York's sovereignty over the Green Mountains, provided New York recognize the New Hampshire land grants. However, when he saw that the neighboring Massachusetts colonists were organizing a militia that also defied British rule, Allen decided to take a tougher stand. After the battles at Lexington and Concord, he called a convention in the town of Bennington, where he was officially elected the commander of the Green Mountain Boys. He then made plans to capture Fort Ticonderoga near the south end of Lake Champlain, which was the most likely staging area for a British or New York attack on the Green Mountain territory.

Meanwhile, Ethan's brothers Heman and Levi had traveled back to Connecticut to arrange financial support for the attack. With the help of a Connecticut patriot leader, Benedict Arnold, they prevailed upon the Hartford Committee of Correspondence to give them £300, which the Committee had recently borrowed from the Connecticut colonial treasury. Arnold also volunteered to join the expedition, as did fifty Minutemen from Williamstown and Pittsfield in western Massachusetts. With some of the money obtained in Hartford, one of the volunteers rented two large boats from a British fort at Crown Point, an outpost ten miles north of Fort Ticonderoga on Lake Champlain. These preliminary activities took place within a three-day period and remained a secret to Captain William De la Place, the British commander of the fort.

In the early morning hours of May 10, 1775, Ethan Allen, Benedict Arnold and an army of three hundred Green Mountain Boys and Minutemen gathered on the western shore of Lake Champlain across from Fort Ticonderoga. However, only eighty-five of the men were able to cross the lake in the rented boats. They were sufficient to overwhelm a surprised garrison of fifty British soldiers guarding the fort. After taking nearly all the guards prisoner, Allen knocked on the door of the headquarters. Lieutenant Jocelyn Feltham, the assistant commander of the fort, opened the door, looked at the intruder and asked under whose authority he was acting. Allen replied that he had come "in the name of the Great Jehovah and the Continental Congress!"[23] When Captain De

Fig. 8
ETHAN ALLEN DEMANDS THE SURRENDER OF FORT TICONDEROGA

la Place finally came to the door, Allen demanded his surrender. The captain had no choice but to comply.

Several days later, the Green Mountain Boys captured two smaller forts at Crown Point and St. Jean and thereby gained control of all of Lake Champlain. The news of these events lifted the spirits of all the colonists who were resisting British tyranny. On July 4, 1775, Ethan Allen appeared before his former enemies in the New York Assembly in Albany and persuaded them to recognize his authority throughout the Green Mountain territory. In return, his Green Mountain Boys joined the New York militia.

E. The Second Continental Congress

On May 10, 1775, the same day the Green Mountain Boys were attacking Fort Ticonderoga, the Second Continental Congress convened in Philadelphia. The agenda included raising an army and a navy, sending diplomatic agents to Europe, and establishing relations with various Indian tribes. This time the representatives met in the Pennsylvania State House, where the colony's legislature had met. The building was later renamed "Independence Hall."

However, the members of the Congress were not quite ready to declare their independence at this meeting. Instead, they adopted a Declaration of the Causes and Necessity of Taking Up Arms, in which they said,

> [W]e mean not to dissolve that union which has so long and so happily subsisted between us, and which we sincerely wish to see restored. . . . We have not raised armies with ambitious designs of separation from Great Britain, and establishing independent states. We fight not for glory or for conquest.

They said they were taking up arms only to defend themselves:

> We have received certain intelligence, that General Carlton, the Governor of Canada, is instigating the people of that province and the Indians to fall upon us; and we have but too much reason to apprehend, that schemes have been formed to excite domestic enemies against us. In brief, a part of these colonies now feel, and all of them are sure of feeling, as far as the vengeance of administration can inflict them, the complicated calamities of fire, sword, and famine. We are reduced to the alternative of choosing an unconditional submission to the tyranny of irritated ministers, or resistance by force.--The latter is our choice.[24]

The Congress then resolved to raise a Continental Army, with both regular army soldiers and militia units from each colony. It chose George Washington to be the army's commander. It also sent another letter to the people of Québec, encouraging them to join "in the defence of our common liberty."[25]

F. Bunker Hill

Meanwhile, the Massachusetts Provincial Army had managed to cordon off the city of Boston, confining General Gage's army of ten thousand soldiers to the peninsula on which the city was located, with no means of escape except by sea. On June 17, Gage ordered his troops to attack a colonial entrenchment on Breed's Hill, which faced the harbor between Charlestown and Boston. The battle that followed was called the "Battle of Bunker Hill," after the larger hill that stood behind Breed's Hill. The British captured both Breed's Hill and Bunker Hill, but they suffered 1054 casualties out of twenty-two hundred soldiers engaged, while the colonists lost 441 soldiers out of thirty-two hundred engaged.[26] One of the colonists killed was the president of the Massachusetts Provincial Congress, Dr. Joseph Warren, who had drafted the Suffolk Resolves and had organized the Minutemen. Bunker Hill was a technical victory for the British but a moral victory for the new Continental Army. The colonists had shown themselves and the British that they could hold their own in battle, even before their new commander George Washington had arrived.

G. Another Petition and More Fighting

Even after Lexington, Concord, Fort Ticonderoga and Bunker Hill, most colonists still wanted to avoid an all-out war against the British. In July 1775, the Continental Congress sent an Olive Branch Petition to the king, asking him to interpose his authority so that both sides could reach a "happy and permanent reconciliation."[27] The king refused to receive the petition. On August 23, 1775, he issued a Proclamation for Suppressing Rebellion and Sedition. On December 22, 1775, Parliament passed a law prohibiting "all manner of trade and commerce" with the rebellious colonies. It also declared that all colonial ships, civilian and military, were lawful prize and their crews were subject to impressment in the British navy.[28]

Although the capture of Fort Ticonderoga had boosted their morale, the colonists faced the difficult task of defending the Lake Champlain region. The British had recaptured Fort St. Jean at the north end of the lake. The Continental Congress therefore authorized a counterattack into the Québec territory. In November 1775, General Richard Montgomery led a force of a thousand New England soldiers, including Ethan Allen and his Green Mountain

Boys, on a march to the British fort at Montréal. Along the way, they convinced 250 French Canadians to join them.

Montgomery's men recaptured Fort St. Jean, but most of the French Canadians deserted and Ethan Allen was captured. Meanwhile, the British elected to evacuate Montréal, so they could consolidate their defenses at their Québec fortress to the northeast.

Confident of victory, the Americans pursued the retreating British army. On reaching Québec, they were joined by six hundred more New Englanders, who had come from Boston through the Maine wilderness under the command of Benedict Arnold. However, the British had eighteen hundred men guarding the fortress. The New Englanders attacked on December 31, 1775 but were turned back in a bloody battle that cost them forty-eight dead, thirty-four wounded and 372 captured.[29] It was the first major defeat for the Continental Army.

The events to the south were more favorable for the colonists. In the aftermath of the Williamsburg gunpowder incident, several youths had broken into the magazine and were severely wounded by a shotgun that had been rigged to fire at the tripping of the spring. The public had blamed Governor Dunmore for setting the trap. Other acts of violence followed and on June 8, Dunmore fled Williamsburg and boarded the *H.M.S. Magdalen*. Many colonists suspected that he had left because British military forces were preparing to attack them. A period of anarchy followed, during which colonial leaders organized independent companies of soldiers. On July 17, a convention of colonial leaders met in Richmond and declared that Governor Dunmore had abdicated and his power would henceforth reside in an eleven man Committee of Safety. Dunmore responded by organizing a flotilla of British warships, from which he launched attacks on towns and plantations along the Tidewater river banks. He also proclaimed freedom for all black slaves who escaped from their masters and enlisted in a regiment to be called the "Loyal Ethiopians." In September 1775, Dunmore was twice humiliated, once when he was thrown overboard in a hurricane and again when one of his ships ran aground and was captured by colonial land forces. In November, he scored a victory over an inexperienced colonial militia unit at Great Bridge, about ten miles south of Norfolk. The following month, however, he ordered several hundred of his men to attack a nine-hundred-man regiment of colonists commanded by Colonel William Woodford at Long Bridge, about twenty miles south of Norfolk. The governor's British, Loyalist and "Ethiopian" troops had to march in single file up a causeway over a swamp in order to reach Woodford's troops, who were stationed safely behind a loop-holed stockade. The attack was a disaster. Dunmore and the others who were not killed or captured were forced to reboard their ships and head out to sea.[30]

Part of Lord Dunmore's problems stemmed from the small number Virginians who chose to join his army. In North Carolina, however, Governor Josiah Martin had reason to believe that he could recruit more Loyalists. Near Cross Creek on the Cape Fear River was a large colony of emigrants from the Scottish Highlands. One of the leaders of this colony was an experienced soldier, Allan MacDonald, whom Governor Martin had raised to the rank of brigadier general. His wife was the renowned Flora MacDonald, the Jacobite heroine who had helped the royal pretender Bonnie Prince Charlie escape to Skye Island after his defeat at Culloden. After a short stay in the Tower of London, she had married Allan and emigrated to America, where she had voiced her support for the British monarchy during the American colonial disputes. When the fighting in the north broke out, she rode the countryside urging everyone to join her husband's Royal Emigrant Regiment. In response, sixteen hundred local Highlanders enlisted. However, many more men joined the North Carolina Continental Army. In February 1776, at Widow Moore's Creek near Wilmington, the Continentals defeated the governor's forces, including MacDonald's Royal Emigrants, leaving the North Carolina Loyalist movement in disarray.[31]

Meanwhile in New England, George Washington, the new commander of the Continental Army, ordered a siege on the British garrison in Boston. Using the cannon seized at Fort Ticonderoga, the Americans began shelling the garrison from Dorchester Heights on March 2, 1776. On March 17, the British soldiers could take the shelling no longer. They evacuated Boston and fled by sea to Nova Scotia.[32]

In May 1776, General Henry Clinton, the commander of the remaining British forces in the south, left his post in North Carolina in order to attack Charleston, South Carolina. Charleston was guarded by a half-built fort on Sullivan's Island, commanded by William Moultrie, a member of the South Carolina Provincial Congress and a colonel of the South Carolina Regiment. Clinton planned to land his soldiers on Long Island (now the Isle of Palms) and then have them ford the shallow waters separating Long Island from the northeast shore of Sullivan's Island. Meanwhile, Commodore Peter Parker's ships were to fire on the fort, which was at the Southwest end of the island. When Clinton launched his attack on June 28, serious flaws in his plan became apparent. His men were unable to ford the waters between Long Island and Sullivan's Island, because even at low tide they were seven to eight feet deep. At the other end of the island, the waters were too shallow for Parker's ships to get close enough to fire effectively on the fort. By contrast, Colonel Moultrie's guns were able to do them great damage. After several hours, Clinton and Parker gave up, taking their men and ships back to sea.[33] Colonel Moultrie received a hero's welcome in Charleston and the fort was named after him.

The colonists thus accomplished by military force what they had failed to do by negotiation. The people of Boston were finally free and the British soldiers had been driven from all the colonies, least for the time being. On the other hand, the British navy was now blockading all the American ports and the British army was planning to reinvade the colonies by way of New York City.

In spite of these events, the colonists had not declared their independence. Many people forget that independence was not their original goal. Initially, they wanted only to repeal the Intolerable Acts and gain recognition of their English liberties. However, as the war continued and their petitions fell on deaf ears, they lost all hope of settling their differences with the British government. It was only then that they thought seriously of independence.

4

The Declaration of Independence

A. A Call for *Common Sense*

The pamphlet *Common Sense*, published in January 1776 by Thomas Paine, called for the Continental Congress to declare the independence of the American colonies from Great Britain. It also called for the Congress to enact a charter for the new nation, guaranteeing "freedom and property to all men, and above all things the free exercise of religion."

Paine was a Quaker who had come to America from England in November 1774, at the urging of Benjamin Franklin. Franklin had met Paine in London and had been impressed by his literary skills, as well as by his commitment to the colonial cause of freedom. When Paine published *Common Sense*, he more than fulfilled Franklin's expectations. First, he explained the natural law origin of government, much as Locke and Blackstone had done. He said that governments were formed by primitive societies when people relaxed "their duty and attachment to one another," thus creating a need to enforce standards of moral virtue.

Paine also said that the only just form of government was one controlled by a legislature of the people's representatives who were made answerable to the people by frequent elections. In that way, he said, the government "will establish a common interest with every part of the community" and they will mutually support one another. On this, Paine said, "depends the *strength of government, and the happiness of the governed.*" He deplored the European governments controlled by hereditary kings and noblemen, and particularly the English government, "so exceedingly complex, that

Chapter 4 The Declaration of Independence 89

the nation may suffer for years together without being able to discover in which part the fault lies, some will say in one and some in another, and every political physician will advise a different medicine."

Paine then wrote,

> But where says some is the King of America? I'll tell you Friend, he reigns above, and doth not make havock of mankind like the Royal --- of Britain. Yet that we may not appear to be defective even in earthly honors, let a day be solemnly set apart for proclaiming the charter; let it be brought forth placed on the divine law, the word of God; let a crown be placed thereon, by which the world may know, that so far as we approve of monarchy, that in America THE LAW IS KING. For as in absolute governments the King is law, so in free countries the law *ought* to be King; and there ought to be no other. But lest any ill use should afterwards arise, let the crown at the conclusion of the ceremony be demolished, and scattered among the people whose right it is.

On that premise, he made the following plea:

> O ye that love mankind! Ye that dare oppose, not only the tyranny, but the tyrant, stand forth! Every spot of the old world is overrun with oppression. Freedom hath been hunted round the globe. Asia and Africa have long expelled her--Europe regards her like a stranger, and England hath given her warning to depart. O! receive the fugitive, and prepare in time an asylum for mankind.

Finally, he concluded,

> . . . until an independence is declared, the Continent will feel itself like a man who continues putting off some unpleasant business from day to day, yet knows it must be done, hates to set about it, wishes it over, and is continually haunted with the thoughts of its necessity.[1]

In the first three months of 1776, 120,000 copies of *Common Sense* were sold at two shillings a piece. By the end of the year, the sales rose to half a million. Paine assigned his copyright in the pamphlet to the Continental Congress. The royalties provided a large and desperately needed contribution to the Congressional war chest.[2]

B. The People Respond

Paine's *Common Sense* hit the American colonists like a thunderbolt. It came in the midst of news that their Continental Army had forced the British soldiers to flee their cities. No wonder they began clamoring for independence![3]

On May 15, 1776, a convention of former members of the disbanded Virginia House of Burgesses instructed its delegates to the Continental Congress "to declare the United Colonies free and independent states." By the time the Congress met in Philadelphia in June, seven other colonial assemblies had given similar instructions to their delegates. While the delegates from the other five colonies waited for their instructions, a committee of five delegates--Thomas Jefferson, John Adams, Benjamin Franklin, Roger Sherman and Robert Livingston--was appointed to draft a proposed declaration of independence. The committee chose Jefferson to prepare the first draft.

Paine had convinced many Americans that it was in their best interests to declare their independence from Great Britain. However, the Declaration of Independence was designed also to convince the people of the world that the Americans were justified in declaring their independence. If they were to win their struggle for freedom, Jefferson and the other members of the Congress knew they would need the support of many people and nations, including leaders who might think their declaration was an unjustified rebellion against a lawful government. They might view the British government as among "the higher powers" that the apostle Paul had said were entitled to obedience because they were "ordained of God" (Rom. 13:1). Therefore, the Declaration had to explain why that government had lost its God-ordained right to rule its American colonies.

At the age of thirty-three, Jefferson was the perfect man for this task. He could express complicated ideas in simple, graceful language. John Adams said he admired his "peculiar felicity of expression." He was an avid student of classical literature, philosophy, history and law. He had read the ancient works of Plato, Aristotle and Cicero and the modern works of Bacon, Locke, and Blackstone.[4] He showered lavish praise on Bacon and Locke but only grudging praise on Blackstone's *Commentaries* because of its shallow treatment of the law and his disgust with attorneys who relied on no other source. He said that Blackstone's book was "the most elegant and best digested in our catalogue" but it "has been perverted more than all others, to the degeneracy of legal science."[5] During the early 1760s, Jefferson had studied law in Williamsburg under the rigorous mentor George Wythe. As a student, lawyer and politician, he had become familiar with the basic documents of English government, from the Magna Charta to the Declaration of Rights. He claimed that he "turned to neither book nor pamphlet" while writing the Declaration of Independence.[6] In that case, he must have known by heart a few portions of the English Declaration of Rights, Locke's *Second Essay Concerning Civil Government* and Blackstone's *Commentaries*.

Jefferson began "The Unanimous Declaration of the Thirteen United States of America" by saying it had become necessary for the people of those states to

> dissolve the political bands which have connected them with another, and to assume the separate and equal station to which *the Laws of Nature and Nature's God* [emphasis added] entitle them.

That meant that the American colonies were declaring their right to return to the state of nature, described by Locke as the state of being of primitive peoples who had no government except for God's laws of nature.

The document then recognized the need for the American people to "declare the causes which impel them to the separation." It prefaced that list of causes with several philosophical truths, said to be "self-evident."

The first truth was that "all men are created equal." This was a necessary premise to the colonists' argument for independence. If all men were not created equal, then the British king and nobles could claim a natural right to govern others, owing to the superior status given them by God when they were born. The equality of all men is now a well-recognized principle of modern government. However, it was the weakest link in the colonists' argument. In 1776, nearly every nation of the world was organized on a class system in which people of noble or wealthy birth had special legal privileges not shared by all. Many American colonists, including Jefferson, owned black slaves. Some said that their slaves had inferior rights because they were of an inferior race. They also claimed the Indians were inferior and in this way justified taking their land. The equality premise of the Declaration also contradicted the tenets of faith of several early American religious groups, including the New England Puritans and the Dutch Calvinists of New York. Those groups believed that God had predestined only a few chosen people to have the true Christian faith and that therefore those people had been born with the right to govern the other people of their communities.

On the other hand, the enlightened philosophers of the eighteenth century had long argued that all men are entitled to the same opportunities and legal rights. In 1690, John Locke had said there was

> nothing more evident than that creatures of the same species and rank, promiscuously born to all the same advantages of nature and the use of the same faculties, should also be equal one amongst the other without subordination or subjection. (App. F, par. 4)

Therefore, when the Americans used the equality of men to justify their separation from Great Britain, most observers accepted it as the way things ought to be. Since then, people have been trying to make it a reality, by preventing discrimination on account of race, religion, sex and other factors. They should be grateful that the American founders admitted that their right to freedom depended on equality. At his famous March on Washington on August 28, 1963, Martin Luther King said,

> I still have a dream. It is a dream deeply rooted in the American dream that one day this nation will rise up and live out the true meaning of its creed---we hold these truths to be self-evident, that all men are created equal.

The second truth proclaimed by the Declaration was that all men "are endowed by their Creator with certain unalienable rights, that among these are Life, Liberty and the pursuit of Happiness." That means that while men may forego living in a primitive state of nature for the sake of living under the protection of governments, they retain certain rights that they had when they were governed only by God's natural law. In his *Commentaries*, Blackstone said that the rights of life and liberty are among those natural, absolute rights of individuals (BL3, 123-134). The "pursuit of happiness" related to Blackstone's explanation of the origin of all natural law rights. He said that God had built the laws of nature into the order of the universe in such a manner that man must obey them "in order to pursue his own happiness" (BL1, 41), or as Locke said, in order to accomplish "the peace and preservation of all mankind" (App. F, par. 7). Blackstone gave as examples the three basic laws of nature common to all societies and religious beliefs: "that we should live honestly, hurt nobody, and should render to every one its due" (BL1, 40-41). In the Declaration of Independence, the statement that the pursuit of happiness is an inalienable right means that human governments have a duty preserve these basic laws of nature by making their own laws and actions conform to them, so that all people can pursue their happiness.

However, the Declaration did not base man's inalienable rights on the revealed laws of the Christian Bible, as some have asserted.[7] The laws of nature are determined by human observation, experience and reasoning, whereas revealed laws become known only through spiritual faith or spiritual sources such as holy scriptures. Most revealed laws of the world's religions motivate their believers to obey the laws of nature and in that way they enhance these laws.

On the other hand, some revealed laws, such as those proclaiming that certain people are born with a God-given right to govern others, are contrary to the laws of nature. There are also many conflicts between the revealed laws of different religions. Therefore, a government based on the revealed laws of one religion is likely to discriminate against people of other religions and violate their natural law rights.

The Declaration's third truth was that governments derive their powers "from the consent of the governed." That was the consent given when primitive men formed governments by the social contracts described by Locke. He said, "the people [cannot] be bound by any laws but such as are enacted by those whom they have chosen and authorized to make laws for them" (App. F, par. 141). Alexander Hamilton said in *The Farmer Refuted* that this precept of government differs from that of Thomas Hobbes, who held that government derives its power from the need that a few good people impose their will on a morally degenerate population. However, Locke's precept does not conflict with the revealed law of the apostle Paul, who said that human governments are "ordained of God" (Rom. 13:1). According to the Bible, God's ordination is in response to the people electing or contracting to have a government. God ordained King Saul to be the first king of Israel in response to the people's request for a king (1 Sam. 8:6, 12:13).

The fourth and last truth of the Declaration was that when a government formed by the consent of the people destroys their natural law rights, then they have the right "to alter or abolish it, and to institute a new government, laying its foundation on such principles, and organizing its powers in such form, as to them shall seem most likely to effect their safety and happiness." That means the principles of natural law are so essential to the very being of government that its right to rule ceases when it violates these principles. Locke said that governments can be dissolved when "the legislative acts against the trust reposed in them." That occurs "when they endeavor to invade the property of the subject, and to make themselves or any part of the community masters or arbitrary disposers of the lives, liberties, or fortunes of the people." He also said,

> When any one or more shall take upon them to make laws, whom the people have not appointed so to do, they make laws without authority, which the people are not therefore bound to obey; by which means they come again to be out of subjection and may constitute to themselves a new legislative as they think best, being in full liberty to resist the force of those who without authority would impose anything upon them.[8]

Therefore, when a government arbitrarily takes away the lives, liberties and fortunes of people, those people have the right to abolish that government and to form a new one that will protect their safety and their ability to pursue happiness through obedience to God's laws of nature.

After reciting these premises, the Declaration listed the many ways by which the British government violated the colonists' natural law rights of life, liberty and the pursuit of happiness. In making this list, Jefferson had the perfect document to guide him, namely the English Declaration of Rights passed by Parliament in 1689 (App. E). That document had been drawn up after King James II had been overthrown in the Revolution of 1688. The causes of that revolution were the king's loyalty to the Roman pope and his persecution of English Protestants. The main difference between that situation and the one confronting the American colonists in 1776 was the colonists were seeking to free themselves from the British king and not the pope.

Several clauses in the Declaration of Independence are almost identical to clauses in the English Declaration of Rights. The latter accused James II of subverting the laws and liberties of the kingdom by "assuming and exercising a power of dispensing with and suspending the laws and the execution of laws without the consent of Parliament." The American Declaration said that George III "has refused his Assent to Laws, the most wholesome and necessary for the public good." The English Declaration attacked James II for "raising and keeping a standing army within this kingdom in time of peace without the consent of Parliament, and quartering soldiers contrary to law." The Declaration of Independence said that George III "has kept among us in times of peace, Standing Armies without the Consent of our legislatures," and has been "quartering large bodies of troops among us."

Other clauses in the Declaration of Independence said that the king of Great Britain had deprived the colonists "of the benefits of trial by jury" and had transported colonists "beyond the seas to be tried for pretended offenses." According to Blackstone, these actions violated the right of personal liberty (BL3, 130-131, 133). Concerning the trial by jury, he said that it "is the most transcendent privilege which any subject can enjoy, or wish for, that he cannot be affected either in his property, his liberty, or his person, but by the unanimous consent of twelve of his neighbors and equals."[9]

The Declaration said that the king had imposed taxes on the colonists without their consent. According to Blackstone, this violated their right of property (BL3, 135).

Another clause said that the king has "dissolved representative houses repeatedly, for opposing, with manly firmness, his invasions on the rights of the people." This was a violation of the right of petitioning the king for redress of grievances, which Blackstone said was among the auxiliary rights for the protection of life, liberty and property (BL3, 138-139).

One of the violations listed by Jefferson in his original draft of the Declaration was that the king had "determined to keep open a market where men should be bought and sold." This statement was stricken because it embarrassed and angered most of the southern delegates and it would have sidetracked the Congress from the more immediate issue of independence from Great Britain. The statement was also hypocritical, coming from Jefferson who owned slaves himself. Nevertheless, slavery weighed heavily on the consciences of many Americans. At least the delegates admitted that their fundamental rights were based on the principle that all men are created equal, even if they did not put that principle into practice throughout the United States.

The Declaration's list of violations ended with five paragraphs of actions by the king of Great Britain since he began his armed attacks on the colonists. These actions included plundering the sea vessels of the colonists, ravaging their coasts, burning their towns, destroying their lives, sending large armies of foreign mercenaries against them, capturing their merchant ships on the high seas and impressing their crews into service against their fellow colonists, inciting colonists loyal to the crown to mount insurrections against the colonial legislatures and enlisting savage Indians to attack colonists of all ages and sexes.

After listing these acts of destruction and tyranny, the Declaration recited the repeated attempts of the colonial representatives to settle their differences with their "British brethren." The Declaration also said that the British have been "deaf to the voice of justice and consanguinity." That was a reminder to the British government that most of the colonists were transplanted Englishmen and that all they wanted were the same rights that their English brothers were enjoying.

The Declaration concluded with a paragraph in which the representatives, "appealing to the Supreme Judge of the world for the rectitude of their intentions," declared "that these United Colonies are, and of Right ought to be, Free and Independent States; . . . ." In support of that declaration, they said, "with a firm reliance on the Protection of Divine Providence, we mutually pledge to each other our lives, our Fortunes and our sacred Honor."

On July 2, 1776, the Congressional delegates from twelve colonies voted to declare their independence. The New York delegates abstained because their colony's assembly had not yet voted on the issue.

Then, on July 4, 1776, the Continental Congress adopted the Declaration of Independence, with only a few changes to Jefferson's original draft. On the same day, the document was engrossed by the clerk of the Congress and signed by the presiding delegate, John Hancock. Some other delegates may have signed the original as well. Copies were then sent to the state legislatures and to Washington's army headquarters.

On July 8, the Declaration was read to a large, cheering crowd gathered outside the State House in Philadelphia. During the following week, it was read in cities and towns throughout the country. Some of the celebrations became riots. In New York City, a gilded lead statue of George III was pulled down and its gold leaf scraped off. The lead was then melted down for musket balls. In Boston, a shield bearing the king's arms over the State House door was torn down and burned. In Savannah, King George was burned in effigy.

Meanwhile, the Congress ordered that an official, engraved copy of the Declaration be prepared, to be signed by all the delegates. When the news arrived on July 19 that the New York assembly had voted in favor of independence, the Congress instructed the engraver to change the heading from "A Declaration by the Representatives of the United States in General Congress Assembled" to "The Unanimous Declaration of the Thirteen United States of America."

On August 2, 1776, fifty delegates to the Congress met and signed the official, engraved copy of the Declaration. The remaining six delegates signed it on later dates.

5

The War of Independence

The story of why the American colonists went to war would not be complete without the story of the war itself. We cannot know the value that these people placed on their freedom without knowing what they sacrificed. This story should also help us understand the motivations and frustrations of people who have recently been fighting for their freedom in Bosnia, Chechnya, Somalia, Rwanda and other places.

Most Americans call this war "The American Revolution." John Adams wrote that the war was the result of a "Revolution in the minds and hearts of the people." However, the war itself did not cause a political revolution, because the class structure of American society remained the same after the war. What the war did cause was the birth of a new nation that was independent of the British Empire but based on principles of government inherited from the English common law, described in Blackstone's *Commentaries*. Therefore, "The War of Independence" is the more appropriate name.

A. Patriots and Loyalists

The War of Independence arose from a dispute over whether the British government could rule its American colonists absolutely, according to any whim or purpose, or whether it should respect the inalienable rights of the colonists. In America as well as England, people were divided on this issue.

In England, the Parliament itself was divided. Many members, including William Pitt, Edmund Burke and Charles James Fox, sympathized with the colonists' demands. They belonged to the reform-minded Whig party, but they were in the minority. The conservative Tories who controlled Parliament were opposed to making concessions. The British army and navy were also divided. Lord Jeffrey Amherst, who had commanded the British army when it took Canada from the French in 1758-60, refused an offer by King George to resume his American post, saying he would not fight against his own countrymen. Admiral Augustus Keppel refused a naval command for the same reason. Many soldiers and sailors of lesser rank also refused to support the American war. In April 1779, sixty Scots of the 71st Highlanders mutinied when they learned of their orders to fight in America.[1] Perhaps they were thinking of their ancestors who had fought for freedom under William Wallace and Robert the Bruce.

In America, the people who supported the American fight for independence called themselves "Patriots"; those who supported the British called themselves "Loyalists." The Patriots preferred to call the Loyalists by a more derisive term, "Tories," after the British political party that was their main opponent. In his *History of the United States*, James Truslow Adams said that there were violent factions on both the Patriot and Loyalist sides, but there were also between these factions "the vast mass of Americans who wanted above all else to be allowed to live their lives and earn their bread in peace, unmolested by new and annoying British laws or the violence of American radical mobs."[2] However, as the war progressed and its battles and raids affected almost every community in every state, nearly all Americans were forced to take sides. Most of them became Patriots.

According the historian Samuel Eliot Morison, nearly 50 percent of the Americans at the start of the war were neutral, while 40 percent were Patriots and 10 percent were Loyalists. These percentages varied from state to state. Massachusetts, Connecticut and Virginia had smaller percentages of Loyalists; New York was about 50 percent Loyalist.[3] In upstate New York, many tenant farmers were Loyalists because they were upset by the landlord-tenant laws passed by the New York assembly. The Patriots were most numerous in New England, because those states had been hardest hit by the British Coercive Acts. The Green Mountain settlers of the future state of Vermont were nearly 100 percent Patriot because of the British ruling against them in their land dispute with New York.

In North Carolina, support for the cause of independence was complicated by a war that broke out in 1776 between small farmers in the western counties, who called themselves "Regulators," and the large eastern landowners who controlled the state legislature and supported the Patriot cause. The Regulators' main complaints were the state's unfair methods of assessing and collecting taxes, the lack of justice in the state's courts and the high fees charged by lawyers in small claims lawsuits. The eastern Patriot farmers won this war and kept North Carolina loyal to their cause, but there remained a serious question of whether the state's western farmers would support the war against the British.

The Loyalists had the advantage of fighting on the side of the British Empire, the world's most powerful empire at the time. At the beginning of the war, the only advantage the Patriots had was their zeal for freedom. In the course of the war, however, the Patriots received help from other nations and individual foreign military leaders. France signed a treaty of alliance with the United States in 1778 and supplied soldiers, naval ships, supplies and money, without which the Patriots would have certainly lost the war. Spain and the Netherlands also helped the Patriots before and after they respectively declared war on Great Britain in 1779 and 1780. The foreign military leaders, who came at their own expense because they believed in the Patriot cause, included the Marquis de Lafayette and Chevalier du Plessis from France, Johann von Kalb ("Jean de Kalb") and Friedrich von Steuben from Germany and Tadeusz Kosciuszko and Casimir Pulaski from Poland. Perhaps if the British had known the Patriots would receive all this help, they would have fought the earlier part of the war with a greater sense of urgency.

B. The War and the Soldiers

The early battle successes of the American soldiers probably did more harm than good in preparing them for the remainder of the long war against the British. In 1776, George Washington faced huge problems in organizing his army. Most of his soldiers were raw recruits who had signed up for only six months, expecting the war to be won by the end of the year. He had no uniforms for them and most states fell far short of their manpower quotas assigned by the Continental Congress.

Washington also had to contend with a Congress divided by regional disputes over how to run the war. There were jealousies between the various state delegations over which general from which state should receive a certain command. The Congressmen from one state or region would often criticize the generals from other states or regions. Washington's harshest critics were Sam Adams and John Adams of Massachusetts.

As the War of Independence proceeded, soldier enlistments became longer. However, many volunteers treated their obligations rather casually, going home when the crops were ready for harvest and not returning until the end of the following spring planting season. Morale was bad because American merchants often refused to honor the Continental script that was printed to pay the soldiers and to buy supplies and food. Not only did the soldiers often have to forage for their food, but they were hampered in their efforts by Loyalist farmers who chased them away. To make matters worse, the food, clothing and money shortages caused several mutinies and attempted mutinies by enlisted men against their regimental commanders.

Because the British also had trouble recruiting soldiers to fight on their side, King George III made arrangements with his German relatives to hire soldiers from various German principalities and duchies. He hired about seventy-five hundred Germans initially and seventy-five hundred more during the war.[4] Because more than half of these soldiers were supplied by the Landgrave of Hesse-Cassel, the Americans called them all "Hessians."

Washington and his subordinate commanders were often able to supplement their forces with Patriot militia units from the region in which they were fighting. However, these militia soldiers usually appeared only when the regular Continental troops were winning battles. The British also enlisted their own militia from Loyalist Americans. These Loyalist troops came mainly from New York and later from South Carolina and Georgia, where the British were able to secure strong seaport bases. The British were also aided by Loyalists from Québec to the north and Florida to the south.

As with most wars, the War of Independence lasted much longer than either side expected. The survivors on both sides grieved over the loss of thousands of soldiers who were killed, as well as over thousands more who were wounded.[5] In addition, the soldiers feared the possibility of capture almost as much as they feared death or maiming. The way both sides treated each other's prisoners was horrendous, even by eighteenth-century standards. In the American camps, the prisoners were often crowded into huts containing thirty to forty people. In the British camps, hundreds were crowded into poorly ventilated rooms.[6] The worst prisons were the British prison ships that housed captured American civilians who were accused of piracy and hijacking British ships. Most prisoners suffered from starvation and disease and many died slow, painful deaths.

An often forgotten part of the War of Independence was the contribution of black slaves and some free black men who served in the Continental Army. In Virginia, all black slaves who enlisted were granted their freedom at the end of the war. Rhode Island purchased black slaves to fill its manpower quota. General Washington's records indicate that in August 1778, there were 755 black soldiers in his fourteen-brigade army. That meant an average of fifty-four black soldiers in each brigade of approximately fifteen hundred men.[7]

C. Long Island and Manhattan Island

After the British evacuated Boston in March 1776, General William Howe replaced General Gage as commander of the British army in America. Howe stationed the main body of his army in Halifax, Nova Scotia, while he awaited reinforcements from Europe. Meanwhile, General Washington moved the major part of his army down to New York City. Its population of twenty-two thousand was second only to that of Philadelphia and its strategic location made it a likely point of attack by the British. Washington placed some of his troops in New York City, at the south end of Manhattan Island, but he placed most of his eighteen thousand men across the East River on Long Island, where they fortified a row of hills south of the Brooklyn Heights on the Upper New York Bay.

On July 3, 1776, General Howe arrived on Staten Island with an army of nine thousand men. Soon after, his brother Admiral Sir Richard Howe arrived from England with a naval force of ten ships of the line, twenty frigates holding twelve hundred guns and hundreds of army transport ships. It was at the time the largest armada ever assembled by the British Empire.[8] In addition, Admiral Howe brought more British soldiers, as well as newly hired Hessian mercenaries. Meanwhile, Sir Henry Clinton and Lord Charles Cornwallis arrived with more troops from Cape Fear, North Carolina, and Charleston, South Carolina, bringing the total number of soldiers on the British side to over thirty thousand.

While gathering these forces for his grand attack on New York, General Howe sent several emissaries to Washington's headquarters for a final attempt to make peace with the Americans. However, the only agreement that Howe was authorized to offer was a guarantee of pardons to the leading conspirators, in exchange for recognition of Britain's absolute right to govern its American colonies in any way that it pleased. Of course, Washington declined the offer.

Therefore, on August 22, 1776, with the ink barely dry on the Declaration of Independence, Howe began moving his soldiers across the Narrows Strait to Long Island. His grand army, nearly twice the size of the American army, seemed destined to drive a mortal stake into the heart of the rebellion.

The ensuing battle on August 27 resulted in an easy and decisive victory for the British. The American commanders made the mistake of standing their ground on the plain below the hills they had fortified, the kind of terrain best suited for the European method of fighting. They also left their eastern flank unguarded. Part of Howe's army marched around this flank and forced the American soldiers into a state of disarray and confusion. For most of these soldiers, this was their first military battle. When they began seeing their comrades die, they panicked and ran, some drowning in swamps and ponds. In the chaos, many of the wounded also died when they were left unattended. Various accounts of the battle estimate the number of American casualties at between one and five thousand. The British and Hessians lost only a few hundred.[9]

However, General Howe failed to pursue the routed Americans. He chose to wait for reinforcements and heavy artillery, in order to avoid the chance of another British blood-bath like the one at Bunker Hill. Howe's delay allowed the retreating Americans to reorganize themselves and dig into fortifications. The Americans were also fortunate that on the following day, torrential rains interrupted Howe's preparations for his next attack.

When the rains began to subside on August 29, Washington decided that he could no longer defend his position. He ordered his men to move back to Manhattan Island and join the rest of his army. That night, nine thousand American soldiers, with provisions, artillery, cattle, horses and wagons, crossed the East River using an assortment of small boats manned by two Massachusetts regiments of seagoing soldiers from Marblehead and Salem. Because of the rain and fog, no one from the British army or navy saw them. The next morning, when thirty thousand British and Hessian soldiers began the charge that was sure to end the American rebellion, the enemy trenches were empty.

In spite of their dramatic escape, the Americans would have still been pinned in a difficult position had General Howe pursued them across the East River. However, he waited over two weeks, believing the Continental Army to be so weak and ill-prepared that it was sure to surrender sooner or later. During the interval, he made another peace offer, this time directly to the Continental Congress. Once again, he was rebuffed. Although many members of the Congress were discouraged, they were not quite ready to give up, either on their general whose tactics they were questioning, or on the cause for which they were fighting.

General Washington used the time given by Howe to reorganize his army and deploy it for a temporary defense of Manhattan Island. He divided his army into three divisions, one, commanded by General Israel Putnam, to guard New York City at the south end of the island, and the other two at the north end of the island, General Joseph Spencer's division at Harlem Heights and General William Heath's division at King's Bridge. He also convinced the Continental Congress that he did not have adequate troops for a permanent defense of New York City. The Congress therefore approved his evacuation of the city in the most expedient manner possible.

On September 15, Howe ferried the major part of his army across the East River to Kip's Bay on the east side of Manhattan Island, near the present 34th Street. Much to General Washington's anger, the American troops defending Kip's Bay fled, allowing the British to land without opposition. Fortunately for the Americans, Howe ordered his troops to set up their camps where they landed, rather than march immediately across the island to the Hudson River. That move would have cut off Putnam's division in New York City from Washington's other two divisions at the north end of the island. While Howe was camping, Putnam was able to march his division north and join it with Spencer's division in Harlem Heights. The next day, two British light infantry battalions encountered 150 Connecticut Rangers and three companies of Virginia riflemen defending the Harlem Heights. The Americans stood their ground this time and beat back the British, giving Washington's whole army a great morale lift.

In spite of the Harlem Heights episode, General Howe was still satisfied with his progress. He had slowly but steadily secured strong footholds on Manhattan Island, Staten Island and the western end of Long Island. He did not seem bothered by the fact that he had missed several chances to destroy his enemy and end the war. His failure to seize these opportunities has drawn much criticism, both from his contemporaries and later historians.

On the other hand, Howe's deliberate, slow movements were typical of the way eighteenth-century European generals operated. The object of most fighting in Europe was to take possession of land with as few casualties as possible. When land was conquered, the farmers who worked the land were also conquered. Usually, the new land and its farmers meant more wealth and power for the king of the conquering army. Therefore, there was seldom any reason to pursue enemy troops already fleeing the conquered land. To give chase would merely risk the lives of the king's soldiers who were needed to guard his new lands and insure his future profits.

What General Howe and other British commanders failed to understand was that the American War of Independence was not a war between kings for the possession of land. It was a war to decide the relationship between the American people and their government. Would these people continue to be the tools of labor and profit for a government having unrestrained power, like the governments of most of the people of the world? Or would they be able to establish a government that was their tool, guarding their security, their liberty and their property? The soldiers of George Washington's army lacked experience and training and they were underfed, underclothed and underpaid, but they had a great mission and each soldier had a personal stake in the success of that mission.

On September 22, 1776, General Howe was able to see an example of one of the many dedicated men who were part of Washington's army. The general's aides brought before him a young man who had been arrested on a street in Brooklyn posing as a Dutch school teacher. A Loyalist sympathizer had informed the arresting British officers that the man was really his cousin and was an officer in the Continental Army. Upon questioning, the man admitted that he was indeed Lieutenant Nathan Hale of the Continental Army and that he had been gathering information concerning British troop movements and reporting those movements to his superior officers. General Howe ordered an immediate public hanging without a trial. As the noose was place around his neck, near what is now the intersection of 63rd Street and First Avenue, Lieutenant Hale announced, "I only regret that I have but one life to lose for my country." General Howe should have realized that it was not enough to kill but one person who was willing to lose his life that others might gain their freedom. He would have to kill them all.

One of the excuses that Howe later gave for his failure to pursue the American army on Manhattan Island was the fires that erupted in New York City on the morning of September 21. A large part of the city, about five hundred buildings, burned to the ground. No evidence was ever found to determine how the fires started, but the British claimed that either Washington's soldiers or Patriot civilians were to blame, because most of the burned buildings were occupied either by the British army or by their Loyalist followers.

D. White Plains, Fort Lee and Fort Washington

Washington had hoped to keep the British navy from sailing up the Hudson River by establishing two forts on the river near the north end of Manhattan Island. The forts were named Fort Washington and Fort Lee, the latter after Washington's second in command, General Charles Lee. However, the fact that gunfire from British warships severely damaged these forts raised serious questions about their ability to stop the British. Washington therefore moved the main body of his army, about fourteen thousand men, north to Westchester County; by setting his troops up there, he hoped to stop any northward advance by the British army. Meanwhile, Howe moved the main body of his army by boat up the East River past the Throg's Neck and landed at Pell's Point. From there he moved to the high ground at East Chester. Washington's objective was another area of high ground further north at

White Plains. To reach that point, however, he had to march his tired army dangerously close to Howe's higher position at East Chester. Fortunately, Howe failed to take advantage of Washington's vulnerable flank and let the Americans march past him. In fact, the British army dallied almost a week waiting for reinforcements to arrive. By the time Howe had caught up to Washington's army, he found it firmly entrenched on most of the high ground in the White Plains area.

It was now late October and morning frosts were becoming common. The American soldiers were still dressed in light summer clothing. One of them, Private Joseph Martin, wrote the following in his diary:

> I have often while upon guard lain on one side until the upper side smarted with cold, then turned that side down to the place warmed by my body, and let the other side take its turn at smarting. . . . In the morning the ground was white as snow with hoar frost. Or perhaps it would rain all night like a flood; all that could be done in that case was to lie down (if one could lie down), take our musket in our arms and place the lock (firing device) between our thighs and "weather it out!"[10]

On October 28, the battle lines were drawn at White Plains. Washington ordered the American infantry to attack first. The British countered with heavy artillery fire. An American soldier recalled that one cannonball

> first took off the head of Smith, a stout heavy man, and dashed it open, then took Taylor across the bowels. It then struck Sergeant Garrett of our company on the hip [and] took off the point of the hip bone . . . What a sight it was to see within a distance of six rods those men with their legs and arms and guns and packs all in a heap.[11]

Once again, the war nearly ended. Howe outmaneuvered Washington, turning his right flank. However, the British general again failed to close in on his enemy. Perhaps the heavy rains stopped him. Washington was therefore able to evacuate his army to Northcastle, five miles to the north of White Plains.

At Northcastle, Washington worried that Howe might march south and attack his twin forts on the Hudson River, Fort Washington and Fort Lee. He therefore took twenty-five hundred men across the Hudson River to help strengthen Fort Lee, leaving General Charles Lee in command of eleven thousand men in Westchester County.

When he arrived at Fort Lee on November 13, Washington had expected to receive five thousand fresh militia promised by the State of New Jersey, but the actual number was only a small fraction of that total. That meant that the entire American force at the two forts, including the twenty-five hundred arriving with Washington, consisted of only about six thousand men. They were no match for the thirteen thousand British and Hessian soldiers who attacked Fort Washington on November 16. The British captured not only the fort but also three thousand American soldiers, 160 cannon and a large supply of food and ammunition. Then, the British crossed the Hudson and captured Fort Lee. Fortunately, the Americans guarding that fort were able to escape.

The British capture of Forts Lee and Washington was a devastating defeat for the Americans. The loss of so many Americans and their equipment depleted their already undermanned army. Washington was also forced to abandon the New York City area, giving the British sole possession of the most strategic port on the American seaboard. However, the Americans still had eleven thousand soldiers in Westchester County, three thousand soldiers in northern New Jersey and thirty-four hundred soldiers at Fort Ticonderoga in northern New York State.

E. Trenton and Princeton

Having secured New York City, Howe considered whether his next move should be to march up the Hudson River Valley and join forces with a Canadian army. That would give the British control of a region extending all the way from New York City to Montréal, thereby isolating the radical New England colonists from other Patriots who appeared to be less enthusiastic about the war.

However, he decided that the quickest way to end the rebellion would be to take control of the rebel headquarters at Philadelphia.

Washington learned of Howe's plan and resolved to defend Philadelphia as well as he could. As he marched across New Jersey with his beaten army, now under three thousand men, General Cornwallis was close behind him with five thousand British and Hessian soldiers. Both armies were headed toward the Delaware River at Trenton, but the Americans reached the river first and crossed into Pennsylvania on December 7 and 8. As they crossed, they commandeered all the boats on the river within twenty miles of Trenton and took them to the Pennsylvania side. Because there were no bridges, the wide river thus became a serious obstacle to a British attack on Philadelphia.

One of the reasons why the Americans reached the Delaware first was that General Howe had ordered Cornwallis to wait for him in New Brunswick so he could bring more troops. Howe had every reason to be confident that the war was over. The Americans had suffered heavy losses in New York and most of their enlistments were due to expire at the end of the year. He became even more confident when Washington's second in command, General Charles Lee, was captured near Morristown, trying to lead a division across New Jersey to reinforce Washington's troops in Pennsylvania. As the British marched across New Jersey, many colonists greeted them with cheers and hospitality.

As a final gesture of goodwill, Howe distributed notices throughout New Jersey offering pardons to all who pledged their allegiance to the king within the next sixty days. In the meantime, he received word from England that he had been knighted for his victorious campaign. With the cold winter setting in, Howe decided to give his men and himself a break. On December 17 he returned to New York City, where his mistress, Betsy Loring, awaited his company. While the general entertained himself, his army was spread in a chain of posts between New York and Philadelphia, except for a detachment of six thousand men he had sent to Rhode Island.

General Washington, on the other hand, had no intention of bedding down for the winter. He was planning a Christmas day attack on a Hessian brigade stationed in Trenton--a daring plan that would mean the end of the war if it failed but a tremendous boost of morale if it succeeded. Its codeword was "Victory or Death."

On December 23, Washington formed his army of twenty-five hundred regular soldiers into ranks, so they could hear their commanders read to them the first issue of Tom Paine's newspaper, *The American Crisis*. Paine had traveled with the soldiers across New Jersey and had seen their wounded bodies and spirits. The lead story of his newspaper read,

> These are the times that try men's souls. The summer soldier and the sunshine patriot will, in this crisis, shrink from the service of his country; but he that stands it now, deserves the love and thanks of man and woman. Tyranny, like hell, is not easily conquered; yet we have this consolation with us, that the harder the conflict, the more glorious the triumph. What we obtain too cheap we esteem too lightly: 'Tis dearness only that gives everything its value. Heaven knows how to put a proper price upon its goods; and it would be strange indeed if so celestial an article as Freedom should not be highly rated.

At seven o'clock on Christmas night, Washington's army began crossing the Delaware to the north of Trenton, ferried by the soldier-sailors of the 14th Massachusetts (Marblehead) Regiment. For eight hours they endured falling snow and sleet and howling winds; large chunks of ice rocked against the boats. When they reached the shore at three o'clock in the morning, one division marched nine miles down the river road to attack Trenton from the west, while another division took a back road so it could attack from the east. The hard ice broke through the shoes of the marching soldiers, which left trails of blood on the white landscape. Both columns reached Trenton at daybreak, just before eight in the morning.

"Der Feind! Heraus! Heraus!" the Hessian guards shouted. By that time, the Americans had already positioned their cannon at the end of each street. As the Hessians rose from bed and tried to form

Fig. 9: WASHINGTON CROSSING THE DELAWARE

their ranks, they were met with cannon balls fired at point blank range. Of the fifteen hundred Hessians, 920 surrendered. "This is a glorious day for our country," Washington beamed.[12] Among the American soldiers was a nineteen-year-old artillery captain, Alexander Hamilton. An eighteen-year-old infantry lieutenant, James Monroe, was wounded.

After the Trenton victory, Washington was able to convince half the men whose enlistments were up to re-enlist. He also added a force of thirty-five hundred militia, mostly from Pennsylvania. Still, Washington had only five thousand men, while Cornwallis was coming toward him with seven thousand British soldiers.

Cornwallis, however, came from the same military school as General Howe. On January 2, 1777, his army was marching against Washington's army, now trapped by the Delaware River to the rear and by two tributary rivers on the flanks, but he suddenly ordered his men to bed down for the night. That allowed Washington to move his army across a bridge and toward a British rear guard stationed near Princeton.

The next morning, the fighting began on the outskirts of Princeton. The British gained an early advantage and had the

Americans running from their positions. General Washington then rode his white horse among the retreating soldiers and convinced most of them to turn around and begin a counterattack. They chased the British into Princeton and the adjacent college campus. One British regiment barricaded itself in a college hall, but the soldiers surrendered when American cannon began shelling the building. Meanwhile, the remainder of the British army retreated to New Brunswick.

After the Princeton battle, Washington moved his army to Morristown, New Jersey. From there he launched a series of raids, capturing Hackensack, Elizabethtown and Newark. From the high ground at Morristown, Washington was able to attack the flank of any of Howe's men who tried to march to or from New York City. Howe was thus forced to keep most of his army in New York. Reports of the American victories spread throughout the states. The Patriots now sensed that the tide of the war had turned and that the cause of liberty was no longer hopeless.

F. Lake Champlain, Bennington, Fort Stanwix and Saratoga

After their unsuccessful attack on Québec, the New England troops commanded by Richard Montgomery and Benedict Arnold returned to Lake Champlain, leaving Canada under British control. In 1776, the Governor-General of Canada, Sir Guy Carleton, prepared to attack the Patriot forces camped on the shores of Lake Champlain. During the summer, he had his men build a navy of twenty-four small gunboats, two huge gunboats, two schooners and five hundred flat-bottomed infantry transport boats, all from seasoned wood shipped from Montréal and Québec. The boats were outfitted with a total of eighty-two guns. Meanwhile, the Americans, under the command of Benedict Arnold, built a navy at the south end of the lake from green timber cut from the surrounding trees. It consisted of five galleys and eight flat-bottomed "gundelos," all of Arnold's own design. Then they added three schooners and a sloop captured from the British. In all, the American ships carried about sixty guns. Arnold knew that with so few boats and no experienced sailors, he could not defeat the British navy. However, he thought he could hold off its attack on the American headquarters at Fort Ticonderoga until the winter came.

On October 5, 1776, Carleton's massive fleet finally left its northern port. Meanwhile, Arnold had sailed northward and positioned his ships in a channel between Valcour Island and the west shore of the lake, about half way up. On October 11, the British fleet passed Valcour Island and Arnold's small fleet sailed out to meet it. The battle lasted six hours. Both sides lost several boats, but the British had far more to spare than the Americans. When the autumn sun set, the battle ended, which was fortunate for the Americans because they were running out of ammunition. The next day, there was more fighting, during which several American ships gallantly held off British attacks. Finally, Arnold led his damaged navy to safety by taking advantage of a hole in the British ranks and sailing against the wind. When the Americans landed, they burned what was left of their ships, as well as the fort at Crown Point. Then, they slowly made their way to Fort Ticonderoga. By the time the British regrouped and repaired their ships, October was nearly over. Because of the winter storms were approaching, Carleton decided that he would not risk an attack on Fort Ticonderoga. So he led his men and ships back to Canada.

In 1777, the British Secretary for American Affairs, Lord George Germain, decided that gaining control of the Hudson River and Lake Champlain must be a top priority. He thought that dividing the New Englanders from the rest of the colonists was the key to winning the war. Germain was not happy with Carleton's uninspiring naval escapades the previous year. For the new task, therefore, he picked a dashing cavalry leader, General John Burgoyne, known as "Gentleman Johnny" by his soldiers, female companions and other admirers. Germain assigned Burgoyne four thousand British regulars, three thousand Hessians and one thousand Canadian militia. He also told him to enlist as many Indians as possible and he ordered General Howe to send reinforcements from New York. The New York forces were to clear out the rebel garrisons on the Hudson River and then join Burgoyne's army when it attacked the thirty-five hundred Americans at Fort Edward on the northern hook of the Hudson River.

At first, the British campaign went rather well. Leaving the St. Lawrence River in early June, Burgoyne's men sailed down Lake Champlain and reached Fort Ticonderoga on July 2. There they surprised an inferior American force under the command of General Arthur St. Clair. However, St. Clair was able to evacuate the fort with relatively few losses and join the main body of Americans at Fort Edward.

Burgoyne chased St. Clair's retreating forces by sailing his men down Lake Champlain. Then when they reached the southern end of the lake, he marched them across a sixteen-mile portage toward the Hudson River. Because the trail was rugged and thickly wooded, his army slowed to a near halt. A group of Americans led by Benedict Arnold had blocked the trail by felling trees, diverting swamp water and destroying all the bridges. His progress was also hampered by local militia who harassed the British with ambush fire. With his baggage train of 180 Canadian batteaux and 130 heavy cannon, all pulled by oxen and horses, Burgoyne's trip across the portage took nearly a month.

When Burgoyne finally reached Fort Edward, he found it vacated: the Americans under General Philip Schuyler had moved further south. Rather than pursue them, he sent an expedition to Vermont to collect food, horses and cattle. The expedition was led by Hessian Lieutenant Colonel Friedrich Baum and consisted of 375 dismounted Hessian dragoons and a total of three hundred Canadian soldiers and Indians. On August 16, just before reaching the Vermont border, they were stopped. A regiment of Green Mountain Rangers commanded by Colonel Seth Warner of New York, along with militia units from western Massachusetts and a company of Stockbridge Indians, met Baum's raiding party on a field a few miles northwest of Bennington, Vermont. Holding his Hessians in reserve, Colonel Baum placed his Canadians and Indians on the front line. However, the Hessians immediately began receiving fire from what they had thought to be their own rear guard. This rear guard turned out to be a detachment of Green Mountain Boys who had posed as Loyalist volunteers. Caught between two lines of fire, Baum's Canadian and Indian soldiers fled, but the 375 Hessians stayed and fought for two hours. All but nine were either killed or captured. Then, the Americans attacked another party of 650 Hessians, sent by Burgoyne in answer to Baum's plea for help. Again, the Americans won, inflicting 230 casualties. In both battles, thirty Americans died and forty others were wounded.

Burgoyne experienced another setback in western New York. He had sent Colonel Barry St. Leger with a column of British regulars, Canadians and Hessians up the St. Lawrence River to Oswego on Lake Ontario. From there they were to march east along the Oswego River, Lake Oneida, and the Mohawk River to Albany, where they were to join the main British force. On his way toward the headwaters of the Mohawk, St. Leger enlisted Mohawk Indians and Loyalists. Then, with a combined force of eighteen hundred men, he attacked Fort Stanwix,[13] guarding the headwaters of the Mohawk River. To his surprise, he found the fort manned by six hundred New York militia. He also heard reports that eight hundred more militia, commanded by the General Nicholas Herkimer, were on their way to help defend the fort.

St. Leger sent a detachment of four hundred Mohawk Indians and Tory Rangers to ambush Herkimer's force on a field near Oriskany, about ten miles east of Fort Stanwix. However, impatient Mohawk Indians attacked prematurely and allowed some of the Americans to escape. The remaining Americans, including Herkimer himself, fought off the Indians in a six-hour battle. Both sides suffered heavy losses. Meanwhile, some of the New York militia at Fort Stanwix attacked St. Leger's camp, routing his men and carting off camp equipment, clothing and money and leaving St. Leger in a weakened position.

Several days later, Benedict Arnold arrived with another relief force of twelve hundred Massachusetts militia. Arnold had also organized an advance party of Indian scouts who had arrived before him and told St. Leger's Indians about the awesome power of the new army they were about to face, as well as about the supernatural powers that Arnold himself possessed. The stories scared St. Leger's Indians so much that they abandoned their positions and returned to their home camps. The defection of these Indians left St. Leger's remaining forces too weak to mount a siege on Fort Stanwix. Finally, on August 22 St. Leger gave up and led his men back to Canada.

Back on the Hudson River, the main body of the American army was camped at Bemis Heights, near Saratoga Springs, about twenty-five miles north of Albany. On August 4, the Continental Congress had appointed General Horatio Gates commander of this army because it thought General Schuyler's retreat from Fort Edward showed him to be prone to retreating prematurely.

While Burgoyne was regrouping his forces at Fort Edward, Gates took the opportunity to build entrenchments at Bemis Heights. He also enlarged his sixty-five-hundred-man army with several hundred Green Mountain Boys who had been encouraged to enlist after their victory over the Hessians at Bennington. Also, more reinforcements arrived in the form of Daniel Morgan's Virginia Rifle Brigade, which Washington had dispatched from his New Jersey headquarters.

When Burgoyne arrived with his army at Bemis Heights on September 19, he tried to occupy a hill overlooking the American entrenchments. Arnold, who by that time had returned from Fort Stanwix, pleaded with Gates to allow him to intercept Burgoyne's troops. At first, Gates was against the idea, but he finally agreed. Taking command of Morgan's Rifles and a regiment of New England militia, Arnold attacked the center of Burgoyne's army on a field called Freeman's Farm. The battle lasted for four hours. One British sergeant recorded, "The conflict was dreadful, . . . Men, and particularly officers, dropped every moment on each side." An American officer wrote, "Nothing could exceed the bravery of Arnold on this day. . . . He seemed the very genius of war. Infuriated by the conflict, maddened by Gates's refusal to send reinforcements which he repeatedly called for, and knowing he was meeting the brunt of the battle, he seemed inspired with the fury of a demon."[14] When the fighting ended, a thousand dead or badly wounded soldiers lay on the field. The British regiments suffered worse, losing nearly a third of their men.

If Gates had given Arnold the reinforcements he had needed, the Americans might have ended the British invasion right then and there. Instead, Burgoyne was able to hold his position. Both Gates and Burgoyne decided not to attack one another until they received reinforcements. However, Gates did send General Benjamin Lincoln and four thousand New England militia around Burgoyne's rear, where they recaptured Fort Ticonderoga, cutting off Burgoyne's line of retreat. Gates also received his expected reinforcements, bringing his total strength to twelve thousand at Bemis Heights, in addition to Lincoln's four thousand at Ticonderoga. Burgoyne, however, did not receive any reinforcements from New York. His six thousand men were surrounded by sixteen thousand Americans. In addition, his soldiers were beginning to desert him, especially the Hessians.

On October 7, Burgoyne tried to salvage his campaign by attacking the left side of the American lines. In this Second Battle of Freeman's Farm, Arnold again led a group of Morgan's Rifles and New England militia against the attacking British and Hessians. Arnold was badly wounded but his men overwhelmed their enemies. Burgoyne was forced to retreat to a nearby hill. After a week-long stalemate, with his troops demoralized and their food running out, the British commander finally sent a flag of truce to the Americans. Gates could have taken the six thousand British and Hessian soldiers captive, but they would have been more of a burden than they were worth. Instead, he allowed them to return to England on the promise that none of them, including Burgoyne, would return to America.

The American victory at Saratoga was a stunning blow to the British effort to regain control of their colonies. Not only were the British and American people surprised, but all of Europe was shocked on hearing the news. Among the reasons why the British invasion failed, the most obvious was the failure of General Howe to send Burgoyne the help he had been promised from New York.

Howe claimed that he did not receive his instructions from London to send reinforcements until August 2, 1777, over two months after Burgoyne had begun marching southward from Canada. Then General Clinton, whom Howe appointed to command the reinforcements, did not leave New York until October 2. By then, Burgoyne had already been pinned in a hopeless position at Saratoga.

Another reason for Burgoyne's defeat was his reliance on the support of Loyalist tenant farmers in upstate New York, who were supposedly ready to take up arms against their Patriot landlords. Some historians, including Howard Zinn, have dwelled on the anti-Patriot class struggle that was taking place during the War of Independence, citing the New York tenant farmers as a prime example of those opposing the Patriot cause.[15] However, when the battle for the control of their land took place, few Loyalist farmers came forward, while the Patriot militia came out in large numbers and played a major role in the defeat of the British. In fact, the New York and western New England militia made such an impression on the British commanders that for the remainder of the war, they never attempted another invasion of the interior of a northern state. Instead, they confined their armies to seaport bases, in the faint hope that American Patriot sentiment might wane. It was a hope that was never realized.

G. Brandywine, Germantown and Valley Forge

While General Burgoyne was fighting for control of the upper Hudson Valley, General Howe was occupied with plans for what he considered a more important mission, namely the capture of the rebel capital of Philadelphia. The capital was the largest of the American cities, having forty thousand residents, almost double that of the second largest city, New York.

Before attacking Philadelphia, Howe spent the months of May and June of 1777 feigning a series of attacks and retreats in northern New Jersey, hoping to lure Washington's army into a vulnerable position. He hoped to force Washington into a decisive battle that would end the American rebellion. However, Washington had failed to take the bait. So all that Howe accomplished was to confuse and anger his soldiers, while they were marching back and forth, enduring the hot summer sun and occasional rounds of Patriot sniper fire. The men vented their anger by looting and burning various homes and barns. As a result, Loyalist sentiment in New Jersey faded fast.

With Washington's army of fourteen thousand still on the loose and his own army of sixteen thousand backed against the New Jersey coast,[16] Howe withdrew his men, horses and equipment to Staten Island, from where he loaded them onto his brother's ships. The 260-ship armada then headed out to sea on July 23.

For several weeks, Washington did not know where his enemy was headed. At first, he thought they might be planning to sail up the Hudson River to help Burgoyne. Another possibility was that they would attack Charleston, South Carolina. Most likely, he decided, they would try to take Philadelphia, which proved to be the case. However, Howe surprised Washington by sailing all the way south to Norfolk and then back up the Chesapeake Bay to get there. He could have simply sailed around the south end of New Jersey and then up the Delaware River, but one of his ship captains gave him an exaggerated report on the difficulties of navigating the Delaware River and unloading troops on its marshy shores.

After thirty-two days at sea, Howe finally unloaded his army at the Head of Elk, Maryland, at the north end of the Chesapeake Bay. His horses were so hungry that they gorged themselves and hundreds of them died. His men were hungry, angry and restless. Again they vented their frustration by looting and burning houses and barns, encouraging more Americans to take up arms against them.

Meanwhile, Washington had his army camped at Neshaminy Creek, thirty miles north of Philadelphia. Upon hearing of Howe's landing, he immediately moved south to meet them. The two armies met on September 11 at Brandywine Creek, twenty-five miles southwest of Philadelphia and just north of the Delaware border. Howe caught Washington off-guard by sending the main body of his army around the American flank. For two hours, the Americans held on, even though their flank had been turned and they were nearly surrounded. As the sun set, the Americans fell back, allowing the British to march on to Philadelphia. The British casualties were about six hundred, while the Americans lost over one thousand. To make matters worse, about ten days later, the British surprised an American division, under the command of Anthony Wayne, at a place called Paoli's Tavern. The massacre cost Wayne four hundred men: three hundred casualties and one hundred taken prisoner.

General Howe marched his army into Philadelphia on September 26, 1777. He set up his headquarters in Germantown, to the northwest of Philadelphia. He also sent out expeditions to capture several American forts on the Delaware River and released three thousand men to guard his supply trains coming from his brother's ships on the Chesapeake Bay. That left Howe with only nine thousand men at Germantown.

Meanwhile, Washington regrouped his forces at Skippack Creek, northwest of Germantown. With new reinforcements, he now had eight thousand regular troops and three thousand militia, perhaps enough to retake Philadelphia. In the early morning hours of October 4, Washington attacked Howe's Germantown headquarters. At first, the attack went surprisingly well, forcing the British front lines to retreat. As the Americans pursued, they seemed to be on the verge of victory. However, they were delayed along the way by plunging fire from the remnants of six British companies that had barricaded themselves in a huge stone mansion owned by Pennsylvania Chief Justice Benjamin Chew. During the attempt to take over this makeshift fortress, more American troops came on the scene and tried to help, while the pursuit of the retreating enemy was put on hold. When the Americans finally resumed their forward attack, they were hampered and confused by the foggy weather and the smoke of the battle. Meanwhile, three fresh British battalions arrived from Philadelphia and Howe was able to launch a counterattack that sent the Americans retreating. The British lost seventy killed and 420 wounded. The Americans suffered 150 killed, 520 wounded and four hundred captured. The British thus won another battle and were able to hold on to Philadelphia.

In order to feel secure in his Philadelphia headquarters, Howe decided that he had to capture the American forts that guarded the Delaware River on the south side of the city. The forts were part of an impressive system of fortifications designed by a Polish army engineer, Tadeusz Kosciuszko, and built under the supervision of a French army engineer, Chevalier du Plessis. Both men had served in the French army and had volunteered to help the Americans in their fight for freedom. The main components of the fortifications were Fort Mifflin on Mud Island near the Pennsylvania side of the river[17] and Fort Mercer, slightly up-river at Red Bank on the New Jersey side. On October 22, two thousand Hessian soldiers tried to capture Fort Mercer, manned by four hundred Rhode Island regulars, but they failed miserably, losing seven hundred casualties and two British warships, while the Americans suffered only thirty-seven casualties. However, on November 10, the British successfully bombarded Fort Mifflin, forcing the Americans to evacuate. The defeat was so demoralizing that the commander of Fort Mercer also ordered his men to evacuate.

After the British victories at Brandywine, Germantown and the Delaware River forts, Washington had to decide where his beleaguered army would spend the winter. He wanted to remain close to Philadelphia so that he could intercept any movement that the British might make. He chose Valley Forge, a two-mile-long wooded slope on the south bank of the Schuykill River, about twenty miles northwest of Philadelphia. Initially, the conditions of the encampment were cold but bearable. However, by Christmastime, it had already become the one of the most miserable winters spent by any army in the history of warfare. The problem was the lack of food and clothing. The local farmers would not sell their produce for the near worthless Continental script. Also, because of the war, clothing prices had risen so much that merchants were refusing to accept anything less than a 1,000 percent profit on their merchandise. Furthermore, the army's supply system was ridden with inefficiencies, bureaucratic red tape, theft and graft. An

American officer wrote the following of the conditions at Valley Forge:

> Here comes a soldier, his bare feet are seen through his worn-out shoes, his legs nearly naked from the tattered remains of an only pair of stockings, his breeches not sufficient to cover his nakedness, his shirt hanging in strings, his hair disheveled, his face meager. His whole appearance pictures a person foresaken and discouraged. He comes and crys with an air of wretchedness and despair: "I am sick, my feet lame, my legs are sore, my body covered with this tormenting itch" (an affliction common in the camp).[18]

The horses received even less food than the men. Many died of starvation and the stench and disease of their carcasses added to the deplorable conditions of the camp.

In February 1778, a strange diversion allowed the soldiers to enjoy a respite from their misery. A man calling himself Lieutenant General Friedrich Ludolf Gerhard Wilhelm Augustin von Steuben arrived at Valley Forge, wearing a uniform full of Prussian army decorations and accompanied by three servants, a cook and three French aides. In fact, he was an impostor. His real name was Steube and he was not from a noble family, as the prefix "von" implied. Although he had served in the Prussian army, he had never risen above the rank of captain. However, he knew and appreciated the fine art of military discipline because he had been educated at a Jesuit school and then progressed through the ranks of the Prussian army to a minor position on the staff of the Prussian king, Frederick the Great.

The self-styled Prussian general also knew how to sell himself. He impressed Benjamin Franklin, when Franklin was in Paris trying to negotiate a treaty with France, and he also impressed the French minister of war. With those contacts, he gained the financial and manpower support that he needed to travel to Valley Forge in royal style. Von Steuben then sold General Washington on a plan for training his army according to Prussian organization and discipline. First, he composed a set of close order drill instructions, which he wrote in French and had one of his French aides translate into

Fig. 10: THE WINTER AT VALLEY FORGE

English. Two officers on Washington's staff, Nathaniel Greene and Alexander Hamilton, then translated the Frenchman's English into a form more recognizable to American ears. Von Steuben began by drilling a platoon of model soldiers from each of the Continental Army's fourteen brigades, showing them how to stand straight at attention and perform all the standard marching moves. He also taught them a twelve-step manual of arms in which the soldiers actually fired their weapons. His drills amused everyone in the army, because he treated the platoon like a group of raw recruits, cursing them in three languages. On one occasion, he exclaimed to a fellow officer, "Viens, Valkaire, mon ami, mon bon ami! Sacre! Goddam de guacheries of dese badouts. Je ne puis plus. I can gurse dem no more!"[19]

The drills were exactly what the American army needed. When the model soldiers returned to their brigades, everyone was eager to learn the new commands. The new drill instructors imitated their teacher, shouting, "Vorwaarts, march! Vun-doo-dree-four! Doo der rear, march! Golumn left, march! Halt! Vun-doo!" They also practiced deploying themselves and changing formations under combat conditions. After four weeks, Washington was amazed. His men now looked like European soldiers, except for their ragged clothes and bleeding feet.

Von Steuben was also impressed that the Americans could work so hard while living under such horrible conditions. He admired the American soldier's free spirit, because he saw that the American's devotion to freedom was why his endured miseries that no European soldier would have tolerated.[20] However, von Steuben found this free spirit very frustrating at times. He said that if he told a European soldier, "Do this," he did it, but with an American he was obliged to say first, "This is the reason why you ought to do this."

The winter at Valley Forge was especially difficult for General Washington because of a plot by several of his subordinate generals to have him dismissed as commander-in-chief. The ring-leaders were General Thomas Conway, who had fought under Washington at Brandywine and Germantown, and General Gates, who had commanded the northern army that had defeated the British at Saratoga. Indeed, a number of members of the Congress, including John Adams and Samuel Adams of Massachusetts, Richard Henry Lee of Virginia and Thomas Mifflin of Pennsylvania, had openly criticized Washington's failures at Brandywine and Germantown and had contrasted them with the success of General Gates at Saratoga. Their feelings against Washington ran particularly high after they had to transfer their Congressional meetings from Philadelphia to York, Pennsylvania, after the battle of Germantown. On the other hand, Conway and Gates wrote letters that were more than critical of their commander: they showed contempt for his leadership as well. When the news of the letters reached Washington, he openly confronted the two men. Both tried to retract their statements and Gates even claimed that one of his letters was a forgery. Conway tried to solve his predicament by offering his resignation, but to his surprise, Congress accepted it. The crowning blow to the plot came when Daniel Morgan, the commander of Morgan's Rifles, arrived at Valley Forge and reported that the true hero of Saratoga was Benedict Arnold and that he would serve under no commander-in-chief except General Washington. From that point on, Washington's critics, both in the army and in Congress, managed to keep their opinions to themselves.

H. The French Alliance

The American victory at Saratoga had thrown the British government into "a state of great distraction," as one official confided to Edmund Burke. Nearly forty thousand British and Hessian soldiers had spent a year and a half fighting against a much smaller number of poorly trained Americans. Not only had they failed to end the rebellion, but they had suffered a shocking number of casualties: they now feared that the American army might soon be able to overpower them. A major reason for that fear lay in rumors of a possible American-French alliance. Lord North therefore decided that he had to make a bold move. In November 1777, he introduced a bill in Parliament calling for a new peace initiative, to be delivered to the American Congress by a royal commission. This commission would have authority to agree to repeal the Coercive Acts and to recognize most of the rights that the Americans had asserted in their Declaration of Independence, except their right to be independent of British rule. Unfortunately, the Christmas season was approaching and Parliament adjourned without taking action on the bill.

Meanwhile, Benjamin Franklin was in Paris negotiating the very treaty that Lord North was fearing. Franklin had come to France hailed as the American republican diplomat, displaying simple clothing and unpretentious manners and living according to the practical rules that he had published in his *Way to Wealth* and *Poor Richard's Almanack*. He was seen as the standard bearer of a new kind of society that most Europeans could only dream of having. The French intellectuals who had studied Rousseau, Voltaire and Montesquieu saw America as the perfect place where people could practice the ideals of an enlightened, reformed society, free of decadent patriarchal estates and oppressive church and state overlords. They thought that if the Americans could throw off the

Fig. 11: FRANKLIN IS PRESENTED TO KING LOUIS XVI
AND QUEEN MARIE ANTOINETTE OF FRANCE

yoke of British rule, they might be able to form such a society. The American model would show the world the superiority of an enlightened government that recognized the principles of equality, liberty and the other natural rights of man. There would then be an overwhelming clamor for the same kind of government in France.

The French king Louis XVI and his ministers were also eager to form a partnership with the Americans. A free United States of America would weaken France's main enemy, the British Empire, and would partly compensate for France's loss of Québec to Britain during the Seven Years' War. Also, French companies would be able to trade with the Americans, which they had not been able to do because of the trade restrictions imposed by the British Parliament. However, the French government had been reluctant to form an alliance with the Americans because they feared that Britain might easily crush the American rebellion and engage France in another costly war.

The American victory at Saratoga changed France's view of the war. It was now worried that Britain might make new peace efforts, resulting in a settlement that would create a British Empire more powerful than ever. One way to prevent that would be to formally ally themselves with the American rebels.

Before 1778, France had sent munitions and clothing to the Americans and had allowed American commercial and military ships to use its seaports. The British government suspected that at least two hundred French army soldiers fought with the Americans at Saratoga.[21] According to some estimates, France had supplied the Americans with 80 percent of their gunpowder--no less than the world's highest quality powder from the French Gunpowder Administration, directed by the renowned chemist Antoine-Laurent Lavoisier. France and Spain had also sent about a million livres ($250,000) to the American Congress. That was all the result of Benjamin Franklin's patient diplomacy. However, it was done secretly. The French ministers delivered their assistance through a clever arrangement with the firm of Hortalez et Cie, managed by the French playwright Caron de Beaumarchais. Publicly, France remained neutral.

In addition to the French government's unofficial help, several French army officers had taken leaves of absence and joined the American army. They included the Delaware River fort engineers Kosciuszko and du Plessis, as well as a young French nobleman, the Marquis Gilbert de Lafayette, who had joined the American army as a major general in the summer of 1777. Although only twenty years old, Lafayette had already demonstrated outstanding leadership while serving in the French army. He had also brought with him sixteen other French officers, as well as a German officer, Jean de Kalb.[22] To maintain its show of neutrality, the French government claimed that it had never authorized Lafayette or the other officers to go to America.

On February 6, 1778, the French foreign minister, the Comte de Vergennes, officially abandoned his position of neutrality by signing two treaties with the United States. One was for a military alliance that was conditioned on Britain declaring war on France, which both parties were sure would happen once the British learned of the agreement. Under the alliance, France promised to recognize the independence of the United States and to continue its war with Britain until Britain recognized that independence. In return, the United States pledged to defend the French West Indies from British attack and not to enter into a peace agreement with Great Britain without the consent of France. The agreement also provided that France would not try to seize Canada. The United States in turn recognized France's right to its West Indian islands. In the other treaty, France recognized the right of the United States to trade with any nation that it pleased. Each nation also granted the other a most favored nation status, which meant that any tariffs and trade restrictions imposed by one nation on the goods of the other would be at least as favorable as the tariffs and trade restrictions imposed on the goods of any third nation.

Meanwhile, Lord North's bill to send a peace offer to America was delayed by long debates in Parliament. Finally, on February 17, 1777, the bill passed and North's peace delegates set sail for America. By the time they arrived in Philadelphia, however, news of the French treaties had reached the American Congress. Its members therefore gave their British visitors a very cool reception. As Henry Laurens, president of the Congress, remarked, if the British peace offer had come sooner, it would have been received with joy. However, as in many human relationships that gradually deteriorate, the Americans and the British had fought each other so hard and for so long that reconciliation was now impossible. Furthermore, the Americans had found a new marriage partner in France and both partners had agreed not to make peace with Britain without the other's permission.

I. Philadelphia and Monmouth Court House

While Lord North was struggling in London to solve the political problems of the American war and Washington's army was suffering at Valley Forge, the British and Hessian soldiers occupying Philadelphia were having a jolly good winter. General Howe set the standard by engaging in a *ménage à trois* relationship with Betsy Loring and her husband John, both of whom he had invited live with him.[23] Francis Hopkinson, a signer of the Declaration of Independence, wrote of them,

> Sir William he, snug as a flea,
> Lay all the time a'snoring,
> Nor dreamed of harm as he lay warm
> In bed with Mrs. Loring.

The British army managed to alienate both the Patriot and the Loyalist residents of Philadelphia. They left artillery weapons and other equipment strewn all over the city's parks and lawns; they chopped down fences, trees and vacant houses for firewood and shoveled their horse manure through holes cut in the floors of buildings, so that it lay festering in the basements. After a few months, the entire city was a stinking mess. The Loyalists were particularly upset because they thought that the British army should have been out pursuing Washington's men rather than allowing them to regroup and gather reinforcements. One Loyalist wrote of the British commander,

> Awake, arise Sir Billy,
> There's forage on the plain.
> Ah, leave your little filly,
> And open the campaign.[24]

The problem was that Sir Billy had grown tired of the war and no longer desired to continue his command. He asked to be relieved and in April 1778 his request was granted. After an extravagant farewell party in May, General Henry Clinton took command of the British army in North America.

Upon Clinton's appointment, Lord Germain, the secretary for American affairs, immediately ordered Clinton to evacuate Philadelphia and consolidate his forces in New York City so that he could defend that city against a French naval attack. Britain had now declared war on France, and a French naval fleet of twelve large warships and a squadron of frigates carrying four thousand infantry was on its way to America.

Clinton chose to move his army to New York City by land because he feared that if he took the sea route the British navy would not be able to defend his army against the French. On June 18, 1778,' Clinton began shipping his fifteen-thousand-man army across the Delaware River. On reaching the other side, the soldiers began a difficult march through the New Jersey countryside. Each man had to carry a hundred-pound backpack under the hot summer sun. The march was especially hard on the Hessians because of their woolen uniforms. They also had to contend with sniper fire from American soldiers and Patriot farmers.

Meanwhile, the main body of the Continental Army had broken its camp at Valley Forge and was in hot pursuit of its moving enemy. Washington had totally reorganized the eleven-thousand-man army and, thanks to von Steuben's training, the men were marching and executing orders with a discipline that rivaled that of the British soldiers. With the help of the French, most of the soldiers now had new clothes and many were wearing new buff and blue uniforms that looked as impressive as the redcoats of the British. More importantly, they showed a renewed spirit, knowing that they had survived one of the toughest winter encampments experienced by any army.

For nine days, the two armies marched on parallel paths across New Jersey toward the ocean port of Sandy Hook, just south of the New York harbor. Clinton planned to load his army on British ships there, for a short cruise across the harbor to New York City. However, before reaching Sandy Hook, Clinton halted his exhausted troops near the Monmouth County Court House to allow them to rest. When he heard the news of the British bivouac, Washington seized the opportunity and ordered an attack on Clinton's army on the morning of June 28, 1778.

Unfortunately, Washington entrusted his attacking corps of five thousand men to the incompetent General Charles Lee, who had recently been released by the British in a high-level prisoner exchange. At first, Lee's forces caught the rear guard of the British army by surprise and gained a tactical advantage. However, their attack was completely disorganized because Lee had failed to

Fig. 12: MOLLY PITCHER TAKES OVER FOR HER FALLEN HUSBAND

communicate any orders or plans to his subordinate commanders. Then, in the middle of all the confusion, he ordered a retreat, for which Washington severely reprimanded him on the battlefield, in front of many witnesses. The retreat allowed Clinton to gather his forces and mount a counterattack against the main body of the Continental Army. The ensuing battle lasted almost the whole day and turned out to be the longest sustained fighting of the whole war. The new training of the American soldiers was evident as they met every one of Clinton's maneuvers with an appropriate counter-maneuver and beat back every British attack.

During the battle, Mary Hayes, the tobacco-chewing wife of a young American private, stepped into the fray and brought pitchers of cold water to the thirsty men of her husband's artillery unit. Then, when her husband was killed, she took over his position and helped fire his cannon. Because of the water she had given them, the soldiers nicknamed her "Molly Pitcher" and she became a legendary hero of the war.

When nightfall came, neither army had gained an advantage over the other. The British therefore marched back to their camp and packed their belongings as quickly as they could. Before sunrise the next morning, Clinton had his army marching again toward Sandy Hook. This time, it was the British who had cause to be thankful for their narrow escape from what might have been a very decisive victory for the Americans. Even so, the British losses were extremely heavy. They reported sixty-five dead, 160 wounded and sixty-four missing. However, the Americans said that they found hundreds of British corpses on the battlefield. In addition, Clinton lost 136 British and 440 Hessian soldiers who deserted him during the tough march from Philadelphia. The American casualties were sixty-nine dead, 161 wounded and 130 missing.[25]

After the battle of Monmouth Court House, the British were able to reach New York City without further interference from the Continental Army. To contain the British in the New York City area, Washington deployed his army in a semi-circle around its north side and established his headquarters at White Plains.

J. The War at Sea

Admiral Jean-Baptiste d'Estaing commanded the naval fleet that France sent to America after its treaties with the Americans in February 1778. D'Estaing's original plan was to attack the British naval fleet that was anchored in Delaware Bay between the south end of New Jersey and the state of Delaware. He expected then to sail north and capture New York City. However, d'Estaing's fleet did not reach Delaware Bay until July 8 and the British fleet had already left the bay by that time. It had sailed north to Sandy Hook, where it intended to pick up Clinton's army and ferry it up to New York City.

D'Estaing therefore sailed from Delaware Bay up to the New York harbor, hoping to intercept the British fleet while it was ferrying Clinton's army. Even if he arrived too late, he planned to attack the British fleet impose a blockade on the harbor. With Washington's army blocking all the land routes to New York City, d'Estaing's blockade would cut the supply lines to all the British land and naval forces in the New York area. However, this plan also failed because d'Estaing's fleet arrived too late to intercept the British fleet and the captains of the larger French naval vessels would not sail into the New York harbor. They were afraid of grounding their ships on the sand bar at the south end of the harbor. Some Americans thought that the real reasons for the French failure to attack New York were that they were unsure of their ability to overpower the British navy and that they did not want a quick end to the American war, for fear that the British would initiate a war of vengeance upon the French people.[26]

Washington and d'Estaing then decided to try to chase the British off the naval base at Newport, Rhode Island. Washington sent a force of ten thousand men to attack Newport by land, half under the command of General Greene and half under General Lafayette. Meanwhile, d'Estaing carried four thousand French soldiers by sea to Newport for an amphibious landing. General Clinton countered by sending five thousand British soldiers to reinforce the three thousand already at Newport. In addition, Admiral Howe sailed to Newport with a fleet that was reinforced by the fleet of Commodore John Byron, recently arrived from England. Just as d'Estaing was about to unload the French soldiers at Newport on August 11, a strong gale forced his ships back out to sea, where he was forced contend with the arriving fleets of Howe and Byron. The winds grew into a violent storm that scattered the ships of both navies and forced both sides to withdraw to make repairs. The French fleet sailed to Boston and the British fleet went back to New York.

Meanwhile, the failure of the French soldiers to make their landing so disgusted Greene's and Lafayette's men that half of them quit and went home. The others went back to New York. When the Frenchmen arrived in Boston, some were attacked by dockworkers loyal to Sam Adams because of their failure to help the American forces at Newport.

After the Newport fiasco, there was a long stalemate; Washington's depleted army was too weak to attack the British stronghold at New York and the British army was afraid to launch any inland expeditions. This stalemate lasted in the north for the remainder of the war.

Lord Germain instructed General Clinton to confine his northern operations to raiding American seaports and destroying Patriot property. In 1778 and 1779, the British army and navy embarked on a series of raids on the coastal towns of New England, New Jersey and the Chesapeake Bay. They looted and burned buildings, captured American ships and completely destroyed the town of Fairfield, Connecticut. They burned so much property in Connecticut that the state later compensated the victims by giving them property in the "firelands" section of its Western Reserve, which now comprises the northeastern part of the state of Ohio.

In response to the British naval raids, the American Congress decided to retaliate with raids of its own. Before 1778, the small American navy had accomplished very little, except for Commodore Esek Hopkins' capture of the town of New Providence (Nassau) in the Bahamas in 1776. Most of the ships commissioned by the Congress had been confined to their harbors by the British navy and many of those had been destroyed, either by the British or by the Americans themselves when they feared that the British would capture them. The most successful American activity on the high seas had been carried out by private ship owners and seamen whom the Congress had allowed to privateer--to intercept any British naval or merchant vessel and keep any property they could grab, including the ship itself. During the war these privateers seized about fifteen hundred British ships and captured more than twelve thousand British seamen.[27]

The small Continental Navy also engaged in raids similar to those of the privateers, but its sailors did not seek booty or other prizes. The most successful commander in this navy was the Scots sailor John Paul Jones. He became a first lieutenant in December 1775 and was promoted to captain in August 1776. During the year 1776 he captured sixteen British ships, destroying eight of them and sending the rest back to their ports. By 1778, he had become well known for his heroic deeds on the high seas. Benjamin Franklin therefore prevailed on the Congress to send him on an expedition to England and Scotland to retaliate for the British naval raids on the American ports. On the first voyage, commanding the ship *Ranger*, Jones attacked Whitehaven in northern England and burned all the ships in the port. He also captured the *H.M.S. Drake* off the coast of Scotland.

In 1779, Franklin arranged for the French admiralty to outfit Jones with a fleet of five ships. Jones renamed his flagship the *Bonhomme Richard*, after Franklin's popular *Poor Richard's Almanack*. The *Bonhomme Richard* carried a crew of 380 men of eleven different nationalities, including English and Scots. Most of the officers besides Jones were Americans.

After raiding the English town of Newcastle and the Scottish capital of Edinburgh, Jones's fleet was challenged one evening by two British warships off Flamborough Head, a new fifty-gun ship called the *Serapis* and a twenty-gun sloop called the *Countess of Scarborough*. The *Bonhomme Richard* quickly became locked in a battle with the *Serapis*. At first, it appeared that the British ship would surely win. Some of the *Richard's* heavy guns burst, killing crew members and blowing up parts of a deck. Then Jones pulled the *Richard* so close to the side of the *Serapis* that his crew was able to lash the masts of the ships together. For two and a half hours in the moonlight, the ships fired broadsides at each other at point-blank range. The *Richard* showed its age, as its rotten timbers splintered under the heavy gun fire. Most of its guns were knocked out and the ship began leaking badly. However, Jones exhorted his crew to fight on. The tide of the battle turned when French sailors on the *Richard's* rigging cleared the British sailors from their rigging by hand-to-hand combat and cleared the decks of the *Serapis* using grenades and other explosives. The battle ended when another American ship, the *Alliance*, hit the *Serapis* with enough gun fire to force the British commander to surrender. Because the *Bonhomme Richard* was sinking fast, Jones transferred his crew to the *Serapis* and sailed her to The Texel, a neutral port on the coast of Holland. He also took with him the *Countess of Scarborough*, which had been captured by another ship in his fleet, the *Pallas*.

The battle between the *Bonhomme Richard* and the *Serapis* had little to do with the outcome of the war, but it was yet another victory that added to the pride and confidence in their cause that Americans were gaining.

In addition to harassment by John Paul Jones and American privateers, British navy had to contend with French navy as well as the Spanish navy, after the Spanish declared war on Britain in June 1779, and the Dutch navy, after the Dutch joined the alliance in 1780. In July 1779, French and Spanish naval fleets attacked a British fleet stationed in the English Channel. Fortunately for the British, a bad storm prevented them from landing of fifty thousand French soldiers on the south coast of England. Meanwhile, the British navy continued to control the entire American coastline.

K. The Western Front

The news of the shots fired at Lexington and Concord reached Fort Pitt and the village of Pittsburgh on May 16, 1775. That same day, the villagers pledged their resistance to the "invaders of American rights and privileges."[28]

On the western front, the War of Independence was very similar to the French and Indian War that had been fought twenty years earlier. The main difference was that instead of French soldiers inciting otherwise peaceful Indians to attack British traders and settlers on the river banks west of the Appalachian Mountains, British soldiers, having replaced the French at Fort Detroit, were inciting the same Indian tribes to attack the same settlements near Fort Pitt. Another difference was that the number of settlers had substantially increased. The relatively small number of British soldiers at Fort Detroit therefore found it even more necessary to supplement their forces with Indian raiders. The American settlers had tried at the beginning of the war to convince the Indians to stay neutral and remain innocent bystanders. Only after many of them began helping the British did they enlist other Indians to fight on their side.

Chapter 5 *The War of Independence* 139

The settlers in the Fort Pitt area as well as in Kentucky and western Maryland were divided by disputes over shortages in food and ammunition, as well as by political questions, such as conflicting claims to their region by the states of Virginia and Pennsylvania. Based on their charters, the Virginians had the best argument for controlling the whole region, including what is now western Pennsylvania. The situation was further complicated by the Illinois-Wabash Company, whose private investors had bought large tracts of land from the western Indians and were lobbying the Congress to take direct jurisdiction over the region and authenticate their land titles. These problems so overwhelming that six different men commanded the fort between 1775 and 1783.

Under such an unstable government, the Americans probably would have lost control of most of the land west of the Appalachian Mountains had not another American hero intervened. He was George Rogers Clark, a Virginia frontier explorer. At the beginning of the war, Clark had persuaded the Virginia Assembly to designate the state's lands west of the Appalachian Mountains as the County of Kentucky and place him in charge of the county's defense against the British and Indians. In 1777, he traveled to Fort Pitt and obtained supplies and men for an expedition to the Mississippi River by way of the Ohio River Valley.

The next summer, with 150 frontiersmen and twenty families of settlers, Clark traveled to the Mississippi. There he captured two British posts, Kaskaskia and Cahokia, located in the present state of Illinois. With the help of his friend Pierre Gibault, he induced the French community of Vincennes, in the present state of Indiana on the Wabash River, to change its allegiance from British to American. He and his followers then withdrew for the winter to Fort Nelson, on the site of the present city of Louisville, Kentucky.

Meanwhile, in December 1778, the British recaptured Vincennes in a raid led by Colonel Henry "the Hair Buyer" Hamilton, named for his collection of American and French scalps that he had bought from the Indians. Hamilton then persuaded some of these Indians to raid ships on the Ohio River that were carrying supplies from the Spaniards in New Orleans to the American settlers at Fort Pitt. The

Spaniards were helping the American rebels, even though a few months remained before Spain would declare war on Great Britain.

When he heard of the Hair Buyer's raids, Clark went back to Kaskaskia in February 1779 and organized a party of 130 American and French soldiers to attack the British base at Vincennes, from where the raids were being launched. On their way, they traveled through 150 miles of flooded plains and marshes, sometimes with icy water up to their chests. When they arrived at Vincennes, seeing that his men were greatly outnumbered by Hamilton's soldiers and Indians, Clark ordered his men to march laterally as well as forward to give the impression of superior numbers. That maneuver fooled most of the Indians and they fled. His sharpshooters then picked off enough British guards to force Hamilton to ask for a peace conference. Before agreeing to the conference, Clark paraded before Hamilton five Indians who had been holding white men's scalps when they were captured. He then had the Indians executed on the spot, using tomahawks. Hamilton immediately surrendered Vincennes and retreated to his headquarters at Fort Detroit.

For the remainder of the war, Clark and his small band of men controlled the Ohio River region. That enabled the Congress to negotiate a peace treaty at the end of the war that gave the United States all the land previously controlled by the British west of the Appalachians and south of the Great Lakes.

L. Savannah, Charleston and Camden

In the fall of 1778, General Clinton decided to launch a major offensive on southern states. In November, he sent a force of thirty-five hundred British regulars and Loyalist militia to attack Savannah, Georgia from the sea. The city was guarded by only seven hundred Continental Army regulars and 150 local militia, under the command of Major General Robert Howe. In addition, the commander of the British forces, Colonel Archibald Campbell, was aided by more British troops that came up from northeast Florida, under the command of General Augustine Prevost. The outmanned Americans fell quickly, suffering five hundred casualties.

The fall of Savannah allowed General Prevost to clear all the American troops out of Georgia. For a while, it appeared that he might control South Carolina as well. However, his attack on Charleston in the spring of 1779 failed, mainly because the American commander Benjamin Lincoln was assisted by a legion of two hundred cavalry led by the Polish count Casimir Pulaski.

In September 1779, Admiral d'Estaing tried to retake the city by sailing up the Savannah River with thirty-five hundred French soldiers. He was joined by Pulaski's cavalry legion and six hundred Continental Army regulars and 150 militia commanded by General Lincoln. That should have been sufficient to overpower the twenty-four hundred British in Savannah, most of whom were Loyalist militia. However, d'Estaing was forced to launch a premature assault after hearing that a British naval squadron was on its way to block his passage out of the river. Furthermore, a sergeant-major of the Charleston grenadiers defected and gave the British all of d'Estaing's assault plans. Consequently, the attack on Savannah failed miserably and the casualties were heavy. Count Pulaski was killed and Admiral d'Estaing was wounded. The French navy then sailed back to France to tend to its wounded.

Meanwhile, General Clinton was planning an active winter. On December 26, 1779, he sailed from New York with ninety transport ships carrying eighty-five hundred British, Hessian and Loyalist infantrymen, plus several cavalry and artillery units, and five large warships and nine frigates carrying 650 guns and five thousand sailors and marines. On February 11, 1780, after a stormy voyage, he landed most of his army thirty miles south of Charleston, South Carolina and prepared to launch a combined land and sea attack on the city. After increasing his troop strength to thirteen thousand with more divisions arriving from New York, he moved the entire force onto the narrow peninsula that led to Charleston. Then on April 10, with the British navy controlling the surrounding water, he demanded the surrender of the fifty-five hundred American soldiers commanded by General Lincoln.

The South Carolina Assembly had resolved to fight "until the last extremity" before allowing Charleston to be taken. Governor John Rutledge (later a U. S. Supreme Court justice) and General Lincoln were of the same mind. They had six hundred black slaves build elaborate fortifications and a moat across the peninsula to block the British advance. After receiving Lincoln's refusal to surrender, Clinton attacked and destroyed these defenses, slowly and methodically. Several more times he demanded surrender; each time, Lincoln refused. All the while, the residents of the town suffered the bombardment of the British artillery. Finally, the Americans could withstand the siege no longer and on May 12 they surrendered. The British took all fifty-five hundred soldiers prisoner and confiscated their six thousand muskets, 391 artillery pieces and huge stores of ammunition and powder. They also captured three ships of the Continental navy. Fortunately, only ninety Americans were killed and 150 were wounded.

Clinton remained in Charleston several months longer to establish a Loyalist government and issue an order that everyone in the state declare his loyalty to his government or be punished as a rebel. Faced with that choice, many who had remained neutral joined either the Loyalist militia or the Patriot militia. In fact, the entire state became bitterly divided between Loyalist and Patriot camps, who wreaked awful acts of terror and destruction on each other's families and property. One reason for this violence was the brutality of a Loyalist cavalry legion commanded by Colonel Banastre Tarleton, who was assigned to enforce Clinton's demand for loyalty and to root out all remaining rebel forces in the state. Early in that campaign, Tarleton's legion massacred over a hundred Continental Army soldiers after they had been beaten in a battle and had raised a white flag, asking for mercy. Because of his failure to give quarter on that occasion, the cry "Tarleton's Quarter" became a call for revenge among the American soldiers.

In June 1780, Clinton put General Cornwallis in charge of a force of four thousand British soldiers and sailed back to New York with the rest of his army. These soldiers as well as the Loyalists commanded by Tarleton then proceeded to subdue the entire state of South Carolina, in spite of brave opposition from Patriot militia units, led by Thomas Sumter, Thomas Butler, Andrew Pickens and the "Ole Swamp Fox," Francis Marion.

Meanwhile, General Washington had sent Lafayette's friend General Jean de Kalb south with the Maryland and Delaware Line units to help Lincoln defend Charleston. However, when the Congress heard that Charleston had fallen, they superseded Washington's orders and appointed General Horatio Gates to command the American troops in the south.

At Hillsboro, North Carolina, Gates took command of the Maryland and Delaware Lines and several militia units and marched them south to Camden, South Carolina. Unfortunately, he chose a route through pine forests, where there were no crops to forage. By the time they reached Camden after an all night march, his three thousand soldiers were not only tired and hungry but suffering from dysentery as well. At daybreak on August 16, they encountered a force of two thousand British and Loyalists under the command of General Cornwallis. Even though their total number was less, the British had more regular army soldiers on their side. The battle was fierce and bloody and the Americans fought gallantly, but their endurance ran out. While hundreds of his men were being killed and captured, Gates himself mounted his horse and galloped north to Charlotte, North Carolina. It was the last time he saw action during the war. About 650 Maryland and Delaware regulars were killed or captured, while about a hundred North Carolina militia were killed or wounded and three hundred more were captured. General de Kalb, hit eleven times, lived for three days before dying of his wounds.

M. The Treason of Benedict Arnold

The British were now in control of both Georgia and South Carolina. The year 1780 was not going well for the United States. To make matters worse, in September, General Washington discovered that one of his top officers, General Benedict Arnold, the hero of Saratoga no less, had been spying for the British for over a year and was about to defect.

After the Americans regained control of Philadelphia in June of 1778, Washington appointed Arnold military governor of the city. Soon after arriving, Arnold met and fell in love with Peggy Shippen, the daughter of a wealthy financier and jurist, Judge Edward Shippen. Like many of the wealthy families of Philadelphia, the Shippens had Loyalist sympathies, although they stood aloof from engaging in Loyalist activities. Initially, Arnold remained committed to the Patriot cause, even after he married Peggy Shippen in April 1779.

In addition to marrying a Loyalist, Arnold mingled with the high society of Philadelphia and invited many Loyalists to lavish parties. However, he also entertained many wealthy contributors to the American cause, including Philadelphia financier Robert Morris and New York conservatives John Jay and Gouverneur Morris. The most visible part of Arnold's high life style was the ornate carriage that carried him around the city. He believed that his battlefield successes had entitled him to live like a king. Furthermore, he paid all his expenses from his own funds, which he had earned as a successful merchant before entering the army. Like Washington and many other generals on the American side, he had suffered huge out-of-pocket expenses while leading his troops and he never received any pay for his military service.

The common people of Philadelphia did not view the matter in the same way as Arnold did. When they saw his aristocratic style of living, they wondered whether they were fighting the war simply to replace one regal dictator with another. Actually, the mere presence of any American military government would have caused some people to raise that issue, although most of them realized that it was merely a wartime necessity.

Seeing the public resentment caused by Arnold's behavior, Joseph Reed, chairman of the Pennsylvania Executive Council and the virtual dictator of the Commonwealth, decided that the time was ripe to have Arnold removed from office. Reed was a devout Calvinist and an ardent advocate of clean, unpretentious living. He was also an avid Patriot who wanted to hang all the Loyalists and confiscate their property. He had been upset with Arnold since the general had first arrived and thwarted his plans to persecute the Loyalists. Such persecutions, Arnold said, would have violated both Washington's order and a Congressional resolution stating that no person was to be molested nor was his property to be confiscated because of his political beliefs. In retaliation, Reed researched Arnold's service record and brought a number of charges against him relating to his use of his command position to do favors for friends, his appropriation of army manpower and property for personal use, his demeaning of militiamen by imposing menial duties on them and, the most serious charge, Arnold's orders to close the shops of Philadelphia so he could buy the goods himself at a cheap price and then sell them at a huge profit.

Arnold tried to have these charges referred to a court martial, where he thought he would have the best chance of a fair trial. However, Reed persuaded the Congress to take jurisdiction. It appointed a committee, headed by William Paca of Delaware, to investigate the charges. Clearing Arnold of six of the eight charges, the committee forwarded the other two to Washington for handling by a court martial. These were the charges relating to the use of army wagons and the demeaning of militiamen. Arnold was overjoyed, confident that his battle was over. A military court, he thought, was sure to acquit him of the remaining charges. He resigned his post as military governor of Philadelphia in order to take a rest.

However, Arnold's joy was short-lived. He was furious when he learned that Reed had talked the Congress into modifying the committee findings by adding to more charges to the court martial order relating to the use of other military property and the order to close the Philadelphia shops. He appealed to the Congress for reconsideration. Meanwhile, a public movement rose in support of Arnold's cause. Fearing that the Congress might be influenced by this movement, the president of the Pennsylvania Commonwealth, one of Reed's puppets, wrote several Congressmen a letter saying that if they took any action favorable to Arnold, they faced "a melancholy prospect of perpetuated disunion between this and the other United States." Because of this threat that Pennsylvania might secede from the union, the Congress transferred Arnold's appeal to another committee, where it lay buried.

The letter from the Pennsylvania president showed the difficulty that some American leaders had in practicing the principles of freedom for which they were fighting. How, after all the injustices suffered at the hands of the British, could the chief official of an American state use the threat of secession, much less any other threat, to deny someone a fair trial or hearing? Yet that is exactly what happened in Philadelphia, less than three years after the Declaration of Independence had been signed in the same city.

Reed compounded his felony when he wrote Washington a threatening letter: if the military court dismissed the charge that Arnold had misappropriated army wagons, he said, the Continental Army would receive no more transport vehicles from Pennsylvania. He also prevailed upon Washington to postpone the trial from its scheduled date of May 1, 1779, in order to give himself more time to gather witnesses.

When Arnold's trial was finally held on December 23, 1779, he was acquitted of all charges except that of misappropriating military property, including army wagons. Although he was sentenced only to a reprimand from General Washington, he was extremely upset upon hearing the verdict.

During the time Arnold was preparing for his court martial, he realized that his battlefield successes were not being appreciated by his compatriots. With his wife's prodding, he also decided that the cause of American freedom was no longer worth the fight. He therefore began sending secret messages to General Clinton stating that he would be willing to transfer his service to the British army, provided he was compensated for the American property he was likely to lose.

Clinton, of course, was only too happy to have Arnold defect, but he also wanted Arnold to help him capture the American fort at West Point, about fifty miles up the Hudson River from New York

City. He reasoned that if he could take West Point, he could break the northern stranglehold that Washington had on his army.

After his court martial, therefore, Arnold requested Washington to put him in charge of West Point. Washington was somewhat confused by Arnold's sudden interest in such an uninteresting, secluded post. Also, he had better use for Arnold. He put him in command of one of the wings of a force that he was sending to defend Newport, Rhode Island from a British sea invasion. The British had abandoned Newport the previous year but now they wanted it back. However, at the last moment, Clinton changed his mind and decided to concentrate on improving his situation in New York. Washington therefore disbanded his Rhode Island force and assigned Arnold to command West Point on August 3, 1780.

All the while, from the summer of 1779 through the summer of 1780, Arnold was negotiating the terms of his defection with Clinton and sending him American military secrets to show his sincerity.

Finally, in September 1780, Clinton decided to make his move on West Point, using information supplied by Arnold and relying on him to make conditions at West Point easy for takeover. However, Clinton was worried about the possibility that an impostor was sending Arnold's messages in an elaborate scheme to trick him or that Arnold himself was deceiving him. Therefore he sent his adjutant general, John André, to meet Arnold personally, aboard a boat on the Hudson River near West Point. The rendezvous took place without difficulty, but on the way back to New York, André was met at the Pine Bridge over the Croton River by several Patriots standing guard. In spite of his pass from General Arnold, the guards were suspicious and searched André. They found three papers tucked in the bottom of his sock that cast suspicion on Arnold's loyalty.

The guards delivered André to Lieutenant Colonel Jameson, commander of the Northcastle outpost. Jameson decided to send a messenger with André's papers to intercept Washington, whom he thought was on the Danbury Road, traveling by coincidence to a meeting with Arnold at West Point. He then sent André under an armed guard to South Salem, near the Connecticut border. The leader of the guard detail then rode to West Point with a letter written by Jameson that presented certain facts to General Arnold, so that he might explain them.

Washington, however, had taken a different road to West Point, so the messenger with the André papers did not catch up to him until he had reached West Point. Meanwhile, the guard with Jameson's letter had arrived at West Point, before Washington got there. Upon seeing the letter and realizing that his plan had failed and that he was in deep trouble, Arnold quickly saddled his horse and rode off, barely escaping an embarrassing meeting with Washington. By the time Washington arrived and received the André papers, Arnold was sailing safely down the Hudson River to his new employer. When Arnold reported the news of André's capture to Clinton, the British commander was so grief-stricken that he hardly acknowledged Arnold's presence. Indeed, he had good reason to be upset. On October 2, his adjutant general was hanged as a spy.

Benedict Arnold's treason and defection to the British was a sad end to what had been an illustrious career as a leader in the American fight for independence. Knowing that one of their most valiant and respected leaders would do such a thing to hurt their cause was also a blow to the morale of the loyal soldiers who were still on the battlefields fighting for their freedom. Another unfortunate part of this scenario was the conduct of Joseph Reed. His name should also live in infamy for his selfish, divisive campaign against Arnold, during which he violated the very principles of freedom and justice that were motivating most other Americans to carry on their war against the British.

N. King's Mountain, Cowpens and Guilford Court House

After his victory at Camden on August 16, 1780, Cornwallis began reporting directly to the American secretary Lord Germain in London, creating an almost independent command in the South. Germain was gaining more trust in Cornwallis while his trust in

Clinton was waning. With Germain's approval, Cornwallis marched north to take over North Carolina and Virginia. His first mistake was appointing a cocky lieutenant colonel, Patrick Ferguson, to lead an attack with four thousand South Carolina Loyalists. Ferguson thought that he could carry out his mission with only a few more than a thousand of these men, leaving the rest behind to guard his headquarters at the village of Ninety-Six, South Carolina. Apparently, he was counting on many Loyalists to come forward and help him, because he was traveling into western North Carolina, where the Regulators had rebelled against their Patriot government in 1776. He also believed that he could scare away the Patriot militia in the area by issuing intimidating threats. First he sent a captured Patriot militiaman over the Blue Ridge Mountains into the Tennessee territory to tell Colonel Isaac Shelby, a local Patriot militia leader, that if he did not surrender, the British would come over the mountains and burn his whole country. When he reached the North Carolina border, he broadcast the following notice:

> Unless you wish to be eaten up by an inundation of Barbarians . . . if you wish to be pinioned, robbed and murdered, and see your wives and daughters, in four days, abused by the dregs of mankind---or in short, if you wish or deserve to live and bear the name of men, grasp your arms in a moment and run to camp.[29]

Hardly any Loyalists responded to these threats. Instead, about fourteen hundred very angry Patriot militiamen gathered from all over the Carolinas, Virginia and the Tennessee territory. Most of them came on horseback with rifles. When Ferguson heard they were chasing him, he set up a defense on King's Mountain, just south of the border between North and South Carolina and thirty miles west of Charlotte.

On October 7, 1780, the Patriots surrounded the mountain and a bloody battle raged. As in the Civil War, it was brother fighting brother. Colonel Ferguson was the only foreign soldier there. Five times the Patriot riflemen charged up the mountain and four times they were driven back by Loyalist bayonets. The fifth time they reached the top and surrounded Ferguson and his men. Ferguson refused to surrender and was instantly killed. Other Loyalists tried to surrender, but the Patriot hearts were filled with vengeance. "Tarleton's quarter!" some shouted as they chased down their neighbors, calling them by name before they killed them. At the end of the hour-long battle, 157 Loyalists were dead, 167 were badly wounded and left to die on the mountain and the other seven hundred surrendered. The Patriot casualties were twenty-eight dead and sixty-two wounded.

After the battle, the Patriots marched their prisoners down to Gilberttown, where they held a war crimes trial. About thirty to forty were convicted of various crimes they had allegedly committed in the course of raiding and burning the South Carolina countryside. Twelve were condemned to death but only nine were actually hanged, because one escaped and two were pardoned.

In December 1780, Washington appointed General Nathaniel Greene, a Rhode Island veteran of Bunker Hill, to take over the southern theatre of the Continental Army. When he arrived at Charlotte, he found that his army consisted of only 950 Continental regulars, about four hundred infantry militia, ninety cavalrymen and sixty artillery cannoneers. They were starving, poorly clothed and in a poor state of morale and discipline. Greene therefore bided his time by sending them out in small guerrilla bands to harass the flanks of Cornwallis's army. Their raids were successful and helped lift their morale and discipline; they also allowed them to forage for food in areas far from their camp. Morale was raised higher when reinforcements arrived from the north, including Light Horse Harry Lee's experienced calvary legion.

Greene then took the risky step of dividing his outnumbered army in two. He stayed with half his men on the east side of Charlotte, while he gave his western column to the newly promoted General Daniel Morgan, who had commanded Morgan's Rifles at the battle of Saratoga. Cornwallis had also received reinforcements from Clinton in New York and responded to Greene's moves by dividing his much larger army into three parts. He hoped to knock out both of Greene's columns with his own flanking columns, while he led his center column unopposed into North Carolina. He ordered Tarleton's western column of eleven hundred men to attack Morgan's column, while he told General Alexander Leslie to keep his eastern column in Camden.

On January 17, 1781, Morgan stood his ground against Tarleton at Cowpens, South Carolina, an area of sandy hills twenty-five miles west of King's Mountain. He designed a series of complicated maneuvers to fool Tarleton, taking advantage of the British leader's tendency to overreact, especially when he saw a retreating enemy. First, one of his lines would fight and then move off to the side and appear to retreat, while another line took its place. Tarleton's men took the bait and kept charging into traps while pursuing their "retreating" enemy. The result was a great victory for the Americans. Almost a thousand of Tarleton's eleven hundred men were either killed or captured.

In spite of his devastating defeats at King's Mountain and Cowpens, Cornwallis was determined to keep moving toward Virginia. His opponent Greene was also hoping he would move north, so that he would extend his supply lines and weaken his hold on South Carolina. After consolidating his remaining forces, Cornwallis tried to chase down Morgan's column, which was headed north toward a Catawba River crossing in North Carolina. However, he soon realized he would never catch Morgan because of the heavy guns and equipment he was trying to drag with him. So he stopped at Ramsour's Mills and burned his excess baggage, including his tents and his casks of rum. His men were so upset about the rum that 250 of them deserted.

Meanwhile, Greene also consolidated his two columns and headed for the Dan River near the Virginia border. Cornwallis chased after him but was delayed by icy, rain-swollen rivers that his men had to cross. At the Catawba River crossing, eight hundred North Carolina militia commanded by General William Davidson pummeled Cornwallis's troops with sniper fire. Unfortunately, Davidson himself was killed by a bullet to the heart. The British were further harassed by a detachment of elite troops commanded by Colonel Otho Williams, which Greene had dispatched from his main army on February 8 after reaching Guilford Court House. Cornwallis mistook these soldiers for the lead guard of Greene's army and therefore thought he had a chance of reaching the Dan River before Greene.

However, the main body of Greene's army was well ahead of Cornwallis and crossed the Dan River into Virginia on February 13, using boats that had been gathered by an advance guard. When the British arrived in hot pursuit, there were no more boats and the river was much too deep to ford. Cornwallis was stuck. He was over two hundred miles from his base in Charleston and running low on food and supplies; he had burned most of his provisions at Ramsour's Mills. He therefore had to pull his army back to Hillsboro, where his soldiers forced local people to contribute food and supplies to their cause.

In the meantime, Williams' detachment rejoined Greene, with additional North Carolina militia picked up along the way. Reinforcements also arrived from the north, bringing Greene's total strength to about forty-four hundred men, while the British were down to under twenty-five hundred men. Cornwallis pleaded for Loyalists to come forth and join him, but to no avail. He wrote to Lord Germain that he was "amongst timid friends and adjoining to inveterate Rebels."[30]

Greene realized that he would soon have to end his retreat and take a stand against Cornwallis or the British would take over all the southern states. His first move in that direction was to send General Andrew Pickens with a Maryland regiment and Light Horse Harry Lee's cavalry on a police mission against the British and Loyalist soldiers who were out gathering food and supplies. By accident, some of Lee's men encountered two Loyalist militiamen; the Loyalists mistook Lee for Tarleton because they wore similar uniforms. They told Lee they were part of a regiment of Loyalists commanded by Colonel John Pyle. The regiment, they said, was coming up the road and would be arriving momentarily. Lee sent one of the Loyalists to tell his commander that Tarleton's men were coming through and to draw his men to the side of the road to allow them to pass. Pyle obeyed and Lee's cavalry rode by with drawn swords and cocked pistols, while Pyle's infantry stood by with their rifles and muskets on their shoulders. Just as Lee halted to shake hands with Pyle, one of Pyle's men spotted the Maryland infantry coming up the road and fired his weapon. Lee's men reacted by wheeling their horses toward Pyle's men and charged them, firing their pistols and swinging their swords. It was a horrible massacre. Of Pyle's four hundred Loyalists, ninety were killed and all the rest were wounded.

In early March, Greene moved the main body of his army back across the Dan to Guilford Court House, near the present city of Greensboro. There, he deployed his men and waited for the British to attack. Cornwallis and his army arrived on March 15, 1781. The front lines immediately engaged one another and the battle that followed was one of the bloodiest of the war. Although the British were outnumbered two to one, they managed to force the Americans to retreat. One reason was that many American soldiers, particularly the militia, panicked and ran. The British also benefited from Greene's failure to launch a counterattack when he might have. Greene feared that if he were not successful, his army would have been badly beaten. If it were, certainly the whole South and perhaps the whole war might have been lost.

For the British soldiers, battle of Guilford Court House was a superb victory. Although heavily outnumbered, they were not outmanned. They displayed a level of prowess and bravery that British historians have praised ever since. However, they lost a quarter of their rapidly diminishing army, with ninety-three dead and 439 wounded, compared to seventy-three dead and 183 wounded Americans. Furthermore, Cornwallis was in such desperate need of food and supplies that he had to pull his army back to Wilmington, a small North Carolina shipping port near the South Carolina border. In England, the Whig leader Charles James Fox remarked, "Another such victory would destroy the British army."[31]

O. Victory at Yorktown

While the British forces in the South were in disarray, the main body of their army in New York was in good condition, particularly by comparison to the Continental Army. In fact, the condition of the Continental Army was so bad that Washington wrote in April 1781, "We are at the end of our tether . . . Now or never our deliverance must come."[32] The deliverance that he had in mind was more aid from the king of France.

Washington's problems stemmed from the continued failure of the various states to contribute enough supplies and equipment. His army was also suffering because the Congress had been unable to obtain more foreign loans and France had been sending less aid during the previous year. Thus, the American soldiers were starving for lack of rations, their clothes were in shreds and most had not been paid in over a year. In protest against their wretched condition, the Pennsylvania and New Jersey Lines had mutinied in January 1781. Fortunately, Washington had been able to restore discipline among these troops, at least temporarily.

In desperation, Washington sent his own personal emissary to the court at Versailles. He was Colonel John Laurens of South Carolina, the twenty-six-year-old son of Henry Laurens, the former president of the Congress who had refused the British peace offer in 1778. Unfortunately, Henry Laurens had been captured by the British while sailing to Holland and was at the moment sitting in the Tower of London awaiting possible execution for treason. Upon arriving in France, John Laurens met with the Marquis de Castries, the minister of marine, and demanded that he dispatch a large fleet to the United States. The marquis replied that his ships had already been sent to attack the British in the West Indies, not in the United States.

Laurens then went to the foreign minister, the Comte de Vergennes, and demanded an immediate loan of twenty-five million livres, worth about five million dollars at the time. During the entire month of April and early May of 1781, Laurens made repeated calls on the foreign minister, explaining the plight of his nation and its sick, starving soldiers. However, all Vergennes would promise was six million livres, an amount already promised to Benjamin Franklin. So the brash young officer obtained a personal audience with King Louis XVI and handed him a written petition. The next day, the French director of finance told Laurens that the French would send the United States supplies worth 2.3 million livres and another 2.3 million livres in cash. He would also arrange for a Dutch loan of ten million livres, to be guaranteed by the French government. In addition, Laurens later learned that the large French fleet bound for West Indies would be redirected to the United States. That fleet was carrying an army of over six thousand soldiers.

While Colonel Laurens was in France, more battles were being fought in the United States. In early April, General Greene marched his troops south to try to recapture South Carolina. His first destination was Camden, which was being defended by nine hundred British and Loyalist soldiers under the command of Lord Francis Rawdon. By the time the news of Greene's march reached Cornwallis at Wilmington on the coast, the British commander realized that he could never reach Camden in time to help Rawdon. On April 25, he began marching his army north to Virginia, which he had always thought a more important objective than the Carolinas. He hoped that his movement might persuade Greene to abandon Camden and head north to defend Virginia. As valid as that reasoning might have been, Cornwallis took a bold step by going to Virginia; Clinton, who was still in theory his superior commander, had told him not to go to Virginia until he had cleared the Carolinas of all American forces and had firmly established British control in those states. On the other hand, Cornwallis had been making most of his reports directly to Lord Germain in London. There were also rumors that the British ministers wanted to replace Clinton with Cornwallis and were simply waiting for Clinton to make an error that would give them a good excuse to do that.

Another reason why Cornwallis should not have gone to Virginia was the fact that Clinton had already sent over four thousand soldiers there and they were gaining control of that state without Cornwallis's help. On December 30, 1780, the traitor Benedict Arnold had landed at Hampton Roads with sixteen hundred men. For four months, Arnold's British regulars and four hundred Loyalist volunteers had roamed the countryside, burning tobacco and military supplies. They had even raided Richmond, the state capital, causing Governor Thomas Jefferson to flee the city. Washington had then sent three light infantry regiments under the command of General Lafayette and they had recaptured Richmond on April 29. However, another British force of twenty-five hundred men commanded by General William Phillips had arrived several days earlier from New York and had joined Arnold's two thousand men in Petersburg, posing a serious threat to Lafayette's army of one thousand Continentals and one to three thousand untested militia in Richmond.

Cornwallis finally arrived at Petersburg on May 20 with 1,435 very tired, hungry soldiers. There he learned that matters had not gone well for the British forces in Virginia. Soon after his arrival, General Phillips had caught malaria and died. Then General Arnold had assumed command of the entire force, over the objections of the men who had served under Phillips. Meanwhile, Lafayette's army was still sitting unmolested up the road in Richmond.

For some unknown reason, Cornwallis elected not to attack Lafayette right away, in spite of his now overwhelming force of seven thousand men, including an additional seventeen hundred men from New York who had just landed at the mouth of the James River. If he had attacked Lafayette at that time, he probably would have beaten him decisively or at least chased him out of Virginia. Either way, he would have controlled the whole region, thus separating the southern states from their northern neighbors. That might well have ended the war in favor of the British. Instead, Cornwallis sent Tarleton's cavalry up to Charlottesville, where Governor Jefferson and the Virginia Assembly had fled after Arnold had raided Richmond. When Tarleton arrived in Charlottesville, most of the assemblymen fled over the Blue Ridge Mountains to Staunton, but some were captured. Jefferson was nearly captured again, because he had remained at his home at Monticello in order to look through his spyglass at the British riding into the city below him.

Meanwhile, Cornwallis also sent a detachment of rangers, commanded by Lieutenant Colonel John Simcoe, to attack a Continental Army supply depot at Point of Fork on the James River. The depot was guarded by General von Steuben and about a thousand Continental regulars and militia. Von Steuben immediately fled the scene with his men, thinking that Cornwallis's whole army was attacking him.

Finally, after these diversions, Cornwallis went after Lafayette in Richmond. The Frenchman withdrew his men to the north and executed a series of moves that confused both Cornwallis and Tarleton's cavalry. Then, on June 10, with his army camped at the Raccoon ford on the Rapidan River, Lafayette finally received some of the aid that he had been hoping would come. General Anthony Wayne arrived with three regiments of the Pennsylvania Line--nine hundred soldiers in all. With his improved strength, Lafayette advanced against Cornwallis, who, again for some unknown reason, did not stand to fight but withdrew southward. Lafayette received more help when von Steuben's brigade arrived, raising his total strength to almost five thousand men. Feeling even more confident, Lafayette attacked again, this time chasing Cornwallis all the way back to Richmond. Several days later, Cornwallis evacuated Richmond and moved his entire army down the peninsula between the York and James rivers, burning tobacco and military stores on the way. At the end of June, the British general arrived at Williamsburg and stationed his army there for a short time before transporting it across the James River to Portsmouth.

While the British were en route to Portsmouth, Lafayette ordered Wayne to attack them at a plantation called Green Spring Farm. Due to his own miscalculation, Lafayette's whole army was nearly trapped and captured. After their miraculous escape, Lafayette was content to keep his army at a safe distance from the enemy and simply monitor its movements.

Fortunately for Lafayette, Cornwallis made no move against him but simply transported his army back across the James River to Yorktown, on the south shore of the mouth of the York River. At Portsmouth, Cornwallis had received a letter from Clinton chastising him for leaving Williamsburg without his permission and telling him to go back to the same area and establish a base at Yorktown. Cornwallis therefore spent the month of August building a fortified camp and naval base at Yorktown, using black slaves that he had procured for the job.

One reason why Cornwallis had to establish a strong sea base in Virginia was that he had been cut off from his Charleston base by Nathaniel Greene. Between the middle of April and late June, Greene's army of fourteen hundred men had forced all British and Loyalist forces out of the northern half of South Carolina, as well as northern Georgia. True to form, Greene had done this without winning a single major battle and technically losing two at Camden and Ninety-Six. Each time, he had failed to dislodge the enemy troops but had left them in such a weakened and isolated condition that they had to abandon their positions. Thus, with Greene's army at large in the Carolinas and "inveterate Rebels" ready to mobilize their militias at a moment's notice, Cornwallis had no sure way of obtaining supplies overland from Charleston, nor could he be assured of a route of retreat if Lafayette were to force him to move in that direction.

While Cornwallis was moving about Virginia in the summer of 1781, Washington was making plans to attack Clinton's army in New York, using the large French fleet and army that the French government had promised to send from the West Indies. He also planned to use the forty-eight-hundred-man French army and eight French ships that were stationed at Newport, Rhode Island, as well as his own army of seven thousand men, which he planned to supplement with militia recruited from New England. General Jean Baptiste Rochambeau, the commander of the French army at Newport, tried to talk Washington into attacking Cornwallis's army in Virginia, pointing out that Clinton had almost fifteen thousand men in New York guarded by the British navy, while Cornwallis had only eight thousand men guarded by no navy. However, Washington did not like the idea of such a battle because in order for the plan to succeed he would have to march most of his army from New York to Virginia, leaving himself vulnerable to Clinton either chasing his rear or marching up the Hudson River and isolating the New England states.

In June, Rochambeau transferred about four thousand of his men from Newport to White Plains. While waiting to hear when the French fleet would be leaving the West Indies, he tried to persuade Washington that their attack should be on Cornwallis, but Washington remained committed to his New York plan. Then, on August 13, one of Rochambeau's aides informed Washington that the frigate *La Concorde* had arrived in Newport the day before with a message that the French fleet was scheduled to leave the West Indies on that very day, August 13, but it would be bound for Virginia, not New York. Furthermore, Admiral Francois de Grasse, the fleet commander, had reported that he could stay only a month and a half on the American continent. Washington was furious when he heard this news and had a long private meeting with the French aide. Afterward, the American commander-in-chief appeared calmer and wrote in his journal,

> Matters having now come to a crisis and a decisive plan to be determined on, I was obliged, from the shortness of Count de Grasse promised stay on this Coast, the apparent disinclination in their Naval Officers to force the harbour of New York and the feeble compliance of the States to my requisitions for Men . . . to give up all idea of attacking New York; and instead thereof to remove the French Troops and a detachment from the American army . . . to Virginia.[33]

Accordingly, Washington sent a message to Lafayette informing him of the plan to attack Cornwallis and telling him to prevent the British from moving south into North Carolina. He also sent General Louis Duportail on a ship to intercept de Grasse and have him send transport ships to the north end of Chesapeake Bay as soon as he arrived, so that they could carry the French and American soldiers marching from New York the rest of the way to southern Virginia. Then he sent another message to the Comte de Barras, the French naval commander at Newport, instructing him to sail his fleet of eight ships, loaded with siege guns, to meet de Grasse's fleet near the mouth of the Chesapeake Bay.

Washington knew that it would take at least a month to assemble all these forces and prepare them for an attack. Thus, the British would certainly know of the attack long before it was launched. On the other hand, news of the Franco-American departure from New York might be delayed by a clever ruse, so that Clinton would be unable to react until it was too late. Washington therefore ordered several regiments to camp on the New Jersey side of the Hudson River and make visible preparations for an attack on New York from the west. He also arranged to have thousands of loaves of bread baked in New Jersey, enough to feed ten thousand French and American soldiers while they were camped there. In addition, known Loyalist spies were given information confirming the plans to attack New York.

Surprisingly, the ruse worked perfectly. On August 21, about four thousand Frenchmen and three thousand Americans left White Plains, leaving behind only four thousand Americans to protect the New York countryside from Clinton's army, which had now grown to over seventeen thousand men with the arrival of more Hessians. However, because of the diversionary activities carried on by the Americans in New Jersey, Clinton did not learn where these troops were headed until September 2. By that time, the French and American armies had already passed through Philadelphia. Furthermore, Clinton had no way of sending reinforcements to Cornwallis; he had sent most of his navy to the Chesapeake Bay area after hearing that two French fleets were headed there. His remaining ships he had given to Benedict Arnold, whom Cornwallis had sent back to New York shortly after arriving in Virginia. In order to rid himself of Arnold, Clinton had sent him to raid his home town of New London, Connecticut. When he finally realized that the French and Americans were organizing a combined land and sea attack on Yorktown, all he could do, or at least all he chose to do, was to send a warning to Cornwallis and wait in his New

York headquarters, hoping the reports from Yorktown would be favorable.

The reports from Yorktown were not favorable. On September 5, the nineteen ships that Clinton had sent to the Chesapeake Bay under Admiral Samuel Graves encountered the fleet of Admiral de Grasse at the mouth of the Chesapeake Bay. De Grasse had recently arrived at the bay and had put ashore three infantry regiments of three thousand soldiers and a cargo of heavy siege cannon. He had been on his way out of the bay to meet Barras's fleet sailing from Newport, when he was surprised by the British fleet. Although nearly trapped in the fifteen-mile wide entrance to the bay between Cape Henry and Cape Charles, de Grasse was able to extricate himself from his vulnerable position by tacking back and forth against the wind, a process that took an excruciatingly long time. Fortunately, the British commander Graves simply waited until the French ships cleared the passage between the capes and formed their battle array. If Graves had attacked when he first saw the French fleet, he probably would have scored an important victory and would have been able to restore naval protection to Cornwallis's army at Yorktown. Instead, the two-hour battle that followed was inconclusive and took a heavy toll on both sides. The British suffered 336 casualties and six badly damaged ships. The French lost 209 casualties and four of their ships were damaged, but not as badly as the British ships. The fighting continued for two more days and de Grasse was able to lure Graves southward toward Cape Hatteras, North Carolina. On September 9, de Grasse suddenly disengaged his fleet from the battle and headed back to the mouth of the Chesapeake, where he joined forces with Barras's fleet, raising his total strength to thirty-five ships, counting the three he had left on the York River. With many of his British ships in bad need of repair, Graves was now in no position to challenge the French again. He headed back to New York, leaving Cornwallis and his eight-thousand-man army sitting isolated in Yorktown.

Clinton also received more bad news from South Carolina. On September 8, while the Battle of the Capes was ending, Nathaniel Greene sent a force of twenty-four-hundred men, including North and South Carolina militia, to attack two thousand British soldiers near Eutaw Springs, South Carolina. Again, Greene's men fought bravely and inflicted heavy casualties on the British but were forced to withdraw. Because the Americans had attacked the British and had then withdrawn, they technically lost the battle. However, the British suffered 866 casualties, compared to 522 American casualties, and the British commander Lord Rawdon was forced to consolidate all his troops at his base in Charleston. Now, except for Charleston and Savannah, the Carolinas and Georgia were now completely free of British soldiers.

Meanwhile, Washington and Rochambeau continued marching their armies south toward the Head of Elk, at the north end of the Chesapeake Bay. As they were greeted in Philadelphia and Baltimore by the cheering crowds, both the French and American soldiers sensed they were marching toward a decisive battle that would win the war. However, the French soldiers were not as exuberant as the Americans. Although they were well-fed and dressed in beautiful uniforms, they were still peasant subjects of an autocratic king and they envied the American soldiers who were about to win their freedom. Rochambeau had to double his guard to prevent his men from escaping into the countryside. The American soldiers were under-fed, wore their own clothing and had not been paid in over a year. Nevertheless, one of Rochambeau's aides, Baron Ludwig von Closen, was impressed by the size, physical strength and military bearing of most of the American soldiers, particularly those of the Rhode Island regiment who were three-quarters black. Von Closen said that regiment was "the most neatly dressed, the best under arms, and the most precise in its maneuvers."[34]

At Chester, just south of Philadelphia, a courier's message told Washington that de Grasse's fleet had arrived in the Chesapeake Bay. The general's face lit with joy. Then, when the French-American army reached the Head of Elk, news of the French naval victory arrived. Everyone cheered as they boarded boats that would carry them down the Chesapeake to Williamsburg on the

Chapter 5   The War of Independence   163

James River. One of Washington's generals said that they knew then that they had Cornwallis "handsomely in a pudding bag."[35]

Washington and Rochambeau arrived at Williamsburg with their armies in the middle of September. With Lafayette's men and the French soldiers de Grasse brought from the West Indies, the French and American infantry in southern Virginia now totaled nearly sixteen thousand men, including over seven thousand Frenchmen and nearly nine thousand Americans. Among the Americans were thirty-two hundred Virginia militia. They were supported by a thirty-five-ship French naval fleet and hundreds of French naval and land artillery pieces. All these forces would soon be ready to attack the eight thousand British soldiers at Yorktown.

Still, there was a chance that the British might extricate themselves. Clinton had ordered Admiral Graves to depart the New York harbor for Yorktown as soon as possible with twenty-three ships and seven thousand infantrymen. Admiral de Grasse sent a note to Washington saying that he was planning to return to the West Indies before the battle began because he was concerned about the coming fall storm season. Fortunately, Washington was able to persuade de Grasse to stay at Yorktown until after the battle and the British fleet never set sail until October 19. The British delay was caused by a combination of bad weather and a long period of preparation by Graves, who was concerned that if he lost a major battle to de Grasse, he would be unable to defend the British position in the West Indies.

Another fortunate event for the French and Americans occurred when Cornwallis withdrew his men from his outer trenches on September 30. He had received word that reinforcements were on their way from New York. By consolidating his forces, he decided he had a better chance of withstanding the coming attack until help arrived. However, the French and Americans immediately moved their cannon into the abandoned trenches. Then they spent the next week digging more trenches for their cannon.

On October 9, the allied forces began firing their cannon at Yorktown, as well as at the British ships on the York River. For eight days, they bombarded the British, progressively moving their cannon closer to the town, until they were only three hundred yards away from the forward British positions. Meanwhile, various infantry and cavalry units attacked the British front lines, capturing several fortifications. On October 16, 350 British troops retaliated in a valiant counterattack but they were driven back. Then, on October 17, the French and Americans stepped up the intensity of their fire, but the British could not answer. They had no more ammunition. Cornwallis had no choice but to surrender.

At a noon ceremony on October 19, 1781, Brigadier General Charles O'Hara, acting on behalf of General Cornwallis, who claimed to be ill, handed his commander's sword to General Lincoln. Washington had appointed Lincoln to receive it because he was the American second-in-command and therefore O'Hara's equal. The American soldiers proudly watched the symbolic gesture with their French allies. Eight thousand British and Hessian soldiers then walked forward and placed their weapons in huge piles. Many wept and could not believe what was happening as they were led off to prison camps. According to one account of the ceremony, the British musicians played "The World Turned Upside Down."

P. The Conclusion of the War

The British surrender at Yorktown did not result in the immediate end of the war. There were still seventeen thousand British and Hessian soldiers occupying New York City, as well as small British garrisons at Penobscot Bay in Maine, Wilmington in North Carolina, Charleston in South Carolina and Savannah in Georgia. However, the Yorktown defeat destroyed the British will to continue the war. When Lord North heard the news on November 25, he exclaimed, "Oh God! It is all over!" He submitted his resignation to George III in order to pave the way for a Whig ministry that would settle the war and grant America its independence. However, the king refused to accept North's resignation. North was his ally in Parliament and the king knew that his own power was at stake as well. In fact, he made a personal address to

Parliament, urging it to continue the war. It was to no avail. Finally, after several months of bitter speeches in the House of Commons, in which the Whigs severely criticized the Tory ministry's handling of the war, the king backed down and accepted North's resignation in March 1782. He was extremely despondent after the defeat and it probably contributed to the fits of madness that he suffered during the remaining thirty-eight years of his life.

The Marquess of Rockingham, who had served once before as prime minister in the 1760s, was elected to replace Lord North. He immediately sent representatives to Paris to negotiate a peace treaty with Benjamin Franklin and others representing the United States. Unfortunately, Rockingham died only a few months after taking office, on July 1, 1782. That was bad news for the Americans, because Lord Henry Shelburne, who succeeded Rockingham, was not as willing to agree to Franklin's peace proposals. The matters in dispute concerned the boundaries of the new nation, fishing rights and the question of whether the United States should restore the property taken from Loyalists. The most difficult issue was whether the United States and Great Britain should conclude their own peace treaty, independent of Britain's disputes with France, Spain and the Netherlands. France in particular was opposed to such a treaty.

Franklin told the British negotiator Richard Oswald that the United States wished to create an enduring, general peace among all the nations then at war. Oswald wrote that both Franklin and the French Foreign Minister Vergennes believed that the United States Congress might be able to guarantee such a general peace. For instance, if two or more of the major European powers were at war with one another, the Congress might end such a conflict merely by declaring its opposition to one of the warring nations, thereby forcing that nation to the settlement table. Oswald agreed that this view had merit, because many Europeans would be flocking to the United States to enjoy the freedoms proclaimed in the American Declaration of Independence. That would enable the United States to become a great world power. Furthermore, many progressive Europeans were already hailing the United States as a symbol of the freedom that people would soon be enjoying in all the nations of Europe.

However, these head-swelling thoughts bore little relation to the actual circumstances in America in 1782. While the negotiations in Paris dragged on and philosophers were speculating on the nature of a new world order, the American war continued. Washington had moved his army back to its position guarding the north side of New York City, which remained under the firm control of the British army. Low pay, low morale and desertions continued to plague the general. Also, the French navy's return to the West Indies had allowed the British navy to regain control of the Atlantic coast and capture American merchant and fishing ships, as well as ships engaged in privateering. In the west, the British enlisted the help of more Indians. On June 4, 1782, a group of Loyalists and Indians ambushed a party of Americans, killing forty to fifty of them, on the Olentangy River near the present cities of Galion and Bucyrus in north central Ohio. The Loyalists then induced Shawnee Indians to raid settlements in Pennsylvania, western Virginia and Kentucky. To stop these raids, on November 10, 1782 George Rogers Clark led a force of eleven hundred cavalry against the Shawnee, burning a number of their villages and a British trading post called Loramie's Store, about thirty miles south of the present city of Lima in western Ohio. It was the last battle of the war that had begun seven years before in Lexington, Massachusetts.

The United States and Great Britain signed a preliminary treaty of peace in Paris on November 30, 1782. More treaties between the United States, Great Britain, France, Spain and the Netherlands were signed February 3, 1783. By these treaties, the United States was recognized as the sovereign of nearly all the land east of the Mississippi River, between the present Georgia-Florida border and the present United States-Canada border. United States citizens were also allowed to fish off the coast of Newfoundland, a right that New Englanders had enjoyed since the Pilgrims landed. The United States refused to agree to restore Loyalist property confiscated by its member states, because it said that was a matter for each state to decide. However, it did agree that no future confiscations would be made and that it would "earnestly recommend" to its member states that they restore the confiscated property.

Because of the time required for all the nations to ratify the treaties, the last British troops did not leave New York City until November 25, 1783. General Washington and his top officers bid farewell to one another on December 4, 1783, at a dinner at Fraunces Tavern near the present corner of Pearl and Broad Streets in New York City.

On his way home to Mount Vernon, Washington stopped to address the United States Congress, which was meeting at Annapolis, Maryland. Many people had suggested that he assume control of the weak national government. The Congress was struggling with huge war debts and other problems. There was a growing feeling that he was the only man who could provide the leadership to deal with these problems. One of his officers had asked if he would consider becoming, "King George I of America." Another army general might have done that, as most generals of other nations have done in similar situations. However, Washington knew that such a move would have defeated the very principles of government for which he and his soldiers had been fighting. On December 23, 1783, he told the Congress,

> Having now finished the work assigned me, I retire from the great theatre of action, and bidding an affectionate farewell to this august body under whose orders I have so long acted, I here offer my commission, and take my leave of all the employments of public life.

While the congressmen and spectators wept, Washington took his commission from his breast pocket and surrendered it to the Congress president, Thomas Mifflin.

Q. The War and the People

The war was over and the Americans had won their independence. However, the costs were great, not only for the soldiers and their families, but for all the people living in America. By one estimate, over twenty-five thousand Americans, about one percent of the total population, lost their lives in the course of the war. Many of them were civilians.[36]

One of the people living in America at the time of the War of Independence was a young boy named Obed Macy. He lived on Nantucket Island, off the southern coast of Cape Cod, Massachusetts. Near the end of his life in 1835, he published *The History of Nantucket*, in which he wrote,

> If we could justify any war, it would be that of the Revolution. Repeated injuries were heaped upon the colonists, which, we allow, it was their duty to notice, in a firm and decided manner. Respecting, as we do, and that most sincerely, the rights of man, we have little sympathy with those who supinely submit to unprovoked injuries. In the dignity of Christian charity we bear and forbear, but our endurance then is a defence which even tyranny will eventually respect. To feel an injury, and to revenge it, are very different things: the highest merit of forbearance consists in the keenest sense of wrong. While then we would bear testimony against all wars, and every species of violence between man and man, we would encourage all to defend their social and individual rights, to cherish self-respect, and maintain their independence; and we believe that there are ample means for this purpose, without resort to blood, and that wars and fightings are the causes, rather than the remedies of oppression. A course of proceeding which throws two nations into mourning over the harm which they have reciprocally done to each other, seems a strange way of deciding between right and wrong. Let the consequences of war be considered apart from the vain glory, and martial equipments, and mighty enterprises, and great talents, and enthusiastic excitement, which are associated with it; let plunder, and rapine and death; let ghastly wounds, mutilated limbs, loathsome disease, and famine and poverty; let the widow, the childless, the orphan; let the crimes of lawless passion, and the permanent injury to moral and christian[sic] virtues, be considered, and who will say that wars are the best means, nay who will say that they should ever be resorted to, for the purpose of deciding a national dispute? Who is there, that, clothed with the spirit of christianity[sic], can justify war; when, before it commences, we are sensible of the

destruction and misery that must ensue? Alas for man that he is blinded to his best interest![37]

Both sides permitted Nantucket neutral status during the War of Independence. Everyone recognized that the islanders could not defend themselves because of their isolated location, twenty miles off the coast of Cape Cod. Nantucket was of no strategic value to either side. Nevertheless, the war had a severe impact on the island's main industry, which was catching and processing whales. While they were at sea, the whaling ships were treated by the British like all other colonial ships. When captured, they were impounded and their crews impressed in the British navy or confined aboard prison ships. The same was true of any ships and crews that attempted to carry whale products from Nantucket to the mainland. Although a few Nantucket ships were able to operate in spite of these conditions, the whaling business and the entire economy of the island came to a virtual standstill during the war. Macy wrote,

> Provision, notwithstanding what was raised on the island, or brought from the continent, was at times very scarce and dear; and many suffered by want, having no means to buy and no employment by which to earn any thing. After a few years of the war had expired, those who had property left did not care to risk it abroad, finding that the danger of capture had materially increased; thus a large number were left in a state of inactivity. Many of the middle class, at the commencement of the war, had some hundreds of dollars by them, which they had saved out of their earnings; but they were now under the necessity of disposing of their past savings for the support of their families. Some of this class became exhausted by the middle, others by the latter part of the war.[38]

Macy also reported that occasionally British ships would land at Nantucket and, against orders, plunder its communities, robbing them of the few provisions they had.[39]

On the mainland, the American people faced similar problems. For instance, during the British occupation of New Jersey in the winter of 1776-77, Hessian mercenary soldiers looted homes and shops throughout the countryside, even the ones belonging to large numbers of people who had signed oaths of loyalty to the British government. The problem was that the Hessians could not read English and so they could not decipher the protection papers that British officers had given the people. Women were particularly upset when the Hessians paraded their camp followers down their streets in the fine apparel that the soldiers had stolen from their homes. As a result, the state of New Jersey, initially in danger of becoming a Loyalist stronghold, was gradually won over to the Patriot cause.

British and Hessian soldiers continued their rude conduct toward the New Jersey people when they marched from Philadelphia back to New York in June 1778. Joseph Martin, a member of an American militia brigade sent to track them down, gave this account of what he saw:

> We had ample opportunity to see the devastation they made in their rout; cattle killed and lying about the fields and pastures, some just in the position they were in when shot down others with a small spot of skin taken off their hind quarters and a mess of steak taken out; household furniture hacked and broken to pieces; wells filled up and mechanics' and farmers' tools destroyed. It was the height of the season of the cherries; the innocent industrious creatures could not climb the trees for the fruit, but universally cut them down.[40]

Many British soldiers considered any American woman fair game for rape. They had a polite way of describing the activity. They called it the sport of "ravishing." Lord Francis Rawdon wrote the following description of how they entertained themselves on Staten Island:

> The fair nymphs of this isle were in wonderful tribulation, as the fresh meat our men have got here has made them riotous as satyrs. A girl cannot step into the bushes to pluck a rose without running the most imminent risk of being ravished, and they are so little accustomed to these vigorous methods that they don't bear them with the proper resignation, and of consequence we have most entertaining court-martials every day.[41]

These war crimes were not confined merely to a few regions of the young nation. Nearly every locality suffered at least one raid or battle and every major city except Baltimore was occupied by the British at one time or another.

The most devastating raids occurred when the British employed Indians to help them. In 1779, the British general Augustine Prevost led a raid through South Carolina using Cherokee Indians along with Florida and Georgia Loyalists. According to the historian Samuel Eliot Morison, their looting, vandalism and savagery caused far more destruction than Sherman's march through Georgia during the Civil War.[42] On July 4, 1778, a date chosen to mock American independence, several Loyalist militia groups sent five hundred Seneca Indians to massacre hundreds of people living in the Wyoming Valley, near the present city of Scranton, Pennsylvania. Some men were burned at the stake and others were beheaded, while their families looked on in horror. Later the same year, another Patriot settlement in Cherry Valley in northern New York suffered a similar Indian attack.

One the other hand, the war was very hard on many Indians, because the Americans sought revenge against them. The year after the Wyoming Valley and Cherry Valley raids, Washington sent five thousand men under General John Sullivan into the same regions, where they destroyed about forty Indian villages, as well as crops, granaries and orchards. The following winter, hundreds of the Indian families who had lived in these towns died of starvation.

Some Indian tribes, particularly the ones living on the western front between Fort Pitt, controlled by the Americans, and Fort Detroit, controlled by the British, did not know which side to support. The Indians who allied themselves with the British suffered attacks by the Americans, while those friendly to the Americans were attacked by the British. Those who tried to remain neutral were harassed by both sides, each side suspecting they were collaborating with the other.

Several groups of Indians on the Tuscarawas River, in what is now eastern Ohio, tried to remain neutral. German missionaries under the leadership of the Reverend David Zeisberger of the

Moravian Church had converted these Indians to Christianity and had taught them to live as white frontier people, in communities of neatly arranged log cabins. There were three such communities: Schoenbrunn, Gnadenhutten and Salem.

In August 1781, British troops from Fort Detroit, accompanied by two chiefs of the Delaware tribe, discovered these Christian Indian settlements. The British took the missionary leaders to Detroit and moved the Indians to an area near port Sandusky on Lake Erie. They reasoned that if these Indians were loyal to their side, they would need to move there to be safe from raids by rebel troops from Fort Pitt, but if they were friends of the rebels, then they ought to be moved to keep them from collaborating with the enemy.

The captured Indians had to leave behind all the corn that was to feed them during the winter. The British therefore allowed about 150 of them to return to their settlements to pick their corn. They were still living in there in March of 1782, when a detachment of American soldiers from Fort Pitt came upon the Gnadenhutten settlement. The soldiers confused these Indians with others who had recently attacked their villages near Fort Pitt. As part of a retaliation plan, they told Indians they would protect them and convinced them to send a messenger to the Salem settlement have those Indians come and join them. After the messenger left, the soldiers tied up the remaining Indians, crowding the men into one house and the women into another. When the Salem Indians arrived with the messenger, the soldiers imprisoned them as well. In all, they imprisoned about ninety Indians. The soldiers then held a meeting and voted to put all the Indians to death, including the women and children. With guns, spears, tomahawks and scalping knives, they killed every one, except for two boys who managed to escape and spread the word of the bloody massacre. Upon hearing of the Gnadenhutten massacre, Americans everywhere were outraged at what their fellow countrymen had done, but they could not undo the atrocity.[43]

The economic hardships suffered by all Patriots and Loyalists, the sexual abuse of American women by British soldiers, the killing and wounding of thousands of soldiers and civilians and the murders of innocent people like the Gnadenhutten Indians were heavy prices to pay, even for the great cause of freedom. Were they worth it? Were the sacrifices necessary?

Most Americans view the War of Independence as one that had to be fought to secure the personal freedoms that they enjoy today--the cherished rights that now make the United States a free country. However, other British colonies were able to gain their independence by more peaceful means. One of those former colonies, the Republic of India, won its independence because one man, Mahatma Gandhi, amazed the world with the effects of his non-violent demonstrations. The black people of America, inspired by Gandhi's example, gained recognition of their civil rights by non-violent demonstrations led by Martin Luther King. More recently, black South Africans, led by Nelson Mandela and Bishop Desmond Tutu, have gained full citizenship and a constitution with a bill of rights, without resorting to a full-scale civil war.

On the other hand, it is not fair to compare those twentieth-century campaigns for independence and freedom with the American colonial efforts of the eighteenth century. The wars in the intervening years, with their increasing tolls of human suffering, have caused people to search harder for ways to avoid war. Also, people on both sides of the American-British dispute tried to negotiate a peaceful settlement. Their desire for peace was evident from the gradual way the War of Independence began. In the early battles, the colonists were trying to defend themselves and force the British to recognize their rights as free Englishmen. Compromise seemed a real possibility, but that was part of the problem. Most of the people on both sides did not realize how fast the chances of compromise were slipping away. They were busy flexing their muscles and trying to establish better negotiating positions. The separation of the American colonies from Great Britain and the War of Independence were not planned events. They happened, and the Declaration of Independence was an explanation of why they happened, not a decision to make them happen.

6

The New Nation Struggles

A. The Articles of Confederation

During the War of Independence and for a few years after the war, the Articles of Confederation defined the powers of the national government of the United States. The Articles were adopted by the Continental Congress on November 15, 1777, when it was meeting in York, Pennsylvania, while the British army was in Philadelphia. The Articles were then ratified by the legislatures of all the states except Maryland in 1778 and 1779. Maryland ratified them on March 1, 1781.

In the midst of fighting for their freedom, the Americans wanted to make sure that their new national government would be tightly controlled by the people and would have only the most limited, essential powers. As a result, the Articles of Confederation gave the national government so little power and made its decision making so difficult that it was practically no government at all. What the Americans had was a mutual defense treaty between thirteen separate states, shown by the following Article III:

> The said States hereby severally enter into a firm league of friendship with each other, for their common defense, the security of their liberties, and their mutual and general welfare, binding themselves to assist each other, against all force offered to, or attacks upon them, or any of them, on account of religion, sovereignty, trade, or any pretense whatever.

The Articles provided for a government to be run by the Congress, which was to consist of delegations sent by the various states, each state being required to send no less than two nor more than seven delegates. All the delegates from each state had to agree on every issue, because each state delegation had only one vote. When the Congress was not in session, the government was managed by the Committee of the States, consisting of one delegate from each state appointed by the whole Congress. Most of the important powers of the government could be exercised only by the whole Congress. Nine states had to vote affirmatively on any bill for it to become a law.

The four decisions requiring a vote by nine states were to wage war against foreign nations, to borrow and appropriate money to pay the government's debts, to make treaties and alliances with foreign nations and to coin money and regulate the value of money coined by the national government and by the state governments.

The main difficulty faced by the Congress was that it had no power to levy direct taxes to carry on these activities. Even tariffs on imported goods were left to the exclusive power of the states. The Congress could raise money only by assessing each state its portion of the needs of the national treasury, that portion to be determined by the state's total assessed land value in relation to the land value of all the states combined. However, the Articles were silent on what could be done if a state did not pay its assessment. A similar problem existed with respect to the Congress's war powers. It could build and equip its own navy, provided the states paid their assessments, but it had to rely on state militia units for its land forces. These units were to be requisitioned according to quotas based on the number of white inhabitants of each state. Again, the Articles were silent on what could be done when states did not provide their militia quotas.

The Congress also had the power to settle disputes between states over boundaries, jurisdiction and other matters. However, that power could be exercised only after the states had attempted to settle their disputes on their own, using arbitrators agreed upon by all parties involved. Even when the matter did finally come before the Congress, it had to be tried by a court of judges chosen by a very complicated procedure. In fact, the entire settlement procedure was so complicated and time consuming that it proved to be totally unworkable.

B. The Problems of Government under the Articles

The deficiencies in the powers of the national government under the Articles were apparent to some degree during the War of Independence. Consider the difficulties Washington experienced because the states did not fulfill their manpower quotas. However, these deficiencies caused more serious problems after the war was over. The biggest problem was the huge debt incurred by the United States during the war. That debt included large amounts of back pay owed to the soldiers who had fought in it. In March 1783, several senior army officers almost succeeded in a plot to take over the Congress by force in order to obtain the back pay and redress other grievances. General Washington had to personally intervene with a passionate plea not to destroy the democratic government that they had fought to establish. Only then was the military coup averted.[1]

At the end of the war, the national debt was forty million dollars, mainly because the states had given the Congress only 15 percent of what they had been assessed. Fortunately, a group of Dutch bankers made a timely loan that kept the new nation's treasury from going bankrupt.[2] However, the states continued to be delinquent in paying their assessments after the war. This inability of the Congress to raise money prevented it from building a navy that could protect its merchant ships. As a result, the American merchant ships were easy prey to pirates. On the Mediterranean Sea in particular, American seamen were routinely captured and held as hostages. Spain refused to allow American merchants to navigate the Mississippi River, and without a navy the Congress was helpless to stop the Spanish interference.[3]

Another trade problem was caused by the discriminatory tariffs and other trade barriers that Great Britain imposed on American goods exported to England and other parts of the British Empire. The Congress had no means of retaliating with similar tariffs against

British goods imported to the American states. Only the states could levy tariffs, and British companies were able to negotiate favorable trade deals by playing the competing interests of the states against one another.[4]

Along with these trade and financial problems were embarrassing internal fights between the states. Pennsylvania and Virginia had conflicting claims to the Pittsburgh region. Connecticut settlers attempting to locate near the present city of Scranton were driven out by gunfire from Pennsylvanians who also claimed the area. Settlers in western Virginia threatened to secede and form their own state of Kentucky, and several of them concocted a secret plot to turn over the Kentucky territory to Spain. A similar movement in western North Carolina resulted in the independent state of Franklin, which was later dissolved and superseded by the state of Tennessee. Meanwhile, settlers in the Vermont region, led by Ethan Allen and his Green Mountain Boys, set up their own regional government, defying the authority of the state of New York. They threatened to secede if the Continental Congress did not recognize Vermont as a separate state. They even threatened to annex themselves to Canada if their demand for statehood were not met, in spite of their fierce loyalty to the Patriot cause during the War of Independence.

The most distressing problem was the great depression caused by the heavy taxes that the states were levying to pay back their war debts. Many small farmers, having incurred large personal debts during the war, found it impossible to pay their debts because of the taxes levied to pay state-owed debts. Most states passed laws forcing creditors to extend their payment dates or to accept near-worthless script that the states issued to the farmers. However, in Massachusetts the Puritan aristocracy insisted on sound financial practices in all dealings. "A bargain's a bargain," they said. As a result, large numbers of peasants lost their farms and many were thrown into crowded and disease-ridden debtor prisons.

In the fall of 1786, a group of farmers in western Massachusetts led by Daniel Shays took up arms and forced a number of county courts to close down so that the judges could not order any more foreclosures. Their plan was to keep the courts closed until the next election, in which they expected they would be able to elect a legislature that would extend the terms of their loans. The mob almost succeeded in capturing the state supreme court in Springfield so that its leaders could not be indicted for treason. However, the state militia was able to break up the insurrection. Further uprisings were prevented only because the state authorities were fairly lenient with the captured leaders. The next session of the state Assembly also granted many of the farmers' demands for debt reform.[5]

When Shays and his followers took over the Massachusetts courts, the state authorities had requested help from the United States Army. However, the Congress had been unable to respond. In fact, with its limited powers, the Congress could only watch helplessly as chaos increased all over the thirteen states. In some respects, the country resembled the Israelite nation under the judges, when "every man did that which was right in his own eyes" (Judges 21:25). On the other hand, the unfair tax foreclosures suffered by the peasant farmers of Massachusetts resembled the oppressive conditions of Roman-controlled Judea at the time of Christ. Americans suffered under both anarchy and tyranny. They had to find a better way to govern themselves.

7

The United States Constitution

A. The Annapolis Meeting

While the Shays rebellion was taking place in Massachusetts, the leaders of several states were meeting in Annapolis, Maryland to resolve serious interstate trade problems. The organizers of the meeting, James Madison, age thirty-five, of Virginia, and Alexander Hamilton, age thirty-one, of New York, had invited delegates from all the states, but only New York, New Jersey, Pennsylvania, Delaware and Virginia were represented. The main reason for the meeting was to discuss a plan to dig a series of canals from the Shenandoah and Ohio River valleys to the Potomac River in order to open commerce between those regions and the east coast. The plan also involved building a series of locks on the Potomac. The states through which the waterways flowed were to agree to allow citizens of all states free navigation rights. Most affected by this waterway system would be Virginia, Maryland and Pennsylvania. However, Madison and Hamilton were hoping to negotiate a broader agreement that would address all trade difficulties between the states. Thus, Madison and Hamilton were trying to accomplish by their *ad hoc* meeting what the Congress had been unable to do, namely, establish interstate cooperation so that American businesses in different states could carry on their trade more efficiently, both with each other and with foreign businesses. With improved trade, it was hoped, Americans could put an end to their economic depression and the prevailing chaos.

The fact that only five states had sent delegates to Annapolis did not discourage Madison and Hamilton. On the contrary, they were excited when Abraham Clark told them that his New Jersey delegation was prepared to consider not only commercial matters but other matters pertaining to the "common interest and personal harmony of the several states." Tench Coxe of Pennsylvania said that there should be a "blending of interests" to "cement the union of the states." Hamilton also favored a stronger union of the states and drafted a resolution calling for a convention of all the states at the State House in Philadelphia on the second Monday of May of 1787, "to devise such further provisions as shall appear to them necessary to render the constitution of the Federal Government adequate to the exigencies of the Union." The resolution was signed by all twelve delegates from the five states attending the meeting.

The Americans had barely won their independence, yet by 1786, their economy was mired in debt and commerce was stagnant. No one trusted anyone. The Shays uprising was a frustrated peasant response to Puritanical leaders who were taking an every-man-for-himself approach to the post-war economic problems. Other people throughout the loose federation of states had the same attitude, reflected in the armed fights over state boundaries and the private deals to transfer land to other nations for quick profit. The Annapolis resolution was a call for an end to that nonsense.

The Annapolis resolution was not the first time anyone had suggested the need for a stronger federal government. However, it was the first time anyone had taken action to solve the problem. The resolution was well received. People ignored the fact that the twelve men who had signed the resolution represented only five of the thirteen states and were not acting on behalf of the Congress. In fact, any twelve citizens could have met in a tavern and signed the resolution and it would have carried as much legal weight. The Congress did not vote in favor of the Constitutional Convention until February 21, 1787, five months after the Annapolis resolution. By that time, however, the legislatures of New Jersey, Pennsylvania, Virginia and South Carolina had already appointed their delegates to the Convention and other arrangements were well under way.

B. The Constitutional Convention

Because of heavy rains, the Convention did not open until May 25, 1787. Even then only seven states were represented, a bare quorum: Massachusetts, New York, Pennsylvania, Delaware, Virginia, South Carolina and Georgia. Some state delegations did not arrive until weeks later and the Rhode Island delegation never did come. At the first session, George Washington was chosen the Convention chairman and he opened the meeting with the words, "Let us raise a standard to which the wise and honest can repair! The event is in the hands of God."

On May 29, Edmund Randolph, the thirty-three-year-old governor of Virginia,[1] the largest and most populous state, introduced a series of resolves that called for a plan of government devised by the state's delegates, primarily James Madison. The government was to have three branches: a legislative branch, an executive branch and a judicial branch. Although the branches were to be separate, each was to have some power to regulate the other two so that powerful political interest groups would have difficulty controlling the whole government. Madison believed that if the new government fell under such control, even its democratically elected officials would become tyrants.[2]

According to the Virginia plan, the legislative branch would have two houses, each comprising a number of representatives from each state based either on the amount of taxes paid from the state to the national government or on the number of free people in the state. The members of the first house would be elected by the people, while the members of the second house would be chosen by the first house from lists of nominees made by the state legislatures. The powers of this legislature were to be spelled out in the new articles: they were to include the power to pass laws covering all situations in which the states were incompetent. The legislature would also have the power to veto state laws deemed contrary to the new articles and to choose the head of the executive branch and the supreme court and inferior court judges of the judicial branch.

On the next day, May 30, most of the Convention delegates were still studying the Virginia resolves when Governor Randolph introduced another resolution that spoke of a "a national government consisting of a supreme legislative, executive and judiciary." The words "national" and "supreme" alarmed many delegates. They had thought that the purpose of the Convention was merely to make minor changes in the Articles of Confederation. Randolph's words sounded like a proposal to make the state governments subservient to a supreme, national government in all respects. Randolph answered emphatically that was not the intention. Gouverneur Morris, representing Pennsylvania, then rose and explained that a "federal" government was merely an agreement among member states to cooperate with one another if and when the need arose, whereas a "national" government had defined powers that it was compelled to exercise on a continuing basis. Morris said that the nation needed an operating national government in order to solve its problems. He added that the word "supreme" meant only that the national government would be supreme in those areas in which it was given power to act. Morris then moved that the Convention adopt Randolph's resolution. The motion passed, six states to one. The majority of Morris' fellow delegates from Pennsylvania cast the only votes against the resolution.

In the following weeks, more state delegations arrived and the primary topic of discussion was the Virginia resolves. On June 20, the Convention voted to delete the word "national" from the Randolph resolution because it conveyed a feeling of a government that was too powerful. However, the Convention retained the concept of a United States government that was "supreme" when operating within its defined sphere of power. That concept became embodied in Article VI, clause 2, which said that the Constitution and the laws and treaties of the United States made pursuant to the Constitution were the supreme law of the land.[3] The powers of the national government and their relation to the powers of the states were clarified in 1791, when the Tenth Amendment to the Constitution declared, "The powers not delegated to the United States by the Constitution, nor prohibited by it to the States, are reserved to the States respectively, or to the people." Thus, in Article VI, clause 2, the Convention gave the United States government its sphere of power, namely the supreme power to carry out the acts specifically authorized by the other provisions of the Constitution, while the Tenth Amendment made clear that the states and the people retained all the powers that were not specifically granted to the United States government by the Constitution.

In addition to the Virginia plan, the Convention considered other plans of government proposed by other state delegations. On June 15, William Paterson of New Jersey (later a U. S. Supreme Court justice) introduced a plan that called for merely revising the Articles of Confederation to give the Congress more power, including the power to levy certain direct taxes on the people and to regulate interstate trade. The plan also called for placing the executive department under a committee, instead of a single president. The organization of the Congress would remain substantially the same: a single house of representatives chosen by the state legislatures, each state having the same number of representatives. That was in contrast to the Virginia plan, which called for the Congress to be divided into two houses, each having a number of representatives from each state proportional to the state's population and no representatives chosen by the state legislatures.

The New Jersey plan was favored by the delegates from most of the smaller states. They said that in the interest of state sovereignty, the national government should serve the interests of the states first and the interests of the people only indirectly through the states. Elbridge Gerry of Massachusetts feared that if the people voted for congressmen directly, they might be easily misled into voting for candidates who made false promises. However, the delegates from the two largest states, Virginia and Pennsylvania, disagreed. George Mason of Virginia argued that a congress elected by the people would be more responsive to their rights. James Madison said that such a congress would rest "on the solid foundation of the people themselves" and provide the greatest security from majority coalitions trampling on the rights of minority groups.[4]

Finally, on July 16, the delegates agreed to a compromise proposed by the Connecticut delegation, whereby the new congress would have two houses: a house of representatives in which each state had a number of representatives proportional to its population (Article I, Section 2[3]) and a senate in which each state had two senators (Article I, Section 3[1]). Also, the members of the house of representatives would be elected directly by the people (Article I, Section 2[1]).

The Convention had trouble deciding how the senators should be elected. James Wilson of Pennsylvania (later a U. S. Supreme Court justice) argued that they should be elected in the same way as the representatives, but Madison said the house of representatives should elect the senators. John Dickinson of Delaware proposed that each state legislature pick the senators. This plan prevailed, because the Convention agreed that it was the best way of assuring that the senators would be wise, experienced aristocrats, similar to the members of the British House of Lords.[5] The Convention thus provided in Article I, Section 3[1] that the senators were to be chosen by the state legislatures; it also provided in Article V that the manner of electing senators could not be changed before 1808. Article V also said that no amendment to the Constitution could deprive any state of having as many senators as any other state without the consent of the state being so deprived. Dickinson's method of choosing senators remained in effect until 1912, when the Seventeenth Amendment provided for the direct election of senators by the people of each state. However, because of Article V, the Constitution will never likely be amended to give the people, rather than the states, equal representation in the Senate.

While the Convention was debating the composition of the legislative branch, it was also considering what kind of executive branch would be best. Should it be headed by a single president or a plurality of executives? Which kind of executive would be the least likely to abuse its power? Would a plurality of executives have difficulty making decisions? Many points of view were expressed with regard to these questions. The Convention voted seven states to three to have a single president.

The Convention also debated the manner of electing the single president. Wilson and Morris argued against the Virginia plan, which called for a president chosen by the legislature. They said that the people ought to elect the president directly. Mason answered that the people would not be well enough informed to choose the president; it would be like asking a blind man to pick out colors. Madison said that if the people elected the president, they would vote for the candidate from their own state, giving the larger states an unfair advantage. Finally, a few days before the end of the Convention, the delegates agreed to a college of electors appointed by the states to elect the president (Article II, Section 1, clauses 2, 3 and 4).

Another issue was whether the president should be able to veto legislation passed by the congress. Franklin did not think the president should have that power because when Pennsylvania had been a colony, one governor had used his veto power to extort salary increases from the legislature. The Convention compromised by giving the president veto power and Congress the power to override the veto by a two-thirds majority of both houses (Article I, Section 7[2]).

Many observers thought the Convention gave the president too much power, making him another king. It made him commander-in-chief of the armed forces and gave him the power to grant reprieves and pardons for offenses against the United States (Article II, Section 2[1]). It also gave him the power to make treaties, provided two-thirds of the senators present concurred, and to appoint all judges and other officers of the United States, with the advice and consent of the senate (Article II, Section 2[2]). To prevent the abuse of these and other powers, the Convention provided that the president, as well as all other government officers, could be removed from office by the legislative branch, on impeachment for and conviction of "Treason, Bribery, or other high Crimes and Misdemeanors" (Article II, Section 4). The House of Representatives was given the power of impeachment (Article I,

Section 2[5]) and the Senate was given the power to try all impeachments and to convict those adjudged guilty (Article I, Section 3[6]).

On July 26, the Convention took a ten-day recess, during which a Committee of Detail drew up a first draft of the Constitution based on the resolutions that had passed at that time. The Committee also added many details that had not been voted upon by the whole Convention. One important detail added was Article III, which said in Section 1, "The judicial Power of the United States shall be vested in one Supreme Court and in such inferior Courts as Congress may from time to time ordain and establish." Section 2 of Article III then set forth a list of powers that these courts were to have. They included the power to decide all cases arising under the Constitution and the laws and treaties of the United States, as well as the power to decide disputes between states and between citizens of different states. Article III was approved by the Convention substantially as proposed by the Committee of Detail.

The Committee of Detail also added in Article I, Section 8 a long list of powers of Congress. This list was adopted by the Convention substantially as written. Clause 1 of Section 8 gave Congress the power to collect taxes and tariffs in order to pay the debts and provide for the common defense and general welfare of the United States. Clause 3 gave Congress the power to regulate foreign and interstate commerce, clause 5 gave it the power to coin money and clause 8 gave it the power to grant patents and copyrights. Clauses 12 and 13 gave Congress the power to raise a national army and navy and clause 18 gave it the power to make all laws necessary and proper for carrying into execution all its other powers. These clauses and the others of Article I, Section 8 have become very important because they define the sole law-making powers of the national government. These clauses are also important because Article VI states that the laws "made pursuant to the Constitution," that is, laws within the powers prescribed by the clauses of Article I, Section 8, are part of the supreme law of the land. Therefore, the states cannot pass laws or take other actions that conflict with these laws.

In addition, the Convention inserted several clauses that insured that the new government would respect certain rights of the people, including a number that had been violated by the British government in the years leading up to the War of Independence. They include the right to a jury trial in criminal cases (Article III, Section 2[3]) and the right of a prisoner to demand a judicial hearing by a writ of habeas corpus to determine whether he is lawfully detained (Article I, Section 9[2]). According to Blackstone, these rights were recognized in England (BL3, 130-131). Hamilton quoted Blackstone's rationale for the writ of habeas corpus in his Federalist Paper No. 84. Article I, Section 9[3] prohibits Congress from passing *ex post facto* laws that declare past acts of people to be crimes when they were not crimes at the times they were committed. Blackstone explained the injustice of such laws in the first volume of his *Commentaries* (BL1, 46). Article I, Section 9[3] also forbids bills of attainder, which are laws that pronounce specific people guilty of high crimes and political offenses without trials and impose sentences of death, forfeiture of property and corruption of blood (forfeiture of descendants' rights). Article VI, clause 3 gives the people some measure of religious liberty by outlawing religious tests as a qualification for holding office in the national government. Article III, Section 3[1] restricts the definition of treason, stating that it shall consist only in levying war against the United States or in giving aid and comfort to its enemies. Thus, no group or faction of people can punish its opposition simply by attaining a majority of votes in Congress and then changing the definition of treason to include its opposition's acts or beliefs.

The Convention imposed several restrictions on the state governments, forbidding them to pass bills of attainder, *ex post facto* laws and laws impairing the obligation of contracts (Article I, Section 10[1]). It also bound the states together by a pledge to recognize the validity of each other's public acts, records and judgments, saying that "[f]ull Faith and Credit shall be given to the Public Acts, Records and judicial Proceedings of every other State" (Article IV, Section 1). In addition, it required that the states not discriminate against each other's citizens, saying, "The citizens of each State shall be entitled to all privileges and immunities of citizens in the several States" (Article IV, Section 2[1]). Blackstone said that a person's absolute rights comprised his civil privileges and private immunities. He said that a person's immunities were "that *residuum* of natural liberty, which is not required by the laws of society to be sacrificed to public convenience" and his privileges were those rights "which society hath engaged to provide, in lieu of the natural liberties so given up by individuals" (BL3, 125).[6] Because Article IV, Section 2[1] allows each state to determine which of its residents are citizens, each state that allowed slavery before the Civil War had the power to deny citizenship to its slaves and thereby exclude them from the privileges and immunities enjoyed by people who are citizens of that state or other states.

There was strong sentiment in the north for a provision in the Constitution that would outlaw slavery. John Jay, who later became the first chief justice of the United States Supreme Court, was the president of the New York antislavery society. Franklin was the president of the Pennsylvania antislavery society; one of his last acts before he died was to sign a petition to Congress for the abolition of slavery. Unfortunately, at the Constitutional Convention, Jay, Franklin and other delegates of like opinion were reluctant to push the slavery issue because they feared that a debate on the subject would divide the delegates so much that they would not agree to any constitution.[7]

Therefore, the Convention not only allowed the states to treat some residents as slaves and others as citizens, but Article IV, Section 2[3] provided that any slave escaping from one state to another had to be returned to his original state. In addition, the Constitution prohibited Congress from passing any law against the migration or importation of slaves until the year 1808 (Art. I, Sec. 9[1]). Only after the Civil War was the Constitution amended to correct these injustices. The Thirteenth Amendment outlawed slavery in all the states. The Fourteenth Amendment took away the states' ability to determine which of their residents are citizens, by saying, first, that all persons born or naturalized in the United States are automatically "citizens of the United States and of the State wherein they reside." Secondly, it said, "No State shall make or enforce any law which shall abridge the privileges or immunities of citizens of the United States." The Fourteenth Amendment also said no state could "deprive any person of life, liberty or property without due process of law; nor deny any person within its jurisdiction the equal protection of the laws." Thus, the Fourteenth Amendment finally forced the states to recognize the premises of the Declaration of Independence that "all men are created equal" and are all entitled to the "unalienable rights" of "Life, liberty and the Pursuit of Happiness." The Fifteenth Amendment prevented the federal and state governments from denying anyone the right to vote "on account of race, color, or previous condition of servitude."

One of the most important issues before the Convention was how the provisions of the Constitution would be enforced. What if one of the branches of the United States government were to overstep the powers given it by the Constitution? What if one of the states were to violate a provision of the Constitution? Who should decide whether that occurred and what should be done about it? The most controversial question was what should be done when Congress made a law that the Constitution did not permit it to make. Some people argued that Congress could be relied upon to police its own obedience to the Constitution.

The Convention answered those questions in Article VI, clause 2 and Article III, Section 2[1]. Article VI, clause 2 said,

> This Constitution, and the Laws of the United States which shall be made in Pursuance thereof; and all Treaties made, or which shall be made, under the Authority of the United States, shall be the supreme Law of the Land; and the Judges of every State shall be bound thereby, any Thing in the Constitution or laws of any State to the Contrary notwithstanding.

This "supremacy clause" was similar to one that Jay had proposed to the old Congress in order to give that body more power under the Articles of Confederation. Paterson's New Jersey Plan had also contained such a clause. However, Luther Martin of Maryland drafted the final form that was adopted by the Convention.

To understand the duty that the supremacy clause places on the state judges, one must understand that every judge has a duty to enforce only those rules and laws made by government agencies acting within the authority given them. For instance, if a local school board were to pass a law setting a speed limit for vehicles traveling on an interstate highway, no responsible judge would enforce such a law, without first determining whether the school board had the power to set a speed limit on an interstate highway. To determine whether the school board had that power, the judge would examine all superior laws and constitutions that would give or take away the school board's power.

The Convention made the U. S. Constitution the supreme law above all other laws and constitutions. It also said that the laws and treaties made pursuant to the U. S. Constitution are supreme above all other laws.[8] Finally, it told the state judges that they are bound by those supreme laws. Therefore, a state judge cannot enforce a state law unless he makes sure that his action would not violate a provision of the United States Constitution or a law or treaty of the United States made pursuant to the Constitution.

The Convention also provided in Article III, Section 2[1] that

> [t]he judicial Power shall extend in all Cases, in Law and Equity, arising under this Constitution, the Laws of the United States, and Treaties made, or which shall be made, under their authority; . . . .

By extending the judicial power to all cases arising under the Constitution, the Convention made the new nation's Supreme Court the final authority in deciding all cases involving alleged violations of the Constitution. Therefore, if a state judge tried to enforce a law that was contrary to the Constitution, his decision could be reversed by the United States Supreme Court. Also, Article III, Section 2[1] meant that the Supreme Court and other United States courts had the power to decide whether a law of Congress was made pursuant to the Constitution or whether an act of any person, corporation or government body violated the

Constitution or any United States law or treaty made pursuant to the Constitution.

Madison said that the judicial branch of the new government had the power to declare void any law "violating a constitution established by the people themselves."[9] In Federalist Paper No. 48, Madison gave examples of how the legislative and executive branches of the Virginia and Pennsylvania state governments had often violated the limits of their constitutional powers. He concluded that "independent tribunals of justice will consider themselves in a peculiar manner the guardian of those rights; they will be an impenetrable bulwark against every assumption of power in the Legislative or Executive. . . ."[10]

Alexander Hamilton explained the need for judges to examine the constitutionality of laws in Federalist Paper No. 78:

> There is no position which depends on clearer principles, than that every act of a delegated authority, contrary to the tenor of the commission under which it is exercised, is void. No legislative act, therefore, contrary to the Constitution, can be valid. To deny this, would be to affirm, that the deputy is greater than his principal; that the servant is above his master; that the representatives of the people are superior to the people themselves; that men acting by virtue of powers, may do not only what their powers do not authorize, but what they forbid.
>
> If it be said that the legislative body are themselves the constitutional judges of their own powers, and that the construction they put upon them is conclusive upon other departments, it may be argued that this cannot be the natural presumption, where it is not to be collected from any particular provisions in the Constitution. It is not otherwise to be supposed, that the Constitution could intend to enable the representatives of the people to substitute their *will* to that of their constituents. It is far more rational to suppose, that the courts were designed to be an intermediate body between the people and the legislature, in order, among other things, to keep the latter within the limits assigned to their authority. The interpretation of the laws is the proper and peculiar province of the courts. A constitution is, in fact, and must be regarded by the judges, as a fundamental law. It therefore belongs to them to ascertain its meaning, as well as the meaning of any particular act proceeding from the legislative body. If there should happen to be

an irreconcilable variance between the two, that which has the superior obligation and validity ought, of course, to be preferred; or, in other words, the Constitution ought to be preferred to the statute, the intention of the people to the intention of their agents.

Nor does this conclusion by any means suppose a superiority of the judicial to the legislative power. It only supposes that the power of the people is superior to both; and that where the will of the legislature, declared in its statutes, stands in opposition to that of the people, declared in the Constitution, the judges ought to be governed by the latter rather than the former. They ought to regulate their decisions by the fundamental laws, rather than by those which are not fundamental.

Another reason why the courts must have the power to determine the constitutionality of acts by the other branches is that they are the first and most important line of defense against the possibility of armed rebellion. Blackstone said in his *Commentaries*,

> [T]o vindicate these rights [of personal security, liberty and property], when actually attacked, the subjects of England are entitled, in the first place, to the regular administration and free course of justice in the courts of law; next to the right of petitioning the king and parliament for redress of grievances; and lastly to the right of having and using arms for self-preservation and defense. (BL3, 140)

If the courts were not able to judge the legality of the laws or other acts of government agencies, then it would be futile for people to apply to them for redress when their security, liberty or property is wrongfully taken. Therefore, the alternative, short of armed rebellion, would be to petition the legislative or executive branches. Many such petitions would be filed every day, all directed to the very people who were responsible for the grievances. Very likely, as the American colonists found, those petitions would fall on deaf ears and then the people would have no choice but to start an armed rebellion, unless they were willing to endure more mistreatment.

The Supreme Court's authority under Article III, Section 2[1] to decide all cases arising under the Constitution also prevents Congress from passing laws that would overrule the Court's interpretation of the Constitution. In 1993, Congress passed the Religious Freedom Restoration Act with the stated purpose of overruling the Court's interpretation of the First Amendment's free exercise of religion clause. In *Bourne v. Flores*, 117 S.Ct. 2157 (1997), the Supreme Court ruled that the Religious Freedom Restoration Act was invalid because it attempted to forbid the states from restricting a person's exercise of religion in situations in which the Supreme Court had ruled that the states had the power to enforce such restrictions.[11]

C. The United States Government Compared to the British Government

The new government proposed by the Convention resembled the British government in one respect. The United States House of Representatives was similar to the British House of Commons. Each house was the lower house of a two-house legislature, and the members of both were elected by voters from a large segment of the population, although one limited to male property owners.

However, there were three major differences between the two governments. First, the United States government was to have no hereditary officials. The upper house of the United States Congress was to comprise senators chosen by the state governments, rather than bishops and hereditary noblemen as in the British House of Lords. Instead of Britain's hereditary king, the president of the United States was to be chosen by a college of electors who in turn were to be chosen by the state governments. These changes put many of the common people a step closer to direct control of their government, but they also showed that the Convention delegates were far from ready to put their complete trust in the kind of democratic government that now exists in the United States, where senators are elected by the people (according to the Seventeenth Amendment) and people of all races and colors and both sexes are able to vote (according to the Fifteenth and Nineteenth Amendments). When Franklin was asked what kind of government the Convention had devised for the nation, he answered, "A republic, if you can keep it." A republic is not necessarily a democracy, but it is a government controlled by a large segment of the population, through elected representatives and other elected officials--none hereditary. Article IV, Section 4 of the Constitution confirmed the Convention's commitment to a republican government by saying, "The United States shall guarantee to every State in this Union a Republican Form of Government."

The second major difference between the two governments was creation of the judiciary as a separate branch of the United States government. In Britain, the judges of the King's Bench and lower courts were part of the executive branch and the House of Lords was both the supreme court and the upper house of Parliament.

The third major difference between the two governments was the very document drafted by the Convention, the United States Constitution. Unlike the English constitution, which consists of traditions proclaimed in the Magna Charta and other sources, all of which can be superseded by Parliamentary fiat, the United States Constitution proclaimed itself to be the supreme law of the land. Thus, it still stands today as a permanent barrier that defines the limits of government power and protects the rights of the people.

D. Federalists and Antifederalists

On September 17, 1787, the Convention adopted the Constitution and sent it to state conventions for ratification. These conventions were special assemblies consisting of delegates elected by the people of each state for the sole purpose of deciding whether their state would ratify the Constitution.

The leading advocates of ratification were Hamilton, Jay and Madison. They wrote a series of articles, later compiled in a book called *The Federalist*, which they sent to various newspapers. These articles explained the Constitution and the need for a federal government that had adequate but limited powers. They used the term "federal government" because it conveyed the concept of a federation of states and was therefore less offensive to people than the idea of a "national government."

Although public sentiment generally favored the Constitution, many people found fault with various provisions. The opponents of the Constitution were called "antifederalists." Luther Martin, a Maryland delegate to the convention, was a leading antifederalist. He wrote a series of letters to various Baltimore newspapers, later compiled in a book called *The Genuine Information*, which criticized the broad powers given the federal courts by Article III of the Constitution. Martin contended that the state courts could handle most of these powers and that clauses such as those of Article III would pave the way for a huge government bureaucracy far removed from the common people.

Martin also criticized Article VI, clause 3 of the Constitution, which said "no religious Test shall ever be required as a qualification to any office or public trust under the United States." He sarcastically observed that this provision had been passed over the objections of

> some members *so unfashionable* as to think that a *belief of the existence of a Deity*, and of a *state of future rewards and punishments* would be some security for the good conduct of our rulers, and that, in a Christian country, it would be *at least decent* to hold out some distinction between the professors of Christianity and downright infidelity or paganism.[12]

However, the prohibition against religious tests did not concern many people. A more common objection was that the Constitution made the president, senators and judges too far removed from the control of the people, because they were not to be elected directly by the people. Many feared that a powerful national government would become a tool of oppression by the aristocracy against the common people. Amos Singletary, a Massachusetts antifederalist, said

> [t]hese lawyers and men of learning and money men that talk so finely, and gloss over matters so smoothly, to make us poor illiterate people swallow down the pill, expect to get Congress themselves; they expect to be the managers of this Constitution, and get all the power and all the money into their own hands, and then they will swallow up us little

folks like the great *Leviathan*. Yes, just as the whale swallowed Jonah.[13]

The most common criticism of the Constitution was that it had very few clauses protecting the basic rights that Americans had fought so hard to win. Many state governments had recognized more of these rights in their state constitutions or in separate declarations. Mason, who wrote the Virginia Declaration of Rights, said that if the national Constitution and laws were supreme over the state constitutions and laws, then the various declarations of rights adopted by the states would be jeopardized. He had proposed to the Convention that the Constitution include a bill of rights, but his motion had been defeated. Madison said that a list of specifically defined rights would be mere parchment barriers that would be disregarded. Furthermore, he thought that such a list of rights would allow their detractors the opportunity of giving them overly limited interpretations. After the Constitution was ratified, however, Jefferson, who was in Paris serving as the United States minister to France, wrote a letter to Madison pressuring him to propose a bill of rights amendment to the Constitution, saying that he had overlooked an important advantage such a bill, namely "the legal check which it puts into the hands of the judiciary."[14]

Hamilton defended the Constitution against Mason's attack by arguing that the federal government would have only those powers specifically given to it by the Constitution. Therefore, because the Constitution did not give Congress the power to deprive people of certain rights, such as freedom of the press, there was no need to state those rights in the affirmative (Federalist Paper No. 84).

The weakness of Hamilton's argument was that there are many clauses in the Constitution that give Congress broad powers that could be interpreted as superior to the personal freedoms guaranteed by the state constitutions. The power of Congress to regulate interstate commerce under Article I, Section 8[3] might be construed to include the power to stop the shipment of religious pamphlets from one state to another, in spite of the freedoms of religion and press guaranteed by most state constitutions.

Another of Hamilton's arguments was that the Constitution did forbid bills of attainder, ex post facto laws, titles of nobility and the suspension of the writ of habeas corpus except in cases of rebellion or invasion of the public safety. It also required a jury trial for all crimes except impeachment. Nevertheless, most people thought that the Constitution ought to enumerate other rights rather than trust them to be safeguarded by the Congress. As Hamilton himself said, "the Constitution ought to be preferred to the statute, the intention of the people to the intention of their agents" (Federalist Paper No. 78). If one of the purposes of the Constitution were to safeguard the intention of the people from the intention of their elected agents, then surely any rights valued by the people ought to be spelled out in the Constitution.

On the other hand, the need for a stronger national government was growing by the day. If the Constitutional Convention were to reconvene to consider amendments guaranteeing people's rights, the delegates would be obliged to consider other amendments as well. A second convention could easily last as long as the first. Hamilton's best argument for adopting the Constitution without amendment was "that I should esteem it the extreme of imprudence to prolong the precarious state of our national affairs, and to expose the Union to the jeopardy of successive experiments, in the chimerical pursuit of a perfect plan. I never expect to see a perfect work from imperfect man" (Federalist Paper No. 85).

E. The Constitution Becomes the Law of the Land

During the last months of 1787 and the year 1788, the state conventions debated whether to ratify the Constitution. Article VII of the Constitution said that nine states would have to ratify it in order for it to be established as a constitution between those states. Some states considered making their ratification conditioned upon a bill of rights being added to the Constitution, but no state actually did that. By July 1788, eleven states had ratified the Constitution as it had been adopted by the Convention. However, several states, including Massachusetts, New York, Maryland and Virginia, strongly recommended that as soon as possible a bill of rights be added to the Constitution. The last two states to ratify, North Carolina and Rhode Island, delayed their ratification until they were certain that a bill of rights would be added.

The new government began operating on March 4, 1789, governing the eleven states that had ratified the Constitution at that time. The first Congress then considered a number of bill of rights amendments to the Constitution, proposed by Madison. To make these amendments effective, Congress and the states would have to follow the procedure prescribed in Article V of the Constitution, which said that an amendment could be proposed either by a two-thirds vote of both houses of Congress or by a convention called by Congress upon the application of the legislatures two-thirds of the states. The amendment would then be effective when it was ratified by three-fourths of the state legislatures or state conventions, depending on the mode of ratification specified by the Congress.

On September 25, 1789, Congress proposed twelve amendments to the Constitution. Eight of these amendments guaranteed that the federal government would respect certain basic rights of the people. These rights included the ones that the British had violated before the Declaration of Independence, as well as other rights, explained in Chapters 8 through 11, that Congress deemed to be fundamental to the freedom of all people.

By December 15, 1791, the required three-fourths of the state legislatures had ratified the eight amendments that guaranteed the rights of the people. They had also ratified two other amendments proposed by Congress.[15] The Ninth Amendment said that the "enumeration in the Constitution of certain rights, shall not be construed to deny or disparage others retained by the people." The Tenth Amendment said that the "powers not delegated to the United States by the Constitution, nor prohibited by it to the States, are reserved to the States respectively, or to the people."

The new federal government thus had three separate branches with carefully defined powers, including the power to control each other's actions. The powers of these branches were also held in check by a jurisdictional fence defined by the rights of the people.

8

Religious Freedom

A. The Development of Religious Freedom in the Thirteen Colonies

In his explanation of the American struggle for freedom, John Adams said "[t]he Revolution was in the minds and hearts of the people; a change in their religious sentiments of their duties and obligations."[1] The American people were changing not only their sentiments toward the British government but their sentiments toward their own churches and communities. While they were gaining a better appreciation of their rights of life, liberty and property, they were discovering that religious freedom was among the most important of those rights.

Most of the British colonies in America were founded in the 1600s, when Europe was still in the throes of the Protestant Reformation. The nations of northern Europe had broken their alliances with the Roman Catholic Church and had established various Protestant sects as their official, government-supported religions. Many people resented the new Protestant religions thrust upon them and wanted to return to the Catholic faith of their forefathers. Others joined new religious sects because they thought their nations' official Protestant churches were not reformed enough. In the nations that remained loyal to the Catholic Church, the people who had joined Protestant religions were tortured, burned and hanged (BL5, 44-50). Amid this turmoil, England endured two armed rebellions: the Puritan revolt of the 1640s against King Charles I, head of the Protestant Church of England, and the revolt of 1688 against the Catholic king, James II. On the

Continent, Protestant and Catholic kingdoms and duchies fought each other for the control of central Europe in the devastating Thirty Years War that lasted from 1618 to 1648, and, by one estimate, took the lives of 10 percent of the German people.[2] Because of these intolerable conditions, thousands of Europeans fled to America, looking for a place where they could live in peace and worship according to their own religious beliefs.

However, most American colonies also had established religions and laws that discriminated against people of other religions. Except for Catholic Maryland before 1689, all American colonies excluded Catholics and non-Christians from public office. In many colonies, these people were not even allowed to vote. Although they sought religious freedom for themselves, most early Americans had a very limited idea of what that freedom meant. Only by a gradual process did America become, as James Madison said in his 1785 Memorial and Remonstrance against Religious Assessments, the "[a]sylum to the persecuted and oppressed of every Nation and Religion" that "promised a lustre to our country." (App. M, Par. 9).

The thirteen colonies that became the United States of America had a variety of religious histories. The development of religious freedom in these colonies can be studied best by looking first at the religious history of each colony before a spiritual revival known as the "Great Awakening" swept through all the colonies during the middle of the eighteenth century.

A.1. Virginia

Virginia, the first of the American colonies, was settled by the English in 1607. From that time until the War of Independence, the Church of England was Virginia's official, tax-supported church. The parish boundaries of this "Anglican" church were the same as the county boundaries of the civil government, except in more densely populated regions where there were several parishes to a county. In the main town of each parish, the local church was the center of community life as well as religious worship. Until the mid-1700s, all members of Virginia society belonged to their local

Anglican church and nearly every community leader served on his church's lay governing board, called the "vestry." The colony's House of Burgesses passed laws that required all colonists to attend their local Anglican churches and punished blasphemy, sacrilege and criticism of the Trinity doctrine.[3]

The parsons of the local Anglican churches were paid in tobacco rather than money because nearly every parishioner earned his income directly or indirectly from tobacco farming. The county sheriff or his deputy was responsible for collecting this tobacco and paying it to the local parson or parsons. The amount of tobacco paid the parsons, the same throughout the colony, was fixed by the House of Burgesses. In 1696, the parsons complained that they were not being paid enough, but the House of Burgesses rejected their petition, saying the complaint was a "malicious, Scandalous and an unjust reflection on the House."[4] This tension between the House of Burgesses and the parsons continued until well into the eighteenth century. In 1758, the House passed the Two-Penny Act that reduced the parsons' pay. That resulted in the famous *Parson's Case* defended by Patrick Henry, described in Chapter 1, Section B.

The lay vestries of the parishes controlled the Anglican churches of America because the country had no Anglican bishop. The bishop of London supposedly supervised all these Anglican churches, but such supervision was a practical impossibility. Although every church was required by English law to base its worship services on the Anglican liturgy and the Book of Common Prayer, the Virginia worship services were more informal than the services held in England. Less important holy days were often not observed. One reason was the geography of the large, sparsely settled Virginia parishes. Because many people had to travel ten or more miles to church, they did not go every Sunday, in spite of the fines that they might incur. They were therefore not as familiar as English Anglicans with church doctrines or with official worship procedures and sanctuary furnishings. Even when they knew better, the lay vestries and parsons of Virginia were less likely than the English bishops to correct errors in such matters.

The type of sermon preached by a Virginia parson often determined the type of tobacco with which he was paid. In some parishes, the tobacco was sweeter than in others and was therefore worth more. Such parishes became known as "sweet parishes," and each new parson soon realized that if he wanted to have a sweet parish, he had better preach sweet sermons. When salvation from hell was preached in colonial Virginia, it was most often the community leaders telling the parsons how to be saved.

A.2. New England

The settlement of New England began with the arrival of the Pilgrims at Plymouth Rock in 1620. Between 1620 and 1638, seven colonies were established along the New England coastline. They included Maine, New Hampshire, Massachusetts Bay, Plymouth, Rhode Island and Providence Plantations, Connecticut and New Haven. In 1664, New Haven was united with Connecticut. In 1677, Maine was united with Massachusetts Bay and remained that way until it became a separate state in 1820. In 1691, Plymouth, which included Cape Cod and other lands east of Rhode Island, was united with Massachusetts Bay.

Like Virginia, the New England colonies were settled mainly by people from England. However, most of them were Puritans who had broken their relations with the Anglican Church. Everywhere except in Rhode Island the Puritans established their own churches. They interpreted the Bible according to the Calvinist tradition, following simple life styles and strict standards of morality and discipline. Their reason for coming to America was to establish a Bible commonwealth, or "a city on a hill," as Governor John Winthrop called his Massachusetts Bay Colony. The Puritans wanted to show the world what could be achieved by a society in which everyone followed the commandments of the Lord as revealed in the Christian Bible. Accordingly, the Massachusetts Body of Liberties prescribed the punishment of death not only for murder and treason but also for blasphemy, worshipping false gods, witchcraft and adultery. For each offense, one or more Bible passages were cited that commanded the same extreme punishment (App. C, sec. 94).

The Puritans organized "Congregational" churches, named because the ultimate decision-making power in all matters of church government resided in the voting members of each congregation. The congregation of a church could, in theory, call a minister of any Christian theology or denomination that it desired. However, as a practical matter, the New England Congregational churches always elected ministers holding strong Puritan beliefs until the Great Awakening period of the mid-1700s, because church membership was very tightly controlled by the Puritan leaders of each congregation. They usually required that each applicant for membership convince the leaders of his Christian faith by recounting an experience that showed how God had chosen him to be saved from the penalty of his sins on account of his faith.

The Congregational ministers were supported primarily by voluntary contributions. However, if these contributions were insufficient, the ministers were paid by taxes assessed on all citizens, including those who did not belong to a Congregational church. The voluntary contributions were usually not sufficient, so religious taxes were levied in nearly every community. In Massachusetts, only Congregational church members could vote for public officials. In Connecticut, voters could belong to any church but they were required to declare their faith in the Trinitarian God (the Father, the Son and the Holy Spirit). As a gesture of separation of church and state, Congregational ministers were forbidden from holding civil office. However, the civil leaders almost always followed the advice of the leading ministers and they often enacted laws exactly as written by the ministers.

The cornerstone of the Puritan legal system was the principle that everyone was both morally and legally bound by the absolute truths of the Bible, which included not only the Bible's rules for preserving civil order but also its instructions for worshipping God and attaining salvation and everlasting life. However, in the mid-1630s, barely five years after the Massachusetts Bay Colony was founded, several citizens challenged their leaders' interpretations of these Biblical truths. They included Anne Hutchinson and the Reverend Roger Williams.

Williams was the pastor of the Congregational Church of Salem, Massachusetts, best known as the place of the infamous witchcraft trials of the 1690s. However, the Salem community deserves a better place in history. The first Christian sermons on religious freedom were preached there in the 1630s. Williams told his congregation that everyone was under the direct control of God and that no group of people, whether organized as a church or a state, had the right to judge God's relations with His people. The reason, he said, was because the Christian churches of the middle ages had betrayed God's trust by forcing millions of unrepentant sinners into membership, through fear of punishment by church and civil authorities. Therefore, those churches had broken any possible chain of succession between the true churches established by Christ's apostles and the modern churches.

Williams was even more adamant concerning the power of civil government. He said that the civil authorities of Massachusetts Bay were acting contrary to the will of God when they punished people for violating the first four of the Ten Commandments, because those commandments related only to God's relationship with His people and that relationship had to be voluntary, not forced. He also attacked the practice of using tax revenues to support ministers and churches, again because a person's gifts to God had to be voluntary. The Puritan leaders of the colony tolerated Williams' sermons for a while, but they finally summoned him before the General Court. Their charges against him are not clear from the existing records, but he was sentenced to banishment from the colony in 1635.

The next year Williams and his followers traveled to the Narragansett Bay area, purchased land from the Indians and established the colony of Rhode Island and Providence Plantations. From the colony's beginning, its laws guaranteed religious freedom to all inhabitants. In 1663, Williams obtained a charter from King Charles II that confirmed this guarantee and Rhode Island became the first American colony to recognize the right of people to worship according to the dictates of their own consciences. Although this charter did not specifically guarantee that there would be no established church, the colonial government of Rhode Island did not give financial support to any church or show favor toward any religious belief.

Anne Hutchinson was a member of the Boston Congregational Church. She gained notoriety among her fellow church members when she began telling of her extraordinary communications with God's Holy Spirit at weekly meetings of her prayer group. She said that everyone should strive to receive these communications because they and not the outward deeds of obedience and signs of sanctification emphasized by most Puritan preachers were the true evidence of God's saving grace. She called these communications with the Holy Spirit "the covenant of grace" and contrasted them with the outward deeds of obedience and signs of sanctification, which she called "the covenant of works." According to the apostle Paul's letters in the Bible, she said, the covenant of grace, not the covenant of works, was the way to salvation.

The Puritan church authorities charged Anne Hutchinson with preaching false doctrines, undermining the authority of the clergy and violating the commandment to honor her father and mother, which they interpreted as including the elders of her community as well. At separate trials before the General Court in Cambridge and the leaders of her Boston Church, Hutchinson was found guilty and sentenced to banishment from the colony in 1638. She and her family then moved to the Rhode Island colony.

Anne Hutchinson's case showed the inconsistency of government-supported Christianity, and her case and Williams' case showed its evil effects. As Anne Hutchinson pointed out, the Christian Bible teaches that God judges people by their inborn faith and communication with the Holy Spirit rather than by their outward deeds of reverence. If that is true, then how can a civil government claim a Christian purpose when it forces people to show outward reverence to God or reduces their outward reverence to a mere community tradition? Williams preached that civil government violates the will of God when it forces people to set money upon His altars and compels them to worship Him.

Of all the New England Puritan colonies, the Plymouth colony had the most liberal and tolerant leaders. One of those leaders was Edward Winslow, who in 1645 wrote to Governor Winthrop of Massachusetts Bay that most of the deputies of the Plymouth General Court wanted

> to allow and maintaine full and free tollerance of religion to all men that would preserve the civill peace and submit unto government; and there was no limitation or exception against Turke, Jew, Papist, Arian, Socinian, Nocholytan, Familist, or any other, etc.[5]

Governor William Bradford of Plymouth did not allow the deputies' motion to come to a vote. However, this episode showed that at least some of the early New England Puritans had a broader view of religious freedom, as well as of religion itself, than the views held by many twentieth-century Christians. One of the sects that Winslow said they proposed to tolerate was the Familists, or "The Family of Love," a Dutch society whose members called themselves Christians but who believed that religion consisted wholly in loving one another and not in obedience to laws, spiritual truths or creeds.[6] The Plymouth deputies' proposal to tolerate the Familists did not mean they agreed with the religious views of these people, but they recognized the Familists's right to practice their religion, "without limitation or exception," as long as they obeyed the government and the laws enacted to maintain the peace of their society.

A possible reason why Governor Bradford did not allow the deputies of the Plymouth Colony to vote on their motion was the pressure he was receiving from the other New England Puritan colonies, particularly Massachusetts Bay, to help prevent the spread of "error and blasphemy" throughout the region. People with diverse religious views, such as those held by Williams and Hutchinson, were continuing to migrate to the region and were causing increasing trouble. The attitude of most New England Puritans was that if these new immigrants did not wish to conform to the established religious beliefs and practices of their communities, they should settle elsewhere. They had sailed across thousands of miles of ocean and had settled on a small spot in the vast American wilderness, so they could live in communities where everyone sought the same will of God and were committed to living their lives according to that will. If there were ever a place where people could justify such a merger of church and state government, colonial New England would have been that place.

However, the New England Puritans were not the only Puritans on the face of the earth. Most Puritans still lived in England, where they were the ones in the minority who had to contend with the religious laws and traditions of the official Church of England. Thus, when a number of New Englanders, including the Browne brothers, Robert Child, Samuel Gorton and John Clark, told people in England of the fines, whippings and banishments administered by the Massachusetts Bay courts to Baptists and other dissenters,[7] the English Puritans were greatly embarrassed. They pressured their American brothers to allow other religious groups the same freedom that they were demanding of the Church of England. It was a classic case of Golden Rule at work.

When the Puritan leader Oliver Cromwell took over the English government in 1649, the Puritans in both England and New England were able to ignore the Golden Rule. Englishmen on both sides of the ocean were fined and imprisoned for failing to conform to Puritan beliefs. As Cromwell's power increased, the Puritan persecution grew more extreme. Between 1658 and 1661, four Quakers were hung in Massachusetts Bay because they had been returned to the colony after being banished for preaching their religious views. When the Cromwell regime ended in 1660, the Quakers petitioned the restoration king Charles II, who ordered an end to these hangings.

During Cromwell's rule, the Puritan leaders of Connecticut were somewhat more tolerant than those of Massachusetts Bay. In 1659, a Jewish "minyan," a congregation that required least ten Jewish men, was known to have worshipped in Connecticut without harassment.[8] Beginning in the 1660s, Anglicans were also allowed to worship in their own churches. However, everyone still had to pay taxes to the Congregational churches and only their members were able to vote for public officials. Connecticut also punished people for transporting Quakers into the colony and for entertaining the Quakers who were already there. The Quakers themselves were whipped for meeting in private houses and committing other similar offenses.

The Connecticut and Massachusetts Puritans also persecuted men and women of all religions who were accused of violating their Bible-based laws against witchcraft. Many women confessed to being "witches" and many men confessed to being "wizards." Those convicted of this crime were sentenced to death by hanging. Some accused "witches" and "wizards" deliberately acted out their roles, trying to cast evil spells on other people. Some were probably mentally ill. However, most witchcraft accusations arose when a so-called "victim" experienced an injury or mishap that appeared to be the work of a supernatural spirit. For instance, the people of that time often blamed illnesses, particularly mental illnesses, on supernatural causes. When a child became afflicted, any parent, nurse or caretaker who displayed the slightest abnormal behavior might be suspected of causing the child's illness by practicing witchcraft. In the New England theocracy, "witches" and "wizards" had to be put to death, because that was the command of the Bible in Exodus 22:18 and Leviticus 20:27 [App. C, sec. 94(2)]. Between 1647 and 1662, eight people convicted of witchcraft were hung in Connecticut and six were hung in Massachusetts.

The witchcraft accusations subsided for a while, but they arose again in 1692 in Salem, Massachusetts, where they grew to epidemic numbers. The cause of these accusations was material from *Memorable Providences*, a book written by the renowned Puritan preacher Cotton Mather. Here, Mather described a case of witchcraft that he had witnessed in his Boston parish. He also described the symptoms of witchcraft and the ways one could detect whether a child was pretending to have the symptoms. Unfortunately, Mather's book fell into the hands of several young girls in Salem who used its instructions to fool their parents and community leaders into believing that they had been victimized by witches. Other children copied the girls and the results were disastrous. Fourteen women and five men were tried and hung for practicing witchcraft. When the community leaders came to their senses, eight more people had been sentenced to die, 150 were in prison awaiting trial and hundreds of others had been accused.[9] In fact, everyone in the region feared that they would be next, including the community leaders themselves. Finally, Increase Mather, the father of Cotton Mather and president of Harvard College, where the colony's ministers were trained, told a gathering of ministers that much of the evidence against those accused of witchcraft should not be allowed at the trials, and he questioned whether the juries were exercising enough care in deciding the cases. He said, "It were better that ten suspected witches should escape, than one innocent person should be condemned."[10] Shortly after Mather's speech, the governor of Massachusetts ordered the trials stopped and forbade further imprisonments for the crime of witchcraft. The Salem community then realized to their horror what had taken place, but they could not bring the innocent back to life. The colony's ministers, including Increase and Cotton Mather, helped put an end to the trials, but the episode was a great blow to their reputations because their sermons against witchcraft had been the cause of the trials.

The Puritan clergy suffered another setback when several new laws required them to tolerate other religions. By the 1680s, they had already become more tolerant of some religious groups, including the Baptists and the Quakers. However, the English Toleration Act of 1689 (BL5, 53) said that all English subjects, including those living in the American colonies, were to be allowed to worship according to their own religious beliefs, provided they acknowledged the supremacy of the English king, renounced allegiance to the pope, did not deny the trinity and attended a registered church that kept its doors open at all times. Also, the Massachusetts Bay charter of 1691, which united the Plymouth Colony with the Massachusetts Bay Colony, provided that there be "a liberty of Conscience allowed in the Worshipp of God to all Christians (Except Papists)."

The New England Puritan leaders were thus no longer able to require that all people worship according to specific religious beliefs other than the doctrine of the trinity. They nevertheless clung to the vision of a united society that was a "city on a hill," in which all people worshipped and acted according to common beliefs in God. Cotton Mather and his fellow ministers resolved this apparent conflict by preaching toleration, but within the broader framework of a religious establishment. They asserted that while the civil government should tolerate other Protestant religions, it should also enforce all of God's commandments according to their Puritan interpretation. Those were the commandments relating to the worship of only one God and the duties owed to that one God. These were translated into laws that forbade blasphemy and idolatry and required observance of the Sabbath, attendance at a Protestant church and tax payments to Congregational churches. According to Mather, there was no difference between a judge's power to enforce such laws, which he called the laws of "the first table," and the laws of "the second table" that dealt with murder, adultery, lying and stealing.[11] He did not see the distinction, made by Locke and later by Blackstone, between the absolute duties that a person owes to God, which human governments have no power to enforce, and relative duties owed by people to each other, which are the province of human government (JL, par. 135, and *Letter Concerning Toleration*; BL3, 119-120 and BL5, 41-42). Mather and his fellow preachers also did not see the distinction between God's revealed law and God's natural law, namely that revealed law cannot be determined logically but must be accepted on the faith of a particular religion, while natural law can be determined logically by the "pursuit of happiness" test and is therefore common to people of all religions, including those having no revealed law.

In 1697, the Connecticut General Court enacted a law that required that each town collect taxes from its citizens for the support of the colony's official churches. Then in 1708, the

General Court adopted the Saybrook Platform, which spelled out the various religious doctrines, disciplines and worship practices that every church had to follow. The Platform also required

> that all the churches within this government that are or shall be thus united in doctrine, worship, and discipline, be, and for the future shall be owned and acknowledged established by law.

In practice, these established churches were the Congregational churches that had been organized by the colony's Puritan founders. The General Court also passed a toleration law in 1708 that allowed dissenters "full liberty of worship" in their own churches, but that law did not exempt the dissenters from the taxes imposed by the 1697 law for the support of the official Congregational churches.

In 1727, the Connecticut General Assembly made a slight concession to the growing number of Anglicans in the colony, after the bishop of London intervened on their behalf. The bishop reminded the Assembly that the Anglican church was the established church throughout the entire kingdom, including all its colonies. Rather than argue with the bishop, which it could have done based on the colony's charter, the Assembly passed a law stipulating that the religious taxes collected from an Anglican could be rebated to his own minister, provided he regularly attended services at an Anglican church. Initially, this law had little practical effect because the Anglican church in Stratford was the only one in the entire colony. However, during the next twenty years the number of Anglican churches in Connecticut increased to fourteen.

After the Anglicans gained relief from Connecticut's religious taxes, the Baptists and the Quakers applied for similar relief. In 1729, the General Assembly exempted them from religious taxes, provided they could produce certificates from their own churches proving that they regularly attended worship services there. Like the Anglicans, most Baptists and Quakers were not able to take immediate advantage of their exemption privileges because they had so few churches in Connecticut. The number of their churches increased later on. The Congregationalists remained the only people in Connecticut who did not have to prove anything to anyone in order to give exclusive support to the religion of their choice.

Massachusetts did not proclaim its religious establishment as openly as Connecticut did with its Saybrook Platform. In 1692, the Massachusetts General Court passed a law that provided for the support of "able, learned and orthodox" ministers, except in Boston, where voluntary contributions were sufficient to maintain all the Congregational ministers. A number of ministers thought that the Massachusetts establishment should be defined in greater detail because there were several towns that did not support any orthodox minister. They petitioned the General Court to provide "Methods for the Establishment of the Christian Religion" in such towns. However, the General Court did not want to proclaim the colony's establishment in detail because they were worried about the Anglican bishops in England who wanted to make their religion the established religion in all the American colonies. The civil and religious leaders of Massachusetts therefore described their establishment in very general terms, so that it appeared to include all Christians. In 1725, Benjamin Colman, a leading member of the Brattle Street Church in Boston, gave the following explanation of the extent of their tolerance to the bishop of Peterborough in England:

> . . . when I say that our Churches and Ministers here are established by the King's Laws, I would pray your Lordship not to understand me in Opposition to the Church of England, for so they are not; but if any Town will chuse a Gentleman of the Church of England for their Pastor or Rector they are at their Liberty, and he is their Minister by the Laws of our Province, as much as any Congregational Minister among us is so. So far is our Establishment from excluding others from the common Rights of men and Christians.[12]

Nevertheless, the Massachusetts Christian establishment remained for many years a *de facto* establishment of the Puritan Congregational religion because in every parish, the Congregationalists were in the majority; therefore the religious tax revenues went to their churches. Like Connecticut, Massachusetts passed a law in 1727 that allowed religious taxes collected from an Anglican to be paid to his own church, but the law provided that the church had to be within five miles of his home and had to be one where he regularly worshipped. And like Connecticut, Massachusetts exempted Baptists and Quakers in 1728 from paying for the support of the ministers elected by their towns. Then in 1731 and 1735, each of these groups was exempted from paying taxes to build new churches for their towns. Of course, these exemptions were unnecessary in Boston, where all churches of every denomination, including Congregationalists, Anglicans, Baptists and Quakers, were fully supported by voluntary contributions. In other towns, each person wishing to avoid paying taxes to the town's Congregational church had to prove that he worshipped regularly at a church of his own denomination. Massachusetts had more Anglican, Baptist and Quaker churches than did Connecticut, but it put more legal red tape in the way of these groups. Local officials also often ignored the new tolerance laws and refused to grant exemptions to Baptists and Quakers, even when they met all the legal requirements.[13]

The religious tax situation in New Hampshire resembled the one in Massachusetts. A 1693 law enabled the landowners of every town to elect a minister, to be paid from religious tax assessments. At that time, only five churches existed in New Hampshire and all were Congregational. However, when a group of Presbyterians formed the town of Londonderry in 1719, they elected a Presbyterian minister. Soon after that, minority groups who attended Presbyterian, Anglican, Baptist and Quaker worship services received either tax exemptions or the right to have their religious taxes paid to their own churches. In many towns, all Protestants were often excused from paying their religious taxes; few or no questions were asked concerning their church attendance.

The signs of religious tolerance were in fact beginning to appear in New England in the early 1700s, but the Puritans still clung to their idea that government should establish the proper religion for people. Connecticut had an established Congregational church whose basic tenets of faith were fixed by the colony's Saybrook Platform. Except for the city of Boston, Massachusetts had a general Christian establishment that required the taxpayers of each town to support the Protestant religion--almost always Congregational--selected by a majority of voters. Both Connecticut and Massachusetts had laws that attempted to enforce the first table of the Ten Commandments by forbidding such acts as blasphemy and Sabbath-breaking. However, these colonies allowed freedom of worship to the people of most religions, including Jews, although Catholic worship was not tolerated because it required that people swear allegiance to the pope, who was regarded as a dangerous and foreign military dictator. Only Protestants were allowed to vote or hold public office.

The residents of Rhode Island and New Hampshire and the city of Boston enjoyed the greatest religious freedom in New England. Rhode Island proudly guaranteed religious free exercise to almost everyone, including Jews and Catholics, and it refused to give support or preference to any religion. It also did not discriminate against any religion, except in one or two instances. During the middle 1700s and possibly for some time after that, the Jews of Newport were denied the rights to vote and hold public office. Roman Catholics also may have been denied these rights, but the documents relating to their situation are still being scrutinized.[14]

Although New Hampshire had a religious tax system similar to that of Massachusetts, its tax exemptions were usually so easy to obtain that, for most practical purposes, the support of religion in that colony, like the support given in Boston, was on a voluntary basis. However, in both New Hampshire and all of Massachusetts, Catholics were not guaranteed freedom of worship, nor could they vote or hold public office.

A.3 New York

Prior to its control by the English, New York City was controlled by the Dutch and was called "New Amsterdam." The city was the capital of the New Netherland colony, founded by the

Dutch West India Company in 1624. The territory that the Dutch claimed for this colony now comprises the states of New York, New Jersey, Pennsylvania and Delaware.

The Dutch Reformed Church was the established, tax-supported church in both the Dutch homeland, the Netherlands, and its New Netherland colony. Like the Puritans, the members of the Dutch Reformed Church generally followed the teachings of the Protestant reformer John Calvin. However, they were more tolerant of people of other religions than were the New England Puritans. One reason was the difficulty they had enticing their own people to come to their American colony. In order to obtain enough workers to till their land, they had to recruit people of various religions from all over Europe, including Catholic Walloons from the southern Netherlands, Huguenots from France, Quakers and Anglicans from England, Lutherans from Denmark and a few Catholics and Jews from Spain, Portugal and Italy. In 1642, a Jesuit missionary, Isaac Jogues, counted eighteen languages spoken among a sampling of four hundred people in New Netherland.[15]

The Dutch West India Company appointed "the classis," a governing board of pastors and elders of the Dutch Reformed Church in Amsterdam, to oversee the religious affairs of New Netherland. This board sent ministers to the colony to organize Dutch Reformed churches there. These ministers also became very active in local politics. They pressured the colony's leaders to make and enforce laws against various kinds of sin, as defined by the Biblical commandments. Their efforts met with varying degrees of success. For instance, Peter Minuit, a French Huguenot who directed the colony from 1626 to 1632, paid no attention to the ranting of the Reverend Jonas Michaëlius, who campaigned for laws against blasphemy, Sabbath-breaking and the like. On the other hand, Peter Stuyvesant, the tyrannical, peg-legged director-general who ruled from 1647 to 1664, was the son of a Dutch Reformed minister and he believed that it was his duty to enforce God's laws. He was also intolerant of other religious groups.

Among those Stuyvesant tried to intimidate were the Jews. About two dozen Sephardic Jews of Spanish and Portuguese ancestry landed in New Amsterdam in the fall of 1654.[16] Their spokesman was Asser Levy van Swellem. At first, Stuyvesant refuse to let them get off their ship, but Levy became emotional and threatened to report his treatment to several influential friends in Amsterdam. Stuyvesant backed down and the Jews came ashore. The next year, Stuyvesant refused to allow Jews to serve in the army that he was sending to take over several Swedish settlements on the Delaware River. Instead, he required that every able-bodied Jew pay a monthly fee for a service exemption. Levy refused to pay. The same year, Levy petitioned the colony's council for the right of Jews to stand guard as town burghers. Stuyvesant, furious, told Levy that if the Jews did not like the way things were in his colony, they should leave; he even offered to raise money for their voyage. In the following years, Levy challenged Stuyvesant on other issues and filed a number of complaints in the Dutch courts, where he usually won. In 1657, he won the right of Jews to carry on retail trading. Following that judgment, he and several other Jews fared very well in the real estate, river transport and slaughterhouse businesses. However, throughout the period of the Dutch rule, the Jews remained few in number and confined their worship to private homes.

Not liking the Quakers any more than he did the Jews, Stuyvesant ordered them banned from the colony. In 1657, the freemen of the town of Flushing on Long Island protested the Quaker banishment and issued a "Flushing Remonstrance," proclaiming that they would welcome not only Quakers but any "sons of Adam who came in love among us." Another champion of the Quaker cause was John Bowne, who was arrested for allowing Quakers to worship in his home. In 1663, Bowne obtained a judgment in the Amsterdam Chamber of the Dutch West India Company, freeing a person who had been arrested for proclaiming his religious views. The Chamber declared that "the consciences of men, at least, ought to be free."[17]

The settlements on the Hudson and Delaware Rivers remained under Dutch control for forty years. However, in 1664 the English asserted that these settlements belonged to them and that the Dutch were trespassers. James Stuart, the Duke of York and brother of England's King Charles II, as well as commander of the English royal navy, sent a fleet of ships into the harbor south of New Amsterdam and demanded that the Dutch surrender. Stuyvesant was completely unprepared for this invasion and was forced to hand the reins of government to the English without a fight.

The English changed the name of the parts of New Netherland along the Hudson River and on Long Island to "New York"; New Amsterdam became "New York City." Under the Articles of Capitulation of 1664, the English recognized all titles to property that had been granted by the Dutch government and they guaranteed that Dutch property owners would have a voice in the new government. The Dutch inhabitants were also guaranteed the right to worship in their own Dutch Reformed churches. Dutch cultural traditions continued to dominate the region for many years after the English took control. The Dutch tradition of "Sinter Klaas" (Dutch for "St. Nicholas"), a bearded man in red clothes who brought gifts to children at Christmas time, spread throughout all the colonies. English-speaking children pronounced the man's name "Santy Claus" and then "Santa Claus." Many Puritan, Anglican and other religious leaders tried unsuccessfully to discourage the Santa Claus tradition because they thought that it detracted from the real meaning of Christmas.

Technically, the Anglican Church was the established church of the New York colony because the Anglican governor was charged with overseeing the religious affairs of the colony and protecting the interests his church. Although all Anglican churches were tax-supported, there were very few of them; the majority of the churches in New York City were Dutch Reformed, but they had to maintain themselves with voluntary contributions. The Dutch Reformed ministers complained of the difficulty of collecting these contributions, but the Anglican ministers did not fare much better because people were delinquent in paying their government-imposed religious taxes.

Along the Hudson River between New York City and Albany, most of the land remained under the control of Dutch patroons, each of whom was like a feudal lord, governing a tract of land the size of a township or larger. Because these patroons exercised both spiritual and temporal control over their workers, the established religion in the Hudson River patroonships remained Dutch Reformed.

On Long Island, where religious diversity was the greatest, a code of laws called the "Duke's Laws" guaranteed the right of free exercise of religion to all Christians. The majority of residents of each town also had the right to select their own tax-supported Protestant religion. Although very few towns chose the Anglican religion, the Anglican church was referred to in many documents as the established church of the New York colony.

In 1683, the New York Assembly enacted a Charter of Liberties that applied the religious provisions of the Duke's Laws to the entire colony, except that a two-thirds majority of each town was required to determine which religion would be tax-supported. The Duke of York approved the Charter. However, before it took effect, his brother died and he ascended the throne as King James II. James had become a Catholic convert and one of his first acts was to try to secure toleration for Catholics. Many people thought that he was trying to replace the Church of England with the Roman Catholic Church as the established church in England and all its colonies. In the political turmoil, the New York Charter of Liberties was ignored by all government officials.

Most New Yorkers probably enjoyed all the religious freedom they wanted during the 1680s. In 1682, the Duke of York gave the following instructions to the Catholic Governor Thomas Dongan of New York:

> You shall permit all persons of what Religion soever quietly to inhabit within your Government without giving them any disturbance or disquiet whatsoever for or by reason of their differing Opinions in matters of Religion, Provided they give no disturbance to ye public peace, nor do molest or disquiet others in ye free exercise of their religion.[18]

This directive appeared to say that all the world's religions were to be tolerated anywhere in the colony. A number of them, in fact, were. In 1687, the governor of New York wrote that his state

> . . . has first a chaplain belonging to the Fort, of the Church of England; secondly, a Dutch Calvinist; thirdly a French Calvinist; fourthly, a Dutch Lutheran. Here be not many of the Church of England; few Roman Catholics; abundance of Quaker preachers, men, and women especially; Singing Quakers; Ranting Quakers; Sabbatarians; Anti-Sabbatarians; some Ana-baptists; some Jews; in short all sorts of opinion there are some, and the most part none at all.[19]

These diverse religious groups received a severe setback when James II was removed from the throne by the Revolution of 1688. The New York Assembly passed a new toleration law, but the law denied toleration to Catholics. It appeared to allow religious freedom to Quakers, but they were often forbidden to meet, fined for performing marriages, and prevented from voting because they would not subscribe to oaths of allegiance.

The Jews, however, were treated more tolerantly during this period. In 1685, they obtained the right to worship publicly and a few years later they built their first synagogue in New York City.[20]

In 1693, the new royal governor of New York, Benjamin Fletcher, vowed to strengthen the establishment of the Anglican church. He chided the New York Assembly for failing to pass a bill for "the settling of a ministry in this province." Later the same year, the Assembly enacted the Ministry Act, which provided for "settling a ministry" in the counties of Westchester, New York, Kings and Queens and, to support this ministry, for collecting taxes from all the inhabitants of these counties. In 1694, the New York City vestry asked the Assembly if the Ministry Act allowed it to call a minister of a religion other than Anglican. The Assembly replied that such an action was allowed, because the word "ministry" in the act referred to any ministry, not simply an Anglican ministry. Governor Fletcher was furious. First, he said, the Assembly had no power to interpret its own laws and, secondly, the terms "church-warden" and "vestrymen" in the act clearly indicated that the only ministry allowed was the Anglican ministry.

For two years, the governor and the legislature debated the intent of the Ministry Act. The dispute was resolved in 1696 when the Anglicans of New York City made a deal with the Dutch Reformed, whereby each group received a charter for a tax-supported church. However, the charter for the Anglicans' Trinity Church stated that it was the established church, although it remained for a number of years the only Anglican church in New York City. In a report to the bishop of London in 1704, the Trinity Church rector William Vesey named only three other Anglican ministers in the entire colony and listed only himself and one other minister as rectors of churches. Another report in 1714 said there were only twelve hundred Anglicans in the colony, of whom 450 were communicants. The Anglicans may have been established in New York, but they were but a small fraction of the colony's total population, estimated at twenty thousand in 1698 and forty thousand in 1723.[21]

In 1699, the New York Assembly passed a law that allowed each town to tax its residents for the purpose of building and maintaining its public buildings, including the churches of the town's preferred religion. However, many towns had difficulty in employing ministers of their own choice. That is because several New York governors in the early 1700s asserted the right to approve or disapprove the appointments of all the colony's ministers, whether or not they were Anglican. One of these governors, Lord Cornbury, said "I do hereby License & Tollerate you" whenever he approved a minister called by one of the towns. The Dutch Reformed ministers objected to this licensing practice, claiming that it violated their liberty of conscience and made a futile request to the classis in Amsterdam to have the English ambassador to the Netherlands intervene. The controversy subsided after Governor Cornbury left office, because later governors involved themselves in the affairs of non-Anglican churches only when they were called upon to resolve disputes. This allowed the Dutch Reformed to maintain their religious freedom by resolving their disputes themselves rather than appealing to the Anglican government.

The Dutch Reformed were not the only people to dispute the New York government's authority over their churches. In his book entitled *The First Freedoms, Church and State in America to the Passage of the First Amendment,* Dr. Thomas Curry describes several conflicts that arose between New York's non-Anglican religious groups and their Anglican government.[22] In 1707, a Presbyterian missionary, Francis Makemie, applied for a license to preach in New York, but Governor Cornbury refused to give him one. Makemie then held a religious service in a private home and was arrested because he had no license. At the trial, Makemie's attorney argued that there was no need for a license or grant of toleration, because the English penal statutes, from which the licenses exempted the ministers, did not apply in the American colonies. In his written account of the trial, Makemie wrote that there was "no particular Persuasion established by law" in New York. The jury found Makemie not guilty, but in an odd ruling, the judge ordered the acquitted defendant to pay the costs of the trial.

Curry also reports that in 1703 and 1704, Governor Cornbury took the church and parsonage away from the Presbyterians of the town of Jamaica, gave both buildings to the Anglicans and directed that their taxes be paid to an Anglican minister rather than a Presbyterian one. The Presbyterians refused to pay. In 1710, they took possession of the parsonage, installed their own minister and paid him from the town's ministerial tax funds. In 1719, a new Anglican minister, Thomas Poyer, secured a court order to have the townspeople pay his wages, but many refused to comply with the order. In 1727, the Presbyterians filed a lawsuit and secured a court order to have the Anglicans return the town church to them. As a result, the Presbyterians gained control of both the church and the parsonage and many continued to withhold their payments to Poyer. When Poyer died in 1731, the Anglicans built their own church with their own money, and for a while at least, the Presbyterians and Anglicans lived together peacefully under an arrangement in which the Presbyterians controlled the original church and parsonage, built with public funds, while the Anglican minister received the town's ministerial taxes.

As Curry points out, the Jamaica events were atypical; most New York towns were able to settle their religious differences quietly and without controversy. However, these events show that when religious groups are allowed to vie for the power of civil government to gain advantage over one another, people can easily lose sight of God's commandment to "love thy neighbor."

Another controversy shows that New Yorkers still had different opinions in the 1750s regarding the nature of their religious establishment. The New York Assembly authorized public funds for founding the King's College (now Columbia University), but the Trinity Church Anglicans asserted that they had the right to control the school because they had been granted "a preference by the Constitution of the Province."[23] William Livingston, a future signer of the United States Constitution, headed a group of three authors of a pamphlet entitled *The Independent Reflector* who argued that the Anglican Church was not the established church of New York. They said the Establishment Act of 1693, by which the ministers of each town were "inducted and established" by the choice of the people, "restricted no particular Protestant Denomination whatsoever." Thus, they said, the Anglican Church had been given no legal preference whereby it would have the right to control the new college. However, the New York Assembly did not agree and gave the Anglicans control of the King's College.

A.4. Pennsylvania, Delaware and New Jersey

The Pennsylvania colony was founded in 1681 by the Quaker leader William Penn. The Quakers themselves were founded in England in 1648 by George Fox. Their movement grew rapidly and large numbers of Quakers began migrating to America in 1652, settling in every colony from New Hampshire to South Carolina. Everywhere they settled, they demanded religious freedom, not only for themselves but for all other people, because religious freedom was an integral part of their faith.

The basic tenet of the Quaker religion was, and still is, a heartfelt commitment to friendship with Jesus Christ, based on Jesus' sermon to His disciples in John 15:6-15. The Quakers of colonial America told their fellow colonists that their first allegiance was to the kingdom of God rather than to the kingdoms of man. That remains their belief today, as does their belief that God reveals His will directly to all people rather than through church or government leaders. They worship in meeting houses instead of churches, and during their services, members often stand and gave spontaneous prayers and witness testimony. However, the Quakers believe this group worship is not as important as each person's private communications with God, in which he must listen for God's still, inner voice. The formal name of the Quakers is "The Society of Friends," but everyone began calling them Quakers after an English judge referred to them by that name. When he appeared before the judge, Fox told him that he should tremble, or "quake," when he heard God speaking to him.

In the colonies that had established churches, the Quakers aroused the anger of community leaders by their proselytizing. They stopped people on the street and told them about religious freedom, the importance of God's kingdom, the relative unimportance of man's kingdoms and the fact that a person should learn God's will by listening to His voice from within rather than to some church or government official. The New England Puritans reacted fiercely. First they put them in jail, but when the Quakers continued to preach from the windows of their jail cells, the Puritan officials had them tied to carts and dragged through the streets. Finally, they banished them from their colonies. As mentioned earlier, when some Quakers returned, the Puritans executed four of them between 1658 and 1661.

Many Quakers in England were also sent to prison for writing and preaching about Quaker beliefs and religious freedom. Penn was one of the most prolific Quaker writers and was sent to prison three times between 1668 and 1671. He wrote many of his pamphlets while he was in prison. He said that civil leaders should give up trying to force people into a uniform religious belief;

instead, they should set an example of "practical religion" by their own Christian action and good works.

In 1677, Penn traveled with Fox to the Netherlands and to Germany, where he met many Quakers who were interested in moving to America to gain religious freedom. He also knew of other Quakers in England who were making plans to join their countrymen in America. Aware that these people were likely to meet the same persecution in America as they were enduring in Europe, Penn got the idea of establishing an American colony where religious freedom was guaranteed. So he asked King Charles II to repay a large debt to his deceased father by giving him land in America.

In 1681, King Charles granted Penn's request by giving him a charter that made him proprietor of the land on the west side of the Delaware River, to be called "Pennsylvania." The only religious provision of the charter gave any group of twenty settlers the right to call an Anglican minister, who was to be allowed to live in the colony without molestation. In 1682, Penn drew up a Frame of Government in which he declared, in paragraph 35,

> [t]hat all persons living in this province, who confess and acknowledge the one Almighty and eternal God, to be the Creator, Upholder and Ruler of the world; and that hold themselves obliged in conscience to live peaceably and justly in civil society, shall, in no ways be molested or prejudiced for their religious persuasion, or practice, in matters of faith and worship, nor shall they be compelled, at any time, to frequent or maintain any religious worship, place or ministry whatever.[24]

The Pennsylvania Assembly passed Penn's Frame of Government and from that time on, the colony's government held firmly to Penn's principles of religious freedom. That was not easy: Pennsylvania Anglicans tried hard to get the Assembly to pass laws that would provide tax support to Anglican ministers and deprive Catholics of their freedom of worship.

The early Pennsylvania view of religious freedom was extensive but had several limitations. The Charter of Privileges passed by the

Pennsylvania Assembly in 1701 required that public officeholders state their belief in Christ, by oath or affirmation. Quaker judges allowed only affirmations and refused to administer oaths because oaths were contrary to their religious beliefs. The Pennsylvania Assembly also passed laws against swearing, drinking healths, playing cards and dice and performing stage plays and cock fights, because they "excite the people to rudeness, cruelty, looseness and irreligion." Penn himself said that these laws were necessary because "wildness and looseness of the people provoke the indignation of God." Neither Penn nor his fellow colonists saw any inconsistency in a government that based its laws on a belief in God and even required public officials to believe in Christ, but also guaranteed that no one would be forced to support a religious ministry or denied the right to believe and worship God as his conscience dictated.

As soon as William Penn publicized his charter, people began migrating to his colony by the thousands, including Quakers from England and Wales, Baptists from Wales, Presbyterians from Scotland and Mennonites from the Rhine valley in Germany. In 1700, the colony's population was about twenty thousand. By 1750, the number had grown to over a hundred thousand, with the migration of many more Germans, including members of the Lutheran and Reformed denominations and Amish people from Switzerland. Many came to escape religious persecution, but they also sought other benefits. The land was very cheap. The initial price was only a hundred pounds for five thousand acres, plus a quitrent of a shilling per hundred acres per year; alternatively, people could rent the land for a penny per acre per year. One of Penn's pamphlets also promised that "The air is sweet and clear, the Heavens serene, like the South-parts of France, rarely Overcast."

In 1701, the Assembly delegates from the three lower counties, which lay along the western shore of the bay at the mouth of the Delaware River, refused to meet with of the rest of the colony's delegates. Originally, the Delaware Bay counties had enjoyed equal representation with the upper counties around Philadelphia, but in the 1690s more upper counties were added. The Bay county delegates then saw themselves as a shrinking minority in an Assembly that had no interest in the concerns of their region. They prevailed upon Penn, therefore, to allow them meet in a separate legislature and pass laws for their own counties. The Delaware Assembly began meeting in 1704, but both Pennsylvania and Delaware had a common governor until they became separate states in 1776. During this period, Penn and his heirs remained the proprietors of Delaware as well as Pennsylvania.

Delaware continued to adhere to the principles of religious freedom delineated of Penn's original Frame of Government. Its population included not only most of the religious groups that had come to Pennsylvania, but also Swedish Lutheran, Dutch Reformed and Jewish immigrants and their descendants, who had established settlements there before Penn's charter was granted. In 1638, Swedish colonists had established New Sweden, on the lower Delaware River near the northern border of the region that was to become the Delaware colony. The Frenchman Peter Minuit, who had headed the New Netherlands colony, was elected the first leader of New Sweden.

New Jersey originally consisted of East Jersey and West Jersey. In the 1660s, the Duke of York gave these territories to two courtiers, John Lord Berkeley and George Carteret. Berkeley took West Jersey, facing the Delaware River and Carteret took East Jersey, facing the Hudson River and the Atlantic Ocean. Berkeley sold West Jersey to two Quakers, John Fenwick and Edward Byllinge, who induced a number of English Quakers to settle there. Carteret's widow sold East Jersey to a syndicate of twelve men. Some Quakers bought land from this syndicate, but most of the settlers were Puritans and Presbyterians from New England and Scotland. Both Jerseys also attracted a number of Irish Catholics, French Huguenots, German Protestants and some Jews.

In 1683, each of the Jerseys adopted constitutions with religious freedom provisions similar to those of Pennsylvania. They said that those who believed in God were to be allowed freedom of worship and that no one was to be "compelled to frequent and maintain any Religious Worship, Place or Ministry." When several Jersey towns began violating their constitution by giving tax support to their chosen religious ministers, the Quakers launched a successful campaign against "Tythes, Militia, and great Taxes." One of the major Quaker victories came in 1697, when the East Jersey Assembly rejected a proposal to allow towns to choose their own tax-supported ministry, similar to the system that had begun in New York under the Duke's Laws.

However, in 1699, the East Jersey Assembly modified its religious liberty guarantees by excluding Catholics and preventing them from holding public office. In 1702, when the two Jersey colonies were merged to form the single colony of New Jersey, the East Jersey rules against Catholics were applied throughout West Jersey as well. In 1722, the New Jersey Assembly passed a law authorizing justices of the peace to require everyone to swear an oath of allegiance to the English king and the Church of England. Quakers were allowed to substitute affirmations. Those who would not comply were deemed "Popish recusants" and subject to the English penal laws against Catholics (BL5, 54-57). Although few if any New Jersey Catholics were punished under these laws, they were forced to practice their religion inconspicuously, by worshipping in buildings that could not be identified as places of Catholic worship. The New Jersey colonists did keep tax-supported ministries out of their colony, but their prejudice against Catholics prevented the kind of religious freedom enjoyed in Pennsylvania, Delaware and Rhode Island.

A.5. Maryland

Maryland was founded by Cecil Calvert, the second Lord Baltimore, pursuant to a charter granted to his father, George Calvert, shortly before the latter's death in 1632. George Calvert had been Secretary of State under James I and had then converted to Catholicism, as had his son Cecil before him. Because of their close friendship with the royal family, the Calverts enjoyed a toleration of religion not accorded most English Catholics.

Although Cecil Calvert was a devout Catholic, he had no intention of spreading the establishment of the Catholic Church to Maryland or anywhere else in the world. He viewed religion as a private matter for each person to keep to himself. He thus envisioned Maryland as a place where Catholics and Protestants could live together in harmony, without government favor to either group. At the same time, his charter gave him personal powers far greater than those given to the later proprietors of Pennsylvania, Delaware and New Jersey. Like a feudal prince, he alone had the power to make laws, although they were subject to the approval his colonial assembly.

The people of Maryland, however, could not understand the ways of a prince who refused to be a religious ruler as well. They also resented the fact that he tried to governed his colony from his home in England, with his brother Leonard acting as his resident agent.

The Calverts' initial conflicts were with the Jesuit priests who had come on the first ships carrying Catholics and Protestants to Maryland. The Jesuits thought that because the colony was governed by a Catholic, the Catholic Church should enjoy privileges similar to those that it had in the Catholic countries of Europe, including being exempt from all taxes and having its own law courts with the power to decide all disputes over Church matters. They also wanted the right to make land contracts with the Indians without the governor's consent. Cecil Calvert summarily denied all their requests for these privileges. He also decreed a Statute of Mortmain, copied from a similar English law, which severely restricted the conditions under which churches could receive grants of land. In addition, he ordered the judges of his colony to impose severe punishments on people who disparaged the religious beliefs of others. Accordingly, the overseer of a Jesuit plantation was fined in 1638 for making unkind remarks to his Protestant workers concerning their religious beliefs. In 1642, a Catholic official was punished for locking Protestants out of a building they had used for worship.

In spite of Cecil Calvert's efforts to treat people of all religions fairly, Maryland gained the reputation of being a land of "papist devils" and "recusants." Those were the words of two Virginians, William Claiborne and Richard Ingle, who led a raid into Maryland in 1645, plundering homes and seizing control of large tracts of land. Fortunately, Leonard Calvert was able to restore order with the aid of troops sent by Governor William Berkeley of Virginia.

In 1647, Leonard Calvert died and Cecil appointed William Stone of Virginia to be the first Protestant governor of Maryland. He told Stone that his main job was to bring more settlers to the colony, advertising it as a place where all Christians could enjoy religious freedom. He also required Stone and his councilors to take oaths promising not to disturb Christians, especially Catholics, in the free exercise of their religion.

In 1649, Calvert sent the Maryland Assembly a religious freedom decree, which it approved. Although it was titled the Maryland Toleration Act, its first paragraph did not express much tolerance. It said,

> whatsoever person or persons within this Province . . . shall from henceforth blaspheme God, . . . or shall deny our Saviour Jesus Christ to bee the sonne of God, or shall deny the holy Trinity the ffather sonne and holy Ghost, or the Godhead of any of the said Three persons of the Trinity or the Unity of the Godhead . . . shall be punished with death and confiscation or forfeiture of all his or her lands. . . .

However, the second paragraph proclaimed

> that noe person or persons . . . professing to believe in Jesus Christ, shall from henceforth bee any waies troubled, Molested or discountenanced for or in respect of his or her religion nor in the free exercise thereof . . . nor any way compelled to the beleife or exercise of any other Religion against his or her consent, soe as they be not unfaithful to the Lord Proprietary, or molest or conspire against the civill Government established or to bee established in this Province under him or his heires.

The Act also provided that anyone who should "presume willfully ... to wronge disturbe trouble or molest any person ... professing to believe in Jesus Christ for or in respect of his or her religion or the free exercise thereof" would be compelled to pay treble damages and a fine of twenty shillings. Offenders who could not pay the damages or the fine were to be punished by public whipping and imprisonment.

Unfortunately, the year of the Toleration Act, 1649, was also the year that Oliver Cromwell beheaded Charles I and established Puritan rule in England. In 1650, Parliament sent a commission to force Virginians and Marylanders to swear allegiance to the new Puritan regime. For a while, Maryland was ruled jointly by Governor Stone and members of the commission. However, Stone was deposed in 1654 when he tried to assert that under the Maryland charter he was the sole governor answerable only the proprietor Cecil Calvert. The commissioners then forced the Maryland Assembly to repeal the Toleration Act and decree that no Catholic in the colony was entitled to the protection of the laws of England. During the remainder of Cromwell's rule, Maryland Catholics were subjected to a vicious reign of terror. All the Catholic priests fled to Virginia, Catholic property was confiscated and four Catholics were hanged. After six other Catholics were condemned to die, Cecil Calvert persuaded Oliver Cromwell to order the Puritan commissioners to end the persecution. In 1658, Calvert regained control of the Maryland government and reinstated the Toleration Act of 1649.

For the next thirty years, Maryland was ruled by Cecil Calvert and then his son Charles, who became the proprietor when Cecil died in 1675. Both the father and the son held firm to the principles of the Toleration Act, but tension between Protestants and Catholics continued to increase. One reason was the government was controlled by Catholics, even though Protestants outnumbered them by a ratio that was estimated between eight to one and thirty to one in a population of twenty-five thousand.[25] More Protestants than Catholics had responded to Calvert's call to come to Maryland to enjoy religious freedom, but the Calverts had appointed their

Catholic relatives and friends to most of the government positions. This entrenched Catholic aristocracy was preventing Protestants who had become successful in business from obtaining the political influence that they believed they had earned.

Another reason for the religious tension was that the Catholics were better organized than the Anglicans, who constituted the majority of the Maryland Protestants. Unlike the English Catholics who had come to Maryland, the Anglicans were not accustomed to supporting their churches voluntarily. In 1678, Mary Taney of Calvert Town sent a petition to the archbishop of Canterbury in England asking that her town be granted maintenance for an Anglican minister. Its residents were too poor to support one on their own and she feared that without a minister her children would "be condemned to infidelity and apostacy."[26] However, poverty alone did not explain why there were so few Anglican church-goers in Maryland. The Anglicans simply exercised their freedom of religion by practicing no religion at all, while the Catholics, rich and poor alike, attended their churches regularly and supported a large contingent of priests and Jesuit missionaries. Thus, in spite of the Calverts' refusal to grant the Catholic Church any legal preferences, it became, in appearance, the official church of Maryland.

Another source of tension was the fear of a French and Indian invasion from the western frontier. The Maryland Protestants believed that French Catholic soldiers and traders living on their western border were recruiting Indians to help them march in and overthrow their government. They also believed that the Catholic aristocracy of their colony had formed an alliance with these French people.

Because of these concerns, many Maryland Protestants petitioned the English government to make the Church of England the established church of Maryland so they could rid the colony of all Catholics. In 1681, Maryland authorities uncovered a plot by two Anglicans, John Coode and Josiah Fendall, to overthrow the Calvert government and replace it with an Anglican government. In separate trials, Fendall's jury found him guilty and he was sentenced to prison, but Coode's jury found him innocent. In 1689, Coode led another rebellion, riding the coattails of the Glorious Revolution that sent the Catholic king James II into exile. As Protestants all over America rejoiced on hearing the news from England, the Catholic leaders of Maryland submitted to Coode's forces. The Calvert experiment with religious freedom died quietly.

The new king William III endorsed the Coode rebellion and sent a royal governor to manage the colony. A new Protestant assembly passed a series of laws that made the Church of England the established church of Maryland. The king's Privy Council, however, rejected some of these laws because they attempted to affirm the colonists' rights and liberties as free Englishmen. Finally in 1702, the Privy Council itself drafted an establishment law and the Maryland assembly passed it. The law extended the English Toleration Act of 1689 to Maryland and allowed Quakers to substitute a solemn affirmation for an oath so they could hold public office without violating their religious belief against oaths. The 1702 law also required every inhabitant, regardless of his religion, to pay forty pounds of tobacco per year for the support of an Anglican minister.

Maryland thus became an Anglican colony with a religious establishment similar to that of Virginia. The relationship between the Anglican clergy and the Maryland Assembly bore a striking resemblance to what was happening in Virginia. The clergy complained of being underpaid, while the assembly firmly replied that the ministers were being paid well enough. The legislators in turn were pressured by people of all religions who were upset about the high cost of supporting the Anglican clergy. The Anglicans had rejoiced when their victory over the Catholics made their church the established religion, but their mood turned sour when they had to pay the taxes required to maintain their establishment. Of course, the Catholics were even more unhappy, because they had to contribute to the Anglican ministers' salaries while voluntarily supporting their own clergy. They were also forbidden to hold public office, unlike the Quakers, whose position was otherwise similar to that of the Catholics. The Quakers complained the loudest about the Anglican establishment and their loss of religious freedom.

In the early 1700s, Benedict Calvert, the son of Charles Calvert and the fourth Lord Baltimore, renounced his Catholic faith and joined the Church of England. Because of Benedict's conversion, King George I returned Maryland to the Calvert family. Benedict's son Charles became the proprietor in 1715. The English religious laws against Catholics (BL5, 54-57) remained in effect. Meanwhile, all kinds of non-Anglican Protestants enjoyed religious freedom, including the Scotch and German Protestants who were migrating across the border from Pennsylvania. In 1756, the Maryland Assembly passed a law that required all Catholics to pay double taxes because it feared their allegiance with French Catholics during the French and Indian War.

A.6. The Carolinas and Georgia

In 1663, Charles II granted eight of his courtiers an American territory that bore the Latin form of his name, "Carolina." The grant included all the land between the southern Virginia boundary and a line sixty-five miles south of St. Augustine, Florida. The southern part of this territory was also claimed by Spain. At the time of the grant, some Anglicans and Quakers had already migrated across the Virginia border and settled in the Albemarle Sound region, which later became part of North Carolina. Afterward, more Virginians moved south into Carolina.

The next permanent settlers were Anglicans who came in the 1670s from the Barbados Islands. They were lured to Carolina by the glowing reports of a Barbadian ship captain, William Hilton. When they arrived, they laid out large plantations on the banks of the Ashley and Cooper Rivers and established the port of Charles Town, later called "Charleston," where the Ashley and Cooper flow together into the Atlantic Ocean. Soon afterward, the Barbadian Anglicans were joined by Presbyterians and Baptists from England and Huguenots from France. The Huguenots were seeking refuge from the persecution of Louis XIV, who had revoked his grandfather's tolerance law, the Edict of Nantes, in 1685.

Throughout the colonial period, the Anglican Church was, in theory, the established church in the entire Carolina region. However, the Anglican establishment in the northern part was so weak that it was practically non-existent. In the southern part, where it was strong, its churches were totally supported by public taxes. Nevertheless, other Protestant groups outnumbered the Anglicans in both the northern and southern parts of the region.

The problems faced by the Anglican establishment in Carolina resulted from difficulties experienced by the proprietors when they tried to form a stable civil government. The Carolina charter gave the proprietors the powers of feudal lords, very similar to the powers of the Maryland proprietor, Cecil Calvert. However, Carolina had eight proprietors, all living in far-away England. They devised an elaborate system of government and land ownership, with themselves at the top of a class pyramid. Directly under the proprietors were noble landowners who held permanent seats in the colony's legislative assemblies. The land was divided into two counties, one in the northern Albemarle Sound region and the other in the southern Charles Town region. Each county had a resident governor and an assembly that included the governor, the deputies of the proprietors, the noble landowners and elected representatives of the common people. The governor was appointed by the proprietors and he had the power to approve or disapprove all laws passed by the assembly. However, any decision by the governor could be reversed by any proprietor or his resident deputy.

This system proved to be extremely confusing and unworkable; colonists in both counties complained often to the proprietors in England. Part of the problem was the corruption and incompetence of the governors, who failed to provide adequate protection against Spanish, Indian and pirate raids. Between 1664 and 1689, the Albemarle colonists had to organize their own defenses against these raids and they forced five governors to resign. In 1691, the proprietors tried to solve the problem by appointing a single governor to manage the entire colony from his residence in Charles

Town, assisted by a deputy governor in Albemarle County. Because the proprietors also made concessions to the colonists, by 1700 there were no noblemen holding vested seats in the legislatures. The colony's form of government and land ownership began to resemble that of Virginia.

In 1712, the proprietors divided Carolina into two colonies, North Carolina and South Carolina, each with its own governor and legislative assembly. In 1719, after the proprietors had rejected a number of laws proposed by the South Carolina Assembly, the legislators asked King George I to buy the colony from the proprietors. The king granted their request and the first royal governor of South Carolina arrived in 1721. In 1729, North Carolina also became a royal colony.

The North Carolina Anglicans were very slow to organize because of the turmoil in their early government. The Quakers became the strongest religious group in the region, taking advantage of the tolerance allowed by the proprietors. The original Carolina charter allowed non-Anglicans "such Indulgences and Dispensations" as the proprietors "shall, in their discretion think fit and reasonable." A 1696 law guaranteed all Christians, except Catholics, "full liberty of conscience." Thus, in 1700, there were three gatherings of Quakers, each led by a lay minister, but there is no record of any Anglican congregation at that time.[27]

In 1701, the legislature of the northern Carolina county passed a law requiring all the inhabitants of each parish to pay their local Anglican minister £30 per year. When the Quakers gained control of the assembly in 1703, they vowed to repeal the law, but before they could act, the proprietors voided the law on the ground that the pay was inadequate. The next year, the Quakers lost their seats in the assembly because a new governor required all officeholders to subscribe to an oath of allegiance, which the Quakers refused to take because of their religious beliefs. With the Anglicans once again in control, the legislature passed a law in 1715 requiring all inhabitants to pay the salaries of the colony's Anglican ministers. However, this law had little effect because so few Anglican ministers were willing to settle in the region. In a book about North Carolina, William Byrd II of Virginia wrote in 1728,

> this is the only Metropolis in the Christian or Mahometan World, where there is neither Church, Chappel, Mosque, Synagogue, or any other Place of Publick Worship of any Sect or Religion whatsoever. What little Devotion there may happen to be is much more private than their vices. The People seem easy without a Minister, as long as they are exempted from paying Him. Sometimes the Society for propagating the Gospel has had the Charity to send over Missionaries to this Country; but unfortunately the Priest has been too Lewd for the people, or, which oftener happens, they too lewd for the Priest. For these Reasons these Reverend Gentlemen have always left their Flocks as arrant Heathen as they found them.[28]

Even by 1765, North Carolina had only five Anglican ministers and they were still having difficulty collecting the taxes for their salaries.[29]

The South Carolina Anglicans were also slow to organize. Their first church, St. Philip's in Charles Town, was built in 1682, but it was still the only Anglican church in the colony in 1698 when the local assembly conferred a £50-a-year maintenance on its minister. In 1701, the legislature enacted several laws that declared the Church of England to be "Settled and Established," required all members of the assembly to be Anglicans, established six parishes and provided that the ministers of these parishes were to be supported from an existing tax on imported goods, authorized each Anglican vestry to tax all parish inhabitants in order to pay church expenses of up to £100 per year, gave the members of each Anglican church the power to elect their own minister and set up a commission of twenty laymen who could remove any minister accused by his parish vestry of immoral or imprudent conduct.

The non-Anglicans, led by the Presbyterians, sued to have these laws voided by the House of Lords and hired Daniel Defoe to argue their case. He said the laws discouraged trade with non-Anglican nations and pointed out that by giving a lay commission the power to dismiss ministers, the laws deprived the bishop of London of his ecclesiastical jurisdiction. The House of Lords agreed voided the 1701 laws.

In 1706, the legislature in Charles Town passed another law that did not require that its members be Anglicans and did not give the lay commissioners the power to remove ministers. The new law divided the colony into ten parishes, each of whose ministers were to be elected by Anglican church members. The ministers' salaries and the costs of building the parish churches were to be paid from the general tax revenues of the colony. The legislature passed another law in 1710 that allowed each parish vestry to draw up to £40 per year from the public treasury for church maintenance. South Carolina thus became the first and only colony to support its established churches from its general tax revenues rather than from specific religious tax assessments. This feature helped to quiet the dissenters. For many years afterward, the tax-supported Anglican churches of South Carolina operated comfortably and without public outcry.

Another reason why religious tensions eased in South Carolina was the tolerance allowed to non-Anglican Protestants. In 1712, Governor Charles Craven pledged to protect the Church of England, while showing "the greatest tenderness to those who are under the misfortune of dissenting from her." Under this policy, the dissenting churches grew even faster than the Anglican churches. In 1710, South Carolina had eight Anglican ministers and eight ministers of other Protestant denominations, but in 1720 the Anglicans had dropped to seven, while the number of non-Anglican ministers had increased to eleven.[30]

In 1732, the year of George Washington's birth, King George II granted a charter for the Georgia colony to a group of prominent Englishmen led by James Oglethorpe. The colony was to be located on land that was originally part of the Carolina county, between the Savannah River and the Spanish settlements on the Florida peninsula. The founders had two missions, one of which was to provide a military buffer zone against attacks from the Spanish settlements. The other, designed to remedy the deplorable conditions of the overcrowded British debtor prisons, was to provide a place where indigent debtors could be rehabilitated. The founders wanted to give the prisoners an opportunity to work off their debts in open farmlands where they could establish new lives for themselves.

The Georgia charter provided that Oglethorpe and his associates were to serve as trustees of the colony for twenty-one years. Because of the missionary nature of the colony, the trustees provided Anglican ministers for the prisoners and other settlers, but they also helped people of other religions to settle in the colony. In 1753, the trustees were relieved of their duties and the colony became a royal one. In 1758, the Georgia Assembly made the Church of England the established church of the colony. However, even by the time of the War of Independence, Georgia had only two Anglican churches. They were maintained by revenues from a special tax on liquor, which would probably be known today as a "sin tax." Because of the nature of this tax, dissenting religious groups were not in a good position to complain about the financial burden of the Anglican establishment. On the other hand, the Anglican establishment was not in a good position to complain about the amount of liquor people were drinking.

A.7. The "Great Awakening" Revival

In 1720, a Dutch Reformed minister, Theodore Jacobus Freylinghuysen, came to the Raritan Valley of New Jersey, west of the southern tip of Staten Island, and began preaching that everyone should have a conversion experience that would transform his moral behavior. He said the churches of America had fallen into lax worship practices, emphasizing form over substance and intellectual reasoning over spiritual vitality. Americans, he said, ought to realize their sinfulness, stand in terror before the law of God, feel His unmerited grace and experience the birth of the Holy Spirit within them.

Meanwhile, the Irish-born Gilbert Tennent was realizing the same need for spiritual revival in his father's log cabin, nicknamed the "Log College," a rustic Presbyterian seminary in Neshaminy, Pennsylvania, northeast of Philadelphia. After graduating in 1725, Tennent became pastor of a Presbyterian church in New Brunswick, New Jersey, in the heart of the Raritan Valley where Freylinghuysen was preaching. He became a close friend and protege of Freylinghuysen and was soon preaching his own fiery sermons, exhorting sinners to repent and become reborn. Although these sermons brought him many devoted followers, many also criticized him. They disliked his showmanship and they did not appreciate his implication that they were not Christians unless they had experienced a dramatic rebirth in their relationships with God. Tennent exacerbated the controversy by attacking his critics, not only in sermons in his own church but in sermons that he preached in other churches throughout the valley. The debate reached a climax in 1740 when he delivered his famous Nottingham Sermon, calling his opponents hypocrites. The next year, he and his followers left the New Brunswick Presbytery and formed an independent church.

However, Tennent soon realized that he had made a mistake. In 1743, therefore, he became pastor of a Presbyterian church in Philadelphia and spent the rest of his life unsuccessfully trying to heal the breach that he had caused among Presbyterians. Other Presbyterian ministers, as well as those of other denominations, had been copying Tennent's old, fiery preaching style. Now, each had his own following of people who had been spiritually reborn. The Presbyterians of this "Great Awakening" movement called themselves "New Side" Presbyterians.

Most Great Awakening ministers did not confine their preaching to one congregation but traveled from church to church instead. The most widely traveled preacher was George Whitefield, a close friend of John and Charles Wesley, the founders of the Methodist movement. In 1738, Whitefield left his native England and traveled to Georgia as a Methodist missionary. The Methodists at that time were a society within the Church of England that emphasized a methodical way of living according to the teachings of the Bible. Whitefield also believed in the need of every person to experience a new birth of spirit, in the manner told by Jesus to Nicodemus in

John 3:1-21. He had experienced such a rebirth in his college days at Oxford.

In 1739, Whitefield traveled back to England and counseled John Wesley through a spiritual renewal that the latter had sought after a difficult time in his life. He then returned to America and spent most of the next thirty years traveling the American coast from Georgia to Massachusetts, converting people of all Christian denominations to a new, reborn relationship with God. Whitefield also converted many Americans to the Methodist way of living according to God's plan and laid the groundwork for making the Methodists a separate denomination apart from the Anglicans after the War of Independence.

The intellectual leader of the Great Awakening was Jonathan Edwards, who preached at the Congregational church in Northampton, Massachusetts from 1726 to 1750, first as an assistant to his grandfather and then as the pastor after his grandfather died in 1729. Edwards became famous for sermons that struck terror in the hearts of his listeners, such the sermon in 1741 entitled "Sinners in the Hands of an Angry God." In spite of his emotional delivery, Edwards' sermons were also high in intellectual content. He became regarded as the chief apologist of the Great Awakening, showing how Locke's thesis that man is vested by God with rights to life, liberty and property is consistent with the Biblical teaching that man is totally dependent on God. He also showed how Newton's laws of physics prove the supremacy of God and the helplessness of man when he tries by himself to cope with matters that lie beyond his control. In addition, he embraced several theological doctrines previously touted in New England only by dissenters, namely God's justification by faith and grace alone, which was Anne Hutchinson's message, and the necessity that a person exercise his own God-given free will in order to have a conversion experience, as Roger Williams had preached.

Under the leadership of Edwards, the Great Awakening preachers shook the foundation of the New England Puritan establishment. Their dramatic style and different ideas impressed many people. However, some rejected their doctrines and resented their ways of preaching, saying the preachers were egocentric, judgmental and insincere. Members of many Congregational churches became divided between "New Lights" who supported the Great Awakening and "Old Lights" who adhered to conventional Puritan theology and ways of preaching. Although Presbyterians and other Protestants in New Jersey, New York and Pennsylvania were divided on the same issues, the New England debates were far more heated because they resulted in contests over whose preachers should receive the religious taxes assessed by each town.

In 1742, the Connecticut Assembly, which was dominated by Old Lights, passed a law that tried to extinguish the New Lights by forbidding any minister to preach in a parish unless he was the tax-supported minister of the parish or had the permission of the parish's tax-supported minister and the majority of his parishioners. The law threatened the New Light movement because most of its preachers were gaining their following by traveling from parish to parish at the invitations of people who represented only a minority of their town's parishioners.

Elisha Williams, a former president of Yale College and a defender of the Great Awakening, challenged the Connecticut law in a 1744 pamphlet, saying that it violated the natural right of every person to follow the dictates of his own conscience or judgment. Williams based his argument on Locke's *Second Essay Concerning Civil Government*, which said that government power is limited to preserving the life, liberty and property of people. According to Locke, "nobody can transfer to another more power than he has in himself" and "having in the state of nature no arbitrary power over the life, liberty, or possession of another, but only so much as the law of nature gave him for the preservation of himself and the rest of mankind, this is all he does or can give up to the commonwealth, and by it to the legislative power, so that the legislative power can have no more than this" (App. F, par. 135). Williams observed, as Locke did in his *Letter Concerning Toleration* (App. F), that a person's religious beliefs and practices are, under ordinary circumstances, no threat to the life, liberty or property of other people. Therefore, he said, the people cannot give their government the power to control each other's religions, because they cannot give up what they never had in the first place.[31]

While Williams staunchly defended the free exercise of religion as a natural right of man, his pamphlet also said that government ought to support an established religion. He also justified the denial of religious freedom to Catholics on the ground that they were enemies of the "Protestant State." The tax support of religion was necessary, he believed, because the civil authorities had a duty to be "Nursing Fathers" of "Schools and the Gospel Ministry." Williams thus ignored the fact that part of a person's exercise of religion is the freedom to decide the nature of the gifts he should make to God for the support of his religious beliefs. He did not appreciate the fact that when the civil government makes that decision for people, it deprives them of the free exercise of their religion. Williams also did not seem concerned that the Great Awakening was being impeded not only by laws that denied people the right to worship as they pleased, but also by laws that gave the Old Lights a political advantage because of their government-supported churches. Rather than destroy that government support, he and other New Lights sought to gain control of it for their own political advantage.

The New Lights were eventually able to elect their own preachers to the tax-supported pulpits of many towns in Massachusetts. This created a checkerboard pattern of New Light and Old Light parishes across the colony. In addition, the New Lights preached a theology that tore away the old Puritan vision of a united, worldly "city on a hill." In 1748, the New Light leader Nathaniel Eells told the Connecticut Assembly that the Kingdom of Christ is not of this world. It is "purely spiritual," he said.[32]

While the complexion of the New England establishment was changing, an even greater transformation was taking place in the Virginia churches. Before 1730, no British colony in America was more homogeneous than Virginia, both in culture and religion. Nearly all white people in the colony were transplanted Englishmen and their only church was the Church of England. In the 1730s, however, Scotch and Irish immigrants began arriving from New York, Pennsylvania and New Jersey and settling in the western counties of Virginia, where they organized Presbyterian churches. Many of these churches were of the "born again," New Side branch of that denomination. The Anglican leaders of the state welcomed these frontier settlers and tolerated their different forms of worship, because they provided a buffer against the intrusion of French explorers from the west. In the 1740s, however, the religion and culture of the western Presbyterians began to clash with that of the eastern Anglicans.

The problems started in Hanover County, north of Richmond, where a bricklayer, Samuel Morris, began holding revival meetings. The meetings drew large crowds of working people like himself, who came to hear him read sermons published by George Whitefield and other Great Awakening preachers. When the demand for more meetings grew, the organizers went to the mountains of southwest Virginia and asked a New Side Presbyterian preacher, William Robinson, to come and help them lead their movement. Other New Side preachers followed, and they traveled the countryside attracting large crowds. They criticized the Anglican Church and suggested that the bishop of London might be "an unconverted man."[33]

The Anglican Reverend Patrick Henry, uncle of the famous Patriot of the same name, asked the Virginia colonial government to stop these itinerant preachers from spreading their subversive doctrines. The governor and his council responded by calling on local authorities to restrain "all Itinerant Preachers." The authorities arrested a number of them and charged them with "vilifying the Established Religion" and preaching at unlicensed places of worship. Some were found guilty and fined. The major newspapers of the colony tried to discredit them, saying they "have turn'd the world upside down."[34]

One of the arguments used during these trials was that the preachers were not entitled to toleration under the English Act of Toleration because they preached at no settled, licensed places of worship. The leaders of the revival movement therefore asked the New York Presbyterian synod to send them a qualified minister who could obtain licenses for their meeting houses. The synod sent

Samuel Davies, a New Side minister who had trained at Samuel Blair's "Log College" in Fogg's Manor, Pennsylvania. In April 1747, Davies applied for and obtained licenses for four meeting houses in Hanover, Goochland, Caroline and Louisa Counties. He proved to be an able leader and his emotional sermons caused many more people to join the New Side Presbyterians, or "New Lights," as they also called themselves. The Anglican gentry became more alarmed. In 1750, the Virginia Council revoked a license that had been granted for a fifth meeting house in New Kent County. Davies was extremely upset. He said the Council was trying to thwart his missionary work in violation of the Act of Toleration. He appealed their decision to the Lords of Trade in England, and in 1751, the Lords ruled in Davies' favor, saying,

> as Toleration and a Free Exercise of Religion is so valuable a branch of true liberty, and so essential to the enriching and improving of a Trading Nation, it should ever be held sacred in His Majesties Colonies.[35]

In spite of his demands for religious freedom, Davies firmly believed that Virginia ought to have a religious establishment. He simply wanted his New Lights to be part of that establishment. During the French and Indian War in the late 1750s, he preached sermons that roused the people to defend their frontier during the French and Indian War, arguing that the war against the evil French Catholics was a test of their Protestant faith in God. He and his fellow preachers also stopped their attacks on the Anglican church and toned down their emotional rhetoric. As a result, the New Lights gradually gained acceptance among the leading members of Virginia society.

Another major change brought by the Great Awakening was the growth in the number of independent Baptist churches. The American Baptist movement had started in Rhode Island in the mid-1600s, under the leadership of Roger Williams and his associate John Clark. Clark was the pastor of the colony's first Baptist church in Newport and, like Williams, a strong advocate of religious freedom. He organized his church as an alternative to the government-supported Congregational churches of the neighboring Puritan colonies. His tenets of faith were the same as those of the Baptist churches that had been organized in the Netherlands and England: each adult person should have the freedom to read and interpret the Bible as the Holy Spirit leads him, and infant baptism is wrong because a person should be baptized only when he is able to make a conscious, free-will decision to repent of his sins and accept Jesus Christ as his Lord and Saviour. They did not believe that membership in a community of believers, signified by infant baptism, was as important as a person's free-will, private relationship with God, which only adult baptism can signify.

During the latter half of the 1600s, the Baptist movement grew at a moderate pace in New England. Meanwhile, English Baptists settled in Pennsylvania and South Carolina. Many New Englanders were drawn to the Baptist churches because of controversies within the Congregational churches over the question of infant baptism. By 1727, the number of Baptists in Massachusetts and Connecticut had grown so large that they were able to get their respective legislatures to pass laws exempting them from paying taxes to support the Congregational churches.

One of the differences between the Baptists and most other Christian groups was their lack of central authority. Each Baptist church employed its own ministers, conducted worship services and managed itself without direction from any superior organization. They formed associations of churches but the only functions of these associations were mutual guidance, fellowship and missionary work. Each Baptist church remained autonomous. Also, the freedom of the individual Baptist to decide what he believed was a cherished part of his religion. The only requirements of his faith were that he make a conscious, free-will decision to repent of his sins, accept Jesus Christ as his Lord and Saviour and be baptized.

The Great Awakening drew many people to the Baptist faith because the Awakening's "born again" message fit so well with the Baptist view that only adults should be baptized. When Protestant churches became divided by the "born again" issues of the Great Awakening, thousands of people left those churches and became

Baptists. They found fellowship with others who shared their views on baptism and conversion and they found the freedom they were seeking concerning other matters of faith. During the Great Awakening, the Baptists increased in greatest number in the southern colonies, where they drew mainly from the Anglican churches.

While the Great Awakening increased the number of "born again" Christians in America, it caused others to join a liberal counter movement, led by two Boston Congregational ministers. One was Jonathan Mayhew, called "The Father of Civil and Religious Liberty in Massachusetts and America" by Robert Treat Paine, one of the four Massachusetts delegates who signed the Declaration of Independence. The other minister was Dr. Charles Chauncy, pastor of the "Old Brick" First Church of Boston from 1727 to 1787. In his later years, Chauncy was the unofficial mentor of many younger Boston ministers, including Mayhew. He was also the most outspoken critic of Jonathan Edwards, saying that his sermons were too emotional and theatrical. Chauncy and Mayhew criticized the New Light emphasis on religious dogma and its vision of people as depraved, sinful creatures who needed conversion experiences to prove that they were chosen to be saved from the hands of an angry God. Chauncy said that God was benevolent and intended that each person enjoy happiness while he grew in religious faith by an ordered, rational process.

Mayhew went further and denied many of the doctrines of the Catholic and Calvinist creeds, including the doctrine of the Trinity. He laid the groundwork for the unitarian and universal salvation movements that took place in various Congregational churches in the late 1700s. One movement led to the founding of an independent Universalist Church in Gloucester, Massachusetts in 1779. Beginning in 1819, many Congregational churches switched their allegiance to a new Unitarian denomination. Both the Unitarians and the Universalists believed in living according to Christian moral values, but they rejected the idea that people had to adhere to dogmatic statements of faith, or even believe in God, in order to practice these values.

Mayhew often preached on civil liberty as well as religious liberty. His most famous sermon was on civil liberty, delivered at Boston's West Church on January 30, 1750, under the title, "A Discourse concerning Unlimited Submission and Non-Resistance to the Higher Powers." Following Locke's view of the basis of civil government, Mayhew said "[t]he only reason for the institution of civil government, and the only rational ground for submission to it, is the common safety and utility." Mayhew's sermons inspired the Patriot leaders of Massachusetts who opposed the British acts of tyranny during the 1760s. John Adams, Sam Adams and James Otis were among his closest friends. On June 8, 1766, only six weeks before his death, Mayhew wrote a letter to Otis suggesting that the colonial assemblies correspond with one another on a regular basis, so they could monitor the injustices inflicted upon each other by the British government. The Patriot committees of correspondence were probably the result this suggestion.

The religious concerns of the colonists were a major reason why they took such a firm stand against the British with respect to their other rights. John Adams wrote that one of the reasons for their opposition to the Stamp Act was that

> if Parliament could tax us, they could establish the Church of England here with all creeds, articles, tests, ceremonies, and tythes, and prohibit all other churches, as conventicles and schism-shops. [36]

However, the colonial legislatures, not Parliament, were depriving the colonists of their religious freedom. In 1774, a Baptist minister, Isaac Backus, led a protest against the Massachusetts religious laws. Eighteen Baptists from Warwick had been thrown into cold jails in the dead of winter, forty miles from home, for failing to pay religious taxes. Backus said the legal certificate that these people needed to prove their tax-exempt status cost four pence, while the British tax on tea was only three pence per pound. He claimed that "[a]ll America are alarmed at the tea tax; though, if they please, they can avoid it by not buying tea, but we have no such liberty." He also claimed the certificate tax was illegal because government had no authority to regulate people's religion.[37] In September 1775, he told the Massachusetts Assembly,

> We have no desire of representing this government as the worst of any who have imposed religious taxes; we fully believe the contrary. Yet, as we are persuaded that an entire freedom from being taxed by civil rulers to religious worship is not a mere favor from any man or men in the world but a right and property granted us by God, who commands us to *stand fast in it*, we have not only the same reason to refuse acknowledgment of such a taxing power here, as America has the above said power [to tax people who are not represented], but also, according to our present light, we should not wrong our consciences in allowing that power to men, which we believe belongs only to God.[38]

By the time of the Declaration of Independence, most Americans realized that their own religious penalties and establishments were as much a violation of their fundamental liberties as the laws passed by Parliament. When their legislatures met in 1776 to organize their new state governments, they took a fresh look at the religious laws that they had inherited. Every state had inherited laws that penalized the people of one or more religions (Table 1, p. 250). No state allowed people other than Protestant Christians to hold public office, Catholics were not guaranteed the right to worship anywhere except Rhode Island, Pennsylvania and Delaware and all the states except New Jersey, Rhode Island, Pennsylvania and Delaware taxed their citizens to support the ministers of one or more religions.

B. The Expansion of Religious Freedom between 1775 and 1790

Between 1775 and 1790, every American state broadened its guarantee of religious freedom. (Table 2 on page 251 shows the condition of religious freedom in the original thirteen states and Vermont in 1790. The improvements made by each state between 1775 and 1790 are in bold print. Tables 1 and 2 also show this was a period of huge population growth, due in part to more Europeans immigrating to the United States after the War of Independence.)

In 1775, each New Hampshire town imposed a tax for the support of its official church; in all but fifteen towns, where the Presbyterians were in the majority, that church was Congregational. Minority Protestants who supported their own churches were usually, but not always, exempted from this tax. Unlike Massachusetts and Connecticut, New Hampshire had no uniform system for verifying that those who failed to pay such taxes were in fact supporting another church. Few objected to these taxes, therefore, and the New Hampshire constitution of 1776 did not even mention religious taxes or rights. However, in 1784, after the Baptists complained that several towns had refused to give them tax exemptions, the state adopted another constitution with a bill of rights guaranteeing that no person of one Protestant sect would be forced to pay to support another sect. On the other hand, the new constitution also gave the state legislature the power to authorize each town to provide for "public protestant teachers of piety, religion, and morality." The New Hampshire towns thus maintained their authority to collect religious taxes, but each citizen had the right to insist that his taxes be paid only to the church of his choice. The constitution also retained the requirement that only Protestants could hold public office. In 1790, the people of New Hampshire rejected an amendment to their constitution that would have granted religious tax exemptions to persons who could certify that they worshipped according to a minority religion. The same amendment would have allowed people other than Protestants to hold public office.

Vermont became the fourteenth state on February 18, 1791 and on November 3, 1791, it ratified the first ten amendments, including the First Amendment that guaranteed religious freedom. Because its ratification was necessary for the adoption of this amendment, Vermont's religious history is relevant to the development of religious freedom in the United States prior to the amendment.

The Vermont territory was settled primarily by Congregational farmers from New Hampshire, Connecticut and Massachusetts. The Baptists were the main minority group. The bill of rights of Vermont's 1777 constitution proclaimed in Article III

Table 1
Religious Freedom in the Thirteen Colonies in 1775

Colony	Population in 1770*	Religions Tolerated+	Nature of **Religious Establishment in 1775**
New Hampshire	62,400	Protestant+	Each town chose its tax-supported Protestant religion, usually CONGREGATIONAL, sometimes Presbyterian; members of other Protestant churches usually not taxed or taxes went to own churches.
Massachusetts incl. Maine	297,900	Protestant+	Each town chose its tax-supported Protestant religion, which with rare exception was CONGREGATIONAL; no religious tax in Boston; Anglican taxes went to their churches; Quakers & Baptists tax exempt, sometimes.
Connecticut	183,900	Protestant+	Tax support of all churches adhering to CONGREGATIONAL Saybrook Platform; Anglican taxes went to their churches; Quakers & Baptists usually tax exempt.
Rhode Island	58,200	all religions	No government support of any religion, but Jews and possibly Catholics could not vote or hold public office.
New York	162,900	Protestant+	ANGLICAN OFFICIALLY; some government preferences to Anglicans, but each town chose its tax-supported Protestant religion, which was usually not Anglican; some towns supported Anglican + another Prot. religion.
New Jersey	117,400	belief in God except Catholic	No government support of any religion, but Anglican Church could not be criticized; only Protestants could hold public office.
Pennsylvania	240,100	belief in God	No government support of any religion; but only Protestants could hold public office.
Delaware	35,500	belief in God	No government support of any religion; but only Protestants could hold public office.
Maryland	202,600	Protestant+	ANGLICAN; all people taxed to maintain the Anglican churches; the colony's many Catholics paid double taxes and could not hold public office.
Virginia	447,000	Protestant+	ANGLICAN; all people taxed to maintain the Anglican churches; preachers of other Protestant religions had to obtain licenses.
North Carolina	197,200	Protestant+	ANGLICAN; however, a weak religious tax collection system; only five Anglican churches in 1765.
South Carolina	124,200	Protestant+	ANGLICAN; its churches supported from the general tax revenues.
Georgia	23,400	Protestant+	ANGLICAN; only two Anglican churches in 1776, funded by a liquor tax.
Total Pop.	2,152,700		

* Population figures are U.S. Census estimates published in *The World Almanac 1994*, 359.
+ In practice, anyone other than a Catholic could worship freely, as long as he did not criticize the Anglican or other established church. However, only Protestants could hold public office.

Table 2
Religious Freedom in the Thirteen States and Vermont in 1790
(changes from 1775 printed in bold)

State	Population in 1790*	Religions Tolerated	Nature of Religious Establishment in 1790
New Hampshire	142,000	belief in God incl. Catholic	Each town chose tax-supported Protestant religion, usually CONGREGATIONAL, sometimes Presbyterian; **1784 Constitution guaranteed that no person of one Protestant sect be forced to pay to support another sect, but towns had duty to support Protestant ministers.** Public office limited to Protestants.
Vermont	85,000	belief in God	Towns could support a Prot. church, usually CONGREG'L, if 2/3 majority approved, but members of other churches could get tax exemptions. Practice discontinued after 1795. Public office limited to Protestants.
Massachusetts incl. Maine	476,000	belief in God incl. Catholic	Each town chose tax-supported Protestant religion, which with rare exception was CONGREG'L; no rel. tax in Boston; **each taxpayer could designate own Prot. church to receive taxes;** Publ. office lim. to Protestants.
Connecticut	238,000	all Christians + incl. Catholic	Tax support of all "established Societies," (e.g. CONGREGATIONAL churches); **other Protestant churches could issue tax exemption certificates to their members.**
Rhode Island	69,000	all religions	No government support of any religion; Catholics could hold public office, but not Jews.
New York	340,000	all religions excl. Catholic	**Repealed all laws "as may be construed to establish or maintain any particular denomination of Christians."** Catholics excluded from public office.
New Jersey	184,000	belief in God incl. Catholic	No government support of any religion; no establishment of one religious sect in preference to another; Only Protestants were guaranteed the right to hold public office.
Pennsylvania	434,000	belief in God	No government support of any religion; **Catholics and Jews**, as well as Protestants, **could hold public office**.
Delaware	59,000	belief in God	No government support of any religion; Catholics, as well as Protestants, could hold public office.
Maryland	320,000	all Christians + incl. Catholic	State legislature controlled the EPISCOPAL Church, but old religious tax law was repealed; new religious tax law defeated; Catholics, as well as Protestants, could hold public office.
Virginia	748,000	all religions	Virginia Statute of 1786 said, "no man shall be compelled to frequent or support any religious worship, place, or ministry whatsoever," and guaranteed that people of all religions could hold public office.
North Carolina	394,000	all religions	**Constitution of 1776 declared there "shall be no establishment of any religious church or denomination . . . in preference to any other,"** but continued to restrict public office to Protestants.
South Carolina	249,000	all religions	Constitution of 1790 guaranteed free exercise of religion, without discrim. or preference, to all mankind.
Georgia	83,000	all religions	Constitution said no one should have to support ministers "except those of their own profession."
Total Pop.	3,821,000		No general religious assessment law ever enacted. Only Protestants could hold public office.

* 1790 U.S. Census figures published in *Historical Statistics of the United States* (Washington, D.C.: Bureau of Census, 1976), 25-36 (Table A195-209).
+ In practice, Jews and people of other religions were allowed freedom of worship. Possibly, in Connecticut, they could also hold public office.

> that no man ought, or of right can be compelled to attend any religious worship, or erect or support any place of worship, or maintain any minister, contrary to the dictates of his conscience; . . . and that no authority can, or ought to be vested in, or assumed by, any power whatsoever, that shall, in any case, interfere with, or in any manner controul, the rights of conscience, in the free exercise of religious worship.

However, the same article also said that

> every sect or denomination of people ought to observe the Sabbath, or the Lord's day, and keep up, and support some sort of religious worship, which to them shall seem most agreeable to the revealed word of God.

It also limited its guarantee of civil rights to Protestants, saying,

> [no] man *who professes the protestant religion,* [emphasis added] be justly deprived or abridged of any civil right, as a citizen, on account of his religious sentiment, or peculiar mode of religious worship, ...[39]

Pursuant to these somewhat conflicting constitutional provisions, the Vermont legislature passed a law in 1783 that gave towns the power to tax their residents for the support of one church, provided two-thirds of the voters consented. A person attending another church could be exempted from the tax if he produced a certificate of attendance signed by an officer of that church. It was not clear whether that other church had to be Protestant or whether it could be any of the world's religions, including Roman Catholic. In 1785, a general tax levy was proposed for the benefit of all churches. However, the Baptists raised a loud protest and the proposal died.[40]

In 1786, Vermont amended its constitution and guaranteed civil rights to people of all religions by deleting the words, "who profess the protestant religion" from the civil rights clause of Article III. However, its constitution too kept the requirement that office holders had to be Protestant. The amended Article III also limited the Sabbath-keeping and religious worship requirements to

Christians by substituting "every sect or denomination of Christians" in place of "every sect or denomination of people." It also deleted the words "and support" from that provision, which raised the question of how the Sabbath-keeping and worship requirements were to be met. In towns that continued to assess religious taxes, the Baptists argued that the new constitution invalidated the 1783 law giving towns the power to assess such taxes. However, after 1795 few if any towns chose to assess these taxes, and the Baptists dropped their complaints.[41]

Although the new constitution gave non-Christians greater freedom by guaranteeing their civil rights and limiting the requirements of Sabbath-keeping and religious worship to Christians, it raised other issues that might have caused controversy. If the state and local governments of Vermont had the power to tell Christians not to break the Sabbath and "keep up some sort of worship," they could have prescribed exactly what people had to do to follow those commandments. That would have certainly drawn protests, not only from the Baptists but from all other Christians.

The state of Massachusetts inherited a religious tax system that was designed to support its Congregational churches. The Baptist leader Isaac Backus wrote that in 1774 he heard John Adams say of his fellow colonists, "we might as well expect a change in the solar system, as to expect they would give up their establishment."[42] During the War of Independence, some leaders of the Massachusetts Assembly tried to determine a way to give up their establishment but at the same time require people to support some kind of Protestant worship. If they could accomplish that, they thought, they could quiet the Baptists and other complaining religious groups while preserving their publicly supported religious ministries. The Assembly leaders thought they had found the solution in Articles II and III of their state's new bill of rights, which was adopted in 1780 as part of the first Massachusetts Constitution.

Article III, clause 5, of the bill of rights declared that

> every denomination of Christians, demeaning themselves peaceably, and as good subjects of the common-wealth, shall be equally under the

protection of the law: and no subordination of any one sect or denomination to another shall ever be established by law.

This provision was designed to end the state's religious establishment. It also ended the old tax system criticized by the Baptists under which many faithful Protestants were denied tax exemptions and thereby forced to support Congregational or Anglican churches to which they did not belong.

Article II of the bill of rights set the stage for the new religious tax system by proclaiming that it was "the right as well as the duty of all men in society, publicly and at stated seasons, to worship the Supreme Being, the great Creator and Preserver of the universe." Article III, clause 1 then authorized the new tax system, by directing the town governments

> to make suitable provision, at their own expense, for the institution of the public worship of God, and for the support and maintenance of public Protestant teachers of piety, religion, and morality, in all cases where such provision shall not be made voluntarily.[43]

In order to comply with clauses 1 and 5 of Article III, the Massachusetts towns changed their religious tax laws so that each taxpayer was allowed to designate any local Protestant church as a recipient of his tax money. If a taxpayer did not designate such a church, then his taxes were to be paid to the church chosen by the majority of the townspeople, which, in all but a few Anglican towns, was Congregational. In the opinion of the state's Congregational leaders, this new tax system did not create a religious establishment, because all Protestant sects were treated equally and none was subordinated to another.

The Massachusetts Baptists did not share that opinion. While they agreed that people should be required to worship according to some Protestant faith, provided no preference was given to the tenets of one particular faith, they disagreed about the tax. One of the Baptist beliefs was that a person's gift of alms to God had to be voluntary and that it was against God's will for government to force people to contribute money to the support of any church, even the church they chose to attend. Because the Congregationalists felt that their churches should be supported because of the essential role they played in the well-being of society, the Baptists claimed that religious taxation was an endorsement of the Congregational tenet of faith. Therefore, they said, it subordinated all other denominations to the Congregational way of worship, in violation of Article III, clause 5 of the Massachusetts constitution.

Instead of resolving the issues, the religious provisions of the 1780 bill of rights intensified the debate between the Congregational and Baptist leaders. Even before the bill of rights was passed, Isaac Backus speculated that the state's religious taxes would be of no benefit to the Baptist churches because their ministers would be forced by their religious convictions to refuse all money that people had been legally required to contribute. Most of the tax money collected from the Baptists would therefore be paid to the Congregational churches. Thus, he said, the new tax system, like the old one, discriminated against the Baptists and denied them their religious freedom. The Congregational ministers replied that the new tax system did not deny anyone freedom of worship, nor was it a "civil establishment," because it supported all Protestant worship and no "particular mode of public worship" was "established by law."[44] The Massachusetts Supreme Court never ruled on this issue directly, but in a 1786 opinion relating to the right of Universalists to have their taxes paid to their own churches, Chief Justice William Cushing (later a U. S. Supreme Court justice) spoke of sects that were not part of "the regular establishment, if it may be so termed."[45]

The Massachusetts debate over religious taxes continued into the early 1800s. Both sides eventually agreed that the taxes constituted a religious establishment. The question of whether or not the establishment was good for society was decided in 1833, when it was abolished.

Connecticut also refused to abolish its religious tax system, which forced everyone, except Anglicans and some Quaker and Baptist groups, to pay taxes to churches that abided by the

Congregational Saybrook Platform. However, unlike the Massachusetts Congregationalists, the Connecticut leaders always admitted that they had a religious establishment. In 1777, members of eleven Baptist churches, calling themselves "Separate Baptists" because they had recently separated from Congregational churches, petitioned the state General·Assembly asking that "the liberty which the bible grants may take place through this State" and that all citizens be allowed to worship "in the manner that they think is most agreeable to the gospel." The Assembly responded with a law that avoided the general issues raised by the petition and simply exempted the Separate Baptists from the religious taxes, provided they obtained certificates attesting to their support of their own churches. Pressed by continued complaints from other religious groups, the legislature enacted another law in 1784 that gave the same exemption to

> all denominations of Christians differing in their religious Sentiments from the People of the established Societies in this State, whether of the Episcopal Church, ... Separates, ... or Baptists, ... or Quaker, or any other Denomination ....[46]

Although this language appeared to include Catholics, a later section of the statute referred only to "all protestant churches as dissent from the worship and ministry established as aforesaid."

In spite of these more tolerant laws, the Connecticut people continued to debate whether they infringed on their religious freedom. In 1776, Congregational minister Judah Champion summed up the arguments for preserving the laws:

> As our civil liberties ... are nearly connected with ... our religious ... so our religious privileges are not inferior to our civil. Every one has God's word, may read and judge for himself. ... Every ecclesiastical society may chuse its own minister, and provide for his support. Happily delivered from Romish superstition ... and that ecclesiastical hierarchy, which neither we, nor our fathers were able to bear--we may serve God without fear. Difference of sentiment respecting the non-essentials of religion, seems to be one of the unavoidable consequences

of man's dreadful apostasy. None may impose for doctrine, the commandments of men; or force others to believe with them. Surely the sacred rights of conscience, are ever to be treated with utmost delicacy. But if any under pretence of conscience, sap the foundation of civil society . . . they are to be restrained by the civil arm. Civil rulers are God's ministers for good . . . [and] a terror to evil works. . . . In favor of virtue, to suppress immorality, and support religion, we have a system of excellent laws enacted, while different persuasions enjoy the most generous liberty and freedom. What greater civil or christian liberty can be enjoyed, or even wish'd for, than the inhabitants of this colony are indulged?[47]

Champion's rhetorical question was answered in a 1791 letter by a Connecticut dissenter, John Leland, who pointed out that heathens, deists, Jews and Catholics were not exempted from the state's religious taxes. Leland asked whether a Jew should be forced to support the "religion of Jesus Christ, when he really believes that he was an impostor." He also asked, "Must the Papist be forced to pay men for preaching down the supremacy of the Pope, who they are sure is the head of the Church?" Religious establishments, he said, are made by "fallible men" who "make their own opinions tests of orthodoxy, and use their own systems, as Procrustes used his iron bedstead, to stretch and measure the consciences of all others by." Finally, Leland asserted,

[t]he certificate law supposes . . . that the legislature have the power to establish a religion; this is false. Second, that they have authority to grant indulgence to non-conformists; this is also false, for a religious liberty is a right and not a favor.[48]

Rhode Island was the one New England colony that always recognized the right of people of all religions, including Jews and other non-Christians, to worship as their own consciences dictated. There was never any government support of religious worship or teaching. However, Jews and possibly Catholics were not permitted to vote or hold public office. The law excluding Catholics, if it ever existed, was apparently repealed shortly after the Declaration of Independence.[49] However, the law excluding Jews was unfortunately not repealed until the nineteenth century.

New York adopted a constitution in 1777 that said that all parts of the common law and all statutes that formed the law of the state on April 19, 1775, were to continue in force, except those parts of the common law and statutes "as may be construed to establish or maintain any particular denomination of Christians or their ministers . . . are, abrogated and rejected."[50] New York thus abolished what was left of its Anglican establishment and the taxes that its towns had levied to maintain their various Protestant churches. Although the constitution appeared to permit a general tax for the benefit of all Christian denominations, the state Assembly never passed such a tax. The constitution also guaranteed the "free exercise and enjoyment of religious profession and worship, without discrimination or preference." However, it required that foreigners applying for citizenship renounce all foreign powers "ecclesiastical as well as civil," thereby excluding Catholics who acknowledged religious allegiance to the pope. A 1788 law prevented Catholics from holding public office by requiring all office holders to renounce both ecclesiastical and civil foreign powers. On the other hand, the constitution and laws of New York appear to have allowed Jews and other non-Christians, in addition to Protestants, to become citizens and hold public office.

In 1776, New Jersey adopted a constitution that guaranteed the right to worship to everyone, including Catholics, but only Protestants were guaranteed the right to hold public office. Articles XVIII and XIX read as follows:

> XVIII. That no person shall ever, within this Colony, be deprived of the inestimable privilege of worshipping Almighty God in a manner agreeable to the dictates of his own conscience; nor, under any pretence whatever, be compelled to attend any place of worship, contrary to his own faith and judgment; nor shall any person, within this Colony, ever be obliged to pay tithes, taxes, or any other rates, for the purpose of building or repairing any other church or churches, place or places of worship, or for the maintenance of any minister or ministry,

contrary to what he believes to be right, or has deliberately or voluntarily engaged himself to perform.

XIX. That there shall be no establishment of any one religious sect in this Province, in preference to another; and that no Protestant inhabitant of this Colony shall be denied the enjoyment of any civil right, merely on account of his religious principles; but that all persons, professing a belief in the faith of any Protestant sect, who shall demean themselves peaceably under the government, as hereby established, shall be capable of being elected into any office of profit or trust, or being a member of either branch of the Legislature, and shall fully and freely enjoy every privilege and immunity, enjoyed by others their fellow subjects.[51]

Although Article XIX limited the prohibition against religious establishments to "the establishment of one sect . . . in preference to another," the last clause of Article XVIII appeared to forbid a general tax assessment for the benefit of all sects of any category, such as all Protestant sects, unless members of other kinds of sects were exempted.

Pennsylvania adopted a constitution in 1776 that guaranteed the same broad religious rights in Article II of its Declaration of Rights that had been guaranteed in its original 1682 charter. All people believing in God were guaranteed the right to worship according to the dictates of their own consciences and no one could "be compelled to attend any religious worship, or maintain any ministry, contrary to, or against, his own free will and consent." Nor could any man who acknowledged a belief in God be deprived of any civil right as a citizen.[52] However, the constitution also imposed a requirement that office holders acknowledge a belief in God and the Old and New Testaments. That allowed both Protestants and Catholics to hold public office, but not Jews. After the Jews complained, a new constitution adopted in 1790 simply required that office holders acknowledge a belief in God and a "future state of rewards and punishments."[53] Now not only Jews but Moslems and a few other non-Christians were allowed to hold public office in Pennsylvania.

Delaware's 1776 constitution contained no bill of rights but said in Article 29 that there was to be "no establishment of any one religious sect in preference to another." That left open the question of whether there might be a general tax for the support of all religious sects. The 1776 constitution also opened public office to Catholics but still required that all office holders profess "faith in God the Father, and in Jesus Christ His only Son, and in the Holy Ghost, one God, blessed for evermore."[54] Technically, these two provisions represented the condition of religious freedom in Delaware when the Bill of Rights of the United States Constitution became effective in 1791. However, in June 1792, Delaware adopted a new constitution that said in Article I,

> Section 1. Although it is the duty of all men frequently to assemble together for the public worship of the Author of the universe, and piety and morality, on which the prosperity of communities depends, are thereby promoted; yet no man shall or ought to be compelled to attend any religious worship, to contribute to the erection or support of any place of worship, or to the maintenance of any ministry, against his own free will and consent; and no power shall or ought to be vested in or assumed by any magistrate that shall in any case interfere with, or in any manner control, the rights of conscience, in the free exercise of religious worship, nor a preference be given by law to any religious societies, denominations, or modes of worship.
> Section 2. No religious test shall be required as a qualification to any office, or public trust, under this State.[55]

Delaware thus acknowledged that all men have a duty to gather to worship God and that the prosperity of society depends on their obeying that duty; at the same time, it acknowledged that it had no power to enforce that duty.

In its preamble, the 1792 Delaware constitution declared that their religious freedom went hand-in-hand with their rights of life, liberty and property and, "in general, of attaining objects suitable to their condition without injury by one to another":

> Through divine goodness all men have, by nature, the rights of worshipping and serving their Creator according to the dictates of their

consciences, of enjoying and defending life and liberty, of acquiring and protecting reputation and property, and, in general, of attaining objects suitable to their condition, without injury by one to another; and as these rights are essential to their welfare, for the due exercise thereof, power is inherent in them; and, therefore, all just authority in the institutions of political society is derived from the people, and established with their consent, to advance their happiness; and they may, for this end, as circumstances require, from time to time, alter their constitution of government.

Maryland adopted a constitution in 1776 that said in Article XXXIII of its bill of rights that no person should

> be compelled to frequent or maintain, or contribute, unless on contract, to maintain any particular place of worship, or any particular ministry;
> [56]
> . . . .

However, the next clause of the Article said

> the Legislature may, in their discretion, lay a general and equal tax, for the support of the Christian religion; leaving to each individual the power of appointing the payment over of the money, collected from him, to the support of any particular place of worship or minister, or for the benefit of the poor of his own denomination, or the poor in general of any particular county: . . . .

Apparently, the words of the first clause, "particular place of worship" and "particular ministry" meant only that the legislature could not compel a person to support a place of worship and ministry selected by the legislature (for example, the Anglican Church). On the other hand, the legislature could, as provided in the second clause, tax a person for the support of Christianity in general and, in particular, for the support of a Christian place of worship and ministry that the person himself selected.

The opening clauses of Article XXXIII that guaranteed religious liberty were also confusing because they did not state clearly whether religious liberty was guaranteed to all persons or merely all Christians. They said

[t]hat, as it is the duty of every man to worship God in such manner as he thinks most acceptable to him; all persons, professing the Christian religion, are equally entitled to protection in their religious liberty; wherefore no person ought by any law to be molested in his person or estate on account of his religious persuasion or profession, or for his religious practice.

Article XXXIII specified that the tax support of ministers of the Anglican Church, known as the Episcopal Church after the separation from Great Britain, was to terminate effective November 1776, but that taxes for church building projects approved earlier were to remain in effect until the projects were completed. Nevertheless, the Maryland legislature continued to control the internal affairs of these churches long after their public tax support had ended. In 1779, it specified in its Vestry Act who could serve on Episcopal vestries, how Episcopal ministers were to be chosen and what penalties could be imposed upon Episcopal church members who were elected to vestries but refused to serve.

In 1784, a bill was introduced in the Maryland legislature proposing that a religious tax of unspecified amount be assessed on all citizens, except those declaring themselves to be "Jews or Mahometans" or not believers "in the Christian religion." Each taxpayer could designate the Christian church to which his taxes were to be paid, but the church had to have thirty adult men living within "a reasonable distance." The bill caused a debate in the House of Representatives so divisive that the members decided to refer it to a vote by the general public. Opponents of the bill pointed out that it was sponsored by the Episcopal churches, who were to be its main beneficiaries because of their majority status. They also objected that because the amount of the tax was not specified, the taxes could be increased indefinitely. On January 20, 1785, the *Maryland Gazette* criticized the bill's "unnecessary parade about the usefulness of morality and religion," and asserted that the legislature was trying to become the judge of acceptable religious worship. On March 25, 1785, the *Baltimore Advertiser* printed a signed petition to the legislature, saying the bill was not in the "spirit of the Christian religion," which "needs not the power of rules to establish, but only to protect it." The petition also said,

> [i]n the opinion of all men of discernment, the law proposed for the support of the clergy, is intended to give one church a preeminence above others, else why are some societies compelled to pay for the support of the clergy, who do not desire it?[57]

Because of the overwhelming public criticism of the tax bill, it was never submitted to the voters. In the following election, candidates who opposed the bill gained an overwhelming majority in the state legislature and the bill was defeated in the next session, forty one to twenty one.[58] In the following years, several other religious tax plans were proposed but none became law. In 1810, the Maryland Declaration of Rights was amended to delete the clause giving the legislature power to lay a tax for the support of the Christian religion.[59]

In 1776, North Carolina adopted a constitution that declared in Article XIX of its bill of rights

> [t]hat all men have a natural and unalienable right to worship Almighty God according to the dictates of their own consciences.

The constitution also terminated the establishment of the Anglican Church, declaring in Article XXXIV

> [t]hat there shall be no establishment of any one religious church or denomination in this State, in preference to any other; neither shall any person, on any pretence whatsoever, be compelled to attend any place of worship contrary to his own faith or judgment, nor be obliged to pay, for the purchase of any glebe, or the building of any house of worship, or for the maintenance of any minister or ministry, contrary to what he believes right, or has voluntarily and personally engaged to perform; but all persons shall be at liberty to exercise their own mode of worship:--*Provided*, That nothing herein contained shall be construed to exempt preachers of treasonable or seditious discourses, from legal trial and punishment.[60]

Although the words "in preference to any other" in the first clause of the article appeared to open the door for a general tax for the support of all religious churches and denominations, the next clause closed that door by declaring that no person could be forced to pay for the support of any ministry. Most people in North Carolina had not paid religious taxes even when they had been required to do so, and they worshipped freely when they pleased and where they pleased. Therefore, their 1776 constitution's declaration of religious rights merely guaranteed that their common practice would continue.

The only religious clause in the North Carolina constitution that caused any controversy was Article XXXII requiring that office holders not deny the truth of the Protestant religion:

> . . . no person, who shall deny the being of God or the truth of the Protestant religion, or the divine authority either of the Old or New Testaments, or who shall hold religious principles incompatible with the freedom and safety of the State, shall be capable of holding any office or place of trust or profit in the civil department within this State.

The debate over this article was not strenuous, probably because it required no affirmative declaration of religious belief. Although the prohibition remained in the constitution for many years, Jews and Catholics who kept their religious beliefs to themselves were able to hold public office in North Carolina.[61]

South Carolina's first constitution, adopted in 1776, allowed the state to continue to support its Anglican churches from its general tax revenues. Other religious groups led by the Presbyterians and Baptists therefore petitioned the legislature in 1777 to terminate the Anglican establishment. Written by William Tennent, a Presbyterian minister from Charleston, the petition asked "[t]hat there never . . . be any establishment of any one religious denomination or sect of Protestant Christians in this state by way of preference to another." In a speech to the South Carolina Assembly, Tennent criticized an alternative proposal "to establish all denominations by law and pay them all equally," calling it a scheme to divide the dissenters by pacifying some of them. He said it was "absurd[,] as the establishment of all religions would in effect be no establishment at all," and "every plan of establishment must operate as a plan of injustice and oppression."

Shortly afterward, however, Tennent discovered a plan of establishment he thought acceptable. There would be no harm if "Christianity itself is the established religion of the state," he declared, provided all churches were fully supported by the voluntary contributions of their members. Under Tennant's plan, all Christian churches and societies would be eligible for incorporation as religious societies, provided they met certain requirements. These societies would then enjoy certain civil rights, such as freedom from being disturbed or molested during their worship services and freedom from being the object of abusive and hateful language.[62]

South Carolina's constitution of 1778 adopted the substance of Tennant's plan, except that its establishment privileges were available only to all Protestants, rather than to all Christians. Article XXXVIII declared "[t]he Christian Protestant religion shall be deemed, and is hereby constituted and declared to be, the established religion of this State." Any group of fifteen or more adult male persons professing the Christian Protestant religion could be "incorporated and esteemed as a church of the established religion of this State," provided it agreed to the following articles:

    1st.   That there is one eternal God, and a future state of rewards and punishments.
    2d. That God is publicly to be worshipped.
    3d. That the Christian religion is the true religion.
    4th.   That the holy scriptures of the Old and New Testaments are of divine inspiration, and are the rule of faith and practice.
    5th.   That it is lawful and the duty of every man being thereunto called by those that govern, to bear witness to the truth.

Furthermore, each minister chosen to lead an incorporated church had to make certain promises. Among other claims, he had to say

[t]hat he is determined by God's grace out of the holy scriptures, to instruct the people committed to his charge, and to teach nothing as required of necessity to eternal salvation but that which he shall be persuaded may be concluded and proved from the scripture; . . . .

Article XXXVIII also listed these benefits of becoming part of the state's religious establishment:

[n]o person shall disturb or molest any religious assembly; nor shall use any reproachful, reviling, or abusive language against any church, that being the certain way of disturbing the peace, and of hindering the conversion of any to the truth, by engaging them in quarrels and animosities, to the hatred of professors, and that profession which otherwise they might be brought to assent to.

For religious groups unable to comply with all the requirements for incorporation, Article XXXVIII guaranteed

[t]hat all persons and religious societies who acknowledge that there is one God, and a future state of rewards and punishments, and that God is publicly to be worshipped, shall be freely tolerated.

In addition, it said that

[n]o person shall, by law, be obliged to pay towards the maintenance and support of a religious worship that he does not freely join in, or has not voluntarily engaged to support.[63]

The provisions of Article XXXVIII raised little controversy, and most Protestant churches in South Carolina joined the state's religious establishment by becoming incorporated. Several proposals were made for taxing people to support their respective established churches, but the legislature did not act on them. Little practical value was therefore attached to a church's becoming incorporated, other than being able to proclaim that it was part of the state's legal establishment.

In 1790, South Carolina adopted another constitution that deleted all the establishment provisions of the old one and simply provided in Article VIII that

> [t]he free exercise and enjoyment of religious profession and worship, without discrimination or preference, shall forever hereafter be allowed within this State to all mankind: *Provided*, That the liberty of conscience thereby declared shall not be so construed as to excuse acts of licentiousness, or justify practices inconsistent with the peace or safety of this State.[64]

The new constitution also deleted all religious requirements for holding public office.

Georgia's first constitution adopted in 1777 declared in Article LVI that

> [a]ll persons whatever shall have the free exercise of their religion; provided it be not repugnant to the peace and safety of the State; and shall not, unless by consent, support any teacher or teachers except those of their own profession.[65]

This clause, like South Carolina's religious freedom clause, allowed the legislature to pass a tax levy that would have forced people to support the churches of their own choice. However, it appeared to prevent the legislature from continuing the liquor tax for the support of churches, unless the liquor could be taxed only if it were sold exclusively by each church to its own members or there were some other arrangement whereby the tax was directed to the church of one's choice.

In 1785, the Georgia legislature passed a law that allowed counties with more than thirty families to levy a tax for the support of a Christian minister chosen by the people. The preamble of the law said of the Christian religion that "its regular establishment and support is among the most important objects of legislative determination." However, no county ever levied a tax under the law.[66] If it had, it likely would have violated Article LVI of the Georgia constitution, because the tax was to be paid not only by the ones who had voted in favor of the minister but by all the people.

The original Georgia constitution also required that all office holders profess the Protestant religion. That requirement was stricken from the state's 1789 constitution, but the religious freedom guarantee of the first constitution remained substantially the same.[67]

C. The Virginia Statute for Religious Freedom

In the mid 1760s, while Virginia Anglicans were still recovering from the loss of many members to the New Light Presbyterians, Separate Baptist preachers began arriving from New England. The Separate Baptists angered the Virginia Anglicans even more than did the New Lights because they attacked the social customs and materialistic ways of the Anglican gentry, such as their custom of bringing horses and other goods to sell on church grounds after Sunday worship services. The Baptist preachers also refused to obtain licenses because they claimed that God had given them a natural right to roam the countryside, preaching to anyone at any time and any place.

The Baptist challenge came at a time when the Virginia Anglicans were dealing with serious internal problems. Many of their members were complaining of the poor quality and low moral conduct of their ministers. The ministers, for their part, were complaining of low pay and lack of job security. They suffered because the local vestries who employed them were usually dominated by the most wealthy and powerful gentlemen of the parishes; these gentlemen generally thought their ministers were paid well enough. They were also critical of the ministers' performance, and the slightest action or statement by a minister deemed offensive to the parish leaders was apt to lead to his dismissal.

Many Virginia Anglicans believed that these problems could be solved by a strong resident bishop who would control the appointments of the ministers and oversee their performance. However, they were reluctant to insist that such a bishop be appointed, because he would have to have been nominated by the king of England, the same king whom they were currently accusing of tyranny and corruption. The conditions of Anglican disarray therefore persisted, and many left their Anglican churches to join the new Baptist congregations. At first, only common people were persuaded to leave, but by the early 1770s, the Baptist congregations included people from all levels of Virginia society, including gentlemen who were qualified to serve on Anglican vestries.

The frustrated Anglican authorities tried hard to control the Baptist movement. They sought grand jury indictments against former Anglicans who had converted, charging that they were violating laws that required them to worship at Anglican churches. Between 1765 and 1771, at least twenty Baptists were imprisoned for preaching at unlicensed meeting places, in violation of the English Act of Toleration.[68] By 1776, that number had reached almost fifty.[69] In other cases, corporal punishment was administered on the spot, as related in this 1771 diary account:

> Brother Waller Informed us . . . [that] about 2 Weeks ago on the Sabbath day Down in Caroline County he Introduced the Worship of God by Singing . . . While he was Singing the Parson of the Parish [who had ridden up with his clerk, the sheriff and some others] would Keep Running the End of his Horsewhip in [Waller's] Mouth, Laying his Whip across the Hym Book, &c. When done Singing [Waller] proceeded to Prayer. In it he was Violently Jerked off the Stage, [they] caught him by the Back part of his Neck[,] Beat his head against the ground, some Times Up[,] Sometimes down, they Carried him through a Gate that stood some Considerable Distance, where a Gentleman [the sheriff] Give him . . . Twenty Lashes with his Horse Whip. . . . Then B[rother] Waller was Released, Went Back Singing praise to God, Mounted the Stage & preached with a Great Deal of Liberty.[70]

The mistreatment of the Baptists angered young James Madison while he was living at his family home in Orange County at the foot of the Blue Ridge Mountains. Madison had returned home in 1772 after graduating from Princeton, where he had studied political theory, including "The Law of Nature and of Nations."[71] He had wanted to enter politics but was forced to delay that plan by ill health that lasted for several years. In January 1774, he wrote to a friend,

> I have indeed as good an Atmosphere at home as the Climate will allow: but have nothing to brag of as to the State of Liberty in my Country. Poverty and Luxury prevail among all sorts: Pride ignorance and Knavery among the Priesthood and Vice and Wickedness among the Laity. This is bad enough But It is not the worst I have to tell you. That diabolical Hell conceived principle of persecution rages among some and to their eternal Infamy the Clergy can furnish their quota of Imps for such business. This vexes me the most of any thing whatever. There are at this [time] in the adjacent County not less than 5 or 6 well meaning men in close Goal for publishing their religious Sentiments which in the main are very orthodox. I have neither patience to hear talk or think any thing relative to the matter, for I have squabbled and scolded abused and ridiculed so long about it, [to so lit]tle purpose that I am without common patience. So I [leave you] to pity me and pray for Liberty of Conscience [to revive among us.][72]

The root of the conflict between the Baptists and Anglicans did not lie so much in their differing theologies as it did in their differing views of the role of churches in their society. The Baptists worshipped in simple dwellings and warehouses--any place where they could come together to strengthen their love of God, family members and neighbors. On the other hand, the Anglicans met in church sanctuaries that were designed not only for worship but for reminding everyone of their respective places in society. The ground floor of each sanctuary was divided into cubicles, most of which were reserved for the important families of the parish, and the oldest and most important families sat closest to the pulpit and the altar. The common people sat either in the rear cubicles or in the balconies. The slaves usually sat in the balcony farthest from the altar. In this setting, the words of the prescribed Book of Common Prayer "evoked postures of deference and submission" not only to God but to the people of superior rank who sat in front of the worshipper.[73] Positions on the church vestry were held by the community leaders; when a leader retired from the vestry he would name his own successor. Community leaders thus passed their mantles of leadership from one generation to the next through their church offices. The church vestries decided which aged and sick people in the community were deserving of the church's financial help. In that manner, the community leaders became the patrons of the poorer people.[74] For the average working person, the grace received from God was embodied in the grace received from the church and community leaders.

The Baptist success in drawing people away from the Anglican churches therefore alarmed many Anglican leaders. They saw the movement as a threat the colony's social structure. However, all attempts to stop the Baptists were failing. When community leaders charged Baptist preachers with disturbing the peace, the judges usually dismissed the charges because the Baptists met in places where no one was disturbed. They tried to use the English Act of Toleration to confine Baptist worship to registered meeting places. However, they were complaining against British tyranny at the same time and the lawyers and judges were therefore questioning whether any English law could be enforced in the colonies. In 1772, members of the House of Burgesses tried to solve this problem by introducing a Virginia bill patterned after the English toleration law. Some conservatives thought the bill was not strong enough and proposed amendments that would ban night meetings and forbid proselytizing to slaves without their owner's permission. However, the liberal House members opposed the bill because it simply tolerated a few dissenters. They said the time had come to recognize the right of every person to complete and unconditional freedom of worship.[75]

The debate over the bill became heated when the temporary rector of the Bruton Parish Church in Williamsburg, the Reverend Samuel Henley, threw himself into the conflict. Because there was no local bishop, Henley's position as rector in the capital city made him the nominal head of the Anglican Church in Virginia. However, Henley was also a professor of moral philosophy at William and Mary College and he did not subscribe to the orthodox theology normally held by people of his position. He criticized Christian dogma, including the doctrine of the trinity, saying, "I shall ever consider universal Love as the first Principle of Religion, that which infinitely supersedes all Knowledge and Orthodoxy. . . . If this be Heresy, I glory in it!"[76] He also denounced the proposed licensing bill in a speech to the House of Burgesses, charging that the "votaries" of intolerance were more "impious" than "the idolators of Moloch." He went on to say that

> [a]s Society cannot be injured but by actions which violate its property or peace, those who demean themselves honestly and orderly ought not to be molested, on account either of their sentiments, or worship. If these sentiments and this worship be the efflux of sincerity and devotion, absurd as they may be, God will approve them. The more such persons abound in every community, the better that community become. . . . Would Legislators maintain the cause of Religion, let them shew its influence on their conduct.[77]

Henley's speech set off an emotional debate with Robert Carter Nicholas, treasurer of the colony and chairman of the Committee for Religion of the House of Burgesses. When the permanent rector of Bruton Parish Church died in 1773, Henley, the temporary rector, would have been the logical choice to take his place. However, the members of the Bruton Church were divided over his qualifications. He was finally dismissed in June 1773, primarily because of his liberal theology and opposition to the pending licensing bill. Nevertheless, he continued to teach at the College of William and Mary and continued to debate his political opponents.

The House of Burgesses became so divided over the licensing bill that no one dared to bring it to a vote. Meanwhile, Anglican rectors and officials in other parishes continued to harass the Baptist preachers. In 1775, Henley moved to England because he could not support the call to take up arms against the British government. Several young Patriot leaders, however, took over his campaign for religious freedom. Among them were Thomas Jefferson, age thirty two, and his friend James Madison, age twenty four.

In June 1776, while the Continental Congress was preparing the Declaration of Independence in Philadelphia, a convention in Williamsburg was drafting a Declaration of Rights for the new state of Virginia. Unfortunately, Jefferson could not attend this convention because he could not be in Philadelphia and Williamsburg at the same time. However, James Madison attended and was able to influence the language of the Declaration's religious freedom article. George Mason, the principal draftsman of the Declaration, had written that "all Men should enjoy the fullest Toleration in the Exercise of Religion, according to the dictates of Conscience . . . ." Those words were designed to end the persecution of the Baptists and other religious groups while allowing the Anglican Church (not yet known as the "Episcopal Church") to continue as the state's official, tax-supported church. Madison proposed that Mason's language be changed to say that "all men are equally entitled to the full and free exercise of religion . . . ." and that the article also provide that "no man or class of men ought, on account of religion, to be invested with any peculiar emoluments or privileges; nor subjected to any penalties or disabilities unless, under color of any religion, any man disturb the peace, the happiness, or safety of society."[78] The second clause would have severely reduced the power of the Anglican-Episcopal establishment. However, seeing that it had no chance of being adopted, Madison withdrew the clause to be sure of gaining approval of his "equal . . . free exercise" clause, so that the Declaration would at least limit the ways by which the state could support its established church. The final article became Article 16 of the Declaration:

> That religion, or the duty which we owe to our Creator, and the manner of discharging it, can be directed only by reason and conviction, not by force or violence; and therefore all men are equally entitled to the free exercise of religion, according to the dictates of conscience; and that it is the mutual duty of all to practise Christian forebearance, love, and charity towards each other.[79]

While he was in Philadelphia working on the Declaration of Independence, Thomas Jefferson also drafted a proposed Virginia state constitution, sending it to Williamsburg in early June. Jefferson's religious freedom article would have ended all religious taxes:

> [a]ll persons shall have full and free liberty of religious opinion; nor shall any be compelled to frequent or maintain any religious service or institution.[80]

In September 1776, Jefferson resigned from the Continental Congress and was elected a member of Virginia's new state legislature, the Virginia General Assembly. When he returned home, he was dismayed to learn that the Virginia Declaration of Rights had no guarantee that people would not be compelled to support a religious service or institution. He was also upset upon learning that when the General Assembly had repealed all acts of Parliament relating to religious crimes, it had left in tact Virginia's own laws punishing heresy and blasphemy.[81]

Other Virginians also believed that their state constitution should have included a broader religious freedom guarantee. The Baptists, Presbyterians and Lutherans sent the Assembly petitions calling for the end of the state's "ecclesiastical establishment." These petitions included a "ten thousand name" Baptist petition. However, the House of Delegates of the General Assembly merely passed a series of resolutions saying that these dissenting groups would no longer be molested. The resolutions also confirmed the Episcopal establishment by declaring that "proper provision should be made for continuing the succession of the clergy and superintending their conduct" and that "public assemblies of societies for divine worship ought to be regulated."[82]

Jefferson responded to these resolutions with several resolutions that proclaimed religious freedom and called for an end to Virginia's religious establishment. He later described the fight over these resolutions as "the severest contests" of his career. He said, "Our greatest opponents were [Edmund] Pendleton and Robert Carter Nicholas, honest men, but zealous churchmen."[83] In his speeches on the House floor, Jefferson relied heavily on Locke's *Second Essay Concerning Civil Government* and *Letter Concern-*

ing Toleration (App. F). He argued that people have given up only those freedoms necessary for the proper function of civil government, while retaining all others, including their religious freedom. He said, "If [there] is [any] unalienable right, it is religious."[84] When he published these arguments in his *Notes on the State of Virginia*, he said,

> ... our rulers can have authority over such natural rights only as we have submitted to them. The rights of conscience we never submitted, we could not submit. We are answerable for them to our God. The legitimate powers of government extend to such acts only as are injurious to others. But it does me no injury for my neighbour to say there are twenty gods, or no god. It neither picks my pocket nor breaks my leg.[85]

Although Jefferson's argument was based on Locke's principles of civil government, his statement concerning "twenty gods, or no god" showed that he did not agree with Locke's exclusion of atheists from toleration or with Locke that atheistic beliefs lead people to violate their civil duties and thus destroy the religions of other people (App. F).

As 1776 was drawing to a close, and while Washington was preparing his troops for their "victory or death" crossing of the Delaware River, the Virginia General Assembly made another attempt to quiet the groups opposed to religious taxation. It amended the state's religious tax law to exempt people of all dissenting religions. However, the amendment also mentioned the possibility of a future general assessment for the support of some denominations. It concluded with the statement, "[t]hat nothing in this act contained shall be construed to affect or influence the said question of general assessment, or voluntary contribution, in any respect whatsoever."[86] At the same time, the amendment created a big loophole in the current tax law. Even Episcopalians could avoid the tax simply by declaring they were dissenters. The legislators therefore suspended the collection of religious taxes until they could agree on a better solution.

In 1777, the General Assembly considered several proposals for a general tax whose proceeds would be distributed to all religious denominations, or at least all Christian denominations. Jefferson countered these proposals with a "Bill for Establishing Religious Freedom" which said that "no man shall be compelled to frequent or support any religious worship, place, or ministry whatsoever, ..." (App. N). In 1779, both Jefferson's bill and a tax bill for the support of designated sects of the "Christian Religion" were submitted to the Assembly. Neither passed. The *Virginia Gazette* favored the tax bill and defended its exclusion of "Jews, Mahomedans, Atheists or Deists" on the ground that because the overwhelming majority of people were Christians, they had the right to define what was good for themselves and for all others as well. People of minority religions who opposed the bill, it said, were no different from people who opposed bridge construction projects designed for the common good.[87]

From 1780 through 1782, disruptions caused by the War of Independence prevented Virginians from continuing their debate over the religious taxes. However, after peace was secured in 1783, the General Assembly received several new petitions asking that a religious tax law be enacted. A typical petition from Isle of Wight County argued "that the prosperity and happiness of this country essentially depends on the progress of religion" and "whatever is to conduce equally to the advantage of all should be borne equally by all." Even the Hanover Presbytery, which had previously opposed all religious taxes, submitted a petition in October 1784 saying that because religion was important for the public welfare and for maintaining morality, a general tax plan would be justified, provided it was consistent with the state's Declaration of Rights, did not support religion as a "spiritual system," did not impose articles of faith "not essential to the preservation of society," did not interfere with the internal government of religious societies and did not "render the ministers of religion independent of the will of the people whom they serve."[88] George Washington also expressed his support for a tax to aid all Christian denominations in a 1785 letter to George Mason. He said, however, that people who declare themselves "Jews, Mahometans or otherwise" should "obtain proper relief" from the tax.[89] Apparently Washington did not consider the difficulty of enforcing a tax law with such an exemption.

In December 1784, a select committee of the General Assembly's House of Delegates introduced A Bill Establishing a Provision for Teachers of the Christian Religion (App. M). The bill provided for the collection of a property tax and gave each property owner the ability to designate the Christian society to which his tax was paid. Each Christian society, except Quakers and Mennonites, was allowed to use the tax money only for paying a minister or teacher of the Gospel or for providing a place of divine worship. The Quakers and Mennonites were allowed to use the money in any manner that conformed to their mode of worship. Because the committee that introduced the bill had been appointed to prepare it pursuant to a motion that passed the House by a vote of forty seven to thirty two, the bill seemed assured of being passed. However, after it was introduced, a series of dramatic events followed that was to change the way most Virginians saw the relationship between religion and civil government.

Orchestrating these events was James Madison. In 1783, he had returned to the Virginia House of Delegates after serving in the Continental Congress. Meanwhile, Jefferson had gone to Paris to negotiate commercial treaties and had stayed there to serve as ambassador to France. Madison therefore led the opposition to the Virginia religious tax bill. Although not a lawyer, he proved to be very adept at debating legal issues and planning legislative strategy. The tax bill, he saw, would probably pass by a small margin if were brought to an early vote, so he moved to delay its final reading. In support of his motion, he pointed out that if the bill became law in its current form, judges would have difficulty determining what a "society of Christians" was and what religious doctrines would qualify a society as "Christian." He asked if the Bible were to be the authority on such matters and, if so, which translation would be used. He also asked which books of the Bible would be taken as canonical and which would be discarded as apocryphal, when

Catholics and various Protestant denominations disagreed. Madison was able to convince a small number of the bill's supporters that these issues ought to be resolved before the bill was presented for a vote. On Christmas eve 1784, the House therefore voted to postpone the bill's final reading until November 1785, by a vote of forty-five to thirty-eight.[90]

After the postponement of the tax bill, Madison met with two of his allies, George and Wilson Nicholas, who happened to be sons of Jefferson's adversary Robert Carter Nicholas, to decide how to take advantage of their extra time. The Nicholas brothers suggested that Madison compose a petition detailing his arguments against the bill. They would then circulate copies of the petition throughout the state and encourage local church and civic groups to sign them and send them to the General Assembly. They hoped these petitions would show the General Assembly that a majority of Virginians were opposed to any kind of religious tax.

Madison agreed with the plan and drafted a petition entitled "A Bill of Memorial and Remonstrance against Religious Assessments" (App. M). He began the bill by reciting the opening clause of Article 16 of the Virginia Bill of Rights, which said that religion "can be directed only by reason and conviction and not by force or violence." In the first paragraph, he argued that

> [t]he Religion then of every man must be left to the conviction and conscience of every man; and it is the right of every man to exercise it as these may dictate. This right is in its nature an unalienable right. It is unalienable; because the opinions of men, depending only on the evidence contemplated by their own minds, cannot follow the dictates of other men: It is unalienable also; because what is here a right towards men, is a duty towards the Creator. It is the duty of every man to render to the Creator such homage, and such only, as he believes to be acceptable to him.

In the second paragraph, Madison stated the importance of preserving not only the right of religious freedom but all other rights as well:

[t]he preservation of a free government requires not merely, that the metes and bounds which separate each department of power may be invariably maintained; but more especially, that neither of them be suffered to overleap the great Barrier which defends the rights of the people. The Rulers who are guilty of such an encroachment, exceed the commission from which they derive their authority, and are Tyrants. The People who submit to it are governed by laws made neither by themselves, nor by an authority derived from them, and are slaves.

In the third paragraph, he answered the argument that the Virginia government's support of Christianity was justified because nearly everyone in the state was a Christian:

[w]ho does not see that the same authority which can establish Christianity, in exclusion of all other Religions, may establish with the same ease any particular sect of Christians, in exclusion of all other Sects? That the same authority which can force a citizen to contribute three pence only of this property for the support of any one establishment, may force him to conform to any other establishment in all cases whatsoever?

In the fourth paragraph, he argued that religious freedom applies equally to all believers and non-believers:

[w]hilst we assert for ourselves a freedom to embrace, to profess and to observe the Religion which we believe to be of divine origin, we cannot deny an equal freedom to those whose minds have not yet yielded to the evidence which has convinced us. If this freedom be abused, it is an offence against God, not against man: To God, therefore, not to men, must an account of it be rendered.

In the ninth paragraph, he answered those who argued that the proposed tax was but a minor imposition for the sake of future safety and freedom:

[w]hat a melancholy mark is the bill of sudden degeneracy? Instead of holding forth an asylum to the persecuted, it is itself a signal of persecution. It degrades from the equal rank of Citizens all those whose opinions in Religion do not bend to those of the Legislative authority.

Distant as it may be, in its present form, from the Inquisition it differs from it only in degree. The one is the first step, the other the last step in the career of intolerance.

In the fifteenth and last paragraph, Madison said the free exercise of religion is "a gift of nature" which government cannot take away:

> ... "the equal right of every citizen to the free exercise of his Religion according to the dictates of conscience" is held by the same tenure with all our other rights. If we recur to its origin, it is equally the gift of nature; if we weigh its importance, it cannot be less dear to us; if we consult the Declaration of those rights which pertain to the good people of Virginia, as the "basis and foundation of Government," it is enumerated with equal solemnity, or rather studied emphasis. Either then, we must say, that the will of the Legislature is the only measure of their authority; and that in the plentitude of this authority, they may sweep away all our fundamental rights; or, that they are bound to leave this particular right untouched and sacred: Either we must say, that they may controul the freedom of the press, may abolish the trial by jury, may swallow up the Executive and Judiciary Powers of the State; nay that they may despoil us of our very right of suffrage, and erect themselves into an independent and hereditary assembly: or we must say, that they have no authority to enact into law the Bill under consideration.

Because of more pressing legislative business, Madison did not complete his Memorial and Remonstrance petition until June 20, 1785. George Nicholas then circulated it throughout the central Piedmont region and the Shenandoah Valley, while George Mason took care of the eastern, Tidewater area of the state.

The response was overwhelming. The General Assembly received over one hundred petitions, ninety opposing the tax and only eleven supporting it. Nearly eleven thousand people signed petitions rejecting it. Nearly half of those people signed twenty-eight Baptist petitions that relied on Bible passages for their arguments. The Presbyterians also submitted petitions voicing their opposition. Most petitioners wrote their own objections to the tax. However, thirteen petitions were exact copies of Madison's

Memorial and Remonstrance bill. The petitioners from Dinwiddie County said that because they had seen other petitions opposing the bill, they were now "as decidedly opposed to a General assessment, as they were formerly in favour of it." Petitioners from Amherst County said they had previously supported the tax proposal only as "[o]ne step at least towards Opening a Way for Obtaining a Supply of ministers who might be Instrumental . . . in Stoping the Prevailing Torrent of Iniquity," but they had changed their minds on seeing how the tax bill "has Distressed . . . many . . . in Different Parts of the State who have Advanced Reasons . . . against it of no Small Weight and Importance." The bill, they claimed, has "bothered the minds and consciences of every pious people." They also pointed out the unfairness of taxing non-Christians for the support of Christianity.[91]

When stacks of petitions against the tax bill arrived in the halls of the General Assembly, its sponsors realized that their cause was hopeless. They did not even call for a vote. In December, Madison sealed the victory for the opposition when he resurrected Jefferson's Bill for Establishing Religious Freedom, which guaranteed "[t]hat no man shall be compelled to frequent or support any religious worship, place, or ministry, whatsoever, ..." Some House members tried to replace his long preamble with Article 16 of the Bill of Rights, but their motion failed, thirty-six to sixty-six. The next day, December 17, Jefferson's bill passed the House with only a few minor changes to the preamble, as indicated in Appendix N. The vote was seventy-four to twenty. The Senate also voted in favor of the bill, but its version contained Article 16 of the Bill of Rights instead of Jefferson's preamble. However, the House reinstated Jefferson's language, fifty-six to thirty-five. In joint negotiations led by Madison, the Senate agreed to the House version and the bill became law on January 19, 1786, bearing the title, "The Virginia Statute for Religious Freedom" (App. N).

Virginia was not the first state to guarantee its citizens freedom from taxes for the support of religious worship, places or ministries. That freedom had already existed for a long time in Rhode Island, New Jersey, Pennsylvania and Delaware. However, by proclaiming that people's religion "shall in no way diminish, enlarge, or affect their civil capacities," Virginia became the first state to guarantee that no person would be denied the right to hold public office because of his religious beliefs. Virginia also became the first state to forbid laws against blasphemy and the like, because its Statute for Religious Freedom guaranteed that no man "shall be forced, restrained, molested, or burthened in his body or goods, nor shall otherwise suffer on account of his religious opinions or belief." In addition, Virginia became the first state to recognize these rights as the natural rights of mankind. The Virginia Statute was not part of the state's constitution, and the General Assembly that enacted it admitted that other assemblies might repeal the law. However, the General Assembly more than made up for that deficiency when it proclaimed at the end of the Statute,

> we are free to declare, and do declare, that the rights hereby asserted are of the natural rights of mankind, and that if any act shall be hereafter passed to repeal the present, or to narrow its operation, such act will be an infringement of natural right.

Only ten years before, Virginia, the largest and most populous American state, had determined that it would maintain the Anglican (Episcopal) Church as its established, state-supported church. No other state had insisted on maintaining such a narrow establishment. Now, Virginia had not only thrown off that establishment, but it had set new standards of religious freedom and proclaimed those standards to be natural rights--rights that all states therefore ought to recognize.

D. Religious Freedom According to the First Amendment

When the new federal Constitution was sent to the states for ratification in 1787, the main criticism of the document was that it had no bill of rights. All the states except Rhode Island had adopted constitutions with their own declarations of rights and they all had at least one provision relating to religious freedom. These states had also given their people broader guarantees of religious freedom than their corresponding colonial government had given, as shown in Tables 1 and 2, pages 250-251. Therefore, when citizens of the various states referred to their own bills of rights as examples of what the federal Constitution ought to have, religious freedom was one of the more frequently mentioned rights. A Pennsylvania writer named "Centinel" complained that the new federal Constitution failed to guarantee that "no man ought, or of right be compelled to attend any religious worship, or erect or support any place of worship." That was a reference to Article II of the Pennsylvania Declaration of Rights. "Sydney" and "Timoleon" of New York also spoke of the need for a rights-of-conscience guarantee in the federal Constitution. Timoleon argued that without such a guarantee, the federal government could use its power to impose taxes for the general welfare in order to establish religious uniformity throughout the United States. Two Pennsylvania writers, "An Old Whig" and "Deliberator," made the same point.[92]

Ironically, some critics of the Constitution objected to the one provision that guaranteed a form of religious freedom. Article VI, clause 3 forbade religious tests for officers of the federal government. Most states still imposed such tests, requiring that state office holders profess a Protestant faith in God or at least a Christian faith in God. The Virginia Statute for Religious Freedom was the only state law that forbade religious tests for officeholders.

In the ratification debates in the state conventions, there were many speeches in favor of a religious freedom amendment. In Virginia, Patrick Henry said the amendment should state that "no particular sect or society ought to be favored or established, by law, in preference to others." The Reverend Francis Cummins of South Carolina spoke against "religious establishments; or of states giving preference to any religious denomination." Maryland delegates proposed that "there be no National Religion established by Law." The New Hampshire convention proposed an amendment saying, "Congress shall make no Laws touching Religion, or to infringe the rights of Conscience." The Virginia convention's proposed amendment declared "all men have an equal, natural and unalienable right to the free exercise of religion according to the dictates of conscience, and . . . no particular religious sect or society ought to be favored or established by Law in preference to others." New York's convention proposed an amendment that said, "no Religious Sect or Society ought to be favored or established by Law in preference to any others."[93]

Soon after the new federal government began operating on March 4, 1789, Congressman James Madison of Virginia introduced in the House of Representatives a number of proposed Bill of Rights amendments to the Constitution. In his fourth and fifth amendments related to religious freedom, he said

> [t]hat in article 1st, section 9, between clauses 3 and 4, [are to] be inserted these clauses, to wit:
>
> The civil rights of none shall be abridged on account of religious belief or worship, nor shall any national religion be established, nor shall the full and equal rights of conscience be in any manner, or on any pretext, infringed. . . .
>
> . . . [and] in article 1st, section 10, between clauses 1 and 2, [are to] be inserted this clause, to wit:
>
> No State shall violate the equal rights of conscience.[94]

On July 21, 1789, the House of Representatives appointed a select committee to consider Madison's proposed Bill of Rights amendments as well as those submitted by some of the state conventions that had ratified the Constitution. Madison was one of its eleven members. On July 28, the committee submitted its report to the House, with a modified form of Madison's first religious freedom amendment:

> [4] Art. 1, Sec. 9--Between Par. 2 and 3 insert, "No religion shall be established by law, nor shall the equal rights of conscience be infringed."

The committee report also included Madison's second amendment that forbade the states from violating the equal rights of conscience, but it changed the wording to include other rights as well:

> [12] Art. 1, Sec. 10, between the 1st and 2d Par. insert, "No state shall infringe the equal rights of conscience, nor the freedom of speech, nor of the press, nor of the right of trial by jury in criminal cases."[95]

The House of Representatives then modified the first religious freedom amendment according to the following version proposed by Fisher Ames of Massachusetts:

> Article the Third. Congress shall make no law establishing religion, or to prevent the free exercise thereof, or to infringe the rights of conscience.

This version made it clear that the amendment was a limitation only on the federal Congress and not on the state governments. However, the second religious freedom amendment specifically applied to the states. The House changed that amendment to read,

> Article the Fourteenth. No State shall infringe the right of trial by Jury in criminal cases, nor the equal rights of conscience, nor the freedom of speech or of the press.[96]

The House sent both of these amendments to the Senate on August 24. On September 7, the Senate rejected the second amendment that limited the power of the states, but recorded no comment or reason. On September 9, the Senate approved a modified version of the first religious freedom amendment, which read,

> Congress shall make no law establishing articles of faith or a mode of worship, or prohibiting the free exercise of religion, ...[97]

On September 25, the Senate and House agreed on twelve amendments to be submitted to the states for ratification. The first two clauses of the amendment that became the First Amendment read,

> Congress shall make no law respecting an establishment of religion, or prohibiting the free exercise thereof; . . . .

When these clauses became part of the Constitution, most Americans were satisfied that they had guaranteed themselves the kind of religious freedom they wanted. For over a century and a half, there was very little debate over the meaning of these clauses. In 1947, however, the Supreme Court of the United States ruled, in *Everson v. Board of Education*, 330 U.S. 1 at 15-16 (1947), that

> [t]he "establishment of religion" clause of the First Amendment means at least this: Neither a state nor the Federal Government can set up a church. Neither can pass laws which aid one religion, aid all religions, or prefer one religion over another. Neither can force or influence a person to go to or to remain away from church against his will or force him to profess a belief or disbelief in any religion. No person can be punished for entertaining or professing religious beliefs or disbeliefs, for church attendance or non-attendance. No tax in any amount, large or small, can be levied so support any religious activities or institutions, whatever they may be called, or whatever form they may adopt to teach or practice religion. Neither a state nor the Federal Government can, openly or secretly, participate in the affairs of any religious organizations or groups and *vice versa*. In the words of Jefferson, the clause against establishment of religion by law was intended to erect "a wall of separation between church and State." *Reynolds v. United States, supra* (98 U.S. at 164, 25 L.ed. 249).

The issue in the *Everson* case was whether a New Jersey school board could use public tax dollars to reimburse parents for their cost of transporting their children to various public and private schools, including Catholic schools, or whether such a use of public money was an "establishment of religion" forbidden by the First Amendment. To answer that question, the Supreme Court applied the above interpretation and ruled that the New Jersey board's program did not violate the First Amendment. Although the

Supreme Court thus ruled that the establishment clause had not been violated in the *Everson* case, many people were upset because they thought the Court had announced an interpretation of the establishment clause that was too broad. This interpretation is still being debated because the Supreme Court has relied on it in subsequent cases, in the course of ruling that other government laws and actions did violate the establishment clause of the First Amendment.

One controversial part of the Court's interpretation of the establishment clause was its statement that the clause applied to the states as well as the federal government. Speaking for the Court, Justice Hugo Black cited previous cases in which it had ruled that states must observe other First Amendment freedoms because the Fourteenth Amendment says that no state shall "deprive people of their life, liberty or property, without due process of law." (The reasons why this "life, liberty and property" clause forces the states to observe people's First Amendment rights will be covered in Chapter 9, Section *B.1* and Chapter 10, Section *D.4*.)

Another controversial part of the Court's *Everson* interpretation was the statement that no government "can pass laws which . . . aid all religions . . . ." Black cited the Virginia Statute for Religious Freedom, which declared "[t]hat no man shall be compelled to frequent or support any religious worship, place, or ministry whatsoever, . . ." He then described how this law was the result of an effort led by Thomas Jefferson and James Madison to prevent the enactment of a tax for the support of all Christian religions in Virginia, which at that time accounted for virtually all religious ministries in the state. In an appendix to his opinion, Black included the complete text of Madison's Bill of Memorial and Remonstrance Against Religious Assessments (App. M). Because Madison also played a key role in the adoption of the First Amendment, Black said that the First Amendment, like the Virginia Statute, was intended to prevent government from forcing people to pay taxes in support of not only one religion but all religions.

Critics of the Supreme Court's opinion in the *Everson* case argue that the First Amendment was intended to prevent only the establishment of one national church or the establishment of one religious sect in preference to others. They point out that when a religious freedom amendment was proposed during the Constitutional ratification debates, some state delegates called for a prohibition against a national religion or a guarantee that no particular sect be established in preference to others. They also point out that Madison's first proposal for a religious freedom amendment said that no "national religion [shall] be established." Another point they make is that after the select committee of the House of Representatives deleted the word "national" from Madison's proposal, several members of the House expressed concern that the amendment might threaten the religious tax systems that still existed in all the New England states except Rhode Island. It was in response to that concern, they say, that Madison suggested inserting "national" back in the amendment.[98]

However, these House proceedings do not show that Madison wanted the amendment to forbid only the establishment of a single national church. That intention would have been inconsistent with Madison's statement in his Bill of Memorial and Remonstrance that a general Christian establishment violates religious freedom because "the same authority which can establish Christianity, in exclusion of all other Religions, may establish with the same ease any particular sect of Christians, in exclusion of all other Sects" (App. N, par. 3). The House proceedings show only that Madison suggested adding the word "national" in order to allay the fear of other Congressmen that the amendment might interfere with the establishments of religion by the various state governments. For that reason, no one, including Madison, suggested putting the word "national" back in the amendment after it was changed to apply only to laws of Congress.

Some critics also point to the Senate debates on the amendment, during which a motion was made to change the House's version to read, "Congress shall make no law establishing one Religious Sect or Society in preference to others, or to infringe the rights of conscience." That motion was defeated twice and then a third time in a slightly modified form. Another motion proposed that the amendment read, "Congress shall make no law establishing any particular denomination of religion in preference to another, or prohibiting the free exercise thereof, nor shall the rights of conscience be infringed." That motion was also defeated but it passed after the words "nor shall the rights of conscience be infringed" were deleted. However, the "particular denomination of religion in preference to another" language was left out in the Senate's final proposal, which read, "Congress shall make no law establishing articles of faith or a mode of worship, ..."[99]

These proceedings show that some Senators wanted the amendment to forbid the establishment of a particular religious denomination in preference to others. We might infer that they wanted this language so that Congress could support multiple religions or all religions. However, if we accept that inference, we must also explain why these Senators, after finally succeeding with their motion to insert the "preferential" language in the amendment, allowed the final version to pass without the language and without the record showing a fight to keep it. Either these Senators did not attach the significance to their "preferential" language that the critics of the *Everson* opinion attach to it, or their bid to limit the scope of the First Amendment was rejected by both houses of Congress. The fact remains that, for one reason or another, the amendment that was added to the Constitution does not read "Congress shall make no law establishing one Religious Sect or Society in preference to others." Rather, it reads, "Congress shall make no law respecting an establishment of religion, ..."

The Supreme Court itself is split over the issue of whether government can give non-preferential support to all religion, although a solid majority of the Court continues to hold that such support is not permitted. Chief Justice William Rehnquist is among the minority on the Court who have filed dissenting opinions on this point. In one of those opinions, before he had been promoted to chief justice, he attacked the majority opinion in *Wallace v. Jaffree*, 472 U.S. 38 (1985), which ruled that an Alabama school prayer law was unconstitutional. He argued that all the Alabama law did was to promote prayer and that government ought to be able to promote prayer in public schools. He refused to test the prayer law against the provisions of the Virginia Statute for Religious Freedom because, he said, the First Amendment did not embody the broad ideology of that Statute. He said that the record is clear that Madison

> saw the First Amendment as designed to prohibit the establishment of a national religion, and perhaps prevent discrimination among sects. He did not see it as requiring neutrality on the part of government between religion and irreligion. Thus the Court's opinion in *Everson*--while correct in bracketing Madison and Jefferson together in their exertions in their home State leading to the enactment of the Virginia Statute of Religious Liberty--is totally incorrect in suggesting that Madison carried these views onto the floor of the United States House of Representatives when he proposed language which would ultimately become the Bill of Rights. (472 U.S. at 98-99)

Thus, Justice Rehnquist said that the Supreme Court should read back into the First Amendment the "national" and "preference" language that was considered but rejected by the Congress that passed the amendment. He also suggested that Madison was willing to give Congress more power over religious matters than the Virginia Statute for Religious Freedom had given to the Virginia General Assembly. By taking that position, he put Madison in the role of a man who gave every ounce of his energy to have his fellow Virginians recognize as a natural right the broadest form of religious freedom ever recognized by any government, only to turn around and allow the federal government to trample that same freedom enjoyed by those same Virginians, under the guise of protecting the general welfare of the United States. Rehnquist's opinion shows us that Madison's original fear of putting a bill of rights in the Constitution was well founded. He feared "that a positive declaration of some of the most essential rights could not be obtained in the requisite latitude" and that "enumerating particular exceptions to the grant of power" might "disparage those rights which were not placed in that enumeration."[100]

The evangelist Pat Robertson has attacked the *Everson* opinion with an argument that conflicts with the one advanced by Rehnquist. In his book *America's Dates with Destiny*, published in 1986, Robertson recognizes that "[t]he important truths of conscience determined by Virginia's Declaration of Religious Freedom became a part of this nation's Constitution and the core of the First Amendment in the Bill of Rights." However, in summarizing the effect of this Virginia law, he says, "We [the Baptist ministers and their fundamentalist friends] are and will always be opposed to the establishment of one church *over any other* [emphasis added] by civil authorities."[101] Thus, Robertson and his followers apparently believe that the Virginia Statute's command that "no man shall be compelled to frequent or support any religious worship, place or ministry whatsoever" protects a man only from being compelled to support one form of religious worship, place or ministry in preference to others. In his 1993 book *The Turning Tide*, Robertson criticized two Supreme Court rulings that held that government could not prescribe Bible reading and prayer for ceremonies held at the opening of each public school day.[102] He therefore believes that taxing a person to finance a school that leads children in daily prayer and Bible reading is not the same as compelling him "to support a religious worship, place or ministry," as written in the Virginia Statute and embodied in the First Amendment.

A critical problem with both the Rehnquist and Robertson interpretations of the First Amendment is the difficulty of giving non-preferential government aid to all religions, except by religious tax credits and other programs that allow each citizen to determine the religion that receives his portion of the aid. Any government-controlled aid to religion necessarily prefers some religions over others, because there is no religious belief or practice that is common to all of them. Each is characterized by a different revelation concerning the fundamental nature and origin of the universe. Some hold that the universe is governed by many gods, some by one god and some by no god. Some hold that the creator of the universe is a separate and supreme governor of his creation, while others believe that all spiritual beings are inseparable parts of the physical universe. Some hold that all religions are manifestations of the same truth, or that all religions sprang from Hindu metaphysics,[103] while others hold that their revealed truths are based on unique revelation and that all other religions are false. Some hold that people must be legally bound to contribute to their ministries, but others hold that all religious support must be voluntary. Every religion includes a form of worship, but some worshippers must pray to a god who transcends nature while others must meditate in communion with nature. If a government were to try give non-preferential aid to all these conflicting beliefs and practices, it would be faced with the impossible task of bestowing equal benefits upon all of them. Even if it tried to accomplish that task, it would be hard pressed to show that the tax dollars it had spent served a valid governmental purpose.

The only principles common to all religions are the laws of nature that most members of society strive to obey for the sake of their own happiness and the happiness of other people. These are the same laws of nature that John Locke said protected the life, liberty and property of each person when he was living in a state of nature; he said it was to preserve these laws that men formed civil governments. The Declaration of Independence confirmed that governments are instituted among men to preserve these laws and the rights that flow from them. Blackstone said that the Roman Emperor Justinian had reduced the laws necessary for people to pursue their happiness to three general precepts: that we should live honestly, should hurt nobody, and should render to everyone his due. Therefore, these are the laws that government must enforce for the good order of society. On the other hand, people have come to recognize that each person must also govern his own life according to additional values for the pursuit of his own personal and social happiness. These values include kindness, discipline, hard work, courage, commitment and self-respect. Together, these public laws and individual values form a body of natural law that is found in all societies, all cultures and all religions because, as Blackstone explained, God has "so inseparably interwoven the laws of eternal justice with the happiness of each individual, that the latter cannot be attained but by observing the former; and, if the former be punctually obeyed, it cannot but induce the latter" (BL1, 40). Therefore, although these laws of nature appear in many sources of God's revealed law and are often recognized as coming from God, people do not have to know God's revelation to discover them. They do not even have to believe in God in order to discover them. They can find them by applying the following rational test: "if this or that action tends to man's real happiness, the performance of it is part of the law of nature; if, on the other hand, this or that action is destructive of man's real happiness, the law of nature forbids it" (BL1, 41).

The unique revealed laws of each religion and its revealed modes of worship serve to motivate its believers to obey the laws of nature. Revealed laws also provide the spiritual strength that a person needs to cope with hard times and to meet the challenges of life. Religion therefore consists of both revealed law and natural law. However, natural law without revealed law is not religion; it is simply philosophy.

One might ask why government should be concerned only with the natural-law part of religion. Why should it not be concerned with both the natural law of human interaction, which it must enforce to maintain civil order, and the revealed law that gives people the strength and motivation to obey that natural law? The answer is that neither the spiritual nor the rational mind of a person can be subject to the power of civil government. Only his external relations with other people can be subject to that power. As Jefferson said in the preamble of the Virginia Statute for Religious Freedom,

> almighty God hath created the mind free; that all attempts to influence it by temporal punishments or burthens, or by civil incapacitations, tend only to beget habits of hypocrisy and meanness, and are a departure from the Holy author of our religion, who being the Lord both of body and mind, yet chose not to propagate it by coercions on either, as was his Almighty power to do; . . . . (App. N)

The truth of this statement is revealed in the Christian scriptures, which report that Jesus instructed His disciples,

> Ye know that the princes of the Gentiles exercise dominion over them, and they that are great exercise authority upon them. But it shall not be so among you: but whosoever will be great among you, let him be your minister; And whosoever will be chief among you, let him be your servant: Even as the Son of man came not to be ministered unto, but to minister, and to give his life a ransom for many. (Matt. 20:25-28)

This truth can also be determined by historical observation and reason, as Madison showed when he wrote in his Memorial and Remonstrance,

> [w]hat influence in fact have ecclesiastical establishments had on Civil Society? In some instances they have been seen to erect a spiritual tyranny on the ruins of Civil authority; in many instances they have been seen upholding the thrones of political tyranny; in no instance have they been seen the guardians of the liberties of the people. Rulers who wished to subvert the public liberty may have found an established clergy convenient auxiliaries. A just government, instituted to secure & perpetuate it, needs them not. Such a government will be best supported by protecting every citizen in the enjoyment of his Religion with the same and equal hand which protects his person and his property; by neither invading the equal rights of every Sect, nor suffering any Sect to invade those of another. (App. M, par. 8)

The principles of religious freedom are therefore natural law rights that every just government must observe. Locke explained why that was so in his Letter Concerning Toleration (App. F). Elisha Williams relied on Locke's Letter when he claimed the Connecticut law forbidding people to preach without licenses was a violation of natural law. Madison confirmed in his Bill of Memorial and Remonstrance that religious freedom was "equally a gift of nature" with all the other natural rights asserted by the American people (App. M, par. 15). Then, the Virginia Statute for Religious Freedom concluded, "the rights hereby asserted are of the natural rights of mankind."

Chapter 8   Religious Freedom

In many states, the struggle for religious freedom was long and painful, but by the time the First Amendment was ratified, all Americans were enjoying new laws that guaranteed them greater religious freedom (see Table 2, page 251). There were also movements under way in most states to expand this freedom even more. Delaware removed religious tests for officeholders in 1792, Georgia guaranteed in 1798 that none of its citizens would be forced to pay for the maintenance of any church or ministry, and in 1810 Maryland deleted the clause in its Declaration of Rights that had given the legislature the power to lay a tax for the support of the Christian religion.[104] New Englanders were also campaigning to dismantle their religious tax systems. They were eliminated in Connecticut in 1818, in New Hampshire in 1819 and in Massachusetts in 1833.

In 1790, Pennsylvania adopted a new constitution that reaffirmed its long-standing commitment to religious freedom with the following words:

> That all men have a natural and indefeasible right to worship Almighty God according to the dictates of their own consciences; that no man can of right be compelled to attend, erect or support any place of worship or maintain any ministry, against his consent; that no human authority can, in any case whatever, control or interfere with the rights of conscience, and no preference shall ever be given by law, to any religious establishments or modes of worship.

When Americans moved westward after adopting their federal Constitution and Bill of Rights, many of their new state constitutions proclaimed these same "natural and indefeasible" rights of conscience, using almost exactly the same words as Pennsylvania had used in its 1790 constitution. Following suit were the constitutions of Kentucky in 1792, Tennessee in 1796, Ohio in 1802, Indiana in 1816, Illinois in 1818, Missouri in 1820, Arkansas in 1836, Kansas in 1855 and Nebraska in 1866.[105]

9

The Bill of Rights

> "Liberty finds no refuge in a jurisprudence of doubt."
> --Justices Sandra Day O'Connor, Anthony Kennedy and David Souter, *Planned Parenthood of Southeastern Pennsylvania v. Casey*, 505 U.S. 833, 844 (1992)

A. The Absolute Rights of Life, Liberty and Property

The first ten amendments to the Constitution contain the "Bill of Rights." The Tenth Amendment says that "[t]he powers not delegated to the [federal government] by the Constitution, nor prohibited by it to the states, are reserved to the states respectively or to the people" (App. O). (The effect of that amendment was covered in Chapter 7, Section B.) The other nine amendments deal exclusively with the rights of the people.

James Madison, who wrote most of the provisions of the Bill of Rights, initially opposed this kind of written list because, he said, "there is great reason to fear a positive declaration of some of the most essential rights could not be made in the requisite latitude," and "by enumerating particular exceptions to the grant of power, it would disparage those rights which were not placed in that enumeration." Madison led the campaign for a bill of rights in spite of these concerns because Jefferson convinced him that "[h]alf a loaf is better than no bread. If we cannot secure all our rights, let us secure what we can."[1]

In his proposed bill of rights, Madison tried to alleviate his concerns by suggesting this clause that became the Ninth Amendment:

> The enumeration in the Constitution, of certain rights, shall not be construed to deny or disparage others retained by the people.

Chapter 9 The Bill of Rights 297

He also proposed the following general guarantee that became part of the Fifth Amendment:

> [n]o person shall . . . be deprived of life, liberty, or property, without due process of law; . . . .²

In addition, Madison said in the preamble to his proposed Bill of Rights:

> That all power is originally vested in, and consequently derived from, the people.
> That government is instituted, and ought to be exercised for the benefit of the people; which consists in the enjoyment of life and liberty, with the right of acquiring and using property, and generally of pursuing and obtaining happiness and safety.
> That the people have an indubitable, unalienable and indefeasible right to reform or change their government, whenever it be found adverse or inadequate to the purposes of its institution.

Madison's preamble was similar to the preambles of several bills of rights amendments that had been proposed by the state conventions that ratified the Constitution. Virginia's proposed preamble said

> there are certain natural rights of which men, when they form a social compact cannot deprive or divest their posterity, among which are the enjoyment of life and liberty, with the means of acquiring, possessing and protecting property, and pursuing and obtaining happiness and safety.

The preamble proposed by the New York convention said that

> all power is originally vested in and consequently derived from the People, and that Government is instituted by them for their common Interest, Protection and Security.
> That the enjoyment of Life, Liberty and the pursuit of Happiness are essential rights which every Government ought to respect and preserve.³

All of these preambles, however, were rejected by the House of Representatives for various technical reasons. Congressman Thomas Tucker of South Carolina said a preamble could not change the meaning of the Constitution and it would therefore not be appropriate to add one in an amendment. Tucker's fellow congressman from South Carolina, Thomas Sumter, thought that a preamble might subvert the meaning of other amendments. Roger Sherman of Connecticut said that another preamble would be redundant in view of the preamble of the original Constitution.[4]

Although Madison's preamble was thus rejected, his broad guarantee that "[n]o person shall . . . be deprived of life, liberty, or property, without due process of law" became part of both the original Bill of Rights amendments, which bound powers of the federal government, and the Fourteenth Amendment, which was adopted after the Civil War and bound the powers of the state governments. The meaning of this broad guarantee has become particularly important in cases involving the powers of the state governments over people's life, liberty and property, because the Constitution contains no list of specific rights guarantees binding on the states similar to the Bill of Rights guarantees binding on the federal government.

As shown earlier, the founding fathers understood that the rights of life, liberty and property embodied the fundamental principles upon which all valid government authority is based. These rights were guaranteed to free Englishmen by the Magna Charta in 1215 (App. A), by subsequent charters and then by the Petition of Right in 1628 (App. B). In his *Second Essay Concerning Civil Government* in 1690, John Locke said that all governments derive their just powers from these basic rights and that all governments owe their obedience to them (App. F, par. 135).

William Blackstone explained the details of the rights of life, liberty and property in the first volume of his *Commentaries on the Laws of England*, published in 1765. In 1788, Mercy Otis Warren quoted from these *Commentaries* in her anti-federalist pamphlet, saying "[t]hat the principal aim of society is to protect individuals in the absolute rights which were vested in them by the immediate laws of nature, but which could not be preserved in peace, without the mutual intercourse which is gained by the institution of friendly and social communities."[5] (BL3, 120)

In her pamphlet, Warren complained that the original Constitution did not guarantee these absolute rights. She was especially concerned that it did not guarantee freedom of the press, freedom from general warrants and the right of trial by jury. She said the right of trial by jury was, in the words of Blackstone, "coeval with the first rudiments of civil government."[6]

In Chapter 1 of Book 1, entitled "The Absolute Rights of Individuals," Blackstone said that each person has two sets of rights and duties: first, the absolute rights and duties that he has because he is an individual person; and second, the relative rights and duties that he has because he is a member of a society of people. In a state of nature without government, a person's absolute rights comprise his "natural liberty" to defend his life, liberty and property from invasion by other people. In a civil society, Blackstone said these absolute rights are restricted by a "civil liberty" which

> is no other than natural liberty so far restrained by human laws (and no farther) as is necessary and expedient for the general advantage of the public. Hence we may collect that the law, which restrains a man from doing mischief to his fellow citizens, though it diminishes the natural, increases the civil liberty of mankind: but every wanton and causeless restraint of the will of the subject, whether practiced by a monarch, a nobility, or a popular assembly, is a degree of tyranny. (BL3, 121-122)

A causeless restraint of a person's liberty occurs when government attempts to enforce an absolute duty. "But with regard to absolute *duties*," Blackstone said,

> which man is bound to perform considered as a mere individual, it is not to be expected that any human municipal laws should at all explain or enforce them. For the end and intent of such laws being only to

regulate the behaviour of mankind, as they are members of society, and stand in various relations to each other, they have consequently no business or concern with any but social or relative duties. (BL3, 119-120)

He also said,

[T]hat constitution or frame of government, that system of laws, is alone calculated to maintain civil liberty, which leaves the subject the entire master of his own conduct, except in those points wherein the public good requires some direction or restraint. (BL3, 122)

In his 1772 pamphlet, *The Rights of the Colonists*, Sam Adams claimed that

[t]he natural liberty of men by entering into society is abridged or restrained so far only as is necessary for the great end of society, the best good of the whole. (App. J)

Therefore, when the founding fathers declared in the Fifth Amendment that "[n]o person shall be . . . deprived of life, liberty or property without due process of law," they were saying that government shall not take away a person's life, liberty or property except when it determines, by due process of law, that such action is required for the good of society. This determination is made when government legislatures enact laws that are within their law-making powers, giving due respect to people's absolute rights of life, liberty and property. It is also made when courts enforce these laws according to procedures that are recognized as necessary for the protection of people's life, liberty and property. The rights of the people to their life, liberty and property are therefore of paramount importance. They are the foundation of the social contract, by which people give up some of their natural law rights so that government can provide for the good of society and enforce the relative rights and duties that prevent people from harming one another. The people do not give government the power to make "wanton or causeless" restraints, such as those relating to their absolute duties, which have nothing to do with their being members of society but only with their being individual people.

After describing the basic premise of government authority, Blackstone said,

> Thus much for the *declaration* of our rights and liberties. The rights themselves thus defined by these several statutes, consist in a number of private immunities; which will appear, from what has been premised, to be indeed no other, than either that *residuum* of natural liberty, which is not required by the laws of society to be sacrificed to public convenience; or else those civil privileges, which society hath engaged to provide, in lieu of the natural liberties so given up by individuals. (BL3, 125)

He then explained that these immunities may be reduced to three principle articles, namely "the right of personal security, the right of personal liberty; and the right of private property" (BL3, 125), as well as "certain other auxiliary subordinate rights of the subject which serve principally as barriers to protect and maintain inviolate the three great and primary rights, of personal security, personal liberty, and private property" (BL3, 136). He also laid out the rules of due process that government must follow in order to judge a person guilty of violating the law of the land, or that body of relative duties it has imposed on all people for the good of society and for preserving everyone's life, liberty and property. If the government does not follow these rules of due process, then it cannot inflict a punishment that deprives anyone of his personal security, his personal liberty or his private property.

A.1. The Right of Personal Security

The general right of personal security is often abbreviated as "the right of life." Blackstone explained that this right is much broader than the right of life; it "consists in a person's legal and uninterrupted enjoyment of his life, his limbs, his body, his health, and his reputation" (BL3, 125). He said that even when government passes laws for the public good that restrict these rights, the government's power is limited in this regard. For instance, government cannot impose sentences of death, maiming or torturing, "unless upon the highest necessity," such as when a person is adjudged guilty of the crime of murder (BL3, 129). Before the War of Independence, the issue of whether the death penalty was too severe arose when the British government threatened to impose that sentence on the colonists who had destroyed the British ship *Gaspée*. To insure that the death penalty is administered only "upon the highest necessity" and that other punishments are administered only when they fit the crime committed, the Eighth Amendment to the U. S. Constitution provides that "cruel and unusual punishments" shall not be inflicted. The Supreme Court of the United States ruled in *Wilkerson v. Utah*, 99 U.S. 130 (Oct. term, 1878) and *Gregg v. Georgia*, 428 U.S. 153 (1976) that the Eighth Amendment prevents a person from being maimed or tortured, no matter what crime he has committed. It does not, however, prevent government from imposing the death penalty in those extreme cases when it is warranted. Blackstone said that the English statutes and common law never inflicted any punishment extending to life or limb "unless upon the highest necessity" and that the great charters of England provide that "no man shall be forejudged of life or limb" or "put to death, without being brought to answer by due process of law" (BL3, 129-130).

Blackstone also said that "the life and limbs of a man are of such high value, in the estimation of the law of England, that it pardons even homicide" if committed in self defense, or in order to preserve them (BL3, 126). However, there is no specific guarantee of the right of self defense in the United States Constitution. Therefore, if a court were to fail to recognize this right, a criminal defendant would have to assert that his general right of life had been violated.

Blackstone also mentioned the following civil privilege encompassed by the right of personal security:

> [t]he law not only regards life and member, and protects every man in the enjoyment of them, but also furnishes him with everything necessary for their support. For there is no man so indigent or wretched, but

he may demand a supply sufficient for all the necessities of life, from the more opulent part of the community. (BL3, 127)

There is no specific guarantee of this right in the United States Constitution, and the U. S. Supreme Court has never ruled that a person has a constitutional right to these basic necessities of life. However, the Court has ruled that government can fix the maximum working hours and minimum wages of laborers as part of its function of regulating the relative rights and duties of people for the protection of their life and health [*Bunting v. Oregon*, 243 U.S. 426 (1917) regarding maximum working hours, and *West Coast Hotel Co. v. Parrish*, 300 U.S. 379 (1937) regarding minimum wages].

Perhaps the Supreme Court should have considered whether a child's right to a quality education is one of the basic necessities of life when it decided the case of *San Antonio Independent School District v. Rodriguez*, 411 U.S. 1 (1973). The Court ruled that education was not a fundamental right in respect of a person's equal protection under the Fourteenth Amendment.[7] However, it did not consider whether a substandard education might violate a person's rights of life, liberty and property. In his *Notes on the State of Virginia*, Jefferson said, "An amendment of our [state] constitution must here come to the aid of public education." He suggested that every county be laid out in school districts five or six miles square, each having a school to which every person was entitled to send his children for three years free of charge.[8] In today's technical world, a person needs much more formal education than he did in Jefferson's day. On the other hand, the Bill of Rights of the U.S. Constitution does not prescribe any positive duties for government, such as the duty of providing a public education that Jefferson suggested for the Virginia Constitution. The U. S. Constitution says only what the federal and state governments cannot do: deprive any person of his life, liberty or property (App. O, Amendments 5 and 14). To guarantee the positive right to the necessities of life, including education, the Constitution would have to be amended to include both that right and a statement of exactly what those necessities are.

A.2. The Right of Liberty

Blackstone said that the general right of liberty "consists in the power of loco-motion, of changing situation, or removing one's person to whatsoever place one's own inclination may direct; without imprisonment or restraint, unless by due course of law" (BL3, 130). He took the words "by due course of law" from the Magna Charta's proclamation of the rights of life, liberty and property. These words mean that government can take away a person's liberty only when he is accused of a crime or found guilty of a crime by procedures that are fundamental to a just society. Blackstone said these procedures are the following:

(1) before being detained in prison, the accused person must be informed of the nature of the charge so that he can respond to it (BL3, 131);

(2) if he believes that he is being improperly detained, the accused may obtain a writ of *habeas corpus*, which requires that the detaining authorities bring him before a judge having jurisdiction over the matter and prove to the judge that they have cause for holding him in prison, but this right may be suspended by Parliament for limited periods of time when national security is threatened (BL3, 131, 132);

(3) to make an imprisonment lawful, "it must either be by process from the courts of judicature, or by warrant from some legal officer, having authority to commit to prison; which warrant must be in writing, under the hand and seal of the magistrate, and express the causes of the commitment; in order to be examined into (if necessary) upon a *habeas corpus*" (BL3, 132-133);

(4) except when the accused is charged with murder or another very serious crime, he must be released while awaiting trial provided he posts bail, which cannot be excessive (BL3, 131);

(5) the accused has the right to be tried by a jury of his equals (BL3, 131) and, according to Blackstone's chapter on jury trials, these trials must be open to the public and all felons should be tried soon after their arraignment;[9]

(6) no person living in England can be taken to a foreign land against his will and, therefore, an Englishman accused of a crime must be tried in England (BL3, 133-134);

(7) all criminal proceedings against an accused must be conducted in public, because "confinement of the person, by secretly hurrying him to gaol, where his sufferings are unknown or forgotten; is a less public, a less striking, and therefore a more dangerous engine of arbitrary government" (BL3, 132).

Blackstone's third requirement of a proper warrant has always been important to Americans. Before the War of Independence, the British government arrested the English political leader John Wilkes pursuant to a general warrant that did not specify who was to be arrested. The American colonists sympathized with Wilkes because they had to endure searches and seizures of their property under general warrants. The Fourth Amendment to the U.S. Constitution now requires that all warrants particularly describe the places to be searched and the persons or things to be seized.

The American colonists were particularly jealous of Blackstone's fifth and sixth requirements, namely the right of trial by jury and the right to be tried in one's own homeland, if that is where the alleged crime was committed. One of their complaints against the Stamp Act and the Townshend Acts was that these laws deprive people of their right to jury trials. After the ship *Gaspée* was burned, the colonists complained when British officials announced that persons accused of the crime would be taken to England for non-jury trials. They also protested the Administration of Justice Act that was passed after the Boston Tea Party because that law required that all colonists accused of capital crimes be taken across the sea and tried in England. The Sixth Amendment to the U. S. Constitution now guarantees that "[i]n all criminal prosecutions, the accused shall enjoy the right to a . . . trial, by an impartial jury of the State and district wherein the crime shall have been committed, ..."

The U. S. Constitution also guarantees the other four due process requirements that Blackstone said were essential to "personal liberty." The Sixth Amendment says that a person accused of a crime has the right "to be informed of the nature and cause of the accusation; . . . ." Article I, Section 9[2] says, "The Privilege of the Writ of Habeas Corpus shall not be suspended, unless when in Cases of Rebellion or Invasion the public Safety may require it." The Eighth Amendment says, "Excessive bail shall not be required, ..." Finally, the Sixth Amendment says, "In all criminal prosecutions, the accused shall enjoy the right to a . . . public trial, ..."

The Bill of Rights also guarantees several procedural rights that Blackstone did not list among the rights of personal liberty. One of these is the Fifth Amendment guarantee that "[n]o person shall be held to answer for a capital, or otherwise infamous crime, unless on presentment or indictment of a Grand Jury, except in cases arising in the land or naval forces, or in the Militia, when in actual service in time of War or public danger; . . . ." However, Blackstone covered this right in his chapter, "Of the Several Modes of Prosecution." He said that the only way of charging a person with a crime, other than by a hearing and indictment by grand jury, was by an accusation without a hearing (an "information") filed by the king's attorney general, his coroner or the master of the crown-office in the court of king's bench. He also said ". . . these informations (of every kind) are confined by the constitutional law to mere misdemesnors only: for, wherever any capital offence is charged, the same law requires that the accusation be warranted by the oath of twelve men [of a grand jury], before the party shall be put to answer it."[10]

The Fifth Amendment also says that no person shall "be subject for the same offense to be twice put in jeopardy of life or limb; . . . ." Blackstone said in his chapter, "Of Courts of a Criminal Jurisdiction," "[I]t is contrary to the genius and spirit of the law of England, to suffer any man to be tried twice for the same offence in a criminal way, especially if acquitted upon the first trial; . . . ." In his chapter, "Of Plea, and Issue," he said that a person accused of a crime could defend an indictment on the ground that he had already been tried and acquitted. His plea of *auterfoits acquit* was "grounded on the universal maxim of the common law of England, that no man is to be brought into jeopardy of his life, more than once, for the same offence." Blackstone also said in his chapter "Of Trial, and Conviction" "[i]f the jury therefore find the prisoner not guilty, he is then for ever quit and discharged of the accusation; except he be appealed of felony within the time limited by law."[11]

Another Fifth Amendment guarantee is that no person "shall be compelled in any criminal case to be a witness against himself." After the English Civil War in 1649, the Levellers petitioned unsuccessfully to have Cromwell's government remove all penalties for a person refusing to testify against himself (App. D, par. XVI). Their purpose was to end the inquisitions that had been used to wring confessions from people accused of preaching heresy or rebellion. Such inquisitions were common not only during the English Civil War but during the entire European Reformation and Counter-Reformation. The American colonists who had fled from these inquisitions believed very strongly that no person should be convicted of a crime by forcing him to admit his guilt. By the time of the War of Independence, the British had also eliminated forced confessions and had adopted the rule, stated by Blackstone, that "no man is to be examined to prove his own infamy."[12]

The Sixth Amendment says, "In all criminal prosecutions, the accused shall enjoy the right to a speedy . . . trial, ..." In "Of Trial, and Conviction," Blackstone said, "it is there usual to try all felons immediately, or soon after their arraignment."[13] Chapter 40 of the Magna Charta was more emphatic. It said, "To none will we sell, to none will we deny, to none will we delay right or justice" (App. A).

The Sixth Amendment guarantees that in all criminal prosecutions, the accused shall have the right "to be confronted with the witnesses against him; to have compulsory process for obtaining witnesses in his favor, and to have the Assistance of Counsel for his defence." Blackstone said in "Of Trial, and Conviction" that for a long time in England, "counsel was not allowed to any prisoner accused of a capital crime, so neither should he be suffered to exculpate himself by the testimony of any witness." This practice did not end in respect of witnesses until 1702, when Parliament passed a law declaring that in all cases of treason and felony, the accused was entitled to have witnesses testify for him under oath, and in like manner the witnesses against the accused were to testify under oath.[14] Persons accused of capital crimes were still not allowed to be represented by counsel when Blackstone published the fourth volume of *Commentaries* in 1769. That caused Blackstone to make one of his few criticisms concerning the state of English law at that time. He said that the rule "seems to be not at all of a piece with the rest of the humane treatment of prisoners by the English law. For upon what face of reason can that assistance be denied to save the life of a man, which yet is allowed him in prosecutions for every petty trespass?"[15] When the American people added the Sixth Amendment to the Constitution, they wanted to make sure that their new federal government did not continue this injustice that had existed for so long in the British legal system.

These are the procedural rules that the U. S. Constitution says must be followed whenever a person is accused of a crime. Sometimes they pose difficulties for police and prosecutors who are trying to protect the public. When they cannot overcome these difficulties, it is possible that a guilty person will be set free. Nevertheless, the rules of due process must be followed because, as Blackstone explained in connection with one of the rules of criminal evidence,

> [a]ll presumptive [circumstantial] evidence of felony should be admitted cautiously: for the law holds, that it is better that ten guilty persons escape, than that one innocent suffer.[16]

As noted earlier, the Puritan leader Increase Mather gave the same reason when he warned the Massachusetts Bay ministers that evidence was being improperly admitted at the Salem witchcraft trials.[17]

A.3. The Right of Property

Blackstone said that the general right of property, inherent in every Englishman, "consists in the free use, enjoyment, and disposal of all his acquisitions, without any control or diminution, save only by the laws of the land" (BL3, 134). He cited the Magna Charta and other English charters that said before a person could have his property taken for violating the law of the land, he must be "duly brought to answer, and be forejudged by course of law." The words "course of law" refer to the same "due course of law" requirements that he listed under the right of liberty.

Blackstone said that the right of property was also expressed in a statute of Edward III, which provided that "no man's lands or goods shall be seized into the king's hands, against the great charter, and the law of the land" (BL3, 134). In the 1765 case of *Entick v. Carrington and Three Other King's Messengers*,[18] the House of Lords ruled that English government officials had wrongfully seized a person's goods when they used general warrants to enter his house and break open his desks and boxes of papers. The warrants were defective because they did not describe the place to be searched or the goods to be seized. Three years before, James Otis had argued to the Massachusetts Superior Court that the same kind of warrants violated the English Constitution. The Fourth Amendment to the U. S. Constitution now guarantees that "no warrants shall issue, but upon probable cause, supported by Oath or affirmation, and particularly describing the place to be searched."

In certain situations the government must take away people's property for the public good, such as when it builds a road, a public building or a utility line. Blackstone said that when this happens, the people have the right to be compensated for the property they have lost (BL3, 135). In these situations, the property owner is seldom compensated fully, because there is no way of measuring accurately the inconvenience that people suffer when they must vacate their homes. The U. S. Constitution guarantees this right in the last clause of the Fifth Amendment, which says that private property shall not "be taken for public use, without just compensation."

Another basic right of property relates to the power of government to take away a person's property by taxing him. Blackstone said, "no subject of England can be constrained to pay any aids or taxes, even for the defence of the realm or the support of government, but such as are imposed by his own consent, or that of his representatives in parliament" (BL3, 135). A major complaint by the American colonists was that they were being taxed by the laws of the English Parliament, in which they had no elected representatives. The drafters of the U.S. Constitution appear to have had this right in mind when they provided in Article I, Section 2[3] that "Representatives and direct Taxes shall be apportioned among the several States which may be included within the Union, according to their respective Numbers, ..." However, Article I, Section 8[1] gave Congress the power to lay and collect other kinds of taxes, including "Duties, Imposts and Excises" that did not have to be apportioned among the states in the same manner as the Representatives in Congress. In the case of *Loughborough v. Blake*, 18 U.S. (5 Wheaton) 317 (1820), the Supreme Court ruled that Congress had the power to impose a direct tax on the people of the District of Columbia, who had no representation in Congress. Chief Justice John Marshall distinguished that situation from the colonial protests of taxation without representation, saying

> [t]he difference between requiring a continent, with an immense population, to submit to be taxed by a government having no common interest with it, separated from it by a vast ocean, restrained by no principle of apportionment, and associated with it by no common feelings; and permitting the representatives of the American people, under the restrictions of our constitution, to tax a part of the society, which is either in a state of infancy advancing to manhood, looking forward to complete equality so soon as that state of manhood shall be attained, as is the case with the territories; or which has voluntarily relinquished the right of representation, and has adopted the whole body of Congress for its legitimate government, as is the case with the district, is too obvious not to present itself to the minds of all. (Ibid., 324)

In 1913, the Sixteenth Amendment to the Constitution further restricted the meaning of Article I, Section 2[3] by giving Congress the power to levy income taxes without apportionment among the states. The Constitution therefore has no guarantee that the people of the District of Columbia and the United States territories cannot be taxed by the federal government, even though they have no representation in Congress. At the present time, the federal tax laws, including the income tax laws, do not generally extend to people who are living and working in the United States territories. Therefore, except for those who voluntarily choose to live in the District of Columbia, very few Americans have reason to echo the colonial complaint of "taxation without representation."

One property right that Blackstone did not list among the absolute rights of Englishmen, but which the Petition of Right declared in 1628, is that "[n]o soldier shall be quartered on the subject without his consent." Blackstone mentioned this right in his chapter, "Of the Civil State."[19] During the colonial period, this right was infringed by two quartering laws, one passed by Parliament in 1765 and one that was part of the Coercive Acts of 1774. Under the 1765 act, two British regiments were quartered in New York City and four British regiments were quartered in Boston. Under the 1774 act, four thousand British soldiers were quartered in Boston. The Third Amendment of the U.S. Constitution now guarantees that "[n]o Soldier shall, in time of peace be quartered in any house without the consent of the Owner, nor in time of war, but in a manner to be prescribed by law."

Blackstone mentioned another property right in his chapter, "Of Judgment and its Consequences," namely that excessive fines ought not to be imposed.[20] This right was first guaranteed in the English Declaration of Rights (App. E); the Eighth Amendment of the U.S. Constitution guarantees the same right.

A.4. Auxiliary Rights for Protection of Life, Liberty and Property

After explaining the principal rights of personal security, personal liberty and private property, Blackstone listed five auxiliary rights that are necessary to prevent violations of these principal rights. Two of these rights relate to the composition and powers of Parliament and the limitations of the king's powers. The U.S. Constitution secures similar rights in Articles I and II, which specify the composition and powers of the legislative and executive branches and the checks and balances between the two. (The differences and similarities between these aspects of American and British government were discussed in Chapter 7, Section C).

Blackstone said the third auxiliary right "is that of applying to the courts of justice for redress of injuries" (BL3, 137-138). This right, including the right of having those civil claims tried by a jury, is guaranteed by the Seventh Amendment to the U.S. Constitution. All English civil cases, he said, were to be tried by jury, except for six very limited species of trials, including trials to determine the existence of a public record and trials to determine the age of a person or whether he is dead or alive.[21]

The Seventh Amendment also provides that no fact tried by a jury "shall be otherwise re-examined in any Court of the United States, than according to the rules of the common law." When that amendment was adopted, those rules of common law were the English rules explained in Blackstone's *Commentaries*. For a hundred years after that, Blackstone's *Commentaries* continued to be the leading authority on the common law that was applied in most of the states.

The fourth auxiliary right described by Blackstone is that of "petitioning the king, or either house of parliament, for the redress of grievances" (BL3, 138-139). The American colonists tried many times to exercise this right. In 1768, the Massachusetts House of Representatives sent King George a petition complaining that the Townshend Acts violated their rights. The British government responded by threatening to dissolve the Massachusetts House and sending four British regiments to occupy Boston. In 1775, the Continental Congress sent an Olive Branch Petition to the king, asking him to interpose his authority so that both sides could reach a "happy and permanent reconciliation." Parliament punished the colonists for sending that petition by passing a law that forbade "all manner of trade and commerce" between the colonies and the rest of the empire. The law also declared that all colonial ships were lawful prize and that their crews were subject to impressment in the British navy.

The right to petition the king or Parliament existed in England at least as early as 1640 (BL3, 139) and probably much earlier. The king or Parliament had no duty to act on the petition, but the right at least gave the petitioner an opportunity to publicize his grievance. Before 1694, there was no general right of free press in England, because all publishers had to obtain licenses in order to publish their books (BL6, footnote [a]). Public speech was also regulated, such as by the statute of 1 Mary st.2. c.12, which allowed the police to disperse public gatherings formed "with intention to offer violence to the privy council, or to change the laws of the kingdom, or for certain other specific purposes."[22] Thus, the right to petition the king, guaranteed in the English Declaration of Rights in 1689, was the first recognition by an English or British government of a limited right of free speech and press.

The American colonists had a much broader view of the right of free speech and press than their British governors. They asserted the right to publicize their grievances against the British government in public speeches as well as newspapers and pamphlets, without any restraint whatsoever. Therefore, when they formed their new nation, they provided in the First Amendment to the U.S. Constitution that "Congress shall make no law . . . abridging the freedom of speech, or of the press; or the right of the people peaceably to assemble, and to petition the government for the redress of grievances."

Blackstone's fifth and last auxiliary right is that of people "having arms for their defence, suitable to their condition and degree, and such as are allowed by law." He said this is "of the natural right of resistance and self preservation, when the sanctions of society and laws are found insufficient to restrain the violence of oppression" (BL3, 139). The Massachusetts Minutemen exercised this right when the British blockaded Boston, threatening the lives of the people of that city. Accordingly, the Second Amendment to the U.S. Constitution says "[a] well regulated Militia, being necessary for the security of a free state, the right of the people to keep and bear Arms, shall not be infringed." The Supreme Court has ruled that this amendment does not give individual people the right to bear arms. It gives only the state governments the right to maintain their state militias (*U. S. v. Cruikshank*, 92 U.S. 542 [Oct. term, 1875]; *U. S. v. Miller*, 307 U.S. 174 [1939]).

The right to bear arms guaranteed by the Second Amendment is narrower than the right described by Blackstone, because he said it was "a natural right of resistance and self preservation" when government protection was lacking. Therefore, if the Supreme Court were to accept Blackstone's definition of this right and recognize it as one of the rights of life, liberty and property guaranteed by the Fifth and Fourteenth Amendments, those amendments would give people the private right to have arms to protect themselves when their government fails to protect them. Those conditions might exist in an urban area where crime is rampant or in a remote area where the police are far away. They might also exist when the government threatens the security of people, such as when the British blockaded Boston. The Supreme Court has not only refused to apply Blackstone's definition of the right to bear arms, but it has held that this Second Amendment guarantee is binding only on the federal government. It is not one of the basic rights protected from state invasion by the life, liberty and property clause of the Fourteenth Amendment (*Presser v. Illinois*, 116 U.S. 252 [1886]).

Blackstone's broader right of having firearms would not preclude the state or federal government from regulating their ownership and use. A primary purpose of government is to insure the safety of all people. Therefore, it must be able to require people to register their firearms, to prevent children and convicted felons from having them, to require owners to be trained in their use and safety and to prevent people from having arms of greater firepower than necessary to protect their families and property. Some of these regulations may be inconvenient to gun owners, but they are justified even if they cause only a slight deterrent to violent crime.

The right to bear arms has never been recognized as a right to own weapons for recreational purposes, such as hunting or gun collecting. The right to own and use such weapons is one of many rights within the general right of owning and using property. Like these property rights, the right to bear arms must always be subject to laws that protect the health and safety of the general public.

The right to bear arms does not give any person or group of people the right to set up a government that is independent of the established federal and state governments. In recent years, groups of people in the United States have organized their own militia units and some have set up independent governments. They claim they have the same right as the American colonists to do this because their basic rights have been violated. However, there is one important difference. These people are trying to form governments that co-exist with the established state and federal governments, with each person having the option of giving allegiance to the government of his choice. That is not possible. If two independent governments were to try to govern the same territory, the result would be chaos. Because American colonists knew this, they tried to settle their disputes with the British government by petitions and negotiations. When they finally declared their independence, they knew they would have fight a war to make that independence a reality. The militia units that are now defying the orders of state and federal judges should ask themselves whether they are prepared to fight the same kind of war. If they are, they should declare that they are the rightful governors of this nation and that everyone must pay taxes to them and obey their laws. Every person in the United States would then have to choose whether to fight on the side of this new government or on the side of the established government, as they had to do during the War of Independence and the Civil War. If the militia units are not prepared to fight such a war, they should abandon their spurious governments and take their complaints to the established courts and government agencies.

A.5. Summary

Most of the specific rights guaranteed in the Bill of Rights of the U.S. Constitution are described by Blackstone in his chapter "Of the Absolute Rights of Individuals." These rights include procedural rights of a person accused of a crime, including the Sixth Amendment rights to be informed of the nature of the charge against him and the right to a public jury trial in the place where the crime was committed, the Fourth Amendment right of a person to a warrant before being committed to prison or having his goods seized and the Eighth Amendment the right to reasonable bail. They also include the Fifth Amendment right to just compensation for property taken for public use, the First Amendment right to petition the government for redress of grievances and the Second Amendment right to keep and bear arms. Blackstone supports the Eighth Amendment guarantee against cruel and unusual punishment in his statement that the death penalty can be imposed only upon "the highest necessity." He also showed how these specific rights relate to the general rights of life, liberty and property that are guaranteed by the Fifth and Fourteenth Amendments.

Blackstone said in other parts of his *Commentaries* that the common law of England included the Third Amendment right against quartering of soldiers, the Fifth Amendment rights of an accused to a grand jury indictment, to be free of his life being put twice in jeopardy for the same offense and to refuse to testify against himself, the Sixth Amendment rights of an accused to a speedy trial and to compel the appearances of witnesses, both those in his favor and those who had spoken against him, the Eight Amendment right against excessive fines and, with some exceptions, the Seventh Amendment right to jury trials in civil cases. He also criticized the failure of the English common law to allow the accused to be represented by counsel in all cases, which is guaranteed by the Sixth Amendment.

On the other hand, Blackstone had a very limited view of the First Amendment freedoms of religion, speech, press and assembly, even though they appear to fall within the "*residuum* of natural liberty that he said "is not required by the laws of society to be sacrificed to public convenience" (BL3, 125). He also said the laws of society can have "no business or concern with any but social or relative duties." "[W]ith regard to absolute duties, which man is bound to perform as a mere individual," he said "it is not to be expected that any human municipal laws should at all explain or enforce them" (BL3, 119-120). However, Blackstone argued that the English limits on the freedoms of religion, speech, press and assembly were justified because of certain relative, social duties that people had toward one another. The American people obviously did not agree with these arguments. The following sections of this chapter will explain this disagreement.

B. The Absolute Duties of People

B.1. Religious Duties

Blackstone said in Book IV, Chapter 2 of his *Commentaries*, entitled, "Of Offences against God and Religion" that

> [i]t was observed, in the beginning of this book, that crimes and misdemesnors are a breach and violation of the public rights and duties, owing to the whole community, considered as a community, in it's aggregate capacity. And in the very entrance of these commentaries it was shewn, that human laws can have no concern with any but social and relative duties; being intended only to regulate the conduct of man, considered under various relations, as a member of civil society. All crimes ought therefore to be estimated merely according to the mischiefs which they produce in civil society: and, of consequence, private vices, or the breach of mere absolute duties, which man is bound to perform considered only as an individual, are not, cannot be, the object of any municipal law; any farther than as by their evil example, or other pernicious effects, they may prejudice the community, and thereby become a species of public crimes. (BL5, 41)

He then explained why, in spite of this limit on its power, the English government could enforce laws made for the protection of the Christian religion and the established Church of England. These laws punished the crimes of (1) apostasy, which he said was a denial of either a belief in God or a belief in the Christian religion by a person who had once professed the "true religion"; (2) heresy, defined as a denial of an essential tenet of Christianity, such as the doctrine of the trinity; (3) the act of reviling the ordinances, sacraments and prayer book of the Church of England; (4) failure to attend the Church of England or a licensed Protestant church; and (5) blasphemy, defined as a denial of the being or providence of God, "contumelious reproaches" of Jesus Christ, "profane scoffing" at the holy scripture, or "exposing it to contempt or ridicule" (BL5, 59). Blackstone said that these offenses against God and religion are not private vices or breaches of absolute duties, because they openly transgress "the precepts of religion, either natural or revealed; and mediately, by their bad example and consequence, the law of society also; . . ." (BL5, 43). He also justified the laws punishing offenses against God and religion because they were necessary for the protection of the established Church of England:

> . . . undoubtedly all persecution and oppression of weak consciences, or the score of religious persuasions, are highly unjustifiable upon every principle of natural reason, civil liberty, or sound religion. But care must be taken not to carry this indulgence into such extremes, as may endanger the national church: there is always a difference to be made between toleration and establishment. (BL5, 51)

One important English crime against God and religion, essential to the protection of the established Church of England, was that of failing to pay tithes and other dues owed to that church. Blackstone covered this crime in Chapter 3, Book II, entitled "Of Real Property; and, first, of Corporeal Hereditaments." One hereditament was the ancient custom of paying a tenth of profits from the sale of all farm products, as well as a tenth of the profits from all manual occupations, trades and fisheries, to the local parish minister. The most current law that Blackstone could cite as authority for collecting these tithes was an edict by the Saxon king Athelstan in the year 930 AD.[23] Yet the ecclesiastical courts of England were still enforcing this law when Blackstone published Book II of his *Commentaries* in 1766. He gave the following justification for the law:

> . . . besides the positive precepts of the new testament, natural reason will tell us, that an order of men, who are separated from the world,

and excluded from other lucrative professions, for the sake of the rest of mankind, have a right to be furnished with the necessaries, conveniences, and moderate enjoyments of life, at their expense, for whose benefit they forego the usual means of providing them.[24]

When the American states declared their independence, many had laws similar to these English laws that were designed for the protection of their established churches. However, they were not as oppressive as the English laws, mainly because the Americans held a more liberal view of what was needed to uphold a religious establishment. As described in Chapter 8, Section B, Massachusetts, New Hampshire and New York allowed each town to select its own tax-supported Protestant church and members of other Protestant churches often received tax exemptions. Most American states further liberalized their religious establishment laws shortly after the Declaration of Independence. In spite of John Adams' 1774 prediction in that "we might as well expect a change in the solar system, as to expect [the people of Massachusetts] would give up their establishment,"[25] they did change their religious tax law in 1780 to allow each taxpayer to designate any local Protestant church as a recipient of his tax money. That touched off a debate between the Congregationalists and the Baptists on the question of whether that eliminated the state's religious establishment. In 1786, Chief Justice Cushing skirted the issue when he said that certain sects were not part of "the regular establishment, if it be so termed."[26] In 1778, the new South Carolina consitution said, "The Christian Protestant religion shall be deemed, and is hereby constituted and declared to be, the established religion of this state."[27]

We may wonder how the Americans justified their establishment laws. The New Hampshire constitution of 1784 prefaced its religious tax provision with the statement that "morality and piety, rightly grounded on evangelical principles, will give the best and greatest security to government, and will lay in the hearts of men the strongest obligations of due subjection."[28] The 1780 Massachusetts constitution simply said that it was "the right as well as the duty of all men in society, publicly and at stated seasons, to worship the Supreme Being, the great Creator and Preserver of the universe."[29]

However, in spite of these arguments, there was a strong movement under way to eliminate all forms of religious establishment in the United States. Rhode Island, New Jersey, Pennsylvania and Delaware had never imposed any religious taxes. In Virginia, the 1785 Memorial and Remonstrance against Religious Assessments declared that "the same authority which can establish Christianity, in exclusion of all other Religions, may establish with the same ease any particular sect of Christians, in exclusion of all other sects" (App. M, par. 3). Based on that reasoning, the Virginia Assembly passed a Statute for Religious Freedom, guaranteeing "[t]hat no man shall be compelled to frequent or support any religious worship, place, or ministry, whatsoever, . . ." and declaring that this was among "the natural rights of mankind" (App. N) In 1790, Pennsylvania declared in its new constitution "[t]hat all men have a natural and indefeasible right to worship God according to the dictates of their own consciences; that no man can be compelled to attend, erect or support any place of worship or maintain any ministry, against his consent: . . . ."[30] Then in 1791, all the states declared in the U. S. Constitution's Bill of Rights that Congress had no power to make a law "respecting an establishment of religion, or prohibiting the free exercise thereof. . . . ." Between 1791 and 1866, many new states joining the union made the same declarations in their bills of rights that Pennsylvania had made in its 1790 constitution. After 1800, only New Hampshire, Massachusetts, and Connecticut retained their previous religious establishments and all these were abolished by 1833.

The American people thus rejected the English view that "there is always a difference to be made between toleration and establishment" (BL5, 51). They apparently did not agree with the arguments that had been advanced for this distinction: that government has the power to prevent people from setting bad examples for one another in matters of religious belief (BL3, 43) or that the revelations of a particular religion will give the greatest security to government. The First Amendment guarantee against religious establishment is based instead on the proposition that a person's religious duties, or the duties he owes to himself or to a spritual power, are among the absolute duties that government cannot enforce.

B.2. The Equivalent Protection Principle

The rights of life, liberty and property are based on an equivalent protection principle, which Blackstone announced when he said that civil liberty "is no other than natural liberty so far restrained by human laws (and no farther) as is necessary and expedient for the general advantage of the public" (BL3, 121). Article III of the New Hampshire Bill of Rights explained the same principle, saying, "When men enter into a state of society, they surrender up some of their natural rights to that society, in order to insure the protection of others; and, without such an equivalent, the surrender is void."[31]

The United States Supreme Court confirmed this equivalent protection principle when it invalidated a Pennsylvania law that required a woman to inform her husband of her intent to have an abortion. Speaking for the Court's majority in *Planned Parenthood of Southeastern Pennsylvania v. Casey*, 505 U.S. 833 (1992), Justices Sandra Day O'Connor, Anthony Kennedy and David Souter said in a joint opinion, quoting Justice John Marshall Harlan's dissent in *Poe v. Ullman*, 367 U.S. 497 at 543 (1961),

> "[t]he full scope of liberty guaranteed by the Due Process Clause [the life, liberty and property clause] . . . is a rational continuum which, broadly speaking, includes a freedom from all substantial arbitrary impositions and purposeless restraints, . . . and which also recognizes, what a reasonable and sensitive judgment must, that certain interests require particularly careful scrutiny of the state needs asserted to justify their abridgment." (505 U.S. at 848)

By recognizing Harlan's concept of liberty, the Supreme Court departed from its previous method of analysis, in which government to had show a "compelling state interest" only when it proposed to restrain a liberty that was "so rooted in the traditions and conscience of our people as to be ranked as fundamental" (*Palko v. Connecticut*, 302 U.S. 319, 325 [1937]). For other restraints on people's liberty, this method required only "a rational relationship to some colorable state interest." (*Sherbert v. Verner*, 374 U.S. 398, 406 [1963]). In the *Planned Parenthood* case, the Supreme Court recognized that people have a right to be free, as Harlan said, "from all substantial arbitrary impositions and purposeless restraints." To determine whether the Pennsylvania husband notification requirement was such an imposition or restraint, the Court weighed the state's interest, namely the husband's concern for his potential offspring, against the restraint on the wife's right to have an abortion. It ruled that this balance fell in the favor of the woman's right, but it might have ruled otherwise had it followed its previous method of analysis and asked whether wife's right to have an abortion was fundamental or had a strong historical tradition. On the other hand, the Court's analysis was consistent with Blackstone's definition of civil liberty and the New Hampshire Bill of Rights, which said that government can require a person to surrender some of his natural liberty only when it provides an equivalent protection.

B.3. *The Control of What Goes In the Mind and Body*

As the *Planned Parenthood* case shows, religious freedom is not the only inalienable right that derives from the equivalent protection principle. Various rights of privacy are also among these inalienable rights. Blackstone gave an example when he said that a person has the right to become drunk in the privacy of his home:

> [l]et a man therefore be ever so abandoned in his principles, or vitious in his practice, provided he keeps his wickedness to himself, and does not offend against the rules of public decency, he is out of the reach of human laws. But if he makes his vices public, though they be such as seem principally to affect himself, (as drunkenness, or the like) they then become, by the bad example they set, of pernicious effects to society; and therefore it is then the business of human laws to correct them. Here the circumstance of publication is what alters the nature of the case. *Public* sobriety is a relative duty, and therefore enjoined by our laws: *private* sobriety is an absolute duty, which whether it be

performed or not, human tribunals can never know; and therefore they can never enforce it by civil sanction. (BL3, 120)

If a man has the right to become drunk at home, does he also have the right to fulfill his lustful desires there? The United States Supreme Court said that he does. In *Stanley v. Georgia*, 394 U.S. 557 (1964), the Court ruled that a person has the right to keep obscene materials in his home for his own viewing. On the other hand, in *Redrup v. New York*, 386 U.S. 767 (1967) and *Ginsberg v. New York*, 390 U.S. 629 (1968), the Court said that government can stop a person from producing, transporting, mailing and selling obscene materials. Those are business activities that the state has an interest in controlling because they induce other people to become addicted to self-destructive pleasures.

There are also limits on a person's right to do what he pleases in his home. Government can stop someone from using a potent narcotic that causes him to become addicted and lose the ability to make reasonable decisions. Under the influence of such a narcotic, he is likely to commit violent crimes or become destitute and burden the public welfare system. Cocaine, heroine and peyote are examples of such narcotics. In *Employment Division, Oregon Department of Human Resources v. Smith*, 494 U.S. 872 (1990), the U. S. Supreme Court ruled that the state of Oregon could forbid the possession and use of peyote, including its use as a religious sacrament by the Native American Church. Thus, the government's interest in protecting people from addiction by dangerous narcotics justifies laws that limit both their private activities and their free exercise of religion.

American courts have disagreed on whether marijuana is an addictive narcotic that induces criminal behavior. In *Ravin v. State of Alaska*, 537 P.2d 494 (1975), the Alaska Supreme Court held a state law against marijuana possession invalid because it violated a person's right of privacy. On the other hand, the Hawaii Supreme Court held that a similar law was valid in *Hawaii v. Kantner*, 493 P.2d 306 (1972). In *Leary v. United States*, 383 F.2d 851 (1967), the U. S. Court of Appeals for the Fifth Circuit upheld a federal law against marijuana possession because of expert witness testimony before Congress that the drug's use is dangerous and is accompanied by criminal episodes of terrible character (Ibid., 869).

If marijuana can be classified as a dangerous narcotic, can beer, wine or liquor also be classified as such? The test is whether these alcoholic beverages destroy people's ability to control their lives and thereby makes them dangerous to society. They have that effect on many people, but most people are able to control their alcoholic consumption. Perhaps for that reason, the prohibition amendment to the Constitution forbade only the manufacture, sale or transportation of intoxicating liquors. It did not forbid their private possession or consumption (App. O, Amend. XVIII).

Although the prohibition amendment was repealed by the Twenty-First Amendment, federal and state governments may still pass laws that forbid the manufacture, transportation or sale of alcoholic beverages. Many state and local governments currently have such laws. Because they regulate business activities that induce people to form self-destructive habits, these laws are justified. Governments may also pass laws that punish people for being drunk in public places or while operating automobiles. Blackstone said that these kinds of laws were needed to prevent people from setting bad examples for one another (BL3, 120), but he also used that reason to justify laws that limited people's freedoms of religion, speech and press. The real justification for laws that control public drinking is the danger that drunken people pose to other people's lives, liberty and property, particularly when they are driving. People who become drunk in public are also an unsightly, pungent nuisance, similar to litter, garbage, smoke and loud noise.

B.4. The Control of Body Integrity

Other absolute duties that government cannot enforce are those that relate to the integrity of a person's body. Blackstone said that the right of personal security "consists in a person's legal and uninterrupted enjoyment of . . . his body" (BL3, 125), subject to reasonable government laws for the protection of everyone's life, liberty and property. However, what a person does with his or her body does not ordinarily affect the life, liberty or property of other people. There are no laws in America that prevent a person from having his body tattooed, from piercing his ears or other body parts or from having plastic surgery.

People are also free to donate their organs to other people. Most people applaud the willingness of one person to give an organ to save the life of another. However, some have questioned the ethics of organ transplant operations, particularly when they have a low chance of success. The expense of these operations puts a great strain on the health care system. If their use continues to increase, a few recipients might become a combination of body parts that bear little resemblance to the person whom God created. Many people believe that a transplant of a life-saving organ is wrong because it is an attempt to thwart the natural destiny of a person's life.

In spite of these beliefs, there is no reason why government should have the power to stop a person from giving or receiving a transplant, provided that the donor is of sound mind and gives his consent and that the cost is funded privately. When that is the case, transplant operations do no injury to society or to any person. On the other hand, many transplant operations are being performed today without the donor's consent. The doctors are acting on only the consent of the donor's next of kin. This practice should be outlawed. Blackstone said that person's right of security includes the right have his limbs remain in-tact (BL3, 126). That right should cover his organs as well and should continue even after the person dies. Therefore, a person's organs should not taken from his body and recombined with those of other people, unless he has given his permission, such as by an organ donor card.

People also have the right to choose whether to be sexually sterilized, such as by vasectomy or salpingectomy. The Supreme Court has allowed only one exception to this rule. In *Buck v. Bell*, 274 U.S. 200 (1927), it upheld a Virginia law that authorized the sterilization of mental patients afflicted with certain hereditary forms of insanity. This may be regarded as simply another instance in which the state may make decisions for people who are unable to make sound judgments that are in either their own best interests or those of society. Some states have enacted laws prescribing sterilization as punishment for certain kinds of habitual criminals. However, the Supreme Court ruled in *Skinner v. Oklahoma*, 316 U.S. 535 (1942) that such a law violated a person's right to equal protection of the laws, because there was no reasonable basis for its application to some kinds of habitual criminals and not to others. In a concurring opinion in that case, Chief Justice Harlan Fiske Stone questioned the validity of any law that prescribed sterilization as punishment for a crime, because it was impossible to ascertain "that the criminal tendencies of any class of habitual offenders are transmissible regardless of the varying mental characteristics of its individuals" (Ibid., 544).

A person's Constitutional rights are also violated when the police probe inside his body for evidence of a crime. In *Rochin v. California*, 342 U.S. 165 (1952), the police saw a man suspected of carrying narcotics swallow two capsules. They arrested him and took him to a hospital, where they forced an emetic into his stomach without his consent. After he vomited the capsules, they tested them and found they contained morphine. The capsules and test results were introduced into evidence at the man's trial and he was convicted of illegal possession of narcotics. The U. S. Supreme Court reversed the conviction, ruling that the capsule evidence had been obtained illegally because the police had violated the man's right of privacy.

Another body integrity issue arises when a woman chooses to have an abortion. In *Roe v. Wade*, 410 U.S. 113 (1973), the United States Supreme Court ruled that a woman's right of privacy and dominion over her body includes her right to decide whether to have an abortion, until she is six months pregnant. The state attorney in that case had argued that the fetus should be regarded as a separate person that had gained a right to life when it was conceived. The Supreme Court rejected that argument, saying that an unborn fetus is not a person whose rights are protected by the U. S. Constitution. Therefore, the mother's Constitutional right of dominion over her body is superior to any right that a state law might try to give the fetus.

In his *Commentaries*, Blackstone tried to show that the absolute rights of Englishmen include a fetus's right to life. He said, "Life is the immediate gift of God, a right inherent by nature in every individual; . . . ." By describing life as an "immediate gift of God," that is, a gift that begins at conception, he was apparently stating his own religious belief, or perhaps that of the established Church of England, because he admitted that life "begins in contemplation of [English] law as soon as an infant is able to stir in the mother's womb." Also, he said that although the ancient Roman law regarded the killing of a fetus as homicide or manslaughter, "at present it is not looked upon in quite so atrocious a light, though it remains a very heinous misdemesnor" (BL3, 125-126). The right of fetal life described by Blackstone was therefore conditioned upon the fetus being able to flex its muscles and, when that right was violated, the offense was treated only as a misdemeanor.

To support his argument that a fetus was regarded as a separate person under English law, Blackstone cited several statutes that enabled a father to bequest equitable property rights to his child in the event that he died before his child was born (BL3, 126). However, those laws did not enable the child to receive property under the bequest until after it was born alive. Americans today can also create trusts for the benefit of unborn children, even those not yet conceived, but a child cannot receive property from the trust until after it is born alive. Because these property rights do not depend on whether the fetus has been conceived and cannot vest until after it is born alive, they are not relevant to the question of whether a fetus has a right to life while it is in its mother's womb and unable to survive outside of it.

What is relevant is the definition of a "person" with respect to the rights guaranteed in by the United States Constitution. Speaking for the Supreme Court in *Roe v. Wade*, Justice Harry Blackmun said that the word "person" does not include a fetus in its mother's womb. He cited eight previous cases in which a court had considered this question and had reached the same conclusion (Ibid., 158).

The state attorney argued that even if the fetus cannot be regarded as a person with its own constitutional rights, government has an interest in protecting all human life, including the life of a fetus. Like his first argument, this argument was based on the proposition that life begins when a fetus is conceived. Justice Blackmun said the Court could not base its decision on that proposition because there had never been a consensus on when life begins, at least among those trained in the respective disciplines of medicine, philosophy and theology (Ibid., 159-161). He said that Jewish and Christian theologians had given many different answers, including conception, a forty/eighty day ensoulment rule,[32] quickening, viability and live birth. One problem with the conception answer, Blackmun said, was that recent medical evidence had shown that conception occurs over a period of time and some birth control techniques, such as the "morning-after pill," took effect during that time. The Court therefore concluded that government cannot arbitrarily adopt one of these theories of life in order to deny the right of a pregnant woman to control her body.

On the other hand, the Court said government has legitimate interests in protecting the health of a pregnant woman and the potentiality of human life at some point during fetal development. Its interest in protecting the woman's health becomes legitimate at approximately the end of the third month of pregnancy, when the maternal health risks of abortion increase above those of normal childbirth. The state's interest in protecting the potentiality of life becomes legitimate at approximately the end of the sixth month of pregnancy, which is approximately when the fetus becomes viable, that is, able to live outside the mother's womb.

In *Planned Parenthood of Southeastern Pennsylvania v. Casey*, supra at 860, the Supreme Court abandoned this six-month rule, because advances in neonatal care had moved the point of viability to an earlier time. The Court said the actual point of viability should therefore determine when government has the power to protect the potential life of a fetus. Although the Court did not say so, this point of viability may also occur after six months or it may never occur if the fetus is seriously deformed.

In *Roe v. Wade*, Justice Blackmun said that government has a legitimate interest in protecting the life of a fetus after it becomes viable because it is then capable of meaningful life outside the mother's womb (Ibid., 163). He did not explain why government has no such interest before the fetus became viable, but there are sound medical reasons for this conclusion. In the early stages of pregnancy, the fetus is in every respect an integral part of its mother's body. Its living tissues rely as much on the mother's life support organs as the living tissues of any other part of her body, including her arms, legs and even the uterus that carries the fetus. Whatever the fetus needs in the way of nutrition, oxygen and other necessities of life, the mother's life support organs must answer the call. When a fetal organ is not working properly, the mother's life support organs try to correct the problem. The mother's body must accept this added burden. There is no alternative. The fetus cannot live except by what it receives from the mother. The fetus may have a life of its own, according to some philosophical views, but that life is an inextricable part of the mother's life. The fetus is part of the single living system that is the mother's body. Under these conditions, government should not have the power to step into the middle of the mother's body and establish rights for one part of her body that override her inalienable right to be the master of her whole body.

The situation is different when the fetus is able to live outside the mother's womb. Although the mother's life support organs continue to supply what the fetus needs, this burden on the mother's body is no longer an absolute necessity. A live birth can happen at any time. The potentiality of another life is at a much higher level--so high that any intentional destruction of the fetus under normal circumstances would be tantamount to murder. The only possible reason for taking a viable fetus from its womb would be to relieve the mother, the fetus or both from a serious medical danger. In these situations, government ought to be able to make sure that, as a first priority, everything is done to reduce the danger to the mother, and, as a second priority, everything is done to reduce the danger to the fetus. Government has an interest in protecting the future life of a viable fetus, but even that interest must be subservient to its interest in protecting the mother's present life.

The rising abortion rate in America since the *Roe v. Wade* decision should be of concern to all people, regardless of whether they agree with this decision. The formation of a new human being is an awe-inspiring process. Everyone should mourn when that process is aborted, either by a natural cause or by the mother's decision. Yet many women mistakenly think that the *Roe v. Wade* decision means that their society does not care whether they abort their pregnancies. They think that only a radical few right-to-life advocates believe that a woman has an obligation to herself and to God to carry her fetus until it is born, if she can do so without serious risk to her health. They do not realize that many pro-choice advocates hold the same belief. The only reason they support a woman's right to choose is the one given by the Supreme Court in *Roe v. Wade*, namely that woman has the right to control her own body and her non-viable fetus is an integral part of her body. She is the sovereign of her body, provided she does not place an undue risk on her own health and safety. Only she can decide what her duty to her fetus should be.

In spite of this sovereignty, most people believe that they should fulfill their duties to themselves and to God, even though their government cannot enforce these duties. A pregnant woman should hold herself no more absolved from her duty to her body, including her fetus, than a sovereign government should hold itself absolved from its duties to its citizens. The woman's duty is not an easy to fulfill. Her fetus places a great strain on her body. A normal pregnancy causes pain and health risk to even the most physically fit young woman. For an older woman, the pain is harder to bear and the health risk is greater. A pregnancy near the time of menopause may well threaten the life of a woman. In a pregnant woman of any age, complications can arise that threaten her life and the life of her fetus. Fortunately, her government does not tell her what to do. Fortunately or unfortunately, she is the sovereign.

Although state and federal governments cannot restrain the freedom of women to have abortions, the Supreme Court has ruled that impoverished women have no constitutional right to have the taxpayers pay for them. In *Maher v. Roe*, 432 U.S. 464 (1977), a woman complained that her right to an abortion had been denied because a Connecticut Welfare Department regulation limited state Medicaid benefits for first trimester abortions to those that were medically necessary. In *Harris v. McRae*, 448 U.S. 297 (1980), a woman complained that her right to have an abortion had been denied by the so-called Hyde Amendment to a federal Health, Education and Welfare Department appropriation bill, forbidding the use of that department's funds for abortions, except when the life of the mother would be endangered if the fetus were carried to full term or when the mother was the victim of rape or incest. In each case, the Supreme Court ruled that the woman's constitutional rights had not been violated.

The *Maher* case was relatively easy for the Court to decide, because the woman was asking for special welfare treatment. She wanted the government to finance an abortion that was not medically necessary, from a fund that was established to reimburse people only for operations that were medically necessary. However, the Hyde Amendment attacked in the *Harris* case raised several equal protection issues. That amendment created a special exception for abortions for all federal government welfare programs that reimbursed impoverished pregnant women for their medical expenses. To be reimbursed for medical expenses other than abortions, the woman had to show only that the medical procedure was necessary to protect her health, but for abortions she had to show that her life was in danger. Speaking for the Court's five-justice majority, Justice Potter Stewart said this exception was justified "because no other procedure [beside an abortion] involves the purposeful termination of a potential life." On the other hand, Justices William Brennan, Harry Blackmun, Thurgood Marshall and John Paul Stevens dissented, primarily for the following reason stated by Justice Marshall:

> [t]he government's interest in protecting human fetal life is not a legitimate one when it is in conflict with "the preservation of the life or health of the mother," *Roe v. Wade*, 410 U.S., at 165, and when the

> Government's effort to make serious health damage to the mother "a more attractive alternative than abortion," *ante*, at 325, does not rationally promote the governmental interest in encouraging normal childbirth. (Ibid., 345)

An often overlooked aspect of the *Roe v. Wade* decision is that it was not based on a ruling that life begins at live birth. The Supreme Court said that "when those trained in the respective disciplines of medicine, philosophy, and theology are unable to arrive at any consensus, the judiciary, at this point in the development in man's knowledge, is not in a position to speculate as to the answer" (Ibid., 159). It was on that basis that the Court concluded, "we do not agree that by adopting one theory of life, Texas may override the rights of the pregnant woman that are at stake" (Ibid., 162).

The converse reasoning should apply when the government proposes to tax people to pay for other people's abortions. The theory that life begins at conception is entitled to as much respect as the theory that life begins when the baby is born alive. Therefore, people who believe that all fetuses are live babies should not be forced to pay for what they view is murder, nor for counseling women to abort their babies simply because they do not want them. Unless the mother's health is in danger, an abortion must be viewed as optional surgery, and that surgery must be viewed as one that destroys life when taxpayers are asked to pay for it. When the courts are confronted with laws that provide public funds for abortions, they should ask, "What business does government have in participating in such an enterprise?"

B.5. *The Control of Life and Death*

Blackstone said that a person committing suicide

> is guilty of a double offence; one spiritual, in invading the power of the Almighty, and rushing into his immediate presence uncalled for; the other temporal, against the king, who hath an interest in the preservation of all his subjects; the law has therefore ranked this among the

highest crimes, making it a peculiar species of felony, a felony committed on oneself.[33]

Blackstone's words raise the question of how "a felony committed on oneself" can violate a relative duty to others or to society. The spiritual nature of the offense, namely, "invading the power of the Almighty," refers to an absolute duty. The temporal nature of the offense, that of depriving the king of the life of his subject, may have given rise a valid claim by an eighteenth-century king who was deemed to be the owner of his subjects, but no modern democratic government can make such a claim on its citizens.

On the other hand, people do have an interest in preserving each other's lives. Blackstone said that governments exist because people choose to stay together "out of the sense of their weakness and imperfection" (BL1, 47). When some one shows his weakness and imperfection by committing suicide, he strikes a blow to the basic purpose of a civil society. He also shows that he has lost the ability to make decisions that are in his own best interests. Therefore, as it must for children, mentally ill people and drug addicts, government must protect suicidal people from their bad judgment. John Locke said, "nobody has an absolute arbitrary power over himself, or over any other, to destroy his own life or take away the life or property of another." That was the basis of his conclusion that government can receive no more power from the people than they have over themselves. Therefore, it cannot arbitrarily take away their life, liberty or property. It can do so only for the good of society (App. F, par. 135).

The main problem with suicide has been how to punish the offender, who has put himself beyond the reach of human laws. Blackstone said that the English laws

> can only act on what he has left behind him, his reputation and his fortune: on the former, by an ignominious burial in the highway, with a stake driven through his body; on the latter, by a forfeiture of all his goods and chattels to the king: hoping that his care for either his reputation, or the welfare of his family, would be some motive to restrain him from so desperate and wicked an act.[34]

These were the English penalties that the American states theoretically inherited when they declared their independence. However, the American colonial courts had not enforced these penalties very often. Most states abolished the penalties soon after the War of Independence. They did not do so because suicide was beyond their control but because the English penalties missed the mark by punishing the innocent, bereaved heirs of the deceased. On the rare occasions when these penalties were enforced, they might have been attacked because they were cruel and unusual. No state today demands forfeiture of the estates of people who commit suicide, nor does any state condemn the bodies of these people to ignominious burials or exhibitions.[35]

In his proposed revision of Virginia's criminal code published in 1787, Thomas Jefferson classified suicide with apostasy, heresy and excusable homicide as acts "to be pitied, not punished."[36] The modern view is that a suicidal person should be counseled and helped rather than punished. Most states, therefore, do not make suicide or attempted suicide a crime. Some even allow recovery of insurance benefits when a person commits suicide, because a suicidal person is not capable of rational judgment and should not be held accountable for trying to destroy himself. However, government should protect a suicidal person from others who would take advantage of his vulnerable condition. Many states therefore have laws that make it a crime to assist others in committing suicide.[37]

The situation is different when a person has succumbed to a persistent vegetative state or has a terminal illness that has caused his health to deteriorate so that he has no reasonable hope of reaping any further enjoyment of life. Many terminally ill people must endure excruciating pain and humiliation while they await their slow, certain deaths. Some people think that choosing to end one's life under these conditions is the wrong decision. Their religious beliefs tell them that they must continue to live in their pain until they die of a natural cause. They believe that any act that would shorten life, such as refusing medical treatment, refusing food and water or taking lethal drugs would be a violation of God's will. On the other hand, many people have decided that if they are ever in this situation, they want to die immediately and they have signed living wills stating that wish. These people are capable of acting in their own best interests. They have a right to die and to have others help them. A person's decision to end his life under these conditions should not be deemed suicidal. It is a rational decision, not one caused by depression or other mental illness. Society has no right to force some dying people to prolong their agony because of the religious beliefs of other people. The weakness and imperfection of society is increased, not diminished, when it forces rational people to stay alive after they have decided to die.

In the mid-1970s, the right to die became a subject of national debate because of a twenty-two-year old New Jersey woman named Karen Quinlan. Karen had suffered severe brain damage as the result of anoxia and was in a persistent vegetative state. Her father applied to a local court for approval to disconnect the respirator on which her body depended for life support. This case was appealed to the New Jersey Supreme Court, which held that Karen's father could have her respirator disconnected because of her right of privacy under the life, liberty, and property clause of the Fourteenth Amendment (*In re Quinlan*, 355 A.2d 647 [1976]). The most difficult issue was whether Karen herself really wanted the respirator disconnected. She had never told anyone what she would have wanted to do under these circumstances. The court resolved the issue by holding that the "only practical way" to prevent the loss of Karen's privacy right was to allow her father and family decide "whether she would exercise it in these circumstances" (Ibid., 664).

Since the *Quinlan* decision, the courts of most states have required better evidence of what an incompetent patient would have wanted to do had he been able to speak for himself. Many states have enacted laws that allow people to decide to refuse medical treatment by signing living wills. However, if an incompetent patient has signed no living will, most of these states require convincing evidence that the patient would have wanted to terminate his treatment if he had been competent and able to communicate his wishes. In *Cruzan v. Missouri Department of Health*, 497 U.S. 261 (1990), the U.S. Supreme Court ruled that the State of Missouri could force an incompetent patient without a living will to continue receiving life sustaining treatment unless there was "clear and convincing evidence" that she did not want such treatment. Speaking for the Court, Chief Justice William Rehnquist stated the common law rule that informed consent is required for all medical treatment. He quoted former Supreme Court Justice Benjamin Cardozo who had said, while sitting on the New York Court of Appeals,

> "Every human being of adult years and sound mind has a right to determine what shall be done with his own body; and a surgeon who performs an operation without his patient's consent commits an assault, for which he is liable for damages." *Schloendorff v. Society of New York Hospital*, 105 N.E. 92, 93 (1914).

Rehnquist said that a corollary to this rule is that "the patient generally possesses the right not to consent, that is, to refuse treatment" (Ibid., 269-270). He also said this is not only a common law right, but also "a constitutionally protected liberty interest..... [F]or the purposes of this case, we assume that the United States Constitution would grant a competent person a constitutionally protected right to refuse lifesaving hydration and nutrition" (Ibid., 278, 279). However, because Cruzan was not competent to make this decision, the Supreme Court ruled that the state of Missouri had a paramount interest in protecting life and was therefore justified in presuming that the person wants to live unless there was clear and convincing evidence to the contrary (Ibid., 280-285).

Although the Supreme Court acknowledged in *Cruzan* that a terminally ill, competent person has the right to end his life by refusing medical treatment, it has now ruled that this right to die does not extend to "assisted suicide," which occurs when a competent, terminally ill person has a doctor assist him in taking a lethal medical treatment.

In *Washington v. Glucksburg*, 117 S.Ct. 2258 (1997), three terminally ill people in the state of Washington wanted their doctors to prescribe lethal drug doses for them. They wanted to die quickly and with the least possible amount of suffering. However, Washington had a law that forbade doctors from giving any assistance to people who wanted to commit suicide. One of these people was a sixty-nine-year-old retired pediatrician who had suffered from cancer for six years. The cancer had metastasized throughout her skeleton. She had benefited temporarily from chemotherapy and radiation but the cancer's remission had ended and was in its final phase. Since June 1993, she had been bedridden and in constant severe pain due to swollen legs, bed sores, poor appetite, nausea, vomiting, impaired vision and incontinence of the bowel. In November 1993, she had been placed in a hospice care facility designed for patients with less than six months life expectancy. The second person was a forty-four-year-old artist dying of AIDS. Since 1991, he had suffered two bouts of pneumonia, severe chronic skin and sinus infections, grand mal seizures and extreme fatigue. He had lost 70 percent of his vision to cytomegalovirus retinitis, a degenerative disease that had destroyed his ability to paint. The third person was a sixty-nine-year-old retired salesman suffering from emphysema, which was causing a constant sensation of suffocating. He had to be connected to an oxygen tank at all times and take morphine to calm his panic reaction associated with his feeling of suffocation. He also suffered from heart failure that obstructed the flow of blood to his extremities, causing him severe leg pain. There was no known cure for either his heart condition or his lung condition. In *Vacco v Quill*, 117 S.Ct. 2293 (1997), three New York state residents in similar situations wanted to die, but a New York law forbade doctors to assist them.

The nine Supreme Court justices unanimously agreed that the Washington and New York laws did not violate the Constitution. However, they had different reasons for reaching this conclusion. In the Court's opinions in both cases, Chief Justice Rehnquist said there was no fundamental right to assisted suicide. He rejected Justice Souter's contention in *Planned Parenthood v. Casey*, supra, that a person's right of life, liberty and property includes a freedom from all "arbitrary impositions" or "purposeless restraints" (Ibid., 2268). He insisted that unless government violates a fundamental right "deeply rooted in our legal tradition," it need show only a "reasonable relation to a legitimate state interest" to justify its action. "The history of the law's treatment of assisted suicide in this country," he said, "has been and continues to be one of the rejection of nearly all efforts to permit it" (Ibid., 2271).

Oddly enough, Rehnquist contrasted assisted suicide with the fundamental right to use contraceptives, established in *Griswold v. Connecticut*, 381 U.S. 479 (1965), and the fundamental right of black and white people to marry each other, established in *Loving v. Virginia*, 388 U.S. 1 (1967)] (Ibid., 2267). Those cases, however, showed that the bans on contraceptives and black and white marriages were as much a part of American history and tradition as the bans on assisted suicide that Rehnquist reviewed in the *Washington v. Glucksburg* case.

Nevertheless, Rehnquist proceeded to list the state interests, which he said need only be reasonably related to assisted suicide (Ibid., 2268) and "[w]e need not weigh exactingly the relative strengths" of these interests (Ibid., 2275). He had good reason to discourage such an analysis. He said one state interest was "the unqualified interest in the preservation of human life," quoting his own statement in the *Cruzan* case, 497 U.S. at 282 (Ibid., 2272). However, that statement referred to the state's concern for the life of a comatose person who was unable to tell people whether she wanted to die. Rehnquist had prefaced that statement with the assumption "that the United States Constitution would grant a competent person a constitutionally protected right to refuse life saving hydration and nutrition" (497 U.S. at 279). He did not explain why a state's unqualified interest in preserving human life was not sufficient to deny a competent person the right to end his life by refusing life-saving hydration and nutrition but was sufficient to deny him the right to end his life by another means.

Rehnquist said that another state interest lies in protecting the integrity and ethics of the medical profession. He quoted the American Medical Association statement that "[p]hysician assisted suicide is fundamentally incompatible with the physician's role as a healer" (117 S.Ct. at 2273). However, most doctors do not agree with that statement. In a recent poll of Oregon doctors, 60 percent of the respondents said that physician-assisted suicide should be legal in appropriate circumstances. That figure was 70 percent in a poll of Michigan doctors. In a survey by the American Society for Internal Medicine, one doctor in five said he had assisted in a patient's suicide. Many of these doctors have published articles in medical journals confirming that they have administered drugs to their patients in order to hasten their deaths.[38] This evidence shows that most doctors regard assisted suicide in the same category as abortion and the removal of life saving hydration and nutrition from terminally ill patients. Each doctor must decide for himself what is ethical. There are no universal rules in the medical profession that govern these situations.

Another state interest, according to Rehnquist, lies "in protecting vulnerable groups--including the poor, the elderly, and disabled persons--from abuse, neglect, and mistakes" (Ibid., 2273). He said these people are subject to coercion by their relatives and "[i]f physician-assisted suicide were permitted, many might resort to it to spare their families the substantial financial burden of end-of-life health care costs." However, these fears appear to be based on mere speculation. Although many states do not forbid competent, terminally ill people to get medical help in taking lethal drugs, Rehnquist cited no evidence that vulnerable people in these states are particularly susceptible to coercion in these situations. The same pressures would appear to be present in respect of people terminating or refusing life support systems, but again he cited no evidence that these pressures have produced the feared results.

The most convincing state interest presented by Rehnquist is the possible practical difficulty of limiting the right of assisted suicide to competent people suffering a terminal illness who had freely chosen to end their lives. He cited reports of the Dutch experience after assisted suicide was legalized. Despite the Dutch government's rules and reporting procedures, there were more than one thousand cases of euthanasia in 1990 in which there was no evidence that the patient had made an explicit request, and there were an additional 4,941 cases where physicians administered lethal morphine overdoses without the patient's explicit consent. These may have included many cases of elderly people suffering from dementia. Based on the Dutch experience, a New York task force concluded that assisted suicide and euthanasia are closely linked and that the risk of abuse is neither speculative nor distant (Ibid., 2274-75).

Justices Antonin Scalia, Clarence Thomas, Anthony Kennedy and Sandra Day O'Connor joined in Chief Justice Rehnquist's opinions. The fact that Kennedy and O'Connor joined Rehnquist may indicate they no longer agree with Harlan's statement that the Constitution guarantees "a freedom from all substantial arbitrary impositions and purposeless restraints," which they had endorsed in *Planned Parenthood v. Casey*, 505 U.S. at 848. Rehnquist specifically rejected Harlan's statement in his opinions. O'Connor concurred, saying that she agreed "there is no generalized right to 'commit suicide.'" However, she also said she saw "no need to address the narrower question of whether a competent person experiencing great suffering has a constitutionally congnizable interest in controlling the circumstances of his or her imminent death" (Ibid., 2303). That may indicate she did not agree with all of Rehnquist's opinions. She based her opinion on the risk that a dying patient's request for life-ending assistance might not be truly voluntary and the fact the New York and Washington laws permitted doctors to hasten a person's death by the use of pain-killing drugs, rather than drugs designed only to kill.

Justice Ruth Bader Ginsberg concurred in the Court's judgments substantially for the reasons given by Justice O'Connor.

Justice Souter wrote a concurring opinion based on the Harlan/*Planned Parenthood* method of analysis rather than the Rehnquist method. He was impressed that the Dutch were not able to limit assisted suicide to competent people suffering a terminal illness who had made conscious decisions to end their lives. Souter said the New York and Washington bans on assisted suicide were therefore justified until the existence of this apparent difficulty was resolved. He concluded, "While I do not decide for all time that respondents' claim should not be recognized, I acknowledge the legislative institutional competence as the better one to deal with that claim at this time" (Ibid., 2293).

Justice Stephen Breyer questioned whether there was any practical difference between the Harlan analysis that recognized that "certain interests require particularly careful scrutiny of the state needs" and the Rehnquist emphasis on "fundamental liberties." He said Harlan's "certain interests" may well be identical to Rehnquist's "fundamental liberties" (Ibid., 2311). However, Rehnquist would probably not agree with Breyer's statement that American legal traditions may support a fundamental "right to die with dignity" that would include "personal control over the manner of death, professional medical assistance, and the avoidance of unnecessary and severe physical suffering--combined." Breyer said the Court did not have to decide whether such a fundamental right existed in the instant cases, because the Washington and New York laws did not prevent these patients from receiving adequate pain-relieving drugs.

Justice John Paul Stevens concurred in the Court's judgment but only because the Washington and New York cases were declaratory judgment actions brought by groups of people who feared they might be charged with crimes. Therefore, he said these groups had to prove the assisted suicide laws were unconstitutional in all or most cases in which they might be applied. Stevens said they had failed to do that, but the result might be different in a criminal case involving certain ideal facts:

> Although there is no absolute right to physician-assisted suicide, *Cruzan* makes it clear that some individuals who no longer have the option of deciding whether to live or to die because they are already on the threshold of death have a constitutionally protected interest that may outweigh the State's interest in preserving life at all costs. . . . I agree that the State has a compelling interest in preventing persons from committing suicide because of depression, or coercion by third parties. But the State's legitimate interest in preventing abuse does not apply to an individual who is not victimized by abuse, who is not suffering from depression, and who makes a rational and voluntary decision to seek assistance in dying. . . . [A] State's prohibition of assisted suicide is justified by the fact that the "'ideal'" case in which "patients would be screened for depression and offered treatment, effective pain

medication would be available, and all patients would have a supportive committed family and doctor" is not the usual case. . . . . (Ibid., 2307, 2308, 2309)

The opinions of Justices O'Connor, Ginsberg, Souter, Breyer and Stevens indicate that the Supreme Court may review again the right to doctor-assisted suicide. In a future case, a party asserting a such a right might be able to show that, despite the Dutch experience, there are ways to limit this right to competent people suffering a terminal illness who have freely chosen to end their lives. Such a party might be hooked to a life-support system and might argue that he would choose to have it removed were it not for the pain it would cause him before he died. He might also argue that there were no adequate pain relief medications available. The Supreme Court might also reconsider the distinctions many of the justices made between killing patients by terminating their life-sustaining hydration and nutrition, killing patients by giving them overdoses of pain relievers and killing patients by giving them non-pain killing, lethal drug medications. They might consider what purpose these distinctions serve, except to limit arbitrarily the ways that competent, suffering, terminally ill people can choose to die.

Until the Supreme Court reviews the right-to-die issue again, the people of each state will be deciding whether the terminally-ill patients in their state should be allowed to have doctors assist them in taking lethal drug medications. The state of Michigan provides an interesting example of how some of these decisions might be made. In 1994, the Michigan Supreme Court ruled in *People v. Kevorkian*, 527 N.W.2d 714 (S.Ct. Mich. 1994) that the well-known Dr. Jack Kevorkian had to stand trial for violating Michigan's doctor-assisted suicide law. That court said that a terminally ill patient had no constitutional right to have others assist him in ending his life. However, since that ruling, the courts of Michigan have tried Dr. Kevorkian on three separate occasions. In each case, the jury found him not guilty of violating either the state's doctor-assisted suicide law or its common law rule against assisted suicide. Perhaps the members of these juries do not agree with the ruling by the

Michigan Supreme Court or with the more recent ruling by the U.S. Supreme Court.

B.6. The Control of People's Sex Lives

Americans may be free to become drunk in their living rooms, but their bedroom activities have not escaped the watchful eyes of their lawmakers.

At one time, most states had laws that banned the use of birth control devices. However, in 1965, the U. S. Supreme Court ruled in *Griswold v. Connecticut*, 381 U.S. 479 that these laws violated the privacy rights of married people. In the 1972 case of *Eisenstadt v. Baird*, 405 U.S. 438, the Supreme Court also ruled that these laws violated the privacy rights of unmarried people.

The U. S. Supreme Court has never ruled on whether government should be able to forbid people to have sexual relations. Many states have laws that forbid unmarried people to have sex, but they seldom try to enforce these laws. One New Jersey prosecutor did try to enforce his state's anti-fornication law, but the New Jersey Supreme Court ruled in 1977 that the law violated people's right of privacy under the Fourteenth Amendment. In *State v. Saunders*, 381 A.2d 333 at 342-343, the court said,

> Fornication may be abhorrent to the morals and deeply held beliefs of many persons. But any appropriate "remedy" for such conduct cannot come from legislative fiat. Private personal acts between two consenting adults are not to be lightly meddled with by the State. The right of personal autonomy is fundamental to a free society. Persons who view fornication as opprobrious conduct may seek strenuously to dissuade people from engaging in it. However, they may not inhibit such conduct through the coercive power of the criminal law. As aptly stated by Sir Francis Bacon, "[t]he sum of behavior is to retain a man's own dignity without intruding on the liberty of others." The fornication statute mocks the dignity of both offenders and enforcers. Surely police have more pressing duties than to search out adults who live a so-called "wayward" life. Surely the dignity of the law is

undermined when an intimate personal activity between consenting adults can be dragged into court and "exposed." More importantly, the liberty which is the birthright of every individual suffers dearly when the State can so grossly intrude on personal autonomy.

Private sex between consenting adults should not be confused with prostitution. That involves the public solicitation of sexual favors for a price. The Court of Appeals for the District of Columbia ruled in *United States v. Moses*, 339 A.2d 46 (D.C. App., 1975) that a law forbidding prostitution does not violate the privacy of either the prostitute or the patron. Government can forbid prostitution for the same reason that it can forbid the sale of obscene materials. It must be able to insulate the public from prostitutes who induce people to become addicted to a self-destructive pleasure. Their street solicitations are also a public nuisance. Government must also be able to stop the pimps and patrons of these prostitutes. The pimps hold the prostitutes in bondage by intimidation and force, while the patrons contribute to this bondage.

Many state legislatures have tried to deter people of different races from having sex by forbidding them to marry. Before 1967, most southern states had laws that banned marriages between white people and people of other races. The U. S. Supreme Court ruled in *Loving v. Virginia*, 388 U.S. 1 (1967), that these laws interfered with people's freedom to marry, a basic civil right that is fundamental to their very existence and survival. Speaking for the unanimous Court, Chief Justice Earl Warren said this freedom could not be limited by racial classifications that were "directly subversive to the principle of equality at the heart of the Fourteenth Amendment" (Ibid., 12). Therefore, he said, they violated both the life, liberty and property clause and the equal protection clause of the Fourteenth Amendment.

Some state laws regulate the kind of sexual activity that two people can have in their bedroom. These laws ban any activity in which the mouth or anus of one person contacts the genitalia of the other person. This activity is sometimes referred to as a "crime against nature" or "deviate sexual intercourse." The laws against this activity usually apply whether the people are of the same or different sexes and whether they are married or unmarried.

Blackstone said that a crime against nature was to be punished in England by hanging the offenders, because it violates "the express law of God" (Lev. 20:13, 15). Thus, it was one of the English offenses against God and religion. Blackstone did not say whether the English law applied only to homosexual relationships or to heterosexual and married relationships as well.[39]

Another word for a crime against nature is "sodomy," because of the Biblical story about the men of Sodom who surrounded Lot's house and demanded that he bring his male house guests out to them "that we may know them" (Gen. 19:5). The house guests were angels sent by God and they certainly would not have consented to the wishes of the men of Sodom. That raises the question of whether sodomy really occurs when both people consent to the activity. In practice, however, most laws against sodomy apply only when both people consent. In cases where one person forces himself on another person, as the men of Sodom tried to do, another law applies that imposes a more severe penalty on that person and no penalty on his victim.

The original thirteen states all had laws forbidding crimes against nature or deviate sexual intercourse. In 1868, when the Fourteenth Amendment became effective and forbade the states from depriving people of their life, liberty and property, thirty-two of the thirty-seven states had laws forbidding such sexual relations. In 1951, all fifty states had these laws. In 1985, only twenty-four states and the District of Columbia had still had laws of this kind (*Bowers v. Hardwick*, 478 U.S. at 192-194). As of 1998, the number of states has dropped to twenty and the District of Columbia no longer has such a law. In five of these twenty states, namely Kansas, Missouri, Montana, Tennessee and Texas, the law against deviate sexual intercourse applies only to homosexual people. In Alabama, the law applies only to unmarried people. In the other fourteen states, namely Arizona, Georgia, Idaho, Louisiana, Maryland, Michigan, Minnesota, Mississippi, North Carolina, Oklahoma, Rhode Island, South Carolina, Utah and Virginia, the law applies to any couple, whether of the same or different sex, whether married or unmarried. In some of these states, the law has been construed to cover only homosexual people. In most states, it is seldom or never applied to anyone except homosexual people.

In *People v. Onofre*, 415 N.E.2d 936 (1980), the highest court of the state of New York, the Court of Appeals, held that New York's anti-sodomy law violated the rights of privacy of homosexual people. The court said that the state

> has failed to demonstrate how government interference with the practice of personal choice in matters of intimate sexual behavior out of view of the public and with no commercial component will serve to advance the cause of public morality or do anything other than restrict individual conduct and impose a concept of private morality chosen by the State. (Ibid., 941)

However, in 1986, the U. S. Supreme Court ruled that a similar anti-sodomy law of the state of Georgia did not violate the privacy rights of homosexual people. In *Bowers v. Hardwick*, 478 U.S. 186, the Court said that the law was justified because of the state's power to forbid immoral conduct. In the Court's majority opinion, Justice Byron White did not distinguish between the state's well recognized interest in maintaining public morality and its questionable interest in regulating private morality, as the New York Court of Appeals had. He also relied on the long history of anti-sodomy laws in America to show that there was no deeply rooted right to engage in such conduct. On the other hand, four of the nine justices of the Court dissented from White's majority opinion. Justice Blackmun, writing on behalf of the dissenting justices, said that

> [c]ertainly some private behavior can affect the fabric of society as a whole. Reasonable people may differ about whether particular sexual acts are moral or immoral, but "we have ample evidence for believing that people will not abandon morality, will not think any better of murder, cruelty or dishonesty, merely because some private sexual practice which they abominate is not punished by the law." H. L. A.

Hart, Immorality and Treason, reprinted in the Law as Literature 220, 225 (L. Blom-Cooper ed. 1961). Petitioner and the Court fail to see the difference between laws that protect public sensibilities and those that enforce private morality....

This case involves no real interference with the rights of others, for the mere knowledge that other individuals do not adhere to one's value system cannot be a legally cognizable interest, cf. *Diamond v. Charles*, 476 U. S. 54, 65-66 (1986), let alone an interest that can justify invading the houses, hearts, and minds of citizens who choose to live their lives differently. (Ibid., 212-213)

Perhaps the next time this issue is reviewed by the Supreme Court, the majority will see the logic of Justice Blackmun's dissent.

Justice Potter Stewart wrote in his dissent in *Griswold v. Connecticut*, supra, that a Connecticut law banning the use of contraceptives was "an uncommonly silly law," perhaps "even asinine" (Ibid., 527). He said, however, that he could not join with the majority of the Court in ruling that law unconstitutional, because he could find no clause in the Constitution that gave people the right to use contraceptives while having sex. Perhaps if he had read the preamble to the New Hampshire bill of rights (quoted above in Section *B.1*), he would have found that the right to be free of "silly" or "asine" laws was covered by the life, liberty and property clauses of the Fifth and Fourteenth Amendments. The New Hampshire preamble explained that a person cannot be forced to surrender his natural rights of life, liberty or property unless the government gives him an equivalent protection in the form of other rights. Blackstone said,

> [T]hat constitution or frame of government, that system of laws is alone calculated to maintain civil liberty, which leaves the subject entire master of his own conduct, except in those points wherein the public good requires some direction or restraint (BL3, 122).

Locke said,

> A man, as has been proved, cannot subject himself to the arbitrary power of another; and having, in the state of Nature, no arbitrary

power over the life, liberty, or possession of another, but only so much as the law of Nature gave himself and the rest of mankind, this is all he doth, or can give the commonwealth, and by it to the legislative power, so that the legislative can do no more than this" (App. F, par. 135).

These statements describe the social contract basis of government. In his majority opinion in *Munn v. Illinois*, 94 U.S. 113 at 124 (Oct. term, 1876), Chief Justice Morrison Waite of the U.S. Supreme Court confirmed that the right of privacy is derived from this social contract when he said,

> "A body politic," as aptly defined in the preamble of the Constitution of Massachusetts, is a social compact by which the whole people covenants with each citizen, and each citizen with the whole people, that all shall be governed by certain laws for the common good." This does not confer power upon the whole people to control rights that are purely and exclusively private, *Thorpe v. R. & B. Railroad Co.*, 27 Vt. 143; but it does authorize the establishment of laws requiring each citizen to so conduct himself, and so use his own property, as not unnecessarily to injure another.

Therefore, government cannot pass "silly" or "asinine" laws that punish a person for his private conduct.

Some people argue that laws that prevent people from using birth control devices are not silly or asinine, nor are laws that forbid abortion, assisted suicide or unnatural sexual activity. They say that society suffers when people are allowed to do these things, even privately. They say the harm is in the collective moral degeneration of society, caused by the bad examples that people set for one another. However, the private duties that a person owes to himself are essentially the same as the private duties he owes to a spiritual authority. For many people, these duties are exactly the same. Whether or not they are the same, government has no basis for defining or enforcing such duties. If it cannot establish a religion that determines what private conduct contributes to the moral degeneration of society, then it should not be able to accomplish the same result by another means.

When government punishes people for setting bad examples for one another, it not only deprives them of their right of privacy; it also deprives them of their freedom of speech and press. Blackstone showed why this is true when he said that if a man keeps his vices to himself, human laws cannot punish him, "[b]ut if he makes his vices public . . . they become, by the bad example they set, of pernicious effects to society. . . . Here the circumstance of publication is what alters the nature of the case" (BL3, 120). He used the same reasoning to justify the English limits on freedom of the press, saying that government could punish a person for any writings judged to be "of a pernicious tendency" (BL6, 152). That was contrary the American view of free speech and press, as the next section of this chapter will show.

C. Free Speech and Press

C.1. Early Struggles for the Right of Free Speech and Press

Bertrand Russell, the world's most outspoken atheist, said, "In a democracy it is necessary that people should learn to endure having their sentiments outraged."[40] That is so because outrage alone does not deprive a person of his life, liberty or property. As noted earlier in Chapter 8, Section C (p. 275), Thomas Jefferson said,

> The legitimate powers of government extend to such acts only as are injurious to others. But it does me no injury for my neighbour to say there are twenty gods, or no god. It neither picks my pocket nor breaks my leg.[41]

Therefore, government cannot forbid a person from doing something that merely causes outrage in the minds of other people or sets a bad example. We have seen how this principle applies to a person's religious freedom and his right of privacy. Now we will see how it applies to his right of free speech and press.

Americans did not always cherish the right of free speech and press the way they do today. In 1670, Governor William Berkeley of Virginia wrote, "I thank God there are no free schools nor printing, and I hope we shall not have them these hundred years; for learning has brought disobedience into the world, and printing has divulged them, and libels against the best governments. God keep us from both!"[42]

In New England, however, public education was not seen as a threat to government authority. Many Puritan communities established public schools during the 1600s. However, they agreed with the other colonial leaders that the printing business should be tightly controlled. As a result, very few colonial books, pamphlets or newspapers dared to criticize government leaders.

One of the first newspapers that did criticize the government was the *New-England Courant*, a Boston newspaper begun in 1721 by James Franklin. In 1722, Franklin was sent to prison for criticizing the failure of the General Assembly to control piracy. So his sixteen-year-old brother Benjamin took over the paper. Benjamin, more discreet than his brother, wrote philosophical dissertations relevant to current events but allowed his readers to figure out the connection. Shortly after his brother was imprisoned, he published the following quotation from a Trenchard and Gordon *Cato Letter* (Chapter 1, Section C) that had appeared in a London newspaper:

> "[w]ithout freedom of thought, there can be no such thing as wisdom; and no such thing as public liberty without freedom of speech; which is the right of every man, as far as by it he does not hurt or controul the right of another; and this is the only check it ought to suffer and the only bounds it ought to know.
>
> "This sacred privilege is so essential to free government, that the security of property, and the freedom of speech always go together; and in those wretched countries where a man cannot call his tongue his own, he can scarce call any thing else his own. Whosoever would overthrow the liberty of a nation must begin by subduing the freeness of speech; a terrible thing to public traitors."[43]

In 1733, a German immigrant, John Peter Zenger, began publishing the *New York Weekly Journal*, a paper that was highly critical of the corrupt practices of New York governor William

Cosby. Zenger did not write many articles himself because of his poor knowledge of English. Most of his articles were letters written by Cosby's political opponents, including council president Rip Van Damm and Lewis Morris, a former chief justice who had been removed by Cosby. They attacked Cosby's moral character and misuse of power. Because of these attacks, Zenger was arrested in 1734 and charged with seditious libel.

At the jury trial the following year, the main issue was whether truth could be a defense to seditious libel. Zenger's attorney, the renowned Philadelphia lawyer Andrew Hamilton, admitted in his opening statement that his client had printed the offending papers. The New York attorney general answered that the jury must therefore find a verdict for the king, "for supposing they were true, the law says that they are not the less libelous for that; nay, indeed, the law says their being true is an aggravation of the crime." Hamilton responded,

> It is said and insisted upon by Mr. Attorney that government is a sacred thing . . . and if those in the Administration . . . must have all their conduct censured by private men, government cannot subsist. This is called a licentiousness not to be tolerated. It is said that it brings the ruler of the people into contempt . . . and so in the end the laws cannot be put into execution. . . . But I wish it might be considered at the same time how often it has happened that the abuse of power has been the primary cause of these evils; that it was the injustice and oppression of these great men which has commonly brought them into contempt with the people.

In his summation at the end of the trial, Hamilton told the jury there was more at stake than his client's own interests:

> [t]he question before the Court and you, Gentlemen of the jury, is not of small or private concern. It is not the cause of a poor printer, nor of New York alone, which you are now trying. No! It may in its consequences affect every freeman that lives under British government on the main of America! It is the best cause. It is the cause of liberty! And I make no doubt that your upright conduct of this day will not only entitle you to the love and esteem of your fellow citizens, but

every man who prefers freedom to a life of slavery will bless and honor you, as men who have baffled the attempt of tyranny, and by an impartial and incorrupt verdict have laid a noble foundation for securing to ourselves, our posterity, and our neighbors that to which nature and the laws of our country have given us a right---the liberty both of exposing and opposing arbitrary power---in these parts of the world, at least, by speaking and writing the truth![44]

The jury acquitted Zenger and a great celebration followed at the Black Horse Tavern. Unfortunately, Zenger could not attend because his jailers would not release him until he paid the room and board for his nine-month-long stay in jail. He had chosen to stay there rather than post the exorbitant bail that had been required for his release while awaiting trial. Afterward, Zenger published an account of his trial, which caused many American colonists to become more aware of their rights and liberties, not only freedom of speech and press, but freedom from excessive bail, the right to trial by jury and other rights. The jury-trial issue had arisen because the New York attorney general had tried to have the judge decide whether Zenger was guilty.

During the events that led to the War of Independence, the colonists relied on their rights of free speech and press to communicate their grievances to the British government and to each other. Their petitions to Parliament, their newspapers and their pamphlets were the means by which they campaigned for all their liberties as free Englishmen. Their freedom of press was attacked when taxes on newspapers levied by the Stamp Act forced some publishers to suspend publication. The colonists also identified their fight for liberty with that of the English politician John Wilkes, who had been imprisoned for publishing a newspaper that criticized the king and his ministers. When Massachusetts Governor Francis Bernard asked the colony's House of Representatives to punish Dr. Joseph Warren for publishing a letter characterizing him as "totally abandoned to wickedness," the House replied that "[a]lthough defaming a man, public or private, is certainly an outrage, yet freedom of the newspapers to tell lies on public men is so associated with their power to tell the truth that we think it impolitic to attempt by law to punish such lying."[45]

However, the right of free speech and press was not among the fundamental rights of life, liberty and property listed by Blackstone. He covered freedom of the press in his chapter "Of Offenses against the Public Peace" (BL6), but he showed that the English had a very narrow view of that right. He said,

> The liberty of the press is indeed essential to the nature of a free state; but this consists in laying no *previous* restraints on publications, and not in freedom from censure for criminal matter when published. Every freeman has an undoubted right to lay what sentiments he pleases before the public: to forbid this, is to destroy the freedom of the press: but if he publishes what is improper, mischievous, or illegal, he must take the consequences of his own temerity. To subject the press to the restrictive power of a licenser, as was formerly done, both before and since the revolution, is to subject all freedom of sentiment to the prejudices of one man, and make him the arbitrary and infallible judge of all controverted points of learning, religion, and government. But to punish (as the law does at present) any dangerous or offensive writings, which, when published, shall on a fair and impartial trial be judged of a pernicious tendency, is necessary for the preservation of peace and good order, of government and religion, the only solid foundations of civil liberty.

According to Blackstone, the English common law recognized there could be no prior government restraint that prevented a person from publishing anything he desired. However, after a person circulated his publication, Blackstone said he could be punished for saying not only things found to be "illegal" or "dangerous," but also things found to be "improper," "mischievous" or "offensive," provided a jury or judge found them to be of a "pernicious tendency."

The American colonists who demanded that the British king recognize their natural rights and liberties did not agree with these limitations on freedom of the press. By the 1760s, most Americans agreed with Benjamin Franklin and Andrew Hamilton, who had told them that the right of free speech and press was a fundamental right essential to protecting all the other rights of life, liberty and property. They had to speak and to publish in order to assert these other rights. They also had to speak and to publish in order to practice their various religions. They had a natural right to speak and to publish anything that did not interfere with other people's enjoyment of their life, liberty or property. The Continental Congress gave this definition of freedom of the press when it listed the "five great rights" in a letter to the inhabitants of Québec, dated October 26, 1774:

> [t]he last right we shall mention, regards freedom of the press. The importance of this consists, besides the advancement of truth, science, morality, and arts in general, in its diffusion of liberal sentiments on the administration of Government, its ready communication of thoughts between subjects, and its consequential promotion of union among them, whereby oppressive officers are shamed or intimidated, into more honorable and just modes of conducting affairs.[46]

Between 1776 and 1784, all the American states except Connecticut and Rhode Island adopted new constitutions. Eight of those constitutions proclaimed a list of people's rights that included freedom of the press. Article 12 of Virginia's Declaration of Rights said

> [t]hat freedom of the press is one of the great bulwarks of liberty, and can never be restrained but by despotick governments.

Pennsylvania was the only state to mention freedom of speech as part of the right of free press, in Article XII of its bill of rights:

> . . . the people have a right to freedom of speech, and of writing, and publishing their sentiments; therefore the freedom of the press ought not to be restrained.

The Vermont territorial constitution of 1786 also declared in Article XV that free speech was part of the right of a free press:

> ... the people have a right of freedom of speech and of writing and publishing their sentiments, concerning the transactions of government--and therefore the freedom of the press ought not to be restrained.

In 1792, Delaware joined the list of states guaranteeing freedom of the press when its new constitution proclaimed in Section 5 of its bill of rights that

> ... [t]he press shall be free to every citizen who undertakes to examine official conduct of men acting in a public capacity; and any citizen may print on any subject, being responsible for the abuse of that liberty. In prosecutions for publications investigating the proceedings of officers, or where the matter published is proper for public information, the truth thereof may be given in evidence; and in all indictments for libels, the jury may determine the facts and the law, as in other cases.

When the state of Connecticut adopted its first constitution in 1818, its declaration of rights included the following provisions:

> Sec. 5. Every citizen may freely speak, write, and publish his sentiments on all subjects, being responsible for the abuse of that liberty.
> Sec. 6. No law shall ever be passed to curtail or restrain the liberty of speech or of the press.
> Sec. 7. In all prosecutions or indictments for libels, the truth may be given in evidence, and the jury shall have the right to determine the law and the facts, under the direction of the court.

Section 20 of the bill of rights of Rhode Island's first constitution, adopted in 1842, said that

> [t]he liberty of the press being essential to the security of freedom of a state, any person may publish his sentiments on any subject, being responsible for the abuse of that liberty: and in all trials for libel, both civil and criminal, the truth, unless published from malicious motives, shall be sufficient defence to the person charged.

In addition to guaranteeing the right of free speech and press, the first constitutions of Connecticut, Maryland, Massachusetts,

New Hampshire, North Carolina, Pennsylvania, Rhode Island and Vermont guaranteed the right to petition the legislature. Except for Maryland, those states also guaranteed the right of peaceable assembly. Section XIX of the 1780 Massachusetts constitution had a typical provision:

> [t]he people have a right, in an orderly and peaceable manner, to assemble to consult upon the common good: give instructions to their representatives, and to request of the legislative body, by the way of addresses, petitions, or remonstrances, redress of wrongs done them, and of grievances they suffer.

New York did not guarantee freedom of speech or press in its 1777 constitution. However, the New York convention that ratified the U. S. Constitution proposed an amendment that said "[t]hat the Freedom of the Press ought not to be violated or restrained." The Virginia ratifying convention proposed a similar amendment saying "[t]hat the people have a right to freedom of speech, and of writing and publishing their Sentiments; but the freedom of the press is one of the greatest bulwarks of liberty and ought not to be violated." Madison's proposed bill of rights amendments included almost the same language as the Virginia convention proposal and added the rights of peaceable assembly and petition for redress of grievances:

> [t]he people shall not be deprived or abridged of their right to speak, to write, or to publish their sentiments; and the freedom of the press, as one of the great bulwarks of liberty, shall be inviolable.
> The people shall not be restrained from peaceably assembling and consulting for their common good; nor from applying to the legislature by petitions, or remonstrances for redress of their grievances.

When the first Congress approved the Bill of Rights amendments to the Constitution, it rewrote Madison's free speech and press guarantees and the following words became part of the First Amendment:

Congress shall make no law . . . abridging the freedom of speech, or of the press; or the right of the people to peaceably assemble, and to petition the government for a redress of grievances.

In 1794, Madison gave a speech to the U. S. House of Representatives in which he summed up the philosophy underlying the right of free speech and press. He said, "If we advert to the nature of Republican Government, we shall find that the censorial power is in the people over the Government, and not in the Government over the people."[47]

The Constitution's free speech and press guarantee received its first major assault in 1798, when Americans became alarmed by the expansion of French power in Europe. Napoleon had annexed nearly all of Europe to the French Empire; Great Britain and Russia were the only major nations that remained independent. Meanwhile, twenty-five thousand Frenchmen had emigrated to the United States. Some had come to escape persecution by the French government but others were plotting to expand French power in America. Congress reacted by passing the Alien and Sedition Acts. The Alien Act gave the president the power to expel suspicious foreigners by executive decree. The Sedition Act made it a crime, punishable by a fine of up to $5,000 and five years in prison, for any person to

> write, print, utter or publish . . . any false, scandalous and malicious writing or writings against the government of the United States, or either house of the Congress . . . , or the President . . . , with the intent to defame . . . or to bring them, or either of them, into contempt or disrepute; or to excite against them, or either or any of them, the hatred of the good people of the United States.

In spite of its requirement that the words be "false" and "malicious," many Americans condemned the Sedition Act because, they said, it violated the rights of free speech and press. About twenty-five men were arrested and ten were convicted under the Act, among them, a member of Congress and several newspaper editors. David Brown of Massachusetts received the longest jail term, four years, for his speech encouraging people to erect a liberty pole, similar to the kind displayed during the French Revolution.[48] These infringements upon the right of free speech and press spurred the Virginia and Kentucky state legislatures to pass resolutions declaring both the Alien Act and the Sedition Act void. Jefferson drafted the Kentucky resolution. The Virginia resolution was drafted by Madison and said

> [t]hat this state having, by its Constitution which ratified the Federal Constitution, expressly declared that, among other essential rights, "the liberty of conscience and of the press cannot be canceled, abridged, restrained or modified by any authority of the United States," and from its extreme anxiety to guard these rights from every possible attack of sophistry and ambition, having, with other states, recommended an amendment for that purpose, which amendment was in due time annexed to the Constitution,---it would mark a reproachful inconsistency and criminal degeneracy, if an indifference were now shown to the palpable violation of one of the rights thus declared and secured, and to the establishment of a precedent which may be fatal to the other.[49]

Maryland and many states north of Maryland passed their own resolutions protesting the ones passed by Virginia and Kentucky. These resolutions said that a state legislature had no authority to declare an act of Congress unconstitutional. Rhode Island and New Hampshire said that the federal Constitution gave the judicial department of the United States the exclusive power to declare a law in violation of that document.[50]

The Sedition Act expired in 1801 without being tested in the courts. When Jefferson became president, he pardoned everyone who had been imprisoned or fined under the law. He also said that he considered the law a nullity, "as absolute and as palpable as if Congress had ordered us to fall down and worship a golden image." In 1836, Senator John C. Calhoun of South Carolina said that he assumed that the invalidity of the Sedition Act was a matter "which no one now doubts." In 1840, Congress directed that all fines levied by the Sedition Act be repaid.[51]

The next attack on the right of free speech and press came when the southern states passed laws that banned antislavery speeches and publications. The First Amendment guarantee applied only to Congress, but all the southern states had guaranteed freedom of the press in their own constitutions. Under Jefferson and Madison's leadership, Virginians had come to appreciate the importance a broad right of free speech and press. However, in 1836, the year that Madison died, the Virginia legislature made it a crime for a member of an "abolition" society to enter the state and "advocate or advise the abolition of slavery."[52] Later it passed a law requiring postmasters to open mail to search for anti-slavery publications. In 1859, a Virginia postmaster banned the *New York Tribune* after finding it offensive.

Many other southern states passed laws requiring postmasters to search mail for anti-slavery materials. They also made it a felony to distribute literature that denied a master's right of property in his slaves. Other laws penalized people who spoke or wrote words that tended to produce discontent among free blacks or cause insubordination among slaves. In North Carolina, Daniel Worth was sentenced to twelve months in prison for distributing an anti-slavery book, *The Impending Crisis*, by Hinton R. Helper. The Republican Party had published the book as a campaign document. The North Carolina Supreme Court rejected Worth's defense that he had given the book only to white people. The court said that the intent to propagate the book's ideas was criminal, whether it be among white or black people.[53]

In the Kansas territory, after the pro-slavery candidates won control of the territorial assembly, the assembly passed laws that made it a felony "to assert that persons have not the right to hold slaves in said Territories," and a felony to circulate any writing containing sentiments calculated to induce slaves to escape from their masters. In 1856, Congressman John Bingham attacked these laws in a speech to the House of Representatives, claiming that the Bill of Rights of the federal Constitution applied to U. S. territorial governments. He said the Kansas laws violated the First Amendment, arguing that it would be a felony there to utter strong words of Algeron Sidney, "resistance to tyrants is obedience to God"; . . . a felony to read in the hearing of one of those fettered bondsmen the words of the Declaration, "All men are born free and equal, and endowed by their Creator with the unalienable rights of life and liberty"; . . . a felony to harbor a slave escaping from his thralldom; a felony to aid freedom in its flight. . . . Before you hold this enactment to be law, burn our immortal Declaration and our free-written Constitution, fetter our free press, and finally penetrate the human soul and put out the light of understanding which the breath of the Almighty hath kindled.[54]

C.2. Political Speech versus the Protection of Government

After the Civil War, the Thirteenth Amendment to the Constitution eliminated slavery and the Fourteenth Amendment said that no state shall deprive any person of life, liberty or property, without due process of law. However, it was not until 1927 that the U. S. Supreme Court ruled that the rights of life, liberty and property include the right of free speech and press. In *Fiske v. Kansas*, 274 U.S. 380 (1927), the Court overturned a state's criminal conviction of Fiske for teaching certain socialist ideas. The only evidence offered by the state prosecutor at the trial was that Fiske had publicly advocated

> "[t]hat the working class and the employing class have nothing in common, and that there can be no peace so long as hunger and want are found among millions of working people and the few who make up the employing class have all the good things of life. . . . Between these two classes a struggle must go on until the workers of the World organize a class, take possession of the earth, and the machinery of production and abolish the wage system. . . . Instead of the conservative motto, 'A fair day's wages for a fair day's work,' we must inscribe on our banner the revolutionary watchword, 'Abolish the wage system.' By organizing industrially we are forming the structure of a new society within the shell of the old." (Ibid., 382-383)

The state prosecutor charged that by uttering these words, Fiske had violated the Kansas law against "criminal syndicalism," which was defined as the advocacy of crime, physical violence or other unlawful acts as a means of accomplishing industrial or political ends. Although the prosecutor admitted that Fiske's words did not specifically advocate these violent acts, he argued that the jury could infer from his words that he advocated such violence. Speaking for a unanimous Court, Justice Edward Sanford said there was nothing in Fiske's words by which such a meaning could be inferred. Therefore, his conviction violated his right of free speech under the life, liberty and property clause of the Fourteenth Amendment.

Sanford distinguished Fiske's words from those at issue in the 1925 case of *Gitlow v. New York*, 268 U.S. 652. Gitlow had been convicted of violating New York's law against "Criminal Anarchy," defined as advocating "that organized government should be overthrown by force or violence, or by assassination of the executive head or of any of the executive officials of government, or by any unlawful means." He had published a "Left Wing Manifesto," in which he touted the doctrine of Revolutionary Socialism:

> Revolutionary Socialism . . . insists that the democratic parliamentary state can never be the basis for the introduction of Socialism; that it is necessary to destroy the parliamentary state, and construct a new state of the organized producers, which will deprive the bourgeoisie of political power, and function as a revolutionary dictatorship of the proletariat. . . . Revolutionary socialism alone is capable of mobilizing the proletariat for Socialism, for the conquest of the power of the State, by means of mass action and proletarian dictatorship. . . . The revolution starts with strikes of protest, developing into mass political strikes and then into revolutionary mass action for the power of the state. Mass action becomes political in purpose while extra-parliamentary in form; it is equally a process of revolution and the revolution itself in operation. The final objective of mass action is the conquest of the power of the state, the annihilation of the bourgeois parliamentary state and the introduction of the transition proletarian state, functioning as a revolutionary dictatorship of the proletariat. . . .

The proletariat revolution and the Communist reconstruction of society---*the struggle for these*---is now indispensable. . . . The Communist International calls the proletariat of the world to the final struggle!

Justice Sanford also wrote the majority opinion in this case. He said that Gitlow's conviction did not violate his right of free speech, because his Manifesto "is not the expression of philosophical abstraction, the mere prediction of future events; it is the language of direct incitement" (Ibid., 665).

Justices Oliver Wendell Holmes and Louis Brandeis dissented in this case because they believed the test of whether words can be forbidden by government is whether they create "a clear and present danger" that they will bring about the evils that government has a right to prevent." Holmes reasoned,

> If the publication of this document had been laid as an attempt to induce an uprising against government at once and not at some indefinite time in the future it would have presented a different question. The object would have been one with which the law might deal, subject to the doubt whether there was any danger that the publication could produce any result, or in other words, whether it was not futile and too remote from possible consequences. But the indictment alleges the publication and nothing more. (Ibid., 673)

Holmes had used this "clear and present danger test" in his majority opinion in *Schenck v. United States*, 249 U.S. 47 (1919), in which the Supreme Court upheld the conviction of a man for mailing leaflets to men who had passed the draft exemption boards, urging them to avoid the draft. He had also filed a dissent based on the lack of a "clear and present danger" in *Abrams et al. v. United States*, 250 U.S. 616 (1919) and both Holmes and Brandeis had dissented for the same reason in *Schaefer v. United States*, 251 U.S. 466 (1920). However, Justice Sanford rejected the "clear and present danger" test in the *Gitlow* case, relying on the following quotation from the Illinois Supreme Court in *People v. Lloyd*, 304 Ill. at 35:

"Manifestly, the legislature has the authority to forbid the advocacy of a doctrine designed and intended to overthrow the government without waiting until there is a present and imminent danger of the success of the plan advocated. If the State were compelled to wait until the apprehended danger became certain, then its right to protect itself would come into being simultaneously with the overthrow of the government, when there would be neither prosecuting officers nor courts of enforcement of the law." (268 U.S. at 669-670)

Based on Justice Sanford's reasoning in the *Gitlow* case, many courts ruled that state laws against "criminal syndicalism" did not violate the right of free speech and press, even when "criminal syndicalism" was defined as merely "advocating . . . the duty, necessity, or propriety of crime, sabotage, violence, or unlawful methods of terrorism as a means of accomplishing industrial or political reform" (Ohio Revised Code Annotated, §2923.13). Some judges claimed to adopt Holmes's "clear and present danger" test, but they interpreted the test so that it covered speech that attempted "to induce an uprising against government at some indefinite time in the future," which was the very kind of speech that Holmes said did not give rise to "a clear and present danger" when he coined the phrase (268 U.S. at 673).

In 1969, the U. S. Supreme Court put an end to this confusion in the case of *Brandenburg v. Ohio*, 395 U.S. 444. Brandenburg was judged guilty of violating the Ohio law against criminal syndicalism because he made the following statement at a Klu Klux Klan rally near Cincinnati:

We're not a revengent organization, but if our President, our Congress, our Supreme Court, continues to suppress the white, Caucasian race, it's possible that there might have to be some revengeance taken. (Ibid., 446)

In a unanimous, joint opinion, the Supreme Court ruled that Brandenburg's conviction violated his right of free speech because he was punished for merely advocating violence, as distinguished from "incitement to imminent lawless action" (Ibid., 448-449). The "incitement to imminent lawless action" test thus apparently replaced the "clear and present danger" test. Justices Black and William O. Douglas said in concurring opinions that because of the distorted meanings it had been given, the "clear and present danger" test should have no place in the interpretation of the First Amendment.

C.3. Prior Restraint and Post Publication Liability

Blackstone said that freedom of the press meant that government could lay "no *previous* restraints" on a person's ability to publish; all it could do was punish the person after he had published forbidden material (BL6). In the 1931 case of *Near v. Minnesota*, 283 U.S. 697, the U.S. Supreme Court was confronted with a Minnesota law that allowed government officials to shut down the publication of any newspaper, magazine or other periodical found to be (a) "obscene, lewd and lascivious" or (b) "malicious, scandalous and defamatory." The defendant Near had been found guilty of violating section (b) of that law and had been enjoined from publishing his newspaper, the *Saturday Press*. He had run a series of articles about a Jewish gangster who carrying on gambling, bootlegging and racketeering operations in Minneapolis. The articles charged that the local law enforcement people were ignoring these crimes because they were being paid by the gangster, and that the mayor and the county prosecutor were derelict in their duties for allowing these things to happen.

The Supreme Court ruled that section (b) of the Minnesota law was unconstitutional because it violated Near's freedom of press under the life, liberty and property clause of the Fourteenth Amendment. Chief Justice Charles Evans Hughes, writing for the majority of the Court, said the law's injunctive remedy had imposed a prior restraint that violated a fundamental principle of freedom of press. Hughes acknowledged that this immunity from prior restraint was not absolute. In *Schenck v. United States*, supra, the Court had approved an injunction against exhorting men to avoid the draft during wartime. In *Patterson v. Colorado*, 205 U.S. 454, it had approved an order enjoining people from interfering with the discharge of judicial orders. These prior restraints were designed to protect the proper administration of government. However, that purpose is not served when people are restrained from criticizing public officials for the way they do their jobs. Hughes said,

> While reckless assaults upon public men, and efforts to bring obloquy upon those who are endeavoring faithfully to discharge official duties, exert a baleful influence and deserve the severest condemnation in public opinion, it cannot be said that this abuse is greater, and it is believed to be less, than that which characterized the period in which our institutions took shape. Meanwhile, the administration of government has become more complex, the opportunities for malfeasance and corruption have multiplied, crime has grown to most serious proportions, and the danger of its protection by unfaithful officials and of the impairment of the fundamental security of life and property by criminal alliances and official neglect, emphasizes the primary need of a vigilant and courageous press, especially in great cities. The fact that the liberty of the press may be abused by miscreant purveyors of scandal does not make any the less necessary the immunity of the press from previous restraint in dealing with official misconduct. Subsequent punishment for such abuses as may exist is the appropriate remedy, consistent with constitutional privilege. (283 U.S. at 719-720)

The attorneys for the state of Minnesota had argued that the law did not violate the right of free press because it allowed the accused the defense that his words were true and they were written with good motives, for justifiable ends. Hughes rejected that argument, saying that if such a law can be enforced,

> the legislature may provide machinery for determining in the complete exercise of its discretion what are justifiable ends and restrain publication accordingly. And it would be but a step to a complete system of censorship. The recognition of authority to impose previous restraint upon publication in order to protect the community against the circulation of charges of misconduct, and especially of official misconduct, necessarily would carry with it the admission of the authority of the censor against which the constitutional barrier was erected. The preliminary freedom, by virtue of the very reason for its

existence, does not depend, as this Court has said, on proof of truth. *Patterson v. Colorado, supra.* (Ibid., 721)

As Blackstone had pointed out, the rule that government cannot impose a prior restraint on publication does not absolve a person from liability when he circulates a publication that injures the rights of other people. And there are exceptions to the prior restraint rule, such as when a person threatens to overthrow the government by force or exhorts people to interfere with the operation of government.

In more recent years, the U. S. Supreme Court has broadened the right to criticize government officials to include immunity from post-publication liability in certain situations. In *New York Times Co. v. Sullivan*, 376 U.S. 254 (1964), a group called the "Committee to Defend Martin Luther King and the Struggle for Freedom in the South" placed a full-page advertisement in the *New York Times* saying that non-violent civil rights demonstrations in the south were being met by "an unprecedented wave of terror by those who would deny and negate" the Bill of Rights. This statement was followed by ten paragraphs of specific charges, two of which read as follows:

> In Montgomery, Alabama, after students sang "My Country, 'Tis of Thee" on the State Capitol steps, their leaders were expelled from school, and truckloads of police armed with shotguns and tear-gas ringed the Alabama State College Campus. When the entire student body protested to state authorities by refusing to re-register, their dining hall was padlocked in an attempt to starve them into submission. . . .
>
> Again and again the Southern violators have answered Dr. King's peaceful protests with intimidation and violence. They have bombed his home almost killing his wife and child. They have assaulted his person. They have arrested him seven times---for "speeding," "loitering," and similar "offenses." And now they have charged him with "perjury"---a *felony* under which they could imprison him for *ten years*. . . . . (Ibid., 257-258)

L. B. Sullivan, a Montgomery city commissioner who supervised the police department, filed an action for civil libel against the New

York Times and some of the people who signed the advertisement. At the trial, Sullivan's attorneys submitted undisputed evidence that (1) the student leaders were not expelled for singing on the state capitol steps but for demanding service at a lunch counter in the Montgomery County Courthouse on another day; (2) the students did not protest by refusing to register but by boycotting classes on a single day; (3) the police never surrounded the campus but large numbers of police were deployed near the campus on three occasions; (4) the police were not called to the campus in connection with the demonstration on the capitol steps, as the advertisement implied; (5) the campus dining hall was never padlocked and the only students barred from the hall were those who neither preregistered nor requested temporary meal tickets; and (6) Dr. King had been arrested only four times, not seven. There was evidence that the advertisement contained other errors, but some of that evidence was contested. Sullivan asserted that because the false statements mentioned the police and spoke of arrests, his reputation as police commissioner had been damaged. He also charged that the Times was negligent in not checking the facts before running the advertisement. He proved the newspaper had information in its own files showing the statements were false. The jury agreed and awarded him $500,000 damages.

The U. S. Supreme Court ruled that this verdict violated the defendants' right of free press under the life, liberty and property clause of the Fourteenth Amendment. Speaking for the Court, Justice William Brennan said that when people who criticize government officials are held liable for damages unless they can prove the truth of their statements, they will "tend to make only statements which 'steer far wider of the unlawful zone.' *Speiser v. Randall, supra.*, 357 U.S. at 526. The rule thus dampens the vigor and limits the variety of public debate" (Ibid., 279). Therefore, said Brennan, when a government official brings a civil libel action, he must prove that the offending statement was not only false but made with "actual malice" (Ibid., 280-281). In the case of Sullivan, the Court said there was no evidence that the defendants made their statements with malice toward him. Justices Black, Douglas and

Arthur Goldberg concurred in Brennan's opinion but said the guarantee of free press ought to be even broader, so that people can make any statements about the conduct of government, including those that are malicious as well as false. They pointed out that the Sedition Act of 1798 punished only people who made false and malicious statements, yet that law was severely criticized by many of the nation's early leaders, including Jefferson, Madison and Calhoun. Congress later agreed with these leaders and refunded all fines imposed under the law. Black, Douglas and Goldberg could have also cited the 1768 statement of the Massachusetts House of Representatives, mentioned in Section *C.1* above, that freedom of newspapers "to tell lies on public men is so associated with their power to tell the truth that we think it impolitic to attempt by law to punish such lying."[55]

The right to criticize government officials is one aspect of the right of free speech and press that is not based on the fact that no other person is injured. Government officials can be injured when false statements are made about them. However, these injuries are an essential part of the price of the public trust that they have sought and gained. Blackstone said that one of the auxiliary rights that people have for the protection of their life, liberty and property is the right to petition the government for the redress of grievances (BL3, 138-139). When a person criticizes a government official, he is essentially doing no more than petitioning for a redress of grievances.

The reason for the broad right to criticize government officials does not apply to criticism of other people. If a person makes a false statement about a private person that injures his reputation, he will be liable for damages. However, the Supreme Court has not clearly indicated what kinds of statements people can or cannot make about public celebrities who do not work for the government. *Hustler Magazine and Larry Flynt v. Jerry Falwell*, 485 U.S. 46 (1988) concerned a parody published by Flynt's *Hustler* magazine implying that Falwell had had sexual intercourse with his mother in an outhouse. Falwell sued Flynt, claiming libel and intentional infliction of emotional distress. Although the jury found no libel because no one could have reasonably believed the parody described actual facts, it awarded Falwell damages for his emotional distress. Flynt appealed the verdict to the U.S. Supreme Court, which ruled that the jury's award for emotional distress violated Flynt's right of free speech. Speaking for the Court, Chief Justice Rehnquist said that claims allowed for emotional distress based on words not judged to be defamatory or libelous would stifle debate on public issues concerning public figures. On the other hand, the Court probably would have ruled against Flynt had the jury not rejected Falwell's libel claim. No public interest was served by Flynt's parody, which was simply a malicious, sleazy story. Such statements are usually held to be libelous, even when directed toward public celebrities, provided the celebrities do not work for the government.

In addition to libel actions, other exceptions to the right of free speech include liability for damages if a person's words incite a riot or induce others to breach their contracts. An advertiser can be liable for publishing false or misleading statements about a competitor's product. An author can be liable for copying words written by another person in violation of the federal copyright laws. A person can be held accountable for publicizing the private affairs of ordinary people without their consent or for using the names or pictures of famous people for commercial gain without their consent. A person can be subject to criminal penalties if he publishes obscene materials or if he distributes unauthorized copies of video or sound recordings. Except for government criticism, the right of free speech and press extends only to communications that do not injure the life, liberty or property of other parties.

C.4. The Right of Peaceable Assembly

The right of people to assemble peaceably to express their views is part of the right of free speech and press. In *DeJonge v. Oregon*, 299 U.S. 353 (1937), the U. S. Supreme Court ruled that a state cannot deprive people of this right because it is guaranteed by the life, liberty and property clause of the Fourteenth Amendment.

Dirk DeJonge had been convicted of assisting in the conduct of a Communist Party meeting, in violation of Oregon's law against criminal syndicalism. Criminal syndicalism was defined as behavior that involved advocating crime, physical violence, sabotage or other unlawful acts in order to accomplish industrial or political change. There was no evidence that the DeJonge or anyone else advocated those things at the meeting; the evidence showed only that the Communist Party had distributed literature that advocated those things. Speaking for the Court, Chief Justice Hughes said that DeJonge's right of peaceable assembly had been violated because

> [i]f the persons assembling have committed crimes elsewhere, if they have formed or are engaged in a conspiracy against the public peace and order, they may be prosecuted for their conspiracy or other violation of valid laws. But it is a different matter when the State, instead of prosecuting them for such offenses, seizes upon the mere participation in a peaceable assembly and a lawful public discussion as the basis for a criminal charge. (Ibid., 365)

C.5. Fighting Words and Hate Speech

The right of free speech does not include "fighting words" or "hate speech" directed at people who would with good reason respond with violence. The leading case on this subject is *Chaplinsky v. New Hampshire*, 315 U.S. 568 (1942). In that case, Chaplinsky told the marshall of Rochester, New Hampshire, "You are a damned racketeer . . . a damned Fascist and the whole government of Rochester are Fascists or agents of Fascists." Chaplinsky had confronted the marshall with those words on a public street after being arrested by another police officer. That officer had arrested him for causing a disturbance at a busy traffic intersection while distributing Jehovah's Witness literature. However, Chaplinsky's conviction was based on the words he used to the city marshall, not on the disturbance at the traffic intersection. The marshall testified that Chaplinsky had also said, "You are a God damned racketeer." His conviction was based on the fact that he had violated a state law that forbade a person to call another person by an offensive or derisive name or making a noise or exclamation with the intent to deride, offend or annoy a person or prevent him from pursuing his lawful occupation.

Chaplinsky claimed the New Hampshire law violated his right of free speech under the life, liberty and property clause of the Fourteenth Amendment. The U. S. Supreme Court did not agree. Speaking for a unanimous Court, Justice Frank Murphy said that a state could protect the public by preventing people from saying "insulting or 'fighting' words---those which by their very utterance inflict injury to tend to incite an immediate breach of the peace."

A significant aspect of the *Chaplinsky* case was that no breach of the peace actually occurred. It was sufficient that the words tended to incite an immediate breach of the peace. In effect, the Supreme Court said that violent words alone can constitute an assault by one person upon another person. Like other forms of criminal assault, it does not matter whether the victim retaliated or simply turned the other cheek.

However, a person can use hate speech if he is speaking at a closed meeting of people who would not be offended by the speech. That rule was established in *Terminello v. Chicago*, 337 U.S. 1 (1949). Terminello was a Catholic priest from Alabama who had been placed under suspension by his bishop. He addressed a convention of the Christian Veterans of America in a Chicago auditorium that was filled to capacity and surrounded on the outside by a crowd of angry demonstrators. Terminello and the Christian Veterans held views that were extremely right wing, closely resembling Fascism, although Terminello claimed that he was not a Fascist. The people outside were at the opposite end of the political spectrum and possibly included Communists. Terminello called the people outside "slimy scum," and said that possibly "some of the scum got in by mistake." He then quoted Communist literature that said the nature of their movement was "not mere talk, but an all embracing blood-soaked reality." The Democratic administration in Washington, he claimed, was allied with this movement and "Queen Eleanor [Roosevelt] is now one of the world's communists." He then attacked the Jews:

I am going to talk about some Jews. . . . Now this danger we face--let us call them Zionist Jews if you will, let's call them aetheistic, communistic Jewish or Zionist Jews, then let us not fear to condemn them. You remember the Apostles when they went into the upper room after the death of their Master, they went in there, after locking the doors; they closed the windows. (Ibid., 20)

At the trial, Terminello testified that before the meeting started, he had seen a number of windows broken by stones and the mob outside pushing in the back door. He said this violence continued during the meeting and that "[p]olice were rushing in and out of the front door protecting the front door, and there was general commotion, all kinds of noises and violence--all from the outside" (Ibid., 15-16). Apparently because of this violence, Terminello ended his speech with these words:

Those mobs are chanting; that is the caveman's chant. They were trained to do it. They were trained this afternoon. They are being led; there will be violence.

That is why I say to you, men, don't you do it. Walk out of here dignified. The police will protect you. Put the women on the inside, where there will be no hurt to them. Just walk; don't stop and argue. . . . They want to picket our meetings. They don't want us to picket their meetings. It is the same kind of tolerance, if we said there was a bedbug in bed, "We don't care for you," or if we looked under the bed and found a snake and said, "I am going to be tolerant and leave the snake there." We will not be tolerant of that mob out there. We are not going to be tolerant any longer.

We are strong enough. We are not going to be tolerant of their smears any longer. We are going to stand up and dare them to smear us.

So, my friends, since we spent much time tonight trying to quiet the howling mob, I am going to bring my thoughts to a conclusion, and the conclusion is this. We must be like the Apostles before the coming of the Holy Ghost. We must not lock ourselves in the upper room for fear of the Jews. I speak of the Communistic Zionistic Jew, and those are not American Jews. We don't want them here; we want them to go back where they came from. (Ibid., 21)

After his speech, Terminello was charged with violating a Chicago ordinance that forbade a noise or disturbance "tending to a breach of the peace." The jury found him guilty after the judge had said that the ordinance prohibited speech that "stirs the public to anger, invites dispute, brings about a condition of unrest, or creates a disturbance."

By a five-to-four majority, the U. S. Supreme Court ruled that Terminello's right of free speech had been violated because, according to the judge's instructions, his only crime was stirring up "anger" and "dispute" and creating "unrest" and "disturbance." Speaking for the majority, Justice Douglas said that

> a function of free speech under our system of government is to invite dispute. It may indeed best serve its high purpose when it induces a condition of unrest, creates dissatisfaction with conditions as they are, or even stirs people to anger. Speech is often provocative and challenging. It may strike at prejudices and preconceptions and have profound unsettling effects as it presses for acceptance of an idea. (Ibid., 4)

Douglas then applied the "clear and present danger" test that Justice Holmes had advocated in his majority opinion in *Schenck v. United States*, supra, and in his dissenting opinion in *Gitlow v. New York*, supra. In order to be punished, Douglas said, the offending speech must be shown "likely to produce a clear and present danger of a serious substantive evil that arises far above public inconvenience, annoyance, or unrest" (Ibid., 4).

Chief Justice Frederick Vinson and Justice Felix Frankfurter dissented on the ground that the Court should have ignored the faulty jury instruction--Terminello's attorneys had not objected to it or mentioned it in any of their appeal briefs, either in the Illinois appellate courts or in the Supreme Court of the United States. Justices Robert Jackson and Harold Burton dissented on the ground that the jury instruction had to be interpreted in the light of the angry and turbulent crowd that was already in a rioting mood. They said that under these circumstances there was a clear and present danger that Terminello's epithets of "slimy scum," "snakes" and "bedbugs" would cause even more violence than was already occurring outside the meeting place.

The *Chaplinsky* and *Terminello* decisions appear in one respect to be difficult to reconcile. The words uttered in both cases were equally hateful and insulting and were calculated to provoke angry responses. However, Chaplinsky was talking face-to-face to the person he was insulting. Terminello was speaking in a closed hall at a rally for people who agreed with his views. The only people offended by his racial slurs and epithets were gate crashers and people who were already rioting outside the hall where he was speaking. They had no right to be within listening range of his speech. The rights of free speech and assembly surely ought to include the right of a group of people with common hatreds to gather in a closed meeting place to vent their anger and discuss their hatreds, no matter how obnoxious those opinions might be to other people. The riot that occurred before, during and after Terminello's speech was the sole work of his detractors and was without justifiable provocation.

Although government can outlaw hate speech designed to provoke violence, it cannot single out certain kinds of hate speech for punishment. In *R.A.V. v. St. Paul*, 505 U.S. 377 (1992), the U. S. Supreme Court invalidated a St. Paul, Minnesota ordinance that forbade the use of fighting words that the city deemed particularly offensive, namely words that insult or provoke violence "on the basis of race, color, creed or gender." The Court ruled that the city was not forbidding hate speech but was regulating the content of the speech.

The next year, however, the Supreme Court upheld a Wisconsin law that increased the penalty for certain violent crimes, if they were committed "because of the race, religion, color, disability, sexual orientation, national origin or ancestry" of the victim [*Wisconsin v. Mitchell*, 508 U.S. 476 (1993)]. The Court ruled the law was valid because it regulated violent conduct, not speech. The opponents of the law had claimed that it suppressed people's speech because they would fear that if they criticized one of groups protected by the law, their words might be used to increase their penalty in the event they later committed a crime against a member of that group. Speaking for the Court, Chief Justice Rehnquist said that hypothesis was too speculative. He also pointed out that the right of free speech does not prevent a person's prior statements from being used to establish an element of a crime, nor does it render that criminal element unconstitutional.

C.6. Non-Verbal Communications

Words are not the only means by which a person can express himself. A person can convey his opinions by holding up a flag or other symbol or by doing something to the flag or symbol, such as saluting it or burning it. The U. S. Supreme Court has ruled that these methods of communicating are forms of speech and press and they are protected by the Constitution for the same reasons that words are protected.

In *Stromberg v. California*, 283 U.S. 359 (1931), the defendant Stromberg was convicted of displaying a red flag in opposition to organized government. The Supreme Court ruled that the conviction violated Stromberg's right of free speech under the life, liberty and property clause of the Fourteenth Amendment. His speech was protected, it ruled, because the flag did not necessarily convey a message that threatened the security of organized government.

In *West Virginia State Board of Education v. Barnette*, 319 U.S. 624 (1943), the Board of Education ordered that all public school teachers and students be required to salute the American flag and say the pledge of allegiance in school ceremonies. A student's failure to conform to this order was deemed "insubordination" and was punished by his expulsion from school. The expelled child was then deemed a delinquent; his parents could be subject to a fine of fifty dollars and a prison term of thirty days. To prevent enforcement of this order, several Jehovah's Witnesses sued the Board because they regarded a flag salute as a violation of God's commandment against worshipping graven images.

The U. S. Supreme Court ruled that the Board of Education order violated the U. S. Constitution, but not because it violated the religious freedom of the Jehovah's Witnesses. The Court ruled that the order violated everyone's right of free speech, thereby overruling its previous decision in *Minersville School District v. Gobitis*, 310 U.S. 586 (1940), in which it had upheld a similar flag salute requirement. Justice Felix Frankfurter had said in the Court's opinion in *Minersville* that "[n]ational unity is the basis of national security" and therefore government authorities could adopt compulsory measures to achieve national unity, such as by ordering school children and teachers to salute the flag. In the *Barnette* case, however, the Court admitted that Frankfurter's reasoning was flawed. Speaking for the Court, Justice Robert Jackson said that national unity could be achieved only by persuasion and example, not by coercion. After reviewing the efforts of previous nations to compel patriotic unity, including the Roman Empire's campaign to force Christians to acknowledge "Caesar is Lord" and the Christian inquisitions during the Middle Ages, he concluded that

> [c]ompulsory unification of opinion achieves only the unanimity of the graveyard. . . . We can have intellectual individualism and the rich cultural diversities that we owe to exceptional minds only at the price of occasional eccentricity and abnormal attitudes. When they are so harmless to others or to the State as those we deal with here, the price is not too great. But freedom to differ is not limited to things that do not matter much. That would be a mere shadow of freedom. The test of its substance is the right to differ as to things that touch the heart of the existing order.
>
> If there is any fixed star in our constitutional constellation, it is that no official, high or petty, can prescribe what shall be called orthodox in politics, nationalism, religion, or other matters of opinion and force citizens to confess by word or act their faith therein. If there are any circumstances which permit an exception, they do not now occur to us. (Ibid., at 641-642)

A person not only has the right express his opinion by displaying a red flag or refusing to salute the American flag, he also has the right to disfigure or burn his own flag. In *Spence v. State of*

Washington, 418 U.S. 405 (1974), Harold Spence had taped a peace symbol to his American flag in violation of a Washington state law. In *Texas v. Johnson*, 491 U.S. 397 (1989), Gregory Johnson had burned his American flag in violation of a Texas state law. In neither case did the state offer any proof that the defendant's conduct had caused a fight, breached the peace or harmed other people. In both cases, the state asserted that its action was justified because of its interest in preserving the American flag as "an important symbol of nationhood and unity." In both cases, the Supreme Court ruled the defendant's right of free speech had been violated because he had a right to question whether the flag was such a symbol and to question the supposed truth represented by the symbol. In the Court's majority opinion in the *Texas v. Johnson* case, Justice Brennan relied on Justice Jackson's reasoning in the *Barnette* case, quoted earlier. In his concurring opinion in *Texas v. Johnson*, Justice Kennedy addressed the concerns of war veterans who marched with the flag in battle while defending America's freedom:

> I agree that the flag holds a lonely place of honor in an age when absolutes are distrusted and simple truths are burdened by unneeded apologetics.
>
> With all respect to those views, I do not believe the Constitution gives us the right to rule as the dissenting Members of the Court urge, however painful this judgment is to announce. Though symbols often are what we ourselves make of them, the flag is constant in expressing beliefs Americans share, beliefs in law and peace and that freedom which sustains the human spirit. The case here today forces recognition of the costs to which those beliefs commit us. It is poignant but fundamental that the flag protects those who hold it in contempt. (Ibid., 421)

The Supreme Court decided the *Texas v. Johnson* case by a five-to-four vote. Chief Justice Rehnquist and Justices White, O'Connor and Stevens dissented. They believed that the American flag deserved an honored status as a symbol of the nation's heritage and that federal and state governments should be allowed to protect that honored status by punishing those who desecrate the flag. Since this case, many people have campaigned for an amendment to the Constitution that would nullify the Court's ruling. In the 1992 and 1996 presidential campaigns, the Republican candidates George Bush and Bob Dole supported an anti-flag-desecration amendment to the Constitution.

The people who support the anti-flag-desecration amendment do not seek to protect the life, liberty or property of people, nor the security or property of government. They seek to protect the patriotic ideal represented by the flag---the ideal of a nation with a great heritage of fighting for freedom and justice and a people who are united and dedicated to carrying on that fight. They say this patriotic ideal is not like any of the other noble ideals by which people should live their lives. Rather, they say, it is of such great importance that it deserves special treatment. In the past they have tried to give the ideal special treatment by making all school children salute the flag and say the pledge of allegiance. Now they are trying to limit the means by which people can oppose the ideal.

Only a few people in America would challenge this ideal. That should not detract from the rights of these people to express their opinions in any way that does not endanger the safety or property of others. The constitutions of several former Communist nations show why the right of free speech and press cannot tolerate exceptions of the kind represented by the anti-flag-desecration amendment. The Rumanian Constitution of 1965 guaranteed freedom of speech and press, equal rights for all people, freedom of religion, freedom of assembly, freedom from arbitrary arrest and many other freedoms. However, it also said that the freedom of speech and press "cannot be used for aims hostile to the socialist system and to the interests of the working people." The Czechoslovak Constitution of 1960, the Hungarian Constitution of 1949 and the Soviet Union Constitution of 1936 guaranteed the same freedoms, but in each case the freedom of speech and press was limited by words similar to the ones of the Czechoslovak Constitution: "consistent with the interests of the working people."[56] This exception gave the Communist leaders a pretense for denying the right of free speech and press in nearly every case when people tried to use it. Because the people had no right of free speech and press, the leaders were able to ignore all the other rights of people without being criticized.

The Communist experience teaches us that the only secure right of free speech and press is one that is free of ideological exceptions, including the very ideology on which the government is founded. The United States government was founded on the ideal of freedom and justice for all--an ideal that embodies the right of free speech and press. People should be able to exercise this right by any means of expression, provided they do not endanger the safety or property of others.

C.7. The Right of the Public to Attend Criminal Trials

Newspapers, television stations and other news media organizations have long asserted that their right of free speech and press includes not only their right to publicize what they already know but also the right to gather the information they want to publicize. There is no basis for that assertion. The U. S. Constitution does not obligate a person to answer questions asked of him by a news reporter, nor does it guarantee news reporters and photographers the right to pursue and harass famous celebrities.

However, in a democratic society, many government proceedings should be open to the general public, including the news media. In the United States, most of the proceedings of Congress, the various federal-rule making agencies, and most state and local law-making bodies are open to the public. Article I, Section 5[3] of the U. S. Constitution says that each house of Congress "shall keep a Journal of its Proceedings, and from time to time publish the same, ..." with the exception, the Constitution adds, of "such Parts as may in their Judgment require Secrecy." That appears to give Congress wide discretion in determining when its own doors or that of any federal agency can be closed to the public. State and local legislatures would appear to have the same discretion without violating the U. S. Constitution.

That discretion does not apply to the judicial branches of the state and federal governments. The U. S. Supreme Court has said that when a court of law is conducting a criminal trial, the public has a right under the U. S. Constitution to attend that trial. In *Richmond Newspapers, Inc. v. Virginia*, 448 U.S. 555 (1980), the Supreme Court said that the public's right to attend a criminal trial stems from its Anglo-American history. Since the Magna Charta, an accused person has been able to demand a jury trial to determine whether he should be punished by having his life, liberty or property taken from him (BL3, 130-131, 134). In his chapter, "Of the Trial by Jury," Blackstone said this jury trial must be open to the public:

> This open examination of witnesses *viva voce*, in the presence of all mankind, is much more conducive to the clearing up of truth, than the private and secret examination taken down in writing before an officer, or his clerk, in the ecclesiastical courts, and all others that have borrowed their practice from the civil law: where a witness may frequently depose that in private, which he will be ashamed to testify in a public and solemn tribunal.[57]

The Sixth Amendment to the U. S. Constitution guarantees the right of an accused person to a public trial. The U. S. Supreme Court ruled in *In re Oliver*, 333 U.S. 257 (1948) that the life, liberty and property clause of the Fourteenth Amendment requires the state courts to observe this right. When the accused person exercises this right, there is no need for other members of the public to demand a public trial. However, the Supreme Court ruled in *Richmond Newspapers, Inc. v. Virginia*, supra, that when the accused person waives his right to a public trial, any member of the public, including a news reporter, can assert his right to have the trial conducted in public. The right of an accused to a fair trial means a trial that is fair to both sides. Therefore, the judge must respect the public's concern that a private hearing might lead to false testimony in favor of the accused. The members of the general public and the victim have the right to assure themselves that the state is properly protecting their rights of life, liberty and property. Chief Justice Warren Burger said in the *Richmond* case that the public has a

> fundamental, natural yearning to see justice done---or even the urge for retribution. The crucial prophylactic aspects of the administration of justice cannot function in the dark; no community catharsis can occur if justice is "done in a corner [or] in any covert manner" *Supra*, at 567. It is not enough to say that results alone will satiate the natural community desire for "satisfaction." A result considered untoward may undermine public confidence, and where the trial has been concealed from public view an unexpected outcome can cause a reaction that the system at best has failed and at worst has been corrupted. (Ibid., 571)

Given this public concern, there should seldom arise a case in which a prosecutor would waive the government's right to a public trial. One of those rare cases might be when the prosecutor needs the testimony of a rape victim and the victim cannot endure the trauma of describing her experience in public. In *Globe Newspaper Co. v. Superior Court for the County of Norfolk*, 457 U.S. 596 (1982), the Globe Newspaper Company, publisher of the *Boston Globe*, was denied access to a trial for the rape of two sixteen-year-old girls and one seventeen-year-old girl. Neither the defense nor prosecuting attorney waived their client's right to a public trial, but a Massachusetts law required the press and the general public to be excluded from all trials for sexual offenses involving a victim under the age of eighteen. The U. S. Supreme Court ruled that this law violated the life, liberty and property clause of the Fourteenth Amendment because it did not allow the judge to determine whether the public and press should be excluded. The Court said that decisions on this issue must be on case-by-case basis, so that the victim, the victim's relatives and the prosecutor have the opportunity to state their wishes concerning public access to the trial.

C.8. Freedom of Speech on the Internet

The Internet has become a major means by which people communicate with one another in modern society. People send messages to one another using E-mail boxes. Mailing list services and mail exploders enable businesses to advertise their products and services to selected potential customers. Newsgroups and chat rooms enable large groups of people to talk among one another. The World Wide Web provides huge libraries of information that everyone can access. Businesses use sites on the Web to advertise their products and services and receive orders from the general public. Stockbrokers have Web sites by which their clients can buy and sell securities. Television and radio stations and newspapers maintain Web sites as a further way of disseminating news and entertainment to the public. These Web sites also allow them to receive feedback from their readers and listeners. Every kind of human interaction and communication known to man now takes place on a larger scale on the Internet, using telecommunication devices better known as computers.

Like all means of communication, the Internet can be used to destroy rather than advance the quality of people's lives. Some people send messages that harass and mislead other people. Sometimes these messages are obscene or are not appropriate for the ears of young children. Preventing this kind of activity has proven very difficult. Computer programs have been designed to deny access to Internet materials that contain certain words or phrases, or to deny access to sources known to transmit inappropriate materials. However, no program has been developed that will block such materials without also blocking large bodies of materials that are not objectionable. There is also no program yet available that will block inappropriate pictures. Because of these difficulties, people have been campaigning for more stringent laws to stop others from sending materials on the Internet that corrupt the minds of children.

In 1996, Congress passed the Communications Decency Act, which had several provisions designed to shield children from these harmful materials.

One of these provisions, 47 U.S.C. §223(a), made it a crime for a person (1) to initiate on a telecommunication device a communication which is obscene or indecent, knowing that the recipient is under eighteen years of age, or (2) to knowingly permit any telecommunications facility under his control to be used for such transmission.

Another provision, 47 U.S.C. §223(d), made it a crime for a person to (1) use an interactive computer service to send or display to a specific person or persons under eighteen years of age any communication that, in context, depicts or describes, in terms patently offensive as measured by contemporary community standards, sexual or excretory activities or organs, or (2) knowingly permit any telecommunications facility under his control to be used for such transmission.

Another provision, 47 U.S.C. §223(e)(5), excused from prosecution any person who has taken, in good faith, reasonable, effective and appropriate actions under the circumstances to restrict or prevent access by minors to the communications prohibited by the first two provisions, and also any person who has restricted access to these communications by requiring use of a verified credit card, debit account, adult access code, or adult personal identification number.

People who used the Internet their businesses were concerned that these provisions would hamper their freedom of speech. The terms "indecent" and "patently offensive" could be interpreted to cover materials that would not be harmful to adults, or even children just under the age of eighteen. The law would limit the transmission of these materials to adults because of the practical difficulties in complying with the child access provisions of §223(e)(5). Immediately after President Clinton signed this law, two lawsuits were filed challenging the constitutionality of these provisions. They were filed by forty-seven plaintiffs, including America On-Line, Inc.; CompuServe Incorporated; Prodigy

Services Company; Apple Computer, Inc.; Microsoft Corporation; the Society of Professional Journalists; the National Writers Union; the Association of Publishers, Editors and Writers; the American Library Association; the Freedom to Read Foundation, Inc.; and the American Civil Liberties Union. The two cases were consolidated and were styled before the U. S. Supreme Court as *Janet Reno, Attorney General of the United States, et al. v. American Civil Liberties Union et al.*, 117 S.Ct. 2329 (1997).

The Supreme Court ruled that the above provisions of the Communications Decency Act (the "CDA") violated the First Amendment, because the terms "indecent" and "patently offensive" were vague. Speaking for the Court, Justice Stevens said these terms were of particular concern because the law was a criminal law that subjected violators to prison terms of up to two years. He said that a criminal law that was difficult to interpret would have a chilling effect on free speech (Ibid., 2344-2345).

Justice Stevens cited cases in which the Supreme Court had ruled that sexual expression that is indecent or offensive but not obscene is protected by the First Amendment, including *Sable Communications of California, Inc. v. FCC*, 492 U.S. 115 at 126 (1989) and *Carey v. Population Services International*, 431 U.S. 678 at 701 (1977)]. He also said the CDA provisions failed the obscenity test established in *Miller v. California*, 413 U.S. 15 (1973), because their coverage was not limited to materials that, taken as a whole, appeal to prurient interests and lack serious literary, artistic or scientific value. For example, the law covered all materials relating to sexual conduct and other subjects of serious biological study, such as excretory organs and processes (Ibid., 2345).

The government emphasized that the CDA provisions were not aimed at restricting communications to adults but only to children under eighteen years of age. Justice Stevens recognized the government's special interest in protecting children. However, regardless of that interest, he said, "the Government may not reduc[e communications to] the adult population . . . to only what is fit for children," quoting *Denver Area Ed. Telecommunications*

Consortium Inc. v. FCC, 116 S.Ct. 2374 at 2393 (1996). "The level of discourse reaching the mailbox," he said, quoting *Bolger v. Youngs Drug Products Corp.*, 463 U.S. 60 at 74-75 (1983), "cannot be limited to that which would be suitable for a sandbox."

The key issue in this case was therefore whether the child access provisions of Section 223(e)(5) of the CDA were sufficient to confine the Act's penalties to communications received by children without diminishing the ability of adults to communicate with one another. Stevens said these provisions were not sufficient, because the District Court had found that there was no effective way for a sender to determine the age of a user who is accessing material through E-mail, mail exploders, newsgroups or chat rooms and that it would be prohibitorily expensive for noncommercial senders, as well as some commercial senders, to verify that users of their Web sites were adults (Ibid., 2347).

The government tried to compare this case to television or radio broadcast cases. These media has had to endure many restrictions on their First Amendment protection. Stevens said that was mainly because warnings cannot adequately protect the listener from unexpected program content. The Internet, he said, was different because of the series of affirmative steps that a user must perform to access specific material. The government also tried to draw an analogy between this restriction and zoning ordinances that restrict adult movie theaters, saying that the CDA was a zoning of cyberspace, or "cyberzoning." Such an analogy could not be made, he said, because the zoning ordinances are aimed not at protecting movie theater customers, but rather at protecting the surrounding property owners from crime and deteriorating property values (Ibid., 2342).

The Supreme Court ruled that the constitutionality of Section 223(a) could be preserved by striking the words "or indecent" from its text, but that Section 223(d) was unconstitutional and could not be saved by severing any of its language.

All nine justices concurred in the Court's judgment in this case. However, Justice O'Connor and Chief Justice Rehnquist dissented from Stevens' rejection of the government's zoning analogy.

Speaking for herself and Rehnquist, O'Connor pointed out that technology was being developed that would enable cyberspace to be zoned. When that happened, Internet users could be stopped from making indecent transmissions, except in "adult only" zones that children could not access. O'Connor also said she would save the constitutionality of Section 223(d) by striking paragraph (B) of the section. She thought paragraph (A) was valid because it forbade only transmissions sent to "a specific person or persons under 18 years of age."

When it becomes technically feasible, cyberspace zoning will solve many problems now experienced by children viewing harmful materials on the Internet. However, this kind of zoning should not be confused with municipal zoning of private property. Cyberspace zoning does not affect the ownership rights of people to their real or personal property. Municipal zoning prevents neighboring landowners from using their respective parcels in ways that harm each other. Cyberspace zoning isolates communication pathways so that respective users cannot possibly interfere with one another. Municipal zoning is the regulation of what people can do with their property. Cyberspace zoning enables the regulation of what people can communicate to one another. The only common element is that people in two fields of endeavor have chosen the same word to describe what they are doing.

D. Summary

The rights proclaimed in the Bill of Rights of the United States Constitution are derived from the fundamental rights of life, liberty and property first proclaimed in the English Magna Charta in 1215. Most of these rights were explained by William Blackstone in his *Commentaries on the Laws of England*, published between 1765 and 1769. The British government violated many of these rights and those violations led the American colonists to declare their independence.

The rights of life, liberty and property include rights that Blackstone listed under the headings of "personal security," "personal liberty," "private property," and "auxiliary rights" for the protection of life, liberty and property. They also include rights derived from the principle that all government restraints on a person's enjoyment of his life, liberty and property must relate to social or relative duties. Government cannot enforce a person's absolute duties to himself or to a spiritual power. The rights derived from this principle include a person's religious freedom, his right of privacy and his right of free speech and press.

On these latter rights, the American founders departed from Blackstone. He said that freedom of the press did not include writings having a "pernicious tendency," and he made a distinction between private thoughts and public speech:

> [n]either is any restraint hereby laid upon freedom of thought and enquiry: liberty of private sentiment is still left; the disseminating, or making public, of bad sentiments, destructive of the ends of society, is the crime which society corrects. (BL5, 152)

By the same reasoning, he defended the English laws that punished offenses against God and religion, because they

> immediately offend Almighty God, by openly transgressing the precepts of religion either natural or revealed; and mediately, by their bad example and consequence, the law of society also; which constitutes that guilt in action, which human tribunals are to censure. (BL4, 43)

He also defended the English laws that regulated the other absolute duties, saying,

> Let a man therefore be ever so abandoned in his principles, or vitious in this practice, provided he keeps his wickedness to himself, and does not offend against the rules of public decency, he is out of the reach of human laws. But if he makes his vices public, though they seem principally to affect himself, (as drunkenness, or the like) they then become, by the bad example they set, of pernicious effects to society. (BL3, 120)

The American people rejected Blackstone's notion that a publication could transform a private act that government could not regulate into a public act that it could regulate, simply because the publication "set a bad example." As colonists, they refused to keep their opinions about their British governors to themselves. They published pamphlets and sent petitions to the king and to Parliament, with copies to their fellow colonists. After they declared their independence, every state enlarged its definition of religious freedom and made no distinction between the public and private practice of religion. Then they proclaimed their freedoms of religion, speech and press in the First Amendment.

The cases presented in this chapter show how some of the rights of life, liberty and property have been applied by the courts to real-life conflicts between people. They show that the Bill of Rights is more than a list of ideals written on a piece of paper. These rights have become the fence that the founding fathers had wanted to erect--the fence that holds the power of government within its rightful boundaries.

10

The Fourteenth Amendment

A. Background

The Fourteenth Amendment is the most controversial part of the U.S. Constitution for two reasons. First, it became part of the Constitution only because the southern states were forced to ratify it after the Civil War, as a condition of having their representatives reinstated in Congress. Secondly, it imposes federal limits on the powers of the state governments that are contrary to the founding fathers' plan of a confederation of essentially sovereign states. The nature and extent of these limits continues to be the subject of an intense, emotional debate.

During the early 1800s, many people thought the states were bound to observe the rights proclaimed in the first eight amendments to the Constitution. However, the First Amendment says only that Congress shall not pass certain laws. The second through eighth amendments do not say whether they are applicable to Congress alone or to state governments as well. In 1833, the U. S. Supreme Court ruled in *Barron v. Baltimore*, 32 U.S. (7 Peters) 243, that the first eight amendments apply only to the federal government and not to the states. In the Court's opinion, Chief Justice John Marshall noted that the main body of the Constitution deals primarily with the powers of the federal government and that all the limitations on the powers of the states were in clauses that expressly mentioned the states. He then concluded, "Had the framers of these amendments intended them to be limitations on the powers of the state governments, they would have imitated the framers of the original constitution, and have expressed that intention" (Ibid., 250).

The Fourteenth Amendment, adopted in 1868, clearly limits the powers of the state governments. Section 1 says,

> All persons born or naturalized in the United States, and subject to the jurisdiction thereof, are citizens of the United States and of the States wherein they reside. No state shall make or enforce any law which shall abridge the privileges or immunities of citizens of the United States; nor shall any State deprive any person of life, liberty, or property, without due process of law; nor deny to any person within its jurisdiction the equal protection of the laws.

These commandments to the states raised again the question of whether they were bound to observe the rights proclaimed in the first eight amendments. Do the words, "nor shall any State deprive any person of life, liberty, or property, without due process of law" mean that the states must observe all or some of these rights? They would appear to mean, at least, that the states must observe those rights embodied within the same words of the Fifth Amendment, which says, "No person shall . . . be deprived of life, liberty, or property, without due process of law." However, Raoul Berger, author of *The Fourteenth Amendment and the Bill of Rights*,[1] says that is not so. The Fourteenth Amendment, he argues, was intended only to give Congress the power to pass the Civil Rights Act of 1866, which forbade the states to treat people unequally with respect to certain rights because of their race, color, or previous condition of slavery. He says the Fourteenth Amendment therefore guarantees no rights except the right of certain people to equal treatment in the specific categories listed in the Civil Rights Act. Other commentators, including Michael Curtis, author of *No State Shall Abridge: The Fourteenth Amendment and the Bill of Rights*,[2] say the Fourteenth Amendment requires the states to recognize all the rights proclaimed in the first eight amendments. This view was first expressed in 1947 by U. S. Supreme Court Justice Hugo Black in his dissenting opinion in *Adamson v. California*, 332 U.S. 46 at 68-123. In 1949, Professor Charles

Fairman of Stanford University rebutted Black's opinion in a law review article, "Does the Fourteenth Amendment Incorporate the Bill of Rights?" 2 *Stanford Law Review* 5 (1949).[3]

The circumstances that led to the adoption of the Fourteenth Amendment are important to understanding the debate over its meaning. Before and during the Civil War, the southern states were violating the rights of free white people as well as black slaves in order to protect the institution of slavery.[4] In 1864, Congressman Isaac Newton Arnold said that before the Civil War "[l]iberty of speech, freedom of the press, and trial by jury had disappeared in the slave States."[5] Other Congressmen complained that the southern states had trampled freedom of religion, freedom of assemblage and freedom from unreasonable searches and seizures.[6] Congressman James Kasson said that slavery "violates more clauses of the Constitution than were violated even by the rebels when they commenced this war."[7]

After the Civil War, the Thirteenth Amendment forced the southern states to stop treating black people as slaves. However, these states enacted "Black Codes" that were designed to maintain the inferior status of black people. These codes denied them the right to buy real estate and limited their right to rent property, their ability to enter into employment contracts and their competence to testify as witnesses in court.

Thus, before and after the Civil War, the southern states were ignoring many of the fundamental rights proclaimed in the first eight amendments to the Constitution. They were able to ignore these rights because the U. S. Supreme Court had ruled that the first eight amendments applied only to the federal government and not to the state governments. The current debate relates to how the Fourteenth Amendment changed that situation.

B. The Adoption of the Fourteenth Amendment

When Congress met after the Civil War on December 4, 1865, the former Confederate states were not represented. The members of Congress appointed a Joint Committee on Reconstruction, comprising six senators and nine representatives, to investigate whether the conditions in these states were made them suitable for regaining representation in Congress. Both Congress and the Joint Committee also considered what other conditions ought to be imposed on the states. Various federal laws and constitutional amendments were proposed containing these conditions. The proposed constitutional amendments were to be in addition to the Thirteenth Amendment, which outlawed slavery and had already been passed by Congress and ratified by most of the states. That amendment had become effective on December 18, 1865.

During the months of December 1865 and January and February 1866, the Joint Committee reviewed several proposals for amending the Constitution to give Congress the power to guarantee to the citizens of each state certain rights, privileges and immunities. On February 26, 1866, Congressman John Bingham of Ohio presented the Committee's proposed amendment to the House of Representatives. It read as follows:

> [t]he Congress shall have power to make all laws which shall be necessary and proper to secure to the citizens of each State all privileges and immunities of citizens in the several States; and to all persons in the several States equal protection in the rights of life, liberty and property.[8]

Many Congressmen praised this proposal, including William Kelley of Pennsylvania, William Higley of California and Frederick Woodbridge of Vermont. However, Congressmen Robert Hale and Giles Hotchkiss of New York criticized it. Hotchkiss suggested that the clause be couched in terms of a prohibition against the states rather than a grant of power to Congress. To give themselves time to resolve this issue, the members of the House postponed further debate on the amendment until April 1866.[9] In the meantime, they turned their attention to a civil rights bill that had been passed by the Senate on February 2, 1866. This bill was designed primarily to stop the southern states from enforcing the Black Codes against former slaves. After several weeks of debate

Chapter 10   The Fourteenth Amendment   393

and amendments, the bill passed the House on March 13. Section 1 said,

> *Be it enacted,* That all persons born in the United States and not subject to any foreign power, excluding Indians not taxed, are hereby declared to be citizens of the United States; and such citizens, of every race and color, without regard to any previous condition of slavery or involuntary servitude, except as a punishment for crime whereof the party shall have been duly convicted, shall have the same right, in every State and Territory in the United States, to make and enforce contracts, to sue, be parties, and give evidence, to inherit, purchase, lease, sell, hold and convey real and personal property, and to full and equal benefit of all laws and proceedings for the security of person and property, as is enjoyed by white citizens, and shall be subject to like punishment, pains and penalties, and to none other, any law, statute, ordinance, regulation, or custom, to the contrary notwithstanding.

However, President Johnson vetoed the bill. He said the Constitution did not give Congress the power to grant citizenship or deny the right of the states to treat black and white people unequally. On April 9, 1866, Congress overrode the president's veto and the new law became known as the Civil Rights Act.[10]

The Joint Committee on Reconstruction then returned to the proposed constitutional amendment that had been tabled in February. Many agreed with President Johnson that the U. S. Constitution did not give Congress the power to pass the Civil Rights Act. That created a renewed sense of urgency to amend the Constitution, so that the Civil Rights Act would clearly fall within the legislative power of Congress.

During the Joint Committee's deliberations, Congressman Bingham introduced another proposal for amending the Constitution. It said,

> No state shall make or enforce any law which shall abridge the privileges or immunities of citizens of the United States; nor shall any State deprive any person of life, liberty or property without due process of law, nor deny to any person within its jurisdiction the equal protection of the laws.

Then on April 30, the Joint Committee submitted its own proposed constitutional amendment to the House of Representatives. The first section was the same as Bingham's proposal except for minor punctuation changes. The other sections dealt with the number of representatives a state would have in Congress, making people who had rebelled against the United States ineligible for federal office, canceling debts incurred in the aid of rebellion against the United States and granting Congress of the power to enforce the provisions of the amendment by appropriate legislation.

In the debate in the House of Representatives, Congressman Bingham explained why his Section 1 should be passed:

> many instances of State injustice and oppression have already occurred in the State Legislation of this Union, of flagrant violations of the guaranteed privileges of citizens of the United States, for which the national Government furnished and could furnish by law no remedy whatever. Contrary to the express letter of your Constitution, "cruel and unusual punishments" have been inflicted under State laws within this Union upon citizens, not only for crimes committed, but for sacred duty done, for which and against which the Government of the United States had provided no remedy and could provide none.... That great want of the citizen and stranger, protection by national law from unconstitutional State enactments, is supplied by the first section of this amendment.[11]

On May 23, Senator Jacob Howard of Michigan introduced the Joint Committee's proposed amendment to the Senate. He said,

> To these privileges and immunities, whatever they may be--for they cannot be defined in their entire extent and precise nature--to these should be added the personal rights guaranteed and secured by the first eight amendments to the Constitution; such as the freedom of speech and of the press; the right of the people peaceably to assemble and petition the Government for a redress of grievances, a right to keep and to bear arms; the right to be exempted from the quartering of soldiers in a house without the consent of the owner; the right to be exempt from unreasonable searches and seizures, and from any search or seizure except by virtue of a warrant issued upon formal oath or

affidavit; the right of an accused person to be informed of the nature of the accusation against him, and his right to be tried by an impartial jury of the vicinage; and also the right to be secure against excessive bail and against cruel and unusual punishments.

Now, sir, here is a mass of privileges, immunities, and rights, some of them secured by the second section of the fourth article of the Constitution, which I have recited, some by the first eight amendments of the constitution; and it is a fact well worthy of attention that the course of a decision of our courts and the present settled doctrine is, that all these immunities, privileges, rights, thus guaranteed by the Constitution or recognized by it, are secured to the citizens solely as a citizen of the United States and a party in their courts. They do not operate in the slightest degree as a restraint or prohibition upon State legislation. States are not affected by them, and it has been repeatedly held that the restriction contained in the Constitution against the taking of private property for public use without just compensation is not a restriction upon State legislation, but applies only to the legislation in Congress.

Now, sir, there is no power given in the Constitution to enforce and to carry out any of these guarantees. They are not powers granted by the Constitution to Congress, and of course do not come within the sweeping clause of the Constitution authorizing Congress to pass all laws necessary and proper for carrying out the foregoing or granted powers, but they stand simply as a bill of rights in the Constitution, without power on the part of Congress to give them full effect; while at the same time the States are not restrained from violating the principles embraced in them except by their own local constitutions, which may be altered from year to year. The great object of the first section of this amendment is, therefore, to restrain the power of the States and compel them at all times to respect these great fundamental guarantees.[12]

After Senator Howard's speech, the president pro tempore of the Senate, Benjamin Franklin Wade of Jefferson, Ohio, suggested that the amendment ought to define those "citizens of the United States" whose privileges or immunities are not to be abridged by the states. Howard therefore moved to insert the following sentence at the beginning of the amendment:

All persons born or naturalized in the United States, and subject to the jurisdiction thereof, are citizens of the United States and of the State wherein they reside.

The Senate and House approved the amendment with this sentence added and sent it to the states for ratification on June 13, 1866. The amendment then became a major issue in the Congressional elections of 1866. The typical race was between a radical Republican and a Copperhead Democrat. The radical Republicans supported the amendment and said that no southern state ought to be represented in Congress until it had established a system of justice guaranteeing to everyone the principles of freedom proclaimed in the U. S. Constitution's Bill of Rights. The Copperhead Democrats opposed the amendment and said the southern states should be represented in Congress immediately.

In the November 1866 elections, the Republicans retained over a two-thirds majority in both houses of Congress--enough to override any presidential veto. However, they were having difficulty getting enough states to ratify their constitutional amendment. Critics claimed that its effects would be far-reaching. Some New Hampshire people said it would destroy the entire constitutional system and that it was "a dangerous infringement upon the rights and independence of the States."[13] A committee of the Texas legislature said the amendment was a virtual repeal of the Tenth Amendment, which reserved to the states or to the people all powers not delegated by the Constitution to the United States nor prohibited by it to the states.[14] A Florida Senate committee said, "From the moment of its engraftment upon the Constitution of the United States, the States would cease to exist as bodies politic . . . ."[15] In the closing weeks of the 1866 Congressional campaign, Orvill Browning, President Johnson's Secretary of the Interior, wrote a long letter in which he said the Fourteenth Amendment would provide power "substantially to annihilate the state judiciary" because all state laws will be "open to criticism, interpretation and adjudication by the federal tribunals, whose judgments and decrees will be supreme and will override the decisions of the State Courts and leave them utterly powerless." According to Joseph James,

Browning's letter "was discussed with great animation in the Democratic press both North and South."[16]

In response to these criticisms, the *Dubuque* [Iowa] *Daily Times* published the following editorial on November 21, 1866:

> [a citizen has] a right to claim privileges and immunities and protection of law. The right to "life, liberty and the pursuit of happiness" is surely his; and the principle of a republican form of government cannot do less than secure him those inherent rights which nature gives. This is the intent of the second clause of the condemned section above quoted. It prohibits any state from making laws to abridge the privileges rightly conferred on every citizen by the federal constitution, which instrument, before, only neglected to define who were entitled to the benefits it conferred.[17]

Governor Jacob Cox of Ohio also defended the amendment:

> [t]he [provisions] consist, first, of the grant of power to the National government to protect the citizens of the whole country in their legal privileges and immunities, should any State attempt to oppress classes of individuals, or deprive them of equal protection of the laws. . . .
>
> A simple statement of these propositions is their complete justification. The first was proven necessary long before the war; when it was notorious that any attempt to exercise freedom of discussion in regard to the system which was then hurrying on the rebellion, was not tolerated in the Southern States; and the State laws gave no real protection to immunities of their kind, which are the very essence of free government.[18]

The first part of Governor Cox's statement gives the impression that he thought the amendment prohibited the states only from treating various classes of people unequally. However, in the second part, he said that the amendment was necessary to stop the states from enforcing laws that violated everyone's right of free speech, not simply the right of a class of people to equal protection of free speech.

By the end of February 1867, twenty of the thirty-six states had ratified the amendment but ten had rejected it. Eight of the rejecting states were former members of the Confederacy. On March 2, 1867, the Republican-controlled Congress passed a law that laid down a list of conditions that had to be met before the representatives of a former Confederate state could be readmitted to Congress. One of these conditions was the state's ratification of the propose Constitutional amendment. As a result of this ultimatum, seven former Confederate states ratified the amendment by the middle of 1868. On July 28, 1868, Congress announced that the required three-fourths of the state legislatures had ratified the amendment and it became the Fourteenth Amendment of the United States Constitution.

C. The Meaning of Section 1

The history of the Fourteenth Amendment shows that both its supporters and opponents knew that it would dramatically limit the powers of the states. Its supporters thought that power should be limited because many states had abused their power for the sake of preserving slavery. Its opponents thought that the Thirteenth Amendment, which had eliminated slavery, was sufficient to correct that abuse of power and that the Fourteenth Amendment would destroy the sovereignty of the states established by the original Constitution. The supporters won the battle.

However, the passage of the Fourteenth Amendment has not deterred its opponents. They have tried in every way to destroy its meaning and effect. In his book, Berger cites Congressman George Latham, who told Congress, "the 'civil rights bill' which is now law . . . covers exactly the same ground as the amendment" and Congressman Martin Thayer, who said, "[I]t is but incorporating in the Constitution the principle of the civil rights bill which has lately become law."[19] Then Berger cites Congressman Samuel Shellabarger, who said the civil rights bill secures "equality of protection in those enumerated civil rights which the States may deem proper to confer upon any races."[20] Taken together, these statements mean that the only effect of the Fourteenth Amendment was to require the states to give people equal protection in those rights that they "may deem proper to confer." We may wonder, if this is what most people thought the amendment meant, why so many opposed it.

The speeches of the legislators who voted on the Fourteenth Amendment show that they had many different opinions concerning its meaning. Even those who compared the amendment to the Civil Rights Act had different views. In the appendix to his dissent in *Adamson v. California*, 332 U.S. 46 at 107-108 (1947), Supreme Court Justice Hugo Black said,

> Some considered that the amendment settled any doubts there might be as to the constitutionality of the Civil Rights Bill. Cong. Globe, 2511, 2896. Others maintained that the Civil Rights Bill would be unconstitutional unless and until the amendment was adopted. Cong. Globe, 2461, 2502, 2506, 2513, 2961. Some thought that amendment was nothing but the Civil Rights "in another shape." Cong. Globe, 2459, 2462, 2465, 2467, 2498, 2502.

These differences of opinion should not be surprising. The amendment was debated in both houses of Congress and sent to over thirty state legislatures for ratification. The most common intent was probably the one shared by the southern legislators, who voted for the amendment because they wanted to get their representatives back into Congress.

To make sense of these diverse opinions and motives, we must consider the rules for determining the intention of a law. During the debates on an early draft of the Fourteenth Amendment, Congressman William Kelley of Pennsylvania defended his view of the Constitution by referring to Blackstone's rules of interpreting a law:

> The fairest and most rational method to interpret the will of the legislator, is by exploring his intentions at the time when the law was made, by *signs* the most natural and probable. And these signs are either the words, the context, the subject matter, the effects and consequence, or the spirit and reason of the law.[21] (BL1, 59)

The specific rules laid out by Blackstone were:

> 1. Words are generally to be understood in their usual and most known signification; . . .
> 2. If the words happen to be still dubious, we may establish meaning from the context; . . .
> 3. As to subject matter, words are always understood as having regard thereto; for that is always supposed to be in the eye of the legislator, and all his expressions directed to that end. . . .
> 4. As to effects and consequence, the rule is, where words bear either none, or a very absurd signification, if literally understood, we must a little deviate from the received sense of them. . . .
> 5. But, lastly, the most universal and effectual way of discovering the true meaning of a law, when the words are dubious, is by considering the reason and spirit of it: or the cause which moved the legislator to enact it. For when this reason ceases, the law itself ought likewise to cease with it. . . .
>
> From this method of interpreting laws, by the reason of them, arises what we call *equity*; which is thus defined by Grotius, "the correction of that, wherein the law (by reason of its universality) is deficient." For since in laws all cases cannot be foreseen or expressed, it is necessary that when general decrees of the law come to be applied to particular cases, there should somewhere be a power vested of excepting those circumstances, which (had they been foreseen) the legislator himself would have excepted. . . . And on the other hand, the liberty of considering all cases in an equitable light may not be indulged too far, lest thereby we destroy all law, and leave the decision of every question entirely in the breast of the judge. And law, without equity, tho' hard and disagreeable, is much more desirable for the public good, than equity without law; which would make every judge a legislator, and introduce most infinite confusion; as there would then be found as many different rules of action laid down in our courts, as there are differences of capacity and sentiment in the human mind. (BL1, 59-62).

Thus, the usual and most known signification of the words of the law is the primary tool for determining the intentions of legislators. The context in which those words are used, the subject matter and the intended effects and consequences of the law may help in this effort. The reason, spirit and cause that moved the legislature to enact the law are also important. Finally, the process should result in an equitable application of the law, especially to facts that were not foreseen by the legislators. However, the desire for an equitable result cannot be pursued to such an extent that the actual words of the law are ignored.

The Ohio Supreme Court added another guideline in the case of *Slingluff v. Weaver*, 66 Ohio St. 621 (1902):

> [t]he province of [statutory] construction is to arrive at the true sense of the language of the act, not to supply language to help out a conjectured intent not to be gathered from the words used. The question is not so much what did the legislature intend to enact, as what did it mean by what it enacted. (Ibid., 628)

The Ohio court confirmed that the intent of the legislators should be examined to resolve doubt about the meaning of a law:

> [b]ut it is equally the law, we suppose, that the court does not possess, and should not attempt to exercise, the power of introducing doubt or ambiguity not apparent in the language, and then resort to verbal modifications to remove such doubt and conform the act to the court's supposition with respect to the intent of the legislature, for it seems well settled, as expressed by Story, J., in *Gardner v. Collins*, 2 Pet. 58: "What the legislative intent was can be derived only from the words they have used; we cannot speculate beyond the reasonable import of those words. The spirit of the act must be extracted from the words of the act, and not from conjectures *aliunde*." (Ibid., 626-627)

Although *Slingluff* opinion is binding only on Ohio courts, it is based on a rule laid down by the United States Supreme Court in the *Gardner v. Collins* case. The reason for looking at the legislature's intent is to illuminate its words, not to contradict them. Otherwise, the legislators might as well dispense with drafting laws. They might simply make a record of their various intentions and tell the judges to sort through them and figure out what they meant the law to be.

To follow these rules of interpretation, we must try to find the usual and most known signification of the words used in the second sentence of Section 1 of the Fourteenth Amendment. This sentence has three clauses. The first says,

> No State shall make or enforce any law which shall abridge the privileges or immunities of citizens of the United States; . . . .

"Citizens of the United States" are defined in the first sentence of Section 1 as, "all persons born or naturalized in the United States, and subject to the jurisdiction thereof, . . ." Naturalized persons would have to be those who are naturalized according to the rules prescribed by Congress, because only Congress has the power to establish a "uniform Rule of Naturalization" (Article I, Section 8[4]). According to the records of Congress, the phrase "subject to the jurisdiction thereof" is intended to exclude children born in the United States who are subject to diplomatic immunity.[22] (The meaning of "privileges or immunities" will be discussed below.)

The second clause says,

> nor shall any State deprive any person of life, liberty, or property, without due process of law; . . . .

(The meanings of "life, liberty, or property" and "due process of law" will be discussed below.)

The third clause says,

> nor deny to any person within its jurisdiction the equal protection of the laws.

(The meaning of "equal protection of the laws" will be discussed in Section E of this chapter.)

"Privileges" and "immunities" appear in Article IV, Section 2[1], and "life, liberty, or property" and "due process of law" appear in the Fifth Amendment. These phrases ought to mean the same in the Fourteenth Amendment as they do in these other parts of the Constitution, unless there is a good reason for a different interpretation.

However, many people have refused to focus on the meanings of these words, especially as they are used in the other parts of the Constitution. They would rather have us look at the Civil Rights Act of 1866, which does not mention "privileges," "immunities" or "due process of law." It refers to some rights of life, liberty and property, but in a very different context. It says that all citizens of the United States of every race and color shall have the same right "to full and equal benefit of all laws and proceedings for the security of person and property, as enjoyed by white citizens." In contrast, the life, liberty and property clause of the Fourteenth Amendment does not say that citizens shall have the *same* rights or *equal* benefit of laws. Rather it says, "nor shall any State deprive any person of life, liberty, or property, without due process of law; . . . ." allowing the subject of equality to be handled by a separate clause.

Applying the rule of the *Slingluff* and *Gardner* cases, we should ask whether the attempts equate the Fourteenth Amendment to the Civil Rights Act merely "supply language to help out a conjectured intent not to be gathered from the words used." They appear to do exactly that. They also add doubt and ambiguity by speculating "beyond the reasonable import" of the amendment's words.

One speech that sheds light on the meaning of "privileges or immunities" is the one that Senator Howard gave when he introduced the Fourteenth Amendment to the Senate. He referred to Article IV, Section 2[1] of the Constitution which said, "The citizens of each State shall be entitled to all Privileges and Immunities of Citizens in the several States." He said that although the U. S. Supreme Court had not defined these privileges and immunities, they had been defined by Supreme Court Justice Bushrod Washington while he was sitting as a District Court judge in the case of *Corfield v. Coryell*, Fed. Case No. 3,230, 6 Fed. Cas. 546 (E.D.Pa., 1823). Senator Howard read the following part of Justice Washington's opinion to the Senate:

> The inquiry is, what are the privileges and immunities of citizens in the several states? We feel no hesitation in confining these expressions to those privileges and immunities which are in their nature fundamen-

tal, which belong of right to the citizens of all free Governments, and which have at all times been enjoyed by the citizens of the several States which compose this Union from the time of their becoming free, independent and sovereign. What these fundamental principles are it would, perhaps be more tedious than difficult to enumerate. They may, however, be all comprehended under the following general heads: protection by the Government, the enjoyment of life and liberty, with the right to acquire and possess property of every kind, and to pursue and obtain happiness and safety, subject nevertheless to such restraints as the Government may justly prescribe for the general good of the whole. The right of a citizen of one State to pass through or to reside in any other State, for the purposes of trade, agriculture, professional pursuits, or otherwise; to claim the benefit of the writ of *habeas corpus*; to institute and maintain actions of any kind in the courts of the State; to take, hold, and dispose of personal property, either real or personal, and an exemption from higher taxes or impositions than are paid by the other citizens of the State, may be mentioned as some of the particular privileges and immunities of citizens which are clearly embraced by the general description of privileges deemed to be fundamental, to which may be added the elective franchise, as regulated and established by the laws or constitution in the State to which it is to be exercised. These, and many others which might be mentioned, are, strictly speaking, privileges and immunities, and the enjoyment of them by the citizens of each State in every other State was manifestly calculated (to use the expressions of the preamble of the corresponding provision of the old Articles of Confederation) "the better to secure and perpetuate mutual friendship and intercourse among the people of the different States of the Union."[23]

Senator Lyman Trumbull and Congressmen James Wilson and Henry Raymond also referred to Justice Washington's definition in the *Coryell* case to explain the meaning of "immunities" in the Civil Rights Bill, before it was amended to delete the words, "There shall be no discrimination in civil rights or immunities among the citizens of the United States."[24]

Senator Howard followed his quotation of Justice Washington by reminding the Senate that the specific privileges and immunities listed in the quote were by way of example only. He said that privileges and immunities also included the rights guaranteed by the first eight amendments to the U. S. Constitution.[25]

We do not know how well Blackstone's *Commentaries* were known to Senator Howard or Justice Washington, but their definitions of "privileges" and "immunities" are very close to this definition found in the *Commentaries*:

> The rights themselves thus defined by these several statutes, consists in a number of private immunities; which will appear, from what has been premised, to be indeed no other, than either that *residuum* of natural liberty, which is not required by the laws of society to be sacrificed to public convenience; or else those civil privileges, which society hath engaged to provide, in lieu of the natural liberties so given up by individuals.... And these may be reduced to three principal or primary articles; the right of personal security, the right of personal liberty; and the right of private property: .... (BL3, 125)

In *Corfield v. Coryell*, supra, Justice Washington said that in their context in Article IV, Section 2[1], each state had the power to determine the particular rights embodied in the words "privileges and immunities." He said that he could not accede to the proposition that, under this provision of the constitution, "the citizens of the several states are permitted to participate in all the rights which belong exclusively to the citizens of any other particular state, merely on the ground that they are enjoyed by those citizens" (Ibid., 552). Fairman and Berger therefore argued that Justice Washington defined "privileges and immunities" as merely equal protection in the rights that a state may wish to confer upon its own citizens. However, Justice Washington said nothing about equal protection in his definition of "privileges and immunities." The only meaning that can be drawn from his opinion is that Article IV, Section 2[1] of the Constitution allows each state to determine which immunities will remain in each citizens' "*residuum* of natural liberty, which is not required by the laws of society to be sacrificed to public convenience," and which privileges it will provide "in lieu of the natural liberties so given up by individuals."

In contrast to Article IV, Section 2[1], the Fourteenth Amendment says, "no state shall abridge the privileges or immunities of the citizens of the United States" and it defines "citizens of the United States" as "all persons born or naturalized in the United States and subject to the jurisdiction thereof." This amendment thus makes United States citizenship independent of citizenship of a particular state. It also guarantees that no state shall abridge the privileges or immunities of these United States citizens. Therefore, under the Fourteenth Amendment, only the United States government can determine who is a citizen of the United States and the privileges and immunities to be enjoyed by those citizens.

According to Justice Washington and Senator Howard, a citizen's privileges and immunities include his "enjoyment of life and property, with the right to acquire and possess property of every kind, and to pursue happiness and safety" (16 Fed. Cas. at 551-552). According to Blackstone, a person's privileges and immunities include his rights of "personal security, personal liberty and private property" (BL3, 125). So there should be little difference between the rights guaranteed by the privileges and immunities clause and the rights guaranteed by the life, liberty and property clause of the Fourteenth Amendment. The major difference between the two is that the former protects only citizens of the United States, whereas the latter protects all persons.

The life, liberty and property clause of the Fourteenth Amendment received very little attention during the amendment's Congressional and state debates. However, Congressman Wilson of Iowa, chairman of the House Judiciary Committee, explained the meaning of "life, liberty and property" in a speech on the Civil Rights Bill in February 1866. He said that bill was designed to protect "the great fundamental civil rights" of people:

> [w]hat are these rights? . . . Blackstone classifies them under three articles, as follows:
>
> 1. The right of personal security; which, he says, "consists in a person's legal and uninterrupted enjoyment of his life, his limbs, his body, his health, and his reputation."

2. The right of personal liberty; and this, he says, "consists in the power of locomotion, of changing situation, or moving one's person to whatever place one's own inclination may direct, without imprisonment or restraint, unless by due course of law."

3. The right of personal property; which he defines to be, "the free use, enjoyment, and disposal of all acquisitions, without any control or diminution, save only by the laws of the land."--*Sharwood's Blackstone*, vol. 1, chap. 1.

In his lecture on the absolute rights of persons, Chancellor Kent (Kent's Commentaries, volume one, page 599) says, "The absolute rights of individuals may be resolved into the right of personal security, the right of personal liberty, and the right to acquire and enjoy property. These rights have been justly considered, and frequently declared, by the people of this country, to be natural, inherent, and inalienable."

Thus, sir, we have the English and American doctrine harmonizing. The great fundamental rights are the inalienable possession of both Englishmen and Americans; and I will not admit that the British constitution excels the American Constitution in the amplitude of its provisions for the protection of these rights.[26]

Senator Trumbull of Illinois, chairman of the Senate Judiciary Committee, also quoted Blackstone's *Commentaries* while explaining the Civil Rights Bill. He was trying to show how the Thirteenth Amendment's prohibition of slavery gave Congress the authority to pass a law that required the states to observe people's civil liberty. He said slavery and liberty are opposite terms and that natural liberty is, according to Blackstone, the

> power of acting as one thinks fit, without any restraint or control, unless by the law of nature, being a right inherent in us by birth, and one of the gifts of God to man in his creation, when he imbued him with the faculty of will. (quoted from BL3, 121)

Senator Trumbull then paraphrased Blackstone, saying,

> . . . every man who enters society gives up a part of this natural liberty, which is the liberty of the savage, the liberty which the wild beast has, for the advantages he obtains in the protection which civil gov-

ernment gives him. Civil liberty, or the liberty which a person enjoys in society, is thus defined by Blackstone:

"Civil liberty is no other than natural liberty, so far restrained by human laws and no further, as is necessary and expedient for the general advantage of the public." (also quoted from BL3, 121)

That is the liberty to which every citizen is entitled; that is the liberty which was intended to be secured by the Declaration of Independence and the Constitution of the United States originally, and more especially by the amendment which has recently been adopted; ....

Later in his speech, Trumbull turned to the privileges and immunities guaranteed by Article IV, Section 2[1]. He quoted Justice Washington's definition in *Corfield v. Coryell*, supra, and said the words mean that a citizen of each state "is entitled to the great fundamental rights of life, liberty, and the pursuit of happiness, and the right to travel, to go where he pleases."[27]

Congressman Wilson and Senator Trumbull therefore understood that the fundamental civil rights of people were the rights that Blackstone described in his chapter "Of the Absolute Rights of Individuals." It is not surprising that Wilson and Trumbull were familiar with Blackstone. His *Commentaries* were the most widely read legal textbooks in America during the nineteenth century. One of Blackstone's biographers, David Lockmiller, said, "it may be safely assumed that practically all lawyers in the United States prior to 1900, at one time or another, read all or parts of the *Commentaries*. Many lawyers read the four books several times and it was studied with interest by laymen."[28] They were a primary source of authority for most American law professors and legal commentators in the nineteenth century, including James Kent and Theodore Dwight of Columbia University, Joseph Story and Theophilus Parsons of Harvard University and Henry Dutton of Yale University. James Kent also served as chief justice of the New York Supreme Court and as chancellor of the New York Court of Chancery. Joseph Story was also a justice of the U. S. Supreme Court. In North Carolina, the *Commentaries* were the standard textbook in law schools conducted by U. S. Supreme Court Justice James Iredell, Judge John Taylor and William Battle.[29] The historian Daniel J. Boorstin said, "Blackstone was to American law what Noah Webster's blue-back speller was to be to American literacy."[30]

The early chapters of this book showed how the American colonists came to appreciate the rights described by Blackstone because they were suffering many violations of the same rights. Chapter 9 showed how both the rights specifically described by Blackstone and those derived from his definition of civil liberty (relating to religion, privacy, speech and press) are now embodied in the Bill of Rights amendments of the United States Constitution. Some are mentioned in the first eight amendments but all are covered by Fifth Amendment general guarantee that no person "be deprived of life, liberty, or property, without due process of law." At one time, only the federal government had to observe that guarantee. However, the Fourteenth Amendment required the states to observe the same guarantee.

D. The Privileges and Immunities and Life, Liberty and Property Clauses

In any lawsuit involving a dispute over the meaning of the Constitution, the Supreme Court of the United States is the final judge (App. O, Article III, Sections 1 and 2). We shall therefore examine the major Supreme Court decisions that have interpreted the privileges and immunities and life, liberty and property clauses of the Fourteenth Amendment. This will be a critical examination, because we will see how the Court rendered the privileges and immunities clause practically meaningless and how it misinterpreted the life, liberty and property clause in many of its early decisions. However, we will also see how it gradually came to realize that a person's right to life, liberty and property includes most of the rights explained in Chapter 9 covering the Bill of Rights. In Section E, we shall examine the equal protection clause of the Fourteenth Amendment in the same critical way.

D.1. The Slaughter-House Decision

In 1873, the U. S. Supreme Court interpreted the Fourteenth Amendment for the first time in the *Slaughter-House Cases*, 83 U.S. (16 Wallace) 36. The Louisiana legislature had passed a law in 1869 granting a private company the exclusive right to maintain livestock slaughter-houses in New Orleans and surrounding counties for a term of twenty-five years. The area of exclusivity was 1154 square miles--only sixty square miles less than the area of Rhode Island. The legislature authorized the private company to conduct its operations on the banks of the Mississippi River below the corporate limits of New Orleans or within certain areas inside those corporate limits. It also required the company to permit any person to use its houses for slaughtering livestock, setting a heavy penalty for each refusal. The legislature also set maximum fees that the company could charge for its services and provided a hundred-dollar penalty for anyone slaughtering an animal in a place not operated by the company.

In many respects, this monopoly resembled the tea monopoly that the British Parliament had granted the East India Company in 1773, which had led to the Boston Tea Party. The butchers in the three colonies affected by the monopoly filed suit to block its enforcement on the ground that it violated the Thirteenth and Fourteenth Amendments of the U. S. Constitution. However, in a five-to-four decision, the Supreme Court ruled that the state of Louisiana had the power to grant the monopoly in order to protect the health, safety and comfort of the general public. Speaking for the Court, Justice Samuel Miller reasoned that because animal slaughtering produces noxious, unsightly wastes, the state had the power to limit the places where it could be performed. One way to do that was to grant a monopoly to one company and limit the places where that company could conduct its slaughtering.

Justice Miller then turned to the provisions of the Thirteenth and Fourteenth Amendments to determine whether the butcher's rights under those amendments had been violated. He quickly rejected the butchers' claim that the Thirteenth Amendment had been violated, saying the only purpose of that amendment was to forbid slavery or the kind of involuntary servitude that binds one person in service to another. He then looked at the privileges and immunities clause of the Fourteenth Amendment in the light of Justice Washington's definition of privileges and immunities in *Corfield v. Coryell,* supra. He said that definition "embraces nearly every civil right for the establishment and protection of which organized government is instituted." However, Justice Miller then reflected on the far-reaching consequences of applying this definition to the privileges and immunities of citizens of the United States guaranteed by the Fourteenth Amendment. He said that if those privileges and immunities were defined that broadly, both the Supreme Court and Congress would have the power to nullify all kinds of state laws whenever they deemed them to be in violation of one of the many rights encompassed by the definition. That would radically change "the whole theory of the relations of the State and federal governments to each other and of both these governments to the people; . . . ." Justice Miller said that because the amendment did not clearly express such a purpose, the majority of the justices were convinced that no such results were intended by Congress or by the ratifying states (Ibid., 78). They apparently reached that conclusion without examining the legislative record of the amendment.

The Supreme Court therefore decided that the privileges and immunities possessed by people because they are citizens of the United States are far more limited that those they have because they are citizens of a particular state. The privileges and immunities of United States citizenship, said Justice Miller, include only those that relate directly to the operation of the federal government, such as a person's right "to assert any claim he may have upon that government, to transact any business he may have with it, to seek its protection, to share its offices, to engage in administering its functions." These rights also include the right to assemble peaceably and petition the federal government for redress of grievances, the right to petition the federal government for a writ of habeas corpus, the right to use the navigable waters of the United States and any rights secured to United States citizens by treaties with foreign nations. In addition, a citizen's privileges and immunities include the right "to demand the care and protection of the federal government over his life, liberty and property when on the high seas or within the jurisdiction of a foreign government" (Ibid., 79). In effect, he said that a citizen of the United States may demand, as one of his privileges and immunities, that the federal government protect his life, liberty and property anywhere in the world, except within the boundaries of a state or territory of the United States.

Justice Miller took a broader view of the life, liberty and property clause of the Fourteenth Amendment. He said that clause imposes the same restrictions on the states that the life, liberty and property clause of the Fifth Amendment imposes on the federal government. However, he said that under past case decisions, the butchers of Louisiana were not deprived of their right of property by the slaughter-house monopoly law. What these past decisions were, why they dictated such a ruling and why the butchers were not deprived of their right of liberty, he did not say (Ibid., 80-81).

Regarding the butchers' claim that their right of equal protection of the laws had been violated, the Supreme Court majority said that clause was designed to prevent the states from discriminating against black people because of their race. Therefore, the butchers' rights of equal protection of the laws had not been violated, because there was no racial discrimination.

Four of the nine judges dissented from Justice Miller's majority opinion. Justice Stephen Field said that he found nothing wrong with the part of the Louisiana law that limited the landing and slaughtering of animals to an area on the Mississippi River below the City of New Orleans, nor did he find anything wrong with the animal inspection part of the law. Those requirements were within the state's power to protect the health and safety of its people. However, he said, the grant of a monopoly to one slaughtering company in a three-county area could not be justified as a health and safety measure or as a right given to a public utility. The slaughtering business is an ordinary trade that any person ought to be able to pursue, in contrast to a public utility that performs work of a governmental nature or requires the use of the state's power of eminent domain. Field also said the slaughtering monopoly was not analogous to a patent monopoly, which is granted to an inventor of a new and useful improvement in exchange for disclosing his invention to the public. A patent monopoly covers only something that would not have existed except for the inventor's work, while the slaughtering monopoly deprived the general public of the right to engage in the well-known and ordinary business of operating animal slaughter-houses, and there was no public benefit gained in return. Only the law's inspection and geographical requirements served the public's interest by protecting its health and safety. Justice Field therefore concluded that the slaughtering monopoly violated the Thirteenth Amendment and the privileges and immunities, life, liberty and property and equal protection clauses of the Fourteenth Amendment.

The privileges and immunities clause of the Fourteenth Amendment, said Justice Field, guaranteed to citizens of the United States the same fundamental rights described by Justice Washington in *Corfield v. Coryell*, supra. He said if that clause

> only refers, as held by the majority of the court in their opinion, to such privileges and immunities as were before its adoption specially designated in the Constitution or necessarily implied as belonging to citizens of the United States, it was a vain and idle enactment, which accomplished nothing, and most unnecessarily excited Congress and the people on its passage. . . . But if the amendment refers to the natural and inalienable rights which belong to all citizens, the inhibition has a profound significance and consequence. (Ibid., 96)

In another dissenting opinion, Justice Joseph Bradley gave this explanation of the Fourteenth Amendment's life, liberty and property clause:

> The people of this country brought with them to its shores the rights of Englishmen; the rights which had been wrested from English sovereigns at various periods of the nation's history. One of these fundamental rights was expressed in these words, found in the Magna Charta: "No freeman shall be taken or imprisoned, or be disseized of his freehold or liberties or free customs, or be outlawed or exiled, or

any otherwise destroyed; nor will we pass upon him or condemn him but by lawful judgment of his peers or by the law of the land." English constitutional writers expound this article as rendering life, liberty, and property inviolable, except by due process of law. This is the very right which the plaintiffs in error claim in this case. Another of these rights was that of habeas corpus, or the right of having any invasion of personal liberty judicially examined into, at once, by a competent judicial magistrate. Blackstone classifies these fundamental rights under three heads, as the absolute rights of individuals, to wit: the right of personal security, the right of personal liberty, and the right of private property. And of the last he says: "The third absolute right, inherent in every Englishman, is that of property, which consists in the free use, enjoyment, and disposal of all his acquisitions, without any control or diminution save only by the laws of the land." (Ibid., 114-115)

He then explained what "privileges and immunities" are:

The privileges and immunities of Englishmen were established and secured by long usage and by various acts of Parliament. But it may be said that the Parliament of England has unlimited authority, and might repeal the laws which have from time to time been enacted. Theoretically this is so, but practically it is not. England has no written constitution, it is true; but it has an unwritten one, resting in the acknowledged, and frequently declared, privileges of Parliament and the people, to violate which in any material respect would produce a revolution in an hour. A violation of one of the fundamental principles of that constitution in the Colonies, namely, the principle that recognizes the property of the people as their own, and which, therefore, regards all taxes for the support of government as gifts of the people through their representatives, and regards taxation without representation as subversive of free government, was the origin of our own revolution.

This, it is true, was the violation of a political right; but personal rights were deemed equally sacred, and were claimed by the very first Congress of the Colonies, assembled in 1774, as the undoubted inheritance of the people of this country; and the Declaration of Independence, which was the first political act of the American people in the independent sovereign capacity, lays the foundation of our National existence on this broad proposition: "That all men are created equal; that they are endowed by the Creator with certain unalienable rights; that among these are life, liberty, and the pursuit of happiness." Here again we have the great threefold division of the rights of freemen, asserted as the rights of man. Rights of life, liberty, and the pursuit of happiness are equivalent to the rights of life, liberty and property. These are the fundamental rights which can only be interfered with, or the enjoyment of which can only be modified, by lawful regulations necessary or proper for the mutual good of all; and these rights, I contend, belong to the citizens of every free government.

For the preservation, exercise, and enjoyment of these rights the individual citizen, as a necessity, must be left free to adopt such calling, profession, or trade as may seem to him most conducive to that end. Without this right he cannot be a freeman. This right to choose one's calling is an essential part of that liberty which it is the object of government to protect; and a calling, when chosen, is a man's property and right. Liberty and property are not protected where these rights are arbitrarily assailed. (Ibid., 115-116)

Although Justice Bradley's words appeared in a dissenting opinion, his interpretation of "life, liberty and property" is very close to the interpretation now made by the majority of justices on the Supreme Court. His interpretation is also supported by Blackstone's description of personal liberty, which he said "consists in the power . . . of changing situation, . . ." and his description of property, which he said "consists in the free use, enjoyment and disposal of all his acquisitions." (BL3, 130, 134)

D.2. Life after the Slaughter-House

Two years after the *Slaughter-House* decision, Justice Miller and the Supreme Court took a broader view of the rights of life, liberty and property. In *The Citizens' Savings & Loan Association of Cleveland, Ohio v. City of Topeka, Kansas*, 87 U.S. (20 Wallace) 655 (Oct. term, 1874), Topeka City had issued $100,000 worth of bonds to help finance the establishment of a local bridge manufacturing company. It was authorized to issue these bonds by the Kansas state legislature to encourage industrial development. After paying the bondholders the interest due on the first coupon, Topeka City defaulted when subsequent coupons became due. The owner of the bonds, the Citizens' Savings & Loan Association, sued to recover the interest. The city claimed that the bonds were void because the law authorizing their issuance was unconstitutional. Its only means of paying the bondholder was to tax its citizens. However, it claimed it could not pay with tax dollars because the debt had not been incurred for a public purpose but rather to give money to a private business.

The U. S. Supreme Court agreed with the city's position and ruled that the Kansas law authorizing the bonds was invalid. As he had in the *Slaughter-House Cases*, Justice Miller wrote majority opinion, but in this case he said,

> It must be conceded that there are such rights in every free government beyond the control of the State. A government which recognized no such rights, which held the lives, the liberty and the property of its citizens subject at all times to the absolute despotism and unlimited control of even the most democratic depository of power, is after all but a despotism. . . .
>
> The theory of our governments, state and national, is opposed to the deposit of unlimited power anywhere. The executive, the legislative and the judicial branches of these governments are all of limited and defined powers.
>
> There are limitations on such power which grow out of the essential nature of all free governments. Implied reservations of individual rights, without which the social compact could not exist, and which are respected by all governments entitled to the name. No court, for instance, would hesitate to declare void a statute that A and B who were husband and wife to each other should be so no longer, but that A should thereafter be the husband of C, and B the wife of D. Or which should enact that the homestead now owned by A should no longer be his, but should henceforth be the property of B. . . .
>
> To lay, with one hand the power of government on the property of the citizen, and with the other bestow it upon favored individuals to aid private enterprises and build up private fortunes, is none the less a robbery because it is done under the forms of law and is called taxation. This is not legislation. It is a decree under legislative forms. . . .

We have established, we think, beyond cavil, that there can be no lawful tax which is not laid for a public purpose. (Ibid., 662-664)

Justice Miller might have also said that there can be no lawful restraint on a person that is not laid for a public purpose. On the other hand, that would have been contrary to his opinion in the *Slaughter-House Cases*, in which he upheld the validity of a law that restrained the general public from operating slaughter-houses in order to give one private company a monopoly.

Miller did not base his decision in the *Topeka* case on a violation of the Fourteenth Amendment or any other part of the U. S. Constitution. Instead, he applied the basic natural law principles concerning the fundamental powers of government. His opinion in the *Slaughter-House Cases* is therefrore difficult to understand. He said in that opinion that none of the three clauses--the privileges and immunities clause, the life, liberty and property clause and the equal protection clause of the Fourteenth Amendment--was broad enough to prevent a state from taking away the general public's right to operate slaughter-houses, in order to give a monopoly to one person. In the *Topeka* decision, however, he said that a state cannot tax the general public in order to give money to one private company; that kind of "unlimited control" over "the lives, the liberty and the property of its citizens . . . is after all but a despotism." One might think he was implying the tax was a violation of the life, liberty and property guarantee of the Fourteenth Amendment, but he never said that.

The *Savings & Loan v. Topeka* decision was not the first time the Supreme Court declared a state law invalid without showing how it violated the U. S. Constitution. In *Calder v. Bull*, 3 U.S. (3 Dallas) 386 (Aug. term, 1798), the Court invalidated a Connecticut law setting aside a court order denying the probate of a will. Justice Samuel Chase said that by so doing, the legislature had arbitrarily taken property from one person and given it to another, which was "contrary to law and reason," though not "expressly restrained" by the Constitution. In *Terrett v. Taylor*, 13 U.S. (9 Cranch) 43 (1815), the Court invalidated a Virginia law taking land away from the Episcopal Church and directing that it be sold and the proceeds given to charity. Justice Joseph Story said, "we think ourselves standing upon the principles of natural justice, upon the fundamental laws of every free government, upon the spirit and letter of the Constitution. . . ." These appear to be the only cases in which the Supreme Court invalidated a state law without ruling that it violated a specific provision of the U. S. Constitution.

In 1876, the year after the *Topeka* decision, the Supreme Court considered for the first time the meaning of "due process of law," in the context of the Fourteenth Amendment's command that no state "shall deprive any person of life, liberty, or property without due process of law." In *Walker v. Sauvinet*, 92 U.S. 90 (Oct. term, 1875), the Court ruled that a person's right to due process of law did not gave him the right to demand a jury in a state civil lawsuit, as he was able to demand in a federal lawsuit under the Seventh Amendment. Speaking for the Court, Chief Justice Morrison Waite said that a state meets the due process of law requirement if the trial "is had according to the settled course of judicial proceedings" and is "process due according to the law of the land." Because this process is determined by the law of the state, he said that each state can determine what is due process in its own courts (Ibid., 93). Waite's ruling, however, raises the following question: if each state can determine the meaning of "due process" within its own boundaries, what is the practical effect of the Fourteenth Amendment's command that no state "shall deprive any person of life, liberty or property without due process of law"?

Chief Justice Waite, Justice Miller and other justices showed a better understanding of the life, liberty and property clause in *Munn v. Illinois*, 94 U.S. 113 (Oct. term, 1876) and *Davidson v. New Orleans*, 96 U.S. 97 (Oct. term, 1877). In both cases, however, the Court ruled that the life, liberty and property clause had not been violated. In the *Munn* case, it ruled that the state could fix the maximum prices charged for storing grain in privately-owned warehouses because these warehouses exercised "a sort of public office" that were in the "gateway of commerce." The Court said the price controls could therefore be justified to protect the commercial flow of public goods. In the *Davidson* case, the Court ruled that a state could tax landowners to pay the cost of hiring a private company to drain a nearby swamp because the tax was for a public purpose.

Although the Supreme Court found no violation of the Constitution in either the *Munn* or the *Davidson* case, these cases are important because the Court recognized that a state regulation must serve the public good order to comply with the life, liberty and property clause of the Fourteenth Amendment. Chief Justice Waite's opinion in the *Munn* case has already been quoted in Chapter 9, Section *B.6* (p. 348), but it bears repeating:

> When one becomes a member of society, he necessarily parts with some rights or privileges which, as an individual not affected by his relations with others, he might retain. "A body politic," as aptly defined in the preamble of the Constitution of Massachusetts, "is a social compact by which the whole people covenants with each citizen, and each citizen with the whole people, that all shall be governed by certain laws for the common good." This does not confer power upon the whole people to control rights which are purely and exclusively private, *Thorpe v. R. & B. Railroad Co.*, 27 Vt. 143; but it does authorize the establishment of laws requiring each citizen to so conduct himself, and so use his own property, as not unnecessarily to injure another. This is the very essence of government, and has found expression in the maxim *sic utere tuo ut alienum non lædas*. From this source come the police powers, which as was said by Mr. Chief Justice Taney in the *License Cases*, 5 How. 583, "are nothing more or less than the powers of government inherent in every sovereignty, . . . that is to say, . . . the power to govern men and things." Under these powers the government regulates the conduct of its citizens one towards another, and the manner in which each shall use his own property, when such regulation becomes necessary for the public good. (Ibid., 124-125)

In the *Davidson* case, Justice Miller said,

> It is easy to see that when the great barons of England wrung from King John, at the point of the sword, the concession that neither their lives nor their property should be disposed of by the crown, except as

provided by the law of the land, they meant by "law of the land" the ancient and customary laws of the English people, or laws enacted by the Parliament of which those barons were a controlling element. It was not in their minds, therefore, to protect themselves against the enactment of laws by the Parliament of England. But when, in the year of grace 1866, there is placed in the Constitution of the United States a declaration that "no State shall deprive any person of life, liberty, or property without due process of law," can a State make any thing due process of law which, by its own legislation, it chooses to declare such? To affirm this is to hold that the prohibition to the states is of no avail, or has no application where the invasion of private rights is effected under the forms of State legislation. It seems to us that a statute which declares in terms, and without more, that the full and exclusive title to a described piece of land, which is now in A., shall be and is hereby vested in B., would, if effectual, deprive A. of his property without due process of law, within the meaning of the constitutional provision. (Ibid., 102)

Justice Miller made one mistake when he said "the law of the land" referred to in the Magna Charta included the laws enacted by Parliament. The first Parliament did not convene until 1265, fifty years after the Magna Charta was signed. Therefore, by "the law of the land," the barons could have meant only the ancient and customary laws of the English people. That resolves Justice Miller's quandary and confirms his opinion that a state cannot declare anything it chooses to be due process of law. Chief Justice Waite had reached the same conclusion in the *Munn* case.

The *Munn* and *Davidson* cases involved property rights. With regard to criminal procedures, however, the Court continued to construe the due process requirement of the life, liberty and property clause very narrowly, each decision raising the question of whether the requirement had any meaning at all. In *Ex parte Wall*, 107 U.S. 265 (1883), the Court ruled that the due process requirement did not prevent a state from convicting a person based on statements that the judge had heard directly from witnesses outside the courtroom. Because none of these witnesses testified in court, the accused was not able to confront and cross examine them. In a federal case, such a conviction would have been illegal under the Sixth Amendment.

In another due process case, *Hurtado v. California*, 110 U.S. 516 (1884), Joseph Hurtado had been tried and convicted of murder and sentenced to die. He claimed that he was being deprived of his life without due process of law in violation of the Fourteenth Amendment because he had been accused merely by a statement signed by a district attorney (an "information") rather than by an indictment signed by a grand jury. However, the Supreme Court ruled that an accusation by an information in a murder trial did not violate the procedural rights of the accused. In the Court's majority opinion, Justice Stanley Matthews said that due process of law did not require the use of all ancient common law procedures. Otherwise, he said, the states would not be able to improve on these procedures (Ibid., 537). However, he did not explain how the substitution of a district attorney's information for a grand jury indictment would improve the handling of murder cases.

Justice Matthews also tried to justify the use of attorney informations on the ground that they had been part of the English common law for a long time. He quoted Blackstone's statement that such informations are "as antient as the common law itself," as well as this statement:

> ". . . as to those offenses, in which informations were allowed as well as indictments, so long as they were confined to this high and respectable jurisdiction, and were carried on in a legal and regular course in his majesty's court of king's bench, the subject had no reason to complain. The same notice was given, the same process was issued, the same pleas were allowed, the same trial by jury was had, the same judgment was given by the same judges, as if the prosecution had originally been by indictment." (Ibid., 538)

However, this passage from Blackstone is misleading in the context of Hurtado's murder trial. Immediately before that passage, Blackstone said,

... these informations (of every kind) are confined by the constitutional law to mere misdemesnors only: for, wherever any capital offence is charged, the same law requires that the accusation be warranted by the oath of twelve men [of a grand jury], before the party shall be put to answer it.[31]

Blackstone also explained how prosecutors had misused informations to harass and vex innocent people.[32]

To justify the Court's ruling, Justice Matthews attacked the historical basis of the trial by jury (Ibid., 529). He said the Latin phrase in the Magna Charta, *nisi per legale judicium parium*, referred only to judges in the Court of Exchequer and *coram regae*. However, the complete phrase in Magna Charta is *nisi per legale judicium parium suorum*, which literally means "unless by legal judgment of his peers" (Chapter 39). Chapter 52 contains the phrase *sine legale judicio parium suorum*, which means literally "without legal judgment of their peers" and the phrase in Chapter 20 is *nisi per sacramentum proborum hominum de visneto*, which means literally, "unless by oath of honest men of the vicinage" (App. A). These chapters may have been loosely interpreted to deprive the common people of their rights during some medieval times, but those errors had long since been corrected by Blackstone's time. Blackstone also said that the trial by jury of twelve equals or peers dated from Saxon England.[33]

Justice Matthews also attacked the historical basis of grand jury indictments. He said that during medieval times, grand juries heard no witnesses and indicted people "upon common fame and general suspicion" (Ibid., 530). However, he neglected to point out that by Blackstone's time, grand juries heard evidence presented by the prosecution, after which, said Blackstone, they "ought to be thoroughly persuaded of the truth of an indictment, so far as the evidence goes; and not to rest satisfied merely with remote probabilities: a doctrine, that might be applied to very oppressive purposes."[34]

Another reason Matthews gave for the Court's ruling was the fact that the Fifth Amendment guaranteed both a grand jury indictment and the right of life, liberty and property. "[A]ccording to a recognized canon of interpretation," he said, there is a presumption that no part of the amendment is superfluous. Therefore, the guarantee in the Fifth Amendment that the federal government shall not deprive a person of life, liberty or property without due process of law cannot include the right to a grand jury, or else the grand jury guarantee would be superfluous. That being the case, Matthews said, the Fourteenth Amendment guarantee that no state shall deprive a person of life, liberty or property without due process of law cannot include the right to a grand jury indictment.

Justice Matthews, however, overlooked the fact that many provisions in the U. S. Constitution are superfluous in some degree with respect to other provisions. The first clause of Article I, Section 8 says that Congress shall have the power to "provide for the common Defence" of the United States. Further on, the same section says that Congress shall have the power "[t]o raise and support Armies," and "[t]o provide and maintain a Navy." Does that mean that providing for the common defense of the United States does not include maintaining an army and a navy? Article III, Section 2[3] says, "The trial of all Crimes, except in Cases of Impeachment, shall be by Jury; and such trial shall be held in the State where the said Crimes shall have been committed; . . ." The Sixth Amendment then says that "[i]n all criminal prosecutions, the accused shall enjoy the right to a speedy and public trial, by an impartial jury of the State and district wherein the crime shall have been committed, . . ." Perhaps the anti-superfluous rule applies only to clauses in the same section of the Constitution. If that is true, then the Supreme Court would be able to say that the life, liberty and property guarantees of the Fifth and Fourteenth Amendments include the jury trial guarantees of Article III and the Sixth Amendment. However, it would not be able to say that the life, liberty and property guarantees include the Fifth Amendment right of a property owner to just compensation when his property is taken for public use.

In 1890, the Supreme Court relied on the anti-superfluous reasoning of the *Hurtado* decision in holding that the life, liberty and property clause of the Fourteenth Amendment did not embody the Eighth Amendment protection against cruel and unusual punishment (*In re Kemmler*, 136 U.S. 436). However, in 1897, the Court ignored the same rule when it said that the life, liberty and property clause of the Fourteenth Amendment prevented a state from taking private property for public use without paying the owner just compensation (*Chicago, Burlington & Quincy Railroad v. Chicago*, 166 U.S. 226 at 241 [1897]). In that case, the Court ruled that the railroad was not deprived of just compensation when it received a jury verdict of only one dollar for the dedication of a new street that crossed its tracks. It said that when a railroad receives a right of way for tracks, an implied condition of that grant is that other rights of way may cross its tracks.

The Supreme Court had, in fact, been giving the life, liberty and property clause a fairly broad meaning in several business regulation cases. In *Yick Wo v. Hopkins*, 118 U.S. 356 (1886), it invalidated an ordinance that had given the San Francisco Board of Supervisors the power to decide who could operate a laundry in a wooden building within the county limits, but it did not prescribe any criteria by which the Board was to make its decisions. The Board could therefore refuse an applicant for any reason, no matter how frivolous. Speaking for the Court, Justice Matthews said the ordinance violated the life, liberty and property clause because

> the very idea that one man may be compelled to hold his life, or the means of living, or any material right essential to the enjoyment of life, at the mere will of another, seems to be intolerable in any country where freedom prevails, being the essence of slavery itself. (Ibid., 370)

The Court also ruled that the Board of Supervisors had denied the petitioners equal protection of the laws. While over two hundred Chinese people had applied for permits to operate laundries, all of them had been turned down, yet the Board had granted permits to eighty other people, none of whom was Chinese.

In another business regulation case, *Allgeyer v. Louisiana*, 165 U.S. 578 (1897), the Court ruled that a Louisiana law violated the life, liberty and property clause because it fined a local citizen for entering into a contract with an New York insurance company relating to property located in Louisiana. The Court ruled that Louisiana had no power to require the New York company to be licensed in its state because the contract was made in New York. The life, liberty and property clause, said the Court, prevents a state from regulating a contract made in another state, even though one of the parties is one of its citizens and the contract relates to property within its jurisdiction.

While the Supreme Court was striking down these state business regulations using a fairly broad interpretation of the Fourteenth Amendment's life, liberty and property clause, it continued to interpret the "due process of law" part of the clause very narrowly when judging the validity of state court procedures. In *Iowa Central Railway v. Iowa*, 160 U.S. 389 at 393 (1896), the Court said that "due process" meant only that a state must adopt a procedure that "gives reasonable notice and affords fair opportunity to be heard before the issues are decided." It therefore ruled that the Iowa Central Railway was not entitled to a jury trial in a state civil trial. The Court continued to rule that "due process" requires only reasonable notice and a fair hearing in *Louisville & Nashville Railroad Company v. Schmidt*, 177 U.S. 230 at 236 (1900), *Hooker v. Los Angeles*, 188 U.S. 314 at 318 (1903) and *Rogers v. Peck*, 199 U.S. 425 at 435 (1905). In *Maxwell v. Dow*, 176 U.S. 581 (1900), the Court ruled that "due process" did not give a criminal defendant the right to a jury trial in a state court, even though the Sixth Amendment guaranteed the right of a jury trial to persons accused of federal crimes and even though this was one of the fundamental rights that the colonists had asserted in their petitions to the British government (Apps. H and K).

The Supreme Court's narrow interpretation of "due process" continued in *Twining v. New Jersey*, 211 U.S. 78 (1908). In that case, the Court ruled that a New Jersey court had not violated a criminal defendant's right of due process when it instructed a jury that it might infer his guilt because he did not testify at his trial. Speaking for the Court, Justice William Moody cited the failure of the English courts to recognize the right of a defendant to avoid this inference and the fact that only four of the original thirteen states recognized the right. Because the Fifth Amendment provides separately for the right not to testify and the right not to be deprived of life, liberty or property without due process of law and because several early state constitutions did the same, he said, "the inference is irresistible that it has been the opinion of constitution makers that the privilege, if fundamental in any sense, is not fundamental in due process of law, nor an essential part of it" (Ibid., 110). Justice Moody thus relied on the same spurious reasoning that the Court had relied on in the *Hurtado* case, supra.

> There can be no doubt, [he added,] so far as the decision in the *Slaughter-House Cases* has determined the question, that the civil rights sometimes described as fundamental and inalienable, which before the war Amendments were enjoyed by state citizenship and protected by state government, were left untouched by this clause of the Fourteenth Amendment. Criticism of this case has never entirely ceased, nor has it ever received universal assent by members of this court. Undoubtedly, it gave much less effect to the Fourteenth Amendment than some of the public men active in framing it intended, and disappointed many others. On the other hand, if the views of the minority had prevailed it is easy to see how far the authority and independence of the States would have been diminished, by subjecting all their legislative and judicial acts to correction by the legislative and review by the judicial branch of the National Government. (Ibid., 96)

However, Justice Moody's reliance on the reasoning of the *Hurtado* and *Slaughter-House* cases appears to conflict with his own statement in another part of his opinion, in which he said

> it is possible that some of the personal rights safeguarded by the first eight Amendments against National action may also be safeguarded against state action, because a denial of them would be a denial of due process of law. *Chicago, Burlington & Quincy Railroad v. Chicago,* 166 U.S. 226. If this is so, it is not because those rights are enumerated in the first eight Amendments, but because they are of such a nature that they are included in the conception of due process of law. (Ibid., 99)

Fortunately, this part of the *Twining* opinion is the one that the Supreme Court relied upon in later cases, including *Powell v. Alabama*, 287 U.S. 45 at 67 (1932) and *Palko v. Connecticut*, 302 U.S. 319 at 326 (1937) (discussed in Section *D.4*).

D.3 The Lochner Era

While the Supreme Court was restricting the meaning of the life, liberty and property clause to uphold the validity of state trial procedures, it began to stretch the meaning of this clause to strike down laws that protected workers from being forced to work for extremely long hours or extremely low pay or from agreeing to other terms of employment that were not in their best interests. In *Lochner v. New York*, 198 U.S. 45 (1905), the Court invalidated a New York law that forbade bakeries to employ people more than ten hours a day or sixty hours a week, on the ground that the life, liberty and property clause protected a businessman's "liberty to contract." Seven years before, in *Holden v. Hardy*, 169 U.S. 366 (1898), the Court had upheld the validity of a Utah law that limited the period of labor in underground mines to eight hours a day. It had ruled that law was within the state's power to interfere "where the parties do not stand upon an equality, or where the public health demands that one party to the contract shall be protected against himself" (Ibid., 397). Speaking for the Court in the *Lochner* case, Justice Rufus Peckham distinguished the New York bakery law from the Utah mining law, which allowed an exception when life or property was in imminent danger. He also said there was no substantial threat to a baker's health in working over ten hours a day, while an underground mine presented a more serious health hazard to workers.

The Supreme Court did not address in the *Lochner* case, as it had in the *Hardy* case, a state's right to intercede when the parties to a contract are in unequal bargaining positions. The New York bakers and the Utah mine workers both appear to have had inferior bargaining positions, yet the Court allowed only the mining workers to be protected by their state's labor laws. By the time of the *Lochner* decision, the majority of justices on the Court had reached the view that government had no legitimate purpose in changing the contractual bargaining power of people. They believed that such interference would violate the "free enterprise" theory of economic justice. One justice who disagreed with this view was Oliver Wendell Holmes. In his dissenting opinion, he wrote that

> [t]he Fourteenth Amendment does not enact Mr. Herbert Spencer's Social Statistics. The other day we sustained the Massachusetts vaccination law. *Jacobson v. Massachusetts*, 197 U.S. 11. United States and state statutes and decisions cutting down the liberty to contract by way of combination are familiar to this court. *Northern Securities Co. v. United States*, 193 U.S. 197. Two years ago we upheld the prohibition of sales of stock on margins or for future delivery in the constitution of California. *Otis v. Parker*, 187 U.S. 606. The decision sustaining an eight-hour law for a miner is still recent. *Holden v. Hardy*, 169 U.S. 366. Some of these laws embody convictions or prejudices which judges are likely to share. Some may not. But a constitution is not intended to embody a particular economic theory, whether of paternalism and the organic relation of the citizen to the State or of *laissez faire*. (Ibid., 75)

The *Lochner* decision began a thirty-year period, called the "Lochner era," during which the Supreme Court invalidated almost two hundred federal and state laws that attempted to regulate business.[35] The Court's position was that these laws had no legitimate governmental purpose and therefore took away people's freedom to negotiate their own contracts. Most of these laws regulated wages and hours of workers, but some regulated other conditions of employment. In *Adair v. United States*, 208 U.S. 161 (1908), the Court ruled that a federal law violated the life, liberty and property clause of the Fifth Amendment because it punished employers who would not hire laborers unless they agreed not to join labor unions. Speaking for the Court, Justice John Marshal Harlan (grandfather of the Justice Harlan mentioned earlier) said the law interfered with the liberty of the employer to choose the kind of employment agreements he would make and there was no valid governmental purpose for this interference. In *Coppage v. Kansas*, 236 U.S. 1 (1915), the Court ruled that a similar Kansas state law violated the Fourteenth Amendment life, liberty and property clause. The Kansas Supreme Court had upheld its state law because "employés, as a rule, are not financially able to be as independent in making contracts for the sale of their labor as are employers in making contracts for the purchase thereof." However, speaking for the U. S. Supreme Court, Justice Mahlon Pitney said it was not within the legitimate power of government to remove "those inequalities that are but the normal and inevitable result" of the freedom to make contracts (Ibid., 17-18).

Although the Supreme Court invalidated many business regulations during the Lochner Era, it actually upheld more laws than it struck down. Such was the case in *Muller v. Oregon*, 208 U.S. 412 (1908), which concerned an Oregon law that limited the hours of employment of women in factories and laundries to ten a day. In the Court's opinion, Justice David Brewer distinguished this law from the law in the *Lochner* case because it protected only female employees who were less able than men to handle strenuous labor. He also said that a woman could not be regarded as the equal of a man in negotiating her contractual rights, because of "her disposition and habits of life which will operate against a full assertion of those rights" (Ibid., 422). He based these findings on a large number of published research reports on female labor, which had been submitted as attachments to a "Brandeis brief," filed by Louis Brandeis, counsel for the defendant in error. The Supreme Court did not usually accept such attachments to briefs. However, Brewer said in this case the Court could rely on the attached reports because they resembled the "state of the art" publications that patent attorneys attached to their briefs in patent infringement lawsuits (Ibid., 419).

The exception that the *Muller* decision created for women was bound to widen. In *Bunting v. Oregon*, 243 U.S. 426 (1917), it widened so much that many thought the Court had overruled the *Lochner* decision. In that case, the Oregon law forbade the employment of any person in any manufacturing plant for more than ten hours a day, excepting watchmen, persons required in emergency situations and persons paid at time-and-a-half their regular wages for every hour over ten, up to a maximum of three additional hours. Speaking for the Court, Justice Joseph McKenna accepted the judgments of Oregon's legislature and supreme court that the law was necessary for the health of manufacturing workers, because no facts were presented to the contrary. He also rejected the contention that the law was really designed to limit wages rather than hours. He therefore ruled that the law was a valid exercise of the state's power to regulate health and safety.

By holding that maximum hour laws were presumed necessary to protect worker health and safety, the *Bunting* decision overruled the *Lochner* requirement that the government show that its law actually protects worker health and safety. However, the Court resurrected this requirement to invalidate a minimum wage law in *Adkins v. Children's Hospital*, 261 U.S. 525 (1923). It struck down a District of Columbia law that established a wage control board with the power to set minimum wages for women and minors. The wages for women were to be based on "the necessary cost of living to any such women workers to maintain them in good health and to protect their morals," and those for minors were to be based on "what wages are unreasonably low for any such minor workers." In the *Adkins* case, a woman had been paid a wage below the minimum set by the board. Felix Frankfurter, the attorney for the District's minimum wage board, submitted a Brandeis brief with many research reports showing that low wages paid to women and children led to child neglect, disease, broken homes, prostitution and death. The reports also cited evidence that minimum wage laws had helped to solve these problems. This data, however, did not impress the majority of the Supreme Court justices. In the Court's opinion, Justice George Sutherland said the improved conditions of working women appeared to result not from the minimum wages set by various laws but from the general improvement of the economy. He said the government had therefore failed to show that a minimum wage law could be justified as a measure for protecting the health and welfare of working women (Ibid., 560). Justice Sutherland also said the employer should be bound to pay only the market value of a worker's services. He should not be responsible for her impoverished condition because he has neither caused nor contributed to that condition. The government, not the employer, should therefore pay the difference between an employee's market value and her minimum subsistence requirements (Ibid., 558-559).

Chief Justice William Howard Taft filed a dissenting opinion in the *Adkins* case, arguing there was no sound distinction between the maximum hours laws, held valid in the *Muller* and *Bunting* cases, supra, and a minimum wage law. The research reports submitted to the Court showed that long hours and low wages are equally harmful to a worker's health (Ibid., 564). In another dissenting opinion, Justice Holmes pointed out that "liberty of contract" is nowhere mentioned in the Constitution. He listed a number of ways that legislatures have limited this so-called liberty, including usury laws and statutes of frauds that restrict many contracts to certain forms. He also cited contract regulations that the Supreme Court had held valid, including insurance rate regulations, laws that regulated the way coal miners are paid and laws that fixed the size of a loaf of bread. Justice Louis Brandeis did not take part in the Court's review of the *Adkins* case.

The *Adkins* case set the stage for many later cases in which the courts invalidated minimum wage laws, maximum price laws and other business regulations. These cases did not present a serious problem during the economic boom times of the 1920s. However, when the Great Depression hit, the precedent set by the *Adkins* and *Lochner* cases hampered the ability of the states and the federal government to deal with the severe economic and social problems of the 1930s. In 1936, the Supreme Court struck down a New York minimum wage law for women in *Morehead v. New York ex rel. Tipaldo*, 298 U.S. 587. This decision came a time when the Supreme Court was invalidating many federal "New Deal" laws on the ground that they regulated local matters and were beyond Congress's power to regulate interstate commerce. President

Roosevelt was campaigning to have the Supreme Court enlarged so he could appoint justices who would have broader views of the Constitutional powers of the federal and state governments to regulate the economy.

Many people, including some of his own Democratic supporters, criticized Roosevelt's plan to "pack" the Supreme Court with his hand-picked justices. The most outspoken critic was Chief Justice Hughes. However, the controversy subsided in the spring of 1937, when the Supreme Court handed down two decisions indicating that the majority of the justices had become more sympathetic to Roosevelt's views on the Constitution. This occurred because Justice Owen Roberts changed his mind on the validity of minimum wage laws, which switched the Court's opinion to a five-to-four vote in favor of their validity. Some people thought that Roberts changed his mind to avoid a confrontation between the Supreme Court and the president. They said it was a "switch in time that saved nine."[36]

The decision on which Roberts switched was *West Coast Hotel v. Parrish*, 300 U.S. 379, handed down on March 29, 1937. The case involved a Washington state minimum wage law for women, very similar to the District of Columbia law that had been struck down by the *Adkins* decision. Chief Justice Hughes, writing the Court's opinion, said the *Adkins* decision "should be, and it is, overruled." He relied heavily on the reasons given in the dissenting opinions filed by Justices Taft and Holmes in the *Adkins* case. With regard to the argument that government should not interfere with the rights of adults to negotiate their own contracts, Hughes said that argument had been met forty years before in *Holden v. Hardy*, supra, when the Supreme Court said,

> "The legislature has also recognized the fact, which the experience of legislators in many States has corroborated, that the proprietors of these establishments and their operatives do not stand upon an equality, and that their interests are, to a certain extent, conflicting. The former naturally desire to obtain as much labor as possible from their employees, while the latter are often induced by the fear of discharge to conform to regulations which their judgment, fairly exercised, would

pronounce to be detrimental to their health and strength. In other words, the proprietors lay down the rules and the laborers are practically constrained to obey them. In such cases self-interest is often an unsafe guide, and the legislature may properly interpose its authority." (Ibid., 393-394, quoting *Holden v. Hardy*, 169 U.S. at 397)

Hughes also answered Justice Sutherland's comment in *Adkins* that the government, not the employer, should be responsible for an employee's impoverished condition. Hughes said, "The community is not bound to provide what is in effect a subsidy for unconscionable employers" (Ibid., 399).

The other Supreme Court decision that pleased President Roosevelt was *National Labor Relations Board v. Jones & Laughlin Steel Corp.*, 301 U.S. 1, made April 12, 1937. In that case, the Court upheld the validity of the National Labor Relations Act, which established the right of employees to form labor unions and to bargain collectively through their chosen representatives. The Act established the National Labor Relations Board and gave it the power to prevent unfair labor practices that affect interstate commerce. It also established procedures for resolving labor disputes and collective bargaining procedures. Among the forbidden labor practices was coercing employees to stay away from unions. Jones & Laughlin Steel Corporation was charged with violating the Act by discriminating against employees at its Aliquippa, Pennsylvania steel plant because they had joined a labor union. Jones and Laughlin contended that the Act violated several sections of the U. S. Constitution, including the interstate commerce clause and the life, liberty and property clause of the Fifth Amendment. Speaking for the majority of the Court, Chief Justice Hughes said Congress had the power to pass the Act under the interstate commerce clause, even though it applied to the laborers who worked exclusively within one state, such as the Jones & Laughlin workers in Aliquippa, Pennsylvania. He said the Aliquippa plant was the focal point of a "stream" or "flow" of commerce that included the interstate movement of iron ore, coal and limestone to the plant and then the movement of steel products to consuming centers across the country. Industrial strife at this plant would cripple this flow of interstate commerce (Ibid., 34-35). Hughes also said the Act did not impose an undue restraint on the contractual liberty of employers in violation of the life, liberty and property clause of the Fifth Amendment. The Act had a valid purpose for its restraints, he said, namely, to give union representatives an opportunity to negotiate with companies in a manner likely to promote industrial peace (Ibid., 45). Another valid purpose, he said, was to enable laborers to bargain through a union because the "union was essential to give laborers the opportunity to deal on an equality with their employer" (Ibid., 33).

The *West Coast* and *National Labor Relations* cases opened an era of government regulation of labor, powerful labor unions and confrontations between the unions and the nation's industrial companies. These cases also ended the *Lochner* era and the paramount importance placed by the courts on "liberty of contract."

The *Lochner* era was an aberration. The United States Constitution does not guarantee an individual the liberty to make contracts according to the conventional common law rules of contracts. Blackstone does not mention such a liberty among the "Absolute Rights of Individuals." He reports that the wages of English laborers were settled by the justices at sessions or the county sheriff.[37] Parliament and the colonial legislatures enacted usury laws that limited the interest that money lenders could charge. The Virginia Colony fixed the wages of parsons and the Massachusetts settlers limited the rates that skilled workmen could charge for their services.[38] These laws were valid because they established the relative rights and duties that governments are organized to establish for the protection of everyone's life, liberty and property. When people submit to civil government instead of living in a state of nature, they seek protection from the brutal, survival-of-the-fittest conditions of nature--both its physical conditions and its economic conditions. They expect the government to protect the physically weak and the economically weak. It is the job of government to provide that protection. That protection includes a law of contracts that, in the judgment of the legislature and not the courts, will achieve economic justice for everyone.

D.4. Liberty beyond Lochner

Although the Supreme Court was preoccupied with contractual liberties during the *Lochner* era, it did address other issues relating to people's life, liberty and property and the due process required to take them away.

In *Moore v. Dempsey*, 261 U.S. 86 (1923), the Court ruled that due process requires at least a semblance of a fair trial. In this case, several Arkansas black men had been arrested for murdering a white man during a confrontation between a crowd of black people and a crowd of white people. While they were in jail awaiting trial, a mob of angry white men marched on the jail and demanded that the prisoners be released so they could lynch them. They were turned away only after officials promised that if the mob would refrain, "the law would be carried out." A month later, the black men were convicted of first degree murder by an all white jury after a trial that lasted only forty-five minutes and a jury deliberation that lasted less than five minutes. Their court-appointed attorney did not consult with them before the trial, nor did he call any of the available witnesses. He did not challenge a juryman nor did he ask for a delay of the trial, for a removal of the trial to another place or for separate trials of each of the accused. Speaking for the Court, Justice Holmes set aside the jury's verdict, ruling that "the whole proceeding is a mask--that counsel, jury and judge were swept to the fatal end by an irresistible wave of public passion, and that the State Courts failed to correct the wrong, . . . " (Ibid., 91).

The right to a fair trial was also the major issue in *Powell v. Alabama*, 287 U.S. 45 (1932), involving the much publicized "Scottsboro boys" trial. Seven black youths were charged with raping two white girls in a gondola car on a moving freight train. Each of the girls later testified that she had been assaulted by six of the seven youths whom they identified. The incident occurred after a fight between a gang of white boys and a gang of black boys that included the seven who were charged with the rape. The fight resulted in all of the white boys except one being thrown off the train. A message was sent ahead to Scottsboro, Alabama, reporting the fight. When the train arrived there, the defendants were arrested and charged. At the opening of their trials two weeks later, no lawyer appeared on their behalf. The judge had appointed all the willing attorneys in the area to represent them at the arraignment. Some attorneys appeared at the arraignment and then helped in preparing the defendants for their trials, but none considered himself officially appointed. The judge finally appointed one of them on the first day of the trial, but it was not clear that the attorney understood he had been officially appointed because he said to the judge, "I will go ahead and help do anything I can do." The juries in all the cases found the defendants guilty and imposed the death penalty on all of them. Speaking for the majority of the Supreme Court, Justice Sutherland said that the defendants had not been adequately represented by counsel. They had therefore been denied due process of law. He said that because the case involved the death penalty and because the defendants were illiterate and ignorant and unable to employ their own attorneys, it was the duty of the court to assign counsel in sufficient time to allow him to prepare for the trials.

In his opinion, Sutherland traced the history of the right to counsel. He said that if the right were to depend on the existence of a similar right under the English common law when the American Constitution was adopted, it would be difficult to maintain it as necessary to due process (Ibid., 60). That was because an Englishman charged with a felony was denied the aid of counsel during the 1700s. However, Sutherland said that in the fourth volume of his *Commentaries*, at page 355, Blackstone had denounced that rule because it was not in keeping with the humane treatment normally accorded prisoners by the English law (Ibid., 60-61). Sutherland also reviewed the history of the right to counsel in each of the thirteen original states. He said that in at least twelve of these states, the right was recognized as essential in all criminal prosecutions, except in one or two instances in which it was limited to capital offenses or more serious crimes (Ibid., 64-65). In addition, he considered the Sixth Amendment guarantee of the right of an accused to counsel in federal criminal cases. The Supreme

Court had said in *Holden v. Hardy*, supra., that the guarantee of a specific right in the Bill of Rights meant that it was not intended to be included as part of the right of life, liberty and property because that right was separately guaranteed in Bill of Rights and the two rights would have been redundant. However, Sutherland pointed out that since the *Holden* case, the Court had made a number of exceptions to that rule, including the right to just compensation for property taken for public use and the rights of free speech and free press. He also quoted Justice Moody's statement in *Twining v. New Jersey*, supra, that "it is possible that some of the personal rights safeguarded by the first eight Amendments against National action may be safeguarded against state action, because a denial of them would be a denial of due process of law" (Ibid., 67). Finally, Sutherland observed that "even the intelligent and educated layman has small and sometimes no skill in the law" and therefore needs "the guiding hand of counsel" (Ibid., 69). He therefore concluded that the right to counsel was essential to due process under the particular circumstances of the *Powell* case.

The Supreme Court continued to expound on the meaning of "due process" in criminal trials in *Mooney v. Holohan*, 294 U.S. 103 (1935). The Court ruled in that case that a person is denied due process if he is convicted on testimony that the prosecuting attorney knows to be a lie. The Court said, "Such a contrivance by the State to procure the conviction and imprisonment of a defendant is as inconsistent with the rudimentary demands of justice as is the obtaining of a like result by intimidation" (Ibid., 112).

In two other criminal due process cases, *Brown v. Mississippi*, 297 U.S. 278 (1936) and *Chambers v. Florida*, 309 U.S. 227 (1940), the Supreme Court ruled that state prosecutors had violated the Fourteenth Amendment by forcing black prisoners to confess to crimes. In the *Brown* case, the prisoners had endured physical torture. Chief Justice Hughes said, "The rack and torture chamber may not be substituted for the witness stand."

In the early 1920s, the Supreme Court invalidated several attempts by states to limit the ability of parents to teach their children about their families' cultural heritage, saying the states had violated their right of liberty under the life, liberty and property clause. In *Meyer v. Nebraska*, 262 U.S. 390 (1923), the state of Nebraska passed a law forbidding the teaching of any modern language other than English to any child in the eighth grade or below in any private, denominational, parochial or public school. It said the purpose of the law was

> to create an enlightened American citizenship in sympathy with the principles and ideals of this country, and to prevent children reared in America from being trained and educated in foreign languages and foreign ideals before they have had an opportunity to learn the English language and observe American ideals. (Ibid., 393-394)

In its appeal brief, the state of Nebraska said that twenty-one other states had enacted similar foreign language laws. The main target of these laws was the German language; their motivation was the recent war against Germany. The states wanted to inhibit parents of German ancestry from passing on to their children the ideals, language and customs of the German Empire, which had recently been defeated by the United States and its allies.

The Supreme Court ruled that the state of Nebraska had arbitrarily interfered with the parents' right to educate their children and teach them foreign languages. The speaking for the Court, Justice James McReynolds said, "Mere knowledge of the German language cannot reasonably be regarded as harmful. Heretofore it has been commonly looked upon as helpful and desirable" (Ibid., 400). He said there was no connection between teaching a foreign language to children and the harm that the states sought to redress, which was children's lack of knowledge of the English language and American ideals. In this case and companion cases, the Supreme Court invalidated the Nebraska foreign language law and the similar laws of several other states [*Bartels v. Iowa, Bohning and Pohl v. Ohio* and *Nebraska District of Evangelical Lutheran Synod v. McKelvie*, 262 U.S. 404 (1923)].

The right of parents to control their children's education was also the issue in *Pierce, Governor of Oregon v. Society of Sisters and Hill Military Academy*, 268 U.S. 510 (1925). In that case, an

Oregon law required the parents of all children between eight and sixteen years to send their children to the state's public schools. The state of Oregon argued that one purpose of the law was to take children off the street and put them in schools so they would not become vagabonds and criminals. It did not explain why state-regulated private and parochial schools would not serve that purpose as well as public schools. It said another purpose of the law was to alleviate suspicions between different religious groups by forcing the children of these groups to mingle during a portion of their education. That would safeguard against future internal dissension and the consequent weakening of the community against foreign dangers (Ibid., 524-525). Justice McReynolds also wrote the Court's opinion in this case. Citing his own opinion in *Meyer v. Nebraska*, supra, he said the Oregon law unreasonably interfered

> with the liberty of parents and guardians to direct the upbringing and education of children under their control. As often heretofore pointed out, rights guaranteed by the Constitution may not be abridged by legislation which has no reasonable relation to some purpose within the competency of the State. The fundamental theory of liberty upon which all governments in this Union repose excludes any general power of the State to standardize its children by forcing them to accept instruction from public teachers only. The child is not the mere creature of the State; those who nurture him and direct his destiny have the right, coupled with the high duty, to recognize and prepare him for additional obligations. (Ibid., 534-535).

During this period, the Supreme Court also considered whether residential-only, municipal zoning violated the life, liberty and property clause of the Fourteenth Amendment. In *Village of Euclid, Ohio v. Ambler Realty Company*, 272 U.S. 365 (1926), the Village of Euclid, Ohio adopted a comprehensive zoning plan designed to control the spread of industrial and commercial development, which had begun to creep over its border from the City of Cleveland. The plan designated large areas of land for residential use only, which was a relatively new zoning concept. All business and trade establishments, as well as hotels and apartment houses, were forbidden in these areas. Ambler Realty filed a lawsuit to enjoin enforcement of this zoning plan, because it owned a sixty-eight-acre tract in one of the newly zoned residential areas. This land was also in the path of the industrial development spreading from Cleveland. Ambler claimed that if it were able to sell its property for industrial development purposes, it could receive about $10,000 an acre, but its residential market value was only about $2,500 an acre.

Speaking for the Court, Justice Sutherland ruled that the Euclid zoning plan did not deprive Ambler of its Fourteenth Amendment property rights because the village had legitimate reasons for adopting the plan. These included the protection of the health and safety of homeowners and their families and the protection of residential areas from traffic congestion, the danger of industrial fires and the "contagion and disorder which in greater or less degree attach to the location of stores, shops and factories." Thus, "[t]he segregation of industries[,] commercial pursuits and dwellings to particular districts in a city, when exercised reasonably, may bear a rational relation to the health, morals, safety and general welfare of the community" (Ibid., 391, 392). Sutherland said the reasonableness of a zoning plan varies with the circumstances and conditions. One that "would be clearly valid as applied to the great cities, might be clearly invalid as applied to rural communities." Recent urban growth had made zoning laws necessary, he observed, while fifty years before, they "probably would have been rejected as arbitrary and oppressive." He maintained that the meaning of the Constitution had not changed; it was simply being applied to new conditions (Ibid., 387).

Between 1927 and 1937, the Supreme Court ruled that the Fourteenth Amendment's life, liberty and property clause requires the states to observe the First Amendment rights of free speech, free press and free assembly. The free speech ruling came in *Fiske v. Kansas*, 247 U.S. 380 (1927), free press in *Near v. Minnesota*, 283 U.S. 697 (1931) and peaceable assembly in *DeJonge v. Oregon*, 299 U.S. 353 (1937). (These cases were discussed in the Chapter 9, Subsections *C.2*, *C.3* and *C.4*.)

Chapter 10   The Fourteenth Amendment   441

In 1937, the Supreme Court ruled in *Palko v. Connecticut*, 302 U.S. 319, that the double jeopardy clause of the Fifth Amendment was not within the life, liberty property guarantee of the Fourteenth Amendment. Justice Benjamin Cardozo reviewed the Court's past decisions in which it had ruled that some rights in the first eight amendments were guaranteed by the Fourteenth Amendment and some were not. The rights not guaranteed were the Fifth Amendment requirements of a grand jury indictment (*Hurtado v. California*, supra) and the right of an accused not to testify against himself (*Twining v. New Jersey*, supra) and the Sixth Amendment requirement of a jury trial in a criminal case (*Maxwell v. Dow*, supra). The rights that were guaranteed were the First Amendment guarantees of the free exercise of religion (*Pierce v. Society of Sisters*, supra) and of free speech, press and assembly (*DeJonge v. Oregon*, supra, and *Near v. Minnesota*, supra) and the Sixth Amendment right of an accused to the benefit of counsel (*Powell v. Alabama*, supra). Justice Cardozo said the difference between these two groups of rights is that the ones within the life, liberty and property guarantee "have been found to be implicit in the concept of ordered liberty, . . ." while the others, he said,

> are not of the very essence of a scheme of ordered liberty. To abolish them is not to violate a "principle of justice so rooted in the traditions and conscience of our people as to be ranked as fundamental." *Snyder v. Massachusetts*, supra, p. 105; *Brown v. Mississippi*, supra, p. 285; *Herbert v. Louisiana*, 272 U.S. 312, 316. (Ibid., 325)

With respect to jury trials, grand jury indictments and immunity from self-incrimination, said Cardozo, "Few would be so narrow or provincial as to maintain that a fair and enlightened system of justice would be impossible without them." He apparently did not consider the fairness of trying an accused by a jury of his fellow citizens instead of by a government-employed judge whose primary interest is in showing the public how well he punishes criminals. For this reason, the right to a jury trial was guaranteed in Chapters 20 and 52 of the Magna Charta, the Petition of Right and the English Declaration of Rights. Blackstone said that the right "seems to have been co-eval with the first civil government" of England, that it has been "looked upon as the glory of English law," and that "it is the most transcendent privilege which any subject can enjoy, or wish for."[39] The colonists asserted their right to jury trials in the Declaration of the Stamp Act Congress and in the Declaration and Resolves of the First Continental Congress. They also said that one of the reasons they were declaring their independence was that King George III had deprived them "of the benefits of Trial by Jury" (App. L). In the light of this history, it seems odd that Justice Cardozo would use the jury trial as an example of a right that is not "so rooted in the traditions and conscience of our people as to be ranked as fundamental."

The *Palko* case, however, was not about jury trials. It was about double jeopardy. The state of Connecticut had appealed Palko's jury verdict of second degree murder. The Connecticut Supreme Court of Errors had then ordered a new trial because some of the state's evidence had been excluded at the first trial. Palko was found guilty of first degree murder at the second trial and sentenced to die. Under the federal rule announced in *Kepner v. United States*, 195 U.S. 100 (1904), the second trial would have violated the Fifth Amendment guarantee against double jeopardy, had this been a federal case. However, this was a state of Connecticut case and Justice Cardozo said the *Kepner* rule was not a fundamental principle of liberty. So the Fourteenth Amendment did not require the state to follow it. He said, "The state is not attempting to wear the accused out by a multitude of cases with accumulated trials. It asks no more than this, that the case go on until there shall be a trial free from corrosion and substantial legal error."

On the other hand, the English courts had always recognized the rule against double jeopardy and they had never granted a new trial after the accused had been acquitted. Blackstone said in his chapter entitled "Of Trial, and Conviction" that an accused could challenge a new indictment on the ground that he had been acquitted of the same offense, because of the "universal maxim of the common law of England, that no man is to be brought into jeopardy of his life, more than once, for the same offense." He also said, "But there hath yet been no instance of granting a new trial, where the prisoner was *acquitted* upon the first. If the jury therefore find the prisoner not guilty, he is then for ever quit and discharged of the accusation;"[40]

The Supreme Court returned to the government's power to regulate business in *United States v. Carolene Products*, 304 U.S. 144 (1938). In that case, the Court upheld the constitutionality of a law that forbade the shipment of filled milk in interstate commerce. "Filled milk" was defined by the law as milk or cream to which had been added a fat or oil other than milk fat. The Supreme Court held that the law was within Congress's power to regulate interstate commerce. It also said that the law did not violate the life, liberty and property clause of the Fifth Amendment because its stated purpose was to protect the public health and to prevent the fraudulent marketing of filled milk as a healthy substitute for pure milk. Also there were reports of legislative hearings at which evidence was presented showing the bad effect on public health when vegetable oils are substituted for natural milk fat. The Court said that even without such evidence, it would presume that the legislature had a rational basis for its judgment that filled milk was injurious to public health (Ibid., 152). It ruled that Carolene Products had not presented sufficient evidence to overcome this presumption.

The Supreme Court's ruling in the *Carolene* case was in line with previous rulings in which the Court had held that similar state laws did not violate the life, liberty and property clause of the Fourteenth Amendment. In *Hebe v. Shaw*, 248 U.S. 297 (1919), the Court had upheld a state law banning the manufacture and sale of filled milk, and in *Powell v. Pennsylvania*, 127 U.S. 678 (1888), it had upheld a state law banning the sale of oleomargarine as a substitute for butter. There was therefore nothing noteworthy about the *Carolene* ruling. In the Court's opinion, however, Justice Harlan Fiske Stone attached a footnote warning that all laws might not be given the same presumption of validity as laws regulating commercial transactions. He gave as examples laws that appear on their face "to be within a specific prohibition of the Constitution, such as those of the first ten amendments, which are deemed equally specific when held to be embraced within the Fourteenth." He also said that the Court might subject "to more exacting judicial scrutiny" laws that restrict voting rights, religious freedom and the freedoms of speech, press and assembly, as well as laws that exhibit "prejudice against discrete and insular minorities" (Ibid., 152-153). Justice Stone thus set the stage for a double standard in the Court's decisions relating to the life, liberty or property clauses of the Fifth and Fourteenth Amendments. Many people believe that the Court has, in fact, applied such a double standard and that it is an arbitrary distinction that has no basis in the words of the Constitution.

Aviam Soifer commented on this footnote in the *Encyclopedia of the American Constitution*:

> Footnote four thus symbolizes the Court's struggle since the late 1930s to confine an earlier, free-wheeling tradition of judicial intervention premised on freedom of contract and substantive due process, on the one hand, while trying, on the other, to create an acceptable basis for active intervention when judges perceive political disadvantages or racial or other invidious discrimination.[41]

There are sound reasons, however, for ruling that government can regulate commerce but cannot limit voting rights, discriminate against minorities or infringe the Bill of Rights. We need only recall the basic nature of government that was envisioned by the American founding fathers. In the Declaration of Independence, they said that people have the right to alter or abolish governments that do not observe the fundamental truths "that all men are created equal," "that they are endowed by their Creator with certain unalienable Rights, that among these are Life, Liberty and the pursuit of Happiness" and, "[t]hat to secure these rights, Governments are instituted among Men, deriving their just powers from the consent of the governed." These truths were well understood by the thousands of Americans who had read Blackstone's *Commentaries* and Locke's *Second Essay Concerning Civil Government*, as illustrated in the New Hampshire Constitution of 1784:

> All men are born equally free and independent; therefore, all government of right originates from the people, is founded in consent, and instituted for the general good.
>
> II. All men have certain natural, essential, and inherent rights; among which are--the enjoying and defending life and liberty--acquiring, possessing and protecting property--and in a word, of seeking and obtaining happiness.
>
> III. When men enter into a state of society, they surrender up some of their natural rights to that society, in order to insure the protection of others; and, without such an equivalent, the surrender is void.
>
> IV. Among the natural rights, some are in their very nature unalienable, because no equivalent can be given or received for them. Of this kind are the RIGHTS OF CONSCIENCE.[42]

In addition to the "rights of conscience" (religious freedom), a person's inalienable rights include his freedom of speech and press and his right to be his own master of his absolute duties.

On the other hand, it is the job of government to define and enforce the relative rights and duties of people, including those relating to their commerce. People are bound by these rights and duties because they surrendered some of their natural rights of life, liberty and property to gain the benefits of a civil society. That is why some of a person's rights of life, liberty and property can be taken by government in exchange for the protection of all people, while other rights remain inalienable. That is the nature of the guarantees of the Fifth and Fourteenth Amendments, that no person shall be deprived of life, liberty or property, without due process of law.

The Fourteenth Amendment also guarantees that no state shall deny to any person the equal protection of the laws, in recognition of the truth proclaimed in the Declaration of Independence that all men are created equal. In addition, the Constitution has been amended to embrace more fully the principle that government derives its just powers from the consent of the governed. The Fifteenth Amendment guarantees that the right to vote shall not be denied or abridged on account of race, color or previous condition of servitude, and the Nineteenth Amendment guarantees that the right to vote shall not be denied or abridged on account of sex. These amendments are the bases of Justice Stone's statements in footnote four of the *Carolene* case.

The long-forgotten privileges and immunities clause of the Fourteenth Amendment resurfaced in *Hague v. C.I.O.*, 307 U.S. 496 (1939). In that case, the leaders of a labor union had been arrested in Jersey City, New Jersey, while attempting to distribute printed leaflets and hold meetings on public property. The leaders had applied for permits to hold such meetings but the city safety director denied the permits. A city ordinance authorized the safety director to refuse permits "for the purpose of preventing riots, disturbances and disorderly assembly." The union and its leaders sued the city officials for damages and an injunction to restrain the violation of their Constitutional rights under the Civil Rights Act of 1871, as amended by the Act of 1911. At the trial there was no evidence that the leaflets or the meetings of the union leaders would cause any riots, disturbances or disorderly conduct. The leaders intended merely to publicize the rights of citizens under the National Labor Relations Act. The evidence showed that the only reason the safety director denied the permits was to prevent the union leaders from accomplishing that purpose. By a majority of five justices to two, the Supreme Court ruled that the labor leaders had been denied their Constitutional rights of free speech and press and peaceable assembly.

However, the five majority justices disagreed on which provision of the Fourteenth Amendment had been violated. Justices Roberts and Black said the privileges and immunities clause had been violated because the purpose of the pamphlets and the meetings was to discuss people's rights under a federal law. They cited the statement by Justice Miller in *The Slaughter-House Cases*, supra at 79, that "the right to peaceably assemble and petition for redress of grievances, . . . are rights of the citizen guaranteed by the federal Constitution" (307 U.S. at 513). Justices Stone and Stanley Reed said that the mere fact that the meetings and pamphlets were designed to inform people about a federal law did not mean that the right to conduct them was a privilege or an immunity of U. S.

citizenship. They also pointed out that the Civil Rights Act gave anyone the right to sue for violation of his constitutional rights. Therefore, the Act did not allow a person to sue for violation of privileges and immunities that were possessed only by U.S. citizens. The only relief the Court could grant was for a violation of the life, liberty and property clause of the Fourteenth Amendment, under the precedents set by *Fiske v. Kansas*, supra, for free speech, *Near v. Minnesota*, supra, for free press and *DeJonge v. Oregon*, supra, for the right of peaceable assembly. Chief Justice Hughes agreed with Justices Roberts and Black that the Jersey City officials had violated the privileges and immunities of the union leaders, but he agreed with Justices Stone and Reed that they could sue only for violations of their rights of life, liberty and property under the Civil Rights Act. The *Hague v. C.I.O.* case made it apparent that there were very few cases in which a court might find that a state had violated the privileges and immunities of a U. S. citizen. That was in spite of Blackstone's assertion that the absolute rights of life, liberty and property "consist of a number of private immunities" which are "either that *residuum* of natural liberty, which is not required by the laws of society to be sacrificed to public convenience; or else those civil privileges, which society hath engaged to provide, in lieu of the natural liberties given up by individuals" (BL3, 125).

The Supreme Court considered the issue of whether a person's rights of life, liberty and property included his right of free exercise of religion in *Cantwell v. Connecticut*, 310 U.S. 296 (1940). A Connecticut state law required that door-to-door solicitors for religious and philanthropic organizations apply for a permit, but only solicitors of organizations deemed to be religious or philanthropic were granted permits. Three Jehovah's Witness ministers, Newton Cantwell and his two sons Jesse and Russell, were convicted of violating the law because they had solicited for their religious group without a permit. Speaking for a unanimous Court, Justice Roberts ruled that the law violated the Cantwells' right to exercise their religious beliefs, because the permits were granted only to those religious organizations that fit the government's definition of religion. The law would have been valid had the permits been based on whether the applicants would be defrauding people, calling at unreasonable times or injuring people in some other way.

In another religious freedom case, the Supreme Court ruled in *Everson v. Board of Education*, 330 U.S. 296 (1946) that states were forbidden by the Fourteenth Amendment to make laws "respecting an establishment of religion." (This case was discussed in Chapter 8, Section D and will be covered further in the discussion of religion in the public schools in Chapter 11.)

By 1946, the Supreme Court had declared that each of the First Amendment rights was within the life, liberty and property guarantee of the Fourteenth Amendment. These rights included the freedoms of speech, press and assembly, right to petition the government for redress of grievances, the free exercise of religion and freedom from government-established religion. It had also ruled that the Fifth Amendment right to just compensation for property taken for public use was a basic right of life, liberty and property that the states had to observe (*Chicago, Burlington & Quincy R. R. v. Chicago*, supra). It had ruled that the states could not take away people's life, liberty or property by arbitrary regulations (*Yick Wo v. Hopkins*, supra, *Meyer v. Nebraska*, supra, and *Pierce v. Society of Sisters*, supra) and, during the *Lochner* era, it had wrestled with the rights of businessmen to make employment contracts.

However, the Court was still taking a narrow view of the procedural rights to be safeguarded from state intrusion by the so-called "due process" clause of the Fourteenth Amendment. It had acknowledged that a state had to inform a person accused of a crime of the nature of the charges against him, as provided in the Sixth Amendment (*Iowa City Ry. Co. v. Iowa*, supra at 393). It had also ruled that people had not received fair trials in a few extreme circumstances (e.g., *Moore v. Dempsey*, supra, *Powell v. Alabama*, supra, and *Brown v. Mississippi*, supra). In most cases however, the Court had rejected the argument that a state's civil or criminal procedures violated a person's right to "due process." These included *Walker v. Sauvinet*, supra, in which a person was denied the Seventh Amendment right of a jury trial in a civil case; *Ex parte Wall*, 107 U.S. 265 (Oct. term, 1882), in which an accused was denied the Sixth Amendment right to confront the witnesses against him; *Hurtado v. California*, supra, in which an accused was denied the Fifth Amendment right of a grand jury indictment; *In re Kemmler*, supra, in which an accused was denied the Eighth Amendment protection against cruel and unusual punishment; *Maxwell v. Dow*, supra, in which an accused was denied the Sixth Amendment right of a jury trial in a criminal case; *Twining v. New Jersey*, supra, in which an accused was denied the Fifth Amendment right to refuse to testify against himself; and *Palko v. Connecticut*, supra, in which an accused was denied the Fifth Amendment right not to have his life be twice put in jeopardy.

D.5. *The Selective Incorporation Era*

In *Adamson v. California*, 332 U.S. 46 (1947), the Supreme Court re-examined the question of whether the states were required to observe the Fifth Amendment right of an accused not to testify against himself. This question had already been decided in *Twining v. New Jersey*, supra, and the Court had ruled that the states were not required to observe this right. The only difference between *Adamson* and *Twining* was that the judge in *Twining* had told the jury that it could consider the fact that the accused had not taken the witness stand and explained why he was innocent in spite of the evidence against him, whereas in *Adamson*, both the judge and the district attorney had commented on the failure of the accused to testify, as specifically allowed by California law. By a five-to-four majority, the Supreme Court in *Adamson* upheld the *Twining* rule and said there had been no violation of the Fourteenth Amendment.

There was nothing surprising in this result. What was surprising was that four of the nine justices dissented and said they believed that the life, liberty and property clause of the Fourteenth Amendment was meant to require the states to observe all the Bill of Rights guarantees of the first eight amendments. Justice Black, joined by Justice Douglas, wrote a dissenting opinion and an appendix that set forth the legislative history of the Fourteenth Amendment. Justices Murphy and Wiley Rutledge joined in a separate dissenting opinion, saying that while they agreed with Black and Douglas they also believed the Fourteenth Amendment covered other procedural rights in addition to the ones specifically stated in the first eight amendments.

Justice Reed wrote the majority opinion in *Adamson*. Justice Frankfurter filed a concurring opinion that sharply criticized the views of the dissenters:

> [a] construction which gives to due process no independent function but turns it into a summary of the specific provisions of the Bill of Rights would, as has been noted, tear up by the roots much of the fabric of law in the several States, and would deprive the States of opportunity for reforms in legal process designed for extending the area of freedom. It would assume that no other abuses would reveal themselves in the course of time than those which had become manifest in 1791. Such a view not only disregards the historic meaning of "due process." It leads inevitably to a warped construction of specific provisions of the Bill of Rights to bring within their scope conduct clearly condemned by due process but not easily fitting into the pigeonholes of specific provisions. (Ibid., 67)

Frankfurter also considered the alternative of "a selective incorporation" of some but not all of the first eight amendments, but rejected that test as too subjective and likely to lead to a selection based on the random preferences of individual justices. He recommended the following test instead:

> [i]n the history of thought "natural law" has a much longer and much better founded meaning and justification that such subjective selection of the first eight Amendments for incorporation into the Fourteenth. . . . We are called upon to apply to the difficult issues of our own day the wisdom afforded by the great opinions in this field, such as those in *Davidson v. New Orleans*, 96 U.S. 97; *Missouri v. Lewis*, 101 U.S. 22; *Hurtado v. California*, 110 U.S. 516; *Holden v. Hardy*, 169 U.S. 366; *Twining v. New Jersey*, 211 U.S. 78, and *Palko v. Connecticut*,

302 U.S. 319. This guidance bids us to be duly mindful of the heritage of the past, with its great lessons of how liberties are won and how they are lost. As judges charged with the delicate task of subjecting the government of a continent to the Rule of Law we must be particularly mindful that it is "a *constitution* we are expounding," so that it should not be imprisoned in what are merely legal forms even though they have the sanction of the Eighteenth century. (Ibid., 65-66)

In his dissenting opinion, Black argued that Congress intended to incorporate the first eight amendments of the Constitution into the Fourteenth Amendment. He relied on the speeches of Senator Howard and Congressman Bingham during the House and Senate deliberations on the Amendment (discussed in Section B of this chapter).[43] In his appendix, Black also quoted Bingham's 1871 speech on a proposed civil rights bill, in which he said that "the privileges and immunities of citizens of the United States, as contradistinguished from citizens of a State, are chiefly defined in the first eight amendments to the Constitution of the United States."[44] Bingham's remarks should be given great weight, he said, because he was the author of Section 1 of the Fourteenth Amendment. Black also replied to Frankfurter's opinion, saying,

> I cannot consider the Bill of Rights to be an outworn 18th Century "strait jacket" as the *Twining* opinion did. Its provisions may be thought outdated abstractions by some. And it is true that they were designed to meet ancient evils. But they are the same kind of human evils that have emerged from century to century wherever excessive power is sought by the few at the expense of the many. In my judgment the people of no nation can lose their liberty so long as a Bill of Rights like ours survives and its basic purposes are conscientiously interpreted, enforced and respected so as to afford continuous protection against old, as well as new, devices and practices which might thwart those purposes. I fear to see the consequences of the Court's practice of substituting its own concepts of decency and fundamental justice for the language of the Bill of Rights as its point of departure in interpreting and enforcing that Bill of Rights. If the choice must be between the selective process of the *Palko* decision applying some of the Bill of Rights to the States, or the *Twining* rule applying none of

them, I would choose the *Palko* selective process. But rather than accept either of these choices, I would follow what I believe was the original purpose of the Fourteenth Amendment--to extend to all the people of the nation the complete protection of the Bill of Rights. To hold that this Court can determine what, if any, provisions of the Bill of Rights will be enforced, and if so to what degree, is to frustrate the great design of the written Constitution. (Ibid., 89)

Although Black's opinion was only a dissent, it fell only a vote short of being the majority opinion and that alarmed many people. In 1949, Professor Charles Fairman of Stanford University challenged Black's analysis of the legislative history of the Fourteenth Amendment in a law review article entitled "Does the Fourteenth Amendment Incorporate the Bill of Rights?" 2 *Stanford Law Review* 5 (1949). That article began the debate that continues to this day.

In spite of their differences over the "incorporation" issue, most of the justices agreed, in a case decided a year after the *Adamson* decision, that one of the essential rights of due process under the Fourteenth Amendment was the Sixth Amendment right of an accused to a public trial. *In re Oliver*, 333 U.S. 257 (1948) involved a person who had been summarily sentenced to sixty days in jail by a Michigan judge who had been acting as a single-person grand jury. In a contempt-of-court hearing, the judge had found the accused guilty of contempt because his testimony did not "jell." The judge had therefore concluded the accused had lied. Neither the single-judge grand jury investigation nor the judge's contempt hearing had been open to the public. The accused did not challenge the propriety of a secret, single-person grand jury investigation; his only complaint was that he had received his contempt citation in a secret hearing. The U. S. Supreme Court ruled that he had a valid complaint.

In the Court's majority opinion, Justice Black did not raise the issue of whether the entire Bill of Rights had been incorporated by the Fourteenth Amendment. He based his opinion solely on the historic roots of the right to a public trial, noting that secret trials had been outlawed in England since the abolition of the Court of

Star Chamber in 1641. He said the distrust of secret trials in America and England was the result of the notorious abuses by the Spanish Inquisition, the English Court of Star Chamber and the French kings' *lettre de cachet*. Black also noted that counsel for the state of Michigan had failed to cite a single, earlier instance of a criminal trial conducted in secret in any federal, state or municipal court during the history of the United States.

Black thus appeared to concede the need for applying the case-by-case standards that the Court's majority had championed in the *Adamson* decision. Perhaps that was because Black was writing a majority opinion for seven justices who represented both sides of the "incorporation" argument. Justice Rutledge, however, was not so constrained in his concurring opinion. He said the secret Michigan proceeding was an example of the excesses prevailing the state courts because the Court had failed to force them to conform to the principles of "ordered personal liberty established by the Bill of Rights" (Ibid., 280).

Even Frankfurter, one of the two dissenting justices in the *Oliver* case, conceded that due process requires a public hearing (Ibid., 284). He dissented in this case only because the secrecy issue had not been raised in the petition for certiorari to the Supreme Court. He joined with Justice Jackson in saying that the proper ruling would have been to remand the case to the state court so that it could rule on the secrecy issue.

In 1949, Frankfurter also acknowledged that the Fourth Amendment guarantee against the unreasonable searches and seizures was one of the "basic rights enshrined in the history and the basic constitutional documents of English-speaking peoples" (*Wolf v. Colorado*, 338 U.S. 25 at 28). Speaking for Court, he said that a violation of this right would "run counter to the guarantee of the Fourteenth Amendment" (Ibid.). However, he said, the Fourteenth Amendment did not embody the federal rule, announced in *Weeks v. United States*, 232 U.S. 383 (1914), that illegally seized evidence could not be used to prove that someone was guilty of a crime. This rule was not essential to due process, he said, because other ways of enforcing the right existed, namely private suits for damages against the officials involved in the search and criminal prosecutions of these officials.

Because of the *Wolf* decision, many states continued to allow illegally seized evidence to be introduced at criminal trials. During the 1950s, some of these states adopted the federal rule because the other remedies for illegal searches were proving ineffective. In 1955, the California Supreme Court ruled in *People v. Cahan*, 44 Cal. 2d, 434 at 455, 282 P. 2d 905 at 911, that illegally seized evidence had to be excluded "because other remedies have completely failed to secure compliance with the constitutional provisions . . ."

Some states, however, Ohio among them, continued to rule that the other remedies were effective guarantees. On May 23, 1957, seven Cleveland, Ohio police officers pried open the back screen door of a private home, broke the glass of the inner door and reached through the broken pane to unlock the door. They were searching for a man whom they wanted to question in connection with a recent bombing; they were also looking for "policy paraphernalia." When they entered the home, the occupant, Miss Mapp, demanded to see a search warrant. A paper was held up to her and she grabbed it and placed it in her bosom. The policemen then reached in, recovered the paper and handcuffed her. One policeman "grabbed" her, "twisted [her] hand," and she "yelled [and] pleaded with him" because "it was hurting." Meanwhile, the other officers searched the entire home. They did not find what they were looking for, but they found obscene materials in a basement trunk. Mapp was tried and convicted of possessing these obscene materials (367 U.S. at 644-645).

Mapp appealed her conviction all the way to the Supreme Court of the United States. In *Mapp v. Ohio*, 367 U.S. 643 at 645 (1961), Justice Tom Clark said in the Court's opinion,

> At the trial no search warrant was produced by the prosecution, nor was the failure to produce one explained or accounted for. At best, "There is, in the record, considerable doubt as to whether there ever was any warrant for the search of defendant's home." 170 Ohio St., at 430, 166 N.E. 2d at 389. The Ohio Supreme Court believed a

"reasonable argument" could be made that the conviction should be reversed "because the 'methods' employed to obtain the [evidence] ... were such as to 'offend "a sense of justice,"'" ....

The Ohio Supreme Court, however, had upheld Mapp's conviction on the ground that the U. S. Supreme Court's ruling in *Wolf v. Colorado* was controlling. It had therefore ruled that the admission of the illegally seized evidence did not violate of Mapp's rights under the Fourteenth Amendment.

On Mapp's appeal to the U. S. Supreme Court, the Court admitted that it had made a mistake in *Wolf v. Colorado*. Justice Clark said the experiences of the state courts since 1949 showed that the only way to protect people from unreasonable searches and seizures was to exclude all illegally seized evidence at criminal trials. The Court therefore ruled, by a five-to-four majority, that the admission of such evidence at Mapp's trial violated her right of due process under the Fourteenth Amendment. Justices Harlan, Frankfurter and Charles Whittaker dissented, saying the Court had been correct in deciding *Wolf v. Colorado*. Justice Stewart filed a memorandum saying the Court should have reversed Mapp's conviction for possessing obscene materials because it violated her right of free thought and expression, not because of the illegally seized evidence.

The *Mapp* decision forced all the states to follow the federal exclusionary rule established in *Weeks v. United States*, supra. In that case, the Court had cited *Boyd v. United States*, 116 U.S. 616 (1886), in which Justice Bradley described the historical background of the Fourth Amendment. Bradley quoted from James Otis's argument against the writs of assistance used by British customs officers. He also told how officials in England had used similar writs to arrest John Wilkes and to seize papers in the case of *Entick v. Carrington* (Ibid., 625-626). After quoting from Lord Camden's opinion in the *Entick* case, Bradley concluded that

> [i]t is not the breaking of his doors, and the rummaging of his drawers, that constitutes the essence of the offence; but it is the invasion of his indefeasible right of personal security, personal liberty and private

property, where that right has never been forfeited by his conviction of some public offence,--it is the invasion of this sacred right which underlies and constitutes the essence of Lord Camden's judgment. Breaking into a house and opening boxes and drawers are circumstances of aggravation; but any forcible and compulsory extortion of a man's own testimony or of his private papers to be used as evidence to convict him of crime or to forfeit his goods, is within the condemnation of that judgment. In this regard the Fourth and Fifth Amendments run almost into each other. (Ibid., 630)

In a concurring opinion, Justice Miller said that Justice Bradley was wrong in equating the Fourth and Fifth Amendments. Miller said the Fifth Amendment prevents the government from forcing a person to testify against himself in all circumstances, whereas the Fourth Amendment prevents only searches and seizures that are unwarranted, that is, without probable cause to believe that a person unlawfully possesses certain goods. However, Bradley's point was that there is no difference between the government's unlawfully breaking into a house and seizing evidence in violation of the Fourth Amendment and the government's using other procedures to force a person to give evidence against himself in violation of the Fifth Amendment. In both cases, the government wrongfully deprives a person of his life, liberty or property when it uses any of these procedures to obtain a criminal conviction.

The *Mapp* decision destroyed the distinction that Justice Frankfurter had made in *Wolf v. Colorado* between a natural-law right and a right to be free from federal intrusion, guaranteed by the Bill of Rights. It also signaled the beginning of a series of cases in which the Supreme Court incorporated into the Fourteenth Amendment nearly all the procedural requirements of the Bill of Rights. In 1962, it held that the words "due process of law" meant that the states could not violate the Eighth Amendment prohibition against cruel and unusual punishments (*Robinson v. California*, 370 U.S. 660). In 1963, it ruled the states had to observe the Sixth Amendment guarantee that the accused shall have the assistance of counsel in all criminal prosecutions (*Gideon v. Wainwright*, 372 U.S. 335). In 1964, it ruled the states had to observe the Fifth

Amendment prohibition against compelling a person in a criminal case to be a witness against himself (*Malloy v. Hogan*, 378 U.S. 1). In 1965, the Court ruled the states had to give the accused the Sixth Amendment right to be confronted with the witnesses against him (*Pointer v. Texas*, 380 U.S. 400). In 1967, it ruled the states had to give the accused a speedy trial, as guaranteed by the Sixth Amendment (*Klopfer v. North Carolina*, 386 U.S. 213). Later the same year, it ruled the states had to guarantee the Sixth Amendment right of an accused to compel witnesses to testify in his favor (*Washington v. Texas*, 388 U.S. 14). In May 1968, it ruled the states could not deny the accused the Sixth Amendment right of a trial by an impartial jury (*Duncan v. Louisiana*, 391 U.S. 145). In June 1968, the Court ruled the states had to recognize that the Fourth Amendment "protects people, not places." Therefore, a state officer could not arrest and search a person on the street unless he had a warrant or probable cause (*Terry v. Ohio*, 392 U.S. 1). In 1969, the Court ruled that the states must observe the Fifth Amendment requirement that no person shall be subject subject to double jeopardy of life or limb for the same offense (*Benton v. Maryland*, 395 U.S. 784).

In 1972, the Supreme Court ruled that the Fourteenth Amendment did not require the states to indict a person by a grand jury before making him stand trial for the capital crime of murder (*Alexander v. Louisiana*, 405 U.S. 625). This is the only rule of criminal procedure guaranteed by the Bill of Rights that the Court has refused to say is covered by the Fourteenth Amendment. The Court cited its ruling in *Hurtado v. California*, supra (Ibid., 633) but did not explain why it summarily accepted that ruling after re-examining its rulings in so many other cases. Perhaps the reason was the Court set aside the Alexander conviction on another ground, namely, that the state had violated the equal protection clause of the Fourteenth Amendment. The defendant was black and the state had deliberately and systematically excluded black persons from the grand jury.

D.6. The Right of a Criminal Suspect to Be Informed of His Rights

In the case of *Miranda v. Arizona*, 384 U.S. 436, decided in 1966, the Supreme Court elaborated on the right to counsel established by *Gideon v. Wainwright* in 1963 and the right against self-incrimination established by *Malloy v. Hogan* in 1964. Before the *Miranda* decision, police were often able to force a confession from a suspect in custody who was not aware that he could refuse to answer their questions or that he could demand to have his attorney present. A common practice of police investigators was to interrogate the suspect in a closed room, sometimes for several days, while he was not allowed to communicate with other people, including his attorney. This practice was known as giving the suspect "the third degree." Of course, the police never told the suspect of his rights. They often told the suspect that if he did not answer their questions, he would appear to be hiding something. In that manner, they misled the suspect into believing that his failure to answer their questions might be used in court as evidence of his guilt. In the *Miranda* case, the Supreme Court outlawed such procedures, ruling that the police must inform a criminal suspect who is in their custody that he has certain basic rights. Otherwise, any statement made by the suspect to the police or other government agents cannot be introduced as evidence at his trial. Speaking for the Court, Chief Justice Earl Warren said,

> Prior to any questioning, the person must be warned that he has a right to remain silent, that any statement he does make may be used as evidence against him, and that he has the right to the presence of an attorney, either retained or appointed. (Ibid., 444)

He also said that if at any time prior to or during the questioning the person indicates that he wishes to remain silent the questioning must cease (Ibid., 473-474). If the interrogation continues without the presence of an attorney and a statement is taken, the government has "a heavy burden" to show that the person "knowingly and intelligently" waived his right against self-incrimination and his right to counsel (Ibid., 475).

Four justices--Clark, Harlan, Stewart and White--dissented from the *Miranda* decision. They said the decision was without precedent and had no historical basis. The majority of the justices, however, saw that a person's constitutional rights to be represented by an attorney and to refuse to testify against himself were based on the assumption that he knew he had these rights. Practical experience had shown this assumption was wrong. The Court therefore ruled that a fundamental attribute of these rights is that a person detained by the police must be informed of them before being questioned. Another attribute is that the person must not be questioned after he has indicated he does not wish to answer more questions.

The *Miranda* decision was sharply criticized when it was announced by the Supreme Court; even today it remains controversial. Many believe that the *Miranda* rule hampers the police in their investigations and that it serves no purpose other than to allow habitual criminals to escape their punishments on a legal technicality. Perhaps that has happened on some occasions. However, the warning required by the *Miranda* rule also helps the person who has been detained by the police for the first time in his life. It tells him some of the facts about the criminal justice system that most habitual criminals already know. A law-abiding citizen may believe that when the police are questioning him about his conduct or what he knows, his best interest lies in telling the police everything he knows. He may believe that in that way he will show the police that he has no guilty conscience and they will be less likely to charge him with a crime, particularly if he cooperates with them to the best of his ability. He may not realize that he might be charged with violating a law that he never heard of and that his ignorance of that law will not exonerate his guilt. He may not fully understand what the police are investigating, even if they give him a brief explanation. Therefore, he may not appreciate the context in which his answers will be understood by the police. He also may not realize that it is natural for an innocent person to be nervous when he is being questioned by the police about a serious crime, particularly if he has never had such an experience before. Under these circumstances, he may make statements that do not represent his true opinions or recollections, or he may give misleading answers because he does not fully understand the questions that the police have asked him. In short, he may not understand that his interests and those of the public are best served when he answers questions only after he has received the advice of an experienced attorney and is confident that he knows the full nature of the police investigation and of all the charges that might be filed against him. Most habitual criminals have learned these things through their past experiences with the criminal justice system. The least that every honest citizen ought to know is "that he has a right to remain silent, that any statement he does make may be used as evidence against him, and that he has the right to the presence of an attorney, either retained or appointed."

Since the *Miranda* case, the Supreme Court has made several exceptions to the requirement that a person detained by the police be told of his rights before being questioned. In *New York v. Quarles*, 467 U.S. 649 (1984), a woman told two police officers that an armed assailant had just raped her and had entered a nearby supermarket. One of the officers ran inside the market and spotted the accused, who fit the description given by the woman. The accused, when captured, was found to be wearing an empty shoulder holster. After handcuffing him but before telling him of his rights, the officer asked the accused where his gun was. The accused nodded toward some empty cartons and said, "The gun is over there." The officer then retrieved the gun from the empty cartons and read the accused his rights. The Supreme Court ruled that the statement by the accused and the gun could be admitted in evidence at his trial for criminal possession of a weapon, it spite of the fact that both were obtained before the accused was told of his rights. Speaking for the Court, Justice Rehnquist said that the rationale of the *Miranda* ruling does not apply to situations in which the police ask questions out of concern for public safety. In this case, the officer had to obtain the gun as soon as possible to prevent it from been found by an accomplice or another person who might use it to endanger the lives of the people in the market shopping their groceries. In *Oregon v. Elstad*, 470 U.S. 298 (1985), the accused made a voluntary confession before being read his rights, and then made the same confession after being read his rights. The Supreme Court ruled that the second confession could be admitted into evidence even though he may have made it because he believed "the cat was already out of the bag" by virtue of his first confession.

D.7. Fundamental Rights Guaranteed in the Main Body of the Constitution

In addition to the rights proclaimed in the first eight amendments, the Constitution guarantees several fundamental rights in its main body. Paragraphs 2, 3 and 8 of Article I, Section 9 place the following restraints on the federal government:

> The Privilege of the Writ of Habeas Corpus shall not be suspended, unless when in Cases of Rebellion or Invasion the public Safety may require it.
> No Bill of Attainder or ex post facto Law shall be passed. . . .
> No Title of Nobility shall be granted by the United States: . . . .

Article I, Section 10[1] places the following restraints on the states:

> No state shall . . . pass any Bill of Attainder, ex post facto Law, or Law impairing the Obligation of Contracts, or grant any Title of Nobility.

These restraints are identical, except the federal government is not forbidden to impair the obligation of contracts and the states are not forbidden to suspend the writ of habeas corpus. However, the Supreme Court ruled in *Calder v. Bull*, 3 Dallas 386 at 388 (1798) that the Constitution does not give Congress the authority to pass "a law that destroys or impairs the lawful private contracts of citizens."

On the other hand, the Supreme Court ruled in *Gasquet v. Lapeyre*, 242 U.S. 367 (1917) that a state can suspend or abolish the writ of habeas corpus for any reason. That is unfortunate. A petition for a writ of habeas corpus is often the only way a prisoner can show a judge that the authorities have no cause for holding him in jail. The English Parliament asserted this valuable right in its Petition of Right of 1628 (App. B, par. 5). The right was more firmly established by the Habeas Corpus Act in the reign of Charles II (31 Car.II. c.2.). Blackstone included the right among the rights of personal liberty in his chapter entitled "Of the Absolute Rights of Individuals" (BL3, 131, 133). In *Corfield v. Coryell*, Justice Washington listed the right among a person's fundamental privileges (6 Fed. Cas. at 552). It is true that if a state prisoner can prove he is being held in violation of a federal Constitutional right, he can obtain a writ of habeas corpus from a federal judge [cf., *Harris v. Nelson*, 394 U.S. 286 (1969)]. However, that is no excuse for a state judge refusing to hear his petition. When an appropriate case is brought again, the U. S. Supreme Court should reconsider whether a state's wrongful suspension of the writ of habeas corpus is a denial of liberty without due process of law, as guaranteed by the Fourteenth Amendment.

D.6. Summary and Further Comments on Incorporation

Table 3 on pages 464 and 465 lists all the rights protected by the Bill of Rights and the Supreme Court decisions that have decided when the life, liberty and property clause of the Fourteenth Amendment forbids the states to violate these rights. The table also shows the historical background of each right in respect of the Magna Charta, the Petition of Right, the Massachusetts Body of Liberties, the proposed Leveller Agreement, the English Declaration of Rights, Blackstone's *Commentaries*, the Declaration of the Stamp Act Congress, the Declaration and Resolves of the First Continental Congress and the Declaration of Independence; it also shows whether the right was asserted by the American colonists. For documents having numbered paragraphs, the table lists the number of the paragraph declaring the right. The numbers in the column, "Colonial Right Assert'd," refer to the year or years in which the colonists asserted the right.

Table 3 shows that by 1972, the U. S. Supreme Court had ruled that the life, liberty and property clause of the Fourteenth Amendment required the states to observe nearly all the guarantees of the Bill of Rights. The exceptions are the following:

(1) the Second Amendment right to bear arms (explained in Chapter 9, Section *A.4*);

(2) the Third Amendment freedom from having soldiers quartered in one's house, but a federal appeals court has ruled this right is guaranteed by the Fourteenth Amendment (*Engblom v. Carey*, 677 F.2d 957 [2nd Cir., 1982]);

(3) the Fifth Amendment right of an accused to a grand jury indictment for a capital or otherwise infamous crime, which the Supreme Court said was not necessary for due process of law in *Alexander v. Louisiana*, 405 U.S. 625 (1972);

(4) the Sixth Amendment right of an accused to a trial in the state and district of the crime, which is derived from the Englishman's right to be tried within the boundaries of England; this right is rarely raised in state courts because the states have no jurisdiction to try people beyond their respective boundaries;

(5) the Seventh Amendment right to a jury trial in a civil case, which the Court said was not to be necessary for due process of law in *Walker v. Sauvinet*, 92 U.S. 90 (Oct. term, 1875);

(6) the Eighth Amendment freedoms from excessive bail and excessive fines; because of the subjective nature of the word "excessive," few appeals are based on these freedoms and none has been taken from a state court to the U. S. Supreme Court.

Two of these exceptions require further comment. The Court's rejection of the Fifth Amendment right to a grand jury indictment in

Table 3

The Historical Background of the Bill of Rights

Right	Mag. Char.	Pet'n of Right	Mass Body Lib's	Level'r Agree-ment	Engl. Decl. Rights	Black-stone's Abs.Rts.	Black-stone's other rts.	Colonial Right Asserted	Stamp Act Res.	Declar. & Res. 1stCon	Dec of Ind.	U. S. Supreme Court's Recognition of Right as One of Life, Liberty and Property
First Amendment												
Religion: No Establmnt				¶XXIII ¶XXIV								*Everson v. Bd. of Ed.*, 330US1(1946)
Religion: Free Exercise				¶X ¶XXVI					X			*Cantwell v. Conn.*, 310US296(1940)
Freedom of Speech												*Fiske v. Kansas*, 247US380(1927)
Freedom of the Press							BL.6					*Near v. Minn.*, 283US697(1931)
Freedom of Assembly			¶95-10					1774		¶8		*DeJonge v. Oregon*, 299US353(1937)
Right to Petition Gov't			¶12 ¶75		X	Aux. Rt.		65,68,74	¶13	¶8	X	*DeJonge v. Oregon*, 299US at 364
Second Amendment												
Right to Bear Arms					X	Aux. Rt.		1774			X	**Rej.** *Presser v. Ill*, 116US252(1886)
Third Amendment												
No Quarter of Soldiers		¶VI					1:400	1774		X	X	**No U.S. Supreme Court Decision***
Fourth Amendment												
No Unreasonable S.& S.						Property		61-67-68				*Mapp v. Ohio*, 367US643(1961)
No Unwarranted Arrest						Liberty	4:288	1768**				*Terry v. Ohio*, 392US1(1968)

* The 2nd Circuit Federal Court of Appeals has held the Third Amendment does apply to the states, *Engblom v. Carey*, 677 F.2d 957 (1982).

** The colonists challenged the use of general warrants to arrest people when they sent a bowl designed by Paul Revere to John Wilkes, engraved with the slogan, "No General Warrants." Wilkes had been unlawfully arrested in England under a general warrant.

Right	Mag. Char.	Pet'n of Right	Mass Body Libs.	Level'r Agree-ment	Eng. Decl. Rights	Black-stone's Abs.Rts.	Black-stone's other rts.	Colonial Right Assert'd	Stamp Act Res.	Declar. & Res. 1stCon	Dec. of Ind.	U. S. Supreme Court's Recognition of Right as One of Life, Liberty & Property
Fifth Amendment												
Grand Jury Indictment							4:305 4:299-300					**Rej** *Alexander v.La.* 405US625(1972)
No Double Jeopardy							4:256, 329, 355					*Benton v. Maryland*, 395US784(1969)
No Self-Incrimination				¶XVI			3:370					*Malloy v. Hogan*, 378US1(1964)
Just Compensation			¶8			Property						*Chic. B&Q v. Chic.*, 166US226(1897)
Sixth Amendment												
Speedy Trial of Crime	¶40		¶41				4:345					*Klopfer v. N. Car.*, 386US213(1967)
Public Trial of Crime						Liberty	3:373					*In re Oliver*, 333US257(1948)
Criminal Trial by Jury	¶20 ¶52	¶ III	¶29	¶XXV	X	Liberty Property	3:349 3:379	65,67,72	¶7			*Duncan v. La.*, 391US145(1968)
Trial in Distr. of Crime	¶20			¶XXV		Liberty		1774		¶5	X	No U.S. Supreme Court Decision***
Informed of Charges		¶ V				Liberty					X	*Iowa C. Ry v. Iowa*, 160US393(1896)
Confront Witnesses	¶38						4:354					*Pointer v. Texas*, 380US400(1965)
Process to Get Witness				¶XXII			4:352-4					*Washington v. Texas*, 388US14(1967)
Right to Counsel			¶26	¶XVII			4:349-50					*Gideon v.W'wright*, 372US335(1963)
Seventh Amendment												
Jury Trial/Civil Action	¶52	¶ III	¶29	¶XXV	X	Property	3:349		¶7	¶5	X	**Rej** *Walker v.Sauvinet*, 92US90(1875)
Eighth Amendment												
No Excessive Bail			¶18		X	Liberty						No U.S. Supreme Court Decision
No Excessive Fines	¶20			¶XXI	X		4:372					No U.S. Supreme Court Decision
No Cruel/Unus. Pun.			¶43 ¶45,46	¶XXI	X	Security		1772				*Robinson v. Cal.*, 370US660(1962)

*** At least two state supreme courts have ruled that states are not required to try crimes in the place where they were committed, *State of Iowa v. Byrnes*, 150 NW 2d 280 (1967) and *State of Maine v. Bowman*, 588 A 2d. 728 (1991).

Alexander v. Louisiana, supra, was based solely on *Hurtado v. California*, 110 U.S. 516 at 538 (1884). Because of the faulty reasoning in the *Hurtado* opinion, including its quotation of Blackstone out of context (see discussion in Section *D.2* of this chapter), the Supreme Court should re-examine this issue.

The Court's rejection of the Seventh Amendment right of a jury trial in a civil case is based solely its early decision in *Walker v. Sauvinet*, supra. In neither that case nor any later case has the Court examined the history and rationale of this right, which is almost co-extensive with the right to a jury trial in criminal cases (Table 3). In the founding fathers' debates over the need for a bill of rights in the Constitution, the right of trial by jury in civil actions received at least as much attention as any other right. One of the concerns of those favoring this right was the need to protect debtors from powerful money lenders, as shown by the following speech by Patrick Henry to the Virginia ratification convention:

> Of what great advantage is it to the American Congress to take away this great and general security? I ask, Of what advantage is it to the public, or to Congress, to drag an unhappy debtor, not for the sake of justice, but to gratify the malice of the plaintiff, with his witnesses, to the federal court, from a great distance? What was the principle that actuated [influenced] the Convention in proposing to put such dangerous powers in the hands of any one? Why is the trial by jury taken away? All the learned arguments that on this occasion do not prove that it [civil trial by jury] is secured [safe without a bill of rights].[45]

In an appropriate case, Supreme Court should reconsider whether due process of law encompasses the right of a civil jury trial.

The other rights of the first eight amendments applied to the states include the freedoms of religion, speech and press guaranteed by the First Amendment. (The histories of these highly-valued rights were explained in Chapter 8 and Sections *B.1* and C of Chapter 9.) Blackstone's absolute rights included the Fourth Amendment freedoms from unreasonable searches, seizures and arrests (explained in connection with the *Mapp v. Ohio* case, supra), as well as the right to just compensation for property taken for public use, the right to a public jury trial, the right of the accused to be informed of the nature and cause his accusation and the freedom from cruel and unusual punishments. The rights of an accused to a speedy trial and to confront the witnesses against him were established by Magna Charta Chapters 40 and 38, respectively. Therefore, the only rights incorporated into the Fourteenth Amendment that require further explanation are the Fifth Amendment freedoms from double jeopardy and self-incrimination and the Sixth Amendment rights of an accused to compulsory process for obtaining witnesses and to the assistance of counsel for his defense.

The freedom from double jeopardy, applied to the states in *Benton v. Maryland*, had its roots in the Greek and Roman civilizations. A law of the East Roman Emperor Justinian said "[t]he governor should not permit the same person to be again accused of crime of which he has been acquitted."[46] In thirteenth century England, an acquittal in a trial by battle precluded a second trial.[47] Blackstone said in his chapter entitled "Of Courts of a Criminal Jurisdiction," "it is contrary to the genius and spirit of the law of England, to suffer any man to be tried twice for the same offence in a criminal way, especially if acquitted upon the first trial; . . . ." In his chapter entitled "Of Plea, and Issue," he said that a person accused of a crime could defend an indictment on the ground that he had already been tried and acquitted. His plea of *auterfoits acquit* was "grounded on the universal maxim of the common law of England, that no man is to be brought into jeopardy of his life, more than once, for the same offence." In his chapter entitled "Of Trial, and Conviction," he said "[i]f the jury therefore find the prisoner not guilty, he is then for ever quit and discharged of the accusation; except he be appealed of felony within the time limited by law."[48] In America, the Massachusetts Body of Liberties of 1641 said in section 42, "No man shall be twise sentenced by Civill Justice to one and the same Crime, offence, or Trespasse" (App. C). Although that did not necessarily preclude a second trial after an acquittal, a Massachusetts law said "everie Action . . . in *criminal* Causes shall be . . . entred in the *rolls* of everie Court . . . that such Actions be not afterwards brought again to the vexation of any man."[49] The courts of colonial Virginia also recognized pleas of former conviction and acquittal.[50]

The freedom from self-incrimination, applied to the states by *Malloy v. Hogan*, was originally a measure designed to protect people from the unjust procedures in medieval courts of inquisition. In 1649, the Levellers included the right in their proposed agreement of the "free people of England." Blackstone said that "no man is to be examined to prove his own infamy."[51] In the *Malloy* case, the Supreme Court relied on Justice Clark's *Mapp v. Ohio* opinion, as well as the opinions of Justice Bradley in *Boyd v. United States* and Lord Camden in *Entick v. Carrington*. The *Entick* case, decided in 1765, had established the British rule against general search warrants. Lord Camden had said,

> "It is very certain that the law obligeth no man to accuse himself; because the necessary means of compelling self-accusation, falling upon the innocent as well as the guilty, would be both cruel and unjust; and it would seem, that search for evidence is disallowed upon the same principle. Then, too, the innocent would be confounded with the guilty." (quoted in *Boyd v. United States*, 116 U.S. at 629)

The *Entick* case had fueled the fire of the colonial complaints against British tyranny, when two years after the *Entick* decision, Parliament passed the Townshend Acts, authorizing the use of the same general warrants that Lord Camden had condemned.

The right of an accused to compel witnesses to testify in his favor was applied to the states in *Washington v. Texas*, supra. In that case, the accused had been convicted of murder, in spite of his testimony that another man had shot the victim after he had run from the scene of the crime. The other man had also been convicted as a co-conspirator in the same crime. The accused had tried to call the other man to testify in order to substantiate his story, but the trial judge had ruled that the other man could not testify because of a Texas law that made co-conspirators ineligible to testify on each other's behalf. Notably, the law allowed a co-conspirator to testify for the prosecutor, even after he had been promised immunity from trial for his own crime.

In his chapter entitled "Of Trial, and Conviction," Blackstone said that for a long time in England, a person accused of a capital crime should not "be suffered to exculpate himself by the testimony of any witness." However, this common law rule was overturned in 1702, when Parliament passed a law declaring that in all cases of treason and felony, the accused was entitled to have witnesses testify for him under oath.[52] In his *Commentaries on the Constitution of the United States*, Joseph Story said that the founding fathers included the right to compel witnesses to testify on his behalf in the Bill of Rights because of the notorious common law rule that had existed in England prior to 1702.[53]

In spite of this history, the U. S. Supreme Court for a long time allowed the federal courts to make an exception to the Sixth Amendment right in the case of co-conspirator witnesses, on the ground they would be likely to perjure themselves for each other's benefit. In 1918, however, the Supreme Court ruled that this exception had no reasonable basis, because "the truth is more likely to be arrived at by hearing the testimony of all persons of competent understanding who may seem to have knowledge of the facts involved in a case, leaving the credit and weight of such testimony to be determined by the jury or by the court . . . ." (*Rosen v. United States*, 245 U.S. 467 at 471). In *Washington v. Texas*, supra, the Supreme Court ruled that this exception also violated a person's Fourteenth Amendment right to life, liberty and property, because of its arbitrary nature. It said "the absurdity of the rule" is shown by the fact that the co-conspirator is considered likely to commit perjury if he testifies for the accused, but not if he agrees to testify for the prosecution in exchange for the favor of not being tried for his own crime.

The right of an accused to the assistance of counsel was applied to the states in *Gideon v. Wainwright*, supra. Blackstone had sharply criticized the English practice of not allowing counsel to persons accused of capital crimes. He said,

> . . . [U]pon what face of reason can that assistance be denied to save the life of a man, which yet is allowed him in prosecutions for every petty trespass? . . . And, to say the truth, the judges themselves are so

sensible of this defect in our modern practice, that they seldom scruple to allow a prisoner counsel to stand by him at the bar, and instruct him what questions to ask, or even to ask questions for him, with respect to matters of fact: for as to matters of law, arising on the trial, they are *intitled* to the assistance of counsel. But still this is a matter of too much importance to be left to the good pleasure of any judge, and is worthy the interposition of the legislature; . . . .[54]

The right to counsel was first established in America by the Puritans of the Massachusetts Bay Colony. They said in paragraph 26 of their Body of Liberties that

[e]very man that findeth himself unfit to plead his own cause in any Court shall have Libertie to imploy any man against whom the Court doth not accept, to help him, Provided he give him noe fee or reward for his paines. (App. C)

The provision that no person, regardless of his wealth, could pay another person to represent him removed the disparity between the ability of the wealthy and the ability of the indigent to defend himself. However, there was still a disparity between the ability of professional government prosecutors and the ability of a person whom a criminal defendant might retain to assist him for no fee.

In the modern world of complex laws and court procedures, the Puritan rule against professional defense counsel is even less practical and fair. On the other hand, allowing defendants to employ professional counsel is fair to some people but not to others. Wealthy defendants can afford the best counsel. That is why it is essential that indigent defendants have the right to be represented by court-appointed counsel.

In *Gideon v. Wainwright*, the defendant Gideon was convicted of breaking into a poolroom with the intent of committing a felony. Under a Florida law, that offense was a felony. Gideon had told the trial judge that he was indigent and had asked for court-appointed counsel. The judge had denied his request, because in Florida the right to appointed counsel was limited to people charged with crimes punishable by death. Gideon had tried to defend himself at his trial but was convicted and sentenced to five years in prison. While in prison, he petitioned the Florida Supreme Court for a writ of habeas corpus, asking to be set free on the ground that he had been denied the assistance of legal counsel. After the Florida Supreme Court denied his petition, he appealed to the U. S. Supreme Court, where he received the assistance of future Supreme Court Justice Abe Fortas and the American Civil Liberties Union.

Gideon's petition appeared to be without merit because of the rule established in *Betts v. Brady*, 316 U.S. 455 (1942). In that case the U. S. Supreme Court had ruled that the denial of legal counsel to an indigent defendant accused of robbery, a crime not punishable by death, was not "a denial of fundamental fairness, shocking to the universal sense of justice" (Ibid., 462). Ten years before, in *Powell v. Alabama*, supra, the Court had ruled that indigent, uneducated black defendants charged with crimes punishable by death had the right to court appointed counsel under the Fourteenth Amendment, but Justice Sutherland had said the Court was not ruling that all indigent defendants necessarily had the right to counsel under all circumstances.

However, on Gideon's appeal to the U. S. Supreme Court in 1963, the Court overruled its decision in the *Betts* case and held that Gideon and all other indigent criminal defendants had a constitutional right to court-appointed counsel. Speaking for the Court, Justice Black said

> From the very beginning, our state and national constitutions and laws have laid great emphasis on procedural and substantive safeguards designed to assure fair trials before impartial tribunals in which every defendant stands equal before the law. This noble ideal cannot be realized if the poor man charged with a crime has to face his accusers without a lawyer to assist him. A defendant's need for a lawyer is nowhere better stated that in the moving words of Justice Sutherland in *Powell* v. *Alabama*:
>
> "The right to be heard would be, in many cases, of little avail if it did not comprehend the right to be heard by counsel. Even the intelligent and educated layman has small and sometimes no skill in the science of

law. If charged with a crime, he is incapable, generally, of determining whether the indictment is good or bad. He is unfamiliar with the rules of evidence. Left without the aid of counsel he may be put on trial without a proper charge, and convicted upon incompetent evidence, or evidence irrelevant to the issue or otherwise inadmissible. He lacks both the skill and knowledge adequately to prepare his defense, even though he have a perfect one. He requires the guiding hand of counsel at every step in the proceedings against him. Without it, though he be not guilty, he faces the danger of conviction because he does not know how to establish his innocence." 287 U.S., at 68-69. (Ibid., 344-345)

The *Miranda* ruling, covered in Section *D.6*, established that the police must inform a criminal suspect of his right to counsel and his right to remain silent before they begin to question him. This right is an attribute of the right to counsel and also the right to refuse to testify against one's self. The Supreme Court has ruled on attributes of other constitutional rights and has given particular attention to the attributes of the right to a jury trial.

Since the Middle Ages, the English had assumed that the right to a jury trial meant a trial by twelve jurors. They had also assumed that the jury's verdict had to be unanimous.[55] Blackstone said that a jury trial

> is the most transcendent privilege which any subject can enjoy, or wish for, that he cannot be affected either in his property, his liberty, or his person, but by the unanimous consent of twelve of his neighbors and equals.[56]

He also said,

> . . . [I]t has been held, that if the jurors do not agree in their verdict before the judges are about to leave the town, though they are not to be threatened or imprisoned, the judges are not bound to wait for them, but may carry them round the circuit from town to town in a cart. This necessity of total unanimity seems to be peculiar to our own constitution; or, at least, in the *nemba* or jury of the antient Goths, there was required (even in criminal cases) only the consent of the major part; and in case of an equality, the defendant was held to be acquitted.[57]

The Supreme Court ruled in *Thompson v. Utah*, 170 U.S. 343 at 349 (1898) that the Sixth Amendment right to a jury trial meant twelve jurors, at least in federal trials. It reaffirmed that ruling in *Patton v. United States*, 281 U.S. 276 at 288 (1930). However, the Court overruled the *Thompson* and *Patton* cases in *Williams v. Florida*, 399 U.S. 78 (1970). In a unanimous decision, it found that the number twelve was a historic accident, citing Lord Coke's explanation that the "number of twelve is much respected in holy writ, as twelve apostles, twelve stones, twelve tribes, etc." (Ibid., 88). It also said the number twelve is not critical to the basic purpose of the jury trial, which is to provide an accused with "an inestimable safeguard against the corrupt or overzealous prosecutor and against the compliant, biased, or eccentric judge" (Ibid., 100, quoting *Duncan v Louisiana*, 391 U.S. at 156). In the *Williams* case, the number of jurors was six, but in *Ballew v. Georgia*, 435 U.S. 223 (1978), the Court ruled that a jury of five was not enough to provide the accused with an adequate safeguard. Justice Louis Powell said the Court had to draw the line somewhere.

In the companion cases of *Johnson v. Louisiana*, 406 U.S. 356 (1972) and *Apodaca v. Oregon*, 406 U.S. 404 (1972), the Supreme Court ruled that the states did not have to require unanimous verdicts, in spite of its previous rulings that federal verdicts did have to be unanimous (cf., *American Publishing Company v. Fisher*, 166 U.S. 464 [1897]). Louisiana allowed a nine-to-three majority and Oregon allowed a ten-to-two majority. Four justices, White, Burger, Blackmun and Rehnquist, thought that "three dissenting votes to acquit raises no question of constitutional substance about either the integrity or the accuracy of the majority verdict of guilt" (Ibid., 360). They favored allowing verdicts by "a substantial majority" of the jurors in both federal and state trials (Ibid., 362). However, Justice Blackmun commented that he would have trouble agreeing to a majority of only seven-to-five (Ibid., 366). Four other justices, Douglas, Brennan, Marshall and Stewart, thought the federal unanimity rule was required to insure the integrity of the verdict and that it should therefore be preserved and applied to the states as well. Only Justice Powell thought the unanimity rule should remain in effect in federal trials but the states should be able to have less-than-unanimous verdicts. He said the framers of the Sixth Amendment intended to force the federal government to observe all the common law attributes of jury trials because they were "in accord both with history and precedent," not because these attributes were "necessarily fundamental to the function performed by the jury" (406 U.S. at 370-371). Oddly enough, even though none of the other justices agreed with his opinion that the rule for federal trials should be different than the one for state trials, Powell's opinion prevailed because a majority of five justices agreed that unanimous verdicts should be required in federal trials and five agreed that the states could have less-than-unanimous verdicts.

The *Johnson* and *Apodaca* decisions were only partially right, according to eight of the nine justices responsible for them. As Justice Douglas pointed out in his dissent in the *Johnson* case, the Court has applied the same standards to both the federal and the state governments in respect of all other rights incorporated by the Fourteenth Amendment (Ibid., 384-386). The reason why is shown in the faulty logic of Justice Powell's opinion. He said the framers of the Bill of Rights intended that the federal government be bound by a unanimity rule that was not "necessarily fundamental to the function performed by the jury." Why would the framers of the Bill of Rights have intended such a thing? They were defining limits of governmental power based on the fundamental laws of nature. If a unanimous verdict is necessary to preserve the integrity and purpose of the jury trial, the Supreme Court should say so and require its use in all state criminal trials.

The record shows that since the 1947 *Adamson* decision, the Supreme Court has adopted neither Frankfurter's applied-history criteria nor Black's view that the Fourteenth Amendment incorporates the entire Bill of Rights. It has chosen instead to examine each right individually, giving more weight to its early historical foundations than to the more recent "wisdom afforded by the great opinions" recommended by Frankfurter. None of the Court's opinions have disputed Cardozo's statement in *Palko* that a restraint on state power must be based on a "principle of justice so rooted in the traditions and conscience of our people as to be ranked as fundamental" (302 U.S. at 325). After the *Adamson* decision the Court simply reached different conclusions on which rights met that criteria. One by one, the Court has ruled that nearly all the procedural rights contained in the Bill of Rights are among the rights of life, liberty and property guaranteed by the Fourteenth Amendment. That should not be surprising. The members of the first Congress who voted for the Bill of Rights probably would have said that all its rights meet Cardozo's criteria. That they thought enough of a right to put it in the Bill of Rights may not be conclusive of its lasting, fundamental importance to American freedom, but it ought to be given some weight. Perhaps even more weight should be given to the reasons why the right is essential to serving justice, which the Supreme Court has always considered when it has ruled that a right is guaranteed by the Fourteenth Amendment.

People have criticized the Supreme Court for departing from the original framework of the Constitution. That is a valid observation, but it is easily explained. The Fourteenth Amendment made the states accountable to the federal government with respect to the powers they exercise over their citizens. It placed a fence around their powers similar to the fence that the Bill of Rights had placed around the federal powers. The Fourteenth Amendment, not the Supreme Court, changed the framework of the Constitution.

E. The Equal Protection Clause

E.1. Background

Some people came to America to escape from kingdoms where they were treated as second-class subjects. Some were forced to come to America as slaves. Some people's families have lived in America for thousands of years but they were treated as second-class people by those who came later. Women have long been treated as second-class people by the world's laws and traditions.

Their backgrounds may be varied, but Americans dislike being treated as second-class people.

The first Europeans who came to America were conscious of their own rights and liberties, but they did not realize that their most important right was equal protection of the laws. In the North as well as the South, the colonists held black people and Indians as slaves. They also disregarded the equal rights of Indians by forcing them off their land.

Equality was not one of the rights that the colonists had been taught to respect when they were in England. The English laws were based on a class system, in which people born of noble rank enjoyed rights and privileges that were denied other people. However, the Americans disavowed that class system when they stated in Article I, Section 9[8] of their federal Constitution that, "No Title of Nobility shall be granted by the United States: . . ." and in Article I, Section 10[1] that "No State shall . . . grant any Title of Nobility."

Another problem with the view that the colonists inherited their unequal laws from the English is that their class system did not force anyone into slavery. Concerning the status of political and civil liberty in England in 1765, Blackstone said that the

> . . . spirit of liberty is so deeply implanted in our constitution, and rooted even in our very soil, that a slave or a negro, the moment he lands in England, falls under the protection of the laws, and with regard to all natural rights becomes *eo instanti* a freeman. (BL3, 123)

Thus, according to Blackstone, if the British government had met the demands of the colonists to extend the absolute rights of Englishmen to America, every colonial slave would have become *eo instanti* a freeman. Perhaps both the War of Independence and the Civil War would have been avoided.

Unfortunately, that did not happen, and slavery continued in America until the end of the Civil War. Even the northern states were slow to abolish it. In 1780, Pennsylvania passed "An Act for the Gradual Abolition of Slavery." It provided that all black and mulatto children born after 1780 were to be freed after serving their mother's masters for twenty-eight years. The Act also required that all slaveholders register their slaves before November 1, 1780. After that date, all unregistered slaves were to be set free.[58] In 1799 and 1804 respectively, New York and New Jersey passed abolition laws similar to the Pennsylvania law.

Massachusetts did not specifically outlaw slavery in its 1780 Declaration of Rights. However, it did proclaim in Article I that

> [a]ll men are born free and equal, and have certain natural, essential, and unalienable rights; among which may be reckoned the right of enjoying and defending their lives and liberties; that of acquiring, possessing, and protecting property; in fine, that of seeking and obtaining their safety and happiness.

The meaning of the statement that "[a]ll men are born free and equal" became an issue in the case of a black slave named Quock Walker. In 1781, Walker escaped from his master, Nathaniel Jennison, and sought refuge on the farm of Seth and John Caldwell. The Caldwells were brothers of Jennison's wife's first husband, who had died. Jennison and some friends went to the Caldwell farm and tried to force Walker to return with them. When Walker resisted, Jennison and his friends beat him and took him back to Jennison's farm. Walker sued Jennison in the nearby city of Worcester, claiming three hundred pounds damages. Jennison's defense was that he was legally entitled to discipline Walker because he was a "proper slave." The jury, however, found that "said Quo[c]k is a Freeman and not the proper Negro slave of the Deft. [defendant]." It awarded Walker £50 in damages. Jennison filed his own lawsuit against the Caldwell brothers, claiming they had seduced Walker to leave his service and illegally employed him for their own benefit. The jury in that case awarded Jennison £25 in damages.

The state attorney general brought criminal charges against Jennison, accusing him of assault and battery. Jennison again argued that he was entitled to punish Walker because he was his slave. The attorney general introduced testimony showing that Walker's former master had promised to free him once he reached the age of twenty-five, that his widow had renewed that promise and that Jennison was aware of the promise before he married the widow. The case was tried in April 1783 before a jury, with all four justices of the Supreme Judicial Court of Massachusetts sitting on the bench. Chief Justice Cushing told the jury that

> [t]he defense set up in this case afforded much scope for discussion and has been fully considered. It is founded on the assumed proposition that slavery had been by law established in this province: that rights to slaves, as property, acquired by law, ought not to be divested by any construction of the Constitution by implication; and that slavery in that instrument is not expressly abolished. . . . But whatever usages formerly prevailed or slid in upon us by the example of others on the subject, they can no longer exist. Sentiments more favorable to the natural rights of mankind, and to that innate desire for liberty which heaven, without regard to complexion or shape, has planted in the human breast---have prevailed since the glorious struggle for our rights began. And these sentiments led the framers of our constitution of government---by which the people of this commonwealth have solemnly bound themselves to each other---to declare---*that all men are born free and equal*; and that *every subject is entitled to liberty*, and to have it guarded by the laws as well as his life and property. In short, without resorting to implication in constructing the constitution, slavery is in my judgment as effectively abolished as it can be by the granting of rights and privileges wholly incompatible and repugnant to its existence. The court are therefore fully of the opinion that perpetual servitude can no longer be tolerated in our government, and that liberty can only be forfeited by some criminal conduct or relinquished by personal consent or contract. And it is therefore unnecessary to consider whether the promises of freedom to Quaco, on the part of his master and mistress, amounted to a manumission or not. The Deft. must be found guilty as the facts charged are not contravened.[59]

After deliberating, the jury found Jennison guilty of assault and battery. Massachusetts thus became the first American state to recognize that black people had the same the constitutional rights of life, liberty and property as white people.

A contemporary abolitionist, the Reverend Jeremy Belknap, said the *Quock Walker* decision "was a mortal wound to slavery in

Massachusetts."[60] In 1795, Judge James Winthrop made the following comment on the *Quock Walker* decision:

> [b]y a construction of our state Constitution, which declares all men by nature free and equal, a number of citizens have been deprived of property formerly acquired under the protection of law.[61]

Table 4 below shows the number of black and white people living in the United States in 1790, according to U. S. Census figures.[62] Of the nearly 760,000 black people in the United States in 1790, less than sixty thousand were free.[63] Nearly all the seven thousand black people in Massachusetts, Vermont and New Hampshire were free. About forty thousand of the sixty-seven thousand black people north of the Mason-Dixon line were free. Virginia and Kentucky had about thirteen thousand free black people and there were about four thousand free black people in the Carolinas, Georgia and Tennessee.[64] Some of these people had escaped from their masters, particularly during the War of Independence. Some had gained their freedom as a reward for fighting

Table 4
Estimated Number of Black and White People
in the United States in 1790 (Rounded to Nearest Thousand)

State	Total People	% Black	Blacks	Whites
New Hampshire	142,000	0.7	1,000	142,000
Vermont Territory	85,000	> 0.5	> 500	85,000
Massachusetts	476,000	1.3	6,000	470,000
Rhode Island	69,000	5.8	4,000	65,000
Connecticut	238,000	2.5	6,000	233,000
New York	340,000	7.6	26,000	314,000
New Jersey	184,000	7.6	14,000	170,000
Pennsylvania	434,000	2.3	10,000	424,000
Delaware	59,000	22.0	13,000	46,000
Maryland	320,000	34.5	111,000	209,000
Virginia	748,000	40.9	306,000	442,000
Kentucky Territory	74,000	17.6	13,000	61,000
North Carolina	394,000	26.9	106,000	288,000
Tennessee Territory	36,000	11.1	4,000	32,000
South Carolina	249,000	43.8	109,000	140,000
Georgia	83,000	36.1	30,000	53,000
Total	3,931,000	19.3	757,000	3,176,000

in that war. Some had bargained for their freedom with their former masters. Some had been set free by masters who believed slavery was morally wrong. Many were freed in Massachusetts because slavery had been declared unlawful in the *Quock Walker* case. However, most states had laws that discriminated against all black people, regardless of whether they were slaves. Until well into the nineteenth century, free black people were excluded from public schools and denied the right to vote in all states except Massachusetts, New Hampshire and Vermont.[65]

In the case of *Dred Scott v. Sandford*, 60 U.S. (19 Howard) 393 (Dec. term, 1856), the U. S. Supreme Court considered the question of whether any black person was entitled to the rights proclaimed by the U. S. Constitution. In 1834, Scott was a black slave owned by Dr. Emerson, a surgeon in the United States Army. In that year, Emerson took Scott from the slave state of Missouri to a military post at Rock Island in the state of Illinois, where slavery was forbidden. In 1836, the Army transferred Emerson to Fort Snelling in the Wisconsin Territory, and Emerson again took Scott with him. A federal law called the Missouri Compromise forbade slavery in the Wisconsin Territory. At Fort Snelling, Scott married Harriet, a black slave whom Emerson had recently purchased from another army officer. The next year, Harriet gave birth to a daughter, Eliza, on the steamship *Gypsy* on the Mississippi River north of the Missouri state line. In 1838, Emerson moved back to Missouri, taking Scott and his wife and child with him. In Missouri, Harriet bore a second child, Lizzie. Emerson then sold Scott, Harriet, Eliza and Lizzie to John Sandford, who held all four of them as slaves in Missouri.

Scott filed two lawsuits against Sandford, one in a Missouri federal court and the other in a Missouri state court. In both suits, Scott alleged that he had become a free person because he and his former master had established residence in Illinois, where slavery was forbidden. He also alleged that he and his wife were free people because they and their former masters had established residence in the Wisconsin Territory, where a federal law forbade slavery. Their daughters Eliza and Lizzie were free because they had been born of free parents.

In the state lawsuit, Scott asked that he and his family be declared free people, because they had gained their freedom in the course of becoming permanent residents of Illinois and Wisconsin, where slavery was forbidden. The jury in that case ruled in Scott's favor. However, the Missouri Supreme Court reversed that decision. It ruled that Missouri law was the controlling law, not federal or Illinois law, and under Missouri law, a slave's previous residence in a free state did not change his status as a slave.

In federal court, Scott charged that Sandford had assaulted him and his family by restraining them and keeping them as slaves. The judge instructed the jury that Scott and his family were Sandford's slaves and that he had a right to restrain them. After the jury ruled in Sandford's favor, Scott appealed to the U. S. Supreme Court, claiming that the jury's instruction was in error.

Scott lost his appeal to the Supreme Court, but for a variety of reasons given by seven justices in separate opinions. Chief Justice Roger Taney (pronounced "Taw'-nee") said the lawsuit should be dismissed because of Scott's black African ancestry. He said that black people, including those who had gained their freedom, were not "people" and they were not "citizens," as those words are used in the U. S. Constitution. Therefore, they could not file a lawsuit in a federal court. Taney said that at the time the Constitution was adopted, black people were

> considered as a subordinate and inferior class of beings, who had been subjugated by the dominant race, and, whether emancipated or not, yet remained subject to their authority, and had no rights or privileges but such as those who held the power and the Government might choose to grant them. . . . They had for more than a century before been regarded as beings of an inferior order, and altogether unfit to associate with the white race, either in social or political relations; and so far inferior, that they had no rights which the white man was bound to respect; and that the negro might justly and lawfully be reduced to slavery for his benefit. He was bought and sold, and treated as an ordinary article of merchandise and traffic, whenever a profit could be made by it. This

opinion was at that time fixed and universal in the civilized portion of the white race. It was regarded as an axiom in morals as well as in politics, which no one thought of disputing, or supposed open to dispute; and men in every grade and position in society daily and habitually acted upon it in their private pursuits, as well as in matters of public concern, without doubting for a moment the correctness of this opinion.

And in no nation was this opinion more firmly fixed or more uniformly acted upon than by the English Government and English people. They not only seized them on the coast of Africa, and sold them or held them in slavery for their own use; but they took them as ordinary articles of merchandise to every country where they could make a profit on them, and were far more extensively engaged in this commerce than any other nation in the world.

The opinion thus entertained and acted upon in England was naturally impressed upon the colonies they founded on this side of the Atlantic. And, accordingly, a negro of the African race was regarded by them as an article of property, and held, and bought and sold as such, in every one of the thirteen colonies which united in the Declaration of Independence, and afterwards formed the Constitution of the United States. The slaves were more or less numerous in different colonies, as slave labor was found more or less profitable. But no one seems to have doubted the correctness of the prevailing opinion of the time. (Ibid., 404-405, 407-408)

Taney then cited the colonial laws of Maryland and Massachusetts that forbade marriages between whites and blacks as evidence that blacks were regarded as inferior. A Massachusetts law also provided that "if any negro or mulatto shall presume to smite or strike any person of the English or other Christian nation, such negro or mulatto shall be severely whipped, at the discretion of the justices before whom the offender shall be convicted." Taney said these laws, still in force when the War of Independence began,

show that a perpetual and impassable barrier was intended to be erected between the white race and the one which they had reduced to slavery, and governed as subjects with absolute and despotic power, and which they then looked upon as so far below them in the scale of created beings, that intermarriages between white persons and negroes or mulattoes were regarded as unnatural and immoral, and punished as crimes, not only in the parties, but in the person who joined them in marriage. And no distinction in this respect was made between the free negro or mulatto and the slave, but this stigma, of the deepest degradation, was fixed upon the whole race. (Ibid., 409)

In many respects, Taney was correct in his assessment of how white Americans viewed black people during the eighteenth century. He was also correct in noting that many colonial laws discriminated against free black people as well as slaves. However, he made several critical errors. He said that the English had treated black Africans as mere articles of merchandise during the American colonial period. He failed to note that by the time of Blackstone's *Commentaries*, the English had declared that every black man who landed on their shores became "*eo instanti* a freeman," so that "the law will protect him in the enjoyment of his person, his liberty, and his property" (BL3, 123; BL4, 412). Taney also said that the treatment of black people as articles of merchandise "was regarded as an axiom in morals as well as in politics, which no one thought of disputing, or supposed open to dispute; . . . ." However, he did not take into account that in 1767, a bill was introduced in the Massachusetts House of Representatives "to prevent the unwarrantable and unlawful Practice or Custom of inslaving Mankind in this Province, and the importation of slaves into the same."[66]

Taney cited the Declaration of Independence as additional evidence that black people were thought of as property and not people. He said that the Declaration's statement that "all men are created equal" could not have meant to include black people. Otherwise, their conduct "would have been utterly and flagrantly inconsistent with the principles they asserted" (Ibid., 410). This view of black people, he claimed, had not changed when the Constitution was adopted. Otherwise, the founding fathers would not have forbidden Congress to prohibit the migration or importation of persons as the states shall deem proper to admit prior to the year 1808, as they did in Article I, Section 9[1]. He did not explain why the deadline of 1808 did not reflect some change in attitude toward slavery, nor why that clause should be construed to apply only to black people. Taney also cited Article IV, Section 2[3], which said that no person held in service or labor in one state shall gain his freedom by escaping to another state. He did not explain why that provision endorsed the concept of slaves as property, rather than the concept of slaves as persons serving under labor contracts (Ibid., 410-412). Taney also did not explain why, if black people were "persons" within the meaning of those sections of the Constitution, they were not "persons" within the meaning of the other sections of the Constitution, such as the Fifth Amendment guarantees that "No person shall . . . be deprived of life, liberty, or property, without due process of law; . . . ."

To support his thesis that even the northern states treated all black people as property and not people, Taney cited several laws of Massachusetts, Connecticut, New Hampshire and Rhode Island that discriminated against free black people (Ibid., 413-416). All these laws had been passed after the War of Independence. The only Massachusetts law was a 1786 statute that declared illegal all marriages between white people and "any negro, Indian, or mulatto, and inflict[ed] a penalty of fifty pounds upon any who shall join them in marriage." He said this law was "a mark of degradation" on negroes, Indians and mulattoes. However, he did not explain why it invalidated the *Quock Walker* decision of 1783, in which the Massachusetts Supreme Court had ruled that black people were covered by the Massachusetts Bill of Rights declaration that "[a]ll men are born free and equal, and have certain natural, essential, and unalienable rights; . . . ." Based on his review of the rights that black people had at the time the U. S. Constitution was adopted, Taney concluded, "It cannot be supposed that [the states] intended to secure to [black people] rights, and privileges, and rank, in the new political body throughout the Union, which every one of them denied within the limits of its own dominion" (Ibid., 416). He was wrong. Quock Walker was a black person who had those rights and privileges, including the right to sue a white person for his freedom. How could Taney deny that Walker and his descendants were citizens and people of the United States? How could he deny that the descendants of other black people like Walker were citizens and people of the United States? There were only a few of them, but if he could not deny that those black people were citizens and persons, how could he discriminate between them and other black people, or even tell them apart?

Taney also ignored the fact that some founding fathers realized that the equality of all people was an essential part of their argument against the arbitrary laws of their British rulers. In his pamphlet, *The Rights of the British Colonies Asserted and Proved* (Boston, 1764), James Otis said,

> The colonists are by the law of nature freeborn, as indeed all men are, white or black. No better reasons can be given for enslaving those of any color than such as Baron Montesquieu has humorously given as the foundation of that cruel slavery exercised over the poor Ethiopians, which threatens one day to reduce both Europe and America to the ignorance and barbarity of the darkest ages. Does it follow that 'tis right to enslave a man because he is black? Will short curled hair like wool instead of Christian hair, as 'tis called by those whose hearts are as hard as the nether millstone, help the argument? Can any logical inference in favor of slavery be drawn from a flat nose, a long or short face? Nothing better can be said in favor of a trade that is the most shocking violation of the law of nature, has a direct tendency to diminish the idea of the inestimable value of liberty, and makes every dealer in it a tyrant, from the director of an African company to the petty chapman in needles and pins on the unhappy coast.[67]

Taney's logic was flawed in other respects. He said the men who framed the Declaration of Independence could not have asserted principles that were inconsistent with those on which they were acting (Ibid., 410). In other words, they were not capable of hypocrisy. He also said that the large slaveholding states would not have acted against their best interests. They would not have consented to a constitution that forced them to recognize that a black citizen visiting from another state was entitled to all the privileges and immunities enjoyed by their own white citizens (Article IV, Section 2[1]). He said that if the slave-holding states had done that, they would have set bad examples for their slaves, thereby disrupting the peace and threatening the safety of their communities. Taney therefore asserted that when the Constitution said "people" or "persons," it meant only white people or persons (Ibid., 416-417), except of course when it spoke of importing persons or catching fugitive persons held in service or labor. Taney thus tried to read into selected sections of the Constitution "language to help out a conjectured intent not to be gathered from the words used," a practice condemned by U. S. Supreme Court in *Gardner v. Collins*, 27 U.S. at 93 (1829), and explained by the Ohio Supreme Court in *Slingluff v. Weaver*, 66 Ohio St. at 628 (1902).

Taney should have recognized that even the great and wise founders of the nation could make mistakes. They could act in ways contrary to their own precepts. They could make agreements that were not in their best interests. He also should have recognized that justice is served only when men are governed by the recognized meanings of words, whether they appear in wills, contracts, regulations, laws, constitutions or international treaties.

Only Justices James Wayne and Peter Daniel agreed with Taney that Scott's lawsuit should be dismissed because he was a black person and therefore a mere piece of property not entitled to the rights of citizens under the Constitution.[68] Scott lost his appeal because a majority of six justices ruled that with respect to his family's residence in the Wisconsin territory, Congress had no power to outlaw slavery in the Missouri Compromise of 1820 and, with respect to his residence in Illinois, the Missouri courts had the power to apply the Missouri rule, by which he remained a slave when he and his master returned to that state. Four justices, Taney, Wayne, Daniel and Robert Grier, said the Compromise was invalid because it forbade citizens to hold slaves as property in a territory of the United States. The law therefore denied those citizens of their property without due process of law, in violation of the Fifth Amendment. Justice John Campbell said the Missouri Compromise was invalid because the slavery issue was a matter for the territorial legislature of a territory to decide, just as it was a matter for the state legislature of a state to decide. Justice John Catron said the Missouri Compromise was invalid because it violated the Louisiana

Purchase Treaty of 1803, which guaranteed to each inhabitant of the territory the free enjoyment of his property, including his slaves.

Justices Benjamin Curtis and John McLean filed dissenting opinions. They said they would have ruled that the Missouri federal court had jurisdiction because the defendant had not raised a timely objection. They also would have ruled that Congress had the power to enact the Missouri Compromise, because there was no universal recognition that slaves are the property of their masters. They are property only when a state law declares them to be property. Other states and the federal government are free to adopt their own rules on that question. Therefore, a slavemaster cannot complain that he has been deprived of his property in other places where slaves are not recognized as property. Because there was no relevant Missouri statute, McLean said the common law controlled the issue of whether the Scotts had surrendered their freedom when they returned to Missouri. He cited cases showing that under this rule they had not surrendered their freedom (Ibid., 550-555) and he pointed out that the Missouri Supreme Court had followed this rule in the past and had not departed from it in Scott's state court action. Instead, that court had simply ignored the Missouri Compromise and the Illinois state constitution (Ibid., 555).

One of the seven justices who ruled against Scott was Justice Samuel Nelson. He said that the Missouri courts had the final say on the applicable law, both in respect of Scott's prior residence in Illinois and in respect of the Scott family's prior residence in the Wisconsin Territory. The Missouri Supreme Court had held that in spite of those facts, the members of the Scott family were still slaves when they returned to Missouri. Therefore, Nelson did not deem it necessary to decide whether the Missouri Compromise was valid or whether Scott was a person who could sue in federal court.

If all seven justices who denied Scott's appeal had agreed with Nelson, few people would have noticed the *Dred Scott* decision. The case would have received no more attention than *Strader v. Graham*, 51 U.S. (10 Howard) 82 (Dec. term, 1850). In that case, an owner had taken his slaves from Kentucky to Ohio and then brought them back to Kentucky. The U. S. Supreme Court had ruled that Kentucky had the right to apply its own law and to decide that the owner had not set his slaves free when he had traveled to Ohio.

However, only Justice Nelson based his opinion solely on the rule laid down in *Strader v. Graham*. Of the other six justices ruling against Scott, Taney, Wayne and Daniel said that no black person could be ever be a person with a right to life, liberty and property under the U. S. Constitution. In the eyes of the federal government, he could never be more than a piece of property. A person owning a black slave therefore had three choices. He could continue to hold on to those slaves, he could sell them to another person or he could abandon them, as a dog owner might abandon his dogs, by leaving them on the roadside to run wild until captured by someone else. In the eyes the federal Government, there could be only be two kinds of black people: slaves and strays.

Individual states could ignore the property theory of slavery and treat black people as property owners or potential property owners, rather than as pieces of property. All the northern states had done that. However, the federal territories, at least those obtained from France by the Louisiana Purchase, were bound by the rule that slaves were property. The territorial legislatures could not change the rule until their territories became states, and then only by amending their state constitutions. By that time, many of their citizens would be slave owners and they would surely oppose any change that would deprive them of their "property." These states would therefore likely continue the federal rule that all black people were property. Together with the Congressmen from the existing slave states, their Congressmen would surely pass more pro-slavery laws similar to the Fugitive Slave Act of 1850, which punished the people of all states who helped slaves escape from their masters.

The *Dred Scott* decision also raised serious doubts concerning the abilities of the anti-slave states to accord their own black people the full status of citizens within their own boundaries. According to Justices Taney, Wayne and Daniel, no black person in any state could be a party in a federal lawsuit or enjoy the other rights of citizens guaranteed by the Constitution. Other justices did not address this issue in the *Dred Scott* case, but they might well agree with them in a later case. The Supreme Court might therefore rule that goods imported by a black person were contraband because his U. S. customs declaration was not signed by a "person." It might also rule that black people were ineligible for U. S. copyrights or patents, because the federal government had the power to grant copyrights and patents only "to Authors and Inventors" (Article I, Section 8[8]). Presumably, a black person could not be an author or an inventor if he were not a person. Issued patents would also be subject to attack, if it were discovered that the inventor or any co-inventor had a black ancestor, because the Court might rule that the black person's contribution was an unpatentable property of nature. All this havoc might occur in the name of preserving the "property" of the southern slave owners.

The *Dred Scott* decision prompted Abraham Lincoln to say on June 17, 1858,

> "A house divided against itself cannot stand."[69] I believe this government cannot endure permanently half slave and half free. I do not expect the Union to be dissolved; I do not expect the house to fall; but I do expect it will cease to be divided. It will become all one thing, or all the other. Either the opponents of slavery will arrest the further spread of it, and place it where the public mind shall rest in the belief that it is in the course of ultimate extinction, or its advocates will push it forward til it shall become alike lawful in all the States, old as well as new, North as well as South.

The majority of Americans agreed with Lincoln and elected him president of the United States in 1860. The southern states responded by seceding from the union and the Civil War followed. After that war, the American people outlawed slavery in the Thirteenth Amendment. Then in the Fourteenth Amendment, they declared, "All persons born or naturalized in the United States, and subject to the jurisdiction thereof, are citizens of the United States and of the State wherein they reside." They also declared, "No state shall . . . deny to any person within its jurisdiction equal protection of the laws."

The concept of equal protection of the laws was new to Anglo-American jurisprudence. When Senator Howard introduced the Joint Committee's proposal to the Senate on May 23, 1866, he said the equal protection clause

> abolishes all class legislation in the States and does away with the injustice of subjecting one caste of persons to a code not applicable to another. It prohibits the hanging of a black man for a crime for which the white man is not hanged. It protects the black man in his fundamental rights as a citizen with the same shield it throws over the white man. Is it not time, Mr. President, that we extend to the black man, I had almost called it the poor privilege of the equal protection of the law? Ought not the time to be now passed when one measure of justice is to be meted out to a member of one caste while another and different measure is meted out to the member of another caste, both castes being alike citizens of the United States, both bound to obey the same laws, to sustain the same Government, and both equally responsible to justice and to God for the deeds done in the body?[70]

The concern for equal protection was not limited to black people. On May 30, 1866, Senator John Conness of California told how the laws of his state had discriminated against Chinese people. He said,

> The Chinese were robbed with impunity, for if a white man was not present no one could testify against the offender. They were robbed and plundered and murdered, and no matter how many of them were present and saw the perpetration of those acts, punishment could not follow, for they were not allowed to testify.... We are entirely ready to accept the provision proposed in this constitutional amendment, that the children born here of Mongolian parents shall be declared by the Constitution of the United States to be entitled to civil rights and to equal protection before the law with others.[71]

The equal protection clause also applies to American Indians. So do the other clauses of the Fourteenth Amendment. During their debates on the amendment, some Senators asked whether Indians living on tribal lands should be excluded from citizenship, because they were not taxed and were treated in other ways as citizens of a foreign nation. The Senate considered changing the first sentence of the amendment to read,

> All persons born in the United States, and subject to the jurisdiction thereof, *excluding Indians not taxed,* [emphasis added] are citizens of the United States and of the State wherein they reside.

However, the motion to add the underlined language was defeated by a vote of thirty nays to ten yeas.[72]

Equal protection of the laws is rooted in two related concepts of government. One is the protection of the law. Blackstone said that the protection of the law is the *"remedial* part of the law," or that part of the law that imposes a remedy when a person's rights are invaded. That remedy consists of action by the government to redress the invasion. The government action might be an order that restores stolen property to its rightful owner or an order to pay damages to an injured person (BL1, 55-56). Equal protection of the laws therefore means that when one person deprives another of his life, liberty or property, the government must give the injured person the same remedy that is available to anyone else deprived of the same right. In a case when the government passes a law that deprives a person of his life, liberty or property, the remedy is the benefit or protection that the law gives people in return for the freedom they have lost. Equal protection of the law then means that the law must give all people the same benefit or protection.

The other concept resides in the nature of government law. Blackstone said that government law, which he called "municipal law,"

> is a *rule*; not a transient sudden order from a superior to or concerning a particular person; but something permanent, uniform, and universal. Therefore a particular act of the legislature to confiscate the goods of Titius, or to attaint him of high treason, does not enter into the idea of municipal law: for the operation of this act is spent on Titius only, and has no relation to the community in general; it is rather a sentence than a law. But an act to declare the crime of which Titius is accused shall

be high treason; this has permanency, uniformity, and universality, and therefore is properly a *rule*. (BL1, 44)

For the same reason, the legislature cannot pass a law that applies only to persons named Titius, unless it has a valid purpose in selecting such people. That is because the permanency, uniformity and universality required of a law exists only when the government has a valid purpose in selecting the people to be covered by the law. In Blackstone's example, the legislature arbitrarily selected one man named Titius, took away his property and left him with no remedy for his loss. It thereby denied him the equal protection of the laws. The same would be true if the legislature arbitrarily selected a group of people and did the same to them. Equal protection would also be denied if the legislature arbitrarily selected a group of people and bestowed on them protections or benefits not bestowed on other people. In that case, the people who were not selected would suffer the loss.

The guarantee of equal protection of the laws is closely related to the rights of life, liberty and property. Most equal protection violations also involve a violation of a right of life, liberty or property. Sometimes a case that begins with an equal protection complaint will be decided on the basis of the life, liberty and property violation and the converse is also true. Equal protection would mean nothing if there were no protection of anyone's life, liberty and property. Conversely, no one can be secure in his enjoyment of life, liberty and property unless all people are entitled to equal protection of the laws. If the laws can favor some people over others, no person favored by today's laws can be sure of keeping his favored status when tomorrow's laws are passed.

E.2. *Equal Protection from the Civil War to World War II*

The first major Supreme Court decision to interpret the equal protection clause was the *Slaughter-House Cases*, 83 U.S. 36 (1873), discussed earlier. Both the majority and dissenting opinions focused on the privileges and immunities clause of the Fourteenth

Amendment. In the majority opinion, Justice Miller summarily dismissed the butchers' claim that their right of equal protection had been violated, saying that clause was intended only to prevent racial discrimination. However, four of the nine justices dissented from this opinion.

In his dissenting opinion, Justice Field cited Connecticut and New York cases that showed that "equality of right among citizens" was a fundamental principle of government that could not be violated. Although he did not refer to the equal protection clause specifically, Field said that this equality of right was now guaranteed by the Fourteenth Amendment:

> In all these cases there is a recognition of the equality of rights among citizens in the pursuit of the ordinary avocations of life, and a declaration that all grants of exclusive privileges, in contravention of this equality, are against common right, and void.
>
> This equality of right, with exemption from all disparaging and partial enactments, in the lawful pursuits of life, throughout the whole country, is the distinguishing privilege of citizens of the United States. To them, everywhere, all pursuits, all professions, all avocations are open without other restrictions than such as are imposed equally upon all others of the same age, sex, and condition. The state may proscribe such regulations for every pursuit and calling of life as will promote the public health, secure the good order and advance the general prosperity of society, but when once proscribed, the pursuit or calling must be free to be followed by every citizen who is within the conditions designated, and will conform to the regulations. This is the fundamental idea upon which our institutions rest; and unless adhered to in the legislation of the country our government will be a republic only in name. The fourteenth amendment, in my judgment, makes it essential to the validity of the legislation of every State that this equality of right should be respected. (Ibid., 109-110)

The first case in which the Supreme Court ruled that a black person had been denied equal protection of the laws was *Strauder v. West Virginia*, 100 U.S. 303 (Oct. term, 1879). In that case, a black man had been convicted of murder in a trial in which only white men were eligible to serve on the jury. Speaking for the Court, Justice William Strong said,

> It is not easy to comprehend how it can be said that while every white man is entitled to a trial by a jury selected from persons of his own race or color, or, rather, selected without discrimination against his color, and a negro is not, the latter is equally protected by the law with the former. (Ibid., 309)

However, he added,

> We do not say that within the limits from which it is not excluded by the amendment a State may not prescribe the qualifications of its jurors, and in so doing make discriminations. It may confine the selection to males, to freeholders, to citizens, to persons within certain ages, or to persons having educational qualifications. We do not believe the Fourteenth Amendment was ever intended to prohibit this. Looking at its history, it is clear it had no such purpose. Its aim was against discrimination because of race or color. (Ibid., 310)

On the other hand, Justice Strong wrote elsewhere in his opinion that

> Blackstone, in his Commentaries, says, "The right of trial by jury, or the country, is a trial by the peers of every Englishman, and is the grand bulwark of his liberties, and is secured to him by the Great Charter." It is also guarded by statutory enactments intended to make impossible what Mr. Bentham called, "packing juries." It is well known that prejudices often exist against particular classes in the community, which may sway the judgment of jurors, and which, therefore, operate in some cases to deny to persons of those classes the full enjoyment of that protection which others enjoy. (Ibid., 309)

In this statement, Strong defined the meaning of "equal protection of the laws" in the context of the facts of the case he was deciding. He did not explain, however, why women, persons without property, non-citizens, persons of certain ages and persons without formal education could not be classes of persons who would be denied equal protection of the laws if they were excluded from juries. There may be valid reasons why, for instance, non-citizens should be excluded from juries, but according to Justice Strong, they could be excluded for no reason at all.

Section 5 of the Fourteenth Amendment gave Congress the power to enforce the provisions of the amendment by appropriate legislation. Before the amendment was passed, Congress had already passed the Civil Rights Act of 1866, which made it a crime for any person, under color of any law or custom, to deprive another person of his right to "equal benefit of all laws and proceedings for the security of person and property, as is enjoyed by white citizens," and to "like punishment, pains and penalties." Some argued that Congress had the power to pass this law under the Thirteenth Amendment, but its validity became more secure after the Fourteenth Amendment was ratified. It covered only actions by government agents that deprived people of their rights to equal legal benefits and punishments. State agents were prohibited from depriving people of these rights by the equal protection clause of the Fourteenth Amendment, and Congress clearly had the power to control the federal agents.

The Civil Rights Act of 1875 presented a more difficult question. In Sections 1 and 2 of that law, Congress made it a crime for any person to deprive another of

> the full and equal enjoyment of the accommodations, advantages, facilities, and privileges of inns, public conveyances on land or water, theatres, and other places of public amusement.

In the *Civil Rights Cases*, 109 U.S. 3 (1883), the Supreme Court ruled that Sections 1 and 2 of the Act of 1875 were unconstitutional because they regulated the actions of private people, and the Fourteenth Amendment does not expressly forbid those kinds of actions. Speaking for the Court, Justice Bradley said that Section 5 of the Fourteenth Amendment

> does not authorize Congress to create a code of municipal law for the regulation of private rights; but to provide modes of redress against the

operation of State laws, and the action of State officers executive or judicial, when these are subversive of the fundamental rights specified in the amendment. Positive rights and privileges are undoubtedly secured by the Fourteenth Amendment; but they are secured by way of prohibition against State laws and State proceedings affecting those rights and privileges, and by power given to Congress to legislate for the purpose of carrying such prohibition into effect; and such legislation must necessarily be predicated upon such supposed State laws or State proceedings, and be directed to the correction of their operation and effect. (Ibid., 11-12)

Bradley also said that Congress had no power under the Thirteenth Amendment to pass the law, even though that amendment "clothes Congress with power to pass all laws necessary and proper for abolishing all badges and incidents of slavery in the United States" (Ibid., 20). He asked,

Can the act of a mere individual, the owner of the inn, public conveyance or place of amusement, refusing the accommodation, be justly regarded as imposing any badge of slavery or servitude upon the applicant, or only as inflicting an ordinary civil injury, properly congnizable by the laws of the State, and presumably subject to redress by those laws until the contrary appears?

After giving to these questions all the consideration which their importance demands, we are forced to the conclusion that such an act of refusal has nothing to do with slavery or involuntary servitude, ... (Ibid., 24)

In *Barbier v. Connolly*, 113 U.S. 27 (1885), and *Yick Wo v. Hopkins*, 118 U.S. 356 (1886), the Supreme Court considered the effect of the equal protection clause on the way state and local governments regulate businesses. Both cases involved the regulation of laundries by the San Francisco County Board of Supervisors. In *Barbier v. Connolly*, a laundry owner argued that his right of equal protection had been violated because San Francisco laundries were forbidden to operate between ten o'clock in the evening and six o'clock in the morning. He said the ordinance discriminated against these laundries because it did not apply to other kinds of businesses or to businesses in other counties. The Supreme Court ruled that this discrimination was permissible because of the government's valid concern for public safety. The laundries used fire to heat their water and it was therefore reasonable that they be required to limit their hours of operation in urban areas where there were many wooden buildings. In *Yick Wo v. Hopkins*, however, the Court ruled that the same Board of Supervisors violated the equal protection clause when it refused permits to operate laundries to two hundred Chinese applicants while granting permits to eighty others who were not Chinese. It also ruled that the Board violated the life, liberty and property clause. (That part of its ruling was covered in Section *D.2* of this chapter.) Speaking for the Court, Justice Stanley Matthews said the Fourteenth Amendment's provisions

> are universal in their application, to all persons within the territorial jurisdiction, without regard to any differences of race, of color, or of nationality; and the equal protection of the laws is a pledge of the protection of equal laws. (Ibid., 369)

During this period, many state and local governments in the South were passing laws that required black people to use public facilities that were separate from those used by white people. They argued that these laws did not violate the equal protection clause, as long as the facilities available to black people were equal to those used by white people. In *Plessy v. Ferguson*, 163 U.S. 537 (1896), the Supreme Court agreed with this argument and upheld a Louisiana law that required railway companies to provide separate but equal coaches for white and black passengers. The law prescribed a twenty-five dollar fine or twenty days in jail for any passenger who insisted on sitting in a coach in which he did not belong because of his race.

The case featured the odyssey of Homer Plessy, a citizen of seven-eighths white ancestry and one-eighth black ancestry. He bought a first-class ticket on the East Louisiana Railway and insisted on sitting in a coach for white people. The police escorted him off the train and threw him in a New Orleans jail. The district attorney charged that Plessy had violated the railway segregation law. Plessy's attorney was unable to persuade the district judge and the Louisiana Supreme Court that the law violated the equal protection clause of the Fourteenth Amendment. So he appealed to the Supreme Court of the United States.

Plessy's main argument was that he had been improperly classed as an inferior black person rather than a member of the dominant white race. He claimed that his skin color was so light that no one could tell that he had black ancestors. Speaking for the Supreme Court, Justice Henry Brown said that if the state had the power to assign black and white people to separate railway coaches, it also had the power to determine who was black and who was white (Ibid., 549).

Plessy's next argument was that if the state had the power to segregate people on the basis of skin color, it also had the power to segregate them on the basis of hair color or nationality, to require that people of different races walk on opposite sides of the street, or to require that white people drive white vehicles and black people black vehicles, on the theory that one side of the street is as good as the other, and one color of vehicle is as good as another. Justice Brown rejected this argument as well:

> [t]he reply to all this is that every exercise of the police power must be reasonable, and extend only to such laws as are enacted in good faith for the promotion of the public good, and not for the annoyance or oppression of a particular class. . . . In determining the question of reasonableness, it [the state] is at liberty to act with reference to the established usages, customs and traditions of the people, and with a view to the promotion of their comfort, and the preservation of the public peace and good order. Gauged by this standard, we cannot say that a law which authorizes or even requires the separation of the two races in public conveyances is unreasonable, or more obnoxious to the Fourteenth Amendment than the acts of Congress requiring separate schools for colored children in the District of Columbia, the constitutionality of which does not seem to have been questioned, or the corresponding acts of state legislatures.

We consider the underlying fallacy of the plaintiff's argument to consist in the assumption that the enforced separation of the two races stamps the colored race with a badge of inferiority. If this be so, it is not by reason of anything found in the act, but solely because the colored race chooses to put that construction on it. (Ibid., 550-551)

Someone should have reminded Justice Brown that Chief Justice Taney had said in the *Dred Scott* case that a Massachusetts law forbidding white people to marry negroes, Indians and mulattoes was "a mark of degradation" on the negroes, Indians and mulattoes (60 U.S. at 413). Brown also said the two races could not be forced to commingle with one another:

[i]f the two races are to meet upon terms of social equality, it must be the result of natural affinities, a mutual appreciation of each other's merits and a voluntary consent of individuals. . . . Legislation is powerless to eradicate racial instincts or to abolish distinctions based upon physical differences, and the attempt to do so can only result in accentuating the difficulties of the present situation. If the civil and political rights of both races be equal one cannot be inferior to the other civilly or politically. If one be inferior to the other socially, the Constitution of the United States cannot put them on the same plane. (Ibid., 551-552)

The problem with this logic is that the Louisiana railway segregation law did not force white and black people to sit together. It forced them to sit apart. If the state forbids different kinds of people to socialize with one another, how can they discover their "natural affinities" and their "mutual appreciation of each other's merits"? How can a Homer Plessy become educated and trained and sell his products and services to others, if his government forbids him to socialize with those people who control his society and are best able to help him achieve those goals? How can a government single out some people, burden them with this disability and then claim that it is giving them equal protection of the laws?

Brown explained that the Louisiana law was reasonable because it promoted "the established usages, customs and traditions of the people . . . their comfort, and . . . the public peace and good order" (Ibid., 550). However, a law is reasonable only if the thing that it promotes is reasonable. During the colonial period, Protestant Americans developed a tradition of shunning and harassing Catholic people. That tradition did not make reasonable the New Jersey law that penalized Catholics for professing their faith, or the Maryland law that subjected Catholic people to double taxation (Chapter 8, Sections *A.4* and *A.5*).

Brown also said the law was reasonable because it preserved the public peace. It is a sad truth that some people hate other kinds of people so much that they threaten to disturb the peace if their government does not insulate them from those people. However, a just and stable government cannot defer to those who threaten civil disorder in order to deprive others of their rights and liberties. It has no choice but to make all people behave themselves.

Justice Brown pointed out that many states had enacted laws requiring that black children attend separate schools. Congress had enacted such a law for the District of Columbia. He said the constitutionality of these laws had not been questioned and they appeared to be at least as obnoxious as the Louisiana railway law (Ibid., 550-551). The relevance of these observations to the merits of the *Plessy* case is not clear, but they indicate the Supreme Court may have been fearing an avalanche of other segregation cases if its ruling had been in Plessy's favor.

In the sole dissenting opinion, Justice John Marshall Harlan said that Plessy had been deprived of his liberty as well as his equal protection of the laws:

> [t]he fundamental objection, therefore, to the statute is that it interferes with the personal freedom of citizens. "Personal liberty," it has been well said, "consists in the power of locomotion, of changing situation, or removing one's person to whatsoever places one's own inclination may direct, without imprisonment or restraint, unless by due course of law." 1 Bl. Com. *134 [BL3, 130]. If a white man and a black man choose to occupy the same public conveyance on a public highway, it is their right to do so, and no government, proceeding alone on grounds of race, can prevent it without infringing the personal liberty of each. (Ibid., 557)

Harlan then predicted that

> ... the judgment this day rendered will, in time prove to be quite as pernicious as the decision made by this tribunal in the *Dred Scott case*. ... What can more certainly arouse race hate, what more certainly create and perpetuate a feeling of distrust between these races, than state enactments, which, in fact, proceed on the ground that colored citizens are so inferior and degraded that they cannot be allowed to sit in public coaches occupied by white citizens? That, as all will admit, is the real meaning of such legislation as was enacted in Louisiana. (Ibid., 559, 560)

For a long time, few people shared Justice Harlan's opinion on the significance of the *Plessy* decision. Americans were deeply divided over the issue of equal rights for black people, but hardly anyone sympathized with Homer Plessy's effort to prove that he was entitled to membership in the white establishment because he was not black. What the leading civil rights advocates did not notice was that because of the *Plessy* ruling, any racial segregation law could meet the equal protection test if it required equal facilities for each race. "Separate but equal" thus became a catch phrase that justified separate schools, separate seats in buses, separate restaurants, separate restrooms, separate neighborhoods, and all kinds of other separations of blacks from whites by government mandate. One example was the case of *Berea College v. Kentucky,* 211 U.S. 45 (1908), in which the U. S. Supreme Court upheld a Kentucky law that forbade black and white students to attend classes together, even though they were enrolled at the same private college. In *Gong Lum v. Rice,* 275 U.S. 78 (1927), the Supreme Court applied the "separate but equal" doctrine to public high schools, when it ruled that a Chinese girl, Martha Lum, was not denied equal protection of the laws when she was excluded from the all white Rosedale Consolidated High School. The Mississippi state constitution provided that "[s]eparate schools shall be maintained for children of the white and colored races." Lum's parents had argued that she was Chinese, not colored. However, the Court reiterated what it had said in *Plessy v. Ferguson*: if the state has the power to assign people of different colors to separate facilities, it also has the power to determine which people are of which color for the purpose of such assignments (163 U.S. at 549).

In one case, however, the "separate but equal" argument failed to convince the Supreme Court. In *Buchanan v. Warley*, 245 U.S. 60 (1917), a Louisville, Kentucky, ordinance forbade a black person to move into any house on a block in which the majority of residents were white. It also forbade a white person to move into any house on a block in which the majority of residents were black. To test the constitutionality of this ordinance, the National Association for the Advancement of Colored People asked a black person named Warley to submit an offer to a white person named Buchanan, to purchase a vacant lot with the following proviso:

> [i]t is understood that I am purchasing the above property for the purpose of having erected thereon a house which I propose to make my residence, and it is a distinct part of this agreement that I shall not be required to accept a deed to the above property or to pay for said property unless I have the right under the laws of the State of Kentucky and the City of Louisville to occupy said property as a residence.

Buchanan accepted Warley's offer, but Warley refused to accept the deed because there were eight white families and only two black families living on the same block. Buchanan therefore sued Warley to compel him to honor the purchase agreement. Warley asserted that he was not bound by the agreement because of the Louisville ordinance that forbade him to occupy the property as a residence. Buchanan replied that the ordinance was not a defense to his action because it violated the Fourteenth Amendment.

The Kentucky Court of Appeals ruled the ordinance was valid and a complete defense to Buchanan's lawsuit. Buchanan then appealed to the Supreme Court of the United States, which reversed the Kentucky decision. Speaking for a unanimous Court, Justice William Rufus Day distinguished the Louisville ordinance from other laws designed to segregate black people from white people. He said the ordinance denied both black and white homeowners of their basic right to transfer their property, including their right of occupancy, to any willing buyer. Although this was a violation of the Fourteenth Amendment's life, liberty and property clause, rather than the equal protection clause, Day said the law's interdiction was "based wholly upon color; simply that and nothing more" (Ibid., 73). Such a law could not be justified, he said, in spite of arguments it would maintain public peace and property values:

> [i]t is urged that this proposed segregation will promote the public peace by preventing race conflicts. Desirable as this is, and important as is the preservation of the public peace, this aim cannot be accomplished by laws or ordinances which deny rights created or protected by the federal Constitution.
> It is said that such acquisitions by colored persons depreciate property owned in the neighbored by white persons. But property may be acquired by undesirable white neighbors or put to disagreeable though lawful uses with like results. (Ibid., 81-82)

Taken together, the *Plessy*, *Berea College* and *Buchanan* cases meant that the rights of black and white people to buy real estate from one another were more fundamental than their rights to sit together on public conveyances or to study together in the same school buildings.

However, the rights of black people to buy real estate in white neighborhoods received a serious setback in *Corrigan and Curtis v. Buckley*, 271 U.S. 323 (1926). In that case, a group of thirty white neighboring home owners in Washington, D. C. executed and recorded an indenture, in which they agreed that no part of their properties should ever be used, occupied by, sold, leased or given to any person of the negro race or blood, and that this covenant should run with the land and bind their respective heirs and assigns for twenty-one years. The following year, one of those home owners, Irene Corrigan, signed an agreement to sell her property to a black woman, Helen Curtis. Another home owner, John Buckley, filed a suit in the Supreme Court of the District of Columbia to enjoin Corrigan from conveying her property to Curtis, because the transfer would violate the neighborhood indenture. Corrigan and

Curtis moved to dismiss Buckley's suit on the ground that the indenture violated the life, liberty and property clause of the Fifth Amendment, the Thirteenth Amendment's prohibition against slavery and involuntary servitude and the privileges and immunities clause, the life, liberty and property clause and the equal protection clause of the Fourteenth Amendment. This motion to dismiss was denied and the denial was affirmed by the Court of Appeals of the District of Columbia. Corrigan and Curtis then appealed to the Supreme Court of the United States. The Supreme Court dismissed their appeal for want of jurisdiction, because it was "entirely lacking in substance or color of merit" (Ibid., 330). The Court said these amendments forbid only actions by federal, state and local governments, not contracts between private persons such as the indenture signed by Corrigan and Buckley.

In 1927, the Supreme Court examined an equal protection issue not related to racial discrimination or business regulation: whether government can order certain kinds of people to be sterilized. In *Buck v. Bell*, 274 U.S. 200, the Court upheld a Virginia law requiring the sterilization of institutionalized mental patients who had been diagnosed with certain genetically transmissible mental deficiencies. The main issue was whether the law violated the life, liberty or property rights of these patients. The Court held that it did not, on the ground that sterilization was in the best interests of both the patient and society. The law also raised an equal protection question because it applied only to people who were patients of mental institutions. Speaking for the Court, Justice Holmes answered, "the law does all that is needed when it does all that it can" (Ibid., 208). Holmes was probably referring to the fact that the state cannot examine a person to determine whether he qualifies for sterilization until he has been placed in an institution.

On the other hand, the Court ruled in *Skinner v. Oklahoma*, 316 U.S. 535 (1942), that an Oklahoma sterilization law did violate a person's right to equal protection. This law imposed sterilization as a penalty for habitual criminals who had been convicted two or more times of crimes "amounting to felonies involving moral turpitude." These felonies included larceny by fraud but not white collar crimes such as embezzlement. Speaking for the Court, Justice Douglas said there was no reasonable distinction between these crimes: the propensity to defraud people of their money and the propensity to embezzle were equal threats to the well being of society and were equally inheritable traits.

E.3. *The Japanese Internment Cases*

After Japan bombed Pearl Harbor on December 7, 1941, many people feared the next attack would be on the west coast of the continental United States. They also feared that Japanese people living on the west coast would assist in this invasion. Various civic and labor organizations called for the federal government to evacuate all people of Japanese ancestry from the states of California, Oregon and Washington. These organizations included the American Legion, the California Joint Immigration Committee, the Native Sons and Daughters of the Golden West, the Western Growers Protective Association, the California Farm Bureau Federation and the Los Angeles Chamber of Commerce. Many newspapers joined the campaign.[73]

Pushed by this public pressure, President Roosevelt issued Executive Order No. 9066 on February 19, 1942, authorizing the secretary of war and his subordinate military commanders to prescribe military areas from which all or any persons may be excluded or restricted in their activities. Then on March 18, 1942, he issued Executive Order No. 9102, which established the War Relocation Authority and authorized the director of that Authority to formulate and carry out a program for the removal, relocation, maintenance and supervision of the persons who had been excluded from military areas under Executive Order No. 9066. On March 21, 1942, Congress passed a law that imposed criminal penalties on anyone who violated a military order issued pursuant to an Executive Order of the President.

Pursuant to Executive Order No. 9066, Lieutenant General J. L. DeWitt, commander of the Western Defense Command, ordered that the states of Washington, Oregon, California and Arizona be divided into two military areas. He proclaimed that after March 27, 1942,

> all alien Japanese, all alien Germans, all alien Italians, and all persons of Japanese ancestry residing or being within the geographical limits of Military Area No. 1 . . . shall be within their place of residence between the hours of 8:00 P. M. and 6:00 A. M., which period is hereinafter referred to as the hours of curfew. (320 U.S. at 88)

General DeWitt also proclaimed that after March 29, 1942, all persons of Japanese ancestry who were within the limits of Military Area No. 1 were forbidden to leave that area until further notice (323 U.S. at 228-229). He then issued Civilian Exclusion Orders that excluded persons of Japanese ancestry from various parts of the Military Areas and required that they report to assembly areas near where they lived. The people reporting were transferred to relocation centers, where they were confined under supervision. Under these Exclusion Orders, nearly all the 112,000 people of Japanese ancestry in California, Oregon, Washington and Arizona were confined in Relocation Centers. About seventy thousand of them were citizens of the United States.

In order to be released from a Relocation Center, each Japanese person had to follow a two-step procedure set up by the War Relocation Authority. First, he had to apply for "leave clearance," which was granted only after an investigation to ascertain "the probable effect upon the war program and upon the public peace and security of issuing indefinite leave" to the applicant (323 U.S. at 292). If he was granted this "leave clearance," an applicant could then apply for "indefinite leave." That would be granted only if he could show that he had a job waiting for him, had adequate financial resources to care for himself, had made living and job search arrangements approved by the War Relocation Authority or was going to live with relatives. In addition, his leave would be granted only if the places where he was going to live and work were not places where "community sentiment" was "unfavorable" (Ibid., 293). These "leave clearance" and "indefinite leave" applications were handled in a leisurely manner. After three years, in the spring of 1945, seventy thousand Japanese people were still interned in relocation centers, held there only because the United States was at war with Japan and because they were of Japanese ancestry.[74] They had not committed any crime.

The first Supreme Court case dealing with these military orders was *Hirabayashi v. United States*, 320 U.S. 81 (1943). Hirabayashi was an American citizen charged with violating the curfew order and for failing to report to an evacuation center in violation of an Exclusion Order. He claimed that these orders violated his Fifth Amendment rights of life, liberty and property, because they discriminated between citizens of Japanese ancestry and citizens of other ancestries. The district judge ruled that the orders did not violate Hirabayashi's rights and the jury found him guilty of violating both orders. He was sentenced to a three-month prison term for each violation, the sentences to run concurrently.

The Supreme Court unanimously upheld the ruling that the curfew order did not violate Hirabayashi's rights, but it declined to rule on the Exclusion Order because Hirabayashi's sentences were concurrent and his prison term was therefore not prolonged by the guilty verdict in respect of the Exclusion Order. The Court acknowledged that, although the Fifth Amendment has no specific equal protection clause, the federal government might be forbidden by the Fifth Amendment to take away a person's life, liberty or property because of his race. However, the Court also said that government officials were entitled to more latitude in respect of the rights of people when the public safety is threatened by foreign invasion. They could therefore discriminate against people if there are "facts and circumstances which indicate that a group of one national extraction may menace that safety more than others,...." (Ibid., 100-101).

Speaking for the Court, Chief Justice Harlan Fiske Stone said that government officials might have considered the following circumstances in judging the threat of Japanese people to national security:

(1) the intense solidarity of Japanese people caused by state laws that prevented them from owning land and marrying

Caucasian people and by private employment discrimination and other practices that isolated them from the mainstream of American society;

(2) the fact that many Japanese parents living in America sent their children to Japanese language classes, which were believed to be sources of Japanese nationalistic propaganda, and some parents sent their children back to Japan for all or part of their education;

(3) the fact that many American citizens of Japanese ancestry were regarded by the Japanese government as retaining their Japanese citizenship; and

(4) the fact that American citizens of Japanese ancestry live among Japanese aliens who are likely to influence their political views (Ibid., 96-98).

Stone added,

> These are only some of the many considerations which those charged with the responsibility for the national defense could take into account in determining the nature and extent of the danger of espionage and sabotage, in the event of invasion or air raid attack. (Ibid., 99)

Perhaps Stone should have listed some of those other considerations in its opinion, because the ones he listed are not convincing. The first was based on speculation that Americans of Japanese ancestry would aid in a Japanese invasion because they had endured previous violations of their civil rights and because they had been isolated by private discrimination. Such unfair treatment seems hardly an excuse for more unfair treatment.

With respect to the second consideration, Japanese parents had a right to teach their children the Japanese language and a right to send them back to Japan for their educations. Those rights had been established in *Meyer v. Nebraska*, 262 U.S. 390 (1923) and *Pierce v. Society of Sisters*, 268 U.S. 510 (1925). There was no evidence that these American citizens were encouraging their children to be disloyal to the United States government. With regard to the third and fourth considerations, many foreign governments at war with the United States have regarded various

American citizens as citizens of their nations also and those citizens have associated with law-abiding aliens from those nations. Except in the case of Japanese-Americans during World War II, those facts have never warranted the presumption that American citizens of a particular ancestry were likely to sabotage the United States government.

In the *Hirabayashi* case, all the Supreme Court justices agreed that the curfew order was a valid exercise of government power. However, when the Court ruled that the Exclusion Order was also valid in *Korematsu v. United States*, 323 U.S. 214 (1944), Justices Roberts, Murphy and Jackson dissented. Justice Black wrote the majority opinion and said that there was little difference between the curfew order and the Exclusion Order, because both had "a definite and close relationship to the prevention of espionage and sabotage" (Ibid., 218). He characterized the Exclusion Order as temporary and said it was justified for the same reasons as given in the *Hirabayashi* case and because approximately five thousand American citizens of Japanese ancestry had, during their confinement, refused to swear unqualified allegiance to the United States and renounce allegiance to the Japanese emperor. Several thousand had requested repatriation to Japan. Apparently, Justice Black did not consider that these people may have been upset over the way the United States government was treating them.

The dissenting justices did not agree that the Exclusion Order was a temporary security measure similar to the curfew order. That was because the Japanese Americans could not leave the areas from which they were excluded. They had to report to assembly areas, from where they were taken to relocation centers, which were, in plain English, prison camps. At the time the *Korematsu* case was decided, December 18, 1944, most of these Japanese-Americans were still confined to these camps and had been living in them for almost three years. Justice Murphy said,

> In adjudging the military action taken in light of the then apparent dangers, we must not erect too high or too meticulous standards; it is necessary only that the action have some reasonable relation to the removal of the dangers of invasion, sabotage and espionage. But the

exclusion, either temporarily or permanently, of all persons of Japanese blood in their veins has no such reasonable relation. And that relation is lacking because the exclusion order necessarily rely for its reasonableness upon the assumption that *all* persons of Japanese ancestry may have a dangerous tendency to commit sabotage and espionage and to aid our Japanese enemy in other ways. It is difficult to believe that reason, logic or experience could be marshaled in support of such an assumption. (Ibid., 235)

In *Ex parte Endo*, 323 U.S. 283 (1944), the United States government gave the real reason why it confined thousands of Japanese Americans to prison camps. In 1942, Mitsuye Endo, an American citizen of Japanese ancestry, was evacuated from her home in Sacramento, California, and taken to Tule Lake War Relocation Center at Newell, Modoc County, California. In July 1942, she filed a petition for a writ of habeas corpus in the local federal district court, asking to be released from the relocation center. In February 1943, she applied for leave clearance and that clearance was granted in August 1943. Instead of applying for indefinite leave, she continued to demand her release through her habeas corpus petition. She claimed she had a right to be set free because her leave clearance proved that she was a loyal citizen and not a threat to government security. The government, however, said that a relocation program based on indefinite leave criteria was necessary to prevent a

> dangerously disorderly migration of unwanted people to unprepared communities; . . . [and] although community hostility toward evacuees has diminished, it has not disappeared and the continuing control of the Authority over the relocation process is essential to the success of the evacuation program. (Ibid., 297)

The Supreme Court granted Endo's petition and unanimously ruled that government had no authority to hold Japanese people in custody after their loyalty had been determined. Speaking for the Court, Justice Douglas said,

> A citizen who is concededly loyal presents no problem of espionage or sabotage. Loyalty is a matter of the heart and mind, not of race,

creed, or color. He who is loyal is by definition not a spy or a saboteur. When the power to detain is derived from the power to protect the war effort against espionage and sabotage, detention which has no relationship to that objective is unauthorized.

Nor may the power to detain an admittedly loyal citizen or to grant him a conditional release be implied as a useful and convenient step in the evacuation program, whatever authority might be implied in the case of those whose loyalty was not conceded or established. If we assume (as we do) that the original evacuation was justified, its lawful character was derived from the fact that it was an espionage and sabotage measure, not that there was community hostility to this group of American citizens. (Ibid., 301)

Like the *Korematsu* case, the *Endo* case was decided December 18, 1944, only a few months before the war ended. For the previous two and a half years, thousands of Japanese Americans had been confined to prison camps, even after the government had determined they were loyal citizens. That was a dark blot on the history of American freedom.

E.4. Past Wrongs Corrected

After the Second World War, many black people were able to secure better jobs and live in better neighborhoods, but they were still hindered by many unjust laws and practices. One such practice was the neighborhood homeowner agreement, whereby groups of white homeowners would agree that no one would sell his home to person who was not white. These agreements were recorded as deed restrictions in the local courts, so that they became binding on subsequent purchasers. In *Shelley v. Kraemer* and *McGhee v. Sipes*, 334 U.S. 1 (1948), people in two communities in Missouri and Michigan had entered into such agreements. The Missouri agreement had been signed in 1911 and had a termination date of 1961. The Michigan agreement had been signed in 1934 and was set to expire in 1960. In each case, an owner sold his property to a black person in violation of the agreement. Neighboring property owners then sued in their local state court to have the sale ruled invalid and the black people's deed transferred back to the original white property owners. The supreme courts of Missouri and Michigan ruled in favor of the neighboring property owners and the deeds were transferred back to the original owners. These cases were then appealed to the Supreme Court of the United States.

Citing *Corrigan v. Buckley*, supra, Chief Justice Vinson said the restrictive agreements did not violate the equal protection clause of the Fourteenth Amendment because they were made by private people, not state governments. However, unlike the black property buyers in *Corrigan v. Buckley*, the buyers in these cases had properly raised the issue of whether the state courts had violated the equal protection clause by enforcing the white-only restrictive agreements. Vinson said, "[B]ut for the active intervention of the state courts, supported by the full panoply of state power, petitioners would have been free to occupy the properties in question without restraint" (Ibid., 19). The Supreme Court therefore ruled that the state courts of Missouri and Michigan had violated the equal protection rights of the black property buyers by taking their deeds away from them.

Hurd v. Hodge, 334 U.S. 24 (1948), also involved a white-only restrictive neighborhood agreement, but one that applied to a Washington, D.C. neighborhood. The federal trial and appellate courts of the District of Columbia enforced the agreement and ruled that the black property owner's deeds were null and void. The equal protection clause of the Fourteenth Amendment applied only to the states. Chief Justice Vinson said, however, that these federal court rulings had violated the Civil Rights Act of 1866. That Act said, "All citizens of the United States shall have the same right, in every state and Territory, as is enjoyed by white citizens thereof to inherit, purchase, lease, sell, hold and convey real and personal property" (Ibid. 31). Vinson said it was therefore not necessary for the Supreme Court to decide whether the D. C. federal courts had violated the Fifth Amendment's life, liberty and property clause (Ibid., 30).

Vinson said the Supreme Court's rulings in *Shelley v. Kraemer*, *McGhee v. Sipes* and *Hurd v. Hodge* were consistent with its ruling in *Corrigan v. Buckley*, when the Court had, twenty-two years before, upheld the right of white property owners to exclude black families from their neighborhoods. However, the facts in all these cases were substantially the same. Vinson distinguished the more recent cases on the ground that the black home buyers in *Corrigan v. Buckley* had not raised the issue of a court's power to enforce an agreement to exclude black people from a neighborhood. Presumably, if those black buyers had raised that issue, and the Supreme Court of 1926 had possessed the same wisdom as the Supreme Court of 1948, all such agreements throughout the United States would have been unenforceable during the intervening twenty-two years.

During this period, more black people were graduating from college, but they were being denied admission to state graduate schools because they were black. In *Missouri ex rel. Gaines v. Canada*, 305 U.S. 337 (1938), *Sipuel v. Oklahoma Board of Regents*, 332 U.S. 631 (1948) and *Sweatt v. Painter*, 339 U.S. 629 (1950), the U. S. Supreme Court ruled that these black people had been denied equal protection of the laws because there were no state-supported schools for black people that were equal to the state-supported, white-only graduate schools. In the *Sweatt v. Painter* case, Sweatt had been denied admission to the University of Texas Law School because he was black. He filed a lawsuit in a Texas state court to compel the school officials to admit him. The judge recognized that he had been denied equal protection of the laws but stayed the proceedings while the state established a law school for black students. After the new law school opened, the judge concluded that it offered "privileges, advantages, and opportunities for the study of law substantially equivalent to those offered by the State to white students at the University of Texas." He therefore refused to order the University of Texas officials to admit Sweatt to their law school. The Texas appellate courts affirmed the judge's decision. However, the Supreme Court of the United States reversed the decision, on the ground that the new black law school was inferior to the University of Texas Law School.

In the Court's opinion, Chief Justice Vinson observed that the black law school was still awaiting full accreditation. It had five full-time professors, twenty-three students and a library of 16,500 volumes. The University of Texas Law School was not only accredited but had an outstanding national reputation. It had a law review, scholarship funds and an Order of Coif chapter for students with superior grade averages. It also had 850 students, sixteen full-time and three part-time professors, some of whom were nationally recognized authorities in their fields, and a library of sixty-five thousand volumes. Vinson said,

> What is more important, the University of Texas Law School possesses to a far greater degree those qualities which are incapable of objective measurement but which make for greatness in a law school. Such qualities, to name but a few, include reputation of the faculty, experience of the administration, position and influence of the alumni, standing in the community, traditions and prestige. It is difficult to believe that one who had a choice between these law schools would consider the question close.
>
> Moreover, although the law is a highly learned profession, we are well aware that it is an intensely practical one. The law school, the proving ground for legal learning and practice, cannot be effective in isolation from the individuals and institutions with which the law interacts. Few students and no one who has practiced law would choose to study in an academic vacuum, removed from the interplay of ideas and the exchange of views with which the law is concerned. The law school to which Texas is willing to admit petitioner excludes from its student body members of racial groups which number 85% of the population of the State and include most of the lawyers, witnesses, jurors, judges and other officials with whom petitioner will inevitably be dealing when he becomes a member of the Texas Bar. (Ibid., 634)

Therefore, the Supreme Court concluded that even under the "separate but equal" doctrine of *Plessy v. Ferguson*, 163 U.S. 537 (1896), the state of Texas had denied Sweatt equal protection of the laws. Vinson said there was thus no need to re-examine the validity of the "separate but equal" rule.

McLaurin v. Oklahoma Board of Regents, 339 U.S. 637 (1950) also involved a state university that discriminated against a black person. G. W. McLaurin was admitted to the University of Oklahoma to pursue a doctor of education degree. However, because he was black, he was required to sit by himself in an anteroom adjoining the classroom, to sit by himself on the mezzanine floor of the school library and to eat by himself in the school cafeteria at different times than when the white students ate. McLaurin petitioned the local federal district court to have these conditions removed. His petition was denied on the ground that these conditions did not violate his right of equal protection of the laws. While McLaurin's appeal to the Supreme Court of the United States was pending, the university modified the conditions of his instruction. He was allowed to sit in the classroom, but in a row designated for black students only. He was allowed to sit on the main floor of the library but at a special table for black students and he was allowed to eat in the cafeteria at the same time as the other students but at a special table.

The U. S. Supreme Court reversed the district court and ruled that the University of Oklahoma had violated McLaurin's right of equal protection. Chief Justice Vinson again wrote the Court's opinion. He said that the restrictions imposed on McLaurin

> impair and inhibit his ability to study, to engage in discussions and exchange views with other students, and, in general, to learn his profession.
>
> Our society grows increasingly complex, and our need for trained leaders increases correspondingly. Appellant's case represents, perhaps, the epitome of that need, for he is attempting to obtain an advanced degree in education, to become, by definition, a leader and trainer of others. Those who will come under his guidance and influence must be directly affected by the education he receives. Their own education and development will necessarily suffer to the extent that his training is unequal to that of his classmates. State-imposed restrictions which produce such inequalities cannot be sustained.
>
> It may be argued that appellant will be in no better position when these restrictions are removed, for he may still be set apart by his

fellow students. This we think irrelevant. There is a vast difference--a Constitutional difference--between restrictions imposed by the state which prohibit the intellectual commingling of students, and the refusal of individuals to commingle where the state presents no such bar. *Shelley v. Kraemer*, 334 U.S. 1, 13-14 (1948). The removal of the state restrictions will not necessarily abate individual and group predilections, prejudices and choices. But at the very least, the state will not be depriving appellant of the opportunity to secure acceptance by his fellow students on his own merits. (Ibid., 641-642)

The Supreme Court's decision in the *McLaurin* case was contrary to its decision in the *Berea College* case, when it upheld a Kentucky law that forbade black and white students to attend classes together, even though they were enrolled at the same college. Vinson's reasoning in both the *Sweatt* and the *McLaurin* cases was also inconsistent with the Court's "separate but equal" reasoning in *Plessy v. Ferguson*, supra. If the Court had applied the *Sweatt* and *McLaurin* logic in the *Plessy* case, then it probably would have ruled that the state of Louisiana had denied Plessy equal protection, because its railway segregation law prevented him from socializing with the people who controlled his society and who could best help him sell his products and services to others. However, the Supreme Court did not mention the *Plessy* case or the *Berea College Case* in its *McLaurin* decision and it refused to overrule the "separate but equal" doctrine.

The logic of the *Sweatt* and *McLaurin* cases was also applicable to public high schools and grade schools. If community reputation and opportunity for student interaction are relevant in judging the equality of segregated university graduate schools, such factors ought to apply as well to in judging the equality of all segregated public schools. On December 9, 10 and 11 in 1952, the Supreme Court heard arguments in five cases from Kansas, South Carolina, Virginia, Delaware and the District of Columbia, filed on behalf of black children who had been forced to attend segregated schools. After hearing the arguments, the Court postponed its decision and scheduled more arguments for the following October. The justices wanted more information on the history of the Fourteenth Amendment in respect of public education and on the possible remedies they might impose should they rule that segregated schools violated that amendment. They may have also wanted to hear the views and recommendations of the new Eisenhower administration that would be taking office on January 20, 1953. Justice Frankfurter gave another reason for the Court's delay in a memorandum to his fellow justices, namely "the ultimate crucial factor . . . [which was] psychological--the adjustment of men's minds and actions to the unfamiliar and unpleasant."[75]

It is possible that the Court was deeply divided over how to decide these cases. Some people believe that Chief Justice Vinson was not in favor of ruling against the segregated school systems, in spite of his opinions in the *Sweatt* and *McLaurin* cases. However, on September 8, 1953, Vinson died of a heart attack. The rearguments were postponed to December and President Eisenhower appointed California governor Earl Warren to replace Vinson as chief justice.

Warren did not ask many questions at the December rearguments, but it soon became evident that he strongly favored a ruling that would declare all segregated schools unconstitutional. He also realized there would a public outcry against such a ruling and enforcement would be difficult. On the other hand, a unanimous ruling might soften the resistance. So he worked to persuade his fellow justices to agree to a unanimous opinion. After several months, all the justices except Jackson and Reed agreed to a draft opinion that Warren had written. Jackson agreed with the decision to end segregated public schools but wanted to write his own opinion. However, he suffered a heart attack and was too ill to write an opinion. Then, Justice Reed agreed to join the majority.[76]

On May 17, 1954, the Court delivered two unanimous opinions, with all nine justices, including the recovering Jackson, sitting on the bench. The first opinion, reported at 347 U.S. 483, applied to the cases of *Brown v. Board of Education of Topeka* from Kansas, *Briggs v. Elliott* from South Carolina, *Davis v. County School Board of Prince Edward County* from Virginia and *Gebhart v.*

Belton from Delaware. The second opinion, reported at 347 U.S. 497, applied to *Bolling v. Sharpe* from the District of Columbia.

In the first opinion, Chief Justice Warren observed that there was almost no mention of public education in the legislative history of the Fourteenth Amendment. He said that was probably because in the 1860s, "the conditions of public education did not approximate those existing today. The curriculum was usually rudimentary, ungraded schools were common in rural areas, the school term was but three months a year in many states and compulsory school attendance was virtually unknown" (Ibid., 490). By contrast, he said,

> Today, education is perhaps the most important function of state and local governments. Compulsory school attendance laws and the great expenditures for education both demonstrate our recognition of the importance of education in our democratic society. It is required in the performance of our most basic public responsibilities, even service in the armed forces. It is the very foundation of good citizenship. Today it is a principal instrument in awakening the child to cultural values, in preparing him for later professional training, and in helping him to adjust normally to his environment. In these days, it is doubtful that any child may reasonably be expected to succeed in life if he is denied the opportunity of an education. Such an opportunity, where the state has undertaken to provide it, is a right which must be made available to all on equal terms.

> We come then to the question presented: Does segregation of children in public schools solely on the basis of race, even though the physical facilities and other "tangible" factors may be equal, deprive the children of the minority group of equal educational opportunities? We believe that it does.

> In *Sweatt v. Painter, supra,* in finding that a segregated law school for Negroes could not provide them equal educational opportunities, this Court relied in large part on "those qualities which are incapable of objective measurement but which make for greatness in a law school." In *McLaurin v. Oklahoma State Regents, supra,* the Court, in requiring that a Negro admitted to a white graduate school be treated like all other students, again resorted to intangible considerations: ". . . his ability to study, to engage in discussions and exchange

views with other students, and, in general, to learn his profession." Such considerations apply with added force to grade and high schools. To separate them from others of similar age and qualifications solely because of their race generates a feeling of inferiority as to their status in the community that may affect their hearts and minds in a way unlikely ever to be undone. The effect of this separation on their educational opportunities was well stated by a finding in the Kansas case by a court which nevertheless felt compelled to rule against the Negro plaintiffs:

> Segregation of white and colored children in public schools has a detrimental effect upon the colored children. The impact is greater when it has the sanction of the law; for the policy of separating the races is usually interpreted as denoting the inferiority of the negro group. A sense of inferiority affects the motivation of a child to learn. Segregation with the sanction of law, therefore, has a tendency to [retard] the educational and mental development of negro children and to deprive them of some of the benefits they would receive in a racial[ly] integrated school system.

Whatever may have been the extent of psychological knowledge at the time of *Plessy v. Ferguson*, this finding is amply supported by modern authority. Any language in *Plessy v. Ferguson* contrary to this finding is rejected. (Ibid., 493-495)

The Supreme Court therefore ruled that the segregated schools of Kansas, South Carolina, Virginia and Delaware violated the equal protection guarantee of the Fourteenth Amendment.

The Supreme Court delivered a separate opinion in the District of Columbia case of *Bolling v. Sharpe* because the segregated schools in that case were operated by the federal government. The Fourteenth Amendment's equal protection clause applies only to state governments and the Constitution does not have a specific equal protection clause that applies to the federal government. In *Bolling v. Sharpe*, Chief Justice Warren explained why that did not matter, because the federally operated segregated schools violated the life, liberty and property clause of the Fifth Amendment. He pointed out that the Court had recognized in the past that the federal government's discrimination "may be so unjustifiable" as to violate the Fifth Amendment rights of life, liberty and property. He cited the Court's statements to that effect in several prior cases, including *Korematsu* and *Hirabayashi* cases, supra, but the Court had not relied on those statements in its rulings.[77] He also cited *Buchanan v. Warley*, supra, in which the Court ruled that a state law forbidding property transfers between black and white people violated the property rights of those people, even though it was also an "unreasonable discrimination" (Ibid., 585). The fact remained that the Court had never ruled that the federal government's discrimination violated the life, liberty and property clause of the Fifth Amendment. As recently as *Hurd v. Hodge*, supra, Chief Justice Vinson had avoided the issue by relying on the Civil Rights Act of 1866, rather than the Fifth Amendment, to rule a restrictive neighborhood covenant unenforceable by the federal courts of the District of Columbia.

In *Bolling v. Sharpe*, however, Chief Justice Warren confronted the issue when he said,

> Although the Court has not assumed to define "liberty" with any great precision, that term is not confined to mere freedom from bodily restraint. Liberty under law extends to the full range of conduct which the individual is free to pursue, and it cannot be restricted except for a proper governmental objective. Segregation in public education is not reasonably related to any proper governmental objective, and thus it imposes on Negro children of the District of Columbia a burden that constitutes an arbitrary deprivation of their liberty in violation of the Due Process [life, liberty and property] Clause. (Ibid., 499-500)

The *Bolling v. Sharpe* case did more than rule that the black children of the District of Columbia had a constitutional right to attend integrated schools. It shed new light on Justice Cardozo's statement in *Palko v. Connecticut* that a right of life, liberty and property had to be "a principle of justice so rooted in the traditions and conscience of our people as to be ranked as fundamental" (302 U.S. at 325). When the Fifth Amendment was adopted in 1791, most of the black people in America were held as slaves, in the

North as well as the South. The Constitution not only permitted these people to be held as slaves, but Article IV, Section 2[3] of the Constitution required that slaves escaping from one state to another had to be returned. In 1793 the U. S. Congress passed the Fugitive Slave Act and in 1850 it amended that law to punish all people in all states who helped fugitive slaves hide or escape from their masters or from federal agents seeking to enforce the law. During that time, the Fifth Amendment's life, liberty and property clause appeared to lay dormant because the Supreme Court ruled in *Bolling v. Sharpe* that it guaranteed the right of black children in the District of Columbia to attend the same schools as their white neighbors. The Court's explanation was that the liberty guaranteed by the clause "extends to the full range of conduct which the individual is free to pursue, and it cannot be restricted except for a proper governmental objective" (Ibid., 499). That was a restatement of the fundamental right of life, liberty and property described by John Locke:

> [a] man, as has been proved, cannot subject himself to the arbitrary power of another; and having in a state of nature no arbitrary power over the life, liberty, or possessions of another, but only so much as the law of nature gave him for the preservation of himself and the rest of mankind, this is all he does or can give up to the commonwealth, and by it to the legislative power, so that the legislative power can have no more that this. Their power, in the utmost bounds of it, is limited to the public good of society. . . . . . (App. F, par. 135)

This basic right of life, liberty and property is therefore "a principle of justice so rooted in the traditions and conscience of our people as to be ranked as fundamental." It is a right that cannot be denied simply because of the hypocritical acts of the founding fathers or their successors. The unanimous *Bolling v. Sharpe* decision thus provided the rationale for the Court's later decisions interpreting the Fourteenth Amendment, particularly those relating to the private acts of people discussed in Chapter 9, Section B.

Although the Supreme Court ruled in *Brown v. Board of Education* and *Bolling v. Sharpe* that segregated public schools could not possibly satisfy the Constitutional right of all people to equal protection of the laws, it did not say that it would be impossible for government to provide other kinds of "separate but equal" facilities. Thus, the Court did not technically overrule its 1896 ruling in *Plessy v. Ferguson*, supra. However, the Court's reliance on intangible factors, such as a black person's inability to interact with white people and his feeling of inferiority caused by forced segregation, sounded the death knell to all kinds of segregated government facilities. In 1955, the Court ruled in *Dawson v. Mayor and City of Baltimore*, 350 U.S. 877, that Baltimore's segregated public recreation facilities violated the rights of black people to equal protection of the laws. The Court ruled the next year that the segregated city buses of Birmingham, Alabama violated the Fourteenth Amendment, in *Gayle v. Browder*, 352 U.S. 903. In 1957, it ruled that a state-operated school for poor young white male orphans in Philadelphia violated the Constitution when it refused to admit poor young black male orphans, in *Pennsylvania v. Board of Directors*, 353 U.S. 230. Then in 1963, it ruled in *Johnson v. Virginia*, 373 U.S. 61, that a traffic judge in Richmond had violated the Constitution when he required a black man to sit on the opposite side of the courtroom from the white people while the man was waiting his turn to appear before the judge.

E.5. The Slow Pace of School Desegregation

In both his *Brown v. Board of Education* and *Bolling v. Sharpe* opinions, Chief Justice Warren announced that the Court would schedule further hearings on whether it should order all black children to be immediately admitted to the school of their choice within their assigned school district, or whether it should order a gradual desegregation of the schools affected by its judgments. The Court said it would also hear arguments on whether, if it chose the latter course of action, it should formulate detailed decrees in each case, and what issues it ought to cover in such decrees. The Court also wanted advice on whether it should appoint a special master to hear evidence and recommend the specific terms of such decrees or

Chapter 10   The Fourteenth Amendment   523

whether it should remand all the cases to the trial court to frame the decrees.

On May 31, 1955, after hearing arguments on these issues, Chief Justice Warren announced the Court's decision (349 U.S. 294). First he commented that substantial progress toward desegregation had already taken place in the Kansas, Delaware and District of Columbia school districts, as well as other school districts across the nation that had filed *amicus curiae* briefs. However, the school districts in Virginia and South Carolina had elected to await the specific terms of the Supreme Court's relief order before taking any action. Warren then announced that the Court had decided to remand the cases to their respective local courts, with directions to formulate desegregation decrees. He said the Court recognized there would be obstacles, because of the physical conditions of school facilities, transportation systems, personnel and the need to revise attendance boundaries. On the other hand, he said school administrators should take into account the public interest in eliminating those obstacles in a systematic and effective manner. Warren directed the district courts to "require that the defendants make a prompt and reasonable start toward full compliance with our May 17, 1954 ruling," and he warned "it should go without saying that the vitality of these constitutional principles cannot be allowed to yield simply because of disagreement with them" (Ibid., 300). Therefore, the district courts were to "enter such orders and decrees consistent with this opinion" as were necessary to desegregate the schools "with all deliberate speed" (Ibid., 301).

Many segregated school districts made good faith efforts to comply with the Supreme Court's 1955 ruling, although the only districts bound by the ruling were the ones who were parties to the cases before the Court. The other districts knew that they would be sued if they did not comply with the ruling. However, the resistance of many communities to the ruling led to violent confrontations, particularly in the southern states.

The most dramatic confrontation occurred in Little Rock, Arkansas, in September 1957. The local school board had adopted a desegregation plan and was planning to take the first step by admitting nine black students to Little Rock Central High School, which had two thousand white students. The high school was located about ten blocks from the Arkansas State Capitol, where the state legislature had just passed a law relieving all school children from compulsory attendance at racially mixed schools. That law had been passed pursuant to a state constitutional amendment adopted in November 1956, commanding the state legislature to oppose "in every Constitutional manner the Unconstitutional desegregation decisions of May 17, 1954 and May 31, 1955 of the United States Supreme Court." On September 2, 1957, the day before the black students were to enter the high school, Governor Orville Faubus dispatched Arkansas National Guard troops to the school grounds and placed the school "off-limits" to black students. This action caused many people who had reluctantly accepted the school board's desegregation plan to come to the high school to protest against the admission of the black students and to show their support for the governor's action. The school board therefore ordered the black students to stay away from the school, and on September 3, it petitioned the local federal judge who had approved the desegregation plan to allow them to delay the first step because of the governor's stationing of National Guard troops. The judge determined that this was not a sufficient reason for postponing the plan and ordered the board to proceed with it immediately. The next day, the nine black children tried to enter the high school, but soldiers of the Arkansas National Guard stood shoulder to shoulder on the school grounds and prevented them from entering. They continued to do so on each school day for the following three weeks.

Meanwhile, the attorney general of the United States petitioned the local federal judge to enjoin the Arkansas governor and the officers of the Arkansas National Guard from interfering with attendance of black students at the Little Rock Central High School. The district judge granted the injunction on Friday, September 20 and on the following Monday, the black students entered the high school under the protection of Little Rock police officers and Arkansas state police officers. However, these officers were unable to control the large crowd of demonstrators who had gathered at the school and they were therefore forced to escort the black students out of the school soon after they had entered. Two days later, President Eisenhower ordered regular U. S. Army troops to the high school and these soldiers were able to secure the permanent admission of the black students. These troops remained at the high school until November 27, 1957, when they were replaced by federalized National Guard troops. The National Guardsmen remained on duty at the high school for the remainder of the school year.

On February 20, 1958, the Little Rock School Board again petitioned the local federal district court to postpone their desegregation program. On June 20, 1958, that court granted the board's petition, because the past year at the Central High School had been attended by conditions of "chaos, bedlam and turmoil," there were "repeated incidents of more or less serious violence directed against the Negro students and their property" and there was "tension and unrest among the school administrators, the class-room teachers, the pupils, and the latter's' parents, which inevitably had an adverse effect upon the educational program." The school district had also suffered a "serious financial burden" because of these events (358 U.S. at 13).

On August 18, 1957, the Fifth Circuit Court of Appeals in New Orleans reversed the district court's ruling but stayed its order pending an appeal to the Supreme Court of the United States. On September 12, 1958, the Supreme Court affirmed the court of appeals' judgment in *Cooper v. Aaron*, 358 U.S. 1. In a joint unanimous opinion by Chief Justice Warren and Justices Black, Brennan, Burton, Clark, Douglas, Frankfurter, Harlan and Whittaker, the Court said,

> The constitutional rights of respondents are not to be sacrificed or yielded to the violence and disorder which have followed upon the actions of the Governor and Legislature. As this Court said some 41 years ago in a unanimous opinion in a case involving another aspect of racial segregation: "It is urged that this proposed segregation will promote the public peace by preventing race conflicts. Desirable as

this is, and important as is the preservation of the public peace, this aim cannot be accomplished by laws or ordinances which deny rights created or protected by the federal Constitution." [Justice William Rufus Day of Ravenna, Ohio, in] *Buchanan v. Warley*, 245 U.S. 60, 81. Thus law and order are not here to be preserved by depriving the Negro children of their constitutional rights. The record before us clearly establishes that the growth of the Board's difficulties to a magnitude beyond its unaided power to control is the product of state action. Those difficulties, as counsel for the Board forthrightly conceded on the oral argument in this Court, can also be brought under control by state action. (Ibid., 16)

Similar problems arose in New Orleans, Louisiana, in 1960 when the state legislature passed a law forbidding school integration. On November 10, Federal District Judge Skelley Wright ruled the law unconstitutional and forbade its implementation. The New Orleans school board then announced plans to transfer five black children to two all-white elementary schools. On November 13, the state legislature seized control of the New Orleans schools, fired the superintendent, and ordered all the schools closed on the next day. Judge Wright immediately ordered the schools to remain open. On November 14, federal marshals escorted four black children to their new schools. A six-year-old girl, Ruby Bridges, was the only black student to enter her school. She had to walk into her school surrounded by armed marshals, while angry white adults shouted hateful words at her and chanted, "Two, four, six, eight, we don't want to integrate!" The next day, eleven white people were arrested in New Orleans for causing various disturbances. On November 17, riots broke out in the city. Meanwhile, the parents of the white children at Ruby's school pulled their children out of the school. Ruby therefore spent most of the year receiving private tutoring in a classroom by herself. The following year, racial tensions eased and Ruby was able to continue her schooling in an integrated classroom.

Rather than challenge the Supreme Court's authority as the Arkansas and Louisiana legislatures did, most state and local governments tried more subtle ways of thwarting the Court's desegregation decree. In *Goss v. Board of Education of Knoxville, Tennessee*, 373 U.S. 683 (1963), the city school board submitted a desegregation plan that rezoned all the districts in the city without regard to race. However, the plan allowed any student who had been transferred from a school where his race was in the majority to a school where his race was in the minority to transfer back to his original school if he so requested. The Supreme Court ruled that this plan was not acceptable, because the transfer provision allowed a student to transfer only from a school where his race was in the minority to a school where his race was in the majority and not vice versa. This kind of transferring would inevitably result in the old system in which students were segregated by race.

The county school board of Prince Edward County was a party to one of the cases decided by the Supreme Court in 1954. It was therefore legally bound to obey the Court's 1955 desegregation order. However, in 1956 the Virginia General Assembly ordered the closing of all public schools in the state attended by white and black children. It also began paying tuition grants to children in non-sectarian private schools and extended. That enabled private individuals to establish schools for white children in those areas where the public schools would be closed, which included Prince Edward County. The General Assembly extended state retirement benefits to teachers in these newly created schools. In 1959, the Virginia Supreme Court of Appeals ruled that the General Assembly's actions had violated the Virginia Constitution [*Harrison v. Day*, 200 Va. 439 (Va. S.Ct., 1959)].

The General Assembly therefore adopted another plan, called "freedom of choice." It repealed the statewide compulsory attendance laws and gave each school district the power to decide what if any local attendance rules would apply. It also made every child in the state, white or black, eligible for a tuition grant to attend a non-sectarian private school or a public school outside his district. For the 1960-61 school year, the grant was $125 per year to an elementary school student and $150 per year to a high school child. Meanwhile, the Prince Edward school board closed all its schools and gave additional tuition grants of $100 to students attending private schools run by the Prince Edward County Foundation, as well as property tax credits of up to 25 percent of contributions made to any non-profit, nonsectarian private school in the county. All these private schools segregated black students from white students. Prince Edward County was the only county in the state where this situation occurred. The public schools continued to operate in all the other counties. In 1963, the U. S. Supreme Court ruled in *Griffin v. County School Board of Prince Edward County*, 377 U.S. 218, that these actions denied the county's black school children equal protection of the laws. Speaking for the Court, Justice Black said,

> Prince Edward's public schools were closed and private schools operated in their place with state and county assistance, for one reason and one reason only: to ensure, through measures taken by the county and the State, that white and colored children in Prince Edward County would not, under any circumstances, go to the same school. Whatever nonracial grounds might support a State's allowing a county to abandon public schools, the object must be a constitutional one, and grounds of race and opposition to desegregation do not qualify as constitutional. (Ibid., 231)

Justice Black then warned the Prince Edward school board, as well as all other school boards, that the time had come for the courts to develop their own desegregation plans in cases where the school boards had failed to present adequate plans. Referring to the Supreme Court's 1955 order that desegregation be accomplished with "all deliberate speed" (349 U.S. at 301), Black said,

> The time for mere "deliberate speed" has run out, and that phrase can no longer justify these Prince Edward County school children their constitutional rights to an educational equal to that afforded by the public schools in the other parts of Virginia. (Ibid., 234)

In 1968, the Supreme Court ruled that segregated school districts could not satisfy their obligation to desegregate their schools simply by allowing the students in the all-white schools the "freedom of choice" to go to an all-black school and vice versa. In the Virginia case of *Green v. County School Board of New Kent County*, 391 U.S. 430, and the Arkansas case of *Raney v. Board of Education of the Gould School District*, 391 U.S. 443, the residents of both districts were approximately 60 percent black and 40 percent white and there was no residential segregation. In both cases, there was one all-white school and one all-black school; each school was a combined elementary and high school until 1965. In that year, the school boards adopted a desegregation plan whereby all students could choose to stay at their present school or go to the other school. As of 1967 in both cases, all the white students had chosen to stay at their present school and approximately 15 percent of the black students had chosen to transfer to the previously all-white school. The Supreme Court unanimously ruled in both cases that this "freedom of choice" plan was not sufficient to comply with the Court's desegregation order in *Brown v. Board of Education*. Speaking for the Court in the Virginia case, Justice Brennan said the Court's order in *Brown v. Board of Education* clearly charged the boards of segregated school districts

> with the affirmative duty to take whatever steps might be necessary to convert to a unitary system in which racial discrimination would be eliminated root and branch. . . . "The time for mere 'deliberate speed' has run out," *Griffin v. County School Board*, 377 U.S. 218, 234; . . . The burden on a school board today is to come forward with a plan that promises realistically to work, and promises to realistically work *now*. . . .
>
> We do not hold that "freedom of choice" can have no place in such a plan. We do not hold that a "freedom of choice" plan might itself be unconstitutional, although that argument has been urged upon us. Rather, all we decide today is that in desegregating a dual system a plan utilizing "freedom of choice" is not an end in itself. (Ibid., 437-440)

In Mississippi, most school districts were still segregated as late as 1969. On July 3, 1969, the federal Court of Appeals for the Fifth Circuit in New Orleans ordered thirty-three Mississippi districts to submit new desegregation plans and have them operating when their schools opened the following September. However, on August 28, the court of appeals suspended its order, after receiving evidence that the time was too short and the administrative problems too difficult to comply with the order (396 U.S. at 1218-1219, 1222). That suspension was appealed to the U. S. Supreme Court, which reinstated the order on October 29. In *Alexander v. Holmes County Board of Education et al.*, 396 U.S. 19 (1969), the Supreme Court ordered all the districts to "begin immediately to operate as unitary school systems within which no person is to be effectively excluded from any school because of race or color." It also ruled that "the Court of Appeals should have denied all motions for extension of time because continued operation of segregated schools under a standard of allowing 'all deliberate speed' for desegregation is no longer permissible" (Ibid., 20).

Two years later, the Supreme Court ruled that when local school districts are guilty of past segregation practices and fail to submit acceptable remedial plans, the local district courts must develop their own plans, which may include busing students to distant schools within the district. In *Swann v. Charlotte-Mecklenburg Board of Education*, 402 U.S. 1 (1971), the Charlotte-Mecklenburg school district comprised the city of Charlotte, North Carolina and its surrounding Mecklenburg County. The district had about sixty thousand white students and twenty-four thousand black students. About twenty-one thousand black students lived in the city of Charlotte and attended schools there. About fourteen thousand of these black students attended schools that were more than 99 percent black. The district judge determined that this segregation was in part the result of the past government action, which included clever locating and sizing of schools and attendance boundaries. He therefore ordered the school board to submit an appropriate desegregation plan. After the board submitted three plans and each was found unacceptable, the judge finally appointed an education expert to draw up a plan. That plan was submitted in February 1970; the school board presented another plan at about the same time.

The plans were substantially the same with respect to the district's high school and junior high attendance zones. Both plans for the ten high schools called for wedged-shaped zones that spread from the center of Charlotte like pieces of a pie. The twenty-one junior high zones were based on a similar concept, except the expert's plan called for nine satellite zones in the suburbs that created better racial mixing. The main difference between the plans were the zones for the seventy-six elementary schools. The board's plan relied entirely on contiguous, gerrymandered zones that left nine schools 86 to 100 percent black and assigned half the white students to zones that were 86 to 100 percent white. The expert's plan called for zones each having two or three outlying schools grouped with a black inner city school. That resulted in every one of the seventy-six schools being within a range of 9 to 38 percent black, but it required a substantial increase in the number of students who had to be bussed long distances to their assigned schools. After several hearings, the district judge directed that the district's desegregation be carried out according to the expert's plan. The Fourth Circuit Court of Appeals in Richmond, Virginia affirmed the judge's order in respect of the high schools and junior high schools, but it vacated his order with respect to the elementary schools on the ground that its busing provisions imposed an unreasonable burden on the students and the school board.

In a unanimous Supreme Court decision, Chief Justice Burger ruled that the Court of Appeals had erred in vacating the district judge's order with respect to the elementary schools. He said the plan did not impose an undue burden because the district judge had determined that the bus trips for the elementary students would average only seven miles and the longest trip would take no more than thirty-five minutes. He noted that compared favorably with the school district's previous transportation system in which 23,600 students on all grade levels were bused an average of fifteen miles each way and spent an average of over an hour on their buses each way. In other situations, however, he said, "An objection to transportation of students may have validity when the time or distance of travel is so great as to either risk the health of children or significantly impinge on the educational process" (Ibid., 30-31).

Burger also said that "schools all or predominantly of one race in a district of mixed population will require close scrutiny to determine that school assignments are not part of state-enforced segregation" (Ibid., 28). In addition, he approved the district judge's limited use of racial quotas as a starting point for developing a desegregation remedy, the optional transfer of students of a majority racial group in one school to another school in which they will be in the minority, and the use of drastically gerrymandered and split attendance zones to accomplish desegregation. With regard to such attendance zones, he said,

> Absent a constitutional violation there would be no basis for judicially ordering assignment of students on a racial basis. All things being equal, with no history of discrimination, it might well be desirable to assign pupils to schools nearest their homes. But all things are not equal in a system that has been deliberately constructed and maintained to enforce racial segregation. The remedy for such segregation may be administratively awkward, inconvenient, and even bizarre in some situations and may impose burdens on some; but all awkwardness and inconvenience cannot be avoided in the interim period when remedial adjustments are being made to eliminate the dual system. . . . When school authorities present a district court with a "loaded game board," affirmative action in the form of remedial altering of attendance zones is proper to achieve truly non-discriminatory assignments. (Ibid., 28)

At time of the *Swann* decision, the Supreme Court also approved desegregation busing orders for Mobile, Alabama and Athens, Georgia (*Davis v. Board of School Commissioners of Mobile County*, 402 U.S. 33, and *McDaniel v. Barresi*, 402 U.S. 39, respectively). Federal district judges then began issuing busing orders to school districts across the nation that had been found guilty of past segregation practices. These districts included Cleveland, Columbus and Dayton, Ohio; Indianapolis, Indiana; Omaha, Nebraska; Austin, Texas; Milwaukee, Wisconsin; Denver,

Colorado; and Seattle, Washington. There was a huge public outcry against these orders, because the busing expenses added to the already severe financial problems of inner city schools, the long bus trips sapped the energy of the younger children, black students continued to suffer discrimination in the integrated schools, racial tensions led to severe discipline problems and the closing of black schools caused many black teachers and principals to lose their jobs. In many cities, black parent groups began to campaign for the return of all-black schools in their own neighborhoods, where they could better monitor faculty hiring and curriculum selection.[78]

The failure of most school busing plans to accomplish their intended purposes has discouraged federal judges from continuing to use this remedy to correct the *de jure* segregation resulting from past discrimination practices. It has also discouraged the use of voluntary busing plans by school districts that were not judged guilty of such past discrimination but wanted to end *de facto* segregation in their all-black neighborhood schools. The Supreme Court has never viewed school busing as being anything but a temporary, last-resort remedy to correct the injustice of past government segregation practices. Experience has raised doubts concerning even that limited utility.

District by district, the desegregation plans ordered by the various courts across the nation are terminating. These plans have enabled thousands of minority children to attend integrated schools. Doubts remain, however, concerning how many of these people have gained better educations, made friends with fellow white students, or now enjoy the same employment opportunities as white people. The court orders have ended most of the blatant, government-sanctioned discrimination that existed at the time of the Supreme Court's *Brown v. Board of Education* decision. Government agencies have now become part of the solution to racial discrimination, rather than part of the problem. However, there is a limit to what government can do to stop racial prejudice, either by white people toward black people and other minorities, or vice versa. There is also a limit to what the courts can do to solve the serious financial and administrative problems of inner city school districts. The right to an equal education means nothing if both sides of the equation are zero.

E.6. The Civil Rights Acts of 1964 and 1968

On December 1, 1955, Rosa Parks, a black woman, was riding on a Montgomery, Alabama, city bus. A white passenger asked her to surrender her seat, but she refused. She was thereupon arrested for violating the city's segregation law. A group of black people responded by organizing the Montgomery Improvement Association. The leader of the group was the twenty-seven-year-old pastor of the Dexter Avenue Baptist Church, Dr. Martin Luther King, Jr. The Association's first project was a boycott of the local transit system in protest of Rosa Parks' arrest. In his first formal address to the group, Dr. King said,

> We have no alternative but to protest. For many years we have shown an amazing patience. We have sometimes given our white brothers the feeling that we liked the way we were being treated. But we come here tonight to be saved from that patience that makes us patient with anything less than freedom and justice.[79]

During the following year, Dr. King led a campaign to desegregate the Montgomery city buses. His home was dynamited and his family's safety threatened in other ways. However, he finally convinced the city leaders to desegregate the buses.

Spurred by this success, King organized the Southern Christian Leadership Conference ("SCLC"), a national organization devoted to gaining civil rights for black people. He traveled across the country giving speeches and conferring with civil rights leaders and ministers about the problems faced by black Americans. In 1959, he traveled to Ghana and India and discussed techniques of nonviolent protest with followers of Mahatma Ghandi. The following year, he moved to Atlanta to resume his previous ministry with his father as co-pastor of the Ebenezer Baptist Church. There he lent the support of the SCLC to local sit-in demonstrations organized by college students.

Chapter 10   The Fourteenth Amendment   535

In October 1960, King was arrested with thirty-three young people at a lunch counter sit-in. Although the charges were dropped, he was sentenced to a state prison farm on the pretext that he had violated his probation on a minor traffic violation. This cruel and unusual punishment by the Georgia authorities caused a nation-wide protest. People urged the Eisenhower administration to intervene, but it failed to do so. Seizing the opportunity, Presidential candidate John F. Kennedy interceded and arranged for King's release. That occurred only days before the election and it may well have given Kennedy the support he needed to defeat Richard Nixon by a narrow margin of victory. The result was a strong political tie between the Kennedy administration and King's civil rights campaign.

In the early 1960s, King led a nationwide campaign to end discrimination in restaurants, business employment and other parts of American society. It culminated in a great civil rights rally of two hundred thousand people gathered in front of the Lincoln Memorial in Washington, D.C. On August 28, 1963, King addressed the gathering with his famous "I have a dream . . ." speech.

Spurred by growing public support for a new civil rights law, President Kennedy sent a proposed bill to Congress on June 19, 1963. Several other bills were introduced. After many hearings, the bills were combined and the Civil Rights Act of 1964 passed on July 2. Most sections of that law are still in effect. Its most significant titles are Title II, which forbids discrimination in places of public accommodation, including places of lodging, eating and entertainment; Title VI, which forbids discrimination by organizations receiving federal money; and Title VII, which forbids employment discrimination.

Immediately after the 1964 Civil Rights Act passed, both the supporters and the opponents of the law were anxious to test its constitutionality. The last major civil rights law, the Civil Rights Act of 1875, had been ruled unconstitutional by the Supreme Court in *The Civil Rights Cases*, supra. The Court had ruled that Congress did not have the power under the Thirteenth and

Fourteenth Amendments to prevent privately owned places of accommodation from discriminating against anyone for whatever reason. However, the Civil Rights Act of 1964 was limited to places of accommodation that affected interstate commerce and was based on Congress's power to regulate interstate commerce under Article I, Section 8[3] of the Constitution. Section 201 of the Act said, in part,

> (a) All persons shall be entitled to the full and equal enjoyment of the goods, services, facilities, privileges, advantages, and accommodations of any place of public accommodation, as defined in this section, without discrimination or segregation on the ground of race, religion, or national origin.
> (b) Each of the following establishments which serves the public is a place of public accommodation within the meaning of this title if its operations affect [interstate or foreign] commerce, or if discrimination or segregation by it is supported by State action:
> (1) any inn, hotel, motel, or other establishment which provides lodging to transient guests, other than an establishment located within a building which contains not more than five rooms for rent or hire and which is actually occupied by the proprietor of such establishment as his residence;
> (2) any restaurant, cafeteria, lunchroom, lunch counter, soda fountain, or other facility principally engaged in selling food for consumption on the premises, including, but not limited to, any such facility located on the premises of any retail establishment; or any gasoline station; . . .
> (c) The operations of an establishment affect [interstate or foreign] commerce within the meaning of this subchapter if (1) it is one of the establishments described in subsection (b) of this section; (2) in the case of an establishment described in paragraph (2) of subsection (b) of this section, it serves or offers to serve interstate travelers or a substantial portion of the food which it serves, or gasoline or other products which it sells has moved in interstate commerce; . . . .[80]

In *Heart of Atlanta Motel Co. v. United States*, 379 U.S. 241 (1964), the Heart of Atlanta Motel argued that Section 201(b)(1) was unconstitutional because it regulated activities that were not interstate commerce. Speaking for the Supreme Court, Justice Tom Clark said that this law, as applied to the Heart of Atlanta Motel, was within Congress's power to regulate interstate commerce. He cited Congressional testimony relating to increased interstate travel by people of all races and the difficulty of black people finding accommodations because of racial discrimination. Congress therefore had the power to relieve this impediment to interstate commerce. Clark did not address the question of whether all non-resident-owned inns or all inns having more than five rooms were part of interstate commerce, because the only issue in this case was whether the Heart of Atlanta Motel could be regulated by Congress. The answer to that question was easy because 75 percent of the Heart of Atlanta guests were from outside the state of Georgia. However, even the broader question would not have been difficult for the Court to answer. In this modern age when the majority of Americans who stay at public inns are interstate travelers, even a small inn will probably serve some guests who have come from beyond its state boundaries.

The case of *Katzenbach v. McClung*, 379 U.S. 294 (1964), presented a more difficult question. The U. S. Attorney General charged that Ollie's Barbecue in Birmingham, Alabama, had violated Section 201 of the Civil Rights Act by refusing to serve black people. Ollie's was probably serving many interstate travelers because of its location in a large city and its seating capacity of 220 customers. However, the Attorney General did not allege that Ollie's was covered by the law because it served or offered to serve interstate travelers [Section 201(c)(2), supra]. He based his case solely on the fact that a substantial portion of the food it served had moved in interstate commerce. Of the $150,000 worth of food purchased by Ollie's during the previous twelve months, $70,000 worth had been purchased from a local supplier who had in turn bought it from an out-of-state supplier. The district court had dismissed the case because "there was no demonstratable connection between food purchased in interstate commerce and sold in a restaurant and the conclusion of Congress that discrimination in the restaurant would affect that commerce" (Ibid., 297).

The Supreme Court reversed the district court's ruling. Speaking for the Court, Justice Clark said,

> A comparison of per capita spending by Negroes in restaurants, theatres, and like establishments indicated less spending, after discounting income differences, in areas where discrimination is widely practiced. This condition, which was especially aggravated in the South, was attributed in the testimony of the Under Secretary of Commerce to racial segregation. See Hearings before the Senate Committee on Commerce on S. 1732, 88th Cong., 1st Sess., 695. This diminutive spending springing from a refusal to serve Negroes and their total loss as customers has, regardless of direct evidence, a close connection to interstate commerce. The fewer customers a restaurant enjoys the less food it sells and consequently the less it buys. (Ibid., 299)

Clark also cited other testimony showing the harmful effect on interstate commerce by racial discrimination in restaurants. However, none of this testimony appears to have separated restaurants serving interstate travelers from those serving only local customers. Thus was no evidence, direct or otherwise, that restaurants who purchased food from interstate commercial suppliers but who served only white customers from their own localities suffered a loss in business or had any impact on interstate commerce. In the absence of such evidence, the Supreme Court should have ruled that Section 201 was unconstitutional insofar as it applied to eating places that were not serving interstate travelers.

Unfortunately, the Supreme Court's faulty reasoning in *Katzenbach v. McClung* is typical of its modern decisions on the interstate commerce clause. As fearless as the Court has been in recent years to protect the Constitutional rights of individual people, it has been reluctant to restrict Congress to its constitutional powers, thereby ignoring the Tenth Amendment rights of the states. The latter subject is beyond the scope of this book, except as it relates to the ideal that all people have an equal opportunity to participate in the life of their society. The civil rights of people are based on this ideal.

Chapter 10   The Fourteenth Amendment   539

By the life, liberty and property and equal protection clauses of the Fifth and Fourteenth Amendments, the United States Constitution prevents the federal and state governments from taking away people's civil rights. By their inherent nature and purpose, Those governments also have a responsibility to require that people respect each other's civil rights. However, many of the responsibilities and powers of civil government in the United States reside in the states, not the federal government. When they adopted the U. S. Constitution, the states delegated some of their responsibilities and powers to the federal government, but the Tenth Amendment says that the states have retained all the powers which they not specifically delegated.

The major obstacle to people's enjoyment of their civil rights has been the failure of state governments to give people equal protection of the laws and to fulfill their responsibilities in respect of other civil rights. The Fourteenth Amendment gave the federal government the power to remove the first obstacle, but the states have ratified no amendment that gives the federal government the power to remove the second obstacle. The best the federal government can do in this situation is to fulfill its own responsibilities by requiring that people respect each others' civil rights in the course of their interstate or foreign commerce or in other matters that Congress has the power to regulate under the Constitution.

The limits on federal power have frustrated many people in their search for ways to solve important national problems such as discrimination based on race, religion or national origin. It is far easier to convince one legislature, the United States Congress, to pass a law than it is to convince fifty state legislatures. The Supreme Court has thus been pressured to stretch the meaning of the Constitution's language to give Congress more power. The *Katzenbach v. McClung* case was one example of how the Supreme Court succumbed to that pressure.

Another example was the case of *Jones v. Alfred H. Mayer Co.*, 392 U.S. 409 (1968). Joseph Lee Jones sued the Alfred H. Mayer Company alleging that Mayer had refused to sell him a home in the Paddock Woods community of St. Louis County, Missouri solely because he was black. He claimed that Mayer had violated a federal law, 42 U.S.C. §1982, which says,

> All citizens of the United States shall have the same right, in every State and Territory, as is enjoyed by white citizens thereof to inherit, purchase, lease, sell, hold, and convey real and personal property.

This law was originally part of Section 1 of the Civil Rights Act of 1866, quoted in Section B of this chapter. The defendant Mayer moved to dismiss Jones's complaint on the ground that the law simply forbade government agencies from discriminating against non-white people. The district judge agreed and dismissed the complaint. The Eighth Circuit Court of Appeals in St. Louis affirmed the decision, but the U. S. Supreme Court reversed, ruling that the law also forbade private individuals from discriminating against non-white people in the sale or lease of their private property. The Court further ruled that Congress had the power forbid such discrimination under its power to enforce the Thirteenth Amendment, which outlawed "slavery" and "involuntary servitude."

In the Court's opinion, Justice Stewart explained why the Thirteenth Amendment gave Congress this power. Quoting from the Congressional debates on the bill that became the Thirteenth Amendment, he said,

> Negro citizens, North and South, who saw in the Thirteenth Amendment a promise of freedom--freedom to "go and come at pleasure" and to "buy and sell when they please"--would be left with "a mere paper guarantee" if Congress were powerless to assure that a dollar in the hands of a Negro will purchase the same thing as a dollar in the hands of a white man. At the very least, the freedom that Congress is empowered to secure under the Thirteenth Amendment includes the freedom to buy whatever a white man buy, the right to live wherever a white man can live. If Congress cannot say that being a free man means at least this much, then the Thirteenth Amendment made a promise the Nation cannot keep. (Ibid., 443)

However, the Thirteenth Amendment promised only to eliminate "slavery" and "involuntary servitude." Senator Trumbull said

Chapter 10   The Fourteenth Amendment   541

during the Senate debates that this amendment would enable Congress to prevent former slaves from being "deprived of the privilege to go and come at pleasure, to buy and sell when they please, [and] to make contracts and enforce contracts,"[81] but there is no indication that he had in mind the privilege of entering into a purchase, sale or contract that was not of the usual, voluntary kind between a willing buyer and a willing seller. Eight years later, Justice Bradley wrote on behalf of the Supreme Court in *The Civil Rights Cases*, supra,

> It would be running the slavery argument into the ground to make [the Thirteenth Amendment] apply to every act of discrimination which a person may see fit to make as to the guests he will entertain, or as to the people he will take into his coach or cab or car, or admit to his concert or theatre, or deal with in matters of intercourse or business. Innkeepers and public carriers, by the laws of all the States, so far as we are aware, are bound, to the extent of their facilities, to furnish proper accommodations to all unobjectionable persons who in good faith apply to them. If the laws themselves make any unjust discrimination, amenable to the prohibitions of the Fourteenth Amendment, Congress has full power to afford a remedy under that amendment and in accordance with it. (109 U.S. at 24-25)

The problem in the *Jones v. Mayer* case was that the law that Jones had charged Mayer with violating was too broad to be based on Congress' power to enforce the Fourteenth Amendment or its power to regulate interstate commerce. Unfortunately, there was no other law in force that would have prevented Mayer from discriminating against Jones.

Coincidentally, two months before the *Jones v. Mayer* decision, Congress had passed a law that would have given Jones a better basis for his complaint, but the law was not to take effect until the next year. That was the Civil Rights Act of 1968, better known as the "Fair Housing Act" or "Open Housing Law." Section 804 of this law, which is still in force, provides that it shall be unlawful:

> (a) To refuse to sell or rent after the making of a bona fide offer, or to refuse to negotiate for the sale or rental of, or otherwise make

available or deny, a dwelling to any person because of race, color, religion, or national origin.

(b) To discriminate against any person in the terms, conditions, or privileges of sale or rental of a dwelling, or in the provision of services or facilities in connection therewith, because of race, color, religion, or national origin.

(c) To make, print, publish, or cause to be made printed, or published any notice, statement, or advertisement, with respect to the sale or rental of a dwelling that indicates any preference, limitation, or discrimination based on race, color, religion, or national origin, or an intention to make any such preference, limitation or discrimination.

(d) To represent to any person because of race, color, religion, or national origin that any dwelling is not available for inspection, sale, or rental when such a dwelling is in fact so available.

(e) For profit, to induce or to attempt to induce any person to sell or rent any dwelling by representations regarding the entry or prospective entry into the neighborhood or a person or persons of a particular race, color, religion, or national origin.

Section 805(a), also still in force, provides:

> It shall be unlawful for any person or other entity whose business includes engaging in residential real estate-related transactions to discriminate against any person in making available such a transaction, or in the terms or conditions of such a transaction, because of race, color, religion, or national origin.

In 1974, Congress amended these sections to forbid discrimination because of a person's sex or familial status and in 1988 it passed the Americans with Disabilities Act, which amended these sections to forbid discrimination because of a person's physical or mental handicap.

Congress intended the Fair Housing Law to apply primarily to people who were in the business of selling or renting real estate or acting as agents of such people. It therefore provided in Section 803(b) that Sections 804(a), (b), (d) and (e) does not apply to resident-owners of single-family houses who are selling their houses themselves without the help of real estate agents. To the extent that the Fair Housing Law regulates only people in the business of selling or renting real estate or acting as agents, it appears to fall within Congress' power to regulate interstate commerce. These people invariably solicit customers in states other than the state where the property is located. Therefore, when they refuse to deal with a person because of his race, color, religion, sex, familial status, handicap or national origin, they are directly affecting the interstate commerce that Congress has the power to regulate.

On the other hand, Section 803(b) of the Fair Housing Law fails to exempt some non-resident home owners who are not doing business in interstate commerce, as well as all resident home owners who post notices under Section 804(c) that indicate a preference, limitation or discrimination based on race, color, religion, sex, familial status, handicap or national origin. In these and other clauses, Congress may have exceeded its powers under the interstate commerce clause. However, no one has seriously challenged the constitutionality of these clauses, mainly because of the Supreme Court's reluctance to rule that Congress has exceeded its powers under the interstate commerce clause. In the unlikely event the Court does invalidate one of these clauses, the main body of the Fair Housing Act would remain in force, as a continuing deterrent to the rampant housing discrimination that prevailed before the law was passed.

Martin Luther King played a major role in the passage of Fair Housing Act. Many of his non-violent rallies and marches were directed against racial discrimination in the sale and rental of housing. The most notable were his 1966 Chicago demonstrations, which resulted in a "Summit Agreement" in which the city leaders promised to increase its enforcement of existing anti-discrimination laws and regulations. However, they reneged on these promises. King meanwhile continued his campaign for a national fair housing law. A bill to enact such a law was introduced in Congress but it was delayed by prolonged debates in both houses in the spring of 1968.

During these debates, the nation was shocked by King's assassination on a motel balcony in Memphis, Tennessee on April 4,

1968. While people mourned and considered King's legacy, Congress received increased pressure to pass the fair housing bill. On April 11, 1968, the bill passed by a narrow margin. No one knows whether King's assassination was the sole work of James Earl Ray, who was convicted of the crime after pleading guilty but later denied his guilt, whether others were involved, or whether someone other than Ray committed the crime. We do know that both King and his assassin(s) played a key role in the passage of the Fair Housing Act--a law that has enabled many of the nation's minories to move into all-white neighborhoods.

E.7. Affirmative Action

Although minories were helped by the passage of the Civil Rights Acts of 1964 and 1968, by the repeal of prejudicial state laws and by the desegregation of many school districts, civil rights advocates argued that they needed more to gain an equal opportunity to participate in American society. Because of past discrimination, they did not have the proper education or training to compete with those who had not suffered discrimination. So the civil rights leaders asked national, state and local governments and private businesses and universities to give preferences to minorities to help them improve their education and obtain better jobs. Beginning in the late 1960s, many of these institutions responded with various kinds of "affirmative action" programs, which resulted in increased minority employment, job promotions and admissions to schools and universities.

Most Americans agreed that some of these programs were warranted, such as aggressive recruiting and remedial training for deserving minority people. However, some programs caused controversy because they set employment or admissions quotas for various minority groups. Non-minority people filed lawsuits, claiming the quotas were "reverse discrimination," which violated their constitutional right to equal protection of the laws, as well as various civil rights laws that forbade racial discrimination.

The U. S. Supreme Court first ruled on the merits of this reverse discrimination claim in *Regents of the University of California v. Bakke*, 438 U.S. 265 (1978). In that case, the medical school of the University of California at Davis operated two admissions programs for its entering class of one hundred students. Its general admissions program was open to everyone, but its special program was open only to "Blacks," "Chicanos," "Asians" and "American Indians" who it had determined were "economically and/or educationally disadvantaged" (Ibid., 274). Applicants who qualified for the special program competed only with each other for sixteen of the one hundred positions in the entering class. They were also not required to have a minimum 2.5 undergraduate grade point average, the requirement for other applicants.

Alan Bakke complained that the medical school's special admissions program resulted in his being denied admission to the school solely because he was white. Bakke had applied for admission to both the 1973 and 1974 entering classes. As the following table shows, his credentials were impressive, but in each year they proved to be insufficient to place him in one of the eighty-four seats allotted to the general admissions program:

Bakke's Scores Compared to the 1973 and 1974 Entering Classes

	Overall Grade Ave.	Science Grade Ave.	MCAT Exam Percentiles			
			Verbal	Math	Sci.	Gen. Inf.
Bakke	3.46	3.44	96	94	97	72
General Program Average, 1973	3.49	3.51	81	76	83	69
General Program Average, 1974	3.29	3.36	69	67	82	72
Special Program Average, 1973	2.88	2.62	46	24	35	33
Special Program Average, 1974	2.62	2.42	34	30	37	18

The major reason why Bakke was not admitted to the 1973 class was the late date of his application. By the time his application was received, the school had stopped accepting applicants who had not scored better than 470 of a possible 500 points on their interviews. Bakke's score was 468 points. After his application was rejected, Bakke wrote a letter to the admissions dean, Dr. George Lowry, in which he criticized the special admissions program and complained that, because of the program, he had been treated unfairly. In 1974, he had the misfortune of having Dr. Lowry conduct his interview and he received a relatively low interview score of 549 of a possible 600 points.

The Supreme Court ruled that the Davis medical school's special admissions program violated Title VI of the 1964 Civil Rights Act, because it excluded Allan Bakke on the sole ground that he was white. A majority of the justices also ruled that Title VI demanded that anyone receiving federal funds must refrain from employing the same racial classifications as the Fourteenth Amendment's equal protection clause demanded of a state or state agency.

In his opinion announcing the Court's decision, Justice Powell recognized that the Davis medical school could consider race in its admission decisions because it had a legitimate interest in admitting a diverse group of students to its entering class. That was because of its "countervailing constitutional interest" under the First Amendment, in selecting "those students who will contribute the most to the 'robust exchange of ideas'" (Ibid., 313). However, Powell said this was

> not an interest in simple ethnic diversity, in which a specified percentage of the student body is in effect guaranteed to be members of selected ethnic groups, with the remaining percentage an undifferentiated aggregation of students. The diversity that furthers a compelling state interest encompasses a far broader array of qualifications and characteristics of which racial or ethnic origin is but a single though important element. Petitioner's special admissions program, focused *solely* on ethnic diversity, would hinder rather than further attainment of genuine diversity. (Ibid., 315)

Justices Brennan, White, Marshall and Blackmun concurred in this ruling, but they said that a racial classification such as the one used by the Davis medical school could be justified if it were needed to overcome the effects of past discrimination by "society at large" (Ibid., 369). Justice Powell disagreed with that opinion because, he said, it would lead to a "two class theory," whereby certain ethnic groups would be given preferred treatment over others on account of past discrimination. He said that would be wrong because

> the white "majority" itself is composed of various minority groups, most of which can lay claim to a history of prior discrimination at the hands of the State and private individuals. Not all of these groups can receive preferential treatment and corresponding judicial tolerance of distinctions drawn in terms of race and nationality, for then the only "majority" left would be a new minority of white Anglo-Saxon Protestants. There is no principled basis for deciding which groups would merit "heightened judicial solicitude" and which would not. Courts would be asked to evaluate the extent of the prejudice and consequent harm suffered by various minority groups. Those whose societal injury is thought to exceed some arbitrary level of tolerability then would be entitled to preferential classifications at the expense of individuals belonging to other groups. Those classifications would be free from exacting judicial scrutiny. As these preferences began to have their desired effect, and the consequences of past discrimination were undone, new judicial rankings would be necessary. The kind of variable sociological and political analysis necessary to produce such rankings simply does not lie within the judicial competence--even if they otherwise were politically feasible or socially desirable.
>
> Moreover, there are serious problems of justice connected with the idea of preference itself. First, it may not be always clear that a so-called preference is in fact benign. Courts may be asked to validate burdens imposed upon individual members of a particular group in order to advance the group's general interest. See *United Jewish Organizations v. Carey,* 430 U.S., at 172-173 (BRENNAN, J., concurring in part). Nothing in the Constitution supports the notion that individuals may be asked to suffer otherwise impermissible burdens in order to enhance the societal standing of their ethnic groups. Second, preferential programs may only reinforce common stereotypes holding

that certain groups are unable to achieve success without special protection based on a factor having no relationship to individual worth. See *DeFunis v. Odegaard*, 416 U.S. 312, 343 (1974) (Douglas, J., dissenting). Third, there is a measure of inequity in forcing innocent persons in respondent's position to bear the burdens of redressing grievances not of their making.

By hitching the meaning of the Equal Protection Clause to these transitory considerations, we would be holding, as a constitutional principle, that judicial scrutiny of classifications touching on racial and ethnic background may vary with the ebb and flow of political forces. Disparate constitutional tolerance of such classifications well may serve to exacerbate racial and ethnic antagonisms rather than alleviate them. *United Jewish Organizations v. Carey, supra*, at 173-174 (BRENNAN, J., concurring in part). Also, the mutability of a constitutional principle, based upon shifting political and social judgments, undermines the chances for consistent application of the Constitution from one generation to the next, a critical feature of its coherent interpretation. *Pollock v. Farmers' Loan & Trust Co.*, 157 U.S. 429, 650-651 (1895) (White, J., dissenting). In expounding the Constitution, the Court's role is to discern "principles sufficiently absolute to give them roots throughout the community and continuity over significant periods of time, and to lift them above the level of pragmatic political judgments of a particular time and place." A. Cox, The Role of the Supreme Court in American Government 114 (1976). (Ibid., 295-299)

Although Justice Powell did not give an example of how a person might be burdened by a preference given to his own ethnic group, he might have used the example of a black person whose credentials, like Bakke's, were just below those required to gain admission to the Davis medical school under its general admissions program. This black person would not have qualified for the special admissions program unless he were "economically and/or educationally disadvantaged," yet he might well have gained admission to the general program had the special program not existed, because his credentials were borderline and the number of seats available to general applicants would have been increased from eighty four to one hundred.

Justice Stevens filed a concurring opinion saying that the question of whether race can ever be a factor in a school admissions policy was not an issue in this case. Joined by Chief Justice Burger and Justices Stewart and Rehnquist, Stevens said the only issue was whether the California Supreme Court had correctly ruled that the Davis medical school had violated Title VI of the 1964 Civil Rights Act. He pointed out that the medical school had conceded that it was operating with federal funds and that its special admissions program may have caused Bakke to be denied admission to the school on account of his race. The school's defense was that Bakke was a member of the majority race and therefore its discrimination carried "no racial stigma" (Ibid., 414). However, Stevens said the legislative history of Title VI of the 1964 Civil Rights Act showed that the intention of the law was to impose an absolute color-blindness test. The law, he said, could not be interpreted to exclude cases in which the discrimination is against the majority race and carries no racial stigma.

The Supreme Court therefore ruled unanimously that the racial quota embodied in the Davis medical school's special admissions program was illegal. However, the Court was deeply divided over the criteria to be applied in judging the validity of affirmative action programs and this division continued in later cases.

The division continued in *Fullilove v. Klutznick*, 448 U.S. 448 (1980), when the justices split four ways on the validity of a federal law that directed that at least 10 percent of the federal government's public works funds be used to procure services or supplies from "minority business enterprises," or "MBE's," defined as enterprises that were at least 50-percent owned by "citizens of the United States who are Negroes, Spanish-speaking, Orientals, Indians, Eskimos, and Aleuts." Prime contractors could obtain waivers of this requirement in respect of their subcontracts upon showing that no MBE's had submitted bids or that the bids of such enterprises were unreasonable (Ibid., 469-470).

Chief Justice Burger and Justices White and Powell said that Congress had the power to remedy the problem of minority businesses having impaired access to government contract work, under both the Constitution's commerce clause (Article I, Section 8[3]) and its enforcement power granted by Section 5 of the Fourteenth Amendment. Burger noted that the law was narrowly tailored to solve this problem and that administrative safeguards prevented minority business enterprises from exploiting the program by charging unreasonable prices. Powell distinguished this case from the *Bakke* case on the grounds that Congress had determined that government contractors had been discriminating against potential minority subcontractors and that the law was narrowly tailored to remedy this problem.

Justices Marshall, Brennan and Blackmun concurred that the law was valid, but they based their opinion on the ground that Congress had a broad power to remedy the effects of past discrimination by society at large.

Justices Stewart and Rehnquist dissented from the majority ruling, saying that the law was invalid because the equal protection clause demands that all laws be color-blind, without exception. Justice Stevens also dissented but said he disagreed with Stewart and Rehnquist because they implied there could never be a valid law classifying people according to race. Stevens said the law in this case was invalid because it was a "slapdash statute" that arbitrarily gave preferences to six racial groups. He asked,

> ... [W]hy are these six racial classifications, and no others, included in the preferred class? Why are aliens excluded from the preference although they are not otherwise ineligible for public contracts? What percentage of Oriental blood or Spanish-speaking skill is required for membership in the preferred class? How does the legacy of slavery and the history of discrimination against the descendants of its victims support a preference for Spanish-speaking citizens who may be directly competing with black citizens in some overpopulated communities? Why is a preference given only to owners of business enterprises and why is that preference unaccompanied by any requirement concerning the employment of disadvantaged persons? Is the preference limited to a subclass of persons who can prove that they are subject to a special disability caused by past discrimination, as the Court's opinion indicates? Or is every member of the racial class entitled to a

preference as the statutory language seems plainly to indicate? Are businesses formed just to take advantage of the preference eligible? (Ibid., 552, n. 30)

The Court also split several ways in *Wygant v. Jackson Board of Education*, 476 U.S. 267 (1986), and arrived at a judgment that seemed to conflict with its judgment in the *Fullilove* case. In *Wygant*, the Board of Education of Jackson, Michigan, entered into a labor agreement with its teachers' union that required that all teacher layoffs be imposed on those with the least seniority, "except," it said, "that at no time will there be a greater percentage of minority personnel laid off than the current percentage of minority personnel employed at the time of layoff." Under this agreement, some non-minority teachers were laid off even though they had greater seniority than some minority teachers who were not. These non-minority teachers sued in their local federal district court, claiming violations of their rights under the equal protection clause of the Fourteenth Amendment and Title VII of the 1964 Civil Rights Act. After the district court and the court of appeals ruled that the teachers' rights were not violated, they appealed to the U. S. Supreme Court.

The high court reversed the lower court rulings and ruled that the school board's layoff plan violated the equal protection clause of the Fourteenth Amendment, but the Court issued no majority opinion. Justice Powell delivered a plurality opinion in which Chief Justice Burger and Justice Rehnquist joined; Justice O'Connor joined in most respects. Powell said,

> This Court never has held that societal discrimination alone is sufficient to justify a racial discrimination. Rather, the Court has insisted upon some showing of prior discrimination by the government unit involved before allowing limited use of racial classifications in order to remedy such discrimination. (Ibid., 274)

The school board tried to justify its preference for minority teachers on the ground that they were needed to serve as role models for the minority students. Powell rejected that argument, primarily because it would have allowed the school to escape completely from the requirement that its racial preference have a remedial purpose. He also said that the role model argument had "no logical stopping point" and could therefore be used by school boards to escape the requirement that their preferences be used only to remedy past employment discrimination. Moreover, said Powell, the role model argument could be used to justify the employment of a very low percentage of black teachers, if a school district had a very low percentage of black students (Ibid., 275-276).

Justice White concurred in the Court's judgment but gave his own reasons. He said the school board's lay-off plan violated the equal protection clause because it amounted to a discharge of white teachers to make room for black teachers, none of whom had been shown to be a victim of racial discrimination.

Justices Marshall, joined by Justices Brennan and Blackmun, dissented from Powell's opinion because, he said, the preference for minority teachers could be justified as a measure to remedy the effects of the turbulent history of attempts to integrate the Jackson public schools. He pointed out that the majority of the justices had ignored this history in their opinions. Justice Stevens also dissented, but on the ground that the school board could have reasonably decided that a diverse ethnic teaching staff would teach the students an important lesson, namely that a person of any ethnic background can do a good job and serve as role model for others. He also pointed out that the teachers themselves attested to the fairness of the lay-off policy when they voted to ratify the agreement signed by their union leaders.

The conflicting signals sent by the Supreme Court in the *Fullilove* and *Wygant* cases were resolved to some extent by its decision in *City of Richmond v. J. A. Croson Co.*, 488 U.S. 469 (1989), in which it invalidated a "Minority Business Utilization Plan" adopted by the city of Richmond, Virginia. This plan required the city's construction contractors to subcontract at least 30 percent of the dollar amount of their contracts to one or more businesses who qualified as "minority business enterprises," or "MBE's," defined as enterprises that were at least 51 percent owned by "[c]itizens of the United States who are Blacks, Spanish-speaking, Orientals, Indians, Eskimos, or Aleuts." The case arose when the City of Richmond failed to award a contract to the J. A. Croson Company to install plumbing fixtures in the city jail, even though Croson had been the sole bidder at the time the sealed bids were opened. The city claimed that Croson had failed to comply with its Minority Business Utilization Plan. Croson, on the other hand, claimed that it had been denied a waiver from the plan unfairly. The only subcontract bid that the city had received from an MBE came twenty-one days after Croson's prime contract bid was due and the MBE's price for fixtures was 7 percent above the current market price, resulting in an increased cost of $7,663.16. Croson had asked that the city give it either a waiver from the Plan so that it to use a different subcontractor or an increased contract price to cover its increased cost of awarding the subcontract to the MBE. The city denied both requests.

Croson therefore sued the City of Richmond, claiming that its Minority Business Utilization Plan violated its right to equal protection of the laws under the Fourteenth Amendment. It argued that, according to the Supreme Court's decision in the *Wygant* case, the city must limit any race-based remedial programs to correcting the effects of its own prior discrimination. Croson claimed there was no evidence of prior discrimination by the city. The city defended its plan on the ground that it was patterned after the federal government's plan approved in the *Fullilove* case. Under the law of that case, the city said, it had the power to remedy the effects of all prior discrimination in its local construction industry. The Supreme Court ruled that the *Wygant* decision was controlling and that the Richmond plan therefore violated the Fourteenth Amendment's equal protection clause.

The Court's ruling against the Richmond plan, which was very similar to the federal government plan upheld in the *Fullilove* case, can be explained in part by the three new justices who had joined the Court in the meantime. President Reagan had promoted Justice Rehnquist to the position of chief justice and had appointed Justices O'Connor, Kennedy and Scalia to replace the retiring Chief Justice

Burger and Justices Stewart and Powell. Burger and Powell had been on the side of the five-justice majority in the *Fullilove* case. O'Connor, Kennedy and Scalia joined White, Rehnquist and Stevens and to form the six-justice majority that invalidated the Richmond plan in the *Croson* case.

Speaking for these justices, O'Connor said the Richmond plan suffered from the same two defects found to be fatal in the *Wygant* teacher lay-off plan: it relied on the general belief that there had been past discrimination in an entire industry, which "provides no guidance for a legislative body to determine the precise scope of the injury it seeks to remedy," and because it had "no logical stopping point" (quoting *Wygant* at 275) it could therefore be used "until the percentage of public contracts awarded to MBE's in Richmond mirrored the percentage of minorities in the population as a whole" (Ibid., 498). She also said,

> While there is no doubt that the sorry history of both private and public discrimination in this country has contributed to the lack of opportunities for black entrepreneurs, this observation, standing alone, cannot justify a rigid racial quota in the awarding of public contracts in Richmond, Virginia. Like the claim that discrimination in primary and secondary schooling justifies a rigid racial preference in medical school admissions, an amorphous claim that there has been past discrimination in a particular industry cannot justify the use of an unyielding racial quota.
>
> It is sheer speculation how many minority firms there would be in Richmond absent past societal discrimination, just as it was sheer speculation how many minority medical students would have been admitted to the medical school at Davis absent past discrimination in educational opportunities. Defining these sorts of injuries as "identified discrimination" would give local governments license to create a patchwork of racial preferences based on statistical generalizations about any particular field of endeavor. (Ibid., 499)

Speaking for only herself, Chief Justice Rehnquist and Justice White, Justice O'Connor distinguished the Richmond plan from the plan adopted by Congress in the *Fullilove* case on the ground that Congress had been granted special powers by Section 5 of the

Fourteenth Amendment to enact laws to secure the guarantees of the Amendment's Section 1. She also pointed out that in the *Fullilove* case, the assumptions made by Congress could be rebutted by a contractor seeking a waiver if he could show that there were no minority businesses bidding who were not trying to exploit the program by charging unreasonable prices (Ibid., 488-489).

Justice Stevens filed a concurring opinion in which he criticized the Richmond Plan for substantially the same reasons as he criticized the Congressional plan in his *Fullilove* dissent.

In another concurring opinion, Justice Kennedy criticized the portion of Justice O'Connor's opinion that said that federal and state laws were subject to different standards of equal protection: "[t]he Fourteenth Amendment ought not to be interpreted to reduce a State's authority [to eradicate racial discrimination and its effects], unless, of course, there is a conflict with federal law or a state remedy is itself a violation of equal protection. The latter is the case presented here" (Ibid., 518). He said the Richmond Plan violated the equal protection clause because the city council failed to evaluate "[t]he nature and scope of the injury that existed; its historical or antecedent causes; the extent to which the city contributed to it, either by intentional acts or by passive complicity in acts of discrimination by the private sector; the necessity for the response adopted, its duration in relation to the wrong, and the precision with which it otherwise bore on whatever injury in fact was addressed" (Ibid., 519).

Justice Scalia also wrote a concurring opinion, in which he endorsed O'Connor's view that state and local governments do not have the same powers as Congress to remedy the effects of past discrimination. He said state and local governments may not discriminate on the basis of race except to eliminate their own systems of unlawful classification.

Justices Marshall, Brennan and Blackmun dissented, saying the city of Richmond had the same power to remedy the effects of past discrimination as Congress had in the *Wygant* case. Marshall said that O'Connor's majority opinion amounted to a ruling that Section

5 of the Fourteenth Amendment pre-empts the states from addressing the problems created by past private discrimination.

In *Metro Broadcasting, Inc. v. F.C.C.*, 497 U.S. 547 (1990), a five-to-four majority of the Supreme Court confirmed that the federal government has special powers not possessed by state and local governments to remedy the effects of past discrimination. The Federal Communications Commission (the "FCC") determined that only 2 percent of the eleven thousand radio and television stations in the United States were owned by people of "minority" groups, defined as "Black, Hispanic Surnamed, American Eskimo, Aleut, American Indian and Asiatic American extraction," even though these groups constituted over 20 percent of the population. Congress and the FCC determined that this situation was a detriment to both minority and non-minority audiences (H. R. Conf. Rep. No. 97-765). Minority audiences suffered because of a lack of stations that served their interests, and non-minority audiences suffered from a lack of exposure to the interests and views of minority groups. The FCC therefore announced that, in the future, when it reviewed mutually exclusive applications for new radio and television stations, it would consider an applicant's minority ownership and management participation as a "plus" factor. It also announced that when a broadcast licensee's qualifications to continue to hold its license were under review, it would make an exception to its policy of refusing to approve an assignment of the license to another party before its review was completed; namely, it would consider approving such an assignment if the assignee were more than 50 percent owned by members of minority groups and the price did not exceed 75 percent of the fair market value of the license.

The *Metro* case was a consolidation of two cases in which these FCC policy changes were challenged on the ground they violated the equal protection rights of applicants for broadcast licenses. In one case, the FCC awarded an Orlando, Florida, television license to Rainbow Broadcasting on the ground that its minority ownership credit outweighed the local residence and civic participation advantage of a competitive applicant, Metro Broadcasting. In the other case, Faith Center had applied to renew its Hartford, Connecticut, television license and Shurberg Broadcasting had applied for a mutually exclusive license. Before the hearing to determine which application should be granted, the FCC approved Faith Center's assignment of its license to Astroline Communications, a minority-owned business.

Justice Brennan wrote the Court's opinion, in which Justices White, Marshall, Blackmun and Stevens joined. He said the FCC's racial preferences did not violate the equal protection clause because they were subject only to only an intermediate standard of scrutiny, not the strict standard applicable to state and local governments. He based that conclusion on Chief Justice Burger's opinion in *Fullilove v. Klutznick*, supra, in which Burger had relied on Congress' special enforcement powers under Section 5 of the Fourteenth Amendment to uphold a federal law designed to remedy discrimination against minority applicants for government subcontracts.

Applying an intermediate standard of scrutiny, which he said the Court had applied in the *Fullilove* case, Brennan said that the federal government had a legitimate interest in increasing the diversity of broadcast programming. He also said Congress and the FCC were qualified to determine that this interest could be served best by licensing policies that gave preferences to minority-owned applicants.

Chief Justice Rehnquist and Justices O'Connor, Scalia and Kennedy dissented. Speaking for all of them, O'Connor said that the federal government's racial preferences should be subject to the same strict scrutiny that was applicable to state government preferences. Applying this strict scrutiny, she said that the government's purpose of promoting broadcast diversity was not compelling because it was too amorphous and too indefinite. It was too amorphous, she said, because there was no way of defining or measuring the diversity of broadcast viewpoints, and it was too indefinite because it would lead to an indefinite use of racial classifications that would, in effect, discriminate against groups "found to contribute to an insufficiently diverse broadcasting spectrum" (Ibid., 614). O'Connor also criticized the FCC's racial preferences because they were not narrowly tailored to achieve the purpose of broadcast diversity and they ignored the more direct means of achieving this diversity, such as regulating the programming of all stations.

Justice O'Connor's statement that the federal government should be bound by the same strict scrutiny as state governments was an apparent contradiction to her Court opinion in the *Croson* case. She had distinguished that case from the *Fullilove* case on the ground that the city of Richmond's power to enforce minority subcontracting rules was not the same as the power that Congress had under Section 5 of the Fourteenth Amendment to enforce similar rules. O'Connor explained in her *Metro* dissent that three of the six justices who had upheld the minority subcontracting rules in *Fullilove* had applied "a most searching examination" but had concluded that "Congress had identified discrimination that had particularly affected the construction industry and had carefully constructed corresponding remedial measures" (Ibid., 607-608). She might have also pointed out that Congress had exercised its Section 5 powers in the *Fullilove* case only to remedy the problem of racial discrimination in the awarding of federal construction contracts, which was a direct violation of the Fourteenth Amendment's equal protection clause. In the *Metro* case, however, the Court applied Section 5 to justify FCC rules that had no remedial purpose but were designed instead to achieve the society-wide goal of greater diversity in television and radio programming. The Court thus overlooked the fact that Congress' enforcement powers under Section 5 of the Fourteenth Amendment were limited to imposing remedies for violations of that amendment. There was no evidence of such a violation in the *Metro* case. There was thus no basis for the Court's ruling that the FCC rules were subject only to an intermediate standard of scrutiny.

Five years later, Justice O'Connor was able to use her dissenting arguments in the *Metro* case to support her majority opinion in *Adarand Constructors v. Peña*, 115 S.Ct. 2097 (1995). O'Connor's job was made easier by the retirements of Justices

Blackmun, Brennan, Marshall and White, all of whom had disagreed with her in the *Metro* case. President Bush had appointed Justices Thomas and Souter to replace Marshall and Brennan and President Clinton had appointed Justices Ginsburg and Breyer to replace Blackmun and White. Of these new justices, only Thomas agreed with O'Connor, but that was enough for Court to repudiate the erroneous portions of its opinion in the *Metro* case.

The *Adarand* case involved a federal law that required most federal agency contracts to contain a clause giving the prime contractor additional payments if it hired subcontractors certified as small businesses controlled by socially and economically disadvantaged people. This clause required the contractor to presume that people were socially or economically disadvantaged if they were "Black Americans, Hispanic Americans, Native Americans, Asian Pacific Americans, and other minorities, or [if they were] any other individual[s] found to be disadvantaged by the [Small Business] Administration pursuant to section 8(a) of the Small Business Act" (Ibid., 2102, citing 15 U.S.C., secs. 637[d][2], [3]). Adarand was the low bidder on a subcontract for the guardrail portion of a Colorado highway construction project. However, the contractor awarded the subcontract to the minority-owned Gonzales Construction Company, in order to qualify for an additional payment under the Small Business Act. Adarand sued the federal government in the local federal district court, claiming that the race-based presumptions under the Small Business Act caused it to lose the subcontract and violated its right of equal protection of the laws. The district court granted the government's motion for summary judgment and the Tenth Circuit Court of Appeals in Denver affirmed, saying that federal racial preferences were subject to only a "lenient standard" of scrutiny under the *Fullilove* and *Metro* cases (Ibid., 2104, citing 16 F.3d at 1544, 1547).

The U. S. Supreme Court reversed the Court of Appeals. Chief Justice Rehnquist and Justices O'Connor, Scalia, Kennedy and Thomas ruled that the same high standard was applicable to all government racial preferences, including those of the federal government. Justices Stevens, Souter, Ginsberg and Breyer opposed that ruling.

Speaking for the Court's five-justice majority, Justice O'Connor distinguished this case from the *Fullilove* decision because a majority of the Court had not applied a lenient standard of scrutiny in that decision. She also attacked the *Metro* decision for being out of step with the Court's previous affirmative action decisions, saying those decisions had established three principles that the Court had undermined in *Metro*. Those principles were skepticism (any racial or ethnic preference is inherently suspect and must receive a most searching examination), consistency (the standard of review under the equal protection clause is not dependent on the race of those burdened or benefited by a particular classification) and congruence (equal protection analysis in respect of the federal government under the Fifth Amendment is the same as the analysis in respect of the states under the Fourteenth Amendment). Accordingly, the Supreme Court vacated the court of appeals' judgment and remanded the case for further proceedings in accordance with O'Connor's opinion.

Justice Scalia concurred with O'Connor in most respects, but he was more emphatic on the subject of consistency, saying,

> Individuals who have been wronged by unlawful racial discrimination should be made whole; but under the Constitution there can be no such thing as a creditor or a debtor race. That concept is alien to the Constitution's focus upon the individual, ... (Ibid., 2118)

In his dissenting opinion, Justice Stevens implied there could in fact be a creditor and a debtor race under the Constitution:

> There is no moral or constitutional equivalence between a policy that is designed to perpetuate a caste system and one that seeks to eradicate racial subordination. Invidious discrimination is an engine of oppression, subjugating a disfavored group to enhance or maintain the power of the majority. Remedial race-based preferences reflect the opposite impulse: a desire to foster equality in society. (Ibid., 2120)

Justice Thomas answered Stevens' argument in his concurring opinion, saying

> [t]hat these programs may have been motivated in part by good intentions cannot provide refuge from the principle that under our Constitution, the government may not make distinctions on the basis of race. As far as the Constitution is concerned, it is irrelevant whether a government's racial classifications are drawn by those who wish to oppress a race or by those who have a sincere desire to help those thought to be disadvantaged....
>
> These programs stamp minorities with a badge of inferiority and may cause them to develop dependencies or to adopt an attitude that they are "entitled" to preferences. Indeed, Justice Stevens once recognized the real harms stemming from seemingly "benign" discrimination. See *Fullilove v. Klutznick*, 448 U.S. 448, 545, 100 S.Ct. 2758, 2809, 65 L.Ed. 902 (1980) (STEVENS, J., dissenting) (noting that "remedial" race legislation is perceived by many as resting on an assumption that those who are granted this special preference are less qualified in some respect that is identified purely by their race").
>
> In my mind, government-sponsored racial discrimination based on benign prejudice is just as noxious as discrimination inspired by malicious prejudice. In each instance, it is racial discrimination, plain and simple. (Ibid., 2119)

In spite of the disagreement among the justices concerning the standard of scrutiny to be applied to government racial preferences, most of them agreed that limited preferences might be valid in some situations. Justice O'Connor said in her majority opinion,

> The unhappy persistence of both the practice and the lingering effects or racial discrimination against minority groups in this country is an unfortunate reality, and government is not disqualified in acting in response to it. As recently as 1987, for example, every Justice of this Court agreed that the Alabama Department of Public Safety's "pervasive, systematic, and obstinate discriminatory conduct" justified a narrowly tailored race-based remedy. See *United States v. Paradise*, 480 U.S., at 167, [190, 196].... (Ibid., 2117)

Justice Souter said in his dissenting opinion that the remand trial of this case should be decided upon "facts about the current effects of past discrimination, the necessity for a preferential remedy, and the suitability of this particular preferential scheme" (Ibid., 2132). Justice Stevens said in his dissenting opinion that diversity could be another justification for a racial classification:

> [t]he majority today overrules *Metro Broadcasting* only insofar as it is "inconsistent with [the] holding" that strict scrutiny applies to "benign" racial classifications promulgated by the federal government. *Ante*, at 2113. The proposition that fostering diversity may provide a sufficient interest to justify such a program is *not* inconsistent with the Court's holding today---indeed, the question is not remotely presented in this case---and I do not take the Court's opinion to diminish that aspect of our decision in *Metro Broadcasting*. (Ibid., 2127-2128)

Diversity and the desire to remedy past discrimination were the main issues in *Hopwood v. Texas*, 78 F. 3rd 932, a case decided by the Fifth Circuit Court of Appeals in New Orleans in 1996. Like the *Bakke* case, supra, this case involved a graduate school admissions program at a state university that gave preferences to people of certain minority backgrounds. The school was the law school at the University of Texas, the same school that had denied admission to a black applicant almost fifty years before and had provoked the Supreme Court to rule in *Sweatt v. Painter*, supra, that a school's reputation must be considered in the "separate but equal" analysis prescribed by the *Plessy v. Ferguson* case, supra. Perhaps that ruling, which came four years before the Court's famous *Brown v. Board of Education* ruling, was the real downfall of the *Plessy* analysis and the real birth of the black civil rights movement. Now the University of Texas Law School was trying to rectify its past mistakes by an admissions program designed to increase its black and Mexican American enrollment.

The Texas law school's high reputation, which had played such an important role in the *Sweatt* decision, had not diminished. In 1995, the *U. S. News and World Report* ranked it seventeenth among the nation's leading law schools.[82] It received over four thousand applications per year, of which nine hundred were accepted. These applications were divided into three groups according to index scores that were composites of the applicants' undergraduate grade averages and Law School Aptitude Test scores. The top group was called the "presumptive-admit" group, the bottom group was the "presumptive-deny" group and those in the middle group were in the "discretionary zone." The applicants in the presumptive-admit group received little review and most were sent offers of admission. The applicants in the presumptive-deny group also received little review and most were sent letters of rejection. Only the applicants in the discretionary zone received an extensive review.

One of the law school's goals was to achieve an entering class enrollment of 10 percent Mexican-Americans and 5 percent blacks, percentages comparable to the percentages of these people graduating from Texas colleges. To reach that goal, the school treated applications from blacks and Mexican-Americans differently from those of other people. In 1992, it placed all black and Mexican-American applicants who had an index score of 189 in the presumptive-admit group, while other applicants needed an index score of 199 for placement in this group. If the other applicants had an index score of 192 or lower, they were placed in the presumptive-deny group, but Black and Mexican-American applicants were placed in that group only if they had index scores of 179 or below. Black and Mexican American applicants in the discretionary zone were reviewed by a subcommittee that was separate from the subcommittees reviewing the other discretionary-zone applicants. The waiting list for marginal black and Mexican-American applicants was also kept separate from the waiting list for the other marginal applicants. Because of this different treatment, all black applicants and 90 percent of the Mexican-American applicants who resided in Texas and had index scores between 189 and 192 received offers of admission, but only 6 percent of the white applicants in that category received offers.

The law school argued that its admissions program favoring black and Mexican-American applicants was justified; the school needed to remedy the effects of past discrimination practiced by the Texas secondary schools, the University of Texas and the law school itself. Speaking for a unanimous three-judge panel of Fifth Circuit Court of Appeals in New Orleans, Judge Jerry Smith said the past discrimination by the law school, illustrated by the *Sweatt v. Painter* case, did not justify its current racial preferences because that discrimination had ended by the 1960s and the school had since then operated an extensive minority recruitment program, which now included a significant amount of scholarship money (Ibid., 953). Smith said the discrimination practiced by the University of Texas and the Texas secondary schools could not be attributed to the law school and was therefore no more relevant than the societal discrimination that the Supreme Court had consistently rejected as a basis for racial classifications.

The most controversial part of Judge Smith's opinion was his answer to the law school's argument that its goal of a more diverse student body justified its classification applicants according to race. He said,

> We agree with the plaintiffs that *any consideration of race or ethnicity by the law school* [emphasis added] for the purpose of achieving a diverse student body is not a compelling interest under the Fourteenth Amendment. (Ibid., 944)

He reached that conclusion because, he said, the Supreme Court's *Metro Broadcasting* decision had been overruled by the *Adarand* decision. The *Metro Broadcasting* case had been the only case in which the Court had ruled that the need for diversity could justify the government's use of race as a factor in judging competing applicants. However, the Court had applied only an intermediate standard of scrutiny in that case, a standard that had been repudiated by the Court in the *Adarand* decision. Judge Smith therefore concluded that the need for diversity could never satisfy the strict standard of scrutiny that the Court ruled in *Adarand* applied to all government racial preferences.

Judge Smith also discounted Justice Powell's statement in the *Bakke* case that a diverse student body might justify a school's use of race as a factor in making admissions decisions. He pointed out that although Powell announced the Court's judgment in the *Bakke* case, no other justices joined in the portion of his opinion in which he made that statement. However, instead of discrediting Powell's opinion and announcing that a diverse student body could never justify the use of race as a factor in judging admissions, Judge Smith might have used Justice Powell's opinion to show why the Texas law school's use of race was as flawed as the use of race by the Davis medical school in *Bakke*. Powell said that a school's compelling interest in having a diverse student body was "not an interest in simple ethnic diversity," but encompassed "a far broader array of qualifications and characteristics of which racial or ethnic origin is but a single though important element." Therefore, he said, a "special admissions program, focused *solely* on ethnic diversity, would hinder rather than further attainment of genuine diversity" (438 U.S. at 315). Like the Davis medical school, the Texas law school had a special admissions program that applied separate standards to black and Mexican American applicants. The program was therefore focused solely on ethnic diversity.

In its petition to have the U. S. Supreme Court review the Fifth Circuit Court's decision, the state of Texas apparently recognized that its law school's admissions policy could not be justified, even as a measure to increase the diversity of the student body. The state admitted this policy "was constitutionally flawed" and that it "has long since been discontinued and will not be reinstated." The state was therefore not challenging the appellate court's judgment but rather its opinion that any consideration of race for the purpose of achieving a diverse student body is not a compelling interest under the Fourteenth Amendment. The Supreme Court denied the Texas petition because, as Justice Souter explained in a special opinion, the Court "reviews judgments, not opinions" (*Texas v. Hopwood*, cert. den., 116 S.Ct. 2580, 2581-2582 [1996]).

Many government-supported colleges and universities are concerned that the Supreme Court might rule in the future that they cannot consider an applicant's race or ethnic background in making their admissions decisions. The Fifth Circuit Court's opinion in the

Hopwood case justifies that concern. However, if a college or university were to use the same review procedure for all applications and consider race as only one of many subjective factors in rating applicants, that procedure ought to withstand even the closest equal protection scrutiny. That is because the only racial preferences found to violate the equal protection clause have been those given to an entire race or group of races. The judges carefully scrutinize these racial preferences because they are contrary to the Constitution's focus on individual rights, as opposed to group rights (e.g., Justice Scalia's opinion in the *Adarand* case, 115 S.Ct. at 2118). Therefore, instead of placing admissions applications in racial groups, government-supported schools should consider judging each applicant individually and according to a "broader array of qualifications and characteristics of which racial or ethnic origin is but a single though important element" (Justice Powell in *Bakke*, 438 U.S. at 315). If they do that, they might well be able to satisfy their legitimate desire for student diversity, free of any restraint imposed by the courts.

The same rationale may not apply to a school's decisions in respect of hiring and discharging faculty members or other employees. That is because these decisions are governed by Title VII of the 1964 Civil Rights Act, which forbids employers to discriminate against a person in the course of such decisions because of his race, color, religion, sex, or nationality. In *Taxman v. Board of Education of the Township of Piscataway*, 91 F.3rd 1547 (1996), the Third Circuit Court of Appeals in Philadelphia ruled that a New Jersey school board had violated Title VII when it laid off Sharon Taxman, a white teacher, and said that it was forced to choose between her and an equally qualified black teacher. The board said it laid off Taxman because she was white and because the black teacher was needed in order to maintain a diverse faculty. However, the court of appeals said the legislative history of Title VII showed that Congress intended that an employer be able to justify its discrimination only by showing that it was needed to remedy the effects of the employer's previous discrimination (Ibid., 1559). Therefore, under Title VII, the school board could not justify its dismissal of a white teacher because of her race because it was trying to maintain a diverse faculty. This case was scheduled to be reviewed by the U. S. Supreme Court in 1998, but the parties settled the case in December 1997. Most observers believe the Supreme Court would not have reversed the court of appeals' decision, even had it decided that the interest of a diverse faculty was a defense under Title VII, because the school board had admitted that it laid off the white teacher solely because of her race. Apparently, that was why the parties settled the case.

The courts have struck down other affirmative action programs because they violated various civil rights laws forbidding racial discrimination. However, these cases are not within the general scope of this book because they do not relate to violations of people's rights under the U. S. Constitution.

E.8. The California Civil Rights Initiative (Proposition 209)

On November 5, 1996, the people of California voted to amend their state constitution to provide that

> [t]he state shall not discriminate against, or grant preferential treatment to, any individual or group on the basis of race, sex, color, ethnicity, or national origin in the operation of public employment, public education, or public contracting.

The proponents of this amendment, known as the "California Civil Rights Initiative" or "Proposition 209," had argued in a pamphlet that

> [a] generation ago, we did it right. We passed civil rights laws to prohibit discrimination. But special interests hijacked the civil rights movement. Instead of equality, governments imposed quotas, preferences, and set-asides.
> And two wrongs don't make it right! Today, students are being rejected from public universities because of their RACE. Job applicants are turned away because their RACE does not meet some "goal"

or "timetable." Contracts are awarded to high bidders because they are of the preferred RACE.

That's just plain wrong and unjust. Government should not discriminate. It must not give a job, a university admission, or a contract based on race or sex. Government must judge all people equally, without discrimination! (Quoted in Ibid., 696-697)

The opponents of Proposition 209 had countered,

California law allows tutoring, mentoring, outreach, recruitment, and counseling to help ensure equal opportunity for women and minorities. Proposition 209 will eliminate affirmative action programs like these that help achieve equal opportunity for women and minorities in public employment, education and contracting. Instead of reforming affirmative action to make it fair for everyone, Proposition 209 makes the current problem worse. (Quoted in Ibid., 697)

An answer to the latter argument was that Proposition 209 would not affect government tutoring, mentoring, outreach, recruitment or counseling programs made available to people based on their educational or economic need rather than their race or sex.

Nearly nine million Californians voted on Proposition 209. Fifty-four percent were in favor and forty-six percent were opposed. The day after the voters approved the amendment, a number of civil rights groups challenged its validity in a complaint filed in the federal District Court for the Northern District of California.

On December 23, 1996, the district judge granted a preliminary injunction forbidding the state to enforce the amendment. He ruled that it imposed an unequal "political structure" that denied women and minorities a right to seek preferential treatment from the lowest level of government, thereby violating the Fourteenth Amendment's equal protection clause. The judge cited two prior U. S. Supreme Court cases in which voters had passed initiatives taking away the power of their local government to remedy earlier racial discrimination. In *Hunter v. Erickson*, 393 U.S. 385 (1969), the Court had invalidated an Akron, Ohio, voter initiative that took away the city council's power to control racial discrimination in the sale or rental of housing without the approval of the Akron voters. In *Washington v. Seattle School District No. 1*, 458 U.S. 457 (1982), the Court had invalidated an initiative passed by the people of the state of Washington barring local school boards from busing students to distant schools for the purpose of desegregation. In both of those cases, the Supreme Court had ruled that the voter initiative had arbitrarily made it more difficult for their government to deal with a racial discrimination problem. The Court had said the initiatives had violated the equal protection rights of people suffering from such discrimination, because they had been denied the same access to a government remedy of their problem that their fellow citizens possessed in respect of their problems. The district judge in this case ruled that the same reasoning applied to the California Civil Rights Initiative and that it therefore violated the Fourteenth Amendment's equal protection clause.

However, on April 8, 1997, in *Coalition for Economic Equity v. Pete Wilson, Governor of California*, 122 F.3rd 692, the Ninth Circuit Court of Appeals in San Francisco reversed the district judge and ruled that the initiative was valid. Speaking for the court's unanimous three-judge panel, Judge Diarmuid O'Scannlain said the California initiative was different from the Akron city and Washington state initiatives because it did not change the rules of access to a government remedy for discrimination. Instead, it forbade all instruments of government in the state from discriminating against or granting preferential treatment to anyone on the basis of race or gender. He explained,

> It is one thing to say that individuals have equal protection rights against political obstructions to equal treatment; it is quite another to say that individuals have equal protection rights against political obstructions to preferential treatment. While the Constitution protects against obstructions to equal treatment, it erects obstructions to preferential treatment by its own terms. (Ibid., 708)

O'Scannlain therefore concluded that California was free to adopt an equal protection standard more strict than the federal standard under the U. S. Constitution. He said, "That the Constitution *permits* the rare race-based or gender-based preference hardly implies that the state cannot ban them altogether" (Ibid.).

Judge O'Scannlain's conclusion has a ring of logic, if one assumes that strictness in respect of equal protection standards is the same as strictness in respect of the standards applied to life, liberty and property rights. A state may bind itself to stricter standards of religious freedom, free speech and press and other rights of life, liberty and property than the standards imposed by the Fourteenth Amendment. That is because there is no conflict with the U. S. Constitution when a state draws an even tighter fence around its powers than the one erected by the Constitution's life, liberty and property guarantee. However, the same is not true of the standard established by the equal protection clause of the Fourteenth Amendment. There can be only one correct standard for determining whether the rights of two people are equal to one another. A standard that is strict in comparison to this correct standard necessarily tilts the scale in favor of one person, while a more liberal standard necessarily tilts the scale in favor of the other person. Both the strict standard and the liberal standard therefore conflict with the correct standard. For example, the Supreme Court has said the equal protection clause of the Fourteenth Amendment allows a state agency the power to remedy the effects of its own past discrimination [*Wygant v. Jackson*, 476 U.S. at 274, citing *Hazelwood School District v. United States*, 433 U.S. 299 (1977)]. Therefore, any state law, initiative or constitutional amendment that attempts to change that standard must be ruled invalid.

The U. S. Supreme Court denied a petition to review the Ninth Circuit Court's ruling upholding the validity of Proposition 209 [118 S.Ct. 397 (1997)]. However, it remains to be seen what meaning the California courts will give to this new law. The main question is whether there will be any difference between the California standard of equal protection and the standard set by the U. S. Supreme Court for the equal protection clause of the Fourteenth Amendment. According to their literature, the people who campaigned for Proposition 209 had views on equal protection that did not conflict with the current rulings of the U. S. Supreme Court. Therefore, Proposition 209 may simply give the California courts an additional tool for enforcing the federal standard of equal protection.

For twenty years, the Supreme Court justices have grappled among themselves to define that federal standard in respect of affirmative action programs. The following principles are now clear:

(1) The U. S. Constitution binds the state and federal governments to the same strict standard of equal protection, and this standard applies equally with respect to all burdens and all preferences to all races (*Adarand Constructors v. Peña*, supra).

(2) No government agency may impose a racial quota, goal or set-aside in the course of making an employment, admission, licensing or contract decision, except as part of a program narrowly tailored to remedy the effects of its own past discrimination (*Wygant v. Jackson*, supra).

(3) No government agency may divide people into racial groups and impose different standards on those groups except as part of a program narrowly tailored to remedy the effects of its own past discrimination (*Regents v. Bakke*, supra).

(4) In the course of making some decisions, a government agency may consider race as a positive factor in the interest of promoting student body diversity, broadcast diversity and perhaps other kinds of diversity (Powell's opinion in *Regents v. Bakke*, supra; *Metro v. F.C.C.*, supra).

E.9. The Equal Rights of Women

The proclamation in the Declaration of Independence that "all men are created equal" raised questions about the status not only of black people but of women as well. In July 1848, a convention at

Seneca Falls, New York adopted a declaration of women's rights that was patterned after the Declaration of Independence (App. P). It began with the same "self-evident" truths as the Declaration of Independence, but said "that all men and women are created equal." It also asserted that

> the history of mankind is a history of repeated injuries and usurpations on the part of man toward woman, having in direct object the establishment of absolute tyranny over her.

The women's declaration then listed a number of injuries by man toward woman. It said that men had denied women their right to vote, monopolized nearly all profitable employments, denied them admission to colleges and excluded them from church ministries. Men had also injured women by passing laws that allowed husbands to deprive their wives of their liberty and property, including their wages, and to "administer chastisement" to them. The declaration also pointed out that "moral delinquencies which exclude women from society, are not only tolerated, but deemed of little account in man."

For the next seventy years, the focus of the women's rights movement was on the right to vote, which was finally secured by the Nineteenth Amendment to the Constitution in 1920. The leaders of this movement included Elizabeth Cady Stanton, Susan B. Anthony and Matilda Joslyn Gage, who together edited the *History of Woman Suffrage*, published in two volumes in 1881 and expanded to a six-volume edition in 1985.[83]

Before the 1970s, women made only minor progress in securing other rights. In 1853, Massachusetts passed a law that enabled a married woman to execute a will without the consent of her husband. New York passed a law in 1860 that gave a married woman the right to own property separately from her husband and to sell her property without his consent.[84] Other rights appeared to be secured by the Fourteenth Amendment's equal protection clause, which was adopted in 1868. However, Congress and the state legislatures continued to pass many laws that discriminated against women. Until 1971, the U. S. Supreme Court consistently ruled that these laws were valid.

Many states discriminated against women through laws and court decisions that deprived married women of their ability to enter into binding contracts, thereby treating them as children. Illinois had such a law and the Illinois Supreme Court ruled that a married woman was therefore not eligible to practice law. The judges based their decision on the fact that she could not have a legally binding relationship with a client. In *Bradwell v. State of Illinois*, 83 U.S. (16 Wallace) 130 (Dec. term, 1873), the U. S. Supreme Court ruled that the state of Illinois did not violate the Fourteenth Amendment by depriving women of their right to practice law, because that right was not one of "privileges and immunities" belonging to citizens of the United States. Speaking for Court's majority, Justice Miller cited the *Slaughter-House Cases*, supra, in which he had recently explained his limited interpretation of "privileges and immunities." Justices Bradley, Field and Noah Swayne had filed vigorous dissents to Miller's *Slaughter-House* opinion, but they concurred with his opinion in the *Bradwell* case. On behalf all three justices, Bradley explained that

> the civil law, as well as nature herself has always recognized a wide difference in the respective spheres and destinies of man and woman. Man is, or should be, woman's protector and defender. The natural and proper timidity and delicacy which belongs to the female sex evidently unfits it for many of the occupations of civil life. The constitution of the family organization, which is founded in the divine ordinance, as well as in the nature of things, indicates the domestic sphere as that which properly belongs to the domain and functions of womanhood. The harmony, not to say identity, or interests and views which belong, or should belong, to the family institution is repugnant to the idea of a woman adapting a distinct and independent career from that of her husband. So firmly fixed was this sentiment in the founders of the common law that it became a maxim of that system of jurisprudence that a woman had no legal existence separate from her husband, who was regarded as her head and representative in the social state; and, notwithstanding some recent modifications of this civil status,

many of the special rules of law flowing from and dependent upon this cardinal principle still exists in full force in most states. . . .

The paramount destiny and mission of woman are to fulfill the noble and benign offices of wife and mother. This is the law of the Creator. (Ibid., 141)

According to Justices Bradley, Field and Swayne, the woman's role as wife and mother was a sacred tradition. Therefore, men should not have to rely exclusively on their private discriminations to preserve it; they should also be able to prop up the tradition with laws that forbade their wives to work in society's better-paying jobs.

Laws designed to keep women in their proper place in the home were enforced until well past the middle of the twentieth century. In *Goesaert v. Cleary*, 335 U.S. 464 (1948), the U. S. Supreme Court upheld a Michigan law that denied bartending licenses to women, except the wives and daughters of male owners of licensed taverns. In the Court's six-to-three majority opinion, Justice Frankfurter referred to the "sprightly and ribald alewife" of Shakespeare's plays as he justified the special treatment of tavern owners' wives and daughters. He said the Constitution does not require legislatures "to reflect sociological insight, or shifting social standards" in the laws they pass (Ibid., 466-467).

In *Hoyt v. Florida*, 368 U.S. 57 (1961), the Supreme Court upheld Florida's volunteer-only system for calling female jurors. Under that system, most women accused of crimes had to stand trial by all-male juries. Nevertheless, the Supreme Court ruled that the exemption of women from jury duty was reasonable because "woman is still regarded as the center of home and family life" (Ibid., 62).

In the 1970s, the U. S. Supreme Court finally began to recognize that government agencies could not arbitrarily discriminate between people on the basis of sex. In *Reed v. Reed*, 404 U.S. 71 (1971), the Court unanimously ruled that an Idaho probate law violated the equal protection clause because it provided that when someone dies without leaving a will and several persons apply who are equally entitled to administer the estate, "males must be preferred to females." The Idaho Supreme Court had ruled that the law was reasonable, because the elimination of females from consideration would "resolve an issue that would otherwise require a hearing as to the merits . . . of the two or more petitioning relatives . . . ." Speaking for the U. S. Supreme Court, Chief Justice Burger said,

> To give a mandatory preference to members of either sex over members of the other, merely to accomplish the elimination of hearings on the merits, is to make the very kind of arbitrary legislative choice forbidden by the Equal Protection Clause of the Fourteenth Amendment; and whatever may be said as to the positive values of avoiding intrafamily controversy, the choice in this context may not lawfully be mandated solely on the basis of sex. (Ibid., 76-77)

Two years later, the Supreme Court ruled that women were entitled to equal protection by the federal government under the Fifth Amendment's life, liberty and property clause. In *Frontiero v. Richardson*, 411 U.S. 677 (1973), the Court ruled that Congress had denied equal protection to women in the armed services when it passed a law that gave all married service men housing allowances and health benefits for their wives but gave the same allowances and benefits to married service women only if they could show they supplied three-fourths of the couple's support. The government conceded that the law's differential treatment toward men and women served no purpose other than the administrative convenience of not having to review the affidavits of the married men, nearly all of whom qualified for the benefits. Eight of the nine justices agreed that this administrative convenience did not justify the different treatment, for the reasons stated in the *Reed* case, supra. Only Justice Rehnquist dissented. Justice Brennan, joined by Justices Douglas, White and Marshall, concluded that classifications based on sex were "inherently suspect" and required "strict judicial scrutiny." Brennan based that conclusion on the fact that "sex, like race and national origin, is an immutable characteristic determined solely by the accident of birth . . . ." Therefore, he said, the imposition of special disabilities upon the members of a particular sex because of their sex would seem to violate "the basic concept of our system that legal burdens should bear some relationship to individual responsibility . . . ." *Weber v. Aetna Casualty & Surety Co.*, 406 U.S. 164, 175 (1972). And what differentiates sex from such nonsuspect statuses as intelligence or physical disability, and aligns it with the recognized suspect criteria, is that the sex characteristic frequently bears no relation to ability to perform or contribute to society. As a result, statutory distinctions between the sexes often have the effect of invidiously relegating an entire class of females to inferior legal status without regard to the actual capabilities of its individual members. (Ibid., 687)

Most of the early Supreme Court decisions against gender discrimination involved laws that favored men over women. The Court seemed reluctant to find fault with laws that favored women over men. In *Kahn v. Shevin*, 416 U.S. 351 (1974), the Court upheld a law that gave a five-hundred-dollar-per-year state property tax credit to widows, blind and totally disabled people but not to widowers. Speaking for the Court, Justice Douglas said the tax credit was a reasonable way of "cushioning the financial impact of spousal loss upon the sex for which that loss imposes a disproportionately heavy burden [because of economic discrimination in most workplaces]" (Ibid., 355). In *Schlesinger v. Ballard*, 419 U.S. 498 (1975), the Court upheld a law that placed male naval officers in a strict "up or out" promotion system but guaranteed female naval officers thirteen years of service before being discharged for lack of promotion. In the Court opinion, Justice Stewart said that the sex distinction was reasonable because it compensated for the fact that female officers had less opportunity than male officers to participate in combat and sea duty and that gave them less opportunity to demonstrate their qualifications for promotion.

The first case in which the Supreme Court invalidated a law that favored women over men was *Weinberger v. Wiesenfeld*, 420 U.S. 636 (1975). A federal social security law gave a death benefit to a widow and her minor children but denied the same benefit to a widower and his minor children. All eight justices who participated in the decision agreed that this law violated the Fifth Amendment. Speaking for the Court, Justice Brennan viewed the law's gender classification as one that primarily discriminated against the deceased wives of the widowers who were unable to collect the death benefit, because it deprived "women of protection for their families which men receive as a result of their employment" (Ibid., 645). However, he also said the

> gender classification discriminates among surviving children solely on the basis of the sex of the surviving parent. Even in the typical family hypothesized by the Act, in which the husband is supporting the family and the mother is caring for the children, this result makes no sense. The fact that a man is working while there is a wife at home does not mean that he would, or should be required to, continue to work if his wife dies. It is no less important for a child to be cared for by its sole surviving parent when that parent is male rather than female. (Ibid., 651-652)

The government tried to justify its gender classification as one that compensated widows for their difficulties arising from economic discrimination, which the Court had recognized was a valid legislative purpose in *Kahn v. Shevin*, supra. Brennan responded that the legislative history of the law showed that

> Congress' purpose in providing benefits to young widows with children was not to provide income to women who were, because of economic discrimination, unable to provide for themselves. Rather §402(g), linked as it is directly to the responsibility for minor children, was intended to permit women who elect to work and to devote themselves to the care of children. Since this purpose in no way is premised upon any special disadvantages of women, it cannot serve to justify a gender-based distinction which diminishes the protection to women who do work. (Ibid., 648)

The equal rights of male and female children the support of their parents was the issue in *Stanton v. Stanton*, 421 U.S. 7 (1975). In that case, the Supreme Court ruled that a Utah law violated the equal protection clause because it required a parent to support an unmarried son until age twenty-one, but an unmarried daughter only until age eighteen. Eight of the justices joined in this decision, while Justice Rehnquist dissented for a procedural reason. Speaking for the eight justices, Justice Blackmun rejected the state of Utah's contention that young men required more time for their education and training to prepare them for their adult responsibilities. He said,

> The presence of women in business, in the professions, in government and, indeed, in all walks of life where education is a desirable, if not always necessary, antecedent is apparent and a proper subject of judicial notice. If a specified age of minority is required for the boy in order to assure him parental support while he attains his education and training, so, too, is it for the girl. To distinguish between the two on educational grounds is to be self-serving: if the female is not to be supported so long as the male, she hardly can be expected to attend school as long as he does, and bringing her education to an end earlier coincides with the role-typing society has long imposed. (Ibid., 15)

The question of whether men and women have an equal right to buy beer was raised in *Craig v. Boren*, 429 U.S. 190 (1976). The Supreme Court ruled that an Oklahoma law violated the equal protection rights of men because it allowed the sale of beer with a 3.2 percent alcohol content to all women over eighteen years of age but required that men be over twenty-one to buy the same beer. The Oklahoma attorney general argued that this gender distinction was reasonably related to the state's interest in traffic safety because statistics showed that substantially more males than females between the ages of eighteen and twenty were arrested for drunk driving, were killed or injured in traffic accidents and were more inclined to drink beer and drive. All the justices except Burger and Rehnquist attacked the relationship between these statistics and a law that forbade the sale but not the possession or consumption of 3.2 percent beer to men between the ages of eighteen and twenty. They pointed out that these men could still obtain the beer from other people, including their female companions. Justice Stewart also said, these statistics "wholly fail to prove or even suggest that 3.2 percent beer is somehow more deleterious when it comes into the hands of a male aged 18-20 than of a female of like age" (Ibid., 215).

Another federal social security law came under fire in *Califano v. Goldfarb*, 430 U.S. 199 (1977). The Court ruled that the law violated the equal protection rights of women because it gave a working man's widow a death benefit regardless of her previous dependency on him but denied the benefit to a working woman's widower unless he could show he had been receiving half his support from his wife. The government argued that the law's gender distinction was justified by the different social welfare needs of widows and widowers, the same justification that the Court recognized as valid in the *Kahn* case, supra. Speaking for himself and Justices White, Marshall and Powell, Justice Brennan said the *Kahn* decision was not relevant because, in this case,

> Congress chose to award benefits, not to widowers who could prove that they are needy, but to those who could prove that they had been dependent on their wives for more than one-half of their support. .... Thus the overall statutory scheme makes actual dependency the general basis of eligibility for OASDI benefits, and the statute, in omitting that requirement for wives and widows, reflects only a presumption that they are ordinarily dependent. At all events, nothing whatever reflects a reasoned congressional judgment that nondependent widows should receive benefits because they are more likely to be needy than nondependent widowers. (Ibid., 213, 214)

Justice Stevens concurred in the judgment of Brennan, White, Marshall and Powell, but gave his own reasons. He said the Court's ruling in the *Kahn* case would have required him to uphold the gender distinction in this case had it not been for the later, conflicting *Wiesenfeld* case. He said that the gender distinction in this case was like the those in the *Kahn* and *Wiesenfeld* cases. He said none of these distinctions was valid because the distinctions were "the accidental byproduct of a traditional way of thinking about females" and were based on archaic, overly broad generalizations (Ibid., 223-224). Justice Rehnquist filed a dissenting opinion, in which Chief Justice Burger and Justices Stewart and Blackmun joined. These justices believed that the gender classification in this case was justified because it eliminated the administrative burden on the Social Security Administration, which would have had to examine millions of applications by widows showing that they had been receiving more than half their support from their husbands. Justice Stevens criticized this justification because the evidence showed that 10 percent of the widows had not been so dependent on their husbands and the government would have therefore saved $750 million a year, "a truly staggering price for a relatively modest administrative gain" (Ibid., 220).

However, the mere fact that a social security law discriminates between men and women does not necessarily mean that it violates the Fifth Amendment. In *Califano v. Webster*, 430 U.S. 313 (1977), decided three weeks after the *Goldfarb* decision, the Supreme Court unanimously upheld a social security law that established a retirement benefit formula for female workers that was more favorable that the one for male workers. According to the Court's opinion,

> the legislative history is clear that the differing treatment of men and women in former §215(b)(3) was not "the accidental byproduct of a traditional way of thinking about females, *Califano v. Goldfarb, ante,* at 223 (STEVENS, J., concurring in judgment), but rather was deliberately enacted to compensate for particular economic disabilities suffered by women. (Ibid., 320)

Chief Justice Burger and Justices Rehnquist, Stewart and Blackmun concurred in this judgment but said they did so for the reasons stated in their dissent in the *Goldfarb* case.

The right of men to collect alimony from their wives was the issue in *Orr. v. Orr*, 440 U.S. 268 (1979). In that case, the Supreme Court ruled that an Alabama law violated the equal protection rights of men because it authorized judges to order husbands to pay alimony to their wives under an appropriate circumstance, but did not authorize the judges to order wives to pay alimony to their husbands under the same circumstances. The

Alabama Civil Court of Appeals suggested that one purpose of the law was to help needy spouses, using sex as a proxy for need. Another purpose was to compensate women for past discrimination during marriage. In the Court opinion, Justice Brennan said these purposes did not justify the law's gender classification because the state's divorce procedure already called for hearings at which evidence of need and discrimination could be presented in each case. He therefore concluded

> [w]here, as here, the State's compensatory and ameliorative purposes are as well served by a gender-neutral classification as one that gender classifies and therefore carries with it the baggage of sexual stereotypes, the State cannot be permitted to classify on the basis of sex. (Ibid., 283)

A law that distinguishes between men and women cannot be justified by making assumptions based on stereotyped images. That was the lesson in *Califano v. Wescott*, 443 U.S. 76 (1979), in which the Supreme Court invalidated a federal public assistance law that gave financial aid to children who were being deprived of basic sustenance because their fathers were unemployed but not to children suffering the same deprivation because their mothers were unemployed. Congress apparently made this distinction for no other reason than it had in mind the traditional family, in which the father was the breadwinner and the mother's employment role, if any, was secondary. Speaking for the Court, Justice Blackmun concluded that the law's gender classification was

> part of the "baggage of sexual stereotypes," *Orr v. Orr*, 440 U.S., at 283, that presumes the father has the "primary responsibility to provide a home and its essentials," *Stanton v. Stanton*, 421 U.S. 7, 10 (1975), while the mother is the "'center of home and family life.'" *Taylor v. Louisiana*, 419 U.S. 522, 534 n. 15 (1975). Legislation that rests on such presumptions, without more, cannot survive scrutiny under the Due Process Clause of the Fifth Amendment. (Ibid., 89)

A law may deny equal protection to the members of one sex even though it does not specifically discriminate against them, if it places people in a classification that consists primarily of people of one sex and there is evidence that the covert purpose of this classification is to discriminate on the basis of sex. Whether there was such a covert purpose was the issue in *Personnel Administrator of Massachusetts v. Feeney*, 442 U.S. 256 (1979). In this case, the Supreme Court ruled that a law that gave promotional and hiring preferences to war veterans did not violate the equal protection clause, even though 98 percent of all war veterans in the state were male. Speaking for the Court, Justice Stewart summarized the relevant case law, saying,

> [A]ny state law overtly or covertly designed to prefer males over females in public employment would require an exceedingly persuasive justification to withstand a constitutional challenge under the Fourteenth Amendment. (Ibid., 273)

Stewart said in this case there was no evidence that the law favoring war veterans was designed for the covert purpose of discriminating against women.

In *Kirchberg v. Feenstra*, 450 U.S. 455 (1981), the Supreme Court invalidated a Louisiana law that was reminiscent the nineteenth-century laws that had provoked the Seneca Falls Declaration to state that a woman's husband had become, "to all intents and purposes, her master--the law giving him the power to deprive her of her property" (App. P). The law gave a husband the unilateral right to dispose of jointly owned community property without his wife's consent, but it did not give the wife the same right. Quoting Justice Stewart in *Personnel Administrator of Massachusetts v. Feeney*, supra, Justice Marshall said,

> [T]he burden remains on the party seeking to uphold a statute that discriminates on the basis of sex to advance an 'exceedingly persuasive justification' for the challenged classification. (Ibid., 461)

Chapter 10   The Fourteenth Amendment   583

Justice Blackmun's statement in the *Westcott* case, Justice Stewart's statement in the *Feeney* case and Justice Marshall's statement in the *Kirchberg* case showed how much the Supreme Court had changed its view of women's rights since the Court ruled in 1961 that exempting women from jury duty was reasonable because "woman is still regarded as the center of home and family life" (*Hoyt v. Florida*, supra., 62).

While the Supreme Court was deciding these cases, the state legislatures of the nation were considering the following Constitutional amendment, proposed by Congress in March 1972:

> Section 1. Equality of rights under the law shall not be denied or abridged by the United States or by any State on account of sex.
> Section 2. The Congress shall have the power to enforce, by appropriate legislation, the provisions of this article.
> Section 3. The Amendment shall take effect two years after the date of ratification.

The original purpose of this "Equal Rights Amendment" was to force the courts to apply a more rigorous test to laws that classified people's rights according to sex. During the 1970s, over half the state legislatures ratified the proposed amendment, but not the three-fourths majority required for its adoption. The amendment was controversial because it became the main focus of a campaign to change the traditional role of women in society.

However, the public debate on the Equal Rights Amendment was pre-empted by the U. S. Supreme Court, because it was already applying a more rigorous test to laws that treated people differently on the basis of sex. People wondered whether the amendment would have any practical effect on the Court's decisions. Its supporters therefore emphasized the symbolic effect it would have on future civil rights legislation, as well as the day-to-day family, social and business relationships between men and women. That argument has not been persuasive enough to change people's minds. The Equal Rights Amendment therefore appears to be a dead issue at the present time.

On the other hand, the campaign to remove gender bias from the nation's laws appears to be alive and well. There is practically no difference between the way the courts now examine laws that classify people according to sex and the way they examine laws that classify people according to race, religion or national origin. All federal, state and local governments must therefore recognize that self-evident truth declared 150 years ago at Seneca Falls, "that all men and women are created equal."

E.10. Homosexual Marriages

The United States has few institutions that are named after married couples. The best known is the College of William and Mary in Williamsburg, Virginia, named after King William and Queen Mary of England. In his *History of the English-Speaking Peoples*, Winston Churchill said of William and Mary,

> William of Orange was fatherless and childless. His life was loveless. His marriage was dictated by reasons of State. . . . Women meant little to him. For a long time he treated his loving, faithful wife with indifference. Later on, towards the end of his reign, when he saw how much Queen Mary had helped him in the English sphere of his policy, he was sincerely grateful to her, as to a faithful friend or Cabinet officer who had maintained the Government. His grief at her death was unaffected. [85]

When most people think of marriage, they think of a mother giving birth to children and a mother and a father caring for these children. However, that was not true of the marriage of William and Mary of England, nor was it true of many other royal marriages, including the marriage of England's famous crusader Richard the Lionhearted to Berengaria of Navarre and the marriage of Frederick the Great of Prussia to Elizabeth Christina of Brunswick-Wolfenbüttel. These were political marriages in which the husband's sexual orientation made it impossible for his wife to bear children.

Although political marriages are no longer common today, there are still many marriages that do not fit the conventional mold. They include older widows and widowers, who want to enjoy married life again but are in no position to have more children, and other men and women who either cannot have blood-related children or do not wish to have them.

Some people are now asking their state governments to recognize another kind of marriage that is not designed for producing and raising blood-related children. These people want to marry other people of the same sex. On December 17, 1990, two women, Ninia Baehr and Genora Dancel, another couple of women, Tammy Rodrigues and Antoinette Pregil, and a couple of men, Pat Lagon and Joseph Melilio, applied for marriage licenses with the Hawaii Department of Health. The department refused to issue them marriage licenses solely because they were same-sex couples and did not meet the requirements of a valid marriage under Section 572-1 of the Hawaii Revised Statutes. They therefore filed a complaint against Director Lewin of the Department of Health in a Honolulu circuit court, asking the court to declare Section 572-1 unconstitutional and enjoin Lewin and his department from withholding marriage licenses solely because the applicants are of the same sex. The circuit judge dismissed the complaint and the couples appealed to the Hawaii Supreme Court.

On May 5, 1993, the Hawaii Supreme Court ruled that the circuit judge should not have dismissed the complaint. The court said that sex is a "suspect category," because Article I, Section 5 of the state's constitution says,

> No person shall be deprived of life, liberty or property without due process of law, nor be denied the equal protection of the laws, nor be denied the enjoyment of the person's civil rights or be discriminated against in the exercise thereof because of race, religion, sex or ancestry.

The court therefore ruled that Section 572-1 is subject to the "strict scrutiny" test and is presumed unconstitutional unless the state "can show that (a) the statute's sex-based classification is justified by compelling state interests and (b) the statute is narrowly drawn to avoid unnecessary abridgments of the applicant couples' constitutional rights" (*Baehr v. Lewin*, 852 P.2d 44 at 67). In accordance with this ruling, the Hawaii Supreme Court remanded the case to the circuit judge for further proceedings in which the state would have the burden of overcoming the presumption that Section 572-1 is unconstitutional.

Judge Steven Levison wrote the court's plurality opinion, in which Acting Chief Judge Ronald Moon joined. Judge James Burns concurred in the result and wrote his own opinion, while Judge Walter Heen wrote a dissenting opinion. Retired Associate Justice Hayashi heard the case but did not participate in the decision because his temporary assignment had expired. In the plurality opinion, Judge Levison said that the state's refusal to allow people of the same sex to marry deprived them of various legal benefits, including state income tax advantages; public assistance advantages; community property rights; dower, curtesy and inheritance rights; various rights relating to divorce and premarital agreements; a real property exemption from writs of attachment or execution and the claim of spousal privilege in court proceedings. He also noted that the plain language of article I, section 5 of the state constitution "prohibits state-sanctioned discrimination against any person in the exercise of his or her civil rights on the basis of sex" (Ibid., 60).

The state defended its policy of denying marriage licenses to same-sex partners on the ground that it was "not the product of impermissible discrimination" against them, but rather "a function of their biologic inability as a couple to satisfy the definition of the status to which they aspire" (Ibid., 61). Judge Walter Heen advanced another argument in his dissenting opinion, saying that Section 572-1 "treats everyone alike and applies equally to both sexes[,]" with the result that "[n]either sex is being *granted* a right or benefit the other does not have, and neither sex is being *denied* a right or benefit that the other has" (Ibid., 71).

In his plurality opinion, Judge Levison answered these arguments with quotations from an opinion by Chief Justice Earl Warren of the U. S. Supreme Court in *Loving v. Virginia*, 388 U.S. 1 (1967). The *Loving* case, discussed in Chapter 9, Section *B.6*, related to laws that forbade people of different races to marry, but Levison said the *Baehr* case was analogous because Article I, Section 5 of the Hawaii Constitution made sex, as well as race, a "suspect category." He said the argument that a same-sex couple could not satisfy the definition of marriage was essentially the same as this one that the trial judge had given in the *Loving* case:

> "Almighty God created the races white, black, yellow, malay and red, and he placed them on separate continents. And but for the interference with this arrangement there would be no cause for such marriages. The fact that he separated the races shows that he did not intend for the races to mix." (Ibid., 62, quoting 388 U.S. at 3)

According to Levison, the trial judge was saying the Virginia law was justified "because it had theretofore never been the 'custom' of the state to recognize mixed marriages, marriage 'always' having been construed to presuppose a different configuration" (Ibid., 63). Levison said that Chief Justice Warren answered that argument when he said,

> "There can be no question but that Virginia's miscegenation statutes rest solely upon distinctions drawn according to race. *The statutes proscribe generally accepted conduct* if engaged in by members of different races. . . . At the very least, the Equal Protection Clause demands that racial classifications . . . be subjected to the "most rigid scrutiny," and, if they are ever to be upheld, *they must be shown to be necessary to the accomplishment of some permissible state objective, independent of the* racial *discrimination which it was the object of the Fourteenth Amendment to eliminate.*" (Ibid., 62, emphasis added by Levison, quoting 388 U.S. at 11)

Levison then addressed Judge Heen's argument that the Hawaii law applied equally to people of both sexes. He said that Chief Justice Warren answered the same argument in the *Loving* case as follows:

"Thus, the State contends that, because its miscegenation statutes punish equally both the white and the Negro participants in an interracial marriage, these statutes, despite their reliance on racial classifications do not constitute an invidious discrimination based upon race.... [W]e reject the notion that the mere 'equal application' of a statute containing racial classifications is enough to remove the classifications from the Fourteenth Amendment's proscriptions of all invidious discriminations.... In the case at bar, ... we deal with statutes containing racial classifications, and the fact of equal application does not immunize the statute from the very heavy burden of justification which the Fourteenth Amendment has traditionally required of state statutes drawn according to race." (Ibid., 68, quoting 388 U.S. at 8)

In other words, if a government forbids a person to do something that he would be allowed to do if he were of a different sex or race, then it is discriminating against him because of his sex or race. Equal protection demands that the government give a good reason for this discrimination.

Judge Burns said in his concurring opinion that he agreed with the court's remand order because the case involved issues of material fact that ought to be heard by the trial court. One of those issues, he said, is whether the word "sex," as used in Article I, Section 5 of the state constitution, includes a person's sexual orientation. Burns said that in his view, "sex" means all aspects of a person's sex that are biologically fated. Therefore, he said that a key issue that the trial court must resolve is whether a person's sexual orientation is biologically fated.

After the Hawaii Supreme Court's remand order, the trial judge held a hearing to determine whether the state had a compelling interest to justify its refusal to issue marriage licenses to same-sex couples. Based on that hearing, the judge ruled in 1996 that the state had failed to show that it had such a interest. He therefore ordered the Hawaii Department of Health to issue marriage licenses to same-sex couples (*Baehr v. Miike*, 1996 WL 694235). However, this order was suspended pending the Department's appeal to the Hawaii Supreme Court. Most observers believe that the Supreme Court will affirm the trial judge's decision.[86]

These observers have also speculated that if and when the state of Hawaii issues marriage licenses to same-sex couples, other states might be forced to recognize these marriages. Article IV, Section 1 of the U. S. Constitution provides that "Full Faith and Credit shall be given in each State to the Public Acts, Records, and judicial Proceedings of every other State" (App. O). That may mean that a marriage that was authorized, performed and recorded in Hawaii must be recognized in every other state, even though it is not the kind of marriage that the other states would have authorized or recorded. The Louisiana courts have ruled that the full faith and credit clause requires that they recognize common law marriages contracted in other states, even though Louisiana law does not recognize or permit the contracting of common law marriages within its boundaries (*Gibbs v. Illinois Central R. Co.*, 125 So. 445 [La. S.Ct., 1929]; *Chivers v. Couch Motor Lines, Inc.*, 159 So.2d 544 [La. Ct. of App., 1964]; and *Parish v. Minvielle*, 217 So.2d 684 [La. Ct. of App., 1969]). However, Louisiana appears to be the only state that has carefully considered the effect of the full faith and credit clause in these situations. Most states recognize marriages performed in other states under their own rules of comity and, under those rules, they usually refuse to recognize marriages that violate their public policy. The Viriginia Supreme Court of Appeals, for instance, has ruled that the principles of comity of that state require its courts to determine the validity of a marriage according to the law of the state where it was performed, unless the marriage violates Virginia public policy (*Toler v. Oakwood Smokeless Coal Corporation*, 4 S.E.2nd 364, 366-67 [1939]). The Virginia high court apparently did not consider whether the U. S. Constitution's full faith and credit clause requires it to recognize marriages performed other states even though they violate Virginia's public policy.

There is also a public policy exception to the full faith and credit clause, but that exception applies only to the laws of other states, not their judgments. The U. S. Supreme Court recently explained this principle in *Baker by Thomas v. General Motors Corporation*,

118 S.Ct. 657 (1998). On behalf of the Court, Justice Ginsburg said,

> A court may be guided by the forum State's "public policy" in determining the *law* applicable to a controversy. See *Nevada v. Hall*, 440 U.S. 410, 421-424, 99 S.Ct. 1182, 118-1190, 59 L.Ed. 416 (1979). But our decisions support no roving "public policy exception" to the full faith and credit due *judgments*. See *Estin*, 334 U.S., at 546, 68 S.Ct., at 1217 (Full faith and Credit Clause "ordered submission . . . even to hostile policies reflected in the judgment of another State, because the practical operation of the federal system, which the Constitution designed, demanded it."); . . . . (Ibid., 664)

This principle may well apply to public records of marriages, even those that are not in the form of judgments.

In 1996, Congress tried to counter the possible effect of the full faith and credit clause on same-sex marriages by passing the Defense of Marriage Act. That law says,

> No State, territory, or possession of the United States, or Indian tribe, shall be required to give effect to any public act, record or judicial proceeding of any other State, territory, possession, or tribe respecting a relationship between persons of the same sex that is treated as a marriage under the laws of such other State, territory, possession, or tribe, or a right or claim arising from such relationship. (28 U.S.C. §1738C)

This law was passed pursuant to Congress's power under the sentence following the full faith and credit clause, which says, "And the Congress may by general Laws prescribe the Manner in which such Acts, Records and Proceedings shall be proved, and the Effect thereof."

However, the U. S. Supreme Court might rule that the Defense of Marriage Act violates the right of people to equal protection of the laws. This law appears to have the same defect as a recent Colorado state constitutional amendment that forbade all government agencies in the state from giving a protected status to people based on their homosexual, lesbian, or bisexual orientation. In

1996, the U. S. Supreme Court ruled in *Romer v. Evans*, 116 S.Ct. 1620, that the Colorado amendment violated people's right to equal protection of the laws. Speaking for himself and Justices Stevens, O'Connor, Souter, Ginsburg and Breyer, Justice Kennedy said,

> First, the amendment has the peculiar property of imposing a broad and undifferentiated disability on a single named group, an exceptional and, as we shall explain, invalid form of legislation. Second, its sheer breadth is so discontinuous with the reasons offered for it that the amendment seems inexplicable by anything but animus toward the class it affects; it lacks a rational relationship to legitimate state interests.
>
> Taking the first point, even in the ordinary equal protection case calling for the most deferential standards, we insist on knowing the relation between the classification adopted and the object attained. The search for the link between classification and objective gives substance to the Equal Protection Clause; it provides guidance and discipline for the legislature, which is entitled to know what sorts of laws it can pass; and it marks the limits of our own authority. In the ordinary case, a law will be sustained if it can be said to advance a legitimate government interest, even if the law seems unwise or works to the disadvantage of a particular group, or if the rationale seems tenuous....
>
> Amendment 2 confounds this normal process of judicial review. It is at once too narrow and too broad. It identifies persons by a single trait and then denies them protection across the board. The resulting disqualification of a class of persons form the right to seek specific protection from the law is unprecedented in our jurisprudence. The absence of precedent for Amendment 2 is itself instructive; "[d]iscriminations of an unusual character especially suggest careful consideration to determine whether they are obnoxious to the constitutional provision." *Louisville Gas & Elec. Co. v. Coleman*, 277 U.S. 32, 37-38, 48 S.Ct. 423, 425, 72 L.Ed. 770 (1928)....
>
> A second and related point is that laws of the kind now before us raise the inevitable inference that the disadvantage imposed is born of animosity toward the class of persons affected. "[I]f the constitutional conception of 'equal protection of the laws' means anything, it must at the very least mean that a bare ... desire to harm a politically unpopular group cannot constitute a *legitimate* governmental interest."

Department of Agriculture v. Moreno, 413 U.S. 528, 534, 93 S.Ct. 2821, 2826, 37 L.Ed.2d 782 (1973). Even laws enacted for broad and ambitious purposes can be explained by reference to legitimate public policies which justify the incidental disadvantages they impose on certain persons. Amendment 2, however, in making a general announcement that gays and lesbians shall not have any particular protections from the law, inflicts on them immediate, continuing, and real injuries that outrun and belie any legitimate justifications that may be claimed for it. We conclude that, in addition to the far-reaching deficiencies of Amendment 2 that we have noted, the principles that it offends, in another sense, are conventional and venerable; a law must bear a rational relationship to a legitimate governmental purpose, *Kadrmas v. Dickinson Public Schools*, 487 U.S. 450, 462, 108 S.Ct. 2481, 2489-2490, 101 L.Ed.2d 399 (1988), and Amendment 2 does not. (Ibid., 1627, 1628-1629)

The state of Colorado said the purposes of Amendment 2 were to give "respect for other citizens' freedom of association, and in particular the liberties of landlords or employers who have personal or religious objections to homosexuality" and to conserve "resources to fight discrimination against other groups." However, Justice Kennedy said, "The breadth of the Amendment is so far removed from these particular justifications that we find it impossible to credit them" (Ibid., 1629).

Justice Scalia, joined by Chief Justice Rehnquist and Justice Thomas, filed a dissenting opinion, saying,

> The constitutional amendment before us is not the manifestation of a "'bare . . . desire to harm'" homosexuals, *ante*, at 1628, but is rather a modest attempt by seemingly tolerant Coloradans to preserve traditional sexual mores against the efforts of a politically powerful minority to revise those mores through the use of laws. (Ibid., 1629)

He also said the majority's decision contradicted the Court's ruling in *Bowers v. Hardwick*, 478 U.S. 186 (1986), that government had a legitimate interest in outlawing conduct that violated traditional sexual mores, in that case sexual intercourse of the kind performed by homosexual people. Justice Scalia was correct in that observation.

The *Romer v. Evans* decision raises serious doubts about the validity of anti-sodomy laws, as well as of all laws that attempt to regulate the kind of private sexual activity discussed in Chapter 9, Section *B.6*. This decision also makes it apparent that a majority of the Supreme Court justices agree with Blackstone's statement that government cannot enforce a person's absolute duties, that is, those duties that he owes only to himself and not to other members of society (BL3, 119-120), but they disagree with Blackstone's statement that absolute duties become a relative duties when a person makes his vices public and sets a bad example (BL3, 120). That is why they do not view the preservation of traditional sexual mores as a legitimate government purpose. As Justice Blackmun said in his dissent in *Bowers v. Hardwick*,

> the mere knowledge that other individuals do not adhere to one's value system cannot be a legally cognizable interest, cf. *Diamond v. Charles*, 476 U. S. 54, 65-66 (1986), let alone an interest that can justify invading the houses, hearts, and minds of citizens who choose to live their lives differently. (478 U.S. at 212-213)

The *Romer v. Evans* decision also sets a high standard for judging the constitutionality of any law that singles out homosexual people and attempts to deprive them of a broad category of rights. The Defense of Marriage Act is such a law because it deprives a couple of the same sex of their right to have their marriage in one state recognized by other states and any "right or claim arising from such relationship." That may not be as broad a spectrum as the preferences attacked by the Colorado amendment of *Romer v. Evans*, but it poses the same kind of difficulty for those trying to show a close relationship between the law's effect and a legitimate government interest.

Therefore, if the Supreme Court follows Justice Kennedy's reasoning in *Romer v. Evans*, it should rule that the Defense of Marriage Act has no effect on the application of the full faith and credit clause to same-sex marriages, because it violates the equal protection rights of same-sex couples. The Court should also rule that there can be no public policy exception to the full faith and credit clause as applied to same-sex marriages, if it follows Justice Ginsburg's opinion in *Baker by Thomas v. General Motors Corporation*. That would mean that, once Hawaii or any other state recognizes same-sex marriages, any same-sex couple would be able to travel to that state, get married there and then take up residence in any other state and demand that their new home state recognize them as a married couple.

There is also a good chance that within the next five years the U. S. Supreme Court will rule that the states that do not grant marriage licenses to same-sex couples are violating the equal protection clause of the Fourteenth Amendment. The logic that the Hawaii Supreme Court applied to its state equal protection clause in the *Baehr v. Lewin* case ought to apply to the Fourteenth Amendment's equal protection clause. The only difference is that the Hawaii Supreme Court ruled that its equal protection clause makes sex a "suspect category" subject to "strict scrutiny," whereas the U. S. Supreme Court has ruled that the Fourteenth Amendment makes sex an intermediate category entitled to "an exceedingly persuasive justification" [*Personnel Administrator of Massachusetts v. Feeney*, 442 U.S. 256 at 273 (1979); *Kirchberg v. Feenstra*, 450 U.S. 455 at 461 (1981)]. This appears to be a minor distinction. Furthermore, the *Romer v. Evans* case shows that even when the U. S. Supreme Court applies a low standard of scrutiny to a law that classifies people according to sexual orientation, the burden of justifying such a law is not easy to overcome.

These predictions presume that the people opposed to same-sex marriages will not reveal a heretofore-unknown, valid governmental purpose for refusing to recognize these marriages. One of the problems in dealing with this issue has been the reluctance of people opposed to same-sex marriages to engage in discussions in which people on both sides have an opportunity to present all the reasons for their respective points of view. Strange as it may seem, this lack of discussion may help the advocates of homosexual rights achieve some of their goals, particularly the one of legalizing same-sex marriages. The critical court hearings on this issue are now under way. The people who have strong opinions but have remained silent should be aware that the time has arrived to speak now or forever hold their peace.

E.11. Summary

Equal protection anchors the fence around the power of government. It insures that the fence remains in the same place for all people. Without equal protection, no one can be secure in the enjoyment of his life, liberty and property. Equal protection means that when government takes away part of a person's life, liberty and property, it must return him the same benefit or protection that it gives any other person. It also means that when government makes distinctions among people because of their race, religion or sex or for any other reason, it must justify that distinction by relating it to a valid governmental purpose. In the history of the United States, these principles have been violated most often by racial discrimination, particularly discrimination against black people. To insure the vitality of the Constitution's equal protection guarantee, America's top priority must be to end that discrimination. However, no person should have to endure a government that gives any kind of arbitrary, preferential treatment to another person.

11

Religion in the Public Schools

This book cannot cover in detail all the rights covered by the Bill of Rights and the Fourteenth Amendment. However, religious freedom merits closer attention than other rights because it has been one of the prime targets of arbitrary government. That has been particularly true of religion in the public schools, where the minds and hearts of tomorrow's leaders are shaped.

The cases on religion in the public schools deal primarily with violations of the First Amendment's establishment clause. They follow the U. S. Supreme Court's interpretation of that clause laid down in *Everson v. Board of Education*, 330 U.S. 1 at 15 (1947):

> Neither a state nor the Federal Government can set up a church. Neither can pass laws which aid one religion, aid all religions, or prefer one religion over another.

As shown in Chapter 8, Section D, the Supreme Court based this interpretation of the establishment clause on the historical events that led to its adoption, including Madison's Memorial and Remonstrance against Religious Assessments (App. M) and the Virginia Statute for Religious Freedom (App. N).

A. Religious Instruction

A year after the *Everson* case, the Supreme Court decided *McCollum v. Board of Education*, 333 U.S. 203 (1948). In that case, religious classes were being taught in the Champaign, Illinois public schools by teachers of Protestant, Catholic and Jewish faiths.

The teachers came from local churches and religious organizations, but not all these organizations were able or willing to furnish teachers. The teachers received their pay from a Council on Religious Education, a local, voluntary association of churches and synagogues, and they were subject to approval and supervision by the school superintendent. The parents decided whether their children would be excused from secular classes during the religious instruction, and if so, which religious classes they would attend.

Speaking for the Court, Justice Black said,

> The foregoing facts . . . show the use of tax-supported property for religious instruction and the close cooperation between school authorities and the religious council in promoting religious education. The operation of the State's compulsory education system thus assists and is integrated with the program of religious instruction carried on by separate religious sects. Pupils compelled by law to go to school for secular education are released in part from their legal duty upon the condition that they attend the religious classes. This is beyond all question a utilization of the tax-established and tax-supported public school system to aid religious groups to spread their faith. (Ibid., 209-210)

Black then quoted the *Everson* decision:

> No tax in any amount, large or small, can be levied to support any religious activities or institutions, whatever they may be called, or whatever form they may adopt to teach or practice religion. (Ibid., 210, quoting from 330 U.S. at 16)

In a concurring opinion, Justice Frankfurter, joined by Justices Jackson, Rutledge and Burton, said the principle of separation of church and state forbids the use of a public school system for the "commingling of sectarian with secular instruction" (Ibid., 201). According to Frankfurter's opinion, the separation of church and state in America grew from the unique needs of diverse peoples, who found they could not reconcile their religious differences in any other way. In the field of public education, that meant that state-run schools had to be confined to non-religious education, while "leaving to the individual's church and home, indoctrination in the faith of his choice" (Ibid., 217). Although the opinion thus reaffirmed that religious establishments were contrary to the American principles of freedom, Frankfurter also said that the separation of church and state was not essential in other free societies (Ibid., 216). He had apparently forgotten that the Virginia Statute for Religious Freedom had declared "the rights hereby asserted are of the natural rights of mankind" and that the constitutions of many other states had declared the same rights to be the "natural and indefeasible" rights of all men (App. N).

The *McCollum* decision, said Frankfurter, should not be taken as binding on other kinds of programs that allow students to be dismissed for religious instruction (Ibid., 231). What programs might be approved by the Court he did not say.

That question was partly answered in *Zorach v. Clauson*, 343 U.S. 306 (1952). In that case, the Supreme Court upheld a New York City released-time program that had all the elements of the *McCollum* program, except that the religious instruction could be given by any "duly constituted religious body" and was given off the school grounds at no expense to the school.

Those program differences, however, were apparently not what Frankfurter had in mind when he wrote his opinion in the *McCollum* case. He filed a dissenting opinion in this case, saying,

> The pith of the case is that formalized religious instruction is substituted for other school activity which those who do not participate in the released-time program are compelled to attend. The school system is very much in operation during this kind of released time. If its doors are closed, they are closed upon those students who do not attend the religious instruction, in order to keep them within the school. That is the very thing which raises the constitutional issue. (Ibid., 321)

The majority of the justices were not impressed by this kind of coercion. Writing for them, Justice Douglas said the New York City program fell in the same category as a school policy that excused students for religious holidays and celebrations (Ibid., 313). He also said,

Chapter 11   Religion in the Public Schools   599

> We are a religious people whose institutions presuppose a Supreme Being. We guarantee the freedom to worship as one chooses. We make room for as wide a variety of beliefs and creeds as the spiritual needs of man deem necessary. We sponsor an attitude on the part of government that allows no partiality to any one group and that lets each flourish according to the zeal of its adherents and the appeal of its dogma. When the state encourages religious instruction or cooperates with religious authorities by adjusting its schedule of public events to sectarian needs, it follows the best of our traditions. For it then respects the religious nature of our people and accommodates the public service to their spiritual needs. To hold that it may not would be to find in the Constitution a requirement that the government show a callous indifference to religious groups. That would be preferring those who believe in no religion over those who do believe. Government may not finance religious groups nor undertake religious instruction nor blend secular and sectarian education nor use secular institutions to force one or some religion on any person. But we find no constitutional requirement which makes it necessary for government to be hostile to religion and to throw its weight against efforts to widen the effective scope of religious influence. The government must be neutral when it comes to competition between the sects. It may not thrust any sect on any person. It may not make a religious observance compulsory. It may not coerce any one to attend church, to observe a religious holiday, or to take religious instruction. But it can close its doors or suspend its operations as to those who want to repair to their religious sanctuary for worship or instruction. No more than that is undertaken here. (Ibid., 313-314)

The Supreme Court thus ruled in the *McCollum* case that a public school may not provide optional religious instruction in its own facilities, even though the teachers are provided at by local religious groups at no expense to the school district. However, under the *Zorach* decision, a public school may excuse students from part of the school day so that they may receive religious instruction off the school grounds and at no public expense.

B. School Prayers and Bible Verses

One way of giving students religious instruction is to teach them to pray. However, prayer goes further than most other religious instruction. It is a way of leading students in the practice of religion. Prayer is a primary way of worshipping God and acknowledging God's power; it is the way people talk to God and the way God talks to them. When a person prays, he expresses the belief that God is listening and will give an appropriate answer.

In *Engel v. Vitale*, 370 U.S. 421 (1962), the New York State Board of Regents composed a prayer and suggested that local school boards require the prayer to be said aloud by each class in the presence of a teacher at the beginning of each school day. The prayer read,

> Almighty God, we acknowledge our dependence upon Thee, and we beg Thy blessings upon us, our parents, our teachers and our Country.

Shortly after the New Hyde Park School District ordered its teachers to begin their class days with this prayer, the parents of ten pupils sued the district and the state to have the prayer reading stopped. They said the prayer was contrary to their religious beliefs and those of their children. They claimed the State Board of Regents had violated the Constitution's establishment clause because they had recommended the prayer to local districts, and the New Hyde Park School District had violated that clause when it ordered its teachers to use the prayer. The New York Court of Appeals ruled that there was no violation of the Constitution, because no pupil was required to join in the prayer over his or his parents' objection. The U. S. Supreme Court reversed the New York court, saying,

> we think that the constitutional prohibition against laws respecting an establishment of religion must at least mean that in this country it is no part of the business of government to compose official prayers for any group of the American people to recite as a part of a religious program carried on by the government. (Ibid., 425)

Chapter 11   Religion in the Public Schools   601

Speaking for the Court, Justice Black answered the arguments of the school board that the prayer was denominationally neutral and voluntary:

> Neither the fact that the prayer may be denominationally neutral nor the fact that its observance on the part of the students is voluntary can serve to free it from the limitations of the Establishment Clause, as it might from the Free Exercise Clause, of the First Amendment. Although these two clauses may in certain instances overlap, they forbid two quite different kinds of government encroachment on religious freedom. The Establishment Clause, unlike the Free Exercise Clause, does not depend upon any showing of direct governmental compulsion and is violated by the enactment of laws which establish an official religion whether those laws operate directly to coerce non-observing individuals or not. This is not to say, of course, that laws officially prescribing a particular form of religious worship do not involve coercion of such individuals. When the power, prestige and financial support of government is placed behind a particular religious belief, the indirect coercive pressure upon religious minorities to conform to the prevailing officially approved religion is plain. But the purposes underlying the Establishment clause go much further than that. Its first and most immediate purpose rested on the belief that a union of government and religion tends to destroy religion. The history of governmentally established religion, both in England and in this country, showed that whenever government had allied itself with one particular form of religion, the inevitable result had been that it had incurred the hatred, disrespect and even contempt of those who held contrary beliefs [Court footnote reference to App. M, par. 13]. That same history showed that many people had lost their respect for any religion that had relied upon the support of government to spread its faith [Court footnote reference to App. M, par. 6, last sentence, and par. 7, first four sentences]. The Establishment Clause thus stands as an expression of principle on the part of the Founders of our Constitution that religion is too personal, too sacred, too holy, to permit its "unhallowed perversion" by a civil magistrate. Another purpose of the Establishment Clause rested upon an awareness of the historical fact that governmentally established religions and religious persecutions go hand in hand. . . .

It has been argued that to apply the Constitution in such a way as to prohibit state laws respecting an establishment of religious services in public schools is to indicate a hostility toward religion or toward prayer. Nothing, of course, could be more wrong. The history of man is inseparable from the history of religion. And perhaps it is not too much to say that since the beginning of that history many people have devoutly believed that "More things are wrought by prayer than this world dreams of." It was doubtless largely due to men who believed this that there grew up a sentiment that caused men to leave the crosscurrents of officially established state religions and religious persecution in Europe and come to this country filled with the hope that they could find a place in which they could pray when they pleased to the God of their faith in the language they chose. And there were men of this same faith in the power of prayer who led the fight for adoption of our Constitution and also for our Bill of Rights with the very guarantees of religious freedom that forbid the sort of governmental activity which New York has attempted here. These men knew that the First Amendment, which tried to put an end to governmental control of religion and prayer, was not written to destroy either. They knew rather that it was written to quiet well-justified fears which nearly all of them felt arising out of an awareness that governments of the past had shackled men's tongues to make them speak only the religious thoughts that government wanted them to speak and to pray only to the God that government wanted them to pray to. It is neither sacrilegious nor antireligious to say that each separate government in this country should stay out of the business of writing or sanctioning official prayers and leave that purely religious function to the people themselves and to those the people choose to look for religious guidance. (Ibid., 430-435)

To answer the argument that the Regents' prayer was a general prayer that did not offend any particular sect, Justice Black quoted James Madison from his Memorial and Remonstrance against Religious Assessments:

"Who does not see that the same authority which can establish Christianity, in exclusion of all other Religions, may establish with the same ease any particular sect of Christians, in exclusion of all other Sects? That the same authority which can force a citizen to contribute three

Chapter 11 Religion in the Public Schools 603

pence only of his property for the support of any one establishment, may force him to conform to any other establishment in all cases whatsoever?" (Ibid., 436, quoting from App. M, par. 3)

In a dissenting opinion, Justice Stewart quoted the speeches of past presidents, including Washington, Adams, Jefferson, Madison, Lincoln, Eisenhower and Kennedy, who had expressed the belief that the successes and adversities of the nation were in the hands of God. He pointed out that the Supreme Court Crier opens each session with the words "God save the United States and this Honorable Court" and both houses of Congress and the legislatures of many states have chaplains who open their sessions with prayers. The armed forces, he said, employ chaplains of various faiths, who minister to the soldiers of those faiths. Stewart also pointed out that since 1865, all United States coins have borne the words "IN GOD WE TRUST" and that a stanza of the national anthem, "The Star Spangled Banner," includes the words "Then conquer we must, when our cause is just, And this be our motto, 'In God is our Trust.'"

However, the religious expressions of government officials and slogans proclaiming a general "trust in God" are not the same as school prayers that train children to worship a specific, supernatural God. A public school teacher who leads children in prayer is performing the same function as a church Sunday School teacher, but the public school teacher is paid by taxpayers who do not necessarily share the religious beliefs expressed in the prayer. Madison campaigned against such tax-supported religious teachers when he wrote the Memorial and Remonstrance against Religious Assessments (App. M). The result of that campaign was the Virginia Statute for Religious Freedom, which declared "That no man shall be compelled to frequent or support any religious worship, place, or ministry whatsoever, . . ." and "that the rights hereby asserted are of the natural rights of mankind, . . ." (App. N). As explained in Chapter 8, Section D, that principle became embodied establishment clause of the First Amendment.

School prayers differ from references to God in other settings because they occur in a teaching environment and because children are more impressionable than adults. In 1983, the U.S. Supreme Court distinguished between school prayers and the prayers of legislative chaplains in *Marsh v. Chambers*, 463 U.S. 783. Speaking for the Court, Chief Justice Burger said of legislative prayers, "Here, the individual claiming injury by the practice is an adult, presumably not readily susceptible to 'religious indoctrination'" (Ibid., 792). That case had been filed by a member of the Nebraska state legislature. The Supreme Court upheld the legislature's practice of opening each session with a prayer led by a state-paid chaplain.

The year after *Engel v. Vitale*, the Supreme Court decided whether a state could require Bible verses to be read in public schools. In *Abington School District v. Schempp*, 374 U.S. 203 (1963), a Pennsylvania law required that

> [a]t least ten verses from the Holy Bible shall be read, without comment, at the opening of each public school on each school day. Any child shall be excused from such Bible reading, or attending such Bible reading, upon the written request of his parent or guardian.

Edward Schempp, his wife Sidney and their children Roger and Donna sued to prevent this law from being enforced on the ground it violated their religious freedom guaranteed by the Fourteenth Amendment. Roger and Donna were students at Abington Senior High School and the family belonged to the Unitarian Church in the Germantown section of Philadelphia, Pennsylvania. Each day during the morning homeroom period at Abington, a student would read ten Bible verses of his own choice over the school intercom system. This Bible reading was followed by the Lord's Prayer, which was recited in unison by the students standing in each classroom. There were never any comments, explanations or questions asked or solicited during this portion of the homeroom period. All parents and students were notified that any student could remain absent from the classroom during these exercises or could choose to remain in the classroom and not participate.

Schempp and his children testified that there were certain religious doctrines purveyed by a literal reading of the Bible "which

Chapter 11 Religion in the Public Schools 605

were contrary to the religious beliefs which they held and to their familial teaching." The children testified that all of these doctrines were read to them at various times in the course of the Abington homeroom Bible readings. Schempp testified that he had considered having his children excluded from these exercises but decided against it because he believed that the children's relations with their teachers and classmates would be adversely affected.

The district judge ruled that the Abington High School Bible reading, the Lord's Prayer exercises and the state law that required these exercises violated the Fourteenth Amendment. He based this ruling on the testimony of two expert witnesses, Dr. Solomon Grayzel, employed by the Schempps, and Dr. Luther A. Weigle, employed by the school district. According to the judge,

> Dr. Grayzel testified that portions of the New Testament were offensive to Jewish tradition and that, from the standpoint of the Jewish faith, the concept of Jesus Christ as the Son of God was "practically blasphemous." He cited instances in the New Testament which, assertedly, were not only sectarian in nature but tended to bring the Jews into ridicule and scorn. Dr. Grayzel gave as his expert opinion that such material from the New Testament could be explained to Jewish children in such a way as to do no harm to them. But if portions of the New Testament were read without explanation, they could be, and in his specific experience with children Dr. Grayzel observed, had been, psychologically harmful to the child and had caused a divisive force within the social media of the school. . . .
>
> On direct examination Dr. Weigle stated that the Bible was non-sectarian. He later stated that the phrase "non-sectarian" meant to him non-sectarian within the Christian faiths. Dr. Weigle stated that his definition of the Holy Bible would include the Jewish Holy Scriptures, but also stated that the "Holy Bible" would not be complete without the New Testament. He stated that the New Testament "conveyed the message of Christians." In his opinion, reading of the Holy Scriptures to the exclusion of the New Testament would be a sectarian practice. Dr. Weigle stated that the Bible was of great moral, historical and literary value. This is conceded by all the parties and is also the view of the court. (Ibid., 209-210)

The district judge therefore ruled that

> [t]he reading of the verses, even without comment, possesses a devotional and religious character and constitutes in effect a religious observance. The devotional and religious nature of the morning exercise is made all the more apparent by the fact that the Bible reading is followed immediately by the recital of the Lord's Prayer. The fact that some pupils, or theoretically all pupils, might be excused from attendance at the exercises does not mitigate the obligatory nature of the ceremony for . . . Section 1516 . . . unequivocally requires the exercises to be held every school day in every school in the Commonwealth. The exercises are held in school buildings and perforce are conducted by and under the authority of the local school authorities and during school sessions. Since the statute requires the reading of the "Holy Bible," a Christian document, the practice . . . prefers the Christian religion. The record demonstrates that it was the intention of . . . the Commonwealth . . . to introduce a religious ceremony into the public schools of the Commonwealth. (Ibid., 210-211)

At the same time it decided the *Abington* case, the Supreme Court also decided *Murray v. Curlett*, a case involving similar facts on certiorari from the Court of Appeals of Maryland, 228 Md. 239. In that case, a Baltimore Board of School Commissioners rule, which had been in force since 1905, required that opening exercises of all city schools consist of "reading, without comment, of a chapter of the Holy Bible and/or the use of the Lord's Prayer." Mrs. Madalyn Murray, a taxpayer, and her son, William J. Murray III, a Baltimore public school student, filed a mandamus petition to compel the school board to rescind this rule. Both Mrs. Murray and her son were atheists. In response to their complaint, the Board had amended its rule to permit students to read from the Catholic Douay version of the Bible in addition to the King James version and to allow a child to be excused from the opening exercise at the request of his parent. However, the Murrays claimed that the rule, even as amended, violated their rights "to freedom of religion under the First and Fourteenth Amendments." They said the rule threatens their religious liberty by placing a premium on belief as against non-belief and subjects their freedom of conscience to the rule of the majority; it pronounces belief in God as the source of all moral and spiritual values, equating these values with religious values, and thereby renders sinister, alien and suspect the beliefs and ideals of your Petitioners, promoting doubt and question of their morality, good citizenship and good faith. (Ibid., 212)

In the Supreme Court's opinion in the *Abington* and *Murray* cases, Justice Clark reviewed the previous cases decided by the Court that had interpreted the First Amendment's establishment and free exercise clauses. He concluded that

the Establishment Clause has been directly considered by this Court eight times in the past score of years and, with only one Justice dissenting on the point, it has consistently held that the clause withdrew all legislative power respecting religious belief or the expression thereof. The test may be stated as follows: what are the purpose and primary effect of the enactment? If either is the advancement or inhibition of religion then the enactment exceeds the scope of the legislative power as circumscribed by the Constitution. That is to say that to withstand the strictures of the Establishment Clause there must be a secular legislative purpose and a primary effect that neither advances nor inhibits religion. . . . The Free Exercise Clause, likewise considered many times here, withdraws from legislative power, state and federal, the exertion of any restraint on the free exercise of religion. Its purpose is to secure religious liberty in the individual by prohibiting any invasions thereof by civil authority. Hence it is necessary in a free exercise case for one to show the coercive effect of the enactment as it operates against him in the practice of his religion. The distinction between the two clauses is apparent--a violation of the Free Exercise clause is predicated on coercion while the Establishment Clause violation need not be so attended. (Ibid., 222-223)

Justice Clark then applied these principles to the facts of the *Abington* and *Murray* cases. He said that in both cases, the Bible readings and prayers were part of the curricular activities of the school and were held in school buildings with the participation of the teachers. Students could be excused from these exercises, but Clark said that establishment clause violations were not predicated on coercion (Ibid., 224-225). In the *Abington* case, the district court had ruled, on the basis of expert testimony, that the state had intended the exercise to be a religious ceremony. It therefore had a religious purpose and a primary effect that advanced religion. In the *Murray* case, the Maryland courts had not made such a finding. The state had argued that its exercise had the secular purposes of promoting moral values, opposing the materialistic trends of our times, the perpetuation of our institutions and the teaching of literature. However, Justice Clark said the provisions of the Baltimore rule showed a contrary purpose:

> Surely the place of the Bible as an instrument of religion cannot be gainsaid, and the State's recognition of the pervading religious character of the ceremony is evident from the rule's specific permission of the alternative use of the Catholic Douay version as well as the recent amendment permitting nonattendance at the exercises. None of these factors is consistent with the contention that the Bible is here used either as an instrument for nonreligious moral inspiration or as a reference for the teaching of secular subjects. (Ibid., 224)

Clark also addressed the school districts' contentions that without religious exercises, a "religion of secularism" is established in the schools and the majority of the students are deprived of the free exercise of their religion. Regarding the "religion of secularism" argument, he said,

> We agree of course that the State may not establish a "religion of secularism" in the sense of affirmatively opposing or showing hostility to religion, thus "preferring those who believe in no religion over those who do not believe." *Zorach v. Clauson, supra*, at 314. We do not agree, however, that this decision in any sense has that effect. In addition, it might well be said that one's education is not complete without a study of comparative religion or the history of religion and its relationship to the advancement of civilization. It certainly may be said that the Bible is worthy of study for its literary and historic qualities. Nothing we have said here indicates that such a study of the Bible

or of religion, when presented objectively as a part of a secular program of education, may not be effected consistently with the First Amendment. (Ibid., 225)

Regarding the free exercise argument, he said,

> While the Free Exercise Clause clearly prohibits the use of state action to deny the rights of free exercise to *anyone*, it has never meant that a majority could use the machinery of the State to practice its beliefs....
> The place of religion in our society is an exalted one, achieved through a long tradition of reliance on the home, the church and the inviolable citadel of the heart and mind. We have come to recognize through bitter experience that it is not within the power of government to invade that citadel, whether its purpose or effect be to aid or oppose, to advance or retard. In the relationship between man and religion, the State is firmly committed to a position of neutrality. (Ibid., 226)

The *Engel, Abington* and *Murray* decisions thus established that public school teachers and administrators cannot lead students in prayer or Bible reading, nor can they assign students to do the same.

In *Stone v. Graham*, 449 U.S. 39 (1980), the Supreme Court addressed the question of whether Bible passages such as the Ten Commandments could be posted on the walls of public schools. A Kentucky law required that the Ten Commandments be posted on the wall of each public school classroom in the state. To determine whether this law violated the establishment clause, the Court applied a three-part test that had been announced in *Lemon v. Kurtzman*, 403 U.S. 602, 612-613 (1971):

(1) Does the law have a secular legislative purpose?

(2) Does the law have a primary effect that neither advances nor inhibits religion? and

(3) Does the law avoid an excessive entanglement with religion?

The Court derived first two parts of this test from Justice Clark's observations in *Abington v. Schempp*, supra, 222-223, based on his review of eight previous Supreme Court decisions interpreting the establishment clause. The third requirement--that there be no excessive entanglement--was taken from Chief Justice Burger's opinion in *Walz v. Tax Commission*, 397 U.S. 664 at 674 (1970). As the historical background described in Chapter 8 showed, the establishment clause is essentially a prohibition against government support of religious ministries. The *Lemon* test is based on the proposition that government does support a religious ministry when it adopts laws or policies that have a religious purpose but no secular purpose, that have the primary effect of advancing or inhibiting religion, or that entangle the government in the religious ministries of other people and organizations.

Applying the *Lemon* test, the Supreme Court ruled in the *Stone* case that the Kentucky law did not have a secular legislative purpose and it therefore violated the establishment clause. The Commonwealth of Kentucky had argued that the law had a secular purpose because it required that each display of the Ten Commandments include the statement, "The secular application of the Ten Commandments is clearly seen in its adoption as the fundamental legal code of Western Civilization and the Common Law of the United States." However, in an opinion by all nine justices, the Supreme Court disagreed; it said

> [t]he pre-eminent purpose for posting the Ten Commandments on schoolroom walls is plainly religious in nature. The Ten Commandments are undeniably a sacred text in the Jewish and Christian faiths, and no legislative recitation of a supposed secular purpose can blind us to that fact. The Commandments do not confine themselves to arguably secular matters, such as honoring one's parents, killing or murder, adultery, stealing, false witness, and covetousness. See Exodus 20:12-17; Deuteronomy 5:16-21. Rather the first part of the Commandments concerns the religious duties of believers: worshipping the Lord God alone, avoiding idolatry, not using the Lord's name in vain, and observing the Sabbath Day. See Exodus 20:1-11; Deuteronomy 5:6-15.

The Court might have also pointed out that if the Kentucky legislature's purpose were to educate students on the fundamental legal codes of western civilization and the common law of the United States, it could have better served that purpose by posting either the secular Hammurabi Code that preceded the Ten Commandments or the secular precepts of the Roman Emperor Justinian--that people should live honestly, hurt nobody and render to everyone its due (BL1, 40).

The Supreme Court said that it did not matter that the posting of the Ten Commandments was financed by private contributions, because "the mere posting of the copies under the auspices of the legislature" violates the establishment clause (Ibid., 42).

In 1985, the Supreme Court considered another school prayer case, *Wallace v. Jaffree*, 472 U.S. 38. In 1978, the Alabama legislature passed a law that required elementary school teachers to announce a period of silence for meditation at the beginning of each day. In 1981, it passed a second law that said that any public school teacher may announce at the beginning of each day a period of silence for meditation or voluntary prayer. In 1982, it passed a third law that said that any teacher or professor of any public educational institution may pray, may lead willing students in prayer or may lead willing students in a specific prayer that began "Almighty God, You alone are our God. We acknowledge You as the Creator and Supreme Judge of the world. . . . ." Ishmael Jaffree filed a lawsuit in the local federal district court, complaining that because of these laws, his kindergarten and second grade children were being subjected to religious indoctrination in violation of the First Amendment, made applicable to the states by the Fourteenth Amendment.

The district court ruled that the 1978 law was valid, because "it is a statute which prescribes nothing more than a child in school shall have the right to meditate in silence and there is nothing wrong with a little meditation and quietness" (*Jaffree v. James*, 544 F.Supp. 727, 732 [S.D. Ala., 1982]). Jaffree did not appeal that ruling. In 1984, the U. S. Supreme Court had unanimously affirmed a Fifth Circuit Court of Appeals ruling that the 1982 law authorizing teacher-led prayers was unconstitutional, citing *Engle v. Vitale* and *Abington v. Schempp* (466 U.S. 924). Therefore, the only issue decided in this 1985 case was the validity of the 1981 law, which authorized teachers to declare a moment of silence for meditation or voluntary prayer.

The Supreme Court ruled that the 1981 law violated the Fourteenth Amendment because it lacked a secular purpose, which was the first requirement of the *Lemon v. Kurtzman* test. Speaking for the Court, Justice John Paul Stevens said,

> even though a statute that is motivated in part by a religious purpose may satisfy the first criterion, see *e.g. Abington School District v. Schempp*, 374 U.S. 203, 296-303, 83 S.Ct. 1560, 1610-1614, 10 L.Ed.2d 844 (1963) (Brennan, J., concurring), the First Amendment requires that a statute must be invalidated if it is entirely motivated by a purpose to advance religion.
>
> In applying the purpose test, it is appropriate to ask "whether government's actual purpose is to endorse or disapprove of religion," *Lynch v. Donnelly*, 465 U.S. at 690 (O'Connor, J., concurring). In this case, the answer to that question is dispositive. For the record not only provides us with an unambiguous affirmative answer, but it also reveals that the enactment of §16-1-20.1 was not motivated by any secular purpose--indeed, the statute had *no* secular purpose.
>
> The sponsor of the bill that became §16-1-20.1, Senator Donald Holmes, inserted into the legislative record--apparently without dissent--a statement indicating that the legislation was an "effort to return voluntary prayer" to the public schools. Later Senator Holmes confirmed this purpose before the District Court. In response to the question whether he had any purpose for the legislation other than returning voluntary prayer to public schools, he stated, "No, I did not have no other purpose in mind" [sic]. The State did not present evidence of *any* secular purpose. (Ibid., 56-57)

Stevens also said the law was obviously designed to return prayer to the public schools, rather than protect the right of students to engage in voluntary prayer, because

> [t]he 1978 statute already protected that right [to engage in voluntary prayer by] . . . containing nothing that prevented any student from

engaging in voluntary prayer during a silent minute of meditation. Appellants have not identified any secular purpose that was not fully served by §16-1-20 before the enactment of §16-1-20.1. Thus, only two conclusions are consistent with the text of §16-1-20.1: (1) the statute was enacted to convey a message of state endorsement and promotion of prayer; or (2) the statute was enacted for no purpose. No one suggests that the statute was nothing but a meaningless or irrational act. (Ibid., 59)

Although the State of Alabama did not identify any secular purpose of the 1981 law that was not served by the 1978 law, there might have been such a purpose. The 1978 law required only elementary school teachers to declare a moment of silence or meditation, whereas the 1981 law allowed all public school teachers to declare a moment of silence or voluntary prayer. Thus, the State might have argued that the 1981 law was designed to extend the moment of silence to middle school and high school students, at the discretion of the teachers at those schools. However, the State still would have had the problem of explaining Senator Holmes' testimony that his only purpose was to return voluntary prayer to the public schools.

Some people have contended that the *Wallace v. Jaffree* ruling forbids periods of silence for meditation or prayer in public schools. They therefore want to amend the Constitution to permit such periods of silence. However, this amendment is not necessary. Under *Wallace v. Jaffree*, any state should be able to pass a valid "period of silence" law, provided its purpose is not to return prayer to the schools, but rather to give students more time for any quiet activity, including the free exercise of religion. That would be a secular purpose because the free exercise of religion is a constitutional, natural law right.

C. The Definition of "Religion"

To determine the proper breadth of religious freedom in public schools as well as other settings, judges are sometimes confronted with the question of what "religion" is.

The Virginia Declaration of Rights of 1776 said that "religion" is "the duty we owe to our Creator and the Manner of discharging it." Madison repeated that definition in Paragraph 1 of his Memorial and Remonstrance against Religious Assessments (App. M). However, this definition was too narrow even at the time it was written. In the 1600s, most deputies to the Plymouth General Court wanted to extend religious tolerance to the Familists, who paid no attention to creeds and spiritual truths and believed that religion consisted wholly in loving one another.[1] Beginning in the 1760s, many Congregationalists in Massachusetts became Universalists and Unitarians and some of them did not view God as the creator and governor of the universe. The first Universalist church was founded in 1776 and the Unitarians started their own churches in the early 1800s. Since then, many religious societies have been founded in the United States that embrace some or all of the tenets of Buddhism, Taoism and other eastern religions that do not require a belief in a Supreme Being or Creator. These events have caused the courts to re-evaluate the conventional definitions of religion that refer to a single God or Supreme Being who is the creator and governor of the universe.

The Third Circuit Federal Court of Appeals in Philadelphia undertook such a re-evaluation in *Malnak v. Yogi*, 592 F.2d 197 (1979). In that case, five New Jersey high schools had offered an elective course in the Science of Creative Intelligence and Transcendental Meditation ("SCI/TM"), funded as a pilot program by the New Jersey State Board of Education and the U. S. Department of Health, Education and Welfare. The course had been taught four or five days a week by teachers specially trained by the World Plan Executive Council--United States, an organization whose object was to disseminate the teachings of SCI/TM. The textbook for the course had been developed by the Maharishi Mahesh Yogi, the founder of the Science of Creative Intelligence. The guardians of several children filed a lawsuit asking that a federal judge enjoin the schools from teaching this course, on the ground that it violated the establishment clause of the First Amendment. The state and federal agencies and the Maharishi argued that there was no violation because SCI/TM was not a religion.

However, both the district judge and the Third Circuit Court of Appeals ruled that SCI/TM was a religion, because of the following features:

> [i]t teaches that "pure creative intelligence" is the basis of life, and that through the process of Transcendental Meditation students can perceive the full potential of their lives.
>
> Essential to the practice of Transcendental Meditation is the "mantra"; a mantra is the sound aid used while meditating. Each meditator has his own personal mantra which is never to be revealed to any other person. It is by concentrating on the mantra that one receives the beneficial effects said to result from Transcendental Meditation.
>
> To acquire his mantra, a meditator must attend a ceremony called a "puja." Every student who participated in the SCI/TM course was required to attend a puja as part of the course. A puja was performed by the teacher for each student individually; it was conducted off school premises on a Sunday; and the student was required to bring some fruit, flowers and a white handkerchief. During the puja the student stood or sat in front of a table while the teacher sang a chant and made offerings to a deified "Guru Dev." Each puja lasted between one and two hours. (Ibid., 198)

The judges ruled that these government sponsored "religious" classes and ceremonies violated the establishment clause because they were similar to ones that the U. S. Supreme Court had forbidden in previous cases. Judge Arlin Adams of the Court of Appeals concurred in this ruling, but he noted that SCI/TM did not concentrate on a supreme being, which was a part of the traditional definition of religion. He therefore though it necessary to explain why SCI/TM was a religion, relying primarily on several U. S. Supreme Court cases in which the definition of religion had been disputed. These included two military conscientious objector cases, *United States v. Seeger*, 380 U.S. 163 (1965) and *Welsh v. United States*, 398 U.S. 333 (1970), and a religious oath case, *Torcaso v. Watkins*, 367 U.S. 488 (1961).

In the conscientious objector cases, the Supreme Court had interpreted Section 6(j) of the Universal Military Service and Training Act, which allowed a person to escape the draft if "by reason of religious training and belief" he is "conscientiously opposed to participation in war in any form." At the time of the facts in both cases, this section read,

> [r]eligious training and belief in this connection means an individual's belief in a relation to a Supreme Being involving duties superior to those arising from any human relation, but does not include essentially political, sociological, or philosophical views or a merely personal moral code.

In the *Seeger* case, Supreme Court Justice Clark said,

> the test of belief "in relation to a Supreme being" is whether a given belief that is sincere and meaningful occupies a place in the life of its possessor parallel to that filled by the orthodox belief in God of one who clearly qualifies for the exemption. Where such beliefs have parallel positions in the lives of their respective holders we cannot say that one is "in a relation to a Supreme Being" and the other is not. (380 U.S. at 165-166)

Clark noted that there had been an ever-broadening understanding of religion in the religious community, quoting the renowned Protestant theologian, Dr. Paul Tillich:

> "In such a state [of self-affirmation] the God of both religious and theological language disappears. But something remains, namely, the seriousness of that doubt in which meaning within meaninglessness is affirmed. The source of this affirmation of meaning within meaninglessness, of certitude within doubt, is not the God of traditional theism but the "God above God," the power of being, which works through those who have no name for it, not even the name God." II Systematic Theology 12 (1957). (Ibid., 180)

Justice Clark also quoted the following from the Vatican II draft declaration on the Roman Catholic Church's relations with non-Christians:

"Ever since primordial days, numerous peoples have had a certain perception of that hidden power which hovers over the course of things and over the events that make up the lives of men; some have even come to know of a Supreme Being and Father. Religions in an advanced culture have been able to use more refined concepts and a more developed language in their struggle for an answer to man's religious questions. . . .

"Nothing that is true and holy in these religions is scorned by the Catholic Church. Ceaselessly the Church proclaims Christ, 'the Way, the Truth, and the Life,' in whom God reconciled all things to Himself. The Church regards with sincere reverence those ways of action and of life, precepts and teachings which, although they differ from the ones she sets forth, reflect nonetheless a ray of that Truth which enlightens all men."[2] (Ibid., 182)

Clark also quoted Dr. David Saville Muzzey, a leader in the Ethical Culture Movement, from his book, *Ethics as a Religion* (1951):

"Everybody except avowed atheists (and they are comparatively few) believes in some kind of God. . . . The proper question to ask, therefore, is not the futile one, Do you believe in God? but rather, What *kind* of God do you believe in?" *Id.*, at 86-87. . . .

"Instead of positing a personal God, whose existence man can neither prove nor disprove, the ethical concept is founded on human experience. It is anthropocentric, not theocentric. Religion, for all the various definitions that have been given it, must surely mean the devotion of man to the highest ideal that he can conceive. And that ideal is a community of spirits in which the latent moral potentialities of men shall have been elicited by their reciprocal endeavors to cultivate the best in their fellow men. What ultimate reality is we do not know; but we have the faith that it expresses itself in the human world as the power which inspires in men moral purpose." At 95.

"Thus the 'God' that we love is not the figure on the great white throne, but the perfect pattern, envisioned by faith, of humanity as it should be, purged of the evil elements which retard its progress toward 'the knowledge, love and practice of the right.'" At 98.

In the *Seeger* case, Seeger stated that his belief that he could not kill another person was a "belief in and devotion to goodness and virtue for their own sakes, and a religious faith in a purely ethical creed" (Ibid., 166). In the *Welsh* case, Welsh crossed out the word "religious" from his application because he did not believe that his belief was religious, according to the traditional definition of that word. The Court of Appeals found that Welsh had "denied that his objection to war was premised on religious belief" and concluded that "[t]he Appeal Board was entitled to take him at his word" (404 F.2d at 1082). However, Supreme Court Justice Black said the Court of Appeals was placing "undue emphasis on the registrant's interpretation of his own beliefs." He said, "very few registrants are fully aware of the broad scope of the word 'religious' as used in § 6(j), and accordingly a registrant's statement that his beliefs are nonreligious is a highly unreliable guide for those charged with administering the objection." Black then noted that the Court of Appeals had said that Welsh held his beliefs "with the strength of more traditional religious convictions." Welsh therefore satisfied the *Seeger* test, because his belief occupied a place in his life parallel to that filled by the orthodox belief in God.

In the *Welsh* case, the Supreme Court was divided over whether the word, "religious," in Section 6(j) of the Universal Military Service and Training Act should be interpreted to include non-theistic religions, because Congress seemed to go out of its way to define "religious training and belief" as a belief in a "Supreme Being." Justice Harlan said the law exempted only people who held theistic beliefs and it was therefore unconstitutional because

> having chosen to exempt, it [Congress] cannot draw the line between theistic or nontheistic religious beliefs on the one hand and secular beliefs on the other. Any such distinctions are not, in my view, compatible with the Establishment clause of the First Amendment. (Ibid., 356)

It appears that Justice Harlan thought the word "religion" in the First Amendment had at least as broad a meaning as Justice Clark's definition of a religious belief "in relation to a Supreme being" in the *Seeger* case. In his concurring opinion in the *Malnak* case, Judge Adams reached the same conclusion. He also cited the

Chapter 11 Religion in the Public Schools

Torcaso case as authority for this broader interpretation of "religion." In the Court's opinion in that case, Justice Black said

> [w]e repeat and again affirm that neither a State nor the Federal Government can constitutionally force a person "to profess a belief or disbelief in any religion." Neither can constitutionally pass laws or impose requirements which aid all religions as against non-believers, and neither can aid those religions based on a belief in the existence of God as against those religions founded on different beliefs. (Ibid., 495)

In a footnote, Black added that

> [a]mong the religions of this country which do not teach what would generally be considered a belief in the existence of God are Buddhism, Taoism, Ethical Culture, Secular Humanism and others. (Ibid., 495)

Judge Adams said that the *Seeger*, *Welsh* and *Torcaso* Supreme Court opinions clearly repudiated the old definition of "religion." However, "the new definition remains not yet fully formed." To rectify that situation, he proposed three indicia for determining whether a supposed religion is in fact a religion, as that word is used in the First Amendment. The first two were the following:

(1) Whether the supposed religion deals with matters of "ultimate concern," such as "the meaning of life and death, man's role in the Universe and the proper moral code of right and wrong" (Ibid., 208--Judge Adams took the phrase "ultimate concern" from Dr. Tillich's statement that the essence of religion is ultimate concern);[3] and

(2) Whether the supposed religion embodies "a comprehensive belief system," as opposed to an answer to one question, such as the "Big Bang" theory of the origin of the Universe (Ibid., 209--Judge Adams quoted St. Thomas Aquinas' statement that the science of theology "commands all other sciences as the ruling science"[4] and said that when scientific theories are combined in a comprehensive belief system, they become a

ruling science that affects a student's approach to several academic disciplines).

Adams said a religion must have these two indicia but the following third indicium was optional. If present, it might be used to resolve doubts about the presence of the first two:

(3) Whether there are "any formal, external, or surface signs that may be analogized to accepted religions. Such signs might include formal services, ceremonial functions, the existence of clergy, structure and organization, efforts at propagation, observation of holidays and other similar manifestations associated with traditional religions" [Ibid., 209--Judge Adams noted that such formal signs were found to be persuasive proofs of religious character in *Washington Ethical Society v. District of Columbia*, 249 F.2d 127 (D.C. Cir., 1957) and *Fellowship of Humanity v. County of Alameda*, 315 P.2d 394 (Cal. App.Ct., 1957), and they were also noted in *Founding Church of Scientology of Washington v. United States*, 409 F.2d 1146 (D.C. Cir., 1969)].

There is another indicium that the courts ought to consider. The main difference between philosophy and religion is that philosophy embodies only natural law, but religion embodies natural law and revealed law. In his chapter "Of the Nature of Laws in General," Blackstone said that natural law consists of "the eternal immutable laws of good and evil, to which the creator himself in all his dispensations conforms; *and which he has enabled human reason to discover*, [emphasis added] so far as they are necessary for the conduct of human actions" (BL1, 40). He also explained that

> if our reason were always, as in our first ancestor before his transgression, clear and perfect, unruffled by passions, unclouded by prejudice, unimpaired by disease or intemperence, the talk would be pleasant and easy; we should need no other guide but this. But every man now finds the contrary in his own experience; that his reason is corrupt, and his understanding full of ignorance and error.

> This has given manifold occasion for the benign interposition of divine providence; which, in compassion to the frailty, the imperfection, and the blindness of human reason, hath been pleased, at sundry times and in divers manners, to discover and enforce it's laws by an immediate and direct revelation. The doctrines thus delivered we call the revealed law or divine law, and they are found only in the holy scriptures. These precepts, when revealed, are found upon comparison to be really a part of the original law of nature, as they tend in all their consequences to man's felicity. But we are not from thence to conclude that the knowledge of these truths was attainable by reason, in it's present corrupted state; since we find that, until they were revealed, they were hid from the wisdom of the ages. As then the moral precepts of this law are indeed of the same original with those of the law of nature, so their intrinsic obligation is of equal strength and perpetuity. Yet undoubtedly the revealed law is (humanly speaking) of infinitely more authority than what we generally call the natural law....
>
> Upon these two foundations, the law of nature and the law of revelation, depend all human laws; that is to say, no human laws should be suffered to contradict these. (BL1, 41-42)

Blackstone said that government must conform to revealed law as well as to natural law because he believed there was only one body of revealed law, namely, the law approved by the official Church of England. However, the religions of the world are each based on a different body of revealed law. The Jews, Christians and Moslems believe in a single, supreme God who created the universe and governs it from above, enforcing His commandments, including the Ten Commandments (Exo. 20:1-18). The Jews believe that their reward for obeying God is the fulfillment of His promise that they will hold the land of Canaan forever (Gen. 17:8, 28:4; Exo. 6:4). The Christian Bible teaches that Jesus Christ is the Son of God, that He died on the cross to save all who believe in Him from the penalty of their sins (John 3:16) and that He said, "I am the way, the truth and the life: no man cometh unto the Father, but by me" (John 14:6). The Moslems call God "Allah" and believe that He revealed a book called the Koran to his prophet Mohammed. The Koran teaches the Moslems to pray, "Praise be to Allah who has never begotten a son; who has no partner in His Kingdom; who needs none to defend Him from humiliation" (17:111). The Koran also teaches that

> [b]ecause of their iniquity, We forbade the Jews good things which were formerly allowed them; because time after time they have debarred others from the path of Allah; because they practice usury--although they were forbidden it--and cheat others of their possessions. (4:160 et seq.)

The Hindu religion is based on the Vedas, which consist of four collections of sacred literature that include stories of celestial gods, hymns, spells, incantations to cure diseases, magical aids to victory in battle and mystic homologies. Asiatic shamanism is based on a belief in celestial gods and in the abilities of certain men and women, called "shamans," to communicate with these gods and enlist their aid to heal people and solve other problems. The Buddhists do not believe in heavenly spirits, but in four holy truths that were revealed to the Buddha Gotama. These truths include the proper way to achieve a state of "nirvana," or cessation of desire. The Sikhs believe in a "revelation in creation" that was described by Guru Nanak. The Jains believe in the "kevela," which is the supreme best knowledge obtained by their founder, Mahavira. The Zoroastrians believe they must choose between the good ways of Ahura Mazda, the god who created heaven and earth, and the ways of the destructive Evil Spirit. The Taoist Canon consists of the "Chuang Tzu," the "Lieh Tzu" and the "Tao Tê Ching." The Chuang Tzu distinguishes between the "lesser knowledge" and the "greater knowledge," the latter being gained while in a trance, a state in which "I lose me." The Shinto worshipper finds the reality of the "kami" by intuition rather than intellect. Confucianism is based on the practical teachings of Confucius and his common sense advice to people regarding their relationships with each other. Confucius also recognized a person's duties to spirits. In his *Analects*, he said, "Of the saying, 'The word "sacrifice" is like the word "present"; one should sacrifice to a spirit as though that spirit was present,' the Master said, If I am not present at the sacrifice, it is as though there were no sacrifice."[5] He also said, "How can

Chapter 11 Religion in the Public Schools

there be any proper service of spirits until the living men have been properly served?"[6]

Like Confucianism, most modern religions focus on common sense, practical rules for every day living, but they too include revealed law beliefs. Dr. Muzzey said of the Ethical Culture Movement that

> [w]hat ultimate reality is we do not know; but *we have the faith* [emphasis added] that it expresses itself in the human world as the power which *inspires* [emphasis added] in men moral purpose... Thus the "God" that we love is not the figure on the great white throne, but the perfect pattern, *envisioned by faith* [emphasis added], of humanity as it should be, purged of the evil elements which retard its progress toward "the knowledge, love and practice of the right."[7]

One modern religion maintains that all its precepts have a rational basis. In its book *What is Scientology?* the Church of Scientology says

> [n]othing in Scientology, however, need be taken on faith. Its truths are self-evident, its principles are easily demonstrable and its technology can be seen at work in any church of Scientology.[8]

However, in its chapter, "The Religious Heritage of Scientology," the Church says

> [t]he knowledge that man is a spirit is as old as man himself. Only recently, with the advent of Western psychology, have notions cropped up that man is merely another animal, a stimulus-response mechanism. Such espousals stand at odds to every religious tradition, which variously speak of the "soul," the "spirit" or the "life force"--to encompass a belief held by all civilized men.
>
> The Scientology religion follows just this tradition of man's search for his spiritual identity. In Scientology, the individual himself is considered to be the spiritual being--a thetan (pronounced "thay'-tn").[9]

The belief that man differs from other animals because he is a spiritual being does not appear to be sustainable by rational proof.

Therefore, even the Scientologists, who pride themselves on their rationality, acknowledge a glimmer of spiritual revelation.

Some modern religions hold that all religions are manifestations of the same truth, that they have the same goal or that they have equal validity. The Baha'is hold such beliefs, but they also believe that the common goal of all religions was fulfilled with the coming of the Baha'u'llah, who died in 1892.[10] The Universalists, who have merged with the Unitarians to form the Unitarian Universalist Church, originally believed in the universal salvation of all people from God's eternal damnation. However, most members of that church now reject the whole idea of salvation and believe instead that all religions offer valid guidance and inspiration.

An article by two Unitarian ministers, Karl M. Chworowsky and Christopher Gist Raible, says that Unitarian Universalists include "agnostics, humanists, even atheists--as well as nature worshipers, pantheists, and those who affirm a personal God."[11] Because of their lack of focus on God, some people contend the Unitarian Universalist Church is a philosophy and not a religion. However, a person's religion consists of more than his beliefs in respect of God, as the following statement illustrates:

> [t]he religion of Jesus, so simply and beautifully expressed in the Sermon on the Mount, remains an ethical ideal for most Unitarian Universalists.[12]

In the Sermon on the Mount, Jesus said, "Blessed are the meek, for they shall inherit the earth" (Matt. 5:5), "Whosoever shall smite thee on the right cheek, turn to him the other also" (Matt. 5:39) and "Love your enemies, bless them that curse you, do good to them that hate you, ..." (Matt. 5:44). There is nothing rational in these commandments. It is natural to love one's friends, but loving one's enemies is against human nature. These commandments are pure revealed law and they convey the heart and soul of the whole Sermon. Who can say that one revealed law is religion and another is not? Who can say that a person who believes in God but refuses to follow these commandments is religious, but a person who denies God but obeys these commandments is not religious?

In a nation that guarantees religious freedom, including freedom from an established religion, government cannot recognize any particular body of revealed law as "of infinitely more authority" than natural law, nor can it conform its laws to any one "law of revelation" (BL1, 42). Instead, government must give equal respect to all revealed law and allow each person to live by the revealed law of his choice. That is one of the meanings of the First Amendment command against laws "respecting an establishment of religion, or prohibiting the free exercise thereof."

Religious freedom therefore means that government laws must be based on human reason alone. At the same time, government must confront Blackstone's statement that man often finds "that his reason is corrupt, and his understanding full of ignorance and error" (BL1, 41). The solution lies in people's opening their minds to criticism and new ideas, admitting their ignorance and correcting their mistakes. The solution does not lie in government laws that force everyone to conform to one revealed law.

Professor Lawrence Tribe and other scholars have expressed concern that a broad definition of "religion" in connection with the prohibition against the establishment of religion would unduly limit "humane" government programs in the fields of psychology, mental health, war and poverty and the like. These scholars therefore believe a broad definition is appropriate for the free exercise guarantee but not for the prohibition against religious establishment. In his opinion in the *Malnak v. Yogi* case, Judge Adams answered this concern:

> [w]ere a school, or government agency, to advance the cause of peace, or opposition to war, such an official position would not qualify as a "religion" even though some citizens might come to adopt that very view because of their own religious beliefs. All programs or positions that entangle the government with issues and problems that might be classified as "ultimate concerns" do not, because of that, become "religious" programs or positions. Only if government favors a comprehensive belief system and advances its teachings does it establish a religion. It does not do so by endorsing isolated moral precepts or by enacting humanitarian economic programs. (592 F.2d at 212)

This concern would be further alleviated by requiring that a supposed religion embody some form of revealed law, in addition to being a comprehensive belief system relating to matters of ultimate concern.

Judge Adams also pointed out that the word "religion" appears only once in the First Amendment. Supreme Court Justice Rutledge said in his dissenting opinion in *Everson v. Board of Education*,

> the word governs two prohibitions and governs them alike. It does not have two meanings, one narrow to forbid "an establishment" and another, much broader, for securing "the free exercise thereof." "Thereof" brings down "religion" with its entire and exact content, no more and no less, from the first into the second guaranty, so that Congress and now the states are as broadly restricted concerning the one as they are regarding the other. (330 U.S. at 32)

D. Religion in Extracurricular Activities

Extracurricular activities are often run by students, with minimal faculty supervision and control. These activities have therefore presented religious freedom issues different from those presented in the course regular classroom instruction. In *Widmar v. Vincent*, 454 U.S. 263 (1981), the state-operated University of Missouri at Kansas City allowed over one hundred student groups to carry on a variety of activities in its buildings. However, it forbade student religious groups to use its buildings or grounds "for purposes of religious worship or religious teaching." The university believed that it had to forbid these activities to maintain the strict separation of church and state required by the establishment clauses of the federal and Missouri constitutions.

In a lawsuit challenging the validity of the university's policy on religious worship and teaching, the Federal District Court for the Western District of Missouri upheld the policy. It said that if the university had allowed religious worship or teaching on its campus, it would have failed the second part of establishment test laid down

Chapter 11   Religion in the Public Schools   627

by the Supreme Court in *Lemon v. Kurtzman*, supra., because it would have allowed its buildings to be used for the advancement of religion. The Eighth Circuit Court of Appeals in St. Louis, however, reversed this judgment and the U. S. Supreme Court upheld the reversal. Speaking for the Supreme Court, Justice Powell said,

> First, an open forum in a public university does not confer any imprimatur of state approval on religious sects or practices. As the Court of Appeals quite aptly stated, such a policy "would no more commit the University . . .[to] religious goals" than it is "now committed to the goals of the Students for a Democratic Society, the Young Socialist Alliance," or any other group eligible to use its facilities. 635 F.2d, at 1317.
>
> Second, the forum is available to a broad class of nonreligious speakers; there are over 100 recognized student groups at UMKC. The provision of benefits to so broad a spectrum of groups is an important index of secular effect. See, *e.g., Wolman v. Walter*, 433 U.S. 229, 240-241 (1977); *Committee for Public Education v. Nyquist, supra*, at 781-782, and n. 38. If the Establishment Clause barred the extension of general benefits to religious groups, "a church could not be protected by the police and fire departments, or have its public sidewalk kept in repair." *Roemer v. Maryland Public Works Bd., supra*, at 747 (plurality opinion); quoted in *Committee for Public Education v. Regan*, 444 U.S., at 658, n. 6. At least in the absence of empirical evidence that religious groups will dominate UMKC's open forum, we agree with the Court of Appeals that the advancement of religion would not be the forum's "primary effect." (Ibid., 274-275)

In a footnote to the first paragraph, Justice Powell said, "University students are, of course, young adults. They are less impressionable than younger students and should be able to appreciate that the University's policy is one of neutrality toward religion" (Ibid., 274, n. 14).

For these reasons, the Supreme Court ruled that the establishment clause did not prevent the University of Missouri from allowing student groups the free exercise of their religion. The university policy therefore violated the rights of the students that were guaranteed by the free speech and the free exercise clauses of the First Amendment. In response to the university's argument that its policy was necessary to comply with the establishment clause of the Missouri constitution, Justice Powell said the requirements of Missouri constitution had to bow to those of the U. S. Constitution (Ibid., 276).

Justice Powell indicated the Supreme Court might have ruled differently had there been "empirical evidence that religious groups will dominate UMKC's open forum" (Ibid., 275). In *Lubbock Civil Liberties Union v. Lubbock Independent School District*, 669 F.2d 1038 (5th Cir., 1982), there was such evidence. That case was the result of a ten-year-long battle between the Civil Liberties Union and the school district of Lubbock, Texas. In 1971, the Civil Liberties Union had complained to the district about school assemblies of "of a Protestant Christian evangelical variety," Bible readings over school public address systems, classroom prayers led by teachers, a period of silent prayer ended by "Amen" over school public address systems and distribution of Gideon Bibles to fifth and sixth grade students. Upon receiving that complaint, the school district agreed to stop these activities. However, the evidence at trial showed that these activities "continued unabated" (Ibid., 1039). In response to public complaints, on January 25, 1979, the board of trustees of the school district adopted "a broad policy regarding religion in the schools." According to the board's minutes, the school administration adopted a procedure that

> provides that we allow student initiated religious activities. *Basically, this will fairly well continue following our present practice* [emphasis added by the court]. You should make the staff aware that we are to comply with the student-centered activity. This provision applies even in the classroom, and teachers are not to promote or initiate the activities. We have the responsibility to provide alternate activities for students who have objections to taking part in any of these programs that we may have. (Ibid., 1040)

In September 1979, the Civil Liberties Union sued the school district, claiming that its policy violated the establishment clause of the First Amendment. In August 1980, the board of trustees responded with a new policy that said that

> [t]he school board permits students to gather at the school with supervision either before or after regular school hours on the same basis as other groups as determined by the school administration to meet for any educational, moral, religious or ethical purposes so long as attendance at such meetings is voluntary. (Ibid., 1041)

The district judge ruled that the January 1979 policy violated the establishment clause of the First Amendment but that the August 1980 policy did not violate the clause. The Fifth Circuit Court of Appeals in New Orleans reversed this ruling with regard to the 1980 policy, holding that it violated all three parts of the *Lemon v. Kurtzman* test. It said the policy had a religious purpose because its statement that students may gather "on the same basis as other groups" indicated it was primarily for the benefit of students who gathered for religious purposes. The policy also had a primary effect of advancing religion because the meetings were timed in association with the beginning or end of the school day and were supervised by school personnel. The Court of Appeals said the *Widmar v. Vincent* ruling did not apply, because the Supreme Court had said in that case that university students were less impressionable than younger students and were therefore able to appreciate that a policy of neutrality toward religion was not an endorsement. The Court of Appeals also said the supervision by school personnel caused an excessive entanglement with religion. In reaching these conclusions, the court was probably influenced by the background and circumstances of the new school board policy, particularly the board's history of using every tactic possible to preserve its program of Christian religious instruction.

In 1984, Congress passed the Federal Equal Access Act, which required public secondary schools that receive federal assistance to provide the same kind of access to religious and political groups that the Supreme Court had said was required by colleges in the *Widmar v. Vincent* case, supra. The Act applied to all secondary schools that received federal assistance and maintained a "limited open forum" by granting "an offering to or opportunity for one or more non-curriculum related student groups to meet on school premises during non-instructional time." It forbade such schools to deny "equal access" to students wishing to meet within the forum because of the "religious, political, philosophical, or other content" of their meetings. The Act provided that a school shall be deemed to offer a fair opportunity to such students if it uniformly provides that the meetings are voluntary and student initiated, are not sponsored by the school or the government, do not interfere with the orderly conduct of the schools educational activities and are not directed, controlled, conducted, or regularly attended by non-school persons. The Act also provided that if the meetings are religious, employees or agents of the school or government may attend only in a "non-participatory capacity."

The Federal Equal Access Act raised two questions: what did the law mean by "non-curriculum related student groups" and did the law violate the establishment clause of the First Amendment? The Supreme Court answered both these questions in *Board of Education of the Westside Community Schools v. Mergens*, 496 U.S. 226 (1990). In that case, the Westside High School in Omaha, Nebraska received federal assistance and maintained about thirty after-school student clubs. They included band and choir clubs; sports clubs; student community volunteer clubs; math, debate and journalism clubs; a chess club and clubs that introduced students to adult occupations, such as the Future Business Leaders of America. The school board recognized all student clubs as a "vital part of the total education program as a means of developing citizenship, wholesome attitudes, good human relations, knowledge and skills" (Ibid., 231).

In January 1985, one of the Westside students, Bridget Mergens, asked the school principal, Dr. Findley, for permission to form a Christian club. She asked that the club be allowed to meet under the same conditions as other clubs, except that it not have a faculty sponsor. Dr. Findley denied Mergens' request. She therefore sued the Westside School District, claiming that the school authorities had violated the Federal Equal Access Act.

In an eight-to-one decision, the Supreme Court ruled that the Equal Access Act, as applied to Westside High School, did not violate the establishment clause of the First Amendment. One of the problems the Court faced in reaching that decision was that it had said in the *Widmar* case that university students were adults and therefore less likely than younger students to mistake a school's equal access policy for an official endorsement of religion. There had also been two recent federal court of appeals rulings that religious meetings in secondary schools violated the First Amendment's establishment clause, at least in some circumstances [*Brandon v. Board of Education of the Guilderland Central School District*, 635 F.2d 971 (1980), decided before the Supreme Court's decision in *Widmar v. Vincent*, and *Lubbock Civil Liberties Union v. Lubbock Independent School District*, supra, decided after *Widmar v. Vincent*]. Those decisions were based in part on the premise that secondary school students were still at impressionable ages.

Speaking for Chief Justice Rehnquist and Justices White and Blackmun, Justice O'Connor said in the Court's plurality opinion that secondary school students were mature enough to understand that "schools do not endorse everything they fail to censor." She cited 92 *Yale Law Journal* 499, 507-509, disclosing research in adolescent psychology, and testimony in the legislative history of the Act that "students below the college level are capable of distinguishing between State-initiated, school-sponsored, or teacher-led religious speech on the one hand and student-initiated, student-led religious speech on the other" (Ibid., 250-251). Therefore, she said, when a secondary school adopts a the limited open forum as defined by the Act, it sends a message of religious neutrality, not endorsement.

Justice Kennedy filed a concurring opinion in which he criticized the "endorsement" test used by Justice O'Connor. He said that a public high school might endorse a religious club

> if the club happens to be one of many activities that the school permits students to choose in order to further the development of their intellect and character in an extracurricular setting. But no constitutional

violation occurs if the school's action is based upon a recognition of the fact that membership in a religious club is one of many permissible ways for a student to further his or her own personal enrichment. The inquiry with respect to coercion must be whether the government imposes pressure upon a student to participate in a religious activity. The inquiry, of course, must be undertaken with sensitivity to the special circumstances that exist in a secondary school where the line between voluntary and coerced participation may be difficulty to draw. No such coercion, however, has been shown to exist as a necessary result of this statute, either on its face or as respondents seek to invoke it on the facts of this case. (Ibid., 261-262)

Justice Scalia joined in Kennedy's opinion.

Justice Marshall filed an opinion concurring in the Court's judgment that the Equal Access Act, as applied to the Westside high school, could avoid violating the establishment clause. However, he expressed serious reservations concerning the fact the Westside board did not recognize any student club that advocates a controversial viewpoint and the fact the board treated its whole student club program as an extension of its educational mission. He said,

> The entry of religious clubs into such a realm poses a real danger that those clubs will be viewed as part of the school's effort to inculcate fundamental values. The school's message with respect to its existing clubs is not one of toleration but one of endorsement. As the majority concedes, the program is part of the "district's commitment to teaching academic, physical, civic, and personal skills and values." *Ante*, at 232. But although a school may permissibly encourage its students to become well rounded as student-athletes, student-musicians, and student-tutors, the Constitution forbids schools to encourage students to become well-rounded as student-worshippers. Neutrality towards religion, as required by the Constitution, is not advanced by requiring a school that endorses the goals of some non-controversial secular organizations to endorse the goals of religious organizations as well. (Ibid., 265-266)

Justice Marshall said the Westside board must therefore do more than comply with the Equal Access Act to avoid violating the establishment clause. Instead of merely prohibiting faculty members from actively participating in the Christian club's meetings, he said

> [i]t must fully disassociate itself from the club's religious speech and avoid appearing to sponsor or endorse the club's goals. It could, for example, entirely discontinue encouraging student participation in clubs and clarify that the clubs are not instrumentally related to the school's overall mission. Or, if the school sought to continue its general endorsement of those student clubs that did not engage in controversial speech, it could do so if it also affirmatively disclaimed any endorsement of the Christian club. (Ibid., 270)

Justice Brennan joined in Marshall's opinion.

The Court also ruled that the Westside High School violated the Equal Access Act, even though its extracurricular clubs were all recognized as a "vital part of the total educational program." Justice O'Connor said the Act applied if a school receiving federal assistance maintained any after-school club whose subject matter was not covered in a class that was taught as part of the school curriculum. That was what the Act meant by a "non-curriculum related student group." Therefore, chess clubs and community service clubs would be "non-curriculum related," unless they covered subjects taught in regular school classes.

Justice Stevens was the lone dissenter in the *Westside* case. He said the Equal Access Act did not apply to Westside because there was no "limited open forum" within the meaning of the Act. He said that Congress intended the Act to apply only to secondary schools that permitted student clubs that had as their purpose "the advocacy of partisan theological, political or ethical views" (Ibid., 276). He also said,

> The Court's construction of this Act, however, leads to a sweeping intrusion by the Federal Government into the operation of our public schools, and does so despite the absence of any indication that Congress intended to divest local school districts of their power to shape the educational environment. If a high school administration continues to believe that it is sound policy to exclude controversial groups, such

as political clubs, the Klu Klux Klan, and perhaps gay rights advocacy groups, from its facilities, it now must also close its doors to traditional extracurricular activities that are non-controversial but not directly related to any course being offered at the school. (Ibid., 290)

The *Westside* case showed the complex problems that result from extending equal access requirements to public secondary schools. High school students can understand that their teachers and administrators do not endorse everything they fail to censor. However, most high school teachers and administrators exercise more control than their college counterparts over the kinds of extracurricular activities that take place in their buildings. In fact, "extracurricular" is not a good description of these high school activities because they are usually viewed as a part of the school curriculum, even though student participation in them is voluntary. Unfortunately, Congress did not show much appreciation for this difference when it passed the Equal Access Act.

On the other hand, public school teachers and administrators must be careful not to violate the religious freedom of their students, even when the Equal Access Act does not apply. They should recognize that they cannot control the religion, or the lack of religion, that students practice in their schools, except when the students interfere with the school's secular educational program or violate secular school regulations. That restraint is not easy for teachers and administrators who are accustomed to exercising tight control over what goes on in their schools.

E. Graduation Prayers

The leading Supreme Court decision on whether school graduation prayers violate the establishment clause is the 1992 case of *Lee v. Weisman*, 505 U.S. 577. Before reviewing that decision, however, we should take a look at several prior lower court decisions that provide a helpful background.

Two of these lower-court cases were consolidated as *Stein and Dahlinger v. Plainwell Community Schools and Portage Public Schools*, 822 F.2d 1406 (6th Cir., 1987). The parents of graduating seniors sued two school districts near Kalamazoo, Michigan, challenging the invocation and benediction prayers at their graduation ceremonies. In both cases, the ceremonies were held at athletic facilities and the graduating seniors were not required to attend the ceremonies to receive their diplomas. At the Plainwell commencement, the invocation and benediction were delivered by honor students who chose the content of their prayers. The Portage commencement was organized and developed by the graduating seniors. For the previous fifteen years, each Portage senior class had chosen to include an invocation and a benediction in its ceremony. Senior class representatives chose local ministers of various Christian denominations to give these prayers.

In 1985, the Plainwell invocation ended with the words, "For it is in giving that we receive; it is in pardoning that we are pardoned and it is in dying that we are born to eternal life." In the same year, the Portage invocation ended with the request, "[W]e ask your blessing upon us now and always through Christ our Lord."

Speaking for the three-judge Federal Court of Appeals in Cincinnati, Judge Gilbert Merritt said these graduation prayers were more like the legislature's prayers in *Marsh v. Chambers*, supra, than the classroom prayers of *Engel v. Vitale* and other school prayer decisions by the U. S. Supreme Court. He said,

> [These] ceremonial invocations and benedictions present less opportunity for religious indoctrination or peer pressure. The potential for coercion in the prayer opportunity was one of the distinctions employed by the Court in *Marsh* to separate legislative prayer from classroom prayer.... Although children are obviously attending the public nature of the proceeding and the usual presence of parents act as a buffer against religious coercion. In addition, the graduation context does not implicate the special nature of the teacher-student relationship--a relationship that focuses on the transmission of knowledge and values by an authority figure. Therefore, the prayer in question here should be analyzed under the *Marsh* standards for ceremonial prayer notwithstanding the fact that a school function is involved. (Ibid., 1409-1410)

However, Judge Merritt ruled that the Plainwell and Portage prayers violated the establishment clause because

> they do not pass the *Marsh* test. They are framed and phrased so that they "symbolically place the government's seal of approval on one religious view"--the Christian view. They employ the language of Christian theology and prayer. Some expressly invoke the name of Jesus as the Savior. They are not "civil" invocations or benedictions used in public legislative and judicial sessions as described in *Marsh*. (Ibid., 1410)

Judge Ted Milburn concurred with Judge Merritt's ruling, but Judge Harry Wellford dissented, on the ground that the Supreme Court had said in *Marsh v. Chambers* that

> "[t]he content of the prayer is not of concern to judges where, as here, there is no indication that the prayer opportunity has been exploited to proselytize or advance any one, or to disparage any other, faith or belief. That being so, it is not for us to embark on a sensitive evaluation or to parse the content of a particular prayer." (Ibid., 1412, citing 463 U.S. at 794-795)

Therefore, Judge Wellford said,

> the question in this case is *not* what kind of invocation or benediction, if any, does the Constitution permit; rather it is whether any invocation or benediction at a public high school commencement in the form of a prayer, or reference to the Deity, the content of which is not officially prescribed, is constitutionally permissible. (Ibid.)

He would have ruled that the Plainwell and Portage prayers did not violate the Constitution because they were composed and delivered by students or their invited guests, not by school administrators or teachers. Although Judge Wellford's opinion was one of dissent, the more recent cases have shown that his focus on the control excercised by the school officials was the correct approach.

In *Jones v. Clear Creek Independent School District*, 930 F.2d 416 (5th Cir., 1991), the Clear Creek, Texas, Board of Trustees adopted the following resolution, drafted by the board's attorney to insure that its graduation ceremonies complied with Judge Merritt's opinion in *Stein v. Plainwell*, supra:

> 1. The use of an invocation and/or benediction at high school graduation exercise shall rest within the discretion of the graduating senior class, with the advice and counsel of the senior class principal;
> 2. The invocation and benediction, if used, shall be given by a student volunteer; and
> 3. Consistent with the principle of equal liberty of conscience[, the invocation and benediction shall be non-sectarian and non-proselytizing. (Ibid., 417)

Following this resolution, the 1986 Clear Creek graduation invocation mentioned, "Lord," "Gospel," "Amen" and God's omnipotence, but did not make the kind of overt references to Christianity that prior invocations had made.

The Federal District Court for the Southern District of Texas ruled that the Constitution's establishment clause did not prohibit the Clear Creek Board from permitting invocations that conform with its resolution. The Fifth Circuit Court of Appeals in New Orleans affirmed that ruling. Judge Thomas Reavley of the Court of Appeals said the resolution met all three parts of the *Lemon* test.

First, Reavley said the resolution had the secular purpose of solemnizing the Clear Creek graduation ceremony. He quoted Supreme Court Justice O'Connor's statement in *Lynch v. Donnelly* that "government acknowledgments of religion serve, in the only ways reasonably possible in our culture, the legitimate purpose[ ] of solemnizing public occasions" (Ibid., 420, quoting 465 U.S. at 693). He rejected the plaintiff's contention that this solemnization purpose was only a pretext for introducing prayer in the public schools. He said that unlike those in prior cases, the students in this case determined whether there would be a prayer and the resolution's nonproselytizing and nonsectarian mandates de-emphasized the religious significance of whatever prayer the students chose. He acknowledged the resolution tolerated invocations to a deity, but he said, we think that this is as consistent with the secular solemnizing purpose as any religious purpose. It is precisely in acknowledging a principle of transcendence, with simple terms of universal understanding--like "God"--that graduation attendees may perceive the profound social significance of the occasion. It is not implausible that Clear Creek's Trustees intended the Resolution to foster just such a perception in many, if not most, attendees. The Resolution's "reason or effect merely happens to coincide or harmonize with the tenets of some . . . religions." *Lynch*, 465 U.S. at 682, 104 S.Ct. at 1364 [citation omitted]. We reject a reading of the First Amendment that would freeze either church and state or religion and politics into perpetually antagonistic postures. (Ibid., 420)

Judge Reavley also said the resolution did not have the primary effect of advancing religion but merely accommodated religion in the manner of the legislature's prayers of *Marsh v. Chambers*, the motto "In God We Trust" on money, and the Pledge of Allegiance to "One nation under God." Graduating seniors, he said, were old enough to understand the difference between daily classroom prayers designed to advance religion and student-initiated, ceremonial graduation prayers that merely accommodate religion.

Reavley said the resolution did not create a government entanglement with religion, because there was no evidence that school administrators chose the students who prepared and presented the prayers nor did they require that there be any prayers. Their only involvement was in screening proposed prayers for sectarianism and proselytization.

A year after the Fifth Circuit's *Clear Creek* decision, the Supreme Court decided *Lee v. Weisman*, supra. In 1989, Robert E. Lee, principal of the Nathan Bishop Middle School in Providence, Rhode Island, invited Rabbi Leslie Gutterman of the Temple Beth El to give the invocation and benediction at the school's graduation ceremony. Lee advised Gutterman that the prayers should be nonsectarian and gave him a pamphlet entitled, "Guidelines for Civic Occasions," prepared by the National Conference of Christians and Jews. The pamphlet recommended that their prayers at nonsectarian civic ceremonies be composed with "inclusiveness and sensitivity," although "[p]rayer of any kind may be inappropriate on some civic occasions" (Ibid., 581).

Four days before the graduation ceremony, Deborah Weisman, a student who was to graduate in the Middle School ceremony, and her father sued the principal in the local federal district court. They asked for an order restraining the principal from including an invocation or benediction in the ceremony. The district judge did not act in time to stop these prayers, but Deborah and her family attended the ceremony and heard the prayers, even though Deborah was not required to attend to receive her diploma. Rabbi Gutterman's invocation began, "God of the Free, Hope of the Brave: For the legacy of America where diversity is celebrated and the rights of minorities are protected, we thank You. . . ." and ended, "May our aspirations for our country and for these young people, who are our hope for the future, be richly fulfilled. Amen." His benediction began "O God, we are grateful to You for having endowed us with the capacity for learning which we have celebrated on this joyous commencement. . . " and ended "We give thanks to You, Lord, for keeping us alive, sustaining us and allowing us to reach this special, happy occasion. Amen." The intermediate parts of both prayers contained the same types of petitions and thanks to God.

After the commencement, the Weismans filed an amended complaint asking that all officials of all the Providence schools be permanently enjoined from inviting clergy to deliver prayers at future graduations. The district judge granted the injunction and the First Circuit Court of Appeals in Boston affirmed the order. The Providence school district then appealed to the Supreme Court of the United States.

By a five-to-four vote, the U. S. Supreme Court affirmed the rulings of the two lower courts. Speaking for the majority, Justice Kennedy said

> [t]hese dominant facts mark and control the confines of our decision: State officials direct the performance of a formal religious exercise at promotional and graduation ceremonies for secondary schools. Even for those students who object to religious exercise, their attendance and participation in state-sponsored religious activity are in

a fair and real sense obligatory, though the school district does not require attendance as a condition for receipt of the diploma. (Ibid., 586)

Justice Kennedy then explained why these activities violated the Constitution:

> [t]he principle that government may accommodate the free exercise of religion does not supersede the fundamental limitations imposed by the Establishment Clause. It is beyond dispute that, at a minimum, the Constitution guarantees that government may not coerce anyone to support or participate in religion or its exercise, or otherwise act in a way which "establishes a [state] religion or religious faith, or tends to do so." *Lynch, supra,* at 678; [other citations omitted] The State's involvement in the school prayers challenged today violates these central principles.
>
> That involvement is as troubling as it is undenied. A school official, the principal, decided that an invocation and a benediction should be given; this is a choice attributable to the State, and from a constitutional perspective it is as if a state statute decreed that the prayers must occur. The principal chose the religious participant, here a rabbi, and that choice is also attributable to the State. . . .
>
> We are asked to recognize the existence of a practice of nonsectarian prayer, prayer within the embrace of what is known as the Judeo-Christian tradition, prayer which is more acceptable than one which, for example, makes explicit references to the God of Israel, or to Jesus Christ, or to a patron saint. There may be some support, as an empirical observation, to the statement of the Court of Appeals for the Sixth Circuit, picked up by Judge Campbell's dissent in the Court of Appeals in this case, that there has emerged in this country a civic religion, one which is tolerated when sectarian exercises are not. *Stein,* 822 F.2d, at 1409; 908 F.2d 1090, 1098-1099 (CA1 1990) (Campbell, J., dissenting) (case below); see also Note, Civil Religion and the Establishment Clause, 95 Yale L. J. 1237 (1986). If common ground can be defined which permits once conflicting faiths to express the shared conviction that there is an ethic and a morality which transcend human invention, the sense of community and purpose of all decent societies might be advanced. But though the First Amendment does not allow

the government to stifle prayers which aspire to these ends, neither does it permit the government to undertake that task for itself.

The First Amendment's Religion Clauses mean that religious beliefs and religious expression are too precious to be either proscribed or prescribed by the State. The design of the Constitution is that preservation and transmission of religious beliefs and worship is a responsibility and a choice committed to the private sphere, which itself is promised freedom to pursue that mission. It must not be forgotten, then, that while concern must be given to define the protection granted to an objector or a dissenting nonbeliever, these same Clauses exist to protect religion from government interference. James Madison, the principal author of the Bill of Rights, did not rest his opposition to a religious establishment on the sole ground of its effect on the minority. A principal ground for his view was: "[E]xperience witnesseth that ecclesiastical establishments, instead of maintaining the purity and efficacy of Religion, have had a contrary operation." . . . [App. M, Par. 7, Kennedy's citations omitted]

These concerns have particular application in the case of school officials, whose effort to monitor prayer will be perceived by the students as inducing a participation they might otherwise reject. Though the efforts of the school officials in this case to find common ground appear to have been a good-faith attempt to recognize the common aspects of religions and not the divisive ones, our precedents do not permit school officials to assist in composing prayers as an incident to a formal exercise for their students. *Engel v. Vitale, supra,* at 425. And these same precedents caution us to measure the idea of a civic religion against the central meaning of the Religion Clauses of the First Amendment, which is that all creeds must be tolerated and none favored. The suggestion that government may establish an official or civic religion as a means of avoiding the establishment of a religion with more specific creeds strikes us as a contradiction that cannot be accepted. (Ibid., 587, 589-590)

One of the school district's arguments was that the Weismans were not injured because Deborah Weisman was not required to attend her graduation ceremony. Justice Scalia based his dissent on this point and he was joined by Chief Justice Rehnquist and Justices White and Thomas. Justice Scalia said the optional nature of these ceremonies made them no different from the numerous government ceremonies at which prayers had been offered since the adoption of the Constitution. Kennedy responded that

> [e]veryone knows that in our society and in our culture high school graduation is one of life's most significant occasions. A school rule which excuses attendance is beside the point. Attendance may not be required by official decree, yet it is apparent that a student is not free to absent herself from the graduation exercise in any real sense of the term "voluntary," for absence would require forfeiture of those intangible benefits which have motivated the student through youth an all her high school years. Graduation is a time for family and those closest to the student to celebrate success and express mutual wishes of gratitude and respect, all to the end of impressing upon the young person the role that it is his or her right and duty to assume in the community and all of its diverse parts. (Ibid., 595)

He also said that when students do attend,

> the school district's supervision and control of a high school graduation ceremony places public pressure, as well as peer pressure, on attending students to stand as a group or, at least, maintain respectful silence during the invocation and benediction. This pressure, though subtle and indirect, can be as real as any overt compulsion. Of course, in our culture standing or remaining silent can signify adherence to a view or simple respect for the views of others. And no doubt some persons who have no desire to join in a prayer have little objection to standing as a sign of respect for those who do. But for the dissenter of high school age, who has a reasonable perception that she is being forced by the State to pray in a manner her conscience will not allow, the injury is no less real. There can be no doubt that for many, if not most, of the students at the graduation, the act of standing or remaining silent was an expression of participation in the rabbi's prayer. That was the very point of the religious exercise. It is of little comfort for the dissenter, then, to be told that for her the act of standing or remaining in silence signifies mere respect, rather than participation. What matters is that, given our social conventions, a reasonable dissenter in this milieu could believe that the group exercise signified her own participation or approval of it.

Finding no violation under these circumstances would place objectors in the dilemma of participating, with all that implies, or protesting. We do not address whether that choice is acceptable if the affected citizens are mature adults, but we think the State may not, consistent with the Establishment Clause, place primary and secondary school children in this position. Research in psychology supports the common assumption that adolescents are often susceptible to pressure from their peers towards conformity, and that the influence is strongest in matters of social convention. . . .

It is, we concede, a brief exercise during which the individual can concentrate on joining its message, meditate on her own religion, or let her mind wander. But the embarrassment and the intrusion of the religious exercise cannot be refuted by arguing that these prayers, and similar ones to be said in the future, are of a *de minimus* character. To do so would be an affront to the rabbi who offered them and to all those for whom the prayers were an essential and profound recognition of divine authority. (Ibid., 593, 594)

Justice Kennedy might have also pointed out to the dissenting justices that Deborah's father Daniel had sued the Providence school board as a taxpayer and that his rights were violated by forcing him to pay taxes to a school system that prescribed religious exercises as a part of its graduation ceremonies. Madison's Memorial and Remonstrance (App. M) showed how those kinds of taxes violated people's religious freedom.[13]

After the *Lee v. Weisman* decision, the Supreme Court vacated the Fifth Circuit Court of Appeals judgment in *Jones v. Clear Creek*, supra, and remanded the case to that court so that it could determine whether its judgment conflicted with *Lee v. Weisman* (505 U.S. 1215 [1992]). On remand, the Fifth Circuit Court of Appeals ruled that its prior decision did not conflict with the Supreme Court's ruling because

[u]nlike the policy at issue in *Lee*, it [the Clear Creek Resolution] does not mandate a prayer. The Resolution does not even mandate an invocation; it merely permits one if the seniors so choose. Moreover, the students present Clear Creek with *their* proposed invocation under

the Resolution, while in *Lee* the school explained its idea for an invocation to a member of an organized religion and directed him to deliver it. -- U.S. at --, 112 S.Ct. at 2652-53, The Resolution is passive compared to the governmental overture toward religion at issue in *Lee*. (977 F.2d 963, 968 [1992])

The plaintiff Merritt Jones asked the Supreme Court to review this decision but his petition was denied (cert. denied, 508 U.S. 967 [1993]).

Since the Fifth Circuit court issued its second opinion in *Jones v. Clear Creek*, other federal appellate and district courts have disagreed with its interpretation of the *Lee v. Weisman* decision. In *Gearon v. Loudoun County School Board*, 844 F.Supp. 1097 (E.D. Va., 1993), a district judge in Alexandria, Virginia, ruled that a school board resolution similar to the *Clear Creek* resolution violated the Constitution. The judge criticized the Fifth Circuit's reasoning in *Clear Creek*, saying, "The notion that a person's constitutional rights may be subject to a majority vote is itself anathema." However, he noted there were factual differences between his case and the *Clear Creek* case, including the fact that the school board in his case had "exhorted" student-sponsored prayers at the district's high school graduation ceremonies (Ibid., 1100). In *Harris v. Joint School District No. 241 and Citizens Preserving America's Heritage*, 41 F.3rd 447 (1994), the Ninth Circuit Court of Appeals in San Francisco also criticized the *Clear Creek* decision when it ruled unconstitutional a Grangeville, Idaho school district policy that allowed graduating seniors to vote on whether to have prayers at their graduation ceremony. This court noted that faculty members and administrators still supervised and controlled the ceremony and the school district assumed the cost of the event. However, the U. S. Supreme Court granted the school district's petition to review this decision and then vacated it and directed the Ninth Circuit Court to dismiss the case as moot [115 S.Ct. 2604 (1995)]. The *Clear Creek* decision was criticized again by a thirteen judge panel of the Third Circuit Court of Appeals in Philadelphia in *ACLU of New Jersey v. Black Horse Pike Regional Board of Education*, 84 F.3rd 1471 (1996). A majority of nine judges ruled unconstitutional a school board policy that allowed graduating students to decide whether prayer would be included in the graduating ceremony as well as the nature of any such prayer. The majority opinion quoted the Ninth Circuit court in the *Harris* case:

> "We cannot allow the school district's delegate to make decisions that the school district cannot make. When the senior class is given plenary power over a state-sponsored, state-controlled event such as a high school graduation, it is just as constrained by the Constitution as the state would be." (Ibid., 1483, quoting 41 F.3rd at 455)

Four of the thirteen judges dissented, saying they would have followed the Fifth Circuit court's reasoning in the *Clear Creek* case. Apparently, no petition was filed asking the U. S. Supreme Court to review this case.

Meanwhile, the Fifth Circuit Court of Appeals in New Orleans has confirmed its opinion in the *Clear Creek* case. In *Ingebretsen v. Jackson Public School District*, 88 F.3rd 274 (1996), the court ruled a Mississippi state law constitutional insofar as it permitted student initiated voluntary prayer at graduation ceremonies, saying in found that portion of the law constitutionally sound under the *Clear Creek* decision (Ibid., 280). The court ruled that the remainder of the law was unconstitutional because it permitted student initiated voluntary prayer at all compulsory and noncompulsory school-related student assemblies. The court distinguished this part of the law from the graduation part because it permitted prayers led not only by students but by teachers and administrators as well, and the prayers could be given at assemblies that all students had to attend as part of their curriculum. The U. S. Supreme Court denied the Mississippi attorney general's petition to review this case [117 S.Ct. 388 (1996)].

In *Adler v. Duval County School Board*, 851 F.Supp. 446 (M.D. Fla., 1994), a Jacksonville, Florida district judge, William Terrell Hodges, upheld the constitutionality of the following school guidelines for graduation ceremonies:

1. The use of a brief opening and/or closing message, not to exceed two minutes, at high school graduation exercises shall rest within the discretion of the graduating senior class;

2. The opening and/or closing message shall be given by a student volunteer, in the graduating senior class, chosen by the graduating senior class as a whole;

3. If the graduating senior class chooses to use an opening and/or closing message, the content of that message shall be prepared by the student volunteer and shall not be monitored or otherwise reviewed by Duval County School Board [sic], its officers or employees. (Ibid., 449)

Judge Hodges said,

> This Court agrees with the Fifth Circuit's analysis in *Jones* [*v. Clear Creek*] that "the graduation prayers permitted by the [guidelines] place less psychological pressure on students than the prayers at issue in *Lee* because all students . . . are aware that any prayers represent the will of their peers, who are less able to coerce participation than an authority figure from the state or clergy." (Ibid., 456, citing 977 F.2d at 971)

On appeal, the Eleventh Circuit Court of Appeals in Atlanta ruled that the *Adler* case should be dismissed for procedural reasons and it therefore declined to rule on the merits of the students' claim that their constitutional rights had been violated (112 F.3d 1475 [1997]).

Of the two lines of lower court decisions on student-initiated graduation prayers, the decisions by the Fifth Circuit and Jacksonville district courts show a better understanding of the Supreme Court's *Lee v. Weisman* decision. The school officials in *Lee v. Weisman* were heavily involved in selecting the graduation prayer (505 U.S. at 590) and that was why the Supreme Court ruled the prayer was a "state-sanctioned religious exercise in which the student was left with no alternative but to submit" (Ibid., 597). Furthermore, the Court gave tacit approval to the Fifth Circuit court's view when it refused to grant a petition for certiorari to review the *Jones v. Clear Creek* and *Ingebretsen v. Jackson* decisions. In its only opportunity to review a contrary decision, the

Court vacated the Ninth Circuit decision in *Harris v. Joint School District No. 241,* 115 S.Ct. 2604 (1995).

The kind of prayer policy adopted by the Duval County, Florida, schools appears to have the best chance of receiving Supreme Court approval. A possible objection to the Clear Creek policy is that it provides that a school principal shall give advice and counsel to the senior class on their use of an invocation and/or benediction. The Duval County policy forbids any monitoring by school employees. Presumably, the Clear Creek Board was concerned that without adult monitoring, the students might give prayers that were proselytizing or sectarian. However, the mere fact that a school administrator has the power to determine what is proselytizing or sectarian might be enough to cause the Supreme Court to rule the process unconstitutional.

In *Marsh v. Chambers,* the Supreme Court approved a state legislature's prayers because the legislators did not exploit the prayer opportunity "to proselytize or advance any one, or to disparage any other, faith or belief" (463 U.S. at 794-795). The decisions approving student-initiated high school graduation prayers are based on the proposition that graduating seniors have the same right as government legislators to have prayers at their respective convocations. That proposition supposes that the graduating seniors can exercise as much restraint as politicians with regard to proselytizing. Perhaps the seniors can be trusted to act more responsibly. There is no basis for ruling that they have a lesser right to pray than a state legislature.

F. Religious Music and Holiday Celebrations

In recent years, officials in many school districts have instructed music teachers to remove all religious music from their courses and choir repertoires. They no longer include religious music in their Christmas holiday celebrations.

The U. S. Supreme Court has not ruled on whether this music violates the establishment clause of the Constitution. However, several lower courts have ruled on the matter and they have all ruled that the religious music does not violate the Constitution. The judges have distinguished this music from prayers and religious classes because its purposes are secular, namely, to teach music skills, to teach an appreciation of music and to celebrate the secular aspects of holidays. Several judges have compared this music to the literary and historic study of the Bible. They have relied on Justice Clark's statement in *Abington v. Schempp* that "[n]othing we have said here indicates that such study of the Bible or of religion, when presented objectively as part of a secular program of education, may not be effected consistently with the First Amendment" (374 U.S. at 225, cited in *Florey v. Sioux Falls School District 49-5*, 619 F.2d at 1315-1316; *Bauchman v. West High School*, 900 F.Supp. at 269; and *Doe v. Duncanville Independent School District*, 70 F.3rd at 407).

In *Florey v. Sioux Falls School District 49-5*, 619 F.2d 1311 (8th Cir., 1980), the school district had received complaints that its Christmas assemblies were religious exercises. The 1977 program at one elementary school featured a responsive discourse between the teacher and the students entitled, "The Beginners Christmas Quiz," which included the following:

Teacher:	Of whom did heav'nly angels sing, and news about his birthday bring?
Class:	Jesus.
Teacher:	Now, can you name the little town where they the Baby Jesus found?
Class:	Bethlehem.
Teacher:	Where had they made a little bed for Christ, the blessed Saviour's head?
Class:	In a manger in a cattle stall.
Teacher:	What is the day we celebrate as birthday of this One so great?
Class:	Christmas.

In response to the complaints, a citizen's committee was appointed to study the matter. The committee formulated a policy statement and a set of rules outlining the bounds of permissible school activity. The school board then adopted the committee's statement and rules, which were as follows:

1. The several holidays throughout the year which have a religious and a secular basis may be observed in the public schools.
2. The historical and contemporary values and the origin of religious holidays may be explained in an unbiased and objective manner without sectarian indoctrination.
3. Music, art, literature and drama having religious themes or basis are permitted as part of the curriculum for school-sponsored activities and programs if presented in a prudent and objective manner and as a traditional part of the cultural and religious heritage of the particular holiday.
4. The use of religious symbols such as a cross, menorah, crescent, Star of David, creche, symbols of Native American religions or other symbols that are a part of a religious holiday is permitted as a teaching aid or resource provided such symbols are displayed as an example of the cultural and religious heritage of the holiday and are temporary in nature. Among these holidays are included Christmas, Easter, Passover, Hannukah, St. Valentine's Day, St. Patrick's Day, Thanksgiving and Halloween.
5. The school district's calendar should be prepared so as to minimize conflicts with religious holidays of all faiths. (Ibid., 1319-1320)

Parents of children attending the Sioux Falls schools filed a lawsuit asking for a declaratory judgment that these rules violated the establishment and free exercise clauses of the First Amendment. South Dakota District Judge Andrew Bogue said the 1977 Christmas program violated the establishment clause. However, he said the new rules, if properly administered and narrowly construed, would not violate the First Amendment. The Eighth Circuit Court of Appeals in St. Louis affirmed Judge Bogue's ruling. In applying the *Lemon* test to determine whether the rules violated the establishment clause, Judge Gerald Heaney said they had a secular purpose:

[w]e view the thrust of these rules to be the advancement of the students' knowledge of society's cultural and religious heritage, as well as the provision of an opportunity for students to perform a full range of music, poetry and drama that is likely to be of interest to the students and their audience. (Ibid., 1314)

Judge Heaney also said the rules did not have the primary effect of advancing religion:

[s]ince all programs and materials authorized by the rules must deal with the secular or cultural basis or heritage of the holidays and since the materials must be presented in a prudent and objective manner and symbols used as a teaching aid, the advancement of a "secular program of education," and not of religion, is the primary effect of the rules. (Ibid., 1317)

The plaintiffs argued that the guidelines required school administrators and teachers to decide what was religious and thereby entangled these government officials with religion. However, Heaney said,

[t]his type of decision inheres in every curriculum choice and would be faced by school administrators and teachers even if the rules did not exist. Indeed, the rules are guidelines designed to aid in the decision-making process. Rather than entangling the schools in religion, the rules provide the means to ensure that the district steers clear of religious exercises. (Ibid., 1318)

Judge Heaney also said there would be no violation of the free exercise clause because the school board provided in its policy statement that students could be excused from activities authorized by the rules (Ibid., 1319).

Holiday displays were the subject of the controversy in *Clever v. Cherry Hill Township Board of Education*, 838 F.Supp. 929 (D. N.J., 1993). A group of New Jersey taxpayers, parents of school children and the American Civil Liberties Union filed a lawsuit challenging the constitutionality of a Cherry Hill school board policy that ordered the display of monthly holiday calendars in elementary and junior high school classrooms. Each month's calendar was to display holidays taken from a district-approved list of holidays that reflected the world's cultural diversity. Next to each calendar was to be posted a list of books and resource materials on each holiday available at the school library. In one year, the November calendar at one school displayed the American Election Day, the American Veteran's day on the eleventh, the birthday of Baha'u'llah of the Baha'i faith on the twelfth, the Hindu holiday Divali on the thirteenth, the Japanese festival Shichi-so-san Seven, Five, Three on the fifteenth, the American Thanksgiving Day and Nanak's birthday of the Sikh faith on the twenty-ninth. Davili and Nanak's birthday were marked by religious symbols. The December calendar included Bodhi Day Buddha's Enlightenment on the eighth, the Jewish Chanukah on the ninth, the American Bill of Rights Day on the fifteenth, Christmas on the twenty-fifth and the African festival Kwanzaa on the twenty-sixth. Except for the Bill of Rights Day, these holidays were marked by religious symbols: a representation of Buddha, a menorah, a nativity scene, and a Kwanzaa candelabra.

The plaintiffs also attacked a school board policy that allowed administrators to set up holiday displays in central school locations. These displays could include religious symbols appropriate for current holidays. The symbols could be displayed for periods not to exceed ten school days. Any religious symbol had to be displayed simultaneously with at least one other religious symbol and at least one cultural and/or ethnic symbol.

Judge Joseph Irenas granted the defendant's motion for summary judgment, ruling that the challenged policy provisions did not violate the establishment clause. Applying the *Lemon* test, he said the provisions had a secular purpose because

> [r]eligion is a pervasive and enduring human phenomenon which is an appropriate, if not desirable, subject of secular study. It is hard to imagine how such study can be undertaken without exposing students to the religious doctrines and symbols of others. Plaintiffs protest that the calendars and central displays are not part of "a planned program of instruction," but the use of appropriate classroom and central

displays is clearly a recognized and legitimate educational technique. If displays are perceived by plaintiffs as capable of conveying unwanted religious messages to the student viewers, surely such displays are capable of having secular educational impact. (Ibid., 939)

He also ruled that the policy provisions did not have a primary effect of advancing or inhibiting religion because of its emphasis on religious diversity. He noted that the policy stated that "[s]chools may teach about but not promote religion" (Ibid., 940). Regarding the plaintiffs' entanglement argument, Judge Irenas said the policy was similar to that of the *Florey* case, supra, and he ruled there was no entanglement for the same reasons as Judge Heaney had given in the *Florey* case (Ibid., 941).

The plaintiffs in the *Clever* case did not attack the Cherry Hill School Board's policy on religious music, which said that

> [a]ny school musical program or concert composed of several choral and instrumental selections, shall have secular educational value and shall not be, nor have the effect of being, religiously oriented or a religious celebration. While individual religious pieces of music may be performed for their musical value, the total effect of a music program or concert may be non-religious. (Ibid., 944)

That policy was more restrictive than the practice allowed in *Doe v. Duncanville Independent School District*, 70 F.3rd 402 (1995). In that case, the Fifth Circuit Court of Appeals in New Orleans ruled that a Texas school district's practice of allowing its employees to supervise and participate in prayers at basketball scrimmages violated the establishment clause. However, the court upheld the district's practice of allowing a school choir to adopt "The Lord Bless You and Keep You" as its theme song. The parties agreed that the establishment clause did not prohibit the choir from singing religious songs as part of a secular music program (Ibid., 497). Judge Eugene Davis said that clause also did not forbid singing one of those songs more frequently as a theme song, for two reasons. First, he said the choir director testified that the song was particularly useful in teaching students to sight read and to sing a capella. Its choice as a theme song therefore had a secular purpose.

Secondly, he said the theme song did not advance or endorse religion because the choir director estimated that

> 60-75 percent of serious choral music is based on sacred themes or text. Given the dominance of religious music in this field, DISD can hardly be presumed to be advancing or endorsing religion by allowing its choirs to sing a religious theme song. As a matter of statistical probability, the song best suited to be the theme song that is religious would force DISD to disqualify the majority of appropriate choral music simply because it is religious. Within the world of choral music, such a restriction would require hostility, not neutrality toward religion. (Ibid., 407-408)

The plaintiffs did not contend that singing a religious song as a theme song transformed the choir's concerts into religious exercises. Judge Davis therefore said in a footnote that there was no entanglement with religion when the school district allowed the choir to perform this theme song at its concerts (Ibid., 407, n. 7).

Bauchman v. West High School, 132 F.3d 542 (10th Cir., 1997), presented more difficult questions than the *Florey, Clever* and *Duncanville* cases. That was because of a choir director's emotional reactions to complaints by one of his students. Rachel Bauchman, a Jewish student at a Salt Lake City high school, charged that her choir director had violated her religious freedom by selecting a repertoire dominated by the music of contemporary Christian songwriters, by requiring her to sing this music and at Christian churches, by criticizing her in front of her classmates for opposing this music and asserting her constitutional rights, by implying she was responsible for cancellation of the choir's 1995 spring tour and by other actions that subjected her to public ridicule.

Bauchman brought a lawsuit against her high school, by and through her mother Cheryl Bauchman, under the Civil Rights Act of 1871 (42 U.S.C. §1983), charging that the school had violated her constitutional rights. The district judge granted the school's motion to dismiss her case on the ground that the choir director's alleged actions, even if proven, would not have violated the establishment clause, nor deprived Bauchman of her free exercise of religion. Two of the three court of appeals judges voted to affirm the district judge's decision.

Speaking for the Tenth Circuit Court of Appeals in Denver, Judge Wade Brorby said there was no establishment clause violation because the choir director had "plausible secular purposes" for selecting some music that was religious and for having the choir perform at churches, among other sites. He said that one such purpose was the director's desire to expose his students to the full array of serious choral music, a major portion of which has religious themes and words. He also noted that most church sanctuaries in the area had better acoustics than high school auditoriums and gymnasiums and provided a better atmosphere for the choral music (Ibid., 554).

Brorby said the primary effect of these concerts was not to advance or endorse religion but to provide programs of secular and religious music that reflect Salt Lake City's culture and heritage (Ibid., 555). He also said these programs did not entangle the West High School with religion, because a reasonable observer would conclude that the selection of religious songs from a body of choral music predominated by such songs and the performance of such music at churches in an area such as Salt Lake City "amount to religiously neutral educational choices" (Ibid., 556).

Regarding the choir director's criticism of Bauchman and his retaliation against her for opposing the religious content of his music, Judge Brorby said the director's conduct was "evidence of a lack of sensitivity, crudeness and poor judgment" but did not violate the student's religious freedom (Ibid.). He also said her right of free exercise of religion had not been denied because she had the option of not participating in any portion of the choir's activities that conflicted with her religious beliefs.

One of Bauchman's main arguments was that the choir director's past conduct over the previous twenty years showed that he chose his choir's music and performance sites for the primary purpose of advancing his religious beliefs. She claimed that the district judge had therefore erred when he limited her pre-trial discovery to the period of time during which she was a choir member. Judge Brorby said the district judge was correct in limiting Bauchman's discovery, because the choir director's purposes had to be determined by his conduct at the time of his activity, not by his "psychological *motives vis á vis* his past conduct" (Ibid., 560). Judge Michael Murphy filed a dissenting opinion, contending that the director's motives could not be distinguished from his purposes and his past conduct was therefore relevant to determining his purposes.

Is a prayer set to music a song or a prayer? That was one of the issues in *Doe v. Aldine Independent School District*, 563 F.Supp. 883 (S.D.Texas, 1982). Aldine High School had an official prayer that was sometimes sung to music. Designed for athletic contests, its words were posted in raised block letters over the gymnasium entrance:

> Dear God, please bless our school and all it stands for. Help keep us free from sin, honest and true, courage and faith to make our school the victor. In Jesus' name we pray, Amen. (Ibid., 884)

The Aldine students often sang this prayer to music played by the school band at athletic contests, pep rallies and graduation ceremonies. Judge John Singleton ruled that both the musical and non-musical versions of the prayer were prayers and that singing the prayer violated the establishment clause, citing *Engel v. Vitale*, *Abington v. Schempp* and other school prayer decisions by the U. S. Supreme Court.

These decisions indicate that religious songs can be sung in public schools in the course of choir concerts, holiday celebrations, graduations and other ceremonies, provided they do not transform these events into religious classes or worship ceremonies. The songs must be presented for their musical, cultural and educational values, not for religious worship. If the songs are merely prayers set to music and their only purpose is to have students pray, a court will probably rule that they violate the establishment clause, as it did in the *Doe v. Aldine* case. School boards, administrators and choir directors should be able to avoid this kind of litigation by following policies similar to the one adopted in *Florey v. Sioux Falls*, supra. If they do, they should be able to continue the religious music that has long been a part America's public school curricula.

G. Evolution and Other Controversial Subjects

G.1. Darwin's Theory

When the English naturalist Charles Darwin published his *Origin of the Species* in 1859, the American people gave it a mixed reaction. Some were angered by his suggestion that the living things of the earth were not created in their present forms but evolved instead from more primitive forms. They thought that Darwin was attacking the validity of the creation story of the Bible. Others found ways to reconcile their religious beliefs with Darwin's theory. Some even praised it as "a remarkable proof of God's wisdom."[14]

In the 1870s, the disagreements over Darwin's theory became entangled with arguments provoked by European Bible scholars who were finding fault with many passages of the Bible. These scholars said that the modern translations of the Bible had come from a combination of sources, some of which were of questionable validity. Some stories in the Bible, they concluded, were not true. They were myths and legends; some were even forgeries. They were not the unerring words of God, as most Christians believed. Many Americans challenged these Bible scholars and claimed that they were corrupting the minds and morals of the general public. Although Darwin was a scientist and had no connection with the Bible scholars, his theory of evolution became the prime target of the counterattack against these scholars. Some preachers and science professors lost their jobs because they approved or taught Darwin's theory. In 1875, Alexander Winchell was dismissed from his geology professorship at Vanderbilt University in Nashville, Tennessee because, the university's governing board said,

> [t]his is an age in which scientific atheism, having divested itself of the habiliments that most adorn and dignify humanity, walks abroad in shameless denudation. The arrogant and impertinent claims of this "science, falsely so called," have been so boisterous and persistent, that the unthinking mass have been sadly deluded; but our university alone has had the courage to lay its young but vigorous hand upon the mane of untamed Speculation and say, "We will have no more of this."[15]

The serious debates over Darwin's theory took place within the scientific community. Around 1900, many scientists had difficulty reconciling Darwin's theory with new discoveries in the field of Mendelian genetics.[16] However, they did not question Darwin's primary thesis that man had evolved from lower life forms. They questioned whether he was correct in saying that this evolution took place by a random selection rather than some other process. By the first decade of the twentieth century Darwin's primary thesis had become accepted in all scientific disciplines. High school biology textbooks therefore began to devote more attention to the theory and most of them presented the subject in a favorable light.

Meanwhile, the critical approach to Bible study was spreading throughout America's theological seminaries. Orthodox Christians reacted by establishing their own Bible schools, such as the Los Angeles Bible Institute, founded in 1907 by the millionaire brothers Lyman and Milton Stewart. In 1910, the Stewart brothers published a series of pamphlets, entitled *The Fundamentals*, which explained the fundamental tenets of the Christian faith. The first tenet was the inerrancy of the Biblical scriptures. The other tenets were based on literal interpretations of those scriptures. The people who read *The Fundamentals* and accepted their tenets became known as "Fundamentalists."[17]

Between 1910 and 1916, the Fundamentalist movement spread across America, backed by the resources of the Stewart brothers and other wealthy Americans, including bankers and businessmen. The movement slowed during the First World War but was rejuvenated in 1919. In that year, a Minnesota Baptist preacher, William Bell Riley, founded the World's Christian Fundamentals

Association. In New York City, John Roach Straton preached in his Calvary Baptist Church that

> [t]he moral decline of the present day started two generations ago when the dark and sinister shadow of Darwinism fell across the fair field of human life . . . America's educational system ultimately will be wrecked if the teaching of evolution is allowed to continue . . . Better wipe out all the schools than undermine belief in the Bible by permitting the teaching of evolution.[18]

Straton campaigned for the removal of a fossil display in New York's American Museum of Natural History because it was "poisoning the minds of school children by false and bestial theories of evolution."[19]

The most colorful speaker against Darwin's theory was William Jennings Bryan, a conservative Presbyterian lay leader and a politician who had three times gained the Democratic nomination for President of the United States. His first nomination had come when he was only thirty-six years old, after his celebrated speech against the gold standard at the 1896 Democratic Convention in Chicago. Before that, he had practiced law in Illinois and Nebraska. After his last unsuccessful bid to be President in 1908, he campaigned for the popular election of U. S. Senators, a federal income tax, a federal department of labor, various anti-trust laws, more publicity for campaign contributions, federal insurance for bank deposits and women's suffrage. His last campaign was against evolution. In 1921, he began a nationwide crusade based on his lecture "The Menace of Darwinism." In 1922, he published a book, *In His Image*, containing a series of lectures he had delivered at Union Theological Seminary in Virginia. In one of the lectures, "The Origin of Man," he said,

> [r]eligion is a matter of the heart, and the impulses of the heart often seem foolish to the mind. Faith is different from and superior to, reason . . . It is better to trust in the Rock of Ages, than to know the ages of the rocks.

In a 1922 article in the *New York Times*, he said,

> The only part of evolution in which any considerable interest is felt is evolution applied to man. A hypothesis in regard to the rocks and plant life does not affect the philosophy upon which one's life is built. Evolution applied to fish, birds and beasts would not materially affect man's view of his own responsibilities . . . The evolution that is harmful . . . is the evolution that destroys man's family tree as taught in the Bible, and makes him a descendant of lower forms of life.[20]

Bryan soon became the leading spokesman in a campaign to stop public school teachers from teaching evolution. Bills outlawing such instruction were introduced in twenty state legislatures. These bills became law in three states, Tennessee, Mississippi and Arkansas. Oklahoma passed a law that forbade the use of textbooks that covered evolution but did not forbid teachers to teach the subject. Florida and Texas adopted resolutions saying that evolution should not be taught in their states' public schools.[21]

G.2. The Monkey Trial

The Tennessee law forbidding the teaching of evolution was called the Butler Act. It forbade any teacher in any public school in the state "to teach any theory that denies the story of the Divine Creation of man as taught in the Bible, and to teach instead that man has descended from a lower order of animals." Teachers who violated the law were subject to a fine of not less than $100 nor more than $500. The Butler Act declared that it was to take effect "from and after its passage." It passed on March 13, 1925 and was approved by Governor Austin Peay on March 21, 1925.

By the first week of May, the public schools in Dayton, Tennessee, had begun their summer recess. With a population of eighteen hundred, Dayton was the county seat of Rhea County, located on the Tennessee River north of Chattanooga. On May 5, the Rhea County School Superintendent Walter White met with his board's attorney, a man named Sue Hicks, to discuss the Butler Act. During their meeting, they walked over to Frank Robinson's drug store in the center of Dayton. Robinson sold not only the normal drug store line of products but school textbooks as well. He was also chairman of the Rhea County School Board.

In the drug store, White and Hicks ordered sodas from Robinson. While they sipped on them, White continued to question Hicks about the Butler Act. Hicks told him not to worry because no one would know what the law meant until it was tested in the courts. White might have dropped the subject at that point if George Rappleyea had not walked in. He said he had just read an article in the *Chattanooga Daily Times*, saying the American Civil Liberties Union was planning a test case of the Butler Act. It was looking for a teacher who was willing to be the defendant and it offered to provide the legal defense for such a teacher, free of charge. Rappleyea suggested that the case could be "right here in Dayton. It would put Dayton on the map!" Hicks liked the idea and so did Robinson. White was not so sure. He wanted to see the law tested and clarified so that it could be enforced, but the school year had just ended.

Rappleyea was the manager of a local coal company. Having moved to Tennessee from New York City, he was one of the few citizens of Dayton opposed to Fundamentalism. The six-year-old son of one of his miners had recently been killed in a car accident. At the funeral, he had overheard the preacher tell the boy's mother that her son was now suffering the flames of Hell because he had never been baptized. Rappleyea had reprimanded the preacher for his cruel remark. Now he wanted to challenge the new Fundamentalist law. He pressured White to agree to a trial. He said that no one would pay attention to the law until it was tested. If White's view of the law prevailed, it would be enforced without any problems. On the other hand, if the law were invalidated, it would be repealed. Everyone in the drugstore was now listening, waiting to hear White's reply. Finally, White accepted the challenge.

Someone asked who the defendant would be. Another person suggested Johnny Scopes, the general science teacher at Dayton High School. He had just completed his first year of teaching and was also the football coach. Everyone liked him and he had become especially popular after Dayton's football team lost to its arch-rival in Chattanooga by its smallest margin of defeat ever. Coincidentally, Scopes had been born and raised in Salem, Illinois, the birthplace of William Jennings Bryan. Bryan had delivered the commencement address at Scopes' high school graduation, just five years before he had come to Dayton.

A student in the drugstore was sent to get Scopes, who was playing tennis with one of his students. When Scopes arrived, still sweating in his tennis clothes, Rappleyea asked him to resolve an argument he had been having. He said his position was that no one could teach biology without teaching evolution. Scopes agreed and said that evolution was an integral part of the textbook, *A Civic Biology*, by George W. Hunter. He had just used the book while substituting for the regular biology teacher, who had become ill during the final two weeks of the school year. He had to review the entire book with the biology students to prepare them for their final exam.

Someone searched the drugstore shelves and found a copy of the Hunter textbook. Scopes thumbed through the pages and read several passages aloud. One passage said,

> We have now learned that animal forms may be arranged so as to begin with very simple one-celled forms and culminate with a group which contains man himself. This arrangement is called the *evolutionary series*. Evolution means change, and these groups are believed by scientists to represent stages of complexity of development of life on earth. Geology teaches that millions of years ago, life upon the earth was very simple, and that gradually more and more complex forms of life appeared, as the rocks formed latest in time show the most highly developed forms of animal life. The great English scientist, Charles Darwin, from this and other evidence, explained the theory of evolution. This is the belief that simple forms of life on earth slowly and gradually gave rise to those more complex and that thus ultimately the most complex forms came into existence.[22]

When Scopes confirmed that he could not have taught biology from Hunter's textbook without teaching evolution, several people exclaimed that he had violated the law. Scopes replied that every other biology teacher in the state must have violated the law because Hunter's textbook had been prescribed by the state government.

Rappleyea then explained to Scopes that the ACLU had offered to defend a test case and that Superintendent White, Board Chairman Robinson and their attorney Hicks wanted to have the case tried in Dayton. He asked if Scopes would agree to be the defendant. Scopes hesitated at first, but the crowd talked him into agreeing. Rappleyea then wired the ACLU in New York City that "Professor J. T. Scopes," a science teacher in Dayton, Tennessee, was about to be arrested and charged with teaching evolution, provided the ACLU would agree to defend him. The ACLU wired back saying it would cooperate "with financial help, legal advice and publicity."

Hicks then drafted a warrant accusing John Scopes of teaching evolution in violation of the Butler Act. Rappleyea signed the warrant and a deputy sheriff called on Scopes to notify him that he was to appear before the justices of the peace on May 9. At the hearing, Rappleyea presented a copy of the Butler Act and read passages from the textbook that Scopes had confessed to using in his biology class. The prosecutor read the charge that on April 24, Scopes taught in the public schools of Rhea County a "certain theory or theories that deny the story of the Divine creation of man as taught in the Bible and did teach [instead] thereof that man had descended from a lower order of animals." The justices bound Scopes over to a grand jury, scheduled to meet in August, and released him on a $1,000 bond.

The news of Scopes' arrest spread quickly. Several Fundamentalist leaders offered to help the prosecution team, which was to be headed by Tom Stewart, attorney general for the Eighteenth Judicial Circuit of Tennessee. William Jennings Bryan heard the news while on a speaking tour. In Memphis, he announced he was willing to help. The World Christian Fundamentals Association wired and asked him to participate on their behalf. Bryan wired back from Pittsburgh that he would. At a speech in West Chester, Pennsylvania on May 13, he said,

> This is a matter for the nation. It is one of the greatest questions ever raised, the question of the right of the people who created and support the schools to control them. If not they--then who?
>
> The Fundamentalists are trying to establish the doctrine the taxpayers have the right to say what shall be taught--the taxpayers and not the scientists.
>
> There are only eleven thousand members of the American Association for the Advancement of Science. I don't believe one in ten thousand should dictate to the rest of us. Can a handful of scientists rob your children of religion and turn them out atheists? We'll find a hundred and nine million Americans on the other side. For the first time in my life I'm on the side of the majority.[23]

When the news of Bryan's interest reached Dayton, Hicks wrote Bryan on behalf of the prosecution team, saying,

> We will consider it a great honor to have you with us in this prosecution. We will have no difficulty in obtaining the consent of the attorney general and the circuit judge for you to appear in the case.[24]

Bryan accepted Hicks' offer.

When Clarence Darrow heard of Bryan's involvement in the case, he said he wanted to represent the other side. At age sixty-eight, Darrow was a renowned criminal defense and labor attorney based in Chicago. He recalled that when he had been a small boy in Kinsman, Ohio, east of Cleveland, his father had held abolitionist meetings in his home.[25] Ten miles away in Andover, where Darrow later began his law practice, John Brown had marshaled his men for their attack on Harper's Ferry. Darrow was nine years old when U. S. Senator Benjamin Wade, of the nearby town of Jefferson, gave a famous speech in support of the Civil Rights Bill of 1866. As president *pro tem* of the Senate, Wade was a leading juror in the impeachment trial of President Andrew Johnson, former governor of Tennessee, and it was in spite of Wade's efforts that Johnson avoided a guilty verdict by one vote. By the early 1880s, Darrow had begun his law practice and was trying lawsuits in the Ashtabula County Courthouse, which was located in Jefferson near the Wade mansion. Darrow became a staunch advocate of the rights guaranteed by the Fourteenth Amendment, which was one of the many Reconstruction laws that Senator Wade had guided through Congress.

In 1885, Darrow moved to Chicago and became a close friend and ally of William Jennings Bryan. He worked with him on labor, farm and banking reform campaigns, as well as on his three campaigns for President of the United States. However, Darrow was an avowed agnostic and he opposed Bryan's Fundamentalist activities. In 1923, he wrote an article for the *Chicago Tribune* in which he challenged Bryan to answer fifty questions on the history of mankind. Bryan responded, "I decline to turn aside to enter into controversy with those who reject the Bible as Mr. Darrow does."[26]

Darrow offered to join the ACLU defense team, free of charge. However, some influential members of the ACLU opposed Darrow's participation because of his unorthodox trial tactics and his representation of criminal defendants whom the public thought were guilty of heinous crimes. The ACLU leaders finally approved Darrow, but only after they were unable to secure a lawyer with a less controversial reputation.[27]

Meanwhile, the local authorities in Dayton were scrambling to make sure that their test case would be the first one. The big city folk in Chattanooga had been organizing another test case to be tried before the Dayton trial. Fortunately, their dastardly plot fell through because the Chattanooga biology teacher denied that he had taught anything about evolution since the Butler Act had passed. The Daytonians were much relieved but still concerned that some other community might pre-empt their trial. Therefore, they pressured Judge John Raulston to move up the trial date. With the consent of both sides, Raulston rescheduled the grand jury hearing for May 25 and set a tentative trial date of July 10.

The grand jury hearing proceeded as planned and Judge Raulston confirmed the trial would start on Friday, July 10. As the great day approached, the Dayton people grew more excited, especially when they began to see famous expert witnesses, lawyers, reporters and spectators arriving from all over the United States. A circus atmosphere prevailed. Bryan and Darrow arrived on different days and each man received a huge ovation. The Dayton Progressive Club sponsored separate banquets to honor them. Meanwhile, Scopes, whose bail had been posted by *The Baltimore Sun*, was almost unnoticed as he helped carry visitors' baggage, serving evolutionists and Fundamentalists with equal courtesy.

The first day of the trial was relatively uneventful. The morning was taken by a second grand jury hearing because there was concern about the legality of the first indictment. Both sides wanted to make sure the irregularities were corrected, so the case would be decided on its major issues. In the afternoon, the prospective jury members were questioned and chosen without a major incident. There were nine farmers on the twelve-man jury. One said he was an active reader and taught grammar school in the winter, three said they read practically nothing except the Bible and one said he could not read anything. Two jury members were landowners who lived off the rents they collected and one was a shipping clerk. Of the jury members who were asked about what they knew of evolution, five said they knew little or nothing about it. One said he had read books about the subject.

During the trial, Bryan and Darrow spoke as much to the public outside the court house as they did to the judge and jury during the trial. Over the weekend of July 11 and 12, they issued a number of statements to reporters. One issue they addressed was whether the Butler Act forbade a teacher to teach a theory that had two characteristics, first, a denial of the story of the Divine Creation of man as taught in the Bible, and, secondly, an affirmation that man has descended from a lower order of animals. The prosecution contended that these two characteristics were one and the same characteristic. Bryan said,

> It [the Butler Act] forbids the teaching of a doctrine that denies the truth of the Bible record of man's creation and, that there may be no misunderstanding of the law, it interprets that language used by speci-

fying the objectionable thing as the doctrine that man is a descendant of some lower form of life, and no scientific specialist could change the law or its meaning, no matter who this specialist might be or how many there might be.

Darrow answered,

> There are two things necessary to crime under the Tennessee statute, one: teaching a theory of creation contrary to the "Divine Account" recorded in Genesis; two: teaching that man evolved from a lower order of animal life. These are purely questions of fact.
>
> With one or two exceptions, every juror in this case has stated he knew little or nothing about evolution. The same thing could be said about almost any jury that would be assembled in any state of the Union.
>
> As there are some thousands of different religions, and some five hundred sects of Christians, naturally there is some difference of opinion as to the divine account as taught in the Bible, and these do not agree. Men have debated a long time as to the meaning of much in the Bible, and especially of the account of creation, and yet a Tennessee jury that has given no attention to evolution is supposed to know, first, what evolution is; secondly, what the Bible teaches in reference to the creation of man; and third, whether these theories and account in the Bible are in conflict. And Mr. Bryan says they should decide all this without evidence. It is obvious that no jury can accomplish any such thing.
>
> The effort to keep the defense from offering evidence in this case is a plain effort to run away from the facts, and is doubtless on account of their inability to get any scientific man in the world to deny the facts that prove the correctness of evolution. This is further shown by the fact that Mr. Bryan delivered a public talk here and said the facts of religion and evolution would at last be brought to light. This Tennessee jury is expected by the state, without any evidence, to find that no man can be a Christian and an evolutionist, and this despite the fact that millions of the ablest men in the world, including a large proportion of the students of religion, are both Christians and evolutionists, and among these are the ablest scientists of the world.

Bryan also defended the right of the people of Tennessee to decide what their public school teachers should teach their children. He said,

> If the people of Tennessee have a right to pass laws for the protection of the religion of their children, then they have the right to determine for themselves, what they consider injurious and dangerous for their children. No specialists from the outside are required to inform the parents of Tennessee as to what is harmful. The testimony of such experts, therefore, is not only incompetent, but would be offensive.
>
> If a law like this were passed in New York and witnesses were called from Tennessee to assure the people of New York that they were unduly alarmed and that there was nothing to fear, their testimony would be objected to as offensive as well as improper. If it would be absurd for Tennessee experts to advise the people of New York and Illinois as to what is helpful or harmful to their children, why is it not absurd to call experts from New York and Illinois to challenge the right of the people of Tennessee to legislate as they please, and according to their own sense of responsibility and their own judgment as to what is harmful and as to what is objectionable from a Bible standpoint?
>
> The people of Tennessee have the right to protect the Bible as they understood it. They are not compelled to consider the interpretations placed upon it by the people of other states, whether Christian or scientific, or both.

Bryan ignored the fact that the Tennessee legislature did not have the power to make themselves religious ministers who interpret the meaning of Biblical scriptures. The state of Tennessee had recognized the natural law right of all people to be free of taxes for the support of religious ministers. The religious freedom guarantee of its constitution was patterned after the 1790 Pennsylvania guarantee (Chapter 8, Section D, page 294) and said that

> . . . all men have a natural and indefeasible right to worship Almighty God according to the dictates of their own conscience; that no man can of right be compelled to attend, erect, or support any place of worship or maintain any minister against his consent; that no human authority can, in any case whatever, control or interfere with the rights

of conscience; and no preference shall ever be given, by law to any religious establishment or mode of worship.

Darrow referred to this section of the Tennessee constitution in his answer to Bryan's speech:

> Mr. Bryan's statements about the rights of Tennessee to protect its religion is ambiguous, if he means that any state has the right to pass a law which prohibits the teaching of any theory that is contrary to any religion, and in doing so he is flying in the face of every state constitution.
>
> The fact that any theory or scientific view may be contrary to any religious idea furnishes no right for a state to prohibit it. If this were true, then most astronomy and geology would fall under the ban. The constitution of Tennessee contains one of the strongest guarantees of religious liberty among all the constitutions of the Union, and no law that would undertake to establish religion or measure conduct would have any validity in this state or any other state without getting rid of the constitutions.
>
> Whether specialists come from Tennessee or outside to tell the meaning of evolution cannot matter. Science is the same everywhere. The Constitution does not permit the legislature to put a Chinese wall around the state of Tennessee, as Mr. Bryan seems to think should be done.
>
> We have no doubt that some scientists will be called from Tennessee, as the statute is so recent that there are still some scientific men here. It is not even sure that the statute would work as Mr. Bryan believes, as all the jurors, with one possible exception, testified that they had never heard of evolution until the law was passed.[28]

When the trial resumed on Monday, July 13, defense attorney John Neal moved to quash the indictment on thirteen grounds. The first twelve related to the Butler Act's violation of various sections of the Tennessee Constitution, including Article I, Section 3 forbidding religious establishments; Article I, Section 19 guaranteeing the right of free speech and press and Article XI; Section 12 which said it was the duty of the state legislature "to cherish literature and science." The thirteenth ground related to the law's violation of the privileges and immunities, life, liberty and property and equal protection clauses of the Fourteenth Amendment to the U. S. Constitution. Darrow gave a three-hour speech explaining the reasons why the indictment should be quashed and presenting the same arguments that he had given the press over the weekend. Hicks and Attorney General Stewart presented the prosecution's arguments, which were essentially the ones that Bryan had made to the press over the weekend.

On Tuesday, while the judge was considering his ruling on the motion to quash, Darrow objected to the daily prayers that were being delivered by members of the clergy. He said he had no objection to an occasional prayer, such as the one delivered at the beginning of the trial, but because the case involved a conflict between science and religion, a daily prayer might influence the jury. Another ACLU attorney, Dudley Malone, pointed out that the prayers already given had been argumentative and were contributing to an atmosphere of hostility toward the defense point of view. Judge Raulston overruled the objection, saying the purpose of the prayers was to invoke divine guidance, not to influence any individual.

Raulston then called a recess so that he could prepare his ruling on the motion to quash the indictment. On Wednesday morning, he announced that the Butler Act was valid, citing the case of *Leeper v. State*, 53 S.W. 962 (1899), in which the Tennessee Supreme Court had upheld a state law requiring uniform textbooks in the public schools. The court in that case had said the state legislature had "the power to prescribe the course of study, as well as the books to be used, and how they shall be obtained and distributed, and its discretion as to methods cannot be controlled by the courts" (Ibid., 969). However, the *Leeper* case did not raise any question concerning the religious freedom guarantees of the Tennessee and United States Constitutions.

On Wednesday afternoon, the attorneys for the prosecution and defense gave their opening statements to the jury. Attorney General Stewart said that Scopes had violated the anti-evolution law by teaching "the theory that mankind is descended from a lower order of animals. Therefore, he has taught a theory which denies the story of the divine creation of man as taught in the Bible."[29]

Speaking for the defense, Malone said that Stewart was mistaken about what he had to prove. He said that to convict his client, he had to prove that Scopes had taught not only that mankind was descended from a lower order of animals, but that he had specifically denied the theory of creation as taught in the Bible. Malone said that the prosecution could not rely on the Fundamentalist view that teaching evolution was necessarily a denial of Biblical teaching. He said the defense would prove

> that there are millions of people who believe in evolution and in the stories of creation as set forth in the Bible, and who find no conflict between the two. The defense maintains that this is a matter of faith and interpretation, which each individual must determine for himself . . . .[30]

Malone said that one of the prosecutors, William Jennings Bryan, had once recognized the right of each person to maintain his own interpretation of the Bible when he praised Jefferson's Virginia Statute for Religious Liberty with these words:

> "He said, too, that there was no earthly judge who was competent to sit in a case and try a man for his religious opinions, for the judgment of the court, he said, would not be a judgment of law but would be the personal opinion of the judge. . . . He pointed out that God had it in his power to control man's mind and body, but that He did not see fit to coerce the mind or body into obedience to even the Divine Will; and that if God Himself was not willing to use coercion to force man to accept certain religious views, man, uninspired and liable to error, ought not use the means that Jehovah would not employ."[31]

After the opening statements, the prosecution put on its witnesses. Superintendent White testified that he had heard Scopes admit that he had taught evolution. Two of Scopes' students confirmed that he had taught the subject to them.

The defense then put on its witnesses. Its first witness was Dr. Maynard Metcalf, a renowned zoology professor from Oberlin

College, about thirty miles southwest of Cleveland, Ohio. He belonged to the Congregational Church in Oberlin and had held various church offices, including Bible-class leader and deacon. He testified that he was acquainted with practically all zoologists, botanists and geologists who had made material contributions to their respective disciplines and that he had personal knowledge that all of these people believed that evolution was a fact. He then began explaining the theory of evolution and the evidence on which it was based. Attorney General Stewart objected that Metcalf's testimony invaded the province of the judge and the jury to decide whether Scopes had violated the law based on the evidence of what he had done. He moved to exclude all of the defense expert testimony "that pertains to evolution or anything that tends to show that there might or might not be a conflict between the story of the divine creation and evolution."[32]

On Thursday, July 16, Judge Raulston listened to the attorneys' arguments for and against Stewart's motion. Darrow said the defense expected to show, first, what the theory of evolution was and, secondly, that no rational interpretation of the Bible was in conflict with this theory. He argued that would prove that Scopes had not taught a theory that denies the creation story of man as taught in the Bible. Therefore, he said, the testimony of science and religious experts, including Dr. Metcalf, was necessary for the defense to prove its case.

The prosecuting attorneys argued that the issue of whether Scopes' actions had violated the Butler Act was one that the jury had to decide by determining from the evidence what Scopes had done and then applying the law to those facts. It was not proper for experts to tell the jury how to do its job. In answer to Darrow's point that experts were needed to tell the jury what a rational interpretation of the Bible was, Bryan said, "More of the jurors are experts on what the Bible is than any Bible expert who does not subscribe to the true spiritual influences or spiritual discernment of what our Bible says."[33]

Bryan's, Stewart's, Darrow's and Malone's speeches consumed the whole day. On Friday, Judge Raulston sustained Stewart's motion "to exclude the expert testimony, the purpose of which is to explain the origin of man and life in this world."[34] He said that under his interpretation of the Butler Act, it was unlawful to teach in the public schools of Tennessee that man descended from a lower order of animals. Therefore, the testimony of the defense experts would be irrelevant. Raulston did, however, grant the defense attorneys' request to place on the record affidavits summarizing the expert testimony that they had planned to present to aid the Tennessee Supreme Court in evaluating the correctness of his decision. These affidavits were to be used solely for that purpose and were not to be given to the jury. The judge then adjourned the trial until Monday morning to give the defense attorneys time to prepare their affidavits.

The trial now appeared to be finished, except for a few formalities. As the principal actors filed out of the courthouse, reporters besieged them with questions. Scopes gave the following statement:

> Of course I was interested in science, but it was more due to my study of Blackstone's *Commentaries* that I disliked this antievolution law. While studying Blackstone at the law classes, while I was a senior at the University of Kentucky, I found that, through the Magna Charta and different bills of rights, one of the great achievements of the English-speaking people was to separate the Church from the courts and legislatures. And, when this law was passed, it seemed to me a violation of the principles that Americans and Englishmen have fought for bitterly for centuries.[35]

Scopes also thanked George Rappleyea for initiating the trial. He added that he was planning to leave Dayton, but the people had been friendly to him and he was sorry go.

On Monday morning, July 20, defense attorney Arthur Garfield Hays submitted twelve affidavits to the judge and summarized their contents. Eight of the affidavits were by scientific experts who explained the evidence of evolution in the fields of geology, anthropology, psychology, zoology and embryology. The other four affidavits were by linguists and theologians who explained the words of the Bible and their translation history.

After lunch, the defense dropped its bombshell. Hays said the defense wished to call William Jennings Bryan to the stand as an expert on the Bible. He said he wished to submit Bryan's testimony along with the affidavits for the purpose of appealing Judge Raulston's ruling. Several prosecuting attorneys objected to one of their own being called to the witness stand, but Bryan himself did not object. He later said that he had wanted to take the stand so that Darrow "might not charge me with unwillingness to face his questions."[36] Judge Raulston said he did not know of a precedent to cover this situation and so he allowed Bryan to testify.

The result was devastating for Bryan. For an hour and a half, Darrow grilled him with questions on his interpretation of the Bible. He asked him about the passage that said that Joshua made the sun stand still. Bryan said he believed the earth moved in respect of the sun but that God may have directed the author of the book of Joshua to use language that could be understood by people who thought the sun traveled around the earth. Therefore, he admitted, the Bible passage could be interpreted to mean the earth stopped spinning on its axis, which was an interpretation that differed from the literal words of the Bible.

Darrow asked, "Do you think the earth was made in six days?" Bryan answered, "Not six days of twenty-four hours." Darrow replied, "Doesn't it say so?" "No, sir," Bryan responded. Darrow asked, "Do you think these were literal days?" Bryan said, "My impression is they were periods, but I would not attempt to argue as against anybody who wanted to believe in literal days." Darrow asked, "Have you any idea of the length of the periods?" Bryan answered, "No, I don't." Darrow asked, "Do you think the sun was made on the fourth day?" "Yes," said Bryan. "And they had evening and morning without the sun?" Bryan began to squirm. "I am simply saying it was a period." Darrow pressed, "They had evening and morning for four periods without the sun, do you think?" Bryan responded, "I believe in Creation as there told and, if I am not able to explain it, I will accept it . . . ."

Darrow continued, "And they had the evening and morning before that time for three days or three periods. All right, that settled it. Now, if you call those periods, they may have been a very long time?" Bryan admitted, "They might have been." Darrow pressed for clarification, asking, "The Creation might have been going on for a very long time?" Bryan answered, "It might have continued for millions of years."

Darrow then turned to the story of Eve's temptation by the serpent. He read Genesis 3:16, in which God told Eve He would punish her by greatly multiplying her child bearing sorrow and making her husband rule over her. Darrow said, "That is right, is it?" Bryan answered, "I accept it as it is." Darrow asked whether Bryan believed that God punished the serpent by making it crawl on its belly, as recorded in Genesis 3:14. Bryan responded, "I believe that." Darrow asked, "Have you any idea how the snake went before that time?" "No, sir," Bryan answered. Darrow asked, "Do you know whether he walked on his tail or not?" Bryan answered, "No sir. I have no way to know."[37] The courtroom erupted in laughter at the idea of a snake walking erect on its tail. Bryan shouted to the crowd, "I want the world to know that this man, who does not believe in a God, is trying to use a court in Tennessee to slur at it and, while it will require time, I am willing to take it!" Darrow responded, "I object to your statement! I am examining you on your fool ideas that no intelligent Christian on earth believes!" The noise in the courtroom grew louder, drowning out the two combatants as they argued and shook their fists at each other. Judge Raulston rapped his gavel and shouted, "Court is adjourned until nine o'clock tomorrow morning!"[38]

The next day, the judge announced that he had reconsidered his decision to allow Bryan to testify and was therefore striking his testimony from the appellate record. He said that Bryan's testimony bore no relevance to the issues of the case. Darrow and Stewart then presented short closing statements. Darrow frankly told the jury that his client wanted a guilty verdict, because the judge had excluded all the evidence that he had wanted to present. His only remedy was to argue the real issues of the case on appeal.

Stewart also asked the jury for a guilty verdict. The jury complied. Before sentencing, Scopes was asked if he had anything to say as to why the Court should not impose punishment upon him. He replied,

> Your honor, I feel I have been convicted of violating an unjust statute. I will continue in the future, as I have in the past, to oppose this law in any way I can. Any other action would be in violation of my ideal of academic freedom--that is, to teach the truth as guaranteed by our Constitution, of personal and religious freedom. I think the fine is unjust.

Judge Raulston fined Scopes $100, the minimum allowed by the law.

On appeal, the Tennessee Supreme Court affirmed Judge Raulston's rulings on the constitutionality of the Butler Act and its interpretation. However, it reversed Scopes' conviction on the ground that the jury, not the judge, should have assessed the fine, as required by Tennessee law. Because Scopes was no longer employed by the state, the Tennessee high court did not remand the case back to the local court. It said there was "nothing to be gained by prolonging the life of this bizarre case" and directed the entry of a *nolle prosequi*, in the interest of "the peace and dignity of the state" (289 S.W. 363 at 367 [1927]). There was thus no basis on which to appeal the case to the Supreme Court of the United States.

Darrow commented in his 1932 autobiography that Tennessee and Mississippi did not insist on the Fundamentalist interpretation of the Bible in all respects because they "both continue to teach that the earth is round and the revolution on its axis brings the day and night, in spite of all opposition."[39] The public consensus was that Darrow had shown that the Fundamentalist interpretation of the Bible had many flaws and that the Tennessee anti-evolution law placed an unfair restriction on public school teachers.

However, the textbook publishers made Bryan the victor, because they reduced their coverage of evolution and treated the subject in a very cursory fashion. They wanted to sell as many books as possible and avoid controversy. As a *Stanford Law Review* article reports, "[t]he absence of controversial material, rather than scientific quality, determined book adoption by many school committees, and antievolutionists had learned to bring effective pressure on them."[40] That policy continued through the 1950s. An entire generation of Americans was thus deprived of an important part of its scientific education because of the antievolutionist movement.

G.3. The Recent Cases

In October 1957, the Russians surprised the world by launching the first man-made satellite to orbit the earth. The Russian "Sputnik" satellite raised concern among Americans that they were losing their technological superiority to a powerful enemy that was a threat to world freedom. In the effort to reverse that trend, American educators began to re-evaluate the nation's high school science courses. In 1959, the National Science Foundation funded the Biological Sciences Curriculum Study at the University of Colorado, which was given the mission to develop and publish new high school biology textbooks. The Study began publishing textbooks in 1963 that were "thoroughly permeated by evolutionary theory."[41] Between 1964 and 1970, nearly half the high schools in America adopted these textbooks.

For the 1965-66 school year, the Little Rock, Arkansas, school administration prescribed one of these biology textbooks. It contained a chapter describing "the theory about the origin . . . of man from a lower form of animal" (*Epperson v. Arkansas*, 393 U.S. 97 at 99 [1968]). Susan Epperson, a tenth-grade biology teacher at Little Rock Central High School, was told to use the textbook. However, a 1928 Arkansas law forbade public school teachers to teach "the theory or doctrine that mankind ascended or descended from a lower form of animals." Epperson was thus confronted with the choice of violating the orders of her superiors or violating the Arkansas law. She therefore filed a petition in the Arkansas Chancery Court asking that the Court declare the Arkansas law void and enjoin the state and the Little Rock school administrators from dismissing her for violating the law. The Chancery Court granted her petition, but the Arkansas Supreme Court reversed, saying the law was "a valid exercise of the state's power to specify curriculum in its public schools" (Ibid., 101, n. 7).

Epperson then appealed to the Supreme Court of the United States. In a unanimous opinion, the nation's high court reversed the Arkansas Supreme Court. Justice Fortas said,

> Arkansas' law cannot be defended as an act of religious neutrality. Arkansas did not seek to excise from the curricula of its schools and universities all discussion of the origin of man. The law's effort was confined to an attempt to blot out a particular theory because of its supposed conflict with the Biblical account, literally read. (Ibid., 109)

Therefore, the law violated First Amendment's prohibition against religious establishment, made applicable to the states by the life, liberty and property clause of the Fourteenth Amendment. Justice Stewart concurred but based his opinion on the free speech clause of the First Amendment. He said,

> It is one thing for a State to determine that "the subject of higher mathematics, or astronomy, or biology" shall not be included in its public school curriculum. It is quite another thing for a State to make it a criminal offense for a public school teacher so much as to mention the very existence of an entire system of respected human thought. That kind of criminal law, I think, would impinge upon the guarantees of free communication contained in the First Amendment, and made applicable to the States by the Fourteenth. (Ibid., 116)

Evolution is not the only subject taught in school that has offended people's religious beliefs. In *Grove v. Mead School District*, 753 F.2d 1528 (9th Cir., 1985), the parents of Cassie Grove in the town of Mead, Washington, objected that she had been assigned to read *The Learning Tree* in her sophomore English literature class. *The Learning Tree* is a novel about a teenage boy in a black, working-class family and it portrays his expectations and outlook on life. The boy's parents are devout Christians but the boy develops a very cynical attitude toward their religion. In one passage, he says to himself,

> The Ten Commandments say we oughn't kill, then we come home from church and wring a chicken's neck for dinner--and Reverend Broadnap eats more'n anybody else. (Ibid., 1545)

Another passage reads,

> "You and your white trash git the hell out'a here!" he shouted. "I don't want no part of you soul savers--bendin' down, like Paw says you do, kissin' the feet of a poor white trash God."

When Cassie and her parents informed the teacher that these and other passages offended their religious beliefs, she was assigned another book and excused from the classroom discussion of *The Learning Tree*. However, the teacher and the school board refused to remove the book from the curriculum. The Groves filed a complaint against the school district in the Spokane Federal District Court, alleging violations of their rights under the Civil Rights Act, 42 U.S.C. §1983. They contended that the use of *The Learning Tree* in Cassie's class violated their rights under the free exercise and establishment clauses of the First Amendment. The school district moved for summary judgment in its favor and the district judge granted the motion and dismissed the complaint. The Groves then appealed to the Ninth Circuit Court of Appeals in San Francisco. The three-judge appellate court unanimously affirmed the district judge.

Judge Eugene Wright of the Court of Appeals said there was no violation of the free exercise clause because Cassie Grove was not required to read the book or participate in its discussion. He also said, "The state interest in providing a well-rounded public education would be critically impeded accommodation of Grove's wishes" (Ibid., 1533). Regarding the establishment clause, Wright said the book did not inhibit the Grove's religion, Fundamentalist Christianity, nor did it advance the religion of secular humanism. Rather, it served a secular function of exposing students to the

Chapter 11   Religion in the Public Schools   679

expectations and orientations of Black Americans. He distinguished the study of *The Learning Tree* in an English literature class from the cases involving school prayer, Bible read[ing and posting the Ten Commandments. Those activities involved, "sponsorship, financial support and active involvement of the sovereign in religious activity" (Ibid., 1534, quoting *Lemon v. Kurtzman*, supra). This case involved the objective study of a book as a piece of literature. Wright noted that

> [t]he Supreme Court has stated clearly that literary and historic study of the Bible is *not* a prohibited religious activity. *Stone*, 449 U.S. at 42, 101 S.Ct. at 194; *Abington School District*, 374 U.S. at 225, 83 S.Ct. at 1573. Not all mention of religion is prohibited in public schools. (Ibid., 1534)

He said that for the same reason the Mead School District's use of *The Learning Tree* as an object of literary study did not violate the establishment clause of the First Amendment.

In a concurring opinion, Judge William Canby explained,

> Were the school board in Cassie's district to require local principals to read over their public address systems a resolution, drawn in words from the book, declaring Jesus Christ to be a "poor white trash God," or "long-legged white son-of-a-bitch," Appendix, *infra* at 1547 and 1549, there would be little doubt that the effect would be to communicate governmental endorsement of anti-Christian sentiments.
>
> By contrast, *The Learning Tree* bears the sole signature of its author, Gordon Parks. It is a work of fiction, not dogmatic philosophy. It is one book, only tangentially "religious," thematically grouped with others in the sophomore literature curriculum. Its purpose and effect is to expose students to the attitudes and outlooks of an important American subculture.
>
> Plaintiffs may be correct in suggesting that the work "hard[ly] . . . constitutes the objective study of Christianity," Appellants' Brief 22, yet objectivity in education need not inhere in each individual item studied; if that were the requirement, precious little would be left to read. Instead, objectivity is to be assessed with reference to the manner in which often highly partisan, subjective material is presented,

handled, and "integrated into the school curriculum, where [even] the Bible may constitutionally be used in an appropriate study of history, civilization, ethics, comparative religion, or the like." *Stone*, 449 U.S. at 42, 101 S.Ct. at 194; *see Abington*, 374 U.S. at 225, 83 S.Ct. at 1573.

Luther's "Ninety-Five Theses" are hardly balanced or objective, yet their pronounced and even vehement bias does not prevent their study in a history class' exploration of the Protestant Reformation, nor is Protestantism "advanced" thereby. The study of Greek mythology does not "advance" pantheism. Teaching about "the divine right of kings" does not endorse a particular dogma, although one is necessarily explored.

Similarly, inclusion of *The Learning Tree* as representative of a particular literary genre neither religiously inhibits nor instills, but simply informs and educates students on a particular social outlook forged in the crucible of black rural life. To include the work no more communicates governmental endorsement of the author's or characters' religious views than to assign *Paradise Lost, Pilgrim's Progress*, or *The Divine Comedy* conveys endorsement or approval of Milton's, Bunyan's, or Dante's Christianity. . . .

Of course, plaintiffs may personally espouse and prefer an unwavering acceptance of a number of the traditional religious doctrines doubted by characters in *The Learning Tree*. The issue, however, is not whether the work disapproves of any particular religious vision, including plaintiffs', but whether its inclusion in the public school curriculum indicates, intentionally or not, that the government joins in that disapproval.

It is true that *The Learning Tree* poses questions and ponders doubts with which plaintiffs may be uncomfortable. Yet to pose questions is not to impose answers. (Ibid., 1540-1541)

The Groves appealed the Ninth Circuit decision to the Supreme Court of the United States, but the high court refused to hear the appeal (474 U.S. 826 [1985]).

After the *Epperson* decision, conservative religious groups began to argue that if a public school teaches evolution, as the Supreme Court ruled that it has a right to do, their views on the matter ought to be given equal time. They also published books that attacked the scientific basis of evolution and promoted their thesis that the creation story of the Bible had a scientific basis that was at least as valid as the basis for evolution. They called the Bible's scientific basis "creation science." Several southern states passed laws that required creation science to be taught whenever evolution was taught in the public schools.

The Louisiana law was challenged by local parents, teachers and religious leaders in *Edwards v. Aguillard*, 482 U.S. 578 (1987). The state defended the lawsuit on the ground that the law protected a legitimate secular interest, namely academic freedom. The district judge granted the plaintiffs' motion for summary judgment, ruling that the law violated the establishment clause. The judge said the law either forbade the teaching of evolution, which the Supreme Court had ruled was unconstitutional in the *Epperson* case, or it required the teaching of creation science with the purpose of advancing a particular religious doctrine (Ibid., 582). The Fifth Circuit Court of Appeals in New Orleans affirmed, explaining that the law's avowed purpose of furthering academic freedom was not consistent with its restriction on teachers that they teach creation science whenever they taught evolution (Ibid.).

The U. S. Supreme Court also affirmed. Speaking for the Court's majority, Justice Brennan addressed the state's new argument that by "academic freedom," it meant the basic concept of "fairness" and "teaching all the evidence" (Ibid., 586). He said

> the goal of basic "fairness" is hardly furthered by the Act's discriminatory preference for the teaching of creation science and against teaching evolution. While requiring that curriculum guides be developed for creation science, the Act says nothing of comparable guides for evolution. La. Rev. Stat. Ann. §17:286.7A (West 1982). Similarly, resource services are supplied for creation science but not for evolution. §17.286.7B. Only "creation scientists" can serve on the panel that supplies the resource services. *Ibid*. The Act forbids school boards to discriminate against anyone who "chooses to be a creation-scientist" or to teach "creationism," but fails to protect those who choose to teach evolution or any other noncreation science theory, or who refuse to teach creation science. §17:286.4C. . . .

The preeminent purpose of the Louisiana Legislature was clearly to advance the religious viewpoint that a supernatural being created humankind. The term "creation science" was defined as embracing this particular religious doctrine by those responsible for the passage of the Creationism Act. Senator Keith's leading expert on creation science, Edward Boudreaux, testified at the legislative hearings that the theory of creation science included belief in the existence of a supernatural creator. (Ibid., 588, 591)

In a concurring opinion, Justice Powell gave some background explaining the nature and origin of creation science:

> The Institute for Creation Research is an affiliate of the Christian Heritage College in San Diego, California. The Institute was established to address the "urgent need for our nation to return to belief in a personal, omnipotent Creator, who has a purpose for His creation and to whom all people must eventually give account." 1 *id.*, at E-197. A goal of the Institute is "a revival of belief in special creation as the true explanation of the origin of the world." Therefore, the Institute is currently working on the "development of new methods for teaching scientific creationism in public schools." *Id.*, at E-197--E-199. the Creation Research Society (CRS) is located in Ann Arbor, Michigan. A member must subscribe to the following statement of belief: "The Bible is the written word of God, and because it is inspired throughout, all of its assertions are historically and scientifically true." 2 *id.*, at E-583. To study creation science at the CRS, a member must accept "that the account of origins in Genesis is a factual presentation of simple historical truth." *Ibid.*

Justice Powell also said,

> That the statute is limited to the scientific evidences supporting the theory does not render its purpose secular. In reaching its conclusion that the Act is unconstitutional, the Court of Appeals "[did] not deny that the underpinnings of creationism may be supported by scientific evidence" 765 F.2d 1251, 1256 (1985). And there is no need to do so. Whatever the academic merit of particular subjects or theories, the Establishment Clause limits the discretion of state officials to pick and choose among them for the purpose of promoting a particular religious

belief. The language of the statute and its legislative history convince me that the Louisiana Legislature exercised its discretion for this purpose in this case. (Ibid., 602, 604)

Chief Justice Rehnquist and Justice Scalia dissented. Scalia filed the only dissenting opinion. He based his dissent on the testimony of legislators and experts that,

(1) There are two and only two scientific explanations for the beginning of life--evolution and creation science. . . .
(2) The body of scientific evidence supporting creation science is as strong as that supporting evolution. . . .
(3) Creation science can and should be presented to children without any religious content. . . .
(4) Although creation science is educationally valuable and strictly scientific, it is now being censored from or misrepresented in the public schools. . . .
(5) The censorship of creation science has at least two harmful effects. First, it deprives students of knowledge of one of the two scientific explanations for the origin of life and leads them to believe that evolution is proven fact; thus, their education suffers and they are wrongly taught that science has proved religious beliefs false. Second, it violates the Establishment Clause. (Ibid., 622-625)

However, this testimony shows a lack of understanding of the academic subject of science, which is more precisely called, "natural science." *Webster's New World Collegiate Dictionary* says that "natural science" is "the systematized knowledge of nature and the physical world."[42] A scientist gains his knowledge of nature and the physical world by observing the things around him. He then forms theories about the nature and behavior of these things and tests these theories by experimentation. In the course of his experiments, the scientist observes and records data, interprets the data and draws conclusions. Sometimes, he concludes that his theory is correct and he formulates a law of nature that describes the behavior of certain things. The process by which he formulates such a law of nature is called inductive reasoning. Scientists and engineers use the laws of nature to predict the future behavior of things and to draw conclusions about their past history. The processes by which they makes these predictions and draw these conclusions are called deductive reasoning. Scientists and engineers also use these laws of nature, predictions and conclusions to help them invent new and useful machines, processes and products.

If a scientist believes in God, and that belief is probably as common among scientists as it is among non-scientists, he might believe that the laws of nature originate from God. Blackstone believed that both the laws of nature in respect of things and the laws of nature in respect of people originate from God (BL1, 38-41). However, a scientist's belief or non-belief in God does not affect the way he investigates and uses the laws of nature. A scientist might believe that God can ruin his experiments by supernatural acts that temporarily suspend the natural laws he is trying to discover. He might believe that God might suspend the laws of nature in the future or that He did suspend them in the past, so that his conclusions about the past and predictions about the future could be wrong. However, the professional scientist does not worry about these possibilities in the course of his work. His job is to improve "the systematized knowledge of nature and the physical world," not to interject his personal religious beliefs or speculate on the possible consequences of supernatural events. No businessman responsible to his investors would employ a scientist to engage in such speculation. No school board or college administration responsible to its students would employ a science teacher who engages in such speculation. That responsibility to students is especially important now because of the recent growth of the biotechnology and health care industries. The knowledge of evolutionary processes is critical to understanding those fields. The young people of today are entitled to science teachers who will teach them the laws of nature without sidetracking them with their religious beliefs concerning the revelations of God and His supernatural acts.

Returning to the first statement in Justice Scalia's opinion, that creation science is one of the two scientific explanations of the beginning of life, that statement is false because creation science is not a scientific explanation. It is based on the revealed tenets of Fundamentalist Christianity, not the natural law investigations of scientists. Those revealed tenets include the belief that "[t]he Bible is the written word of God, and because it is inspired throughout, all of its assertions are historically and scientifically true" (*Edwards v. Aguillard*, 482 U.S. at 602). That means that to a creation scientist, an assertion is "scientifically true" simply because he interprets the Bible as saying it is true. Creation science is therefore not "science" in the academic sense of that word.

The second statement quoted by Justice Scalia is that the scientific evidence supporting creation is as strong as the scientific evidence supporting evolution. However, there are libraries full of the scientific evidence of evolution. It is found in many fields of science, including geology, paleontology, zoology, comparative anatomy, embryology, genetics, biochemistry, molecular biology, physiology and ecology. Paleontologists have studied the fossil remains of animals buried in the earth's rock strata. By radioactive decay and other techniques, they have measured the ages of the rock strata and have found the oldest animal fossils to be small worm-like creatures, with the next oldest branching into more varied forms of life, primarily fishes, followed by forms that included amphibians, then reptiles and finally mammals, including man. Paleontologists have constructed genealogy charts based on the similarities and apparent relationships between these animal remains. Creation scientists have called attention to large gaps in these genealogy charts, but these gaps are gradually being filled as more kinds of fossils are discovered. Embryologists have found that the embryos of mammals pass through fish, amphibian, and reptilian stages during their development, for no apparent functional reason. For instance, human embryos develop fish gills and tails, which are later reduced to non-functional vestiges. Molecular biologists have discovered that each organism's ancestry is recorded in its DNA and the enzymes that govern its life processes. *The New Encyclopaedia Britannica* says in its article on "The Theory of Evolution,"

> [t]he degree of similarity in the sequence of nucleotides or of amino acids can be precisely quantified. For example, cytochrome c (a protein molecule) of humans and chimpanzees consists of the same 104 amino acids in exactly the same order; but differs from that of rhesus monkeys by one amino acid, that of horses by 11 additional amino acids, and that of tuna by 21 additional amino acids. The degree of similarity reflects the recency of common ancestry.

This twenty-nine-page article, written by Francisco Ayala, a biology professor at the University of California, Irvine, summarizes much of the evidence supporting evolution and includes an extensive bibliography.[43] Most of this evidence was not gathered by people who were trying to prove or disprove anything concerning the evolution/creation controversy. It was gathered by scientists who were trying to discover more about the nature of man and his environment so that they and other people could invent solutions to the problems of life on the planet earth.

In contrast, creation scientists rely primarily on the Bible for their "scientific evidence." In his book *The Controversy: Roots of the Creation-Evolution Conflict*, the creation scientist Donald E. Chittick says,

> Part of the data creation science considers are the words God has given to us. They are true data about the universe in the same sense that a sample we would observe in a test tube is also true data about the universe. Evolutionary science ignores or refuses to consider as evidence what God has said. Creation science is not closed to that evidence. Part of the evidence available to scientists are the statements in the Bible about creation. To the extent they are ignored, science will be that much in error about the real situation.[44]

Chittick also cites other evidence, but none that proves that God supernaturally created the living things of the earth in their present forms. He says the genetic codes embedded in DNA and RNA molecules point to the work of an intelligent designer and creator.[45] He also says the extreme complexity of certain animal organs, particularly the eye, show the work of such a creator.[46] These arguments are also presented in Davis and Kenyon's book, *Of*

Chapter 11   Religion in the Public Schools   687

Pandas and People: the Central Question of Biological Origins.[47] They raise serious questions about the most popular theory of how evolution takes place, namely the so-called "synthetic theory," which combines Darwin's random, natural selection principles with Mendel's genetic principles. The synthetic theory attempts to show that all living things evolved by purely natural processes that did not require any intelligent source. However, the possible weakness of that theory does not weaken the contention that evolution has occurred by some means. The mere lack of an adequate or certain explanation of why something happened does not contradict the evidence that it did happen. Perhaps the matter and energy of the universe were pre-programmed to evolve, either by an unknown source or by an everlasting cycle of evolution and involution, or perhaps creation scientists are correct in contending that there is a supernatural power called God who spontaneously created all the species of life in their present forms. The creation scientists, however, have not produced any scientific evidence to support their contention. It remains a contention based solely on one interpretation of the Bible.

Statements (3) and (4) cited by Justice Scalia, that creation science can be presented without any religious content and is strictly scientific, are not true because creation science is based entirely on one particular interpretation of the Bible. Statement (5) is not true because it contains only conclusions based on the supposed truth of the first four statements.

The creation scientists have charged that the general scientific community's heavy opposition to their supernatural creation theory is the result of its "humanistic" bias. If people who confine their professional studies to the laws of nature are humanists, then perhaps most scientists can be called humanists. However, this controversy raises an important religious issue. The creation scientists have, by their numerous arguments based on "Biblical evidence," diverted the true scientists from their study of the laws of nature. They have also spent countless hours of their own time searching for natural evidence of supernatural events. Instead of engaging in those pursuits, the creation scientists might do well to dig deeper into their own religious faith and ask themselves why God has chosen to hide Himself and His miracles from man's rational discovery.

G.4. Science versus Religion

Both science and religion are concerned with questions relating to the nature and origin of the universe and man's place in the universe. However, scientists are concerned exclusively with natural law evidence, as opposed to the revealed law of religious scriptures. In the absence of natural law evidence pointing toward a supernatural event, they would not consider the possibility of such an event in drawing their conclusions. On the other hand, the Bible and other religious scriptures teach that the universe is governed by God, a supernatural being who sometimes suspends the laws of nature and acts in mysterious ways that cannot be discovered by scientists. Given this situation, how can a religious person resolve the conflicts that arise when the conclusions of scientists are at odds with what the scriptures say?

That is a question each person must answer for himself. Some people believe that God created the earth and its living species in their present forms but that He hid His supernatural creation by making these species appear to have evolved from common ancestors. Others believe that the present living species evolved under God's direction. Either He programmed each species' ancestors to evolve or He managed their evolution by divine intervention, or perhaps He did both. Still others believe that evolution has taken place entirely by natural processes, independent of any supernatural action. There are many ways of resolving this conflict.[48] This would be a proper subject of discussion in a comparative religion class, or in a history, literature or philosophy class that covers comparative religion. It would not, however, be a proper subject for a science class.

Chapter 11   Religion in the Public Schools   689

H. Teaching Values

In *Murray v. Curlett (Abington School District. v. Schempp)*, 274 U.S. at 223, the Baltimore City Board of Commissioners argued that its law requiring Bible passages and the Lord's Prayer to be read in city schools promoted moral values. In recent years, many public schools have increased the time they devote to teaching moral values. Sometimes these values are referred to as religious values. However, a closer look shows that nearly all of them are natural law values that human beings of all the world's cultures and religions have come to appreciate by applying principles of common sense to their observations and experiences. They do not belong to the revealed law of only one religion. That does not mean that religious scriptures cannot be cited in the course of teaching these values in public schools. What it does mean is that teachers must take care to promote only the common values and not imply that they reside within the exclusive dominion of any or all religions.

For example, suppose that a public high school teacher wishes to teach his or her students the values adopted by King's Medical Company of Hudson, Ohio. Bill Wooldredge, Vice President of that company, says that its values are based on the following Bible passages:

Mark 9:35--Customers come first;

Proverbs 16:3--Strive for continuous improvement;

John 15:15 and Matthew 28:18-20--Empower our employees;

Proverbs 11:3 and Phillippians 2:14-15--Partnerships are based on integrity;

Matthew 5:44--Respect all individuals;

Daniel 1:5--Train and develop our employees;

Proverbs 12:15--Maintain open communications; and

Matthew 25:27--Give a sound return to our investors.

However, these values are taught by other religions as well. Private companies such as King's Medical may limit their employee instruction to the way these values are taught by one religion, but taxpayer-supported schools cannot do that. They would be giving the impression that these values are the exclusive domain of that religion. They would also be implying that it is the established religion of the school and its government. Public school teachers must therefore teach these values either without reference to any religion or they must show how these values are taught by at least two widely different religions.

By studying the value teachings of two or more religions, public school teachers would not only be complying with the Constitution's establishment clause, but they would also be giving their students a better understanding of the values. Look at the way the King's Medical Company values are illustrated by both the Christian Bible and the *Analects* of Confucius:[49]

Value: Customers come first.

Bible: And he (Jesus) sat down, and called the twelve (disciples), and saith unto them, "If any man desire to be first, the same shall be last of all, and servant of all." (Mark 9:35)

Confucius: Master Tsêng said, Every day I examine myself on these three points: in acting on behalf of others, have I always been loyal to their interests? In intercourse with my friends, have I always been true to my word? Have I failed to repeat the precepts that have been handed down to me? (I, 4)

Value: Strive for continuous improvement.

Bible: Commit thy works unto the Lord, and thy thoughts shall be established. (Proverbs 16:3)

Confucius: The Master said, The words of the *Fa Yü* (Model Sayings) cannot fail to stir us; but what matters is that they should change our ways. The words of *Hsüan Chü* cannot fail to commend themselves to us; but what matters is that we should carry them out. For those who approve but do not carry out, who are stirred, but do not change, I can do nothing at all. (IX, 23)

Confucius: The Master said, In old days men studied for the sake of self-improvement; nowadays men study in order to impress other people. (XIV, 25)

Confucius: The Master said, To have faults and to be making no effort to amend them is to have faults indeed! (XV, 29)

Value: Empower our employees.

Bible: "Henceforth I call you not servants; for the servant knoweth not what his lord doeth: but I have called you friends; for all things that I have heard of my Father I have made known unto you." (Jesus speaking to his disciples, John 15:15)

Bible: And Jesus came and spake unto them, saying, "All power is given unto me in heaven and in earth. Go ye therefore, and teach all nations, baptizing them in the name of the Father, and of the Son, and of the Holy Ghost: Teaching them to observe all things whatsoever I have commanded you alway, even unto the end of the world." Amen. (Matthew 28:18-20)

Confucius: Fan Ch'ih asked about wisdom. The Master said, He who devotes himself to securing for his subjects what it is right they should have, who by respect for the Spirits keeps them at a distance, may be termed wise. He asked about Goodness. The Master said, Goodness cannot be obtained till what is difficult has been duly done. He who has done this may be called Good. (VI, 20)

Confucius: Tzu-kung said, If a ruler not only conferred wide benefits upon the common people, but also compassed the salvation of the whole State, what would you say of him? Surely, you would call him Good? The Master said, It would no longer be a matter of "Good." He would without a doubt be a Divine Sage. Even Yao and Shun could hardly criticize him. As for Goodness--you yourself desire rank and standing; then help others to get rank and standing. You want to turn your own merits to account; then help others to turn theirs to account--in fact, the ability to take one's own feelings as a guide--that is the sort of thing that lies in the direction of Goodness. (VI, 28)

Confucius: The Master said, My friends, I know you think that there is something I am keeping from you. There is nothing at all that I keep from you. I take no steps about which I do not consult you, my friends. Were it otherwise, I should not be Ch'iu. (VII, 23)

Confucius: Tzu-hsia said, A gentleman obtains the confidence of those under him, before putting burdens upon them. If he does so before he has obtained their confidence, they feel that they are being exploited. It is also true that he obtains the confidence (of those above him) before criticizing them. If he does so before he has obtained their confidence, they feel that they are being slandered. (XIX, 10)

Value: Partnerships are based on integrity.
Bible: The integrity of the upright shall guide them: but the perverseness of transgressors shall destroy them. (Proverbs 11:3)
Bible: Do all things without murmurings and disputings: That ye may be blameless and harmless, the sons of God, without rebuke, in the midst of a crooked and perverse nation, among whom ye shine as lights of the world. (Philippians 2:14-15)
Confucius: The Master said, I do not see what use a man can be put to, whose word cannot be trusted. How can a waggon be made to go if it has no yoke-bar or a carriage, if it has no collar-bar? (II, 22)
Confucius: The Master said, A gentleman takes as much trouble to discover what is right as lesser men take to discover what will pay. (IV, 16)
Confucius: The Master said, Man's very life is honesty, in that without it he will be lucky indeed if he escapes with his life. (VI, 17)

Value: Respect all individuals.
Bible: "But I say unto you, Love your enemies, bless them that curse you, do good to them that hate you, and pray for them which despitefully use you, and persecute you." (Jesus' Sermon on the Mount, Matt. 5:44)
Confucius: Tzu-kung asked saying, Is there any single saying that one can act upon all day and every day? The Master said,

Perhaps the saying about consideration: "Never do to others what you would not like them to do to you." (XV, 23)

Value: Train and develop our employees.
Bible: And the king appointed them a daily provision of the king's meat, and of the wine which he drank: so nourishing them three years, that at the end thereof they might stand before the king. (Daniel 1:5)
Confucius: The Master said, From the very poorest upwards--beginning even with the man who could bring no better present than a bundle of dried flesh--none has ever come to me without receiving instruction. (VII, 7)
Confucius: When the Master was going to Wei, Jan Ch'iu drove him. The Master said, What a dense population! Jan Ch'iu said, When the people have multiplied, what next should be done for them? The Master said, Enrich them. Jan Ch'iu said, When one has enriched them, what next should be done for them? The Master said, Instruct them. (XIII, 9)

Value: Maintain open communications.
Bible: The way of a fool is right in his own eyes: but he that hearkeneth unto counsel is wise. (Proverbs 12:15)
Confucius: The Master said, Do I regard myself as a possessor of wisdom? Far from it. But if even a simple peasant comes in all sincerity and asks me a question, I am ready to thrash the matter out, with all its pros and cons, to the very end. (IX, 7)
Confucius: The Master said, It was Hui whom I could count on always to listen attentively to anything I said. (IX, 142)

Value: Give a sound return to our investors.
Bible: "Thou oughtest therefore to have put my money to the exchangers, and then at my coming I should have received mine own with usury." (Jesus' parable of the talents, in which the master chastised his servant who had buried the talent the master had given him, Matthew 25:27)

Confucius: Tzu-kung said, Suppose one had a lovely jewel, should one wrap it up, put it in a box and keep it, or try to get the best price one can for it? The Master said, Sell it! Most certainly sell it! I myself am one who is waiting for an offer. (IX, 12)

The value, "Partnerships are based on integrity," is essentially the same as the natural law precept suggested by the Christian Roman Emperor Justinian, "that we should live honestly" (BL1, 40). Justinian's other two precepts, "[that we] should hurt nobody, and should render to everyone its due," are also found in both the Christian Bible and *The Analects* of Confucius. The precept that we should hurt nobody is a corollary of the broader "golden rule" taught by many religious leaders, including Jesus and Confucius:

Bible: "Therefore all things whatsoever ye would that men should do to you, do ye so to them: for this is the law and the prophets." (from Jesus' Sermon on the Mount, Matthew 7:12)

Confucius: Tzu-kung asked saying, Is there any single saying that one can act upon all day and every day? The Master said, Perhaps the saying about consideration: "Never do to others what you would not like them to do to you." (XV, 23--the same as Confucian rule relating to the value, "Respect for all individuals.")

The precept that we should render to everyone its due is taught in the following passages:

Bible: Render therefore to all their dues; tribute to whom tribute *is due*; custom to whom custom; fear to whom fear; honor to whom honor. (Romans 13:7)

Confucius: The Master said, A young man's duty is to behave well to his parents at home and to his elders abroad, to be cautious in giving promises and punctual in keeping them, to have kindly feelings towards everyone, but seek the intimacy of the Good. If, when all that is done, he has energy to spare, then let him study the polite arts. (I, 6)

Some ethical values may, however, come from the revealed law of only one religion. No philosophy or religion other than Christianity appears to teach people to love enemies who have hurt them. That was how Jesus taught people to apply the value that the King's Medical Company described, "respect [for] all individuals." There is no reason why a person ought to carry this value so far that he would love a stranger who had hurt him. In a case such as this, a public school teacher might point out that the value appears to be unique to a particular religion.

Some ethical values have a logical basis, but not all people agree with the logic. For instance, people disagree on whether adults ought to live together before they are married, whether women should have abortions and whether terminally ill people should take drugs to hasten their deaths. People often base their views of these matters on their religious views. Public school teachers can teach their students about these matters and they can have their students discuss the reasons for and against each point of view. However, they cannot teach students that an ethical rule should be obeyed simply because it is commanded by the scriptures or revealed law of a certain religion.

Ethical values are only one aspect of a person's religious faith and practice. Other aspects of a person's religion are his motivation to do what he knows is right, his desire to go beyond his moral sense of duty and to love other people, his inner strength and perseverance during times of difficulty, pain and sorrow and the spiritual guidance that controls his life's decisions. Psychologists and other advisors can help a person with his motivation, love, inner strength, and decisions, but for many people there is no substitute for religious faith and prayer. Public school teachers can tell their students about these matters, but unlike religious ministers, they cannot tell them there is only one right answer.

I. Establishment of Religion versus Free Exercise of Religion

Americans share no common revealed law. Their families have come from all over the world, bringing diverse cultural traditions and worship practices. What they share is a body of natural law values acquired by observation and reason. They have found that by practicing these values they can improve the quality of their lives. They also share a government that was founded the principles of natural law and the guarantees of life, liberty and property that enable all people to pursue their own happiness.

There is no inherent conflict between people's right to be free from government establishment of religion and their right to exercise their own religious beliefs. School teachers and administrators can avoid violating both rights by applying the following rules:

(1) allow students to pray, worship and/or meditate during their free time, provided they do not interfere with the learning activities of other students;

(2) when the beliefs and practices of a particular religion are discussed in the classroom, treat them as objects of academic study, not as beliefs and practices that students should adopt or reject in their own lives; and

(3) treat all student expressions of religious belief or lack of religious belief with equal respect.

Students should not be forbidden to worship, pray or meditate in public schools, provided they are acting solely on their own initiative. The conflict between religious free exercise and religious establishment occurs only when teachers and administrators try to control the religion practiced by their students.

Some have questioned whether a teacher or administrator has the right practice his religion in the course of his job, as part of his right of religious free exercise. The answer is that he can practice his religion to a limited extent, by applying his beliefs to his own conduct and thus set examples for his students. However, while he is serving the public at taxpayers' expense, he gives up some of the rights that he has when he is acting on his own behalf. One of those rights is the right to be a religious minister to his students.

12

The Nature and Purpose of Government

Since they began petitioning King George III to redress their grievances, Americans have been proclaiming their basic rights as free people. When the colonists' petitions fell on deaf ears, they proclaimed their basic rights in the Declaration of Independence. Then they included bills of rights in their state and federal constitutions. As this book has shown, Americans have continued to proclaim their rights and to debate the meanings of these rights for the past two centuries.

The basic rights proclaimed in constitutions differ from most other legal rights. Constitutional rights do not determine whether a person's conduct is right or wrong. They determine when government has the power to decide whether a person's conduct is right or wrong. The moral standards of society are therefore not relevant to disputes concerning the basic rights that guarantee American freedom.

What is relevant to any discussion of American freedom is an understanding of the nature and purpose of government, because the just powers of government are derived from its nature and purpose. The following is a brief review of that nature and purpose, as envisioned by the early Americans who adopted the Declaration of Independence and Constitution of the United States.

A. The Nature of Government

The second paragraph of Declaration of Independence makes the following three statements about the nature of government:

> We hold these truths to be self-evident: that all men are created equal, that they are endowed by their Creator with certain unalienable Rights, that among these are Life, Liberty and the pursuit of Happiness.--
> That to secure these rights, Governments are instituted among Men, deriving their just powers from the consent of the governed,--
> That whenever any Form of Government becomes destructive of these ends, it is the Right of the People to alter or to abolish it, and to institute a new Government, laying its foundation on such principles and organizing its powers in such form, as to them shall seem most likely to effect their Safety and Happiness. (App. K)

Nearly all the Americans who signed this declaration agreed with the philosophy of government stated by John Locke in his *Second Essay Concerning Civil Government* (1691). Thomas Jefferson, who composed the first draft of the Declaration of Independence, was a great admirer of Locke. The latter's influence on the former may be seen in the following passages from Locke's *Second Essay*:

> [There is] nothing more evident than that creatures of the same species and rank, promiscuously born to all the same advantages of nature and the use of the same faculties, should also be equal one amongst the other without subordination or subjection; . . . (App. F, par. 4)

> The state of nature has a law of nature to govern it, which obliges every one; and reason, which is that law, teaches all mankind who will but consult it that, being all equal and independent, no one ought to harm another in his life, health, liberty, or possessions; . . . (App. F, par. 6)

These passages show the basis of the first statement of the Declaration quoted above, with the exception of "the pursuit of Happi-

Chapter 12   The Nature and Purpose of Government

ness." Jefferson evidently took that phrase from the following explanation of the law of nature by William Blackstone in his *Commentaries*:

> For he [God] has so intimately connected, so inseparably interwoven the laws of eternal justice with the happiness of each individual, that the latter cannot be attained but by observing the former; and, if the former be punctually obeyed, it cannot but induce the latter. In consequence of which mutual connection of justice and human felicity, he has not perplexed the law of nature with a multitude of abstracted rules and precepts, referring merely to the fitness or unfitness of things, as some have vainly surmised; but has graciously reduced the rule of obedience to this one paternal precept, "that man should pursue his own happiness." This is the foundation of what we call ethics, or natural law. For the several articles into which it is branched in our systems, amount to no more than demonstrating, that this or that action tends to man's real happiness, and therefore very justly concluding that the performance of it is a part of the law of nature; or, on the other hand, that this or that action is destructive of man's real happiness, and therefore the law of nature forbids it. (BL1, 40-41)

Although Locke did not use the term "pursuit of happiness," he said the "natural inducement" among men "to love others as themselves" leads men to determine and obey the laws of nature, quoting from *The Laws of Ecclesiastical Polity* by the English theologian and philosopher Richard Hooker (App. F, par. 5-6).

The second statement of the Declaration quoted above says that government derives its just powers from the consent of the governed. Locke explained this concept as follows:

> But I, moreover, affirm that all men are naturally in that state [of nature] and remain so till by their own consents they make themselves members of some politic society; . . . (App. F, par. 15)

> A man, as has been proved, cannot subject himself to the arbitrary power of another; and having in a state of nature no arbitrary power over the life, liberty, or possessions of another, but only so much as the law of nature gave him for the preservation of himself and the rest of

mankind, this is all he does or can give up to the commonwealth, and by it to the legislative power, so that the legislative power can have no more that this. Their power, in the utmost bounds of it, is limited to the public good of society. . . . (App. F, par. 135)

nor can the people be bound by any laws but such as are enacted by those whom they have chosen and authorized to make laws for them.... (App. F, par. 141)

The Declaration's third statement quoted above says that when government becomes destructive of the ends for which it was created, the people may alter or abolish it and create a new government for themselves. Locke confirmed this right in Paragraph 212 of his *Second Essay*:

When any one or more shall take upon them to make laws, whom the people have not appointed so to do, they make laws without authority, which the people are not therefore bound to obey; by which means they come again to be out of subjection and may constitute to themselves a new legislative as they think best, being in full liberty to resist the force of those who without authority would impose anything upon them.[1]

Some philosophers and theologians held a different view of the nature of government. The sixteenth-century Protestant reformer John Calvin said that government leaders receive their authority from God, not from the people. He also said the advantages of the various forms of government--monarchy, aristocracy and democracy--"are so nearly equal that it will not be easy to discover of which the utility preponderates." Therefore, said Calvin, "for private men, who have no authority to deliberate on the regulation of any public affairs, it would surely be a vain occupation to dispute which would be the best form of government in the place where they live." Although he acknowledged that people are most happy under democratic governments that recognize their liberties and said that leaders of such governments have a duty to safeguard these liberties, he also said

Chapter 12   The Nature and Purpose of Government   701

> [I]f those to whom the will of God has assigned another form of government transfer this [duty] to themselves so as to be tempted to desire a revolution, the very thought will be not only foolish and useless, but altogether criminal. If we limit not our views to one city, but look round and take a comprehensive survey of the whole world, or at least extend our observations to distant lands, we shall certainly find it to be a wise arrangement of Divine Providence that various countries are governed by different forms of civil polity, for they are admirably held together with a certain inequality, as the elements are combined in very unequal proportions.[2]

Contrary to the American Declaration, Calvin not only contended that God has willed that some people suffer unequal treatment by their governments and they have no right to overthrow these governments, he also said that people have no ability to discover God's natural law by their own reasoning powers. In his *Confession of Faith which all the citizens and inhabitants of Geneva and the subjects of the country must keep and hold* (1536), he required the Geneva people to acknowledge

> man by nature to be blind, darkened in understanding, and full of corruption and perversity of heart so that of himself he has no power to be able to comprehend the true knowledge of God as is proper, nor to apply himself to good works. But on the contrary, if he is left by God to what he is by nature, he is only able to live in ignorance and to be abandoned to all iniquity. Hence he has need to be illumined by God, so that he come to the right knowledge of his salvation, and thus to be redirected in his affections and reformed to the obedience of the righteousness of God. (Paragraph 4, "Natural Man")

Jefferson proclaimed that he was not a Calvinist in an 1823 letter to John Adams:

> I can never join Calvin in addressing *his god*. He was indeed an Atheist, which I can never be; or rather his religion was Dæmonism. If ever man worshipped a false God, he did. The being described in his 5. points is not the God whom you and I acknolege and adore, the Creator and benevolent governor of the world, but a dæmon of malignant spirit. It would be more pardonable to believe in no god at all,

than to blaspheme him by the atrocious attributes of Calvin. Indeed I think that every Christian sect gives a great handle to Atheism by their general dogma that, without revelation, there would be no sufficient proof of the being of a god.[3]

In the mid-1600s, the English political theorist Robert Filmer said in his book, *Patriarcha, or the Natural Power of Kings*,[4] that every kingdom was a family of people similar to the first family, of which Adam was both father and absolute monarch. According to Filmer, the modern kings had the power of absolute monarchs because they were the eldest heirs of Adam.

A few years after Filmer, the English philosopher Thomas Hobbes agreed that there were no inherent limits on the power of government. However, he did not base his views on the Bible. He said the ideal government was by a "Leviathan," comprised of either a single man or an assembly of men; this "Leviathan" was the ultimate interpreter and enforcer of the laws of society, but was not itself subject to those laws; its only essential quality was its power to compel obedience. Hobbes said that such a Leviathan was necessary to prevent the individual members of society from destroying one another.

During the events leading to the American War of Independence, many defenders of Parliament's power over the colonies appeared to base their arguments on the philosophies of Calvin, Filmer and Hobbes. When the Reverend Samuel Seabury of the Church of England denounced the Continental Congress's claim that the colonies had certain rights of self-government, Alexander Hamilton replied that Seabury's opinions were based on the erroneous assumptions of Hobbes. Hamilton said that Hobbes had held that man was, in a state of nature,

> perfectly free from all restraint of *law* and *government*. Moral obligation, according to him, is derived from the introduction of civil society; and there is no virtue, but what is purely artificial,---the mere contrivance of politicians, for the maintenance of social intercourse. But the reason he ran into this absurd and impious doctrine, was, that he

Chapter 12   The Nature and Purpose of Government   703

disbelieved the existence of an intelligent superintending principle, who is the governor, and will be the final judge of the universe. . . .

Good and wise men, in all ages, have embraced a very dissimilar theory. They have supposed, that the deity, from the relations, we stand in, to himself and to each other, has constituted an external and immutable law; which is, indispensibly, obligatory upon all mankind, prior to any human institution whatever.

This is what is called the law of nature, "which, being coeval with mankind, and dictated by God himself, is, of course, superior in obligation to any other. It is binding over all the globe, in all countries, and at all times. No human laws are of any validity, if contrary to this; and such of them as are valid, derive all their authority, mediately, or immediately, from this original." BLACKSTONE.[5] (BL1, 41)

The view of government expressed by Jefferson, Hamilton and other American founders has been criticized because it ignores the real conditions that have existed throughout the world ever since people gathered in caves. These men, however, were not describing the conditions of the world as it was; they were describing the rightful powers of government and an ideal world that they hoped would some day become real. When Madison said in the preamble to his proposed bill of rights amendments to the U. S. Constitution "[t]hat all power is originally vested in, and consequently derived from, the people," Congressman Gerry of Massachusetts replied,

[T]his holds up an idea that all the governments of the earth are intended for the benefit of the people. Now, I am so far from being of this opinion, that I do not believe that one out of fifty is intended for any such purpose. I believe the establishment of most governments is to gratify the ambition of an individual, who, by fraud, force, or accident, had made himself master of the people. If we contemplate the history of nations, ancient or modern, we shall find they originated either in fraud or force, or both. If this is demonstrable, how can we pretend to say that governments are intended for the benefit of those who are most oppressed by them? This maxim does not appear to me to be strictly true in fact. Therefore I think we ought not insert it in the constitution. I shall therefore propose to amend the clause, by inserting "of right." Then it will stand as it ought. I do not object to the principle, sir. It is a good one, but it does not generally hold in practice.[6]

The American founders thus rejected the *Calvin-and-Hobbes* view of government and adopted the *Locke-and-Blackstone* view, holding that, by the law of nature, government derives its power from the people and so its power is limited to what the people have delegated to it for the good of society. Locke emphasized that natural law is rational, saying that *"reason, which is that law,* [emphasis added] teaches all mankind who will but consult it that, being all equal and independent, no one ought to harm another in his life, health, liberty, or possessions; . . . ." (App. F, par. 6). He also said that all men are equal because they are "of the same species and rank, promiscuously born to all the same advantages of nature and the use of the same faculties" (App. F, par. 4). Blackstone said the law of nature was discoverable by reason alone, through the "pursuit of happiness" test, and that God had made this discovery possible by the way He had "perplexed the law of nature" (BL1, 41). Thus, natural law and revealed law both come from God, but natural law has been made known to all people regardless of their religious beliefs and whether they believe or do not believe in God. This principle is equally religious and secular: as a religious principle it holds that God is the source of both the laws of nature and the rational means by which people determine those laws; as a secular principle it holds that the relative rights and duties that people impose on one another for the sake of each others' happiness can be and ought to be determined rationally--and independently of the revealed law of any religion.

Locke and Blackstone, however, did not believe that government should be based solely on natural law. In his *Letter Concerning Toleration*, Locke had said that atheists were not to be tolerated because "[p]romises, covenants, and oaths, which are the bonds of human society, can have no hold on an atheist," and "those that by their atheism undermine and destroy all religion, can have no pretense of religion whereupon to challenge the privilege of a toleration" (App. F, second excerpt from *Toleration* letter). On the other hand, Jefferson said,

> The legitimate powers of government extend to such acts only as are injurious to others. But it does me no injury for my neighbour to say there are twenty gods, or no god. It neither picks my pocket nor breaks my leg.[7]

Blackstone said that human government should enforce not only God's natural law but also His revealed law as interpreted by the Church of England. He said this revealed law was necessary because man's "reason is corrupt, and his understanding is full of ignorance and error" (BL1, 41). For that reason, and because of the "bad example and consequence" of "openly transgressing the precepts of religion either natural or revealed," he said that government was justified in enforcing laws against heresy, blasphemy, witchcraft, sabbath-breaking and other conduct condemned by the Church of England (BL5, 43-65). The American people, however, established the United States government on a natural-law basis that excludes laws "respecting an establishment of religion, or prohibiting the free exercise thereof; or abridging the freedom of speech, or of the press; . . . ." (U. S. Constitution, First Amendment, App. O).

American government is therefore based on the principles that people have equal rights, that their pursuit of happiness requires them to respect each other's life, liberty and property and that valid government is derived from their common consent. No religious faith is required to accept these principles. They relate to only one aspect of human existence, namely, the way people govern themselves in order to enable each person to pursue his own happiness. These principles are embedded in the United States Constitution, which says in its preamble, "We the People of the United States . . . do ordain and establish this Constitution for the United States of America." The Fifth and Fourteenth Amendments guarantee the rights of life, liberty and property, including religious freedom, freedom of speech and press and equal protection of the laws. Article I establishes a House of Representatives elected by the people. The Seventeenth Amendment says the Senate shall be elected by the people. The Fifteenth and Nineteenth Amendments guarantee the right to vote to people of all races and both sexes. In America, the power of government is derived not from God but from the consent of all the people who stand as equals, regardless of national origin, race, sex or religion.

B. The Purpose of Government

The major clauses of the U. S. Constitution that embody the natural law basis of government are the life, liberty and property clause of the Fifth Amendment and the life, liberty and property and equal protection clauses of the Fourteenth Amendment. These clauses require that government have a valid purpose for taking a person's life, liberty or property and a valid purpose for treating people unequally.[8]

The link between the natural law basis of government and the requirement that it act with a valid purpose was explained in the preamble to the bill of rights of the 1784 New Hampshire Constitution:

> All men are born equally free and independent; therefore, all government of right originates from the people, is founded in consent, and instituted for the general good.
> II. All men have certain natural, essential, and inherent rights; among which are--the enjoying and defending life and liberty--acquiring, possessing and protecting property--and in a word, of seeking and obtaining happiness.
> III. When men enter into a state of society, they surrender up some of their natural rights to that society, in order to insure the protection of others; and, without such an equivalent, the surrender is void.[9]

This defines the social contract that is the only legitimate basis of human government. Like other contracts, the social contract must have a *quid pro quo*, or a something that one party gives the other party in exchange for the something that the other party gives the first party. In contract law, this is known as "consideration." The

Chapter 12 The Nature and Purpose of Government

New Hampshire bill of rights says that when people surrender some of their natural rights to enable their government to function, they must receive something in return from that government, or else the surrender is void.

To give people something in return, government may pass laws designed to stop people from hurting one another with respect to their life, liberty and property. It may also use people's tax revenues to build highways, parks and meeting and entertainment facilities. These are considered to be within the meaning of "the general good" of the public, as that phrase is used the first article of the New Hampshire bill of rights. However, some actions attempted by government do not qualify as being within the general good of the public. In its fourth and fifth articles, the New Hampshire bill says that government cannot regulate people's religion:

> IV. Among the natural rights, some are in their very nature unalienable, because no equivalent can be given or received for them. Of this kind are the RIGHTS OF CONSCIENCE.
>
> V. Every individual has a natural and unalienable right to worship God according to the dictates of his own conscience, and reason; and no subject shall be hurt, molested, or restrained in his person, liberty or estate for worshipping God, in the manner and season most agreeable to the dictates of his own conscience, or for his religious profession, sentiments or persuasion; provided he doth not disturb the public peace, or disturb others in their religious worship.[10]

Government also fails to serve a public good when it regulates the private lives of people. Speaking for the U. S. Supreme Court in 1877, Chief Justice Morrison Waite said in *Munn v. Illinois*, 94 U.S. 113 at 124,

> When one becomes a member of society, he necessarily parts with some rights or privileges which, as an individual not affected by his relations with others, he might retain. "A body politic," as aptly defined in the preamble of the Constitution of Massachusetts, "is a social compact by which the whole people covenants with each citizen, and each citizen with the whole people, that all shall be governed by

certain laws for the common good." This does not confer power upon the whole people to control rights which are purely and exclusively private, *Thorpe v. R. & B. Railroad Co.*, 27 Vt. 143; but it does authorize the establishment of laws requiring each citizen to so conduct himself, and so use his own property, as not unnecessarily to injure another.

These statements give us some idea of what government can and cannot do to fulfill its *quid pro quo* of the social contract. Another possible guide to the purpose of government is the preamble of the U. S. Constitution, which lists the broad purposes of government envisioned by the founding fathers:

> We the People of the United States, in Order to form a more perfect Union, establish Justice, insure domestic Tranquility, provide for the common defence, promote the general Welfare, and secure the Blessings of Liberty to ourselves and our Posterity, do ordain and establish this Constitution for the United States of America. (App. N)

The Constitution's Bill of Rights also helps because it lists some specific acts that are definitely not consistent with the purpose of government. Those acts include laws that deprive people of the free exercise of their religion, laws that forbid speech that does no injury and searches of people's homes without cause for believing they contain evidence of a crime.

However, the Constitution does not contain a comprehensive statement of the purpose of government. Judges must therefore look at other documents to determine whether a government activity has a recognized, valid purpose. Sometimes they must rely on their own understanding of the purpose of government. Judges have therefore been criticized for basing their decisions on their personal political views.

One remedy to this problem would be to amend the Constitution to include a statement regarding the purpose of government. That statement might read as follows:

> The acts of the governments of the United States and the several states shall be limited to the following purposes:

Chapter 12 The Nature and Purpose of Government

1. To provide armed forces and police protection against those who would attack the people, their government or their property;

2. To determine and enforce the relative rights and duties of people concerning their lives, their liberties and their property;

3. To protect the health, safety and natural resources of the people;

4. To preserve the family as the basic unit of society;

5. To protect people who are not competent to act in their own best interests because of immaturity, mental illness, brain damage or chemical addiction;

6. To assist people who are unable to care for themselves, including children, the elderly and the infirm;

7. To provide all people the opportunity to be educated and trained so they can contribute to and benefit from the prosperity of society;

8. To issue money and to establish and regulate banks;

9. To insure that people and business enterprises have access to adequate transportation systems, communications systems, energy and water resources, sanitary and waste disposal systems and places for meeting and recreation;

10. To promote scientific discovery, technical achievement, business enterprise and artistic expression; and

11. To lay and collect taxes, borrow money and pay debts, in order to accomplish the foregoing purposes.

This section shall not be construed as enlarging or diminishing the powers granted the United States government by this Constitution, nor shall it be construed to allow a government of the United States or any state to determine or enforce any private duty that a person may owe to himself or infringe any other right of a person guaranteed by this Constitution.

This statement is intended as only a first draft. It might serve as a starting point for a debate on social ends that justify government's taking away people's life, liberty and property. We live in a society of expanding government regulation, taxation and bureaucracy. The time has come to reflect on the reasons why we need government. Why are we not content to live in a state of nature? Why must we control one another's conduct? The role of government in society should be limited to the answers to that question.

Some might say that government does not need to justify its actions. They would invoke the traditional belief that government has unlimited power. However, that belief should have been dispelled in 1215, when the Magna Charta guaranteed that English landowners known as "freemen" had certain rights the king could not take away. Since then, people have been trying to determine the full scope of these rights and to include every person among the freemen who are entitled to them. At one time, only white, male, Christian landowners were entitled to the rights of freemen. There was no reason why that was so. It was a government-mandated tradition, a tradition that required no reason. That is the crux of the conflict. Government derives its power from the law of nature, and reason *is* the law of nature (App. F, par. 6). The United States Constitution guaranteed the natural law rights of people, in spite of government-mandated traditions that continued to deprive people of these rights. As people have asserted their rights, some of these mandated traditions have been eliminated. As they continue to assert their rights, more such traditions will be eliminated and the voluntary traditions of people will prevail.

In recent years, we Americans have become disillusioned with our government. We are disillusioned because of corrupt officials and miscarriages of justice. That is understandable. We are also disillusioned because our political leaders have misled us into believing that government can rectify most of the evils of our society. When a poll reveals that we are particularly concerned with one of these evils, the politicians promise that government can solve the problem, whether it be race discrimination, drug abuse or a family matter. We therefore think of ourselves as slaves captured by our problems and we seek a larger-than-life Moses who will lead us from our captivity. We forget that we are already a free people. We are the masters of our destinies, particularly in respect of our absolute duties. When our common pursuit of happiness is threatened, we must look primarily to ourselves for the answers. Government can help in some respects, but if we cannot rely on ourselves, we cannot expect the government solutions to work.

Appendices BL, BL1 through BL7 and A through P

Portions of the Appendices in **bold letters**
are those referenced in Chapters 1 to 12.

Appendices BL1 through BL7 are excerpts from
Sir William Blackstone's *Commentaries on the Laws of England*
4 volumes (Oxford, England: Clarendon Press, 1765-69).
Reprints of the entire four volumes may be obtained from
The Legal Classics Library, Birmingham, Alabama

The references in this book to Appendices BL1 to BL7
match the alphanumeric characters
at the bottoms of the pages of these appendices.
For example, in the reference, "(BL1, 130),"
"BL1" means Appendix BL and "130" means page 130
of Blackstone's Book 1.

Appendices BL1, BL2, BL3 and BL4
are from Book 1 of Blackstone's *Commentaries*.
Appendices BL5, BL6 and BL7
are from Book 4 of Blackstone's *Commentaries*.

Table 5
The Relationships between Blackstone's Terms of Art

NATURAL LIBERTY
the unlimited liberty that a person has in a state of nature

In a state of nature, people learn by their reasoning to obey the **LAWS OF NATURE** so that each person may **PURSUE HIS OWN HAPPINESS**.	Because man's reasoning is defective, he also needs **REVEALED LAW** to guide him in the exercise of his natural liberty.

In a civil society, a person gives up his unlimited natural liberty and has instead CIVIL PRIVILEGES and CIVIL LIBERTY, which together comprise his ABSOLUTE RIGHTS:

CIVIL PRIVILEGES (e.g., procedural rights, just compensation) that government must give in return for taking away part of one's natural liberty in order to protect society (which it does by enforcing **RELATIVE RIGHTS** and **RELATIVE DUTIES**)	**CIVIL LIBERTY** (THE *RESIDUUM* OF NATURAL LIBERTY) "natural liberty so far restrained (and no farther) as is necessary . . . for the general advantage of the public" (BL3, 121) (includes freedom to determine **ABSOLUTE DUTIES**)

ABSOLUTE RIGHTS
(PRIVATE IMMUNITIES)

PERSONAL SECURITY RIGHTS	PERSONAL LIBERTY RIGHTS	PRIVATE PROPERTY RIGHTS	AUXILIARY RIGHTS to protect the other rights

BL

A Biography of Sir William Blackstone
and
a Comparison of His Philosophy with That of Jeremy Bentham

Sir William Blackstone, the youngest of four brothers, was born in London on July 10, 1723. His father was a silk merchant who died before William was born. His mother died when he was twelve. He then lived under the care of his uncle, a surgeon, who sent him to the Charterhouse preparatory school. At the age of fifteen, he entered Pembroke College at Oxford University, where he studied the classics and literature. He graduated at the age of eighteen. Near the time of his graduation, Blackstone considered becoming an architect, a drama critic or a poet. He even wrote a treatise entitled *The Elements of Architecture*. However, he decided he could not make enough money in any of those occupations to support himself.

In 1741, Blackstone entered the Middle Temple in London, which was an inn of court, where Englishmen train to become barristers (lawyers). While studying law, he was elected to the All Souls College at Oxford and eventually became a teaching fellow. He took an active interest in the business affairs of the college and supervised the building of the Codrington Library on the All Souls quadrangle. In 1746, he became a barrister but his law practice was not successful. He preferred the academic life at Oxford. In 1750, he earned the degree of Doctor of Civil Law. The following year, he became a judge on the Chancellor's Court in Wallingford, near Oxford, a position that he held until 1759.

In 1753, Blackstone began lecturing on the English common law at Oxford. His lectures were the first ever delivered on that subject at any college. All previous law instruction at the college level had been on the old Roman Law, a body of law that had been largely superseded by the English common law. Because of the eloquence and simplicity of his presentation, Blackstone's lectures were very popular. In 1756, he published *An Analysis of the Laws of England*, to serve as a textbook for his students. In October of 1758, the university created a chair of common law, called the Vinerian professorship, and Blackstone was chosen the first holder of that chair. One of his students in 1759 was John Adams of Massachusetts, who praised his lectures in a letter to a friend, Jonathan Sewell.[1]

In 1761, Blackstone began spending less time in Oxford and more time in London. He began lecturing to law students at the Middle Temple. He was also elected to Parliament, representing Hindon in Wiltshire.

In May 1761, he married Sarah Clitherow and they moved to a house in Wallingford. Soon after the wedding, the couple had a minor conflict concerning the decorating of their house. Blackstone prided himself on his interior design abilities and often became upset when he found that his wife had moved a chair or changed a room in some other way. However, they finally settled on a compromise form of home government. Blackstone took exclusive jurisdiction of his study, while his wife took charge of the rest of the house. Evidently, the ancient principle that "a man's house is his castle" had been superseded by a more modern domestic relations rule.

In July 1761, Blackstone was appointed principal of New Inn Hall. Then in 1763, he was appointed solicitor general to the queen. During this period, he also initiated and directed the building of two new turnpike roads through Wallingford and helped rebuild St. Peter's Church in London.

While lecturing at Oxford, Blackstone had discovered that some students were selling notes of his lectures to others. People outside the school may also have been selling the notes, in which Blackstone noticed many errors. He therefore published his own version of his lectures, his famous *Commentaries on the Laws of England*. They were released in four volumes in 1765, 1766, 1767 and 1769 and totaled 1,886 pages. The books sold extremely well in both England and America because they were the first comprehensive treatise on the English common law. They were purchased by many lay people as well as lawyers, because they were based on lectures designed to teach lay people about the law.

From 1761 to 1770, Blackstone sat in the House of Commons of Parliament. He did not engage actively in Parliamentary politics, except on one occasion in 1769 when he supported the expulsion from Parliament of the notorious troublemaker, John Wilkes. In the debate, he suffered the embarrassment of having his opponent contradict him with a quotation from his own *Commentaries*.

In 1770, Blackstone was knighted by the king for his scholarship and appointed judge of the Common Pleas Court. He also served as judge on the King's Bench, but was then reappointed to the Common Pleas Court. In the late 1770s, his health began to fail and he died on February 14, 1780.

After his death, Blackstone's *Commentaries* continued to be popular, particularly in America, where they became the leading authority on the English common law. For almost a century, the courts of nearly every state followed the rules of common law as explained by Blackstone. Many famous American lawyers, judges and political leaders said that their interest in the law had begun with their reading of Blackstone. During the 1780s, George Wythe, Professor of Law at the College of William and Mary, laid out a study plan for his students that included Blackstone before breakfast. Tuesday was the day he lectured on Blackstone. His students included the future president James Monroe and the future Supreme Court chief justice John Marshall.[2] Abraham Lincoln, according to Carl Sandburg, acted on his dream of becoming a lawyer only after finding a copy of Blackstone's *Commentaries* in a trash barrel. The books seemed to say to him, "Take me and read me; you were made for a lawyer." Lincoln later wrote, "The more I read the more intensely interested I became. Never in my whole life was my mind so thoroughly absorbed. I read until I devoured them."[3]

However, Blackstone's *Commentaries* also received severe criticism, mostly because of its descriptions of the basic divisions and origins of the common law. Very little of this criticism was directed at Blackstone's specific rules of law, such as the rules relating to the absolute rights of Englishmen.

One of the critics of Blackstone's *Commentaries* was the utilitarian philosopher Jeremy Bentham. As a student at Oxford in 1763, he had attended Blackstone's lectures. In 1776, he published a book entitled *Commentaries on the Commentaries*, in which he criticized Blackstone's basic view of English government. Blackstone had painted a picture of a nearly perfect English government whose fundamental laws were derived from those made by God. Bentham argued that there was no such connection, because government laws are made when fallible human judges and juries enforce what they think are the laws by sentences of fine, imprisonment and hanging. On the other hand, God makes His laws by rendering His infallible judgments of eternal damnation upon the offenders. These two spheres of activity are not connected. Therefore, Bentham said, government laws have no divine origin or connection.

The main source of Bentham's irritation with Blackstone was the way his *Commentaries* proudly portrayed not only the divine origin of English laws but their harmony with one another. Bentham had seen many inconsistencies and errors in those laws. His goal was to reform the English legal system, but Blackstone's *Commentaries* gave the public the impression the system needed no reform.

On one point, however, Bentham agreed with Blackstone. Amid hundreds of pages of criticism, he nearly praised one of Blackstone's passages:

> Toward the close of the paragraph, however, I must confess I could not help trembling for our author. It was at seeing [him] within arms length of departing entirely from his character and advancing a proposition that would not only have been intelligible, but fundamentally important, and unquestionably true.

Bentham then rephrased Blackstone's commentary on the pursuit of happiness by deleting the words shown in brackets and adding the words shown in italics in the following:

> This is the foundation of what [we call ethics, or natural law] *may be called Critical Law or Critical Jurisprudence.* [For the] *The* several

articles into which it [is] *might be* branched in our systems[,] amount to no more than demonstrating[,] that this or that [action] *mode of conduct* tends to man's real happiness, and therefore very justly concluding that the [performance] *observance* of it [is a part of the law of nature;] *ought to be either commanded or allow'd of by the Law of the country where it has that tendency:* or, on the other hand, that this or that [action] *mode of conduct* is destructive of man's real happiness, and therefore that [the law of nature forbids it] *(provided the mischief of enforcing the prohibition do not exceed the mischief of the mode of conduct meant to be prohibited) the Law of the country ought to forbid it.*[4]

The principle that Bentham expressed in this rewriting of Blackstone became the foundation of his utilitarian philosophy of government.

The pursuit of happiness was also a key part of the American Declaration of Independence. The American struggle for freedom illustrated the philosophies of both Bentham and Blackstone. According to Bentham's philosophy, the pursuit of happiness motivated the Americans to fight for their freedom. According to Blackstone's philosophy, the pursuit of happiness was a God-given precept that justified their fight for freedom.

BL1

Blackstone on the Nature of Laws

Book 1, Introduction, Section 2,
"Of the Nature of Laws in General"

Law, in it's most general and comprehensive sense, signifies a rule of action; and is applied indiscriminately to all kinds of action, whether animate, or inanimate, rational or irrational. Thus we say, the laws of motion, of gravitation, or optics, or mechanics, as well as the laws of nature and of nations. And it is that rule of action, which is prescribed by some superior, and which the inferior is bound to obey.

Thus when the supreme being formed the universe, and created matter out of nothing, he impressed certain principles upon that matter, from which it can never depart, and without which it would cease to be. When he put that matter into motion, he established certain laws of motion, to which all moveable bodies must conform. And, to descend from the greatest operations to the smallest, when a workman forms a clock, or other piece of mechanism, he establishes at his own pleasure certain arbitrary laws for it's direction; as that the hand shall describe a given space in a given time; to which law as long as the work conforms, so long as it continues to perfection, and answers the end of it's formation.

If we farther advance, from mere inactive matter to vegetable and animal life, we shall find them still governed by laws; more numerous indeed, but equally fixed and invariable. The whole progress of plants, from the seed to the root, and from thence to the seed again; --- the method of animal nutrition, digestion, secretion, and all other branches of vital oeconomy; --- are not left to chance, or the will of the creature itself, but are performed in a wondrous involuntary manner, and guided by unerring rules laid down by the great creator.

This then is the general significance of law, a rule of action dictated by some superior being; and in those creatures that have neither the power to think, nor to will, such laws must be invariably obeyed, so long as the creature itself subsists, for it's existence depends on that obedience. But laws, in their more confined sense, and in which it is our present business to consider them, denote the rules, not of action in general, but of *human* action or conduct: that is, the precepts by which man, the noblest of all sublunary beings, a creature endowed with both reason and freewill, is commanded to make use of those faculties in the general regulation of his behaviour.

Man, considered as a creature, must necessarily be subject to the laws of his creator, for he is entirely a dependent being. A being, independent of any other, has no rule to pursue, but such as he prescribes to himself; but a state of dependence will inevitably oblige the inferior to take the will of him, on whom he depends, as the rule of his conduct: not indeed in every particular, but in all those points wherein his dependence consists. This principle therefore has more or less extent and effect, in proportion as the superiority of the one and the dependence of the other is greater or less, absolute or limited. And consequently as man depends absolutely upon his maker for everything, it is necessary that he should in all points conform to his maker's will.

This will of his maker is called the law of nature. For as God, when he created matter, and endued it with a principle of mobility, established certain rules for the perpetual direction of that motion; so, when he created man, and endued him with freewill to conduct himself in all parts of life, he laid down certain immutable laws of human nature, whereby that freewill is in some degree regulated and restrained, and gave him also the faculty of reason to discover that purport of those laws.

Considering the creator only as a being of infinite *power*, he was able unquestionably to have prescribed whatever laws he pleased to his creature, man, however unjust or severe. But as he is also a being of infinite *wisdom*, he had laid down only such laws as were founded in those relations of justice, that existed in the nature of things antecedent to any positive precept. **These are the eternal, immutable laws of good and evil, to which the creator himself in all his dispensations conforms; and which he has enabled human reason to discover, so far as they are necessary for the conduct of human actions. Such among others are these principles: that we should live honestly, should hurt nobody, and should render to every one it's due; to which three general precepts Justinian[a] has reduced the whole doctrine of law.**

But if the discovery of these first principles of the law of nature depended only upon the due exertion of right reason, and could not otherwise be attained than by a chain of metaphysical disquisitions, mankind would have wanted some inducement to have quickened their inquiries, and the greater part of the world would have rested content in mental indolence, and ignorance it's inseparable companion. As therefore the creator is a being, not only of infinite *power*, and *wisdom*, but also of infinite *goodness*, he has been pleased so to contrive the constitution and frame of humanity, that we should want no other prompter to enquire after and pursue the rule of right, but only our own self-love, that universal principle of action. **For he has so intimately connected, so inseparably interwoven the laws of eternal justice with the happiness of each individual, that the latter cannot be attained but by observing the former; and, if the former be punctually obeyed, it cannot but induce the latter. In consequence of which mutual connection of justice and human felicity, he has not per-**

---

[a] *Juris praecepta sunt haec, honeste vivere, alterum non laedere, suum cuique tribuere. Inst.* 1.1.3.

plexed the law of nature with a multitude of abstracted rules and precepts, referring merely to the fitness or unfitness of things, as some have vainly surmised; but has graciously reduced the rule of obedience to this one paternal precept, "that man should pursue his own happiness." This is the foundation of what we call ethics, or natural law. For the several articles into which it is branched in our systems, amount to no more than demonstrating, that this or that action tends to man's real happiness, and therefore very justly concluding that the performance of it is a part of the law of nature; or, on the other hand, that this or that action is destructive of man's real happiness, and therefore that the law of nature forbids it.

This law of nature, being co-eval with mankind and dictated by God himself, is of course superior in obligation to any other. It is binding over all the globe, in all countries, and at all times: no human laws are of any validity, if contrary to this; and such of them as are valid derive all their force, and all their authority, mediately or immediately, from this original.

But in order to apply this to the particular exigencies of each individual, it is still necessary to have recourse to reason; whose office it is to discover, as was before observed, what the law of nature directs in every circumstance in life; by considering, what method will tend the most effectually to our own substantial happiness. And if our reason were always, as in our first ancestor before his transgression, clear and perfect, unruffled by passions, unclouded by prejudice, unimpaired by disease or intemperance, the talk would be pleasant and easy; we should need no other guide but this. But every man now finds the contrary in his own experience; that his reason is corrupt, and his understanding full of ignorance and error.

This has given manifold occasion for the benign interposition of divine providence; which, in compassion to the frailty, the imperfection, and the blindness of human reason, hath been pleased, at sundry times and in divers manners, to discover and enforce it's laws by an immediate and direct revelation. The doctrines thus delivered we call the revealed or divine law, and they are to be found only in the holy scriptures. These precepts, when revealed, are found upon comparison to be really a part of the original law of nature, as they tend in all their consequences to man's felicity. But we are not from thence to conclude that the knowledge of these truths was attainable by reason, in it's present corrupted state; since we find that, until they were revealed, they were hid from the wisdom of the ages. As then the moral precepts of this law are indeed of the same original with those of the law of nature, so their intrinsic obligation is of equal strength and perpetuity. **Yet undoubtedly the revealed law is (humanly speaking) of infinitely more authority than what we generally call the natural law.** Because one is the law of nature, expressly declared so to be by God himself; the other is only what, by the assistance of human reason, we imagine to be that law. If we could be as certain of the latter as we are the former, both would have an equal authority; but, till then, they can never be put in any competition together.

Upon these two foundations, the law of nature and the law of revelation, depend all human laws; that is to say, no human laws should be suffered to contradict these. There is, it is true, a great number of indifferent points, in which both the divine law and the natural leave a man at his own liberty; but which are found necessary for the benefit of society to be restrained within certain limits. **And herein it is that human laws have their greatest force and efficacy; for, with regard to such points as are not indifferent, human laws are only declaratory of, and act in subordination to, the former. To instance in the case of murder: this is expressly forbidden by the divine, and demonstrably by the natural law; and from these prohibitions arises the true unlawfulness of this crime. Those human laws, that annex a punishment to it, do not at all increase it's moral guilt, or superadd any fresh obligation** *in foro conscientiae* **to abstain from**

it's perpetuation. **Nay, if any human law should allow or injoin us to commit it, we are bound to transgress that human law, or else we must offend both the natural and the divine.** But with regard to matters that are in themselves indifferent, and are not commanded or forbidden by those superior laws; such, for instance, as exporting of wool into foreign countries; here the inferior legislature has scope and opportunity to interpose, and to make that action unlawful which was before not so.

If man were to live in a state of nature, unconnected with other individuals, there would be no occasion for any other laws, that the law of nature, and the law of God. Neither could any other law possibly exist; for a law always supposes some superior who is to make it; and in a state of nature we are all equal, without any other superior but him who is the author of our being. But man was formed for society; and, as is demonstrated by the writers on this subject[b], is neither capable of living alone, nor indeed has the courage to do it. However, as it is impossible for the whole race of mankind to be united in one great society, they must necessarily divide into many; and form separate states, commonwealths, and nations; entirely independent of each other, and yet liable to a mutual intercourse. Hence arises a third kind of law to regulate this mutual intercourse, called, "the law of "nations;" which, as none of these states will acknowledge a superiority in the other, cannot be dictated by either; but depends entirely upon the rules of natural law, or upon mutual compacts, treaties, leagues, and agreements between these several communities: in the construction also of which compacts we have no other rule to resort to, but the law of nature; being the only one to which both communities are equally subject: and therefore the civil law[c] very justly observes, that *quod naturalis ratio inter omnes homines constituit, vocatur jus gentium.*

Thus much I thought it necessary to premise concerning the law of nature, the revealed law, and the law of nations, before

---

[b] Puffendorf, *l.*7. *c.*1. compared with Barbeyrac's commentary.   [c] *Ff.*1.1.9.

I proceeded to treat more fully of the principal subject of this section, municipal or civil law; that is, the rule by which particular districts, communities, or nations are governed; being thus defined by Justinian[d], "*jus civile est quod quisque sibi populus constituit.*" I call it *municipal* law, in compliance with common speech; for, tho' strictly that expression denotes the particular customs of one single *municipium* or free town, yet it may with sufficient propriety be applied to any one state or nation, which is governed by the same laws and customs.

Municipal law, thus understood, is properly defined to be "a "rule of civil conduct prescribed by the supreme power in a state, "commanding what is right and prohibiting what is wrong." Let us endeavor to explain it's several properties, as they arise out of this definition.

And, first, it is a *rule*; not a transient sudden order from a superior to or concerning a particular person; but something permanent, uniform, and universal. Therefore a particular act of the legislature to confiscate the goods of Titius, or to attaint him of high treason, does not enter into the idea of a municipal law: for the operation of this act is spent upon Titius only, and has no relation to the community in general; it is rather a sentence than a law. But an act to declare the crime of which Titius is accused shall be deemed high treason; this has permanency, uniformity, and universality, and therefore is properly a *rule*. It is also called a *rule*, to distinguish it from *advice* or *counsel*, which we are at liberty to follow or not, as we see proper; and to judge upon the reasonableness or unreasonableness of the thing advised. Whereas our obedience to the *law* depends not upon *our approbation*, but upon the *maker's will*. Counsel is only matter of persuasion, law is a matter of injunction; counsel acts only upon the willing, law upon the unwilling also.

[d] *Inst.* 1.2.1.

It is also called a *rule*, to distinguish it from a *compact* or *agreement*; for a compact is a promise proceeding *from* us, law is a command directed *to* us. The language of a compact is, "I will, "or will not, do this;" that of a law is, "thou shalt, or shalt not, do "it." It is true there is an obligation which a compact carries with it, equal in point of conscience to that of a law; but then the original of the obligation is different. In compacts, we ourselves determine and promise what shall be done, before we are obliged to do it; in laws, we are obliged to act, without ourselves determining or promising any thing at all. Upon these accounts law is defined to be "*a rule.*"

Municipal law is also "a rule *of civil conduct.*" This distinguishes municipal law from the natural, or revealed; the former of which is the rule of *moral* conduct, and the latter not only the rule of moral conduct, but also the rule of faith. These regard man as a creature, and point out his duty to God, to himself, and to his neighbour, considered in the light of an individual. But municipal or civil law regards him also as a citizen, and bound to other duties towards his neighbour, that those of mere nature and religion: duties, which he has engaged in by enjoying the benefits of the common union; and which amount to no more, than that he do contribute, on his part, to the subsistence and peace of the society.

It is likewise "a rule *prescribed.*" Because a bare resolution, confined in the breast of the legislator, without manifesting itself by some external sign, can never be properly a law. It is requisite that this resolution be notified to the people who are to obey it. But the manner in which this notification is to be made, is matter of very great indifference. It may be notified by universal tradition and long practice, which supposes a previous publication, and is the case of the common law of England. It may be notified, *viva voce*, by officers appointed for that purpose, as is done with regard to proclamations, and such acts of parliament as are appointed to be publicly read in churches and other assemblies. It may lastly be notified by writing, printing, or the like; which is the general course taken with all our acts of parliament. Yet, whatever way is made use of, it is incumbent on the promulgators to do it in the most public and perspicuous manner; not like Caligula, who (according to Dio Cassius) wrote his laws in a very small character, and hung them up upon high pillars, the more effectually to ensnare the people. **There is still a more unreasonable method than this, which is called making laws *ex post facto*; when *after* and action is committed, the legislator then for the first time declares it to have been a crime, and inflicts a punishment upon the person who has committed it; here it is impossible that the party could foresee that an action, innocent when it was done, should be afterwards converted to guilt by a subsequent law; he had therefore no cause to abstain from it; and all punishment for not abstaining must of consequence be cruel and unjust**[e]. All laws should be therefore made to commence *in futuro*, and be notified before their commencement; which is implied in the term "*prescribed.*" But is then the subject's business to be thoroughly acquainted therewith; for if ignorance, of what he *might* know, were admitted as a legitimate excuse, the laws would be of no effect, but might always be eluded with impunity.

But farther: municipal law is "a rule of civil conduct "prescribed *by the supreme power in a state."* For legislature, as was before observed, is the greatest act of superiority that can be exercised by one being over another. Wherefore it is requisite to the very essence of a law, that it be made by the supreme power. Sovereignty and legislature are indeed convertible terms; one cannot subsist without the other.

---

[e] Such laws among the Romans were denominated *privilegia*, or private laws, of which Cicero *de leg.* 3.19. and in his oration *pro domo*, 17. thus speaks; "*Vetant leges sacratae, vetant duodecim* "*tabulae, leges privatis hominibus irrogari; id enim est privilegium. Nemo unquam tulit, nihil est* "*crudelius, nihil perniciosius, nihil quod minus haec civitas ferre possit.*"

This will naturally lead us into a short enquiry concerning the nature of society and civil government; and the natural, inherent right that belongs to the sovereignty of a state, wherever that sovereignty be lodged, of making and enforcing laws.

The only true and natural foundations of society are the wants and the fears of individuals. Not that we can believe, with some theoretical writers, that there ever was a time when there was no such thing as society; and that, from the impulse of reason, and through a sense of their wants and weaknesses, individuals met together in a large plain, entered into an original contract, and chose the tallest man present to be their governor. This notion, of an actually existing unconnected state of nature, is too wild to be seriously admitted; and besides it is plainly contradictory to the revealed accounts of the primitive origin of mankind, and their preservation two thousand years afterwards; both which were effected by the means of single families. These formed the first society, among themselves; which every day extended it's limits, and when it grew too large to subsist with convenience in that pastoral state, wherein the patriarchs appear to have lived, it necessarily subdivided itself by various migrations into more. Afterwards, as agriculture increased, which employs and can maintain a much greater number of hands, migrations became less frequent; and various tribes, which had formerly separated, reunited again; sometimes by compulsion and conquest, sometimes by accident, and sometimes by compact. **But though society had not it's formal beginning from any convention of individuals, actuated by their wants and their fears; yet it is the *sense* of their weakness and imperfection that *keeps* mankind together; that demonstrates the necessity of this union; and that therefore is the solid and natural foundation, as well as the cement of society. And this is what we mean by the original contract of society; which, though perhaps in no instance it has ever been formally expressed at the first institution of a state, yet in nature and reason must always be understood and implied,**

in the very act of associating together: namely, that the whole should protect all it's parts, and that every part should pay obedience to the will of the whole; or, in other words, that the community should guard the rights of each individual member, and that (in return for this protection) each individual should submit to the laws of the community; without which submission of all it was impossible that protection could be certainly extended to any.

For when society is once formed, government results of course, as necessary to preserve and to keep that society in order. Unless some superior were constituted, whose commands and decisions all the members are bound to obey, they would still remain as in a state of nature, without any judge upon earth to define their several rights, and redress their several wrongs. But, as all the members of society are naturally equal, it may be asked, in whose hands are the reins of government to be entrusted? To this the general answer is easy; but the application of it to particular cases has occasioned one half of those mischiefs which are apt to proceed from misguided political zeal. In general, all mankind will agree that government should be reposed in such persons, in whom those qualities are most likely to be found, the perfection of which are among the attributes of him who is emphatically stiled the supreme being; the three grand requisites, I mean, of wisdom, of goodness, and of power: wisdom, to discern the real interest of the community; goodness, to endeavour always to pursue that real interest; and strength, or power, to carry this knowledge and intention into action. These are the natural foundations of sovereignty, and these are the requisites that ought to be found in every well constituted frame of government.

How the several forms of government we now see in the world at first actually began, is matter of great uncertainty, and has occasioned infinite disputes. It is not my business or intention to enter into any of them. However they began, or by what right soever they subsist, **there is and must be in all of them a supreme, irresistible, absolute, uncontrolled authority, in which the *jura summi imperii*, or the rights of sovereignty, reside.** And this authority is placed in those hands, wherein (according to the opinion of the founders of such respective states, either expressly given, or collected from their tacit approbation) the qualities requisite for supremacy, wisdom, goodness, and power, are the most likely to be found.

The political writers of antiquity will not allow more than three regular forms of government; the first, when the sovereign power is lodged in an aggregate assembly consisting of all the members of a community, which is called a democracy; the second, when it is lodged in a council, composed of select members, and then it is called an aristocracy; the last, when it is entrusted in the hands of a single person, and then it takes the name of a monarchy. All other species of government, they say, are either corruptions of, or reducible to, these three.

By the sovereign power, as was before observed, is meant the making of laws; for wherever that power resides, all others must conform to, and be directed by it, whatever appearance the outward form and administration of the government may put on. For it is at any time in the option of the legislature to alter that form and administration by a new edict or rule, and to put the execution of the laws into whatever hands it pleases: and all the other powers of the state must obey the legislative power in the execution of their several functions, or else the constitution is at an end.

In a democracy, where the right of making laws resides in the people at large, public virtue, or goodness of intention, is more likely to be found, than either of the other qualities of government. Popular assemblies are frequently foolish in their contrivance, and weak in their execution; but generally mean to do the thing that is right and just, and have always a degree of patriotism or public spirit. In aristocracies there is more wisdom to be found, than in other frames of government; being composed, or intended to be composed, of the most experienced citizens; but there is less honesty than in a republic, and less strength than in a monarchy. A monarchy is indeed the most powerful of any, all the sinews of government being knit together, and united in the hand of the prince; but then there is imminent danger of his employing that strength to improvident or oppressive purposes.

Thus these three species of government have, all of them, their several perfections and imperfections. Democracies are usually the best calculated to direct the end of a law; aristocracies to invent the means by which that end shall be obtained; and monarchies to carry those means into execution. And the antients, as was observed, had in general no idea of any other permanent form of government but these three; for though Cicero[f] declares himself of opinion, "*esse* "*optime constitutam republicam, quae ex tribus generibus illis,* "*regali tribus generibus illis, regali, optimo, et populari, sit modice* "*confusa*;" yet Tacitus treats this notion of a mixed government, formed out of them all, and partaking of the advantages of each, as a visionary whim; and one that, if effected, could never be lasting or secure[g].

But happily for us of this island, the British constitution has long remained, and I trust will long continue, a standing exception to the truth of this observation. For, as with us the executive power of the laws is lodged in a single person, they have all the advantages of strength and dispatch, that are to be found in the most absolute monarchy; **and, as the legislature of the kingdom is entrusted to three distinct powers, entirely independent of each other; first, the king; secondly, the lords spiritual and temporal, which is an aristocratical assembly of persons**

---

[f] In his fragments *de rep. l.2.*

[g] "*Cunctas nationes et urbes populus, aut primores, aut singuli regunt: delecta ex his, et constituta* "*reipublicae forma laudari facilius quam evenire, vel, si evenit, haud diuturna esse potest.*" *Ann. l.4.*

selected for their piety, their birth, their wisdom, their valour, or their property; and, thirdly, the house of commons, freely chosen by the people from among themselves, which makes it a kind of democracy; as this aggregate body, actuated by different springs, and attentive to different interests, composes the British parliament, and has the supreme disposal of every thing; there can no inconvenience be attempted by either of the three branches, but will be withstood by one of the other two; each branch being armed with a negative power, sufficient to repel any innovation which it shall think inexpedient or dangerous.

Here then is lodged the sovereignty of the British constitution; and lodged as beneficially as is possible for society. For in no other shape could we be so certain of finding the three great qualities of government so well and so happily united. If the supreme power were lodged in any one of the three branches separately, we must be exposed to the inconveniences of either absolute monarchy, aristocracy, or democracy; and so want two of the three principal ingredients of good polity, either virtue, wisdom, or power. If it were lodged in any two of the branches; for instance, in the king and the house of lords, our laws might be providently made, and well executed, but they might not always have the common good of the people in view: if lodged in the king and commons, we should want that circumspection and mediatory caution, which the wisdom of the peers is to afford: if the supreme rights of the legislature were lodged in the two houses only, and the king had no negative upon their proceedings, they might be tempted to encroach upon the royal prerogative, or perhaps to abolish the kingly office, and thereby weaken (if not totally destroy) the strength of the executive power. But the constitutional government of this island is so admirably tempered and compounded, that nothing can endanger or hurt it, but destroying the equilibrium of power between one branch of the legislature and the rest. For if ever it should happen that the independence of any one of the three should be lost, or that it should become subservient to the views of either of the other two, there would soon be an end of our constitution. The legislature would be changed from that, which was originally set up by the general consent and fundamental act of the society; and such a change, however effected, is according to Mr. Locke[h] (who perhaps carries his theory too far) at once an entire dissolution of the bands of government; and the people would be reduced to a state of anarchy, with liberty to constitute to themselves a new legislative power.

Having thus curiously considered the three usual species of government, and our own singular constitution, selected and compounded from them all, I proceed to observe, that, as the power of making laws constitutes the supreme authority, so wherever the supreme authority in any state resides, it is the ri
ght of that authority to make laws; that is, in the words of our definition, *to prescribe the rule of civil action*. And this may be discovered from the very end and institution of civil states. For a state is a collective body, composed of a multitude of individuals, united for their safety and convenience, and intending to act together as one man. If it therefore is to act as one man, it ought to act by one uniform will. But, inasmuch as political communities are made up of many natural persons, each of whom has his particular will and inclination, these several wills cannot by any *natural* union be joined together, or tempered and disposed into a lasting harmony, so as to constitute and produce that one uniform will of the whole. It can therefore be no otherwise produced than by a *political* union; by the consent of all persons to submit their own private wills to the will of one man, or of one or more assemblies of men, to whom the supreme authority is entrusted: and this will of that one man, or assemblage of men, is in different states, according to their different constitutions, understood to be *law*.

Thus far as to the *right* of the supreme power to make laws; but farther, it is it's *duty* likewise. For since the respec-

---

[h] On government, part 2. Sec. 212.

tive members are bound to conform themselves to the will of the state, it is expedient that they receive directions form the state declaratory of that it's will. But since it is impossible, in so great a multitude, to give injunctions to every particular man, relative to each particular action, therefore the state establishes general rules, for the perpetual information and direction of all persons in all points, whether of positive or negative duty. And this, in order that every man may know what to look upon as his own, what as another's; what absolute and what relative duties are required at his hands; what is to be esteemed honest, dishonest, or indifferent; what degree every man retains of his natural liberty; what he has given up as the price of the benefits of society; and after what manner each person is to moderate the use and exercise of those rights which the state assigns him, in order to promote and secure the public tranquillity.

From what has been advanced, the truth of the former branch of our definition, is (I trust) sufficiently evident; that "*municipal law* "*is a rule of civil conduct prescribed by the supreme power in a* "*state.*" I proceed now to the latter branch of it; that it is a rule so prescribed, "*commanding what is right, and prohibiting what is* "*wrong.*"

Now in order to do this completely, it is first of all necessary that the boundaries of right and wrong be established and ascertained by law. And when this is once done, it will follow of course that it is likewise the business of the law, considered as a rule of civil conduct, to enforce these rights and to restrain or redress these wrongs. It remains therefore only to consider in what manner the law is said to ascertain the boundaries or right and wrong; and the methods which it takes to command the one and prohibit the other.

For this purpose every law may be said to consist of several parts: one, *declaratory*; whereby the rights to be observed, and the wrongs to be eschewed, are clearly defined and laid down:

BL1, 53

another, *directory*; whereby the subject is instructed and enjoined to observe those rights, and to abstain from the commission of those wrongs: a third, *remedial*; whereby a method is pointed out to recover a man's private rights, or redress his private wrongs: to which may be added a fourth, usually termed the *sanction*, or *vindicatory* branch of the law; whereby it is signified what evil or penalty shall be incurred by such as commit any public wrongs, and transgress or neglect their duty.

With regard to the first of these, the *declaratory* part of the municipal law, this depends not so much upon the law or revelation or of nature, as upon the wisdom and will of the legislator. This doctrine, which before was slightly touched, deserves a more particular explanation. **Those rights then which God and nature have established, and are therefore called natural rights, such as are life and liberty, need not the aid of human laws to be more effectually invested in every man than they are; neither do they receive any additional strength when declared by the municipal laws to be inviolable. On the contrary, no human legislature has the power to abridge or destroy them, unless the owner shall himself commit some act that amounts to forfeiture. Neither do divine or natural *duties* (such as, for instance, the worship of God, the maintenance of children, and the like) receive any stronger sanction from being also declared to be duties by the law of the land. The case is the same as to crimes and misdemesnors, that are forbidden by the superior laws, and therefore stiled *mala in se*, such as murder, theft, and perjury; which contract no additional turpitude from being declared unlawful by the inferior legislature. For that legislature in all these cases acts only, as was before observed, in subordination to the great lawgiver, transcribing and publishing his precepts. So that, upon the whole, the declaratory part of the municipal law has no force or operation at all, with regard to actions that are naturally and intrinsically right or wrong.**

But with regard to things in themselves indifferent, the case is entirely altered. These become either right or wrong, just or unjust, duties or misdemesnors, according as the municipal legislator sees proper, for promoting the welfare of the society, and more effectually carrying on the purposes of civil life. Thus our own common law has declared, that the goods of the wife do instantly upon marriage become property and right of the husband; and our statute law has declared all monopolies a public offense: yet that right, and this offense have no foundation in nature; but are merely created by the law, for the purposes of civil society. And sometimes, where the thing itself has it's rise from the law of nature, the particular circumstances and mode of doing it become right or wrong, as the laws of the land shall direct. Thus, for instance, in civil duties; obedience to superiors is the doctrine of revealed as well as natural religion: but who those superiors shall be, and in what circumstances, or to what degrees they shall be obeyed, is the province of human laws to determine. And so, as to injuries or crimes, it must be left to our own legislature to decide, in what cases the seizing another's cattle shall amount to the crime of robbery; and where it shall be a justifiable action, as when a landlord takes them by way of distress for rent.

Thus much for the *declaratory* part of the municipal law: and the *directory* stands much upon the same footing; for this virtually includes the former, the declaration being usually collected from the direction. The law that says, "thou shalt not steal," implies a declaration that stealing is a crime. And we have seen that, in things naturally indifferent, the very essence of right and wrong depends upon the direction of the laws to do or to omit it.

The *remedial* part of a law is so necessary a consequence of the former two, that laws must be very vague and imperfect without it. For in vain would rights be declared, in vain directed

to be observed, if there were no method of recovering and asserting those rights, when wrongfully withheld or invaded. **This is what we mean properly, when we speak of the protection of the law.** When, for instance, the *declaratory* part of the law has said "that the field or inheritance, which belonged to Titius's "father, is vested by his death in Titius;" and the *directory* part has "forbidden any one to enter on another's property without "the leave "of the owner;" if Gaius after this will presume to take possession of the land, the *remedial* part of the law will then interpose its office; will make Gaius restore the possession to Titius, and also pay him damages for the invasion.

With regard to the *sanction* of laws, or the evil that may attend the breach of public duties; it is observed, that human legislators have for the most part chosen to make the sanction of their laws rather *vindicatory* than *remuneratory*, or to consist rather in punishments, than in actual particular rewards. Because, in the first place, the quiet enjoyment and protection of all our civil rights and liberties, which are the sure and general consequence of our obedience to municipal law, are in themselves the best and most valuable of all rewards. Because also, were the exercise of every virtue to be enforced by the proposal of particular rewards, it were impossible for any state to furnish stock enough for so profuse a bounty. And farther, because the dread of evil is a much more forcible principle of human actions than the prospect of good[i]. For which reasons, though a prudent bestowing of rewards is sometimes of exquisite use, yet we find that those civil laws, which enforce and enjoin our duty, do seldom, if ever, propose any privilege or gift to such as obey the law; but do constantly come armed with a penalty denounced against transgressors, either expressly defining the nature and quantity of the punishment, or else leaving it to the discretion of the judges, and those who are entrusted with the care of putting the laws into execution.

---

[i] Locke, Hum. Und. b.2 c.21.

BL1, 56

Of all the parts of the law most effectual is the *vindicatory*. For it is but lost labour to say, "do this, or avoid that," unless we also declare, "this shall be the consequence of your non-compliance." We must therefore observe, that the main strength and force of a law consists in the penalty annexed to it. Herein is to be found the principal obligation of human laws.

Legislators and their laws are said to *compel* and *oblige*; not that by any natural violence they so constrain a man, as to render it impossible for him to act otherwise than as they direct, which is the strict sense of obligation: but because, by declaring and exhibiting a penalty against offenders, they bring it to pass that no man can easily choose to transgress the law; since, by reason of impending correction, compliance is in a high degree preferable to disobedience. And, even where rewards are proposed as well as punishments threatened, the obligation of the law seems chiefly to consist in the penalty: for rewards, in their nature, can only *persuade* and *allure*; nothing is *compulsory* but punishment.

It is held, it is true, and very justly, by the principal of our ethical writers, that human laws are binding upon mens consciences. But if that were the only, or most forcible obligation, the good only would regard the laws, and the bad would set them at defiance. And, true as this principle is, it must still be understood with some restriction. It holds, I apprehend, as to *rights*; and that, when the law has determined the field to belong to Titius, it is matter of conscience no longer to withhold or invade it. So also in regard to *natural duties*, and such offences as are *mala in se*: here we are bound in conscience, because we are bound by superior laws, before those human laws were in being, to perform the one and abstain from the other. But in relation to those laws which enjoin only *positive duties*, and forbid only such things as are not *mala in se* but *mala prohibita* merely, annexing a penalty to non-compliance, here I apprehend conscience is no farther concerned, than by directing a submission to the penalty, in case of our breach of those laws: for otherwise the multitude of penal laws in a state would not only be looked upon as an impolitic, but would also be a very wicked thing; if every such law were a snare for the conscience of the subject. But in these cases the alternative is offered to every man; "either abstain from this, or "submit to such a penalty;" and his conscience will be clear, which ever side of the alternative he thinks proper to embrace. Thus, by the statutes for preserving the game, a penalty is denounced against every unqualified person that kills a hare. Now this prohibitory law does not make the transgression a moral offense: the only obligation in conscience is to submit to the penalty if levied.

I have now gone through the definition laid down of a municipal law; and have shewn that it is "a rule---of civil conduct---prescribed "---by the supreme power of the state---commanding what is right, and "prohibiting what is wrong:" in the explanation of which I have endeavoured to interweave a few useful principles, concerning the nature of civil government, and the obligation of human laws. Before I conclude this section, it may not be amiss to add a few observations concerning the *interpretation* of laws.

When any doubt arose upon the construction of the Roman laws, the usage was to state the case to the emperor in writing, and take his opinion upon it. This was certainly a bad method of interpretation. To interrogate the legislature to decide particular disputes, is not only endless, but affords great room for partiality and oppression. The answers of the emperor were called his rescripts, and these had in succeeding cases the force of perpetual laws; though they ought to be carefully distinguished, by every rational civilian, from those general constitutions, which had only the nature of things for their guide. The emperor Macrinus, as his historian Capitolinus informs us, had once resolved to abolish these rescripts, and retain only the general edicts; he could not bear that the hasty and crude answers of such princes as Commodus and Caracalla should be reverenced as laws. But Justinian thought otherwise[k], and he has preserved them all. In like manner the canon laws, or decretal epistles of the popes, are all of them rescripts in the strictest sense. Contrary to all true forms of reasoning, they argue from particulars to generals.

The fairest and most rational method to interpret the will of the legislator, is by exploring his intentions at the time when the law was made, by *signs* **the most natural and probable. And these signs are either the words, the context, the subject matter, the effects and consequence, or the spirit and reason of the law.** Let us take a short view of them all.

1. Words are generally to be understood in their usual and most known signification; not so much regarding the propriety of grammar, as their general and popular use. Thus the law mentioned by Puffendorf[l], which forbad a layman to *lay hands* on a priest, was adjudged to extend to him, who had hurt a priest with a weapon. Again; terms of art, or technical terms, must be taken according to the acceptation of the learned in each art, trade or science. So in the act of settlement, where the crown of England is limited "to the "princess Sophia, and the heirs of her body, being protestants," it becomes necessary to call the assistance of lawyers, to ascertain the precise idea of the words "*heirs of her body;*" which in a legal sense comprize only certain of her lineal descendants. Lastly, where words are clearly *repugnant* in two laws, the later law takes the place of the elder: *leges posteriores priores contrarias abrogant* is a maxim of universal law, as well as of our own constitutions. And accordingly it was laid down by a law of the twelve tables of Rome, *quod populus postremum jussit, id jus ratum esto.*

[k] *Inst.* 1.2.6.   [l] L. of N. and N. 5.12.3.

2. If words happen to be still dubious, we may establish meaning from the context; with which it may be of singular use to compare a word, or a sentence, whenever they are ambiguous, equivocal, or intricate. Thus the proeme, or preamble, is often called in to help the construction of an act of parliament. Of the same nature and use is the comparison of a law with other laws, that are made by the same legislator, that have som affinity with the subject, or that expressly relate to the same point. Thus, when the law of England declares murder to be felony without benefit of clergy, we must resort to the same law of England to learn what the benefit of clergy is: and, when the common law censures simoniacal contracts, it affords great light to the subject to consider what the canon law has adjudged to be simony.

3. As to subject matter, words are always to be understood as having regard thereto; for that is always supposed to be in the eye of the legislator, and all his expressions directed to that end. Thus, when a law of our Edward III. forbids all ecclesiastical persons to purchase *provisions* at Rome, it might seem to prohibit the buying of grain and other victual; but when we consider that the statute was made to repress the usurpations of the papal see, and that nominations to vacant benefices by the pope were called *provisions*, we shall see that the restraint is intended to be laid upon such provisions only.

4. As to the effects and consequence, the rule is, where words bear either or none, or a very absurd signification, if literally understood, we must a little deviate from the received sense of them. Therefore the Bolognian law, mentioned by Puffendorf[m], which enacted "that whoever drew blood in the streets should be "punished with the utmost severity," was held after long debate not to extend to the surgeon, who opened the vein of a person that fell down in the street with a fit.

[m] *l*.5 *c*.12 sec.8.

5. But, lastly, the most universal and effectual way of discovering the true meaning of a law, when the words are dubious, is by considering the reason and spirit of it; or the cause which moved the legislator to enact it. For when this reason ceases, the law itself ought likewise to cease with it. An instance of this is given in a case put by Cicero, or whoever was the author of the rhetorical treatise inscribed to Herennius[n]. There was a law, that those who in a storm forsook the ship should forfeit all property therein; and the ship and lading should belong entirely to those who staid in it. In a dangerous tempest all the mariners forsook the ship, except only one sick passenger, who by reason of his disease was unable to get out and escape. By chance the ship came safe to port. The sick man kept possession and claimed the benefit of the law. Now here all the learned agree, that the sick man is not within the reason of the law; for the reason of making it was, to give encouragement to such as should venture their lives to save the vessel: but this is a merit, which he could never pretend to, who neither staid in the ship upon that account, nor contributed any thing to its preservation.

From this method of interpreting laws, by the reason of them, arises what we call *equity*; which is thus defined by Grotius[o], "the correction of that, wherein the law (by reason of its "universality) is deficient." For since in laws all cases cannot be foreseen or expressed, it is necessary that when general decrees of the law come to be applied to particular cases, there should somewhere be a power vested of excepting those circumstances, which (had they been foreseen) the legislator himself would have excepted. And these are the cases, which, as Grotius expresses it, "*lex non exacte definit, sed arbitrio boni viri permittit.*"

Equity thus depending, essentially, upon the particular circumstances of each individual case, there can be no established

---

[n] *l.*1 *c.*11.   [o] *de aequitae.*

rules and fixed precepts of equity laid down, without destroying it's very essence, and reducing it to a positive law. **And, on the other hand, the liberty of considering all cases in an equitable light must not be indulged too far, lest thereby we destroy all law, and leave the decision of every question entirely in the breast of the judge. And law, without equity, tho' hard and disagreeable, is much more desirable for the public good, than equity without law; which would make every judge a legislator, and introduce most infinite confusion; as there would then be almost as many different rules of action laid down in our courts, as there are differences of capacity and sentiment in the human mind.**

BL2

Blackstone on
the Countries Subject to the Laws of England

Book 1, Introduction, Section 4,
"Of the Countries Subject to the Laws of England"

This is a reprint of only a portion of Section 4, on pages 104-105.

Besides these adjacent islands, our more distant plantations in America, and elsewhere, are also in some respects subject to the English laws. Plantations, or colonies in distant countries, are either such where the lands are claimed by right of occupancy only, by finding them desart and uncultivated, and peopling them from the mother country; or where, when already cultivated, they have been either gained by conquest, or ceded to us by treaties. And both these rights are founded upon the law of nature, or at least upon that of nations. **But there is a difference between these two species of colonies, with respect to the laws by which they are bound. For it is held[b], that if an uninhabited country be discovered and planted by English subjects, all the English**

       [b] Salk. 4.1.1.666.

laws are immediately there in force. For as the law is the birthright of every subject, so wherever they go they carry their laws with them[c]. But in conquered or ceded countries, that have already laws of their own, the king may indeed alter and change those laws; but till he does actually change them, the antient laws of the country remain, unless such as are against the law of God, as in the case of an infidel country[d].

Our American plantations are principally of this latter sort, being obtained in the last century either by right of conquest and driving out natives (with what natural justice I shall not at present enquire) or by treaties. And therefore the common law of England, as such, has no allowance or authority there; they being no part of the mother country, but distinct (though dependent) dominions. They are subject however to the control of the parliament; though (like Ireland, Man, and the rest) not bound by any acts of parliament, unless particularly named. The form of government in most of them is borrowed from that of England. They have a governor named by the king, (or in some proprietary colonies by the proprietor) who is his representative or deputy. They have courts of justice of their own, from whose decisions an appeal lies to the king in council here in England. Their general assemblies which are their house of commons, together with their council of state being their upper house, with the concurrence of the king or his representative the governor, make laws suited to their own emergencies. But it is particularly declared by statute 7 & 8 W.III. c.22. That all laws, by-laws, usages, and customs, which shall be in practice in any of the plantations, repugnant to any law, made or to be made in this kingdom relative to the said plantations, shall be utterly void and of none effect.

[c] 2 P. W^{ms}. 75.   [d] 7 Rep. 17*b*. Calvin's case. Show. Parl. C.31.

BL3

Blackstone on the Absolute Rights of Individuals

Book 1, Chapter 1,
"Of the Absolute Rights of Individuals"

The objects of the laws of England are so very numerous and extensive, that, in order to consider them with any tolerable ease and perspicuity, it will be necessary to distribute them methodically, under proper and distinct heads; avoiding as much as possible divisions too large and comprehensive on the one hand, and too trifling and minute on the other; both of which are equally productive of confusion.

Now, as municipal law is a rule of civil conduct, commanding what is right, and prohibiting what is wrong; or, as Cicero[a], and after him our Bracton[b], has expressed it, *sanctio justa, jubens honesta et prohibens contraria*; it follows, that the primary and principal objects of the law are RIGHTS, and WRONGS. In the prosecution therefore of these commentaries, I shall follow this very simple and obvious division; and shall in the first place consider the *rights* that are commanded, and secondly the *wrongs* that are forbidden by the laws of England.

Rights are however liable to another subdivision; being either, first, those which concern, and are annexed to the persons of men, and are then called *jura personarum* or the *rights of persons*; or they are, secondly, such as a man may acquire over external objects, or things unconnected with his person, which are stiled *jura rerum* or the *rights of things*. Wrongs also are divisible into, first, *private wrongs*, which, being an infringement merely of particular rights, concern individuals only, and are called civil injuries; and secondly, *public wrongs*, which, being a breach of general and public rights, affect the whole community, and are called crimes and misdemesnors.

The objects of the laws of England falling into this fourfold division, the present commentaries will therefore consist of the four following parts: 1. *The rights of persons*; with the means whereby such rights may be either acquired or lost. 2. *The rights of things*; with the means also of acquiring and losing them. 3. *Private wrongs*, or civil injuries; with the means of redressing them by law. 4. *Public wrongs*, or crimes and misdemesnors; with the means of prevention and punishment.

We are now, first, to consider *the rights of persons*; with the means of acquiring and losing them.

---

[a] 11 *Philipp.* 12.   [b] *l.*1. *c.*3.

Now the rights of persons that are commanded to be observed by the municipal law are of two sorts; first, such as are due *from* every citizen, which are usually called civil *duties*; and, secondly, such as belong *to* him, which is the more popular acceptation of *rights* or *jura*. Both may indeed be comprized in this latter division; for, as all social duties are of a relative nature, at the same time that they are due *from* one man, or set of men, they must also be due *to* another. But I apprehend it will be more clear and easy, to consider many of them as duties required from, rather than as rights belonging to, particular persons. Thus, for instance, allegiance is usually, and therefore most easily, considered as the duty of the people, and protection as the duty of the magistrate; and yet they are, reciprocally, the rights as well as duties of each other. Allegiance is the right of the magistrate, and protection the right of the people.

Persons also are divided by the law into either natural persons, or artificial. Natural persons are such as the God of nature formed us: artificial are such as created and devised by human laws for the purposes of society and government; which are called corporations or bodies politic.

The rights of persons considered in their natural capacities are also of two sorts, absolute and relative. Absolute, which are such as appertain and belong to particular men, merely as individuals or single persons: relative, which are incident to them as members of society, and standing in various relations to each other. The first, that is, absolute rights, will be the subject of the present chapter.

By the absolute *rights* of individuals we mean those which are so in their primary and strictest sense; such as would belong to their persons merely in a state of nature, and which every man is entitled to enjoy whether our of society or in it. But with regard to the absolute *duties*, which man is bound to perform con-

sidered as a mere individual, it is not to be expected that any human municipal laws should at all explain or enforce them. For the end and intent of such laws being only to regulate the behaviour of mankind, as they are members of society, and stand in various relations to each other, they have consequently no business or concern with any but social or relative duties. Let a man therefore be ever so abandoned in his principles, or vitious in his practice, provided he keeps his wickedness to himself, and does not offend against the rules of public decency, he is out of the reach of human laws. But if he makes his vices public, though they be such as seem principally to affect himself, (as drunkenness, or the like) they then become, by the bad example they set, of pernicious effects to society; and therefore it is then the business of human laws to correct them. Here the circumstance of publication is what alters the nature of the case. *Public* sobriety is a relative duty, and therefore enjoined by our laws: *private* sobriety is an absolute duty, which, whether it be performed or not, human tribunals can never know; and therefore they can never enforce it by any civil sanction. But, with respect to *rights*, the case is different. Human laws define and enforce as well those rights which belong to a man considered as an individual, as those which belong to him considered as related to others.

For the principal aim of society is to protect individuals in the enjoyment of those absolute rights, which were vested in them by the immutable laws of nature; but which could not be preserved in peace without that mutual assistance and intercourse, which is gained by the institution of friendly and social communities. Hence it follows, that the first and primary end of human laws is to maintain and regulate these *absolute* rights of individuals. Such rights are social and *relative* result from, and are posterior to, the formation of states and societies: so that to maintain and regulate these, is clearly a subsequent consideration. And therefore the principal view of human laws is, or ought always to be, to explain, protect, and enforce such rights as are

BL3, 120

absolute, which in themselves are few and simple; and, then, such rights as are relative, which arising from a variety of connexions, will be far more numerous and more complicated. These will take up a greater space in any code of laws, and hence may appear to be more attended to, though in reality they are not, than the rights of the former kind. Let us therefore proceed to examine how far all laws ought, and how far the laws of England actually do, take notice of these absolute rights, and provide for their lasting security.

The absolute rights of man, considered as a free agent, endowed with discernment to know good from evil, and with power of choosing those measures which appear to him to be most desirable, are usually summed up in one general appellation, and denominated the natural liberty of mankind. This natural liberty consists properly in a power of acting as one thinks fit, without any restraint or control, unless by the law of nature: being a right inherent in us by birth, and one of the gifts of God to man at his creation, when he endued him with the faculty of freewill. But every man, when he enters into society, gives up a part of his natural liberty, as the price of so valuable a purchase; and, in consideration of receiving the advantages of mutual commerce, obliges himself to conform to those laws, which the community has thought proper to establish. And this species of legal obedience and conformity is infinitely more desirable, than that wild and savage liberty which is sacrificed to obtain it. For no man, that considers a moment, would wish to retain the absolute and uncontrolled power of doing whatever he pleases; the consequence of which is, that every other man would also have the same power; and then there would be so security to individuals in any of the enjoyments of life. **Political therefore, or civil, liberty, which is that of a member of society, is no other than natural liberty so far restrained by human laws (and no farther) as is necessary and expedient for the general advantage of the publick**[c]. Hence we may collect that the law, which restrains a

---

[c] *Facultas ejus, quod cuique facere libet, nisi quid jure prohibetur. Inst.* 1.3.1.

man from doing mischief to his fellow citizens, though it diminishes the natural, increases the civil liberty of mankind: but every wanton and causeless restraint of the will of the subject, whether practiced by a monarch, a nobility, or a popular assembly, is a degree of tyranny.** Nay, that even laws themselves, whether made with or without our consent, if they regulate and constrain our conduct in matters of mere indifference, without any good end in view, are laws destructive of liberty: whereas if any public advantage can arise from observing such precepts, the control of our private inclinations, in one or two particular points, will conduce to preserve our general freedom in others of more importance; by supporting that state, of society, which alone can secure our independence. Thus the statute of king Edward IV[d], which forbad the fine gentlemen of those times (under the degree of a lord) to wear pikes upon their shoes or boots or more than two inches in length, was a law that favoured of oppression; because, however ridiculous the fashion then in use might appear, the restraining it by pecuniary penalties could serve no purpose of common utility. But the statute of king Charles II[e], which prescribes a thing seemingly as indifferent; viz. a dress for the dead, who are all ordered to be buried in woollen; is a law consistent with public liberty, for it encourages the staple trade, on which in great measure depends the universal good of the nation. So that laws, when prudently framed, are by no means subversive but rather introductive of liberty; for (as Mr. Locke has well observed[f]) where there is no law, there is no freedom. **But then, on the other hand, that constitution or frame of government, that system of laws, is alone calculated to maintain civil liberty, which leaves the subject entire master of his own conduct, except in those points wherein the public good requires some direction or restraint.**

The idea and practice of this political or civil liberty flourish in their highest vigour in these kingdoms, where it falls little

[d] 3 Edw.IV. c.5.   [e] 30 Car.II. st.1. c.3.   [f] on Gov. p. 2. Sec. 57.

BL3, 122

short of perfection, and can only be lost or destroyed by the folly or demerits of its owner: the legislature, and or course the laws of England, being peculiarly adapted to the preservation of this inestimable blessing even in the meanest subject. Very different from the modern constitutions of other states, on the continent of Europe, and from the genius of the imperial law; which in general are calculated to vest an arbitrary and despotic power of controlling the actions of the subject in the prince, or a few grandees. **And this spirit of liberty is so deeply implanted in our constitution, and rooted even in our very soil, that a slave or a negro, the moment he lands in England, falls under the protection of the laws, and with regard to all natural rights becomes *eo instanti* a freeman**[g].

The absolute rights of every Englishman (which, taken in a political and extensive sense, are usually called their liberties) as they are founded on nature and reason, so they are coeval with our form of government; though subject at times to fluctuate and change; their establishment (excellent as it is) being still human. At some times we have seen them depressed by overbearing and tyrannical princes; at others so luxuriant as even to tend to anarchy, a worse state than tyranny itself, as any government is better than none at all. But the vigour of our free constitution has always delivered the nation from these embarassments, and, as soon as the convulsions consequent on the struggle have been over, the ballance of our rights and liberties has settled to it's proper level; and their fundamental articles have been from time to time asserted in parliament, as often as they were thought to be in danger.

First, by the great charter of liberties, which was obtained, sword in hand, from king John; and afterwards, with some alterations, confirmed in parliament by Henry the third, his son. Which charter contained very few new grants; but, as sir Edward Coke[h] **observes, was for the most part declaratory of the**

---

[g] Salk. 666.   [h] 2 Inst. proem.

principal grounds of the fundamental laws of England. Afterwards by the statute called *confirmatio cartarum*[i], whereby the great charter is directed to be allowed as the common law; all judgments contrary to it are declared void; copies of it are ordered to be sent to all cathedral churches, and read twice a year to the people; and sentence of excommunication is directed to be as constantly denounced against all those that by word, deed, or counsel act contrary thereto, or in any degree infringe it. Next by a multitude of subsequent corroborating statutes, (sir Edward Coke, I think, reckons thirty two[k],) from the first Edward to Henry the fourth. Then, after a long interval, by *the petition of right*; which was a parliamentary declaration of the liberties of the people, assented to by king Charles the first in the beginning of his reign. Which was closely followed by the still more ample concessions made by that unhappy prince to his parliament, before the fatal rupture between them; and by the many salutary laws, particularly the *habeas corpus* act, passed under Charles the second. To these succeeded *the bill of rights*, or declaration delivered by the lords and commons to the prince and princess of Orange 13 February 1688; and afterwards enacted in parliament, when they became king and queen: which declaration concludes in these remarkable words; "and they "do claim, demand, and insist upon all and singular the premises, "as their undoubted rights and liberties." And the act of parliament itself[l] recognizes "all and singular the rights and "liberties asserted and claimed in the said declaration to be the "true, antient, and indubitable rights of the people of this "kingdom." Lastly, these liberties were again asserted at the commencement of the present century, in the *act of settlement*[m], whereby the crown is limited to his present majesty's illustrious house, and some new provisions were added at the same fortunate aera for better securing our religion, laws, and liberties; which the statute declares to be "the birthright of the people of England;" according to the antient doctrine of the common law[n].

[i] 25 Edw.I.
[k] 2 Inst. proem.
[l] 1 W. and M. st.2. c.2.
[m] 12 & 13 W.III. c.2.
[n] Plowd. 55.

Thus much for the *declaration* of our rights and liberties. The rights themselves thus defined by these several statutes, consist in a number of private immunities; which will appear, from what has been premised, to be indeed no other, than either that *residuum* of natural liberty, which is not required by the laws of society to be sacrificed to public convenience; or else those civil privileges, which society hath engaged to provide, in lieu of the natural liberties given up by individuals. These therefore were formerly, either by inheritance or purchase, the rights of all mankind; but, in most other countries of the world being now more or less debased and destroyed, they at present may be said to remain, in a peculiar and emphatical manner, the rights of the people of England. **And these may be reduced to three principal or primary articles; the right of personal security, the right of personal liberty; and the right of private property:** because as there is no other known method of compulsion, or of abridging man's natural free will, but by an infringement or diminution of one or the other of these important rights, the preservation of these, inviolate, may justly be said to include the preservation of our civil immunities in their largest and most extensive sense.

I. The right of personal security consists in a person's legal and uninterrupted enjoyment of his life, his limbs, his body, his health, and his reputation.

1. Life is the immediate gift of God, a right inherent by nature in every individual; and it begins in contemplation of law as soon as an infant is able to stir in the mother's womb. For if a woman is quick with child, and by a potion, or otherwise, killeth it in her womb; or if any one beat her, whereby the child dieth in her body, and she is delivered of a dead child; this, though not murder, was by the antient law homicide or manslaughter[o]. But at present it is not looked upon in quite so

---

[o] *Si aliquis mulierem praegnantem percusserit, vel ei venenum dederit, per quod fecerit abortivam; si puerperium jam formatum fuerit, et maxime si fuerit animatum, facit homicidium.* Bracton. *l.*3. *c.*21.

atrocious a light, though it remains a very heinous misdemesnor[p].

An infant *in ventre sa mere*, or in the mother's womb, is supposed in law to be born for many purposes. It is capable of having a legacy, or a surrender of a copyhold estate made to it. It may have a guardian assigned to it[q]; and it is enabled to have an estate limited to it's use, and to take afterwards by such limitation, as if it were then actually born[r]. And in this point the civil law agrees with ours[s].

2. A man's limbs, (by which for the present we only understand those members which may be useful to him in fight, and the loss of which only amounts to mayhem by the common law) are also the gift of the wise creator; to enable man to protect himself from external injuries in a state of nature. To these therefore he has a natural inherent right; and they cannot be wantonly destroyed or disabled without a manifest breach of civil liberty.

Both the life and limbs of a man are of such high value, in the estimation of the law of England, that it pardons even homicide if committed *se defendendo*, or in order to preserve them. For whatever is done by a man, to save either life or member, is looked upon as done upon the highest necessity and compulsion. Therefore if a man through fear of death or mayhem is prevailed upon to execute a deed, or do any other legal act; these, though accompanied with all other the requisite solemnities, are totally void in law, if forced upon him by a well-grounded apprehension of losing his life, or even his limbs, in case of his non-compliance[t]. And the same is also a sufficient excuse for the commission of many misdemeanors, as will appear in the fourth book.

---

[p] 3 Inst. 90.

[q] Stat. 12 Car.II. c.24.

[r] Stat. 10 & 11 W.III. c.16.

[s] *Qui in utero sunt, in jure civili intelliguntur in rerum natura esse, cum de eorum commode agatur. Ff.*1.5.26.

[t] 2 Inst. 483.

The constraint a man is under in these circumstances is called in law *duress*, from the Latin *durities*, of which there are two sorts; duress of imprisonment, where a man actually loses his liberty, of which we shall presently speak; and duress *per minas*, where the hardship is only threatened and impending, which is that we are now discoursing of. Duress *per minas* is either for fear of loss of life, or else for fear of mayhem, or loss of limb. And this fear must be upon sufficient reason; "*non,*" as Bracton expresses it, "*suspicio* "*cujuslibet vani et meticulosi hominis, sed talis qui possit cadere in* "*virum constantem; talis enim debet esse metus, qui in se contineat* "*vitae periculum, aut corporis cruciatum*ᵘ." A fear of battery, or being beaten, though never so well grounded, is no duress; neither is the fear of having one's house burnt, or one's goods taken away or destroyed; because in these cases, should the threat be performed, a man may have satisfaction by recovering equivalent damagesʷ: but no suitable atonement can be made for the loss of life, or limb. And the indulgence shewn to a man under this, the principal, sort of duress, the fear of losing his life or limbs, agrees also with that maxim of the civil law; *ignoscitur ei qui sanguinem suum qualiter qualiter redemptum voluit*ˣ.

The law not only regards life and member, and protects every man in the enjoyment of them, but also furnishes him with every thing necessary for their support. For there is no man so indigent or wretched, but he may demand a supply sufficient for all the necessities of life, from the more opulent part of the community, by means of several statutes enacted for the relief of the poor, of which in their proper places. A humane provision; yet, though dictated by the principles of society, discountenanced by the Roman laws. For the edicts of the emperor Constantine, commanding the public to maintain the children of those who were unable to provide for them, in order to prevent the murder and exposure of infants, an institution founded on the same principle as our

---

ᵘ *l.*2. *c.*5.   ʷ 2 Inst. 483.   ˣ *Ff.*48.21.1.

foundling hospitals, though comprized in the Theodosian code[y], were rejected in Justinian's collection.

These rights, of life and member, can only be determined by the death of the person; which is either a civil or natural death. The civil death commences if any man be banished the realm[z] by the process of the common law, or enters into religion; that is, goes into a monastery, and becomes a monk professed: in which cases he is absolutely dead in law, and his next heir shall have his estate. For, such banished man is entirely cut off from society; and such a monk, upon his profession, renounces solemnly all secular concerns: and besides, as the popish clergy claimed an exemption from the duties of civil life, and the commands of the temporal magistrate, the genius of the English law would not suffer those persons to enjoy the benefits of society, who secluded themselves from it, and refused to submit to it's regulations[a]. A monk is therefore accounted *civiliter mortuus*, and when he enters into religion may, like other dying men, make his testament and executors; or, if he makes none, the ordinary may grant administration to his next of kin, as if he were actually dead intestate. And such executors and administrators shall have the same power, and may bring the same actions for debts due *to* the religious, and are liable to the same actions for those due *from* him, as if he were naturally deceased[b]. Nay, so far has this principle been carried, that when one was bound in a bond to an abbot and his successors, and afterwards made his executors and professed himself a monk of the same abbey, and in process of time was himself made abbot thereof; here the law gave him, in the capacity of abbot, an action of debt against his own executors to recover the money due[c]. In short, a monk or religious is so effectually dead in law, that a lease made even to a third person, during the life (generally) of one who afterwards becomes a monk, determines by such his entry into religion: for

[y] *l*.11. *t*.27. [a] This was also a rule in the feodal law, *l*.2. *t*.21. *desiit esse miles seculi,*
[z] Co. Litt. 133. *qui factus est miles Christi; nec beneficium pertinet ad eum qui non debet genere officium.* [b] Litt. Sec. 200. [c] Co. Litt. 133 *b*.

which reason leases, and other conveyances, for life, are usually made to have and to hold for the term of one's *natural* life[d].

This natural life being, as was before observed, the immediate donation of the great creator, cannot legally be disposed of or destroyed by any individual, neither by the person himself nor by any other of his fellow creatures, merely upon their own authority. Yet nevertheless it may, by the divine permission, be frequently forfeited for the breach of those laws of society, which are enforced by the sanction of capital punishments; of the nature, restrictions, expedience, and legality of which, we may hereafter more conveniently enquire in the concluding book of these commentaries. At present, I shall only observe, that whenever the *constitution* of a state vests in any man, or body of men, a power of destroying at pleasure, without the direction of laws, the lives or members of the subject, such constitution is in the highest degree tyrannical: and that whenever any *laws* direct such destruction for light and trivial causes, such laws are likewise tyrannical, though to an inferior degree; because here the subject is aware of the danger he is exposed to, and may by prudent caution provide against it. The statute law of England does therefore very seldom, and the common law does never, inflict any punishment extending to life or limb, unless upon the highest necessity: and the constitution is an utter stranger to any arbitrary power of killing or maiming the subject without the express warrant of law. "*Nullus liber homo*, says the "great charter[e], *aliquo modo destruatur, nisi per legale judicium* "*parium suorum aut per legem terrae.*" Which words, "*aliquo* "*modo destruatur,*" according to sir Edward Coke[f], include a prohibition not only of *killing*, and *maiming*, but also of *torturing* (to which our laws are strangers) and of every oppression by colour of an illegal authority. And it is enacted by the statute 5 Edw.III. c.9. that no man shall be forejudged of life or limb, contrary to the great charter and the law of the land: and again, by statute 28 Ed.III.

[d] 2 Rep. 48. Co. Litt. 132. [e] c.29. [f] 2 Inst. 48.

c.3. **that no man shall be put to death, without being brought to answer by due process of law.**

3. Besides those limbs and members that may be necessary to man, in order to defend himself or annoy his enemy, the rest of his person or body is also entitled by the same natural right to security from the corporal insults of menaces, assaults, beating, and wounding; though such insults amount not to destruction of life or member.

4. The preservation of a man's health from such practices as may prejudice or annoy it, and

5. The security of his reputation or good name from the arts of detraction and slander, are rights to which every man is intitled, by reason and natural justice; since without these it is impossible to have the perfect enjoyment of any other advantage or right. But these three last articles (being of much less importance than those which have gone before, and those which are yet to come) it will suffice to have barely mentioned among the rights of persons; referring the more minute discussion of their several branches, to those parts of our commentaries which treat of the infringement of these rights, under the head of personal wrongs.

II. Next to personal security, the law of England regards, asserts, and preserves the personal liberty of individuals. **This personal liberty consists in the power of loco-motion, of changing situation, or removing one's person to whatsoever place one's own inclination may direct; without imprisonment or restraint, unless by due course of law.** Concerning which we may make the same observations as upon the preceding article; that it is a right strictly natural; that the laws of England have never abridged it without sufficient cause; and, that in this kingdom it cannot ever be abridged at the mere discretion of the magistrate, without the express permission of the laws. **Here again the language of the great charter[g] is, that no freeman shall be taken or imprisoned,**

[g] c.29.

Blackstone on the Absolute Rights of Individuals

but by lawful judgment of his equals, or by the law of the land. And many subsequent old statutes[h] expressly direct, that no man shall be taken or imprisoned by suggestion or petition to the king, or his council, unless it be by legal indictment, or the process of the common law. By the petition of right, 3 Car.I, it is enacted, that no freeman shall be imprisoned or detained without cause shewn, to which he may make answer according to law. **By 16 Car.I. c.10. if any person be restrained of his liberty by order or decree or any illegal court, or by command of the king's majesty in person, or by warrant of the council board, or of any of the privy council; he shall, upon demand of his counsel, have a writ of** *habeas corpus*, **to bring his body before the court of king's bench or common pleas; who shall determine whether the cause of his commitment be just, and thereupon do as to justice shall appertain.** And by 31 Car.II. c.2. commonly called *the habeas corpus act*, the methods of obtaining this writ are so plainly pointed out and enforced, that, so long as this statute remains unimpeached, no subject of England can be long detained in prison, except in those cases in which the law requires and justifies such detainer. And, lest this act should be evaded by demanding unreasonable bail, or sureties for the prisoner's appearance, it is declared by 1 W. & M. st.2. c.2. that excessive bail ought not to be required.

Of great importance to the public is the preservation of this personal liberty: for if once it were left in the power of any, the highest, magistrate to imprison arbitrarily whomever he or his officers thought proper, (as in France it is daily practiced by the crown) there would soon be an end of all other rights and immunities. Some have thought, that unjust attacks, even upon life, or property, at the arbitrary will of the magistrate, are less dangerous to the commonwealth, than such as are made upon the personal liberty of the subject. **To bereave a man of life, or by violence confiscate his estate, without accusation or trial, would be so gross and notorious an act of despotism, as must at once**

---

[h] 5 Edw.III. c.9. 25 Edw.III. st.5. c.4. and 28 Edw.III. c.3.

convey the alarm of tyranny throughout the whole kingdom. But confinement of the person, by secretly hurrying him to gaol, where his sufferings are unknown or forgotten; is a less public, a less striking, and therefore a more dangerous engine of arbitrary government. And yet sometimes, when the state is in real danger, even this may be a necessary measure. But the happiness of our constitution is, that it is not left to the executive power to determine when the danger of the state is so great, as to render this measure expedient. For the parliament only, or legislative power, whenever it sees proper, can authorize the crown, by suspending the *habeas corpus* act for a short and limited time, to imprison suspected persons without giving any reason for so doing. As the senate of Rome was wont to have recourse to a dictator, a magistrate of absolute authority, when they judged the republic in any imminent danger. The decree of the senate, which usually preceded the nomination of this magistrate, "*dent operam consules, nequid* "*respublica detrimenti capiat,*" was called the *senatus consultum ultimae necessitatis.* In like manner this experiment ought only to be tried in cases of extreme emergency; and in these the nation parts with it's liberty for a while, in order to preserve it for ever.

The confinement of the person, in any wise, is an imprisonment. So that the keeping a man against his will in a private house, putting him in stocks, arresting or forcibly detaining him in the street, is an imprisonment[i]. And the law so much discourages unlawful confinement, that if a man is under *duress of imprisonment*, which we before explained to mean a compulsion by an illegal restraint of liberty, until he seals a bond or the like; he may alledge this duress, and void the extorted bond. But if a man be lawfully imprisoned, and either to procure his discharge, or on any other fair account, seals a bond or a deed, this is not by duress of imprisonment, and he is not at liberty to avoid it[k]. **To make imprisonment lawful, it must either be, by process from the courts of judicature, or by warrant from some**

[i] 2 Inst. 589. [k] 2 Inst. 482.

legal officer, having authority to commit to prison; which warrant must be in writing, under the hand and seal of the magistrate, and express the causes of the commitment, in order to be examined into (if necessary) upon a *habeas corpus.* If there be no cause expressed, the goaler is not bound to detain the prisoner[l]. For the law judges in this respect, saith sir Edward Coke, like Festus the Roman governor; that it is unreasonable to send a prisoner, and not to signify withal the crimes alleged against him.

A natural and regular consequence of this personal liberty, is, that every Englishman may claim a right to abide in his own country so long as he pleases; and not to be driven from it unless by the sentence of the law. The king indeed, by his royal prerogative, may issue out his writ *ne exeat regnum,* and prohibit any of his subjects from going into foreign parts without licence[m]. This may be necessary for the public service, and safeguard of the commonwealth. **But no power on earth, except the authority of parliament, can send any subject of England *out of* the land against his will; no not even a criminal. For exile, or transportation, is a punishment unknown to the common law;** and, wherever it is now inflicted, it is either by the choice of the criminal himself, to escape a capital punishment, or else by the express direction of some modern act of parliament. To this purpose the great charter[n] declares that no freeman shall be banished, unless by the judgment of his peers, or by the law of the land. And by the *habeas corpus* act, 31 Car.II. c.2 (that second *magna carta,* and stable bulwark of our liberties) it is enacted, that no subject of this realm, who is an inhabitant of England, Wales, or Berwick, shall be sent prisoner into Scotland, Ireland, Jersey, Guernsey, or places beyond the seas; (where they cannot have the benefit and protection of the common law) but that all such imprisonments shall be illegal; that the person, who shall dare to commit another contrary to this law, shall be disabled from bearing any office, shall incur the penalty of a praemunire, and be incapable of receiving the king's pardon:

---

[l] 2 Inst. 52, 53.   [m] F.N.B. 85.   [n] cap. 29.

and the party suffering shall also have his private action against the person committing, and all his aiders, advisers and abettors, and shall recover treble costs; besides his damages, which no jury shall assess at less than five hundred pounds.

The law is in this respect so benignly and liberally construed for the benefit of the subject, that, though *within* the realm the king may command attendance and service of all his liegemen, yet he cannot send any man *out of* the realm, even upon the public service: he cannot even constitute a man lord deputy or lieutenant of Ireland against his will, nor make him a foreign embassador[o]. For this might in reality be no more than an honorable exile.

III. The third absolute right, inherent in every Englishman, is that of property: which consists in the free use, enjoyment, and disposal of all his acquisitions, without any control or diminution, save only by the laws of the land. The original of private property is probably found in nature, as will be more fully explained in the second book of the ensuing commentaries: but certainly the modifications under which we at present find it, the method of conserving it in the present owner, and of translating it from man to man, are entirely derived from society; and are some of those civil advantages, in exchange for which every individual has resigned a part of his natural liberty. The laws of England are therefore, in point of honor and justice, extremely watchful in ascertaining and protecting this right. **Upon this principle the great charter[p] has declared that no freeman shall be disseised, or divested, of his freehold, or of his liberties, or free customs, but by the judgment of his peers, or by the law of the land. And by a variety of antient statutes[q] it is enacted, that no man's lands or goods shall be seised into the king's hands, against the great charter, and the law of the land; and that no man shall be disinherited, nor put out of his franchises or freehold,**

[o] 2 Inst. 47. [p] c.29. [q] 5 Edw.III. c.9. 25 Edw.III. st.5. c.4. 28 Edw.III. c.3.

unless he be duly brought to answer, and be forejudged by course of law; and if any thing be done to the contrary, it shall be redressed, and holden for none.

So great is the regard of the law of private property, that it will not authorize the least violation of it; no, not even for the general good of the whole community. If a new road, for instance, were to be made through the grounds of a private person, it might perhaps be extensively beneficial to the public; but the law permits no man, or set of men, to do this without the consent of the owner of the land. In vain may it be urged, that the good of the individual ought to yield to that of the community; for it would be dangerous to allow any private man, or even any public tribunal, to be the judge of this common good, and to decide whether it be expedient or no. Besides, the public good is in nothing more essentially interested, than in the protection of every individual's private rights, as modelled by the municipal law. In this, and similar cases the legislature alone can, and indeed frequently does, interpose, and compel the individual to acquiesce. But how does it interpose and compel? Not by absolutely stripping the subject of his property in an arbitrary manner; but by giving him a full indemnification and equivalent for the injury thereby sustained. The public is now considered as an individual, treating with an individual for an exchange. All that the legislature does is to oblige the owner to alienate his possessions for a reasonable price; and even this is an exertion of power, which the legislature indulges with caution, and which nothing but the legislature can perform.

Nor is this the only instance in which the law of the land has postponed even public necessity to the sacred and inviolable rights of private property. **For no subject of England can be constrained to pay aids or taxes, even for the defense of the realm or for the support of government, but such as are imposed by his own consent, or that of his representatives in parliament.** By the statute 25 Edw.I c.5 and 6. it is provided, that the king shall not take any aids or tasks, but by the common assent of the realm. And what that common assent is, is more fully explained by 34 Edw.I. st.4. cap.1. which enacts, that no talliage or aid shall be taken without assent of the arch-bishops, bishops, earls, barons, knights, burgesses, and other freemen of the land[r]: and again by 14 Edw.III. st.2 c.1. the prelates, earls, barons, and commons, citizens, burgesses, and merchants shall not be charged to make any aid, if it be not by the common assent of the great men and commons in parliament. And as this fundamental law had been shamefully evaded under many succeeding princes, by compulsory loans, and benevolences extorted without a real and voluntary consent, it was made an article in the petition of right 3 Car.I, that no man shall be compelled to yield any gift, loan, or benevolence, tax, or such like charge, without common consent by act of parliament. And, lastly, by the statute 1 W. & M. st.2. c.2. it is declared, that levying money for or to the use of the crown, by presence of prerogative, without grant of parliament; or for longer time, or in other manner, than the same is or shall be granted, is illegal.

In the three preceding articles we have taken a short view of the principal absolute rights which appertain to every Englishman. But in vain would these rights be declared, ascertained, and protected by the dead letter of the laws, if the constitution had provided no other method to secure their actual enjoyment. **It has therefore established certain other auxiliary subordinate rights of the subject, which serve principally as barriers to protect and maintain inviolate the three great primary rights, of personal security, personal liberty, and private property. These are,**
    1. The constitution, powers, and privileges of parliament, of which I shall treat at large in the ensuing chapter.

---

[r] See the historical introduction to the great charter, &c. *sub anno* 1297; wherein it is shewn that this statute *de talliago non concedendo*, supposed to have been made in 34 Edw.I, is in reality nothing more than a sort of translation into Latin of the *confirmatio cartarum*, 25 Edw.I., which was originally published in the Norman language.

2. The limitation of the king's prerogative, by bounds so certain and notorious, that it is impossible he should exceed them without the consent of the people. Of this also I shall treat in it's proper place. The former of these keeps the legislative power in due health and vigour, so as to make it improbable that laws should be enacted destructive of general liberty: the latter is a guard upon the executive power, by restraining it from acting either beyond or in contradiction to the laws, that are framed and established by the other.

3. A third subordinate right of every Englishman is that of applying to the courts of justice for redress of injustice. Since the law is in England the supreme arbiter of every man's life, liberty, and the law be duly administered therein. The emphatical words of *magna carta*[s], spoken in the person of the king, who in judgment of law (says sir Edward Coke[t]) is ever present and repeating them in all his courts, are these; "*nulli vendemus, nulli negabimus, aut* "*differemus rectum vel justitiam*: and therefore every subject," continues the same learned author, "for injury done to him *in* "*bonis, in terris, vel persona,* by any other subject, be he "ecclesiastical or temporal without any exception, may take his "remedy by the course of law, and have justice and right for the "injury done to him, freely without sale, fully without any denial, "and speedily without delay." It were endless to enumerate all the *affirmative* acts of parliament wherein justice is directed to be done according to the law of the land: and what that law is, every subject knows; or may know if he pleases: for it depends not upon the arbitrary will of any judge; but is permanent, fixed, and unchangeable, unless by authority of parliament. I shall however just mention a few *negative* statutes, whereby abuses, perversions, or delays of justice, especially by the prerogative, are restrained. It is ordained by

[s] c.29.   [t] 2 Inst. 55.

magna carta[u], that no freeman shall be outlawed, that is put out of the protection and benefit of the laws, but according to the law of the land. By 2 Edw.III. c.8. and 11 Ric.II. c.10. it is enacted, that no commands or letters shall be sent under the great seal, or the little seal, the signet, or privy seal, in disturbance of the law; or to disturb or delay common right: and, though such commandments should come, the judges shall not cease to do right. And by 1 W. & M. st.2 c.2. it is declared, that the pretended power of suspending, or dispensing with laws, or the execution of laws, by regal authority without consent of parliament, is illegal.

Not only the substantial part, or judicial decisions, of the law, but also the formal part, or method of proceeding, cannot be altered but by parliament: for if once those outworks were demolished, there would be no inlet to all manner of innovation in the body of the law itself. The king, it is true, may erect new courts of justice; but then they must proceed according to the old established forms of the common law. For which reason it is declared in the statute 16 Car.I. c.10. upon the dissolution of the court of starchamber, that neither his majesty, not his privy council, have any jurisdiction, power, or authority by English bill, petition, articles, libel (which were the course of proceeding in the starchamber, borrowed from the civil law) or by any other arbitrary way whatsoever, to examine, or draw into question, determine or dispose of the lands or goods of any subjects of this kingdom; but that the same ought to be tried and determined in the ordinary courts of justice, and by *course of law*.

4. If there should happen any uncommon injury, or infringement of the rights beforementioned, which the ordinary course of law is too defective to reach, **there still remains a fourth subordinate right appertaining to every individual, namely, the right of petitioning the king, or either house of parliament, for the**

[u] c.29.

redress of grievances. In Russia we are told[w] that the czar Peter established a law, that no subject might petition the throne, till he had first petitioned two different ministers of state. In case he obtained justice from neither, he might then present a third petition to the prince; but upon pain of death, if found to be in the wrong. The consequence of which was, that no one dared to offer such third petition; and grievances seldom falling under the notice of the sovereign, he had little opportunity to redress them. The restrictions, for some there are, which are laid upon petitioning in England, are of a nature extremely different; and while they promote the spirit of peace, they are no check upon that of liberty. Care only must be taken, lest, under the pretence of petitioning, the subject be guilty of any riot or tumult; as happened in the opening of the memorable parliament in 1640: and, to prevent this, it is provided by the statute 13 Car.II. st.1. c.5. that no petition to the king, or either house of parliament, for any alterations in church or state, shall be signed by above twenty persons, unless the matter thereof be approved by three justices of the peace or the major part of the grand jury, in the country; and in London by the lord mayor, aldermen, and common council; nor shall any petition be presented by more than two persons at a time. But under these regulations, it is declared by the statute 1 W. & M. st.2 c.2 that the subject hath a right to petition; and that all commitments and prosecutions for such petitioning are illegal.

5. The fifth and last auxiliary right of the subject, that I shall at present mention, is that of having arms for their defence, suitable to their condition and degree, and such as are allowed by law. Which is also declared by the same statute 1 W. & M. st.2. c.2. and is indeed a public allowance, under due restrictions, of the natural right of resistance and self-preservation, when the sanctions of society and laws are found insufficient to restrain the violence of oppression.

[w] Montesq. Sp. L. 12.26.

In these several articles consist the rights, or, as they are frequently termed, the liberties of Englishmen: liberties more generally talked of, than thoroughly understood; and yet highly necessary to be perfectly known and considered by every man of rank or property, lest his ignorance of the points whereon it is founded should hurry him into faction and licentiousness on the one hand, or a pusillanimous indifference and criminal submission on the other. And we have seen that these rights consist, primarily, in the free enjoyment of personal security, of personal liberty, and of private property. So long as these remain inviolate, the subject is perfectly free; for every species of compulsive tyranny and oppression must act in opposition to one or other of these rights, having no other object upon which it can possibly be employed. To preserve these from violation, it is necessary that the constitution of parliaments be supported in it's full vigor; and limits certainly known, be set to the royal prerogative. **And, lastly, to vindicate these rights, when actually violated or attacked, the subjects of England are entitled, in the first place, to the regular administration and free course of justice in the courts of law; next to the right of petitioning the king and parliament for redress of grievances; and lastly to the right of having and using arms for self-preservation and defence.** And all these rights and liberties it is our birthright to enjoy entire; unless where the laws of our country have laid them under necessary restraints. Restraints in themselves so gentle and moderate, as will appear upon farther enquiry, that no man of sense or probity would wish to see them slackened. For all of us have it in our choice to do every thing that a good man would desire to do; and are restrained from nothing, but what would be pernicious either to ourselves or our fellow citizens. So that this review of our situation may fully justify the observation of a learned French author, who indeed generally both thought and wrote in the spirit of genuine freedom[y]; and who hath not scrupled to profess, even

[y] Montesq. Sp. L. 11.5.

in the very bosom of his native country, that the English is the only nation in the world, where political or civil liberty is the direct end of its constitution. Recommending therefore to the student in our laws a farther and more accurate search into this extensive and important title, I shall close my remarks upon it with the expiring wish of the famous father Paul to his country, "ESTO "PERPETUA!"

BL4

Blackstone on Slavery

Portions of Book 1, Chapter 13,
"Of the Military and Maritime States," pp. 403-404
and Book 1, Chapter 14,
"Of Master and Servant," pp. 411-413

One of the greatest advantages of our English law is, that not only the crimes themselves which it punishes, but also the penalties which it inflicts, are ascertained and notorious: nothing is left to arbitrary discretion: the king by his judges dispenses what the law previously ordained; but is not himself the legislator. How much therefore is it to be regretted that a set of men, whose bravery has so often preserved the liberties of their country, should be reduced to a state of servitude in the midst of nation of freemen! for sir Edward Coke will inform us[y], that it is one of the genuine marks of servitude, to have the law, which is our rule of action, either concealed or precarious: "*misera est servitus, ubi jus est vagum "aut incognitum.*" Nor is this state of servitude quite consistent with the maxims of sound policy observed by other free nations. For, the greater the general liberty is which any state enjoys, the more cautious has it usually been of introducing slavery in any particular order or profession. These men, as baron Montesquieu observes[z], seeing the liberty

[y] 4 Inst. 332.   [z] Sp. L. 15.12.

BL4, 403

which others possess, and which they themselves are excluded from, are apt (like eunuchs in the eastern seraglios) to live in a state of perpetual envy and hatred towards the rest of the community; and indulge a malignant pleasure in contributing to destroy those privileges, to which they can never be admitted. Hence have many free states, by departing from this rule, been endangered by the revolt of their slaves: while, in absolute and despotic governments where there no real liberty exists, and consequently no invidious comparisons can be formed, such incidents are extremely rare. Two precautions are therefore advised to be observed in all prudent and free governments; 1. To prevent the introduction of slavery at all: or, 2. If it be already introduced, not to intrust those slaves with arms; who will then find themselves an overmatch for the freemen. Much less ought the soldiery to be an exception to the people in general, and the only state of servitude in the nation.

BL4, 404

I. As to the several sorts of servants: I have formerly observed[a] that pure and proper slavery does not, nay cannot, subsist in England; such I mean, whereby an absolute and unlimited power is given to the master over the life and fortune of the slave. And indeed it is repugnant to reason, and the principles of natural law, that such a state should subsist any where. The three origins of the right of slavery assigned by Justinian[b], are all of them built on false foundations. As, first, slavery is held to arise "*jure gentium,*" from a state of captivity in war; whence slaves are called *mancipia, quasi manu capti.* The conqueror, say the civilians, had a right to the life of his captive; and, having spared that, has a right to deal with him as he pleases. But it is an untrue position, when taken generally, that, by the law of nature or nations, a man may kill his enemy: he has only a right to kill him, in particular cases; in cases of absolute necessity, for self-defence; and it is plain this absolute necessity did not subsist, since the victor did not actually kill him, but made him prisoner. **War is itself justifiable only on principles of self-preservation;** and therefore it gives no other right over prisoners, but merely to disable them from doing harm to us, by confining their persons: much less can it give a right to kill, torture, abuse, plunder, or even to enslave, an enemy, when the war is over. Since therefore the right of *making* slaves by captivity, depends on a supposed right of slaughter, that foundation failing, the consequence drawn from it must fail likewise. But, secondly, it is said that slavery may begin "*jure civili;*" when one man sells himself to another. This, if only meant of contracts to serve or

---

[a] pag. 123.

[b] *Servi aut siunt, aut nascuntur: siunt jure gentium, aut jure civili: nascuntur ex ancillis nostris. Inst.* 1.3.4.

work for another, is very just: but when applied to strict slavery, in the sense of the laws of old Rome or modern Barbary, is also impossible. Every sale implies a price, a *quid pro quo*, an equivalent given to the seller in lieu of what he transfers to the buyer: but what equivalent can be given for life, and liberty, both of which (in absolute slavery) are held to be in the master's disposal? His property also, the very price he seems to receive, devolves *ipso facto* to his master, the instant he becomes his slave. In this case therefore the buyer gives nothing, and the seller receives nothing: of what validity then can a sale be, which destroys the very principles upon which all sales are founded? Lastly, we are told, that besides these two ways by which slaves "*siunt,*" or are acquired, they may also be hereditary: "*servi nascuntur;*" the children of acquired slaves are, *jure naturae*, by the negative kind of birthright, slaves also. But this being built upon the two former rights must fall together with them. If neither captivity, nor the sale of oneself, can by the law of nature and reason, reduce the parent to slavery, much less can it reduce the offspring.

Upon these principles the law of England abhors, and will not endure the existence of, slavery within this nation: so that when an attempt was made to introduce it, by statute 1 Edw.VI. c.3. which ordained, that all idle vagabonds should be made slaves, and fed upon bread, water, or small drink, and refuse meat; should wear a ring of iron round their necks, arms, or legs; and should be compelled by beating, chaining, or otherwise, to perform the work assigned them, were it never so vile; the spirit of the nation could not brook this condition, even in the most abandoned rogues; and therefore this statute was repealed in two years afterwards[c]. **And now it is laid down[d], that a slave or negro, the instant he lands in England, becomes a freeman; that is, the law will protect him in the enjoyment of his person, his liberty, and his property. Yet, with regard to any right which the master may have acquired, by contract or the like, to the perpetual service of John or Thomas, this will remain exactly the same**

[c] Stat. 3 & 4 Edw.VI. c.16.   [d] Salk. 666.

state as before: for this is no more than the same state of subjection for life, which every apprentice submits to for the space of seven years, or sometimes for a longer term. Hence too it follows, that the infamous and unchristian practice of withholding baptism from negro servants, lest they should thereby gain their liberty, is totally without foundation, as well as without excuse. The law of England acts upon general and extensive principles: it gives liberty, rightly understood, that is, protection, to a jew, a turk, or a heathen, as well as to those who profess the true religion of Christ; and it will not dissolve a civil contract, either express or implied, between master and servant, on account of the alteration of faith in either of the contraction parties: but the slave is entitled to the same liberty in England before, as after, baptism; and, whatever service the heathen negro owed to his English master, the same is he bound to render when a christian.

BL5

Blackstone on Religion

Book 4, Chapter 4,
"Of Offences against God and Religion,"

In the present chapter we are to enter upon the detail of the several species of crimes and misdemesnors, with the punishment annexed to each by the laws of England. **It was observed, in the beginning of this book**[a]**, that crimes and misdemesnors are a breach and violation of the public rights and duties, owing to the whole community, considered as a community, in it's social aggregate capacity. And in the very entrance of these commentaries**[b] **it was shewn, that human laws can have no concern with any but social and relative duties; being intended only to regulate the conduct of man, considered under various relations, as a member of civil society. All crimes ought therefore to be estimated merely according to the mischiefs which they produce in civil society**[c]**: and, of consequence, private vices, or the breach of mere absolute duties, which man is bound to perform considered only as an individual, are not, cannot be, the object of any municipal law; any farther than as by their evil example, or other pernicious effects, they may prejudice the community, and thereby become a species of public crimes. Thus the vice of drunkenness, if committed privately and alone, is beyond the knowledge and of course beyond the reach of human tribunals: but if committed publicly, in the face of the world, it's evil example makes it liable**

---

[a] See pag. 5.   [b] See Vol.I. pag. 123, 124.   [c] Beccar. ch.8.

to temporal censures. The vice of lying, which consists (abstractly taken) in a criminal violation of truth, and therefore in any shape derogatory from found morality, is not however taken notice of by our law, unless it carries with it some public inconvenience, as spreading false news; or some social injury, as slander and malicious prosecution, for which a private recompense is given. And yet drunkenness and lying are *in foro conscientiae* as thoroughly criminal when they are not, as when they are, attended with public inconvenience. The only difference is, that both public and private vices are subject to the vengeance of eternal justice; and public vices are besides liable to the temporal punishments of human tribunals.

On the other hand, there are some misdemesnors, which are punished by municipal law, that are in themselves nothing criminal, but are made so by the positive constitutions of the state for public convenience. Such as poaching, exportation of wool and the like. These are naturally no offences at all; but their whole criminality consists in their disobedience to the supreme power, which has undoubted right for the well-being and peace of the community to make some things unlawful, which were in themselves indifferent. Upon the whole therefore, though part of the offences to be enumerated in the following sheets are offences against the revealed law of God, others against the law of nature, and some are offences against neither; yet in a treatise of municipal law we must consider them all as deriving their particular guilt, here punishable, from the law of man.

Having premised this caution, I shall next proceed to distribute the several offences, which are either directly or by consequence injurious to civil society, and therefore punishable by the laws of England, under the following general heads: first, those which are more immediately injurious to God and his holy religion; secondly, such as violate and transgress the law of nations; thirdly, such as more especially affect the sovereign executive power of the state, or the king and his government; fourthly, such as more directly infringe the rights of the public or common wealth; and, lastly, such as derogate from those rights and duties, which are owing to particular individuals, and in the preservation and vindication of which the community is deeply interested.

First then, of such crimes and misdemesnors, as more immediately offend Almighty God, by openly transgressing the precepts of religion either natural or revealed; and mediately, by their bad example and consequence, the law of society also; which constitutes that guilt in the action, which human tribunals are to censure.

I. Of this species the first is that of *apostacy*, or a total renunciation of christianity, by embracing either a false religion, or no religion at all. This offence can only take place in such as have once professed the true religion. The perversion of a christian to judaism, paganism, or other false religion, was punished by the emperors Constantius and Julian with confiscation of goods[d]; to which the emperors Theodosius and Valentian added capital punishment, in case the apostate endeavoured to pervert others to the same iniquity[e]. A punishment too severe for any temporal laws to inflict: and yet the zeal of our ancestors imported it into this country; for we find by Bracton[f], that in his time apostates were to be burnt to death. **Doubtless the preservation of christianity, as a national religion, is, abstracted from it's own intrinsic truth, of the utmost consequence to the civil state: which a single instance will sufficiently demonstrate. The belief of a future state of rewards and punishments, the entertaining just ideas of the moral attributes of the supreme being, and a firm persuasion that he superintends and will finally compensate every action in human life (all which are clearly revealed in the doctrines, and forcibly inculcated by the precepts, of our saviour Christ) these are the grand founda-**

[d] Cod.1.7.1.   [e] Ibid. 6.   [f] *l*.3 *c*.9

tion of all judicial oaths; which call God to witness the truth of those facts, which perhaps may be only known to him and the party attending: all moral evidence therefore, all confidence in human veracity, must be weakened by irreligion, and overthrown by infidelity. Wherefore all affronts to christianity, or endeavors to depreciate it's efficacy, are highly deserving of human punishment. But yet the loss of life is a heavier penalty than the offence, taken in a civil light, deserves: and, taken in a spiritual light, our laws have no jurisdiction over it. This punishment therefore has long ago become obsolete; and the offence of apostacy was for a long time the object only of the ecclesiastical courts, which corrected the offender *pro salute animae*. But about the close of the last century, the civil liberties to which we were then restored being used as a cloke of maliciousness, and the most horrid doctrines subversive of all religion being publicly avowed both in discourse and writings, it was found necessary again for the civil power to interpose, by not admitting those miscreants[g] to the privileges of society, who maintained such principles as destroyed all moral obligation. To this end it was enacted by statute 9 & 10 W.III. c.32. that if any person educated in, or having made profession of, the christian religion, shall by writing, printing, teaching, or advised speaking, deny the christian religion to be true, or the holy scriptures to be of divine authority, he shall upon the first offence be rendered incapable to hold any office or place of trust; and, for the second, be rendered incapable of bringing any action, being guardian, executor, legatee, or purchaser of lands, and shall suffer three years imprisonment without bail. To give room however for repentance; if, within four months after the first conviction, the delinquent will in open court publicly renounce his error, he is discharged for that once from all disabilities.

II. A second offence is that of *heresy*; which consists not in a total denial of christianity, but of some of it's essential

---

[g] *Miscroyantz* in our antient law-books is the name of unbelievers.

doctrines, publicly and obstinately avowed; being defined, *"scententia rerum divinarum humano sensu exogitata, palam docta, "et pertinaciter defensa*<u>h</u>*."* And here it must also be acknowleged that particular modes of belief or unbelief, not tending to overturn christianity itself, or to sap the foundations of morality, are by no means the object of coercion by the civil magistrate. What doctrines shall therefore be adjudged heresy, was left by our old constitution to the determination of the ecclesiastical judge; who had herein a most arbitrary latitude allowed him. For the general definition of an heretic given by Lyndewode[i], extends to the smallest deviations from the doctrines of holy church: *"haereticus est qui "dubitat de fide catholica, et qui negligit servare ea, quae Romana "ecclesia statuit, seu servare decreverat."* Or, as the statute 1 Hen.IV. c.15. expresses it in English, "teachers of erroneous "opinions, contrary to the faith and blessed determinations of the "holy church." Very contrary this to the usage of the first general councils, which defined all heretical doctrines with the utmost precision and exactness. And what ought to have alleviated the punishment, the uncertainty of the crime, seems to have enhanced it in those days of blind zeal and pious cruelty. It is true, that the sanctimonious hypocrisy of the canonists went at first no farther than enjoining penance, excommunication, and ecclesiastical deprivation, for heresy; though afterwards they proceeded boldly to imprisonment by the ordinary, and confiscation of goods *in pious usus*. But in the mean time they had prevailed upon the weakness of bigotted princes to make the civil power subservient to their purposes, by making heresy not only a temporal, but even a capital offence: the Romish ecclesiastics determining, without appeal, whatever they pleased to be heresy, and shifting off to the secular arm the odium and drudgery of executions; with which they themselves were too tender and delicate to intermeddle. Nay they pretended to intercede and pray, on behalf of the convicted heretic, *ut citra mortis periculum sententia circa eum moderetur*[k]: well

---

<u>h</u> 1 Hal. P.C. 384.   [i] *cap. de haereticis.*   [k] *Decretal. l.5. t.40 c.27.*

knowing at the same time that they were delivering the unhappy victim to certain death. Hence the capital punishments inflicted on the antient Donatists and Manichaeans by the emperors Theodosius and Justinian[l]: hence also the constitution of the emperor Frederic mentioned by Lyndewode[m], adjudging all persons without distinction to be burnt with fire, who were convicted of heresy by the ecclesiastical judge. The same emperor, in another constitution[n], ordained that if any temporal lord, when admonished by the church, should neglect to clear his territories of heretics within a year, it should be lawful for good catholics to seise and occupy the lands, and utterly to exterminate the heretical possessors. And upon this foundation was built that arbitrary power, so long claimed and so fatally exerted by the pope, of disposing even of the kingdoms of refractory princes to more dutiful sons of the church. The immediate event of this constitution was something singular, and may serve to illustrate at once the gratitude of the holy see, and the just punishment of the royal bigot: for upon the authority of this very constitution, the pope afterwards expelled this very emperor from the kingdom of Sicily, and gave it to Charles of Anjou[o].

Christianity being thus deformed by the daemon of persecution upon the continent, we cannot expect that our own island should be entirely free from the same scourge. And therefore we find among our antient precedents[p] a writ *de haeretico comburendo*, which is thought by some to be as antient as the common law itself. However, it appears from thence, that the conviction of heresy by the common law was not in any petty ecclesiastical court, but before the archbishop himself in a provincial synod; and that the delinquent was delivered over to the king to do as he should please with him; so that the crown had a control over the spiritual power, and might pardon the convict by issuing

---

[l] *Cod. l.1. tit.5.*
[m] *c. de haereticis.*
[n] *Cod.1.5.4.*
[o] Baldus *in Cod.*1.5.4.
[p] F.N.B. 269.

no process against him; the writ *de haeretico comburendo* being not a writ of course, but issuing only by the special direction of the king in council[q].

But in the reign of Henry the fourth, when the eyes of the christian world began to open, and the seeds of the protestant religion (though under the opprobrious name of lollardy[r]) took root in this kingdom; the clergy, taking advantage from the king's dubious title to demand an increase of their own power, obtained an act of parliament[s], which sharpened the edge of persecution to it's utmost keenness. For, by that statute, the diocesan alone, without the intervention of a synod, might convict of heretical tenets; and unless the convict abjured his opinions, or if after abjuration he relapsed, the sheriff was bound *ex officio*, if required by the bishop, to commit the unhappy victim to the flames, without waiting for the consent of the crown. By the statute 2 Hen. V. c.7. lollardy was also made a temporal offence, and indictable in the king's courts; which did not thereby gain an exclusive, but only a concurrent jurisdiction with the bishop's consistory.

Afterwards, when the final reformation of religion began to advance, the power of the ecclesiastics was somewhat moderated: for though what heresy *is*, was not then precisely defined, yet we are told in some points what it *is not*: the statute 25 Hen.VIII. c.14. declaring, that offences against the see of Rome are not heresy; and the ordinary being thereby restrained from proceeding in any case upon mere suspicion; that is, unless the party be accused by two credible witnesses, or an indictment of heresy be first previously found in the king's courts of common law. And yet the spirit of persecution was not then abated, but only diverted into a lay chanel. For in six years afterwards, by statute 31 Hen.VIII. c.14. the bloody law of the six articles was made, which established the six most contested points of popery, tran-

[q] 1 Hal. P.C. 395.   [s] 2 Hen.IV. c.15.

[r] So called not from *lolium*, or tares, (which was afterwards devised, in order to justify the burning of them from Matth. xiii.30.) but from one Walter Lolhard, a German reformer. Mod.Un.Hist. xxvi.13. Spelm. *Gloss.* 371.

substantiation, communion in one kind, the celibacy of the clergy, monastic vows, the sacrifice of the mass, and the auricular confession; which points were "determined and resolved by the "most godly study, pain, and travail of his majesty: for which his "most humble and obedient subjects, the lords *spiritual* and temporal "and the commons, in parliament assembled, did not only render "and give unto his highness their most high and hearty thanks," but did also enact and declare all oppugners of the first to be heretics, and to be burnt with fire; and of the five last to be felons, and to suffer death. The same statute established a new and mixed jurisdiction of clergy and laity for the trial and conviction of heretics; the reigning prince being then equally intent on destroying the supremacy of the bishops of Rome, and establishing all other their corruptions of the christian religion.

I shall not perplex this detail with the various repeals and revivals of these sanguinary laws in the two succeeding reigns; but shall proceed directly to the reign of queen Elizabeth; when the reformation was finally established with temper and decency, unsullied with party rancour, or personal caprice and resentment. By statute 1 Eliz. c.1. all former statutes relating to heresy are repealed, which leaves the jurisdiction of heresy as it stood at common law; *viz.* as to the infliction of common censures, in the ecclesiastical courts; and, in case of burning a heretic, in the provincial synod only[t]. Sir Matthew Hale is indeed of a different opinion, and holds that such power resided in the diocesan also; though he agrees, that in either case the writ *de haeretico comburendo* was not demandable of common right, but grantable or otherwise merely at the king's discretion[u]. But the principal point now gained, was, that by this statute a boundary is for the first time set to what shall be accounted heresy; nothing for the future being to be so determined, but only such tenets, which have been heretofore so declared, 1. By the words of the canonical scriptures; 2. By the first four general councils, or such others

[t] 5 Rep.23. 12 Rep.56.92.   [u] 1 Hal. P.C.405.

as have only used the words of the holy scriptures; or, 3. Which shall hereafter be so declared by the parliament, with the assent of the clergy in convocation. Thus was heresy reduced to a greater certainty than before; though it might not have been the words to have defined it in terms still more precise and particular: as a man continued still liable to be burnt, for what perhaps he did not understand to be heresy, till the ecclesiastical judge so interpreted the words of the canonical scriptures.

For the writ *de haeretico comburendo* still remained in force; and we have instances of it's being put in execution upon two anabaptists in the seventeenth of Elizabeth, and two Arians in the ninth of James the first. But it was totally abolished, and heresy again subjected only to ecclesiastical correction, *pro salute animae,* by virtue of the statute 29 Car.II. c.9. For in one and the same reign, our lands were delivered from the slavery of military tenures; our bodies from arbitrary imprisonment by the *habeas corpus* act; and our minds from the tyranny of superstitious bigotry, by demolishing the last badge of persecution in the English law.

In what I have now said I would not be understood to derogate from the just rights of the national church, or to favor a loose latitude of propagating any crude undigested sentiments in religious matters. Of propagating, I say; for the bare entertaining them, without an endeavor to diffuse them, seems hardly cognizable by any human authority. I only mean to illustrate the excellence of our present establishment, by looking back to former times. Every thing is now as it should be: unless perhaps that heresy ought to be more strictly defined, and no prosecution permitted, even in the ecclesiastical courts, till the tenets in question are by proper authority previously declared to be heretical. Under these restrictions, it seems necessary for the support of the national religion, that the officers of the church should have the power to censure heretics, but not to exterminate or destroy them. **It has also been thought proper for the**

civil magistrate again to interpose, with regard to one species of heresy, very prevalent in modern times: for by statute 9 & 10 W.III. c.32. if any person educated in the christian religion, or professing the same, shall by writing, printing, teaching, or advised speaking, deny any one of the persons of the holy trinity to be God, or maintain that there are more Gods than one, he shall undergo the same penalties and incapacities, which were just now mentioned to be inflicted on apostacy by the same statute. And thus much for the crime of heresy.

III. Another species of offences against religion are those which affect the *established church*. And these are either positive, or negative. Positive, as by reviling it's ordinances: or negative, by non-conformity to it's worship. Of both of these in their order.

1. **And, first, of the offence of** *reviling the ordinances* **of the church. This is a crime of a much grosser nature than the other of mere non-conformity: since it carries with it the utmost indecency, arrogance, and ingratitude: indecency, by setting up private judgment in opposition to public; arrogance, by treating with contempt and rudeness what has at least a better chance to be right, than the singular notions of any particular man; and ingratitude, by denying that indulgence and liberty of conscience to members of the national church, which the retainers to every petty conventicle enjoy.** However it is provided by the statutes 1 Edw. VI. c.1. and 1 Eliz. c.1. that whoever reviles the sacrament of the lord's supper shall be punished by fine and imprisonment: and by the statute 1 Eliz. c.2. if any *minister* shall speak any thing in derogation of the book of common prayer, he shall be imprisoned six months, and forfeit a year's value of his benefice; and for the second offence he shall be deprived.[1] And if *any person* whatsoever shall in plays, songs, or other open words, speak any thing in derogation, depraving, or despising of the said book, he shall forfeit for the first offence an hundred marks; for the second four hundred; and for the

---

[1] Apparently, Blackstone's printer deleted the part of the sentence that told of what the minister was to be deprived.

third shall forfeit all his goods and chattel, and suffer imprisonment for life. These penalties were framed in the infancy of our present establishment; when the disciples of Rome and of Geneva united in inveighing with the utmost bitterness against the English liturgy: and the terror of these laws (for they seldom, if ever, were fully executed) proved a principal means, under providence, of preserving the purity as well as decency of our national worship. Nor can their continuance to this time be thought too severe and intolerant; when we consider, that they are levelled at an offence, to which men cannot now be prompted by any laudable motive; not even any mistaken zeal for reformation: since from political reasons, sufficiently hinted at in a former volume[v], it would now be extremely unadvisable to make any alterations in the service of the church; unless it could be shewn that some manifest impiety or shocking absurdity would follow from continuing in its present form. And therefore the virulent declamations of peevish or opinionated men on topics so often refuted, and of which the preface to the liturgy is itself a perpetual refutation, can be calculated for no other purpose, than merely to disturb the consciences, and poison the minds of people.

2. Non-conformity to the worship of the church is the other, or negative branch of this offence. And for this there is much more to be pleaded than the former; being a matter of private conscience, to the scruples of which our present laws have shewm a very just and christian indulgence. **For undoubtedly all persecution and oppression of weak consciences, on the score of religious persuasions, are highly unjustifiable upon every principle of natural reason, civil liberty, or sound religion. But care must be taken not to carry this indulgence into such extremes, as may endanger the national church: there is always a difference to be made between toleration and establishment.**

Non-conformists are of two sorts: first, such as absent themselves from the divine worship of the established church,

[v] Vol.I. pag.98.

through total irreligion, and attend the service of no other persuasion. These by the statutes of 1 Eliz. c.2. 23 Eliz. c.1. and 3 Jac.I. c.4. forfeit one shilling to the poor every lord's day they so absent themselves, and 20 *l.* to the king if they continue such default for a month together. And if they keep any inmate, thus irreligiously disposed, in their houses, they forfeit 10 *l. per* month.

The second species of non-conformists are those who offend through a mistaken or perverse zeal. Such were esteemed by our laws, enacted since the time of the reformation, to be papists and protestant dissenters: both of which were supposed to be equally schismatics in departing from the national church; with this difference, that the papists divide from us upon material, though erroneous, reasons; but many of the dissenters upon matters of indifference, or, in other words, upon no reason at all. However the laws against the former are much more severe than against the latter; the principles of the papists being deservedly looked upon to be subversive of the civil government, but not those of the protestant dissenters. As to the papists, their tenets are undoubtedly calculated for the introduction of all slavery, both civil and religious: but it may with justice be questioned, whether spirit, the doctrines, and the practice of the sectaries are better calculated to make men good subjects. One thing is obvious to observe, that these have once within the compass of the last century, effected the ruin of our church and monarchy; which the papists have attempted indeed, but have never yet been able to execute.[2] Yet certainly our ancestors were mistaken in their plans of compulsion and intolerance. The sin of schism, as such, is by no means the object of temporal coercion and punishment. If through weakness of intellect, through misdirected piety, through perverseness and acerbity of temper, or (which is often the case) through a prospect of secular advantage in herding with a party, men quarrel with the ecclesiastical establishment, the civil magistrate has nothing to do with it; unless their tenets and practice are such as threaten ruin or dis-

---

[2] Probably a reference to Bonnie Prince Charlie's aborted invasion of England in 1745.

turbance to the state. He is bound indeed to protect the established church, by admitting none but it's genuine members to offices of trust and emolument: for, if every sect was to be indulged in a free communion of civil employments, the idea of a national establishment would at once be destroyed, and the episcopal church would be no longer the church of England. But, this point being once secured, all persecution for diversity of opinions, however ridiculous or absurd they may be, is contrary to every principle of sound policy and civil freedom. The names and subordination of the clergy, the posture of devotion, the materials and colour of the minister's garment, the joining in a known or an unknown form of prayer, and other matters of the same kind, must be left to the option of every man's private judgment.

With regard therefore to *protestant dissenters*, although the experience of their turbulent disposition in former times occasioned several disabilities and restrictions (which I shall not undertake to justify) to be laid upon them by abundance of statutes[w], yet at length the legislature, with a spirit of true magnanimity, extended that indulgence to these sectaries, which they themselves, when in power, had held to be countenancing schism, and denied to the church of England. **The penalties are all of them suspended by the statute 1 W. & M. st.2. c.18. commonly called the toleration act; which exempts all dissenters (except papists, and such as deny the trinity) from all penal laws relating to religion, provided they take the oaths of allegiance and supremacy, and subscribe the declaration against popery, and repair to some congregation registered in the bishop's court or at the sessions, the doors whereof must always be open: and dissenting teachers are also to subscribe the thirty nine articles, except those relating to church government and infant baptism. Thus are all persons, who will approve themselves no papists or oppugners of the trinity, left at full liberty to act as their conscience shall direct them, in the matter of religious worship. But by statute**

---

[w] 31 Eliz. c.1. 17 Car.II c.2 22 Car.II c.1.

5 Geo.I. c.4. no mayor, or principal magistrate, must appear at any dissenting meeting with the ensigns of his office[x], on pain of disability to hold that or any other office: the legislature judging it a matter of propriety, that a mode of worship, set up in opposition to the national, when allowed to be exercised in peace, should be exercised also with decency, gratitude, and humility.

As to *papists*, what has been said of the protestant dissenters would hold equally strong for a general toleration of them; provided their separation was founded only upon difference of opinion in religion, and their principles did not also extend to a subversion of the civil government. If once they could be brought to renounce the supremacy of the pope, they might quietly enjoy their seven sacraments, their purgatory, and auricular confession; their worship of reliques and images; nay even their transubstantiation. But while they acknowlege a foreign power, superior to the sovereignty of the kingdom, they cannot complain if the laws of that kingdom will not treat them upon the footing of good subjects.

Let us therefore now take a view of the laws in force against the papist; who may be divided into three classes, persons professing popery, popish recusants convict, and popish priests. 1. Persons professing the popish religion, besides the former penalties for not frequenting their parish church, are by several statutes, too numerous to be here recited[y], disabled from taking any lands either by descent or purchase, after eighteen years of age, until they renounce their errors; they must at the age of twenty one register their estates before acquired, and all future conveyances and wills relating to them; they are incapable of presenting to any advowson, or granting to any other person any

---

[x] Sir Humphrey Edwin, a lord mayor of London, had the imprudence soon after the toleration-act to go to a presbyterian meeting-house in his formalities: which is alluded to by dead Swift, in his *tale of a tub*, under the allegory of *Jack* getting on a great horse, and eating custard.

[y] See Hawkins's pleas of the crown, and Burn's justice.

BL5, 54

avoidance of the same, in prejudice of the two universities; they may not keep or teach any school under pain of perpetual imprisonment; they are liable also in some instances to pay double taxes; and, if they willingly say or hear mass, they forfeit the one two hundred, the other one hundred marks, and each shall suffer a year's imprisonment. Thus much for persons, who, from the misfortune of family prejudices or otherwise, have conceived an unhappy attachment to the Romish church from their infancy, and publicly profess its errors. But if any evil industry is used to rivet these errors upon them, if any person sends another abroad to be educated in the popish religion, or to reside in any religious house abroad for that purpose, or contributes any thing to their maintenance when there; both the sender, the sent, and the contributor, are disabled to sue in law or equity, to be executor or administrator to any person, to take any legacy or deed of gift, and to bear any office in the realm, and shall forfeit all their goods and chattels, and likewise all their real estate for life. And where these errors are also aggravated by apostacy, or perversion, where a person is reconciled to the see of Rome or procures others to be reconciled, the offence amounts to high treason. 2. Popish recusants, convicted in a court of law of not attending the service of the church of England, are subject to the following disabilities, penalties, and forfeitures, over and above those before-mentioned. They can hold no office or employment; they must not keep arms in their houses, but the same may be seised by the justices of the peace; they may not come within ten miles of London, on pain of 100 *l*; they can bring no action at law, or suit in equity; they are not permitted to travel above five miles from home, unless by licence, upon pain of forfeiting all their goods; and they may not come to court, under pain of 100 *l*. No marriage or burial of such recusant, or baptism of his child, shall be had otherwise than by the ministers of the church of England, under other severe penalties. A married woman, when recusant, shall forfeit two thirds of her dower or jointure, may not be executrix or administratrix to her husband, nor have any part of his goods; and during the coverture may be kept in prison, unless her husband redeems her at the rate of 10 *l.* a month, or the third part of all his lands. And, lastly, as a seme-covert recusant may be imprisoned, so all others must, within three months after conviction, either submit and renounce their errors, or, if required to do so by four justices, must abjure and renounce the realm: and if they do not depart, or if they return without the king's licence, they shall be guilty of felony, and suffer death as felons. There is also an inferior species of recusancy, (refusing to make the declaration against popery enjoined by statute 30 Car.II. st.2. when tendered by the proper magistrate) which, if the party resides within ten miles of London, makes him an absolute recusant convict; or, if at a greater distance, suspends him from having any seat in parliament, keeping arms in his house, or any horse above the value of five pounds. This is the state, by the laws now in being, of a lay papist. But, 3. The remaining species or degree, *viz.* popish priests, are in a still more dangerous condition. By statute 11 & 12 W.III c.4. popish priests or bishops, celebrating mass or exercising any parts of their functions in England, except in the houses of embassadors, are liable to perpetual imprisonment. And by the statute 27 Eliz. c.2. any popish priest, born in the dominions of the crown of England, who shall come over hither from beyond sea, or shall be in England three days without conforming and taking the oaths, is guilty of high treason: and all persons harbouring him are guilty of felony without the benefit of clergy.

This is a short summary of the laws against papists, under their three several classes, of persons professing the popish religion, popish recusants convict, and popish priests. Of which the president Montesquieu observes[z], that they are so rigorous, though not professedly of the sanguinary kind, that they do all the hurt that can possibly be done in cold blood. But in answer to this it may be observed, (what foreigners who only judge from our statute book are not fully apprized of) that these laws

[z] Sp.L. b.19 c.27.

BL5, 56

are seldom exerted to their utmost rigor: and indeed, if they were, it would be very difficult to execute them. For they are rather to be accounted for from their history, and the urgency of the times which produced them, than to be approved (upon a cool review) as a standing system of law. The restless machinations of the jesuits during the reign of Elizabeth, the turbulence and uneasiness of the papists under the new religious establishment, and the boldness of their hopes and wishes for the succession of the queen of Scots, obliged the parliament to counteract so dangerous a spirit by laws of a great, and perhaps necessary severity. The powder-treason, in the succeeding reign, struck a panic into James I, which operated in different ways: it occasioned the enacting of new laws against the papists; but deterred him from putting them in execution. The intrigues of queen Henrietta in the reign of Charles I, the prospect of a popish successor in that of Charles II, the assassination-plot in the reign of king William, and the avowed claim of a popish pretender to the crown, will account for the extension of these penalties at those several periods of our history. But if a time should ever arrive, and perhaps it is not very distant, when all fears of a pretender shall have vanished, and the power and influence of the pope shall become feeble, ridiculous, and despicable, not only in England but in every kingdom of Europe; it probably would not then be amiss to review and soften these rigorous edicts; at least til the *civil* principles of the roman-catholics called again upon the legislature to renew them: for it ought not to be left in the breast of every merciless bigot, to drag down the vengeance of these occasional laws upon inoffensive, though mistaken, subjects; in opposition to the lenient inclinations of the civil magistrate, and to the destruction of every principle of toleration and religious liberty.

In order the better to secure the established church against perils from non-conformists of all denominations, infidels, turks, jews, heretics, papists, and sectaries, there are however two bulwarks erected; called the *corporation* and *test* acts: by the former of which[a] no person can be legally elected to any office relating to the government of any city or corporation, unless, within a twelvemonth before, he has received the sacrament of the lord's supper according to the rites of the church of England: and he is also enjoined to take the oaths of allegiance and supremacy at the same time that he takes the oath of office: or, in default of either of these requisites, such election shall be void. The other, called the test act[b], directs all officers civil and military to take the oaths and make the declaration against transubstantiation, in the court of king's bench or chancery, the next term, or at the next quarter sessions, or (by subsequent statutes) within six months, after their admission; and also within the same time to receive the sacrament of the lord's supper, according to the usage of the church of England, in some public church immediately after divine service and sermon, and to deliver into court a certificate thereof signed by the minister and church-warden, and also to prove the same by two credible witnesses; upon forfeiture of 500 *l*, and disability to hold the said office. And of much the same nature with these is the statute 7 Jac.I. c.2. which permits no persons to be naturalized or restored in blood, but such as undergo a like test: which test having been removed in 1753, in favour of the Jews, was the next session of parliament restored again with some precipitation.

Thus much for offences, which strike at our national religion, or the doctrine and discipline of the church of England in particular. I proceed now to consider some gross impieties and general immoralities, which are taken notice of and punished by our municipal law; frequently in concurrence with the ecclesiastical, to which the censure of many of them does also of right appertain; though with a view somewhat different: the spiritual court punishing all sinful enormities for the sake of reforming the private sinner, *pro salute animae*; **while the temporal courts resent the public affront to religion and morality, on**

---

[a] Stat. 13 Car.II. st.2. c.1.   [b] Stat. 25 Car.II. c.2.

which all government must depend for support, and correcty more for the sake of example than private amendment.

IV. The fourth species of offenses therefore, more immediately against God and religion, is that of *blasphemy* against the Almighty, by denying his being or providence; or by contumelious reproaches of our Saviour Christ. Whither also may be referred all profane scoffing at the holy scripture, or exposing it to contempt and ridicule.[3] These are offences punishable at common law by fine and imprisonment, or other infamous corporal punishment[c]: for christianity is part of the laws of England[d].

V. Somewhat allied to this, though in an inferior degree, is the offence of profane and common *swearing* and *cursing*. By the last statute against which, 19 Geo.II. c.21. which repeals all former ones, every labourer, sailor, or soldier shall forfeit 1 *s.* for every profane oath or curse, every other person under the degree of gentleman 2 *s.* and every gentleman or person of superior rank 5 *s.* to the poor of the parish; and, on a second conviction, double; and, for every subsequent conviction, treble the sum first forfeited; with all charges of conviction: and in default of payment shall be sent to the house of correction for ten days. Any justice of the peace may convict upon his own hearing, or the testimony of one witness; and any constable or peace officer, upon his own hearing, may secure any offender and carry him before a justice, and there convict him. If the justice omits his duty, he forfeits 5 *l.*, and the constable 40 *s.* And the act is to be read in all parish churches, and public chapels, the sunday after every quarter day, on pain of 5 *l.* to be levied by warrant from any justice. Besides this punishment for taking God's name in vain in common discourse, it is enacted by statute 3 Jac.I. c.21. that if in any stage play, interlude, or shew, the name of the holy trinity, or any of the persons therein,

---

[c] 1 Hawk. P.C. 7.   [d] 1 Ventr. 293. 2 Strange, 834.

[3] Blackstone's definition of *blasphemy* is cited as authority for the same definition of that word in *Webster's New Twentieth Century Dictionary of the English Language Unabridged*, 2nd. ed. (New York: The Publishers Guild, Inc., 1966).

be jestingly or profanely used, the offender shall forfeit 10 *l.*, one moiety to the king, and the other to the informer.

VI. A sixth species of offences against God and religion, of which our antient books are full, is a crime of which one knows not well what account to give. I mean the offence of *witchcraft, conjuration, inchantment,* or *sorcery.* To deny the possibility, nay, actual existence, of witchcraft and sorcery, is at once flatly to contradict the revealed word of God, in various passages of both of the old and new testament: and the thing itself is a truth to which every nation in the world hath in it's turn borne testimony, by either examples seemingly well attested, or prohibitory laws, which at least suppose the possibility of a commerce with evil spirits. **The civil law punishes with death not only the sorcerers themselves, but also those who consult them[e]; imitating in the former the express law of God[f], "thou shalt not suffer a witch to live." And our own laws, both before and since the conquest, have been equally penal; ranking this crime in the same class with heresy, and condemning both to the flames[g].** The president Montesquieu[h] ranks them also both together, but with a very different view; laying it down as an important maxim, that we ought to be very circumspect in the prosecution of magic and heresy; because the most unexceptional conduct, the purest morals, and the constant practice of every duty in life, are not a sufficient security against the suspicion of crimes like these. And indeed the ridiculous stories that are generally told, in all ages, are enough to demolish all faith in such a dubious crime; if the contrary evidence were not also extremely strong. Wherefore it seems to be the most eligible way to conclude, with an ingenious writer of our own[i], that in general there has been such a thing as witchcraft; though one cannot give credit to any particular modern instance of it.

[e] *Cod. l.*9. *t.*18
[f] Exod. xxii. 18.
[g] 3 Inst. 44.
[h] Sp. L. b.12. c.5.
[i] Mr. Addison, Spect. No. 117.

Our forefathers were stronger believers, when they enacted by statute 33 Hen.VIII. c.8. all witchcraft and sorcery to be felony without benefit of clergy; and again by statute 1 Jac.I. c.12. that all persons invoking any evil spirit, or consulting, covenanting with, entertaining, employing, feeding, or rewarding any evil spirit; or taking up dead bodies from their graves to be used in any witchcraft, sorcery, charm, or inchantment; or killing or otherwise hurting any person by such infernal arts; should be guilty of felony without benefit of clergy, and suffer death. And, if any person should attempt by sorcery to discover hidden treasure, or to restore stolen goods, or to provoke unlawful love, or to hurt any man or beast, though the same were not effected, he or she should suffer imprisonment and pillory for the first offence, and death for the second. These acts continued in force till lately, to the terror of all antient females in the kingdom: and many poor wretches were sacrificed thereby to the prejudice of their neighbours, and their own illusions; not a few having, by some means or other, confessed to the fact at the gallows. But all executions for this dubious crime are now at an end; our legislature having at length followed the wise example of Louis the XIV in France, who thought proper by an edict to restrain the tribunals of justice from receiving informations of witchcraft[k]. And accordingly it is with us enacted by statute 9 Geo.II. c.5. that no prosecution shall for the future be carried on against any person for conjuration, witchcraft, sorcery, or inchantment. But the misdemeanor of persons pretending to use witchcraft, tell fortunes, or discover stolen goods by skill in the occult sciences, is still deservedly punished with a year's imprisonment, and standing four times in the pillory.

VII. A seventh species of offenders in this class are all *religious imposters:* such as falsely pretend an extraordinary com-

---

[k] Voltaire *Siecl. Louis xiv.* Mod. Univ. Hist. xxv. 215. Yet Vouglans, (*de droit criminel*, 353. 459.) still reckons up sorcery and witchcraft among the crimes punishable in France.

mission from heaven; or terrify and abuse the people with false denunciation of judgments. These, as tending to subvert all religion, by bringing it into ridicule and contempt, are punishable by the temporal courts with fine, imprisonment, and infamous corporal punishment[l].

VIII. Simony, or the corrupt presentation of any one to an ecclesiastical benefice for gift or reward, is also to be considered and an offence against religion; as well by reason of the sacredness of the charge which is thus profanely bought and sold, as because it is always attended with perjury in the person presented[m]. The statute 31 Eliz. c.6. (which, so far as it relates to the forfeiture of the right of presentation, was considered in a former book[n]) enacts, that if any person, for money or other corrupt consideration or promise, directly or indirectly given, shall present, admit, institute, induct, install, or collate any person to an ecclesiastical benefice or dignity, both the giver and taker shall forfeit two years value of the benefice or dignity; one moiety to the king, and the other to any one who will sue for the same. If persons also corruptly resign or exchange their benefices, both the giver and the taker shall in like manner forfeit double the value of the money or other corrupt consideration. And persons who shall corruptly ordain or licence any minister, or procure him to be ordained or licences, (which is the true idea of simony) shall incur a like forfeiture of forty pounds; and the minister himself of ten pounds, besides and incapacity to hold any ecclesiastical perferment for seven years afterwards. Corrupt elections and resignations in colleges, hospitals, and other eleemosynary corporations, are also punished by the same statute with forfeiture of the double value, vacating the place or office, and a devolution of the right of election for that turn to the crown.

[l] 1 Hawk. P.C.7.
[m] 3 Inst. 156.
[n] See Vol. II. pag. 279.

IX. Profanation of the lord's day, or *sabbath-breaking*, is a ninth offence against God and religion, punished by the municipal laws of England. For, besides the notorious indecency and scandal, of permitting any secular business to be publicly transacted on that day, in a country professing christianity, and the corruption of morals which usually follows it's profanation, the keeping one day in seven holy, as a time of relaxation and refreshment as well as for public worship, is of admirable service to the state, considered merely as a civil institution. It humanizes by the help of conversation and society the manners of the lower classes; which would otherwise degenerate into a sordid ferocity and savage selfishness of spirit: it enables the industrious workman to pursue his occupation in the ensuing week with health and chearfulness: it imprints on the minds of the people that sense of their duty to God, so necessary to make them good citizens; but which yet would be worn out and defaced by an unremitted continuance of labour, without any stated times of recalling them to the worship of their maker. And therefore the laws of king Athelstan⁰ forbad all merchandizing on the lord's day, under very severe penalties. And by the statute of 27 Hen.VI. c.5. no fair or market shall be held on the principal festivals, good friday, or any sunday (except the four sundays in harvest) on pain of forfeiting the goods exposed to sale. And, since, by the statute 1 Car.I. c.1. no persons shall assemble, out of their own parishes, shall use any bull or bear baiting, interludes, plays, or other *unlawful* exercises, or pastimes; on pain that every offender shall pay 3 *s.* 4 *d.* to the poor. This statute does not prohibit, but rather impliedly allows, any innocent recreation or amusement, within their respective parishes, even on the lord's day, after divine service is over. But by statute 29 Car.II. c.7. no person is allowed to *work* on the lord's day, or use any boat or barge, or expose any goods to sale; except meat in public houses, milk at certain, and works of ne-

---

⁰ c.24.

cessity or charity, on forfeiture of 5 *s*. Nor shall any drover, carrier, or the like, travel on that day, under pain of twenty shillings.

X. Drunkenness is also punished by statute 4 Jac.I. c.5. with the forfeiture of 5 s.; or the sitting six hours in the stocks: by which time the statute presumes the offender will have regained his senses, and not be liable to do mischief to his neighbors. And there are many wholsome statutes, by way of prevention, chiefly passed in the same reign of king James I, which regulate the licencing of alehouses, and punish persons found tippling therein; or the masters of such houses permitting them.

XI. The last offence which I shall mention, more immediately against religion and morality, and cognizable by the temporal courts, is that of open and notorious *lewdness*: either by frequenting houses of ill fame, which is an indictable offence[p]; or by some grossly scandalous and public indecency, for which the punishment is by fine and imprisonment[q]. In the year 1650, when the ruling powers found it for their interest to put on the semblance of a very extraordinary strictness and purity of morals, not only incest and wilful adultery were made capital crimes; but also the repeated act of keeping a brothel, or committing fornication, were (upon second conviction) made felony without benefit of clergy[r]. But at the restoration, when men from an abhorrence of the hypocrisy of the late times fell into a contrary extreme, of licentiousness, it was not thought proper to renew a law of such unfashionable rigour. And these offences have been ever since left to the feeble coercion of the spiritual court, according to the rules of the canon law; a law which has treated the offence of incontinence, nay even adultery itself, with a great degree of tenderness and lenity; owing perhaps to the celibacy of it's first compilers. The temporal

[p] Poph. 208.
[q] 1 Siderf. 168.
[r] Scobell. 121.

courts therefore take no cognizance of the crime of adultery, otherwise than as a private injury[s].

But, before we quit this subject, we must take notice of the temporal punishment for having *bastard children*, considered in a criminal light; for with regard to the maintenance of such illegitimate offspring, which is a civil concern, we have formerly spoken at large[t]. By the statute 18 Eliz. c.3. two justices may take order for the punishment of the mother and reputed father; but what that punishment shall be, is not therein ascertained: though the contemporary exposition was, that a corporal punishment was intended[u]. By statute 7 Jac.I. c.4. a specific punishment (*viz.* commitment to a house of correction) is inflicted on the woman only. But in both cases, it seems that the penalty can only be inflicted, if the bastard becomes chargeable to the parish: for otherwise the very maintenance of the child is considered as a degree of punishment. By the last mentioned statute the justices may commit the mother to the house of correction, there to be punished and set on work for one year; and, in case of a second offence, till she find sureties never to offend again.

[s] See Vol. III. pag. 139.

[t] See Vol. I. pag. 458.

[u] Dalt. just. ch.11.

BL6

Blackstone on Freedom of the Press

A portion of Book 4, Chapter 9,
"Of Offences against the Public Peace,"
pp. 151-153

In this, and other instances which we have lately considered, where blasphemous, immoral, treasonable, schismatical, seditious, or scandalous libels are punished by the English law, some with a greater, others with a less degree of severity; the *liberty of the press*, properly understood, is by no means infringed or violated. **The liberty of the press is indeed essential to the nature of a free state: but this consists in laying no *previous* restraints upon publications, and not in freedom from censure for criminal matter when published. Every freeman has an undoubted right to lay what sentiments he pleases before the public: to forbid this, is to destroy the freedom of the** press: but if he publishes what is improper, mischievous, or illegal, he must take the consequence of his own temerity. To subject the press to the restrictive power of a licenser, as was formerly done, both before and since the revolution[a], is to subject all freedom of sentiment to the prejudices of one man, and make him the arbitrary and infallible judge of all controverted points in learning, religion, and government. But to punish (as the law does at present) any dangerous or offensive writings, which, when published, shall on a fair and impartial trial be adjudged of a pernicious tendency, is necessary for the preservation of peace and good order, of government and religion, the only solid foundations of civil liberty. Thus the will of individuals is still left free; the abuse only of that free will is the object of legal punishment. Neither is any restraint hereby laid upon freedom of thought or enquiry: liberty of private sentiment is still left; the disseminating, or making public, of bad sentiments, destructive of the ends of society, is the crime which society corrects. A man (says a fine writer on this subject) may be allowed to keep poisons in his closet, but not publicly to vend them as cordials. And to this we may

---

[a] The art of printing, soon after it's introduction, was looked upon (as well in England as in other countries) as merely a matter of state, and subject to the coercion of the crown. It was therefore regulated with us by the king's proclamations, prohibitions, charters of privilege and of licence, and finally by the decrees of the court of starchamber; which limited the number of printers, and of presses which each should employ, and prohibited new publications unless previously approved by proper licensers. On the demolition of this odious jurisdiction in 1641, the long parliament of Charles I, after their rupture with that prince, assumed the same powers as the starchamber exercised with respect to the licensing of books; and in 1643, 1647, 1649, and 1652, (Scobell. i.44,134 ii.88, 230.) issued their ordinances for that purpose, founded principally on the starchamber decree of 1637. In 1662 was passed the statute 13 & 14 Car.II. c.33. which (with some few alterations) was copied from the parliamentary ordinances. This act expired in 1679, but was revived by statute 1 Jac.II. c.17. and continued till 1692. It was then continued for two years longer by statute 4 W. & M. c.24. but, though frequent attempts were made by the government to revive it, in the subsequent part of that reign, (Com. Journ. 11 Feb. 1694. 26 Nov. 1695. 22 Oct. 1696. 9 Feb. 1697. 31 Jan. 1698.) yet the parliament resisted it so strongly, that it finally expired, and the press became properly free, in 1694; and has ever since so continued.

add, that the only plausible argument heretofore used for retraining the just freedom of the press, "that it was necessary to prevent the "daily abuse of it," will entirely lose it's force, when it is shewn (by a seasonable exertion of the laws) that the press cannot be abused to any bad purpose, without incurring a suitable punishment: whereas it never can be used to any good one, when under the control of an inspector. So true will it be found, that to censure the licentiousness, is to maintain the liberty of the press.

BL7

Blackstone on Monopolies

A portion of Book 4, Chapter 12,
"Offences against Public Trade," pp. 159-160

9. Monopolies are much the same offence in other branches of trade, that engrossing is in provisions: being a licence or privilege allowed by the king for the sole buying and selling, making, working, or using, of any thing whatsoever; whereby the subject in general is restrained from that liberty of manufacturing or trading which he had before[n]. These had been carried to an enormous height during the reign of queen Elizabeth; and were heavily complained of by sir Edward Coke[o], in the beginning of the reign of king James the first: but were in great measure remedied by statute 21 Jac.I. c.3. which declares such monopolies to be contrary to law and void; (except as to patents, not exceeding the grant of fourteen years, to the authors of new inventions;) and monopolists are punished with the forfeiture of treble damages and double costs, to those whom they attempt to disturb; and if they procure any action, brought against them for these damages, to be stayed by any extrajudicial order, other than of the court wherein it is brought, they incur the penalties of *praemunire*. Combinations also among victuallers or artificers, to raise the price of provisions, or any commodities, or the rate of labour, are in many cases severely punished by particular statutes; and, in general, by statute 2 & 3 Edw.VI. c.15. with the forfeiture of 10 *l*, or twenty days imprisonment,

[n] 1 Hawk. P.C. 231.   [o] 3 Inst. 181.

with an allowance of only bread and water, for the first offence; 20 *l*. or the pillory, for the second; and 40 *l*. for the third, or else the pillory, loss of one ear, and perpetual infamy. In the same manner, by a constitution of the emperor Zeno[p], all monopolies and combinations to keep up the price of merchandize, provisions, or workmanship, were prohibited upon pain of forfeiture of goods and perpetual banishment.

[p] *Code*. 4.59.1.

A

Selected Chapters of the Magna Charta

Signed and Sealed at Runnymede, England on June 15, 1215.

Translated from the Original Latin Document
that is preserved in the Archives of Lincoln Cathedral.
Printed in London for John Major and Robert Jennings, 1829.
Reprinted by The Legal Classics Library, Division of Gryphon Editions, Ltd., Birmingham, Alabama, 1982.

The pronouns *we* and *our* refer to the king and his officers.

Chapter 20. A freeman shall not be amerced for a small offence, but only according to the degree of the offence; and for a great delinquency, according to the magnitude of the delinquency, saving his contenement: a Merchant shall be amerced in the same manner, saving his merchandise and a villain shall be amerced after the same manner, saving to him his Wainage, if he shall fall into our mercy; and none of the aforesaid amerciaments shall be assessed, but by the oath of honest men of the vicinage.

Chapter 38. No Bailiff, for the future, shall put any man to his law, upon his own simple affirmation, without credible witnesses produced for that purpose.

Chapter 39. No freeman shall be seized, or imprisoned, or dispossessed, or outlawed, or in any way destroyed; nor will we condemn him, nor will we commit him to prison, excepting by the legal judgment of his peers, or by the laws of the land.

Chapter 40. To none will we sell, to none will we deny, to none will we delay right or justice.

Chapter 52. If any have been disseised or dispossessed by us, without a legal verdict of their peers, of their lands, castles, liberties, or rights, we will immediately restore these things to them; and if any dispute shall arise on this head, then it shall be determined by the verdict of the twenty-five Barons, of whom mention is made below, for the security of the peace.--Concerning all those things of which any one hath been disseised or dispossessed, without the legal verdict of his peers by King Henry our father, or King Richard our brother, which we have in our hand, or others hold with our warrants, we shall have respite, until the common term of the Croisaders, excepting those concerning which a plea had been moved, or an inquisition taken, by our precept, before our taking the Cross; but as soon as we shall return from our expedition, or if, by chance, we should not go upon our expedition, we will immediately do complete justice therein.

B

The Petition of Right (1628)

To the King's Most Excellent Majesty

I. Humbly show unto our Sovereign Lord the King, the Lords Spiritual and Temporal, and Commons in Parliament assembled, that whereas it is declared and enacted by a statute made in the time of the reign of King Edward the First, commonly called *Statutum de tallagio no concedendo*, that no tallage or aid shall be laid or levied by the King or his heirs in this realm, without the good will and assent of the Archbishops, Bishops, Earls, Barons, Knights, Burgesses, and other freemen of the commonalty of this realm: and by authority of Parliament holden in the five and twentieth year of the reign of King Edward the Third, it is declared and enacted, that from thenceforth no person shall be compelled to make any loans to the King against his will, because such loans were against reason and the franchise of the land; and by other laws of this realm it is provided, that none should be charged by and charge or imposition, called a Benevolence, nor by such like charge: by which, the statute before-mentioned, and other good laws and statutes of this realm, your subjects have inherited this freedom, that they should not be compelled to contribute to any tax, tallage, aid, or other like charge, not set by common consent in Parliament:

II. Yet nevertheless, of late divers commissions directed to sundry Commissioners in several counties, with instructions, have issued by means whereof your people have been in divers places assembled, and required to lend certain sums of money unto your Majesty, and many of them upon their refusal so to do, have had an oath administered unto them, not warrantable by the laws or statutes of this realm, and have been constrained to become bound to make appearance and give attendance before your Privy Council, and in other places, and others of them have been therefore imprisoned, confined, and sundry other ways molested and disquieted: and divers other charges have been laid and levied upon your people in several counties by Lords Lieutenants, Deputy Lieutenants, Commissioners for Musters, Justices of Peace and others, by command or direction from your Majesty or your Privy Council, against the laws and free customs of this realm.

III. And where also by the statute called, 'The Great Charter of the Liberties of England,' it is declared and enacted, that no freeman may be taken or imprisoned or be disseised of his freehold or liberties, or his free customs, or be outlawed or exiled, or in any manner destroyed, but by the lawful judgment of his peers, or by the law of the land:

IV. And in the eight and twentieth year of the reign of King Edward the Third, it was declared and enacted by authority of Parliament, that no man of what estate or condition that he be, should be put out of his lands or tenements, nor taken, nor imprisoned, nor disinherited, nor put to death, without being brought to answer by due process of law:

V. Nevertheless, against the tenor of the said statutes, and other good laws and statutes of your realm, to that end provided, divers of your subjects have of late been imprisoned without any cause showed, and when for their deliverance they were brought before your Justices, by your Majesty's writs of Habeas Corpus, there to undergo and receive as the Court should order, and their keepers commanded to certify the causes of their detainer; no cause was certified, but that they were detained by your Majesty's special command, signified by the Lords of your Privy Council, and yet were returned back to several prisons, without being charged with anything to which they might make answer according to the law.

VI. And whereas of late great companies of soldiers and mariners have been dispersed into divers counties of the realm, and the inhabitants against their wills have been compelled to receive them into their houses, and there to suffer them to sojourn, against the laws and customs of this realm, and to the great grievance and vexation of the people.

VII. And whereas also by authority of Parliament, in the 25th year of the reign of King Edward the Third, it is declared and enacted, that no man shall be forejudged of life or limb against the form of the Great Charter, and the law of the land; and by the Great Charter and other laws and statutes of this your realm, no man ought to be adjudged to death, but by the laws established in this your realm, either by the customs of the same realm or by Acts of Parliament: and whereas no offender of what kind soever is exempted from the proceedings to be used, and punishments to be inflicted by the laws and statutes of this your realm; nevertheless of late divers commissions under your Majesty's Great Seal have issued forth, by which certain persons have been assigned and appointed Commissioners with power and authority to proceed within the land, according to the justice of martial law against such soldiers and mariners, or other dissolute persons joining with them, as should commit any murder, robbery, felony, mutiny, or other outrage or misdemeanor whatsoever, and by such summary course and order, as is agreeable to martial law, and is used in armies in time of war, to proceed to the trial and condemnation of such offenders, and them to cause to be executed and put to death according to the law martial:

VIII. By pretext whereof, some of your Majesty's subjects have been by some of the said Commissioners put to death, when and where, if by the laws and statutes of the land they had deserved death, by the same laws and statutes also they might, and by no other ought to have been, adjudged and executed:

IX. And also sundry grievous offenders by color thereof, claiming an exemption, have escaped the punishments due to them by the laws and statutes of this your realm, by reason that divers of your officers and ministers of justice have unjustly refused, or forborne to proceed against such offenders according to the same laws and statutes, upon pretence that the said offenders were punishable only by martial law, and by authority of such commissions as aforesaid; which commissions, and all other of like nature, are wholly and directly contrary to the said laws and statutes of this your realm.

X. They do therefore humbly pray your Most Excellent Majesty, that no man hereafter be compelled to make or yield any gift, loan, benevolence, tax, or such like charge, without common consent by Act of Parliament; and that none be called to make answer, or take such oath, or to give attendance, or be confined, or otherwise molested or disquieted concerning the same, or for refusal thereof; and that no freeman, in any such manner as is before-mentioned, be imprisoned or detained; and that your Majesty will be pleased to remove the said soldiers and mariners, and that your people may not be so burdened in time to come; and that the aforesaid commissions for proceeding by martial law, may be revoked and annulled; and that hereafter no commissions of like nature may issue forth to any person or persons whatsoever, to be executed as aforesaid, lest by color of them any of your Majesty's subjects be destroyed or put to death, contrary to the laws and franchise of the land.

XI. All which they most humbly pray of your Most Excellent Majesty, as their rights and liberties according to the laws and statutes of this realm: and that your Majesty would also vouchsafe to declare, that the awards, doings, and proceedings to the prejudice of your people, in any of the premises, shall not be drawn hereafter into consequence or example: and that your Majesty would be also graciously pleased, for the further comfort and safety of your people, to declare your royal will and pleasure, that in the things aforesaid all your officers and ministers shall serve you, according to the laws and statutes of this realm, as they tender the honor of your Majesty, and the prosperity of this kingdom.

C

The Massachusetts Body of Liberties (Selected Sections)

Enacted by the General Court, December 10, 1641
Drafted by the Reverend Nathaniel Ward, Ipswich Congregational Church

Includes References to Similar Provisions of the U.S. Constitution

The free fruition of such liberties Immunities and Privileges as humanitie, Civilitie, and Christianitie call for as due to every man in his place and proportion without the tranquillitie and Stabilitie of Churches and Commonwealths. And the deniall or deprivall thereof, the disturbance if not the ruine of both.

We hould it therefore our dutie and safetie whilst we are about the further establishing of this Government to collect and expresse all such freedoms as for present we foresee may concerne us, and our posteritie after us, And to ratify them with our sollemne consent.

We doe therefore this day religiously and unanimously decree and confirme these following Rites, liberties and privileges concerning our Churches, and Civill State to be respectively impartiallie and inviolably enjoyed and observed throughout our Jurisdiction for ever.

 1. No mans life shall be taken away, no mans honour or good name shall be stayned, no mans person shall be arrested, restrayned, banished, dismembred, nor any wayes punished, no man shall be deprived of his wife or children, no mans goods or estaite shall be taken away from him, nor any way indammaged under colour of law or Countenance of Authoritie, unlesse it be by vertue or equitie of some expresse law of the Country warranting the same, established by a generall Court and sufficiently published, or in case of the defect of a law in any particuler case by the word of god. And in all Capitall cases, or in cases concerning dismembring or banishment, according to that word to be judged by the General Court. (Amends. 5 & 14, "life, liberty or property" clauses)

 2. Every person within this jurisdiction, whether Inhabitant or forreiner shall enjoy the same justice and law, that is generall for the plantation, which we constitute and execute one towards another without partialitie or delay. (Amend. 14, "equal protection" clause)

 3. No man shall be urged to take any oath or subscribe any articles, covenants or remonstrance, of a publique and Civill nature, but such as the Generall Court hath considered, allowed, and required. (Art. VI, cl. 3)

 7. No man shall be compelled to goe out of the limits of this plantation upon any offensive warres which this Commonwealth or any of our friends or confederats shall voluntarily undertake. But onely upon such vindictive and defensive warres in our owne behalfe or the behalfe of our friends and

confederates as shall be enterprized by the Counsell and consent of a Court generall, or by Authority derived from the same.

8. No mans Cattel or goods of what kinde soever shall be pressed or taken for any publique use or service, unlesse it be by warrant grounded upon some act of the generall Court, nor without such reasonable prices and hire as the ordinarie rates of the Countrie do afford. And if his Cattel or goods shall perish or suffer damage in such service, the owner shall be sufficiently recompenced. (Amend. 5, "nor shall private property be taken for public use" clause)

9. No monopolies shall be granted or allowed amongst us, but of such new Inventions that are profitable to the Countrie, and that for a short time.

12. Every man whether Inhabitant or fforreiner, free or not free shall have libertie to come into any publique Court, Councel, or Towne meeting, and either by speech or writeing to move any lawfull, seasonable, and materiall question or to present any necessary motion, complaint, petition, Bill or information, whereof that meeting hath proper congnizance, so it be done in convenient time, due order, and respective manner. (Amend. 1, "right to petition" clause)

17. Every man of or within this Jurisdiction shall have free libertie, not withstanding any Civill power to remove both himselfe, and his familie at their pleasure out of the same, provided there is no legal impediment to the contrarie.

Rites Rules and Liberties concerning Juditiall proceedings.

18. No mans person shall be restrained or imprisoned by any Authority whatsoever, before the law hath sentenced him thereto, If he can put in sufficient securitie, bayle or mainprise, for his appearance, and good behaviour in the meane time, unlesse it be in Crimes Capital, and Contempts in open Court, and in such cases where some expresse act of Court doth allow it. (Amend. 8, "excessive bail" clause)

23. No man shall be adjudged to pay for detaining any debt from any Creditor above eight pounds in the hundred for one yeare, And not above that rate proportionable for all somes what so ever, neither shall this be a coulour or countenance to allow any usurie amongst us contrarie to the law of god.

26. Every man that findeth himself unfit to plead his own cause in any Court shall have Libertie to imploy any man against whom the Court doth not except, to helpe him, Provided he give him noe fee or reward for his paines. This shall not exempt the partie him selfe from Answering such Questions in person as the Court shall thinke meet to demand of him. (Amend. 6, "assistance of counsel" clause)

29. In all Actions at law it shall be the libertie of the plantife and defendant by mutual consent to choose whether they will be tryed by the Bench or by Jurie, unlesse it be where the law upon just reason hath otherwise determined. (Amend. 7) The like libertie shall be granted all persons in Criminall cases. (Art. III, Sec. 3[3] & Amend. 6, "impartial jury" clause)

C: The Massachusetts Body of Liberties

41. Everie man that is to Answere for any Criminall cause, whether he be in prison or under bayle, his cause shall be heard and determined at the next Court that hath proper Cognizance thereof, And may be done without prejudice of Justice. (Amend. 6, "speedy and public trial" clause)

42. No man shall be twise sentenced by Civill Justice for one and the same Crime, offence, or Trespasse. (Amend. 5, "double jeopardy" clause)

43. No man shall be beaten above 40 stripes, nor shall any true gentleman, nor any man equall to a gentleman be punished with whipping, unles his crime be very shamefull, and his course of life vitious andd profligate. (Amend. 8, "cruel and unusual punishments" clause)

45. No man shall be forced by Torture to confesse any Crime against himself nor any other unlesse it be in some Capitall case where he is first fullie convicted by cleare and sufficient evidence to be guilty, After which if the cause be of that nature, That it is very apparent there be other conspiratours, or confederates with him, Then he may be tortured, yet not with such Torture as be Barbarous and inhumane. (Amend. 5, "self incriminataion" and "life, liberty, or property" clauses & Amend. 8, "cruel and unusual punishments" clause)

46. For bodilie punishments we allow amongst us none that are inhumane Barbarous or cruel. (Amend. 8, "cruel and unusual punishments" clause)

47. No man shall be put to death without the testimony of two or three witnesses or that which is equivalent thereto. (Art. III, Sec. 3[1] requires two witnesses to convict a person of treason, a crime usually punishable by death)

53. The age of discretion for passing away lands or such kinde of herediments, or for gieving votes, verdicts or Sentence in any Civill Courts or causes, shall be one and twentie years. (Amend. 26 sets the voting age at 18 years)

Liberties more peculiarlie concerning free men.
(Compare these sections with Amend. 1,
"establishment of religion" and "free exercise" clauses)

58. Civill Authoritie hath power and libertie to see the peace, ordinances and Rules of Christ observed in every church according to his word, so it be done in a Civill and not in an Ecclesiastical way.

59. Civill Authoritie hath power and libertie to deale with any Church member in a way of Civill Justice, notwithstanding any Church relation, office or interest.

60. No church censure shall degrad of depose any man from any Civill dignitie, office, or Authoritie he shall have in the Commonwealth.

61. No Magistrate, Juror, Officer, or other man shall be bound to inform present or reveale any private crime or offence, wherein there is no perill or danger to this plantation or any member thereof, when any necessarie tye of conscience binds him to secresie grounded upon the word of god, unlesse it be in case of testimony lawfully required.

62. No custome or prescription shall ever prevail amongst us in any morall cause, our meaneing is maintaine anythinge than can be proved to bee morrallie sinfull by the word of god.

75. It is and shall be the libertie of any member or members of any Court, Counsell or Civill Assembly in cases of makeing or executing any order or law, that properlie concerne religion, or any cause capitall, or warres, or Subscription to any publique Articles or Remonstrance, in case they cannot in Judgement and conscience consent to that way the Major vote or suffrage goes, to make their contra Remonstrance or protestation in speech and writeing, and upon request to have their dissent recorded in the Rolles of that Court. So it be done Christianlie and respectively for the manner. And their dissent onely be entered without the reasons thereof, for the avoiding of tediousness. (Amend. 1, "free exercise," "freedom of speech" & "petition for redress of grievances" clauses)

Liberties of Children

83. If any parents shall wilfullie and unreasonably deny any childe timely or convenient mariage, or shall exercise any unnaturall severitie towards them, such children shall have free libertie to complaine to Authoritie for redress.

Liberties of Servants

85. If any servants shall flee from the Tiranny and cruelty of their masters to the howse of any freeman of the same Towne, they shall be there protected and susteyned till due order taken for their relise. Provided due notice thereof be speedily given to their maisters from whom they fled. And the next Assistant or Constable where the partie flying is harboured.

86. No servant shall be put out for above a yeare to any other neither in the life time of their maister nor after their death by their Executors of Administrators unlesse it be by consent of Authoritie assembled in some Court or two Assistants.

87. If any man smite out the eye or tooth of his man-servant, or maid-servant, or otherwise mayme or much disfigure him, unless it be by meare casualtie, he shall let them goe free from his service. And shall have such further recompense as the Court shall allow him.

88. Servants that have served diligently and faithfully to the benefit of their maisters seaven years, shall not be sent away emptie. And if any have bene unfaithfull, negligent or unprofitable in their service, notwithstanding the good usage of their maisters, they shall not be dismissed till they have made satisfaction according to the Judgement of the Authoritie.

Liberties of Forreigners and Strangers.

89. If any people of other Nations professing the true Christian Religion shall flee to us from the Tiranny or oppression of their persecutors, or from famyne,

warres, or the like necessary and compulsarie cause, They shall be entertayned and succoured amongst us, according to that power and prudence god shall give us.

90. If any ships or other vessels, be it freind or enemy, shall suffer shipwreck upon our Coast, there shall be no violence or wrong offered to their persons or goods. But their persons shall be harboured, and relieved, and their goods preserved in safety till Authoritie may be certified thereof, and shall take further order therein.

91. There shall never be any bond slaverie, villinage or Captivitie amongst us unles it be lawful Captives taken in just warres, and such strangers was willingly selle themselves or are sold to us. And these shall have all the liberties and Christian usages which the law of god established in Israel concerning such persons doeth morally require. Theis exempts none from servitude who shall be Judged thereto by Authoritie. (Art. IV, Sec 2[3] & Amend. 13)

94. Capitall Laws.

1. If any man after legall conviction shall have or worship any other god, but the lord god, he shall be put to death. *Exo. 22:20; Deut. 13:6, 10; Deut. 17:2, 6.*

2. If any man or woeman be a witch (that is hath or consulteth with a familiar spirit,) They shall be put to death. *Exo. 22:18; Lev. 20:27; Deut. 18:10.*

3. If any man shall Blaspheme the name of god, the father, Sonne or Holie ghost, with direct, expresse, presumptuous or high-handed blasphemie, or shall curse god in the like manner, he shall be put to death. *Lev. 24:15-16.*

4. If any person committ any wilfull murther, which is manslaughter, committed upon premeditated mallice, hatred, or Crueltie, not in mans necessarie and just defense, nor by meere casualtie against his will, he shall be put to death. *Exo. 21:12; Num. 35:13, 14, 30, 31.*

5. If any person slayeth an other suddaienly in his anger or Cureltie of passion, he shall be put to death. *Num. 25:20-21; Lev. 24:17.*

6. If any person shall slay an other through guile, either by poisoning or other such divelish practice, he shall be put to death. *Exo. 21:14.*

7. If any man or woeman shall lyeth with any beaste or bruite creature by Carnall Copulation, They shall surely be put to death. And the beast shall be slaine and buried and not eaten. *Lev. 20:15-16.*

8. If any man lyeth with mankinde as he lyeth with a woeman, both of them have committed abbomination, they shall both surely be put to death. *Lev. 18:20; Lev. 20:19; Deut. 22:23-24.*

9. If any person committeth Adultery with a maried or espoused wife, the Adulterer and Adulteresse shall surely be put to death. *Lev. 18:20; Lev. 20:19; Deut. 22:23-24.*

10. If any man stealeth a man or mankinde, he shall surely be put to death. *Exo. 21:16.*

11. If any man rise up by false witnes, wittingly and of purpose to take away any mans life, he shall be put to death. *Deut. 19:16, 18, 19.*

12. If any man shall conspire and attempt any invasion, insurrection, or publique rebellion against our commonwealth, or shall endeavor to surprize any Towne or Townes, fort or forts therein, or shall treacherously and perfediouslie attempt the alteration and subversion of our frame of politie or Government fundamentallie, he shall be put to death. (Art. III, Sec. 3)

95. A Declaration of the Liberties
the Lord Jesus hath given the Churches.
(Compare Amend. 1, "free exercise" clause)

1. All the people of god within this Jursidiction who are not in a church way, and be orthodox in Judgment, and not scandalous in life, shall have full libertie to gather themselves into a Church Estaite. Provided they doe it in a Christian way, with due observation of the rules of Christ revealed in his word.

2. Every Church hath full libertie to exercise all the ordinances of god, according to the rules of scripture.

3. Every Church hath free libertie and Election and ordination of all their officers from time to time, provided they be able, pious and orthodox.

4. Every Church hath free libertie of Admission, Recommendation, Dismission, and Expulsion, or deposall of their officers and members, upon due cause, with free exercise of the Discipline and Censures of Christ according to the rules of his word.

5. No Injunctions are to be put upon any Church, Church officers or members in point of Doctrine, worship or Discipline, whether for substance or cercumstance besides the Institutions of the lord.

6. Every Church of Christ hath freedome to celebrate dayes of fasting and prayer, and of thanksgiving according to the word of god.

7. The Elders of Churches have free liberty to meete monthly, Quarterly, or otherwise, in convenient numbers and places, for conferences and consultations about Christian and Church questions and occasions.

8. All Churches have libertie to deale with any of their members in a church way that are in hand of Justice. So it be not to retard or hinder the course thereof.

9. Every Church hath libertie to deale with any magistrate, Deputie of Court or other officer what soe ever that is a member in a church way in case of apparent and just offence given in their places, so it be done with due observance and respect.

10. Wee allowe private meetings for edification in religion amongst Christians of all sortes of people. So it be without just offence for number, time, place, and other cercumstances. (Amend. 1, *right of the people to peaceably assemble* clause)

D

Agreement Proposed by the Levellers (Selected Sections)
Tendered in 1647 as a Peace Offering
during the Negotiations between Oliver Cromwell and King Charles I
by John Lilburne, William Walwyn, Thomas Prince, and Richard Overton

We the free People of England, to whom God hath given hearts, means and opportunity to effect the same, do with submission to His wisdom, in His name, and desiring the equity thereof may be to His praise and glory; Agree to ascertain our government, to abolish all arbitrary power, and to set bounds and limits to our supreme, and all subordinate authority, and remove all known grievances.

And accordingly do declare and publish to all the world, that we are agreed as follows,

I. That the supreme authority of England and territories therewith incorporated, shall be and reside henceforward in a Representative of the people consisting of four hundred persons, but no more; in the choice of whom (according to natural right) all men of the age of one and twenty years and upwards (not being servants, or receiving alms, or having served the late King in arms or voluntary contributions) shall have their voices; and be capable of being elected to that supreme trust, those who served the King being disabled for ten years only. All things concerning the distribution of the said four hundred members proportionable to the respective parts of the nation, the several places for election, the manner of giving and taking votes, with all circumstances of like nature, tending to the completing and equal proceedings in elections, as also their salary, is referred to be settled by this present Parliament, in such sort as the next Representative may be in a certain capacity to meet with safety at the time herein expressed: and such circumstances to be made perfect by future Representatives.

IV. That no member of the present Parliament shall be capable of being elected of the next Representative, nor any member of any future Representative shall be capable of being chosen for the Representative immediately succeeding: but are free to be chosen, one Representative having intervened: Nor shall any member of any Representative be made either receiver, treasurer, or other officer during that employment.

VIII. And for the preservation of the supreme authority (in all times) entirely in the hands of such persons only as shall be chosen thereunto---we agree and declare: That the next and all future Representatives, shall continue in full power for the space of one whole year: and that the people shall of course, choose a Parliament once every year, so as all the members thereof may be in a capacity to meet, and take the place of the foregoing Representative: the first Thursday in every August for ever if God so please; Also (for the same reason) that the next or any future Representative being met, shall continue their session day by day without intermission for four months at least; and after that shall be at liberty to adjourn from two months to two months, as they shall see cause until their year be expired, but shall sit no longer than a year upon pain of treason to every member that shall exceed that time: and in times of adjournment shall not erect a Council of State but refer the managing of affairs in the intervals to a Committee of their own members giving such instructions, and publish them, as shall in no measure contradict this agreement.

X. That we do not empower or entrust our said representatives to continue in force, or to make any laws, oaths, or covenants, whereby to compel by penalties or otherwise any person to any thing in or about matters of faith, religion or God's worship or to restrain any person from the profession of his faith, or exercise of religion according to his conscience, nothing having caused more distractions, and heart burnings in all ages, than persecution and molestation for matters of conscience in and about religion.

XIV. We do not empower them to give judgment upon anyone's person or estate, where no law hath been before provided, nor to give power to any other court or jurisdiction so to do, because where there is no law, there is no transgression, for men or magistrates to take cognisance of; neither do we empower them to intermeddle with the execution of any law whatsoever.

We agree and declare,

XVI. That it shall not be in the power of any Representative, to punish, or cause to be punished, any person or persons for refusing to answer to questions against themselves in criminal cases.

XVII. That it shall not be in their power, after the end of the next Representative, to continue or constitute any proceedings in law that shall be longer than six months in the final determination of any cause past all appeal, nor to continue the laws or proceedings therein in any other language than English, nor to hinder any person or person from pleading their own causes, or of making use of whom they please to plead for them.

XXI. That it shall not be in their power to make or continue any law, for taking away any man's life, except in murder, or other like heinous offenses destructive to humane society, or for endeavoring by force to destroy this our Agreement, but shall use their uttermost endeavor to appoint punishments equal to offenses; that so men's lives, limbs, liberties, and estates, may not be liable to be taken away upon trivial or slight occasions as they have been; and shall have special care to preserve, all sorts of people from wickedness, misery, and

D: *Agreement Proposed by the Levellers*

beggary: nor shall the estate of any capital offender be confiscated but in cases of treason only; and in all other capital offenses recompense shall be made to the parties damnified, as well out of the estate of the malefactor, as by loss of life, according to the conscience of his jury.

XXII. That it shall not be in their power to continue or make any law, to deprive any person, in case of trials for life, limb, liberty, or estate, from the benefit of witnesses, on his, or their behalf; nor deprive any person of those privileges, and liberties, contained in the *Petition of Right*, made in the third year of the late King Charles.

XXIII. That it shall not be in their power to continue the grievance of tithes, longer than to the end of the next Representative; in which time, they shall provide to give reasonable satisfaction to all impropriators: neither shall they force by penalties or otherwise, any person to pay towards the maintenance of any ministers, who out of conscience cannot submit thereunto.

XXIV. That it shall not be in their power to impose ministers upon any of the respective parishes, but shall give free liberty to the parishioners of every particular parish, to choose such as themselves approve; and upon such terms, and for such reward, as themselves shall be willing to contribute, or shall contract for. Provided, non be choosers but such as are capable of electing Representatives.

XXV. That it shall not be in their power, to continue or make a law, for any other way of judgments, or conviction of life, limb, liberty, or estate, but only by twelve sworn men of the neighborhood; to be chosen in some free way by the people; to be directed before the end of the next Representative, and not picked and imposed, and not picked and imposed, as hitherto in many places they have been.

XXVI. They shall not disable any person from bearing any office in the Commonwealth, for any opinion or practice in religion, excepting such as maintain the Pope's (or other foreign) supremacy.

E

The English Declaration of Rights (1689)
(to the end of the declaration of the specific grievances and rights)

Clauses relating to grievances in the American Declaration of Independence and/or rights proclaimed in the U. S. Constitution are shown in **bold print**.

Whereas the Lords Spiritual and Temporal and Commons assembled at Westminster, lawfully, fully and freely representing the states of the people of this realm, did upon the thirteenth day of February in the year of our Lord one thousand six hundred eighty-nine present unto their Majesties, then called and known by the names and style of William and Mary, prince and princess of Orange, being present in their proper persons, a certain declaration in writing made by the said Lords and Commons in the words following, viz.:

Whereas the late King James the Second, by the assistance of divers evil counsellors, judges and ministers employed by him, did endeavor to subvert and extirpate the Protestant religion and the laws and liberties of this kingdom;

By assuming and exercizing a power of dispensing with and suspending of laws and the execution of laws without consent of Parliament;

By committing and prosecution divers worthy prelates for humbly petitioning to be excused from concurring to the said assumed power;

By issuing and causing to be executed a commission under the great seal for erecting a court called the Court of Commissioners for Ecclesiastical Causes;

By levying money for and to the use of the Crown by pretence of prerogative for other time and in other manner than the same was granted by Parliament;

By raising and keeping a standing army within this kingdom in time of peace without consent of Parliament, and quartering soldiers contrary to law;

By causing several good subjects being Protestants to be disarmed at the same time when papists were both armed and employed contrary to law;

By violating the freedom of election of members to serve in Parliament;

By prosecutions in the Court of King's Bench for matters and causes cognizable only in Parliament, and by divers other arbitrary and other illegal courses;

And whereas of late years partial corrupt and unqualified persons have been returned and served on juries in trials, and particularly divers jurors in trials for high treason which were not freeholders;

And excessive bail hath been required of persons committed in criminal cases to elude the benefit of the laws made for the liberty of the subjects;

And excessive fines have been imposed;

And illegal and cruel punishments inflicted;

And several grants and promises made of fines and forfeitures before any conviction or judgment against the persons upon whom the same were levied;

All which are utterly and directly contrary to the known laws and statute and freedom of this realm.

E: The English Declaration of Rights

And whereas the said late King James the Second having abdicated the government and the throne being thereby vacant, his Highness the prince of Orange (whom it hath pleased Almighty God to make the glorious instrument of delivering this kingdom from popery and arbitrary power) did (by the advice of the Lords Spiritual and Temporal and divers principal persons of the Commons) cause letters to be written to the Lords Spiritual and Temporal being Protestants, and other letters to the several counties, cities, universities, boroughs and cinque ports, for the choosing of such persons to represent them as were of right to be sent to Parliament, to meet and sit at Westminster upon the two and twentieth day of February of this year one thousand six hundred and eighty nine, in order to such an establishment as that their religion, laws and liberties might not again be in danger of being subverted, upon which letters elections having been accordingly made;

And thereupon the said Lords Spiritual and Temporal and Commons, pursuant to their respective letters and elections, being now assembled in a full and free representative of this nation, taking into their most serious consideration the best means for attaining the ends aforesaid, do in the first place (as their ancestors in like case have usually done) for the vindicating and asserting their ancient rights and liberties declare

That the pretended power of dispensing with laws or the execution of laws by regal authority, as it hath been assumed and exercised of late, is illegal;

That the commissions for erecting the late Court of Commissioners for Ecclesiastical Causes, and all other commissions and courts of like nature, are illegal and pernicious;

That levying money for or to the use of the Crown by pretence of prerogative, without grant of Parliament, for longer time, or in other manner than the same is or shall be granted, is illegal;

That the raising or keeping a standing army within the kingdom in time of peace, unless it be with the consent of Parliament, is against the law;

That the subjects which are Protestants may have arms for their defence suitable to their conditions and as allowed by law;

That election of members of Parliament ought to be free;

That the freedom of speech and debates or proceedings in Parliament ought not to be impeached or questioned in any court or place out of Parliament;

That excessive bail ought not to be required, nor excessive fines imposed, nor cruel and unusual punishments inflicted;

That jurors ought to be duly impanelled and returned, and jurors which pass upon men in trials for high treason ought to be freeholders;

That all grants and promises of fines and forfeitures of particular persons before conviction are illegal and void;

And that for redress of all grievances, and for the amending, strengthening and preserving of the laws, Parliaments ought to be held frequently.

F

Locke on Civil Government and Religion

Second Essay Concerning Civil Government (1690)
Chapters I to IV, IX & XI

CHAPTER I

1. It having been shown in the forgoing discourse:[1]
(1) That Adam had not, either by natural right of fatherhood or by positive donation from God, any such authority over his children or dominion over the world as is pretended.
(2) That if he had, his heirs yet had no right to it.
(3) That if his heirs had, there being no law of nature nor positive law of God that determines which is the right heir in all cases that may arise, the right of succession, and consequently of bearing rule, could not have been certainly determined.
(4) That if even that had been determined, yet the knowledge of which is the eldest line of Adam's posterity being so long since utterly lost that the races of mankind and families of the world there remains not to one above another the least pretense to be the eldest house, and to have the right of inheritance.

All these premises having, as I think, been clearly made out, it is impossible that the rulers now on earth should make any benefit or derive any the least shadow of authority from that which is held to be the fountain of all power: Adam's private dominion and paternal jurisdiction; so that he that will not give just occasion to think that all government in the world is the product only of force and violence, and that men live together by no other rules but that of beasts, where the strongest carries it, and so lay a foundation for perpetual disorder, mischief, tumult, sedition and rebellion--things that the followers of that hypothesis so loudly cry out against--must of necessity find out another rise of government, another original of political power, and another way of designing and knowing the persons that have it than what Sir Robert Filmer has taught us.

2. To this purpose, I think it may not be amiss to set down what I take to be political power; that the power of a magistrate over a subject may be distinguished from that of a father over his children, a master over his servants, a husband over his wife, and a lord over his slave. All of which distinct powers happening sometimes together in the same man, if he be considered under these different relations, it may help us to distinguish these powers one from the other, and show the difference betwixt a rule of a commonwealth, a father of a family, and a captain of a galley.

---

[1] [Locke's *First Treatise Concerning Civil Goverment* (1690)]

3. Political power, then, I take to be a right of making laws with penalties of death and, consequently, all less penalties for the regulating and preserving of property,[2] and of employing the force of the community in the execution of such laws and in the defense of the commonwealth from foreign injury; and all this only for the public good.

CHAPTER II, Of the State of Nature

4. To understand political power right and derive it from its original, we must consider what state all men are naturally in, and that is a state of perfect freedom to order their actions and dispose of their possessions and persons as they think fit, within the bounds of the law of nature, without asking leave or depending upon the will of any other man.

A state also of equality, wherein all the power and jurisdiction is reciprocal, no one having more than another; **there being nothing more evident than that creatures of the same species and rank, promiscuously born to all the same advantages of nature and the use of the same faculties, should also be equal one amongst another without subordination or subjection;** unless the lord and master of them all should, by any manifest declaration of his will, set one above another, and confer on him by an evident and clear appointment an undoubted right to dominion and sovereignty.

5. This equality of men by nature the judicious Hooker looks upon as so evident in itself and beyond all question that he makes it the foundation of that obligation to mutual love amongst men on which he builds the duties we owe one another, from whence he derives the great maxims of justice and charity. His words are:

> The like natural inducement hath brought men to know that it is no less their duty to love others than themselves; for seeing those things which are equal must needs all have one measure; if I cannot but wish to receive good, even as much at every man's hands as any man can wish unto his own soul, how should I look to have any part of my desire herein satisfied unless myself be careful to satisfy the like desire, which is undoubtedly in other men, being of one and the same nature? To have anything offered them repugnant to this desire must needs in all respects grieve them as much as me; so that, if I do harm, I must look to suffer, there being no reason that others should show greater measure of love to me than they have by me showed unto them; my desire therefore to be loved of my equals in nature, as much as possibly may be, imposeth upon me a natural duty of bearing to them-ward fully the like affection; from which relation of equality between ourselves and them that are as ourselves, what several rules and canons natural reason hath drawn, for direction of life, no man is ignorant. (*Eccl. Pol.* lib. i.).

---

[2] [See Section 123, infra, in which Locke says that he calls the "lives, liberties, and estates" of men "by the general name 'property.'"]

6. But though this be a state of liberty, yet it is not a state of license; though man in that state have an uncontrollable liberty to dispose of his person or possessions, yet he is not at liberty to destroy himself, or so much as any creature in his possession, but where some nobler use than its bare preservation calls for it. **The state of nature has a law of nature to govern it, which obliges everyone; and reason, which is that law, teaches all mankind who will but consult it that, being all equal and independent, no one ought to harm another in his life, health, liberty, or possessions;** for men being all the workmanship of one omnipotent and infinitely wise Maker--all the servants of one sovereign master, sent into the world by his order, and about his business--they are his property whose workmanship they are, made to last during his, not one another's pleasure; and being furnished with like faculties, sharing all in one community of nature, there cannot be supposed any such subordination among us that may authorize us to destroy another, as if we were made for one another's uses as the inferior ranks of creatures are for ours. Every one, as he is bound to preserve himself and not to quit his station wilfully, so by the like reason, when his own preservation comes not in competition, ought he, as much as he can, to preserve the rest of mankind, and may not, unless it be to do justice to an offender, take away or impair the life, or what tends to the preservation of the life, the liberty, health, limb, or goods of another.

7. **And that all men may be restrained from invading others' rights and from doing hurt to one another, and the law of nature be observed, which wills the peace and preservation of all mankind, the execution of the law of nature is, in that state, put into every man's hands, whereby everyone has a right to punish the transgressors of that law to such a degree as may hinder its violation;** for the law of nature would, as all other laws that concern men in this world, be in vain if there were nobody that in that state of nature had a power to execute that law and thereby preserve the innocent and restrain the offenders. And if anyone in the state of nature may punish another for any evil he has done, everyone may do so; for in a state of perfect equality, where naturally there is no superiority or jurisdiction of one over another, what any may do in prosecution of that law, everyone must needs have a right to do.

8. And thus in the state of nature one man comes by a power over another; but yet no absolute or arbitrary power to use a criminal, when he has got him in his hands, according to the passionate heats or boundless extravagance of his own will; but only to retribute to him, so far as calm and conscience dictate, what is proportionate to his transgression, which is so much as may serve for reparation and restraint; for these two are the only reasons why one man may lawfully do harm to another, which is that we call punishment. In transgressing the law of nature, the offender declares himself to live by another rule than that of reason and common equity, which is that measure God has set to the actions of men for their mutual security; and so he becomes dangerous to mankind, the tie which is to secure them from injury and violence being slighted and broken by him. Which being a trespass against the whole species and the peace and safety of it provided for by the law of nature, every man upon this score, by the right he has to preserve mankind in general, may restrain, or, where it is necessary, destroy

things noxious to them, and so may bring such evil on any one who has transgressed that law, as may make him repent the doing of it and thereby deter him, and by his example others, from doing the like mischief. And in this case, and upon this ground, *every man has a right to punish the offender and be the executioner of the law of nature.*

9. I doubt not but this will seem a very strange doctrine to some men; but before they condemn it, I desire them to resolve me by what right any prince or state can put to death or punish any alien for any crime he commits in their country. It is certain their laws, by virtue of any sanction they receive from the promulgated will of the legislative, reach not a stranger; they speak not to him, nor, if they did, he is bound to hearken to them. The legislative authority, by which they are in force over the subjects of that commonwealth, has no power over him. Those who have the supreme power of making laws in England, France, or Holland, are to an Indian but like the rest of the world--men without authority; and therefore, if by the law of nature every man has not a power to punish offenses against it as he soberly judges the case to require, I see not how the magistrates of any community can punish an alien of another country, since, in reference to him, they can have no more power than what every man naturally have over another.

10. Besides the crime which consists in violating the law and varying from the right rule of reason, whereby a man so far becomes degenerate and declares himself to quit the principles of human nature and to be a noxious creature, there is commonly injury done to some person or other, and some other man receives damage by this transgression; in which case he who has received any damage has, besides the right of punishment common to him with other men, a particular right to seek reparation from him that has done it; and any other person, who finds it just, may also join with him that is injured and assist him in recovering from the offender so much as may make satisfaction for the harm he has suffered.

11. From these two distinct rights--the one of punishing the crime for restraint and preventing the like offense, which right of punishing is in everybody; the other of taking reparation, which belongs only to the injured party--comes it to pass that the magistrate, who by being magistrate has the common right of punishing put into his hands, can often, where the public good demands not the execution of the law, remit the punishment of criminal offenses by his own authority, but yet cannot remit the satisfaction due to any private man for the damage he has received. That he who has suffered the damage has a right to demand in his own name, and he alone can remit; the damnified person has this power of appropriating to himself the goods or service of the offender by right of self-preservation, as every man has a power to punish the crime to prevent its being committed again, by the right he has of preserving all mankind and doing all reasonable thing he can in order to that end; and thus it is that every man, in the state of nature, has a power to kill a murderer, both to deter others from doing the like injury, which no reparation can compensate, by the example of the punishment that attends it from everybody, and also to secure men from the attempts of a criminal who, having renounced reason--the common rule and measure God has given to mankind--has, by the unjust violence and slaughter he

has committed upon one, declared war against all mankind, and therefore may be destroyed as a lion or a tiger, one of those wild savage beasts with whom men can have no society nor security. And upon this is grounded that great law of nature, "Whoso sheddeth man's blood, by man shall his blood be shed." And Cain was so fully convinced that every one had a right to destroy such a criminal that, after the murder of his brother, he cries out, "Every one that findeth me shall slay me"; so plain was it written in the hearts of mankind.

12. By the same reason may a man in the state of nature punish the lesser breaches of that law. It will perhaps be demanded: with death? I answer: Each transgression may be punished to that degree and with so much severity as will suffice to make it an ill bargain to the offender, give him cause to repent, and terrify others from doing the like. Every offense that can be committed in the state of nature may in the state of nature be also punished equally, and as far forth as it may be in a commonwealth; for though it would be beside my present purpose to enter here into the particulars of the law of nature, or its measures of punishment, yet it is certain there is such a law, and that, too, as intelligible and plain to the rational creature and a studier of that law as the positive laws of commonwealths, nay, possibly plainer, as much as reason is easier to be understood than the fancies and intricate contrivances of men, following contrary and hidden interests put into words; for so truly are a great part of the municipal laws of countries, which are only so far right as they are founded on the law of nature, by which they are to be regulated and interpreted.

13. To this strange doctrine, viz., that in the state of nature every one has the executive power of the law of nature--I doubt not but it will be objected that it is unreasonable for men to be judges in their own cases, that self-love will make men partial to themselves and their friends, and, on the other side, that ill-nature passion, and revenge will carry them too far in punishing others, and hence nothing but confusion and disorder will follow; and that therefore God has certainly appointed government to restrain the partiality and violence of men. I easily grant that civil government is the proper remedy for the inconveniences of the state of nature, which must certainly be great where men may be judges in their own case; since it is easy to be imagined that he who was so unjust as to do his brother an injury will scarce be so just as to condemn himself for it; but I shall desire those who make this objection to remember that absolute monarchs are but men, and if government is to be the remedy of those evils which necessarily follow from men's being judges in their own cases, and the state of nature is therefore not to be endured, I desire to know what kind of government that is, and how much better it is than the state of nature, where one man commanding a multitude has the liberty to be judge in his own case, and may do to all his subjects whatever he pleases, without the least liberty to any one to question or control those who execute his pleasure, and in whatsoever he does, whether led by reason, mistake, or passion, must be submitted to? Much better it is in the state of nature, wherein men are not bound to submit to the unjust will of another; and if he that judges, judges amiss in his own or any other case, he is answerable for it to the rest of mankind.

14. It is often asked as a mighty objection, "Where are or ever were there any men in such a state of nature?" To which it may suffice as an answer at present that since all princes and rulers of independent governments all through the world are in a state of nature, it is plain the world never was, nor ever will be, without numbers of men in that state. I have named all governors of independent communities, whether they are, or are not, in league with others; for it is not every compact that puts an end to the state of nature between men, but only this one of agreeing together mutually to enter into one community and make one body politic; other premises and compacts men may make one with another and yet still be in a state of nature. The promises and bargains for truck, etc., between the two men in the desert island, mentioned by Garcilasso de la Vega, in his history of Peru, or between a Swiss and an Indian in the woods of America, are binding to them, though they are perfectly in a state of nature in reference to one another; for truth and keeping of faith belongs to men as men, and not as members of society.

15. To those that say there were never any men in the state of nature, I will not only oppose the authority of the judicious Hooker, *Eccl. Pol.*, lib. i., sect. 10, where he says,

> The laws which have hitherto been mentioned (i.e., the laws of nature) do bind men absolutely, even as they are men, although they have never any settled fellowship, never anyh solemn agreement amongst themselves what to do, or not to do; but forasmuch as we are not by ourselves sufficient to furnish ourselves with competent store of things needful for such a life as our nature doth desire, a life fit for the dignity of man; therefore to supply those defects and imperfections which are in us, as living singly and solely by ourselves, we are naturally induced to seek communion and fellowship with others. This was the cause of men's uniting themselves at first in politic societies.

But I, moreover, affirm that all men are naturally in that state and remain so till by their own consents they make themselves members of some politic society; and I doubt not in the sequel of this discourse to make it very clear.

CHAPTER III, Of the State of War

16. The state of war is a state of enmity and destruction; and, therefore, declaring by word or action, not a passionate and hasty but a sedate, settled design upon another's life, puts him in a state of war with him against whom he has declared such an intention, as so has exposed his life to the other's power to be taken away by him or anyone that joins with him in his defense and espouses his quarrel; it being reasonable and just I should have a right to destroy that which threatens me with distruction; for, by the fundamental law of nature, man being to be preserved as much as possible when all cannot be preserved, the safety of the innocent is to be preserved; and one may destroy a man who makes war upon him, or has discovered an enmity to his being, for the same reason that he may kill a wolf or a lion, because such men are not under the ties of the common law

reason, have no other rule but that of force and violence, and so may be treated as beasts of prey, those dangerous and noxious creatures that will be sure to destroy him whenever he falls into their power.

17. And hence it is that he who attempts to get another man into his absolute power does thereby put himself into a state of war with him, it being to be understood as a declaration of a design upon his life; for I have reason to conclude that he who would get me into his power without my consent would use me as he pleased when he got me there, and destroy me, too, when he had a fancy to it; for nobody can desire to have me in his absolute power unless it be to compel me by force to that which is against the right of my freedom, i.e., make me a slave. To be free from such force is the only security of my preservation; and reason bids me look upon him as an enemy to my preservation who would take away that freedom which is the fence to it; so that he who makes an attempt to enslave me thereby puts himself into a state of war with me. He that, in a state of nature, would take away the freedom that belongs to any one in that state must necessarily be supposed to have a design to take away everything else, that freedom being the foundation of all the rest; as he that, in the state of society, would take away the freedom belonging to those of that society or commonwealth must be supposed to design to take away from them everything else, and so be looked on as in a state of war.

18. This makes it lawful for a man to kill a thief who has not in the least hurt him, nor declared any design upon his life any farther than, by the use of force, so to get him in his power as to take away his money, or what he pleases, from him; because using force where he has no right to get me into his power, let his pretense be what it will, I have no reason to suppose that he who would take away my liberty would not, when he had me in his power, take away everything else. And therefore it is lawful for me to treat him as one who has put himself into a state of war with me, i.e., kill him if I can; for to that hazard does he justly expose himself whoever introduces a state of war and is aggressor in it.

19. And here we have the plain difference between the state of nature and the state of war which, however som men have confounded, are as far distant as a state of peace, good-will, mutual assistance, and preservation, and a state of enmity, malice, violence, and mutual destruction are from one another. Men living together according to reason, without a common superior on earth with authority to judge between them, is properly the state of nature. But force, or a declared design of force, upon the person of another, where there is no common superior on earth to appeal to for relief, is the state of war; and it is the want of such an appeal [that] gives a man the right of war even against an agrestor, though he be in a society and a fellow subject. Thus a thief, whom I cannot harm but by appeal to the law for having stolen all that I am worth, I may kill when he sets on me to rob me but of my horse or coat; because the law, which was made for my preservation, where it cannot interpose to secure my life from present force, which, if lost, is capable of no reparation, permits me my own defense and the right of war, a liberty to kill the aggressor, because the aggressor allows not time to appeal to our common judge, nor the decision of the law, for remedy in a case where the mischief may be irreparable. Want of a common judge with

authority puts all men in a state of nature; force without right upon a man's person makes a state of war both where there is and is not a common judge.

20. But when the actual force is over, the state of war ceases between those that are in society and are equally on both sides subjected to the fair determination of the law, because then there lies open the remedy of appeal for the past injury and to prevent future harm. But where no such appeal is, as in the state nature, for want of positive laws and judges with authority to appeal to, the state of war once begun continues with a right to the innocent party to destroy the other whenever he can, until the aggressor offers peace and desires reconciliation on such terms as may repair any wrongs he has already done and secure the innocent for the future; nay, where an appeal to the law and constituted judges lies open, but the remedy is denied by a manifest perverting of justice and a barefaced wresting of the laws to protect or indemnify the violence or injuries of some men, or party of men, there it is hard to imagine anything but a state of war; for wherever violence is used and injury done, though by hands appointed to administer justice, it is still violence and injury, however colored with the name, pretenses, or forms of law, the end whereof being to protect and redress the innocent by an unbiased application of it to all who are under it; wherever that is not bona fide done, war is made upon the sufferers, who having no appeal on earth to right them, they are left to the only remedy in such cases--an appeal to heaven.

21. To avoid this state of war--wherein there is no appeal but to heaven, and wherein every the least difference is apt to end, where there is no authority to decide between the contenders--is one great reason of men's putting themselves into society and quitting the state of nature; for where there is an authority, a power on earth from which relief can be had by appeal, there the continuance of the state of war is excluded, and the controversy is decided by that power. Had there been any such court, any superior jurisdiction on earth, to determine the right between Jephthah and the Ammonites, they had never come to a state of war; but we see he was forced to appeal to heaven: "The Lord the Judge," says he, "be judge this day between the children of Israel and the children of Ammon" (Judges xi. 27.), and then prosecuting and relying on his appeal, he leads out his army to battle. And, therefore, in such controversies where the question is put, "Who shall be judge?" it cannot be meant, "who shall decide the controversy"; every one knows what Jephthah here tells us, that "the Lord the Judge" shall judge. Where there is no judge on earth, the appeal lies to the God in heaven. That question then cannot mean: who shall judge whether another has put himself in a state of war with me, and whether I may, as Jephthah did, appeal to heaven in it? Of that I myself can only be judge in my own conscience, as I will answer it, at the great day, to the supreme Judge of all men.

CHAPTER IV, Of Slavery

22. The natural liberty of man is to be free from any superior power on earth, and not to be under the will or legislative authority of man, but to have only the law of nature for his rule. The liberty of man in society is to be under no other

legislative power but that established by consent in the commonwealth, nor under the dominion of any will or restraint of any law but what that legislative shall enact according to the trust put in it. Freedom then is not what Sir Robert Filmer tells us "a liberty for every one to do what he lists, to live as he pleases, and not to be tied by any laws";[3] but freedom of men under government is to have a standing rule to live by, common to every one of that society and made by the legislative power erected in it, a liberty to follow my own will in all things where the rule prescribes not, and not to be subject to the inconstant, uncertain, unknown, arbitrary will of another man; as freedom of nature is to be under no other restraint but the law of nature.

23. This freedom from absolute, arbitrary power is so necessary to, and closely joined with, a man's preservation that he cannot part with it but by what forfeits his preservation and life together; for a man not having the power of his own life cannot by compact or his own consent enslave himself to any one, nor put himself under the absolute arbitrary power of another to take away his life when he pleases. Nobody can give more power than he has himself; and he that cannot take away his own life cannot give another power over it. Indeed, having by his fault forfeited his own life by some act that deserves death, he to whom he has forfeited it may, when he has him in his power, delay to take it and make use of him to his own service; and he does him no injury by it, for whenever he finds the hardship of his slavery outweigh the value of his life, it is in his power, by resisting the will of his master, to draw on himself the death he desires.

24. This is the perfect condition of slavery, which is nothing else but "the state of war continued between a lawful conqueror and a captive"; for if once compact enter between them and make an agreement for a limited power on the one side and obedience on the other, the state of war and slavery ceases as long as the compact endures; for, as has been said, no man can by agreement pass over to another that which he has not in himself--a power over his own life.

I confess we find among the Jews, as well as other nations, that men did sell themselves; but it is plain this was only to drudgery, not to slavery; for it is

CHAPTER IX, Of the Ends of Political Society and Government

123. If man in the state of nature be so free, as has been said, if he be absolute lord of his own person and possessions, equal to the greatest, and subject to nobody, why will he part with his freedom, why will he give up his empire and subject himself to the dominion and control of any other power? To which it is obvious to answer that though in a state of nature he has such a right, yet the enjoyment of it is very uncertain and constantly exposed to the invasion of others; for all being kings as much as he, every man is equal, and the greater part no

---

[3] [Filmer, *Observations upon Aristotle's Politiques Touching Forms of Government* (1652), 55. evident the person sold was not under an absolute, arbitrary, despotical power; for the master could not have the power to kill him at any time whom, at a certain time, he was obliged to let go free out of his service; and the master of such a servant was so far from having arbitrary power over his life that he could not, at pleasure, so much as maim him, but the loss of an eye or tooth set him free (Exod. xxi).

strict observers of equity and justice, the enjoyment of the property he has in this state is very unsafe, very unsecure. This makes him willing to quit a condition which, however free, is full of fears and continual dangers; and it is not without reason that he seeks out and is willing to join in society with others who are already united, or have a mind to unite, for the mutual preservation of their lives, liberties, and estates, which I call by the general name, "property."

124. The great and chief end, therefore of men's uniting into commonwealths and putting themselves under government is the preservation of their property. To which in the state of nature there are many things wanting:

First, there wants an established, settled, known law, received an allowed by common consent to be the standard of right and wrong and the common measure to decide all controversies between them; for though the law of nature be plain and intelligible to all rational creatures, yet man, being biased by their interest as well as ignorant for want of studying it, are not apt to allow of it as a law binding to them in the application of it to their particular cases.

125. Secondly, in the state of nature there wants a known and indifferent judge with authority to determine all differences according to established law; for every one in that state being both judge and executioner of the law of nature, men being partial to themselves, passion and revenge is very apt to carry them too far and with too much heat in their own cases, as well as negligence and unconcernedness to make them too remiss in other men's.

126. Thirdly, in the state of nature there often wants power to back and support the sentence when right, and to give it due execution. They who by any injustice offend will seldom fail, where they are able, by force, to make good their injustice; such resistance many times makes the punishment dangerous and frequently destructive to those who attempt it.

127. Thus mankind, notwithstanding all the privileges of the state of nature, being but in an ill condition while they remain in it, are quickly driven into society. Hence it comes to pass that we seldom find any number of men live any time together in this state. The inconveniences that they are therein exposed to by the irregular and uncertain exercise of the power of every man has of punishing the transgressions of others make them take sanctuary under the established laws of government and therein seek the preservation of their property. It is this makes them so willingly give up every one his single power of punishing, to be exercised by such alone as shall be appointed to it amongst them; and by such rules as the community, or those authorized by them to that purpose, shall agree on. And in this we have the original right of both the legislative and executive power, as well as of the governments and societies themselves.

128. For in the state of nature, to omit the liberty he has of innocent delights, a man has two powers:

The first is to do whatsoever he thinks fit for the preservation of himself and others within the permission of the law of nature, by which law, common to them all, he and all the rest of mankind are one community, make up one society, distinct from all other creatures. And, were it not for the corruption and viciousness of degenerate men, there would be no need of any other, no necessity that men should separate from this great and natural community and by positive agreements combine into smaller and divided associations.

The other power a man has in the state of nature is the power to punish the crimes committed against that law. Both these he gives up when he joins in a private, if I may so call it, or particular politic society and incorporates into any commonwealth separate from the rest of mankind.

129. The first power, viz., of doing whatsoever he thought fit for the preservation of himself and the rest of mankind, he gives up to be regulated by laws made by the society, so far forth as the preservation of himself and the rest of that society shall require; which laws of the society in many things confine the liberty he had by the law of nature.

130. Secondly, the power of punishing he wholly gives up, and engages his natural force--which he might before employ in the execution of the law of nature by his own single authority, as he thought fit--to assist the executive power of the society, as the law thereof shall require; for being now in a new state, wherein he is to enjoy many conveniences from the labor, assistance, and society of others in the same community as well as protection from its whole strength, he is to part also with as much of his natural liberty, in providing for himself, as the good, prosperity, and safety of the society shall require, which is not only necessary, but just, since the other members of the society do the like.

131. But though men when they enter into society give up the equality, liberty and executive power they had in the state of nature into the hands of the society, to be so far disposed of by the legislature as the good of the society shall require, yet it being only with an intention in every one of the better to preserve himself, his liberty and property--for no rational creature can be supposed to change his condition with an intention to be worse--the power of the society, or legislative constituted by them, can never be supposed to extend farther than the common good, but is obliged to secure everyone's property by providing against those three defects above-mentioned that made the state of nature so unsafe and uneasy. And so whoever has the legislative or supreme power of any commonwealth is bound to govern by established standing laws, promulgated and known to the people, and not by extempore decrees; by indifferent and upright judges who are to decide controversies by those laws; and to employ the force of the community at home only in the execution of such laws, or abroad to prevent or redress foreign injuries, and secure the community from inroads and invasion. And all this to be directed to no other end but the peace, safety, and public good of the people.

CHAPTER XI, Of the Extent of the Legislative Power

134. The great end of men's entering into society being the enjoyment of their properties in peace and safety, and the great instrument and means of that being the laws established in that society, the first and fundamental positive law of all commonwealths is the establishing of the legislative power; as the first and fundamental natural law which is to govern even the legislative itself is the preservation of the society and, as far as will consist with the public good, of every person in it. This legislative is not only the supreme power of the

commonwealth, but sacred and unalterable in the hands where the community have once placed it; nor can any edict of anybody else, in what form soever conceived or by what power soever backed, have the force and obligation of a law which has not its sanction from that legislative which the public has chosen and appointed; for without this the law could not have that which is absolutely necessary to its being a law: the consent of the society over whom nobody can have a power to make laws, but by their own consent and by authority received from them.[4] And therefore all the obedience, which by the most solemn ties any one can be obliged to pay, ultimately terminates this supreme power and is directed by those laws which it enacts; nor can any oaths to any foreign power whatsoever, or any domestic subordinate power, discharge any member of the society from his obedience to the legislative acting pursuant to their trust, nor oblige him to any obedience contrary to the laws so enacted, or farther than they do allow; it being ridiculous to imagine one can be tied ultimately to obey any power in the society which is not supreme.

135. Though the legislative, whether placed in one or more, whether it be always in being or only by intervals, though it be the supreme power in every commonwealth, yet:

First, it is not, nor can possibly be, absolutely arbitrary over the lives and fortunes of people. For it being but the joint power of every member of society given up to that person or assembly which is legislator, it can be no more than those persons had in a state of Nature before they entered into society, and gave it up to the community; for nobody can transfer to another more power than he has in himself, and nobody has an absolute arbitrary power over himself, or over any other, to destroy his own life or take away the life or property of another. **A man, as has been proved, cannot subject himself to the arbitrary power of another; and having, in the state of Nature, no arbitrary power over the life, liberty, or possession of another, but only so much as the law of Nature gave him for the preservation of himself and the rest of mankind, this is all he doth, or can give up to the commonwealth, and by it to the legislative power, so that the legislative can have no more than this. Their power in the utmost bounds of it is limited to the public good of the society.**[5] It is a power that hath

---

[4] "The lawful power of making laws to command whole politic societies of men, belonging so properly unto the same entire societies, that for any prince or potentate of what kind soever upon earth to exercise the same of himself, and not by express commission immediately and personally received from God, or else by authority derived at the first from their consent, upon whose persons they impose laws, it is no better than mere tyranny. Laws they are not, therefore, which public approbation hath not made so" (Hooker's *Eccl. Pol.* lib. i. sect. 10).

"Of this point, therefore, we are to note, that such men naturally have no full and perfect power to command whole politic multitudes of men, therefore utterly without our consent we could in such sort be at no man's commandment living. And to be commanded we do consent, when that society whereof we be a part hath at any time before consented, without revoking the same by the like universal agreement. Laws therefore human, of what kind soever, are available by consent" (*Ibid.*).

[5] "Two foundations there are which bear up public societies; the one a natural inclination whereby all men desire sociable life and fellowship; the other an order, expressly or secretly agreed upon, touching the manner of their union in living together. The latter is that which we call the law of a commonweal, the very soul of a politic body, the parts whereof are by law animated, held together,

no other end but preservation, and therefore can never have a right to destroy, enslave, or designedly to impoverish the subjects; the obligations of the law of Nature cease not in society, but only in many cases are drawn closer, and have, by human laws, known penalties annexed to them to enforce their observation. Thus the law of Nature stands as an eternal rule to all men, legislators as well as others. The rules that they make for other men's actions must, as well as their own and other men's actions, be conformable to the law of Nature--i.e., to the will of God, of which that is a declaration--and the fundamental law of nature being the preservation of mankind, no human sanction can be good or valid against it.

136. Secondly, the legislative or supreme authority cannot assume to itself a power to rule by extemporary, arbitrary decrees, but is bound to dispense justice and to decide the rights of the subject by promulgated, standing laws, and knownauthorized judges.[6] For the law of nature being unwritten, and so nowhere to be found but in the minds of men, they who through passion or interest shall miscite or misapply it, cannot so easily be convinced of their mistake where there is no established judge; and so it serves not, as it ought, to determine the rights and fence the properties of those that live under it, especially where every one is judge, interpreter, and executioner of it, too, and that in his own case; and he that has right on his side, having ordinarily but his own single strength, has not force enough to defend himself from his injuries to punish delinquents. To avoid these inconveniences which disorder men's properties in the state of nature, men unite into societies that they may have the united strength of the whole society to secure and defend their properties, and may have standing rules to bound it by which every one may know what is his. To this end it is that men give up all their natural power to the society which they enter into, and the community put the legislative power into such hands as they think fit with this trust, that they shall be governed by declared laws, or else their peace, quiet, and property will still be at the same uncertainty as it was in the state of nature.

137. Absolute arbitrary power or governing without settled standing laws can neither of them consist with the ends of society and government which men would not quit the freedom of the state of nature for, and tie themselves up under, were it not to preserve their lives, liberties, and fortunes, and by stated rules of right and property to secure their peace and quiet. It cannot be supposed that they

---

and set on work in such actions as the common good requireth. Laws politic, ordained for external order and regiment amongst men, are never framed as they should be, unless presuming the will or man to be inwardly obsinate, rebellious, and averse from all obedience to the sacred laws of his nature; in a word, unless presuming man to be, in regard of his depraved mind, little better than a wild beast, they do accordingly provide, notwithstanding, so to frame his outward actions that they be no hindrance unto the common good, for which societies are instituted. Unless they do this, they are not perfect. (Hooker's *Eccl. Pol.* lib. i. sect. 10).

[6] "Human laws are measures in respect of men whose actions they must direct, howbeit such measures they are as have also their higher rules to be measured by, which rules are two, the law of God, and the law of nature; so that laws human must be made according to the general laws of nature, and without contradiction to any positive law of Scripture, otherwise they are ill-made" (Hooker's *Eccl. Pol.* lib. iii. sect. 9). "To constrain men to anything inconvenient doth seem unreasonable" (*Ibid.* lib. i. sect. 10).

should intend, had they a power so to do, to give to any one or more an absolute arbitrary power over their persons and estates and put a force into the magistrate's hand to execute unlimited will arbitrarily upon them. This were to put themselves into a worse condition than the state of nature wherein they had a liberty to defend their right against the injuries of others and were upon equal terms of force to maintain it, whether invaded by a single man or many in combination. Whereas, by supposing they have given up themselves to the absolute arbitrary power and will of a legislator, they have disarmed themselves and armed him to make a prey of them when he pleases, he being in a much worse condition who is exposed to the arbitrary power of one man who has the command of 100,000, than he that is exposed to the arbitrary power of 100,000 single men, nobody being secure that his will, who has such a command, is better than that of other men, though his force be 100,000 times stronger. And, therefore, whatever form the commonwealth is under, the ruling power ought to govern by declared and received laws and not by extemporary dictates and undetermined resolutions; for then mankind will be in a far worse condition than in the state of nature if they shall have armed one or a few men with the joint power of a multitude, to force them to obey at pleasure the exorbitant and unlimited decrees of their sudden thoughts or unrestrained and, till that moment, unknown wills, without having any measures set down which may guide and justify their actions. For all the power the government has, being only for the good of the society, as it ought not to be arbitrary and at pleasure, so it ought to be exercised by established and promulgated laws; that both the people may know their duty and be safe and secure within the limits of the law; and the rulers, too, kept within their bounds, and not be tempted by the power they have in their hands to employ it to such purposes and by such measures as they would not have known, and own not willingly.

138. Thirdly, the supreme power cannot take from any man part of his property without his consent; for the preservation of property being the end of government and that for which men enter into society, it necessarily supposes and requires that the people should have property; without which they must be supposed to lose that, by entering into society, which was the end for which they entered into it--too gross an absurdity for any man to own. Men, therefore, in society having property, they have such right to the goods which by the law of the community are theirs, that nobody has a right to take their substance or any part of it from them without their own consent; without this, they have no property at all, for I have truly no property in that which another can by right take from me when he pleases, against my consent. Hence it is a mistake to think that the supreme or legislative power of any commonwealth can do what it will and dispose of the estates of the subject arbitrarily, or take any part of them at pleasure. This is not much to be feared in governments where the legislative consists, wholly or in part, in assemblies which are variable, whose members, upon the dissolution of the assembly, are subjects under the common laws of their country, equally with the rest. But in governments where the legislative is in one lasting assembly, always in being, or in one man, as in absolute monarchies, there is danger still that they will think themselves to have a distinct interest from teh rest of the community, and so will be apt to increase their own riches and power

by taking what they think fit from the people; for a man's property is not at all secure, though there be good and equitable laws to set the bounds of it between him and his fellow subjects, if he who commands those subjects have the power to take from any private man what part he pleases of his property and use and dispose of it as he thinks good.

139. But government, into whatsoever hands it is put, being, as I have before shown, entrusted with this condition, and for this end, that men might have power to make laws for the regulating of property between subjects one amongst another, yet can never have a power to take to themselves the whole or any part of the subject's property without their own consent; for this would be in effect to leave them no property at all. And to let us see that even absolute power, where it is necessary, is not arbitrary by being absolute, but is still limited by that reason and confined to those ends which required it in some cases to be absolute, we need look no farther than the common practice of martial discipline; for the preservation of the army, and in it of the whole commonwealth, requires an absolute obedience to the command to every superior officer, and it is justly death to disobey or dispute the most dangerous or unreasonable of them; but yet we see that neither the sergeant, that could command a soldier to march up to the mouth of a cannon or stand in a breach where he is almost sure to perish, can command that soldier to give him one penny of his money; nor the general, that can condemn him to death for deserting his post or for not obeying the most desperate orders, can yet, with all his absolute power of life and death, dispose of one farthing of that soldier's estate or seize one jot of his goods, whom yet he can command anything, and hang for the least disobedience. Because such a blind obedience is necessary to that end for which the commander has his power, viz., the preservation of the rest; but the disposing of his goods has nothing to do with it.

140. It is true, governments cannot be supported without great charge, and it is fit every one who enjoys his share of the protection should pay out of his estate his proportion for the maintenance of it. But it must be with his own consent--i.e., the consent of the majority, giving it either by themselves or their representatives chosen by them. For if any one shall claim a power to lay and levy taxes on the people, by his own authority and without such consent of the people, he thereby invades the fundamental law of property and subverts the end of government; for what property have I in that which another may by right take, when he pleases, to himself?

141. Fourthly, the legislative cannot transfer the power of making laws to any other hands; for it being but a delegated power from the people, they who have it cannot pass it over to others. The people alone can appoint the form of the commonwealth, which is by constituting the legislature and appointing in whose hands that shall be. And when the people have said, we will submit to rules and be governed by laws made by such men, and in such forms, nobody else can say other men shall make laws for them; nor can the people be bound by any laws but such as are enacted by those whom they have chosen and authorized to make laws for them. The power of the legislative, being derived from the people by a positive voluntary grant and institution, can be no other than what that positive grant conveyed, which being only to make laws, and not to make legislators, the

legislative can have no power to transfer their authority of making laws and place it in other hands.

142. These are the bounds which the trust that is put in them by the society and the law of God and nature have set to the legislative power of every commonwealth, in all forms of government:

First, they are to govern by promulgated established laws, not to be varied in particular cases, but to have one rule for rich and poor, for the favorite at court and the countryman at plough.

Secondly, these laws also ought to be designed for no other end ultimately but the good of the people.

Thirdly, they must not raise taxes on the property of the people without the consent of the people, given by themselves or their deputies. And this property concerns only such governments where the legislative is always in being, or at least where the people have not reserved any part of the legislative to deputies to be from time to time chosen by themselves.

Fourthly, the legislative neither must nor can transfer the power of making laws to anybody else, or place it anywhere but where the people have.

Letter Concerning Toleration (1689)

First Excerpt from the Main Text:

The commonwealth seems to me to be a society of men constituted only for the procuring, preserving, and advancing their own civil interests.

Civil interests I call life, liberty, health, and indolency of body; and the possession of outward things, such as money, lands, houses, furniture and the like.

It is the duty of the civil magistrate, by the impartial execution of equal laws, to secure unto all the people in general and to every one of his subjects in particular the just possession of these things belonging to this life. If anyone presume to violate the laws of public justice and equity, established for the preservation of those things, his presumption is to be checked by the fear of punishment, consisting of the deprivation or diminution of those civil interests, or goods, which otherwise he might and ought to enjoy. But seeing so man does willingly suffer himself to be punished by the deprivation of any part of his goods, and much less of his liberty or life, therefore, is the magistrate armed with the force and strength of all his subjects, in order to the punishment of those that violate any other man's rights.

Now that the whole jurisdiction of the magistrate reaches only to these civil concernments, and that all civil power, right and dominion, is bounded and confined to the only care of promoting these things; and that it neither can nor ought in any manner to be extended to the salvation of souls, these following considerations seem unto me abundantly to demonstrate.

First, because the care of souls is not committed to the civil magistrate, any more than to other men. It is not committed unto him, I say, by God; because it appears not that God has ever given any such authority to one man over another as to compel anyone to his religion. Nor can any such power be vested in the magistrate by the consent of the people, because no man can so far abandon the care of his own salvation as blindly to leave to the choice of any other, whether prince or subject, to prescribe to him what faith or worship he shall embrace. For no man can, if he would, conform his faith to the dictates of another. All the life and power of true religion consist in the inward and full persuasion of the mind; and faith is not faith without believing. Whatever profession we make, to whatever outward worship we conform, if we are not fully satisfied in our own mind that the one is true and the other well pleasing unto God, such profession and such practice, far from being any furtherance, are indeed great obstacles to our salvation. For in this manner, instead of expiating other sins by the exercise of religion, I say, in offering thus unto God Almighty such a worship as we esteem to be displeasing unto Him, we add unto the number of our other sins those also of hypocrisy and contempt of His Divine Majesty.

In the second place, the care of souls cannot belong to the civil magistrate, because his power consists only in outward force; but true and saving religion consists in the inward persuasion of the mind, without which nothing can be acceptable to God. And such is the nature of the understanding, that it cannot be compelled to the belief of anything by outward force. Confiscation of the estate, imprisonment, torments, nothing of that nature can have any such efficacy as to make men change the inward judgement that they have framed of things.

It may indeed be alleged that the magistrate may make use of arguments, and, thereby; draw the heterodox into the way of truth, and procure their salvation. I grant it; but this is common to him with other men. In teaching, instructing, and redressing the erroneous by reason, he may certainly do what becomes any good man to do. Magistry does not oblige him to put off either humanity or Christianity; but it is one thing to persuade, another to command; one thing to press with arguments, another with penalties. This civil power alone has a right to do; to the other, goodwill is authority enough. Every man has commission to admonish, exhort, convince another of error, and, by reasoning, to draw him into truth; but to give laws, receive obedience, and compel with the sword, belongs to none but the magistrate. And, upon this ground, I affirm that the magistrate's power extends not to the establishing of any articles of faith, or forms of worship, by the force of his laws. For laws are of no force at all without penalties, and penalties in this case are absolutely impertinent, because they are not proper to convince the mind. Neither the profession of any articles of faith, nor the conformity to any outward form of worship (as has already been said), can be available to the salvation of souls, unless the truth of the one and the acceptableness of the other unto God be thoroughly believed by those that so profess and practise. But penalties are no way capable to produce such belief. It is only light and evidence that can work a change in men's opinions; which light can in no manner proceed from corporal sufferings, or any other outward penalties.

In the third place, the care of the salvation of men's souls cannot belong to the magistrate; because, though the rigour of laws and the force of penalties were capable to convince and change men's minds, yet would not that help us all to the salvation of their souls. For there being but one truth, one way to heaven, what hope is there that more men would be led into it if they had no rule but the religion of the court and were put under the necessity to quit the light of their own reason, and oppose the dictates of their own consciences, and blindly to resign themselves up to the will of their governors and to the religion which either ignorance, ambition, or superstition had chanced to establish in countries where they were born? In the variety and contradiction of opinions in religion, wherein the princes of the world are as much divided as in their secular interests, the narrow way would be much straitened; one country alone would be in the right, and all the rest of the world put under an obligation of following their princes in the ways that lead to destruction; and that which heightens the absurdity, and very ill suits the notion of a Deity, men would owe their eternal happiness or misery to the places of their nativity.

These considerations, to omit many others that might have been urged to the same purpose, seem unto me sufficient to conclude that all the power of civil government relates only to men's civil interests, is confined to the care of the things of this world, and hath nothing to do with the world to come.

Second Excerpt from the Main Text:

[Editor's Note: Locke said there were four religious beliefs that civil government did not have to tolerate: (1) beliefs contrary to the moral rules necessary for the preservation of society; (2) belief that a certain sect has the right to overthrow or disobey governments that differ from it in matters of religion; (3) belief in a religion that requires allegiance to a foreign government; and (4) atheism. Locke explained his position regarding atheism in the following paragraph.]

Lastly, those are not at all to be tolerated who deny the being of God. Promises, covenents, and oaths, which are the bonds of human society, can have no hold upon an atheist. The taking away of God, though but even in thought, dissolves all; besides also, those that by their atheism undermine and destroy all religion, can have no pretense of religion whereupon to challenge the privilege of a toleration. As for other practical opinions, though not absolutely free from all error, if they do not tend to establish domination over others, or civil impunity to the Church in which they are taught, there is no reason why they should not be tolerated.

Excerpt from the Postcript:

We are to inquire, therefore, what men are of the same religion. Concerning which it is manifest that those who have one and the same rule of faith and worship are of the same religion; and those who have not the same rule of faith and worship are of different religions. For since all things that belong unto that religion are contained in that rule, it follows necessarily that those who agree in one rule are of one and the same religion, and *vice versa*. Thus Turks and Christians are of different religions, because these take the Holy Scriptures to be the rule of their religion, and those the Alcoran. And for the same reason there may be different religions also even among Christians. The Papists and Lutherans, though both of them profess faith in Christ and are therefore called Christians, yet are not both of the same religion, because these acknowledge nothing but the Holy Scriptures to be the rule and foundation of their religion, those take in also traditions and the decrees of Popes and of these together make the rule of their religion; and thus the Christians of St. John (as they are called) and the Christians of Geneva are of different religions, because these also take only the Scriptures, and those I know not what traditions, for the rule of their religion.

G

Footnote from Memorial by the Massachusetts Assembly on the Absolute Rights of Englishmen (1764)

In response to the Revenue Act passed by Parliament in 1764, the Massachusetts Assembly sent a memorial to its London agent that had been drafted by James Otis. In that memorial, Otis said, "The judges of England have declared that *acts of Parliament against natural equity are void. That acts against the fundamental principles of the British constitution are void.*" To support those statements, Otis attached the following footnote, the first part of which is a quote from De Vattel's *The Law of Nations*:

"A very important question here presents itself. It essentially belongs to society to make laws both in relation to the manner in which it desires to be governed, and the conduct of the citizens: this is called the *legislative power.* The nation may entrust the exercise of it to the prince or an assembly, or to the assembly and the prince jointly, who have then the right of making new and abrogating the old laws. It is here demanded whether if their power extends so far as to the fundamental laws they may change the constitution of the state. The principles we have laid down lead us to decide this point with certainty that the authority of the legislators does not extend so far, and that they ought to consider the funda-mental laws as sacred if the nation has not in very express terms given them that was first established by the nation, which afterwards trusted certain persons with the legislative power, the fundamental laws are excepted from their commission. It appears that the society had only resolved to make provision for the state's being always furnished with laws suited to particular conjunctures, and gave the legislature for that purpose the power of abrogating the ancient and civil political laws that were not fundamental, and of making new ones: but nothing leads us to think that it was willing to submit the constitution itself to their pleasure.

"**When a nation takes possession of a different country and settles a colony there, that country, though separated from the principal establishment, or mother country, naturally becomes a part of the state equally with its ancient possessions. Whenever the political laws or treaties make no distinction between them everything said of the territory of a nation ought also extend to its colonies.**" De Vattel.

"An act of Parliament made against natural equity, as to make a man judge his own cause, would be void; for *jura a naturae sunt immutabilia.*" Hob. 87. Trin[ity Term], 12 Jac. [I], *Day v. Savage*, S. C. and P. [same case in point] cited Arg[uendo] 10 Mod. 115 Hil[ary Term], 11 Anne C.B. [Common Bench] in the case of Thornby and Fleetwood, "but says, that this must be a clear case, and judges will strain hard rather than interpret an act void, *ab initio.*" *This is granted, but still their authority is not boundless if subject to the control of the judges in any case.*

Holt, Chief Justice, thought what Lord Coke said in *Doctor Bonham's Case* a very reasonable and true saying, that if an act of Parliament should ordain that the same person should be both party and judge in his own cause, it would be a void act of Parliament, and an act of Parliament can do no wrong, though it may do several things that look pretty odd; for it may discharge one from the allegiance he lives under and restore to the state of nature, but it cannot make one that lives under a government both judge and party: per Holt C.J., 12 Mod. 687, Hil., 13 Wm. III B.R. [King's Bench] in the case of the *City of London v. Wood*. --It appears in our books that in several cases the common law shall control acts of Parliament and sometimes adjudge them to be utterly void; for when an act of Parliament is against common *right* and *reason*, or repugnant or impossible to be performed, the common law shall control it and adjudge it to be void, and therefore 8 Edw. III c. 30. *Thomas Tregor's Case* upon the statute of Wm. II c. and Art. sup. Cart. 9. Herle said that sometimes statutes are made contrary to law and right, which the makers of them perceiving will not put them in execution. 8 Rep. 118, Hil., 7 Jac. [I], *Dr. Bonham's Case.*

H

Resolutions of the Stamp Act Congress

In Congress at New York, October 19, 1765.

The members of this Congress, sincerely devoted, with the warmest sentiments of affection and duty to His Majesty's person and Government, inviolably attached to the present happy establishment of the Protestant succession, and with minds deeply impressed by a sense of the present and impending misfortunes of the British colonies on this continent; having considered as maturely as time would permit, the circumstances of the said colonies, esteem it our humble opinion, respecting the most essential rights and liberties of the colonists, and of the grievances under which they labor, by reason of several acts of Parliament.

1st. That His Majesty's subjects in these colonies, owe the same allegiance to the Crown of Great Britain, that is owing from his subjects born within the realm, and all due subordination to that august body, the Parliament of Great Britain.

2nd. That His Majesty's liege subjects in these colonies are entitled to all the inherent rights and privileges of his natural born subjects within the kingdom of Great Britain.

3rd. That it is inseparably essential to the freedom of a people, and the undoubted rights of Englishmen, that no taxes should be imposed on them, but with their own consent, given personally, or by their representatives.

4th. That the people of these colonies are not, and from their local circumstances, cannot be represented in the House of Commons in Great Britain.

5th. That the only representatives of the people of these colonies, are persons chosen therein, by themselves; and that no taxes ever have been, or can be constitutionally imposed on them, but by their respective legislatures.

6th. That all supplies to the Crown, being free gifts of the people, it is unreasonable and inconsistent with the principles and spirit of the British constitution, for the people of Great Britain to grant to His Majesty the property of the colonists.

7th. That trial by jury is the inherent and invaluable right of every British subject in these colonies.

8th. That the late act of Parliament, entitled, "An act for granting and applying certain stamp duties, and other duties in the British colonies and plantations in America, etc.," by imposing taxes on the inhabitants of these colonies, and the said act, and several other acts, by extending the jurisdiction of the courts of admiralty beyond its ancient limits, have a manifest tendency to subvert the rights and liberties of the colonists.

9th. That the duties imposed by several late acts of Parliament, from the peculiar circumstances of these colonies, will be extremely burthensome and grievous, and from the scarcity of specie, the payment of them absolutely impracticable.

10th. That as the profits of the trade of these colonies ultimately center in Great Britain, to pay for the manufactures which they are obliged to take from thence, they eventually contribute very largely to all supplies granted there to the Crown.

11th. That the restrictions imposed by several late acts of Parliament, or the trade of these colonies, will render them unable to purchase the manufactures of Great Britain.

12th. That the increase, prosperity and happiness of these colonies, depend on the full and free enjoyment of their rights and liberties, and an intercourse, with Great Britain, mutually affectionate and advantageous.

13th. That it is the right of the British subjects in these colonies to petition the King or either house of Parliament.

Lastly, that it is the indespensable duty of these colonies to the best of sovereigns, to the mother country, and to themselves, to endeavor by a loyal and dutiful address to His Majesty, and humble application to both houses of Parliament, to procure the repeal of the act granting and applying certain stamp duties, of all clauses of any other acts of Parliament, whereby the jurisdiction of the admiralty is extended as aforesaid, and of the other late acts for the restriction of the American commerce.

I

A Vindication of the British Colonies, against the Aspersions of the Halifax Gentleman, in His Letter to a Rhode Island Friend by James Otis (1765), pp. 8-10

Page references are those of Otis to the Halifax gentleman's letter and words in quotations are taken from that letter, unless otherwise noted.

The gentleman is at a loss (p. 8) to "conceive how it comes to pass that the colonies now claim *any other or greater* rights than are expressly granted to them" by charter. Is the gentleman a British-born subject and a lawyer, and ignorant that charters from the crown have usually been given for enlarging the liberties and privileges of the grantees, not for limiting them, much less for curtailing those essential rights which all His Majesty's subjects are entitled to by the laws of God and nature as well as by the common law and by the constitution of their country?

The distinction (p. 8) between personal and political rights is a new invention, and, as applied, has perplexed the author of it. He everywhere confounds the terms rights, liberties, and privileges, which in legal as well as vulgar acceptation denote very different ideas. This is a common mistake with those who cannot see any difference between power and right, between blind, slavish submission and a loyal, generous, and rational obedience to the supreme authority of state.

The rights of men are *natural* or *civil*. Both these are divisible into *absolute* and *relative*. The natural absolute personal rights of individuals are so far from being opposed to political or civil rights that they are the very basis of all municipal laws of any great value. "The absolute liberties of Englishmen, as frequently declared in Parliament, are principally three: the right of *personal* security, personal *liberty*, and private property." [BL3, 125] "Besides these three *primary rights*, there are others which are *secondary* and *subordinate* (to preserve the former from unlawful attacks): (1) The constitution or power of Parliament; (2) The limitation of the King's prerogative (and to vindicate them when actually violated); (3) The regular administration of justice; (4) The right of petitioning for redress of grievances; (5) The right of having and using arms for self-defense." See Mr. Blackstone's accurate and elegant analysis of the laws of England. [BL3, 136-139] The gentleman seems to have taken this and some other of his distinctions from that excellent treatise very ill understood. The analysis had given this general view of the *objects* of the laws of England: I. Rights of persons; II. Rights of things; III. Private wrongs; IV. Public Wrongs. Rights of persons are divided into these: (1) of natural persons; (2) of bodies politic or corporate, i.e. artificial persons or subordinate societies. The rights of these are by the Letter Writer strangely confounded with the political and civil rights of natural persons. And because corporate rights so far as they depend upon charter are matters of the mere favor and grace of the donor or founder, he thence infers (p. 9) that "the colonies have no rights independent of their charters," and that "they can claim no greater than those give them." This is a contradiction to what he admitted in the preceding page, viz., that "by the common law every colonist hath a right to his life, liberty, and property." And he was so vulgar as to call these the "subject's birthright." But what is this birthright worth if it depends merely on a colony charter that, as he says rightly enough, may be taken away by Parliament? I wish the gentleman would answer these questions. Would he think an estate worth much that might be taken from him at the pleasure of another? Are charters from the crown usually given for enlarging the liberties and privileges of the grantees in consideration of some special merit and services done the state, or would he have his readers consider them like the ordinances of a French monarch, for limiting and curtailing those rights which all Britons and all British subjects are entitled to by the laws of God and nature, as well as by the common law and the constitution of their country so admirably built on the principles of the former? By which of these laws in contradistinction to the other are the rights of life, liberty, and estate, personal?

The gentleman's positions and principles that "the several New England charters ascertain, define, and limit the respective *rights* and privileges of each colony," and that "the colonies have no rights independent of their charter," and that "they can claim no greater than those give them," if true, would afford a curious train of consequences. Life, liberty, and property are by the law of nature as well as by the common law secured to the happy inhabitants of South Britain, and constitute their *primary* civil or political rights. But in the colonies these and all other rights, according to our author, depend on charter. Therefore those of the colonies who have no charter have no right to life, liberty, or property. And in those colonies who have charters, these invaluable blessings depend on the mere good will, grace, and pleasure of the supreme power, and all their charters and of course all their rights, even to life, liberty, and property, may be taken away at pleasure. Thus every charter in England may be taken away, for they are but voluntary and gracious grants of the crown of certain limited, local, political privileges superadded to those of the common law. But would it be expedient to strike such a blow without the most urgent necessity? "In all states there is (and must be) an absolute supreme power, to which the right of *legislation* belongs: and which by the singular constitution of these kingdoms is vested in the King, Lords, and Commons" (Blackstone). [BL1, 50-52] Now Magna Carta is but a law of their making, and they may alter it at pleasure; but does it thence follow that it would be expedient to repeal every statute from William the Conquerer to this time? But by the gentleman's principles this may be done wantonly and without any reason at all. Further, by his logic the Parliament may make the monarchy absolute or reduce it to a republic, both which would be contrary to the trust reposed in them by the constitution, which is to preserve, not destroy it; and to this all are sworn, from the King's Majesty in his coronation oath to the meanest subject in the oath of allegiance. Into such absurd and treasonable doctrines must the gentleman run in order to be consistent.

J

The Rights of the Colonists, by Sam Adams
A Declaration by the Boston Committee of Correspondence, November 20, 1772

1st. *The Natural Rights of the Colonists as Men.*
   Among the natural rights of the colonists are these: first, a right to *life*; secondly to *liberty*; thirdly to *property*; together with the right to support and defend them in the best manner they can.---Those are evident branches of, rather than deductions from, the duty of self-preservation, commonly called the first law of nature.
   All men have a right to remain in a state of nature as long as they please; and in case of intolerable oppression, civil or religious, to leave the society they belong to and enter into another.
   When men enter into society, it is by voluntary consent; and they have a right to demand and insist upon the performance of such conditions and previous limitations as form and equitable *original compact*.
   Every natural right not expressly given up or from the nature of a social compact necessarily ceced remains.
   All positive and civil laws should conform as far as possible to the law of natural reason and equity.
   As neither reason requires nor religion permits to the contrary, every man living in or out of a state of civil society has a right peaceably and quietly to worship God according to the dictates of his conscience.
   "Just and true liberty, equal and impartial liberty" in matters spiritual and temporal, is a thing that all men are clearly entitled to, by the eternal and immutable laws of God and nature, as well as by the law of nations, and all well-grounded municipal laws, which must have their foundation in the former.
   In regard to religion, mutual toleration in the different professions thereof is what all good and candid minds in all ages have ever practiced, and both by precept and example inculcated on mankind; and it is now generally agreed among Christians that this spirit of toleration in the fullest extent consistent with the being of civil society "is the chief characteristical mark of the true church" and in so much that Mr. Locke has asserted, and proved beyond the possibility of contradiction on any solid ground, that such toleration ought to be extended to all whose doctrines are not subversive to society. The only sects which he thinks ought to be and which by all wise laws are excluded from such toleration are those who teach doctrines subversive of the civil government under which they live. The Roman Catholics or Papists are excluded by reason of such doctrines as these: that princes excommunicated may be deposed, and those they call heretics may be destroyed without mercy; besides their recognizing the pope in so absolute a manner, in subversion of government, by introducing as far as possible into the states under whose protection they enjoy life, liberty, and
property that solicism in politics, *Imperium in imperio*, leading directly to the worse anarchy and confusion, civil discord, war and bloodshed.

The natural liberty of men by entering into society is abridged or restrained so far only as is necessary for the great end of society, the best good of the whole.

In the state of nature every man is, under God, judge and sole judge of his own rights and the injuries done him. By entering into society he agrees to an arbiter or indifferent judge between him and his neighbors; but he no more renounces his original right than by taking a cause out of the ordinary course of law and leaving the decision to referees or indifferent arbitrations. In the last case he must pay for the references for time and trouble; he should be also willing to pay his just quota for the support of government, the law and constitution, the end of which is to furnish indifferent and impartial judges in all cases that may happen, whether civil, ecclesiastical, marine, or military.

"The natural liberty of man is to be free from any superior power on earth, and not be under the will or legislative authority of man; but only to have the law of nature his rule."

In the state of nature men may, as the patriarchs did, employ hired servants for the defense of their lives, liberty, and property; and they should pay them reasonable wages. Government was instituted for the purposes of common defense; and those who hold the reins of government have an equitable natural right to an honorable support from the same principle "that the laborer is worthy of his hire"; but then the same community which they serve ought to be assessors of their pay: governors have no right to seek what they please; by this, instead of being content with the station assigned them, that of honorable servants of the society, they would soon become absolute masters, despots, and tyrants. Hence, as a private man has a right to say what wages he will give in his private affairs, so has a community to determine what they will give and grant of their substance for the administration of public affairs. And in both cases more are ready generally to offer their service at the proposed and stipulated price than are able and willing to perform their duty.

In short, it is the greatest absurdity to suppose it in the power of one or any number of men at the entering into society to renounce their essential natural rights, or the means of preserving those rights when the great end of civil government from the very nature of its institution is for the support, protection, and defense of those very rights, the principal of which, as is before observed, are life, liberty, and property. If men through fear, fraud, or mistake should *in terms* renounce and give up any essential natural right, the eternal law of reason and the great end of society would absolutely vacate such renunciation; the right to freedom being *the gift* of God Almighty, it is not in the power of man to alienate this gift and voluntarily become a slave.

2nd. *The Rights of Colonists as Christians.*

These may be best understood by reading, and carefully studying the institutes of the great Lawgiver and head of the Christian Church, which are to be found closely written and promulgated in the New Testament.

J: The Rights of the Colonists, Sam Adams

By the act of the British Parliament commonly called the Toleration Act, every subject in England except papists and etc. was restored to, and re-established in, his natural right to worship God according to the dictates of his own conscience. And by the Charter of this province it is granted, ordained, and established (that it is declared as an original right) that there shall be liberty of conscience allowed in the worship of God to all Christians except papists inhabiting or which shall inhabit or be resident within said province or territory. **Magna Charta itself is in substance but a constrained declaration, or proclamation, and promulgation in the name of King, Lords, and Commons of the sense the latter had of their original inherent, indefeasible natural rights, as also those of free citizens equally perdurable with the other. That great author, that great jurist, and even that court writer Mr. Justice Blackstone holds that this recognition was justly obtained of King John sword in hand (BL3, 123-124); and peradventure it must be one day sword in hand again rescued and preserved from total destruction and oblivion.**

3rd. *The Rights of the Colonists as Subjects.*

A commonwealth or state is a body politic or civil society of men united together to promote their mutual safety and prosperity by means of their union.

The *absolute rights* of Englishmen, and all freemen in or out of civil society, are principally: *personal security*, *personal liberty*, and *private property*.

All persons born in the British American colonies are by the laws of God and nature, and by the common law of England, exclusive of all charters from the crown, well entitled, and by the acts of the British Parliament are declared to be entitled to all the natural essential, inherent, and inseparable rights, liberties, and privileges of subjects born in Great Britain or within the realm. Among those rights are the following, which no men or body of men, consistently with their own rights as men and citizens or members of society, can for themselves give up or take away from others:

First, "the first fundamental positive law of all commonwealths or states is the establishing the legislative power; as the first fundamental *natural* law also, which is to govern even the legislative power itself, is the preservation of the society."

Secondly, the legislative has no right to absolute arbitrary power over the lives and fortunes of the people; nor can mortals assume a prerogative, not only too high for men, but for angels, and therefore reserved for the exercise of the Deity alone.

"**The legislative cannot justly *assume* to itself a power to rule by extempore arbitrary decrees; but it is bound to see that justice is dispensed, and that the rights of the subjects be decided by promulgated, standing, and known laws and authorized *independent judges*"**; that is, independent as far as possible of prince or people. "*There shall be one rule of justice for rich and poor; for the favorite in court and the countryman at the plough.*"

Thirdly, the supreme power cannot justly take from any man any part of his property without his consent, in person or by his representatives.

These are some of the first principles of natural law and justice, and the great barriers of all free states, and of the British Constitution in particular. It is utterly irreconcilable to these principles, and to many other fundamental maxims of the common law, common sense, and reason, that a British House of Commons should have a right, at pleasure, to give and grant the property of the colonists. That these colonists are well entitled to all the essential rights, liberties, and privileges of men and freemen born in Britain is manifest, not only from the colony Charter, in general, but acts of the British Parliament. The statute of the 13th of George 2.c.7. naturalizes even foreigners after seven years' residence. The words of the Massachusetts Charter are these: "And further our will and pleasure is, and we do hereby for us, our heirs and successors, grant, establish, and ordain, that all and every of the subjects of us, our heirs and successors which shall go to and inhabit within our said province or territory and every of their children which shall happen to be born there, or one the seas in going thither, or returning from thence shall have and enjoy all liberties and immunities of free and natural subjects with any of the dominions of us, our heirs and successors, to all intents, constructions, and purposes whatsoever as if they and every of them were born within this our realm of England." Now, what liberty can there be where property is taken away without consent? Can it be said with any color of truth and justice that this continent of three thousand miles in length, and of a breadth as yet unexplored, in which, however, it's supposed there are five millions of people, has the least voice, vote, or influence in the decisions of the British Parliament? Have they, all together, any more right or power to return a single member to that House of Commons, who have not inadvertently but deliberately assumed a power to dispose of their lives, liberties, and properties, than to choose an emperor of China! Had the colonists a right to return members to the British Parliament, it would only be hurtful, as from their local situation and circumstances it is impossible they should be ever truly and properly represented there. The inhabitants of this country in all probability in a few years will be more numerous than those of Great Britain and Ireland together; yet it is absurdly expected by the promoters of the present measures that these, with their posterity to all generations, should be easy while their property shall be disposed of by a House of Commons at three thousand miles distant from them, and who cannot be supposed to have the least care or concern for their real interest; who have not only no natural care for their interest, but must be *in effect* bribed against it, as every burden they lay on the colonists is so much saved or gained to themselves. Hitherto many of the colonists have been free from quit rents; but if the breath of a British House of Commons can originate an act for taking away all our money, our lands will go next or be subject to rack rents from haughty and relentless landlords who will ride at ease, while we are trodden in the dirt. The colonists have been branded with the odious names of traitors and rebels, only for complaining of their grievances. How long such treatment will or ought to be borne is submitted.

K

The Declaration and Resolves of the First Continental Congress

(*Note:* All resolutions, except (4) and (6), were adopted unanimously.)

In Congress, at Philadelphia, October 14, 1774.

Whereas, since the close of the last war, the British Parliament, claiming a power of right to bind the people of America, by statute, in all cases whatsoever, hath in some acts expressly imposed taxes on them, and in others, under various pretenses, but it fact for the purpose of raising a revenue, hath imposed rates and duties payable in these colonies, established a board of commissioners, with unconstitutional powers, and extended the jurisdiction of courts of Admiralty, not only for collecting said duties, but for the trial of causes merely arising within the body of a country.

And whereas, in consequence of other statutes, judges, who before held only estates at will in their offices, have been made dependent on the Crown alone for their salaries, and standing armies kept in times of peace:

And whereas, it has lately been resolved in Parliament, that by force of a statute, made in the thirty-fifth year of the reign of King Henry the Eighth, colonists may be transported to England, and tried there upon accusations for treasons, and misprisons, or concealment of treasons committed in the colonies, and by a late statute, such trials have been directed in cases therein mentioned.

And whereas, in the last session of Parliament, three statutes were made, one entitled, "An act to discontinue, in such manner and for such time as are therein mentioned, the landing and discharging, lading, or shipping of goods, wares and merchandise, at the town, and within the harbor of Boston, in the province of Massachusetts Bay, in North America"; another, entitled, "An act for the impartial administration of justice, in the cases of persons questioned for any act done by them in the execution of the law, or for the suppression of riots and tumults, in the province of the Massachusetts Bay, in New England." And another statute was then made, "for making more effectual provision for the government of the province of Quebec, etc." All which statutes are impolitic, unjust and cruel, as well as unconstitutional, and most dangerous and destructive of American rights.

And whereas, assemblies have been frequently dissolved, contrary to the rights of the people, when they attempted to deliberate on grievances; and their dutiful, humble, loyal, and reasonable petitions to the Crown for redress, have been repeatedly treated with contempt by His Majesty's ministers of state:

The good people of the several colonies of New Hampshire, Massachusetts Bay, Rhode Island and Providence Plantations, Connecticut, New York, New

Jersey, Pennsylvania, New Castle, Kent and Sussex on Delaware, Maryland, Virginia, North Carolina, and South Carolina, justly alarmed at these arbitrary proceedings of Parliament and administration, have severally elected, constituted, and appointed deputies to meet and sit in general congress, in the city of Philadelphia, in order to obtain such establishment, as that their religion, laws, and liberties may not be subverted:

Whereupon the deputies so appointed being now assembled, in a full and free representation of these colonies, taking into their most serious consideration, the best means of attaining the ends aforesaid, do, in the first place, as Englishmen, their ancestors in like cases have usually done, for asserting and vindicating their rights and liberties, declare,

That the inhabitants of the English colonies in North America, by the immutable laws of nature, and principles of the English Constitution, and the several charters or compacts, have the following rights:

Resolved, (1) That they are entitled to life, liberty and property, and they have never ceded to any sovereign power whatever, a right to dispose of either without their consent.

Resolved, (2) That our ancestors, who first settled these colonies, were at the time of their emigration from the mother country, entitled to all the rights, liberties, and immunities of free and natural-born subjects, within the realm of England.

Resolved, (3) That by such emigration they by no means forfeited, surrendered, or lost any of those rights, but that they were, and their descendants now are, entitled to the exercise and enjoyment of all such of them, as their local and other circumstances enable them to exercise and enjoy.

Resolved, (4) That the foundation of English liberty, and of all free government, is a right in the people to participate in their legislative council: and as the English colonists are not represented, and from their local and other circumstances, can not properly be properly represented in the British Parliament, they are entitled to a free and exclusive power of legislation in their several provincial legislatures, where their right of representation can alone be preserved, in all cases of taxation and internal polity, subject only to the negative of the sovereign, in such manner as had been theretofore used and accustomed. But, from the necessity of the case, and a regard to the mutual interest of both countries, we cheerfully consent to the operation of such acts of the British Parliament, as are bona fide, restrained to the regulation of our external commerce, for the purpose of securing the commercial advantages of the whole empire to the mother country, and the commercial benefits of its respective members; excluding every idea of taxation, internal or external, for the raising a revenue on the subjects in America, without their consent.

Resolved, (5) That the respective colonies are entitled to the common law of England, and more especially to the great and inestimable privilege of being tried by their peers of the vicinage, according to the course of that law.

Resolved, (6) That they are entitled to the benefit of such of the English statutes as existed at the time of their colonization; and which they have, by experience, respectively found to be applicable to their several local and other circumstances.

Resolved, (7) That these, His Majesty's colonies, are likewise entitled to all the immunities and privileges granted and confirmed to them by royal charters, or secured by the several codes of provincial laws.

Resolved, (8) That they have a right peaceably to assemble, consider of their grievances, and petition the King; and that all prosecutions, prohibitory proclamations, and commitments for the same, are illegal.

Resolved, (9) That the keeping a standing army in these colonies, in times of peace, without the consent of the legislature of that colony, in which such army is kept, is against the law.

Resolved, (10) It is indespensably necessary to good government, and rendered essential by the English constitution, that the constituent branches of the legislature be independent of each other; that, therefore, the exercise of legislative power in several colonies, by a council appointed, during pleasure by the Crown, is unconstitutional, dangerous, and destructive to the freedom of American legislation.

All and each of which the aforesaid deputies, in behalf of themselves and their constituents, do claim, demand, and insist on, as their indubitable rights and liberties; which can not be legally taken from them, altered or abridged by any power whatever, without their own consent, by their representatives in their several provincial legislatures.

In the course of our inquiry, we find many infringements and violations of the foregoing rights, which, from an ardent desire, that harmony and mutual intercourse of affection and interest may be restored, we pass over for the present, and proceed to state such acts and measures as have been adopted since the last war, which demonstrate a system forme to enslave America.

Resolved, That the following acts of Parliament are infringements and violations of the rights of the colonists; and that the repeal of them is essentially necessary in order to restore harmony between Great Britain and the American colonies, viz.:

The several acts of 4 Geo.3. ch.15 and ch.34.--5 Geo.3. ch.25--6 Geo.3 ch.52--7 Geo.3. ch.41, and ch.46--8 Geo.3. ch.22, which impose duties for the purpose of raising revenue in America, extend the powers of the Admiralty courts beyond their ancient limits, deprive the American subject of trial by jury, authorize the judges' certificate to indemnify the prosecutor for damages, that he might otherwise be liable to, requiring oppressive security from a claimant of ships and goods seized, before he shall be allowed to defend his property, and are subversive of American rights.

Also, the 12 Geo.3 ch.24, entitled "An act for the better securing His Majesty's dock-yards, magazines, ships, ammunition, and stores," which declares a new offence in America, and deprives the American subject of a constitutional trial by jury of the vicinage, by authorizing the trial of any person, charged with committing any offence described in the said act, out of the realm, to be indicted and tried for the same in any shire or county within the realm.

Also the three acts passed in the last session of Parliament, for stopping the port and blocking up the harbor of Boston, for altering the charter and government of Massachusetts Bay, and that which is entitled "An act for the better administration of justice," etc.

Also the act passed in the same session for establishing the Roman Catholic religion in the province of Quebec, abolishing the equitable system of English laws, and erecting a tyranny there, to the great danger, from so total a dissimilarity of religion, law, and government of the neighboring British colonies, by the assistance of whose blood and treasure the said country was conquered from France.

Also the act passed in the same session for the better providing suitable quarters for officers and soldiers in His Majesty's service in North America.

Also, that the keeping a standing army in several of these colonies in time of peace, without the consent of the legislature of that colony in which such army is kept, is against the law.

To these grievous acts and measures, Americans can not submit, but in hopes that their fellow subjects in Great Britain will, on a revision of them, restore us to that state in which both countries found happiness and prosperity, we have for the present only resolved to pursue the following peaceable measures:

1st. To enter into a non-importation, non-consumption, and non-exportation agreement or association.

2. To prepare and address to the people of Great Britain, and a memorial to the inhabitants of British America, and

3. To prepare a loyal address to His Majesty; agreeable to resolutions already entered into.

L

The Declaration of Independence

In Congress, July 4, 1776,

The Unanimous Declaration of the Thirteen United States of America,

When, in the course of human events, it becomes necessary for one people to dissolve the political bands which have connected them with another, and to assume, among the powers of the earth, the separate and equal station to which the Laws of Nature and of Nature's God entitle them, a decent respect for the opinions of mankind requires that they should declare the causes which impel them to the separation.--

We hold these truths to be self evident: that all men are created equal; that they are endowed by their Creator with certain unalienable Rights; that among these are life, liberty and the pursuit of Happiness.--

That to secure these rights, Governments are instituted among Men, deriving their just powers from the consent of the governed,--

That whenever any Form of Government becomes destructive of these ends, it is the Right of the People to alter or to abolish it, and to institute a new Government, laying its foundation on such principles and organizing its powers in such form, as to them shall seem most likely to effect their Safety and Happiness. Prudence, indeed, will dictate that Governments long established should not be changed for light and transient causes; and accordingly all experience hath shown, that mankind are more disposed to suffer, while evils are sufferable, that to right themselves by abolishing the forms to which they are accustomed. But when a long train of abuses and usurpations, pursuing invariably the same Object evinces a design to reduce them under absolute Despotism, it is their right, it is their duty, to throw off such Government, and to provide new Guards for their future security.--

Such has been the patient sufferance of these Colonies; and such is now the necessity which constrains them to alter their former Systems of Government. The history of the present King of Great Britain is a history of repeated injuries and usurpations, all having, in direct object, the establishment of an absolute Tyranny over these States. To prove this, let Facts be submitted to a candid world.--

He has refused his Assent to Laws, the most wholesome and necessary for the public good.--

He has forbidden his Governors to pass Laws of immediate and pressing importance, unless suspended in operation till his assent should be obtained; and when so suspended, he has utterly neglected to attend to them.--

He has refused to pass other laws for the accommodation of large districts of people, unless those people would relinquish the right of Representation in the Legislature, a right inestimable to them and formidable to tyrants only.--

He has called together legislative bodies at places unusual, uncomfortable, and distant from the depository of their public Records, for the sole purpose of fatiguing them into compliance with his measures.--

He has dissolved Representative Houses repeatedly, for opposing with manly firmness his invasions on the rights of the people.--

He has refused for a long time, after such dissolutions, to cause others to be elected; whereby the Legislative powers, incapable of Annihilation, have returned to the People at large for their exercise; the State remaining in the mean time exposed to all the dangers of invasion from without, and convulsions within.--

He has endeavored to prevent the population of these States; for that purpose obstructing the Laws of Naturalization of Foreigners; refusing to pass others to encourage their migrations hither, and raising the conditions of new Appropriations of Lands.--

He has obstructed the Administration of Justice, by refusing his Assent to Laws for establishing Judiciary powers.--

He has made Judges dependent on his will alone, for the tenure of their offices, and the amount and payment of their salaries.--

He has erected a multitude of New Offices, and sent hither swarms of Officers to harass our people, and eat out their substance.--

He has kept among us in times of peace, Standing Armies without the Consent of our legislatures.--

He has affected to render the Military independent of and superior to the Civil power.--

He has combined with others to subject us to a jurisdiction foreign to our constitution, and unacknowledged by our laws; giving his Assent to their Acts of pretended Legislation:--

For quartering large bodies of armed troops among us:--

For protecting them, by a mock Trial, from punishment for any Murders which they should commit on the Inhabitants of these States:--

For cutting off our trade with all parts of the world.--

For imposing taxes on us without our consent:--

For depriving us in many cases, of the benefits of Trial by Jury:--

For transporting us beyond the Seas to be tried for pretended offences:--

For abolishing the free System of English Laws in a neighboring Province, establishing therein an Arbitrary government, and enlarging its Boundaries so as to render it at once an example and fit instrument for introducing the same absolute rule in these Colonies:--

For taking away our Charters, abolishing our most valuable Laws, and altering fundamentally the Forms of our Governments:--

For suspending our own Legislatures, and declaring themselves invested with power to legislate for us in all cases whatsoever.--

He has abdicated Government here, by declaring us out of his Protection and waging War against us.--

He has plundered our seas, ravaged our Coasts, burnt our towns, and destroyed the lives of our people.--

He is at this time transporting large Armies of foreign Mercenaries to complete the works of death, desolation, and tyranny, already begun with circumstances of Cruelty & perfidy scarcely paralleled in the most barbarous ages, and totally unworthy the Head of a civilized nation.--

He has constrained our fellow Citizens taken Captive on the high Seas to bear arms against their Country, to become the executioners of the friends and Brethren, or to fall themselves by their Hands.--

He has excited domestic insurrections amongst us, and has endeavored to bring on the inhabitants of our frontiers, the merciless Indian Savages, whose known rule of warfare, is an undistinguished destruction of all ages, sexes, and conditions.--

In every stage of these Oppressions, We have Petitioned for Redress in the most humble terms: Our repeated petitions have been answered only by repeated injury. A Prince, whose character is thus marked by every act which may define a Tyrant, is unfit to be the ruler of a free people.

Nor have we been wanting in attentions to our British Brethren. We have warned them from time to time of attempts by their legislature to extend unwarrantable jurisdiction over us. We have reminded them of the circumstances of our emigration and settlement here. We have appealed to their native justice and magnanimity, and we have conjured them by the ties of our common kindred to disavow these usurpations, which would inevitably interrupt our connections and correspondence. They too have been deaf to the voice of justice and of consanguinity. We must, therefore, acquiesce in the necessity, which denounces our Separation, and hold them, as we hold the rest of mankind, Enemies in War, in Peace, Friends.--

We, therefore, the Representatives of the united States of America, in General Congress, Assembled, appealing to the Supreme Judge of the world for the rectitude of our intentions, do, in the Name, and by the Authority of the good People of these Colonies, solemnly publish and declare, That these United Colonies are, and of Right ought to be, Free and Independent States; that they are Absolved from all Allegiance to the British Crown, and that all political connection between them and the State of Great Britain, is and ought to be totally dissolved; and that as Free and Independent States, they have full Power to levy War, conclude Peace, contract Alliances, establish Commerce, and to do all other Acts and Things which Independent States may of right do.--

And for the support of this Declaration, with a firm reliance on the protection of divine Providence, we mutually pledge to each other our Lives, our Fortunes and our sacred Honor.

[Adopted by the Continental Congress and signed by John Hancock on July 4, 1776; signed by 49 other members of the Continental Congress on August 2, 1776 and by the remaining 6 members on later dates.]

M

A Bill of Memorial and Remonstrance against Religious Assessments
Presented to the Virginia General Assembly (1785)

This bill was prepared by James Madison in June 1785 as a means of opposing a "Bill Establishing a Provision for Teachers of the Christian Religion," which had been introduced in the Virginia General Assembly in December 1984. As a pretext for understanding the 1785 Memorial and Remonstrance Bill, the 1784 Establishment Bill is reprinted first.

A Bill Establishing a Provision for Teachers of the Christian Religion (1784)

Whereas the general diffusion of Christian knowledge hath a natural tendency to correct the morals of men, restrain their vices, and preserve the peace of society; which cannot be effected without a competent provision for learned teachers, who may be thereby enabled to devote their time and attention to the duty of instructing such citizens, as from their circumstances and want of education, cannot otherwise attain such knowledge; and it is judged that such provision may be made by the Legislature, without counteracting the liberal principle heretofore adopted and intended to be preserved by abolishing all distinctions of pre-eminence amongst the different societies or communities of Christians;

Be it therefore enacted by the General Assembly, That for the support of Christian teachers, ... per centum on the amount, or .... in the pound on the sum payable for tax on the property within this Commonwealth, is hereby assessed, and shall be paid by every person chargeable with the said tax at the time the same shall be become due; and the Sheriffs of the several Counties shall have power to levy and collect the same in the same manner and under the like restrictions and limitations, as are or may be prescribed by the laws for raising Revenues of this State.

And be it enacted, That for every sum so paid, the Sheriff or Collector shall give a receipt, expressing therein to what society of Christians the person from whom he may receive the same shall direct the money to be paid, keeping a distinct account thereof in his books. The Sheriff of every County, shall, on or before the ...... day of .... in every year, return to the Court, upon oath, two alphabetical lists of the payments to him made, distinguishing in columns opposite to the names of the persons who shall have paid the same, the society to which the money so paid was by them appropriated; and one column for the names where no appropriation shall be made. One of which lists, after being recorded in a book to be kept for that purpose, shall be filed by the Clerk in his office; the other shall by the Sheriff be fixed up in the Court-house, there to remain for the inspection of all concerned.

And the Sheriff, after deducting five per centum for the collection, shall forthwith pay to such person or persons as shall be appointed to receive the same by the Vestry, Elders, or Directors, however denominated of each such society; or in default thereof, upon the motion of such person or persons to the next or any succeeding Court, execution shall be awarded for the same against the Sheriff and his security, his and their executors or administrators; provided that ten days previous notice be given of such motion. And upon every such execution, the Officer serving the same shall proceed to immediate sale of the estate taken, and shall not accept of security for payment at the end of three months, nor to have the goods forthcoming at the day of sale; for his better direction wherein, the Clerk shall endorse upon every such execution that no security of any kind shall be taken.

And be it further enacted, That the money to be raised by virtue of this Act, shall be by the Vestries, Elders, or Directors of each religious society, appropriated to a provision for a Minister or Teacher of the Gospel of their denomination, or the providing places of divine worship, and to none other use whatsoever; except in the denominations of Quakers and Menonists, who may receive what is collected from their members, and place it in their general fund, to be disposed of in a manner which they shall think best calculated to promote their particular mode of worship.

And be it enacted, That all sums which at the time of payment to the Sheriff or Collector may not be appropriated by the person paying the same, shall be accounted for with the Court in manner as by this Act is directed; and after deducting for his collection, the Sheriff shall pay the amount thereof (upon account certified by the Court to the Auditors of Public Accounts, and by them to the Treasurer) into the public Treasury, to be disposed of under the direction of the General Assembly, for the encouragement of seminaries of learning within the Counties whence such sums shall arise, and to no other use or purpose whatsoever.

THIS Act shall commence, and be in force, from and after the .... day of .... in the year .....

A Bill of Memorial and Remonstrance against Religious Assessments (1785)

To the Honorable the General Assembly of the Commonwealth of Virginia. A Memorial and Remonstrance.

We, the subscribers, citizens of the said Commonwealth, having taken into serious consideration, a Bill printed by order of the last Session of General Assembly, entitled "A Bill establishing a provision for Teachers of the Christian Religion," and conceiving that the same, if finally armed with the sanctions of a law, will be a dangerous abuse of power, are bound as faithful members of a free State, to remonstrate against it, and to declare the reasons by which we are determined. We remonstrate against the said Bill,

1. **Because we hold it for a fundamental and undeniable truth, "that Religion or the duty which we owe to our Creator and the Manner of discharging it, can be directed only by reason and conviction not by force or violence."**[1] The Religion then of every man must be left to the conviction and conscience of every man; and it is the right of every man to exercise it as these may dictate. This right is in its nature an unalienable right. It is unalienable; because the opinions of men, depending only on the evidence contemplated by their own minds, cannot follow the dictates of other men: It is unalienable also; because what is here a right towards men, is a duty towards the Creator. **It is the duty of every man to render to the Creator such homage, and such only, as he believes to be acceptable to him.** This duty is precedent both in order of time and degree of obligation, to the claims of Civil Society. Before any man can be considered as a member of Civil Society, he must be considered as a subject of the Governor of the Universe: And if a member of Civil Society, who enters into any subordinate Association, must always do it with ta reservation of his duty to the general authority; much more must every man who becomes a member of any particular Civil Society, do it with a saving of his allegiance to the Universal Sovereign. We maintain therefore that in matters of Religion, no man's right is abridged by the institution of Civil Society, and that Religion is wholly exempt from its cognizance. True it is, that no other rule exists, by which any question which may divide a Society, can be ultimately determined, but the will of the majority; but it is also true, that the majority may not trespass on the rights of the minority.

2. Because if religion be exempt from the authority of the Society at large, still less can it be subject to that of the Legislative Body. The latter are but the creatures and vicegerents of the former. Their jurisdiction is both derivative and limited: it is limited with regard to the coordinate departments, more necessarily is it limited with regard to the constituents. **The preservation of a free government requires not merely, that the metes and bounds which separate each department of power may be invariably maintained; but more especially, that neither of them be suffered to overleap the great Barrier which defends the rights of the people. The Rulers who are guilty of such an encroachment, exceed the commission from which they derive their authority, and are Tyrants. The People who submit to it are governed by laws made neither by themselves, nor by an authority derived from them, and are slaves.**

3. Because, it is proper to take alarm at the first experiment on our liberties. We hold this prudent jealousy to be the first duty of citizens, and one of [the] noblest characteristics of the late Revolution. The freemen of America did not wait till usurped power had strengthened itself by exercise, and entangled the question in precedents. They saw all the consequences in the principle, and they avoided the consequences by denying the principle. We revere this lesson too much, soon to forget it. **Who does not see that the same authority which can establish Christianity, in exclusion of all other Religions, may establish with the same ease any particular sect of Christians, in exclusion of all other Sects?**

That the same authority which can force a citizen to contribute three pence only of his property for the support of any one establishment, may force him to conform to any other establishment in all cases whatsoever?

4. Because the bill violates that equality which ought to be the basis of every law, and which is more indispensible, in proportion as the validity or expediency of any law is more liable to be impeached. If "all men are by nature equally free and independent,"[2] all men are to be considered as entering into Society on equal conditions; as relinquishing no more, and therefore retaining no less, one than another, of their natural rights. Above all are they to be considered as retaining an "*equal* title to the free exercise of Religion according to the dictates of conscience."[3] **Whilst we assert for ourselves a freedom to embrace, to profess and to observe the Religion which we believe to be of divine origin, we cannot deny an equal freedom to those whose minds have not yet yielded to the evidence which has convinced us. If this freedom be abused, it is an offence against God, not against man: To God, therefore, not to men, must an account of it be rendered.** As the Bill violates equality by subjecting some to peculiar burdens; so it violates the same principle, by granting to others peculiar exemptions. Are the Quakers and Menonists the only sects who think a compulsive support of their religions unnecessary and unwarrantable? Can their piety alone be entrusted with the care of public worship? Ought their Religions to endowed above all others, with extraordinary privileges, by which proselytes may be enticed from all others? We think too favorably of the justice and good sense of these denominations, to believe that they either covet preeminencies over their fellow citizens, or that they will be seduced by them, from the common opposition to the measure.

5. Because the bill implies either that the Civil Magistrate is a competent Judge of Religious truth; or that he may employ Religion as an engine of Civil policy. The first is an arrogant pretension falsified by the contradictory opinions of Rulers of all ages, and throughout the world: The second an unhallowed perversion of the means of salvation.

6. Because the establishment proposed by the Bill is not requisite for the support of the Christian Religion. To say that it is, is a contradiction to the Christian Religion itself; for every page of it disavows a dependence on the powers of this world: it is a contradiction to fact; for it is known that this Religion both existed and flourished, not only without the support of human laws, but in spite of every opposition from them; and not only during the period of miraculous aid, but long after it had been left to its own evidence, and the ordinary care of Providence: Nay, it is a contradiction in terms; for a Religion not invented by human policy, must have pre-existed and been supported, before it was established by human policy. It is moreover to weaken in those who profess this Religion a pious confidence in its innate excellence, and the patronage of its Author; and to foster in those who still reject it, a suspicion that its friends are too conscious of its fallacies, to trust it to its own merits.

7. Because **experience witnesseth that ecclesiastical establishments, instead of maintaining the purity and efficacy of Religion, have had a contrary operation.** During almost fifteen centuries, has the legal establishment of Christianity been on trial. What have been its fruits? More or less in all places, pride and indolence in the Clergy; ignorance and servility in the laity; in both, superstition, bigotry and persecution. Enquire of the Teachers of Christianity for the ages in which it appeared in its greatest lustre; those of every sect, point to the ages prior to its incorporation with Civil policy. Propose a restoration of this primitive state in which its Teachers depended on the voluntary rewards of their flocks; many of them predict its downfall. On which side ought their testimony to have greatest weight, when for or when against their interest?

8. Because the establishment in question is not necessary for the support of Civil Government. If it be urged as necessary for the support of Civil Government only as it is a means of supporting Religion, and it be not necessary for the latter purpose, it cannot be necessary for the former. If Religion be not within [the] cognizance of Civil Government, how can its legal establishment be said to be necessary to civil Government? **What influence in fact have ecclesiastical establishments had on Civil Society? In some instances they have been seen to erect a spiritual tyranny on the ruins of Civil authority; in many instances they have been seen upholding the thrones of political tyranny; in no instance have they been seen the guardians of the liberties of the people. Rulers who wished to subvert the public liberty may have found an established clergy convenient auxiliaries. A just government, instituted to secure & perpetuate it, needs them not. Such a government will be best supported by protecting every citizen in the enjoyment of his Religion with the same equal hand which protects his person and his property; by neither invading the equal rights of any Sect, nor suffering any Sect to invade those of another.**

9. Because the proposed establishment is a departure from that generous policy, which, offering an asylum to the persecuted and oppressed of every Nation and Religion, promised a lustre to our country, and an accession to the number of its citizens. **What a melancholy mark is the bill of sudden degeneracy? Instead of holding forth an asylum to the persecuted, it is itself a signal of persecution. It degrades from the equal rank of Citizens all those whose opinions in Religion do not bend to those of the Legislative authority. Distant as it may be, in its present form, from the Inquisition it differs from it only in degree. The one is the first step, the other the last in the career of intolerance.** The magnanimous sufferer under this cruel scourge in foreign Regions, must view the Bill as a Beacon to our Coast, warning him to seek some other haven, where liberty and philanthropy in their due extent may offer a more certain repose from his troubles.

10. Because, it will have a like tendency to banish our Citizens. The allurements presented by other situations every day thinning their number. To superadd a fresh motive to emigration, by revoking the liberty which they now

enjoy, would be the same species of folly which has dishonoured and depopulated flourishing kingdoms.

11. Because, it will destroy that moderation and harmony which the forbearance of our laws to intermeddle with Religion, has produced amongst its several sects. Torrents of blood have been spilt in the old world, by vain attempts of the secular arm to extinguish Religious discord, by proscribing all difference in Religious opinions. Time has at length revealed the true remedy. Every relaxation of narrow and rigorous policy, wherever it has been tried, has been found to assuage the disease. The American Theatre has exhibited proofs, that equal and compleat liberty, if it does not wholly eradicate it, sufficiently destroys its malignant influence on the health and prosperity of the State. If with the salutary effects of this system under our own eyes, we begin to contract the bonds of Religious freedom, we know no name that will too severely reproach our folly. At least let warning be taken at the first fruits of the threatened innovation. The very appearance of the Bill has transformed that "Christian forbearance,[4] love and charity," which of late mutually prevailed, into animosities and jealousies, which may not soon be appeased. What mischiefs may not be dreaded should this enemy to the public quiet, be armed with the force of a law?

12. Because, the policy of the bill is adverse to the diffusion of the light of Christianity. The first wish of those who enjoy this precious gift, ought to be that it may be imparted to the whole race of mankind. Compare the number of those who have as yet received it with the number still remaining under the dominion of false Religions; and how small is the former! Does the policy of the Bill tend to lessen the disproportion? No; it at once discourages those who are strangers to the light of [revelation] from coming into the Region of it; and countenances, by example the nations who continue in darkness, in shutting out those who might convey it to them. Instead of levelling as far as possible, every obstacle to the victorious progress of truth, the Bill with an ignoble and unchristian timidity would circumscribe it, with a wall of defence, against the encroachments of error.

13. Because attempts to enforce by legal sanctions, acts obnoxious to so great a proportion of Citizens, tend to enervate the laws in general, and to slacken the bands of Society. If it be difficult to execute any law which is not generally deemed necessary or salutary, what must be the case where it is deemed invalid and dangerous? and what may be the effect of so striking an example of impotency in the Government, on its general authority.

14. Because a measure of such singular magnitude and delicacy ought not to be imposed, without the clearest evidence that it is called for by a majority of citizens: and no satisfactory method is yet proposed by which the voice of the majority in this case may be determined, or its influence secured. "The people of the respective counties are indeed requested to signify their opinion respecting the adoption of the Bill to the next Session of Assembly." But the representation must be made equal, before the voice either of the Representatives or of the Counties, will be that of the people. Our hope is that neither of the former will, after due consideration, espouse the dangerous principle of the Bill. Should the

event disappoint us, it will still leave us in full confidence, that a fair appeal to the latter will reverse the sentence against our liberties.

15. Because, finally, "the equal right of every citizen to the free exercise of his Religion according to the dictates of conscience" is held by the same tenure with all our other rights. If we recur to its origin, it is equally the gift of nature; if we weigh its importance, it cannot be less dear to us; if we consult the Declaration of those rights which pertain to the good people of Virginia, as the "basis and foundation of Government,"[5] it is enumerated with equal solemnity, or rather studied emphasis. Either then, we must say, that the will of the Legislature is the only measure of their authority; and that in the plentitude of this authority, they may sweep away all our fundamental rights; or, that they are bound to leave this particular right untouched and sacred: Either we must say, that they may controul the freedom of the press, may abolish the trial by jury, may swallow up the Executive and Judiciary Powers of the State; nay that they may despoil us of our very right of suffrage, and erect themselves into an independent and hereditary assembly: or we must say, that they have no authority to enact into law the Bill under consideration. We the subscribers say, that the General Assembly of this Commonwealth have no such authority; And that no effort may be omitted on our part against so dangerous a usurpation, we oppose to it, this remonstrance; earnestly praying, as we are in duty bound, that the Supreme Lawgiver of the Universe, by illuminating those to whom it is addressed, may on the one hand, turn their councils from every act which would affront his holy prerogative, or violate the trust committed to them: and on the other, guide them into every measure which may be worthy of his [blessing, may re]dound to their own praise, and may establish more firmly the liberties, the prosperity, and the Happiness of the Commonwealth.

Notes

These notes appear in the original document and all refer to the Virginia Declaration of Rights, adopted by the Virginia Convention in 1776.
1. Decl. Rights, Art: 16.
2. Decl. Rights, Art. 1.
3. Art: 16.
4. Art. 16.
5. Decl. Rights-title.

Ye know that the princes of the Gentiles exercise dominion over them, and they that are great exercise authority upon them. But it shall not be so among you: but whosoever will be great among you, let him be your minister; and whosoever will be chief among you, let him be your servant: Even as the Son of man came not to be ministered unto, but to minister, and to give his life a ransom for many.
--Matt. 20:25-28

N

The Virginia Statute for Religious Freedom

Original Bill Introduced by Thomas Jefferson in 1777
Passed by the Virginia General Assembly on January 16, 1786

[*Some words of Jefferson's bill were deleted from the Statute; these words are italicized and in brackets.*]

Whereas [*Well aware that the opinions and belief of men depend not on their own will, but follow involuntarily the evidence proposed to their minds; that*] Almighty God hath created the mind free[, *and manifested his supreme will that free it shall remain by making it altogether insusceptible of restraint*]; that all attempts to influence it by temporal punishments or burthens, or by civil incapacitations, tend only to beget habits of hypocrisy and meanness, and are a departure from the plan of the Holy author or our religion, who being Lord both of body and mind, yet chose not to propagate it by coercions on either, as was in his Almighty power to do[, *but to extend it by his influence on reason alone*]; that the impious presumption of legislators and rulers, civil as well as ecclesiastical, who being themselves but fallible and uninspired men, have assumed dominion over the faith of others, setting up their own opinions and modes of thinking as the only true and infallible, and as such endeavouring to impose them on others, hath established and maintained false religions over the greatest part of the world, and through all time; that to compel a man to furnish contributions of money for the propagation of opinions which he disbelieves [*and abhors*], is sinful and tyrannical; that even the forcing him to support this or that teacher of his own religious persuasion, is depriving him of the comfortable liberty of giving his contributions to the particular pastor, whose morals he would make his pattern, and whose powers he feels most persuasive to righteousness, and is withdrawing from the ministry those temporary rewards, which proceeding from an approbation of their personal conduct, are an additional incitement to earnest and unremitting labours for the instruction of mankind; that our civil rights have no dependence on our religious opinions, any more than our opinions in physics or geometry; that therefore the proscribing any citizen as unworthy the public confidence by laying upon him an incapacity of being called to offices of trust and emolument, unless he profess or renounce this or that religious opinion, is depriving him injuriously of those privileges and advantages to which in common with his fellow-citizens he has a natural right; that it tends only to corrupt the principles of that [*very*] religion it is meant to encourage, by bribing with a monopoly of worldly honours and emoluments, those who will externally profess and conform to it; that though indeed these are criminal who do not withstand such temptation, yet neither are those innocent who lay the bait in their way; [*that the opinions of men are not the object of civil government, nor under its jurisdiction;*] that to suffer the civil magistrate to intrude his powers into the field of opinion, and to restrain the profession or propagation of principles on supposition of their ill tendency, is a dangerous fallacy, which at once destroys all religious liberty, because he being of course judge of that tendency will make his opinions the rule of judgment, and approve or condemn the sentiments of others only as they shall square with or differ from his own; that it is time enough for the rightful purposes of civil government, for its officers to interfere when principles break out into overt acts against peace and good order; and finally, that truth is great and will prevail if left to herself, that she is the proper and sufficient antagonist of error, and has nothing to fear from the conflict, unless by human interposition disarmed of natural weapons, free argument and debate, errors ceasing to be dangerous when it is permitted freely to contradict them:

[*We the General Assembly of Virginia do enact*] Be it enacted by the General Assembly, That no man shall be compelled to frequent or support any religious worship, place, or ministry whatsoever, nor shall be enforced, restrained, molested, or burthened in his body or goods, nor shall otherwise suffer on account of his religious opinions or belief; but that all men shall be free to profess, and by argument to maintain, their opinion in matters of religion, and that the same shall in no way diminish, enlarge, or affect their civil capacities.

And though we well know that this assembly elected by the people for the ordinary purposes of legislation only, have no power to restrain the acts of succeeding assemblies, constituted with powers equal to our own, and that therefore to declare this act to be irrevocable would be of no effect in law; **yet we are free to declare, and do declare, that the rights hereby asserted are of the natural rights of mankind, and that if any act shall be hereafter passed to repeal the present, or to narrow its operation, such act will be an infringement of natural right.**

O

The United States Constitution
(Selected Sections and Amendments Relating to People's Rights and States' Rights)

We the people of the United States, in Order to form a more perfect Union, establish Justice, insure domestic Tranquility, provide for the common defence, promote the general Welfare, and secure the Blessings of Liberty to ourselves and our Posterity, do ordain and establish this Constitution for the United States of America.

Article I
The Legislative Department

Section 8 The Congress shall have the power
1. To lay and collect taxes, duties, imposts and excises, to pay the debts and provide for the common defense and general welfare of the United States, but all duties, imposts and excises shall be uniform throughout the United States;
2. To borrow money on the credit of the United States;
3. To regulate commerce with foreign nations, and among the several States, and with the Indian tribes;
4. To establish a uniform rule of naturalization, and uniform laws on the subject of bankruptcies throughout the United States;
5. To coin money, regulate the value thereof, and of foreign coin, and fix the standard of weights and measures;
6. To provide for the punishment of counterfeiting the securities and current coin of the United States;
7. To establish post offices and post roads;
8. To promote the progress of science and useful arts, by securing for limited times to authors and inventors the exclusive right to their respective writings and discoveries;
9. To constitute tribunals inferior to the Supreme Court;
10. To define and punish piracies and felonies committed on the high seas, and offences against the law of nations;
11. To declare war, grant letters of marque and reprisal, and make rules concerning captures on land and water;
12. To raise and support armies, but no appropriation of money to that use shall be longer than for two years;
13. To provide and maintain a navy;
14. To make rules for the government and regulation of the land and naval forces;
15. To provide for calling forth the militia to execute the laws of the Union, suppress insurrections and repel invasions;

16. To provide for organizing, arming, and disciplining the militia, and for governing such part of them as may be employed in the service of the United States, reserving to the States respectively, the appointment of officers, and the authority of training the militia according to the discipline prescribed by Congress;

17. To exercise exclusive legislation in all cases whatsoever, over such district (not exceeding ten miles square) as may, by cession of particular States, and the acceptance of Congress, become the seat of the government of the United States, and to exercise like authority over all places purchased by the consent of the legislature of the State in which the same shall be, for the erection of forts, magazines, arsenals, dockyards, and other needful buildings; and

18. To make all laws which shall be necessary and proper for carrying into execution the foregoing powers, and all other powers vested by this Constitution in the government of the United States, or in any department or officer thereof.

Section 9

1. The migration or importation of such persons as any of the States now existing shall think proper to admit, shall not be prohibited by the Congress prior to the year one thousand eight hundred and eight, but a tax or duty may be imposed on such importation, not exceeding ten dollars for each person.

2. The privilege of the writ of *habeas corpus* shall not be suspended, unless when in cases of rebellion or invasion the public safety may require it.

3. No bill of attainder or *ex post facto* law shall be passed.

4. No capitation[, or other direct,] tax shall be laid, unless in proportion to the census or enumeration herein before directed to be taken (bracketed portion superseded by the 16th Amendment, giving Congress the power to tax income).

5. No tax or other duty shall be laid on articles exported from any State.

6. No preference shall be given by any regulation of commerce or revenue to the ports of one State over those of another: nor shall vessels bound to, or from, one State be obliged to enter, clear, or pay duties in another.

7. No money shall be drawn from the treasury, but in consequence of appropriations made by law; and a regular statement and account of the receipts and expenditures of all public money shall be published from time to time.

8. No title of nobility shall be granted by the United States: and no person holding any office of profit or trust under them, shall, without the consent of the Congress, accept any present, emolument, office, or title, of any kind whatever, from any king, prince, or foreign State.

Section 10

1. No State shall enter into any treaty, alliance, or confederation; grant letters of marque and reprisal; coin money; emit bills of credit; make anything but gold and silver coin a tender in payment of debts; pass any bill of attainder, *ex post facto* law, or law impairing the obligation of contracts, or grant any title of nobility.

2. No State shall, without the consent of the Congress, lay any imposts or duties on imports or exports, except what may be absolutely necessary for executing its inspection laws; and the net produce of all duties and imposts laid by any State on imports or exports, shall be for the use of the treasury of the United States; and all such laws shall be subject to the revision and control of the Congress.

3. No State shall, without the consent of Congress, lay any duty of tonnage, keep troops, or ships of war in time of peace, enter into any agreement or compact with another State, or with a foreign power, or engage in war, unless actually invaded, or in such imminent danger as will not admit of delay.

Article III
The Judicial Department

Section 1

The judicial power of the United States shall be vested in one Supreme Court, and in such inferior courts and the Congress may from time to time ordain and establish. The judges, both of the Supreme and inferior courts, shall hold their offices during good behavior, and shall, at stated times, receive for their services, a compensation, which shall not be diminished during their continuance in office.

Section 2

1. The judicial power shall extend in all cases, in law and equity, arising under this Constitution, the laws of the United States, and treaties made, or which shall be made, under their authority;--to all cases affecting ambassadors, other public ministers and consuls;--to all cases of admiralty and maritime jurisdiction;--to all controversies to which the United States shall be a party;--to controversies between two or more States;[--between a State and citizens of another State;]--between citizens of different States;--between citizens of the same State claiming lands under grants of different States, and between a State or the citizens thereof, and foreign States, citizens or subjects (bracketed portion superseded by the 11th Amendment).

2. In all cases affecting ambassadors, other public ministers and consuls, and those in which a State shall be a party, the Supreme Court shall have original jurisdiction. In all the other cases before mentioned, the Supreme Court shall have appellate jurisdiction, both as to law and to fact, with such exceptions, and under such regulations as the Congress shall make.

3. The trial of all crimes, except in cases of impeachment, shall be by jury; and such trial shall be held in the State where the said crimes shall have been committed; but when not committed within any State, the trial shall be at such place or places as the Congress may by law have directed.

Section 3

1. Treason against the United States shall consist only in levying war against them, or in adhering to their enemies, giving them aid and comfort. No person shall be convicted of treason unless on the testimony of two witnesses to the same overt act, or on confession in open court.

2. The Congress shall have power to declare the punishment of treason, but no attainder of treason shall work corruption of blood, or forfeiture except during the life of the person attained.

Article IV

Section 1

Full faith and credit shall be given in each State to the public acts, records, and judicial proceedings of every other State. And the Congress may by general laws prescribe the manner in which such acts, records and proceedings shall be proved, and the effect thereof.

Section 2

1. The citizens of each State shall be entitled to all privileges and immunities of citizens in the several States.

2. A person charged in any State with treason, felony, or other crime, who shall flee from justice, and be found in another State, shall on demand of the executive authority of the State from which he fled, be delivered up to be removed to the State having jurisdiction of the crime.

3. No person held to service or labor in one State under the laws thereof, escaping into another, shall, in consequence of any law or regulation therein, be discharged from such service or labor, but shall be delivered up on claim of the party to whom such service or labor may be due (superseded by the 13th Amendment).

Section 3

1. New States may be admitted by the Congress into this Union; but no new State shall be formed or erected within the jurisdiction of any other State; nor any State be formed by the junction of two or more States, or parts of States, without the consent of the legislatures of the States concerned as well as Congress.

2. The Congress shall have power to dispose of and make all needful rules and regulations respecting the territory or other property belonging to the United States; and nothing in this Constitution shall be so construed as to prejudice any claims of the United States, or of any particular State.

Section 4

The United States shall guarantee to every State in this Union a republican form of government, and shall protect each of them against invasion; and on application of the legislature, or of the executive (when the legislature cannot be convened) against domestic violence.

Article V

The Congress, whenever two thirds of both Houses shall deem it necessary, shall propose amendments to this Constitution, or, on the application of the legislatures of two thirds of the several States, shall call a convention for proposing amendments, which in either case, shall be valid to all intents and purposes, as part of this Constitution when ratified by the legislatures of three fourths of the several States, or by conventions of three fourths thereof, as the one or the other mode of ratification may be proposed by the Congress; Provided that no amendment which may be made prior to the year one thousand eight hundred and eight shall in any manner affect the first and fourth clauses in the ninth section of the first article; and that no State, without its consent, shall be deprived of its equal suffrage in the Senate.

Article VI

1. All debts contracted and engagements entered into, before the adoption of this Constitution, shall be as valid against the United States under this Constitution, as under the Confederation.

2. This, Constitution, and the laws of the United States which shall be made in pursuance thereof; and all treaties made, or which shall be made, under the authority of the United States, shall be the supreme law of the land; and the Judges of every State shall be bound thereby, anything in the Constitution or laws of any State to the contrary notwithstanding.

3. The senators and representatives before mentioned, and the members of the several State legislatures, and all executive and judicial officers, both of the United States and of the several States, shall be bound by oath and affirmation to support this Constitution; but no religious test shall ever be required as a qualification to any office or public trust under the United States.

Article VII

The ratification of the conventions of nine States shall be sufficient for the establishment of this Constitution between the States so ratifying the same.

Done in Convention by the unanimous consent of the States present the seventeenth day of September in the year of our Lord one thousand seven hundred and eighty-seven, and of the independence of the United States of America the twelfth. In witness whereof we have hereunto subscribed our names. [Names omitted]

Amendments to the United States Constitution
The first ten amendments were passed by Congress September 25, 1789 and ratified by three fourths of the states December 15, 1791.

First Amendment
Congress shall make no law respecting an establishment of religion, or prohibiting the free exercise thereof; or abridging the freedom of speech, or of the press; or the right of the people peaceably to assemble, and to petition the government for a redress of grievances.

Second Amendment
A well regulated militia, being necessary to the security of a free State, the right of the people to keep and bear arms, shall not be infringed.

Third Amendment
No soldier shall, in time of peace be quartered in any house, without the consent of the owner, not in time of war, but in a manner to be prescribed by law.

Fourth Amendment
The right of the people to be secure in their persons, houses, papers, and effects, against unreasonable searches and seizures, shall not be violated, and no warrants shall issue, but upon probable cause, supported by oath or affirmation, and particularly describing the place to be searched, and the persons or things to be seized.

Fifth Amendment
No person shall be held to answer for a capital, or otherwise infamous crime, unless on a presentment or indictment of a grand jury, except in cases arising in the land or naval forces, or in the militia, when in actual service in time of war or public danger; nor shall any person be subject for the same offence to be twice put in jeopardy of life or limb; nor shall be compelled in any criminal case to be a witness against himself, nor be deprived of life, liberty, or property, without due process of law; nor shall private property be taken for public use without just compensation.

Sixth Amendment
In all criminal prosecutions, the accused shall enjoy the right to a speedy and public trial, by and impartial jury of the State and district wherein the crime shall have been committed, which district shall have been previously ascertained by law, and to be informed of the nature and cause of the accusation; to be confronted with the witnesses against him; to have compulsory process for obtaining witnesses in his favor, and to have the assistance of counsel for his defense.

Seventh Amendment

In suits at common law, where the value in controversy shall exceed twenty dollars, the right of trial by jury shall be preserved, and no fact tried by a jury shall be otherwise reexamined in any court of the United States, than according to the rules of the common law.

Eighth Amendment

Excessive bail shall not be required, nor excessive fines imposed, nor cruel and unusual punishments inflicted.

Ninth Amendment

The enumeration in the Constitution of certain rights shall not be construed to deny or disparage others retained by the people.

Tenth Amendment

The powers not delegated to the United States by the Constitution, nor prohibited by it to the States, are reserved to the States respectively, or to the people.

Eleventh Amendment (ratified January 8, 1798)

The judicial power of the United States shall not be construed to extend to any suit in law or equity, commenced or prosecuted against one of the United States by citizens of another State, or by citizens or subjects of any foreign State.

Thirteenth Amendment (ratified December 18, 1865)

Section 1. Neither slavery nor involuntary servitude, except as punishment for a crime whereof the party shall have been duly convicted, shall exist within the United States, or any place subject to their jurisdiction.

Section 2. Congress shall have the power to enforce this article by appropriate legislation.

Fourteenth Amendment (ratified July 28, 1868)

Section 1. All persons born or naturalized in the United States, and subject to the jurisdiction thereof, are citizens of the United States and of the States wherein they reside. No state shall make or enforce any law which shall abridge the privileges or immunities of the citizens of the United States; nor shall any State deprive any person of life, liberty, or property, without due process of law; nor deny to any person within its jurisdiction the equal protection of the laws.

[The following sections of the Fourteenth Amendment are omitted: Section 2, relating to the apportionment of congressmen among the states, particularly when a state denies the right to vote to any of its male inhabitants over 21 years of age; Section 3, relating to the disability to serve in congress of persons who have engaged in insurrection or rebellion against the United States; and Section

4, relating to the nullification of public debts incurred in aid of insurrection or rebellion against the United States.]

Section 5. The Congress shall have power to enforce, by appropriate legislation, the provisions of this article.

Fifteenth Amendment (ratified March 30, 1870)

Section 1. The right of the citizens of the United States to vote shall not be denied or abridged by the United States or by any State on account of race, color, or previous condition of servitude.

Section 2. The Congress shall have power to enforce this article by appropriate legislation.

Sixteenth Amendment (ratified February 25, 1913)

The Congress shall have power to lay and collect taxes on incomes, from whatever source derived, without apportionment among the several States, and without regard to any census or enumeration.

Seventeenth Amendment (ratified May 31, 1913)

The Senate of the United States shall be composed of two senators from each state, elected by the people thereof, for six years, and each senator shall have one vote. The electors in each State shall have the qualifications requisite for electors of the most numerous branch of the State legislature.

When vacancies happen in the representation of any State in the Senate, the executive authority of such State shall issue writs of election to fill such vacancies: *Provided*, That the legislature of any State may empower the executive thereof to make temporary appointments until the people fill the vacancies by election as the legislature may direct.

This amendment shall not be construed as to affect the election or term of any senator chosen before it becomes valid as part of the Constitution.

Eighteenth Amendment (ratified January 29, 1919)

After one year from the ratification of this article, the manufacture, sale, or transportation of intoxicating liquors within, the importation thereof into, or the exportation thereof from the United States and all territory subject to the jurisdiction thereof for beverage purposes is hereby prohibited.

The Congress and the several states shall have concurrent power to enforce this article by appropriate legislation.

This article shall be inoperative unless it shall have been ratified an an amendment to the Constitution by the legislatures of the several States, as provided in the Constitution, within seven years from the date of the submission hereof to the States by Congress.

O: The United States Constitution

Nineteenth Amendment (ratified August 26, 1920)

The right of citizens of the United States to vote shall not be denied or abridged by the United States or any State on account of sex.

The Congress shall have power by appropriate legislation to enforce the provisions of this article.

Twenty-First Amendment (ratified December 5, 1933)

Section 1. The eighteenth article of amendment to the Constitution of the United States is hereby repealed.

Section 2. The transportation or importation into any State, Territory or possession of the United States for delivery of use therein of intoxicating liquors, in violation of the laws thereof, is hereby prohibited.

Section 3. This article shall be inoperative unless it shall have been ratified an an amendment to the Constitution by convention in the several States, as provided in the Constitution, within seven years from the date of the submission thereof to the States by the Congress.

Twenty-Fourth Amendment (ratified Jan. 23, 1964)

Section 1. The right of citizens of the United States to vote in any primary or other election for President or Vice President, for electors for President or Vice President, or for Senator or Representative in Congress, shall not be denied or abridged by the United States or any State by reason of failure to pay any poll tax or other tax.

Section 2. The Congress shall have power to enforce this article by appropriate legislation.

Twenty-Sixth Amendment (ratified July 1, 1971)

Section 1. The right of citizens of the United States, who are eighteen years of age or older, to vote shall not be denied or abridged by the United States or by any State on account of age.

Section 2. The Congress shall have power to enforce this article by appropriate legislation.

Twenty-Seventh Amendment (ratified May 7, 1992)

No law varying the compensation for the services of the Senators and Representatives, shall take effect, until an election of Representatives shall have intervened.

The Rights of Women

The Seneca Falls Declaration of Sentiments and Resolutions
Seneca Falls, New York, July 19, 1848

Reprinted from *The History of Woman Suffrage*,
Elizabeth Cady Stanton, Susan B. Anthony and Matilda Joslyn Gage, eds., 6 vols. repr. of 2 vol. 1881 ed. (Salem, New Hampshire: Ayer Company, 1985), 1:70-73

1. Declaration of Sentiments

When, in the course of human events, it becomes necessary for one portion of the family of man to assume among the people of the earth a position different from that which they have hitherto occupied, but one to which the laws of nature and nature's God entitle them, a decent respect for the opinions of mankind requires that they should declare the causes that impel them to such a course.

We hold these truths to be self-evident: **that all men and women are created equal;** that they are endowed by their Creator with certain inalienable rights; that among these are life, liberty, and the pursuit of happiness; that to secure these rights governments are instituted, deriving their just powers from the consent of the governed. Whenever any form of government becomes destructive of these ends, it is the right of those who suffer from it to refuse allegiance to it, and to insist upon the institution of a new government, laying its foundation on such principles, and organizing its powers in such form, as to them shall seem most likely to effect their safety and happiness. Prudence indeed, will dictate that governments long established should not be changed for light and transient causes; and accordingly all experience hath shown that mankind are more disposed to suffer, while evils are sufferable, than to right themselves by abolishing the forms to which they are accustomed. But when a long train of abuses and usurpations, pursuing invariably the same object evinces a design to reduce them under absolute despotism, it is their duty to throw off such government, and to provide new guards for their future security. Such has been the patient sufferance of the women under this government, and such is now the necessity which constrains them to demand the equal station to which they are entitled.

The history of mankind is a history of repeated injuries and usurpations on the part of man toward woman, having in direct object the establishment of an absolute tyranny over her. To prove this, let facts be submitted to a candid world.

He has never permitted her to exercise her inalienable right to the elective franchise.

He has compelled her to submit to laws, in the formation of which she has no voice.

He has withheld from her rights which are given to the most ignorant and degraded men--both natives and foreigners.

Having deprived her of this first right of a citizen, the elective franchise, thereby leaving her without representation in the halls of legislation, he has oppressed her on all sides.

He has made her, in the eyes of the law, civilly dead.

He has taken from her all right in property, even to the wages she earns.

He has made her, morally, an irresponsible being, as she can commit many crimes with impunity, provided they be done in the presence of her husband. In the convenant of marriage, she is compelled to promise obedience to her husband, **he becoming, to all intents and purposes, her master--the law giving him power to deprive her of her liberty, and to administer chastisement.**

He has so framed the laws of divorce, as to what shall be the proper causes, and in case of separation, to whom guardianship of the children shall be given, as to be wholly regardless of the happiness of women--the law, in all cases, going upon a false supposition of the supremacy of man, and giving all power into his hands.

After depriving her of all rights as a married woman, if single, and the owner of property, he has taxed her to support a government which recognizes her only when her property can be made profitable to it.

He has monopolized nearly all the profitable employments, and from those she is permitted to follow, she receives but a scanty remuneration. He closes against her all the avenues to wealth and distinction which he considers most honorable to himself. As a teacher of theology, medicine, or law, she is not known.

He has denied her the facilities for obtaining a thorough education, all colleges being closed to her.

He allows her in Church, as well as State, but a subordinate position, claiming Apostolic authority for her exclusion from the ministry, and, with some exceptions, from any public participation in the affairs of the Church.

He has created a false public sentiment by giving to the world a different code of morals for men and women, by which moral delinqencies which exclude women from society, are not only tolerated, but deemed of little account in man.

He has usurped the perogative of Jehovah himself, claiming it as his right to assign for her a sphere of action, when that belongs to her conscience and to her God.

He has endeavored, in every way that he could, to destroy her confidence in her own powers, to lessen her self-respect and to make her willing to lead a dependent and abject life.

Now, in view of this entire disfranchisement of one-half the people of this country, their social and religious degradation--in view of the unjust laws above mentioned, and because women do not feel themselves aggrieved, oppressed, and fraudulently deprived of their most sacred rights, we insist that they have immediate admission to all the rights and privileges which belong to them as citizens of the United States.

In entering upon the great work before us, we anticipate no small amount of misconception, misrepresentation, and ridicule; but we shall use every instrumentality within our power to effect our object. We shall employ agents, circulate tracts, petition the State and National legislatures, and endeavor to enlist the pulpit and the press in our behalf. We hope this Convention will be followed by a series of Conventions embracing every part of the country.

2. Resolutions

WHEREAS, The great precept of nature is conceded to be, that "man shall pursue his own true and substantial happiness." Blackstone in this Commentaries remarks, that this law of Nature being coeval with mankind, and dictated by God himself, is of course superior in obligation to any other. It is binding over all the globe, in all countries and at all times; no human laws are of any validity if contrary to this, and such of them as are valid, derive all their force, and all their validity, and all their authority, mediately and immediately, from this original; therefore,

Resolved, That such laws as conflict, in any way, with the true and substantial happiness of woman, are contrary to the great precept of nature and of no validity, for this is "superior in obligation to any other."

Resolved, That all laws which prevent woman from occupying such a station in society as her conscience shall dictate, or which place her in a position inferior to that of man, are contrary to the great precept of nature, and therefore of no force or authority.

Resolved, That woman is man's equal--was intended to be so by the Creator, and the highest good of the race demands that she should be recognized as such.

Resolved, That the women of this country ought to be enlightened in regard to the laws under which they live, that they may no longer publish their degradation by declaring themselves satisfied with their present position, nor their ignorance, by asserting that they have all the rights they want.

Resolved, That inasmuch as man, while claiming for himself intellectual superiority, does accord to woman moral superiority, it is pre-eminently his duty to encourage her to speak and teach, as she has an opportunity, in all religious assemblies.

Resolved, That the same amount of virtue, delicacy, and refinement of behavior that is required of woman in the social state, should also be required of man, and the same transgressions should be visited with equal severity on both man and woman.

Resolved, That the objection of indelicacy and impropriety, which is so often brought against woman when she addresses a public audience, comes with a very ill-grace from those who encourage, by their attendance, her appearance on the stage, in the concert, or in feats of the circus.

Resolved, That woman has too long rested satisfied in the circumscribed limits which corrupt customs and a perverted application of the Scriptures have marked out for her, and that it is time she should move in the enlarged sphere which her great Creator has assigned her.

Resolved, That it is the duty of the women of this country to secure to themselves their sacred right to the elective franchise.[1]

Resolved, That the equality of human rights results necessarily from the fact of the identity of the race in capabilities and responsibilities.

Resolved, therefore, That, being invested by the creator with the same capabilities, and the same consciousness of responsibility for their exercise, it is demonstrably the right and duty of woman, equally with man, to promote every righteous cause by every righteous means; and especially in regard to the great subjects of morals and religion, it is self-evidently her right to participate with her brother in teaching them, both in private and in public, by writing and by speaking, by any instrumentalities proper to be used, and in any assemblies proper to be held; and this being a self-evident truth growing out of the divinely implanted principles of human nature, any custom or authority adverse to it, whether modern or wearing the hoary sanction of antiquity, is to be regarded as a self-evident falsehood, and at war with mankind.

The 1881 volume 1 records, on page 73, that Lucretia Mott offered and spoke to the following additional resolution:

Resolved, That the speedy success of our cause depends upon the zealous and untiring efforts of both men and women, for the overthrow of the monopoly of the pulpit, and for securing to women an equal participation in various trades, professions, and commerce.

---

[1] The 1881 volume 1 also records on page 73 that, "The only resolution that was not unanimously adopted was the ninth, urging the women of the country to secure to themselves the elective franchise. Those who took part in the debate feared a demand for the right to vote would defeat others they deemed more rational, and make the whole movement ridiculous. But Mrs. Stanton and Frederick Douglass seeing that the power to choose rulers and make laws, was the right by which all others could be secured, persistently advocated the resolution, and at last carried it by a small majority.

Notes

CHAPTER 1

1. "James Otis's Speech Against the Writs of Assistance" in Henry Steele Commager, ed., *Documents of American History*, 5th ed. (New York: Appleton-Century-Crofts, 1949), 45-47, repr. from *The Works of John Adams*, C. F. Adams, ed., v. II, 521 ff.

2. A. J. Langguth, *Patriots: The Men Who Started the American Revolution* (New York: Simon & Schuster, 1989), 22-23.

3. Anson Phelps Stokes, *Church and State in the United States*, 3 vols. (New York: Harper & Brothers, 1950), 1:223. Bernard Bailyn, *The Ideological Origins of the American Revolution*. 2nd ed., rev. and enl. (Cambridge, Mass. and London, Engl.: Belknap Press of Harvard University Press, 1992) quotes an 1815 letter from John Adams to Thomas Jefferson saying "What do we mean by the American Revolution? The War? That was no part of the Revolution; it was only an effect and consequence of it. The Revolution was in the minds of the people, and this was effected, from 1760 to 1775, in the course of fifteen years before a drop of blood was shed at Lexington. The records of thirteen legislatures, the pamphlets, newspapers in all the colonies, ought to be consulted during that period to ascertain the steps by which public opinion was enlightened and informed concerning the authority of Parliament over the colonies."

4. Langguth, *Patriots*, 26-27.

5. Ibid., 47.

6. Ibid., 46.

7. Sir William Blackstone, *Commentaries on the Laws of England*, 4 vols. (Oxford, England: Clarendon Press, 1765-69), reprinted by The Legal Classics Library (Birmingham, Ala.: Gryphon Editions, 1983), 1:38-62, 1:117-141; see Appendices BL1 and BL3.

8. John Locke, *Concerning Civil Government, Second Essay*, appearing in *Great Books of the Western World*, v. 35 (Chicago: Encyclopaedia Britannica, 1952, 28th repr., 1986); John Locke, *Second Treatise of Government*, ed. with introduction by Thomas P. Peardon (New York: The Liberal Arts Press, 1952, repr. 1954); see Appendix F.

9. This is a reference to paragraph 135 in Appendix F.

10. Each reference to one of the Appendices BL1 to BL7 (reprinted from Blackstone's *Commentaries*) consists of the appendix identification, followed by the page number of one of Blackstone's volumes. Blackstone's page numbers are at the bottom of each page of Appendices BL1 to BL7; BL1 to BL4 are from Book 1 of Blackstone's *Commentaries*; BL5 to BL7 are from Book 4 of Blackstone's *Commentaries*.

11. Richard Thomson, *An Historical Essay on the Magna Charta of King John: To Which Are Added, the Great Charter in Latin and English; the Charters of Liberties and Confirmations, Granted by Henry III and Edward I; The*

Original Charter of the Forests; and Various Authentic Instruments Connected with Them (London: John Major and Robert Jennings, 1829), reprinted by The Legal Classics Library, Division of Gryphon Editions, Ltd. (Birmingham, Alabama, 1982), 2.

12. Ibid., 81, 83, 87 for the Magna Charta of King John; 115 for the charter of King Henry III; 154, for the charter of King Edward I.

13. Winston S. Churchill, *A History of the English-Speaking Peoples*, 4 vols. (New York: Dodd, Mead, 1956-58), 2:143.

14. VIII Coke Rep. 114a, 118a-b (K.B., 1610). Coke's opinion in this case is one of the most controversial in the history of English jurisprudence. Most English judges have taken the view that they do not have the power to declare acts of Parliament void, in contrast to American judges who are able to hold acts of their legislatures void for being in conflict with their constitutions. In *Bonham's case*, Chief Justice Coke discussed four previous cases in which English courts had held various acts of Parliament void. *Bonham's case* originated as a complaint of false imprisonment brought by Dr. Bonham against the Royal College of Physicians. The College had fined the doctor and enjoined him from further practice of medicine after finding that he had illegally practiced medicine in London without first obtaining a proper certificate. When Dr. Bonham continued to practice and refused to pay the fine, the college officials imprisoned him. Coke gave five reasons why Dr. Bonham had been wrongfully imprisoned. One of these reasons was based on the College's statute of incorporation, which gave it the power to "regulate all London physicians and punish infractions with fine and imprisonment" and specified that half of each fine collected was to go to the College. Coke said that the College's entitlement to half the fines made it a party to the cases it was judging, thereby violating the common law maxim that no man ought to judge his own case. Therefore, he declared the statute void because it was "against common right and reason." Coke's opinion on this issue did not set a precedent for later cases, because none of the other judges on the court agreed with him that an act of Parliament could be ruled void. Nevertheless, in the years leading to the American War of Independence, American colonial leaders often quoted this opinion in their speeches against acts of Parliament. In 1765, Patrick Henry referred to Coke's opinion in his speech against the Stamp Act in the Virginia House of Burgesses.

15. Bailyn, *Ideological Origins*, 36.

16. Ibid., 84.

17. For an extensive discussion of the colonial pamphlets and their sources, see Bailyn, *Ideological Origins*. A portion of James Otis, *A Vindication of the British Colonies* is reprinted in Appendix H, from Bailyn's, *Pamphlets of the American Revolution*, 4 vols., John Harvard Library (Cambridge, Mass.: Belknap Press of Harvard University Press, 1965), 1:558-560. Sam Adams, *The Rights of the Colonists*, is reprinted in Appendix I. For other collections of colonial pamphlets see *Old South Leaflets*, 8 vols. (Boston: Directors of the Old South Work, Old South Meeting House, n.d.); *The Annals of America*, 21 vols., v. 2, 1755-1783 (Chicago: Encyclopaedia Britannica, Inc., 1968); Saul K.

Padover, ed., *The World of the Founding Fathers: Their Basic Ideas on Freedom and Self-Government* (New York: Thomas Yoseloff, 1960).

18. Charles B. Morris, ed., *Burke's Speech on Conciliation with America* (New York and London: Harper & Brothers, 1945), 31; also George Otto Trevelyan, *The American Revolution*, ed. Richard B. Morris (New York: David McKay, 1964), 58.

19. Lewis Warden, *The Life of Blackstone* (Charlottesville, Va.: The Michie Company, 1938), 320-324. Warden says that several hundred copies of the first 1765 volume were initially sent to America. Orders increased rapidly after that and by the time all four volumes had been published, about a thousand sets had been shipped to America, at £10 per set including shipping costs. Then in 1771, Robert Bell, a Philadelphia bookseller, began publishing the books and selling them at £3 per set. Bell reported, "Booksellers alone took 700 copies, Rivington of New York leading with 200, and Robert Wells of Charleston, South Carolina, coming next with 68. Individual subscriptions exceeded 700. Thus an edition in excess of 1400 copies was called for before the work was printed."

20. Ibid., 327.

21. Daniel J. Boorstin, *The Americans: The Colonial Experience* (New York: Vintage Books, a division of Random House, 1958), 202. Webster's blue-backed speller, referred to in the Boorstin quote, was published in 1783.

22. Churchill, *English-Speaking Peoples*, 3:165; Robert Leckie, *George Washington's War* (New York: HarperCollins, 1992), 39.

23. 19 Howell's State Trials, 1029. A large portion of Lord Camden's opinion in this case, as well as a portion of Otis's argument to the Massachusetts Superior Court and the facts of the Wilkes case, may be found in the U.S. Supreme Court opinion by Justice Bradley in *Boyd v. U.S.*, 116 U.S. 616 at 624-630 (1886).

24. Blackstone, *Commentaries*, 4:288.

25. "The Proclamation of 1763," repr. in Commager, *Documents*, 47-50, and *Annals of America*, 84-86.

26. Thomson, *Historical Essay on the Magna Charta*, 372.

27. Repr. from Bailyn, *Pamphlets*, 1:473-477 (Otis pamplet pp. 69-73).

28. At this point, Thacher cited several English statutes that limited the power of the non-jury admiralty courts to matters done on the sea, including 13 Richard II c.5, "Admirals and their deputies shall not meddle henceforth of anything done within the realm, but only of a thing done upon the sea," and 15 Richard II c.3, providing that in respect of all matters "rising within the bodies of the countries, as well by land as by water, and also of wreck of the sea, the admiral's court shall have no jurisdiction" (Bailyn, *Pamphlets*, 1:726-727, n. 5).

29. Repr. from Bailyn, *Pamphlets*, 1:492-495 (Thacher pamphlet pp. 7-11). Thacher's last statement, that no action shall be maintained if there were no probable cause, probably means no action for damages, not that the claimant would be unable to recover his goods.

30. For reprints of the Bland, Fitch, Otis, Thacher, Hopkins and Fitch pamphlets, see Bailyn, *Pamphlets*, Pamphs. 4, 6, 7, 8 and 9, respectively.

31. By a "sheet," the Stamp Act meant a large sheet of paper of a minimum eighteen by twenty-four inches, usually cut and folded to make eight or sixteen pages of a book or pamphlet or folded in half to make four folio pages of a newspaper. For pamphlets, newspapers and handbills using less that a whole sheet, the tax was less, sometimes only a half penny.

32. John R. Alden, *A History of the American Revolution* (New York: Alfred A. Knopf, 1976), 66; Langguth, *Patriots*, 51.

33. Ibid., 67.

34. Mercy Otis Warren, *History of the Rise, Progress and Termination of the American Revolution*, 3 vols. (Boston: Manning and Loring for E. Larkin, 1805), 1:46, repr. in 2 vols. with annotation by Lester H. Cohen (Indianapolis: Legal*Classics*, 1988), 1:17. Mrs. Warren was the sister of James Otis and the wife of James Warren, a first cousin of Dr. Joseph Warren. James Warren was also leading Patriot. When his cousin Joseph died at Bunker Hill, he succeeded him as president of the Massachusetts Provincial Congress.

35. Langguth, *Patriots*, 52-56.

36. Leckie, *Washington's War*, 49.

37. For the Braintree and Northampton resolutions, see Commager, *Documents*, 56-57, 59.

38. Martin Howard, *A Letter from a Gentleman at Halifax to a Rhode Island Friend* (Halifax, 1765), 12; repr. in Bailyn, *Pamphlets*, Pamphlet 10.

39. Soame Jenyns, *The Objections to the Taxation of Our American Colonies, Briefly Considered* (London, 1765), repr. in part in *Annals of America*, 2:160-161.

40. Bailyn, *Pamphlets*, 601-603, discussing Thomas Whately, *The Regulations Lately Made Concerning the Colonies and the Taxes Imposed upon Them, Considered* (1765) and William Knox, *The Claim of the Colonies to an Exemption from Internal Taxes* (1765).

41. James Otis, *A Vindication of the British Colonies, against the Aspersions of the Halifax Gentleman, in His Letter to a Rhode Island Friend* (Boston, 1765), repr. in Bailyn, *Pamphlets*, Pamphlet 11; Daniel Dulany, *Considerations on the Propriety of Imposing Taxes in the British Colonies, for the Purpose of Raising Revenue, by Act of Parliament* (Annapolis, 1765), repr. in Bailyn, *Pamphlets*, Pamphlet 13.

42. Bailyn, *Pamphlets*, 1:538 (Howard quote), 1:564 (Otis quote).

43. Blackstone, *Commentaries*, 1:166.

44. Commager, *Documents*, 59.

45. Langguth, *Patriots*, 85.

46. *Annals of America*, 156.

47. Commager, *Documents*, 60-61.

48. Blackstone also said that private conduct that does not affect others, such as becoming drunk while in the privacy of one's home, is beyond the reach of human laws (BL3, 120). He also said that laws that restrain conduct in matters of mere indifference, in contrast with laws that further some public good, are destructive of natural liberty (BL3, 122). However, Blackstone made several other statements that could be interpreted as contradicting his statements on pp. 41-43, 119, 120 and 122 of his first volume. He said that in all forms of government, there must be "a supreme, irresistible, absolute, uncontrolled authority," in which the rights of sovereignty reside (BL1, 49). He then defined the sovereign power as the power to make laws, saying that wherever that power resides, all others must conform to it. Because Britain's lawmaking power resides in the king and Parliament (BL1, 50-51), and their power is absolute and uncontrolled, they can apparently make laws that violate God's natural laws. Furthermore, all Englishmen must obey those laws, which appears to be exactly the opposite of what he said at 1:41-43. This apparent conflict may be resolved by interpreting the statements at 1:49 as defining the practical, absolute power that every sovereign government possesses, as long as it has a police force and an army that can enforce its laws. That does not mean that all its laws are necessarily just or within the rightful power of the government. It means only that, as a practical matter, the people must obey a government that violates their rights unless they can either (1) persuade the government stop its illegal activity or (2) overthrow the government and replace it with another that acts with more respect for their rights. The American colonists tried persuasion, until they declared their independence in 1776.

49. Bailyn, *Pamphlets*, 1:535.

50. Ibid., 1:558-560. In fn. 6, 1:760, Bailyn said, "Otis states Blackstone's formulation correctly, but the words he quotes are conflatations and paraphrases of scattered phrases and sentences. He seems to have written this section from notes he had taken of Blackstone's book rather than from the volume itself. He may well have found it difficult to keep a copy of Blackstone at hand to refer to when he was writing the pamphlet since copies of volume I must just then have begun to arrive in the colonies." However, Bailyn says on 1:736 that Otis's pamphlet was published the third week of March 1765, whereas George Wickersham, former U.S. Attorney General, said that the first volume of Blackstone's *Commentaries* was not published until November 1765. That was in a July 1924 speech at the Royal Courts of Justice, at a ceremony dedicating a statute of Blackstone, published as an appendix by David A. Lockmiller, *Sir William Blackstone* (Chapel Hill: University of North Carolina Press, 1938), 266. Blackstone said in the preface of his first volume that he was publishing his *Commentaries* because other people had been circulating unauthorized notes of his lectures and he wanted to set the record straight with his own account of what he was teaching. He had also published *An Analysis of the Laws of England* in 1756, a less comprehensive work that was sold primarily as a textbook for his students. Because Otis's pamphlet was published before Blackstone's *Commentaries*, Otis may have had either a copy of unauthorized notes of Blackstone's lectures or his earlier textbook, which would explain why Otis's quotations, though accurate in general content, appeared to Bailyn to be "conflatations and paraphrases of scattered phrases and sentences" of Blackstone's *Commentar-*

ies. Otis's use of the Blackstonian terms, "personal security" and "personal liberty," in his 1764 letter to the London agent for the Massachusetts House of Representatives, published as an appendix to his pamphlet, *The Rights of the British Colonies Asserted and Proved*, also shows that he may have had either a copy of the unauthorized notes or the earlier textbook.

51. Ibid., 1:541.
52. John Dickinson, "On the Suspension of the New York Assembly," repr. in *Annals of America*, 182-184.
53. Commager, *Documents*, 64.
54. Warren, *American Revolution*, 1:28.
55. Ibid., 3:307 of the original text, 2:630 of the reprint. Mrs. Warren, like her brother, appears to have paraphrased Blackstone. The closest passage of Blackstone I have found, which conveys the thought of Mrs. Warren's quote, is at 3:380, where he said, "Every new tribunal, erected for the decision of facts, without the intervention of a jury, (whether composed of justices of the peace, commissioners of revenue, judges of a court of conscience, or any other standing magistrates) is a step towards establishing aristocracy, the most oppressive of absolute governments. . . . And in every country on the continent, as the trial by peers has been gradually disused, so the nobles have increased in power, till the state has been torn to pieces by rival factions, and oligarchy in effect has been established, though under the shadow of regal government."
56. "Massachusetts Circular Letter," repr. in Commager, *Documents*, 66-67.
57. Langguth, *Patriots*, 99-100.
58. Samuel Eliot Morison, *The Oxford History of the American People*, 3 vols. (New York: Oxford University Press, 1965; reprinted, New York: NAL Penguin, Mentor Books, 1972), 1:261.
59. Langguth, *Patriots*, 95-97. The leader was quoting 1 Kings 12:16 and 2 Chron. 10:16, which described the separation of the kingdom of Israel from the kingdom of Judah: "So when all Israel saw that the king hearkened not unto them, the people answered the king, saying, What portion have we in David? neither *have we* inheritance in the son of Jesse: to your tents, O Israel: now see to thine own house, David. So Israel departed unto their tents."
60. Morrison, *Oxford History*, 1:267.
61. Langguth, *Patriots*, 104.
62. Ibid.
63. Ibid., 111.

CHAPTER 2

1. Langguth, *Patriots*, 169 (chap. 1, n. 2).
2. Quoted in Morison, *Oxford History*, 1:273 (chap. 1, n. 58).
3. Blackstone, *Commentaries*, 3:379 (chap. 1, n. 7).
4. Benjamin Woods Labaree, *The Boston Tea Party* (New York: Oxford University Press, 1964), 58.

5. The anti-monopoly provision, Section 9 of the Massachusetts Body of Liberties, adopted in 1641, reads as follows:

> No monopolies shall be granted or allowed amongst us, but of such new Inventions that are profitable to the Countrie, and that for a short time.

This provision was similar to the English Statute of Monopolies, enacted by Parliament in 1623. Blackstone explained this statute in his *Commentaries*, 4:159-160 (BL7). Both the English statute and the Massachusetts Body of Liberties provision contained an exception allowing the granting of patents on inventions for limited periods of time. However, the Massachusetts statute was broader than the English statute, because the latter prohibited only monopolies on the "buying, selling, making, working or using of anything within this Realme." Technically, it did not prohibit monopolies on the shipping of products to and from England.

6. The requirement that the Company sell its goods at public auction was designed to insulate it from the charge that it had a monopoly on the sale of oriental goods in England. Such a monopoly was prohibited by the Statute of Monopolies.

7. Alden, *American Revolution*, 138 (chap. 1, n. 32).

8. This monopoly violated the spirit of the Statute of Monopolies of 1623 and would have been a direct violation of that law had it applied in America as well as England. The Tea Act also violated the anti-monopoly provision of the Massachusetts Body of Liberties of 1641 and was, to use the words of Chief Justice Coke in *Bonham's Case*, "against common right and reason." When a legislature restrains all business enterprises except one from trading in a certain product, it must show that the restraint is in the best interests of the public. Blackstone said, "[T]hat constitution or frame of government, that system of laws, is alone calculated to maintain civil liberty, which leaves the subject entire master of his own conduct, except in those points wherein the public good requires some direction or restraint" (BL3, 122).

9. The story of the Hutchinson-Oliver letters is told by Catherine Drinker Bowen in *The Most Dangerous Man in America: Scenes from the Life of Benjamin Franklin* (Boston: Little, Brown and Company, 1974), 230-243. Somehow, these private letters fell into Franklin's hands while he was in London and he sent them to his friend Thomas Cushing, speaker of the Massachusetts House of Representatives. He later said his purpose was to ease tensions between the colonists and the British government by showing that it was not the British government but the two local Massachusetts governors, born and raised among the colonists, who were responsible for depriving the colonists of their rights. However, Franklin's plan backfired. In January 1774, he was summoned to a hearing before the Privy Council, where Solicitor General Alexander Wedderburn accused him of stealing the letters and threatened to prosecute him in the Chancery Court. Fortunately, Franklin was never arrested or prosecuted, but the Privy Council refused to dismiss Hutchinson and Oliver from their posts and gave them a staunch vote of support. To this day no one knows how Franklin got hold of the letters.

10. Quoted in Langguth, *Patriots*, 175-176.

11. Langguth, *Patriots*, 178. An audio recreation of this meeting may be heard on earphones installed at the seats of the Old South Meeting House in Boston.

12. Ibid., 179. Hancock was quoting Judges 17:6 and 21:25.

13. There is now a replica of one of the ships from which the Indian masqueraders dumped the tea located next to the Congress Street Bridge and the Boston Children's Museum. Actors on board the replica reenact the event during scheduled hours. Children and their parents may join the actors in dumping crates of that "detested East India tea" into the Boston Harbor.

14. Blackstone, *Commentaries*, 1:400.

15. Quoted in Morison, *Oxford History*, 1:276.

16. Ibid., 1:277.

17. Reprinted in *Annals of America*, 256-257 (chap. 1, n. 17).

18. Reprinted in Merrill D. Peterson, ed., *The Portable Thomas Jefferson* (New York: Viking Penguin, Penguin Books, 1975, reprint, 1977), xvi, 3-21.

19. Ibid., xvi, 3.

20. Reprinted in *Annals of America*, 59-60.

21. Quoted in Leckie, *Washington's War*, 91 (chap. 1, n. 22).

22. For an excellent description of the Continental Association and the debates in the Continental Congress leading to the agreement, see David Ammerman, *In the Common Cause: American Response to the Coercive Acts of 1774* (Charlottesville: University Press of Virginia, 1974).

23. Reprinted in *Annals of America*, 278; Stokes, *Church and State*, 1:262-263 (chap. 1, n. 3).

24. J. Bartlett Brebner, *Canada, a Modern History* (Ann Arbor: University of Michigan Press, 1960), 47.

25. Sir John G. Bourinot, *Canada under British Rule 1760-1900* (Toronto: Copp, Clark, 1901), 186.

26. Brebner, *Canada*, 93.

27. Reprinted in *Annals of America*, 281; Stokes, *Church and State*, 1:263.

28. Reprinted in *Annals of America*, 282.

29. Worthington Chauncey Ford, ed., *Journals of the Continental Congress 1774-1789*, 14 vols. (Washington: Government Printing Office, 1904), 1:107-108.

30. Blackstone, *Commentaries*, 2:78.

31. Because of his Tory sympathies, Seabury lost his church position during the War of Independence. He supported himself by practicing medicine and serving as a chaplain in the British army, ministering to the broken body as well as the broken spirit. After the war, Seabury regained his church position and became the first American bishop of the Church of England in 1784, as well as the presiding officer of the American convention of churches of that denomination. In 1789, Seabury's convention became independent of the Church of

England and changed its name to the "Protestant Episcopal Church in the United States of America." It is now known informally as the "Episcopal Church."

32. Alexander Hamilton, *A Full Vindication of the Measures of Congress* (New York: James Rivington, 1774), 5.

33. Reprinted in *Annals of America*, 289.

34. Alexander Hamilton, *The Farmer Refuted* (New York: James Rivington, 1775), 5-7.

35. Reprinted in *Annals of America*, 289-291.

CHAPTER 3

1. Blackstone, *Commentaries*, 4:149-150 (chap. 1, n. 7).

2. Trevelyan, *The American Revolution*, 129 (chap. 1, n. 18).

3. Quoted in Langguth, *Patriots*, 216 (chap. 1, n. 2).

4. Reprinted in Morris, *Burke's Speech*, 65 (chap. 1, n. 18).

5. Ibid., 74.

6. Ibid., 86.

7. Langguth, *Patriots*, 216.

8. Morison, *Oxford History*, 1: 281 (chap. 1, n. 58); Trevelyan, *American Revolution*, 166-168.

9. Reprinted in *The Annals of America*, 322-323 (chap. 1, n. 17), from the 1817 reconstruction of Henry's speech by William Wirt in *The Life and Character of Patrick Henry* (Philadelphia, n.d.), 137-142. The March 20 Convention, including Henry's speech, is reenacted every Sunday afternoon during the summer months at St. John's Church in Richmond.

10. Langguth, *Patriots*, 223.

11. Christopher Hibbert, *Redcoats and Rebels: The American Revolution through British Eyes* (New York: W. W. Norton & Company, 1990), 28.

12. Christ's Church is also known as The Old North Church and is located at the corner of the present Salem and Tileston Streets in Boston.

13. Henry Steele Commager and Richard B. Morris, *The Spirit of Seventy-Six* (New York: Harper & Row, 1958; revised, 1975), 69-70. The Battle of Lexington is re-enacted every year beginning at 5:30 am, April 19th ("Patriots Day"), on the Battle Green in the center of Lexington. The other Patriots Day events are also re-enacted before crowds totaling about twenty-five thousand people.

14. Ibid., 84.

15. Alden, *American Revolution*, 175 (chap. 1, n. 32).

16. Leckie, *Washington's War*, 115 (chap. 1, n. 22).

17. John E. Selby, *The Revolution in Virginia, 1775-1783* (Williamsburg: The Colonial Williamsburg Foundation, 1988), 1-2.

18. Quoted in Selby, *The Revolution*, 3-4.

19. Selby, *The Revolution*, 4-5.

20. These tracts comprised 129 separate townships at the time, according to Michael Bellisiles, *Revolutionary Outlaws* (Charlottesville: University Press of Virginia, 1993), 41-42.
21. Ibid., 85.
22. Quoted in Bellisiles, *Revolutionary Outlaws*, 86-87.
23. Quoted in Morison, *Oxford History*, 1:287; Langguth, *Patriots*, 261.
24. Ford, *Journals of the Continental Congress*, 2:140 ff. (chap. 2, n. 29).
25. Ibid., 2:68 ff.
26. Morison, *Oxford History*, 1:290.
27. Quoted in Morison, *Oxford History*, 1:290.
28. Morison, *Oxford History*, 1:291.
29. Leckie, *Washington's War*, 213.
30. Selby, *The Revolution in Virginia*, 41-79; Hibbert, *Redcoats and Rebels*, 101-103.
31. Hibbert, *Redcoats and Rebels*, 103-104; for the number of Highlanders in the under MacDonald, see Morision, *Oxford History*, 1:292-293.
32. Hibbert, *Redcoats and Rebels*, 73-75.
33. Ibid., 104-109.

CHAPTER 4

1. Thomas Paine, *Common Sense* (1776), reprinted with intro. by Isaac Krammick (New York: Penguin Books, 1976)
2. Langguth, *Patriots*, 341 (chap. 1, n. 2).
3. Morison (*Oxford History*, 312, chap. 1, n. 58) estimates that 40 per cent of the Americans were "actively Patriot" at the beginning of the war.
4. Willard Sterne Randall, *Thomas Jefferson: A Life*, a John Macrae Book (New York: Henry Holt and Company, 1993), 273.
5. Quoted in Randall, *Thomas Jefferson*, 273.
6. Randall, *Thomas Jefferson*, 272.
7. Pat Robertson, *America's Dates with Destiny* (Nashville, Tenn.: Thomas Nelson, 1986), 66-67.
8. Locke, *Second Treatise*, par. 212, p. 120; par. 221, p. 123 (chap. 1, n. 8).
9. Blackstone, *Commentaries*, 3:379 (see chap. 1, n. 7).

CHAPTER 5

1. Hibbert, *Redcoats and Rebels*, 261 (chap. 3, n. 11).
2. Quoted in Franklin P. Cole, *They Preached Liberty* (Indianapolis: Liberty-*Press*, 1977), 22.
3. Morison, *Oxford History*, 312-313 (chap. 1, n. 58).
4. Leckie, *Washington's War*, 251-252 (chap. 1, n. 22); Hibbert, *Redcoats and Rebels*, 119-121.

5. According to the *1994 World Almanac* (p. 708), 4,435 American soldiers were killed in battle and 6,188 were wounded, but the editors caution that the data for wars prior to World War I are based on incomplete records. There are also no reliable records indicating how many died off the battlefields from disease or wounds. Typically, in wars fought before 1900 that number was much higher than the number of battle deaths.

6. Leckie, *Washington's War*, 460; Hibbert, *Redcoats and Rebels*, 199.

7. Page Smith, *A New Age Now Begins, A People's History of the American Revolution*, vol. 2 (New York: McGraw Hill, 1976), 1806; Leckie, *Washington's War*, 181; Morison, *Oxford History*, 301.

8. Langguth, *Patriots*, 375 (chap. 1, n. 2); Leckie, *Washington's War*, 258.

9. The Americans lost over one thousand, according to Morison (*Oxford History*, 317); they lost 974 killed, wounded or missing and 1,079 captured, according to Leckie (*Washington's War*, 264); the number was two thousand prisoners plus three thousand other casualties, according to Hibbert (*Redcoats and Rebels*, 123).

10. Quoted in Leckie, *Washington's War*, 284.

11. Quoted in Hibbert, *Redcoats and Rebels*, 129.

12. Quoted in Leckie, *Washington's War*, 321.

13. Fort Stanwix is now located in downtown Rome, New York.

14. Quoted in Hibbert, *Redcoats and Rebels*, 185.

15. Howard Zinn, *A People's History of the United States*, Harper Colophon ed. (New York: Harper & Row, 1980), repr., HarperPerennial ed. (New York: HarperCollins, 1990), 63.

16. Morison reports that Washington had twelve thousand men, while Howe had eighteen thousand (*Oxford History*, 1:328). On the other hand, Leckie, says that Washington had fourteen to sixteen thousand, of which eleven to twelve thousand were fit for duty and that Howe had fifteen to eighteen thousand (*Washington's War*, 349-350). According to Hibbert, Howe had only fourteen thousand men (*Redcoats and Rebels*, 155). These discrepancies indicate the margin of error in the reported troop strengths during the battles of the American War of Independence.

17. Mud Island is now part of the mainland; Fort Mifflin now stands on the Pennsylvania bank of the Delaware, between the Philadelphia International Airport and the mouth of the Schuykill River.

18. Quoted in Leckie, *Washington's War*, 436.

19. Ibid., 441.

20. Leckie, *Washington's War*, 440-441.

21. Hibbert, *Redcoats and Rebels*, 207.

22. Leckie, *Washington's War*, 335. De Kalb's real name was "Johann von Kalb." However, he called himself "Jean de Kalb" to fit in better with his French comrades.

23. Ibid., 460. "Ménage à trois" is how Leckie describes this relationship. General Howe invited both Mr. and Mrs. Loring to spend the winter with him in Philadelphia.

24. Quoted in Leckie, *Washington's War*, 461.
25. Leckie, *Washington's War*, 486.
26. Ibid., 492; Morison, *Oxford History*, 336.
27. *The New Encyclopaedia Britannica*, 15th ed., Macropaedia, s.v. "United States of America, History."
28. Quoted in Henry Steele Commager, "Forts in the Wilderness," chap. 1 in Stefan Lorant, *Pittsburgh: The Story of an American City* (Garden City, New York: Doubleday & Company, 1964), 46.
29. Quoted in Leckie, *Washington's War*, 585.
30. Ibid., 612.
31. Quoted in Hibbert, *Redcoats and Rebels*, 306.
32. Ibid., 322.
33. Quoted in Smith, *New Age*, 2:1657-1658.
34. Quoted in Leckie, 641.
35. Ibid., 652.
36. Howard Peckham, ed., *The Toll of Independence* (Chicago: University of Chicago Press, 1974).
37. Obed Macy, *The History of Nantucket*, 2nd ed. (Mansfield, Mass.: Macy & Pratt, 1880; reprint, Ellinwood, Kansas: Macys of Ellinwood, 1985), 84-85.
38. Ibid., 94-95.
39. Ibid., 98.
40. Quoted in Leckie, *Washington's War*, 473.
41. Ibid., 333.
42. Leckie, *Washington's War*, 336.
43. Henry Howe, *Historical Collections of Ohio*, 3 vols. (Columbus, Ohio: Henry Howe & Son, 1891), 3:368-370. The story of Gnadenhutten, Schoenbrunn and Salem Indians is recreated every year in a summer-long play, "Trumpet in the Land," at an outdoor theatre in Schoenbrunn, Ohio, near New Philadelphia.

CHAPTER 6

1. Smith, *A New Age Now Begins*, 1768-1778 (chap. 5, n. 7).
2. Richard B. Morris, *Witnesses at the Creation* (New York: Henry Holt and Company, 1985), 124-125.
3. Ibid., 142-143.
4. Ibid., 123; Morison, *Oxford History*, 1:370 (chap. 1, n. 58).
5. Morison, *Oxford History*, 1:390-393; Morris, *Witnesses*, 169-176.

CHAPTER 7

1. Edmund Randolph was the nephew of Peyton Randolph, the first president of the Continental Congress and the last speaker of colonial Virginia's House of Burgesses.

2. A. E. Dick Howard, "James Madison and the Founding of the Republic" (1985), reprinted in *James Madison on Religious Liberty*, ed. Robert S. Alley (Buffalo, N.Y.: Prometheus Books, 1985), 29.

3. According to Article VI, clause 2, the laws and treaties included within the supreme law are "the laws of the United States which shall be made in pursuance" of the Constitution and "all treaties made, or which shall be made, under the authority of the United States." The reason for this difference in language appears to be the fact that, before the Constitution was adopted, there were existing treaties with foreign nations that the United States had entered into under the Articles of Confederation (see Morris, *Witnesses*, 149, full cite at chap. 6, n. 2). Thus, the Convention delegates worded the supremacy clause so that these prior treaties would also be part of the "supreme law of the land." However, the subsequent treaties, like the subsequent laws, are part of the supreme law of the land only if they are made pursuant to the Constitution.

4. Morris, *Witnesses*, 201-203.

5. Ibid., 203-205.

6. See Chapter 10, Section C, for a further discussion of privileges and immunities of Article IV, Section 2[1], as well as Section 1 of the Fourteenth Amendment.

7. Ibid., 193-194.

8. N. 3, supra.

9. Quoted in Morison, *Oxford History*, 1:401 (chap. 1, n. 58). This is not the rule in England, where "an Act of Parliament can do no wrong, though it can do some things that look pretty odd" (Lord Holt in *City of London v. Wood*, 12 Mod. 669, 687 [1701]). In 1610, Chief Justice Coke had held in *Bonham's case* that an English court could hold an act of Parliament void, when it is "against common right and reason, or repugnant, or impossible to be performed, . . ." VIII Coke Rep. 114a, 118a-b (K.B., 1610). Coke even cited four previous cases in which courts voided acts of Parliament. However, Coke's opinion was not followed by later judges, because he gave four other reasons for his decision and none of the other judges on the court agreed that they could hold an act of Parliament void. Of course, England has never had a written constitution that says that its provisions, and the laws and treaties made pursuant to them, are "the supreme law of the land." Therefore, in England there are no supreme laws except those passed by Parliament. James Madison and Alexander Hamilton led the fight to put the supremacy clause in the Constitution so that courts would have the power to declare acts of Congress unconstitutional.

By coincidence, Madison was the defendant in the case of *Marbury v. Madison*, 5 U.S. (1 Cranch) 137 (Feb. term, 1803), the first case in which the Supreme Court held an act of Congress invalid because it violated the Constitution. Madison was President Jefferson's secretary of state and had refused to deliver letters appointing Marbury to the post of justice of the peace for the District of Columbia. Marbury had been appointed by Jefferson's predecessor, John Adams, just prior to Adams' leaving office. So, he filed a lawsuit in the Supreme Court asking it to grant a writ of mandamus compelling Madison to deliver his letters of appointment. The Supreme Court denied the writ, because, according to Chief Justice John Marshall, the Court did not have the power to grant a writ of mandamus. Marshall said that the law authorizing the Supreme Court to grant such writs was invalid was because the writs were not within the scope of the Supreme Court's jurisdiction defined in the Constitution.

10. Quoted in Howard, "James Madison," reprinted in *James Madison on Religious Liberty*, 31.

11. In 1990, Supreme Court had ruled in *Employment Division, Oregon Department of Human Resources v. Smith*, 494 U.S. 872, that Oregon could forbid the possession and use of peyote by anyone, including members of the Native American Church who wanted to use it as a religious sacrament. Peyote was a harmful drug and the Court ruled that Native American Church members could not claim exemption from an Oregon law of general applicability that had a valid governmental purpose. By same reasoning, in *Boerne v. Flores*, supra, the Supreme Court ruled that the Catholic Church could not claim exemption from a Texas city council's zoning ordinance requiring preapproval of construction affecting historic landmarks. The Court also ruled that Congress had exceeded its powers in passing the Religious Freedom Restoration Act, which would have given the Church such an exemption.

12. Quoted in Morris, *Witnesses*, 220.

13. Ibid., 232-233.

14. Letter from Jefferson to Madison, Paris, March 15, 1789, reprinted in Bernard Schwartz, *The Bill of Rights, A Documentary History*, 2 vols. (New York: Chelsea House Publishers and McGraw Hill, Inc., 1971), 1:620.

15. Of the two additional amendments proposed by Congress on September 25, 1789, one was never ratified and the other took over two hundred years to be ratified. The proposed amendment that was never ratified related to the number of members that the House of Representatives should have in proportion to the population of the United States. The other became the Twenty-Seventh Amendment and provided that no law changing the compensation of Senators and Representatives shall take effect until an election of representatives shall have intervened. This amendment became effective May 19, 1992.

CHAPTER 8

1. Quoted in Stokes, *Church and State*, 1:223 (chap. 1, n. 3).

2. Daniel J. Boorstin, "The Founding Fathers and the Courage to Doubt," *Free Inquiry* 3: no. 3 (Summer 1983) (Free Inquiry, 1983), reprinted in Robert S. Alley, ed., *James Madison on Religious Liberty* (Buffalo, N.Y.: Prometheus Books, 1985), 209. The ten percent death toll for Germans in the Thirty Years War compares to a 1.5 percent American death toll in their Civil War, which was their most devastating war (over five hundred thousand of thirty-five million total population), possibly as high as one percent for Americans in their War of Independence (twenty-five thousand of 2.5 million total population), a 0.3 percent American death toll in World War II (407 thousand of 140 million total population) and a 0.03 percent American death toll for the Viet Nam War (fifty-eight thousand of two hundred million total population). See *World Almanac 1994*, pp. 359-361 for total populations, p. 708 for all war deaths except War of Independence, and Howard Peckham, ed. *The Toll of Independence* (University of Chicago Press, 1974) for rough estimate of War of Independence deaths.

   3. Leonard W. Levy, *The Establishment Clause: Religion and the First Amendment*, 2nd ed. (Chapel Hill: University of North Carolina Press, 1994), 4.

   4. Quoted in Thomas J. Curry, *The First Freedoms, Church and State in America to the Passage of the First Amendment* (New York: Oxford University Press, 1986, paperback ed., 1987), 51.

   5. Quoted in Curry, *The First Freedoms*, 18-19, citing William Hubbard, *A General History of New England* (Boston, 1815; reprint, New York, 1972), 573, and Thomas Hutchinson, ed., *Collection of Original Papers Relative to the History of the Colony of Massachusetts Bay*, 2 vols. (Boston, 1865; reprint, New York, 1967), 1:174.

   6. The Familists originated in Holland in the middle 1500s and their organization had spread to England by the 1600s. The Plymouth colonists probably came into contact with them in both England and Holland. The Puritans accused many other unorthodox religious groups of being Familists. Thus, Winslow's use of the term *Familists* in his letter was probably a reference to all these groups, including the real Familists.

   7. Curry, *The First Freedoms*, 10, 14-15.

   8. Howard Fast, *The Jews: Story of a People*, A Laurel Book (New York: Dell Publishing Company, 1968), 296.

   9. Thomas Jefferson Wertenbaker, *The First Americans: 1607-1690.* Vol. 2 of *A History of American Life*, 12 vols., Arthur M. Schlesinger and Dixon Ryan Fox eds. (New York: The Macmillan Company, 1927), 154; Morison, *Oxford History*, 176-177 (chap. 1, n. 58).

   10. Quoted in Paul Boyer and Stephen Nissenbaum, *Salem Possessed: The Social Origins of Witchcraft* (Cambridge, Mass.: Harvard University Press, 1974), 10.

   11. Curry, *The First Freedoms*, 82-90.

   12. Quoted in Curry, *The First Freedoms*, 108, citing Ebenezer Turell, *The Life and Character of . . . Benjamin Colman* (Boston, 1749), 138-139.

   13. Levy, *The Establishment Clause*, 22.

   14. Curry, *The First Freedoms*, 90-91.

   15. Ibid., 62.

   16. Fast, *The Jews*, 292-295.

   17. Quoted in Stokes, *Church and State*, 1:166.

   18. Ibid.

   19. Ibid., 1:167.

   20. Leo Rosten, ed., *Religions of America: Ferment and Faith in an Age of Crisis*, A Touchstone Book, revision of 1952-63 editions (New York: Simon and Shuster, 1975), 616.

   21. Curry, *The First Freedoms*, 67.

22. Ibid., 68-71; the Jamaica controversy is also described by Levy in *The Establishment Clause*, 14-15.

23. Quoted in Curry, *The First Freedoms*, 122, citing William Smith, *A General Idea of the College of Mirania* (New York, 1753); see also Levy, *The Establishment Clause*, 16.

24. Francis Newton Thorpe, ed., *The Federal and State Constitutions, Colonial Charters, and Other Organic Laws of the States, Territories and Colonies Now or Heretofore Forming The United States of America*, 7 vols. (Published under the Act of Congress of June 30, 1906; reprint, Buffalo, N.Y.: William S. Hein, 1993), 5:3063.

25. Curry, *The First Freedoms*, 44.

26. Quoted in Curry, *The First Freedoms*, 43-44.

27. Curry, *The First Freedoms*, 57.

28. *The American Heritage History of the Thirteen Colonies* (New York: American Heritage Publishing, 1967), 218, quoting William Byrd's *History of the Dividing Line* (1728).

29. Curry, *The First Freedoms*, 151, citing many books and articles including A. Roger Ekirch, *"Poor Carolina" Politics and Society in Colonial North Carolina 1729-1776* (Chapel Hill, 1981), 30.

30. Ibid., 59.

31. Elisha Williams, *The essential Rights and Liberties of Protestants. A seasonable Plea for the Liberty of Conscience, and The Right of private Judgment in Matters of Religion without any Control from Human Authority. Being a Letter, from a Gentleman in the Massachusetts-Bay to his Friend in Connecticut* (Boston, 1744); for a discussion of this pamphlet, see Curry, The First Freedoms, 97-98, citing other discussions, including Shipton, ed., *Sibley's Harvard Graduates*, 5:588-598, and Richard L. Bushman, *From Puritan to Yankee: Character and the Social Order in Connecticut, 1690-1765* (Cambridge, Mass., 1967), 227-230, 136-237.

32. Quoted in Curry, *The First Freedoms*, 98.

33. Quoted in Rhys Isaac, *The Transformation of Virginia 1740-1790* (Chapel Hill: University of North Carolina Press, 1982; reprint, New York: W. W. Norton & Company, 1988), 148.

34. Ibid., 149-150.

35. Ibid., 151-152; also quoted in Curry, *The First Freedoms*, 100, citing William Stevens Perry, *Historical Collection of the Protestant Episcopal Church of Virginia* (privately printed, 1870), 380.

36. Quoted in Curry, *The First Freedoms*, 127, citing William Stevens Perry, *Papers relating to the History of the Church in Massachusetts* (privately printed, 1873), 519; Henry Wilder Foote, *Annals of King's Chapel*, 3 vols. (Boston, 1882), 2:267; Charles Francis Adams, ed., *The Works of John Adams*, 10 vols. (Boston, 1850), 10:187-188.

37. Levy, *The Establishment Clause*, 2.

38. Isaac Backus, "Memorial in Behalf of the Warren Association to the Massachusetts Assembly," *The Annals of America*, v. 2, 1755-1783 (Chicago: Encyclopaedia Britannica, Inc., 1968), 366.

39. Thorpe, *Constitutions*, 6:3740.

40. Curry, *The First Freedoms*, 188-189.

41. Ibid., 189, citing Isaac Backus, *A History of New England with Particular Reference to the Baptists*, 2 vols., David Weston, ed. (Newton, Mass., 1871; reprint, New York, 1969), 2:548-549.

42. Quoted in Curry, *The First Freedoms*, 175, citing William G. McLoughlin, ed., *The Diary of Isaac Backus*, 3 vols. (Providence, 1979), 2:917.

43. Thorpe, *Constitutions*, 3:1889-1890.

44. Quoted in Curry, *The First Freedoms*, 174, citing William Symmes, *A Sermon* (Boston, 1785), 45-56, Chandler Robbins, *A Sermon* (Boston, 1791), 37, and David Tappan, *A Sermon* (Boston, 1792), 23.

45. Ibid., citing John D. Cushing, "Notes on Disestablishment in Massachusetts, 1780-1833," *WMQ* 26 (1969), 180.

46. Ibid., 181, citing *Acts and Laws of the State of Connecticut* (New London, 1784), 21-22, and Isaac Backus, *A History of New England with Particular Reference to the Baptists*, 2 vols., David Weston, ed. (Newton, Mass., 1871, repr. ed., New York, 1969), 2:316-317.

47. Ibid., 179, citing Judah Champion, *Civil and Christian Liberty* (Hartford, 1776), 10-11.

48. Ibid., 182, citing L. F. Greene, ed., *The Writings of John Leland* (New York, 1845; reprint, New York, 1969), 183, 187, 182, 188.

49. Curry, *The First Freedoms*, 162-163, citing J. R. Bartlett, ed., *Colonial Records of Rhode Island* (Providence, 1780-1783), 1:674.

50. Thorpe, *Constitutions*, 5:2635-2636.

51. Ibid., 5: 2597-2598.

52. Ibid., 5:3082.

53. Ibid., 5:3100.

54. Ibid., 1:566-567.

55. Ibid., 1:568.

56. Ibid., 3:1689.

57. Quoted in Curry, *The First Freedoms*, 156.

58. Curry, *The First Freedoms*, 157.

59. Thorpe, *Constitutions*, 3:1705.

60. Ibid., 5:2788, 2793.

61. Curry, *The First Freedoms*, 152; Stokes, *Church and State*, 1:403.

62. Ibid., 149-150, citing Newton B. Jones, ed., "Writings of the Reverend William Tennent," *South Carolina Historical Magazine* 61 (1960), 195, 202-203.

63. Thorpe, *Constitutions*, 6:3255-3257.

64. Ibid., 6:3264.

65. Ibid., 2:785.

66. Curry, *The First Freedoms*, 153, citing Reba Carolyn Strickland, *Religion in the State in Georgia in the Eighteenth Century* (New York, 1939), 164; A. D. Chandler, ed., *Colonial Records of the State of Georgia 1732-1782*, 26 vols. (Atlanta, 1904-16), vol. 19, part 2, 395-398; and A. D. Chandler, ed., *Revolutionary Records of Georgia 1769-1784*, 3 vols. (Atlanta, 1908), 3:141.

67. Thorpe, *Constitutions*, 2:779, 789.

68. Isaac, *Transformation of Virginia*, 193, citing Lewis Peyton Little, *Imprisoned Preachers and Religious Liberty in Virginia* (Lynchburg, Va., 1938), 44-49, 229, 249, 275-276, 312.

69. Curry, *The First Freedoms*, 135.

70. Quoted in Isaac, *Transformation of Virginia*, 162-163, citing John Williams, Journal, MS, May 10, 1771, Virginia Baptist Historical Society, University of Richmond, and Morgan Edwards, "Materials Toward a History of the Baptists in the Province of Virginia, 1772," MS, pp. 75-76, Furman University Library, Greenville, South Carolina.

71. A. E. Dick Howard, "James Madison and The Founding of the Republic" (1985), Alley, *Madison on Religious Liberty*, 21, 23.

72. Letter repr. in Alley, *Madison on Religious Liberty*, 47-48.

73. Isaac, *Transformation of Virginia*, 64.

74. Ibid., 65.

75. Rhys Isaac, "The Rage of Malice of the Old Serpent Devil: The Dissenters and the Making and Remaking of the Virginia Statute for Religious Freedom," printed in *The Virginia Statute for Religious Freedom*, Merrill D. Peterson and Robert C. Vaughan, eds. (Cambridge, Engl. and New York: Cambridge University Press, 1988), 143-144.

76. Quoted in Isaac, *Transformation of Virginia*, 236, citing numerous Henley writings.

77. Ibid., 220, citing Samuel Henley, *The Distinct Claims of Government and Religion Considered in a Sermon Preached before the Honourable House of Burgesses, at Williamsburg, in Virginia, March 1, 1772* (Cambridge, Mass., 1772).

78. Quoted in Lance Banning, "Madison, the Statute, and Republican Convictions," *The Virginia Statute for Religious Freedom*, 112, citing Willliam T. Hutchinson, William M. E. Rachal and Robert A. Rutland, eds., *The Papers of James Madison*, 14 vols. (Chicago and Charlottesville, Va., 1962--), 1:173-175.

79. Henry Steele Commager, ed., *Documents of American History*, 5th ed. (New York: Appleton-Century-Crofts, 1949), 104.

80. Thomas Jefferson, "Draft Constitution for Virginia," printed in Merrill D. Peterson, ed., *The Portable Thomas Jefferson*, Penguin Books (New York: Viking Penguin, Inc., 1975), 249.

81. Jefferson, "Query XVII, Religion," part of his *Notes on the State of Virginia* (1785), Peterson, *The Portable Thomas Jefferson*, 209-210.

82. Quoted in Isaac, *Transformation of Virginia*, 280-281, citing *Journal of the House of Delegates of the Commonwealth of Virginia*, 2d ed. (Richmond,

Va., 1828), 8, 48, 63, 76, 80, 83, 89 and 90.

83. Quoted in Thomas E. Buckley, S.J., "The Political Theology of Thomas Jefferson," *The Virginia Statute for Religious Freedom*, 84, citing *The Works of Thomas Jefferson*, Paul Leicester Ford, ed. (New York, 1904-5), 1:62.

84. Ibid., 86, citing Bernhard Fabian, "Jefferson's *Notes on Virginia:* The Genesis of Query XVII, *The different religions received into that State?,*" 3 *W & M Quarterly* 12 (1955), 129.

85. Jefferson, "Query XVII, Religion," *Notes on the State of Virginia* (1785), *The Portable Thomas Jefferson*, 210.

86. Quoted in Marvin K. Singleton, "Colonial Virginia as First Amendment Matrix: Henry, Madison, and the Assessment Establishment," *A Journal of Church and State* VIII: no. 3 (Autumn 1966), repr. Alley, *Madison on Religious Liberty*, 160.

87. Curry, *The First Freedoms*, 139, citing *Virginia Gazette*, Sept. 18 and Nov. 6, 1979.

88. Quoted in Curry, *The First Freedoms*, 139-141, citing Charles F. James, *Documentary History of the Struggle for Religious Liberty in Virginia* (Lynchburg, 1900; reprint, New York, 1971), 120, 125, 234-235.

89. Curry, *The First Freedoms*, 140, citing Paul F. Boller, Jr., "George Washington on Religious Liberty," *WMQ* 17 (1960), 490.

90. Lance Banning, "James Madison, the Statute for Religious Freedom, and the Crisis of Republican Convictions," *The Virginia Statute for Religious Freedom*, 117; see also "Madison's Notes on Debate," Alley, *Madison on Religious Liberty*, 54.

91. Isaac, "The Rage of Malice of the Old Serpent Devil," *The Virginia Statute for Religious Freedom*, 147, 150 and footnote 22, and Curry, *The First Freedoms*, 143.

92. Curry, *The First Freedoms*, 196-197, citing Herbert J. Storing, ed., *The Complete Anti-Federalist*, 7 vols. (Chicago, 1981), 2:152, 3:36-37, 179, 6:119 and 6:124, and other sources.

93. Quoted in Curry, *The First Freedoms*, 197, citing Jonathan Eliot, ed., *The Debates in the Several State Conventions on the Adoption of the Federal Constitution*, 5 vols. (Washington, D.C., 1836; reprint, New York, n.d.), 4:191, 199, 200, 208, 2:328, 399, and other sources; for amendments proposed by the New Hampshire, Virginia and New York conventions, see Helen E. Veit, Kenneth R. Bowling and Charlene Baugs Bickford, eds., *Creating the Bill of Rights: The Documentary Record from the First Congress* (Baltimore: Johns Hopkins University Press, 1991), 16, 19 and 22.

94. Quoted in Veit, *Creating the Bill of Rights*, 12-13.

95. Ibid., 30-31.

96. Ibid., 38, 41.

97. Ibid., 38, n. 8.

98. Ibid., 158.

99. Quoted in Curry, *The First Freedoms*, 206-207, citing Linda Grant DePauw, ed., *Documentary History of the First Federal Congress of the United*

States of America, 3 vols. to date (Baltimore, 1977-), 1:151, 1:166.

100. Madison letter to Jefferson dated October 17, 1788, section reprinted in Alley, *Madison on Religious Liberty*, 72, and Curry, *The First Freedoms*, 109.

101. Robertson, *America's Dates With Destiny*, 84 (chap. 4, n. 6).

102. Pat Robertson, *The Turning Tide: The Fall of Liberalism and the Rise of Common Sense* (Dallas: Word Publishing, 1993), 274, citing *Engel v. Vitale*, 370 U.S. 421 (1962) and *Murray v. Curlett*, 374 U.S. 203 (1963).

103. Correspondence between John Adams and Thomas Jefferson indicates that both men believed that all religions can be traced to Hindu metaphysics. See J. G. A. Pocock, "Religious Freedom and the Desacralization of Politics: From the English Civil Wars to the Virginia Statute," *The Virginia Statute for Religious Freedom*, 65, citing Lester J. Cappon, ed., *The Adams-Jefferson Letters: The Complete Correspondence Between Thomas Jefferson and Abigail and John Adams* (Chapel Hill, N.C., 1959), 2, passim.

104. For Delaware, see Thorpe, *Constitutions*, 1:568; for Georgia, 2:800-801; for Maryland, 3:1705.

105. For Pennsylvania, see Thorpe, *Constitutions*, 5:3100; for Kentucky, 3:1274; for Ohio, 5:2910; for Indiana, 2:1058; for Illinois, 2:981; for Missouri, 4:2163; for Arkansas, 1:269; for Kansas, 2:1180; and for Nebraska, 4:2350.

CHAPTER 9

1. Madison's letter to Jefferson, Oct. 17, 1788 and Madison's address to the House introducing his proposed bill of rights, June 8, 1789, reprinted in Schwartz, *The Bill of Rights*, 1:615, 2:1031 (chap. 7, n. 14); Jefferson's letter to Madison, Mar. 15, 1789, reprinted in *The Portable Thomas Jefferson*, Peterson, ed., 438 (chap. 8, n. 80).

2. This clause will be referred to in this book as "the life, liberty and property clause" because it guarantees the rights of life, liberty and property. However, most judges and commentators call this "the due process clause" because of the exception made to the guarantee.

3. Quoted in Veit, *Creating the Bill of Rights*, 17, 23 (chap. 8, n. 93).

4. Schwartz, *The Bill of Rights*, 2:1076-1077.

5. Mercy Otis Warren, *Observations on the New Constitution, and on the Federal and State Conventions by a Columbian Patriot* (1788), reprinted with prefatory note by Lawrence W. Towner of the Massachusetts Institute of Technology (Boston, The Old South Association, 1955), 7. Towner says this pamphlet was originally attributed to the Massachusetts political leader Elbridge Gerry but that recent evidence shows Mrs. Warren to be the author; on the other hand, Saul Padover reprinted the pamphlet as Gerry's in *The World of the Founding Fathers: Their Basic Ideas on Freedom and Self-Government* (New York: Thomas Yoseloff, 1960).

6. Ibid., 8; Blackstone, *Commentaries*, 3:349.

7. The plaintiff in *San Antonio v. Rodriguez* argued that the Texas system of allowing each school district to tax its own property owners to raise most of its revenue deprived children in the poorer school districts of equal protection of the law. However, the fact that the governments of different geographical areas tax people in different amounts and provide correspondingly different services does not violate the equal protection clause. The laws and acts of each government subdivision must be judged independently to determine whether that subdivision treats each person equally. By the very nature of government, inequalities are bound to exist between the governments of different geographical areas.

8. Jefferson, "Query XIV, Laws," *Notes on the State of Virginia* (1787), *The Portable Thomas Jefferson*, Peterson, ed., 193, 196-199.

9. Blackstone, *Commentaries*, 3:373, for public nature of jury trials, and 4:345 for trial of felons soon after arraignment (chap. 1, n. 7).

10. Ibid., 4:305.

11. Ibid., 4:256, 4:329, 4:355.

12. Ibid., 3:370; see also 4:350, where Blackstone says the requirement that two witnesses testify to prove treason shall be lifted only if "the party shall willingly and without violence confess the same" and the confession "must be in open court."

13. Ibid., 4:345.

14. Ibid., 4:352-354.

15. Ibid., 4:349.

16. Ibid., 4:352.

17. Boyer, *Salem Possessed*, 10 (chap. 8, n. 10).

18. 19 *Howell's State Trials* 1029.

19. Blackstone, *Commentaries*, 1:400.

20. Ibid., 4:372.

21. Ibid., 3:348; these six species are explained in Blackstone's chapter, "Of the several Species of Trial," 3:325-348.

22. Ibid., 4:142-143.

23. Ibid., 2:26.

24. Ibid., 2:25.

25. Quoted in Curry, *The First Freedoms*, 175 (chap. 8, n. 4), citing McLoughlin, ed., *The Diary of Isaac Backus*, 2:917 (chap. 8, n. 42).

26. Ibid., 174, citing John D. Cushing, "Notes on the Disestablishment in Massachusetts, 1780-1833," *WMQ* 26 (1969), 180.

27. Thorpe, *Constitutions*, 6:3255-3257 (chap. 8, n. 24).

28. Ibid., 4:2453-2454.

29. Ibid., 3:1889.

30. Ibid., 5:3100.

31. Ibid., 4:2453.

32. The ensoulment view, subscribed to by St. Augustine of Hippo in *The City of God*, holds that life begins when the fetus receives its soul, thought to be forty days after conception for males and eighty days after conception for females.

33. Blackstone, *Commentaries*, 4:189.
34. Ibid., 4:190.
35. Thomas J. Marzen, Mary K. O'Dowd, Daniel Crone and Thomas J. Balch, "Suicide: A Constitutional Right?", *Duquesne Law Review*, vol. 24, no. 1 (Fall, 1985), pp. 1-147; see pp. 64-100 for the history of suicide laws in America.
36. Jefferson, "Query XIV, Laws," *Notes on the State of Virginia*, *The Portable Thomas Jefferson*, Peterson, ed., 195.
37. Marzen et al. in "Suicide: A Constitutional Right?" (pp. 97-98) reports that, at the time of this 1985 article, twenty-six states had laws against assisting suicide and a number of other states would probably punish those who assist suicide.
38. For the sources of these statistics, see the Ninth Circuit Court of Appeals' decision in the *Washington v. Glucksburg* case, *Compassion in Dying v. Washington*, 79 F.3d 790 at 811, n. 57, citing "Physician Assisted Suicide and the Right to Die with Assistance," 105 *Harvard L. Rev.* 2021, n. 7 (1992); 79 F.3d at 811, n. 58; 79 F.3d at 828, n. 104, citing Melinda Lee, et al., "Legalizing Assisted Suicide--Views of Physicians in Oregon," 334 *N. Engl. J. Med.* 310 (1996); 79 F.3d at 828, n. 105, citing Jerald G. Bachman, "Attitudes of Michigan Physicians and the Public toward Legalizing Physician-Assisted Suicide and Voluntary Euthanasia," 334 *N. Engl. J. Med.* 303, 305 fig. 1 (1996).
39. Blackstone, *Commentaries*, 4:215-216.
40. From the preface of Harry M. Bracken, *Freedom of Speech, Words Are Not Deeds* (Westport, Conn.: Praeger Publishers, 1994).
41. Jefferson, "Query XVII, Religion," *Notes on the State of Virginia*, *The Portable Thomas Jefferson*, Peterson, ed., 210.
42. Frank B. Latham, *The Trial of John Peter Zenger, August 1735*, A Focus Book (New York: Franklin Watts, Inc., 1970), 15.
43. Ibid., 17; for more details, see the portion of Benjamin Franklin's memoirs reprinted in *Annals of America*, 368-369 (chap. 1, n. 31) or *Memoirs of Benjamin Franklin* (New York, 1839), 1:32-43.
44. Ibid., 48, 55-56; see also 17 Howell's St. Tr. 675 (1735).
45. Langguth, *Patriots*, 104 (chap. 1, n. 2)
46. *Journals of the Continental Congress*, 1:108 (chap. 2, n. 29).
47. *Annals of Congress*, 4:934 (1794), quoted in *New York Times Co. v. Sullivan*, 376 U.S. 254 at 275 (1964).
48. Morison, *Oxford History*, 2:77 (chap. 1, n. 58).
49. Henry Steel Commager, ed., *Documents of American History*, 5th ed. (New York: Appleton-Century-Crofts, Inc., 1949), 182.
50. Ibid., 184-185.
51. *New York Times v. Sullivan*, supra. at 276.
52. Michael Kent Curtis, *No State Shall Abridge: The Fourteenth Amendment and the Bill of Rights* (Durham, N.C.: Duke University Press, 1986), 30, citing C. Eaton, *Freedom of Thought in the Old South* (1964), 127.

53. Ibid., 30-31.
54. Ibid., 53.
55. Langguth, *Patriots*, 104.
56. Amos J. Peaslee, *Constitutions of Nations*, rev. 3rd ed. (The Hague: Martinus Nijhoff, 1968), 3: 232, Art. 28 for Czechoslovakia; 3:443, Art. 55 for Hungary; 3:771-772, Arts. 28-29 for Rumania; 3:1005, Art. 125 for the Soviet Union. Under the new democratic regimes, these exceptions have been removed; see *Constitutions of the Countries of the World*, Albert P. Blaustein and Gilbert H. Flanz, eds. (Dobbs Ferry, N.Y.: Oceana Publications), Czech Republic Constitution of 1993, p. 157, Art. 17 of Charter of Fundamental Rights and Freedoms; Hungarian Constitution of 1990, p. 22, Sec. 61; Rumanian Constitution of 1991, p. 10, Art. 30; Draft Russian Federation Constitution of 1992, p. 9, Art. 43.
57. Blackstone, *Commentaries*, 3:373.

CHAPTER 10

1. Raoul Berger, *The Fourteenth Amendment and the Bill of Rights* (Norman, Okla.: University of Oklahoma Press, 1989); see the Bibliography, *infra*, for more publications by Berger on this subject.
2. Curtis, *No State Shall Abridge* (see chap. 9, n. 49); see the Bibilography, *infra*, for more publications by Curtis on this subject; see also *Encyclopedia of the American Constitution*, Leonard W. Levy, ed., 4 vols. plus supplement (New York: Macmillan Publishing Company, 1986; supplement, 1992), s.v. Leonard W. Levy, "Incorporation Doctrine." See also William Crosskey, "Charles Fairman's 'Legislative History' and the Constitutional Limitations of State Authority," 22 *University of Chicago Law Review* 25 (1954).
3. See also Stanley Morrison, "Does the Fourteenth Amendment Incorporate the Bill of Rights?" 2 *Stanford Law Review* 140 (1949).
4. For violations of freedom of the press by the southern states, see Chapter 9, Section D, pp. 362-63.
5. Curtis, *No State Shall Abridge*, 37, citing *Congressional Globe*, 38th Cong., 1st sess. (1864), 114.
6. Ibid., 37-38, 50, citing *Cong. Globe*, 38th Cong., 1st sess. (1864), 1202, 20.
7. Ibid., 84, citing *Cong. Globe*, 38th Cong., 2nd sess. (1865), 193.
8. *Cong. Globe*, 39th Cong., 1st sess. (1866), 1034.
9. Ibid., 1095.
10. *Documents of American History*, Henry Steele Commager, ed., 2 vols. (New York: Appleton-Century-Crofts, 1949), 2:14-16; *U. S. Statutes at Large*, Vol. XIV, 27 ff.
11. *Cong. Globe*, 39th Cong., 1st sess. (1866), 2542-2543.
12. Ibid., 2765.
13. Quoted in Curtis, *No State Shall Abridge*, 151, citing Joseph James, *Ratification of the Fourteenth Amendment* (1984), 17.

14. Ibid., citing James, *Ratification*, 60.

15. Charles Fairman, "Does the Fourteenth Amendment Incorporate the Bill of Rights?" 2 *Stanford Law Review* 5 (1949), 93.

16. Curtis, *No State Shall Abridge*, 151-152, citing James, *Ratification*, 75.

17. Quoted in Curtis, *No State Shall Abridge*, 132, citing *Dubuque Daily Times*, Nov. 21, 1866 at 2, col. 1.

18. Ibid., 147, citing Fairman, "Does the Fourteenth Amendment," at 96.

19. Berger, *The Fourteenth Amendment*, 40.

20. Ibid., 123.

21. *Cong. Globe*, supra, 1058.

22. Ibid., 2897, including Senator Williams' comments and the defeat of Senator Van Winkle's proposal to have the amendment exclude Indians not taxed from citizenship.

23. Ibid., 2765, citing 16 Fed. Cas. 551-552.

24. Ibid., 474-475 for Senator Trumbull, 1117-1118 for Congressman Wilson and 1269 for Congressman Raymond.

25. Ibid., 2765.

26. Ibid., 1118.

27. Ibid., 474-475.

28. Lockmiller, *Sir William Blackstone*, 177 (chap. 1, n. 50).

29. Ibid., 176.

30. Boorstin, *The Americans: The Colonial Experience*, 202 (see chap. 1, n. 21).

31. Blackstone, *Commentaries*, 4:305 (see chap. 1, n. 7).

32. Ibid., 4:306-307.

33. Ibid., 3:379, 3:349.

34. Ibid., 4:300.

35. Professor Laurence Tribe reports that the Supreme Court invalidated 197 state and federal laws regulating business between 1899 and 1937: Laurence H. Tribe, *American Constitutional Law* (Mineola, N.Y.: The Foundation Press, Inc., 1978, rev'd 1984), 435, fn. 2.

36. Ibid., 449, including fn. 18; Tribe argues that Robert's switch "was not motivated solely by the threat of court-packing" because his private correspondence indicates his shift in thinking evolved over a period of time and he felt the issues had not been properly raised in *Morehead v. New York*, supra.

37. Blackstone, *Commentaries*, 1:414; for English laws against usury, see Blackstone, *Commentaries*, 2:455-458 and 4:156-157.

38. For Virginia parsons' wages, see this book, Chapter 1, Section B and Chapter 8, Section A, and Wertenbaker, *The First Americans*, 120-124 (see chap. 8, n. 9); for Massachusetts skilled labor rates, see Wertenbaker, *The First Americans*, 69.

39. Blackstone, *Commentaries*, 3:349, 3:379.

40. Ibid., 4:329, 4:355; Blackstone followed the words of the second quotation with, "except he be appealed of felony within the time limited by law." An "appeal of felony" was the English term for another suit by the victim of the felony, "demanding punishment on account of the injury suffered, rather than for the offence against the public" (Ibid., 4:308). This action was similar to the recent civil action by the heirs of Ron Goldman and Nicole Brown Simpson against O. J. Simpson, but it allowed the accused to be punished in the same manner as if he had been convicted by indictment. Money damages could also be awarded the victim or heirs. Blackstone said this action dated back to the early Saxon kingdoms and to the Irish Brehon law, but it was currently in very little use in England. An appeal of felony could be filed only before the criminal indictment or upon the accused being acquitted or pardoned by the king. In England as late as the reign of Henry IV (1399-1413), if the defendant were found guilty of murder in such an action, the court might order the relatives of the slain to drag the guilty person to his place of execution. Blackstone said this custom prevailed "even now among the wild and untutored inhabitants of America: as if the finger of nature had pointed it out to mankind, in their rude and uncultivated state" (Ibid., 4:311-312).

41. Aviam Soifer. "United States v. Carolene Products." *Encyclopedia of the American Constitution*. Leonard W. Levy, ed. 4 vols. New York: Macmillan Publishing Company, 1986.

42. Thorpe, *Constitutions*, 4:2453-2454 (see chap. 8, n. 24).

43. For Howard's speech, see *Cong. Globe,* 39th Cong., 1st sess. (1866), 2542-2543; for Bingham's speech, see Ibid., 2765; see also Black's appendix to his *Adamson* opinion, 332 U.S. at 100-103, 104-107.

44. Black's appendix, 332 U.S. at 115; *Cong. Globe*, 42nd Cong., 1st sess. (1871), 81, 83-85.

45. *A Civil Jury Trial*, v. 7 of *The American Heritage History of the Bill of Rights* (Englewood Cliffs, N. J.: Silver Burdett Press, a division of Simon & Schuster, Inc., 1991), 73-74.

46. *Bartkus v. Illinois*, 359 U.S. 121 at 152 (1959), citing *Digest of Justinian*, Digest 48.2.7.2, translated by 11 Scott, *The Civil Law*, 17.

47. Ibid., citing 2 Bracton, *De Legibus et Consuetudinibus Angliae* (Woodbine ed., 1922), 391, 397.

48. Blackstone, *Commentaries*, 4:256, 329, 355.

49. *Bartkus v. Illinois*, 359 U.S. at 153-154, citing Farrand, ed., *The Laws and Liberties of Massachusetts (1648)* (1929), 47.

50. Ibid., 154, citing Scott, *Criminal Law in Colonial Virginia*, 81-82, 102.

51. Blackstone, *Commentaries*, 3:370.

52. Ibid., 4:352-354.

53. 3 Story, *Commentaries on the Constitution of the United States*, Sections 1786-1788 (1833).

54. Blackstone, *Commentaries*, 4:349-350.

55. For the number of jurors, see authorities quoted in *Thompson v. Utah*, 170 U.S. at 349 (1898); according to Justice Douglas' dissent in *Johnson v. Louisiana*, 406 U.S. at 383 (1972), the first reported jury case requiring unanimity was *Anonymous Case*, 41 Lib. Assisarum 11 (1367).

56. Blackstone, *Commentaries*, 3:379.
57. Ibid., 3:376, citing *Lib. Aff. fol.* 40. *pl.* 11, Barrington on the statutes. 17, 18, 19 and Stiernh. *l.*1. *c.*4.
58. A. Leon Higginbotham, Jr., *In the Matter of Color: Race and the Legal Process* (New York: Oxford University Press, 1978), 299-310.
59. Ibid., 94-95.
60. Ibid., 91.
61. Ibid., 96-97.
62. *Historical Statistics of the United States: Colonial Times to 1970* (Washington, D.C.: U.S. Department of Commerce, Bureau of the Census, 1976), 25-36 (Table A195-209). In 1790, Massachusetts included the present state of Maine, which at the time had 97,000 people (1,000 black, 96,000 black), and Virginia included the present state of West Virginia, which at the time had 56,000 people (black and white numbers unavailable).
63. Ibid., 14 (Table A91-104, n. 1).
64. Peter Kolchin, *American Slavery, 1619-1877*, American Century Series (New York: Hill and Wang, a division of Farrar, Straus and Giroux, 1993), 81.
65. Ibid., 82.
66. A. Leon Higginbotham, Jr., *In the Matter of Color: Race and the Legal Process* (New York: Oxford University Press, 1978), 83.
67. Bailyn, *Pamphlets*, 1:439 (repr. of Otis, *The Rights of the British Colonies* [Boston, 1764], 29) (chap. 1, n. 17). In a footnote on Otis' reference to Montesquieu, Bailyn says that Montesquieu cariacatured the presumed arguments of slave traders and owners in *The Spirit of the Laws*, xv, 5, e.g., "Sugar would be too dear if the plants . . . were cultivated by any other than slaves. These creatures are all over black, and with such a flat nose that they can scarcely by pitied. It is hardly to be believed that God, who is a wise Being, should place a soul, especially a good soul, in such an ugly body" (Nugent tr., Franz Neumann, ed., New York, 1949). Bailyn says that some readers actually took Montesquieu's arguments seriously and used them to defend slavery, citing F. T. H. Fletcher, *Montesquieu and English Politics (1750-1800)* (London, 1939), 228-229.
68. Justice Wayne said that he concurred "entirely in the opinion of the court as it has been written and read by the Chief Justice--without any qualification of its reasoning or its conclusions-- . . . ." (Ibid., 454). Justice Daniel said "[t]hat so far as rights and immunities appertaining to citizens have been defined and secured by the Constitution and laws of the United States, the African race is not and never was recognized either by the language or purposes of the former; . . . ." (Ibid., 482).
69. Lincoln was quoting Jesus in Matthew 12:26 and Mark 3:24-25.
70. *Cong. Globe*, supra, 2766.
71. Ibid., 2892.
72. Ibid., 2897.
73. Kenneth L. Karst, "Japanese American Cases," *Encyclopedia of the American Constitution*, citing a list of organizations published by U. S. Attorney

General Francis Biddle.

74. Ibid.

75. Kenneth L. Karst, "Brown v. Board of Education," *Encyclopedia of the American Constitution*, Leonard W. Levy, ed. (New York: Macmillan Publishing Company, 1986).

76. Ibid.

77. The cases cited by Warren were *Gibson v. Mississippi*, 162 U.S. 565, 591 (1896); *Steward Machine Co. v. Davis*, 301 U.S. 548, 585 (1937); *Currin v. Wallace*, 306 U.S. 1, 13-14 (1939); *Detroit Bank v. United States*, 317 U.S. 329 (1942); *Hirabayashi v. United States*, 320 U.S. 1, 100 (1943) and *Korematsu v. United States*, 323 U.S. 214, 216 (1943).

78. Derek A. Bell, "Desegregation," *Encyclopedia of the American Constitution*; see also Derek A. Bell, *Race, Racism and American Law* (Boston: Little Brown, 1973, 1980).

79. David L. Lewis, "King, Martin Luther," *The New Encyclopaedia Britannica*, 15th ed., Macropaedia.

80. The last sentence of Section 201(c) reads, "For purposes of this section, "commerce" means travel, trade, traffic, commerce, transportation, or communication among the several States, or between the District of Columbia and any State, or between any foreign country or any territory or possession and any State, or between any foreign country or any territory or possession and any State or the District of Columbia, or between points in the same State but through any other State or the District of Columbia or a foreign country.

81. *Cong. Globe*, 39th Cong., 1st Sess., 43.

82. "America's Best Graduate Schools," *U. S. News and World Report*, March 20, 1995, p. 84.

83. Stanton, Anthony and Gage, eds., *History of Woman Suffrage*, 6 vols., incl. repr. of 2 vol. set published by Fowler & Wells, New York, 1881 (Salem, New Hampshire: Ayer Company, 1985).

84. Ibid., 1:211 for Massachusetts law, 1:686-688 for New York law.

85. Churchill, *English-Speaking Peoples*, 3:3 (chap. 1, n. 13).

86. *American Bar Association Journal*, Mar. 1998, p. 44.

CHAPTER 11

1. Curry, *The First Freedoms* 18-19 (chap. 8, n. 4), citing William Hubbard, *A General History of New England* (Boston, 1815; reprint, New York, 1972), 573, and Thomas Hutchinson, ed., *Collection of Original Papers Relative to the History of the Colony of Massachusetts Bay*, 2 vols. (Boston, 1865; reprint, New York, 1967), 1:174.

2. Vatican II, *Draft Declaration on the Church's Relations with Non-Christians: Council Daybook*, 3rd Sess., p. 282, N.C.W.C., Washington, D.C., 1965.

3. Citing Paul Tillich, *Dynamics of Faith*, 1-2 (1958).

4. Citing Thomas Aquinas, Prologue to *Commentary of IV Books of Sen-*

tences, repr. in *An Aquinas Reader* (M. Clark, ed., 1972), 41.

5. Arthur Waley, transl. and anno., *The Analects of Confucius* (London: George Allen & Unwin Ltd., 1938), Book III, par. 12, p. 97

6. For more detail on these sources of revelation, see Geoffrey Parrinder, ed., *World Religions, From Ancient History to the Present* (New York: Facts on File, 1983), 385-392 for the Jewish Torah and Talmud, 420-423 for the Christian Bible, 471-475 for the Islamic Koran, 193-216 for the Hindu Vedas, 262-278 for Buddha Gotama's "revealed truth," 252 for Guru Nanak's "revelation in creation," 242 for the Jain *kvela*, 176-181 for the Zoroastrian religion, 328 and 333 for the Taoist Canon, 355 for the Shinto *kami*, and 319-321 for the teachings of Confucius.

7. David Saville Muzzey, *Ethics as a Religion* (1951), 95, 98, quoted in 380 U.S. at 162.

8. Church of Scientology International, *What Is Scientology?* (Los Angeles: Bridge Publications Inc., 1993), 57.

9. Ibid., 7.

10. Muzzey, *Ethics*, 515.

11. Chworowsky and Raible, "What is a Unitarian Universalist?," *Religions of America: Ferment and Faith in an Age of Crisis*, Leo Rosten, ed., a Touchstone Book, revision of 1952-63 editions (New York: Simon and Shuster, 1975), 265.

12. Ibid.

13. When federal and state governments exceed their constitutional powers, a person does not ordinarily have standing to sue based on the fact that he paid taxes to those governments and that his taxes are being misused. The reason was stated in *Frothingham v. Mellon*, 262 U.S. 447, 486-487 (1923): "His interest in the moneys of the Treasury--partly realized from taxation and partly from other sources--is shared with millions of others; is comparatively minute and indeterminable; and the effect on future taxation, of any payment out of the funds, so remote, fluctuating and uncertain, that no basis is afforded for an appeal to the preventive powers of equity." However, as the First Circuit Court of Appeals pointed out in *Donnelly v. Lynch*, 691 F.2d 1029 (1982), rev'd on other grounds, 465 U.S. 668 (1984), this reasoning does not apply when the taxes are paid to local municipalities and school boards.

In *Doremus v. Board of Education*, 342 U.S. 429 (1952), the U. S. Supreme Court did dismiss an appeal by a taxpayer seeking to remove prayer and Bible reading from his local public school on the ground that the taxpayer had no standing to bring such an action. Because of that decision, petitioners complaining of government violations of the establishment clause have been reluctant to rely solely on their taxpayer status. Judges, including Justice Kennedy, have also been reluctant to base their decisions on taxpayer injury. However, the *Doremus* appeal was dismissed because it was poorly presented to the Supreme Court. Apparently for that reason, the Supreme Court failed to consider that the establishment clause is essentially a guarantee against taxes for the support of religion. The whole background of the establishment clause relates to such taxes. Madison's Memorial and Remonstrance was against "religious assessments." The relevant part of the Virginia Statute for Religious Freedom says "[t]hat no man shall be compelled to . . . support any religious worship, place or ministry whatsoever, . . ." (App. N). This, combined with the fact that most establishment clause claims are against local governments, would appear to give any person who pays local taxes used in part for the support of "any religious worship, place or ministry" solid standing to petition either for a decree exempting him from such taxes or an injunction against such further use of his taxes.

14. Jay D. Wexler, "Of Pandas, People and the First Amendment: The Constitutionality of Teaching Intelligent Design in the Public Schools," 49 *Stanford Law Review* 439 (Jan., 1997), 445, citing John R. Cole, "Scopes and Beyond: Antievolutionism and American Culture," *Scientists Confront Creationism*, Laurie R. Godfrey, ed. (1983), 13, 19.

15. Quoted in L. Sprague de Camp, *The Great Monkey Trial* (Garden City, N.Y.: Doubleday & Company, 1968), 25, citing Stewart G. Cole, *The History of Fundamentalism* (New York: Richard R. Smith, Inc., 1931), 41 and Andrew Dickson White, *A History of the Warfare of Science with Theology in Christendom* (New York: Dover Publications, Inc., 1960), 2:315.

16. Wexler, "Of Pandas," 445, citing Ronald L. Numbers, *The Creationists: The Evolution of Scientific Creationism* (1992), 38.

17. de Camp, *Monkey Trial*, 29.

18. Quoted in de Camp, *Monkey Trial*, 30, citing Harbor Allen, "The Anti-Evolution Campaign in America," *Current History*, Sept. 1926, 895, and other sources.

19. Ibid., 30-31.

20. Ibid., 45.

21. *Epperson v. Arkansas*, 393 U.S. 97 at 98, 101 (1968), see notes 1 and 8 on those pages.

22. Quoted in de Camp, *Monkey Trial*, 11-12, quoting George William Hunter, *A Civic Biology* (New York: American Book Co., 1914), 194ff.

23. Ibid., 72, citing *Outlook*, May 17, 1925, p. 131 and *School and Society*, May 23, 1925, p. 616.

24. Ibid., 73-74, citing Bryan and Bryan, Mary Baird, *The Memoirs of William Jennings Bryan* (priv. print., 1925), 483.

25. Kevin Tierney, *Darrow: A Biography* (New York: Thomas Y. Cromwell, 1979), 8-9, citing Clarence Darrow, *Farmington* (Chicago: A. C. McClung & Co., 1904), 268.

26. Quoted in de Camp, *Monkey Trial*, 79.

27. de Camp, *Monkey Trial*, 89-90, 96-99.

28. Quoted in de Camp, *Monkey Trial*, 221-223, citing articles by Charles Michelson in *The Dayton (Ohio) News*, July 12, 1925, p. 2, Forrest Davis in the *New York Herald Tribune*, July 12, 1925, p. 2, and the *New York Times*, July 12, 1925, p. 2.

29. Ibid., 287.

30. Ibid., 289.

31. Ibid., 289-290, citing *Record of the Proceedings of the State of Tennessee vs. John Thomas Scopes, Circuit Court, Rhea County, beginning July 10, 1925, Dayton Tennessee* (Chicago: Maclaskey & Maclaskey, Shorthand Reporting), 277-281.
32. Ibid., 302, citing *Record*, 343-352.
33. Ibid., 326.
34. Ibid., 350.
35. Ibid., 357-358, citing *Chattanooga News*, July 18, 1925 and *Shreveport Times*, July 18, 1925.
36. Ibid., 428.
37. Bryan might have answered that the snake could have had legs before it tempted Eve. However, that might have forced Bryan to admit that the snake "evolved" to its present form.
38. See de Camp, *Monkey Trial*, 383-410, for a more complete excerpt of the transcript of Darrow's interrogation of Bryan.
39. Quoted in U. S. Supreme Court Reports, 393 U.S. at 102, citing Darrow, *The Story of My Life* (1932), 247.
40. Wexler, "Of Pandas," 447, citing Cole, "Scopes and Beyond," 23.
41. Ibid., citing Cole, 24, Edward J. Larson, *Trial and Error: The American Controversy over Creation and Evolution* (1985), 91, 95-98 and Dorothy Nelkin, *The Creation Controversy: Science or Scripture in the Schools* (1982), 44-47.
42. *Webster's New World Collegiate Dictionary*, 3rd ed. (New York: Macmillan USA, 1997), s.v. "natural science."
43. Francisco Jose Ayala, "The Theory of Evolution," *The New Encyclopaedia Britannica*, 15th ed., Macropaedia. Ayala edited *Molecular Evolution* (1976), authored *Population and Evolutionary Genetics: a Primer* (1982) and *Tempo and Mode in Evolution* (Wash., D.C.: National Academy Press, 1995) and co-authored with James W. Valentine *Evolving: The Theory and Processes of Organic Evolution* (1979).
44. Donald E. Chittick, *The Controversy: Roots of the Creation-Evolution Conflict* (Portland, Ore.: Multnomah Press, 1984), 162.
45. Ibid., 67-68.
46. Ibid., 70, citing Robert Jastrow, "Evolution: Selection for Perfection," *Science Digest*, Dec. 1981, 86, who in turn cites William Paley, *Natural Theology* (New York: Harper & Brothers, 1845).
47. Percival Davis and Dean H. Kenyon, *Of Pandas and People: The Central Question of Biological Origins*, 2nd ed. (Richardson, Texas: Foundation for Thought and Ethics, 1993).
48. For different approaches to reconciling science and religion, compare Davis and Kenyon's *Pandas* with Fritjof Capra's *The Tao of Physics*, rev. of Shambhala 1975 publ. (New York: Bantam Books, 1984).
49. Waley, *Analects*. Confucius lived from 551 B.C. to 479 B.C., but Waley reports that many parts of *The Analects* came from later sources (Ibid., 21-23). Copies of the Ku version, from which Waley made his translation, were

alleged to have been found on various dates ranging from 156 B.C. to 87 B.C., but he says this version may not have attained its present form until the second-century AD (Ibid., 23-24). Waley used the Ku version in all but two instances, when he used the Lu version (Ibid., 24).

CHAPTER 12

1. Locke, *Second Treatise*, par. 212, p. 120 (chap. 1, n. 8).
2. John Calvin, *Institutes of the Christian Religion*, Book 4, chap. xx, John Allen's translation reprinted as "On Civil Government" in *Calvin: On God and Political Duty*, John T. McNeill, ed., The Library of Liberal Arts (Indianapolis: Bobbs-Merrill Educational Publishing, 1956), 48, 52-54.
3. *The Adams-Jefferson Letters: The Complete Correspondence between Thomas Jefferson and Abigail and John Adams*, Lester J. Cappon, editor (Chapel Hill: University of North Carolina Press, 1988), 591.
4. Filmer died in 1653 but his book *Patriarcha* was not published until 1680.
5. Hamilton, "The Farmer Refuted," 5-6 (chap. 2, n. 34; see chap. 2, Section G for a longer quotation from this pamphlet).
6. Schwartz, *Bill of Rights*, 2:1076 (chap. 7, n. 14).
7. Jefferson, "Query XVII, Religion," *Notes on the State of Virginia* (1785), reprinted in *The Portable Thomas Jefferson*, Peterson, ed., 210 (chap. 8, n. 85).
8. For life, liberty and property, c.f. *Munn v. Illinois*, 94 U.S. 113 (Oct. term, 1876), *Planned Parenthood of Southeastern Pennsylvania v. Casey*, 505 U.S. 833, 848 (1992) and other cases discussed in Chapter 9, Section C and Chapter 10, Section D; for unequal treatment, c.f. *Skinner v. Oklahoma*, 316 U.S. 535 (1942) and other cases discussed in Chapter 10, Section E.
9. Thorpe, *Constitutions*, 4:2453-2454 (chap. 8, n. 24).
10. Ibid.; see Chapter 9, Section *B.1.* for the subsequent paragraphs of the New Hampshire bill of rights relating to religious freedom.

APPENDIX BL

1. Lockmiller, *Sir William Blackstone*, 169 (chap. 1, n. 51).
2. Joyce Blackburn, *George Wythe of Williamsburg* (New York: Harper & Row, 1975), 104-105; Justice Vernon C. Spratley, "Presentation of the Bust of George Wythe," printed in *Ceremonies in Celebration of the Beginning of the John Marshall Bicentennial Year and the 175th Anniversary of the First Chair of Law in the United States and the Creation of a Chair of Taxation at the College of William and Mary* (Williamsburg, Va., 1954), 50.
3. Lockmiller, *Sir William Blackstone*, 178.
4. Jeremy Bentham, *A Comment on the Commentaries*, edited with introduction by Charles Warren Everett (Oxford, Engl.: Clarendon Press, 1928), 43-44, quoting Blackstone, *Commentaries*, 1:41 (chap. 1, n. 7); Appendix BL3.

Selected Bibliography

Abraham, Henry J. and Barbara A. Perry. *Freedom and the Court: Civil Rights and Liberties in the United States*. 6th ed. New York and Oxford, England: Oxford University Press, 1994.

Adams, Sam. *The Rights of the Colonists*. Boston, 1772. Reprinted Appendix J and in *The Annals of America*. Vol. 2 of 21 vols., 1755-1783. Chicago: Encyclopaedia Britannica, Inc., 1968.

Adler, Mortimer J. "The Constitutional Convention of 1787." "The Federalist and Anti-Federalist Papers." Appendices A and B in *We Hold These Truths*. New York: Macmillan Publishing Company, Collier Books, 1987.

Alden, John R. *A History of the American Revolution*. New York: Alfred A. Knopf, 1976.

Alderman, Ellen and Caroline Kennedy. *In our Defense: The Bill of Rights in Action*. New York: Avon Books, 1991.

Alley, Robert S., ed., *James Madison on Religious Liberty*. Buffalo, N.Y.: Prometheus Books, 1985.

The American Heritage Book of the Revolution. Richard M. Ketchum, ed. New York: American Heritage Publishing Company, Inc., 1958.

The American Heritage History of the Bill of Rights. Englewood Cliffs, New Jersey: Silver Burdett Press, a division of Simon & Schuster, Inc., 1991.

The American Heritage History of the Making of the Nation. 1783-1860. Ralph K. Andrist, ed. New York: American Heritage Publishing Company, Inc., 1968. Revised, New York: American Heritage Publishing Company, Inc., 1987.

The American Heritage History of the Thirteen Colonies. Michael Blow, ed. New York: American Heritage Publishing Company, Inc., 1967.

Ammerman, David. *In the Common Cause: American Response to the Coercive Acts of 1774*. Charlottesville: University Press of Virginia, 1974.

The Annals of America. Vol. 2 of 21 vols., 1755-1783. Chicago: Encyclopaedia Britannica, Inc., 1968.

Ayala, Francisco Jose, "The Theory of Evolution," *The New Encyclopaedia Britannica*, 15th ed., Macropaedia.

Backus, Isaac. "Memorial in Behalf of the Warren Association to the Massachusetts Assembly." *The Annals of America*. Vol. 2, 1755-1783. Chicago: Encyclopaedia Britannica, Inc., 1968.

---. *A History of New England with Particular Reference to the Baptists*. 2 vols. David Weston, ed. Newton, Mass., 1871. Reprint edition, New York, 1969.

Bailyn, Bernard. *Faces of Revolution*. First Vintage Books Edition. New York: Vintage Books, a division of Random House, 1992.

---. *The Ideological Origins of the American Revolution*. 2nd ed., rev. and enl. Cambridge, Mass. and London, Engl.: Belknap Press of Harvard University Press, 1992.

Bailyn, Bernard, ed. *Pamphlets of the American Revolution*. 4 vols. John Harvard Library. Cambridge, Mass.: Belknap Press of Harvard University Press, 1965.

Beccaria, Cesare. *Crimes and Punishment*. 1764.

Bellesiles, Michael A. *Revolutionary Outlaws: Ethan Allen and the Struggle for Independence on the Early American Frontier*. Charlottesville: University Press of Virginia, 1993.

Bentham, Jeremy. *A Comment on the Commentaries: A Criticism of William Blackstone's Commentaries on the Laws of England*. Introduction and notes, Charles Warren Everett. Oxford, England: Clarendon Press, 1928.

Berger, Raoul. *Congress v. The Supreme Court*. Cambridge, Mass.: Harvard University Press, 1969.

---. *Government by Judiciary: The Transformation of the Fourteenth Amendment*. Cambridge, Mass.: Harvard University Press, 1977.

---. "'Government by Judiciary': Judge Gibbons' Argument Ad Hominem," 59 *Boston University Law Review* 783 (1979).

---. "Incorporation of the Bill of Rights in the Fourteenth Amendment: A Nine-Lived Cat," 42 *Ohio State Law Journal* 435 (1981).

---. "Incorporation of the Bill of Rights in the Fourteenth Amendment: A Reply to Michael Curtis' Response," 44 *Ohio State Law Journal* 1 (1983).

---. *The Fourteenth Amendment and the Bill of Rights*. Norman, Okla.: University of Oklahoma Press, 1989.

Blackburn, Joyce. *George Wythe of Williamsburg*. New York: Harper & Row, 1975.

Blackstone, William. *Commentaries on the Laws of England*. 4 vols. Oxford, England: Clarendon Press, 1765-1769. Reprint in The Legal Classics Library. Birmingham, Ala.: Gryphon Editions, 1983.

Bland, Richard. *The Colonel Dismounted: Or the Rector Vindicated*. Williamsburg, 1764. Reprinted in *Pamphlets of the American Revolution*. Vol. 1 of 4 vols. John Harvard Library. Cambridge, Mass.: Belknap Press of Harvard University Press, 1965.

Blaustein, Albert P. and Gilbert H. Flanz, eds. *Constitutions of the Countries of the World*. Dobbs Ferry, N.Y.: Oceana Publications.

Boorstin, Daniel J. *The Americans: The Colonial Experience*. Vintage Books. New York: Random House, 1958.

Bourinot, Sir John G. *Canada under British Rule: 1760-1900*. Toronto: Copp, Clark, 1901.

Bowen, Catherine Drinker. *The Lion and the Throne: The Life and Times of Sir Edward Coke*. An Atlantic Monthly Pressbook. Boston: Little Brown and Company, 1957.

---. *Miracle at Philadelphia: The Story of the Constitutional Convention, May to September 1787*. An Atlantic Monthly Pressbook. Boston: Little Brown and Company, 1966.

---. *The Most Dangerous Man in America: Scenes from the Life of Benjamin Franklin*. Boston: Little, Brown and Company, 1974.

Boyer, Paul and Stephen Nissenbaum. *Salem Possessed: The Social Origins of Witchcraft.* Cambridge, Mass.: Harvard University Press, 1974.

Bracken, Harry M. *Freedom of Speech: Words are not Deeds.* Westport, Conn.: Praeger Publishers, 1994.

Brebner, J. Bartlett. *Canada: A Modern History.* Ann Arbor: University of Michigan Press, 1960.

Bremer, Francis J., ed. *Anne Hutchinson: Troubler of the Puritan Zion.* New York: Robert E. Krieger Publishing Company, 1980.

Brooks, David L., ed. *From Magna Charta to the Constitution: Documents in the Struggle for Liberty.* San Francisco: Fox & Wilkes, 1993.

Burke, Edmund. *Burke's Speech on Conciliation with America.* Charles B. Morris, ed. New York and London: Harper & Brothers, 1945.

Calvin, John. *God and Political Duty.* Bobbs-Merrill, 1956. Reprint, 1980

Capra, Fritjof, *The Tao of Physics.* Revision of Shambhala 1975 publication. New York: Bantam Books, 1984.

Ceremonies in Celebration of the Beginning of the John Marshall Bicentennial Year and the 175th Anniversary of the First Chair of Law in the United States and the Creation of a Chair of Taxation at the College of William and Mary. Williamsburg, 1954.

Church of Scientology International. *What Is Scientology?* Los Angeles: Bridge Publications Inc., 1993.

Churchill, Winston S. *A History of the English Speaking Peoples.* 4 vols. New York: Dodd, Mead, 1956-1958.

Chworowsky, Karl M. and Christopher Gist Raible. "What is a Unitarian Universalist?" *Religions of America: Ferment and Faith in an Age of Crisis.* Leo Rosten, ed. A Touchstone Book. Revision of 1952-63 editions. New York: Simon and Shuster, 1975.

Cobb, Sanford H. *The Rise of Religious Liberty in America.* 3 vols. New York: Burt Franklin, 1902.

Cole, Frank P., ed. *They Preached Liberty.* Indianapolis: Liberty*Press*, 1977.

Cole, John R. "Scopes and Beyond: Antievolutionism and American Culture." *Scientists Confront Creationism*, Laurie R. Godfrey, ed. 1983.

Cole, Stewart G. *The History of Fundamentalism.* New York: Richard R. Smith, Inc., 1931.

Commager, Henry Steele, ed. *Documents of American History.* Crofts American History Series. 5th ed. New York: Appleton-Century-Crofts, 1949.

---. "Forts in the Wilderness." Chap. 1 of Stephan Lorant. *Pittsburgh: The Story of an American City.* Garden City, N.Y.: Doubleday & Company, 1964.

Commager, Henry Steele and Richard B. Morris. *The Spirit of Seventy-Six.* New York: Harper & Row, 1958. Revised, 1975.

Confucius. *The Analects of Confucius.* Arthur Waley, translator. London: George Allen & Unwin Ltd., 1938.

The Congressional Globe. Proceedings of the United States Congress. 38th Cong., 1st and 2nd Sess.; 39th Cong., 1st Sess. Blair and Rives, 1864-1866.

Cord, Robert L. *Separation of Church and State: Historical Fact and Current Fiction.* New York: Lambeth Press, 1982.
Crosskey, William. "Charles Fairman's 'Legislative History' and the Constitutional Limitations of State Authority," 22 *University of Chicago Law Review* 25 (1954).
Curry, Thomas P. *The First Freedoms: Church and State in America to the Passage of the First Amendment.* New York: Oxford Universty Press, 1986. Paperback ed., 1987.
Curtis, Michael Kent. "The Bill of Rights as a Limitation on State Authority: A Reply to Professor Berger," 16 *Wake Forest L. R.* 45 (1980).
---. "Further Adventures of a Nine-Lived Cat: A Response to Mr. Berger on Incorporation of the Bill of Rights," 43 *Ohio State Law Journal* 89 (1982).
---. *No State Shall Abridge: The Fourteenth Amendment and the Bill of Rights.* Durham, N.C.: Duke University Press, 1986.
Darrow, Clarence. *Farmington.* Chicago: A. C. McClung & Co., 1904.
Davis, Percival and Dean H. Kenyon, *Of Pandas and People: The Central Question of Biological Origins.* 2nd ed. Richardson, Texas: Foundation for Thought and Ethics, 1993.
de Camp, L. Sprague. *The Great Monkey Trial.* Garden City, N. Y.: Doubleday & Company, Inc., 1968.
de Vattel, Emmerich. *The Law of Nations.* 1758.
Dulany, Daniel. *Considerations on the Propriety of Imposing Taxes in the British Colonies for the Purpose of Raising Revenue, by Act of Parliament.* Annapolis, 1765. Reprinted in *Pamphlets of the American Revolution.* Bernard Bailyn, ed. Vol. 1 of 4 vols. John Harvard Library. Cambridge, Mass.: Belknap Press of Harvard University Press, 1965.
Encyclopedia of the American Constitution. Leonard W. Levy, ed. 4 vols. plus supplement. New York: Macmillan Publishing Company, 1986; supplement, 1992.
Evans, M. Stanton. *The Theme is Freedom: Religion, Politics and the American Tradition.* Washington, D.C.: Regnery Publishing, 1994.
Fairman, Charles. "Does the Fourteenth Amendment Incorporate the Bill of Rights?" 2 *Stanford Law Review* 5 (1949);
---. "A Reply to Professor Crosskey," 22 *University of Chicago Law Review* 144 (1954).
Fast, Howard. *The Jews: Story of a People.* A Laurel Book. New York: Dell Publishing Co., 1968.
Filmer, Robert. *Patriarcha, or the Natural Power of Kings.* 1680.
Fritz, Jean. *Cast for a Revolution: Some American Friends and Enemies.* Boston: Houghton Mifflin Company, 1972.
---. *Shh! We're Writing the Constitution.* New York: G. P. Putnam's Sons, 1987.
Ginger, Ray. *Six Days or Forever?: Tennessee v. John Thomas Scopes.* New York: Oxford University Press, 1974.
Goodrich, Rev. Charles A. *A History of the United States of America.* New York: George C. Smith & Co., 1829.

Grafton, John. *The American Revolution: A Picture Sourcebook*. Dover Pictorial Archive Series. New York: Dover Publications, 1975.

Grotius, Hugo. *On the Law of War and Peace*. 1625.

Hakim, Joy. *From Colonies to Country*. Book 3 of 10 books, "A History of Us." New York: Oxford University Press, 1993.

Hall, David D., ed. *The Antinomian Controversy: 1636-1638: A Documentary History*. 2nd ed. Durham, N.C.: Duke University Press, 1990.

Hamilton, Alexander. *A Full Vindication of the Measures of Congress*. New York: James Rivington, 1774.

---. *The Farmer Refuted*. New York: James Rivington, 1775.

Hamilton, Alexander, James Madison and John Jay. *Selections from the Federalist*. Ed. Henry Steele Commager. New York: Appleton-Century-Crofts, 1949.

Hibbert, Christopher. *Redcoats and Rebels: The American Revolution through British Eyes*. New York: W. W. Norton & Company, 1990.

Higginbotham, A. Leon, Jr. *In the Matter of Color: Race and the Legal Process*. New York: Oxford University Press, 1978.

Historical Statistics of the United States: Colonial Times to 1970. Washington, D.C.: U.S. Department of Commerce, Bureau of the Census, 1976.

Hobbes, Thomas. *The Leviathan*. 1651.

Hooker, Richard. *The Laws of Ecclesiastical Polity*. 1594, 1597, 1648.

Howard, Martin. *A Letter from a Gentleman at Halifax to a Rhode Island Friend*. Halifax, 1765. Reprinted in *Pamphlets of the American Revolution*. Bernard Bailyn, ed. Vol. 1 of 4 vols. John Harvard Library. Cambridge, Mass.: Belknap Press of Harvard University Press, 1965.

Howe, Henry. *Historical Collections of Ohio*. 3 vols. Columbus: Henry Howe & Son, 1891.

Hutchinson, Thomas, ed. *Collection of Original Papers Relative to the History of the Colony of Massachusetts Bay*. 2 vols. Boston, 1865. Reprint, New York, 1967,

Isaac, Rhys. *The Transformation of Virginia, 1740-1790*. Chapel Hill: University of North Carolina Press, 1982. Reprint, New York and London: W. W. Norton & Company, 1988.

Jastrow, Robert. "Evolution: Selection for Perfection." P. 86 in *Science Digest*, Dec. 1981.

Jefferson, Thomas. *Notes on the State of Virginia*. Paris, 1784; Philadelphia, 1788. Reprinted in *The Portable Thomas Jefferson*, Merrill D. Peterson, ed. New York: Viking Penguin, Penguin Books, 1975. Reprint, 1977.

---. *A Summary View of the Rights of British America*. Williamsburg, Philadelphia and London, 1774. Reprinted in *The Portable Thomas Jefferson*, Merrill D. Peterson, ed. New York: Viking Penguin, Penguin Books, 1975. Reprint, 1977.

Jenyns, Soame. *The Objections to the Taxation of Our American Colonies, Briefly Considered*. London, 1765. Reprinted in part in *Annals of America*. Vol. 1 of 21 vols. Chicago: Encyclopaedia Britannica, Inc., 1968.

Journals of the Continental Congress: 1774-1789. Worthington Chauncey Ford, ed. Vol. 1 of 14 vols. Washington: United States Government Printing Office, 1904.

Karst, Kenneth L. "Brown v. Board of Education." *Encyclopedia of the American Constitution.* Leonard W. Levy, ed. 4 vols. New York: Macmillan Publishing Company, 1986.

---. "The Japanese American Cases." *Encyclopedia of the American Constitution.* Leonard W. Levy, ed. 4 vols. New York: Macmillan Publishing Company, 1986.

Kent, James. *Commentaries on American Law.* 4 vols. 14th ed. Boston: Little, Brown, 1896.

Ketcham, Ralph. *The Anti-Federalist Papers and The Constitutional Convention Debates.* New York: NAL Penguin, 1986.

Kolchin, Peter. *American Slavery, 1619-1877.* American Century Series. New York: Hill and Wang, a division of Farrar, Straus and Giroux, 1993.

Kronenburger, Louis. *The Extraordinary Mr. Wilkes.* Garden City, N.Y.: Doubleday & Company, 1974.

Labaree, Benjamin Woods. *The Boston Tea Party.* New York: Oxford University Press, 1964.

Lacey, Michael J. and Knud Haakonssen, eds. *A Culture of Rights: The Bill of Rights in Philosophy, Politics, and Law--1791 and 1991.* Cambridge, England and New York: Woodrow Wilson International Center for Scholars and Cambridge University Press, 1991.

Langguth, A. J. *Patriots: The Men Who Started the American Revolution.* New York: Simon & Schuster, 1989.

Latham, Frank B. *The Trial of John Peter Zenger, August 1735.* A Focus Book. New York: Franklin Watts, Inc., 1970.

Leckie, Robert. *George Washington's War.* New York: HarperCollins, 1992.

Lewis, David L., "King, Martin Luther," *The New Encyclopaedia Britannica,* 15th ed., Macropaedia.

Levy, Leonard W. *The Establishment Clause: Religion and the First Amendment.* 2nd ed. Chapel Hill: University of North Carolina Press, 1994.

Locke, John. *A Letter Concerning Toleration.* 1689. Reprinted in *Great Books of the Western World.* Vol. 35. Chicago: Encyclopaedia Britannica, 1952, 28th printing, 1986.

---. *Second Essay Concerning Civil Government.* 1690. Reprinted in *Great Books of the Western World.* Vol. 35. Chicago: Encyclopaedia Britannica, 1952, 28th printing, 1986. Also reprinted in *Second Treatise of Government.* Thomas P. Peardon, ed. New York: The Liberal Arts Press, 1952.

Lockmiller, David A. *Sir William Blackstone.* Chapel Hill: University of North Carolina Press, 1938.

Lorant, Stefan. *Pittsburgh: The Story of an American City.* Garden City, N.Y.: Doubleday & Company, 1964.

Macaulay, Catharine. *History of England from the Ascension of James I to That of the Brunswick Line.* 1763-1783.

---. *Address to the People of England, Scotland and Ireland.* 1775.

Macy, Obed. *The History of Nantucket.* 2nd ed. Mansfield, Mass.: Macy & Pratt, 1880. Reprint, Ellinwood, Kansas: Macys of Elinwood, 1985.

McEvedy, Colin. *The Penguin Atlas of North American History to 1870.* New York: Viking Penguin, 1988.

McWhirter, Dariean A. *Equal Protection.* Exploring the Constitution Series. Phoenix, Ariz.: Oryx Press, 1995.

Meltzer, Milton. *The Bill of Rights: How We Got It and What It Means.* New York: Thomas Y. Crowell, 1990.

Miller, John C. *Alexander Hamilton: Portrait in Paradox.* New York: Harper & Brothers, 1959.

Montesquieu, Baron Charles-Louis. *Spirit of Laws.* 1748.

Morgan, Edmund S. *Roger Williams: The Church and the State.* New York: W.W. Norton & Company, 1967.

Morison, Samuel Eliot. *The Oxford History of the American People.* Vol. 1, *Prehistory to 1789.* New York: Oxford University Press, 1968. Reprint, New York: NAL Penguin, Mentor Books, 1972.

Morris, Richard B. *Witnesses at the Creation.* New York: Henry Holt and Company, 1985.

Morris, Richard B. and Henry Steele Commager. *Encyclopedia of History.* 6th ed. New York: Harper & Row, 1982.

Mott, Rodney L. *Due Process of Law.* Indianapolis: The Bobbs-Merrill Company, 1926.

Muzzey, David Saville. *Ethics as a Religion.* 1951.

Nelson, William E. *The Fourteenth Amendment: From Political Principle to Judicial Doctrine.* Cambridge, Mass.: Harvard University Press, 1988.

Nord, Warren A. *Religion and American Education: Rethinking a National Dilemma.* Chapel Hill: University of North Carolina Press, 1995.

O'Brien, David M. *Constitutional Law and Politics.* 2nd ed. 2 vols. New York: W. W. Norton & Company, 1995.

Otis, James. *The Rights of the British Colonies Asserted and Proved.* Boston, 1764. Reprinted in *Pamphlets of the American Revolution.* Bernard Bailyn, ed. Vol. 1 of 4 vols. John Harvard Library. Cambridge, Mass.: Belknap Press of Harvard University Press, 1965.

---. *A Vindication of the British Colonies, against the Aspersions of the Halifax Gentleman, in His Letter to a Rhode Island Friend.* Boston, 1765. Reprinted in *Pamphlets of the American Revolution.* Bernard Bailyn, ed. Vol. 1 of 4 vols. John Harvard Library. Cambridge, Mass.: Belknap Press of Harvard University Press, 1965. Portion also reprinted in Appendix I.

Padover, Saul K., ed. *The World of the Founding Fathers: Their Basic Ideas on Freedom and Self-Government.* New York: Thomas Yoseloff, 1960.

Paine, Thomas. *Common Sense.* 1776. Reprinted with intro. by Isaac Kramnick. New York: Penguin Books, 1976.

Paley, William. *Natural Theology*. New York: Harper & Brothers, 1845.
Parrinder, Geoffrey, ed. *World Religions: From Ancient History to the Present*. New York: Facts on File, 1983.
Peckham, Howard, ed. *The Toll of Independence*. Chicago: University of Chicago Press, 1974.
Peaslee, Amos J. *Constitutions of Nations*. Rev. 3rd ed. The Hague: Martinus Nijhoff, 1968.
Peterson, Merrill D., ed. *The Portable Thomas Jefferson*. New York: Viking Penguin, Penguin Books, 1975. Reprint, 1977.
Pfeffer, Leo. *Church, State and Freedom*. Boston: Beacon Press, 1967.
Priestly, Joseph. *Essay on the First Principles of Government, and on the Nature of Political, Civil and Religious Liberty*. 1769.
Ramsey, David. *The History of the American Revolution*. 2 vols. Philadelphia: R. Aitken, 1789. Reprint with intro. by Lester H. Cohen, Indianapolis: Liberty*Classics*, 1989.
Randall, Willard Sterne. *Thomas Jefferson. A Life*. A John Macrae Book. New York: Henry Holt and Company, 1993.
Robertson, Pat. *America's Dates with Destiny*. Nashville: Thomas Nelson, 1986.
---. *The Turning Tide*. Dallas: Word Publishing, 1993.
Rossiter, Clinton. *The First American Revolution: The American Colonies on the Eve of Independence*. Part 1 of *Seedtime of the Republic*. New York: Harcourt Brace Jovanovich, 1953. Revised, 1956.
Rosten, Leo, ed. *Religions of America: Ferment and Faith in an Age of Crisis*. A Touchstone Book. Revision of 1952-63 editions. New York: Simon and Shuster, 1975.
Rousseau, Jean-Jacques. *Discourse on the Origin of Inequality*. 1755.
---. *The Social Contract*. 1762.
Schwartz, Bernard. *The Bill of Rights: A Documentary History*. 2 vols. New York: Chelsea House Publishers and McGraw Hill, Inc., 1971.
Seabury, Samuel. *Letters from a Westchester Farmer*. New York, 1774-75.
Selby, John E. *The Revolution in Virginia, 1775-1783*. Williamsburg: The Colonial Williamsburg Foundation, 1988.
Sidney, Algeron. *Discourses Concerning Civil Government*. 1698.
Smith, Page. *A New Age Now Begins: A People's History of the American Revolution*. 2 vols. New York: McGraw Hill, 1976.
Soifer, Aviam. "United States v. Carolene Products." *Encyclopedia of the American Constitution*. Leonard W. Levy, ed. New York: Macmillan Publishing Company, 1986.
Spratley, Justice Vernon C. "Presentation of the Bust of George Wythe." *Ceremonies in Celebration of the Beginning of the John Marshall Bicentennial Year . . . at the College of William and Mary*. Williamsburg, 1954.
Stanton, Elizabeth Cady, Susan B. Anthony and Matilda Joslyn Gage. *History of Woman Suffrage*. 6 vols. Salem, New Hampshire: Ayer Company, 1985.

Includes reprint of 2 volumes published by Fowler & Wells, New York, 1881.
Stokes, Anson Phelps. *Church and State in the United States.* 3 vols. New York: Harper & Brothers, 1950.
Stokes, Anson Phelps, and Leo Pfeffer. *Church and State in the United States.* New York: Harper & Row, 1964.
Story, Joseph. *Commentaries on the Constitution of the United States.* 1833.
Trenchard, John and Thomas Gordon. *The Independent Whig.* 1719.
---. *Cato's Letters.* 1720-1723.
Thomson, Richard, *An Historical Essay on the Magna Charta of King John: To Which Are Added, the Great Charter in Latin and English; the Charters of Liberties and Confirmations, Granted by Henry III and Edward I; The Original Charter of the Forests; and Various Authentic Instruments Connected with Them.* London: John Major and Robert Jennings, 1829. Reprinted by The Legal Classics Library, Division of Gryphon Editions, Ltd., Birmingham, Alabama, 1982.
Thorpe, Francis Newton, ed. *The Federal and State Constitutions, Colonial Charters, and Other Organic Laws of the States, Territories and Colonies Now or Heretofore Forming The United States of America.* 7 vols. Published under the Act of Congress of June 30, 1906; repr. Buffalo, N.Y.: William S. Hein, 1993.
Tierney, Kevin. *Darrow: A Biography.* New York: Thomas Y. Cromwell, 1979.
Tillich, Paul. *A History of Christian Thought from its Judaic and Hellenistic Origins to Existentialism.* Carl E. Braaten, ed. A Touchstone Book. New York: Simon and Schuster, 1968.
Trevelyan, George Otto. *The American Revolution.* Ed., Richard B. Morris. New York: David McKay, 1964.
Tribe, Laurence H. *American Constitutional Law.* Mineola, N.Y.: The Foundation Press, Inc., 1978. Revised, 1984.
Vatican II. *Draft Declaration on the Church's Relations with Non-Christians: Council Daybook.* Washington D.C., 1965.
Veit, Helen E., Kenneth R. Bowling and Charlene Baugs Bickford, eds. *Creating the Bill of Rights: The Documentary Record from the First Congress.* Baltimore: Johns Hopkins University Press, 1991.
The Virginia Statute for Religious Freedom. Merrill D. Peterson and Robert C. Vaughan, eds. Cambridge, England; Melbourne, Australia; New York: Cambridge University Press, 1988.
Voltaire. *Lettres Philosophiques.* 1734.
von Pufendorf, Samuel Freiherr. *Of the Law and Nature of Nations.* 1672.
---. *The Whole Duty of Man According to the Law of Nature.* 1673.
Warden, Lewis C. *The Life of Blackstone.* Charlottesville, Va.: The Michie Company, 1938.
Warren, Mercy Otis. *Observations on the New Constitution, and on the Federal and State Conventions by a Columbian Patriot.* 1788. Repr. with

preferatory note by Lawrence W. Towner of the Massachusetts Institute of Technology. Boston: The Old South Association, 1955.

Warren, Mercy Otis. *History of the Rise, Progress and Termination of the American Revolution.* 3 vols. Boston: Manning and Loring for E. Larkin, 1805. Repr. in 2 vols. with annotation by Lester H. Cohen. Indianapolis: Legal*Classics*, 1988.

Wertenbaker, Thomas Jefferson. *The First Americans, 1607-1690.* Vol. 2 of *A History of American Life.* 12 vols. Arthur M. Schlesinger and Dixon Ryan Fox, eds. New York: The Macmillan Company, 1927.

Wexler, Jay D. "Of Pandas, People and the First Amendment: The Constitutionality of Teaching Intelligent Design in the Public Schools," 49 *Stanford Law Review* 439 (Jan., 1997).

White, Andrew Dickson. *A History of the Warfare of Science with Theology in Christendom.* New York: Dover Publications, 1960.

Wright, Louis B. *Magna Carta and The Tradition of Liberty.* Washington, D.C.: The American Revolution Bicentennial Administration, the United States Capitol Historical Society and the Supreme Court Historical Society, 1976.

Zinn, Howard. *A People's History of the United States.* New York: Harper & Row, 1980. Reprint, New York: HarperPerennial, 1990.

Index

A table of all legal cases mentioned in this book appears in the last section of this index. The persons, places and organizations involved in the facts of most of these cases are not listed in any section. Only the case titles, judges and legal principles are listed.

A. People, Groups and Private Organizations

No titles or offices are given, except for kings and judges; unless otherwise noted, "Justice" means a U. S. Supreme Court justice and "Judge" means a federal judge.

Adam (Biblical patriarch), 216, 702
Adams, Judge Arlin, 615, 618-620, 625-626
Adams, John, 9, 24, 32, 43-44, 60, 90-91, 99, 102, 126, 199, 247, 253, 319, 603, 701, 714, 878 (n. 3), 897 (n. 103)
Adams, Sam, 19, 24, 28, 31, 32, 41, 44-47, 48-51, 54-55, 75-76, 102, 126, 247, 300
  Boston resolution, 24
  The Rights of the Colonists, 50-51, 300, 845-848
  "Whippingpost," 24
Aleuts, 549, 552-553, 556
Allen, Ethan, 80-82, 84-85, 177
American Association for the Advancement of Science, 663
American Civil Liberties Union, 384, 628-629, 631, 644, 650-651, 660-662, 664, 669
American colonists, 3-5, 7-9, 19-20, 23-24, 32-41, 49-50, 58, 70, 87, 90, 173, 199-200, 305, 307, 310, 313, 315, 386, 442, 464-465, 476
American Legion, 505
American Museum of Natural History, 658
Americans, 3, 167-174, 295, 308, 310, 317, 319, 320, 349, 352, 475-476, 501, 544, 656, 676, 695-696, 697, 705, 717
Ames, Fisher, 285
Amherst, Lord Jeffrey, 100
Amish people, 225
Anabaptists, 219
André, John, 147-148
Anglican Church (Church of England), 10, 16-17, 62, 66, 200-202, 207, 211-212, 217-222, 227, 231-240, 242-244, 246-247, 250, 254, 258, 261-264, 271-273, 282, 621, 702, 705
  archbishop of Canterbury, 231
  bishop of London, 237, 243
  New York City Vestry, 219
  Society for Propogating the Gospel, 236
Anglicans, 200-202, 211, 213, 215, 217, 231-238, 240, 243-244, 255, 268-273, 282
Anthony, Susan B., 572
antifederalists, 195-197
Anti-Sabbatarians, 219
Aristotle, 91

Arnold, Benedict, 81, 85, 114-119, 143-148, 156, 160
Arnold, Isaac Newton, 391
Asians, 545, 556, 559
Athelstan, king of England, 318
Attucks, Crispus, 47
Augustine of Hippo
  City of God, 898 (n. 32)
Ayala, Francisco
  "The Theory of Evolution," 685-686
Backus, Isaac, 247-248, 253
Bacon, Francis, 91, 343
Baha'is, 624, 654
Bailyn, Bernard, 17
  Ideological Origins of the American Revolution, 17
Baltimore Advertiser, 263
Baltimore Sun, 665
Baptists, 207, 209, 211, 213, 225, 233, 244-247, 249-250, 252-256, 264, 268-274, 280, 291, 657-658
  Separate Baptists, 256, 268
Barras, Comte de, 160-161
Barré, Isaac, 29, 30
Battle, William, 408-409
Baum, Friedrich, 116-117
Beccaria, Cesare, 19
  Crimes and Punishment, 19
Belknap, Jeremy, 478-479
Bell, Robert, 880 (n. 19)
Beneš, Eduard, vi-vii
Bentham, Jeremy, 494, 713, 715-717
  Commentaries on the Commentaries, 716
Berengaria of Navarre, 584
Berger, Raoul, 390, 398-399, 405
Berkeley, John, Lord, 226
Berkeley, William, 229, 349-350
Bernard, Francis, 42, 44-47, 352-353
Bingham, John, 359-360, 392-394
Black, Justice Hugo, 287, 364, 368, 390, 399, 446-447, 449-453, 471-472, 474, 509, 525-526, 528, 597, 601-603, 618-619
black people, 5, 390-393, 398, 402-403, 435-437, 475-490, 493-504, 511-544, 549, 552-553, 556, 559, 563-564

919

slaves, 92, 103, 142, 158, 391-393, 398, 475-489, 496, 520-521
Blackmun, Justice Harry, 327-329, 331-332, 346-347, 473, 547, 550, 552, 555, 557-559, 578-581, 583, 593, 631
Blackstone, William, 12, 19-20, 713-717
An Analysis of the Laws of England, 713
Commentaries on the Laws of England, 6, 12-13, 19-20, 22-23, 35, 37, 41, 43, 49-50, 64-69, 80, 88, 91, 93, 96, 99, 187-188, 192, 210, 292-293, 298-325, 327, 332-333, 344-345, 347-349, 353, 364, 366, 368, 380, 386-388, 399-401, 405-409, 414-415, 421-422, 434, 436, 441-445, 447, 462, 464-470, 472, 476, 483, 491-492, 593, 620-621, 625, 672, 684, 699, 703-705, 714-804, 876, 881-882 (n. 48), 882-883 (n. 50), 898 (ns. 12 & 21), 901-902 (n. 40)
The Elements of Architecture, 713
Blair, Samuel, 244
Bland, Richard
The Colonel Dismounted, 19, 28
Bogue, Judge Andrew, 649
Bonnie Prince Charlie, 86
Boorstin, Daniel J., 20, 409
Boston Gazette, 44-45
Boston Globe, 381
Bowne, John, 216
Bradford, William, 206
Bradley, Justice Joseph, 413-415, 455-456, 468, 495-496, 541, 573-574
Brandeis, Justice Louis, 362, 429, 431
Braxton, Carter, 79
Brennan, Justice William, 331-332, 367-368, 377, 473-474, 525-526, 529, 547-548, 550, 552, 555, 557-559, 577, 579, 581, 612, 633, 681-682
Brewer, Justice David, 429
Breyer, Justice Stephen, 341-342, 559-560, 591
Bridges, Ruby, 526
Brorby, Judge Wade, 654
Brown, David, 358
Brown, Justice Henry, 498-500
Brown, John, 663
Browne brothers, 207
Browning, Orvill, 397
Bryan, William Jennings, 658-659, 661-675
Buddha Gotama, 622, 654
Burger, Chief Justice Warren, 381, 473, 531-532, 549-551, 553-554, 557, 575-576, 578-580, 604, 610
Burgoyne, John, 115-121
Burke, Edmund, 20, 58, 72-73, 127
Burns, James, Hawaii Supreme Court judge, 586, 588
Burton, Justice Harold, vi-vii, 373-374, 525-526, 597
Bute, John Stuart, Lord, 31
Butler, Thomas, 142-143
Byrd, William, II, 236

Byllinge, Edward, 226
Byron, John, 135
Calhoun, John C., 358-359, 368
California Joint Immigration Committee, 505
California Farm Bureau Federation, 505
Calvert, Benedict (4th Lord Baltimore), 233
Calvert, Cecil (2nd Lord Baltimore), 227-231, 234
Calvert, Charles (3rd Lord Baltimore), 230-232
Calvert, Charles (5th Lord Baltimore), 233
Calvert, George (1st Lord Baltimore), 227
Calvert, Leonard, 228-229
Calvin, John, 215, 700-702, 704,
Geneva Confession of Faith, 701
Calvinists, 202, 215, 246
Camden, Lord, 455-456, 468, 880 (n. 23)
Campbell, Archibald, 140-141
Campbell, Justice John, 486
Canby, Judge William, 679-680
Cardozo, Justice Benjamin, 336, 441-442, 474-475, 520
Carleton, Guy, 83, 114-115
Carteret, George, 226
Castres, Marquis de, 154
Catholic Church, v, 62, 199, 214, 228, 231, 246, 252, 278
Jesuits, 124, 215
pope, 95, 214, 258
schools, 286
Catholics, 63, 199-200, 214-215, 218, 219, 226-233, 235, 242, 244, 246, 248, 250-252, 256-260, 264, 278
Walloons, 215
Cato's Letters, 17, 350
Catron, Justice John, 486-487
"Centinal" of Pennsylvania, 283
Charles I, king of England, 199
Charles II, king of England, 17, 204, 207, 217, 224, 233
Champion, Judah, 256-257
Chase, Justice Samuel, 417
Chattanooga Daily Times, 660
Chauncy, Charles, 246
Chew, Benjamin, Pennsylvania chief justice, 122
Chicago Tribune, 664
Chicano people, 545
Child, Robert, 207
Chinese people, 424, 490, 496-497
Chittick, Donald, 686
Church, Benjamin, 24
Chworowski, Karl M., 624
Cicero, 91
Clark, Abraham, 179-180
Clark, George Rogers, 139-140
Clark, John, 207, 244-245
Clark, Justice Tom, 454-455, 459, 468, 525-526, 537-538, 607-609, 616-618, 648
Claiborne, William, 229
Clinton, Henry, 87, 104, 120, 131-136, 140-143, 146-150, 155, 158-161, 163

A. People, Groups and Private Organizations 921

Clinton, William, 383
Clitherow, Sarah, 714
Coke, Edward, English chief justice, 15, 839-840, 879 (n. 14), 890 (n. 9)
Colden, Cadwallader, 35-36
Colman, Benjamin, 212
Columbia University (King's College), 66, 222, 408
committees of correspondence, 49-51, 56, 58, 61, 247
Confucius
  Analects, 622-623, 690-694, 907-908 (n. 49)
Congregationalists, 203-205, 211-214, 240-241, 245-246, 249-251, 253-257, 614, 671
Conness, John, 490
Conway, Thomas, 126
Coode, John, 231-232
Copperhead Democrats, 396
Corbin, Richard, 78-79
Cornbury, Lord (Edward Hyde), 220-221
Cornwallis, Charles, Lord, 104, 111, 142-143, 148-153, 155-161, 163-164
Cosby, William, 350-351
Cox, Jacob, 397
Coxe, Tench, 180
Craven, Charles, 237
Cromwell, Oliver, 66, 207, 307
Cummins, Francis, 283
Curry, Thomas, 221-222
Curtis, Justice Benjamin, 487
Cushing, Justice William (also Massachusetts chief justice), 255, 319, 478
Czech Cultural Garden, v
Daniel, Justice Peter, 486, 488-489, 903 (n. 68)
Darrow, Clarence, 663-666, 668-669, 671, 673-675
Darwin, Charles, 656-658, 687
  Origin of the Species, 656
Davidson, William, 151
Davis, Judge Eugene, 652-653
Davies, Samuel, 11, 243-244
Dawes, William, 75
Day, Justice William Rufus, 502-503, 526
Dayton Progressive Club, 665
d'Estaing, Jean-Baptiste, 134-135
de Beaumarchais, Caron, 129
de Grasse, Francois, 159-163
de Kalb, Jean, 101, 129, 143
De la Place, William, 81-82
de Vattel, Emmerich, 18-19
  The Law of Nations, 18-19, 38, 839
Defoe, Daniel, 236-237
"Deliberator" of Pennsylvania, 283
Democratic Party, 658
DeWitt, J. L., 505-506
Dexter Avenue Baptist Church (Montgomery, Ala.), 534
Dickinson, John, 184
  Letters from a Farmer in Pennsylvania, 19, 40
Dixon, John, 78

Dongan, Thomas, 218-219
Douglas, Justice William O., 364, 368, 373, 449-450, 473-474, 505, 510-511, 525-526, 548, 575-576, 598-599
du Plessis, Chevalier, 101, 123, 129
Dubcek, Alexander, vii
Dubuque [Iowa] *Daily Times*, 397
Dulany, Daniel, 34
Dunmore, John Murray, Earl of, 58, 76, 78, 85-86
Duportail, Louis, 159-160
Dutch patroons, 217-218
Dutch Reformed Church (Calvinist), 92, 215-221
  the classis, 215
Dutton, Henry, 408
Dwight, Theodore, 408
East India Company, viii, 51-55
Ebenezer Baptist Church, 534-535
Edward I, king of England, 14, 23-24
Edward III, king of England, 309
Edward the Confessor, king of England, 14
Edwards, Jonathan, 240-241
Eells, Nathaniel, 242
Eisenhower, Dwight, 517, 525, 535, 603
Elizabeth I, queen of England, 14-15
Elizabeth of Brunswick-Wolfenbüttel, 584
English Protestants, 95
Episcopal Church, 252, 256, 262, 273-274, 282
Episcopalians, 275
Eskimos, 549, 552-553, 556
Ethical Culture Movement, 617, 623
Europeans, v, 165-166, 200
Fairman, Charles, 390-391, 405, 452
Falwell, Jerry, 368-369
Familists, 206, 614, 892 (n. 6)
farmers, Massachusetts, 177-178
Faubus, Orville, 524
federalists, 194-197
Feltham, Jocelyn, 81
Fendall, Josiah, 231-232
Fenwick, John, 226
Ferguson, Patrick, 149-150
Field, Justice Stephen, 412-413, 493, 573-574
Filmer, Robert
  Patriarcha, 702
Fitch, Thomas
  Reasons ... British Colonies Should Not Be Charged with Internal Taxes, 27-28
Fletcher, Benjamin, 219-220
Flynt, Larry, 368-369
Fortas, Justice Abe, 471, 677
Fox, Charles James, 99-100
Fox, George, 222-224
Frankfurter, Justice Felix, 373, 376, 430, 450-451, 453-456, 474, 517, 574, 597-598
Franklin, Benjamin, 36, 73, 88, 90, 124, 127-128, 136-137, 155, 165-167, 185, 188, 193, 350, 353-354, 884-885 (n. 9)
  Way to Wealth, 127
  Poor Richard's Almanack, 127, 137
Franklin, James, 350

Franz Joseph, emperor of Austria, v
Frederick the Great, king of Prussia, 124, 584
French Calvinists, 219
French habitants, 62
French immigrants, 215, 226, 233-234, 357
French intellectuals, 127-128
Freylinghuysen, Theodore, 238-239
Fundamentalist Christians, 657-658, 662, 665, 675, 685
Gage, Matilda Joslyn, 572
Gage, Thomas, 70, 72, 75-76, 83-84, 104
Galloway, Joseph, 61
Gandhi, Mahatma, 173, 534
Gates, Horatio, 118-119, 126, 143
George I, king of Great Britain, 235
George II, king of Great Britain, 79, 237
George III, king of Great Britain, 10, 19-21, 23, 31, 41-42, 54, 56, 59-60, 78, 79, 95-96, 98, 100, 102, 164-165, 312, 442, 697
   Proclamation of 1763, 23
   Proclamation for Suppressing Rebellion and Sedition, 84
Germain, George, Lord, 115, 131, 148-149, 152, 155
German immigrants, 226, 233, 350
German missionaries, 171-172
Gerry, Elbridge, 183, 703-704
Ginsberg, Justice Ruth Bader, 340, 342, 559-560, 590-591, 594
Goldberg, Justice Arthur, 368
Goldwater, Barry, 1
Gordon, Thomas, 17, 19
   Independent Whig, 17
   Cato's Letters, 17, 350
Gorton, Samuel, 207
Graves, Samuel, 161, 163
Greene, Nathaniel, 125, 135, 150-153, 155, 158, 161-162
Grenville, George, 21, 28, 36
Grier, Justice Robert, 486
Grotius, Hugo
   On the Law of War and Peace, 16
Hale, Nathan, 108
Hale, Robert, 392
Hamilton, Alexander, 113, 125, 179-180, 187, 191, 194, 196-197, 702-703
   Federalist Paper 78, 191-192
   Federalist Paper 84, 196
   Federalist Paper 85, 197
   A Full Vindication of the Measures of Congress, 66-67
   The Farmer Refuted, 67-69, 94, 702-703
Hamilton, Andrew, 351-354
Hamilton, Henry "the Hair-Buyer," 139-140
Hancock, John, 43-44, 55, 71, 75-76, 97
Harlan, Justice John Marshall (grandfather), 428-429, 500-501
Harlan, Justice John Marshall (grandson), 321, 340-341, 455, 459, 525-526, 618
Harold, king of England, 14

Harvard University (College), 44, 209, 408
Havlicek, Karl, vii
Hayes, Mary (Molly Pitcher), 133
Hays, Arthur Garfield, 672-673
Heaney, Judge Gerald, 649-650, 652
Heath, William, 106
Heen, Walter, Hawaii Supreme Court judge, 586-587
Henley, Samuel, 271-272
Helper, Hinton R.
   The Impending Crisis, 359
Henry, Patrick, 10-12, 29-30, 51, 73-75, 78-79, 201, 283, 466
Henry, Reverend Patrick, 11, 243
Henry III, king of England, 14
Herkimer, Nicholas, 117
Hesse-Cassel, Landgrave of, 102
Hicks, Sue, 659-660, 662-663, 669
Higley, William, 392
Hillsborough, Wills Hill, Lord, 42, 44, 46
Hilton, William, 233
Hindus, 622, 654
Hispanic people, 556, 559, 563-564
Hitler, Adolph, vii
Hoadley, Bishop Benjamin, 17
Hobbes, Thomas, 67, 94, 702, 704
Hodges, Judge William Terrell, 645-646
Holmes, Justice Oliver Wendell, 362-363, 373, 428, 431-432, 435, 504
Holt, Lord, English ch justice, 839-840, 890 (n. 9)
Hopkins, Esek, 136
Hopkins, Stephen
   The Rights of the Colonies Examined, 27-28
Hooker, Richard
   Laws of Ecclesiastical Polity, 16, 699, 823
Hortalez et Cie, 129
Hotchkiss, Giles, 392
Howard, Jacob, 394-395, 403-406, 490
Howard, Martin
   Halifax Letter, 32, 38-39
Howe, Richard, 104, 121, 135
Howe, Robert, 140-141
Howe, William, 104-109, 111, 113-115, 119-123, 130-131
Hughes, Chief Justice Charles Evans, 364-366, 432-434, 437, 447
Huguenots, 215, 226, 233-234
Hunter, George W.
   A Civic Biology, 661-662
Hustler Magazine, 368-369
Hutchinson, Anne, 31, 203-206, 240
Hutchinson, Thomas, 8-9, 31, 53-55, 884-885 (n. 9)
Illinois Wabash Company, 139
Indians (Native Americans), 4, 37, 83, 92, 97, 139, 166, 171-173, 490-491, 545, 549, 552-553, 556, 559
   Delaware, 172
   Cherokee, 171
   Gnadenhutten, 171-173

A. People, Groups and Private Organizations

Mohawk, 117
Narragansett, 204
Seneca, 171
Shawnee, 166
Ingle, Richard, 229
Iredell, Justice James, 408-409
Irenas, Judge Joseph, 651-652
Irish immigrants, 226, 242-243
Jackson, Justice Robert, 373-374, 376-377, 453, 509, 517, 597
Jains, 622
James, Joseph, 396-397
James II, king of England, 17, 95-96, 199, 217-219, 232
Jameson, Lt. Col., 147-148
Japanese people, 505-514
Jay, Chief Justice John, 62, 144, 188, 189, 194
Jefferson, Thomas, 51, 59-60, 73-74, 156-157, 196, 272-278, 281, 287, 293, 296, 334, 358-359, 368, 603, 670, 701-703, 705, 878 (n. 3), 897 (n. 103)
   drafts Declaration of Independence, 90-97
   Notes on the State of Virginia, 275, 303, 334, 349
   "Summary View of the Rights of British America," 59-60
Jenyns, Soame, 32-34
Jesus Christ, 223, 239-240, 245, 257, 260, 294, 318, 621, 624, 690-695, 863
Jews, 207, 214-216, 219, 250-251, 257-259, 262, 264, 276, 277, 318, 621, 654
Jogues, Isaac, 215
John, king of England, 14, 37, 50
Johnson, Andrew, 393, 397, 663
Jones, John Paul, 136-138
Justinian, Roman emperor, 292
Kasson, James, 391
Kelley, William, 392, 399
Kennedy, John F., 535, 603
Kennedy, Justice Anthony, 296, 321-322, 340, 553-555, 557, 559-560, 591-592, 631-632, 639-643
Kent, James, New York chief justice, 407, 408
   Kent's Commentaries, 407
Keppel, Augustus, 100
Kevorkian, Jack, 342
King, Martin Luther, Jr., 93, 173, 366-367, 534-535, 543
King's College (Columbia University), 66, 222
King's Medical Company, 689-690
Knox, William, 33-34
Kosciuszko, Tadeusz, 101, 123, 129
Lafayette, Gilbert, Marquis de, 101, 129, 135, 143, 156-159, 163
Latham, George, 398-399
Laurens, Henry, 130, 154
Laurens, John, 154-155
Lavoisier, Antoine-Laurent, 129
Lee, Charles, 108, 110-111, 132-133
Lee, Francis Lightfoot, 73-74
Lee, Lighthorse Harry, 150, 152
Lee, Richard Henry, 73-74, 126
Leland, John, 257
Leslie, Alexander, 151
Levellers, 15-16, 307
   agreement proposal, 15-16, 66, 307, 464-465, 468, 815-817
Levison, Steven, Hawaii Supreme Court judge, 586-588
Levy van Swellem, Asser, 215-216
Lincoln, Abraham, 5, 18, 489, 603, 715
   Gettysburg Address, 18
Lincoln, Benjamin, 119, 141-143
Livingston, Robert, 90
Livingston, William, 222
   The Independent Reflector, 222
Locke, John, 12-13, 16-17, 19, 33, 210, 240-242, 247, 274-275, 292, 704
   Letter Concerning Toleration, 210, 241-242, 274-275, 294, 704-705, 837-840
   Second Essay Concerning Civil Government, 12-13, 16, 66-67, 88, 91-95, 210, 241-242, 274-275, 298, 347, 444, 521, 698-700, 704, 820-835
Lockmiller, David, 408
Loring, Betsy, 111, 130-131
Loring, John, 130-131
Los Angeles Bible Institute, 657
Los Angeles Chamber of Commerce, 505
Lot (Biblical character), 345
Louis XVI, king of France, 128, 155
Loyalists, 100-101, 166, 171-173
   number, 100-101
   farmers, 102
   Florida, 171
   Georgia, 171
   New Jersey, 121
   New York City, 108
   New York state, 120
   North Carolina, 149, 152
   Ohio, 166
   South Carolina, 142-143
   Philadelphia, 131, 144
   restoration of property, 165-167
Lutherans, 215, 219, 225-226, 274
Macauley, Catharine, 17-18
   History of England, 17
   Address to the People of England, Scotland and Ireland, 17-18
MacDonald, Alan, 86
MacDonald, Flora, 86
Macy, Obed, 168-169
   The History of Nantucket, 168-169
Madison, James, 179-181, 183-185, 191, 194, 196, 198, 269, 272-273, 277-281, 284-285, 287-288, 290, 294, 296-298, 356-359, 368, 602-603, 614, 703, 890-891 (n. 9)
   Federalist Paper 48, 191

"Memorial and Remonstrance against Religious Assessments," 200, 278-281, 287-288, 294, 643, 856-862
Makemie, Francis, 221
Malone, Dudley, 669-671
Mandela, Nelson, 173
Marie Antoinette, queen of France, 128
Marion, Francis, 142-143
Marshall, Chief Justice John, 20, 310, 715, 890-891 (n. 9)
Marshall, Justice Thurgood, 331-332, 473-474, 547, 550, 552, 555-559, 575, 579, 582-583, 632-633
Martin, Joseph, 109, 170
Martin, Josiah, 86
Martin, Luther, 190, 195
  The Genuine Information, 195
Mary II, queen of England, 584
Maryland Gazette, 29, 262-263
Mason, George, 183, 185, 196, 273, 276, 280
Mather, Cotton, 208-210
  Memorable Providences, 208-209
Mather, Increase, 209, 308
Matthews, Justice Stanley, 421-424, 497
Maury, James, 10-11
Mauduit, Jasper, 24
Mayhew, Jonathan, 246-247
McKenna, Justice Joseph, 430
McLean, Justice John, 487
McReynolds, Justice James, 438-439
Mendel, Gregor, 657, 687
Mennonites, 277
Merritt, Judge Gilbert, 635-637
Metcalf, Maynard, 670-671
Methodists, 239-240
Mexican-Americans, 563-564
Michaëlius, Jonas, 215
Mifflin, Thomas, 126, 167
Milburn, Judge Ted, 636
Miller, Justice Samuel, 410-412, 416-420, 446, 456, 493, 573
minority peoples, 544-571
Minuit, Peter, 215, 226
Mohammed, 621
Monroe, James, 113, 715
Montague, George, 78
Montague, John, 73
Montesquieu, Charles-Louis, Baron, 18, 127, 485, 903 (n. 67)
  Spirit of the Laws, 18, 903 (n. 67)
Montgomery, Richard, 84-85, 114
Montgomery [Alabama] Improvement Association, 534
Moody, Justice William, 425-427, 437
Moon, Ronald, Hawaii Supreme Court judge, 586
Moravian Church, 171-172
Morgan, Daniel, 118-119, 126-127
Morison, Samuel Eliot, 100, 171
Morris, Gouverneur, 144, 182, 185
Morris, Lewis, New York chief justice, 351
Morris, Robert, 144
Morris, Samuel, 243
Moslems (Mahometans), 236, 262, 621-622
Moultrie, William, 87
Muhlenberg, John Peter Gabriel, 75
Murphy, Justice Frank, 371, 450, 509-510
Murphy, Judge Michael, 655
Muzzey, Saville, 617, 623
National Association for the Advancement of Coloerd People (NAACP), 502
National Science Foundation, 676
Native Sons & Daughters of the Golden West, 505
Neal, John, 668-669
Nelson, Justice Samuel, 487-488
Nelson, Thomas, Jr., 79
Nicholas, George, 278, 280
Nicholas, Robert Carter, 78-79, 272, 274, 278
Nicholas, Wilson, 278
Nicodemus (Biblical character), 239-240
Nixon, Richard, 535
New England Courant, 350
New York Times, 366-368, 659
New York Tribune, 359
New York Weekly Journal, 350-351
New Englanders, 166, 202
New Lights, 11, 241-242, 244, 246, 268
Newton, Isaac, 240
non-minority peoples, 544-571
North, Frederick, Lord, 73, 127, 130, 164-165
North Carolina Regulators, 101
Oberlin College, 670-671
O'Connor, Justice Sandra Day, 296, 321-322, 340, 342, 377-378, 385-386, 551, 553-555, 557-561, 591, 612, 631, 633, 637
O'Hara, Charles, 164
O'Scannlain, Judge Diarmuid, 569-570
Oglethorpe, James, 237-238
Old Lights, 241-242
"An Old Whig" of Pennsylvania, 283
Oliver, Andrew, 31, 53-54, 884-885 (n. 9)
Oriental people, 549, 552-553
Oswald, Richard, 165-166
Otis, James, 8-10, 12, 19, 24-26, 28, 34-35, 38-39, 41, 45-46, 247, 455
  Memorial of Massachusetts Assembly, 24-26, 839-840
  Rights of the British Colonies Asserted and Proved, 19, 26, 485
  A Vindication of the British Colonies, 34-35, 38-39, 843-844, 882-883 (n. 50)
Oxford University, 713, 715-716
  All Souls College, 713
  Codrington Library, 713
  Pembroke College, 713
Paca, William, 152
Paine, Robert Treat, 246
Paine, Thomas
  Common Sense, viii, 5, 88-90
  The American Crisis, 112
Parker, Peter, 87

A. People, Groups and Private Organizations

Parks, Rosa, 534
Parsons, Theophilus, 408
Paterson, Justice William, 183, 189-190
Patriots, 100-101, 172-173
  number, 100-101
  New Jersey, 121, 132, 170
  New York City, 108
  New York state, 120, 147, 171
  New England, 100-101, 110, 115
  North Carolina, 149
  Pennsylvania, 171
    Philadelphia, 131
Paul, the apostle, 94, 205
Peay, Austin, 659
Peckham, Justice Rufus, 427
Pendleton, Edmund, 274
Penn, William, 18, 222-226
Pennsylvania Journal and Weekly Advertiser, 29-30
Phillips, William, 156
Pickens, Andrew, 152-153
Pilgrims, 166, 202
Pitcher, Molly (Mary Hayes), 133
Pitney, Justice Mahlon, 429
Pitt, William (the elder), 36, 71-72, 99-100
Plato, 91
Pope, Alexander, 23
Powell, Justice Louis, 473-474, 546-554, 564-566, 579, 627-628, 682-683
Poyer, Thomas, 221-222
Pratt, English Chief Justice, 21
Presbyterians, 213, 221-222, 233, 236, 238-239, 241-244, 249-251, 264-265, 268, 274, 280, 658
  Hanover Presbytery, 276
  New Side (New Light), 239, 244, 268
Prescott, Samuel, 75
Prevost, Augustine, 140-141, 171
Priestly, Joseph
  Essay on First Principles of Government, 17
Princeton College, 114, 269-270
Protestants, 199-200, 210, 213, 214, 218, 222, 226, 228-235, 237, 241-242, 244-245, 248-256, 258-259, 264-266, 268, 278, 283, 500
Pufendorf, Samuel von
  On the Law and Nature of Nations, 16
  The Whole Duty of Man According to the Law of Nature, 16
Pulaski, Casimir, 101
Puritans, 92, 177, 202-215, 217, 240-242, 245
Putnam, Israel, 106
Pyle, John, 152-153
Quakers, 54, 88, 207-209, 211, 213, 215-216, 219, 222-227, 232-233, 235, 250, 255-256, 277
radical Republicans, 396
Raible, Christopher, 624
Randolph, Peyton, 60, 74, 78
Randolph, Edmund, 181-182
Rappleyea, George, 660-662, 672
Raulston, John, Tennessee judge, 664, 669, 671-675
Rawdon, Francis, Lord, 155, 162, 170
Ray, James Earl, 544
Raymond, Henry, 404
Reagan, Ronald, 553-554
Reavley, Judge Thomas, 637-638
Reed, Joseph, 144-146, 148
Reed, Justice Stanley, 446-447, 450, 517
Reformed Church, 225
Rehnquist, Chief Justice William, 289-292, 335-341, 369, 375, 377-378, 385-386, 460, 473, 549-551, 553-555, 557, 559-560, 575, 578-580, 592, 631, 641, 683
Revere, Paul, 42, 54, 61, 75-76
Richard the Lionhearted, king of England, 584
Riley, William Bell, 657-658
Rivington (bookseller), 800 (n. 19)
Robert the Bruce, king of Scotland, 100
Roberts, Justice Owen, 432, 446-448, 509
Robertson, Pat, 291-292
  America's Dates with Destiny, 291
  The Turning Tide, 291
Robinson, Frank, 659-660
Robinson, William, 243
Rochambeau, Jean Baptiste, 158-159, 162-163
Rockingham, Marquess of, 36, 165
Roosevelt, Franklin Delano, 431-433, 505
Rotch, Francis, 54-55
Rousseau, Jean-Jacques, 18, 127
  Discourse on the Origin of Inequality, 18
  The Social Contract, 18
Russell, Bertrand, 349
Russians, vii
Rutledge, Justice John, 142
Rutledge, Justice Wiley, 450, 453, 597, 626
Sabbatarians, 219
St. Clair, Arthur, 116
St. Leger, Barry, 117-118
Sandburg, Carl, 715
Sanford, Justice Edward, 361-363
Saul, king of Israel, 94
Saxon kings, 13-14
Scalia, Justice Antonin, 340, 553-555, 557, 559-560, 566, 592-593, 632, 641-642, 683-687
Schuyler, Philip, 116, 118
Scientologists, 623-624
Scopes, John, 660-662, 669-672, 675
Scotch immigrants, 233, 242-243
Scott, Dred, 480-489, 499
Seabury, Samuel, 885-886 (n. 31)
  "Westchester Farmer" pamphlets, 66-67, 69, 702-703
Sewell, Jonathan, 714
Shays, Daniel, 177-178
Shelburne, Henry, Lord, 165
Shellaberger, Samuel, 398-399
Shelby, Isaac, 149
Sherman, Roger, 90, 298
Sherman, William Tecumseh, 171

Shintos, 622
Shippen, Edward, 144
Shippen, Peggy, 144
Sidney, Algeron, 17, 33
  Discourses Concerning Civil Government, 17
Sikhs, 622, 654
Simcoe, John, 157
Singletary, Amos, 195-196
Singleton, Judge John, 655
Smith, Judge Jerry, 564-565
Soifer, Aviam, 444
Sons of Liberty, 28-31, 35-36, 42, 44-47, 48
Souter, Justice David, 296, 321-322, 337, 340, 342, 559-560, 562, 565, 591
Southern Christian Leadership Conference, 534-535
Spencer, Joseph, 106
Stanton, Elizabeth Cady, 572
Stevens, Justice John Paul, 331-332, 341-342, 377-378, 384-385, 549-552, 554-555, 557, 560-562, 579, 580, 591, 612-613, 633-634
Stewart, Lyman, 657
Stewart, Milton, 657
Stewart, Justice Potter, 331, 347, 459, 473-474, 540-541, 549-550, 553-554, 576, 578-580, 582-583, 603
Stewart, Tom, 662, 669-672, 674-675
Stone, Chief Justice Harlan Fiske, 326, 443-447, 507-509
Stone, William, 229
Story, Justice Joseph, 408, 417-418, 469
  Commentaries on the Constitution of the United States, 469
Straton, John Roach, 658
Strong, Justice William, 494-495
Stuyvesant, Peter, 215-217
Sullivan, John, 171
Sumter, Thomas, 142-143, 298
Sutherland, Justice George, 430-431, 433, 436-437, 440, 471-472
Swayne, Justice Noah, 573-574
Swedish immigrants, 216, 226
"Sydney" of New York, 283
Taft, Chief Justice William Howard, 431-432
Taoists, 622
Tarleton, Banastre, 142-143, 156
Taney, Mary, 231
Taney, Chief Justice Roger, 481-486, 488-489, 499
Taylor, Judge John, 409
Tennent, Gilbert, 238-239
Tennent, William, 264-265
Thacher, Oxenbridge, 800 (ns. 28-29)
  The Sentiments of a British American, 26-28
Thayer, Martin, 398-399
Thomas, Justice Clarence, 340, 559, 561, 592, 641
Thomas Aquinas, 619
Tillich, Paul, 616, 619
"Timoleon" of New York, 283

Tory Party, 100, 165
Townshend, Charles, 40
Trenchard, John, 17, 19
  Independent Whig, 17
  Cato's Letters, 17, 350
Tribe, Laurence, 625, 901 (ns. 35-36)
  American Constitutional Law, 901 (ns. 35-36)
Trumbull, Lyman, 404, 407-408, 540-541
Tucker, Thomas, 298
Tutu, Desmond, 173
Union Theological Seminary, 658
Unitarians, 246, 614, 624
Universalists, 246, 614, 624
Van Damm, Rip, 351
Vanderbilt University, 656-657
Vergennes, Comte de, 129-130, 154-155, 165-166
Vesey, William, 220
Vinson, Chief Justice Frederick, 373, 512-517, 520
Virginia Gazette, 276
Voltaire, 18, 127
  Lettres philisophiques, 18
von Closen, Ludwig, Baron, 162
von Steuben, Friedrich, 101, 124-126, 132, 157
Wade, Benjamin Franklin, 395, 663-664
Waite, Chief Justice Morrison, 348, 419, 707-708
Walker, Quock, 477-480, 484-485
Wallace, William, 100
Waller, Brother, 269
Walloons, 215
Warden, Louis, 20
Warner, Seth, 116-117
Warren, Chief Justice Earl, 344, 458-459, 517-520, 522-523, 525-526, 586-588
Warren, James, 881 (n. 34)
Warren, Joseph, 24, 44-45, 61, 71, 84, 352-353, 881 (n. 34)
Warren, Mercy Otis, 40-41, 298-299, 881 (n. 34), 883 (n. 55), 897 (n. 5)
Washington, Justice Bushrod, 403-405, 411, 413, 462
Washington, George, 73-74, 83-84, 86-87, 97, 102-114, 118, 120-128, 130-135, 143-145, 147-148, 150, 154, 156, 158-160, 162-164, 166-167, 171, 176, 181, 237, 275, 276-277, 603
Wayne, Anthony, 122
Wayne, Justice James, 486, 488-489, 903 (n. 68)
Webster, Noah, 20, 409, 880 (n. 21)
Wellford, Judge Harry, 636
Wells, Robert, 880 (n. 19)
Wenceslas, king of Bohemia, vii
Wentworth, Benning, 79-80
Wesley, Charles, 239
Wesley, John, 239-240
Western Growers Protective Association, 505
Whately, Thomas, 33-34, 54
Whig Party, 99-100, 165

A. People, Groups and Private Organizations 927

White, Justice Byron, 346, 377-378, 459, 473, 547-550, 552, 554-555, 558-559, 575, 579, 631, 641
White, Walter, 659-660, 670
Whitefield, George, 239-240, 243
Whittaker, Charles, 455
Wilkes, John, 20-23, 42, 305, 352, 455, 715
  North Briton No. 45, 21, 42
William and Mary, College of, 271-272, 584, 715
William the Conqueror, king of England, 14, 37
William III, king of England, 16, 232, 584
Williams, Elisha, 241-242, 294
Williams, Otho, 151-152
Williams, Roger, 203-206, 240, 244
Wilson, Justice James, 184, 185
Wilson, James, 404, 406-408
Winchell, Alexander, 656

Winslow, Edward, 206
Winthrop, James, Massachusetts judge, 479
Winthrop, John, 202
Woodbridge, Frederick, 392
Woodford, William, 86
Wooldredge, Bill, 689
World's Christian Fundamentals Association, 657-658
Worth, Daniel, 359
Wright, Judge Eugene, 678-679
Wright, Judge Skelley, 526
Wythe, George, 91, 715
Yale Universtity (College), 44, 241, 408
Zeisberger, David, 171-172
Zenger, John Peter, 350-352
Zinn, Howard, 120
Zoroastrians, 622

B. Places and Events

Alabama
  Montgomery, 534
Appalachian Mountains, 23, 63, 138-140
Arkansas
  antievolution law, 659
  Little Rock school integration protest, 523-526
Bahama Islands
  New Providence (Nassau), 136
Barbados Islands, 233
Bohemia, v, vii
Canada (Québec), 62-63, 84-85, 136
Champlain, Lake, 81-82, 84
Chesapeake Bay, 121, 159-163
  coastal raids by British, 136
Connecticut, 73, 80-81, 100, 202, 208, 210-214, 249, 255-257
  coastal raids by British, 136
  Fairfield, 136
  Hartford, 81
    Committee of Correspondence, 81
  New London, 160
  population, 250-251
    black and white, 479
Connecticut River, 79
Czechoslovakia, vii
  Prague, vii
  Wenceslas Square, vii
Delaware, 121, 134, 215, 225-227, 260-261
  population, 250-251
    black and white, 479
Delaware Bay, 134, 225
Delaware River, 111-113, 121, 132, 216, 225-226, 275
  forts battle, 123, 888 (n. 17)
  Washington's crossing, 112-113, 275
East Jersey, 226-227
England, 8-9, 16-19, 20-23, 119, 202, 225, 231, 233, 234, 239, 245, 714
  civil wars, 15, 66, 199, 307
  Charterhouse school, 713

Flamborough Head, 137
Hastings, Battle of, 14
London, 23, 36, 48, 148, 713, 714
  St. Peter's Church, 714
  Tower of London, 16, 86, 154
Newcastle, 137
Oxford, 713, 715-716
Peterborough, 212
Revolution of 1688, 16, 95, 232
south coast, 138
Wallingford, 713, 714
English Channel, 138
Europe, 165-166, 199-200
  Counter-Reformation, 199-200, 307
  Reformation, 199-200, 307
  First World War, 657
  Second World War, v, 891-892 (n. 2)
  Seven Years War, 7, 21
  Thirty Years War, 200
Florida, 166, 237
  St. Augustine, 233
France, 101, 154, 225, 233
  Paris, 124, 127-128, 165-167, 277
Georgia, 140-141, 143, 158, 166, 171, 237-240, 267-268
  Atlanta, 534-535
    lunch counter sit-in, 535
  Loyalist troops in, 103, 158
  population, 250-251
    black and white, 479
  Savannah, 98, 140-141, 162, 164
Germany, 101, 200
  Rhine Valley, 225
Ghana, 534
Great Lakes, 140
Holland, 154
  The Texel, 137
Hudson River, 110, 115-116, 118, 120, 121, 146-148, 159-160, 216-218, 226
Hungary, Budapest, viii

Illinois, 139-140, 543, 658, 663-664
  Cahokia, 139
  Chicago
    civil rights demonstrations, 543
      Summit Agreement, 543
    Democratic Convention (1896), 658
  Kaskaskia, 139-140
  Salem, 661
India, 534
Indiana
  Vincennes, 139-140
Italy, 19
Judea, Roman controlled, 178
Kentucky, 139, 166
  black and white population, 479
  Ft. Nelson (Louisville), 139
Lake Champlain battle, 114-115, 116
  Valcour Island, 115
Lake Erie, 172
Lake Ontario, 117
Louisiana
  New Orleans, 139
    school integration protest, 526
Maine, 85
  Penobsot Bay, 164
Maryland, 29, 121, 139, 179, 227-233, 261-263
  Annapolis, 167, 179-180
  Baltimore, 162, 171
  Calvert Town, 231
  coastal raids by British, 136
  Head of Elk, 121, 162
  population, 250-252
    black and white, 479
  western settlements, 139
Massachusetts, 73, 100, 203, 207, 212-214, 249, 253-255, 308
  Boston, 8-9, 24, 30-31, 42-47, 87, 135, 312
    Christ's Church, 75
    church contributions, 212, 214
    church controversy, 205
    Beacon Hill, 45
    Blockade, 56-58, 61, 70-71
    Boston Massacre, 47
    Boston Tea Party, viii, 51-56, 73
      ship *Dartmouth*, 54-55
    Brattle Street Church, 212
    British troops in, 45-47, 70-73, 75-76
    Dorchester Heights battle, 86-87
    Griffin's Wharf, 56
    Liberty Tree, 31, 45
    Liberty, seizure of ship, 42-44
    Faneuil Hall, 45, 54
    molasses smuggling, 8
    "Old Brick" First Church, 246
    Old South Meeting House, 54-55
    Stamp Act riots, 30-31, 53-54
    State House, 8, 47, 98
  Cape Cod, 168-169, 202

Charlestown, 75
  Breed's Hill, 83-84
  Bunker Hill battle, 83-84
Concord, 75-76
  North Bridge battle, 76, 78, 84, 138
Gloucester, 246
Lexington battle, viii, 75-77, 78, 84, 138, 166
Marblehead, 71, 105
Nantucket Island, 168-169
  wartime economy, 169
  whaling industry, 169
Northampton, 240
Plymouth Rock, 202
Pittsfield, 81
population, 250-251
  black and white, 479
Salem, 105
  church controversy, 204
  witchcraft trials, 208-209, 308
Shays' rebellion, 177-180
Springfield, 178
Warwick, 247
Williamstown, 81
Michigan
  Ft. Detroit, 138, 140, 171-172
Minnesota, 658
Mississippi River, 139, 166, 176
Mediterranean Sea, 176
Narrows Strait, 105
Netherlands, 215, 245
  Amsterdam, 215
New England, 159
  Baptist growth, 245
  coastal raids by British, 136
  free press status, 350
New Hampshire, 73, 79, 213-214, 248-249
  population, 250-251
    black and white, 479
New Jersey, 110-111, 120-121, 132, 134, 136, 160, 169-170, 215, 226-227, 241, 242-243, 258-259
  coastal raids by British, 136
  Elizabethtown, 114
  Ft. Lee, 108
    capture by British, 110
  Hackensack, 114
  Monmouth Courthouse battle, 132-134
  Morristown, 111, 114
  New Brunswick, 111, 239
  Newark, 114
  population, 250-251
    black and white, 479
  Princeton battle, 113-114
  Raritan Valley, 238-239
  Sandy Hook, 132, 134
  Trenton battle, 111-113
New Netherland, 214-217
  New Amsterdam, 214-217

B. Places and Events 929

New York, 63, 79, 92, 100, 111, 179, 217-222, 227, 241-244, 258, 675
  Albany, 82, 117, 217-218
  Bemis Heights, 118-119
  Cherry Valley Indian raid, 171
  Crown Point, 81-82
  Ft. Edward, 116, 118
  Ft. Stanwix battle, 116-117
  Ft. Ticonderoga, 81-82, 84, 86, 110, 115, 116, 119
    battle, 81-82
  Lake Oneida, 117
  Loyalist troops in, 103
  Long Island, 104-106, 218
    Kings County, 219
      Brooklyn, 107
      Long Island battle, 104-105
    Queens County, 219
      "Flushing Remonstrance," 216
      Jamaica, 221
    Manhattan Island (New York County), 104-108, 110, 219
      Fort Washington, 108
        capture by British, 110
      Harlem Heights, 106-107
      Kip's Bay battle, 106
      King's Bridge, 106
      New York City, 29-32, 35-36, 39-40, 47, 87, 98, 106, 108, 110, 111, 114, 120, 132, 134, 135, 141, 144, 146-147, 156, 158-161, 163, 166-167, 170, 217-220, 222, 352, 658, 660, 662
        Black Horse Tavern, 352
        Cavalry Baptist Church, 658
        East India tea arrives, 53
        Fraunces Tavern, 167
        liberty pole cut down, 47
        Stamp Act riots, 30
        synagogue (first), 219
        Trinity Church, 220, 221
  Mohawk River, 117
  Oriskany battle, 117
  Oswego River, 117
  population, 250-251
    black and white, 479
  Saratoga battle, 118-120, 126, 127, 128, 143, 150
    Freeman's Farm battles, 118-119
  Saratoga Springs, 118
  Staten Island, 104, 106, 121, 170, 238
  West Point, 146-148
  Westchester County, 108, 219
    Croton River Pine Bridge, 147
    East Chester, 108
    Northcastle, 109-110, 147
    Pell's Point, 108
    South Salem, 147-148
    White Plains, 108-109, 134, 159
      battle, 108-109

New York harbor, 132, 134-135, 163
Newfoundland, 10, 73, 167
North Carolina, 87, 101, 149-150, 155, 159, 177, 233, 236, 263-264
  Albemarle Sound, 233-235
  Cape Fear, 104
  Cape Hatteras, 161
  Catawba River crossing, 151
  Charlotte, 143, 149-150
  Cross Creek, 86
  Dan River, 151-153
  Guilford Courthouse, 151-152
    battle, 153
  Greensboro, 153
  Hillsboro, 143, 152
  population, 250-251
    black and white, 479
  Quaker settlements, 233
  Ramsour's Mills, 151-152
  Widow Moore's Creek battle, 86
  Wilmington, 86, 153, 164
Nova Scotia, 73, 87
  Halifax, 32, 45, 47, 104
Ohio
  Andover, 663
  Bucyrus, 166
  Cleveland, v
  Connecticut Western Reserve, 136
    Firelands region, 136
  Galion, 166
  Gnadenhutten massacre, 171-172
  Jefferson, 663-664
    Ashtabula County Courthouse, 664
  Kinsman, 663
  Lima, 166
  Loramie's Store battle, 166
  Olentangy River, 166
  Salem, 171-172
  Sandusky, 172
  Schoenbrunn, 171-172
  Tuscarawas River, 171-172
Ohio River, 63, 139-140, 179
Pennsylvania, 18, 63, 111, 166, 179, 215, 259
  Baptist settlements, 245
  Brandywine Creek battle, 121-123, 126
  Chester, 162
  Ft. Pitt, 138-139, 171-172
  Germantown battle, 122-123
  Neshaminy, 238
    Log College, 238-239
  Neshaminy Creek, 121
  Paoli's Tavern massacre, 122
  Philadelphia, 60, 78, 90, 111, 120-123, 126, 130-131, 144-146, 160-162, 225, 238-239
    East India tea arrives, 53
    Pennsylvania State House (Independence Hall), 82-83, 98, 180-181
  Pittsburgh, 138, 662-663
  population, 250-251

930 Index

black and white, 479
Schuykill River, 123
Scranton, 171, 177
Valley Forge, 123-126, 130, 132
West Chester, 663
Wyoming Valley Indian raid, 171
York, 174
Poland, 101
Potomac River, 179
Québec (Canada), 62-63, 84-85
Ft. St. Jean, 82, 84-85, 136
Montréal fortress, 84-85, 110, 114
Québec fortress, 85, 114
Rhode Island, 32, 73, 111, 202, 204, 214, 227, 244, 257-258
Narragansett Bay, 204
Gaspée ship burned, 48
Newport, 30, 135, 147, 158-161, 214, 244
birth of Baptist movement, 244
naval base, 135, 147, 158
Stamp Act riots, 30
population, 250-251
black and white, 479
St. Lawrence River, 116, 117
Savannah River, 141, 237
Scotland, 225-226
Edinburgh, 137
South Carolina, 140-143, 155, 171, 233-237, 264-267
Ashley River, 233
Baptist settlements, 233, 245
Camden, 155
battles, 143, 148, 158
Charleston, 104, 121, 140-143, 158, 162, 164, 233-235
battle, 141-142
St. Philip's Church, 236
Stamp Act riots, 30
Sullivan's Island battle, 87
East India tea arrives, 53
Cooper River, 233
Cowpens battle, 151
Eutaw Springs battle, 162
Gilberttown, 150
King's Mountain battle, 149-150
Loyalist troops in, 103, 142-143, 149-150, 158
Ninety-Six, 149
battle, 158
population, 250-251
blackand white, 479
Presbyterian settlements, 233
Sweden, 16
Tennessee, 149, 659-675
black and white population, 479
Chattanooga, 659, 661, 664
Memphis, 544, 662
King assassination, 544
Nashville, 656-657
Dayton, 659-675

Tennesse River, 659
Unites States of America, vii-viii, 165-166
Civil War, 5, 298, 315, 389, 891-892 (n. 2)
French and Indian War, 78, 79-80, 100, 138, 244
Great Depression, 930
depression after War of Independence, 177
population, 250-251
black and white, 479
Second World War, v, 891-892 (n. 2)
Viet Nam War, 891-892 (n. 2)
War of Independence, viii, 5-6, 9, 99-173, 177, 253, 302, 315, 350, 476
post-war economic difficulties, 179-180
Vermont, 79-81, 101, 116-117, 249, 251-253
Bennington battle, 116-117
Ft. Dummer, 79
population, 251
black and white, 479
Virginia, 63, 100, 149, 155-164, 166, 179, 200-202, 229-230, 233, 242-243, 268-282, 320, 658
Amherst County, 281
Blue Ridge Mountains, 156
Cape Henry and Cape Charles battle, 161
Charlottesville, 156-157
Dinwiddie County, 281
Doncastle's Ordinary, 78
Fredericksburg, 78
Great Bridge battle, 86
Green Spring Farm, 157
Hampton Roads, 156
Hanover County, 78, 243
Hanover *Parson's Case*, 10-12
Harper's Ferry, 663
James River, 76, 157-158, 162-163
Long Bridge battle, 86
Monticello, 157
Mount Vernon, 167
New Kent County, 244
Norfolk, 86, 121
Petersburg, 156
Piedmont region, 280
Point of Fork, 157
population, 250-251
blackand white, 479
Portsmouth, 157-158
Rapidan River, Racoon Ford, 157
Richmond, 85, 156
St. John's Church, 73-75
Shenandoah Valley, 179, 280
Staunton, 156
Tidewater river banks, 85, 280
Williamsburg, 28-30, 91, 157-158, 163, 273-274
Bruton Parish Church, 271
Gunpowder incident, 76, 77-78, 85
Raleigh Tavern, 58
Virginia Convention, 59-60

B. Places and Events

York River, 78, 157-158, 161, 163
Yorktown, 79, 158, 160-161, 163-164
   battle, 163-164, 180
Wabash River, 139
Wales, 225

Washington, D.C., viii
   Martin Luther King's march, 92-93, 535
West Indies, British, 154
West Indies, French, 130, 158-159, 163
West Jersey, 226

C. Nations, States and Government Agencies, Laws and Documents

Alabama, state
   domestic relations law--sex distinction, 580-581
   Montgomery city bus segregation, 534
Arkansas, state
   anti-school-integration law, 523-527
   religious freedom guarantee, 295
Austrian Empire, v, 7
   Seven Years' War, 7, 21, 128
California, state
   Civil Rights Initiative, 567-571
   University of California, Irvine, 686
   University of California, Davis, 545-549
Canada, 177
Carolina colony, 233-235
   charter, 234-235
   religious liberty law (1696), 235
   religious taxes, 234-237
Colorado, state
   const. amendment--homosexuals, 590-594
   University of Colorado, 676
Connecticut colony, 202, 249
   General Assembly (General Court), 210-212, 242
      religious tax laws, 210-211
         concessions to Anglicans, Baptists and Quakers, 211
      Saybrook Platform, 210-214, 255
      toleration law, 211
   religious freedom, establishment (1775), 250
   treasury, 81
   witchcraft trials, 208
Connecticut, state
   delegates to Const. Convention, 184
   General Assembly, 255-256
      laws discriminating against blacks, 484
   free speech and press guarantee, 355
   right to petition and assemble, 356
   religious establishment abolished, 295, 320
   religious freedom, establishment (1790), 251
   religious taxes and exemptions, 255-257
   territory dispute with Pennsylvania, 177
Czechoslovak constitution (1960)
   free speech and press limitation, 378-379
Delaware, colony, 320
   Assembly, 32, 226
   religious freedom (1775), 250, 281, 320
Delaware, state, 145, 179,
   constitution (1776), 260-261
      free press article, 355

      delegates to Const. Convention, 181, 184
   religious freedom (1790), 251, 260-261
   religious test for officeholders, 260, 295
East Jersey colony, 226
   religious freedom guarantee, 226
Florida Senate response to proposed 14th Amend., 397
France, 7-8, 10, 62
   army, 135, 138, 155, 158-164
   British-American war, 7-8, 79-80, 100, 138, 244
   Edict of Nantes, 233-234
   French Civil Law, 62-63
   Jefferson ambassador to, 277
   minister of war, 124
   navy, 131, 134-135, 138, 154-155, 158-161, 163-164, 166
      La Concorde, ship, 159
   peace treaty with Great Britain, 165-166
   Québec, loss of, 130
   secret aid to U.S., 130, 132
   Seven Years' War, 7, 21, 128
   treaty with U. S., 101, 124, 127-130
   treaty aid, 154-155
Franklin, state, 177
Georgia, colony, 61, 237-238
   Assembly, 31-32, 238
      Church of England established, 238
      religious tax on liquor, 238
   charter, 238
   religious freedom, establishment (1775), 250
Georgia, state, 181
   constitutions, 267-268
   religious freedom, establishment (1790), 251, 267-268
   guarantee against religious taxes (1798), 295
German duchies, v
Great Britain (England), 3-9, 128-131, 216-217
   admiralty courts, 24, 26-29, 31-32, 39-40
   army, 75-76, 81-85, 100, 104-123, 127, 130-136, 138-143, 148-164, 166-167, 169-173
      71st Highlanders, 100
      Canadian militia, 115-117
      Hessian troops, 102, 104-105, 111-113, 115-119, 123, 127, 130, 132, 141, 160, 164, 169-170
      Indians, 115-118, 138-140, 166, 171
         Cherokees, 171
         Delawares, 172

932   *Index*

Mohawks, 117-118
Senecas, 171
Shawnees, 166
Loyalist troops, 86, 103, 117, 141-143, 149-153, 155-156, 171
    Loyal Ethiopians, 85-86
    Royal Emigrant Regiment, 86
    Tarleton's cavalry legion, 142
    raids on civilians, 171
prison camps, 103
Tory Rangers, 117
Board (Lords) of Trade, 79, 244
Chancellor's Court, 713
Charter of Edward I (1297), 14, 23-24
Charter of Henry III (1216), 14
Common Pleas Court, 715
constitution, unwritten, 26, 72
customs officers, 8-9, 22, 40, 43-44, 46
debtor prisons, 237-238
declares war on France, 131
French and Indian War, 7-8, 79-80, 100, 138, 244
King's Bench, 15, 715, 839
king, 69, 80, 92, 95-97, 193
Magna Charta, 14, 24-25, 37-38, 50, 80, 91, 194, 298, 304, 307, 309, 360, 386, 419-420, 422, 464-465, 672, 710, 805
Middle Temple, 713-714
navy, 100, 105, 121, 132, 134-138, 154, 160-161, 163, 169, 217
    prison ships, 103
    raids on civilians, 136, 160, 169
    warships
       Countess of Scarborough, 137
       Fowey, 78
       Gaspée, 48-49, 302
       Magdalen, 76, 85
       Nautilus, 75
       Romney, 42-43
       Serapis, 137-138
New Inn Hall, 714
Parliament, 14-15, 21, 23-41, 47, 48, 51-52, 56, 65-66, 71-74, 99, 127, 130, 164-165, 230, 248, 274, 420
    "Coercive (Intolerable) Acts," 56-65, 71-73, 87
       Administration of Justice Act, 56, 71
       Boston Port Act, 56-58, 71
       Massachusetts Government Act, 56, 71
       Quartering Act (1765), 39-40
       Quartering Act (1774), 56-57
       Québec Act, 18, 56, 62-63
    Declaratory Act, 36-37
    English Declaration of Rights, 16, 91, 95, 313, 462, 464-465, 818-820
    House of Commons, 21-23, 69, 72-73, 165, 193
    House of Lords, 21-23, 69, 71-72, 193, 236-237

    New England Restraining Act, 73
    Petition of Right, 15, 298, 462, 464-466, 806-808
    prohibits all trade and commerce with the colonies, 84, 302-313
    Quartering Act of 1765, 39-40
    Revenue Act of 1764, 23-28
    Stamp Act, 28-32, 247, 881 (n. 31)
    Statute of Monopolies, 15, 803-804, 884 (n. 15)
    Statute of Northampton, 70
    Sugar Act of 1733, 8
    Tea Act of 1773, 52-53
    Toleration Act (1689), 209, 232, 243, 269, 271
    Townshend Acts, 40-41, 44, 47, 48, 52-53, 312
peace treaty with United States, France, Spain and the Netherlands, 165-166
Seven Years' War, 7, 21, 128
Royal Council, 79
Green Mountain government, 80-81, 177
Green Mountain Boys, 80-82, 84-85, 177
Hungary, v
    free speech and press (1949 Const.), 378
Idaho state probate law--sex distinction, 574-575
Illinois religious freedom guarantee, 295
India, Republic of, 173
Indiana religious freedom guarantee, 295
Kansas territory
    antislavery speech and press forbidden, 359-360
Kansas state religious freedom guarantee, 295
Kentucky, state
    religious freedom guarantee, 295
    resolution against Alien & Sedition Acts, 358
    University of Kentucky, 672
Louisiana, state
    anti-school-integration law, 526-527
    law giving only husband right to dispose of jointy owned property, 582-583
Maryland colony, 227-233
    Assembly, 229
    Alien & Sedition Acts counter-resolution, 358
    Church of England established, 232
    religious taxes, 232
    right to petition grievances, 356
    persecution of Catholics, 232-233
    Statute of Mortmain, 228
    Toleration Act (1649), 229-230
    religious freedom, establishment (1775), 250
Maryland, state, 174, 197
    bill of rights, 261-262, 295
    delegates to Const. Convention, 190
    guarantee against religious taxes, 263, 295
    proposed religious tax, 262-263
    religious freedom, establishment (1790), 251
Massachusetts Bay colony, 10, 202, 249, 319
    Body of Liberties, 15, 51, 202-203, 462, 464-465, 809-814, 884 (n. 5)

C. Nations, States, Laws and Documents 933

Boston Committee of Correspondence, 49-50
Boston declaration of rights, 49-50
Braintree resolutions, 32
Charter of 1691, 209-210
  liberty of conscience for Protestants, 209-210
Christianity established, 212
civil authorities, 204
House of Representatives (Assembly, General Court), 9-10, 31-32, 45, 248
  resolutions, 32
  religious tax laws, 212, 214, 247-248, 319
    concessions to Anglicans, Baptists and Quakers, 213
  Revenue Act Memorial, 24-26, 839-840
  Townshend Acts, petition against and confirmation of same, 41-42
labor rate regulation, 434
proposed resolution concerning British troops, 45-46
Provincial Congress, 71, 84
  Committee of Safety, 71
    Minutemen, 71, 75-76, 81, 313
  Provincial Army, 83-84
religious freedom, establishment (1775), 250, 253
religious persecution, 207-209, 247-248
Suffolk County Resolves, 61
Superior Court, 8-9, 31, 53
witchcraft trials, 208-209
Massachusetts, state, 197, 319-320
  Assembly, 178, 253
    hiring law preferring war veterans, 582
    law enabling women to execute will without husband's consent (1853), 572
    law forbidding interracial marriages, 484
    Quock Walker case, 477-479
  constitution and bill of rights (1780), 253-254, 319, 484
    rights to petition and assemble, 356
  courts closed, 177-178
  delegates to Const. Convention, 181, 183
  religious establishment abolished, 255, 295, 320
  religious freedom, establishment (1790), 251
  religious taxes and establishment, 253-255, 319
  Shays rebellion, 178
Michigan, state
  assisted suicide law, 342
  bartender licensing law, 574
Mississippi antievolution law, 659, 675
Missouri religious freedom guarantee, 295
Nebraska religious freedom guarantee, 295
Netherlands (Dutch Republic), 101, 214-217
  courts, 216
  Dutch West India Company, 214-216
    Amsterdam Chamber, 216
  loan to U.S., 155
  navy, 138
  peace treaty with Great Britain, 165-166
  religious tolerance, 216

New Hampshire colony, 202, 319
  Assembly, 32
    religious taxes, 213-214, 248-250, 319
      concessions to Anglicans, Baptists, Presbyterians and Quakers, 213
  Green Mountain land grants, 79-81
  religious freedom, establishment (1775), 250
New Hampshire, state
  Alien & Sedition Acts counter-resolution, 358
  constitutions and bill of rights, 249, 319-322, 347, 495, 706-707
    rights to petition and assemble, 356
  federal anti-establishment proposal, 283
  religious establishment abolished, 295, 320
  religious freedom, establishment (1790), 251
New Haven colony, 202
New Jersey colony
  Assembly, 32, 227
    rejects religious taxes, 227, 248, 250, 281, 320
  anti-Catholic laws, 227
  religious freedom (1775), 250, 281
New Jersey, state, 179-180
  constitution (1776), 258-259
  delegates to Const. Convention, 183, 189-190
  religious freedom (1790), 251, 258-259
  slavery abolition law, 477
New Netherland colony, 214-217
  religious establishment, 215
  religious tolerance, 215-216
New Sweden colony, 216, 226
New York, colony, 61, 79-82, 100, 319
  Articles of Capitulation (1664), 217
    private property rights recognized, 217
    worship freedom guaranteed, 217
  Assembly, 39-40, 82, 97-98, 218-222
    Charter of Liberties, 218
    King's College founding, 222
    landlord-tenant laws, 100
    militia, 82
    Ministry (Establishment) Act (1693), 219-220, 222
    religious tax law (1699), 220, 319
    toleration law, 219
  Duke's Laws, 218, 222
    religious free exercise guarantee, 218
  religious freedom, establishment (1775), 250
  religious taxes, 217-222, 250
  religious tolerance, 217-222
New York, state, 177, 179
  constitution (1777), 258
    Anglican Church disestablished, 258
  delegates to Constitutional Convention, 181, 185, 188
  federal anti-establishment proposal, 284
  federal free press proposal, 356
  law giving women right to own and sell property without husband's consent (1860), 572
  religious freedom (1790), 251, 258

slavery abolition law, 477
North Carolina, colony
  Assembly, 31-32
    Church of England establishment, 236
    religious tax law (1715), 235
  religious freedom, establishment (1775), 250
North Carolina, state
  constitution (1776), 263-264
    Anglican Church disestablished, 263-264
  delays ratifying the Constitution, 198
  religious freedom (1790), 251
  religious test for officeholders, 264
  rights to petition and assemble, 356
Ohio religious freedom guarantee, 295
Oklahoma
  antievolution law, 659
  beer sale law--sex distinction, 578-579
Pennsylvania, colony
  Assembly, 36
    Charter of Privileges, 224-225
      office-holders limited to Christians, 225
    morality laws, 225
  charter, 224, 259
  Frame of Government, 224, 226
    religious freedom, 224, 226, 248, 281
  religious freedom (1775), 250
Pennsylvania, state, 179-180, 191
  constitutions, 259
    religious freedom articles, 259, 295, 667
  delegates to Constitutional Convention, 181-185, 188
  Executive Council, 144
  religious freedom (1790), 251, 259
  slavery abolition law, 476-477
  territory dispute with Connecticut, 177
  territory dispute with Virginia, 139, 177
  threat to secede, 145-146
Plymouth colony, 202
  Great Fundamentals of Government, 15
Protestant Reformation, 199
Prussian Empire, v
  army, 124
  Seven Years' War, 7, 21, 128
Rhode Island and Providence Plantations colony, 202, 204-205, 214
  religious free exercise guarantee, 205, 214, 248, 281
  religious freedom (1775), 250, 257-258
  rights of Catholics and Jews, 257-258
Rhode Island, state, 103, 282
  delays ratifying the Constitution, 198
  free press guarantee, 355
  laws discriminating against blacks, 484
  no delegates to Const. Convention, 181
  religious freedom (1790), 251, 257-258
  rights of Catholics and Jews, 257-258
  rights to petition and assemble, 356
Rumanian Constitution (1965)
  free speech and press limitation, 378

Russian Sputnik sattelite, 676
South Carolina, colony
  Assembly, 42, 58
    Church of England established, 234, 236
  Provincial Congress, 87
  religious freedom, establishment (1775), 250
South Carolina, state, 180-181
  Assembly, 142, 180
  constitutions, 264-267
    Christianity established, 265-266, 319
    Christianity disestablished, 267
  religious freedom (1790), 251
Spain
  aid to U.S., 129, 139-140
  control of Mississippi River, 176
  declares war on Great Britain, 140
  Florida settlements, 233-234
  Kentucky annexation plan, 177
  navy, 138
  peace treaty with Great Britain, 165-166
Tennessee, state, 177, 659-675
  antievolution law (Butler Act), 659-675
  Eighteenth Judicial Circuit, 662, 664-675
  religious freedom guarantee, 295, 667-678
  Rhea County schools, 659-662
Texas state legislature response to proposed 14th Amend., 397
United States of America
  American Civil War, 5, 298, 315, 389, 391, 476, 489, 891-892 (n. 2)
  Articles of Confederation, 174-178, 183
    Committee of the States, 175
    common defense purpose, 174
    tax and war power limitations, 175
    settling disputes between states, 175, 177
    voting by the states, 174-175
  Articles of Confederation Congress, viii, 5, 101-102, 104, 123-124, 126-130, 137, 139-140, 143, 145-146, 154, 167, 174-180, 273-274, 277
    British peace initiatives, 104, 127, 130
    Continental script, 102, 123
    criticism of General Washington, 126
    debt problems, 176
    Declaration of Independence, 3-6, 18, 20, 59, 88-98, 123, 165, 173, 189, 198, 248, 257-258, 273-274, 292, 462, 464-465, 697-700, 717, 853-855
    Dutch bank loan, 176
    military coup averted, 176
    peace treaty with Great Britain, 165-167
    tariffs, lack of power to levy, 175-177
    treaty with France, 101, 124, 127-130
    war debts, 167
  Colonial Congresses
    First Continental Congress, 58-67, 73
      The Continental Association, 61
      address "To the people of Great Britain," 62-63

C. Nations, States, Laws and Documents 935

Declaration and Resolves, 62-63, 70-72, 462, 464-465, 849-852
letter to the people of Québec, 64
Suffolk Resolves adopted, 61
Second Continental Congress, viii, 5, 78, 81-83, 88
Declaration of the Causes and Necessity of Taking Up Arms, 83
letter to the people of Québec, 83, 354
Olive Branch Petition, 84, 312
vote for independence, 97
Stamp Act Congress, 31-32
Resolutions, 32, 36, 462, 464-465, 841-842
Constitution, v, viii, 3, 6, 179-198, 282, 697, 705, 708, 867-875
1st Amendment, 388, 389
establishment of religion, 65, 224, 248-295, 316-317, 320-321, 448, 464, 466, 596-696, 705, 870
legislative history, 282-286
interpretation, 286-295, 596-696
free exercise of religion, 282-286, 316-317, 391, 444-445, 447-448, 464, 466, 609, 626-634, 705, 708 870
legislative history, 282-286
free press, v, 20-23, 44-45, 64-65, 196, 223, 299, 313, 316-317, 349-388, 391, 394, 440, 444-445, 448, 464, 466, 705, 800-802, 870
free speech, v, 3, 7, 223, 313, 316-317, 349-388, 391, 394, 440, 444-445, 448, 464, 466, 546, 705, 708, 870
peaceable assembly, 56, 65, 313, 316-317, 369-370, 391, 394, 440, 448 464, 870
right to petition, 41-42, 65, 69, 96, 312, 313, 316, 394, 464, 766-767, 870
2nd Amend. right to bear arms, 3, 69-71, 83, 313-316, 394, 463,464, 767, 870
3rd Amend., no quartering soldiers, 7, 15, 39-40, 56-57, 62, 65, 95-96, 311, 316, 394, 463, 464, 870
4th Amendment
no unreasonable seach and seizure, 7-9, 22, 309, 316, 391, 394-395, 453-456, 464, 466-467, 708, 762-763, 870
no unwarranted arrest, 21, 304-305, 316 464, 466-467, 760-761, 762, 870
5th Amendment, 390, 705-706
grand jury indictment, 306, 316, 421-423, 449, 457, 463, 465, 466, 870
no double jeopardy, 306-307, 316, 441-443, 449, 457, 465, 467-468, 870
no self-incrimination, 15, 307, 316, 425-427, 449, 455-457, 458-461, 465, 467-468, 870
life, liberty and property, due process, 297, 298, 301, 303, 304, 309, 316, 390, 402, 409, 412, 484, 486, 488, 504, 519-521, 575, 705, 706, 753-769, 870
just compensation, 309-310, 316, 424, 448, 465, 467, 763, 870
6th Amendment
speedy criminal trial, 307, 316, 457, 465, 467, 870
public criminal trial, 305-306, 316, 380, 452-453, 465, 760, 870
criminal trial by jury, 24, 27, 29, 39, 40-41, 42, 48-49, 62, 64-65, 96, 187, 299, 305-306, 316, 380, 391, 395, 425, 441-442, 449, 457, 465, 467, 472-474, 493-495, 758-759, 870
trial in district of crime, 49, 56, 305-306, 316, 395, 463, 465, 761-762, 870
right to be informed of charges, 304, 306, 316, 395, 425, 448, 465, 467, 759, 870
right to confront witnesses, 307-308, 316, 420-421, 449, 457, 465, 467, 870
right of process to get witnesses, 307-308, 316, 457, 465, 467-469, 870
right to counsel, 15, 307-308, 316, 435-437, 456, 458-461, 465, 467, 469-472, 870
7th Amendment
right to civil jury trial, 312, 316, 418, 448-449, 463, 465, 466, 871
8th Amendment
no excessive bail, 304, 306, 316, 395, 463, 465, 759, 871
no excessive fines, 311, 316, 463, 465, 871
no cruel or unusual punishment, 49, 302, 316, 394, 395, 424, 449, 456, 465, 467, 757-758, 871
9th Amend., non-enumerated rights of the people, 98, 296, 871
10th Amend., powers not delegated to U.S. retained by the states and people, 182-183, 296, 538, 871
13th Amend., slavery abolished, 188, 360, 391-392, 398, 489, 495-496, 504, 540-541, 871
14th Amendment, 489
citizenship, 188-189, 395-396, 489, 871
privileges and immunities, 187-189, 393, 395, 402-406, 413-415, 446-447, 492-493, 753, 871
life, liberty and property, due process, 189, 298, 303, 360, 380-381, 393, 406-408, 409-475, 706, 753-769, 871
equal protection, 188-189, 303, 393, 412, 475-595, 705, 706, 871
legislative and ratification history, 391-398
15th Amend., right to vote not denied on account of race, etc., 189, 445, 706, 872
16th Amend., income tax, 311, 872
17th Amend., direct election of senators, 184, 193, 706, 872

936 Index

19th Amend., right to vote not denied on account of sex, 445-446, 706, 873
27th Amend., congressional pay increase limit, 875, 891 (n. 15)
army (I, 8[12]), 186, 865
bill of attainder (I, 9[3] & 10[1]), 187, 197, 461-462, 866
Bill of Rights, 3, 6, 196-198, 282, 296-388, 389, 464-465, 697, 703, 708, 870-871
  proposed preambles, 297-298
commerce (I, 8[3]), 186, 196, 433-434, 443, 536-539, 865
contract obligations, impairment of (I, 10[1]), 185, 461-462, 866
electoral college (II, 1[2-4]), 185
ex post facto laws (I, 9[3] & 10[1]), 187, 197, 461-462, 866
full faith and credit (IV, 1), 185, 589-590, 868
habeas corpus (I, 9[2]), 187, 197, 304, 461-462, 759-760, 866
impeachment and conviction by Congress (II, 4; I, 2[5] & 3[6]), 185-186
judicial power (III, 1, 2), 186, 189-193, 194, 196, 867, 890-891 (ns. 9 & 11)
jury trial (III, 2[3]), 187, 465, 867
law-making power (I, 8[18]), 186, 866
money (I, 8[5]), 186, 865
navy (I, 8[13]), 186, 865
patents and copyrights (I, 8[8]), 186, 489, 865
preamble, 708
presidential powers
  appointment (II, 2[2]), 185
  reprieve (II, 2[1]), 185
  treaty-making (II, 2[2]), 185
  veto (I, 7[2]), 185
privileges and immunities (IV, 2[1]), 187-189, 395, 403-404, 485-486, 868
ratification by the states, 194-198
ratification process (VII), 197
religious test for office (VI, 3), 187, 193, 283, 869
representation--House (I, 2[3]), 184, 705-706
representation--Senate (I, 3[1]), 184
republican government (IV, 4), 194, 868-869
slaves, escaped (IV, 2[3]), 188, 484, 868
supremacy clause (Art. VI[2]), 182-183, 186-190, 194, 196, 869, 890 (n. 3)
taxes (I, 8[1] & 2[3]), 186, 310-311, 865
voting rights (15th, 19th, 24th & 26th Amends.), 189, 872-873
Constitutional Convention, 180-194
  Annapolis resolution, 180
  Connecticut compromise, 184
  executive branch, 184-186
  judicial branch, 186, 189-194
  legislative branch
    one-house proposal, 183
    powers of, 181, 183, 186
    representation by population vs. representation by state, 183-184
    rights of the people, 187-188
    senators, election of, 184
    two-house proposal, 181, 184
  New Jersey plan, 183
  three-branch government, 181, 194
  Virginia plan, 181-183, 185
Continental Army, 83-86, 90, 104-127, 130-136, 140-143, 146, 148-164, 166-168
  black soldiers, 103, 162
  Carolina militia, 149-150
  Connecticut Rangers, 106
  Delaware Line, 143
  Green Mountain Boys, 117, 118
  Green Mountain Rangers, 116
  Indians, 116-118, 138
    Stockbridge, Mass. Indians, 116-117
  militia units, 103, 170
  Marblehead and Salem, Mass. regiments, 105, 112
  Maryland Line, 143
  Maryland regiment, 152-153
  Massachusetts militia, 116-118
  New England militia, 84-85, 118-120
  New Jersey Line, 154
  New York militia, 117, 120
  North Carolina militia, 152, 162
  prison camps, 103
  Pennsylvania militia, 113
  Pennsylvania Line, 154, 157
  raids on Indian villages, 166, 171
  Rhode Island regiment, 162
  soldiers
    desertions, 102, 166
    enlistment periods, 102
    food and health problems, 102, 123-124, 154-155, 162
    morale, 102, 154, 166
    mutinies, 102, 154
    pay, 102, 154, 166, 176 soldiers, state quotas, 102-103, 159, 176
    uniforms, 102, 123-124, 154, 162
  South Carolina militia, 163
  South Carolina Regiment, 87
  Tennessee militia, 149-150
  Valley Forge, 123-126, 130, 132
  Virginia militia, 149-150, 156, 163
  Virginia riflemen, 106
    Morgan's Rifle Brigade, 118-119
Continental Navy, 136-138
  inability to protect merchant ships, 176
  privateering, 136, 166
  warships
    Alliance, 137
    Bonhomme Richard, 137-138
    Pallas, 137
Federal Communications Commission, 556-558

C. Nations, States, Laws and Documents 937

First World War, 657
Louisiana Purchase Treaty (1803), 486-489
Second World War, v, 891-892 (n. 2)
United States Army, 178, 525
United States Congress
   Alien and Sedition Acts, 357-359
   Americans with Disabilities Act (1988), 542
   armed services laws--sex distinctions, 575-576
   Civil Rights Act (1866), 390, 392-393, 402-403, 495, 512, 540, 663
   Civil Rights Act (1875), 495-496, 535-536
   Civil Righst Act (1964), 535-538, 544, 546, 549, 551, 566-567, 904 (n. 80)
   Civil Rights Act (1968), 541-544
   Communications Decency Act, 383-386
   Defense of Marriage Act, 590-591, 593-594
   Fugitive Slave Act (1850), 488
   Joint Committee on Reconstruction, 391-394
   Missouri Compromise (1820), 486-487
   minority business enterprise law, 549-551
   New Deal laws, 431-434
   public assistance law--sex distinction, 581
   Religious Freedom Restoration Act, 193
   Small Business Act, 559
   Social Security laws--sex distinctions, 576-577, 579-580
   United States Supreme Court (not including decisions listed in Section E), 6, 186, 188, 189-194, 193, 409
   Viet Nam War, 891-892 (n. 2)
   War of Independence, viii, 5-6, 9, 99-173, 177, 253, 350, 476, 891-892 (n. 2)
Utah domestice relations law--sex distinction, 577-578
Vermont regional government, 177
Vermont territorial government
   constitution, 249, 252-253
   free speech and press guarantee, 354-356
   rights to petition and assemble, 356
   religious taxes, 252-253
   religious freedom, establishment (1790), 251
Virginia, colony, 10, 229, 243, 349-350
   Albemarle County resolutions, 58-59
   Church of England established, 200-202, 243
      Baptist persecution, 269-270
      Church role in Virginia society, 270-271

      internal difficulties, 268-270
   Committee of Correspondence, 51
   Committee of Safety, 85
   Council, 244
   House of Burgesses, 10, 12, 31-32, 51, 58, 90, 201, 271-272
      Boston Port Act, resolutions against, 58
      Stamp Act, resolutions against, 29-31
      Two-Penny Act, 10-11, 28, 201
   Northampton County resolutions, 32
   Parson's Case, 201
   religious freedom, establishment (1775), 250
   Revolutionary Convention, 59-60, 73-75
Virginia, state, 103, 179-180, 191, 197
   Declaration of Rights, 196, 273, 354, 614
      free speech and press article, 354
      religious freedom article, 273, 614
   delegates to Constitutional Convention, 181-185, 191
   federal anti-establishment proposal, 283-284
   federal free press proposal, 356
   General Assembly, 139, 156
      antislavery speech and press forbidden, 359
      House of Delegates, 274, 277-278
         Bill Establishing Provision for Teachers of the Christian Religion, 276-277, 294-295, 858-859
         Episcopal establishment confirmed, 274, 282
      religious tax law amended, 275
      resolution against Alien & Sedition Acts, 358
      Senate, 281
      Statute for Religious Freedom, 276, 281-283, 290-291, 293-294, 320, 596, 598, 603, 670, 865-866, 905-906 (n. 13)
   Kentucky territory's threat to join Spain, 177
   Memorial and Remonstrance against Religious Assessments, 277-281, 320, 596, 602-603, 614, 643, 859-864, 905-906 (n. 13)
   opposition to establishment, 274-275
   "ten thousand name" Baptist petition, 274
   religious freedom (1790), 251
   Richmond Minority Business Utilization Plan, 552-556
   territory dispute with Pennsylvania, 139, 177
West Jersey colony, 226
   religious freedom guarantee, 226

D. Legal Rights, Philosophies, Religions and Other Subjects

abortion, 3, 326-332
absolute duties, 210, 299, 317-349, 445, 747-748
absolute rights, 13-14, 19, 37-39, 43, 49-50, 68-69, 299-301, 409, 476, 745-769
adultery, 202, 210, 813
affirmative action, 3, 544-571
   broadcasting, 556-559
   public construction work, 549-551, 559-562

public education, 545-549, 551-556, 562-567
summary of affirmative action, 571
alcohol sale and consumption, 322-324
alter or abolish govenment, right to, 94-95, 698, 700-701, 853
Amish religion, 225
Anabaptist religion, 219

938 Index

Anglican denomination, 10, 16-17, 62, 66, 200-202, 207, 211-213, 215, 217-222, 227, 231-240, 242-244, 246-247, 250, 254-255, 258, 261-264, 268-273, 282, 621, 705
Anti-Sabbatarian religion, 219
arms, right to bear, 3, 69-71, 83, 313-316, 464, 766-767, 870
arrest, v, 21, 304-305, 316, 464, 760-761
arrested person's right to be warned, 458-461
atheism, 275-276, 349, 606, 617, 624, 657, 663, 701-702
auxiliary rights, 41-42, 70, 96, 464-465, 765-769
"bad example" justification for laws, 318, 348-349, 387-388, 485-486
Baha'i religion, 624, 651
Baptist denomination, 209, 211, 213, 225, 233, 244-247, 249-250, 252-256, 264, 268-274, 280, 291, 657-658
Bible distribution in public schools, 628
Bible reading in public schools, 604-609
birth control, 343
Black Codes, 391-392
black people, equal rights, 493-496, 497-501, 502-504, 511-544
blasphemy, 201, 202, 206, 210, 214, 215, 274, 282, 705, 793, 813
body integrity, 324-332
boycott agreements, 44-47, 59-61
Brandeis brief, 429-430
Buddhism, 622
business regulation, 424, 443-444, 448, 496-497
capital punishment, 15, 49, 301-303, 757-758, 813-814
Calvinism, 202, 215, 219, 246, 700-702
Catholicism, v, 62-63, 199-200, 214-215, 218-219, 226-233, 235, 242, 244, 246, 248, 250-252, 256-260, 264, 278
Chinese people, equal rights, 490, 497, 501-502
Christianity, 3, 93, 168, 171-172, 195, 236, 277, 294, 621, 624, 660, 690-695, 863
   baptism, 245-246
   Bible, incl. quoted passages, 44, 55, 94, 178, 195-196, 202-204, 208, 215, 223, 239-240, 277-278, 280, 294, 345, 60-4-609, 656-688, 863, 883 (n. 59), 885 (n. 12)
   creation story, 656-677, 680-688
   born again, 238-240, 245-246
   free will, 204, 240, 245
   Holy Spirit, 238, 245, 260
   justification by faith and grace, 205, 240
   Trinitarian God, 207, 246, 272
civil liberty, 246-247, 299-300, 749
circumstantial evidence, 209, 308
colonial officials, pay, appointment, 41, 48, 56
common law, 713-715
Communism, vii, 378-379
confessions, forced, 437
conflict of laws rules, 487-488
Confucianism, 622-623, 690-694

Congregational denomination, 203-205, 211-214, 240-241, 245-246, 249-251, 253-257, 614
consent of the people, government by, 12-13, 66, 94, 698, 699-700, 703, 705, 825, 831-832
contract consideration, 706
contract, liberty of, 427-434, 448
copyrights, viii, 89-90, 489
counsel, right to, 15, 307-308, 316, 435-437, 457-461, 465, 467, 469-472, 870
   right to be warned of right, 458-461
criminal trials, right of public to attend, 379-381
cruel and unusual punishment, 49, 302, 316, 394, 449, 456, 465, 757-758, 871
death penalty, 15, 49, 301-303, 757-758, 813-814
democracy, 194
die, right to, 3, 332-342
double jeopardy, 441-443, 449, 457, 465, 467-468, 870
drug abuse, 323-324
due process of law, 418, 421, 425-427, 435-437, 448-449
Dutch Reformed denomination, 92, 215-221
education, right to, 3, 303
education, parents' right to control, 437-439, 448, 508-509
environmental concerns, 3
Episcopal denomination, 252, 256, 262, 273-275, 282, 885-886 (n. 31)
equal protection, v, 3, 5, 18, 188-189, 303, 392, 393, 397, 475-595, 705, 706, 871
equal rights, 92-93, 821, 475-495, 698, 705
Equal Rights Amendment (proposed), 583-584
equivalent protection principle, 321-322
Ethical Culture Movement, 617, 623
evolution, 656-677, 680-688
fair trial, right to, 435-437, 448
Familist religion, 206, 614
Fascism, viii
fishing rights, 10, 73, 166
flag burning, saluting and display, 3, 375-379
fornication, 343-344
Fundamentalist Christianity, 657-658, 660, 662, 665, 675, 685
gay rights, 3, 344-347, 584-595
Golden Rule, 207
graduation prayers, 634-647
grand jury idictment, 306, 316, 421-423, 449, 465, 664, 665, 870
Great Awakening, 200, 203, 238-248
habeas corpus, writ of, 22, 64, 187, 197, 304, 761-762, 868
heresy, 274, 705, 778-784
Hindu religion, 622
homosexual sex, 344-347
homosexual marriages, 584-595
horses, wartime suffering, 121, 124
Huguenot religion, 215, 226, 233-234
humanism, 4, 687
idolatry, 210

D. Legal Rights, Philosophies, Religions, ect. 939

incorporation of Bill of Rights amendments into 14th Amend. life, liberty and property clause, 449-457
incorporation of equal protection into 5th Amend. live, liberty and property clause, 507, 519-521
Indians, equal rights, 490-491
internal affairs, right of colonists to control, 28, 58-60, 65-66, 95
Internet, freedom of speech on, 382-386
interpretation of laws, 399-401
 rules applied to 14th Amend., 402-409
Islam (Mahometan religion), 236, 262, 621-622
Jainism, 622
Japanese people, equal rights, 505-511
Judaism, 3, 207, 214-216, 219, 250-251, 257-259, 262, 264, 276, 277, 621
jury trial, right to, 24, 27, 29, 39, 40-41, 42, 48-49, 62, 64-65, 96, 187, 299, 305-306, 316, 380, 391, 422, 425, 441-442, 449, 457, 465, 472-474, 493-495, 867, 870, 871
laborers' pay and work conditions, 303, 427-434
legitimate powers of government, 275
liberty, right of, 13, 22, 25, 49-50, 96, 189, 304-308, 386-387, 464-465, 503, 758-762
life, liberty and property, 4-7, 12-20, 25, 38-39, 60, 65-69, 189, 241-242, 292, 296-317, 321, 378, 386, 392-393, 403, 406-408, 698-700, 705-707, 753-769
life, liberty and the pursuit of happiness, 93, 189, 698, 849
"Love thy neighbor" commandment, 222, 272
Lutheran denomination, 215, 219, 225-226, 274
lying, 210, 778, 814
marriage between races, 344
"menace to public peace, safety" justification for discrimination, 499-500, 503, 507-511, 525-526
Methodist denomination, 239-240
morality laws, 225
Moravian religion, 171-172
monopolies, 14-15, 51-53, 59, 803-804
natural law (law of nature), 12-13, 16-20, 38, 66-69, 88, 91-95, 210, 241-242, 280, 282, 292-293, 300, 417, 450-451, 456, 667-668, 698, 703, 705, 710, 718-723, 749, 878
natural liberty, 40, 50, 66-69, 72, 188, 280, 282, 299-301, 316-317, 322, 324-325, 405, 407-408, 733, 749, 753, 827, 830, 846, 881-882 (n. 48)
natural rights, 280, 282, 290
natural science, 683-684, 688
Naziism, viii
necessities of life, 302-303, 755
New Light religion, 11, 241-242, 244, 246, 268
nobility, titles of, 197, 461, 476, 866
non-importation agreements, 44, 47, 59-61
non-violent demonstrations, 173
obscene materials, 323
Old Light religion, 241-242

patents, viii, 14-15, 51-52, 186, 413, 429, 489
peaceable assembly, right of, 56, 65, 313, 316-317, 369-370, 391, 440, 444, 464, 870
personal security, right of, 13, 25, 49, 50, 301-303, 386-387, 464-465, 753-758
petition, right to, 41-42, 65, 69, 96, 369-370
place of trial, right to, 49, 56, 305-306, 316, 465, 761-762, 870
prayer in legislative assemblies, 603-604, 635-636, 638, 647
prayer in public schools, 600-603, 611-614, 634-647
predestination, 92
Presbyterian denomination, 213, 221-222, 233, 236, 238-239, 241-244, 249-251, 264-265, 268, 274, 276, 280
press, freedom of, v, 20-23, 44-45, 64-65, 196, 223, 299, 313, 316-317, 349-388, 391, 440, 464, 705, 800-802, 870
price regulating laws, 410-415, 418-419
privacy, right of, 321-349, 387
privileges and immunities, 187-189, 301, 392-393, 402-406, 753, 871
property, right of, 13, 25, 35, 43, 49, 50, 96, 309-311, 386, 387, 410-420, 464-465, 486, 762-764
prostitution, 344
Protestant religion, 63, 95, 199-200, 210, 213, 214, 218, 222, 226, 228-235, 237, 241-242, 244-245, 248-256, 258-259, 264-266, 268, 278, 283, 500
public office, right to hold, 195, 200, 203, 214, 225, 227, 232-233, 248, 250-252, 257, 260, 264, 267-268, 282, 283, 295
Puritan religion, 92, 177, 202-215, 217, 240-242, 245
pursuit of happiness, 4, 7, 93, 292-293, 698-699, 705, 710, 716-717, 722-723
Quaker religion, 54, 88, 207-209, 211, 213, 215-216, 219, 222-227, 232-233, 235, 250, 255-256, 277
quartering soldiers, 7, 15, 39-40, 56-57, 62, 65, 95-96, 464, 870
quid pro quo, 706-709
race discrimination, 493-495, 497-504, 511-571
racially restrictive housing laws and private covenants, 502-504, 511-513
rape and sex abuse, 170, 172-173
Reformed denomination, 225
relative rights and duties, 13, 210, 300, 317, 322-324, 387, 445, 750
"religion" defined, 613-626
religious freedom, 3, 15, 62-63, 65, 196, 199-295, 317-321, 387, 391, 444-445, 596-696, 705, 707-708, 710, 859-866
religious establishment, freedom from, 65, 224, 248-295, 316-320, 464, 596-696, 705, 859-866, 870

religious holiday assemblies and displays in public schools, 648-652
religious instruction in public schools, 596-600
 in extracurricular activities, 626-634
religious persecution, 207, 223-224, 232-233
religious music in public schools, 647-648, 652-656
religious taxes, 201, 203, 208, 210-214, 217-222, 248-264, 266-268, 273-274
republican government, 193-194
revealed law, 13, 93-94, 210, 292, 723-725
reverse discrimination, 549-571
revolution, right of, 17, 94-95
residuum of natural liberty, 188, 300-301, 316-317, 447, 753
rights of Englishmen, 36-39, 62, 64-66, 72, 87, 97, 745-769
Roman law, 713
Sabbatarian religion, 219
Sabbath observance, 210, 214, 215, 252-253, 797
sacrilege, 201
salvation, 202, 203, 205
Science of Creative Intelligence and Transcendental Meditation (SCI/TM), 614-615
Scientology religion, 623-624
search and seizure, v, 7-9, 22, 43, 309, 316, 391, 464, 708, 762-764, 870
segregation, government forced, 497-503, 505-511, 513-534
 in public schools, 501-502, 513-534
 in other public facilities, 522, 534
self defense, right of, 302, 754
self-incrimination, right against, 15, 425-427, 449, 455-461, 467-468
 right to be warned of right, 458-461
separate but equal, 497-503
separation of powers, 18, 181-182, 194
sex discrimination, 494-495, 571-584, 710, 874-877
Shintoism, 622
Sikh religion, 622
Sinter Klaas (Santa Claus), 217
slavery, 5, 92, 96, 188, 390-391, 476-491, 495, 770-774
social contract, 12-13, 18, 300, 313, 348, 706-709
sodomy, 344-347

speech, freedom of, v, 3, 7, 223, 313, 316-317, 349-388, 391, 397, 440, 444-445, 464, 705, 708, 870
state of nature, 12, 13, 292, 709, 821-825
standing armies, 65, 95
stealing, 210, 813
sterilization of criminals and mental patients, 504-505
suicide, 332-334
Taoism, 622
tax, valid purpose required, 419-420
taxation without representation, 7, 17-18, 23-42, 59-60, 62, 64-65, 72, 96, 310-311, 763
Ten Commandments, 204, 609-611
 honor father and mother, 205
 no adultery, 210, 813
 no graven image (idolatry), 210
 no lying, 210, 778, 814
 no murder, 210, 813
 no other gods or Lord's name in vain (blasphemy), 201, 202, 206, 210, 214, 215, 795, 813
 no stealing, 210, 813
 posting in public schools, 609-611
 Sabbath observance, 210, 214, 215, 252-253, 797
tenures, freedom from oppressive, 64-66
Thirty Years War, 200
treason, 10, 11, 185
Trinitarian God, 203, 246
Unitarian-Universalist religion, 246, 614, 624
usury laws, 434
values, teaching in public schools, 689-695
voting rights, 16, 189, 193, 208, 219, 257, 444
war crimes trial, 150
war, morality of, 168-169
warrants and writs of assistance, 40-42
 arrest, 21, 304-305, 316, 457, 464, 762-763, 870
 general, 9, 21-23, 39, 41-42
 search and seizure, 7-9, 22, 309, 316, 453-456, 464, 762-763
witchcraft, 202, 208-209, 705, 794-795, 813
women, equal rights, 3, 494-495, 571-584, 658, 705, 874-877
"Yankee Doodle" song, 46
zoning, 439-440
Zoroastrianism, 622

E. Table of Cases

Abington Township (Pennsylvania) *School District of, v. Schempp*, 374 U.S. 203 (1963): 604-609, 611-612, 648, 655, 679-680, 689
Abrams et al. v. U.S., 250 U.S. 616 (1919): 362
Adair v. U.S., 208 U.S. 161 (1908): 428-429
Adamson v. California, 332 U.S. 46 (1947): 390-391, 399, 449-452, 474-475
Adarand Constructors v. Peña, 515 U.S. 200, 115 S.Ct. 2097 (1995): 558-562, 564, 566, 571
Adkins v. Children's Hospital, 261 U.S. 525 (1923): 430-431, 432

E. Table of Cases 941

Adler v. Duval County (Florida) *School Board*, 851 F.Supp. 446 (M.D. Fla., 1994), 112 F.3d 1475 (11th Cir., 1997): 645-646
Alexander v. Holmes County (Mississippi) *Board of Education et al.*, 396 U.S. 19 (1969): 529-530
Alexander v. Louisiana, 405 U.S. 625 (1972): 456, 463, 466
Allgeyer v. Louisiana, 165 U.S. 578 (1897): 424-425
American Civil Liberties Union of New Jersey v. Black Horse Pike Regional Board of Education, 84 F.3d 1471 (3rd Cir., 1996): 644-645
American Publishing v. Fisher, 166 U.S. 464 (1897): 473
Apodaca v. Oregon, 406 U.S. 404 (1972): 473-474
Baehr v. Lewin, 852 P.2d 44 (Hawaii S.Ct., 1993): 585-589, 594
Baehr v. Miike, 1996 WL 694235: 588-589
Baker by Thomas v. General Motors Corporation, 118 S.Ct. 657 (1998): 589-590, 594
Ballew v. Georgia, 435 U.S. 223 (1978): 473
Barbier v. Connolly, 113 U.S. 27 (1885): 496-497
Barron v. Baltimore, 32 U.S. (7 Peters) 243 (Jan. term, 1833): 389-390
Bartels v. Iowa, 262 U.S. 404 (1923), 438
Bartkus v. Illinois, 359 U.S. 121 (1959): 902 (ns. 46, 49)
Bauchman v. West High School, 900 F.Supp. 254 (D. Utah, 1995): 648
Bauchman v. West High School, 132 F.3d 542 (10th Cir., 1997): 653-655
Benton v. Maryland, 395 U.S. 784 (1969): 456, 465, 467
Berea College v. Kentucky, 211 U.S. 45 (1908): 501, 503, 516
Betts v. Brady, 316 U.S. 455 (1942): 471-472
Board of Education of the Westside Community Schools v. Mergens, 496 U.S. 226 (1990): 630-634
Boerne v. Flores, 117 S.Ct. 2157 (1997): 193, 893 (n. 11)
Bohning and Pohl v. Ohio, 262 U.S. 404 (1923): 438
Bolger v. Youngs Drug Products Corp., 463 U.S. 60 (1983): 385
Bolling v. Sharpe, 342 U.S. 497 (1954): 518-522
Bolling v. Sharpe II, 349 U.S. 294 (1955): 522-523
Bonham's Case, VIII Coke Rep. 114a (K.B., 1610): 15, 879 (n. 14), 890 (n. 9)
Bourne v. Flores, 117 S.Ct. 2157 (1997): 193
Bowers v. Hardwick, 478 U.S. 186 (1986): 345, 346-347, 592-593
Boyd v. U.S., 116 U.S. 616 (1886), 455-456, 468, 880 (n. 23)
Bradwell v. State of Illinois, 83 U.S. (16 Wallace) 130 (Dec. term, 1872): 573-574
Brandenburg v. Ohio, 395 U.S. 444 (1969): 363-364
Brandon v. Board of Education of the Guilderland (New York) *Central School District*, 635 F.2d 971 (2nd Cir., 1980): 631
Briggs v. Elliott, 347 U.S. 483 (1954): 517-519
Briggs v. Elliott II, 349 U.S. 294 (1955): 521-523
Brown v. Board of Education of Topeka, 347 U.S. 483 (1954): 517-519, 521-522, 533, 562, 904 (n. 75)
Brown v. Board of Education of Topeka II, 349 U.S. 294 (1955): 522-523, 529, 533
Brown v. Mississippi, 297 U.S. 278 (1936): 437, 441, 448
Buchanan v. Warley, 245 U.S. 60 (1917): 502-503, 520, 526
Buck v. Bell, 274 U.S. 200 (1927): 325-326, 504
Bunting v. Oregon, 243 U.S. 426 (1917): 302-303, 429-431
Calder v. Bull, 3 U.S. (3 Dallas) 386 (Aug. term, 1798): 417, 461
Califano v. Goldfarb, 430 U.S. 199 (1977): 578-580
Califano v. Webster, 430 U.S. 313 (1977): 580
Califano v. Wescott, 443 U.S. 76 (1979): 581, 583
Cantwell v. Connecticut, 310 U.S. 296 (1940): 447-448, 464
Carey v. Population Services International, 431 US 678 (1977): 384
Chambers v. Florida, 309 U.S. 227 (1940): 437
Chaplinsky v. New Hampshire, 315 U.S. 568 (1942): 370-371, 374
Chicago, Burlington & Quincy Railroad v. Chicago, 166 U.S. 226 (1897): 424, 426, 448, 465
Chivers v. Couch Motor Lines, Inc., 159 So.2d 544 (La. Ct. of App., 1964): 589
Citizen's Savings & Loan Association of Cleveland, Ohio v. City of Topeka, Kansas, 87 U.S. (20 Wallace) 655 (Oct. term, 1874): 415-417
City of Richmond v. J. A. Croson Co., 488 U.S. 469 (1989): 552-556

City of London v. Wood, 12 Mod. 669 (King's Bench, 1701): 890 (n. 9)
Civil Rights Cases, 109 U.S. 3 (1883): 495-496, 535-536, 541
Clever v. Cherry Hill Township (New Jersey) *Board of Education*, 838 F.Supp. 929 (D. N.J., 1993): 650-652, 653
Coalition for Economic Equity v. Pete Wilson, Governor of California, 122 F.3d 692 (1997), cert. den. 118 S.Ct. 397 (1997): 567-571
Committee for Public Education v. Nyquist, 413 U.S. 756 (1973): 627
Committee for Public Education v. Regan, 444 U.S. 646 (1980): 627
Compassion in Dying v. Washington, 79 F.3d 790 (9th Cir., 1996): 899 (n. 38)
Cooper v. Aaron, 358 U.S. 1 (1957): 523-526
Corfield v. Coryell, Fed. Case No. 3,230, 6 Fed. Cas. 546 (E.D. Pa., 1823): 403-405, 408, 411, 413, 462
Corrigan and Curtis v. Buckley, 271 U.S. 323 (1926): 503-504, 512-513
Craig v. Boren, 429 U.S. 190 (1976): 578-579
Cruzan v. Missouri Department of Health, 497 U.S. 261 (1990): 335-336, 338
Currin v. Wallace, 306 U.S. 1 (1939): 904 (n. 77)
Davidson v. New Orleans, 96 U.S. 97 (Oct. term, 1877): 418-421, 450
Davis v. Board of Commissioners of Mobile County, 402 U.S. 33 (1971): 532
Davis v. County School Board of Prince Edward County (Virginia), 347 U.S. 483 (1954): 517-519
Davis v. County School Board of Prince Edward County (Virignia) *II*, 349 U.S. 294 (1955): 522-523
Dawson v. Mayor and City of Baltimore, 350 U.S. 877 (1955), affirming 220 F.2d 386 (4th Cir., 1955): 522
DeFunis v. Odegaard, 416 U.S. 312 (1974): 548
DeJonge v. Oregon, 299 U.S. 353 (1937): 369-370, 440, 441, 447, 464
Denver Area Educational Telecommunications Consortium v. F.C.C., 116 S.Ct. 2374 (1996), 384-385
Detroit Bank v. U.S., 317 U.S. 329 (1942): 904 (n. 77)
Diamond v. Charles, 476 U.S. 54 (1986): 347, 593
Doe v. Aldine (Texas) *Independent School District*, 563 F.Supp. 883 (S.D. Texas, 1982): 655-656
Doe v. Duncanville (Texas) *Independent School District*, 70 F.3d 402 (5th Cir., 1995): 648, 652-653
Donnelly v. Lynch, 691 F.2d 1029 (1st Cir., 1982), 905 (n. 13)
Doremus v. Board of Education of the Borough of Hawthorne (New Jersey), 342 U.S. 429 (1952): 905 (n. 13)
Dred Scott v. Sandford, 60 U.S. (19 Howard) 393 (Dec. term, 1856): 480-489, 499
Duncan v. Louisiana, 391 U.S. 145 (1968): 456, 465, 473
Edwards v. Aguillard, 482 U.S. 578 (1987): 681-688
Eisenstadt v. Baird, 405 U.S. 438 (1965): 343
Employment Division, Oregon Department of Human Resources v. Smith, 494 U.S. 872 (1990): 323, 891 (n. 11)
Endo, Ex parte, 323 U.S. 283 (1944): 510-511
Engblom v. Carey, 677 F.2d 957 (2nd Cir., 1982): 463, 464
Engel v. Vitale, 370 U.S. 421 (1962): 600-603, 604, 611, 635, 641, 655, 897 (n. 102)
Entick v. Carrington and Three Other King's Messengers, 19 Howell's State Trials 1029 (1765): 22, 309, 455-456, 468, 880 (n. 23)
Epperson v. Arkansas, 393 U.S. 97 (1968): 674-677, 680-681, 906 (n. 21)
Euclid (Ohio), *Village of v. Ambler Realty Company*, 272 U.S. 365 (1926): 439-440
Everson v. Board of Education of the Township of Ewing (New Jersey), 330 U.S. 1 (1947): 286-288, 448, 464, 596, 597, 626
Fellowship of Humanity v. County of Alameda, 315 P.2d 394 (Cal. App.Ct., 1957): 620
Fiske v. Kansas, 274 U.S. 380 (1927): 360-361, 440, 447, 464
Florey v. Sioux Falls (S. Dakota) *School District 49-5*, 619 F.2d 1311 (8th Cir., 1980): 648-650, 652, 653, 655-656
Founding Church of Scientology of Washington v. U.S., 409 F.2d 1146: 620
Frontiero v. Richardson, 411 U.S. 677 (1973): 575-576
Frothingham v. Mellon, 262 U.S. 447 (1923): 905 (n. 13)
Fullilove v. Klutznick, 448 U.S. 448 (1980): 549-551, 552-555, 557-561
Gardner v. Collins, 27 U.S. (2 Peters) 58 (Jan. term, 1829): 401-403, 486
Gasquet v. Lapeyre, 242 U.S. 367 (1917): 461

E. Table of Cases 943

Gayle v. Browder, 352 U.S. 903 (1956), aff'g 142 F.Supp. 707 (M.D. Ala., 1956): 522
Gearon v. Loudoun County (Virginia) *School Board*, 844 F.Supp. 1097 (E.D. Va., 1993): 644
Gebhart v. Belton, 347 U.S. 483 (1954): 517-519
Gebhart v. Belton II, 349 U.S. 294 (1955): 522-523
Gibbs v. Illinois Central Railway Co., 125 So. 445 (La. S.Ct., 1929): 589
Gibson v. Mississippi, 162 U.S. 565 (1896): 904 (n. 77)
Gideon v. Wainwright, 372 U.S. 335 (1963): 456, 458, 465, 469-472
Ginsberg v. New York, 390 U.S. 629 (1968): 323
Gitlow v. New York, 268 U.S. 652 (1925): 361-362, 373
Globe Newspaper Company v. Superior Court for the County of Norfolk (Massachusettes), 457 U.S. 596 (1982): 381
Goesaert v. Cleary, 335 U.S. 464 (1948): 574
Gong Lum v. Rice, 275 U.S. 78 (1927): 501-502
Goss v. Board of Education of Knoxville (Tennessee), 373 U.S. 683 (1963), 527
Green v. County School Board of New Kent County (Virginia), 391 U.S. 430 (1968), 528-529
Gregg v. Georgia, 428 U.S. 153 (1976): 302
Griffin v. County School Board of Prince Edward County (Virginia), 377 U.S. 218 (1963), 528, 529
Griswold v. Connecticut, 381 U.S. 479 (1965), 338, 343, 347
Grove v. Meade (Washington) *School District*, 753 F.2d 1528 (9th Cir., 1985), cert. den., 474 U.S. 826 (1985): 677-680
Hague v. C.I.O., 307 U.S. 496 (1939): 446-447
Harris v. Joint School District No. 241 (Idaho) *and Citizens Preserving America's Heritage*, 41 F.3d 447 (9th Cir., 1994), appeal dismissed, 115 S.Ct.2604 (1995): 644, 646
Harris v. McRae, 448 U.S. 297 (1980): 331-332
Harris v. Nelson, 394 U.S. 286 (1969): 462
Harrison v. Day, 200 Va. 439 (Va. S.Ct., 1959): 527
Hawaii v. Kanter, 493 P.2d 306 (Haw. S.Ct., 1972): 323
Hazelwood School District v. U.S., 433 U.S. 299 (1977): 570
Heart of Atlanta Motel v. U.S., 379 U.S. 241 (1964): 536-537
Hebe v. Shaw, 248 U.S. 297 (1919): 443
Herbert v. Louisiana, 272 U.S. 312 (1926): 441
Hirabayashi v. U.S., 320 U.S. 81 (1943): 507-509, 520, 904 (n. 77)
Holden v. Hardy, 169 U.S. 366 (1898): 427, 428, 432, 433, 450
Hooker v. Los Angeles, 188 U.S. 314 (1903): 425
Hopwood v. Texas, 78 F.3d 932 (5th Cir., 1996), cert. den. 116 S.Ct. 2580, 2581-82 (1996): 562-566
Hoyt v. Florida, 368 U.S. 57 (1961): 574, 583
Hunter v. Erickson, 393 U.S. 385 (1969): 568-569
Hurd v. Hodge, 334 U.S. 24 (1948): 512, 520
Hurtado v. California, 110 U.S. 516 (1884): 421-423, 426, 441, 448, 450, 457, 466
Hustler Magazine and Larry Flynt v. Jerry Falwell, 485 U.S. 46 (1988): 368-369
Ingebretsen v. Jackson (Mississippi) *Public School District*, 88 F.3d 274 (5th Cir., 1996), cert. den. 117 S.Ct. 388 (1996): 645, 646
Iowa v. Byrnes, 150 N.W. 2d 280 (Iowa S.Ct., 1967): 465
Iowa Central Railway v. Iowa, 160 U.S. 389 (1896): 425, 448, 465
Jacobson v. Massachusetts, 197 U.S. 11 (1905): 428
Jaffree v. James, 544 F.Supp. 727 (S.D. Ala., 1982): 611
Johnson v. Louisiana, 406 U.S. 356 (1972): 473-474, 902 (n. 55)
Johnson v. Virginia, 373 U.S. 61 (1963): 522
Jones v. Alfred H. Mayer Company, 392 U.S. 409 (1968): 539-541
Jones v. Clear Creek (Texas) *Independent School District*, 930 F.2d 416 (5th Cir., 1991), remanded 505 U.S. 1215 (1992), rehearing, 977 F.2d 963 (1992): 636-638, 643-647
Kadrmas v. Dickson Public Schools, 487 U.S. 450 (1988): 592
Kahn v. Shevin, 416 U.S. 351 (1974): 576, 577, 579
Katzenbach v. McClung, 379 U.S. 294 (1964): 537-539
In re Kemmler, 136 U.S. 436 (1890): 423-424, 449
Kepner v. U.S., 195 U.S. 100 (1904): 442
Kirchberg v. Feenstra, 450 U.S. 455 (1981): 582-583, 594
Klopfer v. North Carolina, 386 U.S. 213 (1967): 456, 465

944 Index

Korematsu v. U.S., 323 U.S. 214 (1944): 509-510, 511, 520, 906 (n. 77)
Leary v. U.S., 383 F.2d 851 (5th Cir., 1967): 323-324
Lee v. Weisman, 505 U.S. 577 (1992): 634, 638-644, 646
Leeper v. State of Tennessee, 53 S.W. 962 (Tenn. S.Ct., 1899): 669
Lemon v. Kurtzman, 403 U.S. 602 (1971): 609-610, 612, 626-627, 629, 637, 651-652, 678
License Cases, 46 U.S. (5 Howard) 504 (Jan. term, 1847): 419
Lochner v. New York, 198 U.S. 45 (1905): 427-428
London, City of v. Wood, 12 Mod. 669 (1701): 842, 890 (n. 9)
Loughborough v. Blake, 18 U.S. (5 Wheaton) 317 (1820): 310
Louisville & Nashville Railroad Company v. Schmidt, 177 U.S. 230 (1900): 425
Louisville Gas & Electric Company v. Coleman, 277 U.S. 32 (1928): 591
Loving v. Virginia, 388 U.S. 1 (1967): 338, 344, 586-587
Lubbock Civil Liberties Union v. Lubbock (Texas) *Independent School District*, 669 F.2d 1038 (5th Cir., 1982): 628-629, 631
Lynch v. Donnelly, 465 U.S. 668 (1984): 612, 637, 640, 905 (n. 13)
Maher v. Roe, 432 U.S. 464 (1977): 330-331
Maine v. Bowman, 588 A.2nd 728 (Maine S.Ct., 1991): 465
Malloy v. Hogan, 378 U.S. 1 (1964): 456-458, 465, 468
Malnak v. Yogi, 592 F.2d 197 (3rd Cir., 1979): 614-626
Mapp v. Ohio, 367 U.S. 643 (1961): 454-455, 464, 466-467, 468
Marbury v. Madison, 5 U.S. (1 Cranch) 137 (Feb. term, 1803): 890-891 (n. 9)
Marsh v. Chambers, 463 U.S. 783 (1983): 603-604, 635-636, 638, 647
Maxwell v. Dow, 176 U.S. 581 (1900): 425, 441, 449
McCollum v. Board of Education of School District No. 71 (Champaign County, Illinois), 333 U.S. 203 (1948): 596-598
McDaniel v. Barresi, 402 U.S. 39 (1971): 532
McGhee v. Sipes, 334 U.S. 1 (1948): 511, 512
McLaurin v. Oklahoma Board of Regents, 339 U.S. 637 (1950): 515-518
Metro Broadcasting, Inc. v. F.C.C., 497 U.S. 547 (1990): 556-558, 559-560, 562, 564, 571
Meyer v. Nebraska, 262 U.S. 390 (1923): 438-439, 448, 508
Miller v. California, 413 U.S. 15 (1973): 384
Minersville School District v. Gobitis, 310 U.S. 586 (1940): 376
Miranda v. Arizona, 384 U.S. 436 (1966): 458-460, 472
Missouri ex rel. Gaines v. Canada, 305 U.S. 337 (1938): 513
Missouri v. Lewis, 101 U.S. 22 (Oct. term, 1879): 450
Mooney v. Holohan, 294 U.S. 103 (1935): 437
Moore v. Dempsey, 261 U.S. 86 (1923): 435, 448
Morehead v. New York ex rel. Tipaldo, 298 U.S. 587 (1936): 431-432, 903 (n. 36)
Muller v. Oregon, 208 U.S. 412 (1908): 428, 431
Munn v. Illinois, 94 U.S. 113 (Oct.term, 1876): 348, 418-420, 707-708, 908 (n. 8)
Murray v. Curlett, 374 U.S. 203 (1963): 606-608, 689, 897 (n. 102)
National Labor Relations Board v. Jones & Laughlin Steel Corp., 301 U.S. 1 (1937): 433-434
Near v. Minnesota, 283 U.S. 697 (1931): 364-366, 440, 441, 447, 464
Nebraska District of Evangelical Lutheran Synod v. McKelvie, 262 U.S. 404 (1923): 438
Nevada v. Hall, 440 U.S. 410 (1979): 590
New Jersey v. Saunders, 381 A.2d 333 (1977): 343-344
New York v. Quarles, 467 U.S. 649 (1984): 460
New York Times v. Sullivan, 376 U.S. 254 (1964): 366-368, 899 (ns. 47, 51)
Northern Securities v. U.S., 193 U.S. 197 (1904): 428
In re Oliver, 333 U.S. 257 (1948): 380, 452-453, 465
Oregon v. Elstad, 470 U.S. 298 (1985): 460-461
Orr v. Orr, 440 U.S. 268 (1979): 580-581
Otis v. Parker, 187 U.S. 606 (1903): 428
Palko v. Connecticut, 302 U.S. 319 (1937): 321-322, 427, 441-443, 449, 450-451, 452, 474-475, 520
Parish, Wyble, widow of, v. Minvielle, 217 So.2d 684 (La. Ct. of App., 1969): 589
Patterson v. Colorado, 205 U.S. 454 (1907): 362-363
Patton v. U.S., 281 U.S. 276 (1930): 473

E. Table of Cases 945

Pennsylvania v. Board of Directors, 353 U.S. 230 (1957): 522
People v. Cahan, 282 P.2d 905 (Cal. S.Ct., 1955): 454
People v. Kevorkian, 527 N.W.2d 714 (Mich. S.Ct., 1994): 342-343
People v. Lloyd, 304 Ill. 23 (Ill. S.Ct., 1922): 360
People of the State of New York v. Onofre, 415 N.E.2d 936 (N.Y. App.Ct., 1980): 346
Personnel Administrator of Massachusetts v. Feeney, 442 U.S. 256 (1979): 582-583, 594
Pierce, Governor of Oregon v. Society of Sisters and Hill Military Academy, 268 U.S. 510 (1925): 438-439, 441, 448, 508
Planned Parenthood of Southeastern Pennsylvania v. Casey, 505 U.S. 833 (1992): 296, 321-322, 328, 337, 340, 908 (n. 8)
Plessy v. Ferguson, 163 U.S. 537 (1896): 497-502, 503, 514, 516, 519, 522, 562
Poe v. Ullman, 367 U.S. 497 (1961): 321, 340-341
Pointer v. Texas, 380 U.S. 400 (1965): 456, 465
Pollock v. Farmers' Loan & Trust Co., 157 U.S. 429 (1895): 548
Powell v. Alabama, 287 U.S. 45 (1932): 427, 435-437, 441, 448, 471
Powell v. Pennsylvania, 127 U.S. 678 (1888): 443
Presser v. Illinois, 116 U.S. 252 (1886): 314, 464
In re Quinlan, 355 A.2d 647 (N.J. S.Ct., 1976), 335-336
Quock Walker Case (Mass. S.Ct., 1783): 478-479, 484-485
R.A.V. v. St. Paul, 505 U.S. 377 (1992): 374
Raney v. County School Board of Gould School District (Arkansas), 391 U.S. 443 (1968): 528-529
Ravin v. State of Alaska, 537 P.2d 494 (Alaska S.Ct., 1975): 323
Redrup v. New York, 386 U.S. 767 (1967): 323
Reed v. Reed, 404 U.S. 71 (1971): 574-575
Regents of University of California v. Bakke, 438 U.S. 265 (1978): 545-549, 550, 562, 565-566, 571
Reno, Janet v. American Civil Liberties Union, 117 S.Ct. 2329 (1997): 382-386
Richmond (Virginia), City of v. J. A. Croson Co., 488 U.S. 469 (1989): 552-556
Richmond Newspapers, Inc. v. Virginia, 448 U.S. 555 (1980), 380-381
Robinson v. California, 370 U.S. 660 (1962): 456, 465
Rochin v. California, 342 U.S. 165 (1952): 326
Roe v. Wade, 410 U.S. 113 (1973): 326-332
Roemer v. Public Works Board of Maryland, 426 U.S. 736 (1976): 627
Rogers v. Peck, 199 U.S. 425 (1905): 425
Romer v. Evans, 116 S.Ct. 1620 (1996): 590-594
Rosen v. U.S., 245 U.S. 467 (1918): 469
Sable Communications of California v. F.C.C., 492 U.S. 115 (1989): 384
San Antonio Independent School District v. Rodriguez, 411 U.S. 1 (1973): 303, 897-898 (n. 7)
Scott, Dred v. Sandford, 60 U.S. (19 Howard) 393 (Dec. term, 1856): 480-489, 499
Schaeffer v. U.S., 251 U.S. 466 (1920): 363
Schenck v. U.S., 249 U.S. 47 (1919): 359, 361-362, 370
Schlesinger v. Ballard, 419 U.S. 498 (1975): 576
Schloendorf v. Society of New York Hospital, 105 N.E. 92 (1914): 336
School District of Abington Township (Pennsylvania) *v. Schempp*, 374 U.S. 203 (1963): 604-609, 611-612, 648, 655, 679-680, 689
Scopes "Monkey" Trial (Tenn., 18th Cir., 1925): 659-676
Scopes v. State of Tennessee, 289 S.W. 363 (Tenn. S.Ct., 1927), 675
Shelley v. Kraemer, 334 U.S. 1 (1948): 511-512, 516
Sherbert v. Verner, 374 U.S. 398 (1963): 322
Sipuel v. Oklahoma Board of Regents, 332 U.S. 631 (1948): 513
Skinner v. Oklahoma, 316 U.S. 535 (1942): 326, 504-505, 908 (n. 8)
Slaughter-House Cases, 83 U.S. (16 Wallace) 36 (Dec. term, 1872): 410-418, 419, 420, 426, 446, 492-493, 573
Slingluff v. Weaver, 66 Ohio St. 621 (Ohio S.Ct., 1902): 401, 403, 486
Spence v. State of Washington, 418 U.S. 405 (1974): 380
Stanley v. Georgia, 394 U.S. 557 (1969): 323
Stanton v. Stanton, 421 U.S. 7 (1975): 577-578, 581
State of Hawaii v. Kanter, 493 P.2d 306 (Hawaii S.Ct., 1972): 323
State of Iowa v. Byrnes, 150 N.W.2d 280 (Iowa S.Ct., 1967): 465

State of Maine v. Bowman, 588 A.2d 728 (Maine S.Ct., 1991): 465
State of New Jersey v. Saunders, 381 A.2d 333 (1977): 343-344
Stein and Dahlinger v. Plainwell (Michigan) *Community Schools and Portage* (Michigan) *Public Schools,* 822 F.2d 1406 (6th Cir., 1987): 634-637, 640
Steward Machine Co. v. Davis, 301 U.S. 548 (1937): 905 (n. 77)
Stone v. Graham, 449 U.S. 39 (1980): 609-611, 679-680
Strader v. Graham, 51 U.S. (10 Howard) 82 (Dec. term, 1850): 487-488
Strauder v. West Virginia, 100 U.S. 303 (Oct. term, 1879): 493-495
Stromberg v. California, 283 U.S. 359 (1931): 375
Swann v. Charlotte-Mecklenburg (N. Carolina) *Board of Education,* 402 U.S. 1 (1971): 530-532
Sweatt v. Painter, 339 U.S. 629 (1950): 513-514, 516-517, 518, 562, 564
Taxman v. Board of Education of the Township of Piscataway (New Jersey), 91 F.3d 1547 (3rd Cir., 1996): 566-567
Taylor v. Louisiana, 419 U.S. 522 (1975): 581
Terminello v. Chicago, 337 U.S. 1 (1949): 371-374
Terrett v. Taylor, 13 U.S. (9 Cranch) 43 (1815): 417-418
Terry v. Ohio, 392 U.S. 1 (1968): 456, 464
Texas v. Johnson, 491 U.S. 397 (1989): 377-378
Thompson v. Utah, 170 U.S. 343 (1898): 473, 902 (n. 55)
Thorpe v. Rutland & Burlington Railroad Co., 27 Vt. 143 (Vt. S.Ct., 1854): 348, 419, 707-708
Toler v. Oakwood Smokeless Coal Corporation, 4 S.E.2d 364 (1939): 589
Torcaso v. Watkins, 367 U.S. 488 (1961): 615, 618-619
Twining v. New Jersey, 211 U.S. 78 (1908): 425-427, 437, 441, 449, 450
United Jewish Organizations v. Carey, 430 U.S. 144 (1977): 547-548
U.S. v. Carolene Products, 304 U.S. 144 (1938): 443-444, 446, 902 (n. 41)
U.S. v. Cruikshank, 92 U.S. 542 (Oct. term, 1875): 314
U.S. v. Miller, 307 U.S. 174 (1939): 314
U.S. v. Moses, 339 A.2d 46 (D.C. App., 1975), 344
U.S. v. Paradise, 480 U.S. 149 (1987): 561
U.S. v. Seeger, 380 U.S. 163 (1965): 615-619
U. S. Department of Agriculture v. Moreno, 413 U.S. 528 (1973): 591-592
Village of Euclid (Ohio) *v. Ambler Realty Company,* 272 U.S. 365 (1926): 439-440
Vacco v. Quill, 117 S.Ct. 2293 (1997), 337-342
Walker v. Sauvinet, 92 U.S. 90 (Oct. term, 1875): 418, 448-449, 463, 465
Walker, Quock, Case (Mass. S.Ct., 1783): 477-479, 484-485
Wall, Ex parte, 107 U.S. 265 (Oct. term, 1882), 449
Wallace v. Jaffree, 472 U.S. 38 (1985): 289-290, 611-613
Walz v. Tax Commission, 397 U.S. 664 (1970): 610
Washington v. Glucksburg, 117 S.Ct. 2258 (1997): 336-342, 899 (n. 38)
Washington v. Seattle School District No. 1, 458 U.S. 457 (1982): 569
Washington v. Texas, 388 U.S. 14 (1967): 456, 465, 468
Washington Ethical Society v. District of Columbia, 249 F.2d 127 (D.C.Cir., 1957): 620
Weber v. Aetna Casualty & Surety Co., 406 U.S. 164 (1972): 576
Weeks v. U.S., 232 U.S. 383 (1914): 455
Weinberger v. Wiesenfeld, 420 U.S. 636 (1975): 576-577, 579
Welsh v. U.S., 398 U.S. 333 (1970): 615, 618-619
West Coast Hotel v. Parrish, 300 U.S. 379 (1937): 302-303, 432-434
West Virginia State Board of Education v. Barnette, 319 U.S. 624 (1943): 375-376, 377
Widmar v. Vincent, 454 U.S. 263 (1981): 626-628, 629, 631
Wilkerson v. Utah, 99 U.S. 130 (Oct. term, 1878): 302
Williams v. Florida, 399 U.S. 78 (1970): 473
Wisconsin v. Mitchell, 508 U.S. 476 (1993): 374-375
Wolf v. Colorado, 338 U.S. 25 (1949): 453-454, 455, 456
Wolman v. Walter, 433 U.S. 229 (1977): 627
Wygant v. Jackson (Michigan) *Board of Education,* 476 U.S. 267 (1986): 551-555, 570-571
Yick Wo v. Hopkins, 118 U.S. 356 (1886): 424, 448, 496-497
Zenger Case (N.Y. trial ct., 1735): 350-352
Zorach v. Clauson, 343 U.S. 306 (1952): 598-599, 608